June 4–6, 2011
San Jose, California, USA

**Association for
Computing Machinery**

Advancing Computing as a Science & Profession

SPAA'11

Proceedings of the Twenty-Third Annual Symposium on
Parallelism in Algorithms and Architectures

Sponsored by:
ACM SIGACT & ACM SIGARCH

and supported by:
IBM & Akamai

Association for Computing Machinery

Advancing Computing as a Science & Profession

The Association for Computing Machinery
2 Penn Plaza, Suite 701
New York, New York 10121-0701

Notice to Past Authors of ACM-Published Articles

ISBN: 978-1-4503-0743-7

Additional copies may be ordered prepaid from:

ACM Order Department
PO Box 30777
New York, NY 10087-0777, USA

Phone: 1-800-342-6626 (USA and Canada)
+1-212-626-0500 (Global)
Fax: +1-212-944-1318
E-mail: acmhelp@acm.org
Hours of Operation: 8:30 am – 4:30 pm ET

ACM Order Number: 417110

Printed in the USA

Foreword

This volume consists of papers that were presented at the *23rd ACM Symposium on Parallelism in Algorithms and Architectures (SPAA'11)*, held on June 4-6, 2011, in San Jose, USA. It was sponsored by the ACM Special Interest Groups on Algorithms and Computation Theory (SIGACT) and Computer Architecture (SIGARCH) and organized in cooperation with the European Association for Theoretical Computer Science (EATCS). SPAA'11 is part of the *Federated Computing Research Conference (FCRC'11)*. Financial support was provided by Akamai and IBM Research.

The program committee selected the 35 SPAA'11 regular presentations following electronic discussions and a day-long phone conference on March 4, 2011 that was graciously arranged by IBM Research. Of these papers, the paper "Graph Expansion and Communication Costs of Fast Matrix Multiplication" by Grey Ballard, James Demmel, Olga Holtz and Oded Schwartz was selected to receive the best paper award.

The regular presentations were selected out of 116 submitted abstracts. The mix of selected papers reflects the unique nature of SPAA in bringing together the theory and practice of parallel computing. SPAA defines parallelism very broadly to encompass any computational device or scheme that can perform multiple operations or tasks simultaneously or concurrently. The technical papers in this volume are to be considered preliminary versions, and authors are generally expected to publish polished and complete versions in archival scientific journals.

In addition to the regular presentations, this volume includes 15 brief announcements. The committee's decisions in accepting brief announcements were based on the perceived interest of these contributions, with the goal that they serve as bases for further significant advances in parallelism in computing. Extended versions of the SPAA brief announcements and posters may be published later in other conferences or journals. Finally, this year's program also included a panel discussion on teaching parallelism, featuring panelists Guy Blelloch, Charles Leiserson, Paul Petersen, Nir Shavit, and Uzi Vishkin, with Christian Scheideler as moderator.

The program committee would like to thank all who submitted papers and who helped the committee in the review process. The names of these external reviewers appear later in the proceedings. We would very much like to thank the program committee for all of their hard work during the paper selection process. The authors, the external reviewers, and the program committee together made it possible to come up with a great collection of papers for the conference.

Friedhelm Meyer auf der Heide   **Rajmohan Rajaraman**
University of Paderborn, Germany   *Northeastern University, USA*
SPAA 2011 General Chair   *SPAA 2011 Program Chair*

Table of Contents

Session 4: Brief Announcements I

Session Chair: Gopal Pandurangan *(Nanyang Technological University and Brown University)*

Session 5: A Panel Discussion on Teaching Parallelism

Session 6: Coordination Algorithms

Session Chair: Jennifer Welch *(Texas A&M)*

Session 7: Games and Approximation Algorithms

Session Chair: Rohit Khandekar *(IBM T.J. Watson Research Center)*

Session 8: Network and P2P Algorithms

Session Chair: Pierre Fraignaiud *(CNRS and University Paris Diderot)*

Session 9: Brief Announcements II

Session Chair: Geppino Pucci *(University of Padova)*

Session 10: Scheduling and Network Communication

Session Chair: Rajmohan Rajaraman *(Northeastern University)*

Session 11: Brief Announcements III

Session Chair: Jennifer Welch *(Texas A&M)*

Session 12: Concurrency Control

Session Chair: Marcos K. Aguilera *(Microsoft Research)*

Session 13: Cache Hierarchies and Memory Sharing

Session Chair: Susanne Albers *(Humboldt University)*

SPAA 2011 Symposium Organization

General Chair: Friedhelm Meyer auf der Heide (*University of Paderborn, Germany*)

Program Chair: Rajmohan Rajaraman (*Northeastern University, USA*)

Program Committee: Marcos K. Aguilera (*Microsoft Research, USA*)
Susanne Albers (*Humbholdt University, Berlin, Germany*)
Anne Benoit (*ENS Lyon, France*)
Konstantin Busch (*Louisiana State University, USA*)
Shimin Chen (*Intel Research, Pittsburgh, USA*)
Frank Dehne (*Carleton University, Canada*)
Rolf Fagerberg (*University of Southern Denmark, Denmark*)
Pierre Fraigniaud (*CNRS and University Paris Diderot, France*)
Tom Friedetzky (*Durham University, UK*)
MohammadTaghi Hajiaghayi (*AT&T Research and University of Maryland, College Park, USA*)
Idit Keidar (*Technion, Israel*)
Rohit Khandekar (*IBM T.J. Watson Research Center, USA*)
Hsien-Hsin S. Lee (*Georgia Tech, USA*)
Victor Luchangco (*Sun Labs, Oracle, USA*)
Gopal Pandurangan (*Nanyang Technological University, Singapore and Brown University, USA*)
Geppino Pucci (*University of Padova, Italy*)
Andrea Richa (*Arizona State University, USA*)
Christian Schindelhauer (*University of Freiburg, Germany*)
Sivan Toledo (*Tel Aviv University, Israel*)
Roger Wattenhofer (*ETH Zurich, Switzerland*)
Jennifer Welch (*Texas A&M, USA*)

Publicity Chair: Andrea W. Richa (*Arizona State University, USA*)

Treasurer and Registration Chair: David Bunde (*Knox College, USA*)

Secretary: Christian Scheideler (*University of Paderborn, Germany*)

Additional reviewers (continued):

Oved Itzhak
Andreas Jakoby
Thomas Janson
David Johnson
Shoaib Kamil
Howard Karloff
Ian Kash
Barbara Keller
Maleq Khan
Guy Korland
Guy Kortsarz
Kishore Kothapalli
Tobias Langner
Kim Skak Larsen
Jean-Yves L'Excellent
I-Ting Lee
Peng Li
Vahid Liaghat
Chung-Hsiang Lin
Yaroslav Litus
Vahideh Manshadi
Virendra Marathe
Dániel Marx
Shashank Mehta
Alessandro Mei
Remo Meier
Rami Melhem
Maged Michael
Emanuele Milani
Vahab Mirrokni
Kedar Namjoshi
Danupon Nanongkai
Cosmin Oancea
Neil Olver
Christian Ortolf
Mi-Young Park
Francesco Pasquale
Sriram Pemmaraju
Dmitri Perelman
Enoch Peserico
Alberto Pettarin
Andrea Pietracaprina
Rajiv Raman
S.S. Ravi

Paul Renaud-Goud
Matteo Riondato
Yves Robert
Peter Robinson
Scott Roche
Eric Ruppert
Barna Saha
Alfred Samman
Peter Sanders
Amin Sayedi
Christian Scheideler
Stefan Schmid
Johannes Schneider
Michele Scquizzato
Hadas Shachnai
Gokarna Sharma
Xipeng Shen
Tatiana Shpeisman
Mark Silberstein
Francesco Silvestri
Jasmin Smula
Evan Speight
Daniel Spielman
Srivathsan Srinivasagopalan
Ashok Srinivasan
Nikhil Srivastava
Srikanta Tirthapura
Alexander Tiskin
Amitabh Trehan
Bora Ucar
Fabio Vandin
Arne Vater
Francesco Versaci
Saira Viqar
Frédéric Vivien
Berthold Voecking
Richard Vuduc
Johannes Wendeberg
Josef Widder
Bojian Xu
Richard Yoo
Neal Young
Morteza Zadimoghaddam
Oles Zhulyn

SPAA 2011 Sponsors & Supporters

Sponsors:

Supporters:

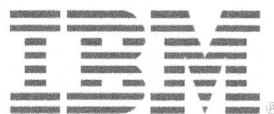

Graph Expansion and Communication Costs of Fast Matrix Multiplication

(Regular Submission)

Grey Ballard[*]
Computer Science
Department
UC Berkeley
Berkeley, CA 94720
ballard@eecs.berkeley.edu

James Demmel[†]
Mathematics Department
and CS Division
UC Berkeley
Berkeley, CA 94720
demmel@cs.berkeley.edu

Olga Holtz[‡]
Departments of Mathematics
UC Berkeley
and TU Berlin
Berkeley, CA 94720
holtz@math.berkeley.edu

Oded Schwartz[§]
Computer Science
Department
UC Berkeley
Berkeley, CA 94720
odedsc@eecs.berkeley.edu

ABSTRACT

The communication cost of algorithms (also known as I/O-complexity) is shown to be closely related to the expansion properties of the corresponding computation graphs. We demonstrate this on Strassen's and other fast matrix multiplication algorithms, and obtain the first lower bounds on their communication costs. For sequential algorithms these bounds are attainable and so optimal.

ACM Classification Keywords: F.2.1

[*]Research supported by Microsoft (Award #024263) and Intel (Award #024894) funding and by matching funding by U.C. Discovery (Award #DIG07-10227).

[†]This material is based on work supported by U.S. Department of Energy grants under Grant Numbers DE-SC0003959, DE-SC0004938, and DE-FC02-06-ER25786, as well as Lawrence Berkeley National Laboratory Contract DE-AC02-05CH11231.

[‡]Research supported by the Sofja Kovalevskaja programme of Alexander von Humboldt Foundation and by the National Science Foundation under agreement DMS-0635607, while visiting the Institute for Advanced Study.

[§]Part of this research was performed while at The Weizmann Institute of Science, and while at Technische Universität Berlin. Research supported by U.S. Department of Energy grants under Grant Numbers DE-SC0003959, by ERC Starting Grant Number 239985, and by the Sofja Kovalevskaja programme of Alexander von Humboldt Foundation.

ACM General Terms: Algorithms, Design, Performance.
Authors Keywords: Communication-avoiding algorithms, Fast matrix multiplication, I/O-Complexity.

1. INTRODUCTION

The communication of an algorithm (e.g., transferring data between the CPU and memory devices, or between parallel processors, a.k.a. I/O-complexity) often costs significantly more time than its arithmetic[1]. It is therefore of interest to obtain lower bounds for the communication needed on the one hand, and to design and implement algorithms minimizing communication[2] and attaining these lower bounds on the other hand.

While Moore's Law predicts an exponential speedup of hardware in general, the annual improvement rate of time-per-arithmetic-operation has, over the years, consistently exceeded that of time-per-word read/write [GSP04]. The fraction of running time spent on communication is thus expected to increase further.

Communication model.

We model communication costs of sequential and parallel architecture as follows. In the sequential case, with two levels of memory hierarchy (fast and slow), communication means reading data items (*words*) from slow memory (of unbounded size), to fast memory (of size M) and writing data from fast memory to slow memory[3]. Words that are stored contiguously in slow memory can be read or written

---

[1]Communication time varies by orders of magnitude, from 0.5×10^{-9} second for L1 cache reference, to 10^{-2} second for disk access. The variation is even more dramatic when communication occurs over networks or the internet [GSP04].

[2]Communication requires much more energy than arithmetic, and saving energy may be even more important than saving time.

[3]See [BDHS10a] for definition of a model with memory hierarchy, and a reduction from the two levels model. All

in a bundle which we will call a *message*. We assume that a message of n words can be communicated between fast and slow memory in time $\alpha + \beta n$ where α is the *latency* (seconds per message) and β is the *inverse bandwidth* (seconds per word). We define the *bandwidth cost* of an algorithm to be the total number of words communicated and the *latency cost* of an algorithm to be the total number of messages communicated. We assume that the input matrices initially resides in slow memory, and is too large to fit in the smaller fast memory. Our goal then is to minimize bandwidth and latency costs.[4]

In the parallel case, we assume p processors, each with memory of size M. We are interested in the communication among the processors. As in the sequential case, we assume that a message of n consecutively stored words can be communicated in time $\alpha + \beta n$. This cost includes the time required to "pack" non-contiguous words into a single message, if necessary. We assume that the input is initially evenly distributed among all processors, so $M \cdot p$ is at least as large as the input. Again, the bandwidth cost and latency cost are the words and messages counts respectively. However, we count the number of words and messages communicated along the critical path as defined in [YM88] (i.e., two words that are communicated simultaneously are counted only once), as this metric is closely related to the total running time of the algorithm. As before, our goal is to minimize the number of words and messages communicated.

We assume that (1) the cost per flop is the same on each processor and the communication costs (α and β) are the same between each pair of processors, (2) all communication is "blocking": a processor can send/receive a single message at a time, and cannot communicate and compute a flop simultaneously (the latter assumption can be dropped, affecting the running time by a factor of two at most), and (3) there is no communication resource contention among processors. For example, if processor 0 sends a message of size n to processor 1 at time 0, and processor 2 sends a message of size n to processor 3 also at time 0, the cost along the critical path is $\alpha + \beta n$. However, if both processor 0 and processor 1 try to send a message to processor 2 at the same time, the cost along the critical path will be the sum of the costs of each message.

The Computation Graph and Implementations of an Algorithm.

The computation performed by an algorithm on a given input can be modeled as a computation directed acyclic graph *(CDAG)* : We have a vertex for each input / intermediate / output argument, and edges according to direct dependencies (e.g., for the binary arithmetic operation $x := y + z$ we have a directed edge from v_y to v_x and from v_z to v_x, where the vertices v_x, v_y, v_z stand for the arguments x, y, z, respectively).

An implementation of an algorithm determines, in the parallel model, which arithmetic operations are performed by which of the p processors. This corresponds to partitioning the corresponding CDAG into p parts. Edges crossing between the various parts correspond to arguments that are in the possession of one processor, but are needed by another processor, therefore relate to communication. In the sequential model, an implementation determines the order of the arithmetic operations, in a way that respects the partial ordering of the CDAG (see Section 3 relating this to communication cost).

Implementations of an algorithm may greatly vary in their communication costs. The *I/O-complexity of an algorithm* is the minimum bandwidth cost of the algorithm, over all possible implementations. The I/O-complexity of a problem is defined to be the minimum I/O-complexity of all algorithms for this problem.

There are quite a few I/O-complexity lower and upper bounds of specific algorithms (see below). These are results of the form: any implementation of algorithm *Alg* requires at least X communication (or: there is an implementation for algorithm *Alg* that requires at most X communication). However, we are not aware of I/O-complexity lower bounds for a *problem*, i.e., of the form: any algorithm for a problem P requires at least X communication. The lower bounds in this paper are for all the *implementations* for a family of algorithms: Strassen-like[5] fast matrix multiplication.

Previous Work.

Consider the classical $\Theta(n^3)$ algorithm for matrix multiplication. While naïve implementations are communication inefficient, communication-minimizing sequential and parallel variants of this algorithm were constructed, and proved optimal, by matching lower bounds [Can69, HK81, FLPR99, ITT04].

In [BDHS10a, BDHS10b] we generalize the results of [HK81, ITT04] regarding matrix multiplication, to obtain new I/O-complexity lower bounds for a much wider variety of algorithms. Most of our bounds are shown to be tight. This includes algorithms for LU factorization, Cholesky factorization, LDL^T factorization, QR factorization, as well as algorithms for eigenvalues and singular values. Thus we essentially cover all direct methods of linear algebra. The results hold for dense matrix algorithms (most of them have $O(n^3)$ complexity), as well as sparse matrix algorithms (whose running time depends on the number of non-zero elements, and their locations). They apply to sequential and parallel algorithms, to compositions of linear algebra operations (like computing the powers of a matrix), and to certain graph theoretic problems[6].

In [BDHS10a, BDHS10b] we use the approach of [ITT04], based on the Loomis-Whitney geometric theorem [LW49, BZ88], by embedding segments of the computation process into a three dimensional cube. This approach, however, is not suitable when distributivity is used, as is the case in Strassen [Str69] and other fast matrix multiplication algorithms (e.g., [CW90, CKSU05]).

While the I/O-complexity of classic matrix multiplication

---

bounds in this paper thus apply to the model with memory hierarchy as well.

[4]The sequential communication model used here is sometimes called the *two-level I/O model* or *disk access machine (DAM)* model (see [AV88, BBF+07, CR06]). Our bandwidth cost model follows that of [HK81] and [ITT04] in that it assumes the block-transfer size is one word of data ($B = 1$ in the common notation). However, our model allows message sizes to vary from one word up to the maximum number of words that can fit in fast memory.

[5]See Section 5 for definition.

[6]See [MPP02] for bounds on graph-related problems, and our [BDHS10b] for a detailed list of previously known and recently designed sequential and parallel algorithms that attain the above mentioned lower bounds.

and algorithms with similar structure is quite well understood, this is not the case for algorithms of more complex structure. Avoiding the communication of parallel classical matrix multiplication was addressed [Can69] almost simultaneously with the publication of Strassen's fast matrix multiplication [Str69]. Moreover, an I/O-complexity lower bound for the classical matrix multiplication algorithm is known for almost three decades [HK81]. Nevertheless, the I/O-complexity of Strassen's fast matrix multiplication and similar algorithms has not yet been resolved.

In this paper we obtain the first communication cost lower bound for Strassen's and other fast matrix multiplication algorithm, in the sequential and parallel models. For sequential algorithms these bounds are attainable and so optimal.

Communication Costs of Fast Matrix Multiplication

Upper bound.

The I/O-complexity $IO(n)$ of Strassen's algorithm (see Algorithm 1, Appendix B), applied to n-by-n matrices on a machine with fast memory of size M, can be bounded above as follows (for actual uses of Strassen's algorithm, see [DHSS94, HLJJ+96, DS04]): Run the recursion until the matrices are sufficiently small. Then, read the two input sub-matrices into the fast memory, perform the matrix multiplication inside the fast memory, and write the result into the slow memory[7]. We thus have $IO(n) \leq 7 \cdot IO\left(\frac{n}{2}\right) + O(n^2)$ and $IO\left(\frac{\sqrt{M}}{3}\right) = O(M)$. Thus

$$IO(n) = O\left(\left(\frac{n}{\sqrt{M}}\right)^{\lg 7} \cdot M\right). \qquad (1)$$

Lower bound.

In this paper, we obtain a tight lower bound:

THEOREM 1. (MAIN THEOREM) *The I/O-complexity $IO(n)$ of Strassen's algorithm on a machine with fast memory of size M, assuming that no arithmetic operation is computed twice[8], is*

$$IO(n) = \Omega\left(\left(\frac{n}{\sqrt{M}}\right)^{\lg 7} \cdot M\right). \qquad (2)$$

It holds for any implementation and any known variant of Strassen's algorithm[9,10]. This includes Winograd's $O(n^{\lg 7})$ variant that uses 15 additions instead of 18, which is the most used fast matrix multiplication algorithm in practice [DHSS94, HLJJ+96, DS04].

For parallel algorithms, using a reduction from the sequential to the parallel model (see e.g., [ITT04] or our [BDHS10b]) this yields:

---

[7] Here we assume that the recursion tree is traversed in the usual depth-first order.

[8] We assume no recomputation throughout the paper.

[9] This lower bound for the sequential case seems to contradict the upper bound from FOCS'99 [FLPR99, BCG+08]), due to a miscalculation [Lei08].

[10] To obtain the lower bounds for latency costs we divide the bandwidth costs by the maximal message length, M. This holds for all the lower bounds here, both in the sequential and parallel models.

COROLLARY 2. *Let $IO(n)$ be the I/O-complexity of Strassen's algorithm, run on a machine with p processors, each with a local memory of size M. Assume that no arithmetic operation is computed twice. Then*

$$IO(n) = \Omega\left(\left(\frac{n}{\sqrt{M}}\right)^{\lg 7} \cdot \frac{M}{p}\right).$$

Note that although recomputation is forbidden here, replication of the input is allowed. Specifically, for multiplying matrices of maximum possible size (i.e., $M = \Theta\left(\frac{n^2}{p}\right)$, a "2D algorithm") we have $IO(n) = \Omega\left(n^2/p^{2-\frac{\lg 7}{2}}\right)$.

We can extend the bounds to a wider class of all Strassen-like fast matrix multiplication algorithms. Let Alg be any Strassen-like matrix multiplication algorithm that runs in time $O(n^{\omega_0})$ for some $2 < \omega_0 < 3$. Then, using the same arguments that lead to (1), the I/O-complexity of Alg can be shown to be $IO(n) = O\left(\left(\frac{n}{\sqrt{M}}\right)^{\omega_0} \cdot M\right)$. We obtain a matching lower bound:

THEOREM 3. *The I/O-complexity $IO(n)$ of a recursive Strassen-like fast matrix multiplication algorithm with $O(n^{\omega_0})$ arithmetic operations, on a machine with fast memory of size M is*

$$IO(n) = \Omega\left(\left(\frac{n}{\sqrt{M}}\right)^{\omega_0} \cdot M\right). \qquad (3)$$

COROLLARY 4. *Let $IO(n)$ be the I/O-complexity of a Strassen-like algorithm (with arithmetic performed as in Theorem 3), run on a machine with p processors, each with a local memory of size M. Assume that no arithmetic operation is computed twice. Then*

$$IO(n) = \Omega\left(\left(\frac{n}{\sqrt{M}}\right)^{\omega_0} \cdot \frac{M}{p}\right).$$

For the "2D" case $M = \Theta\left(\frac{n^2}{p}\right)$ we have $IO(n) = \Omega\left(\frac{n^2}{p^{2-\frac{\omega_0}{2}}}\right)$. Corollaries 2 and 4 can be generalized to other models, such as the heterogenous model (where processors have different memory sizes and communication and computation speeds), and shared memory model. The reduction is achieved by observing the communication of a single processor.

The Expansion Approach

The proof of the main theorem is based on estimating the edge expansion of the computation directed acyclic graph *(CDAG)* of an algorithm. The I/O-complexity is shown to be closely connected to the edge expansion properties of this graph. As the graph has a recursive structure, the expansion can be analyzed directly (combinatorially, similarly to what is done in [Mih89, ASS08, KKK10]) or by spectral analysis (in the spirit of what was done for the Zig-Zag expanders [RVW02]). There is, however, a new technical challenge. The replacement product and the Zig-Zag product act similarly on all vertices. This is not what happens in our case: multiplication and addition vertices behave differently.

The expansion approach is similar to the one taken by Hong and Kung [HK81]. They use the red-blue pebble game to obtain tight lower-bounds on the I/O-complexity of many algorithms, including ordinary matrix multiplication, matrix-vector multiplication, and FFT. The proof is obtained by showing that the size of any subset of the vertices of the CDAG is bounded by a function of the size of its dominator set.

On the one hand, their dominator set technique has the advantage of allowing recomputation of any intermediate value. We were not able to allow recomputation using our edge expansion approach. On the other hand, the dominator set requires large input or output. Such an assumption is not needed by the edge expansion approach, as the bounds are guaranteed by edge expansion of many (internal) parts of the CDAG. In that regard, one can view the approach of [ITT04] (also in [BDHS10a, BDHS10b]) as an edge expansion assertion on the CDAGs of the corresponding classical algorithms.

The study of expansion properties of a CDAG was also suggested as one of the main motivations of Lev and Valiant [LV83] in their work on superconcentrators. They point out many papers proving that classes of algorithms computing DFT, matrix inversion and other problems all have to have good expansion properties, thus providing lower-bounds on the number of the arithmetic operations required.

Other papers study connections between bounded-space computation, and combinatorial expansion-related properties of the corresponding CDAG (see e.g., [Sav94, BP99, BPD00] and their references).

Paper organization.

Section 2 contains preliminaries on the notions of graph expansion. In Section 3 we state and prove the connection between I/O-complexity and the expansion properties of the computation graph. In Section 4 we analyze the expansion of the CDAG of Strassen's algorithm. We present the generalization of the bounds to other fast matrix multiplication algorithms, conclusions and open problems in Section 5.

2. PRELIMINARIES

Edge expansion.

The edge expansion $h(G)$ of a d-regular undirected graph $G = (V, E)$ is:

$$h(G) \equiv \min_{U \subseteq V, |U| \leq |V|/2} \frac{|E(U, V \setminus U)|}{d \cdot |U|} \quad (4)$$

where $E(A, B) \equiv E_G(A, B)$ is the set of edges connecting the vertex sets A and B. We omit the subscript G when the context makes it clear.

Expansion of small sets.

For many graphs, small sets of vertices have better expansion guarantee. Let $h_s(G)$ denote the edge expansion guarantee for sets of size at most s in G:

$$h_s(G) \equiv \min_{U \subseteq V, |U| \leq s} \frac{|E(U, V \setminus U)|}{d \cdot |U|} . \quad (5)$$

In many cases, $h_s(G)$ does not depend on $|V(G)|$, although it may decrease when s increases. One way of bounding $h_s(G)$ is by decomposing G into small subgraphs of large edge expansion.

CLAIM 5. *Let $G = (V, E)$ be a d-regular graph that can be decomposed into edge-disjoint (but not necessarily vertex disjoint) copies of a d'-regular graph $G' = (V', E')$. Then the edge expansion guarantee of G for sets of size at most*

$|V'|/2$ *is* $h(G') \cdot \frac{d'}{d}$, *namely*

$$h_{\frac{|V'|}{2}}(G) \equiv \min_{U \subseteq V, |U| \leq |V'|/2} \frac{|E_G(U, V \setminus U)|}{d \cdot |U|} \geq h(G') \cdot \frac{d'}{d} .$$

See proof in Appendix A.

When G is not regular.

If $G = (V, E)$ is not regular but has a bounded maximal degree d, then we can add $(< d)$ loops to vertices of degree $< d$, obtaining a regular graph G'[11]. Note that for any $S \in V$, we have $|E_G(S, V \setminus S)| = |E_{G'}(S, V \setminus S)|$, as none of the added edges (loops) contributes to the edge expansion of G'.

3. I/O-COMPLEXITY AND EDGE EXPANSION

In this section we recall the computation graph of an algorithm, then show how a partition argument connects the expansion properties of the graph and the I/O-complexity of the algorithm. A similar partition argument already appeared in [ITT04], and then in our [BDHS10b]. In both cases it is used to relate I/O-complexity to the Loomis-Whitney geometric bound [LW49], which can be viewed, in this context, as an expansion guarantee for the corresponding graphs.

The computation graph.

For a given algorithm, we consider the computation (directed) graph $G = (V, E)$, where there is a vertex for each arithmetic operation *(AO)* performed, and for every input element. G contains a directed edge (u, v), if the output operand of the AO corresponding to u (or the input element corresponding to u), is an input operand to the AO corresponding to v. The in-degree of any vertex of G is, therefore, at most 2 (as the arithmetic operations are binary). The out-degree is, in general, unbounded[12], i.e., it may be a function of $|V|$. We next show how an expansion analysis of this graph can be used to obtain the I/O-complexity lower bound for the corresponding algorithm.

The partition argument.

Let M be the size of the fast memory. Let O be any total ordering of the vertices that respects the partial ordering of the CDAG G, i.e., all the edges are going from left to right. This ordering can be thought of as the actual order in which the computations are performed. Let P be any partition of V into segments $S_1, S_2, ...$, so that a segment $S_i \in P$ is a subset of the vertices that are contiguous in the total ordering O.

Let R_S and W_S be the set of read and write operands, respectively (see Figure 1). Namely, R_S is the set of vertices outside S that have an edge going into S, and W_S is the set of vertices in S that have an edge going outside of S. Then the total I/O-complexity due to reads of AOs in S is at least $|R_S| - M$, as at most M of the needed $|R_S|$ operands are already in fast memory when the execution of the segment's

---

[11] Here we use the convention that a loop adds 1 to the degree of a vertex.

[12] As the lower bounds are derived for the bounded out-degree case, we will show how to convert the corresponding CDAG to obtain constant out-degree, without affecting the I/O-complexity too much.

4

AOs starts. Similarly, S causes at least $|W_S| - M$ actual write operations, as at most M of the operands needed by other segments are left in the fast memory when the execution of the segment's AOs ends. The I/O-complexity is therefore bounded below by[13]

$$IO \geq \max_P \sum_{S \in P} (|R_S| + |W_S| - 2M) . \qquad (6)$$

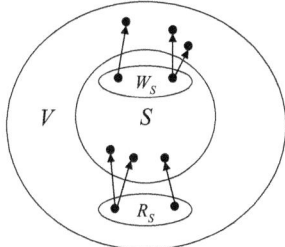

Figure 1: A subset (segment) S and its corresponding read operands R_S, and write operands W_S.

Edge expansion and I/O-complexity.

Consider a segment S and its read and write operands R_S and W_S (see Figure 1). If the graph G containing S has $h(G)$ edge expansion[14], maximum degree d and at least $2|S|$ vertices, then (using the definition of $h(G)$), we have

CLAIM 6. $|R_S| + |W_S| \geq \frac{1}{2} \cdot h(G) \cdot |S|$.

PROOF. We have $|E(S, V \setminus S)| \geq h(G) \cdot d \cdot |S|$. Either (at least) half of the edges $E(S, V \setminus S)$ touch R_S or half of them touch W_S. As every vertex is of degree d, we have $|R_S| + |W_S| \geq \max\{|R_S|, |W_S|\} \geq \frac{1}{d} \cdot \frac{1}{2} \cdot |E(S, V \setminus S)| \geq h(G) \cdot |S|/2$. $\square$

Combining this with (6) and choosing to partition V into $|V|/s$ segments of equal size s, we obtain: $IO \geq \max_s \frac{|V|}{s} \cdot \left(\frac{h(G) \cdot s}{2} - 2M \right) = \Omega(|V| \cdot h(G))$. In many cases $h(G)$ is too small to attain the desired I/O-complexity lower bound. Typically, $h(G)$ is a decreasing function in $|V(G)|$, namely the edge expansion deteriorates with the increase of the input size and with the running time of the corresponding algorithm. This is the case with matrix multiplication algorithms: the cubic, as well as the Strassen and Strassen-like algorithms. In such cases, it is better to consider the expansion of G on small sets only: $IO \geq \max_s \frac{|V|}{s} \cdot \left(\frac{h_s(G) \cdot s}{2} - 2M \right)$. Choosing[15] the minimal s so that

$$\frac{h_s(G) \cdot s}{2} \geq 3M \qquad (7)$$

we obtain

$$IO \geq \frac{|V|}{s} \cdot M . \qquad (8)$$

In some cases, the computation graph G does not fit this analysis: it may not be regular (with vertices of unbounded degree), or its edge expansion may be hard to analyze. In such cases, we may consider some subgraph G' of G instead to obtain a lower bound on the I/O-complexity:

CLAIM 7. *Let $G = (V, E)$ be a computation graph of an algorithm Alg. Let $G' = (V', E')$ be a subgraph of G, i.e., $V' \subseteq V$ and $E' \subseteq E$. If G' is d regular and $\alpha = \frac{|V'|}{|V|}$, then the I/O-complexity of Alg is*

$$IO \geq \frac{\alpha}{2} \cdot \frac{|V|}{s} \cdot M \qquad (9)$$

where s is chosen so that $\frac{h_s(G') \cdot \alpha s}{2} \geq 3M$.

The correctness of this claim follows from Equations (7) and (8), and from the fact that at least an $\alpha/2$ fraction of the segments have at least $\frac{\alpha}{2} \cdot s$ of their vertices in G' (otherwise $V' < \frac{\alpha}{2} \cdot V/s \cdot s + (1 - \frac{\alpha}{2}) \cdot V/s \cdot \frac{\alpha}{2} s < \alpha V$). We therefore have:

LEMMA 8. *Let Alg be an algorithm with $AO(N)$ arithmetic operations (N being the total input size, $N = \Theta(n^2)$ for matrix multiplication) and computation graph $G(N) = (V, E)$. Let $G'(N) = (V', E')$ be a regular constant degree subgraph of G, with $\frac{|V'|}{|V|} = \Theta(1)$. Then the I/O-complexity of Alg[16] on a machine with fast memory of size M is*

$$IO = \Omega\left(|V'| \cdot h_s(G'(N))\right) \quad \text{for } s = AO(M) . \qquad (10)$$

As $AO(N) = \Theta(|V'|)$ and $h_s(G'(N))$ for $s = AO(M)$ is $\Theta(h(G'(M)))$ (recall Claim 5) we obtain, equivalently,

$$IO = \Omega\left(AO(N) \cdot h(G'(M))\right) . \qquad (11)$$

4. EXPANSION PROPERTIES OF STRASSEN'S ALGORITHM

Recall Strassen's algorithm for matrix multiplication (see Algorithm 1 in Appendix B) and consider its computation graph (see Figure 2). Let $H_{\lg n}$ be the computation graph of Strassen's algorithm on input matrices of size $n \times n$. $H_{\lg n}$ has the following structure: encode A: generate weighted sums of elements of A. Similarly encode B. Then multiply the encodings of A and B element-wise. Finally, decode C, by taking weighted sums of the products. This is the structure of all the fast matrix multiplication algorithms that were obtained since Strassen's[17].

Assume w.l.o.g. that n is an integer power of 2. Denote by $Enc_{\lg n} A$ the part of $H_{\lg n}$ that corresponds to the encoding

---

[13]One can think of this as a game: the first player orders the vertices. The second player partitions them into contiguous segments. The objective of the first player (e.g., a good programmer) is to order the vertices so that any consecutive partitioning by the second player leads to a small communication count.

[14]The direction of the edges does not matter much for the expansion-bandwidth argument: treating all edges as undirected, changes the I/O-complexity estimate by a factor of 2 at most. For simplicity, we will treat G as undirected.

[15]The existence of an s that satisfies the condition is not always guaranteed. In the next section we confirm this for

Strassen, for sufficiently large $|V(G)|$ (in particular, $|V(G)|$ has to be larger than M). Indeed this is the interesting case, as otherwise all computations can be performed inside the fast memory, with no communication, except for reading the input once.

[16]In Strassen's algorithm, $N = 2n^2$ is the number of input matrices elements and $T(N) = \Theta(n^{\omega_0}) = \Theta\left(N^{\omega_0/2}\right)$. G' is the graph $Dec_k C$ for $k = \lg M$, see Section 4 for the definition of $Dec_k C$.

[17]Indeed, any fast matrix multiplication algorithm can be converted into one of this form [Raz03].

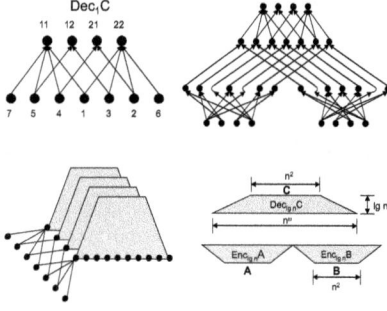

Figure 2: The computation graph of Strassen's algorithm (See Algorithm 1 in Appendix).
Top left: Dec_1C. **Top right:** H_1.
Bottom left: $Dec_{\lg n}C$. **Bottom right:** $H_{\lg n}$.
Vertices drawn with in-degrees larger than 2 indicate a (weighted) summation. A vertex v with l incoming edges represents a full binary tree (not necessarily balanced) with root v and l leaves.

of matrix A. Similarly, $Enc_{\lg n}B$, and $Dec_{\lg n}C$ correspond to the parts of $H_{\lg n}$ that compute the encoding of B and the decoding of C, respectively.

Duplicate Dec_1C 7^i times. Duplicate Dec_iC four times. We next identify the $4 \cdot 7^i$ output vertices of the copies of Dec_1C with the $4 \cdot 7^i$ input vertices of the copies of Dec_iC. Recall that each Dec_1C has four output vertices. The first output vertex of the 7^i Dec_1C graphs are identified with the 7^i input vertices of the first copy of Dec_iC. The second output vertex of the 7^i Dec_1C graphs are identified with the 7^i input vertices of the second copy of Dec_iC. And so on. We make sure that the jth input vertex of a copy of Dec_iC is identified with an output vertex of the jth copy of Dec_1C.

We similarly obtain $Enc_{i+1}A$ from Enc_iA and Enc_1A (and $Enc_{i+1}B$ from Enc_iB and Enc_1B). For every i, H_i is obtained by connecting edges from the jth output vertices of Enc_iA and Enc_iB to the jth input vertex of Dec_iC.

The graph Dec_1C has no vertices which are both input and output, therefore:

FACT 9. *$Dec_{\lg n}C$ is of maximal degree 6.*

However, Enc_1A and Enc_1B have vertices which are both input and output (e.g., A_{11}), therefore $Enc_{\lg n}A$ and $Enc_{\lg n}B$ have vertices of out-degree $\Theta(\lg n)$. All in-degrees are at most 2, as an arithmetic operation has at most two inputs.

As $H_{\lg n}$ contains vertices of large degrees, it is easier to consider $Dec_{\lg n}C$: it contains only vertices of constant bounded degree, yet at least one third of the vertices of $H_{\lg n}$ are in it.

LEMMA 10. (MAIN LEMMA) *The edge expansion of Dec_kC is*

$$h(Dec_kC) = \Omega\left(\left(\frac{4}{7}\right)^k\right)$$

See proof in Section 4.
Assume w.l.o.g. that n is an integer power of $\sqrt{M}$.[18] Then $Dec_{\lg n}C$ can be split into edge-disjoint copies of $Dec_{\frac{1}{2}\lg M}C$.

---

[18] We may assume this, as we are dealing with a lower bound here, so it suffices to prove the assertion for an infinite num-

Using Claim 5, we thus deduce the expansion of $Dec_{\lg n}C$ on small sets:

COROLLARY 11. *$s \cdot h_s(Dec_{\lg n}C) \geq 3M$ for $s = 9 \cdot M^{\lg 7/2}$.*

As $Dec_{\lg n}C$ contains $\alpha = \frac{1}{3}$ of the vertices of $H_{\lg n}$, Lemma 8 now yields Main Theorem 1. Note that $Dec_{\lg n}C$ has no input vertices, so no restriction on input replication is needed.

Dec_1C is presented, for simplicity, with vertices of in-degree larger than two (but constant). A vertex of degree larger than two, in fact, represents a full binary tree. Note that replacing these high in-degree vertices with trees changes the edge expansion of the graph by a constant factor at most (as this graph is of constant size, and connected). Moreover, as there is no change in the number of input and output vertices, the arguments in the following proof of Lemma 10 still hold.

Combinatorial Estimation of the Expansion.

PROOF OF LEMMA 10. Let $G_k = (V, E)$ be Dec_kC, and let $S \subseteq V, |S| \leq |V|/2$. We next show that $|E(S, V \setminus S)| \geq c \cdot d \cdot |S| \cdot \left(\frac{4}{7}\right)^k$, where c is some universal constant, and d is the constant degree of Dec_kC (after adding loops to make it regular).

The proof works as follows. Recall that G_k is a layered graph, so all edges (excluding loops) connect between consecutive levels of vertices. We argue (in Claim 15) that each level of G_k contains about the same fraction of S vertices, or else we have many edges leaving S. We also observe (in Fact 16) that such homogeneity (of a fraction of S vertices) does not hold between distinct parts of the lowest level, or, again, we have many edges leaving S. We then show that the homogeneity between levels combined with the heterogeneity of the lowest level, guarantees that there are many edges leaving S.

Let l_i be the ith level of vertices of G_k, so $4^k = |l_1| < |l_2| < \cdots < |l_i| = 4^{k-i+1}7^{i-1} < \cdots < |l_{k+1}| = 7^k$. Let $S_i \equiv S \cap l_i$. Let $\sigma = \frac{|S|}{|V|}$ be the fractional size of S and $\sigma_i = \frac{|S_i|}{|l_i|}$ be the fractional size of S in level i. Due to averaging, we observe the following:

FACT 12. *There exist i and i' such that $\sigma_i \leq \sigma \leq \sigma_{i'}$.*

From the geometric sum, we now have:

FACT 13.
$$\begin{aligned}
|V| &= \sum_{i=1}^{k+1} |l_i| = \sum_{i=1}^{k+1} |l_{k+1}| \cdot \left(\frac{4}{7}\right)^i \\
&= |l_{k+1}| \cdot \left(1 - \left(\frac{4}{7}\right)^{k+2}\right) \cdot \frac{7}{3} \\
&= \left(\frac{4}{7}\right)^k \cdot |l_1| \cdot \left(1 - \left(\frac{4}{7}\right)^{k+2}\right) \cdot \frac{7}{3}
\end{aligned}$$

so $\frac{3}{7} \leq \frac{|l_{k+1}|}{|V|} \leq \frac{3}{7} \cdot \frac{1}{1-\left(\frac{4}{7}\right)^{k+2}}$, and $\frac{3}{7} \cdot \left(\frac{4}{7}\right)^k \leq \frac{|l_1|}{|V|} \leq \frac{3}{7} \cdot \left(\frac{4}{7}\right)^k \cdot \frac{1}{1-\left(\frac{4}{7}\right)^{k+2}}$.

---

ber of n's. Alternatively, in the following decomposition argument, we leave out a few of the top or bottom levels of vertices of $Dec_{\lg n}C$, so that n is an integer power of $\sqrt{M}$ and so that at most $|S|/2$ vertices of S are cut off.

CLAIM 14. *There exists $c' = c'(G_1)$ so that $|E(S, V \setminus S) \cap E(l_i, l_{i+1})| \geq c' \cdot d \cdot |\delta_i| \cdot |l_i|$.*

PROOF. Let G' be a G_1 component connecting l_i with l_{i+1} (so it has four vertices in l_i and seven in l_{i+1}). G' has no edges in $E(S, V \setminus S)$ if all or none of its vertices are in S. Otherwise, as G' is connected, it contributes at least one edge to $E(S, V \setminus S)$. The number of such G_1 components with all their vertices in S is at most $\min\{\sigma_i, \sigma_{i+1}\} \cdot \frac{|l_i|}{4}$. Therefore, there are at least $|\sigma_i - \sigma_{i+1}| \cdot \frac{|l_i|}{4}$ G_1 components with at least one vertex in S and one vertex that is not. $\square$

CLAIM 15 (HOMOGENEITY BETWEEN LEVELS). *If there exists i so that $\frac{|\sigma - \sigma_i|}{\sigma} \geq \frac{1}{10}$, then*

$$|E(S, V \setminus S)| \geq c \cdot d \cdot |S| \cdot \left(\frac{4}{7}\right)^k$$

where $c > 0$ is some constant depending on G_1 only.

PROOF. Assume that there exists j so that $\frac{|\sigma - \sigma_j|}{\sigma} \geq \frac{1}{10}$. Let $\delta_i \equiv \sigma_{i+1} - \sigma_i$. By Claim 14, we have

$$
\begin{aligned}
|E(S, V \setminus S)| &\geq \sum_{i \in [k]} |E(S, V \setminus S) \cap E(l_i, l_{i+1})| \\
&\geq \sum_{i \in [k]} c' \cdot d \cdot |\delta_i| \cdot |l_i| \\
&\geq c' \cdot d \cdot |l_1| \sum_{i \in [k]} |\delta_i| \\
&\geq c' \cdot d \cdot |l_1| \cdot \left(\max_{i \in [k+1]} \sigma_i - \min_{i \in [k+1]} \sigma_i\right).
\end{aligned}
$$

By the initial assumption, there exists j so that $\frac{|\sigma - \sigma_j|}{\sigma} \geq \frac{1}{10}$, therefore $\max_i \sigma_i - \min_i \sigma_i \geq \frac{\sigma}{10}$, then $|E(S, V \setminus S)| \geq c' \cdot d \cdot |l_1| \cdot \frac{\sigma}{10}$. By Fact 13, $\geq c' \cdot d \cdot \frac{3}{7} \cdot \left(\frac{4}{7}\right)^k \cdot |V| \cdot \frac{\sigma}{10} \geq c \cdot d \cdot |S| \cdot \left(\frac{4}{7}\right)^k$, for any $c \leq \frac{c'}{10} \cdot \frac{3}{7}$. $\square$

Let T_k be a tree corresponding to the recursive construction of G_k in the following way (see Figure 3). T_k is a tree of height $k + 1$, where each internal node has four children. The root r of T_k corresponds to l_{k+1} (the largest level of G_k). The four children of r correspond to the largest levels of the four graphs that one can obtain by removing the level of vertices l_{k+1} from G_k. And so on. For every node u of T_k, denote by V_u the set of vertices in G_k corresponding to u. We thus have $|V_r| = 7^k$ where r is the root of T_k, $|V_u| = 7^{k-1}$ for each node u that is a child of r; and in general we have 4^i tree nodes u corresponding to a set of size $|V_u| = 7^{k-i+1}$. Each leaf l correspond to a set of size 1.

For a tree node u, let us define $\rho_u = \frac{|S \cap V_u|}{|V_u|}$ to be the fraction of S nodes in V_u, and $\delta_u = |\rho_u - \rho_{p(u)}|$, where $p(u)$ is the parent of u (for the root r we let $p(r) = r$). We let t_i be the ith level of T_k, counting from the bottom, so t_{k+1} is the root and t_1 are the leaves.

FACT 16. *As $V_r = l_{k+1}$ we have $\rho_r = \sigma_{k+1}$. For a tree leaf $u \in t_1$, we have $|V_u| = 1$. Therefore $\rho_u \in \{0, 1\}$. The number of vertices u in t_1 with $\rho_u = 1$ is $\sigma_1 \cdot |l_1|$.*

CLAIM 17. *Let u_0 be an internal tree node, and let u_1, u_2, u_3, u_4 be its four children. Then*

$$\sum_i |E(S, V \setminus S) \cap E(V_{u_i}, V_{u_0})| \geq c'' \cdot d \cdot \sum_i |\rho_{u_i} - \rho_{u_0}| \cdot |V_{u_i}|$$

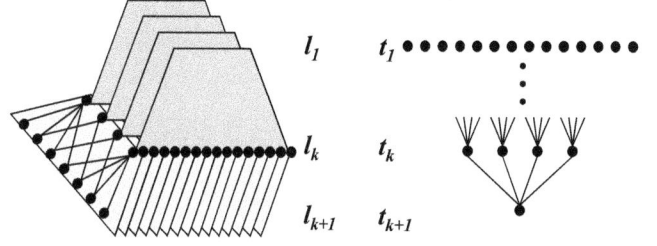

Figure 3: The graph G_k and its corresponding tree T_k.

where $c'' = c''(G_1)$.

PROOF. The proof follows that of Claim 14. Let G' be a G_1 component, connecting V_{u_0} with $\bigcup_{i \in [4]} V_{u_i}$ (so it has seven vertices in V_{u_0} and one in each of $V_{u_1}, V_{u_2}, V_{u_3}, V_{u_4}$). G' has no edges in $E(S, V \setminus S)$ if all or none of its vertices are in S. Otherwise, as G' is connected, it contributes at least one edge to $E(S, V \setminus S)$. The number of G_1 components with all their vertices in S is at most $\min\{\rho_{u_0}, \rho_{u_1}, \rho_{u_2}, \rho_{u_3}, \rho_{u_4}\} \cdot \frac{|V_{u_1}|}{4}$. Therefore, there are at least $\max_{i \in [4]}\{|\rho_{u_0} - \rho_{u_i}|\} \cdot \frac{|V_{u_1}|}{4} \geq \frac{1}{16} \cdot \sum_{i \in [4]} |\rho_{u_i} - \rho_{u_0}| \cdot |V_{u_i}|$ G_1 components with at least one vertex in S and one vertex that is not. $\square$

We have $|E(S, V \setminus S)| = \sum_{u \in T_k} |E(S, V \setminus S) \cap E(V_u, V_{p(u)})|$. By Claim 17, this is at least $\sum_{u \in T_k} c'' \cdot d \cdot |\rho_u - \rho_{p(u)}| \cdot |V_u| = c'' \cdot d \cdot \sum_{i \in [k]} \sum_{u \in t_i} |\rho_u - \rho_{p(u)}| \cdot 7^{i-1} \geq c'' \cdot d \cdot \sum_{i \in [k]} \sum_{u \in t_i} |\rho_u - \rho_{p(u)}| \cdot 4^{i-1}$. As each internal node has four children, this is $c'' \cdot d \cdot \sum_{v \in t_1} \sum_{u \in v \sim r} |\rho_u - \rho_{p(u)}|$, where $v \sim r$ is the path from v to the root r. This is at least $c'' \cdot d \cdot \sum_{v \in t_1} |\rho_u - \rho_r|$, by the triangle inequality for $|\cdot|$. By Fact 16, it is $\geq c'' \cdot d \cdot |l_1| \cdot ((1 - \sigma_1) \cdot \rho_r + \sigma_1 \cdot (1 - \rho_r))$. By Claim 15, w.l.o.g., $|\sigma_{k+1} - \sigma|/\sigma \leq \frac{1}{10}$ and $|\sigma_1 - \sigma|/\sigma \leq \frac{1}{10}$. As $\rho_r = \sigma_{k+1}$, $|E(S, V \setminus S)| \geq \frac{3}{4} \cdot c'' \cdot d \cdot |l_1| \cdot \sigma$, and by Fact 13, $\geq c \cdot d \cdot |S| \cdot \left(\frac{4}{7}\right)^k$, for any $c \leq \frac{3}{4} \cdot c''$. This completes the proof of Lemma 10.

5. CONCLUSIONS AND OPEN PROBLEMS

We obtained a tight lower bound for the I/O-complexity of Strassen's and Strassen-like fast matrix multiplication algorithms. These bounds are optimal for the sequential model with two memory levels and with memory hierarchy. The lower bounds extend to the parallel model and other models. We are not aware of matching upper bounds for the parallel cases. However recently these bounds were attained by 2.5D parallel implementations for Strassen's algorithm and for Strassen-like algorithms [BDH+11].

Strassen-like Algorithms.

A Strassen-like algorithm has a recursive structure that utilizes a base case: multiplying two n_0-by-n_0 matrices using $m(n_0)$ multiplications. Given two matrices of size n-by-n, it splits them into n_0-by-n_0 blocks (each of size $\frac{n}{n_0}$-by-$\frac{n}{n_0}$), and works blockwise, according to the base case algorithm. Additions (and subtractions) in the base case are interpreted as additions (and subtractions) of blocks. These are performed element-wise. Multiplications in the base case are interpreted as multiplications of blocks. These are performed by recursively calling the algorithm. The arithmetic count of the algorithm is then $T(n) = m(n_0) \cdot T\left(\frac{n}{n_0}\right) + O(n^2)$, so $T(n) = \Theta(n^{\omega_0})$ where $\omega_0 = \log_{n_0} m(n_0)$. We further demand that the $Dec_1 C$ is a connected graph.

This class includes Winograd's variant of Strassen's algorithm [Win71], which uses 15 additions rather than 18, but not the cubic algorithm, where $Dec_1 C$ is composed of four disconnected graphs (corresponding to the four outputs). We conjecture that $Dec_1 C$ is connected for all the following fast matrix-multiplication algorithms

and they are all Strassen-like: [Pan80, Bin80, Sch81, Rom82, CW82, Str87, CW87], (see [BCS97] for discussion of these algorithms), as well as [CKSU05], where the base case utilizes a novel group-theoretic approach.

To prove Theorem 3, which generalizes the I/O-complexity lower bound of Strassen's algorithm (Theorem 1) to all Strassen-like algorithms, we note the following:

The entire proof of Theorem 1, and in particular, the computations in the proof of Lemma 10, hold for any Strassen-like algorithm, where we plug in n_0^2, $m(n_0)$, and $\frac{n_0}{m(n_0)}$ instead of $4, 7$, and $\frac{4}{7}$. For bounding the asymptotic I/O-complexity, we do not care about the number of internal vertices of $Dec_1 C$; we need only to know that it is connected, and to know the sizes n_0 and $m(n_0)$. The only nontrivial adjustment is to show the equivalent of Fact 9: that the $Dec_{\log n} C$ graph is of bounded degree.

CLAIM 18. *The $Dec_{\log n} C$ graph of any Strassen-like algorithm is of degree bounded by a constant.*

PROOF. If the set of input vertices of $Dec_1 C$, and the set of its output vertices are disjoint, then $Dec_{\log n} C$ is of constant bounded degree (its maximal degree is at most twice the largest degree of $Dec_1 C$).

Assume (towards contradiction) that the base graph $Dec_1 C$ has an input vertex which is also an output vertex. An output vertex represents the inner product of two n_0-long vectors. The corresponding bilinear polynomial is irreducible. This is a contradiction, since an input vertex represents the multiplication of a (weighted) sum of elements of A with a (weighted) sum of elements of B. □

Other Fast Matrix Multiplication Algorithms.

Another class of matrix multiplication algorithms, the *uniform, non-stationary* algorithms, allows mixing of schemes of the previous (Strassen-like) class. In each recursive level, a different scheme may be used. The CDAG has a repeating structure inside one level, but the structure may differ between two distinct levels. This class includes, for example, algorithms that optimize for input sizes, (for size that is not an integer power of a constant integer). The class also includes algorithms that cut the recursion off at some point, and then switch to the classical algorithm. For these and other implementation issues, see [DHSS94, HLJJ+96] (sequential model) and [DS04] (parallel model). The I/O-complexity lower-bound generalizes to this class, and will appear in a separate note [BDHS11c].

A third class, the *non-uniform, non-stationary* algorithms, allows recursive calls to have different structure, even when they refer to multiplication of matrices in the same recursive level. It is not clear how to analyze the expansion of

the CDAG of an algorithm in the third class, although we are not aware of any algorithm in this class. Such an analysis, applied to the base case of [CKSU05], may improve the I/O-complexity lower bound by a (large) constant.

Multiplication of rectangular matrices have seen a series of increasingly fast algorithms culminating in Coppersmith's algorithm [Cop97]. We suggest the first lower bounds of the communication costs for these algorithms, and show that in some cases they are attainable, and therefore optimal [BDHS11b].

As fast matrix multiplication is a basic building block in many fast algorithms in linear-algebra (e.g., LU, QR, Sylvester equation) their I/O-complexity can in many cases be determined using our approach [BDHS11a].

Other Algorithms, Other Hardware.

Our lower bounds, as well as most of the previous lower bounds deal with linear algebra and numerical analysis algorithms[19]. Our new approach, however, seems general enough to address I/O-complexity lower bounds of other algorithms (recall Lemma 8).

In many cases, the simplest recursive implementation of an algorithm turns out to be communication optimal (e.g., in the cases of matrix multiplication [FLPR99] and Cholesky decomposition [AP00, BDHS10a], but not in the case of LU decomposition [Tol97]). This leads to the question: when is the communication optimality of an algorithm determined by the expansion properties of the corresponding computation graphs? In this work we showed that such is the case for Strassen-like fast matrix multiplication algorithms.

It is of great interest to construct new models general enough to capture the rich and evolving design space of current and predicted future computers. Such models can be *homogeneous*, consisting of many layers, where the components of each layer are the same (e.g., a supercomputer with many identical multi-core chips on a board, many identical boards in a rack, many identical racks, and many identical levels of associated memory hierarchy); or *heterogeneous*, with components with different properties residing on the same level (e.g., CPUs alongside GPUs, where the latter can do some computations very quickly, but are much slower to communicate with).

Some experience has been acquired with such systems (e.g., using GPU assisted linear algebra computation [VD08]). A first step in analyzing such systems has been recently introduced by Ballard, Demmel, and Gearhart [BDG11], where they modeled heterogenous shared memory architectures, such as mixed GPU/CPU architecture, and obtained tight lower and upper bounds for $O(n^3)$ matrix multiplication.

However, there is currently no systematic theoretic way of obtaining upper and lower bounds for arbitrary hardware models. Expanding such results to other architectures and algorithmic techniques is a challenging goal. For example, recursive algorithms tend to be cache oblivious and communication optimal for the sequential hierarchy model. Finding an equivalent technique that would work for an arbitrary architecture is a fundamental open problem.

---

[19]With the exception of a few results related to graph algorithms, e.g., in [MPP02] and in our [BDHS10b].

6. ACKNOWLEDGMENT

We thank Eran Rom, Edgar Solomonik, and Chris Umans for helpful discussions.

7. REFERENCES

[AP00]   N. Ahmed and K. Pingali. Automatic generation of block-recursive codes. In *Euro-Par '00: Proceedings from the 6th International Euro-Par Conference on Parallel Processing*, pages 368–378, London, UK, 2000. Springer-Verlag.

[ASS08]   N. Alon, O. Schwartz, and A. Shapira. An elementary construction of constant-degree expanders. *Combinatorics, Probability & Computing*, 17(3):319–327, 2008.

[AV88]   A. Aggarwal and J. S. Vitter. The input/output complexity of sorting and related problems. *Commun. ACM*, 31(9):1116–1127, 1988.

[Bai88]   D. H. Bailey. Extra-high speed matrix multiplication on the Cray-2. *SIAM J. Sci. Stat. Comput*, 9:603–607, 1988.

[BBF+07]   M. A. Bender, G. S. Brodal, R. Fagerberg, R. Jacob, and E. Vicari. Optimal sparse matrix dense vector multiplication in the I/O-model. In *SPAA '07: Proceedings of the nineteenth annual ACM symposium on Parallel algorithms and architectures*, pages 61–70, New York, NY, USA, 2007. ACM.

[BCG+08]   G. E. Blelloch, R. A. Chowdhury, P. B. Gibbons, V. Ramachandran, S. Chen, and M. Kozuch. Provably good multicore cache performance for divide-and-conquer algorithms. In *SODA '08: Proceedings of the nineteenth annual ACM-SIAM symposium on Discrete algorithms*, pages 501–510, Philadelphia, PA, USA, 2008. Society for Industrial and Applied Mathematics.

[BCS97]   P. Bürgisser, M. Clausen, and M. A. Shokrollahi. *Algebraic Complexity Theory*. Number 315 in Grundlehren der mathematischen Wissenschaften. Springer Verlag, 1997.

[BDG11]   G. Ballard, J. Demmel, and A. Gearhart. Communication bounds for heterogeneous architectures. In *23rd ACM Symposium on Parallelism in Algorithms and Architectures (SPAA 2011)*, 2011. (to appear as a "brief announcement").

[BDH+11]   G. Ballard, J. Demmel, O. Holtz, E. Rom, and O. Schwartz. Communication-Minimizing Parallel Implementation for Strassen's Algorithm. Unpublished, 2011.

[BDHS10a] G. Ballard, J. Demmel, O. Holtz, and O. Schwartz. Communication-optimal parallel and sequential Cholesky decomposition. *SIAM Journal on Scientific Computing*, 32(6):3495–3523, December 2010.

[BDHS10b] G. Ballard, J. Demmel, O. Holtz, and O. Schwartz. Minimizing communication in linear algebra. Submitted. Available from http://arxiv.org/abs/0905.2485, 2010.

[BDHS11a] G. Ballard, J. Demmel, O. Holtz, and O. Schwartz. Minimizing Communication in Fast Linear Algebra. Unpublished, 2011.

[BDHS11b] G. Ballard, J. Demmel, O. Holtz, and O. Schwartz. Revisiting Coppersmith's "Rectangular matrix multiplication revisited" for I/O-Complexity. Unpublished, 2011.

[BDHS11c] G. Ballard, J. Demmel, O. Holtz, and O. Schwartz. The Communication Costs of Hybrid Algorithms for Fast Matrix Multiplication. Unpublished, 2011.

[Bin80]   D. Bini. Relations between exact and approximate bilinear algorithms. applications. *Calcolo*, 17:87–97, 1980. 10.1007/BF02575865.

[BP99]   G. Bilardi and F. Preparata. Processor-time tradeoffs under bounded-speed message propagation: Part II, lower boundes. *Theory of Computing Systems*, 32(5):1432–4350, 1999.

[BPD00]   G. Bilardi, A. Pietracaprina, and P. D'Alberto. On the space and access complexity of computation DAGs. In *WG '00: Proceedings of the 26th International Workshop on Graph-Theoretic Concepts in Computer Science*, pages 47–58, London, UK, 2000. Springer-Verlag.

[BZ88]   Y. D. Burago and V. A. Zalgaller. *Geometric Inequalities*, volume 285 of *Grundlehren der Mathematische Wissenschaften*. Springer, Berlin, 1988.

[Can69]   L. Cannon. *A cellular computer to implement the Kalman filter algorithm*. PhD thesis, Montana State University, Bozeman, MN, 1969.

[CKSU05]   H. Cohn, R. D. Kleinberg, B. Szegedy, and C. Umans. Group-theoretic algorithms for matrix multiplication. In *FOCS*, pages 379–388, 2005.

[Cop97]   D. Coppersmith. Rectangular matrix multiplication revisited. *J. Complex.*, 13:42–49, March 1997.

[CR06]   R. A. Chowdhury and V. Ramachandran. Cache-oblivious dynamic programming. In *SODA '06: Proceedings of the seventeenth annual ACM-SIAM symposium on Discrete algorithm*, pages 591–600, New York, NY, USA, 2006. ACM.

[CW82]   D. Coppersmith and S. Winograd. On the asymptotic complexity of matrix multiplication. *SIAM Journal on Computing*, 11(3):472–492, 1982.

[CW87]   D. Coppersmith and S. Winograd. Matrix multiplication via arithmetic progressions. In *Proceedings of the nineteenth annual ACM symposium on Theory of computing*, STOC '87, pages 1–6, New York, NY, USA, 1987. ACM.

[CW90]   D. Coppersmith and S. Winograd. Matrix multiplication via arithmetic progressions. *J. Symb. Comput.*, 9(3):251–280, 1990.

[DHSS94]   C. C. Douglas, M. Heroux, G. Slishman, and R. M. Smith. GEMMW: A portable level 3 BLAS Winograd variant of Strassen's matrix-matrix multiply algorithm. *Journal of Computational Physics*, 110(1):1–10, 1994.

[DS04] F. Desprez and F. Suter. Impact of mixed-parallelism on parallel implementations of the Strassen and Winograd matrix multiplication algorithms: Research articles. *Concurrency and Computation: Practice and Experience*, 16(8):771–797, 2004.

[FLPR99] M. Frigo, C. E. Leiserson, H. Prokop, and S. Ramachandran. Cache-oblivious algorithms. In *FOCS '99: Proceedings of the 40th Annual Symposium on Foundations of Computer Science*, page 285, Washington, DC, USA, 1999. IEEE Computer Society.

[GSP04] S. L. Graham, M. Snir, and C. A. Patterson, editors. *Getting up to Speed: The Future of Supercomputing*. Report of National Research Council of the National Academies Sciences. The National Academies Press, Washington, D.C., 2004. 289 pages, http://www.nap.edu.

[HK81] J. W. Hong and H. T. Kung. I/O complexity: The red-blue pebble game. In *STOC '81: Proceedings of the thirteenth annual ACM symposium on Theory of computing*, pages 326–333, New York, NY, USA, 1981. ACM.

[HLJJ+96] S. Huss-Lederman, E. M. Jacobson, J. R. Johnson, A. Tsao, and T. Turnbull. Implementation of Strassen's algorithm for matrix multiplication. In *Supercomputing '96: Proceedings of the 1996 ACM/IEEE conference on Supercomputing (CDROM)*, page 32, Washington, DC, USA, 1996. IEEE Computer Society.

[ITT04] D. Irony, S. Toledo, and A. Tiskin. Communication lower bounds for distributed-memory matrix multiplication. *J. Parallel Distrib. Comput.*, 64(9):1017–1026, 2004.

[KKK10] M. Koucky, V. Kabanets, and A. Kolokolova. Expanders made elementary, 2010. In preparation, Available from http://www.cs.sfu.ca/~kabanets/papers/expanders.pdf.

[Lei08] C. E. Leiserson. Personal communication with G. Ballard, J. Demmel, O. Holtz, and O. Schwartz, 2008.

[LV83] G. Lev and L. G. Valiant. Size bounds for superconcentrators. *Theoretical Computer Science*, 22(3):233–251, 1983.

[LW49] L. H. Loomis and H. Whitney. An inequality related to the isoperimetric inequality. *Bulletin of the AMS*, 55:961–962, 1949.

[Mih89] M. Mihail. Conductance and convergence of Markov chains: A combinatorial treatment of expanders. In *Proceedings of the Thirtieth Annual IEEE Symposium on Foundations of Computer Science*, pages 526–Ǔ531, 1989.

[MPP02] J. P. Michael, M. Penner, and V. K. Prasanna. Optimizing graph algorithms for improved cache performance. In *Proc. Int'l Parallel and Distributed Processing Symp. (IPDPS 2002)*, Fort Lauderdale, FL, pages 769–782, 2002.

[Pan80] V. Y. Pan. New fast algorithms for matrix operations. *SIAM Journal on Computing*, 9(2):321–342, 1980.

[Raz03] R. Raz. On the complexity of matrix product. *SIAM J. Comput.*, 32(5):1356–1369 (electronic), 2003.

[Rom82] F. Romani. Some properties of disjoint sums of tensors related to matrix multiplication. *SIAM Journal on Computing*, 11(2):263–267, 1982.

[RVW02] O. Reingold, S. Vadhan, and A. Wigderson. Entropy waves, the zig-zag graph product, and new constant-degree expanders. *Annals of Mathematics*, 155(1):157–187, 2002.

[Sav94] J. Savage. Space-time tradeoffs in memory hierarchies. Technical report, Brown University, Providence, RI, USA, 1994.

[Sch81] A. Schönhage. Partial and total matrix multiplication. *SIAM Journal on Computing*, 10(3):434–455, 1981.

[Str69] V. Strassen. Gaussian elimination is not optimal. *Numer. Math.*, 13:354–356, 1969.

[Str87] V. Strassen. Relative bilinear complexity and matrix multiplication. *Journal für die reine und angewandte Mathematik (Crelles Journal)*, 1987(375–376):406–443, 1987.

[Tol97] S. Toledo. Locality of reference in LU decomposition with partial pivoting. *SIAM J. Matrix Anal. Appl.*, 18(4):1065–1081, 1997.

[VD08] V. Volkov and J. Demmel. Benchmarking GPUs to tune dense linear algebra. In *SC '08: Proceedings of the 2008 ACM/IEEE conference on Supercomputing*, pages 1–11, Piscataway, NJ, USA, 2008. IEEE Press.

[Win71] S. Winograd. On the multiplication of 2 × 2 matrices. *Linear Algebra Appl.*, 4(4):381–388., October 1971.

[YM88] C.-Q. Yang and B.P. Miller. Critical path analysis for the execution of parallel and distributed programs. In *Proceedings of the 8th International Conference on Distributed Computing Systems*, pages 366–373, Jun. 1988.

APPENDIX

A. EXPANSION ESTIMATION BY GRAPH DECOMPOSITION

DEFINITION 1 (GRAPH DECOMPOSITION). *We say that the set of graphs $\{G_i' = (V_i, E_i)\}_{i \in [l]}$ is an edge-disjoint decomposition of $G = (V, E)$ if $V = \bigcup_i V_i$ and $E = \biguplus_i E_i$.*

PROOF. (of Claim 5) Let $U \subseteq V$ be of size $U \leq |V'|/2$. Let $\{G_i' = (V_i, E_i)\}_{i \in [l]}$ be an edge-disjoint decomposition of G, where every G_i is isomorphic to G'. Then

$$
\begin{aligned}
|E_G(U, V \setminus U)| &= \sum_{i \in [l]} |E_{G_i'}(U_i, V_i \setminus U_i)| \geq \sum_{i \in [l]} h(G_i') \cdot d' \cdot |U_i| \\
&= h(G') \cdot d' \cdot \sum_{i \in [l]} |U_i| \geq h(G') \cdot d' \cdot |U| .
\end{aligned}
$$

Therefore $\frac{|E_G(U, V \setminus U)|}{d \cdot |U|} \geq h(G') \cdot \frac{d'}{d}$. □

10

B. STRASSEN'S FAST MATRIX MULTIPLICATION ALGORITHM

Strassen's original algorithm follows [Str69]. See [Win71] for Winograd's variant, which reduces the number of additions.

Algorithm 1 Matrix Multiplication: Strassen's Algorithm

Input: Two $n \times n$ matrices, A and B.

1: **if** $n = 1$ **then**
2:     $C_{11} = A_{11} \cdot B_{11}$
3: **else**
4:     {Decompose A into four equal square blocks $A = \begin{pmatrix} A_{11} & A_{12} \\ A_{21} & A_{22} \end{pmatrix}$
    and the same for B.}
5:     $M_1 = (A_{11} + A_{22}) \cdot (B_{11} + B_{22})$
6:     $M_2 = (A_{21} + A_{22}) \cdot B_{11}$
7:     $M_3 = A_{11} \cdot (B_{12} - B_{22})$
8:     $M_4 = A_{22} \cdot (B_{21} - B_{11})$
9:     $M_5 = (A_{11} + A_{12}) \cdot B_{22}$
10:     $M_6 = (A_{21} - A_{11}) \cdot (B_{11} + B_{12})$
11:     $M_7 = (A_{12} - A_{22}) \cdot (B_{21} + B_{22})$
12:     $C_{11} = M_1 + M_4 - M_5 + M_7$
13:     $C_{12} = M_3 + M_5$
14:     $C_{21} = M_2 + M_4$
15:     $C_{22} = M_1 - M_2 + M_3 + M_6$
16: **end if**
17: **return** C

See [DHSS94, HLJJ$^+$96, Bai88] for implementation issues of Strassen's algorithm.

Near Linear-Work Parallel SDD Solvers, Low-Diameter Decomposition, and Low-Stretch Subgraphs

Guy E. Blelloch   Anupam Gupta   Ioannis Koutis[†]   Gary L. Miller
Richard Peng   Kanat Tangwongsan

Carnegie Mellon University and [†]University of Puerto Rico, Rio Piedras
{guyb, anupamg, i.koutis, glmiller, yangp, ktangwon}@cs.cmu.edu

ABSTRACT

This paper presents the design and analysis of a near linear-work parallel algorithm for solving symmetric diagonally dominant (SDD) linear systems. On input of a SDD n-by-n matrix A with m non-zero entries and a vector b, our algorithm computes a vector $\tilde{x}$ such that $\|\tilde{x} - A^+b\|_A \leq \varepsilon \cdot \|A^+b\|_A$ in $O(m \log^{O(1)} n \log \frac{1}{\varepsilon})$ work and $O(m^{1/3+\theta} \log \frac{1}{\varepsilon})$ depth for any fixed $\theta > 0$.

The algorithm relies on a parallel algorithm for generating low-stretch spanning trees or spanning subgraphs. To this end, we first develop a parallel decomposition algorithm that in polylogarithmic depth and $\tilde{O}(|E|)$ work[1], partitions a graph into components with polylogarithmic diameter such that only a small fraction of the original edges are between the components. This can be used to generate low-stretch spanning trees with average stretch $O(n^\alpha)$ in $O(n^{1+\alpha})$ work and $O(n^\alpha)$ depth. Alternatively, it can be used to generate spanning subgraphs with polylogarithmic average stretch in $\tilde{O}(|E|)$ work and polylogarithmic depth. We apply this subgraph construction to derive our solver.

By using the linear system solver in known applications, our results imply improved parallel randomized algorithms for several problems, including single-source shortest paths, maximum flow, min-cost flow, and approximate max-flow.

Categories and Subject Descriptors

F.2 [**Theory of Computation**]: Analysis of Algorithms and Problem Complexity

General Terms

Algorithms, Theory

Keywords

Parallel algorithms, linear systems, low-stretch spanning trees, low-stretch subgraphs, low-diameter decomposition

---

[1]The $\tilde{O}(\cdot)$ notion hides polylogarithmic factors.

1. INTRODUCTION

Solving a system of linear equations $Ax = b$ is a fundamental computing primitive that lies at the core of many numerical and scientific computing algorithms, including the popular interior-point algorithms. The special case of symmetric diagonally dominant (SDD) systems has seen substantial progress in recent years; in particular, the ground-breaking work of Spielman and Teng showed how to solve SDD systems to accuracy ε in time $\tilde{O}(m \log(1/\varepsilon))$, where m is the number of non-zeros in the $n \times n$-matrix A.[2] This is algorithmically significant since solving SDD systems has implications to computing eigenvectors, solving flow problems, finding graph sparsifiers, and problems in vision and graphics (see [Spi10, Ten10] for these and other applications).

In the sequential setting, the current best SDD solvers run in $O(m \log^2 n (\log \log n)^{O(1)} \log(1/\varepsilon))$ time [KMP10]. However, with the exception of the special case of planar SDD systems [KM07], we know of no previous parallel SDD solvers that perform near-linear[3] work and achieve non-trivial parallelism. This raises a natural question: *Is it possible to solve an SDD linear system in $o(n)$ depth and $\tilde{O}(m)$ work?* We answer this question affirmatively:

Theorem 1.1 *For any fixed $\theta > 0$ and any $\varepsilon > 0$, there is an algorithm* SDDSolve *that on input an $n \times n$ SDD matrix A with m non-zero elements and a vector b, computes a vector $\tilde{x}$ such that $\|\tilde{x} - A^+b\|_A \leq \varepsilon \cdot \|A^+b\|_A$ in $O(m \log^{O(1)} n \log \frac{1}{\varepsilon})$ work and $O(m^{1/3+\theta} \log \frac{1}{\varepsilon})$ depth.*

In the process, we give parallel algorithms for constructing graph decompositions with strong-diameter guarantees, and parallel algorithms to construct low-stretch spanning trees and low-stretch ultra-sparse subgraphs, which may be of independent interest. An overview of these algorithms and their underlying techniques is given in Section 3.

Some Applications. Let us mention some of the implications of Theorem 1.1, obtained by plugging it into known reductions.

— Construction of Spectral Sparsifiers. Spielman and Srivastava [SS08] showed that spectral sparsifiers can be constructed using $O(\log n)$ Laplacian solves, and using our theorem we get spectral and cut sparsifiers in $\tilde{O}(m^{1/3+\theta})$ depth and $\tilde{O}(m)$ work.

— Flow Problems. Daitsch and Spielman [DS08] showed that various graph optimization problems, such as max-flow, min-cost

---

[2]The Spielman-Teng solver and all subsequent improvements are randomized algorithms. As a consequence, all algorithms relying on the solvers are also randomized. For simplicity, we omit standard complexity factors related to the probability of error.
[3]i.e. linear up to polylog factors.

flow, and lossy flow problems, can be reduced to $\tilde{O}(m^{1/2})$ applications[4] of SDD solves via interior point methods described in [Ye97, Ren01, BV04]. Combining this with our main theorem implies that these algorithms can be parallelized to run in $\tilde{O}(m^{5/6+\theta})$ depth and $\tilde{O}(m^{3/2})$ work. This gives the first parallel algorithm with $o(n)$ depth which is work-efficient to within polylog(n) factors relative to the sequential algorithm for all problems analyzed in [DS08]. In some sense, the parallel bounds are more interesting than the sequential times because in many cases the results in [DS08] are not the best known sequentially (e.g. max-flow)—but do lead to the best know parallel bounds for problems that have traditionally been hard to parallelize. Finally, we note that although [DS08] does not explicitly analyze shortest path, their analysis naturally generalizes the LP for it.

2. PRELIMINARIES AND NOTATION

Throughout the paper, we use the notation $\tilde{O}(f(n))$ to mean $O(f(n) \, \text{polylog}(f(n)))$. We use $A \uplus B$ to denote disjoint unions, and $[k]$ to denote the set $\{1, 2, \ldots, k\}$. Given a graph $G = (V, E)$, let $dist(u, v)$ denote the *edge-count distance* (or hop distance) between u and v, ignoring the edge lengths. When the graph has edge lengths $w(e)$ (also denoted by w_e), let $d_G(u, v)$ denote the *edge-length distance*, the shortest path (according to these edge lengths) between u and v. If the graph has unit edge lengths, the two definitions coincide. We drop subscripts when the context is clear. We denote by $V(G)$ and $E(G)$, respectively, the set of nodes and the set of edges, and use $n = |V(G)|$ and $m = |E(G)|$. For an edge $e = \{u, v\}$, the stretch of e on G' is $\text{str}_{G'}(e) = d_{G'}(u, v)/w(e)$. The *total stretch* of $G = (V, E, w)$ with respect to G' is $\text{str}_{G'}(E(G)) = \sum_{e \in E(G)} \text{str}_{G'}(e)$.

Given $G = (V, E)$, a distance function δ (which is either *dist* or *d*), and a partition of V into $C_1 \uplus C_2 \uplus \ldots \uplus C_p$, let $G[C_i]$ denote the induced subgraph on set C_i. The *weak diameter* of C_i is $\max_{u,v \in C_i} \delta_G(u, v)$, whereas the *strong diameter* of C_i is $\max_{u,v \in C_i} \delta_{G[C_i]}(u, v)$; the former measures distances in the original graph whereas the latter measures distances within the induced subgraph. The strong (or weak) diameter of the partition is the maximum strong (or weak) diameter over all the components C_i's.

Graph Laplacians. For a fixed, but arbitrary, numbering of the nodes and edges in a graph $G = (V, E)$, the Laplacian L_G of G is the $|V|$-by-$|V|$ matrix given by

$$L_G(i, j) = \begin{cases} -w_{ij} & \text{if } i \neq j \\ \sum_{\{j,i\} \in E(G)} w_{ij} & \text{if } i = j \end{cases},$$

When the context is clear, we use G and L_G interchangeably. Given two graphs G and H and a scalar $\mu \in \mathbb{R}$, we say $G \preceq \mu H$ if $\mu L_H - L_G$ is positive semidefinite, or equivalently $x^\top L_G x \leq \mu x^\top L_H x$ for all vector $x \in \mathbb{R}^{|V|}$.

Matrix Norms, SDD Matrices. For a matrix A, we denote by A^+ the Moore-Penrose pseudoinverse of A (i.e., A^+ has the same null space as A and acts as the inverse of A on its image). Given a symmetric positive semi-definite matrix A, the A-*norm* of a vector x is defined as $\|x\|_A = \sqrt{x^\top A x}$. A matrix A is symmetrically diagonally dominant (SDD) if it is symmetric and for all i, $A_{i,i} \geq \sum_{j \neq i} |A_{i,j}|$. Solving an SDD system reduces in $O(m)$ work and $O(\log^{O(1)} m)$ depth to solving a graph Laplacian (a subclass of SDD matrices corresponding to undirected weighted graphs) [Gre96, Section 7.1].

Parallel Models. We analyze algorithms in the standard PRAM model, focusing on the work and depth parameters of the algorithms. By *work*, we mean the total operation count—and by *depth*, we mean the longest chain of dependencies (i.e., parallel time in PRAM).

Parallel Ball Growing. Let $B_G(s, r)$ denote the ball of edge-count distance r from a source s, i.e., $B_G(s, r) = \{v \in V(G) : dist_G(s, v) \leq r\}$. We rely on an elementary form of parallel breadth-first search to compute $B_G(s, r)$. The algorithm visits the nodes level by level as they are encountered in the BFS order. More precisely, level 0 contains only the source node s, level 1 contains the neighbors of s, and each subsequent level $i + 1$ contains the neighbors of level i's nodes that have not shown up in a previous level. On standard parallel models (e.g., CRCW), this can be computed in $O(r \log n)$ depth and $O(m')$ work, where m' is the total number of edges encountered in the search. Our applications apply ball growing on r roughly $O(\log^{O(1)} n)$, resulting in a small depth bound. The alternative approach of repeatedly squaring a matrix gives a better depth bound for large r *at the expense* of a much larger work bound (about n^3). The idea of small-radius parallel ball growing has previously been employed in the context of approximate shortest paths (see, e.g., [KS97, Coh00]).

3. OVERVIEW OF OUR TECHNIQUES

In the general solver framework of Spielman and Teng [ST06, KMP10], near linear-time SDD solvers rely on a suitable preconditioning chain of progressively smaller graphs. Assuming that we have an algorithm for generating low-stretch spanning trees, the algorithm as given in [KMP10] parallelizes under the following modifications: (i) perform the partial Cholesky factorization in parallel and (ii) terminate the preconditioning chain with a graph that is of size approximately $m^{1/3}$. The details in Section 6 are the primary motivation of the main technical part of the paper, a parallel implementation of a modified version of Alon et al.'s low-stretch spanning tree algorithm [AKPW95].

More specifically, as a first step, we find an embedding of graphs into a spanning tree with average stretch $2^{O(\sqrt{\log n \log \log n})}$ in $\tilde{O}(m)$ work and $O(2^{O(\sqrt{\log n \log \log n})} \log \Delta)$ depth, where Δ is the ratio of the largest to smallest distance in the graph. The original AKPW algorithm relies on a parallel graph decomposition scheme of Awerbuch [Awe85], which takes an unweighted graph and breaks it into components with a specified diameter and few crossing edges. While such schemes are known in the sequential setting, they do not parallelize readily because removing edges belonging to one component might increase the diameter or even disconnect subsequent components. We present the first near linear-work parallel decomposition algorithm that also gives strong-diameter guarantees, in Section 4, and the tree embedding results in Section 5.1.

Ideally, we would have liked for our spanning trees to have a polylogarithmic stretch, computable by a polylogarithmic depth, near linear-work algorithm. However, for our solvers, we make the additional observation that we do not really need a spanning *tree* with small stretch; it suffices to give an "ultra-sparse" graph with small stretch, one that has only $O(m/\text{polylog}(n))$ edges more than a tree. Hence, we present a parallel algorithm in Section 5.2 which outputs an ultra-sparse graph with $O(\text{polylog}(n))$ average stretch, performing $\tilde{O}(m)$ work with $O(\text{polylog}(n))$ depth. Note that this removes the dependence of $\log \Delta$ in the depth, and reduces both the stretch and the depth from $2^{O(\sqrt{\log n \log \log n})}$ to $O(\text{polylog}(n))$.[5]

---

[4] here $\tilde{O}$ hides $\log U$ factors as well, where it's assumed that the edge weights are integers in the range $[1 \ldots U]$

[5] As an aside, this construction of low-stretch ultra-sparse graphs shows how to obtain the $\tilde{O}(m)$-time linear system solver of Spielman and Teng [ST06] without using their low-stretch spanning trees result [EEST05, ABN08].

When combined with the aforementioned routines for constructing a SDD solver presented in Section 6, this low-stretch spanning subgraph construction yields a parallel solver algorithm.

4. PARALLEL LOW-DIAMETER DECOMPOSITION

In this section, we present a parallel algorithm for partitioning a graph into components with low (strong) diameter while cutting only a few edges in each of the k disjoint subsets of the input edges. The sequential version of this algorithm is at the heart of the AKPW low-stretch spanning tree algorithm [AKPW95].

The outer layer of the AKPW algorithm (cf. Section 5) can be viewed as bucketing the input edges by weight, then partitioning and contracting them repeatedly. In this view, a number of edge classes are "reduced" simultaneously in an iteration. Further, as we are required to output a tree at the end, the components need to have low strong-diameter (i.e., one could not take "shortcuts" through other components). In the sequential case, this requirement is met by removing components one after another; though, this does not parallelize readily. We deal with this issue by growing balls from multiple sites and assigning vertices to the first region that reaches them. With suitable "jitters" in the start time, we can lower the probability of an edge going across two regions. This probability also depends on the number of regions that could reach such an edge. To keep this number small, we use a repeated sampling procedure motivated by Cohen's (β, W)-cover construction [Coh93].

The pseudocode of our algorithm is presented in Algorithm 4.1. For this algorithm, the graph G is unweighted and E is composed of k edge classes $E_1 \uplus \cdots \uplus E_k$. As defined earlier, $dist_{G[C_i]}(\cdot, \cdot)$ measures the edge-count shortest-path distance (i.e., hop count) in the graph induced on the component C_i. We use $dist^{(t)}$ as shorthand for $dist_{G_t}$, and also define $B^{(t)}(u, r) \stackrel{\text{def}}{=} B_{G^{(t)}}(u, r) = \{v \in V^{(t)} : dist^{(t)}(u, v) \le r\}$. (Note that $X^{(t)} = \cup_{s \in S^{(t)}} B^{(t)}(s, r^{(t)} - \delta_s^{(t)})$ in Steps ??–??) We define $E_j^{(t)} := E^{(t)} \cap E_j$ for all $j \in [k]$.

Algorithm 4.1 Partition $(G = (V, E = E_1 \uplus \cdots \uplus E_k), \rho)$ — Partition an input graph G into components of radius at most ρ.

Let $G^{(1)} = (V^{(1)}, E^{(1)}) \leftarrow G$. Define $R = \rho/(2 \log n)$. Create empty collection of components $\mathcal{C}$.

For $t = 1, 2, \ldots, T = 2 \log_2 n$,

1. Randomly sample $S^{(t)} \subseteq V^{(t)}$, where $|S^{(t)}| = \sigma_t = 12 n^{t/T-1} |V^{(t)}| \log n$, or use $S^{(t)} = V^{(t)}$ if $|V^{(t)}| < \sigma_t$.

2. For each "center" $s \in S^{(t)}$, draw $\delta_s^{(t)}$ uniformly at random from $\mathbb{Z} \cap [0, R]$.

3. Let $r^{(t)} \leftarrow (T - t + 1)R$.

4. For each center $s \in S^{(t)}$, compute the ball $B_s^{(t)} = B^{(t)}(s, r^{(t)} - \delta_s^{(t)})$.

5. Let $X^{(t)} = \cup_{s \in S^{(t)}} B_s^{(t)}$.

6. Create components $\{C_s^{(t)} \mid s \in S^{(t)}\}$ by assigning each $u \in X^{(t)}$ to the component $C_s^{(t)}$ such that s minimizes $dist_{G^{(t)}}(u, s) + \delta_s^{(t)}$ (breaking ties lexicographically).

7. Add non-empty $C_s^{(t)}$ components to $\mathcal{C}$.

8. Set $V^{(t+1)} \leftarrow V^{(t)} \setminus X^{(t)}$, and let $G^{(t+1)} \leftarrow G^{(t)}[V^{(t+1)}]$. Quit early if $V^{(t+1)}$ is empty.

If there is some i such that E_i has more than $|E_i| \frac{c_1 \cdot k \log^3 n}{\rho}$ edges between components, restart from the beginning. (Recall that k was the number of edge classes.)

Return $\mathcal{C}$.

The main theorem of this section is the following:

Theorem 4.1 (Parallel Low-Diameter Decomposition) *Given an input graph $G = (V, E_1 \uplus \ldots \uplus E_k)$ with k edge classes and a "radius" parameter ρ, the algorithm* Partition(G, ρ) *outputs a partition of V into components $\mathcal{C} = (C_1, C_2, \ldots, C_p)$, each with center s_i such that*

1. *the center $s_i \in C_i$ for all $i \in [p]$,*

2. *for each i, every $u \in C_i$ satisfies $dist_{G[C_i]}(s_i, u) \le \rho$, and*

3. *for all $j = 1, \ldots, k$, the number of edges in E_j that go between components is at most $|E_j| \cdot \frac{c_1 \cdot k \log^3 n}{\rho}$, where c_1 is an absolute constant.*

Furthermore, Partition *runs in $O(m \log^2 n)$ expected work and $O(\rho \log^2 n)$ expected depth.*

Before proceeding with the analysis, we point out that it is possible for some component $C_s^{(t)}$ to remain empty in Step 6; indeed, because of the "jitter" terms $\delta_i^{(t)}$, some sampled vertex $s \in S^{(t)}$ may be assigned to $C_{s'}^{(t)}$ rather than $C_s^{(t)}$.

We begin by proving properties (1)–(2) of Theorem 4.1. First, we state an easy-to-verify fact:

Fact 4.2 *If vertex u lies in component $C_s^{(t)}$, then $dist^{(t)}(s, u) \le r^{(t)}$. Moreover, $u \in B_s^{(t)}$.*

We also need the following lemma to argue about strong diameter.

Lemma 4.3 *If vertex $u \in C_s^{(t)}$, and vertex $v \in V^{(t)}$ lies on any u-s shortest path in $G^{(t)}$, then $v \in C_s^{(t)}$.*

PROOF. Since $u \in C_s^{(t)}$, Fact 4.2 implies u belongs to $B_s^{(t)}$. But $dist^{(t)}(v, i) < dist^{(t)}(u, i)$, and hence v belongs to $B_s^{(t)}$ and $X^{(t)}$ as well. This implies that v is assigned to *some* component $C_j^{(t)}$; we claim $j = s$.

For a contradiction, assume that $j \ne s$, and hence $dist^{(t)}(v, j) + \delta_j^{(t)} \le dist^{(t)}(v, s) + \delta_s^{(t)}$. In this case $dist^{(t)}(u, j) + \delta_j^{(t)} \le dist^{(t)}(u, v) + dist^{(t)}(v, j) + \delta_j^{(t)}$ (by the triangle inequality). Now using the assumption, this expression is at most $dist^{(t)}(u, v) + dist^{(t)}(v, s) + \delta_s^{(t)} = dist^{(t)}(u, s) + \delta_s^{(t)}$ (since v lies on the shortest u-s path). But then, u would be also assigned to $C_j^{(t)}$, a contradiction. □

Hence, for each non-empty component $C_s^{(t)}$, its center s lies within the component (since it lies on the shortest path from s to any $u \in C_s^{(t)}$), which proves Theorem 4.1(1). Moreover, by Fact 4.2 and Lemma 4.3, the (strong) radius is at most TR, proving Theorem 4.1(2). It now remains to prove the third property, and the work and depth bounds.

Lemma 4.4 *For any vertex $u \in V$, with probability at least $1 - n^{-6}$, there are at most $68 \log^2 n$ pairs[6] (s, t) such that $s \in S^{(t)}$ and $u \in B^{(t)}(s, r^{(t)})$,*

We will prove this lemma in a series of claims.

Claim 4.5 *For $t \in [T]$ and $v \in V^{(t)}$, if $|B^{(t)}(v, r^{(t+1)})| \ge n^{1-t/T}$, then $v \in X^{(t)}$ w.p. at least $1 - n^{-12}$.*

---

[6] In fact, for a given s, there is a unique t—if this s is ever chosen as a "starting point."

15

PROOF. First, note that for any $s \in S^{(t)}$, $r^{(t)} - \delta_s \geq r^{(t)} - R = r^{(t+1)}$, and so if $s \in B^{(t)}(v, r^{(t+1)})$, then $v \in B_s^{(t)}$ and hence in $X^{(t)}$. Therefore, $\mathbf{Pr}\left[v \in X^{(t)}\right] \geq \mathbf{Pr}\left[S^{(t)} \cap B^{(t)}(v, r^{(t+1)}) \neq \emptyset\right]$, the probability that a random subset of $V^{(t)}$ of size σ_t hits the ball $B^{(t)}(v, r^{(t+1)})$. But, $\mathbf{Pr}\left[S^{(t)} \cap B^{(t)}(v, r^{(t+1)}) \neq \emptyset\right] \geq 1 - \left(1 - \frac{|B^{(t)}(v, r^{(t+1)})|}{|V^{(t)}|}\right)^{\sigma_t}$, which is at least $1 - n^{-12}$. $\square$

Claim 4.6 *For $t \in [T]$ and $v \in V$, the number of $s \in S^{(t)}$ such that $v \in B(s, r^{(t)})$ is at most $34 \log n$ w.p. at least $1 - n^{-8}$.*

PROOF. For $t = 1$, the size $\sigma_1 = O(\log n)$ and hence the claim follows trivially. For $t \geq 2$, we condition on all the choices made in rounds $1, 2, \ldots, t-2$. Note that if v does not survive in $V^{(t-1)}$, then it does not belong to $V^{(t)}$ either, and the claim is immediate. So, consider two cases, depending on the size of the ball $B^{(t-1)}(v, r^{(t)})$ in iteration $t - 1$:

— *Case 1.* If $|B^{(t-1)}(v, r^{(t)})| \geq n^{1-(t-1)/T}$, then by Claim 3.5, with probability at least $1 - n^{-12}$, we have $v \in X^{(t-1)}$, so v would *not* belong to $V^{(t)}$ and this means **no** $s \in S^{(t)}$ will satisfy $v \in B^{(t)}(s, r^{(t)})$, proving the claim for this case.

— *Case 2.* Otherwise, $|B^{(t-1)}(v, r^{(t)})| < n^{1-(t-1)/T}$. We have $|B^{(t)}(v, r^{(t)})| \leq |B^{(t-1)}(v, r^{(t)})| < n^{1-(t-1)/T}$ as $B^{(t)}(v, r^{(t)}) \subseteq B^{(t-1)}(v, r^{(t)})$. Now let X be the number of s such that $v \in B^{(t)}(s, r^{(t)})$, so $X = \sum_{s \in S^{(t)}} \mathbf{1}_{\{s \in B^{(t)}(v, r^{(t)})\}}$. Over the random choice of $S^{(t)}$,

$$\mathbf{Pr}\left[s \in B^{(t)}(v, r^{(t)})\right] = \frac{|B^{(t)}(v, r^{(t)})|}{|V^{(t)}|} \leq \frac{1}{|V^{(t)}|} n^{1-(t-1)/T},$$

which gives

$$\mathbf{E}[X] = \sigma_t \cdot \mathbf{Pr}\left[s \in B^{(t)}(v, r^{(t)})\right] \leq 17 \log n.$$

To obtain a high probability bound for X, we will apply the tail bound in Lemma A.1. Note that X is simply a hypergeometric random variable with the following parameters setting: total balls $N = |V^{(t)}|$, red balls $M = |B^{(t)}(v, r^{(t)})|$, and the number balls drawn is σ_t. Therefore, $\mathbf{Pr}[X \geq 34 \log n] \leq \exp\{-\frac{1}{4} \cdot 34 \log n\}$, so $X \leq 34 \log n$ with probability at least $1 - n^{-8}$.

Hence, regardless of what choices we made in rounds $1, 2, \ldots, t-2$, the conditional probability of seeing more than $34 \log n$ different s's is at most n^{-8}. Hence, we can remove the conditioning, and the claim follows. $\square$

Lemma 4.7 *If for each vertex $u \in V$, there are at most $68 \log^2 n$ pairs (s, t) such that $s \in S^{(t)}$ and $u \in B^{(t)}(s, r^{(t)})$, then for an edge uv, the probability that u belongs to a different component than v is at most $68 \log^2 n / R$.*

PROOF. We define a center $s \in S^{(t)}$ as "separating" u and v if $|B_s^{(t)} \cap \{u, v\}| = 1$. Clearly, if u, v lie in different components then there is some $t \in [T]$ and some center s that separates them. For a center $s \in S^{(t)}$, this can happen only if $\delta_s = R - dist(s, u)$, since $dist(s, v) \leq dist(s, u) - 1$. As there are R possible values of δ_s, this event occurs with probability at most $1/R$. And since there are only $68 \log^2 n$ different centers s that can possibly cut the edge, using a trivial union bound over them gives us an upper bound of $68 \log^2 n / R$ on the probability. $\square$

By Markov's inequality and Lemma 4.4, which shows that the premise to Lemma 4.7 holds with probability exceeding $1 - o(1) \geq 1/2$, we have the following corollary:

Corollary 4.8 *With probability at least $1/4$, for all $i \in [k]$, the number of edges in E_i that are between components is at most $|E_i| \frac{136 k \log^2 n}{R}$.*

We now combine these lemmas to prove Theorem 4.1.

Proof of Theorem 4.1: Using $R = \rho/(2 \log n)$ and $c_1 = 136$, Corollary 4.8 gives that the last step should be successful with probability at least $1/4$. Therefore, the algorithm will pass the final check step in 4 rounds in expectation. Now consider the depth/work required each time the algorithm is run from the start to right before the final check step. Each computation of $B^{(t)}(v, r^{(t)})$ can be done using a BFS. Since $r^{(t)} \leq \rho$, the depth is bounded by $O(\rho \log n)$ per iteration. By Lemma 4.4, each vertex is reached by at most $O(\log^2 n)$ starting points, yielding a total work of $O(m \log^2 n)$. ∎

5. PARALLEL LOW-STRETCH SPANNING TREES AND SUBGRAPHS

This section presents parallel algorithms for low-stretch spanning trees and for low-stretch spanning subgraphs. To obtain the low-stretch spanning tree algorithm, we apply the construction of Alon et al. [AKPW95] (henceforth, the AKPW construction), together with the parallel graph partition algorithm from the previous section. The resulting procedure, however, is not ideal for two reasons: the depth of the algorithm depends on the "spread" Δ—the ratio between the heaviest edge and the lightest edge—and even for polynomial spread, both the depth and the average stretch are super-logarithmic (both of them have a $2^{O(\sqrt{\log n \cdot \log \log n})}$ term). Fortunately, for our application, we observe that we do not need spanning trees but merely low-stretch sparse graphs. In Section 5.2, we describe modifications to this construction to obtain a parallel algorithm which computes sparse subgraphs that give us only polylogarithmic average stretch and that can be computed in polylogarithmic depth and $\tilde{O}(m)$ work. We believe that this construction may be of independent interest.

5.1 Low-Stretch Spanning Trees

Using the AKPW construction, along with the `Partition` procedure from Section 4, we will prove the following theorem:

Theorem 5.1 (Low-Stretch Spanning Tree) *There is an algorithm* `AKPW(G)` *which given as input a graph $G = (V, E, w)$, produces a spanning tree in $O(\log^{O(1)} n \cdot 2^{O(\sqrt{\log n \cdot \log \log n})} \log \Delta)$ expected depth and $\tilde{O}(m)$ expected work such that the total stretch of all edges is bounded by $m \cdot 2^{O(\sqrt{\log n \cdot \log \log n})}$.*

Algorithm 5.1 `AKPW` $(G = (V, E, w))$ — a low-stretch spanning tree construction.

---
i. Normalize the edges so that $\min\{w(e) : e \in E\} = 1$.
ii. Let $y = 2^{\sqrt{6 \log n \cdot \log \log n}}$, $\tau = \lceil 3 \log(n)/\log y \rceil$, $z = 4 c_1 y \tau \log^3 n$. Initialize $T = \emptyset$.
iii. Divide E into $E_1, E_2, \ldots$, where $E_i = \{e \in E \mid w(e) \in [z^{i-1}, z^i)\}$.
   Let $E^{(1)} = E$ and $E_i^{(1)} = E_i$ for all i.
iv. For $j = 1, 2, \ldots$, until the graph is exhausted,
   1. $(C_1, C_2, \ldots, C_p) = $ `Partition`$((V^{(j)}, \uplus_{i \leq j} E_i^{(j)}), z/4)$
   2. Add a BFS tree of each component to T.
   3. Define graph $(V^{(j+1)}, E^{(j+1)})$ by contracting all edges within the components and removing all self-loops (but maintaining parallel edges). Create $E_i^{(j+1)}$ from $E_i^{(j)}$ taking into account the contractions.
v. Output the tree T.

Presented in Algorithm 5.1 is a restatement of the AKPW algorithm, except that here we will use our parallel low-diameter decomposition for the partition step. In words, iteration j of Algorithm 5.1 looks at a graph $(V^{(j)}, E^{(j)})$ which is a minor of the original graph (because components were contracted in previous iterations, and because it only considers the edges in the first j weight classes). It uses $\texttt{Partition}((V, \uplus_{j \leq k} E_j), z/4)$ to decompose this graph into components such that the hop radius is at most $z/4$ and each weight class has only $1/y$ fraction of its edges crossing between components. (Parameters y, z are defined in the algorithm and are slightly different from the original settings in the AKPW algorithm.) It then shrinks each of the components into a single node (while adding a BFS tree on that component to T), and iterates on this graph. Adding these BFS trees maintains the invariant that the set of original nodes which have been contracted into a (super-)node in the current graph are connected in T; hence, when the algorithm stops, we have a spanning tree of the original graph—hopefully of low total stretch.

We begin the analysis of the total stretch and running time by proving two useful facts:

Fact 5.2 *The number of edges* $|E_i^{(j)}|$ *is at most* $|E_i|/y^{j-i}$.

PROOF. If we could ensure that the number of weight classes in play at any time is at most τ, the number of edges in each class would fall by at least a factor of $\frac{c_1 \tau \log^3 n}{z/4} = 1/y$ by Theorem 4.1(3) and the definition of z, and this would prove the fact. Now, for the first τ iterations, the number of weight classes is at most τ just because we consider only the first j weight classes in iteration j. Now in iteration $\tau + 1$, the number of surviving edges of E_1 would fall to $|E_1|/y^\tau \leq |E_1|/n^3 < 1$, and hence there would only be τ weight classes left. It is easy to see that this invariant can be maintained over the course of the algorithm. □

Fact 5.3 *In iteration j, the radius of a component according to edge weights (in the expanded-out graph) is at most* z^{j+1}.

PROOF. The proof is by induction on j. First, note that by Theorem 4.1(2), each of the clusters computed in any iteration j has edge-count radius at most $z/4$. Now the base case $j = 1$ follows by noting that each edge in E_1 has weight less than z, giving a radius of at most $z^2/4 < z^{j+1}$. Now assume inductively that the radius in iteration $j - 1$ is at most z^j. Now any path with $z/4$ edges from the center to some node in the contracted graph will pass through at most $z/4$ edges of weight at most z^j, and at most $z/4 + 1$ supernodes, each of which adds a distance of $2z^j$; hence, the new radius is at most $z^{j+1}/4 + (z/4+1)2z^j \leq z^{j+1}$ as long as $z \geq 8$. □

Applying these facts, we bound the total stretch of an edge class.

Lemma 5.4 *For any $i \geq 1$,* $\mathsf{str}_T(E_i) \leq 4y^2|E_i|(4c_1\tau\log^3 n)^{\tau+1}$.

PROOF. Let e be an edge in E_i contracted during iteration j. Since $e \in E_i$, we know $w(e) > z^{i-1}$. By Fact 5.3, the path connecting the two endpoints of e in F has distance at most $2z^{j+1}$. Thus, $\mathsf{str}_T(e) \leq 2z^{j+1}/z^{i-1} = 2z^{j-i+2}$. Fact 5.2 indicates that the number of such edges is at most $|E_i^{(j)}| \leq |E_i|/y^{j-i}$. We conclude that

$$\mathsf{str}_T(E_i) \leq \sum_{j=i}^{i+\tau-1} 2z^{j-i+2}|E_i|/y^{j-i}$$
$$\leq 4y^2|E_i|(4c_1\tau\log^3 n)^{\tau+1}$$

□

Proof of Theorem 5.1: Summing across the edge classes gives the promised bound on stretch. Now there are $\lceil \log_z \Delta \rceil$ weight classes E_i's in all, and since each time the number of edges in a (non-empty) class drops by a factor of y, the algorithm has at most $O(\log \Delta + \tau)$ iterations. By Theorem 4.1 and standard techniques, each iteration does $O(m \log^2 n)$ work and has $O(z \log^2 n) = O(\log^{O(1)} n \cdot 2^{O(\sqrt{\log n \cdot \log \log n})})$ depth in expectation. ∎

5.2 Low-Stretch Spanning Subgraphs

We now show how to alter the parallel low-stretch spanning tree construction from the preceding section to give a low-stretch spanning *subgraph* construction that has no dependence on the "spread," and moreover has only polylogarithmic stretch. This comes at the cost of obtaining a sparse subgraph with $n - 1 + O(m/\operatorname{polylog} n)$ edges instead of a tree, but suffices for our solver application. The two main ideas behind these improvements are the following: Firstly, the number of surviving edges in each weight class decreases by a logarithmic factor in each iteration; hence, we could throw in all surviving edges after they have been whittled down in a constant number of iterations—this removes the factor of $2^{O(\sqrt{\log n \cdot \log \log n})}$ from both the average stretch and the depth. Secondly, if Δ is large, we will identify certain weight-classes with $O(m/\operatorname{polylog} n)$ edges, which by setting them aside, will allow us to break up the chain of dependencies and obtain $O(\operatorname{polylog} n)$ depth; these edges will be thrown back into the final solution, adding $O(m/\operatorname{polylog} n)$ extra edges (which we can tolerate) without increasing the average stretch.

5.2.1 The First Improvement

Let us first show how to achieve polylogarithmic stretch with an ultra-sparse subgraph. Given parameters $\lambda \in \mathbb{Z}_{>0}$ and $\beta \geq c_2 \log^3 n$ (where $c_2 = 2 \cdot (4c_1(\lambda+1))^{\frac{1}{2}(\lambda-1)}$), we obtain the new algorithm $\texttt{SparseAKPW}(G, \lambda, \beta)$ by modifying Algorithm 5.1 as follows:

(1) use the altered parameters $y = \frac{1}{c_2}\beta/\log^3 n$ and $z = 4c_1 y(\lambda+1)\log^3 n$;

(2) in each iteration j, call $\texttt{Partition}$ with at most $\lambda + 1$ edge classes—keep the λ classes $E_j^{(j)}, E_{j-1}^{(j)}, \ldots, E_{j-\lambda+1}^{(j)}$, but then define a "generic bucket" $E_0^{(j)} := \cup_{j' \leq j-\lambda} E_{j'}^{(j)}$ as the last part of the partition; and

(3) finally, output not just the tree T but the subgraph $\widehat{G} = T \cup (\cup_{i \geq 1} E_i^{(i+\lambda)})$.

Lemma 5.5 *Given a graph G, parameters $\lambda \in \mathbb{Z}_{>0}$ and $\beta \geq c_2 \log^3 n$ (where $c_2 = 2 \cdot (4c_1(\lambda+1))^{\frac{1}{2}(\lambda-1)}$) the algorithm $\texttt{SparseAKPW}(G, \lambda, \beta)$ outputs a subgraph of G with at most $n - 1 + m(c_2(\log^3 n/\beta))^\lambda$ edges and total stretch at most $m\beta^2 \log^{3\lambda+3} n$. Moreover, the expected work is $\tilde{O}(m)$ and expected depth is $O((c_1\beta/c_2)\lambda\log^2 n(\log \Delta + \log n))$.*

PROOF. The proof parallels that for Theorem 5.1. Fact 5.3 remains unchanged. The claim from Fact 5.2 now remains true only for $j \in \{i, \ldots, i+\lambda-1\}$; after that the edges in $E_i^{(j)}$ become part of $E_0^{(j)}$, and we only give a cumulative guarantee on the generic bucket. But this does hurt us: if $e \in E_i$ is contracted in iteration $j \leq i + \lambda - 1$ (i.e., it lies within a component formed in iteration j), then $\mathsf{str}_{\widehat{G}}(e) \leq 2z^{j-i+2}$. And the edges of E_i that survive till iteration $j \geq i + \lambda$ have stretch 1 because they are eventually all added to $\widehat{G}$; hence we do not have to worry that they belong to the class $E_0^{(j)}$ for those iterations. Thus, $\mathsf{str}_{\widehat{G}}(E_i) \leq \sum_{j=i}^{i+\lambda-1} 2z^{j-i+2} \cdot |E_i|/y^{j-i} \leq 4y^2(\frac{z}{y})^{\lambda-1}|E_i|$.

Summing across the edge classes gives $\operatorname{str}_{\widehat{G}}(E) \leq 4y^2(\frac{z}{y})^{\lambda-1}m$, which simplifies to $O(m\beta^2 \log^{3\lambda+3} n)$. Next, the number of edges in the output follows directly from the fact T can have at most $n-1$ edges, and the number of extra edges from each class is only a $1/y^\lambda$ fraction (i.e., $|E_i^{(i+\lambda)}| \leq |E_i|/y^\lambda$ from Fact 5.2). Finally, the work remains the same; for each of the $(\log \Delta + \tau)$ distance scales the depth is still $O(z \log^2 n)$, but the new value of z causes this to become $O((c_1\beta/c_2)\lambda \log^2 n)$. □

5.2.2 The Second Improvement

The depth of the SparseAKPW algorithm still depends on $\log \Delta$, and the reason is straightforward: the graph $G^{(j)}$ used in iteration j is built by taking $G^{(1)}$ and contracting edges in each iteration—hence, it depends on all previous iterations. However, the crucial observation is that if we had τ consecutive weight classes E_i's which are empty, we could break this chain of dependencies at this point. However, there may be no empty weight classes; but having weight classes with relatively few edges is enough, as we show next.

Fact 5.6 *Given a graph $G = (V, E)$ and a subset of edges $F \subseteq E$, let $G' = G \setminus F$ be a potentially disconnected graph. If $\widehat{G}'$ is a subgraph of G' with total stretch $\operatorname{str}_{\widehat{G}'}(E(G')) \leq D$, then the total stretch of E on $\widehat{G} := \widehat{G}' \cup F$ is at most $|F| + D$.*

Consider a graph $G = (V, E, w)$ with edge weights $w(e) \geq 1$, and let $E_i(G) := \{e \in E(G) \mid w(e) \in [z^{i-1}, z^i)\}$ be the weight classes. Then, G is called (γ, τ)-*well-spaced* if there is a set of *special* weight classes $\{E_i(G)\}_{i \in I}$ such that for each $i \in I$, (a) there are at most γ weight classes before the following special weight class $\min\{i' \in I \cup \{\infty\} \mid i' > i\}$, and (b) the τ weight classes $E_{i-1}(G), E_{i-2}(G), \ldots, E_{i-\tau}(G)$ preceding i are all empty.

Lemma 5.7 *Given any graph $G = (V, E)$, $\tau \in \mathbb{Z}_+$, and $\theta \leq 1$, there exists a graph $G' = (V, E')$ which is $(4\tau/\theta, \tau)$-well-spaced, and $|E' \setminus E| \leq \theta \cdot |E|$. Moreover, G' can be constructed in $O(m)$ work and $O(\log n)$ depth.*

PROOF. Let $\delta = \frac{\log \Delta}{\log z}$; note that the edge classes for G are $E_1, \ldots, E_\delta$, some of which may be empty. Denote by E_J the union $\cup_{i \in J} E_i$. We construct G' as follows: Divide these edge classes into disjoint groups $J_1, J_2, \ldots \subseteq [\delta]$, where each group consists of $\lceil \tau/\theta \rceil$ consecutive classes. Within a group J_i, by an averaging argument, there must be a range $L_i \subseteq J_i$ of τ consecutive edge classes that contains at most a θ fraction of all the edges in this group, i.e., $|E_{L_i}| \leq \theta \cdot |E_{J_i}|$ and $|L_i| \geq \tau$. We form G' by removing these the edges in all these groups L_i's from G, i.e., $G' = (V, E \setminus (\cup_i E_{L_i}))$. This removes only a θ fraction of all the edges of the graph.

We claim G' is $(4\tau/\theta, \tau)$-well-spaced. Indeed, if we remove the group L_i, then we designate the smallest $j \in [\delta]$ such that $j > \max\{j' \in L_i\}$ as a special bucket (if such a j exists). Since we removed the edges in E_{L_i}, the second condition for being well-spaced follows. Moreover, the number of buckets between a special bucket and the following one is at most $2\lceil \tau/\theta \rceil - (\tau - 1) \leq 4\tau/\theta$. Finally, these computations can be done in $O(m)$ work and $O(\log n)$ depth using standard techniques [JáJ92, Lei92]. □

Lemma 5.8 *Let $\tau = 3\log n/\log y$. Given a graph G which is (γ, τ)-well-spaced, SparseAKPW can be computed on G with $\tilde{O}(m)$ work and $O(\frac{c_1}{c_2}\gamma\lambda\beta \log^2 n)$ depth.*

PROOF. Since G is (γ, τ)-well-spaced, each special bucket $i \in I$ must be preceded by τ empty buckets. Hence, in iteration i

of SparseAKPW, any surviving edges belong to buckets $E_{i-\tau}$ or smaller. However, these edges have been reduced by a factor of y in each iteration and since $\tau > \log_y n^2$, all the edges have been contracted in previous iterations—i.e., $E_\ell^{(i)}$ for $\ell < i$ is empty.

Consider any special bucket i: we claim that we can construct the vertex set $V^{(i)}$ that SparseAKPW sees at the beginning of iteration i, without having to run the previous iterations. Indeed, we can just take the MST on the entire graph $G = G^{(1)}$, retain only the edges from buckets $E_{i-\tau}$ and lower, and contract the connected components of this forest to get $V^{(i)}$. And once we know this vertex set $V^{(i)}$, we can drop out the edges from E_i and higher buckets which have been contracted (these are now self-loops), and execute iterations $i, i+1, \ldots$ of SparseAKPW without waiting for the preceding iterations to finish. Moreover, given the MST, all this can be done in $O(m)$ work and $O(\log n)$ depth.

Finally, for each special bucket i in parallel, we start running SparseAKPW at iteration i. Since there are at most γ iterations until the next special bucket, the total depth is only $O(\gamma z \log^2 n) = O(\frac{c_1}{c_2}\gamma\lambda\beta \log^2 n)$. □

Theorem 5.9 (Low-Stretch Subgraphs) *Given a weighted graph G, $\lambda \in \mathbb{Z}_{>0}$, and $\beta \geq c_2 \log^3 n$ (where $c_2 = 2 \cdot (4c_1(\lambda + 1))^{\frac{1}{2}(\lambda-1)}$), there is an algorithm LSSubgraph(G, β, λ) that finds a subgraph $\widehat{G}$ such that*

1. $|E(\widehat{G})| \leq n - 1 + m \left(c_{LS}\frac{\log^3 n}{\beta}\right)^\lambda$

2. *The total stretch (of all $E(G)$ edges) in the subgraph $\widehat{G}$ is at most by $m\beta^2 \log^{3\lambda+3} n$,*

where $c_{LS} (= c_2 + 1)$ is a constant. Moreover, the procedure runs in $O(\lambda\beta^{\lambda+1} \log^{3-3\lambda} n)$ depth and $\tilde{O}(m)$ work. If $\lambda = O(1)$ and $\beta = \operatorname{polylog}(n)$, the depth term simplifies to $O(\log^{O(1)} n)$.

PROOF. Given a graph G, we set $\tau = 3\log n/\log y$ and $\theta = (\log^3 n/\beta)^\lambda$, and apply Lemma 5.7 to delete at most θm edges, and get a $(4\tau/\theta, \tau)$-well-spaced graph G'. Let $m' = |E'|$. On this graph, we run SparseAKPW to obtain a graph $\widehat{G}'$ with $n - 1 + m'(c_2(\log^3 n/\beta))^\lambda$ edges and total stretch at most $m'\beta^2 \log^{3\lambda+3} n$; moreover, Lemma 5.8 shows this can be computed with $\tilde{O}(m)$ work and $O(\frac{c_1}{c_2}(4\tau/\theta)\lambda\beta \log^2 n) = O(\lambda\beta^{\lambda+1} \log^{3-3\lambda} n)$ depth.

Finally, we output the graph $\widehat{G} = \widehat{G}' \cup (E(G) \setminus E(G'))$; this gives the desired bounds on stretch and the number of edges as implied by Fact 5.6 and Lemma 5.5. □

6. PARALLEL SDD SOLVER

In this section, we derive a parallel solver for symmetric diagonally dominant (SDD) linear systems, using the ingredients developed in the previous sections. The solver follows closely the line of work of [ST03, ST06, KM07, KMP10]. Specifically, we will derive a proof for the main theorem (Theorem 1.1), the statement of which is reproduced below.

Theorem 1.1. For any fixed $\theta > 0$ and any $\varepsilon > 0$, there is an algorithm SDDSolve that on input an SDD matrix A and a vector b computes a vector $\tilde{x}$ such that $\|\tilde{x} - A^+b\|_A \leq \varepsilon \cdot \|A^+b\|_A$ in $O(m \log^{O(1)} n \log \frac{1}{\varepsilon})$ work and $O(m^{1/3+\theta} \log \frac{1}{\varepsilon})$ depth.

In proving this theorem, we will focus on Laplacian linear systems. As noted earlier, linear systems on SDD matrices are reducible to systems on graph Laplacians in $O(\log(m + n))$ depth and $O(m + n)$ work [Gre96]. Furthermore, because of the one-to-one correspondence between graphs and their Laplacians, we will use the two terms interchangeably.

The core of the near-linear time Laplacian solvers in [ST03, ST06, KMP10] is a "preconditioning" chain of progressively smaller graphs $\langle A_1 = A, A_2, \ldots, A_d \rangle$, along with a well-understood recursive algorithm, known as recursive preconditioned Chebyshev method—rPCh, that traverses the levels of the chain and for each visit at level $i < d$, performs $O(1)$ matrix-vector multiplications with A_i and other simple vector-vector operations. Each time the algorithm reaches level d, it solves a linear system on A_d using a direct method. Except for solving the bottom-level systems, all these operations can be accomplished in linear work and $O(\log(m+n))$ depth. The recursion itself is based on a simple scheme; for each visit at level i the algorithm makes at most κ_i' recursive calls to level $i+1$, where $\kappa_i' \geq 2$ is a fixed system-independent integer. Therefore, assuming we have computed a chain of preconditioners, the total required depth is (up to a log) equal to the total number of times the algorithm reaches the last (and smallest) level A_d.

6.1 Parallel Construction of Solver Chain

The construction of the preconditioning chain in [KMP10] relies on a subroutine that on input a graph A_i, constructs a slightly sparser graph B_i which is spectrally related to A_i. This "incremental sparsification" routine is in turn based on the computation of a low-stretch tree for A_i. The parallelization of the low-stretch tree is actually the main obstacle in parallelizing the whole solver presented in [KMP10]. Crucial to effectively applying our result in Section 5 is a simple observation that the sparsification routine of [KMP10] only requires a low-stretch spanning subgraph rather than a tree. Then, with the exception of some parameters in its construction, the preconditioning chain remains essentially the same.

The following lemma is immediate from Section 6 of [KMP10].

Lemma 6.1 *Given a graph G and a subgraph $\widehat{G}$ of G such that the total stretch of all edges in G with respect to $\widehat{G}$ is $m \cdot S$, a parameter on condition number κ, and a success probability $1 - 1/\xi$, there is an algorithm that constructs a graph H such that*

1. $G \preceq H \preceq \kappa \cdot G$, and

2. $|E(H)| = |E(\widehat{G})| + (c_{IS} \cdot S \log n \log \xi)/\kappa$
in $O(\log^2 n)$ depth and $O(m \log^2 n)$ work, where c_{IS} is an absolute constant.

Although Lemma 6.1 was originally stated with $\widehat{G}$ being a spanning tree, the proof in fact works without changes for an arbitrary subgraph. For our purposes, ξ has to be at most $O(\log n)$ and that introduces an additional $O(\log \log n)$ term. For simplicity, in the rest of the section, we will consider this as an extra $\log n$ factor.

Lemma 6.2 *Given a weighted graph G, parameters λ and η such that $\eta \geq \lambda \geq 16$, we can construct in $O(\log^{2\eta\lambda} n)$ depth and $\tilde{O}(m)$ work another graph H such that*

1. $G \preceq H \preceq \frac{1}{10} \cdot \log^{\eta\lambda} n \cdot G$

2. $|E(H)| \leq n - 1 + m \cdot c_{PC}/\log^{\eta\lambda-2\eta-4\lambda}(n)$,
where c_{PC} is an absolute constant.

PROOF. Let $\widehat{G} = \texttt{LSSubgraph}(G, \lambda, \log^\eta n)$. Then, Theorem 5.9 shows that $|E(\widehat{G})|$ is at most

$$n - 1 + m \left(\frac{c_{LS} \cdot \log^3 n}{\beta} \right)^\lambda = n - 1 + m \left(\frac{c_{LS}}{\log^{\eta-3} n} \right)^\lambda$$

Furthermore, the total stretch of all edges in G with respect to $\widehat{G}$ is at most $S = m\beta^2 \log^{\lambda+3} n \leq m \log^{2\eta+3\lambda+3} n$. Applying

Lemma 6.1 with $\kappa = \frac{1}{10} \log^{\eta\lambda} n$ gives H such that $G \preceq H \preceq \frac{1}{10} \log^{\eta\lambda} n \cdot G$ and $|E(H)|$ is at most

$$
\begin{aligned}
& n - 1 + m \cdot \left(\frac{c_{LS}^\lambda}{\log^{\lambda(\eta-3)} n} + \frac{10 \cdot c_{IS} \log^{2\eta+3\lambda+5} n}{\log^{\eta\lambda} n} \right) \\
\leq \quad & n - 1 + m \cdot \frac{c_{PC}}{\log^{\eta\lambda-2\lambda-3k-5} n} \\
\leq \quad & n - 1 + m \cdot \frac{c_{PC}}{\log^{\eta\lambda-2\eta-4\lambda} n}.
\end{aligned}
$$

$\square$

We now give a more precise definition of the preconditioning chain we use for the parallel solver by giving the pseudocode for constructing it.

Definition 6.3 (Preconditioning Chain) *Consider a chain of graphs $C = \langle A_1 = A, B_1, A_2, \ldots, A_d \rangle$, and denote by n_i and m_i the number of nodes and edges of A_i respectively. We say that C is preconditioning chain for A if*

1. $B_i = \texttt{IncrementalSparsify}(A_i)$.

2. $A_{i+1} = \texttt{GreedyElimination}(B_i)$.

3. $A_i \preceq B_i \preceq 1/10 \cdot \kappa_i A_i$, for some explicitly known integer κ_i. [7]

As noted above, the rPCh algorithm relies on finding the solution of linear systems on A_d, the bottom-level systems. To parallelize these solves, we make use of the following fact which can be found in Sections 3.4. and 4.2 of [GVL96].

Fact 6.4 *A factorization $LL^\top$ of the pseudo-inverse of an n-by-n Laplacian A, where L is a lower triangular matrix, can be computed in $O(n)$ time and $O(n^3)$ work, and any solves thereafter can be done in $O(\log n)$ time and $O(n^2)$ work.*

Note that although A is not positive definite, its null space is the space spanned by the all 1s vector when the underlying graph is connected. Therefore, we can in turn drop the first row and column to obtain a semi-definite matrix on which LU factorization is numerically stable.

The routine GreedyElimination is a partial Cholesky factorization (for details see [ST06] or [KMP10]) on vertices of degree at most 2. From a graph-theoretic point of view, GreedyElimination can be viewed as simply recursively removing nodes of degree one and splicing out nodes of degree two. The sequential version of GreedyElimination returns a graph with no degree 1 or 2 nodes. The parallel version that we present below leaves some degree-2 nodes in the graph, but their number will be small enough to not affect the complexity.

Lemma 6.5 *If G has n vertices and $n - 1 + m$ edges, then the procedure GreedyElimination(G) returns a graph with at most $2m - 2$ nodes in $O(n + m)$ work and $O(\log n)$ depth **whp**.*

PROOF. The sequential version of GreedyElimination(G) is equivalent to repeatedly removing degree 1 vertices and splicing out 2 vertices until no more exist while maintaining self-loops and multiple edges (see, e.g., [ST03, ST06] and [Kou07, Section 2.3.4]). Thus, the problem is a slight generalization of parallel tree contraction [MR89]. In the parallel version, we show that while the graph has more than $2m - 2$ nodes, we can efficiently find and eliminate a

---

[7] The constant of $1/10$ in the condition number is introduced only to simplify subsequent notation.

"large" independent set of degree two nodes, in addition to all degree one vertices.

We alternate between two steps, which are equivalent to `Rake` and `Compress` in [MR89], until the vertex count is at most $2m - 2$: Mark an independent set of degree 2 vertices, then

1. Contract all degree 1 vertices, and

2. Compress and/or contract out the marked vertices.

To find the independent set, we use a randomized marking algorithm on the degree two vertices (this is used in place of maximal independent set for work efficiency): Each degree two node flips a coin with probability $\frac{1}{3}$ of turning up heads; we mark a node if it is a heads and its neighbors either did not flip a coin or flipped a tail.

We show that the two steps above will remove a constant fraction of "extra" vertices. Let G is a multigraph with n vertices and $m + n - 1$ edges. First, observe that if all vertices have degree at least three then $n \leq 2(m - 1)$ and we would be finished. So, let T be any fixed spanning tree of G; let a_1 (resp. a_2) be the number of vertices in T of degree one (resp. two) and a_3 the number those of degree three or more. Similarly, let b_1, b_2, and b_3 be the number vertices in G of degree 1, 2, and at least 3, respectively, where the degree is the vertex's degree in G.

It is easy to check that in expectation, these two steps remove $b_1 + \frac{4}{27} b_2 \geq b_1 + \frac{1}{7} b_2$ vertices. In the following, we will show that $b_1 + \frac{1}{7} b_2 \geq \frac{1}{7} \Delta n$, where $\Delta n = n - (2m - 2) = n - 2m + 2$ denotes the number of "extra" vertices in the graph. Consider non-tree edges and how they are attached to the tree T. Let m_1, m_2, and m_3 be the number of attachment of the following types, respectively:

(1) an attachment to x, a degree 1 vertex in T, where x has at least one other attachment.

(2) an attachment to x, a degree 1 vertex in T, where x has no other attachment.

(3) an attachment to a degree 2 vertex in T.

As each edge is incident on two endpoints, we have $m_1 + m_2 + m_3 \leq 2m$. Also, we can lower bound b_1 and b_2 in terms of m_i's and a_i's: we have $b_1 \geq a_1 - m_1/2 - m_2$ and $b_2 \geq m_2 + a_2 - m_3$. This gives

$$
\begin{aligned}
b_1 + \tfrac{1}{7} b_2 &\geq \tfrac{2}{7}(a_1 - m_1/2 - m_2) + \tfrac{1}{7}(m_2 + a_2 - m_3) \\
&= \tfrac{2}{7} a_1 + \tfrac{1}{7} a_2 - \tfrac{1}{7}(m_1 + m_2 + m_3) \\
&\geq \tfrac{2}{7} a_1 + \tfrac{1}{7} a_2 - \tfrac{2}{7} m.
\end{aligned}
$$

Consequently, $b_1 + \frac{1}{7} b_2 \geq \frac{1}{7}(2a_1 + a_2 - 2m) \geq \frac{1}{7} \cdot \Delta n$, where to show the last step, it suffices to show that $n + 2 \leq 2a_1 + a_2$ for a tree T of n nodes. WLOG, we may assume that all nodes of T have degree either one or three, in which case $2a_1 = n + 2$. Finally, by Chernoff bounds, the algorithm will finish with high probability in $O(\log n)$ rounds. $\square$

6.2 Parallel Performance of Solver Chain

Spielman and Teng [ST06, Section 5] gave a (sequential) time bound for solving a linear SDD system given a preconditioner chain. The following lemma extends their Theorem 5.5 to give parallel runtime bounds (work and depth), as a function of κ_i's and m_i's. We note that in the bounds below, the m_d^2 term arises from the dense inverse used to solve the linear system in the bottom level.

Lemma 6.6 *There is an algorithm that given a preconditioner chain* $\mathcal{C} = \langle A_1 = A, A_2, \ldots, A_d \rangle$ *for a matrix A, a vector b, and an error tolerance ε, computes a vector $\tilde{x}$ such that*

$$
\|\tilde{x} - A^+ b\|_A \leq \varepsilon \cdot \|A^+ b\|_A,
$$

with depth bounded by

$$
\left(\sum_{1 \leq i \leq d} \prod_{1 \leq j < i} \sqrt{\kappa_j} \right) \log n \log\left(\tfrac{1}{\varepsilon}\right)
$$

$$
\leq O\left(\left(\prod_{1 \leq j < d} \sqrt{\kappa_j} \right) \log n \log\left(\tfrac{1}{\varepsilon}\right) \right)
$$

and work bounded by

$$
\left(\sum_{1 \leq i \leq d-1} m_i \cdot \prod_{j \leq i} \sqrt{\kappa_j} + m_d^2 \prod_{1 \leq j < d} \sqrt{\kappa_j} \right) \log\left(\tfrac{1}{\varepsilon}\right).
$$

To reason about Lemma 6.6, we will rely on the following lemma about preconditioned Chebyshev iteration and the recursive solves that happen at each level of the chain. This lemma is a restatement of Spielman and Teng's Lemma 5.3 (slightly modified so that the $\sqrt{\kappa_i}$ does not involve a constant, which shows up instead as constant in the preconditioner chain's definition).

Lemma 6.7 *Given a preconditioner chain of length d, it is possible to construct linear operators* solve_{A_i} *for all $i \leq d$ such that*

$$
(1 - e^{-2}) A_i^+ \preceq \mathsf{solve}_{A_i} \preceq (1 + e^2)
$$

and solve_{A_i} *is a polynomial of degree $\sqrt{\kappa_i}$ involving* $\mathsf{solve}_{A_{i+1}}$ *and 4 matrices with m_i non-zero entries (from* `GreedyElimination`*).*

Armed with this, we state and prove the following lemma:

Lemma 6.8 *For $\ell \geq 1$, given any vector b, the vector* $\mathsf{solve}_{A_\ell} \cdot b$ *can be computed in depth*

$$
\log n \sum_{\ell \leq i \leq d} \prod_{\ell \leq j < i} \sqrt{\kappa_j}
$$

and work

$$
\sum_{\ell \leq i \leq d-1} m_i \cdot \prod_{\ell \leq j \leq i} \sqrt{\kappa_j} + m_d^2 \prod_{\ell \leq j < d} \sqrt{\kappa_j}
$$

PROOF. The proof is by induction in decreasing order on ℓ. When $d = \ell$, all we are doing is a matrix multiplication with a dense inverse. This takes $O(\log n)$ depth and $O(m_d^2)$ work.

Suppose the result is true for $\ell + 1$. Then since solve_{A_ℓ} can be expressed as a polynomial of degree $\sqrt{\kappa_\ell}$ involving an operator that is $\mathsf{solve}_{A_{\ell+1}}$ multiplied by at most 4 matrices with $O(m_\ell)$ non-zero entries. We have that the total depth is

$$
\log n \sqrt{\kappa_\ell} + \sqrt{\kappa_\ell} \cdot \left(\log n \sum_{\ell+1 \leq i \leq d} \prod_{\ell+1 \leq j < i} \sqrt{\kappa_j} \right)
$$

$$
= \log n \sum_{\ell \leq i \leq d} \prod_{\ell \leq j < i} \sqrt{\kappa_j}
$$

and the total work is bounded by

$$
\sqrt{\kappa_\ell} m_\ell +
$$

$$
\sqrt{\kappa_\ell} \cdot \left(\sum_{\ell+1 \leq i \leq d-1} m_i \cdot \prod_{\ell+1 \leq j \leq i} \sqrt{\kappa_j} + m_d^2 \prod_{\ell+1 \leq j < d} \sqrt{\kappa_j} \right)
$$

$$
= \sum_{\ell \leq i \leq d-1} m_i \cdot \prod_{\ell \leq j \leq i} \sqrt{\kappa_j} + m_d^2 \prod_{\ell \leq j < d} \sqrt{\kappa_j}.
$$

$\square$

Proof of Lemma 6.6: The ε-accuracy bound follows from applying preconditioned Chebyshev to solve_{A_1} similarly to Spielman and Teng's Theorem 5.5 [ST06], and the running time bounds follow from Lemma 6.8 when $\ell = 1$. ∎

6.3 Optimizing the Chain for Depth

Lemma 6.6 shows that the algorithm's performance is determined by the settings of κ_i's and m_i's; however, as we will be using Lemma 6.2, the number of edges m_i is essentially dictated by our choice of κ_i. We now show that if we terminate chain earlier, i.e. adjusting the dimension A_d to roughly $O(m^{1/3} \log \varepsilon^{-1})$, we can obtain good parallel performance. As a first attempt, we will set κ_i's uniformly:

Lemma 6.9 *For any fixed $\theta > 0$, if we construct a preconditioner chain using Lemma 6.2 setting λ to some proper constant greater than 21, $\eta = \lambda$ and extending the sequence until $m_d \leq m^{1/3-\delta}$ for some δ depending on λ, we get a solver algorithm that runs in $O(m^{1/3+\theta} \log(1/\varepsilon))$ depth and $\tilde{O}(m \log 1/\varepsilon)$ work as $\lambda \to \infty$, where ε is the accuracy precision of the solution, as defined in the statement of Theorem 1.1.*

PROOF. By Lemma 6.1, we have that m_{i+1}—the number of edges in level $i + 1$—is bounded by

$$O\left(m_i \cdot \frac{c_{PC}}{\log^{\eta\lambda - 2\eta - 4\lambda}}\right) = O\left(m_i \cdot \frac{c_{PC}}{\log^{\lambda(\lambda-6)}}\right),$$

which can be repeatedly apply to give

$$m_i \leq m \cdot \left(\frac{c_{PC}}{\log^{\lambda(\lambda-6)} n}\right)^{i-1}$$

Therefore, when $\lambda > 12$, we have that for each $i < d$,

$$m_i \cdot \prod_{j \leq i} \sqrt{\kappa(n_j)} \leq m \cdot \left(\frac{c_{PC}}{\log^{\lambda(\lambda-6)} n}\right)^{i-1} \cdot \left(\sqrt{\log^{\lambda^2} n}\right)^i$$

$$= \tilde{O}(m) \cdot \left(\frac{c_{PC}}{\log^{\lambda(\lambda-12)/2} n}\right)^i$$

$$\leq \tilde{O}(m)$$

Now consider the term involving m_d. We have that d is bounded by $\left(\frac{2}{3} + \delta\right) \log m / \log\left(\frac{1}{c_{PC}} \log n^{\lambda(\lambda-6)}\right)$. Combining with the $\kappa_i = \log^{\lambda^2} n$, we get

$$\prod_{1 \leq j \leq d} \sqrt{\kappa(n_j)}$$

$$= \left(\log n^{\lambda^2/2}\right)^{\left(\frac{2}{3}+\delta\right) \log m / \log\left(c \log n^{\lambda(\lambda-6)}\right)}$$

$$= \exp\left(\log\log n \frac{\lambda^2}{2}\left(\frac{2}{3} + \delta\right) \frac{\log m}{\lambda(\lambda-6)\log\log n - \log c_{PC}}\right)$$

$$\leq \exp\left(\log\log n \frac{\lambda^2}{2}\left(\frac{2}{3} + \delta\right) \frac{\log m}{\lambda(\lambda-7)\log\log n}\right)$$

$$\text{(since } \log c_{PC} \geq -\log n)$$

$$= \exp\left(\log n \frac{\lambda}{\lambda-7}\left(\frac{1}{3} + \frac{\delta}{2}\right)\right)$$

$$= O(m^{\left(\frac{1}{3}+\frac{\delta}{2}\right)\frac{\lambda}{\lambda-7}})$$

Since $m_d = O(m^{\frac{1}{3}-\delta})$, the total work is bounded by

$$O(m^{\left(\frac{1}{3}+\frac{\delta}{2}\right)\frac{\lambda}{\lambda-7}+\frac{2}{3}-2\delta}) = O(m^{1+\frac{7}{\lambda-7}-\delta\frac{\lambda-14}{\lambda-7}})$$

So, setting $\delta \geq \frac{7}{\lambda-14}$ suffices to bound the total work by $\tilde{O}(m)$. And, when δ is set to $\frac{7}{\lambda-14}$, the total parallel running time is bounded by the number of times the last layer is called

$$\prod_j \sqrt{\kappa(n_j)} \leq O(m^{\left(\frac{1}{3}+\frac{1}{2(\lambda-14)}\right)\frac{\lambda}{\lambda-7}})$$

$$\leq O(m^{\frac{1}{3}+\frac{7}{\lambda-14}+\frac{\lambda}{2(\lambda-14)(\lambda-7)}})$$

$$\leq O(m^{\frac{1}{3}+\frac{14}{\lambda-14}}) \quad \text{when } \lambda \geq 21$$

Setting λ arbitrarily large suffices to give $O(m^{1/3+\theta})$ depth. ∎

To match the promised bounds in Theorem 1.1, we improve the performance by reducing the exponent on the $\log n$ term in the total work from λ^2 to some large fixed constant while letting total depth still approach $O(m^{1/3+\theta})$.

Proof of Theorem 1.1: Consider setting $\lambda = 13$ and $\eta \geq \lambda$. Then,

$$\eta\lambda - 2\eta - 4\lambda \geq \eta(\lambda - 6) \geq \frac{7}{13}\eta\lambda$$

We use c_4 to denote this constant of $\frac{7}{13}$, namely c_4 satisfies

$$c_{PC}/\log^{\eta k - 2\eta - 4\lambda} n \leq c_{PC}/\log^{c_4 \eta \lambda} n$$

We can then pick a constant threshold L and set κ_i for all $i \leq L$ as follows:

$$\kappa_1 = \log^{\lambda^2} n, \kappa_2 = \log^{(2c_4)\lambda^2} n, \cdots, \kappa_i = \log^{(2c_4)^{i-1}\lambda^2} n$$

To solve A_L, we apply Lemma 6.9, which is analogous to setting $A_L, \ldots, A_d$ uniformly. The depth required in constructing these preconditioners is $O(m_d + \sum_{j=1}^{L}(2c_4)^{j-1}\lambda^2)$, plus $O(m_d)$ for computing the inverse at the last level—for a total of $O(m_d) = O(m^{1/3})$.

As for work, the total work is bounded by

$$\sum_{i \leq d} m_i \prod_{1 \leq j \leq i} \sqrt{\kappa_j} + \prod_{1 \leq j \leq d} \sqrt{\kappa_j} m_d^2$$

$$= \sum_{i < L} m_i \prod_{1 \leq j \leq i} \sqrt{\kappa_j} + \left(\prod_{1 \leq j < L} \sqrt{\kappa_j}\right) \cdot$$

$$\left(\sqrt{\kappa_L} \sum_{i \geq L} m_i \prod_{L \leq j \leq i} \sqrt{\kappa_j} + m_d^2 \prod_{L \leq j \leq d} \sqrt{\kappa_j}\right)$$

$$\leq \sum_{i < L} m_i \prod_{1 \leq j \leq i} \sqrt{\kappa_j} + \left(\prod_{1 \leq j < L} \sqrt{\kappa_j}\right) m_L \sqrt{\kappa_L}$$

$$= \sum_{i \leq L} m_i \prod_{1 \leq j \leq i} \sqrt{\kappa_j}$$

$$\leq \sum_{i \leq L} \frac{m}{\prod_{j < i} \kappa_i^{c_4}} \prod_{1 \leq j \leq i} \sqrt{\kappa_j}$$

$$= m \sum_{i \leq L} \frac{\sqrt{\kappa_1} \prod_{2 \leq j \leq i} \sqrt{\kappa_{j-1}^{2c_4}}}{\prod_{j < i} \kappa_i^{c_4}}$$

$$= mL\sqrt{\kappa_1}$$

The first inequality follows from the fact that the exponent of $\log^n$ in κ_L can be arbitrarily large, and then applying Lemma 6.9 to the solves after level L. The fact that $m_{i+1} \leq m_i \cdot O(1/\kappa_i^{c_4})$ follows from Lemma 6.2.

Since L is a constant, $\prod_{1 \leq j \leq L} \in O(\text{polylog } n)$, so the total depth is still bounded by $O(m^{1/3+\theta})$ by Lemma 6.9. ∎

7. CONCLUSION

We presented a near linear-work parallel algorithm for constructing graph decompositions with strong-diameter guarantees and parallel algorithms for constructing $2^{O(\sqrt{\log n \log \log n})}$-stretch spanning trees and $O(\log^{O(1)} n)$-stretch ultra-sparse subgraphs. The ultra-sparse subgraphs were shown to be useful in the design of a near linear-work parallel SDD solver. By plugging our result into previous frameworks, we obtained improved parallel algorithms for several problems on graphs.

We leave open the design of a (near) linear-work parallel algorithm for the construction of a low-stretch tree with polylogarithmic stretch. We also feel that the design of (near) work-efficient $O(\log^{O(1)} n)$-depth SDD solver is a very interesting problem that will probably require the development of new techniques.

Acknowledgments. This work is partially supported by the National Science Foundation under grant numbers CCF-1018463, CCF-1018188, and CCF-1016799, by an Alfred P. Sloan Fellowship, and by generous gifts from IBM, Intel, and Microsoft.

References

[ABN08] Ittai Abraham, Yair Bartal, and Ofer Neiman. Nearly tight low stretch spanning trees. In *FOCS*, pages 781–790, 2008.

[AKPW95] Noga Alon, Richard M. Karp, David Peleg, and Douglas West. A graph-theoretic game and its application to the k-server problem. *SIAM J. Comput.*, 24(1):78–100, 1995.

[Awe85] Baruch Awerbuch. Complexity of network synchronization. *J. Assoc. Comput. Mach.*, 32(4):804–823, 1985.

[BV04] S. Boyd and L. Vandenberghe. *Convex Optimization*. Camebridge University Press, 2004.

[Chv79] V. Chvátal. The tail of the hypergeometric distribution. *Discrete Mathematics*, 25(3):285–287, 1979.

[Coh93] E. Cohen. Fast algorithms for constructing t-spanners and paths with stretch t. In *Proceedings of the 1993 IEEE 34th Annual Foundations of Computer Science*, pages 648–658, Washington, DC, USA, 1993. IEEE Computer Society.

[Coh00] Edith Cohen. Polylog-time and near-linear work approximation scheme for undirected shortest paths. *J. ACM*, 47(1):132–166, 2000.

[DS08] Samuel I. Daitch and Daniel A. Spielman. Faster approximate lossy generalized flow via interior point algorithms. *CoRR*, abs/0803.0988, 2008.

[EEST05] Michael Elkin, Yuval Emek, Daniel A. Spielman, and Shang-Hua Teng. Lower-stretch spanning trees. In *Proceedings of the thirty-seventh annual ACM symposium on Theory of computing*, pages 494–503, New York, NY, USA, 2005. ACM Press.

[Gre96] Keith Gremban. *Combinatorial Preconditioners for Sparse, Symmetric, Diagonally Dominant Linear Systems*. PhD thesis, Carnegie Mellon University, Pittsburgh, October 1996. CMU CS Tech Report CMU-CS-96-123.

[GVL96] G. H. Golub and C. F. Van Loan. *Matrix Computations*. Johns Hopkins Press, 3rd edition, 1996.

[Hoe63] Wassily Hoeffding. Probability Inequalities for Sums of Bounded Random Variables. *Journal of the American Statistical Association*, 58(301):13–30, 1963.

[JáJ92] Joseph JáJá. *An Introduction to Parallel Algorithms*. Addison-Wesley, 1992.

[KM07] Ioannis Koutis and Gary L. Miller. A linear work, $O(n^{1/6})$ time, parallel algorithm for solving planar laplacians. In *SODA*, pages 1002–1011, 2007.

[KMP10] Ioannis Koutis, Gary L. Miller, and Richard Peng. Approaching optimality for solving SDD linear systems. In *FOCS*, pages 235–244, 2010.

[Kou07] Ioannis Koutis. *Combinatorial and algebraic algorithms for optimal multilevel algorithms*. PhD thesis, Carnegie Mellon University, Pittsburgh, May 2007. CMU CS Tech Report CMU-CS-07-131.

[KS97] Philip N. Klein and Sairam Subramanian. A randomized parallel algorithm for single-source shortest paths. *J. Algorithms*, 25(2):205–220, 1997.

[Lei92] F. Thomson Leighton. *Introduction to Parallel Algorithms and Architectures: Array, Trees, Hypercubes*. Morgan Kaufmann Publishers Inc., San Francisco, CA, USA, 1992.

[MR89] Gary L. Miller and John H. Reif. Parallel tree contraction part 1: Fundamentals. In Silvio Micali, editor, *Randomness and Computation*, pages 47–72. JAI Press, Greenwich, Connecticut, 1989. Vol. 5.

[Ren01] James Renegar. *A mathematical view of interior-point methods in convex optimization*. Society for Industrial and Applied Mathematics, Philadelphia, PA, USA, 2001.

[Ska09] Matthew Skala. Hypergeometric tail inequalities: ending the insanity, 2009.

[Spi10] Daniel A. Spielman. Algorithms, Graph Theory, and Linear Equations in Laplacian Matrices. In *Proceedings of the International Congress of Mathematicians*, 2010.

[SS08] Daniel A. Spielman and Nikhil Srivastava. Graph sparsification by effective resistances. In *STOC*, pages 563–568, 2008.

[ST03] Daniel A. Spielman and Shang-Hua Teng. Solving sparse, symmetric, diagonally-dominant linear systems in time $O(m^{1.31})$. In *FOCS*, pages 416–427, 2003.

[ST06] Daniel A. Spielman and Shang-Hua Teng. Nearly-linear time algorithms for preconditioning and solving symmetric, diagonally dominant linear systems. *CoRR*, abs/cs/0607105, 2006.

[Ten10] Shang-Hua Teng. The Laplacian Paradigm: Emerging Algorithms for Massive Graphs. In *Theory and Applications of Models of Computation*, pages 2–14, 2010.

[Ye97] Y. Ye. *Interior point algorithms: theory and analysis*. Wiley, 1997.

APPENDIX

A. UTILITY LEMMAS AND THEOREMS

Lemma A.1 (Hypergeometric Tailbound) *Let H be a hypergeometric random variable denoting the number of red balls found in sample of n drawn from a total of N balls of which M are red. Then, if $\mu = \mathbf{E}[H] = nM/N$, then*

$$\Pr[H \geq 2\mu] \leq e^{-\mu/4}$$

PROOF. We apply the following theorem of Hoeffding [Chv79, Hoe63, Ska09]. For any $t > 0$,

$$\Pr[H \geq \mu + tn] \leq \left(\left(\frac{p}{p+t}\right)^{p+t} \left(\frac{1-p}{1-p-t}\right)^{1-p-t} \right)^n,$$

where $p = \mu/n$. Using $t = p$, we have

$$\Pr[H \geq 2\mu] \leq \left(\left(\frac{p}{2p}\right)^{2p} \left(\frac{1-p}{1-2p}\right)^{1-2p} \right)^n$$

$$\leq \left(e^{-p\ln 4} \left(1 + \frac{p}{1-2p}\right)^{1-2p} \right)^n$$

$$\leq \left(e^{-p\ln 4} \cdot e^p \right)^n$$

$$\leq e^{-\frac{1}{4}pn}$$

$\square$

Linear-Work Greedy Parallel Approximate Set Cover and Variants

Guy E. Blelloch   Richard Peng   Kanat Tangwongsan

Carnegie Mellon University

{guyb, yangp, ktangwon}@cs.cmu.edu

ABSTRACT

We present parallel greedy approximation algorithms for set cover and related problems. These algorithms build on an algorithm for solving a graph problem we formulate and study called Maximal Nearly Independent Set (MaNIS)—a graph abstraction of a key component in existing work on parallel set cover.

We derive a randomized algorithm for MaNIS that has $O(m)$ work and $O(\log^2 m)$ depth on input with m edges. Using MaNIS, we obtain RNC algorithms that yield a $(1 + \varepsilon)H_n$-approximation for set cover, a $(1 - \frac{1}{e} - \varepsilon)$-approximation for max cover and a $(4 + \varepsilon)$-approximation for min-sum set cover all in linear work; and an $O(\log^* n)$-approximation for asymmetric k-center for $k \leq \log^{O(1)} n$ and a $(1.861 + \varepsilon)$-approximation for metric facility location both in essentially the same work bounds as their sequential counterparts.

Categories and Subject Descriptors

F.2 [**Theory of Computation**]: Analysis of Algorithms and Problem Complexity

General Terms

Algorithms, Theory

Keywords

Parallel algorithms, approximation algorithms, set cover, max cover, facility location

1. INTRODUCTION

Set cover is one of the most fundamental and well-studied problems in optimization and approximation algorithms. This problem and its variants have a wide variety of applications in the real world, including locating warehouses, testing faults, scheduling crews on airlines, and allocating wavelength in wireless communication. Let $\mathcal{U}$ be a set of n ground elements, $\mathcal{F}$ be a collection of subsets of $\mathcal{U}$ covering $\mathcal{U}$

(i.e., $\cup_{S \in \mathcal{F}} S = \mathcal{U}$), and $c \colon \mathcal{F} \to \mathbb{R}_+$ a cost function. The *set cover problem* is to find the cheapest collection of sets $\mathcal{A} \subseteq \mathcal{F}$ such that $\cup_{S \in \mathcal{A}} S = \mathcal{U}$, where the cost of the solution $\mathcal{A}$ is specified by $c(\mathcal{A}) = \sum_{S \in \mathcal{A}} c(S)$. Unweighted set cover (all weights are equal) appeared as one of the 21 problems Karp identified as NP-complete in 1972 [Kar72]. Two years later, Johnson [Joh74] proved that the simple greedy method gives an approximation that is at most a factor $H_n = \sum_{k=1}^{n} \frac{1}{k}$ from optimal. Subsequently, Chvátal [Chv79] proved the same approximation bounds for the weighted case. These results are complemented by a matching hardness result: Feige [Fei98] showed that unless $\mathsf{NP} \subseteq \mathsf{DTIME}(n^{O(\log \log n)})$, set cover cannot be approximated in polynomial time with a ratio better than $(1 - o(1)) \ln n$. This essentially shows that the greedy algorithm is optimal.

Not only is greedy set cover optimal but it also gives an extremely simple $O(M)$ time algorithm for the unweighted case and $O(M \log M)$ time for the weighted case, where $M \geq n$ is the sum of the sizes of the sets. In addition, ideas similar to greedy set cover have been successfully applied to max k-cover, min-sum set cover, k-center, and facility location, generally leading to optimal or good-quality, yet simple, approximation algorithms.

From a parallelization point of view, however, the greedy method is in general difficult to parallelize, because at each step, only the highest-utility option is chosen and every subsequent step is likely to depend on the preceding one. Berger, Rompel, and Shor [BRS94] (BRS) showed that the greedy set cover algorithm can be "approximately" parallelized by bucketing[1] utility values (in this case, the number of new elements covered per unit cost) by factors of $(1 + \varepsilon)$ and processing sets within a bucket in parallel. Furthermore, the number of buckets can be kept to $O(\log n)$ by preprocessing. However, deciding which sets within each bucket to choose requires some care: although at a given time, many sets might have utility values within a factor of $(1 + \varepsilon)$ of the current best option, the sets taken together might not cover as many *unique* elements as their utility values imply—shared elements can be counted towards only one of the sets. BRS developed a technique to subselect within a bucket by first further bucketing by cost, then set size, and finally element degree, and then randomly selecting sets with an appropriate probability. This leads to an $O(\log^5 M)$-depth and $O(m \log^4 M)$-work randomized algorithm, giving a $((1 + \varepsilon)H_n)$-approximation on a PRAM. Rajagopalan and Vazirani [RV98] improved the

---

[1]The bucketing approach has also been used for other algorithms such as vertex cover [KVY94] and metric facility location [BT10].

depth to $O(\log^3(Mn))$ with work $O(M \log^2 M)$ but at the cost of a factor of two in the approximation (essentially a factor-$2(1 + \varepsilon)H_n$ approximation).

In comparison to their sequential counterparts, none of these previous set-cover algorithms are work efficient—their work is asymptotically more than the time for the optimal sequential algorithm.[2] Work efficiency is important since it allows an algorithm to be applied efficiently to both a modest number of processors (one being the most modest) and a larger number. Even with a larger number of processors, work-efficient algorithms limit the amount of resources used and hence presumably the cost of the computation.

Our Contributions: In this paper, we abstract out the most important component of the bucketing approach, which we refer to as Maximal Nearly Independent Set (MaNIS), and develop an $O(m)$ work and $O(\log^2 m)$ depth algorithm for an input graph with m edges, on an EREW PRAM (*work* is the total operation count, and *depth* the number of steps on the PRAM). The MaNIS problem is to find a subset of sets such that they are nearly independent (their elements do not overlap too much), and maximal (no set can be added without introducing too much overlap). Since we have to look at the input, which has size $O(m)$, the algorithm is work efficient. The MaNIS abstraction allows us to reasonably easily apply it to several set-cover like problems. In particular, we develop the following work-efficient approximation algorithms:

— *Set cover.* We develop an $O(M)$ work, $O(\log^3 M)$ depth (parallel time) algorithm with approximation ratio $(1+\varepsilon)H_n$. For the unweighted case, the same algorithm gives a $(1 + \varepsilon)(1 + \ln(n/\mathsf{opt}))$ approximation where opt is the optimal set-cover cost.
— *Max cover.* We develop an $O(M)$ work, $O(\log^3 M)$ depth prefix-optimal algorithm with approximation ratio $(1 - 1/e - \varepsilon)$. This significantly improves the work bounds over a recent result [CKT10].
— *Min-sum set cover.* We develop an $O(M)$ work, $O(\log^3 M)$ depth algorithm with an approximation ratio of $(4 + \varepsilon)H_n$. We know of no other RNC parallel approximation algorithms for this problem.
— *Asymmetric k-center.* We develop an $O(p(k + \log^* n))$ work, $O(k \log n + \log^3 n \log^* n)$ depth algorithm with approximation ratio $O(\log^* n)$, where $p = n(n-1)/2$ is the size of the table of distances between elements. The algorithm is based on the sequential algorithm of Panigrahy and Vishwanathan [PV98] and we know of no other RNC parallel approximation algorithms for this problem.
— *Metric facility location.* We develop an $O(p \log p)$ work, $O(\log^4 p)$ depth algorithm with approximation ratio $(1.861 + \varepsilon)$, where $p = |F| \times |C|$ is the size of the distance table. The algorithm is based on the greedy algorithm of Jain et al. [JMM+03] and improves on the approximation ratio of $(3 + \varepsilon)$ for the best previous RNC algorithm [BT10].

All these algorithms run on a CRCW PRAM but rely on only a few primitives discussed in the next section, and thus should be easily ported to other models.

2. PRELIMINARIES AND NOTATION

For a graph G, we denote by $\deg_G(v)$ the degree of the vertex v in G and use $N_G(v)$ to denote the neighbor set of

the node v. Furthermore, we write $u \sim v$ for u is adjacent to v. Extending this notation, we write $N_G(X)$ to mean the neighbors of the vertex set X, i.e., $N_G(X) = \cup_{w \in X} N_G(w)$. We drop the subscript (i.e., writing $\deg(v)$, $N(v)$, and $N(X)$) when the context is clear. Let $V(G)$ and $E(G)$ denote respectively the set of nodes and the set of edges. We use the notation $\widetilde{O}(f(n))$ to mean $O(f(n)\,\mathrm{polylog}(n))$ and $[k]$ to denote the set $\{1, 2, \ldots, k\}$. An event happens with high probability (w.h.p.) if it happens with probability exceeding $1 - n^{-O(1)}$. We analyze the algorithms in the PRAM model. We use both the EREW (Exclusive Read Exclusive Write) and CRCW (Concurrent Read Concurrent Write) variants of the PRAM, and for the CRCW, assume an arbitrary value is written. For an input of size n, we assume that every memory word has $O(\log n)$ bits. In our analysis, we are primarily concerned with minimizing the work while achieving polylogarithmic depth and less concerned with polylogarithmic factors in the depth since such measures are typically not robust across models. All algorithms we develop are in NC or RNC, so they have polylogarithmic depth.

The algorithms in this paper are all based on a bipartite graph $G = (A \cup B, E), E \subseteq A \times B$. In set cover, for example, we use A to represent the subsets $\mathcal{F}$ and B for the ground elements $\mathcal{U}$. In addition to operating over the vertices and edges of the graph, the algorithms need to copy a value from each vertex (on either side) to its incident edges, need to "sum" values from the incident edges of each vertex using a binary associative operator, and given $A' \subseteq A$ and $B' \subseteq B$ need to *subselect* the graph $G' = (A' \cup B', (A' \times B') \cap E)$.

For analyzing bounds, we assume that G is represented in a form of adjacency array we refer to as the *packed representation* of G. In this representation, the vertices in A and B and the edges in E are each stored contiguously, and each vertex has a pointer to a contiguous array of pointers to its incident edges. With this representation, all the operations mentioned in the previous paragraph can be implemented using standard techniques in $O(|G|)$ work and $O(\log |G|)$ depth on an EREW PRAM, where $|G| = |A| + |B| + |E|$. The set-cover algorithm also needs the following operation for constructing the packed representation.

Lemma 2.1 *Given a bipartite graph $G = (A \cup B, E)$ represented as an array of $a \in A$, each with a pointer to an array of integer identifiers for its neighbors in B, the packed representation of G can be generated with $O(|G|)$ work and $O(\log^2 |G|)$ depth (both w.h.p.) on a CRCW PRAM.*

PROOF. We note that the statement of the lemma allows for the integer identifiers to be sparse and possibly much larger than $|B|$. To implement the operation use duplicate elimination over the identifiers for B to get a unique representative for each $b \in B$ and give these representatives contiguous integer labels in the range $[|B|]$. This can be done with hashing in randomized $O(|G|)$-work $O(\log^2 |G|)$-depth [BM98]. Now that the labels for B are bounded by $[|B|]$ we can use a bounded integer sort [RR89] to collect all edges pointing to the same $b \in B$ and generate the adjacency arrays for the vertices in B in randomized $O(n)$ work and $O(\log n)$ depth on a (arbitrary) CRCW PRAM. $\square$

We will also use the following.

Lemma 2.2 *If $y_1, \ldots, y_n \in (0, 1]$ are drawn independently such that $\mathbf{Pr}\left[x_i \in \left(\frac{j-1}{n}, \frac{j}{n}\right]\right] \leq \frac{1}{n}$ for all $i, j = 1, \ldots, n$, then*

[2]We note that the sequential time for a weighted $(1 + \varepsilon)H_n$-approximation for set-cover is $O(M)$ when using bucketing.

the keys $y_1, \ldots, y_n$ can be sorted in expected $O(n)$ work and $O(\log n)$ depth on an CRCW *PRAM*

PROOF. Use parallel radix sort to bucket the keys into $B_1, \ldots, B_n$, where B_j contains keys between $\left(\frac{j-1}{n}, \frac{j}{n}\right]$. This requires $O(n)$ work and $O(\log n)$ depth. Then, for each B_i, in parallel, we can sort the elements in the bucket in $O(|B_i|^2)$ work $O(|B_i|)$ depth using, for example, a parallel implementation of the insertion sort algorithm. The work to sort these buckets is $\mathbf{E}\left[\sum_i |B_i|^2\right] \leq 2n$. Furthermore, balls-and-bins analysis shows that for all i, $|B_i| \leq O(\log n)$ with high probability. Thus, the depth of the sorting part is bounded by $\mathbf{E}[\max_i |B_i|] \leq O(\log n)$. $\square$

3. MANIS

We motivate the study of Maximal Nearly Independent Set (MaNIS) by revisiting existing parallel algorithms for set cover. These algorithms define a notion of utility—the number of new elements covered per unit cost—for each available option (set). Each iteration then involves identifying and working on the remaining sets that have utility within a $(1 + \varepsilon)$ factor of the current best utility value—and for fast progress, requires that the best option after an iteration has utility at most a $(1 + \varepsilon)$ factor smaller than before. Among the sets meeting the criterion, deciding which ones to include in the final solution is non-trivial. Selecting any one of these sets leads to an approximation ratio within $(1 + \varepsilon)$ of the strictly greedy algorithm but may not meet the fast progress requirement. Including all of them altogether leads to arbitrarily bad bounds on the approximation ratio (many sets are likely to share ground elements) but does ensure fast progress. To meet both requirements, we would like to select a "maximal" collection of sets that have small, bounded overlap—if a set is left unchosen, its utility must have dropped sufficiently. This leads to the following graph problem formulation, where the input bipartite graph models the interference between sets.

Definition 3.1 ((ε, δ)-MaNIS) *Let $\varepsilon, \delta > 0$. Given a bipartite graph $G = (A \cup B, E)$, we say that a set $J \subseteq A$ is a (ε, δ) maximal nearly independent set, or (ε, δ)-MaNIS, if*

(1) Nearly Independent. The chosen options do not interfere much with each other, i.e.,

$$|N(J)| \geq (1 - \delta - \varepsilon) \sum_{a \in J} |N(a)|.$$

(2) Maximal. The unchosen options have significant overlaps with the chosen options, i.e., for all $a \in A \setminus J$,

$$|N(a) \setminus N(J)| < (1 - \varepsilon)|N(a)|$$

The first condition in this MaNIS definition only provides guarantees on average—it ensures that *on average* each chosen option does not overlap much with each other. It is often desirable to have a stronger guarantee that provides assurance on a per-option basis. This motivates the following strengthened definition, which implies the previous definition.

Definition 3.2 (Ranked (ε, δ)-MaNIS) *Let $\varepsilon, \delta > 0$. Given a bipartite graph $G = (A \cup B, E)$, we say that a set $J = \{s_1, s_2, \ldots, s_k\} \subseteq A$ is a ranked (ε, δ) maximal nearly independent set, or a ranked (ε, δ)-MaNIS for short, if*

(1) Nearly Independent. There is an ordering (not part of the MaNIS solution) $s_1, s_2, \ldots, s_k$ such that each chosen option s_i is almost completely independent of $s_1, s_2, \ldots, s_{i-1}$, i.e., for all $i = 1, \ldots, k$,

$$|N(s_i) \setminus N(\{s_1, s_2, \ldots, s_{i-1}\})| \geq (1 - \delta - \varepsilon)|N(s_i)|.$$

(2) Maximal. The unchosen options have significant overlaps with the chosen options, i.e., for all $a \in A \setminus J$,

$$|N(a) \setminus N(J)| < (1 - \varepsilon)|N(a)|.$$

Under this definition, an algorithm for ranked MaNIS only has to return a set J but not the ordering. Furthermore, the following fact is easy to verify:

Fact 3.3 *If J is a ranked (ε, δ)-MaNIS, then every $J' \subseteq J$ satisfies $|N(J')| \geq (1 - \delta - \varepsilon) \sum_{j \in J'} |N(j)|$.*

Connection with previous work: Both versions of MaNIS can be seen as a generalization of maximal independent set (MIS). Indeed, when $\delta = \varepsilon = 0$, the problem is the maximal set packing problem, which can be solved using a maximal independent set algorithm [KW85, Lub86], albeit with $O(\log n)$ more work than the simple sequential algorithm that solves both versions of MaNIS in $O(|E|)$ sequential time.

Embedded in existing parallel set-cover algorithms are steps that can be extracted to compute MaNIS. We obtain from Berger et al. [BRS94] (henceforth, the BRS algorithm) an RNC^4 algorithm for computing $(\varepsilon, 8\varepsilon)$-MaNIS in $O(|E| \log^3 n)$ work. Similarly, we extract from Rajagopalan and Vazirani [RV98] (henceforth, the RV algorithm) an RNC^2 algorithm for computing *ranked* $(\varepsilon^2, 1 - \frac{1}{2(1+\varepsilon)} - \varepsilon^2)$-MaNIS in $O(|E| \log |E|)$ work.

Unfortunately, neither of the existing algorithms, as analyzed, is work efficient. In addition, the existing analysis of the RV algorithm places a restriction on δ: even when ε is arbitrarily close to 0, we cannot have δ below $\frac{1}{2}$.

3.1 Linear-Work Ranked MaNIS

We present an algorithm for the ranked MaNIS problem. Our algorithm is inspired by the RV algorithm. Not only is the algorithm work efficient but also it removes the $\frac{1}{2}$ restriction on δ, matching and surpassing the guarantees given by previous algorithms. To obtain these bounds, we need a new analysis that differs from that of the RV algorithm. Our algorithm can be modified to compute ranked (ε, δ)-MaNIS for any $0 < \varepsilon < \delta$ in essentially the same work and depth bounds (with worse constants); however, for the sake of presentation, we settle for the following theorem:

Theorem 3.4 (Ranked MaNIS) *Fix $\varepsilon > 0$. For a bipartite graph $G = (A \cup B, E)$ in packed representation there exists a randomized* EREW *PRAM algorithm* MaNIS$_{(\varepsilon, 3\varepsilon)}(G)$ *that produces a ranked $(\varepsilon, 3\varepsilon)$-MaNIS in $O(|E|)$ expected work and $O(\log^2 |E|)$ expected depth.*

Presented in Algorithm 3.1 is an algorithm for computing ranked MaNIS. To understand this algorithm, we will first consider a natural sequential algorithm for $(\varepsilon, 3\varepsilon)$-MaNIS—and discuss modifications that have led us to the parallel version. To compute MaNIS, we could first pick an ordering of the vertices of A and consider them in this order: for

Algorithm 3.1 $\text{MaNIS}_{(\varepsilon, 3\varepsilon)}$ — a parallel algorithm for computing ranked $(\varepsilon, 3\varepsilon)$-MaNIS

Input: a bipartite graph $G = (A \cup B, E)$.

Output: $J \subseteq A$ satisfying Definition 3.2.

Initialize $G^{(0)} = (A^{(0)} \cup B^{(0)}, E^{(0)}) = (A \cup B, E)$, and for each $a \in A$, $D(a) = |N_{G^{(0)}}(a)|$.

Set $t = 0$. Repeat the following steps until $A^{(t)}$ is empty:

1. For $a \in A^{(t)}$, randomly pick $x_a \in_R [0, 1]$

2. For $b \in B^{(t)}$, let $\varphi^{(t)}(b)$ be b's neighbor with maximum x_a

3. Pick vertices of $A^{(t)}$ chosen by sufficiently many in $B^{(t)}$:
$$J^{(t)} = \left\{ a \in A^{(t)} \ \Big| \ \sum_{b \in B^{(t)}} \mathbf{1}_{\{\varphi^{(t)}(b)=a\}} \geq (1 - 4\varepsilon)D(a) \right\}.$$

4. Update the graph by removing J and its neighbors, and elements of $A^{(t)}$ with too few remaining neighbors:
$B^{(t+1)} = B^{(t)} \setminus N_{G^{(t)}}(J^{(t)})$
$A^{(t+1)} = \{a \in A^{(t)} \setminus J^{(t)} : |N_{G^{(t)}}(a) \cap B^{(t+1)}| \geq (1-\varepsilon)D(a)\}$
$E^{(t+1)} = E^{(t)} \cap (A^{(t+1)} \times B^{(t+1)})$

5. $t = t + 1$

Finally, return $J = J^{(0)} \cup \cdots \cup J^{(t-1)}$.

---

each $a \in A$, if a has at least $(1 - 4\varepsilon)D(a)$ neighbors, we add a to the output and delete its neighbors; otherwise, set it aside. Thus, every vertex added certainly satisfies the nearly-independent requirement. Furthermore, if a vertex is not added, its degree must have dropped below $(1 - \varepsilon)D(a)$, which ensures the maximality condition.

Algorithm 3.1 achieves parallelism in two ways. First, we adapt the selection process so that multiple vertices can be chosen together at the same time. Unlike the sequential algorithm, the parallel version can decide whether to include a vertex $a \in A$ without knowing the outcomes of the preceding vertices. This is done by making the inclusion condition more conservative: Assign each $b \in B$ to the first $a \in A$ in the chosen ordering—regardless of whether a will be included in the solution. Then, for each $a \in A$, include it in the solution if enough of its neighbors are assigned to it. This step is highly parallel and ensures that every vertex added satisfies the nearly-independent requirement. Unfortunately, this process by itself may miss vertices that must be included.

Second, we repeat the selection process until no more vertices can be selected but ensure that the number of iterations is small. As the analysis below shows, a random permutation allows the algorithm to remove a constant fraction of the edges, making sure that it will finish in a logarithmic number of iterations. Note that unlike before, the multiple iterations make it necessary to distinguish between the original degree of a vertex, $D(a)$, and its degree in the current iteration (which we denote by $\deg(a)$ in the proof). Furthermore, we need an clean-up step after each iteration to eliminate vertices that are already maximal so that they will not hamper progress in subsequent rounds.

Running Time Analysis: To prove the work and depth bounds, consider the potential function
$$\Phi^{(t)} \stackrel{\text{def}}{=} \sum_{a \in A^{(t)}} |N_{G^{(t)}}(a)|,$$

which counts the number of remaining edges. The following lemma shows that sufficient progress is made in each step:

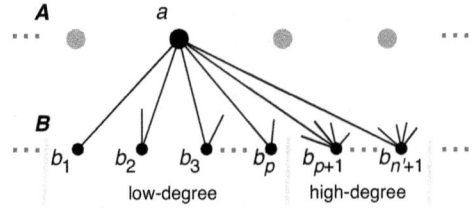

Figure 1: MaNIS analysis: for each $a \in A^{(t)}$, **order its neighbors so that** $N_{G^{(t)}}(a) = \{b_1, \ldots, b_{n'}\}$ **and** $\deg(b_1) \leq \deg(b_2) \leq \cdots \leq \deg(b_{n'})$, **where** $n' = \deg_{G^{(t)}}(a)$.

Lemma 3.5 *For* $t \geq 0$, $\mathbf{E}\left[\Phi^{(t+1)}\right] \leq (1 - c)\Phi^{(t)}$, *where* $c = \frac{1}{4}\varepsilon^2(1 - \varepsilon)$.

Before proceeding with the proof, we offer a high-level sketch. We say a vertex $a \in A^{(t)}$ deletes an edge (a', b) if $a \in J^{(t)}$ and $\varphi^{(t)}(b) = a$. In essence, the proof shows that for $a \in A^{(t)}$, the expected number of edges a deletes, denoted by Δ_a in the proof, is proportional to the degree of a. If a has few neighbors, it suffices to consider the probability that all neighbors select a. Otherwise, the proof separates the neighbors of a into high- and low- degree groups and analyzes Δ_a by averaging over possible values of x_a. In particular, it considers a y_a (i.e., $1 - \varepsilon/\deg(b_p)$ in the proof) such that for all $x_a \geq y_a$, there are likely sufficiently many low-degree neighbors that select a to ensure with constant probability that a is in $J^{(t)}$. Then, the proof shows that there is sufficient contribution to Δ_a from just the high-degree neighbors and just when $x_a \geq y_a$ (that is when a is likely in $J^{(t)}$). This is formalized in the proof below.

PROOF. Consider an iteration t. Let $\deg(x) = \deg_{G^{(t)}}(x)$ and $\Delta_a = \mathbf{1}_{\{a \in J^{(t)}\}} \sum_{b: \varphi^{(t)}(b)=a} \deg(b)$. Thus, when a is included in $J^{(t)}$, Δ_a is the sum of the degrees of all neighbors of a that are assigned to a (by $\varphi^{(t)}$). It is zero otherwise if $a \notin J^{(t)}$. Since $\varphi^{(t)} : B^{(t)} \to A^{(t)}$ maps each $b \in B^{(t)}$ to a unique element in $A^{(t)}$, the sum of Δ_a over a is a lower bound on the number edges we lose in this round. That is,
$$\Phi^{(t)} - \Phi^{(t+1)} \geq \sum_{a \in A^{(t)}} \Delta_a,$$

so it suffices to show that for all $a \in A^{(t)}$, $\mathbf{E}[\Delta_a] \geq c \cdot \deg(a)$.

Let $a \in A^{(t)}$ be given and assume WLOG that $N_{G^{(t)}}(a) = \{b_1, \ldots, b_{n'}\}$ such that $\deg(b_1) \leq \deg(b_2) \leq \cdots \leq \deg(b_{n'})$. (as shown in Figure 1). Now consider the following cases:

— *Case 1. a has only a few neighbors:* Suppose $n' < \frac{2}{\varepsilon}$. Let $\mathcal{E}_1$ be the event that $x_a = \max\{x_{a'} : a' \in N_{G^{(t)}}(N_{G^{(t)}}(A^{(t)}))\}$. Then, $\mathcal{E}_1$ implies that (1) $a \in J^{(t)}$ and (2) $\varphi^{(t)}(b_{n'}) = a$. Therefore,
$$\mathbf{E}[\Delta_a] \geq \mathbf{Pr}[\mathcal{E}_1] \cdot \deg(b_{n'}) \geq \frac{1}{n'} \geq c \cdot \deg(a),$$

because $|N_{G^{(t)}}(N_{G^{(t)}}(A^{(t)}))| \leq n' \cdot \deg(b_{n'})$ and $n' = \deg(a) < 2/\varepsilon$.

— *Case 2. a has many neighbors*, i.e., $n' \geq \frac{2}{\varepsilon}$. Partition the neighbors of a into low- and high- degree elements as follows. Let $p = \lfloor (1 - \varepsilon)\deg(a) \rfloor$, $L(a) = \{b_1, \ldots, b_p\}$, and $H(a) = \{b_{p+1}, \ldots, b_{n'}\}$. To complete the proof for this case, we rely on the following claim.

Claim 3.6 *Let* $\mathsf{select}_a^{(t)} = \{b \in B^{(t)} : \varphi^{(t)}(b) = a\}$, *and* $\mathcal{E}_2$ *be the event that* $|L(a) \setminus \mathsf{select}_a^{(t)}| \le 2\varepsilon|L(a)|$. *Then, (i) for* $\gamma \le \varepsilon/\deg(b_p)$, $\mathbf{Pr}[\mathcal{E}_2|x_a = 1 - \gamma] \ge \frac{1}{2}$; *and (ii) for* $b \in H(a)$ *and* $\gamma \le \varepsilon/\deg(b)$, $\mathbf{Pr}\big[\varphi^{(t)}(b) = a|\mathcal{E}_2, x_a = 1 - \gamma\big] \ge 1 - \varepsilon$.

Note that $\mathcal{E}_2$ implies $|\mathsf{select}_a^{(t)}| \ge n' - \varepsilon n' - 2\varepsilon n' \ge (1 - 4\varepsilon)D(a)$, because $n' \ge (1-\varepsilon)D(a)$. This in turn means that $\mathcal{E}_2$ implies $a \in J^{(t)}$. Applying the claim, we establish

$$\mathbf{E}[\Delta_a] \ge \sum_{b \in H(a)} \deg(b)\mathbf{Pr}\Big[\mathcal{E}_2 \wedge \varphi^{(t)}(b) = a\Big]$$

$$\ge \sum_{b \in H(a)} \int_{\gamma=0}^{\frac{\varepsilon}{\deg(b)}} \deg(b)\mathbf{Pr}\big[\mathcal{E}_2|x_a = 1 - \gamma\big]$$
$$\mathbf{Pr}\Big[\varphi^{(t)}(b) = a|\mathcal{E}_2, x_a = 1 - \gamma\Big]d\gamma$$

$$\ge \sum_{b \in H(a)} \varepsilon\frac{1}{2}(1 - \varepsilon)$$

$$\ge c \cdot \deg(a),$$

where the final step follows because $|H(a)| \ge \varepsilon n' \ge 1$. $\quad\square$

Proof of Claim 3.6: To prove (i), let $X \stackrel{\text{def}}{=} |L(a)\setminus\mathsf{select}_a^{(t)}| = \sum_{j\in L(a)} \mathbf{1}_{\{j\notin\mathsf{select}_a^{(t)}\}}$, so

$$\mathbf{E}[X|x_a = 1 - \gamma] = \sum_{j\in L(a)} \mathbf{Pr}\Big[j \notin \mathsf{select}_a^{(t)}|x_a = 1 - \gamma\Big].$$

Then, note that $j \in \mathsf{select}_a^{(t)}$ iff. $x_a = \max\{x_i : i \in N_{G^{(t)}}(j)\}$. Thus, for $j \in L(a)$,

$$\mathbf{Pr}\Big[j \notin \mathsf{select}_a^{(t)}|x_a = 1 - \gamma\Big] \le 1 - \left(1 - \frac{\varepsilon}{\deg(b_p)}\right)^{\deg(j)} \le \varepsilon,$$

and so $\mathbf{E}[X|x_a = 1 - \gamma] \le \varepsilon|L(a)|$. By Markov's inequality, we have $\mathbf{Pr}[\mathcal{E}_2|x_a = 1 - \gamma] \ge 1 - \frac{\varepsilon}{2\varepsilon} = \frac{1}{2}$.

We will now prove (ii). Consider that for $i \in N_{G^{(t)}}(b)\setminus\{a\}$, $\mathbf{Pr}[x_i > x_a|\mathcal{E}_2, x_a = 1 - \gamma] \le \gamma$. Union bounds give

$$\mathbf{Pr}\Big[\varphi^{(t)}(b) = a|\mathcal{E}_2, x_a = 1 - \gamma\Big] \ge 1 - \sum_{i \in N_{G^{(t)}}(b)\setminus\{a\}} \gamma$$
$$\ge 1 - \varepsilon.$$

$\quad\blacksquare$

Each iteration can be implemented in $O(\Phi^{(t)})$ work and $O(\log \Phi^{(t)})$ depth on an **EREW** PRAM since beyond trivial parallel application and some summations, the iteration only involves the operations on the packed representation of G discussed in Section 2. Since $\Phi^{(t)}$ decreases geometrically (in expectation), the bounds follow. Algorithm 3.1 as described selects random reals x_a between 0 and 1. But it is sufficient for each a to use a random integer with $O(\log n)$ bits such that w.h.p., there are no collisions. In fact, since the x_a's are only compared, it suffices to use a random permutation over A since the distribution over the ranking would be the same.

4. LINEAR-WORK SET COVER

As our first example, in this section, we apply MaNIS to parallelize a greedy approximation algorithm for weighted set cover. Specifically, we prove the following theorem:

Theorem 4.1 *Fix* $0 < \varepsilon < \frac{1}{2}$. *For a set system* $(\mathcal{U}, \mathcal{F})$, *where* $|\mathcal{U}| = n$, *there is a randomized* $(1+\varepsilon)H_n$-*approximation*

Algorithm 4.1 SetCover — parallel greedy set cover.

Input: a set cover instance $(\mathcal{U}, \mathcal{F}, c)$.

Output: a collection of sets covering the ground elements.

i. Let $\gamma = \max_{e\in\mathcal{U}} \min_{S\in\mathcal{F}} c(S)$,
   $M = \sum_{S\in\mathcal{F}} |S|$,
   $T = \log_{1/(1-\varepsilon)}(M^3/\varepsilon)$,
   and $\beta = \frac{M^2}{\varepsilon\cdot\gamma}$.

ii. Let $(\mathcal{A}; A_0, \dots, A_T) = \texttt{Prebucket}(\mathcal{U}, \mathcal{F}, c)$ and $\mathcal{U}_0 = \mathcal{U}$

iii. For $t = 0, \dots, T$, perform the following steps:

1. Remove deleted elements from sets in this bucket:
   $A_t' = \{S \cap \mathcal{U}_t : S \in A_t\}$
2. Only keep sets that still belong in this bucket:
   $A_t'' = \{S \in A_t' : c(S)/|S| > \beta \cdot (1 - \varepsilon)^{t+1}\}$
3. Select a maximal nearly independent set from the bucket:
   $J_t = \texttt{MaNIS}_{(\varepsilon, 3\varepsilon)}(A_t'')$
4. Remove elements covered by J_t:
   $\mathcal{U}_{t+1} = \mathcal{U}_t \setminus X_t$ where $X_t = \cup_{S\in J_t} S$
5. Move remaining sets to the next bucket:
   $A_{t+1} = A_{t+1} \cup (A_t' \setminus J_t)$

iv. Finally, return $\mathcal{A} \cup J_0 \cup \dots \cup J_T$.

---

for (weighted) set cover that runs in $O(M)$ *expected work and* $O(\log^3 M)$ *expected depth on a* **CRCW** *PRAM, where* $M = \sum_{S\in\mathcal{F}} |S|$.

We describe a parallel greedy approximation algorithm for set cover in Algorithm 4.1. To motivate the algorithm, we discuss three ideas crucial for transforming the standard greedy set-cover algorithm into a linear-work algorithm with substantial parallelism: (1) approximate greedy through bucketing, (2) prebucketing and lazy bucket transfer, and (3) subselection via MaNIS. Despite the presence of some these ideas in previous work, it is the combination of our improved MaNIS algorithm and careful lazy bucket transfer that is responsible for better work and approximation bounds.

Like in previous algorithms, bucketing creates opportunities for parallelism at the round level, by grouping together sets by their coverage-per-unit-cost values in powers of $(1-\varepsilon)$. Consequently, there will be at most $O(\log_{1+\varepsilon}\rho)$ buckets (also rounds), where ρ is the ratio between the largest and the smallest coverage-per-unit-cost values. This, however, raises several questions (which are solved by ideas (2) and (3)).

First, *how can we make ρ small and keep the contents of the relevant buckets "fresh" in linear work?* As detailed in Lemma 4.2, the algorithm relies on a subroutine **Prebucket** that first preprocesses the input to keep ρ polynomially bounded by setting aside certain "cheap" sets that will be included in the final solution by default and throwing away sets that will never be used in the solution. It then classifies the sets into buckets $A_0, A_1, \dots A_T$ by their utility; however, this initial bucketing will be stale as the algorithm progresses. While we cannot afford to reclassify the sets in every round, it suffices to maintain an invariant that each set in $S \in A_i$ satisfies $|S \cap \mathcal{U}_t|/c(S) \le \beta \cdot (1-\varepsilon)^i$. Further, we make sure that the bucket that contains the current best option is fresh—and move the sets that do not belong there accordingly.

Second, *what to do with the sets in each bucket to satisfy both the bucket invariant and the desired approximation ratio?* This is where we apply MaNIS. As previously discussed in Section 3, MaNIS allows the algorithm to choose nearly non-overlapping sets, which helps bound the approximation guarantees and ensures that sets which MaNIS leaves out can be moved to the next bucket and satisfy the bucket invariant.

In the following lemma and proof, we use the definitions for γ, M, T, and β from Algorithm 4.1. Further, let **opt** denote the optimal cost.

Lemma 4.2 *There is an algorithm* `Prebucket` *that takes as input a set system* $(\mathcal{U}, \mathcal{F}, c)$ *and produces a set* $\mathcal{A}$ *such that* $c(\mathcal{A}) \leq \varepsilon \cdot$ **opt** *and buckets* $A_0, \ldots, A_T$ *such that*

1. *for each* $S \in \mathcal{F} \setminus \mathcal{A}$, *either* S *costs more than* $M\gamma$ *or* $S \in A_i$ *for which* $c(S)/|S| \in (\beta \cdot (1-\varepsilon)^{i+1}, \beta \cdot (1-\varepsilon)^i]$.

2. *there exists a set cover solution costing at most* **opt** *using sets from* $\mathcal{A} \cup A_0 \cup A_1 \cup \cdots \cup A_T$;

3. *the algorithm runs in* $O(M)$ *work and* $O(\log M)$ *depth on a* CRCW *PRAM.*

PROOF. We rely on the following bounds on **opt** [RV98]: $\gamma \leq$ **opt** $\leq M\gamma$. Two things are clear as a consequence: (i) if $c(S) \leq \varepsilon \cdot \frac{\gamma}{M}$, S can be included in $\mathcal{A}$, yielding a total cost at most $\varepsilon\gamma \leq \varepsilon \cdot$ **opt**. (ii) if $c(S) > M\gamma$, then S can be discarded (S is not part of any optimal solution).

Thus, we are left with sets costing between $\varepsilon \cdot \frac{\gamma}{M}$ and $M\gamma$. Compute $|S|/c(S)$ for each remaining set S, in parallel, and store S in A_i such that $c(S)/|S| \in (\beta \cdot (1-\varepsilon)^{i+1}, \beta \cdot (1-\varepsilon)^i]$. We know that $1/(M\gamma) \leq c(S)/|S| \leq M^2/(\varepsilon\gamma) = \beta$, so the buckets are numbered between $i = 0$ and $i = \log_{1/(1-\varepsilon)}(M^3/\varepsilon) = T$.

Computing M, γ, and $c(S)/|S|$ for all sets S can be done in $O(M)$ work and $O(\log M)$ depth using parallel sums. Once each set knows its bucket based on $c(S)/|S|$, a stable integer sort over integers in the range $[O(\log M)]$ can be used to collect them into buckets with the same work and depth bounds [RR89]. □

Approximation Guarantees: We follow a standard proof in Vazirani [Vaz01]. It should be noted that although we do not mention LPs here, the proof given below is similar in spirit to the dual-fitting proof presented by Rajagopalan and Vazirani [RV98]. Let $p_t = \frac{1}{\beta}(1-\varepsilon)^{-(t+1)}$. For each $e \in \mathcal{U}$, if e is covered in iteration t, define the price of this element to be $p(e) = p_t$. That is, every element covered in this iteration has the same price p_t. Now, Step 2 ensures that if $S \in A_t''$ can cover e, then $c(S)/|S| \leq p(e)$, where $|S|$ is the size of S after Step 2 in iteration t. Let $X_t = \cup_{S \in J_t} S$ be the set of elements covered in iteration t. The near independent property of $(\varepsilon, 3\varepsilon)$-MaNIS indicates that $|X_t| = |N(J_t)| \geq (1-4\varepsilon)\sum_{S \in J_t} N(S)$, where $N(\cdot)$ here is the neighborhood set in A_t''. Thus, $c(J_0 \cup \cdots \cup J_T)$ can be written as

$$\sum_t \sum_{S \in J_t} \frac{c(S)}{|S|} \cdot |S| \leq \sum_t p_t \sum_{S \in J_t} |S| \leq \frac{1}{1-4\varepsilon} \sum_{e \in \mathcal{U}} p(e).$$

Let $\mathcal{O}^*$ be any optimal solution. Consider a set $S^* \in \mathcal{O}^*$. Since all buckets $t' < t$ are empty, we know that $p_t \leq \frac{1}{1-\varepsilon} \min_{S \in A_t''} \frac{c(S)}{|S|}$. Furthermore, for each $e \in S^*$, let t_e denote the iteration in which e was covered. By greedy properties (as argued in [RV98, Vaz01]),

$$\sum_{e \in S^*} \min_{S \in G_{t_e}''} \frac{c(S)}{|S|} \leq \left(1 + \frac{1}{2} + \frac{1}{3} + \ldots \frac{1}{|S^*|}\right)c(S^*).$$

Hence, $c(J_0 \cup \cdots \cup J_T) \leq \frac{1}{1-5\varepsilon} \sum_{S^* \in \mathcal{O}^*} H_{|S^*|} c(S^*) \leq \frac{1}{1-5\varepsilon} H_n \cdot$ **opt** $\leq (1+\varepsilon')H_n \cdot$ **opt** (using $\varepsilon = O(\varepsilon')$), as promised.

Implementation and Work and Depth Bounds: To analyze the cost of the algorithm, we need to be more specific about the representation of all structures that are used. We assume the sets $S \in \mathcal{F}$ are given unique integer identifiers $[|\mathcal{F}|]$, and similarly for the elements $e \in \mathcal{U}$. Each set keeps a pointer to an array of identifiers for its elements, and each bucket keeps a pointer to an array of identifiers for its sets. The sets can shrink over time as elements are filtered out in Step 1 of each iteration of the algorithm. We keep a Boolean array indicating which of the elements from $\mathcal{U}$ remain in $\mathcal{U}_{\sqcup}$. Let $\mathcal{A}^{(t)}$ be the snapshot of A_t at the beginning of iteration t of Algorithm 4.1, and $M_t = \sum_{S \in \mathcal{A}^{(t)}} |S|$.

Claim: Iteration t of Algorithm 4.1 can be accomplished in expected $O(M_t)$ work and $O(\log^2 M_t)$ depth on the randomized CRCW PRAM.

Steps 1 and 2 use simple filtering on arrays of total length $O(M_t)$, which can be done with prefix sums. Step 3 requires converting adjacency arrays for each set in A_t'' to the packed representation needed by MaNIS. The indices of the elements might be sparse, but this conversion can be done using Lemma 2.1. The cost of this conversion, as well as the cost of running MaNIS, is within the claimed bounds. Step 4 and 5 just involve setting flags, a filter, and an append, all on arrays of length $O(M_t)$.

Now there are $O(\log M)$ iterations, and `Prebucket` has depth $O(\log M)$, so the overall depth is bounded by $O(\log^3 M)$. To prove the work bound, we will derive a bound on $\sum_t M_t$. We note that every time a set is moved from one bucket to the next its size decreases by a constant factor, and hence the total work attributed to each set is proportional to its original size. More formally, we have the following claim:

Claim: If $S \in \mathcal{A}^{(t)}$, $|S| \leq c(S) \cdot \beta \cdot (1-\varepsilon)^t$.

This claim can be shown inductively: For any set $S \in \mathcal{F}$, `Prebucket` guarantees that the bucket that S went into satisfies the claim. Following that, this set can be shrunk and moved (Steps 1, 2, and 5). It is easy to check that the claim is satisfied (by noting Steps 2 and 5's criteria and that sets not chosen by MaNIS are shrunk by an ε fraction).

By this claim, the total sum $\sum_t M_t$ is at most

$$\sum_t \sum_{S \in \mathcal{A}^{(t)}} c(S) \cdot \beta \cdot (1-\varepsilon)^t \leq \sum_{S \in \mathcal{F}} \frac{1}{\varepsilon} \cdot c(S)\beta \cdot (1-\varepsilon)^{t_S},$$

where t_S is the bucket index of S in the initial bucketing. Furthermore, Lemma 4.2 indicates that $|S| \geq c(S) \cdot \beta \cdot (1-\varepsilon)^{t_S+1}$, showing that $\sum_t M_t = O(\frac{1}{\varepsilon}M)$ as $\varepsilon \leq \frac{1}{2}$. Since the work on each step is proportional to M_t, the overall work is $O(\frac{1}{\varepsilon}M)$.

5. SET COVERING VARIANTS

Using the `SetCover` algorithm from the previous section, we describe simple changes to the algorithm or the analysis that results in solutions to variants of set cover. In this section, *we will be working with unweighted set cover.*

Ordered vs. Unordered. We would like to develop algorithms for prefix-optimal max cover and min-sum set cover, using our set-cover algorithm; however, unlike set cover, these problems want an ordering on the chosen sets—not

28

just an unordered collection. As we now describe, minimal changes to the `SetCover` algorithm will enable it to output an ordered sequence of sets which closely approximate the greedy behavior. Specially, we will give an algorithm with the following property[3]: Let $\mathcal{T} \subseteq \mathcal{U}$ be given. Suppose there exist ℓ sets covering $\mathcal{T}$, and our parallel algorithm outputs an ordered collection $S_1, \ldots, S_p$ covering $\mathcal{U}$, then

Lemma 5.1 *For any $i \leq p$, the number of elements in $\mathcal{T}$ freshly covered by S_i, i.e., $|S_i \cap R_i|$, is at least $(1-5\varepsilon)|R_i|/\ell$, where $R_i = \mathcal{T} \setminus (\cup_{j<i}S_j)$ contains the elements of $\mathcal{T}$ that remain uncovered after choosing $S_1, \ldots, S_{i-1}$.*

We modify the `SetCover` algorithm as follows. Make `MaNIS` returns a totally ordered sequence, by sorting each $J^{(t)}$ by their x_a's values and stringing together the sorted sequences $J^{(0)}, J^{(1)}, \ldots$; this can be done in the same work-depth bounds (Lemma 2.2) in CRCW. Further, modify `SetCover` so that (1) `Prebucket` only buckets the sets (but will not throw away sets nor eagerly include some of them) and (2) its Step iv. returns a concatenated sequence, instead of a union. Again, this does not change the work-depth bound but outputs an ordered sequence.

Next, we show that the output sequence has the claimed property by proving the following technical claim (variables here refer to those in Algorithm 4.1). Lemma 5.1 is a direct sequence of this claim (note that the sets we output come from $J_0, J_1, \ldots$ in that order).

Claim 5.2 *For all $t \geq 0$, if $\widehat{J}_t \subseteq J_t$ and $\widehat{X}_t = \cup_{S \in \widehat{J}_t} S$, then $|\widehat{X}_t \cap \mathcal{T}| \geq (1-5\varepsilon) \cdot |\widehat{J}_t| \cdot |Q_t|/\ell$, where $Q_t = \mathcal{T} \setminus (\cup_{t' < t} X_{t'})$.*

PROOF. Let $t \geq 0$. By our assumption, there exist ℓ sets that fully cover Q_t. An averaging argument shows that there must be a single set, among the remaining sets, with a coverage ratio of at least $|Q_t|/\ell$. Since at the beginning of iteration t, we have $A_{t'} = \emptyset$ for $t' < t$, it follows that $\tau_t \geq |Q_t|/\ell$, where $\tau_t = \beta \cdot (1-\varepsilon)^t$. Furthermore, all sets $S \in A_t''$ have the property that $|S| \geq \tau_t(1-\varepsilon)$. Furthermore, Fact 3.3 guarantees that $\widehat{J}_t$ covers, among $\mathcal{T}$, at least $|N(\widehat{J}_t)| \geq (1 - 4\varepsilon) \sum_{j \in \widehat{J}_t} |N(j)| \geq (1-4\varepsilon)(1-\varepsilon)\tau_t|\widehat{J}_t| \geq (1-5\varepsilon)|\widehat{J}_t||Q_t|/\ell$, proving the lemma. $\square$

5.1 Max Cover

The max k-cover problem takes as input an integer $k > 0$ and a set system (generally unweighted), and the goal is to find k sets that cover as many elements as possible. The sequential greedy algorithm gives a $(1-1/e)$-approximation, which is tight assuming standard complexity assumptions. In the parallel setting, previous parallel set-covering algorithms do not directly give $(1 - \frac{1}{e} - \varepsilon)$-approximation. But in the related MapReduce model, Chierichetti et al. [CKT10] give a $1 - 1/e - \varepsilon$-approximation, which gives rise to a $O(m \log^3 M)$-work algorithm in PRAM, where $M = \sum_{S \in \mathcal{F}} |S|$. This is not work efficient compared to the greedy algorithm, which runs in at most $O(M \log M)$ time for any k.

In this section, we give a factor-$(1 - \frac{1}{e} - \varepsilon)$ prefix optimal algorithm for max cover. As in Chierichetti et al. [CKT10],

we say that a sequence of sets $S_1, S_2, \ldots, S_p$ covering the whole ground elements is *factor-σ prefix optimal* if for all $k \leq p$, $|\cup_{i \leq k} S_i| \geq \sigma \cdot \mathsf{opt}_k$, where opt_k denotes the optimal coverage using k sets. More specifically, we prove the following theorem:

Theorem 5.3 *Fix $0 < \varepsilon < \frac{1}{2}$. There is a factor-$(1 - \frac{1}{e} - \varepsilon)$ prefix optimal algorithm the max cover problem requiring $O(M)$ work and $O(\log^3 M)$ depth, where $M = \sum_{S \in \mathcal{F}} |S|$.*

PROOF. Use the algorithm from Lemma 5.1, so the work-depth bounds follow immediately from set cover. To argue prefix optimality, let k be given and $OPT_k \subseteq \mathcal{F}$ be an optimal max k-cover solution. Applying Lemma 5.1 with $\mathcal{T} = OPT_k$ gives that $|R_{i+1}| \leq |R_i|(1 - \frac{1}{k}(1 - 5\varepsilon))$ and $|R_1| = |OPT_k|$. Also, we know that using $S_1, \ldots, S_k$, we will have covered at least $OPT_k - |R_{k+1}|$ elements of OPT_k. By unfolding the recurrence, we have $OPT_k - |R_{k+1}| \geq OPT_k - OPT_k \cdot \exp\{-(1 - 5\varepsilon)\}$. Setting $\varepsilon = \frac{e}{5}\varepsilon'$ completes the proof. $\square$

5.2 Special Case: Unweighted Set Cover

When the sets all have the same cost, we can derive a slightly different and stronger form of approximation guarantees for the same algorithm. We apply this bound to derive guarantees for asymmetric k-center in Section 5.4. The following corollary can be derived from Lemma 5.1 in a manner similar to the max-cover proof; we omit the proof in the interest of space.

Corollary 5.4 *Let $0 < \varepsilon \leq \frac{1}{2}$. For an unweighted set cover instance, set cover can be approximated with cost at most $\mathsf{opt}(1+\varepsilon)(1+\ln(n/\mathsf{opt}))$, where opt is the cost of the optimal set cover solution.*

5.3 Min-Sum Set Cover

Another important and well-studied set covering problem is the min-sum set cover problem: given a set system $(\mathcal{U}, \mathcal{F})$, the goal is to find a sequence $S_1, \ldots, S_{n'}$ to minimize the cost $cost(\langle S_1, \ldots, S_{n'} \rangle) \stackrel{\text{def}}{=} \sum_{e \in \mathcal{U}} \tau(e)$, where $\tau(e) \stackrel{\text{def}}{=} \min\{i : e \in S_i\}$. Feige et al. [FLT04] (also implicit in Bar-Noy et al. [BNBH+98]) showed that the standard set cover algorithm gives a 4-approximation, which is optimal unless $\mathsf{P} = \mathsf{NP}$. The following theorem shows that this carries over to our parallel set cover algorithm:

Theorem 5.5 *Fix $0 < \varepsilon \leq \frac{1}{2}$. There is a parallel $(4 + \varepsilon)$-approximation algorithm for the min-sum set cover problem that runs in $O(M)$ work and $O(\log^3 M)$ depth.*

PROOF. Consider the modified algorithm in Lemma 5.1. Suppose it outputs a sequence of sets $\mathsf{Alg} = \langle S_1, S_2, \ldots, S_{n'} \rangle$ covering $\mathcal{U}$, and an optimal solution is $\mathcal{O}^* = \langle O_1, \ldots, O_q \rangle$. Let $\alpha_i = S_i \setminus (\cup_{j<i} S_j)$ denote the elements freshly covered by S_i and $\beta_i = \mathcal{U} \setminus (\cup_{j<i} S_j)$ be the elements not covered by $S_1, \ldots, S_{i-1}$. Thus, $|\beta_i| = |\mathcal{U}| - \sum_{j<i} |\alpha_j|$. Following Feige et al. [FLT04], the cost of our solution is $cost(\mathsf{Alg}) = \sum_{i>0} i \cdot |\alpha_i| = \sum_{i>0} |\beta_i|$, which can be rewritten as $\sum_{i>0} \sum_{e \in \alpha_i} \frac{|\beta_i|}{|\alpha_i|} = \sum_{e \in \mathcal{U}} p(e)$, where the price $p(e) = \frac{|\beta_i|}{|\alpha_i|}$ for i such that $e \in \alpha_i$. We will depict and argue about these costs pictorially as follows. First, the "histogram" diagram (below) is made up of $|\mathcal{U}|$ horizontal columns, ordered from left to right in the order the optimal solution covers them.

---

[3]This is the analog of the following fact from the sequential greedy algorithm [You95, PV98]: if there exist ℓ sets covering $\mathcal{T}$, and greedy picks sets $\chi_1, \ldots, \chi_p$ (in that order) covering $\mathcal{U}$, then for $i \leq p$, the number of elements in $\mathcal{T}$ freshly covered by χ_i is at least $|R_i|/\ell$, where $R_i = \mathcal{T} \setminus (\cup_{j<i}\chi_j)$.

The height of column $e \in \mathcal{U}$ is its $\tau(e)$ in the optimal solution. Additionally, the "price" diagram is also made up of $|\mathcal{U}|$ columns, though ordered from left to right in the order our solution covers them; the height of column e is $p(e)$.

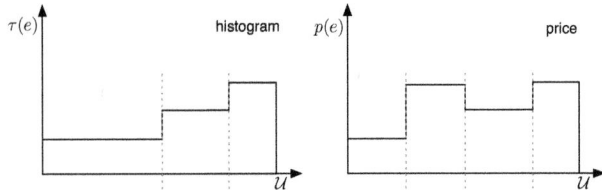

We can easily check that (1) the histogram curve has area opt $= cost(\mathcal{O}^*)$ and (2) the price curve has area $cost(\mathsf{Alg})$. We will show that shrinking the price diagram by 2 horizontally and θ vertically (θ to be chosen later) allows it to lie completely inside the histogram when they are aligned on the bottom-right corner. Let $p = (x, y)$ be a point inside (or on) the price diagram. Suppose p lies in the column $e \in \alpha_i$, so $y \leq p(e) = |\beta_i|/|\alpha_i|$—and p is at most $|\beta_i|$ from the right.

When shrunk, p will have height $h = p(e)/\theta$ and width—the distance from the right end—$r = \frac{1}{2}|\beta_i|$. We estimate how many elements inside β_i are covered by the optimal solution using its first h sets. Of all the sets in $\mathcal{F}$, there exists a set S such that $|S \cap \beta_i| \geq |O_j^* \cap \beta_i|$ for all $j < i$.

Arguing similarly to previous proofs in this section, we have that $|\alpha_i| \geq (1 - 5\varepsilon)|S|$, so at this time, the optimal algorithm could have covered at most $h \cdot \frac{1}{1-5\varepsilon}|\alpha_i|$. Setting $\theta = \frac{2}{1-5\varepsilon}$ gives that the first h sets of $\mathcal{O}^*$ will leave $|\beta_i| - \frac{1}{2}|\beta_i| \geq \frac{1}{2}|\beta_i| = r$ elements of β_i remaining. Therefore, the scaled version of p lies inside the histogram, proving that the algorithm is a 2θ-approximation. By setting $\varepsilon = \frac{1}{40}\varepsilon'$, we have $2\theta = \frac{4}{1-5\varepsilon} \leq 4 + \varepsilon'$, which completes the proof. $\square$

5.4 Application: Asymmetric k-Center

Building on the set cover algorithm we just developed, we present an algorithm for asymmetric k-center. The input is an integer $k > 0$ and a distance function $d \colon V \times V \to \mathbb{R}_+$, where V is a set of n vertices; the goal is to find a set $F \subseteq V$ of k centers that minimizes the objective $\max_{j \in V} \min_{i \in F} d(i, j)$, where $d(x, y)$, which needs not be symmetric, denotes the distance from x to y. The distance d, however, is assumed to satisfy the triangle inequality, i.e., $d(x, y) \leq d(x, z) + d(z, y)$. For symmetric d, there is a 2-approximation for both the sequential [HS85, Gon85] and parallel settings [BT10]. This result is optimal assuming $\mathsf{P} \neq \mathsf{NP}$. However, when d is not symmetric—hence the name asymmetric k-center, there is a $O(\log^* n)$-approximation in the sequential setting, which is also optimal unless $\mathsf{NP} \subseteq \mathsf{DTIME}(n^{O(\log \log n)})$ [CGH+05], but nothing was previously known for the parallel setting.

In this section, we develop a parallel factor-$O(\log^* n)$ algorithm for this problem, based on the (sequential) algorithm of Panigrahy and Vishwanathan [PV98]. Thier algorithm consists of two phases: recursive cover and find-and-halve.

Recursive Cover for Asymmetric k-Center. The recursive cover algorithm of Panigrahy and Vishwanathan [PV98] (shown below) is easy to parallelize given the set cover routine from Corollary 5.4. Here, V is the input set of vertices.

Set $A_0 = A$ and $i = 0$. While $|A_i| > 2k$, repeat the following:

1. Construct a set cover instance $(\mathcal{U}, \mathcal{F})$, where $\mathcal{U} = A_i$ and $\mathcal{F} = \{S_1, \ldots, S_{|V|}\}$ such that $S_x = \{y \in A_i : d(x, y) \leq r\}$.

2. $B = \mathsf{SetCover}(\mathcal{U}, \mathcal{F})$.

3. $A_{i+1} = B \cap A$ and $i = i + 1$.

Let $n = |A|$. Assuming d is given as a distance matrix, Step 1 takes $O(n^2)$ work and $O(\log n)$ depth (to generate the packed representation). In $O(n^2)$ work and $O(\log^3 n)$ depth, Steps 2 and 3 can be implemented using the set-cover algorithm (Section 5.2) and standard techniques. Following [PV98]'s analysis, we know the number of iterations is at most $O(\log^* n)$. Therefore, this recursive cover requires $O(n^2 \log^* n)$ work and $O(\log^* n \log^3 n)$ depth.

Next, the find-and-halve phase will be run sequentially beyond trivial parallization. We have the following theorem:

Theorem 5.6 *Let $\varepsilon > 0$. There is a $O(n^2 \cdot (k + \log^* n))$-work $O(k \cdot \log n + \log^3 n \log^3 n)$-depth factor-$O(\log^* n)$ approximation algorithm for the asymmetric k-center problem*

Note that the algorithm performs essentially the same work as the sequential one. Furthermore, for $k \leq \log^{O(1)} n$, this is an RNC algorithm. As suggested in [PV98], the recursive cover procedure alone yields a bicriteria approximation, in which the solution consists of $2k$ centers and costs at most $O(\log^* n)$ more than the optimal cost. This bicriteria approximation has $O(\log^{O(1)} n)$ depth for any k.

6. GREEDY FACILITY LOCATION

Metric facility location is a fundamental problem in approximation algorithms. The input consists of a set of *facilities* F and a set of *clients* C, where each facility $i \in F$ has cost f_i, and each client $j \in C$ incurs $d(j, i)$ to use facility i—and the goal is to find a set of facilities $F_S \subseteq F$ that minimizes the objective function $\Phi_{\mathsf{F}}(F_S) = \sum_{i \in F_S} f_i + \sum_{j \in C} d(j, F_S)$. The distance d is assumed to be symmetric and satisfy the triangle inequality. This problem has an exceptionally simple factor-1.861 greedy algorithm due to Jain et al. [JMM+03], which has been parallelized by Blelloch and Tangwongsan [BT10], yielding an RNC $(6 + \varepsilon)$-approximation with work $O(p \log^2 p)$, where $p = |F| \times |C|$.

Using ideas from previous sections, we develop an RNC algorithm with an improved approximation guarantee, which essentially matches that of the sequential version.

Theorem 6.1 *Let $\varepsilon > 0$ be a small constant. There is a $O(p \log p)$-work $O(\log^4 p)$-depth factor-$(1.861 + \varepsilon)$ approximation algorithm for the (metric) facility location problem.*

We need the following definition for the algorithm:

Definition 6.2 (Star, Price, and Maximal Star) *A star $\mathcal{S} = (i, C')$ consists of a facility i and a subset of clients $C' \subseteq C$. The price of $\mathcal{S}$ is $\pi(\mathcal{S}) = (f_i + \sum_{j \in C'} d(j, i))/|C'|$. A star $\mathcal{S}$ is said to be maximal if all strict super sets of C' have a larger price, i.e., for all $C'' \supsetneq C'$, $\pi((i, C'')) > \pi((i, C'))$. Let $\mathsf{best}(i)$ be the price of the lowest-priced maximal star centered at i (on the current/remaining instance).*

Presented in Algorithm 6.1 is a parallel greedy approximation algorithm for metric facility location. The algorithm closely mimics the behaviors of Jain et al.'s algorithm, except the parallel algorithm is more aggressive in choosing the stars to open. Consider the natural integer-program formulation of facility location for which the relaxation yields the pair of

Minimize	$\sum_{i\in F, j\in C} d(j,i)x_{ij} \;+\; \sum_{i\in F} f_i y_i$		**Maximize**	$\sum_{j\in C} \alpha_j$	
Subj. to: $\begin{cases}\end{cases}$	$\sum_{i\in F} x_{ij} \;\geq\; 1$ $y_i - x_{ij} \;\geq\; 0$ $x_{ij} \geq 0,\; y_i \geq 0$	for $j \in C$ for $i \in F, j \in C$	**Subj. to:** $\begin{cases}\end{cases}$	$\sum_{j\in C} \beta_{ij} \;\leq\; f_i$ $\alpha_j - \beta_{ij} \;\leq\; d(j,i)$ $\beta_{ij} \geq 0,\; \alpha_j \geq 0$	for $i \in F$ for $i \in F, j \in C$

Figure 2: The primal (left) and dual (right) programs for metric (uncapacitated) facility location.

Algorithm 6.1 Parallel greedy algorithm for metric facility location.

Set $F_A = \emptyset$. For $t = 1, 2, \ldots$, until $C = \emptyset$,

  i. Let $\tau^{(t)} = (1+\varepsilon) \cdot \min\{\mathsf{best}(i) : i \in F\}$ and $F^{(t)} = \{i \in F : \mathsf{best}(i) \leq \tau^{(t)}\}$.

 ii. Build a bipartite graph G from $F^{(t)}$ and $N(\cdot)$, where for each $i \in F^{(t)}$, $N(i) = \{j \in C : d(j,i) \leq \tau^{(t)}\}$.

iii. While $(F^{(t)} \neq \emptyset)$, repeat:

  1. Compute $\Delta J^{(t)} = \mathsf{MaNIS}_{(\varepsilon, 3\varepsilon)}(G)$ and $J^{(t)} = J^{(t)} \cup \Delta J^{(t)}$

  2. Remove $\Delta J^{(t)}$ and $N(\Delta J^{(t)})$ from G, remove the clients $N(\Delta J^{(t)})$ from C, and set $f_i = 0$ for all $i \in \Delta J^{(t)}$.

  3. Delete any $i \in F^{(t)}$ such that $\pi((i, N(i))) > \tau^{(t)}$.

---

primal (left) and dual (right) programs shown in Figure 2. We wish to give a dual-fitting analysis similar to that of Jain et al.

Their proof shows that the solution's cost is equal to the sum of α_j's over the clients, where α_j is the price of the star with which client j is connected up. Following this analysis, we set α_j to $\tau^{(t)}/(1+\varepsilon)$ where t is the iteration that the client was removed. Note that stars chosen in $F^{(t)}$ may have overlapping clients. For this reason, we cannot afford to open them all, or we would not be able to bound the solution's cost by the sum of α_j's. This situation, however, is rectified by the use of MANIS, allowing us to prove Lemma 6.5, which relates the cost of the solution to α_j's. Before we prove this lemma, two easy-to-check facts are in order:

Fact 6.3 In the graph G constructed in Step 2, for all $i \in F^{(t)}$, $\pi((i, N(i))) \leq \tau^{(t)}$.

Fact 6.4 At any point during iteration t, $\mathsf{best}(i) \leq \tau^{(t)}$ if and only if $\pi((i, N(i))) \leq \tau^{(t)}$.

Lemma 6.5 The cost of the algorithm's solution $\Phi_\mathsf{F}(F_A)$ is upper-bounded by $\frac{1}{1-5\varepsilon} \sum_{j\in C} \alpha_j$.

PROOF. Let $t > 0$ and consider what happens inside the inner loop (Steps iii.1—iii.3). Each iteration of the inner loop runs MANIS on $F^{(t)}$ with each $i \in F^{(t)}$ satisfying $\tau^{(t)} \geq \pi((i, N(i))) = (f_i + \sum_{j\in N(i)} d(j,i))/|N(i)|$, so

$$|N(i)| \geq \frac{1}{\tau^{(t)}}\Big(f_i + \sum_{j\in N(i)} d(j,i)\Big).$$

Because of Fact 6.3 and Step iii.3, the relationship $\tau^{(t)} \geq \pi((i, N(i)))$ is maintained throughout iteration t. Running a $(\varepsilon, 3\varepsilon)$-MANIS on $F^{(t)}$ ensures that each $\Delta J^{(t)}$ satisfies

$|N(\Delta J^{(t)})| \geq (1-4\varepsilon) \sum_{i\in \Delta J^{(t)}} |N(i)|$. Thus,

$$\sum_{j\in \Delta J^{(t)}} \alpha_j = \frac{\tau^{(t)}}{1+\varepsilon} |N(\Delta J^{(t)})| \geq \frac{\tau^{(t)}}{1+\varepsilon}(1-4\varepsilon) \sum_{i\in \Delta J^{(t)}} |N(i)|$$

$$\geq (1-5\varepsilon) \sum_{i\in \Delta J^{(t)}} \Big(f_i + \sum_{j\in N(i)} d(j,i)\Big),$$

which is at least

$$(1-5\varepsilon)\Big(\sum_{i\in \Delta J^{(t)}} f_i + \sum_{j\in N(\Delta J^{(t)})} d(j, \Delta J^{(t)})\Big).$$

Since every client has to appear in at least one $J^{(t)}$, summing across the inner loop's iterations and t gives the lemma. $\square$

In the series of claims that follows, we show that when scaled down by a factor of $\gamma = 1.861$, the α setting determined above is a dual feasible solution. We will assume without loss of generality that $\alpha_1 \leq \alpha_2 \leq \cdots \leq \alpha_{|C|}$. Let $W_i = \{j \in C : \alpha_j \geq \gamma \cdot d(j,i)\}$ for all $i \in F$ and $W = \cup_i W_i$.

Claim 6.6 For any facility $i \in F$ and client $j_0 \in C$,

$$\sum_{j\in W : j \geq j_0} \max(0, \alpha_{j_0} - d(j,i)) \;\leq\; f_i.$$

PROOF. Suppose for a contradiction that there exist client j and facility i such that the inequality in the claim does not hold. Let t be the iteration such that $\alpha_{j_0} = \tau^{(t)}/(1+\varepsilon)$. Let $\widehat{C}^{(t)}$ be the set of clients j's such that $\alpha_{j_0} - d(j,i) > 0$ that remain at the beginning of iteration t. Thus, by our assumption and the fact that $\{j \in W : j \geq j_0 \wedge \alpha_{j_0} > d(j,i)\} \subseteq \widehat{C}^{(t)}$, we establish $\sum_{j\in \widehat{C}^{(t)}} \alpha_{j_0} - d(j,i) = \sum_{j\in \widehat{C}^{(t)}} \max(0, \alpha_{j_0} - d(j,i)) \geq \sum_{j\in W : j \geq j_0} \max(0, \alpha_{j_0} - d(j,i)) > f_i$. It follows that $\alpha_{j_0} > \frac{1}{|\widehat{C}^{(t)}|}(f_i + \sum_{j\in \widehat{C}^{(t)}} d(j,i))$. Hence, $\tau^{(t)}/(1+\varepsilon) = \alpha_{j_0} > \frac{1}{|\widehat{C}^{(t)}|}(f_i + \sum_{j\in \widehat{C}^{(t)}} d(j,i)) \geq \mathsf{best}(i) \geq \tau^{(t)}/(1+\varepsilon)$ since $\tau^{(t)}/(1+\varepsilon)$ is the minimum of the best price in that iteration. This gives a contradiction, proving the claim. $\square$

Claim 6.7 Let $i \in F$, and $j, j' \in W$ be clients. Then, $\alpha_j \leq \alpha_{j'} + d(i, j') + d(i, j)$.

PROOF. If $\alpha_j \leq \alpha_{j'}$, the proof is trivial, so assume $\alpha_j > \alpha_{j'}$. Let i' be any facility that removed j' (i.e, $i' \in \Delta J^{(t)}$ such that $j \in N(i')$). It suffices to show that $\alpha_j \leq d(i', j)$ and the claim follows from triangle inequality. Since $\alpha_j > \alpha_{j'}$, in the iteration t where $\alpha_j = \tau^{(t)}/(1+\varepsilon)$, we know that $f_{i'}$ has already been set to 0, so $\mathsf{best}(i') \leq d(j, i')$. Furthermore, in this iteration, $\alpha_j \leq \mathsf{best}(i')$ as $\alpha_j = \min\{\mathsf{best}(i)\}$, proving the claim. $\square$

These two claims are sufficient to set up a factor-revealing LP identical to Jain et al.'s. Therefore, the following lemma follows from Jain et al. [JMM+03] (Lemmas 3.4 and 3.6):

Lemma 6.8 The setting $\alpha'_j = \frac{\alpha_j}{\gamma}$ and $\beta'_{ij} = \max(0, \alpha'_j - d(j,i))$ is a dual feasible solution, where $\gamma = 1.861$.

Combining this lemma with Lemma 6.5 and weak duality, we have the promised approximation guarantee.

Running time analysis: Fix $\varepsilon > 0$. We argue that the number of rounds is upper bounded by $O(\log p)$. For this, we need a preprocessing step which ensures that the ratio between the largest τ and the smallest τ ever encountered in the algorithm is $O(p^{O(1)})$. This can be done in $O(p)$ work and $O(\log(|F| + |C|))$ depth, adding $\varepsilon \cdot \mathbf{opt}$ to the solution's cost [BT10]. Armed with that, it suffices to show the following claim.

Claim 6.9 $\tau^{(t+1)} \geq (1 + \varepsilon) \cdot \tau^{(t)}$.

PROOF. Let $\mathsf{best}^{(t)}(i)$ denote $\mathsf{best}(i)$ at the beginning of iteration t. Let i^* be the facility whose $\mathsf{best}^{(t+1)}(i^*)$ attains $\tau^{(t+1)}/(1 + \varepsilon)$. To prove the claim, it suffices to show that $\mathsf{best}^{(t+1)}(i^*) \geq \tau^{(t)}$, as this will imply $\tau^{(t+1)} \geq (1 + \varepsilon) \cdot \tau^{(t)}$. Now consider two possibilities.
— *Case 1.* i^* was part of $F^{(t)}$, so then either i^* was opened in this iteration or i^* was removed from $F^{(t)}$ in Step 3.iii. If i^* was opened, all clients at distance at most $\tau^{(t)}$ from it would be connected up, so $\mathsf{best}^{(t+1)}(i^*) \geq \tau^{(t)}$. Otherwise, i^* was removed in Step iii.3, in which case $\mathsf{best}^{(t+1)}(i^*) \geq \tau^{(t)}$ by the removal criteria and Fact 6.4.
— *Case 2.* Otherwise, i^* was not part of $F^{(t)}$. This means that $\mathsf{best}^{(t)}(i^*) > \tau^{(t)}$. As the set of unconnected clients can only become smaller, the price of the best star centered at i^* can only go up. So $\mathsf{best}^{(t+1)}(i^*)$ will be at least $\tau^{(t)}$, which in turn implies the claim. $\square$

Thus, the total number of iterations (outer loop) in the algorithm is $O(\log p)$. We now consider the work and depth of each iteration. Step 1 involves computing $\mathsf{best}(i)$ for all $i \in F$. This can be done in $O(p)$ work and $O(\log p)$ depth using a prefix computation and standard techniques (see [BT10] for details). Step 2 can be done in the same work-depth bounds. Inside the inner loop, each MANIS call requires $O(p')$ work and $O(\log^2 p')$ depth, where m' is the number of edges in G. Steps iii.2–3 do not require more than $O(p')$ work and $O(\log p')$ depth. Furthermore, note that if $i \in F^{(t)}$ is not chosen by MANIS, it loses at least an ε fraction of its neighbors. Therefore, the total work of in the inner loop (for each t) is $O(\varepsilon^{-1} p)$, and depth $O(\log^3 p)$. Combining these gives the theorem.

7. CONCLUSION

We formulated and studied MANIS—a graph abstraction of a problem at the crux of many (set) covering-type problem. We gave a linear-work RNC solution to this problem and applied it to derive parallel approximation algorithms for several problems, yielding RNC algorithms for set cover, (prefix-optimal) max cover, min-sum set cover, asymmetric k-center, and metric facility location.

Acknowledgments. This work is partially supported by the National Science Foundation under grant number CCF-1018188 and by generous gifts from IBM, Intel, and Microsoft. We thank Anupam Gupta for valuable suggestions and conversations.

References

[BM98] Guy E. Blelloch and Bruce M. Maggs. *Handbook of Algorithms and Theory of Computation*, chapter Parallel Algorithms. CRC Press, Boca Raton, FL, 1998.

[BNBH+98] Amotz Bar-Noy, Mihir Bellare, Magnús M. Halldórsson, Hadas Shachnai, and Tami Tamir. On chromatic sums and distributed resource allocation. *Inform. and Comput.*, 140(2):183–202, 1998.

[BRS94] Bonnie Berger, John Rompel, and Peter W. Shor. Efficient *NC* algorithms for set cover with applications to learning and geometry. *J. Comput. Syst. Sci.*, 49(3):454–477, 1994.

[BT10] Guy E. Blelloch and Kanat Tangwongsan. Parallel approximation algorithms for facility-location problems. In *SPAA*, pages 315–324, 2010.

[CGH+05] Julia Chuzhoy, Sudipto Guha, Eran Halperin, Sanjeev Khanna, Guy Kortsarz, Robert Krauthgamer, and Joseph Naor. Asymmetric k-center is log* n-hard to approximate. *J. ACM*, 52(4):538–551, 2005.

[Chv79] V. Chvatal. A greedy heuristic for the set-covering problem. *Mathematics of Operations Research*, 4(3):pp. 233–235, 1979.

[CKT10] Flavio Chierichetti, Ravi Kumar, and Andrew Tomkins. Max-cover in map-reduce. In *WWW*, pages 231–240, 2010.

[Fei98] U. Feige. A threshold of ln n for approximating set cover. *J. ACM*, 45(4):634–652, 1998.

[FLT04] Uriel Feige, László Lovász, and Prasad Tetali. Approximating min sum set cover. *Algorithmica*, 40(4):219–234, 2004.

[Gon85] Teofilo F. Gonzalez. Clustering to minimize the maximum intercluster distance. *Theoret. Comput. Sci.*, 38(2-3):293–306, 1985.

[HS85] Dorit S. Hochbaum and David B. Shmoys. A best possible heuristic for the k-center problem. *Mathematics of Operations Research*, 10(2):180–184, 1985.

[JMM+03] Kamal Jain, Mohammad Mahdian, Evangelos Markakis, Amin Saberi, and Vijay V. Vazirani. Greedy facility location algorithms analyzed using dual fitting with factor-revealing LP. *Journal of the ACM*, 50(6):795–824, 2003.

[Joh74] David S. Johnson. Approximation algorithms for combinatorial problems. *J. Comput. System Sci.*, 9:256–278, 1974.

[Kar72] R. M. Karp. Reducibility Among Combinatorial Problems. In R. E. Miller and J. W. Thatcher, editors, *Complexity of Computer Computations*, pages 85–103. Plenum Press, 1972.

[KVY94] Samir Khuller, Uzi Vishkin, and Neal E. Young. A primal-dual parallel approximation technique applied to weighted set and vertex covers. *J. Algorithms*, 17(2):280–289, 1994.

[KW85] Richard M. Karp and Avi Wigderson. A fast parallel algorithm for the maximal independent set problem. *Journal of the ACM*, 32(4):762–773, 1985.

[Lub86] Michael Luby. A simple parallel algorithm for the maximal independent set problem. *SIAM J. Comput.*, 15(4):1036–1053, 1986.

[PV98] Rina Panigrahy and Sundar Vishwanathan. An $O(\log^* n)$ approximation algorithm for the asymmetric p-center problem. *J. Algorithms*, 27(2):259–268, 1998.

[RR89] Sanguthevar Rajasekaran and John H. Reif. Optimal and sublogarithmic time randomized parallel sorting algorithms. *SIAM J. Comput.*, 18(3):594–607, 1989.

[RV98] Sridhar Rajagopalan and Vijay V. Vazirani. Primal-dual *RNC* approximation algorithms for set cover and covering integer programs. *SIAM J. Comput.*, 28(2):525–540, 1998.

[Vaz01] Vijay V. Vazirani. *Approximation algorithms.* Springer-Verlag, Berlin, 2001.

[You95] Neal E. Young. Randomized rounding without solving the linear program. In *SODA*, pages 170–178, 1995.

Parallelism in Dynamic Well-Spaced Point Sets

Umut A. Acar
Max-Planck Institute for
Software Systems
Kaiserslautern, Germany
umut@mpi-sws.org

Andrew Cotter
Toyota Technological Institute
Chicago, IL
cotter@ttic.edu

Benoît Hudson
Autodesk, Inc.
Montreal, QC, Canada
benoit.hudson@autodesk.com

Duru Türkoğlu
Dept. of Computer Science
University of Chicago
Chicago, IL
duru@cs.uchicago.edu

ABSTRACT

Parallel algorithms and dynamic algorithms possess an interesting duality property: compared to sequential algorithms, parallel algorithms improve run-time while preserving work, while dynamic algorithms improve work but typically offer no parallelism. Although they are often considered separately, parallel and dynamic algorithms employ similar design techniques. They both identify parts of the computation that are independent of each other. This suggests that dynamic algorithms could be parallelized to improve work efficiency while preserving fast parallel run-time.

In this paper, we parallelize a dynamic algorithm for well-spaced point sets, an important problem related to mesh refinement in computational geometry. Our parallel dynamic algorithm computes a well-spaced superset of a dynamically changing set of points, allowing arbitrary dynamic modifications to the input set. On an EREW PRAM, our algorithm processes batches of k modifications such as insertions and deletions in $O(k \log \Delta)$ total work and in $O(\log \Delta)$ parallel time using k processors, where Δ is the geometric spread of the data, while ensuring that the output is always within a constant factor of the optimal size. EREW PRAM model is quite different from actual hardware such as modern multiprocessors. We therefore describe techniques for implementing our algorithm on modern multi-core computers and provide a prototype implementation. Our empirical evaluation shows that our algorithm can be practical, yielding a large degree of parallelism and good speedups.

Categories and Subject Descriptors

F.2.2 [**Analysis of Algorithms and Problem Complexity**]: Nonnumerical Algorithms and Problems—*Geometrical problems and computations*

General Terms

Algorithms, Theory, Performance, Experimentation

Keywords

Well-spaced point sets, Voronoi diagrams, mesh refinement, parallel batch dynamic updates, self-adjusting computation, multithreading

1. INTRODUCTION

In many applications, algorithms are repeatedly invoked on sequences of data that are related to or derived from each other. For example, in computer aided design, one might create an incrementally evolving model which undergoes relatively small changes at each iteration. After adjusting the design, the user may invoke features that send the design as input to an algorithm that requires expensive computations, e.g., a geometric algorithm such as a mesh generator. To take advantage of the resulting similarity between the inputs, researchers have developed so called *dynamic algorithms* that update the output by performing significantly less work than a complete re-computation. Except for a few (e.g., [19, 25]), dynamic algorithms are typically sequential (see [11, 14, 13] for some surveys) and allow the input to undergo only a single modification, e.g., insertion or deletion, at a time.

The interaction between parallel and dynamic algorithms is not well understood, but appears to be strong. For example, they are duals in terms of their effect on work and run-time: when compared to sequential algorithms, parallel algorithms improve parallel run-time but not the work (total computation), whereas dynamic algorithms improve work by only updating parts of the output affected by a change, but offer no parallelism. The design and analysis of parallel and dynamic algorithms are also deeply related. Both parallel and dynamic algorithms identify independent parts of the computation in order to achieve either a high degree of parallelism or efficient dynamic updates when the input is modified. These relationships suggest that dynamic and parallel algorithms may be designed to improve both work and parallel run-time. Such algorithms accept arbitrarily changing input data sets (as opposed to permitting single, unitary changes to the input), and respond to them in both work-optimal and parallel-time-optimal fashion by performing only the amount of work necessary to update the previous output in accordance with the modified input.

In this paper, we present parallel construction and parallel dynamic update algorithms for the *well-spaced point-sets problem*. Given an input set of points N, the problem requires computing the asymptotically smallest *well-spaced* superset M ⊃ N by inserting additional so called *Steiner points*, to ensure that the Voronoi cells of the final Voronoi diagram all have bounded aspect ratio (Section 2). Well-spaced point sets are closely related to mesh generation, an important problem in computational geometry [10, 6, 21, 27, 16], where the goal is to cover a domain with simplices (i.e. triangles in 2D and tetrahedra in 3D) such that all simplices have good quality, in the sense that their face and dihedral angles are bounded away from 0° and 180°. Well-spaced point sets directly yield quality meshes in 2D, and can be used to obtain quality meshes in 3D with the help of a sliver removal algorithm [9].

Our construction algorithm builds a well-spaced superset of a given point set, and our dynamic algorithm updates it as the input is modified. Both return well-spaced point sets that are *size-optimal*, in the sense that their size is within a constant factor of the size of the smallest well-spaced superset. Our dynamic update algorithm allows arbitrary modifications to the input, e.g., single or batch insertions, or deletions, or their combinations. We present our algorithms in the EREW PRAM model, where no concurrent memory accesses take place. Our construction algorithm matches the best prior parallel off-line algorithms [17] in efficiency: it builds a superset of a given set of n points in $O(n \log \Delta)$ work and $O(\log \Delta)$ parallel time using n processors, where Δ is the *geometric spread*, defined as the ratio of the diameter to the closest pair distance of the input set. Our update algorithm performs a batch of k updates (insertions and deletions) in $O(k \log \Delta)$ work and $O(\log \Delta)$ parallel time using k processors. These bounds assume that vertex coordinates fit inside a machine word, and that common arithmetic operations on these words require only constant time.

The starting point for our algorithms is the aforementioned similarity between the design of dynamic and parallel algorithms: that the very independence exploited by a dynamic algorithm may be utilized to extract parallelism. Indeed, we start with a previously proposed dynamic algorithm for well-spaced point sets [4] and parallelize it for the EREW PRAM model (Section 4). Parallelization of the dynamic algorithm involves some major modifications to the quadtree data structure used for point location (Section 3) and careful exploitation of locality properties of the geometric operations used by the dynamic algorithm. This yields a parallel dynamic update algorithm that accepts arbitrary modifications to the input and updates the output correctly and efficiently. To support such parallel dynamic updates, we utilize a *computation graph* to represent the dependencies in the computation, allowing quick identification and re-use of those tasks which are unaffected by a modification. We show that it is possible to provide lock-free mutually exclusive access to the computation graph by taking advantage of certain locality properties (Section 5).

The approach of developing a construction algorithm and then providing a dynamic update algorithm based on change propagation is inspired by recent advances on self-adjusting computation (e.g., [2, 15, 20]). In self-adjusting computation, programs can respond automatically to modifications

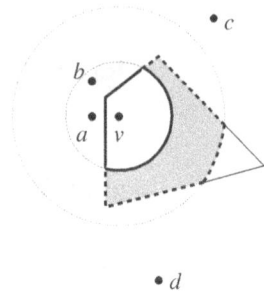

Figure 1: M $= \{a, b, c, d, v\}$ NN$_M(v) = |va|$. **Thick solid and dashed boundaries display** Vor$_M^\rho(v)$ **and** Vor$_M^\beta(v)$. **Shaded region is the** (ρ, β) **picking region.** c **and** d **are** β**-clipped but not** ρ**-clipped Voronoi neighbors of** v.

to their data by invoking a general-purpose change propagation algorithm [1]. The data structures required by change propagation can be constructed automatically by observing execution. Our computation graphs are abstract representations of these data structures. Similarly our dynamic update algorithm is an adaptation of the change propagation algorithm for the problem of well-spaced point sets. Nearly all of that work, however, consider sequential computations. The results in this paper show that they can effectively be parallelized in this particular problem. Previous work applied these techniques effectively to other computational geometry problems such as kinetic three-dimensional convex hulls [3] and sequential dynamic and kinetic well-spaced point sets [4, 5]. Our approach can also be viewed as a dynamization technique, which has been used effectively for a relatively broad range of algorithms (e.g., [26, 8, 12, 24]).

Since our algorithms are based on the EREW PRAM model, and since our bounds are asymptotic, it is not directly clear if our algorithms yield the desired efficiency in practice, e.g., on modern multi-core computers with a modest number of processors. For example, in the EREW PRAM model, processors execute in lockstep, emulation of which in multi-core systems would require global synchronization. Similarly, in our EREW algorithms, exclusivity of memory accesses is ensured at the cost of a large amount of sequentialization, although much less suffices in practice, largely because concurrent reads are permissible. We therefore present practical adaptations of our construction and dynamic update algorithms to multi-core systems (Section 6). We also provide prototype implementations. Our experiments with 2D and 3D synthetic and real-world data sets give some evidence that the proposed techniques work effectively in practice (Section 7).

2. PRELIMINARIES

Our algorithms maintain a well-spaced superset M of a set of input points N that can be dynamically modified by insertion/deletion of a set of points N*. Without loss of generality, we scale and shift the point set N such that $B = [0, 1]^d$ becomes a bounding box. We use the term *point* to refer to any point in B and *vertex* to refer to the input and output points. For any vertex set M ⊂ B, the *Voronoi cell* of v in M, written Vor$_M(v)$, consists of points $x \in B$ such that for all $u \in$ M, $|vx| \leq |ux|$. The *nearest-neighbor distance* of v, written NN$_M(v)$, is the distance from v to the nearest other vertex in M. Following Talmor [27], a vertex is ρ-*well-spaced* if its Voronoi cell is contained within the ball of radius ρ NN$_M(v)$ centered at v; M is ρ-well-spaced if every vertex in M is ρ-well-spaced. The β-*clipped Voronoi cell* of v, written Vor$_M^\beta(v)$, is the intersection of Vor$_M(v)$ with the ball of radius β NN$_M(v)$ centered at v [18]. For any $\beta > \rho$, we define the (ρ, β) *picking region* of v, written Vor$_M^{(\rho,\beta)}(v)$, as

$\mathrm{Vor}_{\mathsf{M}}^{\beta}(v) \setminus \mathrm{Vor}_{\mathsf{M}}^{\rho}(v)$, the region of the Voronoi cell bounded by concentric balls of radius $\rho \mathrm{NN}_{\mathsf{M}}(v)$ and $\beta \mathrm{NN}_{\mathsf{M}}(v)$. A vertex u is a *(β-clipped) Voronoi neighbor* of v if the (β-clipped) Voronoi cell of v contains a point equidistant from v and u. Figure 1 illustrates these definitions.

3. QUADTREE

To permit the rapid calculation of such things as nearest neighbors and clipped Voronoi cells, we use a point location data structure based on the balanced quadtree of Bern, Eppstein, and Gilbert [6]. In two dimensions, under the assumptions that every vertex coordinate is a b-bit integer and that arithmetic and bitwise operations on b-bit integers require constant time, earlier work [7] has shown how to construct a balanced quadtree on a set of n vertices in $O(n \log n)$ work and $O(\log n)$ parallel time on an EREW PRAM, assuming that $b \in O(\log n)$. We extend this construction to arbitrary dimensions, and describe how k *dynamic vertices* may be inserted into (or deleted from) an existing quadtree in $O(k \log \Delta)$ work and $O(\log \Delta)$ parallel time, with the assumption that $b \in O(\log \Delta)$, which states that we do not use much higher arithmetic precision than is necessary to distinguish the input points.

We define a d-dimensional balanced quadtree to be the *minimal* quadtree which satisfies the following properties:

- Crowding: every leaf node of the quadtree contains at most one vertex, and if it does, none of its neighbors contains a vertex.

- Grading: all neighbors of any internal node must exist in the quadtree.

Here, we define the *neighbors* of a quadtree node to be the nodes in each of the $3^d - 1$ cardinal and diagonal directions, at the same level. To support fast traversals and access, a quadtree node keeps pointers to its parent, children, and neighbors. Additionally, every leaf node, which we refer to as a *square*, contains a pointer to an input vertex it may contain, and a list of Steiner vertices. In a balanced quadtree satisfying these properties, the set of squares partitions the space defined by the quadtree in such a way that two adjacent squares (i.e, two squares that share a common border) are either neighbors, or at consecutive levels.

Our quadtree supports the `QTClippedVoronoi`(v, β) function, which returns the β-clipped Voronoi cell of v in $O(1)$ time [18] and the `QTInsert` and `QTDelete` operations for modifying the vertex set. Each takes as input a balanced quadtree on a set of vertices N, and a set N^* of k *dynamic vertices* to either insert into, or delete from, this quadtree. `QTInsert` and `QTDelete` return the set of leaf nodes of the original quadtree that are internal nodes of the resulting quadtree and the leaf nodes that are removed from the original quadtree respectively. Our main result about this data structure, which we give without proof due to space limitations, states that the `QTInsert` and `QTDelete` functions may be effectively parallelized.

THEOREM 3.1. *Given a set N^* of k vertices and a quadtree Q, the functions QTInsert and QTDelete update the quadtree by performing $O(k \log \Delta)$ work in $O(\log \Delta)$ parallel time on an EREW PRAM.*

The `QTInsert` and `QTDelete` functions start by constructing, in Bern et al.'s terminology [7], a "framework" (a hypothetical quadtree) on N^*, the primary purpose of which is to define an "ownership" relation between dynamic vertices and quadtree nodes such that every node containing a dynamic vertex is "owned" by exactly one dynamic vertex. The functions then insert/delete the vertices N^* into/from the quadtree and finish by enforcing the crowding, grading and minimality properties in several passes, each of which is performed in parallel.

To repair the quadtree, we use k processors, each of which is identified with a dynamic vertex $p \in \mathsf{N}^*$. As we prove in lemmas 3.2 and 3.3, insertion or deletion of a vertex p only affects a local neighborhood of the quadtree nodes which contain p. Each processor is responsible for repairing the portion of the quadtree affected by its vertex, potentially in all b levels. The ownership relation defined by the framework, and a careful ordering on parallel operations defined by a coloring scheme, ensure exclusive accesses to memory, and that each affected node will be repaired by only one processor. By ensuring that there are a constant number of colors, and permitting no two operations of different colors to execute concurrently, these passes satisfy the requirements of an EREW PRAM model, with only a constant factor overhead in runtime.

Framework construction. The construction of the framework, which is performed at the start of every `QTInsert` and `QTDelete` operation, is very similar to the unbalanced quadtree construction of Bern et al. (section 2 of [7]).

We begin by sorting the dynamic vertices N^* in Morton's Z-order [23, 7]. Using this sorted list, we will define an auxiliary data structure for each vertex which contains the information needed by the framework.

We say that a dynamic vertex "owns" a quadtree square if it is the first dynamic vertex (in the sorted array N^*) which is contained within the boundaries of this square. Every dynamic vertex owns at least one square, but a vertex may own multiple squares–in particular, if it owns a square at level ℓ, then it owns a smaller square at every level $\ell' > \ell$. Similarly, we say that one dynamic vertex p is a "parent" of p' if p is the owner of the parent square (in the quadtree) of the minimum-level square owned by p'.

The framework keeps track of this parent-child relationship between vertices. For convenience, we will treat this data structure as a set of fields vertices themselves, although its lifetime is only that of the insertion or deletion operation, not of the quadtree itself:

- Level: Level (in the quadtree) of the minimum-level square owned by this vertex.

- Parent: Index of the parent vertex in the sorted list N^*.

- Nodes: Array of pointers, indexed by level, to the quadtree squares owned by this vertex. Initialized to *null*.

The level of the ith dynamic vertex is the number of high-order bits of the coordinates of $\mathsf{N}[i]$ and $\mathsf{N}[i-1]$ which are identical, plus one. The first vertex in the sorted list is at level 0. Once the levels have been found, the *parent* fields may be populated. One may verify that the parent index i of a vertex at index j is the largest $i < j$ such that $\mathsf{N}[i].level < \mathsf{N}[j].level$.

The final step in this construction is to "link up" this framework to the quadtree proper by populating the *nodes* fields. This is accomplished using a set of parallel processes, one for each dynamic vertex, which execute in lockstep.

Each iterates through the levels of the quadtree in a top-down manner (from the root towards the leaves), and finds the quadtree node owned by its dynamic vertex at the current level by inspecting the children (in the quadtree) of the node owned by its *parent* dynamic vertex at the previous level. If a `QTInsert` operation is being performed, then the new dynamic vertices are inserted into the appropriate leaf nodes once they are encountered, and these leaves split as necessary in order to ensure that each leaf node contains at most one vertex. If a `QTDelete` operation is being performed, then the dynamic vertices are removed from these leaf nodes, but no quadtree nodes are merged–minimality will be enforced later.

During this top-down pass, we use a coloring scheme (described in detail below) to ensure that concurrent memory accesses cannot occur. During a `QTDelete` operation, two processes could access the same memory location only if they simultaneously work on nodes which share a parent. The fact that `QTSplit` is called during a `QTInsert` operation slightly complicates things, since we must update neighbor pointers when nodes are split, making it necessary for us to choose a coloring scheme which guarantees that no two processes may concurrently work on nodes whose parents share a neighbor.

Crowding and Grading Passes. The sole purpose of the framework is to make it possible to iterate, in parallel, over the quadtree nodes owned by dynamic vertices. With the framework in place, we repair the quadtree in a series of top-down and bottom-up passes over the quadtree. During these passes, a distinct process is associated with each dynamic vertex. These processes then, in lockstep, iterate through first the levels, and then the colors. In parallel, each performs a local constant-time operation on a node which it owns at the current level, if it is of the current color.

The coloring scheme is of vital importance to ensuring that concurrent memory accesses cannot occur during a pass over the quadtree. We assign a color to each quadtree node by taking each coordinate of the node modulo κ. Two nodes at the same level which are of the same color will be at least $\kappa - 1$ squares away from each other. ، The following two lemmas show that a small constant κ (7, in fact) suffices, when enforcing the crowding and grading properties.

LEMMA 3.2. *Let φ be a node that is must be split due to crowding. Then there is a vertex $p \in \mathsf{N}^*$ that lies either inside φ or one of its neighbors.*

PROOF. Follows immediately from the definition of the crowding property. □

LEMMA 3.3. *(Lemma 1 of Moore [22]) Let φ be a node that is split due to grading. Then a descendant of one of its neighbors must have been split due to crowding.*

Due to space limitations, we omit details on the passes which are performed in order to enforce the crowding, grading and minimality properties after some number of insertions or deletions. Briefly, we proceed by first enforcing the crowding property in a single top-down pass. We then perform a bottom-up pass in which it is determined which nodes must be split or merged in order to satisfy the grading property and minimality, and finally a top-down pass in which these splits/merges are actually performed.

4. PARALLEL ALGORITHM

Given a set of vertices N, we can construct a ρ-well-spaced superset of N by repeatedly "filling" the vertices until the set becomes ρ-well-spaced. To fill a vertex v, we apply a *fill* operation to v that inserts Steiner vertices within the (ρ, β) picking region of v (Figure 1), making v ρ-well-spaced. This approach, while correct, is not efficient because we may fill vertices many times.

To create an efficient parallel algorithm, we first notice that the Steiner vertices inserted when filling a vertex are always at least ρ times the nearest neighbor distance from the vertex, and therefore that inserting a Steiner vertex does not affect the well-spacedness of those vertices with nearest neighbor distances less than ρ times that of the vertex being filled. We can thus partition the vertices into groups, called *ranks*, such that vertices with nearest neighbor distances within a factor of ρ of each other are in the same rank. The vertices will then be filled in rank order. We observe that the vertices in each rank need not be filled sequentially, because filling a vertex only affects a local neighborhood. This allows us to partition the vertices in each rank into a constant number of *colors*, in such a way that we can fill vertices of the same color in parallel, while sequentially ordering the vertices of different colors. Each processor maintains an independent queue of pending operations, and fills the vertices sequentially in rank and color order. We show that the ranks and colors can be carefully picked to ensure that all memory reads and writes are exclusive.

This partial ordering takes advantage of independence of operations. We make this independence concrete by recording dependencies between vertices in a computation graph. In order to handle batch dynamic updates to the input, we employ a change-propagation mechanism that updates parts of the computation affected by dynamic modifications.

Construction Algorithm. The construction algorithm (Figure 2) revolves around two operations, `Fill` and `Dispatch`. As was briefly described above, the `Fill` operation inserts Steiner vertices to make a vertex ρ-well-spaced. A `Dispatch` operation computes the rank of a vertex, which we define as the base ρ logarithm of its nearest neighbor distance, and keeps it up to date as Steiner vertices are inserted. We say both operations *act on* a vertex (the first argument). The unique dispatch operation acting on a vertex v runs before the fill operations acting on v, and schedules fill operations for the vertex and its β-clipped Voronoi neighbors at the current rank, ensuring correct ordering of fill operations. We define *time* as a triple consisting of a rank, a flag indicating a dispatch (D) or fill (F), and a color.

Given a set of input vertices N, we assign one processor to each vertex $p \in \mathsf{N}$, each of which locally maintains an operation array Ω indexed by time, and executes `ParallelWS` in order to construct a ρ-well-spaced superset of its input N. `ParallelWS` starts by constructing a quadtree in parallel by inserting vertices into an empty quadtree. It then enqueues a dispatch operation for its assigned vertex p and proceeds by, at each rank, iterating through each color, executing the dispatch operations for that color, and then doing the same for the rank's fill operations. Both sets of operations use κ_O colors; we discuss the choice of κ_O in detail later in this section. The dispatch and fill operations also modify the computation graph. Consider a dispatch or a fill operation acting on a vertex v at time t, represented by the node (v, t); this operation inserts edges $((v, t), (w, t_w))$ as described in

```
ParallelWS (p, N) =
  QTInsert(p, N, nil)
  t_p ← Enqueue(p, |square of p|, D, Ω)
  Add edge (p, 0) ⟶ (p, t_p)
  for r = rank of t_p to ⌊log_ρ √d⌋ do
    for c = 1 to κ_O^d do
      t ← (r, D, c)
      for each v ∈ Ω[t] do Dispatch(v, t, Ω)
    for c = 1 to κ_O^d do
      t ← (r, F, c)
      for each v ∈ Ω[t] do Fill(v, t, Ω)

Dispatch (v, t, Ω) =
  (u, CV) ← QTClippedVoronoi(v, β, t)
  t_v ← Enqueue(v, |vu|, F, Ω)
  Add edge (v, t) ⟶ (v, t_v)
  for each CV-neighbor w of v do
    t_w ← Enqueue(w, |wv|, F, Ω)
    Add edge (v, t) ⟶ (w, t_w)

Fill (v, t, Ω) =
  (u, CV) ← QTClippedVoronoi(v, β, t)
  while v is not ρ-well-spaced do
    Pick w ∈ CV s.t. |vw| ≥ ρ · |vu|
    Insert w as a Steiner vertex
    t_w ← Enqueue(w, |wv|, D, Ω)
    Add edge (v, t) ⟶ (w, t_w)
    Update CV with w

Enqueue (v, nnv, T, Ω) =
  r_v ← ⌊log_ρ nnv⌋,  c_v ← color(v, r_v)
  t_v ← (r_v, T, c_v)
  if ∄ edge · ⟶ (v, t_v) then
    Ω[t_v] ← Ω[t_v] ∪ {v}
  return t_v
```

Figure 2: The pseudo-code of the parallel algorithm.

the pseudo-code. Here t_w is the time of the (potential) operation scheduled to act on w. In order to keep track of dependencies through the quadtree, a `QTClippedVoronoi` call executed by the operation acting on v records the node (v, t) in every square s that it accesses.

Dynamic Update Algorithm. We describe our parallel algorithm (pseudo-code in Figure 3) for updating the well-spaced output after a batch insertion/deletion of vertices into/from the input. Given a set of dynamic vertices N^* to be inserted or deleted, we assign one processor to each vertex $p \in N^*$, each of which participates in the dynamic update by executing `Insert/Delete` and then `Propagate`. Each processor locally maintains three arrays of operations $\Omega^\ominus, \Omega^\oplus, \Omega^\otimes$ that hold (respectively) the obsolete, fresh, and inconsistent operations, which are (respectively) to be deleted, executed, and re-executed. The `Insert` and `Delete` functions take a set of vertices N^* along with the quadtree Q, and insert/delete N^* into/from Q, receiving a set of obsolete squares $\Sigma^\ominus$. Next, each enqueues the dispatch operation for the vertex p assigned to its processor into the obsolete or fresh operation arrays, and proceeds to execute `Propagate`. This function starts by inserting the readers of the obsolete squares into the array of inconsistent operations by iterating through each quadtree depth, using κ_S colors (details later in this section) in order to ensure that the operation queues

of different processors are disjoint. It then enqueues an obsolete dispatch operation for each vertex contained in an obsolete square, and enqueues a fresh dispatch operation for the same vertex at the new square. After the initializations, `Propagate` proceeds in time order. At each rank, it starts by fixing the dispatch operations. Iterating through colors, `Fix` undoes the operations in the obsolete and inconsistent arrays, and updates the inconsistent operation array by removing the obsolete operations. It then finishes fixing the dispatch operations by performing those in the inconsistent and fresh arrays. Next, `Propagate` fixes the fill operations by having `Fix` undo and perform them in a similar fashion. For fill operations, `Fix` also marks readers of those squares whose Steiner vertex lists have changed to be inconsistent.

During the update, the dispatch and fill operations, as well as the undo operations, all maintain the computation graph. Undos remove the edges originating from the vertex on which these operations act. In order to propagate and repair the effects of inconsistencies that arise while inserting or removing Steiner vertices, we rely on the `MarkReaders` operation. `MarkReaders` marks dispatch and fill operations that are scheduled in the future, and whose clipped Voronoi computations access the inconsistent square, to be inconsistent themselves.

Coloring for Dynamism and Parallelism. To update the output when the input point set changes, our dynamic algorithm identifies the operations made inconsistent by the changes, and re-executes them. When an operation is re-executed, it can make another operation inconsistent by inserting a Steiner vertex. For efficient updates, it is therefore crucial that such dependency chains be short–of no more than logarithmic length. Since there are logarithmically many ranks, it suffices to ensure that the dependencies between operations in the same rank are of constant length. At any given rank r, both dispatches and fills access only the quadtree squares within a ball of radius $O(\rho^r)$. Their modifications to the computation graph are local as well, since they insert edges only towards vertices within this ball. This allows us to partition the work at a given rank into a constant number of color classes in such a way that dependencies occur only between the operations of different colors, guaranteeing efficient dynamic updates as well as exclusive reads and writes: operations at the same color class are independent, in that they neither access the same quadtree squares nor access the same nodes in the computation graph.

More formally, we define two squares of the same size to be *related* if there is a dispatch or fill operation that accesses both of them. We show that there exists a constant number of colors (κ_S^d) coloring squares of the same size such that no two squares are related if they have the same color

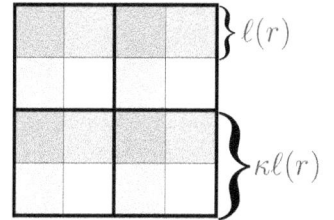

Figure 4: Illustration of a coloring scheme ($\kappa = 2$).

(Lemma 5.2). This ensures that in the initialization of the dynamic update, different processors do not simultaneously mark operations reading an obsolete square to be inconsistent. We say that two dispatch or fill operations executed at the same rank *interfere* if the squares accessed by the operations are related. We disallow interference by using a *coloring scheme* that partitions the space based on a param-

```
Fix (r, T) =
  for c = 1 to κ_O^d do
    t ← (r, T, c)
    for each v ∈ Ω^⊖[t] do Undo(v, t)
    Remove unflagged vertices from Ω^⊗[t]
    for each v ∈ Ω^⊗[t] do Undo(v, t)
    for each v ∈ Ω^⊕[t] ∪ Ω^⊗[t] do
      if T = D then Dispatch(v, t, Ω^⊕)
      if T = F then
        Fill(v, t, Ω^⊕)
        for each inserted Steiner w do
          MarkReaders(square of w, t)

Undo (v, t) =
  Unflag v at time t
  for each edge (v, t) ⟶ (w, t_w) do
    Remove edge (v, t) ⟶ (w, t_w)
    if ∄ edge · ⟶ (w, t_w) then
      Ω^⊖[t_w] ← Ω^⊖[t_w] ∪ {w}
      if t = (·, F, ·) then
        MarkReaders(square of w, t)
      Delete w from its square

MarkReaders (s, t) =
  for each v reading s at time t' > t do
    if v at time t' is not flagged then
      Flag v at time t'
      Ω^⊗[t'] ← Ω^⊗[t'] ∪ {v}
```

```
Insert (p, N*, Q) =
  Ω^⊖, Ω^⊕, Ω^⊗ ← ∅
  Σ^⊖ ← QTInsert(p, N*, Q)
  t_p ← Enqueue(p, |square of p|, D, Ω^⊕)
  Add edge (p, 0) ⟶ (p, t_p)

Delete (p, N*, Q) =
  Ω^⊖, Ω^⊕, Ω^⊗ ← ∅
  Σ^⊖ ← QTDelete(p, N*, Q)
  Remove edge (p, 0) ⟶ (p, ·)
  Enqueue(p, |square of p|, D, Ω^⊖)

Propagate (p, Σ^⊖) =
  for each quadtree depth ℓ do
    for c = 1 to κ_S^d do
      for each s ∈ Σ^⊖ at depth ℓ do
        if color of s is c then
          MarkReaders(s, 0)
  for each s ∈ Σ^⊖ and v ≠ p ∈ s do
    if v is an input vertex then
      Remove edge (v, 0) ⟶ (v, ·)
      Enqueue(v, |s|, D, Ω^⊖)
      t_v ← Enqueue(v, |square of v|, D, Ω^⊕)
      Add edge (v, 0) ⟶ (v, t_v)
  r_min ← min rank in Ω^⊖ ∪ Ω^⊕ ∪ Ω^⊗
  for r = r_min to ⌊log_ρ √d⌋ do
    Fix(r, D), Fix(r, F)
```

Figure 3: The pseudo-code of the parallel dynamic update algorithm.

eter κ_O and a real valued function $\ell(r)$ defined on ranks. At each rank r, we partition the space into d-dimensional hypercubes or *tiles* with side length $\ell(r)$. We color tiles such that they are colored periodically in each dimension with period κ_O, using κ_O^d *colors* in total. An operation at rank r that acts on a vertex v has color $c \in \{1, 2, \ldots, \kappa_O^d\}$ if v lies in a c colored tile. Figure 4 illustrates a coloring scheme in 2D. By choosing $\ell(r)$ small enough and κ_O large enough, we prove that two operations at the same rank do not interfere with each other if they have the same color (Lemma 5.3).

5. PARALLEL WORK AND DEPTH

We show that the work is efficiently distributed among the processors, of which there is one for each input vertex (construction), or each dynamic vertex being inserted or deleted (dynamic update). First, we prove that our parallel algorithms can be implemented on an EREW PRAM, i.e., the operations executed at any time step perform only exclusive reads and writes (Lemma 5.4). Then, we prove that a processor performs operations only on the vertices that are relatively close to its input vertex (Lemma 5.5). Taking advantage of this property, we prove that each processor spends $O(1)$ time at each time-step.

The design of the parallel algorithms we present in Section 4 is inspired by the algorithms developed by Acar et al. [4]. Some of their results are useful in proving the results we state here. In particular, they prove that the nearest neighbor distance of a vertex at rank r is bounded below by $\Omega(\rho^r)$ and that any operation acting on that vertex accesses

a region within a ball of radius at most $O(\rho^r)$. These bounds allow us to show the existence of a constant size coloring scheme and that our algorithms are suitable for the EREW PRAM model. For construction and dynamic updates, the theorems on correctness follow similarly.

THEOREM 5.1. *The superset of points that* ParallelWS *constructs and that* Insert *and* Delete *maintains are ρ-well-spaced and size-optimal.*

PROOF. The major difference between our algorithms and the algorithms of Acar et al. is the order in which the vertices are processed, due to difference in the coloring schemes. This does not affect the correctness of our algorithms, so the correctness theorems of Acar et al. [4] continue to apply. □

LEMMA 5.2. *We can color the squares of a given size with $\kappa_S^d \in O(1)$ colors in such a way that two squares are not related if they have the same color.*

PROOF. Hudson and Türkoğlu prove that once the vertices the nearest neighbors of which are within distance $O(\rho^r)$ are ρ-well-spaced the clipped Voronoi cell computations only read squares s that have side length $|s| \in \Omega(\rho^r)$ and within distance $O(\rho^r)$ of v [18]. The balanced condition on the quadtree ensures that these squares have side lengths of size $O(\rho^r)$, thus, $\Theta(\rho^r)$. In other words, squares of a certain size ℓ can be read by operations at constantly many different ranks; let the maximum of those be r. Since any operation at rank r reads squares within a hypercube whose size (side length) is $O(\rho^r)$, in every dimension, a constant number of squares of size ℓ cover this hypercube. Setting κ_S to be this constant completes our proof. □

LEMMA 5.3. *There exists a coloring scheme with $\ell(r) \in \Omega(\rho^r)$ and $\kappa_O \in O(1)$ such that any two dispatch or fill operations executed at the same time step do not interfere.*

PROOF. Consider an operation op acting on v at rank r. Consider another operation op' acting on a vertex w at rank r' that reads a common square. Assuming that the set of squares op' reads is $\mathcal{S}$, we would like to show that there is no vertex $v' \neq v$ at the same time step as v that reads a square from $\mathcal{S}$. The arguments used in the proof of Lemma 5.2 show us $|ws| \in O(\rho^{r'}) = O(\rho^r)$ and $|vs| \in O(\rho^r)$. Using the triangle inequality, we get $|wv| \leq \alpha\rho^r$ for some constant α. Acar et al. proves that the nearest neighbor distance of v is bounded from below by $\Omega(\rho^r)$ [4], let $\ell(r)$ be this bound. To ensure independence, a coloring scheme with $(\kappa_O - 1)\ell(r) > 2\alpha\rho^r$ suffices because any vertex v' that could interfere with v has to be within $2\alpha\rho^r$ distance of v. Since $\ell(r) \in \Omega(\rho^r)$, there exists a coloring parameter $\kappa_O \in O(1)$ that satisfies the above inequality. $\square$

LEMMA 5.4. *The `ParallelWS`, `Insert` and `Delete` functions perform exclusive reads and exclusive writes at every parallel step.*

PROOF. The `Insert` and `Delete` functions start by modifying the quadtree. Theorem 3.1 ensures that the quadtree modifications obey the restrictions of the EREW PRAM model. These functions then call `Propagate`. The initial loop iterates over each quadtree depth ℓ (or size) and square color c and marks the readers of the squares (at depth ℓ and color c) of every processor. Since the square lists $\Sigma^\ominus$ of each processor are disjoint, Lemma 5.2 ensures that two squares at the same depth and color are not related, guaranteeing exclusive memory accesses. The next loop satisfies the EREW conditions by disjointness of the squares.

We are left to prove that the main loop performs operations in an exclusive manner. We show this in two parts: first we prove that two distinct operations executing at the same time do not interfere with each other, second that multiple processors do not try to execute the same operation. For the first part, we observe that fill, dispatch, and undo operations only read squares visited by its `QTClippedVoronoi` call and may only enqueue operations that read a common square. The definition of operation interference captures this observation: two independent operations cannot read or write into the same memory locations. Lemma 5.3 shows the existence of a coloring scheme that enables us to process only independent operations at each time step.

The second part is more technical. In order to ensure that no two distinct processors enqueue the same operation into their schedule, we check the existence of edges in the computation graph. Consider an operation op acting on w at time t_w that is already scheduled in $\Omega^\oplus$. We guarantee that no other processor schedules the same vertex at the same time by checking incoming edges onto (w, t_w). If one exists, we do not schedule. For undo operations, we follow a similar pattern, and do not schedule an operation acting on w at time t_w to be undone until all edges towards (w, t_w) are cleared. Hence, obsolete and fresh operation arrays on all processors contain at most one copy of any vertex. For the inconsistent lists we ensure the same property using flags: the only function that enqueues into inconsistent lists makes sure that the same vertex is not scheduled into two different inconsistent lists. These arguments complete our proof. $\square$

LEMMA 5.5. *Given the operation schedule Ω associated with an input vertex p, each vertex v scheduled in Ω at rank r satisfies $|vp| \in O(\rho^r)$.*

PROOF. We prove our claim using induction on the order our algorithm enqueues vertices into the schedule Ω. For each rank r, we show that there exists a constant α such that for every vertex v scheduled at rank r, we have $|vp| < \alpha\rho^r$. Initially, a vertex v scheduled in Ω either lies inside a square in $\Sigma^\ominus$ or there is an operation acting on it reading a square from $\Sigma^\ominus$. Using the Lemmas 3.2 and 3.3 and the fact that each operation at rank r reads squares within $O(\rho^r)$ distance, we prove the base case, that $|vp| \in O(\rho^r)$. For the inductive step, we assume that any vertex v at rank $r' < r$ is within $\alpha\rho^{r'}$ distance of p. By the locality of the operations, we know that any vertex scheduled for a dispatch or a fill operation at rank r is within distance $O(\rho^r)$ of a vertex in Ω at an earlier rank $r' < r$ or at rank r but an earlier color. Since there is a constant number of colors, any vertex v is within distance $O(\rho^r)$ of another vertex w at rank $r' < r$; let α' be the constant in the asymptotic notation. By inductive hypothesis, we have $|wp| < \alpha\rho^{r'}$. Setting $\alpha = \rho\alpha'/(\rho-1)$, and using the triangle inequality, we prove that $|vp| < \alpha\rho^r$. $\square$

THEOREM 5.6. *Given a set of k vertices N^*, `Insert` and `Delete` update the previous input N to N' by inserting or deleting N^*, and update the previous output to a size-optimal ρ-well-spaced superset of N' in $O(k \log \Delta)$ work and $O(\log \Delta)$ parallel time on an EREW PRAM.*

PROOF. Theorem 3.1 shows that the quadtree can be modified in $O(\log \Delta)$ parallel time using k processors on an EREW PRAM. Lemma 5.4 shows that the `Insert` and `Delete` algorithms can be implemented on an EREW PRAM without extra overhead. For the processor associated with a vertex $p \in \mathsf{N}^*$, Lemma 5.5 shows that any vertex $v \in \Omega$ at rank r is of distance $O(\rho^r)$ away from p. Acar et al. prove a lower bound on the nearest neighbor distance of a vertex v at rank r: $\mathrm{NN}_\mathsf{M}(v) \in \Omega(\rho^r)$ [4]. Thus, a packing argument bounds the number of the vertices in Ω at rank r by a constant. Furthermore, Acar et al. prove that each vertex can be processed in $O(1)$ time. The fact that there are $O(\log \Delta)$ ranks proves our claim on parallel runtime. Observing that there are k processors completes the proof. $\square$

6. A PRACTICAL ALGORITHM

The algorithm that we present in Section 4 assumes an execution model in which processors execute each instruction in lockstep; in practice, this requires global synchronization after every instruction. The algorithm also relies on a large number of colors to ensure exclusive accesses to memory. Although we prove (section 5) the existence of a constant number of colors guaranteeing independence, thus ensuring a high degree of parallelism, we believe the constants may be too large for many practical input sizes. It is therefore not clear if the EREW algorithm can be implemented efficiently on actual hardware, such as contemporary multi-core computers, on which asymptotic benefits may not be realized.

In this section, we describe some key ingredients of a practical implementation of our algorithms on contemporary multi-core machines. We identified the modifications that would be most helpful in attaining such an algorithm by implementing a sequential version of our EREW algorithm, profiling it extensively, and developing an implementation that is tailored not to the asymptotic case, but instead to commodity multi-core machines, and to real-world datasets sampled from the literature. Broadly, the modifications consist of a simplification that permits sequentializing much of the algorithm, elimination of EREW requirements in favor of judicious use of locks, and establishment of a trade-off between number of colors and the parallelism, enabling us to use far fewer colors.

Sequential Operations and Locks. Our EREW algorithm prevents all concurrent reads and writes. On multi-core machines, concurrent reads cause no problems, although concurrent writes must be prevented. This can be accomplished through the use of locks, especially when data is accessed by a small number of processors, each of which holds the lock briefly. Simple experiments with a single-threaded prototype implementation indicate that upwards of 70% of program runtime is spent performing geometric computations in 2D, and significantly more in 3D. The remaining runtime is split between quadtree construction, operation queues, the computation graph, and other bookkeeping tasks. Hence, our primary goal must be to effectively distribute `Dispatch` and `Fill` operations, which perform these geometric operations, across processors. Unless there are a very large number of processors, the vital portions of the minor components of the algorithm may be protected with locks, or even performed sequentially. The `QTInsert` and `QTDelete` quadtree operations fit into this category, since although their theoretical cost is asymptotically significant, it may be, in practical terms, neglected. These operations may therefore be performed sequentially. The computation graph is also inexpensive enough to maintain that it may be protected by a single global lock.

There is little practical benefit to explicitly partitioning pending operations across processors. Instead, it is simplest to use a global priority queue for the `Dispatch` and `Fill` operations, protected by a lock. In addition to simplifying the algorithm, this approach postpones the decision of on which processor each operation will be scheduled from when it is created, to when it is performed, potentially resulting in a better-balanced workload.

The lists of Steiner vertices which are maintained on the leaves of the quadtree may be accessed concurrently by multiple `Fill` operations, and must therefore be protected with locks. The locality of operations (lemma 5.5) implies that only "nearby" operations could potentially access the same list, and therefore that there will be little contention. Our experiments confirm this intuition.

Coloring Scheme. The EREW algorithm uses colors to ensure exclusive memory accesses. Since `Dispatch` operations write only to the computation graph, which can be protected with a lock, we can perform all dispatches at each rank in parallel–no coloring scheme is necessary. In contrast, since `Fill` operations insert Steiner vertices, the order in which they are executed will affect their results, implying that they cannot be executed entirely in parallel. We therefore continue to use a coloring scheme to ensure correctness.

The coloring scheme we propose is a variant of that described in section 4. In both schemes, the goal is to identify independent operations so that they may be executed in parallel, although the definition of "independent" is subtly different. For the EREW algorithm, we ensure that no two processes access related quadtree squares. In practice, the computation graph and the quadtree squares are pro-

tected by locks, so it is sufficient to guarantee that two `Fill` operations, executing in parallel, cannot affect each others' Steiner vertex choices. Specifically, if there are two concurrently-executing `Fill` operations acting on vertices u and v at rank r, then that acting on u may not insert a Steiner vertex which would be a β-clipped Voronoi neighbor of v (and vice-versa). Because any Steiner vertex inserted by the operation acting on u will be inserted within a radius of $\beta \rho^{r+1}$, and all β-clipped Voronoi neighbors of v must be within $2\beta \rho^{r+1}$, it suffices to ensure that concurrently-executing `Fill` operations are more than $3\beta \rho^{r+1}$ apart.

As in section 4, we partition space into a grid of tiles of side length $\ell(r)$. The "color" of each tile will be determined by taking its coordinates modulo κ_O, and the "color coordinate" by taking the integer quotients with κ_O. The "color" and "color coordinate" of an operation are those of the tile containing the vertex on which the operation acts. While, for the EREW algorithm, $\ell(r)$ was chosen to be small enough that each tile could contain at most one operation, we will, for reasons which will be explained shortly, here relax this restriction. Instead, if there are multiple operations scheduled at the same color and color coordinate (i.e. within the same tile), then they will be executed sequentially by the same processor. As before, operations of different colors will be executed sequentially, and operations of the same color *but different color coordinates* will be executed in parallel. To ensure independence, we must choose $(\kappa_O - 1)\ell(r) > 3\beta \rho^{r+1}$.

The operation queues are prioritized by (in order), rank, color and color coordinate. At each rank and color, each processor locks the queue, and takes possession of the top operations of the same color coordinate. After releasing the lock, it then performs these operations sequentially. This approach comes at a cost, in terms of parallelism: the larger $\ell(r)$ is, the more steps must be taken while sequentially executing all of the operations within one tile. Conversely, the larger κ_O is, the more colors there will be, and the more sequential steps will be performed while iterating over the possible colors. Experimentally, we have found that the latter consideration wins out. When finding well-spaced supersets of 2D and 3D uniformly random datasets of 10000 points, the parallel depth of the computation increases monotonically with κ_O for all $\kappa_O > 3$. For this reason, in our implementation, we fix $\kappa_O = 3$.

7. EXPERIMENTS

We have implemented two versions of the proposed algorithms (Section 6), one sequential and one parallel, and performed an experimental analysis using both synthetic and real datasets with parameters $\rho = \sqrt{2}$, and $\beta = 2$ in 2D or $\beta = 2\sqrt{2}/\sqrt{3}$ in 3D. Our experiments confirm our asymptotic bounds and give strong evidence that they can be realized efficiently in practice.

The Implementations. The sequential implementation, while computing the well-spaced superset of the input set, also calculates the work and depth of the computation. Although experiments with the sequential implementation confirm that our asymptotic bounds apply to real-world data, they give no indication as to what the constant factors may be. To resolve this, we have completed a multi-threaded implementation[1] along the lines of that described in Section 6.

---

[1] http://nagoya.uchicago.edu/~cotter/projects/dynamic_wsp

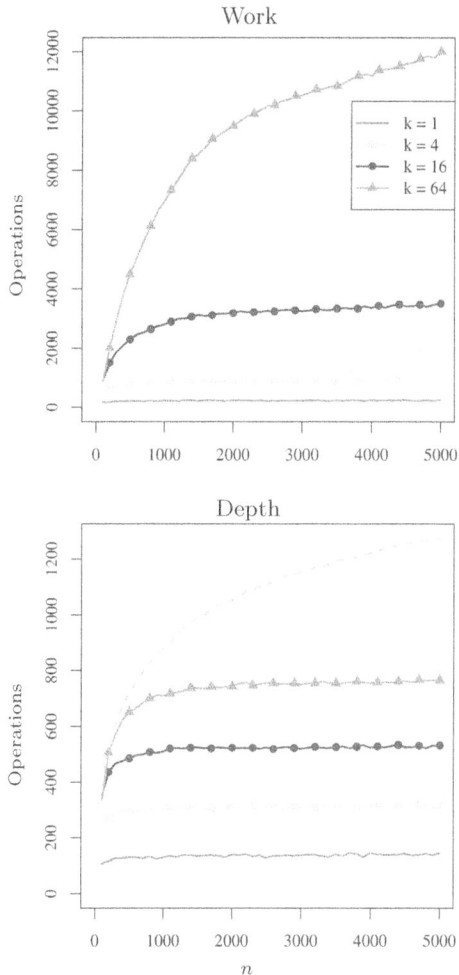

Figure 5: Measured work and depth versus input size n, for two sets of k changes. The dashed curve in the depth plot is twice the depth of a from-scratch run, and is an upper bound on the depth due only to `Dispatch` and `Fill` operations, neglecting undos.

Work and Depth. The *work* and *depth* numbers reported by the sequential implementation are the numbers of operations executed in total, and along the maximum length path in the computation. Alternatively, they measure the single processor and multiprocessor (on an idealized infinitely-parallel machine) times, respectively. Figure 5 shows the work and depth which result from erasing k random vertices from an existing well-spaced point set of size n, updating the set of Steiner vertices, then inserting k vertices, and updating again. We average over 16 runs on each of 16 different size-n input vertex sets (for a total of 256 runs per plotted point). All vertices have floating-point coordinates, and are chosen uniformly at random from the unit square, in two dimensions. The plot on the left shows that the total work required for these two sets of size-k changes is roughly proportional to our $O(k \log \Delta)$ bound (Theorem 5.6). The right hand plot shows that the depths resulting from these changes do not appear to meet our expected $O(\log \Delta)$ upper bound–there appears to be a k dependence. The reason for this is that our upper bound is tight only when operations are scheduled at all ranks and colors. In practice, the

proportion of ranks and colors which are occupied decreases as k decreases, resulting in observed depths outperforming the upper bound by increasing amounts for smaller k. The relative magnitudes of the work and depth numbers show that there is significant parallelism in this algorithm even with the relatively small inputs considered.

Table 1 shows results of computations of well-spaced supersets of a number of well-known 2D and 3D datasets, all of which are significantly larger than the synthetic datasets of the previous experiments. "Simulated" work and depth numbers are calculated as before. On these real-world datasets, there appears to be significant available parallelism–the minimum work-to-depth ratio is 60 (on the Stanford bunny).

Timings and Speedups. Using our parallel implementation, we have measured the actual run-times for finding well-spaced supersets of each of these real datasets, which are also reported in Table 1. Our testing machine has an Intel Core i5 750 CPU, 8G of memory, and runs Ubuntu 10.04. This is a four-core processor.

In the first set of experiments, we calculated a well-spaced point set for each dataset, from scratch, for each number of threads, and averaged the wall-clock times over 10 runs. Each "Speedups" column reports the ratio of the average time taken by the t-thread runs to that of the 1-thread runs.

Our second set of experiments were designed to test the multi-threaded performance of localized dynamic changes. In these experiments, we first created a well-spaced point set on all of the points of a dataset *except* for those within a random ball of radius 0.01 in 2D or 0.1 in 3D. The "k" column in Table 1 contains the number of points in each of these balls. We then measured the time required to insert the "missing" points and update the well-spaced point set on each number of threads, averaged over 10 runs. The reported speedups are the ratios of these average runtimes to that required to find a well-spaced point set from scratch on a single thread. They therefore measure the performance improvement due *both* to dynamism and parallelism. The performance improvement due *only* to dynamism is the 1-thread speedup, while the parallel speedups of the dynamic algorithm may be recovered by taking the ratios of the k-thread and 1-thread speedups. The tested changes are fairly large, because our focus is on the performance impact of parallelism. There is an appealing synergy between dynamism and parallelism when viewed from a performance standpoint: dynamic updates are most efficient when the change set is small and the dataset is two dimensional, whereas parallel speedups are most pronounced when the change set is large and the dataset is three dimensional.

8. CONCLUSION

We presented a parallel and dynamic algorithm for well-spaced point sets, a fundamental problem directly related to meshing in 2D and 3D. The algorithm combines the best characteristics of parallel and dynamic algorithms: as a parallel algorithm, it delivers fast response on parallel computers, and as a dynamic algorithm, it does so by performing minimally necessary work by taking advantage of the similarity between inputs. When the input is modified by k insertions and/or deletions the algorithm performs $O(k \log \Delta)$ work and requires $O(\log \Delta)$ time using k processors on an EREW PRAM. We also presented an adaptation of the algorithm for modern multi-core systems and experimental results suggesting that the algorithm can be made practical.

Table 1: Simulated work and depth numbers, and actual speedups observed, on real-world data. The "Speedups" columns show the parallel speedups observed when calculating well-spaced supersets from scratch. The "Dynamic Speedups" columns show the speedups observed when performing k localized dynamic insertions relative to the time for calculating a well-spaced superset from scratch using a single thread.

Application			Simulated		Speedups		Dynamic Speedups			
Data Set	d	n	Work	Depth	2 cores	4 cores	k	1 core	2 cores	4 cores
New Zealand	2	18595	194838	1650	1.7×	2.9×	463	49×	74×	98×
Cape Cod	2	20930	170588	1330	1.7×	2.9×	83	144×	188×	200×
Lake Superior	2	33487	318484	1622	1.7×	2.8×	296	102×	150×	189×
SF Bay	2	85910	681506	2000	1.7×	2.7×	322	196×	299×	408×
Stanford Bunny	3	35947	289860	4779	1.9×	3.6×	657	9.3×	16×	26×
Armadillo	3	172974	1214280	7539	1.9×	3.6×	4242	14×	25×	42×

9. REFERENCES

[1] U. A. Acar. *Self-Adjusting Computation*. PhD thesis, Department of Computer Science, Carnegie Mellon University, May 2005.

[2] U. A. Acar, G. E. Blelloch, M. Blume, and K. Tangwongsan. An experimental analysis of self-adjusting computation. In *Programming Language Design and Implementation*, 2006.

[3] U. A. Acar, G. E. Blelloch, K. Tangwongsan, and D. Türkoğlu. Robust kinetic convex hulls in 3D. In *European Symposium on Algorithms*, September 2008.

[4] U. A. Acar, A. Cotter, B. Hudson, and D. Türkoğlu. Dynamic well-spaced point sets. In *SCG '10: the 26th Annual Symposium on Computational Geometry*, 2010.

[5] U. A. Acar, B. Hudson, and D. Türkoğlu. Kinetic mesh refinement in 2d. In *SCG '11: the 27th Annual Symposium on Computational Geometry*, 2011.

[6] M. Bern, D. Eppstein, and J. R. Gilbert. Provably Good Mesh Generation. *J. Computer and System Sciences*, 48(3):384–409, 1994.

[7] M. W. Bern, D. Eppstein, and S.-H. Teng. Parallel construction of quadtrees and quality triangulations. *International Journal of Computational Geometry and Applications*, 9(6):517–532, 1999.

[8] J.-D. Boissonnat, O. Devillers, R. Schott, M. Teillaud, and M. Yvinec. Applications of random sampling to on-line algorithms in computational geometry. *Discrete Computional Geometry*, 8:51–71, 1992.

[9] S.-W. Cheng, T. K. Dey, H. Edelsbrunner, M. A. Facello, and S.-H. Teng. Silver exudation. *J. ACM*, 47(5):883–904, 2000.

[10] L. P. Chew. Guaranteed-quality triangular meshes. Technical Report TR-89-983, Department of Computer Science, Cornell University, 1989.

[11] Y.-J. Chiang and R. Tamassia. Dynamic algorithms in computational geometry. *Proceedings of the IEEE*, 80(9):1412–1434, 1992.

[12] K. L. Clarkson, K. Mehlhorn, and R. Seidel. Four results on randomized incremental constructions. *Computational Geometry Theory and Application*, 3:185–212, 1993.

[13] C. Demetrescu, I. Finocchi, and G. Italiano. *Handbook on Data Structures and Applications*, chapter 36: Dynamic Graphs. 2005.

[14] L. Guibas. Modeling motion. In J. Goodman and J. O'Rourke, editors, *Handbook of Discrete and Computational Geometry*, pages 1117–1134. Chapman and Hall/CRC, 2nd edition, 2004.

[15] M. A. Hammer, U. A. Acar, and Y. Chen. CEAL: A C-based language for self-adjusting computation. In *Programming Language Design and Implementation*, June 2009.

[16] B. Hudson, G. Miller, and T. Phillips. Sparse voronoi refinement. In *Proceedings of the 2006 International Meshing Roundtable*, 2006.

[17] B. Hudson, G. Miller, and T. Phillips. Sparse Parallel Delaunay Mesh Refinement. In *SPAA*, 2007.

[18] B. Hudson and D. Türkoğlu. An efficient query structure for mesh refinement. In *Canadian Conference on Computational Geometry*, 2008.

[19] H. Jung and K. Mehlhorn. Parallel algorithms for computing maximal independent sets in trees and for updating minimum spanning trees. *Inf. Process. Lett.*, 27:227–236, April 1988.

[20] R. Ley-Wild, U. A. Acar, and M. Fluet. A cost semantics for self-adjusting computation. In *Principles of Programming Languages*, 2009.

[21] G. L. Miller, D. Talmor, S.-H. Teng, N. Walkington, and H. Wang. Control Volume Meshes Using Sphere Packing: Generation, Refinement and Coarsening. In *Fifth Intl. Meshing Roundtable*, pages 47–61, 1996.

[22] D. Moore. The cost of balancing generalized quadtrees. In *SMA '95: symposium on Solid modeling and app.*, pages 305–312, New York, NY, USA, 1995. ACM.

[23] G. M. Morton. A computer oriented geodetic data base; and a new technique in file sequencing. Technical report, IBM, Ottowa, CA, 1966.

[24] K. Mulmuley. *Computational Geometry: An Introduction Through Randomized Algorithms*. Prentice Hall, 1994.

[25] S. Pawagi and O. Kaser. Optimal parallel algorithms for multiple updates of minimum spanning trees. *Algorithmica*, 9:357–381, 1993.

[26] O. Schwarzkopf. Dynamic maintenance of geometric structures made easy. In *32nd Annual Symposium on Foundations of Computer Science*, pages 197–206, October 1991.

[27] D. Talmor. *Well-Spaced Points for Numerical Methods*. PhD thesis, Carnegie Mellon University, August 1997. CMU-CS-97-164.

A Study of Transactional Memory vs. Locks in Practice

Victor Pankratius
Karlsruhe Institute of Technology
76131 Karlsruhe, Germany
www.victorpankratius.com
victor.pankratius@kit.edu

Ali-Reza Adl-Tabatabai
Programming Systems Lab
Intel Corporation
Santa Clara, California
ali-reza.adl-tabatabai@intel.com

ABSTRACT

Transactional Memory (TM) promises to simplify parallel programming by replacing locks with atomic transactions. Despite much recent progress in TM research, there is very little experience using TM to develop realistic parallel programs from scratch. In this paper, we present the results of a detailed case study comparing teams of programmers developing a parallel program from scratch using transactional memory and locks. We analyze and quantify in a realistic environment the development time, programming progress, code metrics, programming patterns, and ease of code understanding for six teams who each wrote a parallel desktop search engine over a fifteen week period. Three randomly chosen teams used Intel's Software Transactional Memory compiler and Pthreads, while the other teams used just Pthreads. Our analysis is exploratory: Given the same requirements, how far did each team get? The TM teams were among the first to have a prototype parallel search engine. Compared to the locks teams, the TM teams spent less than half the time debugging segmentation faults, but had more problems tuning performance and implementing queries. Code inspections with industry experts revealed that TM code was easier to understand than locks code, because the locks teams used many locks (up to thousands) to improve performance. Learning from each team's individual success and failure story, this paper provides valuable lessons for improving TM.

Categories and Subject Descriptors: D.1.3 [Programming Techniques]: Concurrent Programming — Parallel programming. **General Terms:** Human Factors.

1. INTRODUCTION

Multicore is a challenge for software engineering, and we need mainstream languages that support productive and robust parallel programming in the large. In response to the problems of parallel programming with locks, Transactional Memory (TM) has been proposed as an alternative synchronization mechanism. Several new parallel programming languages such X10, Fortress, Chapel, and Clojure, all provide transactions in-lieu of locks as the primary concurrency control mechanism. Other research systems have extended existing languages such as C++ [21], Java [4], Haskell [12], and ML [23] with support for Transactional Memory.

Despite the recent advances in TM research, there is little experience using TM to develop more realistic parallel programs from scratch. Recent discussions [24] of TM versus locks focused on small, mostly numerical programs or micro-benchmarks to evaluate the worst case performance, but none of them took into account more complex applications and software engineering aspects such as the productivity of programmers over a longer period of time; the time needed for design, implementation, testing and debugging; the ease of code understanding; or problems with the usage of parallel language constructs. Other work studying the conversion of locks programs to TM failed to shed light on the issues encountered when parallelizing with TM from scratch [34].

This paper addresses a novel research question in an exploratory case study: How exactly do individuals program in parallel with locks and TM, given the same programming problem *specification*? Using diverse, real cases, we aim to analyze in-depth how the use of TM or lock-based constructs influence parallel programming and the resulting program. This approach differs from previous work providing a locks-versus-TM performance comparison on the same exact program. Moreover, we focus on learning from individual approaches rather than on testing hypotheses on statistically aggregated data.

We study graduate-level student programmers tasked with developing a parallel desktop search engine from scratch under realistic time pressures. The study was organized as a one-semester graduate-level computer science course. All subjects received the same four-week training at the start of the semester. The programming part of the project spanned ten weeks starting after the training. The study randomly assigned twelve graduate students to six teams. Three of the teams (teams L1, L2, and L3) had to use locks, while the other three teams (TM1, TM2, and TM3) had to use TM language constructs provided by the Intel C++ Software Transactional Memory (STM) compiler [21] – one of the most advanced STM compilers built on top of Intel's production C++ compiler.

The case study shows that TM was indeed applicable to a more complex, non-numerical program, and that a combination of TM with locks is useful and came out of necessity in practice. Locks teams spent more time on debugging due to segmentation faults than TM teams. TM teams, however, spent more time on performance-related issues than locks teams. The parallel programs of TM teams were easier to understand, according to code inspections done jointly with industry compiler experts. Locks teams tended to have more complex parallel programs by employing up to *thousands* of locks to achieve scalability. The paper also shows that TM does not solve all concurrency control problems, and thus is not a silver bullet. In particular, both the locks and TM teams had data races because they used incorrect double-checked locking patterns [5].

The paper is a summarized version of [22] and makes the following contributions: (1) it is the first study to document how several teams wrote a realistic application from scratch using TM and locks over an extended period of time; (2) it provides insights by analyzing a combination of quantitative and qualitative data on performance, hours spent on various development phases, code metrics, ease of code understanding, and subjective psychological issues; (3) it shows that TM is indeed a valuable approach for parallel programming, although with an immature tool chain; (4) it provides evidence that it was beneficial to use TM and locks in combination, thus leveraging the advantages of both programming models; and (5) it collects evidence falsifying opinions that TM does not help building real-world parallel applications.

Empirical studies with human subjects are vital for assessing the true value of parallel programming proposals in practice and exposing problems and new directions to the research community. Unfortunately, case studies like this one are rare because they are costly, risky, and require a long time to conduct.

The paper is organized as follows. Section 2 presents the project requirements, the STM compiler, and collected evidence. Section 3 presents code metrics focusing on productivity and the use of parallelism constructs. Section 4 discusses the results of code inspections for all the programs. Section 5 breaks down the effort each team spent on parallelization, tuning, and debugging. Section 6 measures the performance of each team's search engine. Section 7 summarizes key results from our study. Section 8 discusses potential threats to validity. Section 9 contrasts related work. Section 10 provides our conclusion.

2. CASE STUDY DESIGN

Every team developed a desktop search engine based on the following requirements:

Indexing. The search engine works on text files only. It starts crawling in a pre-defined directory and recursively in all subdirectories. The index does not have to persist on disk. Different strategies for index creation may be employed (e.g., division into several sub-indices). All non-alphanumeric characters are treated as word separators. Case and hyphens between words are ignored. A progress indicator for indexing must show bytes and files processed so far, words found so far, and the number of words in the index. The number of indexing threads must be configurable via a command line parameter.

Search. The search must allow different types of queries: (1) queries for coherent text passages (e.g., "this is a test"); (2) queries with wildcard at the beginning or the end of a word (e.g.,"hou*" or "*pa"); (3) queries containing several words representing *AND* concatenation (e.g., "tree house garden"); (4) queries with word exclusion (e.g., "-fruit").

Queries must be allowed to execute while indexing is in progress, but it is not required to run more than one query at a time in parallel. It was up to the teams to decide whether to parallelize each query; the number of query threads was not required to be configurable from the command line, but the teams had to provide a reasonable default for the benchmarking. We assume that the files to be indexed do not change while the desktop search engine executes. In addition, no files are deleted and no new files are added. Features that are *not* required are an "OR" operator in queries, stemming or word similarity search, and regular expressions.

Output. Files for which the query is true must be output in a sorted order according to a primary and secondary criterion: (1) the sum of occurrences of all query words, needed if several criteria exist, such as in AND queries; and (2) alphabetically by file name. The default output of a query consists of the first 50 paths and files sorted as mentioned before, the total number of files matching a query, and the query time.

Scenario. To simulate a real-world industry scenario, we allowed the teams to use any data structures that they wanted. To be even more realistic, we allowed them to reuse any library or open-source code from the Web. This diversity was intentional because it helped find out which approaches worked and which did not work. All students had Bachelor-equivalent degrees in computer science and were pursuing Master's degrees in computer science. Students with inappropriate skills were not accepted in the project, and all accepted students received the same training on TM and locks prior to project start. All teams except team TM3 had one member with course experience on parallelism. More details on the experience profiles, which differ for each team, are shown in [22].

Before the study started, we gave the same parallel programming training to all students covering common parallel programming issues such as race conditions and deadlocks. We also conducted a feasibility study to make sure that the timeframe set for all teams is sufficient to finish the project and implement all features.

Compiler. The TM teams were required to use Intel's STM compiler, an industrial-strength C/C++ compiler that has been extended with a prototype implementation of transactional language constructs for C++ [21]. We used the first version of this compiler when it was available for download from Intel's website. We decided not use a library based approach [6] because we felt a language-based approach was more productive and less error prone. The Intel STM compiler provides new statements that allow the programmer to define and abort transactions easily. The `__tm_atomic` keyword defines an atomic block of statements that will execute as a transaction. Atomic blocks can be nested, and the effects of inner transactions are visible only when the outer transaction commits. The `__tm_abort` statement rolls back a transaction and reverses the effects to the state that existed on the entry to the innermost transaction enclosing the abort statement. The compiler extensions also include annotations to functions and classes to mark functions that will be called inside transactions. The `__tm_callable` annotation marks functions that can be called inside transactions and instructs the compiler to generate a transactional clone with the necessary instrumentation on shared memory accesses. The instrumentation calls into the STM run-time, which tracks conflicts between transactions. On detecting a conflict, the run-time rolls back the effects of a transaction and retries it. The `__tm_pure` annotation marks functions that the compiler does not need to instrument; the programmer must make sure that such functions can be safely called inside transactions without instrumentation.

The TM teams were allowed to use Pthreads in combination with the TM extensions so that they could create and manage threads. It is technically possible to use locks, semaphores, and condition variables in combination with transactions, and subjects were allowed to do so.

Throughout this study, we followed the recommendations of [25, 32, 33] and used several sources of qualitative and quantitative evidence: (1) The teams used diaries to take notes, track progress, explain ideas and successful or unsuccessful approaches, document technical or non-technical problems, and capture events that had an impact on the work. (2) A time report sheet capturing effort on a daily basis, split according to predefined task categories. Section 5 analyzes these times reports. (3) Notes from weekly (semi-structured) interviews [25] asking open-ended questions about current status, problems, and plans without requiring any particular format in the response. Tables 1 and 2 summarize the interviews starting on the fourth week of the project, which was the first week with clearly visible progress. (4) A post-project questionnaire, filled out individually by each student. The detailed questions and all answers are listed in [22]. (5) The source code produced by each team. (6) The subversion repository that all teams were required to use. (7) Personal observations of the instructor.

3. CODE METRICS

This section presents measurements of objective code metrics gathered from all programs.

Summary of insights. The results show that in this study, the locks-based programs were more complex parallel programs, because the locks programmers tended to use many locks; our code inspections in Section 4 reinforce with additional observations that locks programs were more complex. Although the locks and TM teams programmed parallel search engines with similar functionality, the TM teams used fewer critical sections that often had fewer lines of code than the critical sections of the locks teams.

The results also show that two of the TM teams combined TM with Pthreads synchronization primitives, and that the TM teams rarely used the more advanced TM language constructs – only one team used the `__tm_pure` keyword, and only one team used the `__tm_abort` keyword. Our code inspections, presented in Section 4, provide further insight into these results. Inspections revealed that the Pthreads synchronization primitives were used for I/O and producer-consumer co-ordination. Inspections further revealed that `__tm_pure` was used for printing debug messages and optimizing access to immutable data, and that `__tm_abort` was used incorrectly in a racy fashion to optimize performance instead of being used for failure atomicity.

Figure 1 shows the total lines of code (LOC) produced by all teams, excluding comments, blank lines, or code from foreign libraries. All teams produced about the same amount of code; on average, locks teams produced 2160 LOC, and TM teams produced 2228 LOC.

TM teams have a higher standard deviation of LOC compared to locks teams, which can be explained by the fact that team TM1 (the most inexperienced team) had incomplete code that did not work on the final benchmark. On the other hand, team TM3 had more code than any other team, because they decided to implement themselves many thread-safe helper functions due to lacking library support for TM programs.

3.1 Usage of parallel constructs

Locks and TM teams clearly differ in how many lines of code contain parallel constructs (Figure 1). Between 5% and 11% of the locks teams code had parallel constructs (179 LOC on average). By contrast, between 2% and 5% of TM teams code had parallel constructs (83 LOC on average).

All locks teams used condition variables, but none of the TM teams did. Two of the TM teams used Pthread constructs in addition to the constructs for thread creation or destruction: As will be discussed in Section 4, team TM2 used one lock to protect a large critical section containing I/O, and team TM3 used two semaphores for producer-consumer synchronization.

Synchronization constructs were rarely lexically nested, with at most one level of lexical nesting. Later code inspections revealed for all TM teams that the nesting of their nested transactions was not necessary.

The special-purpose TM constructs offered by Intel's compiler were used very differently. Team TM2 used the `__tm_callable` annotation in 2 lines of code, but team TM3 used it in 115 lines. Team TM2 were the only team that used the `__tm_pure` annotation; later code inspections show that one usage of `__tm_pure` was for a declaration of `printf` so that they could debug the program. This is evidence that we need better debugging tools for TM. Only team TM1 used the `__tm_abort` construct, but as later code inspections show, they did not use it as it was intended to be used for failure atomicity – most of the time they used it incorrectly to optimize performance and implemented a racy double-checking pattern [5].

3.2 Comparison of critical sections

The critical sections differ for locks teams and TM teams. Figure 2 shows details on how many critical sections each team had and the cumulative lines of code. We see, for example, that team L2 has 25 critical sections with a size less than or equal to 1 LOC, 36 critical sections with a size less than or equal to 4 LOC, and so on.

We statically approximated a lower bound on the length of critical sections by manually counting the LOC enclosed by lock/unlock operations, semaphore operations, or *atomic* blocks, and excluding comments and blank lines. Information from code inspections shows that some locks teams had arrays with thousands of locks, but these lock definitions showed up as just one line of code; we counted a function call within a critical section as one LOC and omitted dynamic analyses.

A key observation is that most critical sections are short. TM teams have fewer critical sections than locks teams, even though all teams implement similar functionality. The locks teams have many critical sections with just one line of code, which could have been easily expressed as atomic blocks.

4. CODE INSPECTIONS

In this section, we present observations from code inspections. The authors and leading industry compiler experts inspected each team's code in detail, but in an anonymized

	Locks Teams			TM Teams		
	L1	L2	L3	TM1	TM2	TM3
Total Lines of Code (excl. comments, blank lines)	2014	2285	2182	1501	2131	3052
	avg: 2160 stddev: 137			avg: 2228 stddev: 780		
LOC pthread*	157	261	120	17	23	12
	8%	11%	5%	1%	1%	0%
LOC tm_*	0	0	0	36	22	139
				2%	1%	5%
LOC with paral. constr. (pthread* + tm_*)	157	261	120	53	45	151
	8%	11%	5%	4%	2%	5%
	avg: 179 stddev: 73			avg: 83 stddev: 59		
Total effort in pers. hours	151	334	208	208	261	141
Productivity in person hours/LOC	0.07	0.15	0.10	0.14	0.12	0.05
	avg: 0.105 stddev: 0.037			avg: 0.102 stddev: 0.049		

	Locks Teams			TM Teams		
	L1	L2	L3	TM1	TM2	TM3
Selected details on Pthreads constructs						
LOC pthread_create*	8	13	8	6	3	3
LOC pthread_cond*	10	18	6	0	0	0
LOC sem_*	0	0	0	0	0	10
LOC pthread_mutex_t*	14	28	9	0	1	0
LOC pthread_mutex_lock*	43	45	24	0	1	0
LOC pthread_mutex_unlock*	43	49	34	0	2	0
Average LOC per critical section	7.1	3.1	9.2		85	4.5
- no. of crit. sect. with nested locks (levels)	1 (1)	0	1(1)			
Selected details on Transactional Memory constructs						
LOC tm_atomic (= #atomic blocks)				12	17	24
- average LOC per atomic section				5.9	3.5	6.4
- no of nested atomic sections (level)				0	2 (1)	1 (1)
LOC tm_callable				18	2	115
LOC tm_pure				0	3	0
LOC tm_abort				6	0	0

Figure 1: Code metrics for the parallel desktop search engines of all teams.

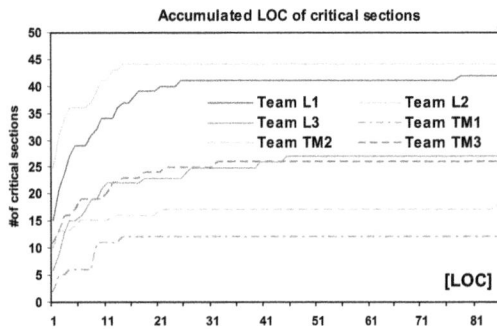

Figure 2: Code distribution in critical sections.

form. These inspections allow us to analyze the use of constructs, the kinds of parallel programming mistakes, and code and bug patterns. We present selected highlights from each team on architecture, major data structures, synchronization, ease of code understanding, and problems.

Summary of insights. The code inspections revealed several interesting usages of the parallelism primitives. First, the lock-based programs used many fine-grain locks to get scalability, and the use of fine-grained locks was difficult to validate by code inspection. Second, code inspections revealed why the TM teams combined Pthreads synchronization with atomic blocks, and how they used the more advanced TM language constructs: Realistic TM programs require producer-consumer synchronization, perform I/O, and need ways to optimize access to immutable data.

Despite being taught otherwise, our inspections revealed that all teams – both locks and TM teams – incorrectly assumed in several places that it is safe to read shared data without synchronization and had obvious data races due to racy double-checked locking patterns [5].

4.1 Code inspections for locks teams

In general, all locks teams parallelized the indexing using a crawler thread to generate work for a set of worker threads that created the index in parallel. The granularity of work differed between the teams: In team L2's program the crawler thread generated work at the granularity of files, while in team L1's and L3's programs the crawler thread parsed each file and generated work at the granularity of words. All teams could query at the same time as indexing, but team L3 did not parallelize the query itself. All teams had a shared index data structure that was updated in parallel by the indexing worker threads and concurrently read by a query thread.

The code inspections show that realistic programs may require many fine-grain locks in order to have scalable performance. All teams attempted fine-grain locking of the index data structure to allow concurrent access to disjoint parts of the index structure; to protect the index structure, team L2 used 1600 (!) locks, team L3 used 80 locks, and team L1 used 54 locks. Team L2's program, which had the largest number of locks, was the only locks program to scale on indexing. Locks are mostly used in a block-structured manner; however, team L2 and L3 have cases where unlocking is performed in both *then* or *else* statements due to a function return from the middle of a critical section (explaining why there are more unlock operations than lock operations in Figure 1). Many locks are created dynamically, so the total number of locks is larger than the count of lines of code count containing the `pthread_mutex_t` construct.

Some locks teams used the high number of locks to compensate for their insecurity when writing complex parallel programs. Team L2, for example, emulated the Java synchronized construct. They introduced a lock for every object knowing that they would sacrifice performance, yet they still had races. Most teams made the common mistake of believing that unprotected reading of shared state is safe (despite being taught otherwise), thus they had races. Only team L1 had critical sections protecting a single shared variable read.

Team L1 has index data structure consisting of an array of sub-indices for every character. Each sub-index consists of a map storing all words starting with the particular character of that sub-index. They use a lock to protect the work queue, several locks to protect code that displays information, and two arrays of locks and two additional locks protecting accesses to the two sub-index arrays. Each lock in these two arrays of locks protects a different character in one of the two sub-index arrays, so there are 54 (27 x 2) locks protecting the index structure. The number of dynamic lock instances is therefore greater than in Figure 1. To avoid deadlocks, the team specified an order for acquiring locks in these lock arrays, documented as comments in a header file. This protocol is not complete, however, because it misses some locks that are acquired in a nested fashion; in addition, the code violates the protocol in at least one place. The team also used a copy-and-paste approach for many critical sections.

Team L2 used an inverted index data structure in which stored words are accessed using the first two characters. They don't speed up wildcard searches using a reverse index. The team assumes 40 possible characters and creates $40 \times 40 = 1600$ disjoint map structures, each of which maps a word to the document and position within the document. With this many maps, they hope to insert and access the index in parallel without causing much conflict. It is difficult to spot the high number of locks in the code of the indexing data structure:

```
//vocabulary.h:
 class Vocabulary {
 private:
    std::map<std::string, InvertedList> invertedLists;
    pthread_mutex_t access_mutex;
...
//bigvocabulary.cc
...
characters="abcdefghijklmnopqrstuvwxyzäöüSS0123456789"
// creates the index-structure
 for(int i=0; i < (int)characters.length();i++){
    std::map<std::string,Vocabulary>tmp_map;
    for(int j=0; j < (int)characters.length();j++){
      Vocabulary tmp_voc;
      tmp_voc.initialize();  ...
```

Later on, this nested loop creates 1600 vocabulary objects, each of which contains a lock and the map. Team L2's code has clear data races. The getter accessor functions on most classes don't use locks while updater functions do, so this team assumes that writing to a shared data structure must be protected by a lock, but reading does not.

Team L3 used a BurstTrie based on [13] for their index data structures, a more complex tree-based data structure compared to the maps used by teams L1 and L2. This team used an array of 40 locks at the root of the index data structure, and 40 at the root of the reverse index. The locks are acquired depending on the first letter of the word to be indexed. An insertion into the index requires acquiring two locks. This leads to the same scalability problems as for team L1, which is lots of contention for words with a frequent first letter. They also have racy code:

```
//called by each indexer thread
void BurstTrie::Insert(...) {
  ...
  if(rootNode == NULL){
  rootNode = new BurstNode(); //unprotected
  rootNodeReverse = new BurstNode(); //unprotected
  ...
  }
```

4.2 Code inspections for TM teams

Like some of the locks teams, teams TM1 and TM3 implemented a crawler thread that produced a list of files to index into a shared work queue from which a pool of indexer threads grabbed work. Except for team TM1, none of the TM teams parallelized queries. Unlike all of the other teams, team TM2 used a persistent index on disk and ran queries in a separate program that read the on-disk index.

The code inspections show that realistic TM programs need to perform producer-consumer synchronization. Team TM3 used a semaphore. Team TM2 avoided producer-consumer synchronization because each indexing thread performed part of the crawling. Team TM1 did not consider producer-consumer synchronization because an indexer thread exits once it detects an empty work queue. The C++ TM model must therefore either be extended to handle these operations, or TM must be allowed to be combined with other lock-based primitives.

In addition, realistic TM programs need to do I/O and optimize access to immutable data inside transactions. Team TM2 used a global lock in a critical section that performed many I/O operations. They also used `__tm_pure` to optimize comparisons of immutable strings inside of a transaction. It was hard for the code reviewers to validate the correct usage of `__tm_pure`. A compiler-enforceable approach would clearly have been better.

Like the locks teams, TM teams incorrectly assumed that unprotected reading of shared state is safe. Most teams systematically tried to optimize transaction performance by first checking a condition outside a transactions and then checking it inside, similar to incorrect implementations of the double-checked locking pattern [5].

Team TM1 used a two-level index based on linked lists. On the first level there is an entry for each character a word can start with. For each of these entries, there is a list of characters a word can end with on the second level. Attached to each entry on the second level is a list of all words (with document positions) that start and end with a certain character. Team TM1's code has clear data races. The `__tm_atomic` construct mostly protects short code passages. The `__tm_abort` construct was used six times. In five times, they used it incorrectly to implement a racy double-checking pattern:

```
while (added == 1) {
 //check outside atomic
 if (dokulist->get_counter() < DOKU_NUM) {
 __tm_atomic { //check inside atomic
   if (dokulist->get_counter() >= DOKU_NUM) {
     __tm_abort; }
   else {dokulist->add_to_DokuNode(newDoku,newPosi);
     added = 0;}}}}
```

Team TM2, unlike all other teams, does not have a crawler thread. Instead, each indexer thread updates a shared directory stack that keeps track of the current directory to crawl. This is also the only team to store the index on disk. This team used a modified B-tree according to the approach described in [18]. They incorrectly tried to avoid transaction overhead in a double-checked locking style:

```
//bufferload.c
...
if (dl->length < DLCHUNK) { //check outside
__tm_atomic {
 if (dl->length < DLCHUNK) { //check inside
  dl->entry[dl->length].docid = docid;
  dl->entry[dl->length].freq = 1;dl->length++;
  return 0;} }
```

Team TM2 also assumed that reading shared variables without protection is safe, thus introducing data races:

```
//bufferload.c
...
while (word = getWord(p)) {
  node = findBufferWord(&b, word);
  __tm_atomic {
    node = findBufferWord(node, word);  ...
```

Team TM3 used a crawler thread that goes breadth-first through the directories and produces a list of files to be indexed into a single work queue. A pool of indexer threads each opens the files, invokes a lexer to produce term-frequency pairs, and updates the shared index. For the index data structure, they use a vocabulary trie as in [7], which is a tree-like data structure with nodes representing shared prefixes of index terms. Two semaphores, `fillcount` and `emptycount` are used in the thread pool for producer-consumer synchronization. `__tm_atomic` mostly protects short code passages. They used several small transactions back-to-back instead of big transactions to optimize performance. Their indexer code has a race as it uses an incorrect variant of double-checked locking [5]. They check outside a transaction if their stack of files is empty, and then perform a *pop* operation inside a transaction. To work correctly, both operations should be inside the same transaction:

```
while(true){ //consumer
 sem_wait(&fillcount);
 if (new_files->is_empty()) {break;}
 __tm_atomic {filename = new_files->pop();}
 sem_post(&emptycount);  ...
```

5. PROGRAMMING EFFORT

Throughout the project, each team filled out a form tracking how many hours they spent per day on a certain task category. Figure 3 summarizes the overall results (the complete form is shown in [22]). TM teams spent less total effort than the locks teams. In particular, TM teams spent 28 hours less on reading documentation, 80 hours less on implementation, and 14 hours less on debugging than the locks teams. However, TM teams also implemented fewer query types, as shown in Figure 4.

Another source of evidence of programming effort is the interview results shown in Tables 1 and 2. We first summarize the results of the interviews and then analyze the efforts on parallelization, tuning, and debugging using both the data from Figure 3 and the interview data.

5.1 Interviews

Locks teams. In the eighth week, two weeks before the deadline, all locks teams had parallel implementations, but none of them could show a full demonstration. In the ninth week all teams had running search engines, but two of them appeared experimental: Team L1's program was unstable, and team L2's had segmentation faults. Team L3 focused on performance testing, but in the following week they found a bug. By the end of the project in the tenth week, team L1 had run out of time and skipped performance tests, team L2 was not finished with performance tests, and team L3 had discovered a concurrency bug that they were trying to fix before submission.

TM teams. In the eighth week, team TM1 had just a serial program, team TM2 had an incomplete parallel indexer and no queries working, while team TM3 had a full-fledged working demo. In the ninth week, team TM1 was still incomplete, team TM2 had a running, but buggy parallel program with bad performance, and team TM3 fixed many bugs in their search engine. By the end of the project in the tenth week, team TM1's program failed on the final benchmark, team TM2 had parallel indexing and queries working with reasonable performance, and team TM3 had an even more improved search engine.

Teams TM1 and TM2 procrastinated parallelization due to various reasons. Team TM1 lacked experience; both students were hesitant and insecure, especially during implementation. Team TM2 procrastinated parallelization because they wanted to have a more or less perfect sequential program as a basis on which to introduce transactions. Despite being the most experienced team in the study, they thought that query implementation would be trivial and underestimated its complexity. It appears that TM encourages the procrastination of parallelization in cases such as those of TM1 and TM2. All TM teams reported that it was difficult to find out where and how to apply atomic blocks and TM function annotations in a larger code base. In addition, TM performance was hard to predict. We need better tools to simplify these tasks.

Interestingly, even though teams TM2 and TM3 complain about difficulties in using TM constructs late into the project, the evidence shows that these teams merely had the impression that they could not make good progress and were hampered by TM constructs — the objective data shows that they did pretty well, even better compared to the locks teams.

5.2 Parallelization

TM teams spent in total about half as much time as the locks teams on writing parallel code (see [22] for details). TM allowed the experienced TM teams more time to think sequentially, which is backed up by (1) the hours spent on sequential code versus parallel code, and (2) the time lag between the first day of work on sequential code and the first day of work on parallel code. The locks teams had a shorter time lag between the first day of work on sequential code and the first day of work on parallel code: team L1, 1 day; team L2, 13 days; and team L3, 19 days. By contrast, TM teams have larger time lags: team TM3, 19 days; team TM2, 23 days; and team TM1, 29 days.

The effort data generally backs up several of our observations related to parallelization from the interviews. First, the larger time lags for teams TM1 and TM2 back up our observations that these teams procrastinated parallelization. Team TM3, who were also the first to have a working parallel version, started parallelization after locks teams L1 and L2. The locks teams L1 and L2 were the first to start parallelizing, whereas the teams TM1 and TM2 were the last to start parallelization.

5.3 Performance tuning

The collected effort data shows that TM teams had more problems with performance tuning than the locks teams. Late into the project, the TM teams had to experiment with performance and restructure their programs to deal with performance problems. Refactoring effort increased for all TM teams by the end of the project. Team TM2 mentioned during the interviews that they had to split up large transactions into smaller ones, pointing to a late restructuring problem for TM programs. In order to understand TM performance, all TM teams had sharp increases of effort by the end of the project to do performance experiments with smaller programs. All these results suggest that further research is needed into developing performance analysis tools and refactoring techniques for TM-based programs. In addition, research on programming patterns or anti-patterns for TM can help reduce performance problems.

Total Effort (Person Hours)

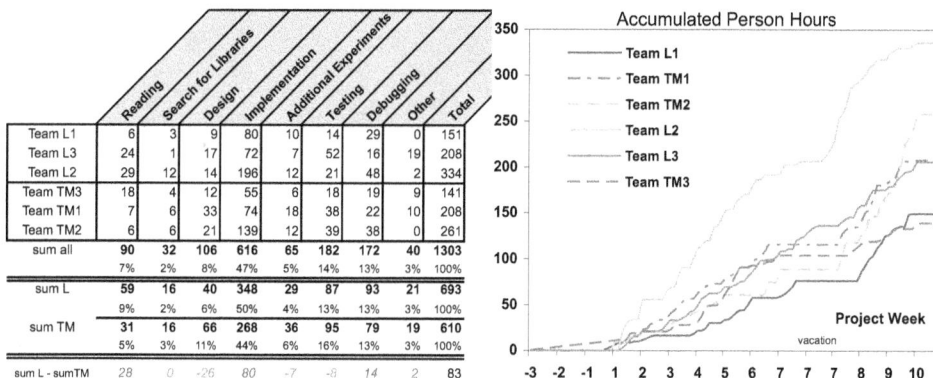

	Reading	Search for Libraries	Design	Implementation	Additional Experiments	Testing	Debugging	Other	Total
Team L1	6	3	9	80	10	14	29	0	151
Team L3	24	1	17	72	7	52	16	19	208
Team L2	29	12	14	196	12	21	48	2	334
Team TM3	18	4	12	55	6	18	19	9	141
Team TM1	7	6	33	74	18	38	22	10	208
Team TM2	6	6	21	139	12	39	38	0	261
sum all	90	32	106	616	65	182	172	40	1303
	7%	2%	8%	47%	5%	14%	13%	3%	100%
sum L	59	16	40	348	29	87	93	21	693
	9%	2%	6%	50%	4%	13%	13%	3%	100%
sum TM	31	16	66	268	36	95	79	19	610
	5%	3%	11%	44%	6%	16%	13%	3%	100%
sum L - sumTM	28	0	-26	80	-7	-8	14	2	83

Figure 3: Total effort of all teams in person hours.

Prj. Week	
4	• **L1:** The team discussed the index design and the placement of locks, but did not have any code running yet. • **L2:** The team finished a sequential indexer and assessed its performance. They were the first team to elaborate thoughts on how threads might traverse the index in parallel. • **L3:** The team did not have a running program yet. The team discussed indexing strategies and data structures choices, but had no code running.
5	• **L1:** The team assessed two prototypes for parallel indexing in various experiments. First, they used one global mutex, which yielded bad performance. Then, they decided to go for several independently locked sub-indexes. • **L2:** The team implemented a rudimentary parallel indexer. • **L3:** The team had implemented a sequential prototype with an index structure, and they were testing the performance. They had a customized, small benchmark that was unrelated to the case study benchmark.
6	• **L1:** The team had a prototype of parallel indexing and parallel queries working, but the prototype had performance problems. The file crawler – a key component for indexing – was not implemented, but just simulated. • **L2:** Parallel indexing worked. Queries could be executed while indexing was in progress. • **L3:** Parallel indexing worked. Queries were implemented in a rudimentary way.
7	• **L1:** Parallel indexing and parallel queries still worked with the simulated file crawler. They were working on query result ranking but were not finished yet. • **L2:** The team has made little progress due to problems with C. • **L3:** The team showed how they used the Linux system monitor for performance testing and debugging. There was not much other progress to see.
8	• **L1:** The team had finished all components except the file crawler, but they hadn't tested it yet on the real benchmark. • **L2:** The team found out that they had problems compiling their code on other machines and were about to fix that. • **L3:** Parallel indexing and parallel search worked, but only on a subset of the case study benchmark.
9	• **L1:** The team finished implementing the file crawler. Parallel indexing and parallel queries worked, but were unstable. • **L2:** Parallel indexing parallel queries worked. The team fixed segmentation faults and did performance tests. • **L3:** Parallel indexing and queries worked. The team continued with performance testing.
10	• **L1:** The team still had not tested performance on the given benchmark. • **L2:** The team was about to test performance on the given benchmark. • **L3:** The team was about to fix a bug with the file statistics update of their indexer.

Table 1: Progress summary from locks teams interviews.

5.4 Debugging

The total time for debugging was higher for locks teams than for TM teams (93 hours vs. 79 hours, respectively). Debugging due to segmentation faults was the major debugging cause for all teams. In total, locks teams spent 55 hours (59%) of debugging time on segmentation faults, whereas TM teams spent 23 hours (29%) of debugging time [22]. The time for debugging unexpected program behavior, was comparable for locks and TM teams; locks teams spent 20 hours (22%) of debugging time, and TM teams spent 16 hours (20%) of debugging time.

The effort spent on debugging segmentation faults seems to be influenced by the number of lines of code containing parallel constructs. Teams L3 and TM2 spent the least effort (4 hours) on debugging segmentation faults [22]. According to Figure 1, team L3 had the lowest number of lines of code with parallel constructs among the locks teams (120 LOC; 5% of the code); similarly, team TM2 had the lowest number of lines of code with parallel constructs among the TM teams (45 LOC; 2% of the code). By contrast, team L2 spent most effort on debugging segmentation faults (35 hours) and had the most lines of code (261 LOC; 11% of code) with parallel constructs. In addition, team L2 had the most extensive usage of condition variables, and team L3 the least among the locks teams. If future empirical studies confirm these observations, then TM programs requiring fewer parallel constructs than comparable locks programs will have an advantage in the debugging phase, as there would be a reduced probability for mistakes.

In the questionnaire responses, the TM teams felt that they had many segmentation faults and unexplainable crashes compared to the locks teams. Objective data shows, however, that the TM teams spent less effort than the locks teams on fixing segmentation faults [22].

6. PERFORMANCE MEASUREMENTS

Figure 4 shows the indexing and query performance for each team's programs. It shows what was possible for the subjects to achieve in a realistic programming environment with freedom of design decisions, but given the same programming problem, the same limited amount of development time, and the same starting conditions for all teams.

Prj.Week	
4	• **TM1:** The team discussed design alternatives. • **TM2:** The team was about to implement their index data structure and planned to have an executable version in 1–2 weeks. • **TM3:** The team had a rudimentary indexer. They had problems understanding and applying TM constructs.
5	• **TM1:** The team was testing a first sequential indexer. They had not thought how to parallelize or how to use TM. • **TM2:** The team implemented sequential index reading and writing operations. No thoughts on parallelism. • **TM3:** This was the first team of all with a working parallel indexer. Performance tests are done on the final benchmark. Segmentation faults appeared due to missing thread-safe TM libraries; they start implementing low-level functions by themselves.
6	• **TM1:** The team's entire code was sequential and incomplete. They had no new thoughts on parallelism or TM; many of their ideas were not well-developed. They planned to parallelize their program the following week. They were worried about the performance of their sequential program and hoped that parallelism would make it faster. The memory consumption of their program began to grow. • **TM2:** The team's entire code was still sequential. Neither of them had thought of parallelism or transactions yet. • **TM3:** The team's parallel indexing worked. A rudimentary query could execute while indexing was in progress.
7	• **TM1:** The team had made some unsuccessful parallelization attempts. They tested their program with just one of the files from the benchmark. They had memory leaks they couldn't find. • **TM2:** The team evaluated the TM annotations for functions on the their index. Part of the sequential code for insertions had to be restructured. They developed a strategy to minimize transaction overhead. Search was not implemented yet; they assumed it was trivial, though in the end almost no query worked. • **TM3:** The team finished implementing their thread-safe library functions.
8	• **TM1:** The team had procrastinated much of the parallelization work; indexing was serial. The few parallelization attempts were superficial. The memory leak was still there. Only one word could be used in a query. • **TM2:** The team had not yet finished parallel indexing. No performance tests had yet been done. Queries did not work yet. • **TM3:** The team showed a full-fledged working demo of parallel indexing and search. They used compiler statistics (such as #TMaborts, #TMretries, etc.) for performance optimization.
9	• **TM1:** The team' parallel indexing and queries were almost finished. Queries allowed just the inclusion or exclusion of one word. • **TM2:** The team's indexing and queries worked in parallel, but were not error-free. The program performance was still bad. Too much of the code was enclosed by atomic blocks. They started a lot of non-trivial refactoring to shrink the size of atomic blocks. • **TM3:** The team fixed a segmentation fault and many bugs.
10	• **TM1:** The team's indexing did not work for the case study benchmark, due to the memory leak they did not fix. Turning on compiler optimizations caused segmentation faults, which was a bug in the compiler. • **TM2:** The team's parallel indexing and queries worked. Turning on compiler optimizations caused segmentation faults. The frustrated team said that TM did not really relieve them from their problems, but just shifted them to transactions. They had problems understanding the performance overhead of _tm_atomic blocks; they were more expensive than expected. • **TM3:** The team's search engine was complete. They used TM frequently, but the team said it was difficult and tedious to find the places where to employ the _tm_callable function annotation.

Table 2: Progress summary from TM teams interviews.

Performance measurements were done by instructors on a Dell eight core machine with a dual-socket Intel Quadcore E5320 QC processor, clocked at 1.86 GHz, with 8 GB of RAM, and running Ubuntu Linux 2.6. Each point represents the average of five measurements. Only results of correctly working features are shown. All teams were requested to provide a configurable command line parameter to specify the number of indexing threads, and only this parameter was varied when measuring performance. All source codes were compiled with Intel's C compiler, using STM extensions for the TM teams. All source codes were inspected to ensure that they measure execution time in the same way; `printf` statements within time measurement blocks were commented out. The input file set used for benchmarking consists of directories containing a diverse selection of ASCII text files (50,887 files, 742 MB MB in total). It includes the Calgary Text Compression Corpus (which is used to evaluate compression programs), one big text file, four larger files, and many small files [22].

Team TM3 had the best indexing performance of all teams, completing the benchmark in 178 seconds. Compared to the fastest locks team on indexing (team L2) that finished in 532 seconds, TM was three times faster. TM teams had the best execution times for half of the queries; they were 13%–95% lower than the fastest locks team. Despite differing program designs, the measurements of the submitted search engines represent counter-examples that contrast the literature overgeneralizing that Software Transactional Memory always performs poorly [9].

Except for team TM1 who had memory consumption problems not fixed until the deadline, all teams had executable parallel programs at the final deadline. No search engine was perfect, however, as all implementations had queries that were either too slow, missing, or executing incorrectly. The number of working queries was the only difference in feature completeness, which is rather minimal considering the complexity of the overall project. Out of 18 queries, locks teams implemented 18 (L1), 17 (L3), and 10 (L2), while TM teams implemented 14 (TM3), 4 (TM2), and 0 (TM1). The locks teams implemented more queries than the TM teams, though locks team's queries were slow in many cases (see Figure 4). Our observations suggest that locks teams implemented more queries by skipping thorough software engineering practices such as testing and debugging (i.e., they risked that their features might not work). We assume that the effort gap between locks and TM teams would be even wider than in Figure 3 if the locks teams had tested their programs in a fashion comparable to the TM teams.

7. KEY RESULTS

The case study shows in the given setting that TM was indeed applicable to a more complex, non-numerical program. The results also show that TM needs better mechanisms for coordination and better handling of I/O. Programmer-initiated aborts were almost never used, and when used, they were used mostly incorrectly. We provide evidence that a combination of TM with locks is needed in practice and discovered real use cases of how locks and TM need to be combined: Two of the TM teams used TM as well as locks in the same program. One team combined TM with semaphores for producer-consumer coordination, and another team combined TM with a lock to protect a critical section that performed many I/O operations. This is an important insight because TM and locks were used as complementary approaches, not as alternatives excluding each other. This is a new point of view that has not been fully explored in the literature so far. While TM implementations have used locks under the covers (e.g., the STM runtime used in the Intel STM compiler [21]), researchers have not fully explored programming models that provide both

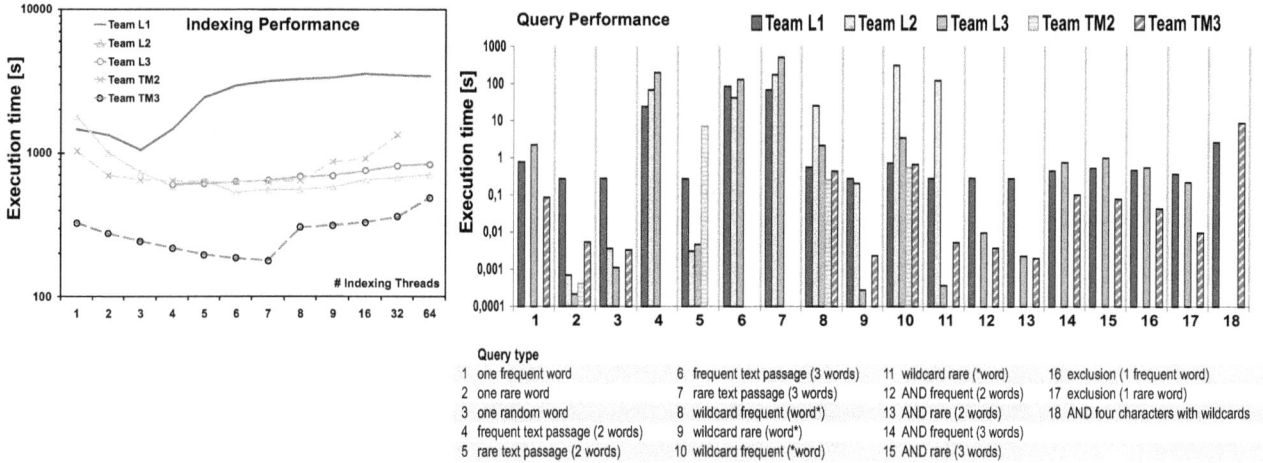

Figure 4: Indexing and query performance. The right graphs excludes for each team the queries that are not implemented or not executing correctly.

locks and atomic blocks with clear semantics. Intel's recent Draft Specification of Transactional Language Constructs for C++ [3] allows locks inside of atomic blocks. The authors of this specification were in large part influenced by the results of this study.

TM team's program performance was not bad compared to the locks teams. Team L1 was the only team to have implemented all queries, but they had the worst indexing performance and a slow search. Locks teams spent more time on debugging due to segmentation faults than TM teams. TM teams, however, spent more time on performance-related issues than locks teams, which also indicates that we need better TM performance tuning tools.

The parallel programs of TM teams were easier to understand, according to code inspections done jointly with industry compiler experts. Although all teams implemented similar program functionality, all TM teams used significantly fewer parallel constructs than the locks teams. Locks teams tended to have more complex parallel programs by employing many locks, sometimes *thousands* of locks due to the indexing data structure. All teams had races that were detected after the project by code inspection.

We detected differences in how teams perceived their progress by comparing subjective data from the questionnaire and interviews with objective data from the code and time report sheets. Team TM3, for example, thought that they were not advancing fast enough because they had to use transactions, but at the same time they had the first working parallel program and least effort of all teams. By contrast, locks teams subjectively believed they made good progress but actually needed more effort.

The study also shows that TM is not a silver bullet for parallel programming. The most inexperienced team using TM (TM1) did not produce a working program; parallel programming remains difficult.

8. THREATS TO VALIDITY

A case study provides detailed insights on one case being studied [25]. Our study describes observations and explores a variety of previously unknown issues when programmers with different experience use TM and locks in the realistic environment of a large project. It is easy to disprove general statements even with a small number of subjects, but difficult to prove general statements. By contrast, experiments would require a totally controlled environment (at the expense of realism) and a very narrow and previously known hypothesis to test. Even though the study focuses on just one type of application, it is possible that results differ for other applications; however, many of the encountered problems are representative and occur in other contexts as well. Such effects can be compensated by triangulating data from several sources. Internal validity is created by triangulating multiple sources of evidence and different types of data to reduce bias. In addition, we employed randomization in two places: once when creating the student teams, and once when assigning the programming model to the teams. Before the study started, we gave the same parallel programming training to all students to create similar starting conditions. We conducted a feasibility study to make the sure that the amount of time should suffice to complete the project in the given time. Even if we assume teams L2 and TM2 were outliers (the teams with the highest efforts), the study results would still lead to the same conclusions that the total implementation and debugging effort for locks teams is higher.

The employed STM compiler was a prototype and had some bugs, sometimes producing crashes when compiling with optimizations. However, this was the most advanced C++ STM compiler available at the time of the study. Other studies reported similar problems [34]. Due to the different types of collected data (e.g., interviews, questionnaire, personal observations), we were able to isolate situations in which the experienced problems were due to compiler bugs.

9. RELATED WORK

Empirical studies for parallel programming with TM are scarce. This is supported by a comprehensive overview of the TM literature [2]. Various Transactional Memory implementations have been proposed based on hardware [14, 20], software [4, 6, 15, 21, 28], or a hybrid of the two [10, 17]. These studies have either used small programs that exercise lists, hash tables, and other data structures, or have transformed lock-based benchmarks into TM programs [16, 34] –

for example, the Stanford ParalleL Applications for SHared memory (SPLASH-2) [31], the PARSEC benchmark suite [8], or SPEC OMP [29]. In addition, TM-specific benchmark suites have been developed, such as the Stanford Transactional Applications for Multi-Processing (STAMP) [19]. All of these benchmarks consist mostly of numerical applications. Various case studies have assessed the performance of non-trivial applications using TM (e.g., Lee's algorithm for circuit routing [1], the Linux sendmail application [26], among others [27, 11, 30]). These studies did not pay attention to software engineering aspects of TM.

Rossbach et al. [24] looked at errors in the programs of a larger number of undergraduate students from different classes, but has serious methodological shortcomings, which we avoided in our study. In [24], the groups of students and the employed STM implementations are changed over time, which does not ensure continuity. In addition, [24] is flawed because the students were asked to assign themselves to groups, and students wrongly assigned themselves and ended up in groups of different sizes, which should have been all equally sized. Moreover, our study is conducted with graduate students, an advanced industrial-strength C++ STM compiler (rather than a Java API), and a complex application (rather than a toy program). Our study has new sources of evidence (Section 2) that provide more detailed insights into how the TM language constructs were used, the thought processes of each programmer, and the actual program performance (not discussed in [24]). We also show actual examples of code patterns and anti-patterns.

10. CONCLUSION

This is the first case study to provide insights for TM programming from a variety of data, including code quality and metrics, performance, effort, and subjective programmer impressions. The study provides evidence for the necessity to employ TM and locks in a complementary way, and that they should not be considered as alternatives excluding each other. Our evidence also shows that to realize fully the benefits of TM in C++ we need language refinements supporting condition synchronization, and better debugging and performance tuning tool support. The lessons learned from this study significantly influenced the development of Intel's new generation STM Compiler. Even with TM, however, parallel programming remains difficult, so the quest for new parallel programming language features must continue.

Acknowledgements. We thank Frank Otto for helping with lab organization, and Matthias Dempe and Nikolay Petkov for assisting with performance measurements. We thank the Intel STM team, Ravi Narayanaswamy, Yang Ni, Tatiana Shpeisman, Xinmin Tian, and Adam Welc for help with code inspections. We thank Chris Vick at Sun Labs for feedback.

11. REFERENCES

[1] M. Ansari et al. Lee-TM: A non-trivial benchmark suite for transactional memory. In *Algorithms and Architectures for Parallel Processing*, pages 196–207, 2008.

[2] TM bibliography. http://www.cs.wisc.edu/trans-memory/biblio/index.html, March 2011.

[3] A.-R. Adl-Tabatabai and T. Shpeisman (editors). Draft specification of transactional language constructs for C++ (v.1.0), 2009.

[4] A.-R. Adl-Tabatabai et al. Compiler and runtime support for efficient software transactional memory. In *Proc. ACM PLDI '06*, pages 26–37, 2006.

[5] D. Bacon et al. The "double-checked locking is broken" declaration. http://www.cs.umd.edu/~pugh/java/memoryModel/DoubleCheckedLocking.html, Dec. 2010.

[6] W. Baek et al. The OpenTM transactional application programming interface. In *Proc. ACM PACT '07*, 2007.

[7] R. Baeza-Yates and B. Ribeiro-Neto. *Modern Information Retrieval.* Addison-Wesley, May 1999.

[8] C. Bienia et al. The PARSEC benchmark suite: characterization and architectural implications. In *Proc. ACM PACT '08*, pages 72–81, 2008.

[9] C. Cascaval et al. Software transactional memory: why is it only a research toy? *Commun. ACM*, 51(11):40–46, 2008.

[10] P. Damron et al. Hybrid transactional memory. In *Proc. ACM ASPLOS-XII*, pages 336–346, 2006.

[11] R. Guerraoui et al. STMBench7: a benchmark for software transactional memory. *SIGOPS OSR*, 41(3), 2007.

[12] T. Harris et al. Composable memory transactions. In *Proc. ACM PPoPP '05*, pages 48–60, 2005.

[13] S. Heinz et al. Burst tries: a fast, efficient data structure for string keys. *ACM Trans. Inf. Syst.*, 20(2):192–223, 2002.

[14] M. Herlihy and J. E. B. Moss. Transactional memory: architectural support for lock-free data structures. In *Proc. ACM ISCA '93*, pages 289–300, 1993.

[15] Intel. Intel C++ STM compiler prototype edition 2.0. language extensions and user's guide, 2008.

[16] C. J.Rossbach et al. Txlinux: using and managing hardware transactional memory in an operating system. In *Proc. ACM SOSP '07*, pages 87–102, 2007.

[17] S. Kumar et al. Hybrid transactional memory. In *Proc. ACM PPoPP '06*, pages 209–220, 2006.

[18] N. Lester et al. Efficient online index construction for text databases. *ACM Trans. Database Syst.*, 33(3):1–33, 2008.

[19] C. C. Minh et al. STAMP: Stanford transactional applications for multi-processing. In *Proc. IISWC*, 2008.

[20] K. Moore et al. LogTM: log-based transactional memory. In *Proc. HPCA '06*, pages 254–265, 2006.

[21] Y. Ni et al. Design and implementation of transactional constructs for C/C++. In *Proc. ACM OOPSLA*, 2008.

[22] V. Pankratius et al. Does transactional memory keep its promises? Results from an empirical study. Technical report, 2009-12, University of Karlsruhe, Germany, 2009.

[23] M. F. Ringenburg and D. Grossman. AtomCaml: first-class atomicity via rollback. In *Proc. ACM ICFP*, 2005.

[24] C. J. Rossbach et al. Is transactional programming actually easier? In *Proc. ACM PPoPP*, 2010.

[25] P. Runeson and M. Höst. Guidelines for conducting and reporting case study research in software engineering. *Empirical Software Engineering*, 14(2):131–164, 2009.

[26] B. Saha et al. McRT-STM: a high performance software transactional memory system for a multi-core runtime. In *Proc. ACM PPoPP '06*, pages 187–197, 2006.

[27] M. Scott et al. Delaunay triangulation with transactions and barriers. In *Proc. IEEE IISWC*, 2007.

[28] N. Shavit and D. Touitou. Software transactional memory. *Distributed Computing*, V10(2):99–116, 1997.

[29] Standard Performance Evaluation Corporation. SPEC OpenMP Benchmark Suite. www.spec.org/omp, 2009.

[30] I. Watson et al. A study of a transactional parallel routing algorithm. In *Proc. ACM PACT '07*, pages 388–398, 2007.

[31] S. C. Woo et al. The SPLASH-2 programs: characterization and methodological considerations. In *ACM ISCA*, 1995.

[32] R. K. Yin. *Case Study Research: Design and Methods.* Sage Publications, Inc, 3rd edition, 2002.

[33] C. Zannier et al. On the success of empirical studies in the International Conference on Software Engineering. In *Proc. ACM ICSE '06*, pages 341–350, 2006.

[34] F. Zyulkyarov et al. Atomic quake: using transactional memory in an interactive multiplayer game server. In *Proc. ACM PPoPP '09*, pages 25–34, 2009.

Optimizing Hybrid Transactional Memory:
The Importance of Nonspeculative Operations

Torvald Riegel
Technische Universität
Dresden, Germany
torvald.riegel@tu-
dresden.de

Martin Nowack
Technische Universität
Dresden, Germany
martin.nowack@tu-
dresden.de

Christof Fetzer
Technische Universität
Dresden, Germany
christof.fetzer@tu-
dresden.de

Patrick Marlier
Université de Neuchâtel,
Switzerland
patrick.marlier@unine.ch

Pascal Felber
Université de Neuchâtel,
Switzerland
pascal.felber@unine.ch

ABSTRACT

Transactional memory (TM) is a speculative shared-memory synchronization mechanism used to speed up concurrent programs. Most current TM implementations are software-based (STM) and incur noticeable overheads for each transactional memory access. Hardware TM proposals (HTM) address this issue but typically suffer from other restrictions such as limits on the number of data locations that can be accessed in a transaction.

In this paper, we present several new *hybrid TM* algorithms that can execute HTM and STM transactions concurrently and can thus provide good performance over a large spectrum of workloads. The algorithms exploit the ability of some HTMs to have both speculative and nonspeculative (nontransactional) memory accesses within a transaction to decrease the transactions' runtime overhead, abort rates, and hardware capacity requirements. We evaluate implementations of these algorithms based on AMD's Advanced Synchronization Facility, an x86 instruction set extension proposal that has been shown to provide a sound basis for HTM.

Categories and Subject Descriptors

D.1.3 [**Programming Techniques**]: Concurrent Programming

General Terms

Algorithms, Performance

Keywords

Transactional Memory

1. INTRODUCTION

Today's multicore and manycore CPUs require parallelized software to unfold their full performance potential. Shared-memory synchronization plays a big role in parallel software, either when synchronizing and merging results of parallel tasks, or when parallelizing programs by speculatively executing tasks concurrently.

Until now, most concurrent programs have been programmed using lock-based synchronization. Yet, locks are considered difficult to use for the average programmer, especially when locking at a fine granularity to provide scalable performance. This is particularly important when considering that large classes of programs will have to be parallelized by programmers who are not well trained in concurrent programming. Transactional memory (TM) is a promising alternative for synchronization because programmers only need to declare *which* regions in their program must be atomic, not *how* atomicity will be implemented. Unfortunately, current software transactional memory (STM) implementations have a relatively large performance overhead. While there is certainly room left for further optimizations, it is believed by many that only hardware transactional memory (HTM) implementations can have a sufficiently good performance for TM to become widely adopted by developers.

Of the many published HTMs, only two designs have been proposed by industry for possible inclusion in high-volume microprocessors: Sun's Rock TM [10] and AMD's Advanced Synchronization Facility (ASF) [1]. While these HTMs have notable differences, they are both based on simple designs that provide best-effort HTM in the sense that only a subset of all reasonable transactions are expected to be supported by hardware. They have several limitations (e. g., the number of cache lines that can be accessed in a transaction can be as low as four) and have to be complemented with software fallback solutions that execute in software the transactions that cannot run in hardware. A simple fallback strategy is to execute software transactions serially, i.e., one at a time. However, this approach limits performance when software transactions are frequent. It is therefore desirable to develop *hybrid* TM (HyTM) in which multiple hardware and software transactions can run concurrently.

Most previous HyTM proposals have assumed HTMs in which every memory access inside a transaction is speculative, that is, it is transactional, isolated from other threads until transaction commit and will be rolled back on abort. In contrast, ASF provides selective annotation, which means that nonspeculative memory accesses are supported within transactions (including nonspeculative atomic instructions) and speculative memory accesses have to be explicitly marked as such.

Technique	Explained in
1. Monitor metadata but read data nonspeculatively.	Sec. 3
2. Use nonspeculative atomic read-modify-write operations to send synchronization messages.	Sec. 3 & 4
3. Validate hardware transactions against software synchronization messages.	Sec. 4

Table 1: General-purpose synchronization techniques enabled by the availability of nonspeculative operations in hardware transactions.

Contributions.

In this paper, we present a family of *novel HyTM algorithms* that use AMD's ASF as HTM. We make heavy use of nonspeculative operations in transactions to construct efficient HyTM algorithms that improve on previous HyTMs. In particular, they decrease the runtime overhead, abort rates, and HTM capacity requirements of hardware transactions, while at the same time allowing hardware and software transactions to run and commit concurrently (this is further discussed in Section 2.2 and Table 3).

Our HyTM algorithms use two state-of-the-art STM algorithms from different research groups, LSA [25] and NOrec [8], for software transactions. LSA and NOrec focus on different workloads in their optimizations, e.g., a higher level of concurrency vs. lower single-thread overheads. The resulting HyTM compositions provide the same guarantees as the respective STMs.

We evaluate the performance of our algorithms on a near-cycle-accurate x86 simulator with support for several implementations of ASF [5] that differ notably in their capacity limits. Our HyTMs are embedded into a full TM software stack for C/C++.

Nonspeculative operations are useful beyond HyTM optimizations. Table 1 shows three *general-purpose synchronization techniques* that we present in this paper, which are all combinations of both transaction-based synchronization and classic nontransactional synchronization using standard atomic instructions. The first technique can reduce HTM capacity requirements and has similarities to lock elision [22], whereas the other two are about composability with nontransactional synchronization. We will explain the techniques further in Sections 3 and 4. To make them applicable, the HTM does not only have to allow nonspeculative operations but it must also provide certain ordering guarantees (see Section 2.1).

The rest of the paper is organized as follows. In Section 2, we provide background information about ASF and TM in general, and we discuss related work on HyTM designs. We present our new HyTM algorithms in Sections 3 and 4, evaluate them in Section 5, and conclude in Section 6.

2. BACKGROUND AND RELATED WORK

Our objective is to investigate the design of *hybrid transactional memory algorithms* that exploit hardware facilities for decreasing the overhead of transactions in good cases while composing well with state-of-the-art software transactional memory algorithms. We assume that the TM runtime system is implemented as part of a library with a well-specified interface for starting, committing, and aborting transactions, as well as performing transactional memory accesses (loads and stores).

We focus on C/C++ and use a full TM stack [5] consisting of a TM library and a transactional C/C++ compiler. This implementation complies with the specification of C++ support for TM constructs [15], which includes ensuring privatization safety for trans-

---

Algorithm 1 Common transaction start code for all HyTMs.

```
 1:  hytm-start()_p:
 2:    if hytm-disabled()_p then
 3:      goto line 7
 4:    s ← SPECULATE                    ▷ start hardware transaction
 5:    if s ≠ 0 then                    ▷ did we jump back here after an abort?
 6:      if fallback-to-stm(s) then     ▷ retry in software?
 7:        stm-start()_p                ▷ we are in a software transaction
 8:        return false                 ▷ execute STM codepath
 9:      goto line 4         ▷ restore registers, stack, etc. and retry
10:    htm-start()_p                    ▷ we are in a hardware transaction
11:    return true                      ▷ execute HTM codepath
```

actions, whereas publication safety [18] as required by the specification [15] is basically the responsibility of the programmer (i.e., C/C++ source code must be race-free) and the compiler (i.e., it must not introduce race conditions). Informally, C++ transactions are guaranteed to execute virtually sequentially and in isolation as long as the program is race-free in terms of the upcoming C++ memory model [16] extended with specific rules for transactions.

The compiler generates separate STM and HTM code paths for each transaction. A common transaction start function (see Algorithm 1) takes care of selecting STM or HTM code at runtime. A transaction first tries to run in hardware mode using a special ASF SPECULATE instruction (line 4). This instruction returns a non-zero value when jumping back after an abort, similarly to setjmp/-longjmp in the standard C library. If the transaction aborts and a retry is unlikely to succeed (as determined on line 6, for example, because of capacity limitations or after multiple aborts due to contention), it switches to software mode. After this has been decided, only STM or HTM code will be executed (functions starting with stm- or htm-, respectively) during this attempt to execute the transaction.

In the rest of this section, we give an overview of the hardware TM support used for our hybrid algorithms and we discuss related work.

2.1 Advanced Synchronization Facility

AMD's Advanced Synchronization Facility (ASF) is a proposal [1] of hardware extensions for x86_64 CPUs. It essentially provides hardware support for the speculative execution of regions of code. These speculative regions are similar to transactions in that they take effect atomically. We have shown in a previous study [5] that ASF can be used as an efficient pure HTM in a realistic TM software stack. The HyTM algorithms that we present in this paper are based on ASF and rely on a similar software stack.

AMD has designed ASF in such a way that it would be feasible to implement ASF in high-volume microprocessors. Hence, ASF comes with a number of limitations [1, 11, 6]. First, the number of disjoint locations that can be accessed in a transaction is limited either by the size of speculation buffers (which are expensive and thus have been designed with small capacity) or by the associativity of caches (when tracking speculative state in caches). Second, ASF transactions are not virtualized and therefore, abort on events such as context switches or page faults. These limitations illustrate that HyTM will be required to build a feature-rich TM for programmers.

In contrast to several other HTM proposals, ASF provides *selective annotation* for speculative memory accesses. Speculative regions (SRs, the equivalent of transactions) are demarcated with new SPECULATE and COMMIT CPU instructions. In an SR, speculative/protected memory accesses, in the form of ASF-specific LOCK MOV CPU instructions, can be mixed with nonspeculative/unprotected accesses, i.e., ordinary load/store instructions (MOV) as well as atomic instructions such as compare-and-set (CAS). Selective annotation requires more work on the compiler side, but allows the

CPU A mode	CPU A operation	CPU B cache line state	
		Prot. Shared	Prot. Owned
Speculative region	LOCK MOV (load)	OK	*B aborts*
Speculative region	LOCK MOV (store)	*B aborts*	*B aborts*
Speculative region	LOCK PREFETCH	OK	*B aborts*
Speculative region	LOCK PREFETCHW	*B aborts*	*B aborts*
Speculative region	COMMIT	OK	OK
Any	Read operation	OK	*B aborts*
Any	Write operation	*B aborts*	*B aborts*
Any	Prefetch operation	OK	*B aborts*
Any	PREFETCHW	*B aborts*	*B aborts*

Table 2: Conflict matrix for ASF operations ([1], §6.2.1).

TM to use speculative accesses sparingly and thus preserve precious ASF capacity. Second, the availability of nonspeculative atomic instructions allows us to use common concurrent programming techniques during a transaction, which can reduce the number of transaction aborts due to benign contention (e. g., when updating a shared counter). In an SR, nonspeculative loads are allowed to read state that is speculatively updated in the same SR, but nonspeculative stores must not overlap with previous speculative accesses. Conflict detection for speculative accesses is handled at the granularity of a cache line.

ASF also provides CPU instructions for monitoring a cache line for concurrent stores (LOCK PREFETCH) or loads and stores (LOCK PREFETCHW), for stopping monitoring a cache line (RELEASE), and for aborting a SR and discarding all speculative modifications (ABORT).

Conflict resolution in ASF follows the "requester wins" policy (i. e., existing SRs will be aborted by incoming conflicting memory accesses). Table 2 summarizes how ASF handles contention when CPU A performs an operation while CPU B is in a SR with the cache line protected by ASF [1]. These conflict resolution rules are important for understanding how our HyTM algorithms work and why they perform well.

The ordering guarantees that ASF provides for mixed speculative and nonspeculative accesses are important for the correctness of our algorithms, and are required for the general-purpose synchronization techniques listed in Table 1 to be applicable or practical. In short, aborts are instantaneous with respect to the program order of instructions in SRs. For example, aborts are supposed to happen before externally visible effects such as page faults or nonspeculative stores appear. A consequence is that memory lines are monitored early for conflicting accesses (i. e., once the respective instructions are issued in the CPU, which is always before they retire). After an abort, execution is resumed at the SPECULATE instruction. Further, atomic instructions such as compare-and-set or fetch-and-increment retain their ordering guarantees (e. g., a CAS ordered before a COMMIT in a program will become visible before the transaction's commit). This behavior illustrates why speculative accesses are also referred to as "protected" accesses.

2.2 Previous HyTM Designs

Table 3 shows a comparison of our HyTM algorithms (second and third row) with previous HyTM designs. The columns list HyTM properties that have a major influence on performance.

First, at least first-generation HTM will not be able to run all transactions in hardware. Thus there likely will be software transactions, which should be able to run concurrently with hardware transactions (see column two[1]). Second, HyTMs should not introduce additional runtime overhead for hardware transactions, which would decrease HTM's performance advantage compared to STM.

Third, HTM capacity for transactional memory accesses is scarce, so HyTM should require as little capacity as possible[2]. Furthermore, HyTM algorithms that do not guarantee privatization safety for software transactions have to ensure this using additional implementation methods (see Section 3), resulting in additional runtime overhead. Visible reads are often more costly for STMs than invisible reads and can introduce artificial conflicts with transactional HTM reads (e. g., if the STM updates an orec).

In phased TM [17], the implementation mode for transactions is switched globally and (i. e., only software or hardware transactions are running at a time)[3]. This leads to no HyTM overhead when in hardware mode, but even a single transaction that has to run in software reduces overall performance to the level of STM. The phased TM approach is orthogonal to hybrid TM.

Similarly, the HyTM [14] presented by Hofmann et al. uses a simple global lock as software fallback mechanism instead of an STM that can run several software transactions concurrently. Hardware transactions wait for a software transaction to finish before committing, but are not protected from reading uncommitted and thus potentially inconsistent updates of software transactions ("dirty reads"). Note that with ASF, hardware transactions are not completely sandboxed. For example, page faults due to inconsistent snapshots will abort speculative regions but will also be visible to the operating system.

Kumar et al. describe a HyTM [24] based on an object-based STM design with indirection via locator objects, which uses visible reads and requires small hardware transactions even for software transactions. Recent research has shown that STM algorithms with invisible reads and no indirection have significantly lower overhead (e.g., [9, 20, 8]).

Damron et al. present a HyTM [21] that combines a best-effort HTM with a word-based STM algorithm that uses visible reads and performs conflict detection based on ownership records. The HTM does not use selective annotation and thus hardware transactions have to monitor application data and TM metadata (i. e., ownership records) for each access, which significantly increases the HTM capacity required to successfully run transactions in hardware. Likewise, visible reads result in significant overheads for STMs. This HyTM is also used in a study about the HTM support in Rock [10].

The hardware-accelerated STM algorithms (HASTM) by Saha et al. [3] are based on ownership records[4] (like LSA but unlike NOrec). HASTM in cautious mode monitors application data and does read logging, whereas our hybrid LSA algorithms (see Section 3 and row three) monitor ownership records and do not log reads. HASTM in aggressive mode monitors both application data and ownership records, thus suffering from higher HTM capacity requirements (evaluated in Section 5). Thus, only our hybrid LSA algorithms can change the ownership-record-to-memory mapping to achieve a larger effective read capacity. Transactional stores in HASTM are not accelerated but executed in software only. Furthermore, HASTM in cautious mode as presented in the paper does not prevent dirty reads[5], which can crash transactions in unmanaged environments such as C/C++.

---

[1]"Yes" means that non-conflicting pairs of software/hardware transactions can run concurrently.

[2]"Orecs" are ownership records (i. e., TM metadata with an M:N mapping from memory locations to orecs). "Data" refers to the application data accessed in a transaction.

[3]The serial irrevocable mode that is present in most current STMs is a special case of the phased approach, as it can be used as a very simple software fallback for HTMs

[4]We consider its cacheline-based variants.

[5]It first checks the version in an ownership record and then loads data speculatively. Executing these steps in reverse order fixes this problem.

HyTM	HW/SW concurrency	HW txn load/store runtime overheads	HW capacity used for	Privatization safety (SW)	Invisible reads (SW)	Remarks
HyNOrec-2	Yes, SW commits stall other HW/SW ops	Very small	Data	Yes	Yes	See Algorithm 7
HyLSA (eager)	Yes	Small (load orec)	Orecs and data updates	No	Yes	See Algorithm 3
Phased TM [17]	No	None	Data	N/A	N/A	Can use any STM
Hoffman et al. [14]	Little	None	Data	Yes	No	Dirty reads not prevented
Kumar et al. [24]	Yes	High (indirection)	Data	Yes	No	
Damron et al. [21]	Yes	Small (load orec)	Data and orecs	Yes	No	
HASTM [3] cautious	Yes	Medium (load+log orec)	Read data	No	Yes	Stores in SW only
HASTM aggressive	Yes	Small (load orec)	Read data and orecs	No	Yes	Stores in SW only
HyNOrec-DSS [8]	Partial, SW commits abort HW txns	None, but concurrent commits abort each other	Data and 2 locks	Yes	Yes	
HyNOrec-DSS-2 [7]	Yes, SW commits stall other HW/SW ops	Very small, concurrent commits can still abort each other (but less likely)	Data and 3 locks/counters	Yes	Yes	This information is about their best-performing algorithms

Table 3: Overview of HyTM designs.

Spear et al. propose to use Alert-On-Update (AOU) [19] to accelerate snapshots by reducing the number of necessary software snapshot validations in STMs based on ownership records. However, our LSA STM algorithm already has efficient time-based snapshots due to its use of a global time base, whereas AOU uses a commit counter heuristic, which can suffer from false positives that lead to costly re-validations. The details of the AOU algorithm are not presented, thus it is difficult to assess the remaining HyTM aspects and overheads (and we do not include it in Table 3).

Dalessandro et al. informally describe a HyTM [8] based on the NOrec STM ("HyNOrec-DSS"). It features low runtime overheads and capacity requirements but it shows less scalability because (1) commits of software transactions abort hardware transactions and (2) concurrent commit phases of hardware transactions can abort each other as well. We discuss and evaluate this in detail in Sections 4 and 5.

In concurrent work [7] that has been published after our first results [12], Dalessandro et al. describe optimizations of HyNOrec-DSS ("HyNOrec-DSS-2", last row) and evaluate them on Rock [10] and on ASF. They try to reduce conflicts on metadata (NOrec's global lock, see Section 4) by distributing commit notifications using speculative stores over several counters, which leads to additional runtime overhead for software transactions because they then have to validate all these counters (and at least two) after each transactional load. In contrast, our HyTMs use nonspeculative read-modify-write operations for such notifications (the second technique in Table 1), which enables software transactions to validate using only a single counter. Their algorithms also use nonspeculative loads to validate during a hardware transaction's runtime ("lazy subscription", the third technique in Table 1) but still use speculative reads for validation during commit, and thus require more HTM capacity than our algorithm. Furthermore, they propose an optimization similar in spirit to phased TM, but embedded into the HyTM algorithms ("SWExists"), which avoids commit-time synchronization with software transactions if none is running. However, this requires speculative accesses to one further location (thus increasing HTM capacity requirements), and only helps in workloads in which software transactions are rare. SWExists could be applied to our algorithms as well and could increase scalability if mostly hardware transactions execute. Their evaluation results on Rock cannot be easily compared with ours because Rock is fairly limited compared to ASF. On ASF, they only show results for one ASF implementation, LLB256 (see Section 2.1), which has sufficient capacity to run almost all transactions in hardware and represents the best case in terms of HTM capacity. Other ASF implementations with reduced capacity (e. g., because of cache associativity or a smaller LLB) might be more likely to appear in real hardware but in turn make extra speculative accesses for HyTM

metadata much more costly. Furthermore, the choice of LLB256 makes it more difficult to compare their optimizations in detail to ours because, as we show in Section 5, the interesting behavior of HyTMs (and arguably, the target workload for best-effort HTM) appears with workloads in which software transactions are *not* rare.

As shown in Table 3, the new HyTM algorithms that we present in this paper improve on previous designs. In the class without orecs, HyNOrec-2 provides a high level of concurrency and good scalability while not wasting HTM capacity and requiring only a very small runtime overhead. For HyTMs with orecs, HyLSA features either lower HTM capacity requirements or a smaller runtime overhead.

3. THE HYBRID LAZY SNAPSHOT ALGORITHM

Our first algorithm extends the lazy snapshot algorithm (LSA) first presented in [25]. LSA is a time-based STM algorithm that uses on-demand validation and a global time base to build a consistent snapshot of the values accessed by a transaction. The basic version of the LSA algorithm is shown in Algorithm 2 and briefly described below (please refer to the original paper for further details [25]).[6]

Transaction stores are buffered until commit. The consistency of the snapshot read by the transaction is checked based on versioned locks (ownership records, or *orecs* for short) and a global time base, which is typically implemented using a shared counter. The orec protecting a given memory location is determined by hashing the address and looking up the associated entry in a global array of orecs. Note that, in this design, an orec protects multiple memory locations.

To install its updates during commit, a transaction first acquires the locks that cover updated memory locations (line 38) and obtains a new commit time from the global time base by incrementing it atomically (line 43). The transaction subsequently validates that the values it has read have not changed (lines 45 and 53–57) and, if so, writes back its updates to shared memory (lines 48–49). Finally, when releasing the locks, the versions of the orecs are set to the commit time (lines 51–52). Reading transactions can thus see the virtual commit time of the updated memory locations and use it to check the consistency of their read set. If all loads did not virtually happen at the same time, the snapshot is inconsistent.

A snapshot can be extended by validating that values previously read are valid at extension time, which is guaranteed if the versions

---

[6]Because of our efforts to present algorithms using a common notation, the presentation of LSA and NOrec [8] differ slightly from the versions found in the original papers. Notice that we use the notation cas(*addr* : *expected-val* → *new-val*) for the compare-and-set operation.

Algorithm 2 LSA STM algorithm (encounter-time locking/write-back variant) [13]

```
 1: Global state:
 2:    clock ← 0                                          ▷ global clock
 3:    orecs: word-sized ownership records, each consisting of:
 4:       locked: bit indicating if orec is locked
 5:       owner: thread owning the orec (if locked)
 6:       version: version number (if ¬locked)

 7: State of thread p:
 8:    lb: lower bound of snapshot
 9:    ub: upper bound of snapshot
10:    r-set: read set of tuples ⟨addr, val, ver⟩
11:    w-set: write set of tuples ⟨addr, val⟩

12: stm-start()_p:
13:    lb ← ub ← clock
14:    r-set ← w-set ← ∅

15: stm-load(addr)_p:
16:    ⟨orec, val⟩ ← ⟨orecs[hash(addr)], *addr⟩        ▷ post-validated atomic read [13]
17:    if orec.locked then
18:       if orec.owner ≠ p then
19:          abort()                                       ▷ orec owned by other thread
20:       if ⟨addr, new-val, *⟩ ∈ w-set then
21:          val ← new-val                                 ▷ update write set entry
22:    else
23:       if orec.version > ub then                        ▷ try to extend snapshot
24:          ub ← clock
25:          if ¬validate() then
26:             abort()                                     ▷ cannot extend snapshot
27:       val ← *addr
28:       r-set ← r-set ∪ {⟨addr, val, orec.version⟩}      ▷ add to read set
29:    return val
```

```
30: stm-store(addr, val)_p:
31:    orec ← orecs[hash(addr)]
32:    if orec.locked then
33:       if orec.owner ≠ p then
34:          abort()                                        ▷ orec owned by other thread
35:    else
36:       if ⟨addr, *, ver⟩ ∈ r-set ∧ ver ≠ orec.version then
37:          abort()                                        ▷ read different version earlier
38:       if ¬cas(orecs[hash(addr)] : orec → ⟨true, p⟩) then
39:          abort()                                        ▷ cannot acquire orec
40:       w-set ← w-set \ {⟨addr, *⟩} ∪ {⟨addr, val⟩}       ▷ add to write set

41: stm-commit()_p:
42:    if w-set ≠ ∅ then                                    ▷ is transaction read-only?
43:       ub ← atomic-inc-and-fetch(clock)                  ▷ commit timestamp
44:       if ub ≠ lb + 1 then
45:          if ¬validate() then
46:             abort()                                      ▷ cannot extend snapshot
47:       o-set ← ∅                                          ▷ set of orecs updated by transaction
48:       for all ⟨addr, val⟩ ∈ w-set do                    ▷ write updates to memory
49:          *addr ← val
50:          o-set ← o-set ∪ {hash(addr)}
51:       for all o ∈ o-set do
52:          orecs[o] ← ⟨false, ub⟩                          ▷ release orecs

53: validate()_p:
54:    for all ⟨addr, val, ver⟩ ∈ r-set do                  ▷ Are orecs free and version unchanged?
55:       orec ← orecs[hash(addr)]
56:       if (orec.locked ∧ orec.owner ≠ p) ∨
             (¬orec.locked ∧ orec.version ≠ ver) then
57:          abort()                                         ▷ inconsistent snapshot
```

in the associated orecs have not changed. LSA tries to extend the snapshot when reading a value protected by an orec with a version number more recent than the snapshot's upper bound (line 25), as well as when committing to extend the snapshot up to the commit time, which represents the linearization point of the transaction (line 45).

We now describe the hybrid extensions of LSA using eager conflict detection (shown in Algorithm 3). A variant with lazy conflict detection is presented in the companion technical report [23]. Note that the HyTM decides at runtime whether to execute in hardware or software mode, as explained in Section 2 and Algorithm 1.

Transactional loads first perform an ASF-protected load of the associated orec (line 6). This operation starts monitoring of the

Algorithm 3 HyLSA — Eager variant (extends Algorithm 2)

```
 1: State of thread p:                                    ▷ extends state of Algorithm 2
 2:    o-set: set of orecs updated by transaction

 3: htm-start()_p:
 4:    o-set ← ∅

 5: htm-load(addr)_p:
 6:    LOCK MOV: orec ← orecs[hash(addr)]                 ▷ protected load
 7:    if orec.locked then
 8:       ABORT                                           ▷ orec owned by (other) software transaction
 9:    val ← addr                                         ▷ nonspeculative load
10:    return val

11: htm-store(addr, val)_p:
12:    LOCK MOV: orec ← orecs[hash(addr)]                 ▷ protected load
13:    if orec.locked then
14:       ABORT                                           ▷ orec owned by (other) software transaction
15:    LOCK PREFETCHW orec                                ▷ watch for concurrent loads/stores
16:    LOCK MOV: addr ← val                               ▷ speculative write
17:    o-set ← o-set ∪ {hash(addr)}

18: htm-commit()_p:
19:    if o ≠ ∅ then                                      ▷ is transaction read-only?
20:       ct ← atomic-inc-and-fetch(clock)                ▷ commit timestamp
21:       for all o ∈ o-set do
22:          LOCK MOV: orecs[o] ← ⟨false, ct⟩
23:    COMMIT                                             ▷ commit hardware transaction
```

orec for changes and will lead to an abort if the orec is updated by another thread. If the orec is not locked, the transaction uses a *nonspeculative* load operation (line 9) to read the target value. Note that ASF will start monitoring the orec before loading from the target address (see Section 2.1). If the transaction is not aborted before returning a value, this means that the orecs associated with this address and all previously read addresses have not changed and are not locked, thus creating an atomic snapshot.

This represents an application of the first of the synchronization techniques listed in Table 1: We only monitor metadata (i.e., the orec) but read application data nonspeculatively. This enables the HyTM to influence the HTM capacity required for transactions via its mapping from data to metadata, which in turn can make best-effort HTM useable even if transactions have to read more application data than provided by the HTM's capacity. In turn, the HTM has to guarantee that the monitoring starts before the nonspeculative load.

Transactional stores proceed as loads, first monitoring the orec and verifying that it is not locked (lines 12–14). The transaction then watches the orec for reads and writes by other transactions (PREFETCHW on line 15). The operation effectively ensures *eager* detection of conflicts with concurrent transactions. Finally, the updated memory location is speculatively written (line 16).

Upon commit, an update transaction first acquires a unique commit timestamp from the global time base (line 20). This will be ordered after the start of monitoring of previously accessed orecs, but will become visible to other threads before the transaction's commit (see Section 2.1). Next, it speculatively writes all updated orecs (lines 21–22), and finally tries to commit the transaction (line 23). Note that these steps are thus ordered in the same way as the equivalent steps in a software transaction (i.e., acquiring orecs or recording orec version numbers before incrementing *clock*, and validating orec version numbers or releasing orecs afterwards). If the transaction commits successfully, then we know that no other transaction performed conflicting accesses to the orecs (representing data conflicts). Thus, the hardware transaction could have equally been

57

a software transaction that acquired write locks for its orecs and or validated that their version numbers were not changed. If the hardware transaction aborts, then it only might have incremented *clock*, which is harmless because other transactions cannot distinguish this from a software update transaction that did not update any values that have they have read.

By nonspeculatively incrementing *clock* (line 20), a hardware update transaction *sends a synchronization message* to software transactions, notifying them that they might have to validate due to pending hardware transaction commits. It is thus an application of the second general-purpose technique in Table 1. Because ASF provides nonspeculative atomic read-modify-write (RMW) operations, hardware transactions can very efficiently send such messages. In contrast, using speculatively stores would lead to frequent aborts caused by consumers of those messages. If using just nonspeculative stores instead of RMW operations, concurrent transactions would have to write to separate locations to avoid lost updates, which in turn would require observers to check many different locations. In the case of HyLSA, this would also prevent the efficiency that is gained by using a single global time basis. The ordering guarantees that ASF provides for nonspeculative atomic RMW operations are essential because it allows hardware transactions to send messages after monitoring data and before commit or monitoring further data.

To ensure privatization safety for the hybrid LSA algorithm, we use a typical STM quiescence-based protocol (not shown in the pseudo-code). Basically, update transactions potentially privatize data, so they have to wait until concurrent transactions that might have accessed the updated locations have finished or have extended their snapshot far enough into the future (so that they would have observed the updates). Because hardware transactions will be aborted immediately by conflicting updates, their snapshot is always most recent and we do not need to wait for them.

4. THE HYBRID NOREC ALGORITHMS

In this section, we take another algorithm from the literature, NOrec [8], and discuss how to turn it into a scalable HyTM for ASF. Roughly speaking, NOrec uses a single orec (a global versioned lock) and relies on value-based validation (VBV) in addition to time-based validation. The basic version of the NOrec algorithm and its original hybrid variant (HyNOrec-DSS), as informally described by Dalessandro et al. [8], are briefly summarized here and further described in a companion technical report [23]. To simplify the presentation, we will show these algorithms embedded in or as a modification of our initial HyTM algorithm. NOrec is basically the STM code in Algorithm 4 when discarding *esl*.

The NOrec algorithm is quite similar, when ignoring VBV, to timestamp-based TMs like TL2 [9] or LSA [25]. The main difference with the description given in Section 3 is that NOrec uses a single orec (*gsl*, line 2) and does not acquire the lock before attempting to commit a transaction. As a consequence, it yields a very simple implementation and allows for a few optimizations. In particular, it is not necessary to track which locks are covering loads or stores, and the lock itself can serve as time base (lines 30/36, 13, and 40). However, such a design would not scale well when update transactions commit frequently because timestamp-based validation would also fail frequently (e. g., in the checks on lines 21 and 30). Therefore, NOrec attempts value-based validation (lines 42–44) whenever timestamp-based validation is not successful (lines 22 and 31).

With VBV, the consistency of a transaction's read set is verified on the basis of the values that have been loaded instead of the versions of the orecs. The disadvantage of using values is that one has

---

Algorithm 4 HyNOrec-0: STM acquires locks separately

```
 1:  Global state:
 2:      gsl: word-sized global sequence lock, consisting of:
 3:          locked: most significant bit, true iff locked
 4:          clock: clock (remaining bits)
 5:      esl: extra sequence lock

 6:  State of thread p:
 7:      sl: thread-local sequence lock
 8:      r-set: read set of tuples ⟨addr, val⟩
 9:      w-set: write set of tuples ⟨addr, val⟩
10:      update: are we in an update transaction?

11:  stm-start()_p:
12:      repeat
13:          sl ← gsl                              ▷ get the transaction's start time
14:      until ¬ sl.locked                        ▷ wait until concurrent commits have finished
15:      r-set ← w-set ← ∅

16:  stm-load(addr)_p:
17:      if ⟨addr, new-val⟩ ∈ w-set then          ▷ read after write?
18:          val ← new-val                        ▷ return buffered value
19:      else
20:          val ← *addr
21:          while sl ≠ gsl do                    ▷ timestamp-based validation
22:              sl ← validate()                  ▷ value-based validation
23:              val ← *addr
24:          r-set ← r-set ∪ {⟨addr, val⟩}
25:      return val

26:  stm-store(addr, val)_p:
27:      w-set ← w-set ∪ {⟨addr, val⟩}            ▷ updates are buffered

28:  stm-commit()_p:
29:      if w-set ≠ ∅ then                        ▷ is transaction read-only?
30:          while ¬ cas(gsl : sl → ⟨true, sl.clock⟩) do   ▷ acquire commit lock
31:              sl ← validate()                  ▷ value-based validation
32:          esl ← ⟨true, sl.clock⟩               ▷ also acquire extra lock (no need for cas)
33:          for all ⟨addr, val⟩ ∈ w-set do       ▷ write updates to memory
34:              *addr ← val
35:          esl ← ⟨false, sl.clock + 1⟩          ▷ release locks and increment clock
36:          gsl ← ⟨false, sl.clock + 1⟩

37:  validate()_p:
38:      repeat
39:          repeat
40:              c ← gsl                          ▷ get current time
41:          until ¬ c.locked                     ▷ wait until concurrent commits have finished
42:          for all ⟨addr, val⟩ ∈ r-set do
43:              if *addr ≠ val then              ▷ value-based validation
44:                  abort()                      ▷ inconsistent snapshot
45:      until c = gsl
46:      return c

47:  htm-start()_p:
48:      LOCK MOV : l ← esl                       ▷ protected load (monitor extra lock)
49:      if l.locked then                         ▷ extra lock available?
50:          ABORT                                ▷ no: spin by explicit self-abort
51:      update ← false                           ▷ initially not an update transaction

52:  htm-load(addr)_p:
53:      LOCK MOV : val ← addr                    ▷ protected load
54:      return val

55:  htm-store(addr, val)_p:
56:      LOCK MOV : addr ← val                    ▷ speculative write
57:      update ← true                            ▷ we are in an update transaction

58:  htm-commit()_p:
59:      if update then
60:          LOCK MOV : l ← gsl
61:          if l.locked then                     ▷ main lock available?
62:              ABORT                            ▷ no: we will be aborted anyway
63:          LOCK MOV : gsl ← ⟨false, l.clock + 1⟩   ▷ release lock, incr. clock
64:      COMMIT                                    ▷ commit hardware transaction
```

---

to potentially track more data in the read set because several addresses often map to the same orec. VBV is typically paired with serialized commit phases. In NOrec, this is enforced on lines 14 and 41.

Our implementation of NOrec differs in a few points from the original implementation [8]. Notably, in our implementation, when writing back buffered updates upon commit, we only write to pre-

Algorithm 5 HyNOrec-DSS: HyTM by Dalessandro et al. [8] (extends Algorithm 4)

```
 1:  stm-acquire-locks()_p :
 2:     SPECULATE                          ▷ start hardware transaction (retry code omitted)
 3:     LOCK MOV : l ← gsl
 4:     if l = sl then
 5:        LOCK MOV : gsl ← ⟨true,sl.clock⟩      ▷ try to acquire commit lock
 6:        LOCK MOV : esl ← ⟨true,sl.clock⟩      ▷ also acquire extra lock
 7:     COMMIT
 8:     return l = sl                       ▷ true ⇔ locks were acquired atomically

 9:  stm-commit()_p :                       ▷ replaces function of Algorithm 4
10:     if w-set ≠ ∅ then                   ▷ is transaction read-only?
11:        while ¬ stm-acquire-locks() do   ▷ acquire gsl and esl atomically
12:           sl ← validate()
13:        for all ⟨addr,val⟩ ∈ w-set do    ▷ write updates to memory
14:           *addr ← val
15:        esl ← ⟨false,sl.clock + 1⟩        ▷ may abort hardware transaction
16:        gsl ← ⟨false,sl.clock + 1⟩        ▷ release lock and increment clock

17:  htm-store(addr,val)_p :                ▷ replaces function of Algorithm 4
18:     LOCK MOV : addr ← val               ▷ speculative write

19:  htm-commit()_p :                       ▷ replaces function of Algorithm 4
20:     LOCK MOV : l ← gsl
21:     LOCK MOV : gsl ← ⟨false,l.clock + 1⟩  ▷ release lock and increment clock
22:     COMMIT                              ▷ commit hardware transaction
```

Algorithm 6 HyNOrec-1: HTM writes gsl nonspeculatively (extends Algorithm 4)

```
 1:  htm-start()_p :                        ▷ replaces function of Algorithm 4
 2:     wait until ¬ esl.locked             ▷ spin while extra lock unavailable
 3:     LOCK MOV : l ← esl                  ▷ protected load
 4:     if l.locked then                    ▷ extra lock available?
 5:        ABORT                            ▷ no: explicit self-abort
 6:     update ← false                      ▷ initially not an update transaction

 7:  htm-commit()_p :                       ▷ replaces function of Algorithm 4
 8:     if update then
 9:        l ← atomic-fetch-and-inc(gsl) ▷ increment gsl.clock (gsl.locked is MSB)
10:        if l.locked then
11:           ABORT                ▷ main lock unavailable, we will be aborted anyway
12:     COMMIT                              ▷ commit hardware transaction
```

cisely those bytes that were modified by the application, whereas the original implementation always performs updates at the granularity of aligned machine words. This more complex bookkeeping introduces higher runtime overheads but is required for the STM to operate correctly according to the C/C++ TM specification [15].

The reason for creating a hybrid extension to NOrec is that this algorithm can potentially provide better performance for low thread counts because it does not have to pay the runtime overheads associated with accessing multiple orecs. In turn, LSA is expected to provide better scalability with large thread counts or frequent but disjoint commits of software transactions. Therefore, both algorithms are of practical interest depending on the target architecture and workload.

The main approach of HyNOrec-DSS (Algorithm 5) is to use two global sequence locks, gsl and esl. Software transactions acquire both locks on commit and increment their version numbers after committing, whereas hardware transactions monitor esl for changes and increment only gsl's version on commit. Thus, software transactions are notified about data updates using gsl, and will use esl to abort hardware transactions and prevent them from executing during software commits. From the perspective of software transactions, committed hardware transactions are thus equivalent to software transactions that committed atomically.

The major problem of HyNOrec-DSS is that it does not scale well in practice (see Section 5). For example, Dalessandro et al. assume [8] that the update of the contended gsl by every hardware transaction (line 21 in Algorithm 5) is not a performance problem because it would happen close to the end of a transaction. However, we observed in experimental evaluation a high rate of aborts and poor overall performance for this algorithm.

In what follows, we will construct a new algorithm, HyNOrec-2, which performs much better while being no more complex. gsl and esl are used by software and hardware transactions to synchronize with each other, so our key approach is to apply the last two techniques from Table 1 and use nonspeculative operations to let hardware transactions synchronize more efficiently via these variables. To better explain and evaluate the different optimizations involved, we additionally show two intermediate algorithms.

Algorithm 4 shows our first (intermediate) NOrec-based HyTM, this time considering the addition of esl, which will serve as the basis for the other two variants. As a first straightforward opti-

mization, a hardware transaction has to update gsl only if it will actually update shared state on commit (line 59).

Second, we do not need to use a small hardware transaction to update both gsl and esl in stm-commit. This is not necessary because esl is purely used to notify hardware transactions about software commits[7] and can only be modified by a software transaction that previously acquired gsl (line 30). In contrast to Algorithm 5, this allows hardware transactions to try to commit at a time where gsl has been acquired but esl has not yet been updated (which would have aborted the hardware transaction). However, this case can be handled by just letting the hardware transaction abort if gsl has been locked (line 62).

This second change is not about performance but it allows us to have a software fallback path in the HyTM that does not depend on HTM progress guarantees (e. g., no spurious aborts), which are surprisingly difficult to implement [11]. Also, programs can use the software path in the HyTM as is on hardware that does not support ASF.

Algorithm 4 can still suffer from conflicts on gsl if updating hardware transactions commit frequently. Algorithm 6 shows that we can replace the speculative update of gsl with a *nonspeculative* atomic fetch-and-increment instruction (line 9),[8] which allows hardware transactions that access disjoint data to not abort each other anymore and makes the algorithm scale better. This is an application of our second general-purpose technique and has similarities to acquiring a commit time nonspeculatively in HyLSA (see Section 3 for a detailed discussion).

To understand why this is possible, consider possible orderings of the hardware transaction's fetch-and-increment and a software transaction's compare-and-set (CAS) on gsl. If the increment gets ordered first, the CAS will fail and will cause a software transaction validation. If the software transaction accesses during validation any updates of the hardware transaction before the former can commit, it will abort the hardware transaction, making the situation look like if some transaction committed without updating anything. If in contrast the CAS comes first, the hardware transaction will notice that gsl was locked before it incremented gsl and will abort. The hardware transaction's update to gsl is harmless because no transaction interprets gsl.clock if gsl is locked.

Additionally, hardware transactions spin nonspeculatively if esl is locked before accessing it speculatively to avoid unnecessary aborts (line 2).

---

[7] As a matter of fact, esl.clock can contain any value as long as the lock bit is updated properly because such an update will abort hardware transactions monitoring esl.

[8] Note that the fetch-and-incremented will be ordered before the commit of the transaction. Also, using a typical compare-and-set loop instead of the fetch-and-increment yields lower performance according to our experiments.

Algorithm 7 HyNOrec-2: HTM does not monitor *esl* (extends Algorithm 4)

```
 1: htm-start()_p:                         ▷ replaces function of Algorithm 4
 2:   update ← false              ▷ initially not an update transaction

 3: htm-load(addr)_p:                       ▷ replaces function of Algorithm 4
 4:   LOCK MOV : val ← addr                            ▷ protected load
 5:   wait until ¬ esl.locked          ▷ spin while extra lock unavailable
 6:   return val

 7: hytm-commit()_p:                       ▷ replaces function of Algorithm 4
 8:   if update then
 9:     atomic-inc(gsl)            ▷ increment gsl.clock (gsl.locked is MSB)
10:     wait until ¬ gsl.locked
11:   COMMIT                               ▷ commit hardware transaction
```

Benchmark	Range	Commits on hardware code path (%)		
		LLB8	LLB8L1	LLB256
SkipList-Large	8192	< 1%	Figure 1	100%
SkipList-Small	1024	< 1%	HyLSA: 90–95%	100%
			HyNOrec: 95–100%	
RBTree-Large	8192	0–2%	HyLSA: 70–90%	100%
			HyNOrec: 95–100%	
RBTree-Small	1024	2–10%	HyLSA: 85–95%	100%
			HyNOrec: 100%	
HashTable	128000	100% (except HyLSA-* on LLB8-L1: 95%)		
LinkedList-Large	512	1–3%	Figure 1	100%
LinkedList-Small	28	30–60%	100%	100%

Table 4: IntegerSet microbenchmarks and approximate ratio of HTM commits to total number of commits.

The remaining problem of Algorithm 5 is that committing a software transaction aborts *all* hardware transactions that execute concurrently. One might see this as a minor issue assuming that, typically, software transactions are much longer than hardware transactions, but this is not necessarily the case. There are several reasons why a transaction cannot use ASF, for example because it contains instructions that are not allowed in ASF speculative regions (e. g., rdtsc), or because its access pattern quickly exceeds the associativity of the cache used to track the speculative loads, hence leading to capacity aborts after only few accesses.

Fortunately, software transactions can commit without having to abort nonconflicting hardware transactions. The key insight to understand this second extension is that the monitoring in hardware transactions is like an over-cautious form of continuous value-based validation (any conflicting access to a speculatively accessed cache line will abort a transaction). In NOrec, software transactions tolerate concurrent commits of other transactions by performing value-based validation when necessary.

Our final optimization is shown in Algorithm 7. Hardware transactions do not monitor *esl* using speculative accesses anymore. The purpose of *esl* is to prevent hardware transactions from reading inconsistent state such as partial updates by software transactions. To detect such cases and thus still obtain a consistent snapshot, hardware transactions first read the data speculatively (line 4) and then wait until they observe with *nonspeculative* loads that *esl* is not locked (line 5). If this succeeds and the transaction reaches line 6 without being aborted, it is guaranteed that it had a consistent snapshot valid at line 5 at a time when there were no concurrent commits by software transactions. Again, note that ASF will have started monitoring the data before performing the subsequent nonspeculative loads.

The reasoning for waiting until *gsl* is not locked on line 10 is similar and just applied to the commit optimization in HyNOrec-1. Waiting for *gsl* is as good as waiting for *esl* because *esl* will be locked iff *gsl* is locked (see Algorithm 4).

Thus, hardware transactions essentially *validate against commit messages by software transactions* (the third general-purpose technique in Table 1). This consists of the nonspeculative spinning on *esl* (reading commit messages by software transactions) combined with the implicit value-based validation performed by ASF monitoring the data accessed by the hardware transaction. The nonspeculative accesses allow hardware transactions to observe and tolerate software commits that create no data conflicts (i. e., pass value-based validation).

Note that *esl* could be removed and replaced by just *gsl*. A downside of this approach is that it would increase the number of cache misses on line 5 because both hardware and software commits would update the same lock. Therefore, we keep the separation between *gsl* and *esl*.

5. EVALUATION

To evaluate the performance of our HyTMs, we use a similar experimental setup as in a previous study [5]. We simulate a machine with sixteen x86 CPU cores on a single socket, each having a clock speed of 2.2 GHz. The simulator is near-cycle-accurate (e. g., it simulates details of out-of-order execution). We evaluate three ASF implementations. Two of them, "LLB8" and "LLB256" can track/ buffer speculative loads and store in a fully-associative buffer that holds up to 8 or 256 distinct cache lines. "LLB8L1" is a variant which uses only buffers for speculative stores but uses the L1 cache to track transactional loads. We show these ASF implementations because they have different costs when implemented in a microprocessor (e. g., required chip area). LLB8 will have to resort to the STM code path often because most transactions will exceed its capacity. LLB256 is sufficient to run almost all transactions in our benchmarks in the HTM code path, but is more expensive. LLB8L1 represents a middle ground. Its capacity for loads is limited by either the cache's size (1024 lines) or its associativity (2-way).

In order to get the best performance, the compiler links in the TM library statically and optimizes the code by inlining TM functions. The STM implementations that we compare against are "LSA" (a version of TinySTM [20] using write-through mode, eager conflict detection, and ensuring privatization-safety, similar to Algorithm 2) and "NOrec" [8] (similar to the STM code in Algorithm 4). The baseline HTM ("HTM") uses serial-irrevocable mode as simple software fallback. The HyTM implementations have the same names as the respective algorithms (e. g., Algorithm 7 is denoted "HyNOrec-2") and use the LSA and NOrec implementations for their software code paths.

As benchmarks, we use selected applications from the STAMP TM benchmark suite [4] and the typical integer set microbenchmarks (IntegerSet). The latter are implementations of a sorted set of integers based on a skip list, a red-black tree, a hash table, and a linked list. During runtime, several threads use transactions to repeatedly execute insert, remove, or contains operations on the set (operations and elements are chosen randomly). All set elements are within a certain key range, and the set is initially half full. Table 4 shows the configurations that we consider. In HashTable all transactions are update transactions (insert or remove operations), in all other benchmarks the update rate is 20%. However, these operations only insert (remove) an element if it is absent from (part of) the set, so the actual percentage of update transactions can be smaller. We use the Hoard memory allocator [2] in HashTable and glibc 2.10 standard malloc in the other benchmarks.

Because we do not have enough space to show all measurements in the same level of detail, we first present a few interesting cases. Table 4 shows which percentage of transaction commits happen on the hardware code path in comparison to the total number of

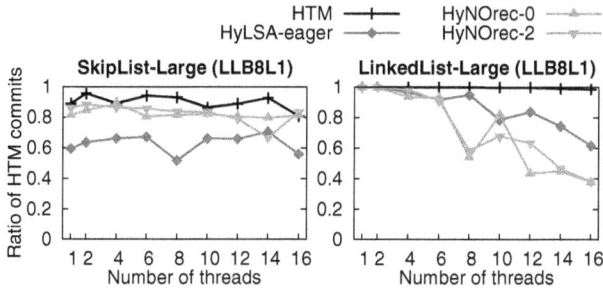

Figure 1: Ratio of HTM commits to total number of commits.

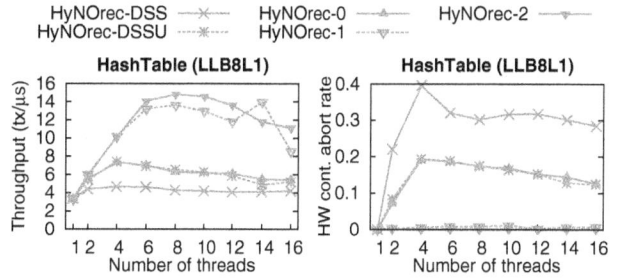

Figure 2: Comparison of HyNOrec algorithms. The hardware contention abort rate is the number of aborts due to ASF contention per transaction that commits in hardware or switches to the software codepath.

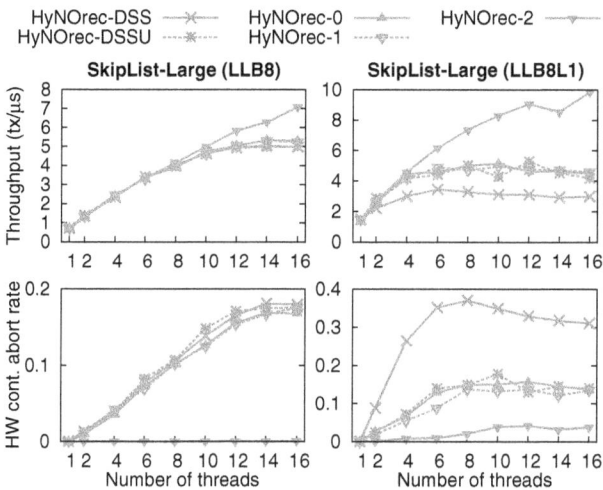

Figure 3: Comparison of HyNOrec algorithms (HashTable).

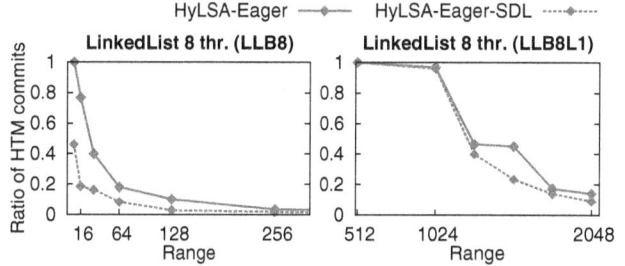

Figure 4: Ratio of HTM commits to total number of commits for 8 threads and read-only LinkedList of various sizes (range), when accessing data speculatively (SDL) or not.

commits. LLB256 provides sufficient capacity to execute all transactions in our IntegerSet configurations in hardware. In contrast, LLB8's capacity is most often too small. Note that in our implementations, only permanent ASF abort reasons like exceeding ASF's capacity make the HyTM switch to the software code path. Contention will not result in such a switch unless a transaction suffers from a high number of retries (100 in our experiments). Therefore, the ratio of HTM's commits that we show is essentially independent of the level of contention in a workload.

Figure 2 shows a comparison between the HyNOrec algorithms for the same SkipList benchmarks but with two different ASF implementations. With LLB8 (left side), all transactions have to fall back to software executions (see Table 4), but interestingly HyNOrec-2 is able to scale better than the other algorithms. The abort rate due to contention shows that this is because hardware transactions in the other HyNOrec variants suffer from contention aborts before they notice a capacity abort, which makes them switch to software execution. Because HyNOrec-2 does not monitor esl, it will not be aborted by commits of nonconflicting software transactions, and will find out quickly that it should switch to software, then taking advantage of STM scalability.

When using LLB8L1 (right side), many transactions can execute in hardware (see Table 4 and Figure 1). HyNOrec-2 also scales much better in this case, showing that its ability to survive commits of nonconflicting software transactions (e. g., in contrast to

HyNOrec-1) is beneficial even when the majority of transactions execute in hardware. Furthermore, HyNOrec-DSS suffers from many more aborts than the other TMs. To explain this, we show results for HyNOrec-DSSU, which is like HyNOrec-DSS but only updates gsl when update transactions commit, thus reducing the number of speculative updates to gsl (SkipList has 20% update transactions). HyNOrec-DSSU performs similar to HyNOrec-0, indicating that this part of the HyNOrec-0 optimizations is crucial. HyNOrec-DSS never performed better than HyNOrec-0 in any of our benchmarks and often performed significantly worse. It does not scale beyond 4 to 6 threads in IntegerSet unless transactions execute the software code path most of the time. Therefore, we discard HyNOrec-DSS from now on.

Figure 3 shows HashTable, which runs short and mostly update transactions. HyNOrec-1 performs and scales much better than HyNOrec-0 and suffers from very few aborts, whereas the rate of aborts due to contention is still significant for HyNOrec-0. This shows that updating gsl nonspeculatively is an important optimization, especially if commits of update transactions are frequent. Second, it highlights that updating gsl speculatively can indeed lead to contention.

ASF capacity requirements for execution under the HyNOrec TMs are similar to HTM. However, even though HyNorec-2 does not access more data speculatively than an HTM, it can effectively reach capacity limits earlier. It has to always check esl, which keeps esl in the cache and can thus reduce the capacity limit by one, which can matter if the effective limit is the cache associativity.

After looking at the HyNOrec algorithms, let us now focus on HyLSA[9]. Its capacity requirements are different than those of Hy-NOrec. HyLSA buffers updates speculatively and thus, for stores,

---

[9] Unfortunately, the current version of the ASF simulator does not provide the ASF ordering guarantees for nonspeculative accesses in all cases. To be able to run the same HyLSA TMs in all benchmarks, we had to add memory barriers (i. e., an `lfence` instruction)

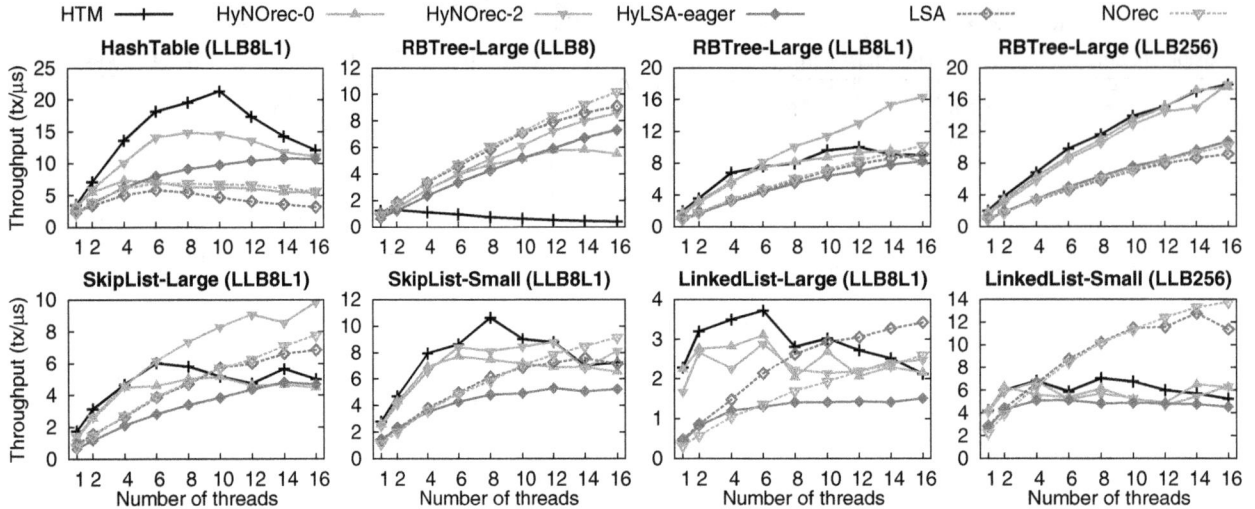

Figure 5: Overview of scalability of TMs with IntegerSet.

needs ASF capacity for both data and orecs. However, for loads, only orecs are accessed speculatively, and the hash function that maps data to orecs influences capacity requirements. In our implementations, word-sized data are mapped to word-sized orecs (i.e., we discard the lower three bits of an address and select with the remaining bits a slot in an array with 2^{20} orecs). Orecs are not cache-line padded because padding would likely increase capacity requirements for HyLSA unless more than one adjacent cache line maps to the same orec. Without padding, hardware transactions detect conflicts on cacheline granularity, whereas STM transactions can detect conflicts on word-size granularity and can thus potentially scale better in high-contention workloads.

Table 4 and Figure 1 show that HyLSA is already more likely to hit capacity limitations than HyNOrec just because it needs twice the capacity for stores, so it is important for HyLSA to read data nonspeculatively. Figure 4 illustrates this point further, showing that when accessing data and orecs speculatively (HyLSA-eager-SDL), less transactions can execute the hardware code path. HASTM in aggressive mode and the HyTM by Damron et al. also suffer from this (see Table 3).

Figure 5 presents a concluding overview of TM performance with the integer set microbenchmarks. We show configurations that are representative or that highlight interesting properties. Hash-Table performs similar on all ASF implementations and scales very well, but ultimately suffers from external bottlenecks (e.g., the memory allocator). LLB8 is (on all other benchmarks) not sufficient to run many transactions in hardware, and STMs perform slightly better than HyTMs because the latter try to first execute in hardware (unsuccessfully).

HyNOrec-2 has very good overall performance, especially on scalable workloads. It is not aborted by nonconflicting concurrent commits of software transactions, which is one of the reasons why it performs better than HyNOrec-0 (e.g., in SkipList-Large on LLBL1, see Figure 1 for HTM ratio). Pure HTM has the lowest overhead but its simple fallback mode (serial execution) can quickly decrease its performance. HyLSA has higher runtime overhead than HyNOrec but typically scales well.

In the small LinkedList on LLB256, all transactions can execute in hardware but HyTMs and HTM do not scale. The reason for

this behavior is that ASF's conflict detection is on the granularity of cache lines, whereas STMs can use smaller granularities (word-sized in LSA, value-based validation in NOrec), which can be beneficial in high-contention workloads with a high level of false sharing. As explained before, HyLSA could use the indirection of the orecs and the memory-to-orec hash function to emulate a smaller granularity for conflict detection. However, this will waste ASF capacity and thus does not seem to be a generally useful strategy. Instead, a HyTM should perhaps switch proactively to software to try to employ a more contention-resistant STM algorithm.

To conclude the evaluation, we show performance results for selected applications from STAMP (see Table 5) in Figure 6. We chose benchmarks that are stable and have parallelism in their workloads, and executed them using STAMP's standard parameter configurations for simulator environments. LLB256 is again sufficient to execute all transactions in hardware. SSCA2 and KMeans have small transactions, but interestingly HyNOrec-0 seems to require just a little too much capacity (in contrast to the other HyNOrec TMs, it accesses *esl* and *gsl* speculatively). Genome on LLB8 also exhibits this behavior. HyLSA's larger capacity requirements for stores decrease the HTM ratio as well.

HyNOrec-2 performs best among the HyTMs most of the time and is often close to or better than HTM. Its performance suffers in Genome due to its software fallback (NOrec) performing worse than LSA. It often performs much better than HyNOrec-0

Benchmark	LLB8	LLB8-L1	LLB256
Genome	HTM, HyNOrec-2: 65% HyNOrec-1: 60% HyNOrec-0: 50% HyLSA: 38–42%	HTM: 90–95% HyNOrec: 85–90% HyLSA: 75%	100%
KMeans-Hi KMeans-Lo	HTM, HyNOrec-{1|2}: 100% HyLSA, HyNOrec-0: 25%	95–100%	100%
Vacation-Hi	0%	HTM: 13–14% HyNOrec: 9–12% HyLSA: 3–5%	100%
Vacation-Lo	0%	HTM: 8–11% HyNOrec: 6–9% HyLSA: 1–2%	100%
SSCA2	99–100%		

Table 5: Approximate ratio of HTM commits to total number of commits in STAMP.

between the speculative load of an orec and the nonspeculative load of data (e.g., lines 6 and 9 in Algorithm 3).

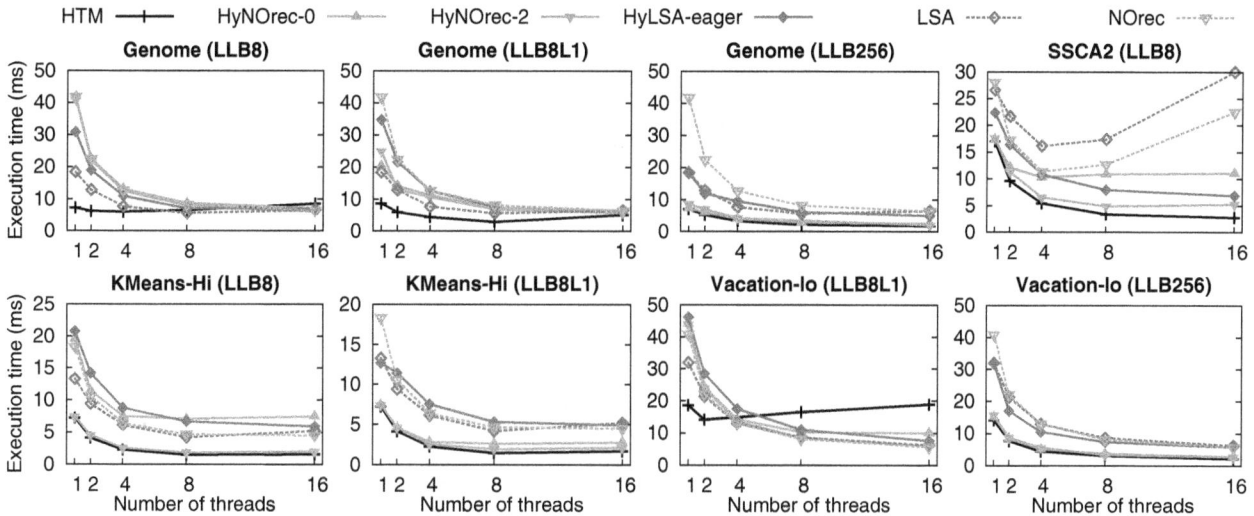

Figure 6: Overview of scalability of TMs in selected STAMP benchmarks. SSCA2 performs similar on all ASF implementations. KMeans-Lo performs roughly similiar to KMeans-Hi, and KMeans-Hi on LLB8L1 is similar to LLB256. Vacation-Hi performs similar to Vacation-Lo, and Vacation-Lo on LLB8 is similar to LLB8L1.

(and HyNOrec-DSS), thus demonstrating the benefits of our optimizations. HyLSA has higher runtime overhead than HyNOrec but scales well.

6. CONCLUSION

In this paper, we have proposed and evaluated novel hybrid software/hardware transactional memory algorithms. As shown in Table 3, they improve upon previous HyTM algorithms by either allowing for a larger level of concurrency between hardware and software transactions, by reducing runtime overhead of hardware transactions, or by requiring less HTM capacity and thus allowing more transactions to run with hardware acceleration. We confirmed this through experimental evaluation on a near-cycle-accurate x86 simulator with support for AMD's ASF hardware extensions.

While previous HyTM designs have used nonspeculative memory accesses inside of hardware transactions, we show that this has a much larger potential and importance if algorithms also make use of nonspeculative atomic read-modify-write instructions. We also found it very useful that ASF monitors speculatively accessed locations eagerly for conflicting accesses by other threads. We believe that the general-purpose techniques that we used in our algorithms (Table 1) apply not just to HyTM but can be useful in general for concurrent algorithms based on new synchronization hardware like ASF.

Acknowledgements. We would like to thank Stephan Diestelhorst of AMD for his clarifications regarding the ASF specification, and Tim Harris for his suggestions in improving this paper. The research leading to these results has received funding from the European Community's Seventh Framework Programme (FP7/2007-2013) under grant agreement N° 216852.

7. REFERENCES

[1] Advanced Micro Devices, Inc. *Advanced Synchronization Facility - Proposed Architectural Specification*, 2.1 edition, Mar. 2009.

[2] E. D. Berger, K. S. McKinley, R. D. Blumofe, and P. R. Wilson. Hoard: a scalable memory allocator for multithreaded applications. In *Proceedings of the ninth international conference on Architectural support for programming languages and operating systems*, ASPLOS-IX, pages 117–128, New York, NY, USA, 2000. ACM.

[3] Bratin Saha, Ali-Reza Adl Tabatabai, and Quinn Jacobson. Architectural Support for Software Transactional Memory. In *International Symposium on Microarchitecture (MICRO'06)*, 2006.

[4] C. Cao Minh, J. Chung, C. Kozyrakis, and K. Olukotun. STAMP: Stanford Transactional Applications for Multi-Processing. In *IISWC '08: Proceedings of The IEEE International Symposium on Workload Characterization*, September 2008.

[5] D. Christie, J.-W. Chung, S. Diestelhorst, M. Hohmuth, M. Pohlack, C. Fetzer, M. Nowack, T. Riegel, P. Felber, P. Marlier, and E. Riviere. Evaluation of AMD's Advanced Synchronization Facility Within a Complete Transactional Memory Stack. In *EuroSys '10: Proceedings of the 5th European conference on Computer systems*, pages 27–40, New York, NY, USA, 2010. ACM.

[6] J. Chung, D. Christie, M. Pohlack, S. Diestelhorst, M. Hohmuth, and L. Yen. Compilation of Thoughts about AMD Advanced Synchronization Facility and First-Generation Hardware Transactional Memory Support. In *TRANSACT*, 2010.

[7] L. Dalessandro, F. Carouge, S. White, Y. Lev, M. Moir, M. L. Scott, and M. F. Spear. Hybrid NOrec: A Case Study in the Effectiveness of Best Effort Hardware Transactional Memory. In *Architectural Support for Programming Languages and Operating Systems (ASPLOS)*, Mar. 2011.

[8] L. Dalessandro, M. F. Spear, and M. L. Scott. NOrec: streamlining STM by abolishing ownership records. In *PPoPP '10: Proceedings of the 15th ACM SIGPLAN symposium on Principles and practice of parallel programming*, pages 67–78, New York, NY, USA, 2010. ACM.

[9] David Dice, Ori Shalev, and Nir Shavit. Transactional Locking II. In S. Dolev, editor, *DISC*, volume 4167 of

Lecture Notes in Computer Science, pages 194–208. Springer, 2006.

[10] D. Dice, Y. Lev, M. Moir, and D. Nussbaum. Early experience with a commercial hardware transactional memory implementation. In *ASPLOS '09: Proceeding of the 14th international conference on Architectural support for programming languages and operating systems*, pages 157–168, New York, NY, USA, 2009. ACM.

[11] S. Diestelhorst, M. Pohlack, M. Hohmuth, D. Christie, J.-W. Chung, and L. Yen. Implementing AMD's Advanced Synchronization Facility in an out-of-order x86 core. In *TRANSACT*, 2010.

[12] P. Felber, C. Fetzer, P. Marlier, M. Nowack, and T. Riegel. Brief Announcement: Hybrid Time-Based Transactional Memory. In N. Lynch and A. Shvartsman, editors, *Distributed Computing*, volume 6343 of *Lecture Notes in Computer Science*, pages 124–126. Springer Berlin / Heidelberg, 2010. The full version is available as technical report TUD-FI10-06-Nov.2010.

[13] P. Felber, C. Fetzer, P. Marlier, and T. Riegel. Time-based Software Transactional Memory. *IEEE Trans. Parallel Distrib. Syst.*, 21:1793–1807, December 2010.

[14] O. S. Hofmann, C. J. Rossbach, and E. Witchel. Maximum benefit from a minimal HTM. In *ASPLOS '09: Proceeding of the 14th international conference on Architectural support for programming languages and operating systems*, pages 145–156, New York, NY, USA, 2009. ACM.

[15] Intel. *Draft Specification of Transactional Language Constructs for C++*. Intel, IBM, Sun, 1.0 edition, Aug. 2009.

[16] ISO. *Programming Languages — C++*, ISO/IEC JTC1 SC22 WG21 N 3092 edition, Mar. 2010.

[17] Y. Lev, M. Moir, and D. Nussbaum. PhTM: Phased Transactional Memory. In *TRANSACT '07: 2nd Workshop on Transactional Computing*, aug 2007.

[18] V. Menon, S. Balensiefer, T. Shpeisman, A.-R. Adl-Tabatabai, R. L. Hudson, B. Saha, and A. Welc. Practical Weak-Atomicity Semantics for Java STM. In *SPAA '08: Proceedings of the twentieth annual symposium on Parallelism in algorithms and architectures*, pages 314–325, New York, NY, USA, 2008. ACM.

[19] Michael F. Spear, Arrvindh Shriraman, Luke Dalessandro, Sandhya Dwarkadas, and Michael L. Scott. Nonblocking Transactions Without Indirection Using Alert-on-Update. In *19th ACM Symposium on Parallelism in Algorithms and Architectures (SPAA)*, 2007.

[20] Pascal Felber, Christof Fetzer, and Torvald Riegel. Dynamic Performance Tuning of Word-Based Software Transactional Memory. In *Proceedings of the 13th ACM SIGPLAN Symposium on Principles and Practice of Parallel Programming (PPoPP)*, 2008.

[21] Peter Damron, Alexandra Fedorova, Yossi Lev, Victor Luchangco, Mark Moir, and Daniel Nussbaum. Hybrid transactional memory. In *ASPLOS-XII: Proceedings of the 12th international conference on Architectural support for programming languages and operating systems*, pages 336–346, New York, NY, USA, 2006. ACM Press.

[22] R. Rajwar and J. R. Goodman. Speculative lock elision: enabling highly concurrent multithreaded execution. In *MICRO 34: Proceedings of the 34th annual ACM/IEEE international symposium on Microarchitecture*, pages 294–305, Washington, DC, USA, 2001. IEEE Computer Society.

[23] T. Riegel, P. Marlier, M. Nowack, P. Felber, and C. Fetzer. Optimizing Hybrid Transactional Memory: The Importance of Nonspeculative Operations. Technical Report TUD-FI10-06-Nov.2010, Technische Universität Dresden, November 2010. Full version of the DISC 2010 brief announcement.

[24] Sanjeev Kumar, Michael Chu, Christopher J. Hughes, Partha Kundu, and Anthony Nguyen. Hybrid transactional memory. In *PPoPP '06: Proceedings of the eleventh ACM SIGPLAN symposium on Principles and practice of parallel programming*, pages 209–220, New York, NY, USA, 2006. ACM Press.

[25] Torvald Riegel, Pascal Felber, and Christof Fetzer. A Lazy Snapshot Algorithm with Eager Validation. In *20th International Symposium on Distributed Computing (DISC)*, September 2006.

Flat-Combining NUMA Locks

Dave Dice
Oracle Labs
dave.dice@oracle.com

Virendra J. Marathe
Oracle Labs
virendra.marathe@oracle.com

Nir Shavit
Oracle Labs
nir.shavit@oracle.com

ABSTRACT

Multicore machines are growing in size, and accordingly shifting from simple bus-based designs to NUMA and CC-NUMA architectures. With this shift, the need for scalable hierarchical locking algorithms is becoming crucial to performance. This paper presents a novel scalable hierarchical queue-lock algorithm based on the flat combining synchronization paradigm. At the core of the new algorithm is a scheme for building local queues of waiting threads in a highly efficient manner, and then merging them globally, all with little interconnect traffic and virtually no costly synchronization operations in the common case. In empirical testing on an Oracle SPARC Enterprise T5440 Server, a 256-way CC-NUMA machine, our new flat-combining hierarchical lock significantly outperforms all classic locking algorithms, and at high concurrency levels, provides up to a factor of two improvement over HCLH, the most efficient known hierarchical locking algorithm.

Categories and Subject Descriptors

D.1.3 [**Programming Techniques**]: Concurrent Programming

General Terms

Algorithms, Design, Experimentation, Performance

Keywords

hierarchical locks, queue locks, flat combining

1. INTRODUCTION

Queue locks [1, 2, 3, 4], and in particular the CLH [2, 3, 4] and MCS [3] locks, have long been the algorithms of choice for locking in many high performance systems. They are known to reduce the overall cache coherence traffic by forming queues of threads, each spinning on a separate memory location as they await their turn to access the critical section.

Current trends in multicore architecture design imply that in coming years, there will be an accelerated shift towards distributed nonuniform memory-access (NUMA) and cache-coherent NUMA (CC-NUMA) architectures. Such architectures, examples of which include Intel's 4 chip/32 way Nehalem-based systems and Oracle's 4 chip/256 way Niagara-based systems, consist of collections of computing cores with fast local memory (as found on a single multicore chip), communicating with each other via a slower (inter-chip) communication medium. Access by a core to the local memory, and in particular to a shared local cache, can be several times faster than access to the remote memory located on another chip [5].

Radović and Hagersten [5] were the first to show the benefits of designing locks that improve locality of reference on CC-NUMA architectures by developing *hierarchical locks*: general-purpose mutual-exclusion locks that encourage threads with high mutual memory locality to acquire the lock consecutively, thus reducing the overall level of cache misses when executing instructions in the critical section.

Radović and Hagersten introduced the hierarchical back-off lock (HBO): a *test-and-test-and-set* lock augmented with a new *backoff scheme* to reduce contention on the lock variable. Their hierarchical backoff mechanism allows the back-off delay to be tuned dynamically, so that when a thread notices that another thread from its own local cluster owns the lock, it can reduce its delay and increase its chances of acquiring the lock consecutively. However, because the locks are test-and-test-and-set locks, they incur invalidation traffic on every modification of the shared global lock variable, which is especially costly on NUMA machines. In their work [5], Radović and Hagersten did introduce a heuristic technique to throttle inter-chip coherence traffic. However, as we show in our evalution (Section 3), it does not necessarily translate to better scalability. Moreover, the dynamic adjustment of backoff delay time in the lock introduces significant starvation and fairness issues: it becomes likely that two or more threads from the same cluster will repeatedly acquire a lock while threads from other clusters starve. Radović and Hagersten also introduced a heuristic to improve fairness, but this requires fine tuning of the backoff parameters, which can change with the underlying application's characteristics.

Luchangco et al. [6] overcome these drawbacks by introducing a hierarchical version of the CLH queue-locking algorithm (HCLH). Their HCLH algorithm collects requests on each chip into a local CLH style queue, and then has the thread at the head of the queue integrate each chip's queue into a single global queue in a highly effective manner. This avoids the overhead of spinning on a shared location and eliminates fairness and starvation issues. The algorithm's drawback is that it forms the local queues of waiting threads by having each thread perform an atomic *register-to-memory-swap* (SWAP) operation[1] on the shared head of the local queue. These SWAPs to a shared location cause a bottleneck and introduce an overhead, implying that the thread merging the local queue into the global one must either wait for a long period (10s of microseconds) or globally merge an unacceptably short local queue. Furthermore, HCLH has complex condition checks along its critical execution path in order to determine if a thread must perform the operations of merging local CLH queues with the global queue. All of these drawbacks result in performance degradation, which takes away some of the benefits of the HCLH lock's locality of reference for operations in the critical section. Nevertheless, as we show empirically, the HCLH algorithm can improve on the original MCS and CLH locks, as well as the HBO lock, by a factor of 2 to 3.

This paper presents the *flat-combining MCS lock* (FC-MCS), a new hierarchical queue-lock design based on a combination of the flat-combining synchronization paradigm [7] and the MCS lock algorithm [3]. Flat combining is a novel mutual-exclusion based client-server style synchronization paradigm introduced to speed up operations on shared data structures. In this paper, we provide the first use of flat combining to add scalability to locks.

The key algorithmic breakthrough in our work is a new efficient way for threads to use a flat-combining methodology to build MCS-style local queues of waiting threads, each spinning on its own node, and then splice them seamlessly into a global MCS queue. In our new algorithm, threads spin on their local nodes while attempting to select one thread as a designated combiner. This combiner in turn constructs a local queue by collecting the requests of all spinning threads, and then splices this queue into the global one.

The use of the combiner approach at high concurrency levels allows our algorithm to overcome the main drawback of HCLH: threads are collected into the local queue quickly by allowing threads to post requests in parallel using only a simple write (without even a write-read memory barrier) to an unshared location, as opposed to using sequences of SWAP operations on a shared location to create the local queues in HCLH. This allows the combiner thread, the one putting together the local queue, to form relatively long local queues (empirically we found them to contain 90% of locally waiting threads), and to do so with little delay. Moreover, the common case critical path in the new algorithm is significantly shallower than HCLH, which, as is typical with locking algorithms, has a measurable effect on performance.

In a set of tests conducted on an Oracle SPARC Enterprise T5440 Server, a 256-way CC-NUMA multicore machine, we found that our new FC-MCS hierarchical locking algorithm significantly outperforms all prior locking algorithms. In particular FC-MCS can outperform the previous best hierarchical lock, the HCLH lock, by a factor of 2 at high concurrency levels.

The one drawback of our new FC locking algorithm is that unlike prior hierarchical locks, the use of the flat combining structure is not memory efficient: if multiple locks are being

accessed, a thread will have to keep a node per lock for any lock it is repeatedly accessing, and these nodes will be recycled only after a thread has ceased to access a given lock. Our new FC-based locks are therefore unsuited for applications in which memory resources are limited.

We describe our algorithm in detail in Section 2. This includes our basic algorithm that combines flat combining and MCS lock algorithms, and a key optimization that enables good performance at low contention levels. Section 3 presents our experimental results which show that our FC-MCS lock can outperform the best of existing locks by up to a factor of 2. We conclude in Section 4.

2. THE NEW HIERARCHICAL LOCK ALGORITHM

In this section, we describe our new flat-combining based hierarchical locking algorithm in detail. We assume that the system is organized into clusters of computing cores, each of which has a large cache that is shared among the cores local to that cluster, so that inter-cluster communication is significantly more expensive than intra-cluster communication. We use the term cluster to capture the collection of cores, and to make clear that they could be cores on a single multicore chip, or cores on a collection of multicore chips that have proximity to the same memory or caching structure; it all depends on the size of the NUMA machine at hand. We will also assume that each cluster has a unique *cluster id* known to all threads on the cluster.

Hendler et al. [7] showed how, given a sequential data structure, one can design a *flat combining* (henceforth FC) concurrent implementation of the structure that incurs very low synchronization overheads. The FC implementation uses mutual exclusion to repeatedly pick a unique "combiner" thread that will apply all other threads' operations to the structure. In our new FC-MCS algorithm we devise a simplified and streamlined variant of the FC algorithm and use it to effectively construct a local queue among threads in a given cluster. Combiners from various clusters will then repeatedly merge their local queues into a single global queue that will have virtually the same efficient handover structure as an MCS queue lock [3]. As we show, the use of flat combining will allow us to reduce overheads and introduce parallelism into the local queue creation process, and this parallelism, in turn, allows us to deliver improved performance.

2.1 Flat-Combining Local Queues

Our hierarchical FC-MCS lock consists of a collection of local flat-combining queues (FCQueues), one per cluster, and a single global queue (GlobalQueue). Figure 1 depicts an example of our lock construction for two clusters. We begin by describing the key elements of our algorithm, whose pseudocode appears in Figures 2 and 3. For the sake of clarity, some of the details presented here are omitted from the pseudocode.

As seen in Figure 1, each instance of a FCQueue consists of: a local FCLock, a *count* of the number of combining passes, a pointer to the *head* of a *publication list*, and pointers to the localHead and localTail of a sub-list. The publication list consists of thread specific nodes of a size proportional to the number of threads that are concurrently accessing the lock. Though one could implement the list in an array,

---

[1]On some architectures the SWAP operation is emulated using repeated *compare-and-swap* operations in a loop.

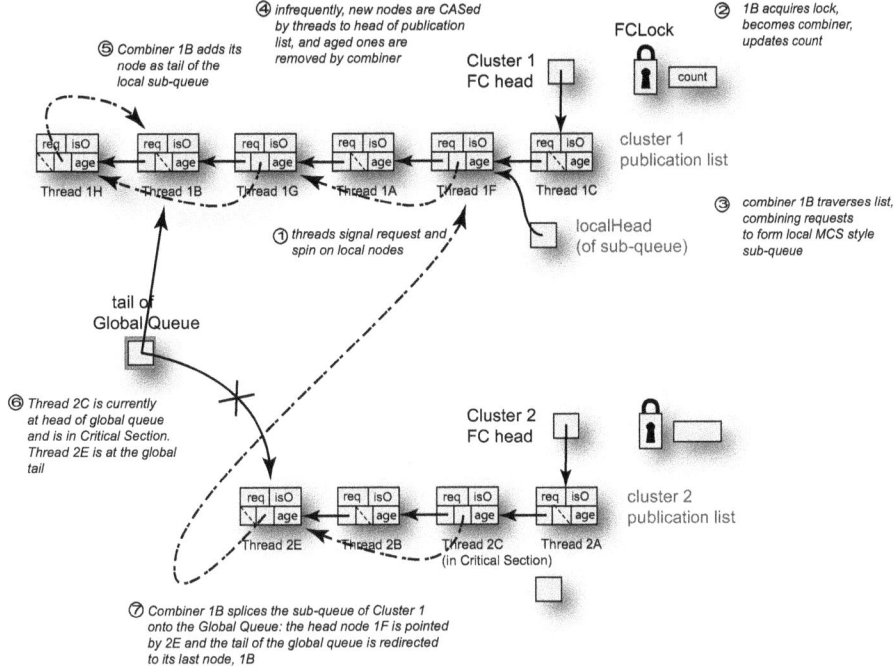

Figure 1: A Hierarchical FC Queue Lock for two clusters. At the start of the depicted scenario, Thread 2C is in the critical section. Upon release it will update the isOwner (isO in the figure) field of node 2E, which is at the tail of the global queue. The scenario starts when Thread 1B becomes a combiner in Cluster 1, collects a local list consisting of nodes 1F, 1G, and 1H. It then adds its own node 1B as the last in the sublist. Finally, it splices this sublist onto the global queue by setting node 2E to point to its local list head node 1F, and setting the globalTail to 1B. The global queue at the end of the scenario is the one along the dotted pointers.

the dynamic publication list using thread specific pointers is necessary for a practical solution because the number of potential threads is unknown, and is typically much greater than the array size. Using an array one would have forced us to solve a renaming problem [8] among the threads accessing it. This would imply a CAS per location, which would give us little advantage over existing techniques. We therefore have a list rather than an array.

Moreover, in our case, using the list has an important secondary advantage: the same nodes used in the flat combining publication list will be used in the sub-list of the MCS-style queue locking algorithm. This means that threads will spin on the same nodes in both the combining and lock-awaiting phases.

Each thread t accessing the local FCQueue in a cluster executes the following sequence of steps, which allows the construction of a local list of threads, each spinning on a given node, waiting for its predecessor to notify it that the critical section is free. The following then is the local FC-Queue algorithm for a given thread t:

1. Thread t first indicates its lock acquisition request in the requestReady field of its thread specific publication node (no need to use a load-store memory barrier). If t's thread specific publication node is marked as active, t continues to step 2, otherwise it continues to step 5.

2. t checks if the local FCLock is taken. If so (another thread is an active combiner), t spins on the requestReady field waiting for a response to the lock acquisition request (one can add a yield at this point to allow other threads on the same core to run). Once in a while, while spinning, t checks to see if the lock is still taken and that its publication node is active. If the node is inactive, t proceeds to step 5. Once the response is available (in the form of requestReady getting reset to false), t proceeds to spin on its isOwner field, waiting for it to be set by its predecessor thread in the queue.

3. If the local FCLock is not taken, t attempts to acquire it and become a combiner. On failure it returns to spinning in step 2.

4. Otherwise, t holds the FCLock and is the combiner. Thereafter, t

   - increments the combining pass *count* by one.
   - traverses the publication list (our algorithm guarantees that this is done in a wait-free manner) from the publication list head, combining all "ready" (indicated via the requestReady flag) acquisition requests into an ordered logical queue (pointed to by the localHead and localTail from Figure 2), setting the *age* of each of these nodes to the current *count*, and resetting the requestReady fields after notifying each thread who its successor in the list is, that is, the node it must notify upon leaving the global critical section.

```
myFCNode.isOwner = false;
myFCNode.canBeGlobalTail = false;
myFCNode.requestReady = true;

FCNode localTail = NULL;
FCNode localHead = NULL;

// lock acquire code
while (true) {
  if (myFCNode is inActive) {
    InsertFC(myFCNode);
  }
  if (FCQueue.FCLock not Acquired) {
    if (CAS(FCQueue.FCLock, Free, Acquired)) {
      if (myFCNode.requestReady) {
        // become the flat combiner
        FCQueue.count++;
        for MaxCombiningIterations do {
          for each FCNode in FCQueue do {
            if (FCNode.requestReady == true
                && FCNode != myFCNode) {
              // add FCNode to the local wait queue
              if (localHead == NULL) {
                localHead = FCNode;
                localTail = FCNode;
              } else {
                localTail.next = FCNode;
                localTail = FCNode;
              }
              FCNode.age = FCQueue.count;
              FCNode.requestReady = false;
            } else {
              if (FCQueue.count - FCNode.age >
                  threshold) {
                remove FCNode from FCQueue;
              }
            }
          }
        }
        // add combiner's FCNode to the local
        // wait queue
        localTail.next = myFCNode;
        localTail = myFCNode;
        myFCNode.canBeGlobalTail = true;
        myFCNode.requestReady = false;
        // splice the local wait queue into
        // the global wait queue
        prevTail= SWAP(globalTail, localTail));
        if (prevTail != NULL) {
          prevTail.next = localHead;
        } else {
          localHead.isOwner = true;
        }
      }
      // release the FCQueue.FCLock
      FCQueue.FCLock = Free;
    }
  }
  if (myFCNode.requestReady == false) {
    break;
  }
}
// wait to become the lock owner
while (myFCNode.FCLock.isOwner == false);
```

Figure 2: Acquiring an FC Hierarchical Lock.

- At the end of the traversal, t enqueues its node at the localTail of the local queue, and sets its node's canBeGlobalTail flag. As we describe later, this flag is used by the lock releaser to determine if it needs to read the globalTail during the lock

```
if (myFCNode.canBeGlobalTail == true) {
  while (true) {
    if (globalTail == myFCNode) {
      if (CAS(globalTail, myFCNode, NULL) == true) {
        // cleanup CAS succeeded
        break;
      }
    } else {
      // lock handoff
      if (myFCNode.next != NULL) {
        myFCNode.next.isOwner = true;
        break;
      }
    }
  }
} else {
  // lock handoff
  myFCNode.next.isOwner = true;
}
```

Figure 3: Releasing an FC Hierarchical Lock.

release operation. (In Figure 1, Thread 1B becomes a combiner in cluster 1, collects a local list consisting of nodes 1F, 1G, and 1H. It then adds its own node 1B as the last in the sublist.)

- If the *count* is such that a cleanup needs to be performed, t, during its traversal of the publication list, starting from the second item (as we explain below, we always leave the item pointed to by the *head* in the list), removes from the publication list all nodes whose *age* is much smaller than the current *count*. This is done by removing the node and marking it as inactive.

- Thread t releases the FCLock.

5. If thread t has no thread specific publication node, it allocates one, marked as active. If it already has one marked as inactive, it marks it as active. Thread t then executes a store-load memory barrier, and proceeds to insert its node into the head of the FC publication list by repeatedly attempting to perform a successful CAS on it. If and when t succeeds, it proceeds to step 1.

The combiner pass creates the local queue. As seen in cluster 1 in Figure 1, this local queue does not necessarily include all the nodes in the publication list. For example, node 1A is in the publication list but not in the local queue.

Notice that nodes are added to the publication list using a CAS only at the head of the list, and so a simple wait-free traversal by the combiner is trivial to implement [9]. Thus, the removal will not require any synchronization as long as it is not performed on the node pointed to from the head: the continuation of the list past this first node is only ever changed by the thread holding the global lock. Note that the first item is not an anchor or dummy node, we are simply not removing it. Once a new node is inserted, if it is unused it will be removed, and even if no new nodes are added, leaving it in the list will not affect performance.

The common case for a thread is that its node is active in the publication list and some other thread is the combiner, so it completes in step 2 after having only performed a store and a sequence of loads ending with a single cache miss. The end result is that there is a lot of parallelism, and little synchronization overhead, in the process of collecting nodes into the local queue, which in turn translates into reduced access time and longer local queues, giving our algorithm its advantage over the HCLH algorithm.

2.2 The Global Queue

Our global queue works in MCS style as opposed to the CLH style of HCLH. By this we mean that a thread spins on a field of its own node, notifies its successor upon leaving the critical section, and re-uses its own node in the next access attempt. This is in contrast with HCLH and CLH, where threads spin on the nodes of their predecessors, update their own node, and using their predecessor's released node in the next attempt. The choice of an MCS style lock is necessary and serves several roles in our algorithm: in the FC publication list, the lock access list, and the global queue. In order to remain in the publication list, a thread must use its own node repeatedly in all accesses, a property that holds for queuing in MCS style but not CLH style.

Our splicing approach into the global queue will create an MCS global queue, spanning all the clusters' local queues, in which each thread knows only of its immediate successor, and yet all nodes are ordered in a global way that enhances chances that nodes from a given cluster follow one another. As in the HCLH algorithm, this is key to our algorithm's ability to exploit data locality to achieve better performance. If one can form large collections of requests from the same cluster, the algorithm can minimizes the lock handoff intervals.

To create the global queue, each combiner splices the node pointed by the localTail of its local queue into the node at the global queue's (globalTail), logically moving an entire collection of nodes into the global queue. After splicing the sub-queue into the global queue, the combiner spins on its node's isOwner flag.

In the original MCS lock algorithm, a lock releaser checks the globalTail to determine if its node is the last in the MCS queue, and if so, CASes globalTail to null. We note that this lookup of globalTail may lead to a cache miss and a bus transaction if globalTail was last modified by a remote cluster thread. Furthermore, we also observe that in our algorithm, since the local queue combiner is at the localTail, no other node in that local queue can be the last node in the global MCS queue. Hence, none of the intermediate nodes in the sub-queue needs to make the above mentioned check of globalTail. We use the canBeGlobalTail field to indicate to a thread if its node can possibly be the last node in the global MCS queue. The combiner sets its node's canBeGlobalTail field to true, and then checks the globalTail in its lock release operation. All other threads do not need to do the check.

If the lock releaser's node has a successor, the releaser sets the successor's isOwner field to true, thus handing over the lock ownership.

2.3 Adjustments for Low Concurrency

The scheme we describe above works exceptionally well at high concurrency levels. However, at low concurrency levels, combining of requests into sufficiently large sub-queues becomes impossible, leaving the unwanted overhead of attempting to combine. Our solution is a simple one: at low concurrency levels let threads skip the attempt to combine and access the global queue directly. The elegant part in the FC-MCS algorithmic design is that the batches of nodes are added by combiners seamlessly, still maintaining the properties of an MCS queue with respect to all others, which allows

individual threads to access the global queue and add themselves to it in a straightforward manner. In the combined algorithm, threads can apply a simple local test to determine of they should combine or attempt to access the queue directly. Our choice was to have threads count the size of the sub-queue when they were last combiners, and if the size is low several times, they switch to direct access with high probability. If in some access the combined queue is large, they switch back.

In summary, our new FC hierarchical locking algorithm creates an MCS style global queue which, at high concurrency levels, builds long sublists of adjacent local nodes, delivering good locality of reference for threads accessing the critical section. It does so in a highly efficient way by parallelizing the process of creating the local sub-queues on each cluster using flat combining.

2.4 Comparison to HCLH

At a high level, the design of FC-MCS is very similar to that of HCLH: Build local wait queues. Designate a "master" for each local queue, which splices the local queue in the global queue. Finally, let each thread spin on its node (or its node's predecessor) to determine if the thread has acquired the lock.

However, we observe that there are two key differences between FC-MCS and HCLH:

- The methods of building the local queues are drastically different in HCLH and FC-MCS. The HCLH local queue is pretty much a CLH queue, where each thread atomically (using the SWAP instruction) adds itself in the queue. This leads to contention on the tail of the CLH queue, which, as we will see in Section 3, becomes a performance bottleneck. The FC-MCS local queue, however, is built by the combiner by simply perusing through the flat combining list. As a result, there is almost no synchronization required to build local queues; the exception being the atomic operation needed to determine the combiner thread (essentially a test-and-test-and-set lock acquisition). All the non-combiner threads simply post their requests (using a store instruction, without any store-load barriers) in their respective flat combining request nodes. This design methodology eliminates the contention bottleneck we observe in HCLH and all the other queue based locks, thus enabling greater parallelism in the local queue building process.

- In HCLH, after a thread enqueues its request in the local CLH queue, it spin waits on its node's predecessor to determine if it has become the lock owner. Because each thread needs to know if it is the local queue master the spin waiting logic is quite complicated, leading to several checks that appear in the critical path of the algorithm. This clearly adds to the latency of the lock handoff operation. On the other hand, the spin waiting of threads in FC-MCS is just like that of the MCS lock. The thread spins on its node's isOwner flag. This enables a much more streamlined and efficient lock handoff for FC-MCS.

Both the key differences, especially the first one, contribute to the drastically better performance (as we shall see in Section 3) of FC-MCS over HCLH.

3. EMPIRICAL EVALUATION

This section presents an empirical comparison of our new FC-MCS algorithm with the most efficient known locking algorithms, the CLH [2, 4] and MCS [3] queue locks, the HBO hierarchical backoff lock [5] and the HCLH hierarchical queue-lock [6]. Our collected data clearly shows that our algorithm outperforms all prior algorithms.

3.1 Methodology

We implemented all algorithms in C++, and compiled them with the Oracle Sun Studio 12.1 C++ compiler at optimization level xO5. The experiments were conducted on an Oracle T5440 series machine, which consists of 4 Niagara II chips, each chip containing 8 cores, and each core containing 8 hardware thread contexts, for a total of 256 hardware thread contexts running at a 1.4 GHz clock frequency. Each chip has an on board 4MB L2 cache, and each core has a shared 8KB L1 data cache.

To emphasize the impact of locality on these algorithms, we ensured that the threads in all workloads were evenly distributed among the 4 chips. For instance, for a test involving 32 threads, 8 threads were bound to each chip. This thread binding also helps ensure that the thread distribution is maintained throughout the runs. In all our tests, the main thread fires off a group of threads, each of which executes a critical region 100,000 times. Each iteration consists of a critical and a non-critical region, both of which can be configured differently to capture the behaviors of a diverse set of workloads.

We implemented our own versions of the mcs lock, clh lock, hbo lock, and naturally new-fc-mcs lock, and borrowed the highly tuned original hclh lock code developed by its authors [6].

3.2 Common Case: Scalability Under Standard Conditions

We first report the scalability results of a workload where each thread executes a counter increment (essentially a single read and a single write) in its critical region. Such short critical regions routinely occur in realistic workloads. The non-critical region consists of an idle spin loop for a randomly selected interval between 0 and 4 microseconds. This reflects a fair amount of work done between consecutive critical region executions, as is the case with most realistic applications.

Figure 4 depicts the performance of all the locking algorithms. Clearly, beyond 32 threads, the new-fc-mcs lock scales significantly better than all the others, improving on the mcs and clh locks by a factor of 4, and on hclh by a factor of 2 at high thread counts. Note that contrary to earlier results for the hclh lock [6], reported on a Sun E25K distributed memory machine, on our 256 way multicore architecture hclh significantly outperforms clh. We conjecture that this is due to threads sharing an L2 cache in our architecture, and therefore having a big win from locality of reference. As expected, at low thread counts, all the algorithms perform poorly because of the lack of pipelining in performing various synchronization operations. The non-critical region is large, and so throughput can only improve as concurrency increases since threads overlap executing the critical region with the lock acquisition operations and with execution of the non-critical region. As can be seen, below 32 threads, the new-fc-mcs lock performs similarly to the

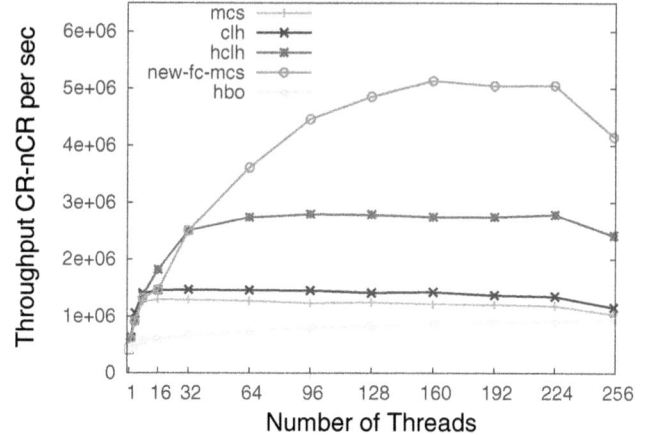

Figure 4: Average throughput in terms of number of critical and non-critical regions executed per second. In each critical region a thread increments a globally shared counter, while in the non-critical region it spins for a randomly selected interval of 0 to 4 microseconds.

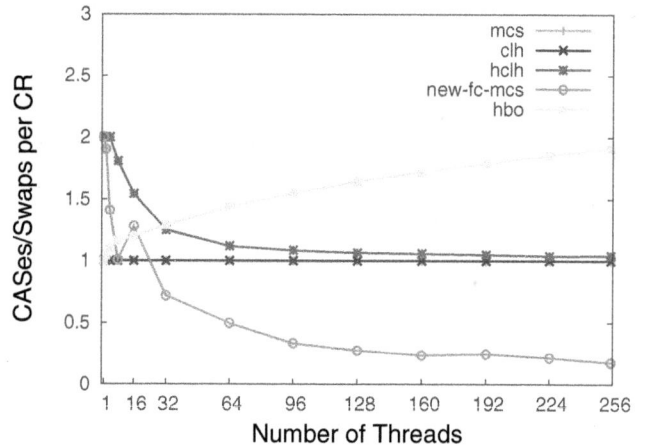

Figure 5: Average number of atomic CAS/SWAP instructions per critical region.

mcs lock: the low level of combining brings the adaptation mechanism into play, with threads skipping the combining attempts and directly accessing the global MCS lock.

Figures 5 and 6 help explain the superior performance of new-fc-mcs at high thread counts. The atomic read-modify-write operations (CAS and SWAP instructions) in all the algorithms are executed on shared locations and are thus indicative of bottlenecks. The average number of atomic read-modify-write instructions per critical region is drastically lower in new-fc-mcs compared to all other algorithms (Figure 5). In the mcs, clh, and hbo locks, all operations are applied sequentially on the same global location. The hbo algorithm suffers from increased CAS failures to an extent that overshadows the wins from improved cache locality. In the hclh lock, there is parallelism among local queues, but the building of the local CLH queues requires atomic oper-

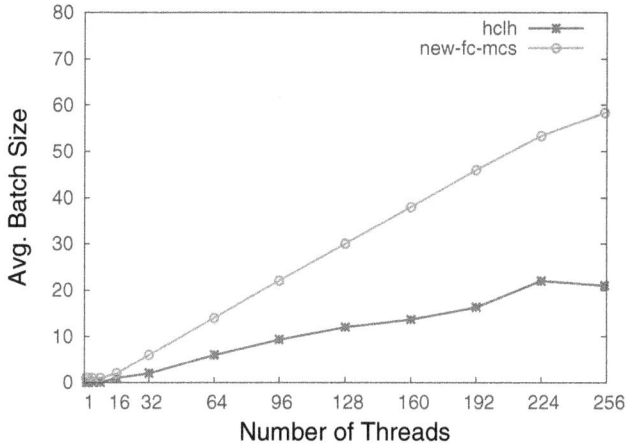

Figure 6: The average number of lock acquisition requests batched together by the combiner/master of each cluster. At low levels, we turned off the option to skip batching to expose the "natural" batching level. Since there is no batching of requests in mcs, clh, and hbo, we do not represent them in this graph.

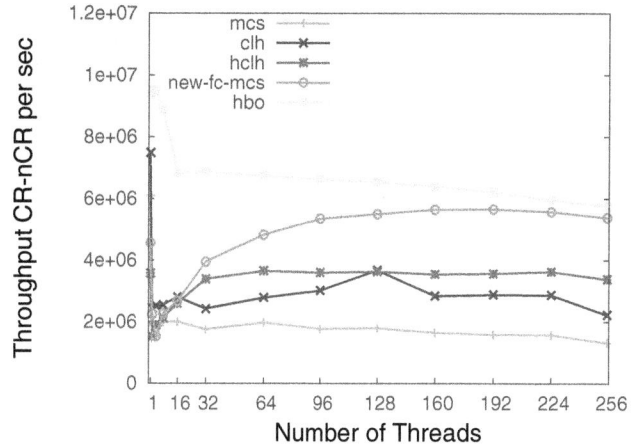

Figure 7: Average throughput of critical and non-critical region executions. Each thread's critical region and non-critical region are empty.

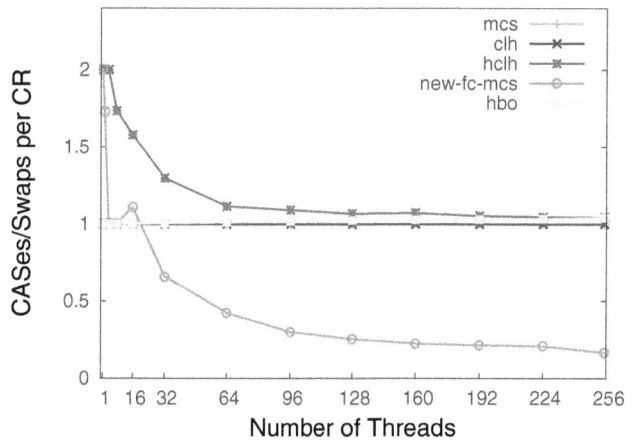

Figure 8: Average number of atomic CAS/SWAP instructions. Each thread's critical region and non-critical region are empty.

ations on the local queue's Tail pointer, which introduces a sequential bottleneck in the buildup of the local CLH queue. This bottleneck, as witnessed in Figure 6, results in smaller "batches" of local CLH queue nodes in the global CLH queue (the alternative of improving the batch size by having the local CLH queue master wait for longer intervals to get a decent sized batch, does not help noticeably improve latency either).

In new-fc-mcs, there is no bottleneck in posting requests, as threads apply simple write operations in parallel, which the combiner then picks up. The result, as witnessed in Figure 6, is a high level of batching where close to 90% of requests are batched, which explains the factor-of-two better performance of new-fc-mcs over hclh. At lower concurrency levels (see Figure 6), obtaining large batches is impossible. However, our low contention adaptation mechanism helps the threads "bypass" the flat combining phase and directly enqueue their requests into the global queue. As a result, we observe that new-fc-mcs tracks the performance of mcs at low threading levels, and thus continues to be competitive.

3.3 Stress Test: Scalability with Empty Critical and Non-Critical Regions

In order to stress-test all the locking algorithms, we ran an experiment with empty critical and non-critical regions. All threads essentially acquire and release the lock for a 100,000 times. Although the experiment is not a realistic workload, it helps us avoid the issue of non-critical work masking any lock operation latencies, thus enabling us to do a "bare bones" comparison between the different algorithms.

Figures 7, 8, and 9 depict the performance of all the locks in this workload. The performance trend is somewhat different than before: hbo outperforms all the other locks. We were initially surprised by this finding. However, on second thought this behavior makes sense: because remote threads have a bigger backoff range, the lock, upon being taken by a thread from a cluster, tends to remain in the cluster for

long intervals. In our experiments, we observed that the threads in a cluster are typically successful in locally acquiring and releasing the lock for about 10,000 times before a remote thread is able to acquire the lock. More importantly, because the non-critical region of this benchmark is empty, a lock releaser tends to quickly return to re-acquire the lock. As a result, the number of local lock acquisition requests, and their corresponding success rates (because of the backoff bias towards local threads), remain high at all times. This same behavior of hbo did not manifest itself in our earlier benchmark because of the non-zero duration of the non-critical region. This non-zero duration spaces apart the re-acquisition attempts of threads, and as a result, the number of local acquisition requests remains relatively low, and hence the chance of remote threads acquiring the lock increases.

For the remaining algorithms, as concurrency increases, mcs scales worst, followed by clh, followed by hclh, and fi-

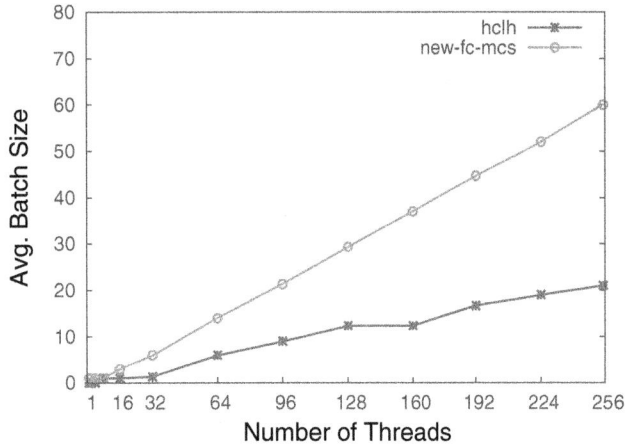

Figure 9: Average number of lock acquisition requests batched together by the combiner/master of each cluster. Since there is no batching of requests in mcs, clh, and hbo, we do not represent them in this graph.

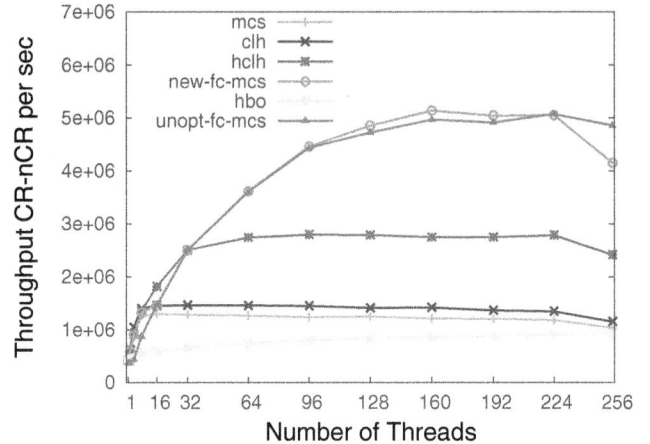

Figure 10: The throughput graph from Figure 4 with the curve for the unopt-fc-mcs variant of our algorithm.

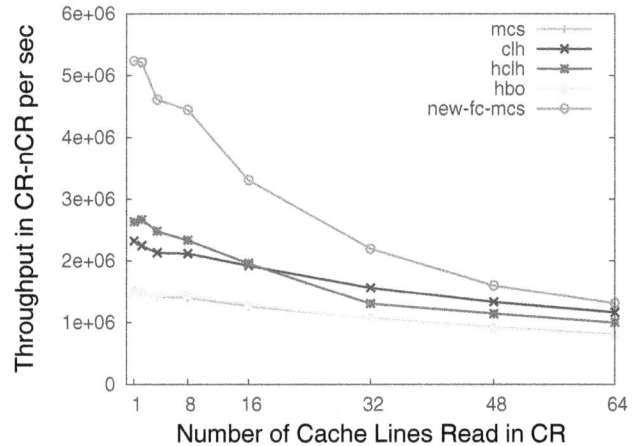

Figure 11: The effect of growing the footprint of the read-only critical region. The number of threads per test in this experiment was fixed at 248.

nally new-fc-mcs, which performs best. We attribute this to the same reasons as in the prior sub-section – lower numbers of atomic operations, and quicker batching of lock acquisition requests. It is interesting that even at this very high load, new-fc-mcs continues to deliver very large batch sizes (Figure 9) because of lower number of atomics (Figure 8), while the batch size of hclh drops because of relatively higher number of atomic operations.

We would like to mention an implementation detail of our algorithm that appears to be relevant here. During our experiments, we noticed that the effectiveness of the flat combining operation is sensitive to the arrival rate of the threads. If the thread arrival rate is low, the flat combiner must iterate more times through the flat combining queue in order to batch together sufficiently many requests. However, we must be careful to prevent the combiner from iterating through the flat combining queue too many times in order to avoid an increase in the latency of the locking operation. This involves a delicate dance to dynamically adapt the combiner's iteration limit (if the limit is N, the combiner iterates through the flat combining queue N times) to the underlying workload. To that end, we have implemented a simple heuristic that appears to do very well for the workloads we tested: after a flat combining operation, if the combiner determines that the ratio of the number of requests (batched together by the combiner) to the size of the flat combining queue is below a particular threshold (50% in our tests), the combiner increments the iteration limit. This increment is subject to a maximum ceiling (128 in our tests). Similarly, if the ratio goes beyond a particular threshold (90% in our tests), the iteration limit is decremented by the combiner if it is greater than 1.

3.4 Impact of Our Low Concurrency Optimization

As discussed at the end of Section 2, the basic FC-MCS lock suffers from significant overheads at low thread counts, which we avoid by switching to applying operations directly

to the global queue at low thread counts. Figure 10 shows the impact of not using our optimization, that is, always executing the combining operation, even in the absence of contention, on the same workload discussed in Section 3.2. Without the optimization (unopt-fc-mcs), the overhead of trying to combine dominates performance because there are not enough threads to combine. With the optimization, at low thread counts new-fc-mcs mimics the mcs lock behavior and continues tracking the performance of an unopt-fc-mcs at higher thread counts. Our optimization appears to be surprisingly effective for a wide range of workloads.

3.5 The Critical Region Footprint Effect

Our last set of experiments tests the effect of increasing the footprint of the critical region on the performance of the locks. We present results for two slightly different experiments. In both experiments, the footprint of the critical region increases from 1 cache-line to 64 cache-lines. In the

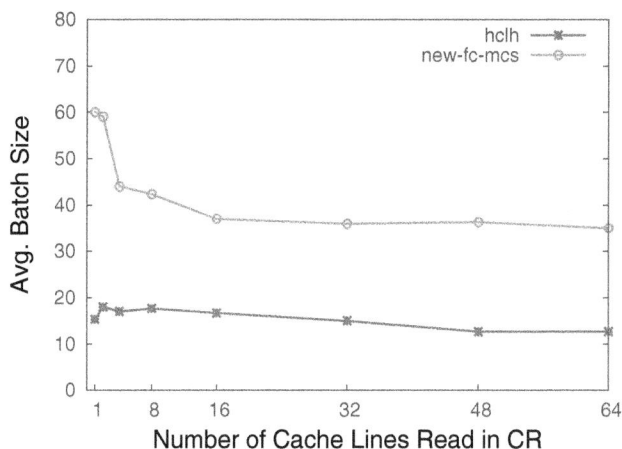

Figure 12: Average number of lock acquisition requests batched together by the combiner/master of each cluster for the growing read-only critical region. We represent data for only new-fc-mcs and hclh.

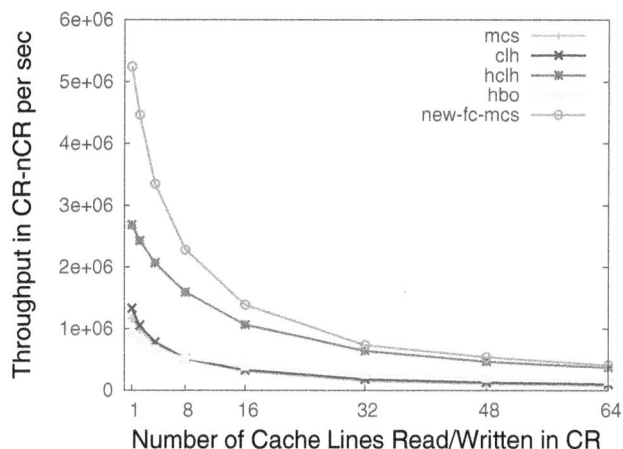

Figure 13: Effect of growing the footprint of the read-write critical region. The number of threads per test in this experiment was fixed at 248.

first experiment, the critical region only reads the shared variables (an integer counter on each cache line), whereas in the second experiment, the critical region both reads and writes the shared variables (incrementing an integer counter on each cache line). Each data point in the graphs represents a test run consisting of 248 threads, each repeatedly executing the critical region for 100,000 times. The non-critical region consists of an idle loop in which the thread spins for a randomly chosen interval between 0 and 4 microseconds.

Read-only Critical Regions.

Figure 11 depicts the effect of the growing footprint of the read-only critical region on the performance of all the locks. The new-fc-mcs lock continues to significantly outperform all other locks, starting with twice the performance of the other locks for small critical regions (1-4 cache lines). Notice however, that this performance gap dwindles as the critical region footprint (and consequently length) increases. We believe this is an expected result: Because the critical region is read-only, we expect all the cache-lines touched by it to be resident in host thread's L1 cache. Additionally, the locality benefits of new-fc-mcs and hclh, which remain more or less constant because the critical region is read-only, decline in a relative sense because the critical region length (and hence execution time) increases significantly (eventually its size becomes the dominating performance factor). Nevertheless, we observe that critical region lengths are typically small in real world applications, and new-fc-mcs is very effective in delivering much better throughput in that range – it outperforms all alternatives by a factor of 1.5 to 2 in the 1 to 16 read-only cache line range.

Figure 12 shows the average batching sizes of the new-fc-mcs and hclh locks for the tests reported in Figure 11. As in our previous experiments, new-fc-mcs is much more effective than hclh in batching lock acquisition requests. Notice the drop in batching size for new-fc-mcs. This is expected because as the length of the critical region increases, the interval between two lock acquisition attempts for each thread increases, and hence fewer threads are batched together by

the flat combiner. The batching size remains more or less constant for larger critical regions. We believe the heuristic we applied – to dynamically re-adjust the combiner's combining iterations based on the batching size – helps new-fc-mcs maintain the constant batching size. The batching size of hclh remains more or less constant.

Also notice that clh begins to outperform hclh at around 32 cache line sized critical regions. We believe that since the locality benefits of hclh become increasingly insignificant (given the increasing size of the read-only critical region), the expensive lock handoff operation in hclh (consisting of multiple conditional checks) starts to become an important performance concern. The lock handoff operation of clh is much more streamlined and efficient, which helps it outperform hclh for larger critical regions.

Because of the contention on the central test-and-test-and-set (TATAS) lock, hbo is unable to leverage any significant locality benefits, and ends up performing similar to mcs. To its credit, hbo significantly improves scalability over a simple TATAS lock (not shown here), enabling performance comparable to that of mcs.

Read-Write Critical Regions.

Figure 13 depicts the effect on throughput of the growing footprints of critical regions that modify the cache lines they access. As in the read-only experiment, new-fc-mcs outperforms all other locks for all critical region sizes. However, the pattern of the graphs is significantly different than that of the read-only experiment (Figure 11).

First, all the non-hierarchical locks incur huge performance costs compared to new-fc-mcs and hclh because of the coherence traffic generated by the continuously modified cache lines in the critical region. The new-fc-mcs and hclh locks significantly reduce the coherence traffic by effectively batching together lock acquisition requests coming from the same cluster. The hbo lock continues to suffer from contention on its central TATAS lock, and hence performs comparably to the non-hierarchical locks.

Second, although new-fc-mcs outperforms hclh by a factor of 2 with 1 cache line, this performance gap narrows rather

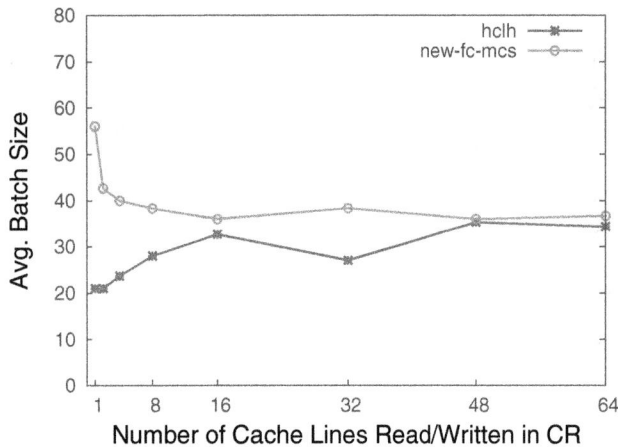

Figure 14: Average number of lock acquisition requests batched together by the combiner/master of each cluster for the growing read-write critical region. We represent data for only new-fc-mcs and hclh.

quickly as the number of lines is increased (with a difference of just about 25% at 16 cache lines, which dwindles down to about 10% at 64 cache lines). The explanation for this behavior appears in Figure 14 – the average batching size of new-fc-mcs decreases (much like in the read-only experiment), but more interestingly, the average batching size of hclh increases.

Reduction in the batching size of new-fc-mcs can be attributed to the increase in critical region length. However, the batching size increase for hclh appears to be counterintuitive. The explanation of this rather contradictory behavior of hclh lies in its implementation details: The hclh code is the original highly tuned implementation of hclh [6], which contains an interesting heuristic to help the master thread determine the amount of time it has to wait for more threads to join the local CLH queue. If the master determines that there was no other thread in its cluster that acquired the lock between its current and previous lock acquisition attempts, it halves the waiting time, assuming that the lock is lightly contended. Otherwise, if the master determines that no batching happened, it doubles the waiting time limit, assuming that it can do better batching the next time around. There are of course lower and upper bounds on the waiting time limits. What happens in the tests depicted in Figure 13 is that, since threads arrive at the lock (to acquire it) more slowly, the waiting time for the master effectively increases to a point where batching becomes more effective. This increase in batching size leads to better data locality, which helps "improve" the performance of hclh compared to that of new-fc-mcs. Note that since this is a read-write intensive critical region, data locality plays a critical role in a lock's performance. Thus, the benefits of better locality (achieved by better batching) outweigh the cost of waiting for longer durations in hclh.

Based on our finding, a natural question to ask is: Can we increase the waiting time for smaller critical regions to get better batching for hclh so as to get better locality and performance? Unfortunately that seems not be the case. Our testing indicates that hclh has to maintain a delicate balance

between the amount of waiting and the resulting batching sizes to guarantee the best possible performance. If the waiting time is too long, the master ends up worthlessly waiting for new threads that never show up in the duration, thus compromising some of the benefits of better locality. The hclh authors have developed a highly tuned implementation that takes all these factors into account.

In any case, we observe that new-fc-mcs performs substantially (a factor of 1.5 to 2 times) better than hclh for what we consider to be critical regions with reasonably large read-write memory footprints (1 to 4 cache lines).

4. CONCLUSION

The growing size of multicore machines is likely to shift the design space in the NUMA and CC-NUMA direction, requiring the development of appropriate concurrent algorithms and synchronization mechanisms. This paper tackles the most basic of the multicore synchronization algorithms, the lock, presenting a new NUMA directed algorithm. The new lock is based on a combination of the flat combining synchronization paradigm and the MCS lock that adapts and scales significantly better than any of the prior locks on a wide range of workloads. We hope this paper will help to revive the line of research on locks and synchronization structures directed at NUMA architectures.

5. REFERENCES

[1] Anderson, T.: The performance implications of spin lock alternatives for shared-memory multiprocessors. IEEE Trans. Parallel and Distributed Systems **1**(1) (1990) 6–16

[2] Craig, T.: Building FIFO and priority-queueing spin locks from atomic swap. Technical Report TR 93-02-02, University of Washington, Dept of Computer Science (1993)

[3] Mellor-Crummey, J., Scott, M.: Algorithms for scalable synchronization on shared-memory multiprocessors. ACM Trans. Computer Systems **9**(1) (1991) 21–65

[4] Magnussen, P., Landin, A., Hagersten, E.: Queue locks on cache coherent multiprocessors. In: Proc. 8th International Symposium on Parallel Processing (IPPS). (1994) 165–171

[5] Radović, Z., Hagersten, E.: Hierarchical Backoff Locks for Nonuniform Communication Architectures. In: HPCA-9, Anaheim, California, USA (2003) 241–252

[6] Victor Luchangco and Dan Nussbaum and Nir Shavit: A Hierarchical CLH Queue Lock. In: Proceedings of the 12th International Euro-Par Conference. (2006) 801–810

[7] Hendler, D., Incze, I., Shavit, N., Tzafrir, M.: Flat Combining and the Synchronization-Parallelism Tradeoff. In: Proceedings of the 22nd ACM Symposium on Parallelism in Algorithms and Architectures. (2010) 355–364

[8] Attiya, H., Bar-Noy, A., Dolev, D., Peleg, D., Reischuk, R.: Renaming in an Asynchronous Environment. J. ACM **37**(3) (1990) 524–548

[9] Herlihy, M., Shavit, N.: The Art of Multiprocessor Programming. Morgan Kaufmann (2007)

Location-Based Memory Fences

Edya Ladan-Mozes   I-Ting Angelina Lee

MIT CSAIL
32 Vassar Street, Cambridge, MA 02139
{edya, angelee}@csail.mit.edu

Dmitry Vyukov*

OOO Google
7 Balchug Street, Moscow, 115035, Russia
dvyukov@google.com

ABSTRACT

Traditional memory fences are program-counter (PC) based. That
is, a memory fence enforces a serialization point in the program
instruction stream — it ensures that all memory references before
the fence in the program order have taken effect before the execution continues onto instructions after the fence. Such PC-based
memory fences always cause the processor to stall, even when the
synchronization is unnecessary during a particular execution. We
propose the concept of *location-based memory fences*, which aim
to reduce the cost of synchronization due to the latency of memory
fence execution in parallel algorithms.

Unlike a PC-based memory fence, a location-based memory
fence serializes the instruction stream of the executing thread T_1
only when a different thread T_2 attempts to read the memory location which is guarded by the location-based memory fence. In
this work, we describe a hardware mechanism for location-based
memory fences, prove its correctness, and evaluate its potential
performance benefit. Our experimental results are based on a software simulation of the proposed location-based memory fence, and
thus expected to incur higher overhead than the proposed hardware mechanism would. Nevertheless, our software experiments
show that applications can benefit from using location-based memory fences, but they do not scale as well in some cases, due to the
software overhead. These results suggest that a hardware support
for location-based memory fences is worth considering.

Categories and Subject Descriptors: C.1.m [Processor Architec-
tures]: Miscellaneous; D.1.3 [Programming Techniques]: Concurrent Programming—*Parallel programming*

General Terms: Design, Performance, Theory

Keywords: location-based memory fences, memory fences, asymmetric synchronization, the Dekker duality, the Dekker protocol,
biased locks

---

*This work was conducted by the author outside of Google.

This research was supported in part by the National Science Foundation
under Grant CNS-1017058 and in part by the Angstrom Project funded by
the Defense Advanced Research Projects Agency UHPC program under
Agreement Number HR0011-10-9-0009.

```
                   Initially L1 = L2 = 0;

        Thread 1                      Thread 2
T1.1   L1 = 1;              T2.1   L2 = 1;
T1.2   if(L2 == 0) {        T2.2   if(L1 == 0) {
T1.3     /* critical        T2.3     /* critical
T1.4       section */       T2.4       section */
T1.5   }                    T2.5   }
T1.6   L1 = 0;              T2.6   L2 = 0;
```

Figure 1: A simplified version of the Dekker protocol (omitting the mechanism to allow the threads to take turns), assuming sequential consistency.

1. INTRODUCTION

On many modern multicore architectures, threads [1] typically
communicate and synchronize via shared memory. Classic synchronization algorithms such as Dekker [10], Dijkstra [9], Lamport
(Bakery) [18], and Peterson [22] use simple load-store operations
on shared variables to achieve mutual exclusion among threads. All
these algorithms employ an idiom, referred as the ***Dekker duality*** [6], in which every thread writes to a shared variable to indicate
its intent to enter the critical section and reads the other's variable
to coordinate access to the critical section.

Crucially, the correctness of such idiom rely on that the memory
model exhibits ***sequential consistency*** (SC) [19], where all processors observe the same sequence of memory accesses, and within
this sequence, the accesses made by each processor appear in its
program order. While the SC memory model is the most intuitive
to the programmer, existing systems typically implement weaker
memory models that relax the memory ordering to achieve higher
performance. The reordering does not affect the correctness of software execution for the most part, but in some cases, such as in the
Dekker duality, it is important that the execution follows the program order, and the processors observe the relevant accesses in the
same relative order.

Consider the following code segment shown in Figure 1, which
is a simplified version of the Dekker protocol [10][2] using the idiom
to synchronize access to the critical section among two threads.
If the read in line T1.2 gets reordered with the write in line T1.1
(and similarly for Thread 2), or if Thread 1 and Thread 2 observe
different order of when the writes (lines T1.1 and T2.1) occur, an

---

[1] Throughout the paper, we use the terms thread and processor interchangeably. In particular, we use thread in the context of describing an algorithm
and processor in the context of describing hardware features.
[2] This simplified version is vulnerable to livelock, where both threads simultaneous try to enter the critical section — each thread sets its own flag, reads
the other thread's flag, retreats, and retries. Without some way of breaking
the tie, the two threads can repeatedly conflict with each other and retry
perpetually. The full version is augmented with mechanism to allow the
threads to take turns and thus guarantees progress. For the sake of clarity,
we present the simplified version here.

incorrect execution may result, causing the two threads to enter the critical section concurrently.

To ensure a correct execution in such cases, these architectures provide serializing instructions and memory fences to force a specific memory ordering when necessary. Thus, a correct implementation of the Dekker protocol for such systems would require a pair of memory fences between the write and the read (between lines T1.1 and T1.2, and lines T2.1 and T2.2 in Figure 1), ensuring that the write becomes visible to all processors before the read is executed. Memory fences are costly, however, taking many more cycles to complete than regular reads and writes. Furthermore, a memory fence incurs overhead on the program execution even when the program is executed serially, or when the synchronization is unnecessary. For instance, the overhead incurred by the fence is unnecessary if only one thread intends to enter the critical section, and its write eventually becomes visible before another thread tries to enter the critical section.

Traditional implementation of memory fences is program-counter (PC) based. One cannot avoid the overhead incurred by a PC-based memory fence: upon execution the processor must stall, waiting for all outstanding writes before the fence in the instruction stream to become globally visible. The stalling is unnecessary, however, when no other threads are performing a read on these updated memory locations. In this work, we propose a **location-based memory fence**, which causes the executing thread to "serialize" only when another thread tries to access the memory location associated with the memory fence. Location-based memory fences aim to reduce the latency in program execution incurred by memory fences. Unlike a PC-based memory fence, a location-based memory fence is *conditional* and *remotely enforced* — whether the executing thread serializes the memory accesses or not depends on whether there exists another thread that attempts to access the memory location associated with the memory fence.

Applications that employ the Dekker duality can benefit from location-based memory fences. While the Dekker duality seems to apply only to applications that synchronize between two threads, the idiom is commonly used to optimize applications involving multiple threads that exhibit **asymmetric synchronization patterns**, where one thread, the **primary thread**, enters a particular critical section much more frequently than the other threads running in the same process, referred as the **secondary threads**. Such applications typically employ an augmented version of the Dekker protocol: the secondary threads first compete for the right to synchronize with the primary thread (by grabbing an ordinary lock); once obtaining the right, the winning secondary thread then synchronizes with the primary thread using the Dekker protocol. The augmented Dekker protocol intends to speedup the execution path of the primary thread, even at the expanse of the secondary threads; therefore, it is particularly desirable to optimize away the overhead of memory fences on the primary thread's execution path, when the application executes serially or when there is no contention.

Many examples of such applications exist. For example, Java Monitors are implemented with biased locking [7, 16, 21], which uses an augmented version of the Dekker protocol to coordinate between the bias-holding thread (primary) and a revoker thread (secondary). Java Virtual Machine (JVM) employs the Dekker duality to coordinate between mutator threads (primary) executing outside of JVM (via Java Native Interface) and the garbage collector (secondary) [7]. In a runtime scheduler that employs a work-stealing algorithm [2–5, 11, 12, 17], the "victim" (primary) and a given "thief" (secondary) coordinate the steal using an augmented Dekker-like protocol. Finally, in network package processing applications, each processing thread (primary) maintains its own data

structures for its group of source addresses, but occasionally, a thread (secondary) might need to update data structures maintained by a different thread [23].

Such applications motivate our study of location-based memory fences. In these applications, we would like to tune the algorithm so that the primary thread operates on the fast path and avoid the overhead of memory fences when possible; only when a secondary thread attempts to enter the critical section, the secondary thread takes measures to ensure that the primary thread serializes, thereby achieving synchronization.

To evaluate the feasibility of location-based memory fences, we use a software prototype to simulate the effect of location-based memory fences and evaluate two applications with the software prototype. While the software implementation incurs higher overhead than the proposed hardware mechanism would, our experiments show that applications still benefit from the software implementation. These results suggest that a hardware support for location-based memory fences is worth considering.

The rest of the paper is organized as follows. Section 2 gives a abbreviated background on why reordering occurs in architectures that support a weaker memory model. Section 3 presents the proposed hardware mechanism for location-based memory fences. Section 4 formally defines the specification of location-based memory fences, proves that the proposed hardware mechanism implements the specification, and lastly shows that the Dekker protocol using location-based memory fences provides mutual exclusion. Section 5 evaluates the feasibility of location-based memory fences using a software prototype implementation with two applications. Section 6 gives a brief overview on related work. Finally, Section 7 draws concluding remarks.

2. STORE BUFFERS AND MEMORY ACCESSES REORDERING

In this section, we briefly review features of modern architecture design, which are necessary for our proposed hardware mechanism for location-based memory fences. In particular, throughout the rest of the paper, we assume that the target architecture implements either the Total-Store-Order (TSO) model (implemented by SPARC-V9 [24]) or the Process-Ordering (PO) model (implemented by Intel 64, IA-32 [15], and AMD64 architectures [1]). We also describe how **memory reordering** can occur, i.e., how the observable order in which memory locations are accessed can differ from the program order. Memory reordering can be introduced either by the compiler or the underlying hardware. Compiler fences that prevent the compiler from reordering have relatively small overhead, whereas the memory fences that prevent the reordering at the hardware level are much more costly. In this section, we focus on the reordering at the hardware level.

The target architecture we are considering supports out-of-order execution, but "commits" executed instructions in order. While the underlying hardware can freely reorder instructions, the result of committed instructions must still obey rules defined by the memory model implemented by the hardware. Specifically, the TSO and PO models conform to the following ordering principles for regular reads and writes issued by a given processor:[3]

1. Reads are not reordered with other reads;
2. Writes are not reordered with older reads;

---

[3]There are more ordering principles when one considers the interleaving of memory accesses issued by multiple processors and when one accounts for serializing instructions and memory fences; for the purpose of explaining the hardware mechanism, we only include a relevant subset. We refer interested readers to [1, 15, 24] for full details.

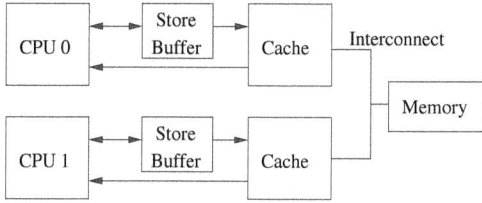

Figure 2: A simplified illustration of the relationship between the CPUs, the store buffers, and the memory hierarchy. Each CPU is connected with its own private cache. In addition, a store buffer is placed between the CPU and the cache, so that a write issued by the CPU is first stored in the store buffer and flushed out to the cache at later time. A read may be served by the cache, or by the store buffer if the store buffer contains a write to the same target address as the read.

3. Writes are not reordered with other writes; and

4. Reads may be reordered with older writes if they have different target locations (but they are not reordered if they have the same target location).

Principle 4 violates the Dekker duality, because it allows the read in line T1.2 of Figure 1 to appear to Thread 2 as if it has occurred before line T1.1, even though it appears as executed in order for Thread 1. The reason behind Principle 4 is to allow a typical optimization that modern architectures implement — writes performed by the processing unit are queued up in a private store buffer, which is a first-in-first-out (FIFO) queue instead of being written out to the memory hierarchy.

Figure 2 is a simplified illustration of the relationship between the processors (CPUs), the store buffers, and the memory hierarchy. Though not explicitly shown in Figure 2, the memory hierarchy in modern architectures typically consists of several levels of private and shared caches and the main memory. The further away the memory hierarchy is from the processor, the higher the latency it incurs. The use of a store buffer improves the performance of the program, because writing to a store buffer avoids the latency incurred by writing out to the cache. A write in the store buffer is only visible to the executing processor but not to other processors, however. Thus, from other processors' perspective, it appears as if the read has taken place before the older write (in program order). On the contrary, assuming that a cache coherence protocol is employed, a write becomes globally visible once its written to the cache, since the coherence protocol mandates accesses to data and enforces sequentially consistent view of the accessed data among the caches of all processors. As required by the proposed hardware mechanism for location-based memory fences, we assume that the target architecture employs the MESI cache coherence protocol [15], although the mechanism can be adapted to other variants such as MSI [13] and MOESI [1].

Now we define more precisely what we mean by committing the executed instructions in order. A read instruction is considered to be **committed** once the data is available (in at least Shared state) in the processor's private cache. A read may be speculatively executed out of order, but it must be committed in order. That is, the processor may perform a speculative read and fetch the cache line early, but if the cache line gets invalidated between the speculative read and when the read should commit in program order, the processor must reissue the read and fetch the cache line again. Once a read is committed successfully, the read value can be used in subsequent instructions.

A write instruction, on the other hand, has two phases: "committed" and "completed." A write is considered to be **committed** once it is written to the store buffer, although its effect is not yet visible by other processors. A write is considered to be **completed**,

when it is flushed from the store buffer and written to the processor's cache. Once a write is completed, its effect becomes globally visible, since the cache coherence protocol ensures that all processors have a consistent view (the processor must gain Exclusive state on the flushed location before it update the value in the cache).

Since the guarantee is only that instructions must be committed in order, once the write is committed, the processor is free to continue executing subsequent instructions. A subsequent read instruction (with a different target address) may freely commit, even though an older write may still be in the store buffer. Thus, the resulting behavior observable by the other processors is that the read appears to have taken place before the older write.

The executing processor does not observe this reordering and always sees its own write, however, since the hardware employs **store-buffer forwarding**, so that a read with a target address that appears in the store buffer is serviced by the store buffer instead of by the cache. The store-buffer forwarding also enforces the ordering principle that a read is not reordered with an older write if they have the same target address. Furthermore, due to store-buffer forwarding, when two writes from two processors, say P_1 and P_2, interleave, the write ordering observed by P_1 may differ from the write ordering observed by P_2, because each processor always sees its own write as soon as it commits, but not the write performed by the other processor until the write reaches the cache.[4]

Whenever the system bus is available, the store buffer flushes the oldest entry to memory, so that each write becomes complete in FIFO order, ensuring that a write is never reordered with other writes (Principle 3). In the event that a context switch, an interrupt, or a serializing instruction (e.g., a memory fence) is encountered, the entire store buffer is drained as well, stalling the processor until all writes in the store buffer become globally visible.

3. LOCATION-BASED MEMORY FENCES

In this section, we describe location-based memory fences, or `l-mfence` in detail, including its informal specification, usage, and a proposed hardware implementation. The formal specification, as well as a correctness proof, is presented in Section 4. The proposed hardware mechanism that implements the `l-mfence` assumes an underlying architecture as described in Section 2.

Informal Specification and Usage of l-mfence

To describe the informal specification of `l-mfence`, we need to digress a bit and first describe the specification of an ordinary memory fence, or `mfence`. In Section 4 we give a formal definition of these ordering before we formally define the specification of the `l-mfence`.

The `mfence` instruction can be used to prevent other processors from observing reordering of the executing processor's instruction stream, at the point of a `mfence` execution — `mfence` simply forces the processor to stall until its store buffer is drained, flushing all its entries out to the cache in FIFO order. We say that the executing processor "serializes" its instruction stream at the point of `mfence`, meaning that the executing processor completes all the memory accesses prior to `mfence`, before executing instructions after `mfence`.

An `l-mfence`, unlike an ordinary memory fence, executes a memory fence "on demand." It takes in two inputs: a location l guarded by the fence and a value v to store in l (see Figure 3(a)), and it serializes the instruction stream of the executing processor only when another processor attempts to access the guarded memory location.

---

[4]While P_1 and P_2 may observe different orders, the other processors in the system will observe a consistent ordering of the two writes.

	Primary Thread		Secondary Thread

```
K1   l-mfence(&L1,1);        J1   L2 = 1;
K2   if(L2 == 0) {           J2   mfence();
K3       /* critical         J3   if(L1 == 0) {
K4          section */        J4       /* critical
K5   }                       J5          section */
K6   L1 = 0;                 J6   }
                             J7   L2 = 0;
```

(a)

Instruction translation for l-mfence(L1,1) (line K1 in Thread 1)

```
K1.1   MOV LEBit <- 1         //set LEBit
K1.2   MOV LEAddr <- &L1      //LEAddr gets addr of l
K1.3   LE  &L1                //load l in E mode
K1.4   ST  [&L1] <- 1         //store l=v
K1.5   BNQ LEBit, 0, DONE     //Go to DONE if LEBit != 0
K1.6   MFENCE                 //else execute mfence
K1.7   DONE:
K1.8   //the rest of the program (line K2)
```

(b)

Figure 3: (a) The asymmetric Dekker protocol using location-based memory fences. The code for the primary thread is shown in lines K1–K6, and the code the secondary thread is shown in lines J1–J7. (b) The instructions generated for l-mfence shown in line K1 in the code for the primary thread in (a).

The serialization of P's instruction stream enforces a relative ordering between the store S associated with the execution of l-mfence and the other accesses performed by P. The ordering between S and an access A are observed consistently across processors, including the processor executed the l-mfence and A. That is, from P's perspective, if P executed S before (after) A, all processors observe that S "happened" before (after) A. The serialization does not enforce any relative ordering between accesses that happen before (after) S, however, meaning that the l-mfence ensures that all processors (including P) consistently observe that A_1 and A_2 happened before (after) S, but they may not have a consistent view of the relative ordering between A_1 and A_2. The relative ordering between these accesses is still defined by the TSO / PO memory model.

The use of l-mfence is very similar to the use of mfence, except that the l-mfence is associated with a specific store. A in mfence, when l-mfence is used in the program, an implicit compiler fence should be inserted in place to prevent reordering at the compiler level. Threads synchronizing via l-mfence need to coordinate with each other and be careful as to where to place the l-mfence and which memory location to guard / read after. Since a l-mfence does not guarantee atomic read-modify-write operation, its correct usage typically involves single writer only. Note that l-mfence prevents other processors from observing the reordering of the executing processor's instruction stream, but it does not prevent the executing processor from observing reordering of other processors' instruction streams. Therefore, correct usages of l-mfence typically consist of a pair of memory fences. For instance, to ensure correct execution in the case of the Dekker protocol, it is crucial that *both* processors insert memory fences between the write and the read, to prevent the other processor from observing reordering. For l-mfence, the pairing can be with either another l-mfence or an ordinary mfence.

Hardware Implementation of l-mfence

Our proposed implementation of l-mfence requires a new hardware mechanism, called *load-exclusive / store*, or *LE/ST*. Conceptually, the LE/ST mechanism allows the processor to setup a "link" to keep track of the status of the store associated with the l-mfence (i.e., whether the store to guarded location is committed

or completed as defined in Section 2). It also allows the processor to coordinate with the cache controller to monitor attempts to access the guarded location. Another processor's attempt to access the guarded location causes the processor to clear the link and triggers actions necessary to serialize the instruction stream. On the other hand, if the store becomes complete before another processor attempts to access the guarded location, the processor clears the link and thus stops guarding the location.

LE/ST requires one new instruction and two additional hardware registers. The new instruction, LE, takes one operand — the location of the variable to load, and obtains Exclusive state on that location. Therefore, once LE is *committed*, the processor has the location in its cache in Exclusive state, and no other processors have a valid copy of the location in their cache. Since LE is very similar to a regular load, except the requirement for Exclusive state on the location, it can be easily implemented by modern architectures using the MESI coherency protocol. The two additional hardware registers are LEBit and LEAddr, both readable and writable by the processor, and readable by the cache controller. The processor must update these register to enable the link and guard the memory location specified by the l- mfence. First we describe how the processor updates these registers to setup the link, and then we describe how the processor and the cache controller coordinate with each other to guard the memory location.

Figure 3(b) presents the assembly-like translation for the l-mfence(l,v) where $l == L1$ and $v == 1$.[5] Initially, LEBit and LEAddr are cleared. As part of the l-mfence(&L1,1), the processor starts to create the link to the guarded location by setting the LEBit with 1 and LEAddr with L1 (lines K1.1 and K1.2 in Figure 3(b)). Next, the LE instruction in line K1.3 loads L1 into the cache in Exclusive state, so that no other processor holds a copy of L1 in its cache. At this point we say that the link is set. The ST instruction in line K1.4 stores the value 1 to L1, committing it into the store buffer. If for any reason the link is broken, implied by the zero value in LEBit (line K1.5), the processor executes a MFENCE (line K1.6). The MFENCE causes the processor to serialize its execution — it flushes the store buffer, and by that it completes the store of the guarded location, making it globally observable by other processors. If the link is not broken when the ST in line K1.4 commits, the processor may continue without flushing the store buffer.

We now explain how the cache controller interacts with the processor to guard the location stored in LEAddr. Whenever both LEBit and LEAddr are set, the cache controller listens to cache coherency traffic, and notifies the processor if any request requires the controller to either (1) downgrade the cache line corresponding to the memory location stored in LEAddr from Exclusive state; or (2) evicts the cache line. The cache controller then waits for the processor's response before it takes any actions regarding the guarded location, since these events break the link to the guarded location.

When the processor receives the notification from the cache controller, it clears the LEBit and LEAddr, flushes the store buffer, and replies to the cache controller. At the time the processor replies the cache controller, the most up-to-date value of the guarded location is already in the cache. When the cache controller gets the processor's reply, it resumes the actions it needs to take regarding the guarded location. By clearing the LEBit, the processor remembers that the link to the guarded location is broken. In the event that the link is broken before ST (line K1.4) was committed, the code for

---

[5]The code shown is not strictly assembly. First, we are not using a particular instruction set. Second, for the sake of clarity, we choose to use the store instruction (line K1.4) instead of using the regular move instructions to specify instructions that write to memory (i.e., non registers).

l-mfence takes the branch that executes an MFENCE, causing the store buffer to flush (line K1.5) after the store commits.

The link remains set for as long as the primary processor still has the cache line, until the corresponding store to the guarded location is complete. When the corresponding store in the store buffer is flushed, possibly due to other internal reasons (for instance, the store is naturally flushed as the oldest entry in the buffer, the buffer is full, or a context switch occurs), upon completing the store, the processor also clears LEBit and LEAddr. The guarded location can still remain in the cache in Exclusive (or Modify) state if there is no request to evict or downgrade it.

In the context of the Dekker protocol, since LE ensures that the primary processor has the cache line for L1 in Exclusive state before the ST in line K1.4, its cache controller must receive a downgrade request from a secondary processor before the secondary processor can access L1. Furthermore, since the cache controller of the primary processor cannot respond to the downgrade request until the primary processor replies, the secondary processor will see the most up-to-date value of L1. Essentially, we piggyback on the cache coherence protocol to detect another processor's attempt to access the guarded location. We also rely on the coherency protocol to deliver the most up-to-date value to the other processor, since the store buffer is flushed before the cache controller replies to the secondary processor. It is necessary for the cache controller to notify the processor when it needs to evict the cache line, since the cache controller can no longer help guarding the memory location, if the given cache line is evicted.

The design of this hardware mechanism is intended to be lightweight and efficient. Since we assume only one pair of LEBit and LEAddr are allocated per processor, if a processor encounters a second LE/ST while the link from the first LE/ST is still in effect, the processor must flush the store buffer, clear LEBit and LEAddr, before it can proceed with the second LE/ST. *unless* the second LE/ST has the same target load address as the first LE/ST.

Expected Overhead of the LE/ST Mechanism

The LE/ST mechanism ensures that the primary processor, when running alone, will not execute any memory fences, and perform only regular stores; it still needs to perform LE regardless, but that should not incur much overhead — the hope is that the target cache line of LE stays in the primary processor's cache. Furthermore, the target cache line of LE only gets invalidated whenever the secondary processor attempts to enter the critical section. Assuming the secondary processor synchronizes infrequently, the target cache line stays in primary processor's cache between the secondary processor's synchronization attempts. Finally, the primary processor flushes the store buffer only when the secondary processor attempts to enter the critical section when the link is in effect, so the primary processor should perform regular store for the most part. On the other hand, the secondary processor could stall for a while when waiting for the primary processor to flush its store buffer, but the assumption is that the secondary processor can incur overhead if it improves the performance of the primary processor.

If the secondary processor synchronizes frequently, each use of l-mfence may result in one store buffer flush, which is comparable to a regular mfence. There is once case in which the /Fast processor will flush the buffer twice – if a downgrade request (due to a secondary processor attempts to access the guarded memory location) arrives at the primary processor between the commit of LE (line K1.3) and ST (line K1.4). The first flush is performed when the processor is notified, and the second flush is performed after the ST commits, via taking the branch (lines K1.5 and K1.6). During the first flush, the guarded location is not committed to the store buffer yet. We choose to flush the store buffer at this point, because it results a more intuitive specification for the l-mfence. The second flush, on the other hand, is essential to guarantee correctness. Without the second flush, one could construct a scenario in which the secondary processor enters the critical section twice, once before the primary processor commits its store to L1 and once after, wrongfully allowing both processors to execute in the critical section concurrently. Even though the processor flushes the store buffer twice, the second flush contains only on location, the guarded location.

Lastly, the cache controller needs to compare the incoming request from cache coherence traffic against the address stored in LEAddr when the LE/ST mechanism is in effect. We believe that this comparison can be done in parallel with other operations that the cache controller already performs to handle the request, and thus it should not incur additional performance penalty.

4. FORMAL SPECIFICATION AND CORRECTNESS OF L-MFENCE

In this section, we formally define the specification of l-mfence and prove that the hardware mechanism described in Section 3 implements the specification.[6] Then, based on the specification of l-mfence, we prove that the asymmetric Dekker Protocol using l-mfence (as shown in Figure 3(a)) achieves mutual exclusion.

Formal Specification of l-mfence

To formally define the specification of l-mfence, we first define the *serialization order* for a given memory location.

DEFINITION 1. *Given a memory location l, the **serialization order** of accesses to l performed by all processors is as follows.*

 1. *A load L from location l is **serialized after** a store S of v to l if and only if L observes v.*
 2. *A store S of v to location l performed by a processor P is **serialized after** a store S' of v' to l if at the time of **completion** of S, had P executed a load, the load would have observed v' from S'.*
 3. *A load L from l is **serialized before** a store S of v to l if there exists a store S' to l such that L is serialized after S', and S is also serialized after S'.*

Note that the serialization order involving stores are defined by the time of completion, not commit. To complete a store of v to l, the executing processor P must gain Exclusive state on l, and thus it can be viewed as if the store was preceded by a load from l, since the value of l exists in P's cache in Exclusive state. Furthermore, since the serialization order on a location l is defined by the completion time of stores, all processors agree on a single serialization order.

Definition 1 defines the serialization order on a given memory location that is globally consistent. *Program order*, on the other hand, is defined for a given processor, which is the order of memory accesses occurred in a processor P's instruction stream from P's perspective. If we consider all memory accesses from every processor to every memory location, there exists a global *visibility order* on these accesses (a posteriori), where the visibility order is consistent with the serialization order for each memory location and the ordering priciples defined by the TSO / PO model relative to each processor's program order.

---

[6]The definitions we describe in this section in order to formally define the specification for l-mfence are similar to certain definitions described in [14], although we use different notations and terminology, and define only the terms we need.

Given the visibility order of a particular execution, we say that a memory access A_1 **happened before (after)** another access A_2 if A_1 precedes (follows) A_2 in the visibility order, or $A_1 < A_2$. From P's perspective, we say that a memory access A_1 **occured before (after)** another access A_2 if A_1 precedes (follows) A_2 in P's program order, or $A_1 \ll A_2$.

Now we define the specification of l-mfence formally.

DEFINITION 2. *Given a store S associated with* l-mfence *executed by a processor P, and an access A also performed by P, the* l-mfence *enforces that if $A \ll S$ then $A < S$, and vice versa, without breaking the TSO / PO ordering principles.*

An l-mfence(l,v) performed by processor P executes a store S of v to l, and enforces a happened-before (after) relation between S and any other access A performed by P that is consistent with S and A's relative ordering in P's program order. That is, if access A occurred before (after) l-mfence in P's instruction stream, A appears to all processors that it has happened before (after) S in the global visibility order.

Correctness Proof of the LE/ST Mechanism

We start by some definition and lemmas that will help us show that the LE/ST mechanism (which includes the code sequence shown in Figure 3(b)) implements the specification of l-mfence.

DEFINITION 3. *Given the LE/ST mechanism and a particular instance of* l-mfence(l,v), *a link for the* l-mfence *is* **set** *if LEBit contains 1, LEAddr contain l, and the cache line for l is in the executing processor's private cache in Exclusive or Modified state. If any of these conditions is not met, the link is* **clear**.

LEMMA 1. *Given a particular instance of* l-mfence(l,v), *if LEBit contains 1 when the store commits (line K1.4), the link must be set.*

PROOF. By committing instructions shown in lines K1.1–K1.3, the executing processor set up the link. Since LEBit is set as the **first** instruction of the l-mfence execution, if the link was broken at any point before the commit of ST in line K1.4, the LE/ST mechanism clears LEBit as part of breaking the link. Once the link is broken, LEBit is never set again until the next instance of l-mfence. □

LEMMA 2. *The LE/ST mechanism maintains the ordering principles defined by the TSO / PO memory model.*

PROOF. The LE/ST mechanism uses regular loads[7], stores, and memory fences, which maintains the FIFO ordering in the store buffer and the fact that instructions are committed in order. Thus, the TSO / PO principles are maintained. □

LEMMA 3. *The LE/ST mechanism ensures that, before P_1 commits the next instruction following* l-mfence(l,v), *either the store S to l in line K1.4 is already complete, or any other access to l from another processor P_2 must happen after S.*

PROOF. There are two cases to consider — either the link is clear at the time when S commits (Case 1), or the link is still set (Case 2).

Case 1: By Lemma 1, we know that if the link is clear, the LEBit must be 0. Therefore, by the code for LE/ST mechanism (Figure 3(b)), the condition for the branch (line K1.5) is false, and thus

---

[7]As explained in Section 2, the LE instruction is very similar to a regular load and can be implemented using the existing architecture and cache coherency protocol.

P_1 must execute the MFENCE in line K1.6, causing S to complete before the next instruction (line K2 in Figure 3(a)) commits.

Case 2: If the link is set, by Definition 3, we know that P_1 has l in Exclusive / Modify state. Therefore, any processor P_2 will issue coherence traffic to P_1 before P_2 can commit a load from l or complete a store to l (a store must acquire Exclusive state on the location before it can complete). Since the link is set, P_1's cache controller will notify the processor when such request arrives. By the LE/ST mechanism upon notification, P_1 clears the link, flushes its store buffer to complete S, and replies to the cache controller. Only after that, the cache controller responds to P_2's request. Thus, P_2's access to l happened after S. □

THEOREM 4. *The LE/ST mechanism implements the specification of* l-mfence *as defined in Definition 2.*

PROOF. To show that the LE/ST mechanism implements the specification of l-mfence, we show that l-mfence enforces that if $A \ll S$ then $A < S$ and vice versa. By Lemma 2, we know that the LE/ST mechanism maintains the TSO / PO principles. Thus, the case where $A \ll S$ (for A being either a load or a store) is trivially true. Similarly, the case where $S \ll A$ where A is another store to a different location is also trivially true. Moreover, since the visibility order is always consistent with the serialization order to a given location, the case where $S \ll A$ where A loads from or stores to the same target location as S, is also trivially true. Thus, the only case we need to analyze is $S \ll A$, where A is a load with a different target location, and we show that $S < A$.

Let P_1 be the processor executing the l-mfence(l_1,v), and its program order dictates that the store S to l_1 (associated with the l-mfence) happened before a load A from location l_2. Assume for the purpose of contradiction, that some processor P_2 observes that S happened after A. The only way that P_2 can observe such happened-after relation is if P_2 performs some operations B accessing l_2 and C accessing l_1 in such way that S is forced to happen after A. That is, based on the TSO / PO principles and the serialization order observed by P_2 during execution, S cannot happen before A.

We consider possible candidates for B and C. In order to enforce an ordering on B and C in visibility order, we cannot have B being a store and C being load, because the TSO / PO principles does not enforce that $B < C$ if $B \ll C$. We will not consider B being a load, because we wish to enforce a visibility order between A (also a load) and B based on the serialization order of l_2, which is determined by stores completed on l_2. Involving an additional store on l_2 to force a serialization order between A and B is essentially the same effect as simply choosing B as a store. Thus, we only consider the case in which both B and C are store operations.

With B storing to l_2 and C storing to l_1, we construct a scenario to obtain the visibility order $A < B < C < S$. Since $B \ll C$ in P_2's program order, we have $B < C$ as dictated by the TSO / PO model (Principle 3 in Section 2). We can obtain $A < B$ via the serialization order, since they both operate on memory location l_2 (assuming B is serialized after A). Similarly, we can obtain $C < S$ via the serialization order, since they both operate on memory location l_1.

Given this visibility order, we know that A (a load) must commit before B completes, otherwise A would observe the value stored by B and therefore serialize after B. Similarly, C must complete before S completes, otherwise S would serialize before C. We also know that B must complete before C completes, by the TSO / PO principles. That means, A must commit before S completes. There are two cases to consider here.

Case 1: The link for the l-mfence that S is associated with is clear when A commits. By Lemma 3, since S must complete before

the next instruction (following `l-mfence`) commits, we know that this visibility order cannot occur, and $S < A$.

Case 2: The link is set when A commits. In this case, S is committed but not yet complete when A commits. Let's name the next immediate access to l_1 that completes as D (possibly from any processor). By Lemma 3, D must happen after S, i.e., $S < D$. If D turns out be C, then $S < C$, and there is no reason why we cannot rearrange the visibility order to obtain $S < A < B < C$, since there is no ordering constraint that prevents S from moving upward. If D is not C, then C must complete and happen after D, so we still have $S < C$. With the same reasoning, we can rearrange the visibility order to obtain $S < A < B < C$.

In both cases, we have $S < A$, which agrees with P_1's program order, $S \ll A$. □

Theorem 4 proves that the LE/ST mechanism correctly implements the specification of `l-mfence`. In the following subsection, we prove that this specification is sufficient to guarantee mutual exclusion if it is used by the primary thread in the asymmetric Dekker protocol.

Correctness Proof of the Asymmetric Dekker Algorithm using l-mfence

We now prove that the `l-mfence(l,v)` specification is sufficient for achieving mutual exclusion when it is used in the asymmetric Dekker protocol, such as shown in Figure 3(a). The proof is based on two lemmas, each shows that if one thread is running in its critical section, the other one is prevented from entering it. For brevity, we name the primary thread executing the `l-mfence` $T1$ (lines K1–K6 in Figure 3(a)) and the secondary thread $T2$ (lines J1–J7 in Figure 3(a)).

LEMMA 5. *Assuming both $T1$ and $T2$ are concurrently attempting to enter the critical section. If $T1$ reads that $L2 == 0$ in line K2 and is therefore entering the critical section, $T2$ will not enter the critical section.*

PROOF. If $T1$ reads that $L2 == 0$ in line K2, we know that the load in line K2 must have committed before the store in line J1 completed. That is, the load in line K2 happened before the store in line J1. Since $T2$ uses an `mfence` (line J2) between lines J1 and J3, the load in line J3 cannot execute until the store in line J1 completes. Thus, the load in line K2 must also have happened before the load in line J3. By the specification of `l-mfence` (Definition 2), since the store to $L1$ associated with the `l-mfence` in line K1 must appear to happen before the load in line K2 to all processors, $T2$ must observe that the store in line K1 happened before the load in line K2, which happened before the load in line J3. Therefore, when $T2$ executes the load in line J3, it must observe the store performed in line K1, read $L1 == 1$ (assuming $T1$ has not left the critical section), and refrain from entering the critical section. □

LEMMA 6. *Assuming both $T1$ and $T2$ are concurrently attempting to enter the critical section. If $T2$ reads that $L1 == 0$ in line J3 and is entering the critical section, $T1$ will not enter the critical section.*

PROOF. If $T2$ reads that $L1 == 0$ in line J3, we know that the load in line J3 must have been serialized before the store that is associated with the `l-mfence(L1, 1)`. Thus, the load in line J3 happened before the the store for `l-mfence(&L1, 1)` in line K1. By the specification of `l-mfence` (Definition 2), $T2$ must observe that the store associated with line K1 happened before the load in line K2, so the load in line J3 must also have happened before the load in line K2. Since $T2$ uses an `mfence` (line J2) between lines J1

and J3, the load in line J3 cannot execute until the store in line J1 completes, and thus the store in line J1 must also have happened before the load in line K2. Thus, when $T1$ executes the load in line K2, $T1$ must observe $T2$'s store to $L2$ and read $L2 == 1$ (assuming $T2$ has not left the critical section), and refrain from entering the critical section. □

THEOREM 7. *The asymmetric Dekker protocol using `l-mfence` allows at most one thread to execute in the critical section at any given time.*

PROOF. Follows form Lemmas 5 and 6. □

As we have shown, the asymmetric Dekker protocol shown in Figure 3(a) guarantees mutual exclusion. Nonetheless, it requires additional tie-breaking code (similar to the original Dekker protocol) to avoid live lock situations in which both threads are kept outside their critical sections.

The asymmetric Dekker protocol is designed to optimize away the overhead incurred onto the primary thread at the expanse of additional overhead on the secondary thread, which is advantageous for applications that exhibit asymmetric synchronization patterns. Hence, we use an `mfence` in the secondary thread instead of `l-mfence` to avoid incurring additional overhead on the primary thread. If the secondary thread was using an `l-mfence`, the primary thread may need to wait for the secondary thread to flush its store buffer when it attempts to read $L2$ in line K2. Nevertheless, the secondary thread has the option of executing the mirrored code (using `l-mfence(&L2,1)` in line J2), and the protocol still provides mutual exclusion in such case.

5. EVALUATION

To evaluate the feasibility of location-based memory fences, we have implemented a software prototype of location-based memory fences using signals. The idea of using signals to cause a thread to serialize has been proposed by Dice et al. in [6], but was not evaluated. We implemented the signal-based serialization method similar to what [6] proposed, and use it as a basis for evaluating the expected performance of the hardware mechanism for location-based memory fences. We incorporate the software prototype of the fences into two applications. In this section, we briefly summarize the software prototype, the experimental setup, and the results of our evaluation.

Software Prototype of l-mfence

The software prototype must correctly capture two main effects. First, the primary thread must not reorder the write and the read at the compiler level. We achieve this simply by inserting a compiler fence at the appropriate place. Second, before the secondary thread attempts to read the primary thread's flag, it must cause the primary thread to serialize, and only proceed to read the flag when it knows that the primary thread has performed serialization. We achieve this via signals — a software signal generates an interrupt on the processor receiving the signal, and the processor flushes its store buffer before calling the signal handling routine. Thus, the secondary thread sends a signal to the primary thread and waits for an acknowledgment by spinning on a shared variable.[8] Upon receiving the signal (which implicitly flushes the store buffer), the primary thread executes a user-defined signal handler, which sets the shared variable as an acknowledgment, thereby allowing the secondary thread to resume execution.

---

[8]This is assuming that the signaling succeeds; the signaling would fail if the primary thread has already terminated.

This software prototype implementation incurs overhead that the proposed hardware mechanism would not. First, since the signal handler is user-defined, upon receiving the signal, the primary thread would need to cross between kernel and user modes four times, which incurs high overhead. The same overhead is incurred on the secondary thread as well, since the secondary thread must wait for the primary thread to acknowledge receiving the signal. Second, the secondary thread may observe some latency if the primary thread is de-scheduled from the processor.[9] The proposed hardware mechanism would not observe these overheads.

On the other hand, in the software implementation, the fences incur virtually no overhead on the primary thread when there is no contention. This is not the case for the hardware mechanism, which incurs a small overhead on the primary thread. This overhead results from the registers setup, the branch to check LEBit, and the wait for Exclusive state on the guarded location. When there is no contention, however, most of this overhead is eliminated by the successful branch prediction and the fact that the location stays in the primary thread cache in Exclusive or Modified state, because no other thread is trying to access it. When there is contention, we speculate that the signal handling overhead associated with the software implementation are much higher compared to the hardware mechanism. Even though the software implementation does not faithfully simulate the overhead of the hardware mechanism, it nonetheless gives us some idea as to whether the hardware mechanism is worth investigating.

Experimental Setup

We incorporate the software prototype of the fences into two applications — the asymmetric Cilk-5 runtime system and an asymmetric multiple-readers single-writer lock.

For the first application, we have modified the open-source Cilk-5 runtime system [11][10] to incorporate the location-based memory fence into its Dekker-like protocol employed by the runtime work stealing scheduler, referred as the *ACilk-5 runtime*. In ACilk-5 runtime, when a thief (the secondary thread) needs to find more work to do, it engages in the asymmetric Dekker-like protocol with a given victim (the primary thread) in order to "steal" work from the victim's "deque." If there are more than two thieves attempt to steal from the same victim, the thieves must first compete for the right to engage the victim via a lock acquisition, so that only a single thief would engage in the Dekker protocol with the victim at any given moment. Assuming the application contains ample parallelism, a victim would access its own deque much more frequently than a thief, because steal occurs infrequently.

For the second application, we have designed an *asymmetric multiple-readers single-writer lock*, where the lock is biased towards the readers, henceforth referred as the *ARW lock*. From time to time, a reader (the primary thread) turns into a writer (the secondary thread), and attempts to acquire the ARW lock in write mode by engaging in the asymmetric Dekker protocol with each of the registered readers. Similarly to ACilk-5, if there are more than one writer at a given moment, the writers compete for permission to write by first acquiring a lock, and only the winning writer is allowed to engage in the Dekker protocol with the readers.

We ran all experiments on an AMD Opteron system with 4 quad-core 2 GHz CPU's having a total of 8 GBytes of memory. Each core

---

[9]The correctness of the protocol is not affected by the primary thread being de-scheduled, because the de-scheduling constitutes a context switch, which requires the store buffer to drain before the de-scheduling.

[10]The open-source Cilk-5 system is available at http://supertech.csail.mit.edu/cilk/cilk-5.4.6.tar.gz.

Application	Input	Description
cholesky	4000/40000	Cholesky factorization
cilksort	10^8	Parallel merge sort
fft	2^{26}	Fast Fourier transform
fib	42	Recursive Fibonacci
fibx	280	Alternate between fib(n-1) and fib(n-40)
heat	2048×500	Jacobi heat diffusion
knapsack	32	Recursive knapsack
lu	4096	LU-decomposition
matmul	2048	Matrix multiply
nqueens	14	Count ways to place N queens
rectmul	4096	Rectangular matrix multiply
strassen	4096	Strassen matrix multiply

Figure 4: The 12 benchmark applications.

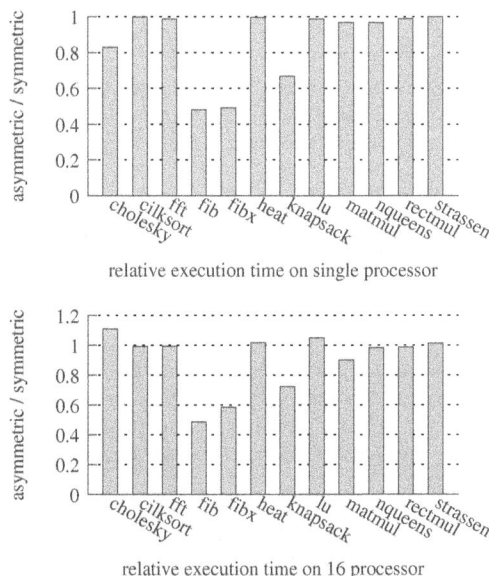

relative execution time on single processor

relative execution time on 16 processor

Figure 5: (a) The relative serial execution time of the ACilk-5 runtime system compared to the original Cilk-5 runtime system for 12 Cilk benchmarks. (b) The relative execution time of the ACilk-5 runtime system compared to the original Cilk-5 runtime system for 12 Cilk benchmarks on 16 cores. A value below 1 means that the application runs faster on ACilk-5 than on Cilk-5; a value above 1 means the other way around. Each value is calculated by normalizing the execution time of the benchmarks on ACilk-5 with that on Cilk-5.

on a chip has a 64-KByte private L1-data-cache and a 512-KByte private L2-cache, but all cores on a chip share a 2-MByte L3-cache.

Evaluation Using ACilk-5

To evaluate the effect of location-based memory fences, we compare the execution time of applications running on ACilk-5 versus running on Cilk-5 across 12 benchmarks. Figure 4 provides a brief description of each benchmark.

Figure 5(a) compares the performance of the benchmarks run on ACilk-5 and Cilk-5 when executed serially. Figure 5(b) shows a similar performance comparison when executed on 16 cores. For each measurement, we took the mean of 10 runs (with standard deviation of less than 3%). A value below 1 means that the application runs faster on ACilk-5 than on Cilk-5. Not surprisingly, when executed serially, ACilk-5 runs faster, because the victim executes on the fast path with virtually no overhead from memory fences. The improvement that ACilk-5 exhibits over Cilk-5 when running a given benchmark is directly related to the number and the granularity of tasks that the benchmark generates. Since ACilk-5 saves the overhead of executing the memory fence whenever the victim accesses its deque, the more frequently a victim accesses its own deque, the more overhead ACilk-5 saves compared to Cilk-5.

Figure 5(b) shows the same performance comparison when executed on 16 cores. For most benchmarks, the execution time follows the same trend, where the normalized execution time is comparable between the serial execution versus the parallel execution; thus, the scalability of the two systems are comparable. The only obvious differences are in cholesky and lu, which do not scale as well under ACilk-5.

In the software implementation, the scalability of a benchmark under ACilk-5 is correlated with the ability to amortizes the overhead for sending / handling signals against successful steals. While the analysis of the work-stealing algorithm (referred as the "work-first" principle [11]) dictates that one should put the scheduling overhead onto the steal path (thief's path) instead of onto the work path (victim's path), one must be able to amortize the overhead against successful steals in order to obtain good performance. In all benchmarks besides cholesky and lu, at least 90% of the signals sent by the thieves realize to successful steals, while in the case of cholesky, the signals-to-successful-steals ratio is only 53.6%, and in the case of lu, the ratio is only 72.8%. This means that high percentage of the signaling overhead in these two benchmarks cannot be accounted towards successful steals, and thus the performance suffers. With hardware support, the overhead in such case would be similar to a cache miss for the victim and an ordinary memory fence for the thief. Therefore we believe that the hardware mechanism would scale better even for these applications.

Evaluation Using ARW Lock

We evaluate the effect of location-based memory fences by comparing the read throughput of a microbenchmark using the ARW lock to the read throughput using its symmetric counterpart: the same design but uses the original symmetric Dekker protocol instead of the asymmetric Dekker protocol, henceforth referred as the **SRW lock**. Each thread performs read operations most of the time, and only occasionally it performs a write. In the tests, the threads read from and write to an array with 4 elements. The read-to-write ratio is an input parameter to the microbenchmark: assuming the ratio is $N : 1$, and there are P threads executing, then for every N/P reads, a thread performs a write. With each configuration, we run the microbenchmark for 10 seconds, calculate the read throughput, and compare the throughput using the ARW lock against the throughput using the SRW lock.

Figure 6(a) shows the throughput comparison between the ARW lock and the SRW lock. In the software prototype of location-based memory fences, since a request for serialization translates to a signal, the writer ends up signaling a list of readers and waiting for their responses one by one, which becomes a serializing bottleneck. This is particularly inefficient when the thread counts is high, and the read-to-write ratio is low.

We speculate that the lack of scalability is again due to the overhead of sending signals in the software implementation. To confirm this, we devised an ARW lock that implements a *waiting heuristic*: when a writer wants to write, instead of sending signals to the readers immediately, it first indicates intent to write and spin-waits to see if any reader responds, acknowledging the writer's intent to write. Only after spin-waiting for a while, the writer sends signals to readers who have not acknowledged. We refer to the ARW lock with this heuristic as the **ARW+ lock**.

Figure 6(b) shows the throughput comparison between the ARW+ lock and the SRW lock. A value above 1 means that the ARW+ lock performs better. There are two main trends to notice. First, as the number of threads increases, the ARW+ locks consis-

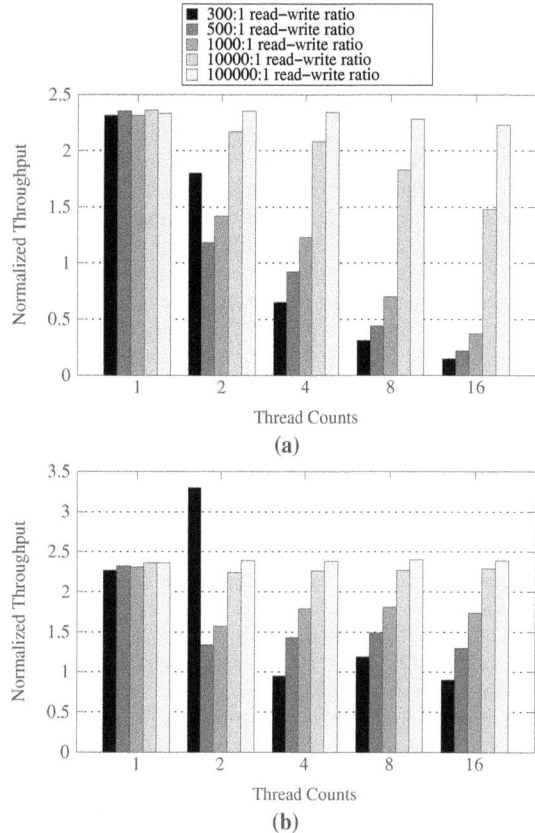

Figure 6: (a) The relative read throughput of execution using the ARW lock compared to that using the SRW lock. (b) The relative throughput of execution using the ARW+ lock (i.e., the ARW lock with the waiting heuristics) compared to that using the SRW lock. Since we are comparing the relative throughput, a value above 1 means that the ARW lock / ARW+ lock performs better; a value below 1 means that the SRW lock performs better. Each value is calculated by normalizing the read throughput from the execution using the ARW lock by that using the SRW lock.

tently have higher throughput compared to the SRW locks for each specific read/write ratio, except for the 300 : 1 ratio. Second, as the ratio between read and writes increases for a given thread count, the ARW+ consistently outperforms SRW, with one noticeable outliner: the data point for ratio of 300 : 1 with two threads. This can be explained by the fact that when there are only two threads, the writer end up receiving the acknowledgment most of the times and does not need to send signals. While the heuristic seems to work well in the microbenchmarks, if the reader does not acquire/release locks frequently in practice, the waiting heuristic would not help as much, since a thread would only get a chance to check for pending intent during lock acquire and release. With that in mind, the results inspire some confidence that ARW should exhibit good performance when implemented with hardware support for location-based memory fences.

6. RELATED WORK

Our work is closely related to studies performed on biased locks and asymmetric synchronization, so we focus on these in the section. Several researchers studied this area, mainly in the context of improving performance for Java locks.

[23] describes a fast biased lock algorithm, which allows the primary thread to avoid executing memory fences, until a secondary thread attempts to enter the critical section. In which case, the sec-

ondary thread must wait for the primary thread to grant access in order to continue execution. While this request and grant protocol is performed via shared variables and therefore fairly efficient, this implementation can potentially deadlock if the biased lock is nested within another lock (or any resource that can block).

The studies in [7] and [21] describe similar biased lock implementations, where the owner of the lock is on the fast path for accessing the lock, and other threads need to revoke it and compete for ownership, and the lock ownership may transfer. Both algorithms use the "collocation" trick, where the status field and the lock field are allocated on the same word. They first write to one field and then the whole word is read. The correctness of the algorithm depends on the fact that hardware typically does not reorder read before older write when the addresses overlap. This collocation trick, while interesting, is not guaranteed to be safe, and on systems which this trick works correctly, the collocation always forces a memory fence to be issued regardless of whether there is contention [8].

Serialization using signal and notify was proposed in [6], as well as other more heavy-weight serialization mechanisms. Their work focus on software means to cause serialization in another thread, while decreasing synchronization overhead on the primary thread in applications that exhibit asymmetric synchronization patterns.

Finally, in [20], Lin et al. propose a hardware mechanism for conditional memory fences, whose aim is also to reduce the overhead of memory fences when synchronization is unnecessary. In [20], however, the assumption is that the compiler would automatically insert memory fences in order to enforce sequential consistency everywhere, and there may be multiple outstanding memory fences for a given thread at a given moment. Thus, their hardware mechanism is much more heavyweight compared to ours, so as to handle multiple outstanding fences at a given moment. Our mechanism is designed for applications that are hand-tuned with manually inserted fences, and we aim to provide a lightweight solution which does not handle multiple outstanding fences.

7. CONCLUSION

In this work, we propose location-based memory fences, which aim to reduce the overhead incurred by memory fences in parallel algorithms. Location-based memory fences are particularly well-suited for algorithms that exhibit asymmetric synchronization patterns. We describe a hardware mechanism to support location-based memory fences, proved its correctness and evaluate the feasibility of the fences using a software prototype. Our evaluation with the software prototype inspires confidence that the suggested LE/ST mechanism for supporting location-based memory fences in hardware is worth considering.

Finally, location-based memory fences lend itself to a different way of viewing programs compared to the traditional PC-based memory fences. It would be interesting to investigate what other algorithms can benefit from location-based memory fences, as well as other mechanisms that exploit the location-based model.

8. ACKNOWLEDGMENTS

We like to thank Joel Emer of Intel Corporation and MIT, David Dice of Oracle Labs, and William Hasenplaugh, Charles Leiserson, Jim Sukha, and other members of the SuperTech Group at MIT CSAIL for helpful discussions.

9. REFERENCES

[1] Advanced Micro Devices. *AMD64 Architecture Programmer's Manual Volume 2: System Programming*, June 2010.

[2] Nimar S. Arora, Robert D. Blumofe, and C. Greg Plaxton. Thread scheduling for multiprogrammed multiprocessors. In *SPAA '98*, pages 119–129, June 1998.

[3] Robert D. Blumofe, Christopher F. Joerg, Bradley C. Kuszmaul, Charles E. Leiserson, Keith H. Randall, and Yuli Zhou. Cilk: An efficient multithreaded runtime system. In *PPoPP '05*, pages 207–216, July 1995.

[4] Robert D. Blumofe and Charles E. Leiserson. Scheduling multithreaded computations by work stealing. *JACM*, 46(5):720–748, September 1999.

[5] Robert D. Blumofe and Dionisios Papadopoulos. Hood: A user-level threads library for multiprogrammed multiprocessors. Technical Report, University of Texas at Austin, 1999.

[6] Dave Dice, Hui Huang, and Mingyao Yang. Asymmetric dekker synchronization. Technical report, Sun Microsystems Inc., July 2001.

[7] Dave Dice, Mark Moir, and William Scherer III. Quickly reacquirable locks. Technical report, Sun Microsystems Inc., 2003.

[8] David Dice. David Dice's Weblog: http://blogs.sun.com/dave/entry/biased_locking_in_hotspot#comments, 2006.

[9] E. W. Dijkstra. Solution of a problem in concurrent programming control. *Communications of the ACM*, 8(9):569, September 1965.

[10] E. W. Dijkstra. Co-operating sequential processes. In *Programming Languages*. 1968.

[11] Matteo Frigo, Charles E. Leiserson, and Keith H. Randall. The implementation of the Cilk-5 multithreaded language. In *PLDI '98*, pages 212–223, 1998.

[12] Robert H. Halstead, Jr. Multilisp: A language for concurrent symbolic computation. *ACM TOPLAS*, 7(4):501–538, October 1985.

[13] John L. Hennessy and David A. Patterson. *Computer Architecture: a Quantitative Approach*. Morgan Kaufmann, San Francisco, CA, fourth edition, 2007.

[14] Intel Corporation. *A Formal Specification of Intel Itanium Processor Family Memory Ordering*, October 2011.

[15] Intel Corporation. *Intel® 64 and IA-32 Architectures Software Developer's Manual Volume 3A: System Programming Guide, Part 1*, January 2011.

[16] Kiyokuni Kawachiya, Akira Koseki, and Tamiya Onodera. Lock reservation: Java locks can mostly do without atomic operations. In *OOPSLA '02*, pages 130–141, 2002.

[17] David A. Kranz, Robert H. Halstead, Jr., and Eric Mohr. Mul-T: A high-performance parallel Lisp. In *PLDI '89*, pages 81–90, June 1989.

[18] Leslie Lamport. A new solution of dijkstra's concurrent programming problem. *Communications of the ACM*, 17(8):453–455, 1974.

[19] Leslie Lamport. How to make a multiprocessor computer that correctly executes multiprocess programs. *IEEE Transactions on Computers*, C-28(9):690–691, September 1979.

[20] Changhui Lin, Vijay Nagarajan, and Rajiv Gupta. Efficient sequential consistency using conditional fences. In *PACT '10*, pages 295–306, 2010.

[21] Tamiya Onodera, Kiyokuni Kawachiya, and Akira Koseki. Lock reservation for java reconsidered. In *ECOOP '04*, pages 559–583, 2004.

[22] G. L. Peterson. Myths about the mutual exclusion problem. *Information Processing Letters*, 12(3):115–116, June 1981.

[23] Nalini Vasudevan, Kedar S. Namjoshi, and Stephen A. Edwards. Simple and fast biased locks. In *PACT '10*, pages 65–74, 2010.

[24] David L. Weaver and Tom Germond, editors. *The SPARC Architecture Manual, Version 9*. PTR Prentice Hall, 1994.

Filtering: A Method for Solving Graph Problems in MapReduce

Silvio Lattanzi*
Google, Inc.
New York, NY, USA
silviolat@gmail.com

Benjamin Moseley†
University of Illinois
Urbana, IL, USA
bmosele2@illinois.edu

Siddharth Suri
Yahoo! Research
New York, NY, USA
ssuri@yahoo-inc.com

Sergei Vassilvitskii
Yahoo! Research
New York, NY, USA
sergei@yahoo-inc.com

ABSTRACT

The MapReduce framework is currently the *de facto* standard used throughout both industry and academia for petabyte scale data analysis. As the input to a typical MapReduce computation is large, one of the key requirements of the framework is that the input cannot be stored on a single machine and must be processed in parallel. In this paper we describe a general algorithmic design technique in the MapReduce framework called *filtering*. The main idea behind filtering is to reduce the size of the input in a distributed fashion so that the resulting, much smaller, problem instance can be solved on a single machine. Using this approach we give new algorithms in the MapReduce framework for a variety of fundamental graph problems for sufficiently dense graphs. Specifically, we present algorithms for minimum spanning trees, maximal matchings, approximate weighted matchings, approximate vertex and edge covers and minimum cuts. In all of these cases, we parameterize our algorithms by the amount of memory available on the machines allowing us to show tradeoffs between the memory available and the number of MapReduce rounds. For each setting we will show that even if the machines are only given substantially sublinear memory, our algorithms run in a constant number of MapReduce rounds. To demonstrate the practical viability of our algorithms we implement the maximal matching algorithm that lies at the core of our analysis and show that it achieves a significant speedup over the sequential version.

Categories and Subject Descriptors

F.2.2 [**Analysis of Algorithms and Problem Complexity**]: Nonnumerical Algorithms and Problems

---

*Work done while visiting Yahoo! Labs.
†Work done while visiting Yahoo! Labs. Partially supported by NSF grants CCF-0728782 and CCF-1016684.

General Terms

Algorithms, Theory

Keywords

MapReduce, Graph Algorithms, Matchings

1. INTRODUCTION

The amount of data available and requiring analysis has grown at an astonishing rate in recent years. For example, Yahoo! processes over 100 billion events, amounting to over 120 terabytes, daily [7]. Similarly, Facebook processes over 80 terabytes of data per day [17]. Although the amount of memory in commercially available servers has also grown at a remarkable pace in the past decade, and now exceeds a once unthinkable amount of 100 GB, it remains woefully inadequate to process such huge amounts of data. To cope with this deluge of information people have (again) turned to parallel algorithms for data processing. In recent years MapReduce [3], and its open source implementation, Hadoop [20], have emerged as the standard platform for large scale distributed computation. About 5 years ago, Google reported that it processes over 3 petabytes of data using MapReduce in one month [3]. Yahoo! and Facebook use Hadoop as their primary method for analyzing massive data sets [7, 17]. Moreover, over 100 companies and 10 universities are using Hadoop [6, 21] for large scale data analysis.

Many different types of data have contributed to this growth. One particularly rich datatype that has captured the interest of both industry and academia is massive graphs. Graphs such as the World Wide Web can easily consist of billions of nodes and trillions of edges [16]. Citation graphs, affiliation graphs, instant messenger graphs, and phone call graphs have recently been studied as part of social network analysis. Although it was previously thought that graphs of this nature are sparse, the work of Leskovec, Kleinberg and Faloutsos [14] dispelled this notion. The authors analyzed the growth over time of 9 different massive graphs from 4 different domains and showed that graphs become denser. Specifically, if $n(t)$ and $e(t)$ denote the number of nodes and edges at time t, respectively, they show that $e(t) \propto n(t)^{1+c}$, where $1 \geq c > 0$. They lowest value of c they find is 0.08, but they observe three graphs with $c > 0.5$. The algorithms we present are efficient for such dense graphs, as well as their sparser counterparts.

Previous approaches to graph algorithms on MapReduce attempt to shoehorn message passing style algorithms into the framework

[9, 15]. These algorithms often require $O(d)$ rounds, where d is the diameter of the input graph, even for such simple tasks as computing connected components, minimum spanning trees, etc. A round in a MapReduce computation can be very expensive time-wise, because it often requires a massive amount of data (on the order of terabytes) to be transmitted from one set of machines to another. This is usually the dominant cost in a MapReduce computation. Therefore minimizing the number of rounds is essential for efficient MapReduce computations. In this work we show how many fundamental graph algorithms can be computed in a constant number of rounds. We use the previously defined model of computation for MapReduce [13] to perform our analysis.

1.1 Contributions

All of our algorithms take the same general approach, which we call *filtering*. They proceed in two stages. First, the algorithms use the parallelization of MapReduce to selectively drop, or *filter*, parts of the input with the goal of reducing the problem size so that the result is small enough to fit into a single machine's memory. In the second stage the algorithms compute the final answer on this reduced input. The technical challenge is to choose enough edges to drop but still be able to compute either an optimal or provably near optimal solution. The filtering step differs in complexity depending on the problem and takes a few slightly different forms. We exhibit the flexibility of this approach by showing how it can be used to solve a variety of graph problems.

In Section 2.4 we apply the filtering technique to computing the connected components and minimum spanning trees of dense graphs. The algorithm, which is much simpler, and more efficient algorithm than the one that appeared in [13], partitions the original input and solves a subproblem on each partition. The algorithm recurses until the data set is small enough to fit into the memory of a single machine.

In Section 3, we turn to the problem of matchings, and show how to compute a maximal matching in three MapReduce rounds in the model of [13]. The algorithm begins by solving a subproblem on a small sample of the original input. We then use this interim solution to prune out the vast majority of edges of the original input, thus dramatically reducing the size of the remaining problem, and recursing if it is not small enough to fit onto a single machine. The algorithm allows for a tradeoff between the number of rounds and the available memory. Specifically, for graphs with at most n^{1+c} edges and machines with memory at least $n^{1+\epsilon}$ our algorithm will require $O(c/\epsilon)$ rounds. If the machines have memory $O(n)$ then our algorithm requires $O(\log n)$ rounds.

We then use this algorithm as a building block, and show algorithms for computing an 8-approximation for maximum weighted matching, a 2-approximation to Vertex Cover and a $3/2$-approximation to Edge Cover. For all of these algorithms, the number of machines used will be at most $O(N/\eta)$ where N is the size of the input and η is the memory available on each machine. That is, these algorithms require just enough machines to fit the entire input on all of the machines. Finally, in Section 4 we adapt the seminal work of Karger [10] to the MapReduce setting. Here the filtering succeeds with a limited probability; however, we argue that we can replicate the algorithm enough times in parallel so that one of the runs succeeds without destroying the minimum cut.

1.2 Related Work

The authors of [13] give a formal model of computation of MapReduce called $\mathcal{MRC}$ which we will briefly summarize in the next section. There are two models of computation that are similar to $\mathcal{MRC}$. We describe these models and their relationship to

$\mathcal{MRC}$ in turn. We also discuss how known algorithms in those models relate to the algorithms presented in this work.

The algorithms presented in this paper run in a constant number of rounds when the memory per machine is superlinear in the number of vertices ($n^{1+\epsilon}$ for some $\epsilon > 0$). Although this requirement is reminiscent of the semi-streaming model [4], the similarities end there, as the two models are very different. One problem that is hard to solve in semi-streaming but can be solved in $\mathcal{MRC}$ is graph connectivity. As shown in [4], in the semi-streaming model, without a superlinear amount of memory it is impossible to answer connectivity queries. In $\mathcal{MRC}$, however, previous work [13] shows how to answer connectivity queries when the memory per machine is limited to $n^{1-\epsilon}$, albeit at the cost of a logarithmic number of rounds. Conversely, a problem that is trivial in the semi-streaming model but more complicated in $\mathcal{MRC}$ is finding a maximal matching. In the semi-streaming model one simply streams through the edges, and adds the edge to the current matching if it is feasible. As we show in Section 3, finding a maximal matching in $\mathcal{MRC}$ is a computable, but non-trivial endeavor. The technical challenge for this algorithm stems from the fact that no single machine can see all of the edges of the input graph, rather the model *requires* the algorithm designer to parallelize the processing[1].

Although parallel algorithms are gaining a resurgence, this is an area that was widely studied previously under different models of parallel computation. The most popular model is the PRAM model, which allows for a polynomial number of processors with shared memory. There are hundreds of papers for solving problems in this model and previous work [5, 13] shows how to simulate certain types of PRAM algorithms in $\mathcal{MRC}$. Most of these results yield $\mathcal{MRC}$ algorithms that require $\Omega(\log n)$ rounds, whereas in this work we focus on algorithms that use $O(1)$ rounds. Nonetheless, to compare with previous work, we next describe PRAM algorithms that either can be simulated in $\mathcal{MRC}$, or could be directly implemented in $\mathcal{MRC}$. Israel and Itai [8] give an $O(\log n)$ round algorithm for computing maximal matchings on a PRAM. It could be implemented in $\mathcal{MRC}$, but would require $O(\log n)$ rounds. Similarly, [19] gives a distributed algorithm which yields constant factor approximation to the weighted matching problem. This algorithm, which could also be implemented in $\mathcal{MRC}$, takes $O(\log^2 n)$ rounds. Finally, Karger's algorithm is in $\mathcal{RNC}$ but also requires $O(\log^2 n)$ rounds. We show how to implement it in MapReduce in a constant number of rounds in Section 4.

2. PRELIMINARIES

2.1 MapReduce Overview

We remind the reader about the salient features of the MapReduce computing paradigm (see [13] for more details). The input, and all intermediate data, is stored in $\langle key; value \rangle$ pairs and the computation proceeds in rounds. Each round is split into three consecutive phases: map, shuffle and reduce. In the map phase the input is processed one tuple at a time. All $\langle key; value \rangle$ pairs emitted by the map phase which have the same key are then aggregated by the MapReduce system during the shuffle phase and sent to the same machine. Finally each key, along with all the values associated with it, are processed together during the reduce phase.

Since all the values with the same key end up on the same machine, one can view the map phase as a kind of routing step that determines which values end up together. The key acts as a (logi-

---

[1]In practice this requirement stems from the fact that even streaming through a terabyte of data requires a non-trivial amount of time as the machine remains IO bound.

cal) address of the machine, and the system makes sure all of the $\langle key; value \rangle$ pairs with the same key are collected on the same machine. To simplify our reasoning about the model, we can combine the reduce and the subsequent map phases. Looking at the computation through this lens, every round each machine performs some computation on the set of $\langle key; value \rangle$ pairs assigned to it (reduce phase), and then designates which machine each output value should be sent to in the next round (map phase). The shuffle ensures that the data is moved to the right machine, after which the next round of computation can begin. In this simpler model, we shall only use the term machines as opposed to mappers and reducers.

More formally, let ρ_j denote the reduce function for round j, and let μ_{j+1} denote the map function for the following round of an $\mathcal{MRC}$ algorithm [13] where $j \geq 1$. Now let $\phi_j(x) = \mu_{j+1} \odot \rho_j(x)$. Here ρ_j takes as input some set of $\langle key; value \rangle$ pairs denoted by x and outputs another set of $\langle key; value \rangle$ pairs. We define the $\odot$ operator to feed the output of $\rho_j(x)$ to μ_{j+1} one $\langle key; value \rangle$ pair at a time. Thus ϕ_j denotes the operation of first executing the reducer function, ρ_j, on the set of values in x and then executing the map function, μ_{j+1}, on each $\langle key; value \rangle$ pair output by $\rho_j(x)$ individually. This syntactic change allows the algorithm designer to avoid defining mappers and reducers and instead define what each machine does during each round of computation and specify which machine each output $\langle key; value \rangle$ pair should go to.

We can now translate the restrictions on ρ_j and μ_j from the $\mathcal{MRC}$ model of [13] to restrictions on ϕ_j. Since we are joining the reduce and the subsequent map phase, we combine the restrictions imposed on both of these computations. There are three sets of restrictions: those on the number of machines, the memory available on each machine and the total number of rounds taken by the computation. For an input of size N, and a sufficiently small $\epsilon > 0$, there are $N^{1-\epsilon}$ machines, each with $N^{1-\epsilon}$ memory available for computation. As a result, the total amount of memory available to the entire system is $O(N^{2-2\epsilon})$. See [13] for a discussion and justification. An algorithm in $\mathcal{MRC}$ belongs to $\mathcal{MRC}^i$ if it runs in worst case $O(\log^i N)$ rounds. Thus, when designing a $\mathcal{MRC}^0$ algorithm there are three properties that need to be checked:

- **Machine Memory:** In each round the total memory used by a single machine is at most $O(N^{1-\epsilon})$ bits.

- **Total Memory:** The total amount of data shuffled in any round is $O(N^{2-2\epsilon})$ bits[2].

- **Rounds:** The number of rounds is a constant.

2.2 Total Work and Work Efficiency

Next we define the amount of work done by an $\mathcal{MRC}$ algorithm by taking the standard definition of work efficiency from the PRAM setting and adapting it to the MapReduce setting. Let $w(N)$ denote the amount of work done by an r-round, $\mathcal{MRC}$ algorithm on an input of size N. This is simply the sum of the amount of work done during each round of computation. The amount of work done during round i of a computation is the product of the number of machines used in that round, denoted $p_i(N)$, and the worst case running time of each machine, denoted $t_i(N)$. More specifically,

$$w(N) = \sum_{i=1}^{r} w_i(N) = \sum_{i=1}^{r} p_i(N) t_i(N). \qquad (1)$$

---

[2]In other words, the total amount of data shuffled in any round must be less than the total amount of memory in the system.

```
Algorithm: MST(V,E)
1:  if |E| < η then
2:      Compute T* = MST(E)
3:      return T*
4:  end if
5:  ℓ ← Θ(|E|/η)
6:  Partition E into E₁, E₂, ..., Eℓ where |Eᵢ| < η using a
        universal hash function h : E → {1, 2, ..., ℓ}.
7:  In parallel: Compute Tᵢ, the minimum spanning tree on
        G(V, Eᵢ).
8:  return MST(V, ∪ᵢTᵢ)
```

Figure 1: Minimum spanning tree algorithm

If the amount of work done by an $\mathcal{MRC}$ algorithm matches the running time of the best known sequential algorithm, we say the $\mathcal{MRC}$ algorithm is *work efficient*.

2.3 Notation

Let $G = (V, E)$ be an undirected graph, and denote by $n = |V|$ and $m = |E|$. We will call G, c-dense, if $m = n^{1+c}$ where $0 < c \leq 1$. In what follows we assume that the machines have some limited memory η. We will assume that the number of available machines is $O(m/\eta)$. Notice that the number of machines is just the number required to fit the input on all of the machines simultaneously. All of our algorithms will consider the case where $\eta = n^{1+\epsilon}$ for some $\epsilon > 0$. For a constant ϵ, the algorithms we define will take a constant number of rounds and lie in $\mathcal{MRC}^0$ [13], beating the $\Omega(\log n)$ running time provided by the PRAM simulation constructions (see Theorem 7.1 in [13]). However, even when $\eta = O(n)$ our algorithms will run in $O(\log n)$ rounds. This exposes the memory vs. rounds tradeoff since most of the algorithms presented take fewer rounds as the memory per machine increases. We now proceed to describe the individual algorithms, in order of progressively more complex filtering techniques.

2.4 Warm Up: Connected Components and Minimum Spanning Trees

We present the formal algorithm for computing minimum spanning trees (the connected components algorithm is identical). The algorithm works by partitioning the edges of the input graph into subsets of size η and sending each subgraph to its own machine. Then, each machine throws out any edge that is guaranteed not to be a part of any MST because it is the heaviest edge on some cycle in that machine's subgraph. If the resulting graph fits into memory of a single machine, the algorithm terminates. Otherwise, the algorithm recurses on the smaller instance. We give the pseudocode in Figure 1.

We assume the algorithm is given a c-dense graph; each machine has memory $\eta = O(n^{1+\epsilon})$, and that the number of machines $\ell = \Theta(n^{c-\epsilon})$. Thus the algorithm only uses enough memory, across the entire system, to store the input. We show that every iteration reduces the input size by $n^{c/\epsilon}$, and thus after $\lceil c/\epsilon \rceil$ iterations the algorithm terminates.

LEMMA 2.1. *Algorithm MST(V,E) terminates after $\lceil c/\epsilon \rceil$ iterations and returns the Minimum Spanning Tree.*

PROOF. To show correctness, note that any edge that is not part of the MST on a subgraph of G is also not part of the MST of G by the cycle property of minimum spanning trees.

It remains to show that (1) the memory constraints of each machine are never violated and (2) the total number of rounds is limited. Since the partition is done randomly, an easy Chernoff argument shows that no machine gets assigned more than η edges with high probability. Finally, note that $|\bigcup_i T_i| \leq \ell(n-1) = O(n^{1+c-\epsilon})$. Therefore after $\lceil c/\epsilon \rceil - 1$ iterations the input is small enough to fit onto a single machine, and the overall algorithm terminates after $\lceil c/\epsilon \rceil$ rounds. $\square$

LEMMA 2.2. *The MST(V,E) algorithm does $O(\frac{cm}{\epsilon}\alpha(m,n))$ total work.*

PROOF. During a specific iteration, randomly partitioning E into $E_1, E_2, \ldots, E_\ell$ requires a linear scan over the edges which is $O(m)$ work. Computing the minimum spanning tree M_i of each part of the partition using the algorithm of [2] takes $O(\ell\frac{m}{\ell}\alpha(m,n))$ work. Computing the MST of G_{sparse} on one machine using the same algorithm requires $\ell(n-1)\alpha(m,n) = O(m\alpha(m,n))$ work. $\square$

For constant ϵ the $\mathcal{MRC}$ algorithm uses $O(m\alpha(m,n))$ work. Since the best known sequential algorithm [11] runs in time $O(m)$ in expectation, the $\mathcal{MRC}$ algorithm is work efficient up to a factor of $\alpha(m,n)$.

3. MATCHINGS AND COVERS

The maximum matching problem and its variants play a central role in theoretical computer science, so it is natural to determine if is possible to efficiently compute a maximum matching, or, more simply, a maximal matching, in the MapReduce framework. The question is not trivial. Indeed, due to the constraints of the model, it is not possible to store (or even stream through) all of the edges of a graph on a single machine. Furthermore, it is easy to come up with examples where the partitioning technique similar to that used for MSTs (Section 2.4) yields an arbitrarily bad matching. Simply sampling the edges uniformly, or even using one of the sparsification approaches [18] appears unfruitful because good sparsifiers do not necessarily preserve maximal matchings.

Despite these difficulties, we are able to show that by combining a simple sampling technique and a post-processing strategy it is possible to compute an unweighted maximal matching and thus a 2-approximation to the unweighted maximum matching problem using only machines with memory of size $O(n)$ and $O(\log n)$ rounds. More generally, we show that we can find a maximal matching on c-dense graphs in $O(c/\epsilon)$ rounds using machines with $\Omega(n^{1+\epsilon})$ memory; only three rounds are necessary if $\epsilon = 2c/3$. We extend this technique to obtain an 8-approximation algorithm for maximum weighted matching and use similar approaches to approximate the vertex and edge cover problems. This section is organized as follows: first we present the algorithm to solve the unweighted maximal matching, and then we explain how to use this algorithm to solve the weighted maximum matching problem. Finally, we show how the techniques can be adapted to solve the minimum vertex and the minimum edge cover problems.

3.1 Unweighted Maximal Matchings

The algorithm works by first sampling $O(\eta)$ edges and finding a maximal matching M_1 on the resulting subgraph. Given this matching, we can now safely remove edges that are in conflict (i.e. those incident on nodes in M_1) from the original graph G. If the resulting filtered graph, H is small enough to fit onto a single machine, the algorithm augments M_1 with a matching found on H. Otherwise, we augment M_1 with the matching found by recursing on H. Note that since the size of the graph reduces from round to round, the effective sampling probability increases, resulting in a larger sample of the remaining graph.

Formally, let $G(V,E)$ be a simple graph where $n = |V|$ and $|E| \leq n^{1+c}$ for some $c > 0$. We begin by assuming that each of the machines has at least η memory. We fix the exact value of η later, but require that $\eta \geq 40n$. We give the pseudocode for the algorithm below:

1. Set $M = \emptyset$ and $\mathcal{S} = E$.

2. Sample every edge $(u,v) \in \mathcal{S}$ uniformly at random with probability $p = \frac{\eta}{10|\mathcal{S}|}$. Let E' be the set of sampled edges.

3. If $|E'| > \eta$ the algorithm fails. Otherwise give the graph $G(V,E')$ as input to a single machine and compute a maximal matching M' on it. Set $M = M \cup M'$.

4. Let I be the set of unmatched vertices in G. Compute the subgraph of G induced by I, $G[I]$, and let $E[I]$ be the set of edges in $G[I]$. If $|E_i| > \eta$, set $\mathcal{S} = E[I]$ and return to step 2. Otherwise continue to step 5.

5. Compute a maximal matching M'' on $G[I]$ and output $M = M \cup M''$

To proceed we need the following technical lemma, which shows that with high probability every induced subgraph with sufficiently many edges, has at least one edge in the sample.

LEMMA 3.1. *Let $E' \subseteq E$ be a set of edges chosen independently with probability p. Then with probability at least $1 - e^{-n}$, for all $I \subseteq V$ either $|E[I]| < 2n/p$ or $E[I] \cap E' \neq \emptyset$.*

PROOF. Fix one such subgraph, $G[I] = (I, E[I])$ with $|E[I]| \geq 2n/p$. The probability that none of the edges in $E[I]$ were chosen to be in E' is $(1-p)^{|E[I]|} \leq (1-p)^{2n/p} \leq e^{-2n}$. Since there are at most 2^n total possible induced subgraphs $G[I]$, the probability that there exists one that does not have an edge in E' is at most $2^n e^{-2n} \leq e^{-n}$. $\square$

Next we bound the number of iterations the algorithm takes. Note that, the term iteration refers to the number of times the algorithm is repeated. This does not refer to a MapReduce round.

LEMMA 3.2. *If $\eta \geq 40n$ then the algorithm runs for at most $O(\log n)$ iterations with high probability. Furthermore, if $\eta = n^{1+\epsilon}$, where $0 < \epsilon < c$ is a fixed constant, then the algorithm runs in at most $\lfloor c/\epsilon \rfloor$ iterations with high probability.*

PROOF. Fix an iteration i of the algorithm and let p be the sampling probability for this iteration. Let E_i be the set of edges at the beginning of this iteration, and denote by I the set of unmatched vertices after this iteration. From Lemma 3.1, if $|E[I]| \geq 2n/p$ then an edge of $E[I]$ will be sampled with high probability. Note that no edge in $E[I]$ is incident on any edge in M'. Thus, if an edge from $E[I]$ is sampled then our algorithm would have chosen this edge to be in the matching. This contradicts the fact that no vertex in I is matched. Hence, $|E[I]| \leq 2n/p \leq \frac{20n|E_i|}{\eta}$ with high probability.

Now consider the first iteration of the algorithm, let $G_1(V_1, E_1)$ be the induced graph on the unmatched nodes after the first step of the algorithm. The above argument implies that $|E_1| \leq \frac{20n|E_0|}{\eta} \leq \frac{20n|E|}{\eta} \leq \frac{|E|}{2}$. Similarly $|E_2| \leq \frac{20n|E_1|}{\eta} \leq \frac{(20n)^2|E_0|}{\eta^2} \leq \frac{|E|}{2^2}$. So after i iterations $|E_i| \leq \frac{|E|}{2^i}$. The first part of the claim follows.

To conclude the proof note that if $\eta = n^{1+\epsilon}$, we have that $|E_i| \leq \frac{|E|}{n^{i\epsilon}}$, and thus the algorithm terminates after $\lfloor c/\epsilon \rfloor$ iterations. $\square$

We continue by showing the correctness of the algorithm.

THEOREM 3.1. *The algorithm finds a maximal matching of* $G = (V, E)$ *with high probability.*

PROOF. First consider the case that the algorithm does not fail. Assume, for the sake of contradiction, that there exists an edge $(u, v) \in E$ such that neither u nor v are matched in the final matching M that is output. Consider the last iteration of the algorithm. Since $(u, v) \in E$ and u and v are not matched, $(u, v) \in E[I]$. Since this is the last run of the algorithm, a maximal matching M'' of $G[I]$ is computed on one machine. Since M'' is maximal, either u or v or both must be matched in it. All of the edges of M'' get added to M in the last step, which gives our contradiction.

Next, consider the case that the algorithm failed. This occurs due to the set of edges E' having size larger than η in some iteration of the algorithm. Note that $\mathbf{E}[|E'|] = |\mathcal{S}| \cdot p = \eta/10$ in a given iteration. By the Chernoff Bound it follows that $|E'| \geq \eta$ with probability smaller than $2^{-\eta} \leq 2^{-40n}$ (since $\eta \geq 40n$). By Lemma 3.2 the algorithm completes in at most $O(\log n)$ rounds, thus the total failure probability is bounded by $O(\log n 2^{-40n})$ using the union bound. □

Finally we show how to implement this algorithm in MapReduce.

COROLLARY 3.1. *The Maximal Matching algorithm can be implemented in three MapReduce rounds when* $\eta = n^{1+2c/3}$. *Furthermore, when* $\eta = n^{1+\epsilon}$ *then the algorithm runs for* $3\lfloor c/\epsilon \rfloor$ *rounds and* $O(\log n)$ *rounds when* $\eta \geq 40n$.

PROOF. By Lemma 3.2 the algorithm runs for one iteration with high probability when $\eta = n^{1+2c/3}$, $\lfloor c/\epsilon \rfloor$ iterations when $\eta = n^{1+\epsilon}$. Therefore it only remains to describe how to compute the graph $G[I]$. For this we appeal to Lemma 6.1 in [13], where the set S_i are the edges incident on node i, and the function f_i drops the edge i if it is matched and keeps it otherwise. Hence, each iteration of the algorithm requires 3 MapReduce rounds. □

LEMMA 3.3. *The maximal matching algorithm presented above is work efficient when* $\eta = n^{1+\epsilon}$ *where* $0 < \epsilon < c$ *is a fixed constant.*

PROOF. By Lemma 3.2 when $\eta = n^{1+\epsilon}$ there are at most a constant number of iterations of the algorithm. Thus it suffices to show that $O(m)$ work is done in a single iteration. Sampling each edge with probability p requires a linear scan over the edges, which is $O(m)$ work. Computing a maximal matching on one machine can be done using a straightforward, greedy semi-streaming algorithm requiring $|E'| \leq \eta \leq m$ work. Computing $G[I]$ can be done as follows. Load M' onto m^ϵ machines where $0 < \epsilon < c$ and partition E among those machines. Then, if an edge in E is incident on an edge in M' the machines drop that edge, otherwise that edge is in $G[I]$. This results in $O(m)$ work to load all of the data onto the machines and $O(m)$ work to compute $G[I]$. Since $G[I]$ has at most m edges, computing M'' on one machine using the best known greedy semi-streaming algorithm also requires $O(m)$ work. □

Since the vertices in a maximal matching provide a 2-approximation to the vertex cover problem, we get the following corollary.

COROLLARY 3.2. *A 2-approximation to the optimal vertex cover can be computed in three MapReduce rounds when* $\eta = n^{1+2c/3}$. *Further, when* $\eta = n^{1+\epsilon}$ *then the algorithm runs for* $3\lfloor c/\epsilon \rfloor$ *rounds and* $O(\log n)$ *rounds when* $\eta \geq 40n$. *This algorithm does* $O(m)$ *total work when* $\eta = n^{1+\epsilon}$ *for a constant* $\epsilon > 0$.

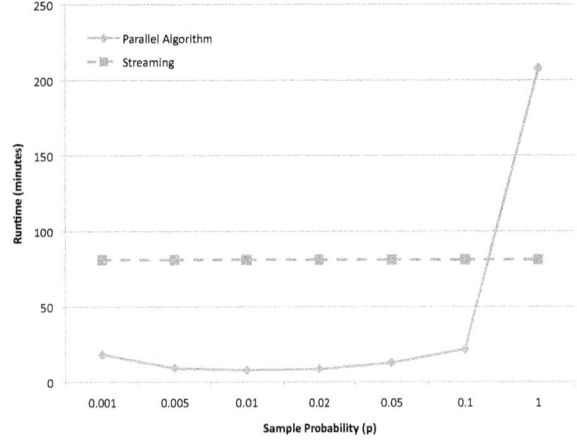

Figure 2: The running time of the MapReduce matching algorithm for different values of p, as well as the baseline provided by the streaming implementation.

3.1.1 Experimental Validation

In this Section we experimentally validate the above algorithm and demonstrate that it leads to significant runtime improvements in practice. Our data set consists of a sample of a graph of the twitter follower network, previously used in [1]. The graph has 50,767,223 nodes, 2,669,502,959 edges, and takes about 44GB when stored on disk. We implemented the greedy streaming algorithm for maximum matching as well as the three phase MapReduce algorithm described above. The streaming algorithm remains I/O bounded and completes in 81 minutes. The total running times for the MapReduce algorithm with different values for the sampling probability p are given in Figure 2.

The MapReduce algorithm achieves a significant speedup (over 10x) over a large number of values for p. The speed up is the result of the fact that a single machine never scans the whole input. Both the sampling in stage 1 and the filtering in stage 2 are performed in parallel. Note that the parallelization does not come for free, and the MapReduce system has non-trivial overhead over the straightforward streaming implementation. For example, when $p = 1$, the MapReduce algorithm essentially implements the streaming algorithm (since all of the edges are mapped onto a single machine), however the running time is almost 2.5 times slower. Overall these results show that the algorithms proposed are not only interesting from a theoretical viewpoint, but are viable and useful in practice.

3.2 Maximum Weighted Matching

We present an algorithm that computes an approximation to the maximum weighted matching problem using a constant number of MapReduce rounds. Our algorithm takes advantage of both the sequential and parallel power of MapReduce. Indeed, it will compute several matchings in parallel and then combine them on a single machine to compute the final result. We assume that the maximum weight on an edge is polynomial in $|E|$ and we prove an 8-approximation algorithm. Our analysis is motivated by the work of Feigenbaum et al. [4], but is technically different since no single machines sees all of the edges.

The input of the algorithm is a simple graph $G(V, E)$ and a weight function $w : E \rightarrow \mathbb{R}$. We assume that $|V| = n$ and $|E| = n^{1+c}$ for a constant $c > 0$. Without loss of generality, assume that $\min\{w(e) : e \in E\} = 1$ and $W = \max\{w(e) : e \in E\}$. The algorithm works as follows:

1. Split the graph G into $G_1, G_2, \cdots, G_{\lceil \log W \rceil}$, where G_i is the graph on the set V of vertices and contains edges with weights in $(2^{i-1}, 2^i]$.

2. For $1 \leq i \leq \lceil \log W \rceil$ run the maximal matching algorithm on G_i. Let M_i be the maximal matching for the graph G_i.

3. Set $M = \emptyset$. Consider the edge sets sequentially, in descending order, $M_{\lceil \log W \rceil}, \ldots, M_2, M_1$. When considering an edge $e \in M_i$, we add it to the matching if and only if $M \cup \{e\}$ is a valid matching. After all edges are considered, output M.

LEMMA 3.4. *The above algorithm outputs an 8-approximation to the weighted maximum matching problem.*

PROOF. Let OPT be the maximum weighted matching in G and denote by $V(M_i)$ the set of vertices incident on the edges in M_i. Consider an edge $(u, v) = e \in$ OPT, such that $e \in G_j$ for some j. Let i^* be the maximum i such that $\{u, v\} \cap V(M_{i^*}) \neq \emptyset$. Note that i^* must exist, and $i^* \geq j$ else we could have added e to M_j. Therefore, $w(e) \leq 2^{i^*}$.

Now for every such edge $(u, v) \in$ OPT we select one vertex from $\{u, v\} \cap V(M_{i^*})$. Without loss of generality, let that v be the selected vertex. We say that v is a *blocking vertex for e*. For each blocking vertex v, we associate its incident edge in M_{i^*} and call it the *blocking edge for e*. Let $V_b(i)$ be the set of blocking vertices in $V(M_i)$, we have that

$$\sum_{i=1}^{\lceil \log W \rceil} 2^i |V_b(i)| \geq \sum_{e \in \text{OPT}} w(e).$$

This follows from the fact that every vertex can "block" at most one $e \in$ OPT and that OPT is a valid matching. Note also that from the definition of *blocking vertex* if $(u, v) \in M \cap M_j$ then $u, v \notin \cup_{k<j} V_b(k)$.

Now suppose that an edge $(x, y) \in M_k$ is discarded by step 3 of the algorithm. This can happen if and only if there is an edge already present in the matching with a higher weight adjacent to x or y. Formally, there is a $(u, v) \in M$, $(u, v) \in M_j$ with $j > k$ and $\{u, v\} \cap \{x, y\} \neq \emptyset$. Without loss of generality assume that $\{u, v\} \cap \{x, y\} = x$ and consider such an edge (x, v). We say that (x, v) killed the edge (x, y) and the vertex y. Notice that an edge $(u, v) \in M$ and $(u, v) \in M_j$ kills at most two edges for every M_k with $k < j$ and kills at most two nodes in $V_b(k)$. Finally we also define $(u, v)_b$ as the set of *blocking vertices* associated with the *blocking edge* (u, v).

Now consider $V_b(k)$, each blocking vertex was either killed by one of the edges in the matching M, or is adjacent to one of the edges in M_k. Furthermore, the total weight of the edges in OPT with that were blocked by a *blocking vertex* killed by (u, v) is at most

$$\sum_{i=1}^{j-1} 2^i \big| \{V_b(i) \text{ killed by } (u,v)\} \big| \leq \sum_{i=1}^{j-1} 2^{i+1} \leq 2^{j+1} \leq 4w((u,v)).$$
(2)

To conclude, note that each edge in OPT that is not in M was either blocked directly by an edge in M, or was blocked by a vertex that was killed by an edge in M. To bound the former, consider an edge $(u, v) \in M_j \cap M$. Note that this edge can be incident on at most 2 edges in OPT, each of weight $2^j \leq 2w((u,v))$, and thus the weight in OPT incident on an edge (u, v) is $4w((u, v))$.

Putting this together with Equation 2 we conclude:

$$8 \sum_{(u,v) \in M} w((u,v)) \geq \sum_{e \in \text{OPT}} w(e).$$

$\square$

Furthermore we can show that the analysis of our algorithm is essentially tight. Indeed there exists a family of graphs where our algorithm finds a solution with weight $\frac{w(OPT)}{8-o(1)}$ with high probability. We prove the following lemma in Appendix A.

LEMMA 3.5. *There is a graph where our algorithm computes a solution that has value $\frac{w(OPT)}{8-o(1)}$ with high probability.*

Finally, suppose that the weight function $w : E \to \mathbb{R}$ is such that $\forall e \in E, w(e) \in O(poly(|E|))$ and that each machine has memory at least $\eta \geq \max\{2n \log^2 n, |V| \lceil \log^2 W \rceil\}$. Then we can run the above algorithm in MapReduce using only one more round than the maximal matching algorithm. In the first round we split G into $G_1, \ldots, G_{\lceil \log W \rceil}$; then we run the maximal matching algorithm of the previous subsection in parallel on $\lceil \log W \rceil$ machines. In the last round, we run the last step on a single machine. The last step is always possible because we have at most $|V| \lceil \log W \rceil$ edges each with weights of size $\log W$.

THEOREM 3.2. *There is an algorithm that finds a 8-approximation to the maximum weighted matching problem on a c dense graph using machines with memory $\eta = n^{1+\epsilon}$ in $3\lfloor c/\epsilon \rfloor + 1$ rounds with high probability.*

COROLLARY 3.3. *There is an algorithm that, with high probability, finds a 8-approximation to the maximum weighted matching problem that runs in four MapReduce rounds when $\eta = n^{1+2/3c}$.*

To conclude the analysis of the algorithm we now study the work amount of the maximum matching algorithm.

LEMMA 3.6. *The amount of work performed by the maximum matching algorithm presented above is $O(m)$ when $\eta = n^{1+\epsilon}$ where $0 < \epsilon < c$ is a fixed constant.*

PROOF. The first step of the algorithm requires $O(m)$ work as it can be done using a linear scan over the edges. In the second step, by Lemma 3.3 each machine performs work that is linear in the number of edges that are assigned to the machine. Since the edges are partitioned across the machines, the total work done in the second step is $O(m)$. Finally we can perform the third step by a semi-streaming algorithm that greedily adds edges in the order $M_{\lceil \log W \rceil}, \ldots, M_2, M_1$, requiring $O(m)$ work. $\square$

3.3 Minimum Edge Cover

Next we turn to the minimum edge cover problem. An edge cover of a graph $G(V, E)$ is a set of edges $E^* \subseteq E$ such that each vertex of V has at least one endpoint in E^*. The minimum edge cover is an edge cover E^* of minimum size.

Let $G(V, E)$ be a simple graph. The algorithm to compute a edge cover is as follows:

1. Find a maximal matching M of G using the procedure described in Section 3.1.

2. Let I be the set of uncovered vertices. For each uncovered vertex, take any edge incident on the vertex in I. Let this set of edges be U.

3. Output $E^* = M \cup U$.

Note that this procedure produces a feasible edge cover E^*. To bound the size of E^* let OPT denote the size of the minimum edge cover for the graph G and let OPT_m denote the size of the maximum matching in G. It is known that the minimum edge cover of a graph is equal to $|V| - \text{OPT}_m$. We also know that $|U| = |V| - 2|M|$. Therefore, $|E^*| = |V| - |M| \leq |V| - \frac{1}{2}\text{OPT}_m$ since a maximal matching has size at least $\frac{1}{2}\text{OPT}_m$. Knowing that $\text{OPT}_m \leq |V|/2$ and using Corollary 3.1 to bound the number of rounds we have the following theorem.

THEOREM 3.3. *There is an algorithm that, with high probability, finds a $\frac{3}{2}$-approximation to the minimum edge cover in MapReduce. If each machine has memory $\eta \geq 40n$ then the algorithm runs in $O(\log n)$ rounds. Further, if $\eta = n^{1+\epsilon}$, where $0 < \epsilon < c$ is a fixed constant, then the algorithm runs in $3\lfloor c/\epsilon \rfloor + 1$ rounds.*

COROLLARY 3.4. *There is an algorithm that, with high probability, finds a $\frac{3}{2}$-approximation to the minimum edge cover in four MapReduce rounds when $\eta = n^{1+2/3c}$.*

Now we prove that the amount of work performed by the edge cover algorithm is $O(m)$.

LEMMA 3.7. *The amount of work performed by the edge cover algorithm presented above is $O(m)$ when $\eta = n^{1+\epsilon}$ where $0 < \epsilon < c$ is a fixed constant.*

PROOF. By Lemma 3.3 when $\eta = n^{1+\epsilon}$ the first step of the algorithm can be done performing $O(m)$ operations. The second step can be performed by a semi streaming algorithm that requires $O(m)$ work. Thus the claim follows. □

4. MINIMUM CUT

Whereas in the previous algorithms the filtering was done by dropping certain edges, this algorithm filters by contracting edges. Contracting an edge, will obviously reduce the number of edges and may either keep the number of vertices the same (in the case we contracted a self loop), or reduce it by one. To compute the minimum cut of a graph we appeal to the contraction algorithm introduced by Karger [10]. The algorithm has a well known property that the random choices made in the early rounds succeed with high probability, whereas those made in the later rounds have a much lower probability of success. We exploit this property by showing how to filter the input in the first phase (by contracting edges) so that the remaining graph is guaranteed to be small enough to fit onto a single machine, yet large enough to ensure that the failure probability remains bounded. Once the filtering phase is complete, and the problem instance is small enough to fit onto a single machine, we can employ any one of the well known methods to find the minimum cut in the filtered graph. We then decrease the failure probability by running several executions of the algorithm in parallel, thus ensuring that in one of the copies the minimum cut survives this filtering phase.

The complicating factor in the scheme above is contracting the right number of edges so that the properties above hold. We proceed by labeling each edge with a random number between 0 and 1 and then searching for a threshold t so that contracting all of the edges with label less than t results in the desired number of vertices. Typically such a search would take logarithmic time, however, by doing the search in parallel across a large number of machines, we can reduce the depth of the recursion tree to be constant. Moreover, to compute the number of vertices remaining after the first t edges are contracted, we refer to the connected components algorithm in Section 2.4. Since the connected components algorithm uses a small number of machines, we can show that even with many parallel invocations we will not violate the machine budget. We present the algorithm and its analysis below. Also, the algorithm uses two subroutines, Find_t and Contract which are defined in turn.

Algorithm 1 MinCut(E)

1: **for** $i = 1$ to n^{δ_1} (in parallel) **do**
2:     tag $e \in E$ with a number r_e chosen uniformly at random from $[0, 1]$
3:     $t \leftarrow \text{Find}_t(E, 0, 1)$
4:     $E_i \leftarrow \text{Contract}(E, t)$
5:     $C_i \leftarrow$ min cut of E_i
6: **end for**
7: **return** minimum cut over all C_i

4.1 Find Algorithm

The pseudocode for the algorithm to find the correct threshold is given below. The algorithm performs a parallel search on the value t so that contracting all edges with weight at most t results in a graph with n^{δ_3} vertices. The algorithm invokes n^{δ_2} copies of the connected components algorithm, each of which uses at most $n^{c-\epsilon}$ machines, with $n^{1+\epsilon}$ memory.

Algorithm 2 $\text{Find}_t(E, \min, \max)$

1: {Uses $n^{\delta_2 + c/\epsilon}$ machines.}
2: $\gamma \leftarrow \frac{\max - \min}{n^{\delta_2}}$
3: **for** $j = 1$ to n^{δ_2} (in parallel) **do**
4:     $\tau_j \leftarrow \min + j\gamma$
5:     $E_j \leftarrow \{e \in E \mid r_e \leq \tau_j\}$
6:     $cc_j \leftarrow$ number of connected components in $G = (V, E_j)$
7: **end for**
8: **if** there exists a j such that $cc_j = n^{\delta_3}$ **then**
9:     **return** j
10: **else**
11:     **return** $\text{Find}_t(E, \tau_j, \tau_{j+1})$ where j is the smallest value s.t. $cc_j < n^{\delta_3}, cc_{j+1} > n^{\delta_3}$
12: **end if**

4.2 Contraction Algorithm

We state the contraction algorithm and prove bounds on its performance.

Algorithm 3 Contract(E, t)

1: $CC \leftarrow$ connected components in $\{e \in E \mid r_e \leq t\}$
2: let $h : [n] \rightarrow [n^{\delta_4}]$ be a universal hash function
3: map each edge (u, v) to machine $h(u)$ and $h(v)$
4: map the assignment of node u to its connected component $CC(u)$, to machine $h(u)$
5: on each reducer rename all instances of u to $CC(u)$
6: map each edge (u, v) to machine $h(u) + h(v)$
7: Drop self loops (edges in same connected component)
8: Aggregate parallel edges

LEMMA 4.1. *The Contract algorithm uses n^{δ_4} machines with $O(\frac{m}{n^{\delta_4}})$ space with high probability.*

PROOF. Partition V into parts $P_j = \{v \in V \mid 2^{j-1} < \deg(v) \leq 2^j\}$. Since the degree of each node is bounded by n, there are at most $\log n$ parts in the partition. Define the *volume* of part j as $V_j = |P_j| \cdot 2^j$. Parts having volume less than $m^{1-\epsilon}$ could all be mapped to one reducer without violating its space restriction. We now focus on parts with $V_j > m^{1-\epsilon}$, and so let P_j be such a part. Thus P_j contains between $\frac{m^{1-\epsilon}}{2^j}$ and $\frac{2m^{1-\epsilon}}{2^j}$ vertices. Let ρ

be an arbitrary reducer. Since h is universal, the probability that any vertex $v \in P_j$ maps to ρ is exactly $n^{-\delta_4}$. Therefore, in expectation, the number of vertices of P_j mapping to ρ is at most $\frac{2m^{1-\epsilon}}{2^j n^{\delta_4}}$. Since each of these vertices has degree at most 2^j, in expectation the number of edges that map to ρ is at most $\frac{2m^{1-\epsilon}}{n^{\delta_4}}$. Let the random variable X_j denote the number of vertices from P_j that map to ρ. Say that a bad event happens if more than $\frac{4m^{1-\epsilon}}{2^j}$ vertices of V_j map to ρ. Chernoff bounds tell us that the probability of such an event happening is $O(1/n^{2\delta_4})$,

$$\Pr\left[X_j > \frac{10m^{1-\epsilon}}{n^{\delta_4}}\right] < 2^{-\left(\frac{10m^{1-\epsilon}}{n^{\delta_4}}\right)} < \frac{1}{n^{2\delta_4}}. \tag{3}$$

Taking a union bound over all n^{δ_4} reducers and $\log n$ parts, we can conclude that the probability of any reducer being overloaded is bounded below by $1 - o(1)$. $\square$

4.3 Analysis of the MinCut Algorithm

We proceed to bound the total number of machines, maximum amount of memory, and the total number of rounds used by the MinCut algorithm.

LEMMA 4.2. *The total number of machines used by the MinCut algorithm is $n^{\delta_1}\left(n^{\delta_2+c-\epsilon} + n^{\delta_4}\right)$.*

PROOF. The algorithm begins by running n^{δ_1} parallel copies of a simpler algorithm which first invokes Find_t, to find a threshold t for each instance. This algorithm uses n^{δ_2} parallel copies of a connected component algorithm, which itself uses $n^{c-\epsilon}$ machines (see Section 2.4). After finding the threshold, we invoke the Contract algorithm, which uses n^{δ_4} machines per instance. Together this gives the desired number of machines. $\square$

LEMMA 4.3. *The memory used by each machine during the execution of MinCut is bounded by $\max\{n^{2\delta_3}, n^{1+c-\delta_4}, n^{1+\epsilon}\}$.*

PROOF. There are three distinct steps where we must bound the memory. The first is the the searching phase of Find_t. Since this algorithm executes instances of the connected components algorithm in parallel, the results of Section 2.4 ensure that each instance uses at most $\eta = n^{1+\epsilon}$ memory. The second is the contraction algorithm. Lemma 4.1 assures us that the input to each machine is of size at most $O(\frac{m}{n^{\delta_4}})$. Finally, the last step of MinCut requires that we load an instance with n^{δ_3} vertices, and hence at most $n^{2\delta_3}$ edges onto a single machine. $\square$

LEMMA 4.4. *Suppose the amount of memory available per machine is $\eta = n^{1+\epsilon}$. MinCut runs in $O(\frac{1}{\epsilon\delta_2})$ number of rounds.*

PROOF. The only variable part of the running time is the number of rounds necessary to found a threshold τ so that the number of connected components in Find_t is exactly n^{δ_3}. Observe that after the kth recursive call, the number of edges with threshold between min and max is $\frac{m}{n^{\delta_2 k}}$. Therefore the algorithm must terminate after at most $\frac{1+c}{\delta_2}$ rounds, which is constant for constant δ_2. $\square$

We are now ready to prove the main theorem.

THEOREM 4.1. *Algorithm MinCut returns the minimum cut in G with probability at least $1 - o(1)$, uses at most $\eta = n^{1+\epsilon}$ memory per machine and completes in $O(\frac{1}{\epsilon^2})$ rounds.*

PROOF. We first show that the success probability is at least

$$1 - \left(1 - \frac{n^{2\delta_3}}{n^2}\right)^{n^{\delta_1}}.$$

The algorithm invokes n^{δ_1} parallel copies of the following approach: (1) simulate Karger's contraction algorithm [10] for the first $n - n^{\delta_3}$ steps resulting in a graph G_t and (2) Identify the minimum cut on G_t. By Corollary 2.2 of [12] step (1) succeeds with probability at least $p = \Omega(n^{2\delta_3-2})$. Since the second step can be made to fail with 0 probability, each of the parallel copies succeeds with probability at least p. By running n^{δ_1} independent copies of the algorithm, the probability that all of the copies fail in step (1) is at most $1 - (1-p)^{n^{\delta_1}}$.

To prove the theorem, we must find a setting of the parameters $\delta_1, \delta_2, \delta_3$, and δ_4 so that the memory, machines, and correctness constraints are satisfied.

$$\max\{n^{2\delta_3}, n^{1+c-\delta_4}\} \le \eta = n^{1+\epsilon} \qquad \text{Memory}$$

$$n^{\delta_1}\left(n^{\delta_2+c-\epsilon} + n^{\delta_4}\right) = o(m) = o(n^{1+c}) \qquad \text{Machines}$$

$$\left(1 - \frac{n^{2\delta_3}}{n^2}\right)^{n^{\delta_1}} = o(1) \qquad \text{Correctness}$$

Setting $\delta_1 = 1 - \epsilon/2$, $\delta_2 = \epsilon$, $\delta_3 = \frac{1+\epsilon}{2}$, $\delta_4 = c$ satisfies all of them. $\square$

Acknowledgments

We would like to thank Ashish Goel, Jake Hofman, John Langford, Ravi Kumar, Serge Plotkin and Cong Yu for many helpful discussions.

5. REFERENCES

[1] E. Bakshy, J. Hofman, W. Mason, and D. J. Watts. Everyone's an influencer: Quantifying influence on twitter. In *Proceedings of WSDM*, 2011.

[2] Bernard Chazelle. A minimum spanning tree algorithm with inverse-Ackerman type complexity. *Journal of the ACM*, 47(6):1028–1047, November 2000.

[3] Jeffrey Dean and Sanjay Ghemawat. MapReduce: Simplified data processing on large clusters. In *Proceedings of OSDI*, pages 137–150, 2004.

[4] Joan Feigenbaum, Sampath Kannan, Andrew McGregor, Siddharth Suri, and Jian Zhang. On graph problems in a semi-streaming model. *Theoretical Computer Science*, 348(2–3):207–216, December 2005.

[5] Michael T. Goodrich. Simulating parallel algorithms in the mapreduce framework with applications to parallel computational geometry. Second Workshop on Massive Data Algorithmics (MASSIVE 2010), June 2010.

[6] Hadoop Wiki - Powered By. http://wiki.apache.org/hadoop/PoweredBy.

[7] Blake Irving. Big data and the power of hadoop. Yahoo! Hadoop Summit, June 2010.

[8] Amos Israel and A. Itai. A fast and simple randomized parallel algorithm for maximal matching. *Information Processing Letters*, 22(2):77–80, 1986.

[9] U Kang, Charalampos Tsourakakis, Ana Paula Appel, Christos Faloutsos, and Jure Leskovec. HADI: Fast diameter estimation and mining in massive graphs with hadoop. Technical Report CMU-ML-08-117, CMU, December 2008.

[10] David R. Karger. Global min-cuts in $\mathcal{RNC}$ and other ramifications of a simple mincut algorithm. In *Proceedings of SODA*, pages 21–30, January 1993.

[11] David R. Karger, Philip N. Klein, and Robert E. Tarjan. A randomized linear-time algorithm for finding minimum spanning trees. In *Proceedings of the twenty-sixth annual ACM symposium on Theory of computing*, Proceedings of STOC, pages 9–15, New York, NY, USA, 1994. ACM.

[12] David R. Karger and Clifford Stein. An $\tilde{O}(n^2)$ algorithm for minimum cuts. In *Proceedings of STOC*, pages 757–765, May 1993.

[13] Howard Karloff, Siddharth Suri, and Sergei Vassilvitskii. A model of computation for MapReduce. In *Proceedings of SODA*, pages 938–948, 2010.

[14] Jure Leskovec, Jon Kleinberg, and Christos Faloutsos. Graphs over time: Densification laws, shrinking daimeters and possible explanations. In *Proc. 11th ACM SIGKDD International Conference on Knowledge Discovery and Data Mining*, 2005.

[15] Jimmy Lin and Chris Dyer. *Data-Intensive Text Processing with MapReduce*. Number 7 in Synthesis Lectures on Human Language Technologies. Morgan and Claypool, April 2010.

[16] Grzegorz Malewicz, Matthew H. Austern, Aart J.C. Bik, James C. Dehnert, Ilan Horn, Naty Leiser, and Grzegorz Czajkowski. Pregel: A system for large-scale graph processing. In *Proceedings of SIGMOD*, pages 135–145, Indianapolis, IN, USA, June 2010. ACM.

[17] Mike Schroepfer. Inside large-scale analytics at facebook. Yahoo! Hadoop Summit, June 2010.

[18] Daniel A. Spielman and Nikhil Srivastava. Graph sparsification by effective resistances. In *Proceedings of STOC*, pages 563–568, New York, NY, USA, 2008. ACM.

[19] Mirjam Wattenhofer and Roger Wattenhofer. Distributed weighted matching. In *Proceedings of DISC*, pages 335–348. Springer, 2003.

[20] Tom White. *Hadoop: The Definitive Guide*. O'Reilly Media, 2009.

[21] Yahoo! Inc Press Release. Yahoo! partners with four top universities to advance cloud computing systems and applications research. http://research.yahoo.com/news/2743, April 2009.

APPENDIX

A. WEIGHTED MATCHING LOWER BOUND

LEMMA A.1. *There is a graph where our algorithm compute a solution that has value $\frac{w(OPT)}{8-o(1)}$ with high probability.*

PROOF. Let $G(V,E)$ a graph on n nodes and m vertices, and fix a $W = 2^{\lceil \log m \rceil}$. We say that a bipartite graph $G(V, E_1, E_2)$ is balanced if $|E_1| = |E_2|$. Consider the following graph: there is a central balanced bipartite clique, B_1, on $\frac{n}{2 \log W}$ nodes and all the edges of the clique have weight $\frac{W}{2} + 1$. Every side of the central bipartite clique is also part of other $\log W - 1$ balanced bipartite cliques. We refer to those cliques has $B_2^{E_1}, B_3^{E_1}, \cdots, B_W^{E_1}, B_2^{E_2}, B_3^{E_2}, \cdots, B_W^{E_2}$. In both $B_i^{E_1}$ and $B_i^{E_2}$ we have that the weight of the edges in them have weight $\frac{W}{2^i} + 1$. Furthermore every node in B_1 is also connected with an additional node of degree one with an edge of weight W, and every node in $B_i^{E_1} \setminus B_1$ and $B_i^{E_2} \setminus B_1$ is connected to a node of degree one with an edge of weight $\frac{W}{2^{i-1}}$. Figure 3 shows the subgraph composed by B_1 and the two graphs $B_i^{E_1}$ and $B_i^{E_2}$.

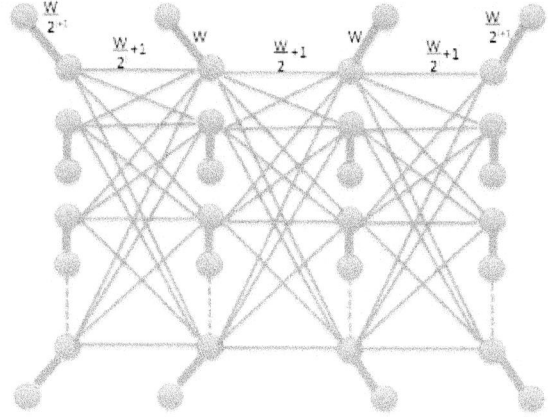

Figure 3: **The subgraph(we have drawn only the edges of weight W, $\frac{W}{2} + 1$, $\frac{W}{2^{i+1}}$ and $\frac{W}{2^i} + 1$) of the graph of G for which our algorithm finds a solution with value $\frac{w(OPT)}{8-o(1)}$ with high probability.**

Note that the optimal weighted maximum matching for this graph is the one that is composed by all the edges incident to a node of degree one and its total value is

$$2W \cdot \frac{n}{2 \log W} + W \cdot \frac{n}{2 \log W} + \frac{W}{2} \cdot \frac{n}{2 \log W} + \cdots + \frac{n}{2 \log W}$$

$$= 2W \frac{n}{2 \log W} \sum_{i=0}^{W} \frac{1}{2^i}$$

$$= 2W \frac{n}{2 \log W} \cdot \frac{1 - 2^{W+1}}{1 - 2^{-1}}$$

$$= (4 - o(1))W \frac{n}{2 \log W}.$$

Now we will show an upper-bound on the performance of our algorithm that holds with high probability. Recall that in step one our algorithm splits the graph in $G_1, \cdots, G_W$ subgraph where the edges in G_i are in in $(2^{i-1}, 2^i]$ then it computes a maximal matching on G_i using the technique shown in the previous subsection. In particular the algorithm works as follows: it samples the edges in G_i with probability $\frac{1}{|E_i|^\epsilon}$ and then computes a maximal matching on it, finally it tries to match the unmatched nodes using the edges between the unmatched nodes in G_i.

To understand the value of the matching returned by the algorithm, consider the graph G_i note that this graph is composed only by the edges in $B_i^{E_1}$, $B_i^{E_2}$ and the edges connected to nodes of degree one with weight $\frac{W}{2^{i-1}}$. We refer to those last edges as the heavy edges in G_i. Note that the heavy edges are all connected to vertices in $B_i^{E_1} \setminus B_1$ and $B_i^{E_2} \setminus B_1$. Let s be the number of vertices in a side of $B_i^{E_1}$, note that G_i, for $i > 1$ has $6s$ nodes and $s^2 + 2s$ edges.

Recall that we sample an edges with probability $\frac{1}{C|V_i|^\epsilon} = \frac{1}{C(6s)^\epsilon}$, so we have that in expectation we sample $\Theta\left(2s \frac{1}{(2s)^\epsilon}\right) = \Theta\left((2s)^{1-\epsilon}\right)$ heavy edges, thus using the Chernoff bound we have that the probability that the number of sampled heavy edges is bigger or equal than $\Theta\left(3(6s)^{(1-\epsilon)}\right)$ is $e^{-3(6s)^{(1-\epsilon)}}$. Further notice that by lemma 3.1 for every set of node in $B_i^{E_1}$ or $B_i^{E_2}$ with $(6s)^{1+2\epsilon}$ edges we have at least an edge in it with probability $e^{-\sqrt{6s}\left(\frac{1}{C}(6s)^\epsilon - \log(6s)\right)}$.

Thus the maximum number of nodes left unmatched in $B_i^{E_1}$ or $B_i^{E_2}$ after step 2 of the maximal matching algorithm is smaller then $(6s)^{\frac{1+2\epsilon}{2}} + \Theta\left(3(6s)^{(1-\epsilon)}\right)$ so even if we matched those nodes with the heavy edges in G_i we use at most $(6s)^{\frac{1+2\epsilon}{2}} + \Theta\left(3(6s)^{(1-\epsilon)}\right)$ of those edges. Thus we have that for every G_i, for every $i > 1$ the maximal matching algorithm uses at most $\Theta\left(6(6s)^{(1-\epsilon)} + (6s)^{\frac{1+2\epsilon}{2}}\right) = o\left(\frac{s}{\log^2 s}\right)$ heavy edges with probability $\left(1 - 2e^{-\sqrt{6s}\left(\frac{1}{C}(6s)^\epsilon - \log(6s)\right)}\right)$.

With the same reasoning, just with different constant, we notice that the same fact holds also for G_1. So we have that for every G_i we use only $o\left(\frac{|V_i|}{\log^2 |V_i|}\right)$ heavy edges with probability $\left(1 - 2e^{-\Theta(\sqrt{|V_i|})}\right)$, further notice that every maximal matching that the algorithm computes it always matches the nodes in B_1, because it is alway possible to use the edges that connect those nodes to the nodes of degree 1.

Knowing that we notice that the final matching that our algorithm outputs is composed by the maximal matching of G_1 plus all the heavy edges in maximal matching of $G_2, \cdots, G_W$. Thus we have that with probability $\prod_i \left(1 - 2e^{-\Theta(\sqrt{|V_i|})}\right) = 1 - o(1)^3$ the total weight of the computed solution is upper-bounded by $\left(\frac{W}{2} + 1\right)\frac{n}{2\log W} + W \log W \cdot o\left(\frac{s}{\log^2 s}\right) = \frac{W}{2}\frac{n}{2\log W} + o(W)$ and so the ratio between the optimum and the solution is

$$\frac{(4 - o(1))W\frac{n}{2\log W}}{\frac{W}{2}\frac{n}{2\log W} + o(W)} = \frac{1}{8 - o(1)}.$$

Thus the claim follows. $\square$

---

[3] Note that every $|V_i| \in \Theta\left(\frac{n}{\log W}\right)$

Parallelism and Data Movement Characterization of Contemporary Application Classes

Victoria Caparrós Cabezas
IBM Research — Zürich
Säumerstrasse 4, 8803 Rüschlikon, Switzerland
vca@zurich.ibm.com

Phillip Stanley-Marbell
IBM Research — Zürich
Säumerstrasse 4, 8803 Rüschlikon, Switzerland
pst@zurich.ibm.com

ABSTRACT

This paper presents a framework for characterizing the distribution of fine-grained parallelism, data movement, and communication-minimizing code partitions. Understanding the spectrum of parallelism available in applications, and how much data movement might result if such parallelism is exploited, is essential in the hardware design process because these properties will be the limiters to performance scaling of future computing systems. The framework is applied to characterizing 26 applications and kernels, classified according to their dominant components in the Berkeley dwarf/computational motif classification.

The *distributions* of ILP and TLP over execution time are studied, and it is shown that, though mean ILP is high, available ILP is significantly smaller for most of the execution. The results from this framework are complemented by hardware performance counter data on two RISC platforms (IBM Power7 and Freescale P2020) and one CISC platform (Intel Atom D510), spanning a broad range of real machine characteristics. Employing a combination of these new techniques, and building upon previous proposals, it is demonstrated that the similarity in available ideal-case parallelism and data movement within and across the dwarf classes, is limited.

Categories and Subject Descriptors

C.1.4 [**Computer Systems Organization**]: Processor Architectures—*Parallel Architectures*; C.4 [**Computer Systems Organization**]: Performance of Systems—*Measurement Techniques*; I.6.6 [**Computing Methodologies**]: Simulation and Modeling—*Simulation Output Analysis*

General Terms

Algorithms, Measurement, Performance.

Keywords

Instruction-level parallelism, basic-block-level parallelism, data movement, Berkeley computational motifs.

1. INTRODUCTION

For many technology generations, increases in performance were achieved via higher clock speeds and aggressive exploitation of instruction-level parallelism, through the use of wide superscalar out-of-order issue architectures. In the last decade, clock frequencies have stagnated, largely due to the inability to cope with the associated high power dissipation, which increases approximately linearly with clock speed. In large-scale systems, the integral of this power dissipation over time (i.e., energy) has monetary costs over the first few years of deployment that may surpass hardware purchase costs. Further associated challenges include the supply of required power, and the removal of generated heat. Thus, there has been an increasing shift to achieving improved performance by harnessing parallelism by means of new parallel and distributed algorithms, parallelizing compilers [17], or parallel hardware architectures, such as multi-core and multi-processor architectures.

The appropriate combination of superscalar architecture width, multithreading, multi-core, and multiplicity of processors, will depend on the availability of the corresponding granularities of parallelism in applications. Harnessing parallelism however results in dependences that previously existed within a monolithic execution grouping, to be exposed, in one form or another, as data movement across the parallelized partitions. Understanding limit-case *hardware-extractable parallelism* and *data movement* in modern applications is hence a necessary step to reason about properties of future computing platforms.

This paper presents a framework that enables the analysis of the distribution of parallelism over the entire execution, rather than simply reporting average values of available parallelism as in previous limit-case parallelism studies [18, 21, 19, 23, 26, 29]. By analyzing the cumulative distribution of the potential instruction- and thread-level parallelism[1] over execution, it is demonstrated that 80% of the execution time for most applications has available parallelism that is smaller than the mean values previously reported, in some cases up to 1000× smaller.

The *Berkeley dwarf classification* [2], is *intended* to categorize computational motifs according to their communication and computation patterns. The motifs cover a broad spectrum of workloads, from scientific applications, whose numerical kernels have traditionally been the target of high-performance computing systems, to modern applications, such as machine learning or database software, that are supposed to be promising areas for future computing systems. This paper shows, quantitatively, that applications that are dominated by the same computational motif do not necessarily have similar amounts of machine-extractable instruction- or thread-

---

[1]In the rest of the paper, thread-level parallelism (TLP) refers to basic-bock-granularity TLP, which can be exploited by speculative multithreaded architectures.

level parallelism and data movement characteristics. The main contributions are:

- a quantitative study of the available parallelism and data movement requirements across parallel partitions, at the instruction- and basic-block-level, for applications covering the Berkeley computational motifs;

- new insight into the amount of limit-case instruction- and thread-level parallelism, by studying the distribution and the cumulative distribution over execution cycles;

- a new execution-driven approach to identifying the ideal task partitioning that minimizes data movement due to true dependences, along with a method to identify regions with potential data-level parallelism;

- IPC trends on a range of state-of-the-art RISC and CISC architectures, using hardware performance counter data, to complement the ideal-case ILP analyses presented.

An overview of relevant related research is presented in Section 2. It is followed by a description of the techniques employed in characterizing instruction- and basic-block-level parallelism, as well as the ideal code partitioning into communicating tasks (Section 3) and data movement properties (Section 4). Section 5 then presents the results of the foregoing parallelism and data movement analysis techniques for a collection of 26 applications spanning the Berkeley dwarf classification, along with complementary hardware performance counter measurements. A summary of the results and new insights, along with directions for further investigation, is presented in Section 6, which concludes.

2. RELATED RESEARCH

Properties of application behavior (e.g., memory access patterns) across different sets of workloads, from HPC to commercial applications, have been extensively characterized in the literature. Although most of these studies are based on simulations or measurements from actual performance counters, some focus on upper bound analyses and characterize ideal-case properties.

Most of the related research on ideal-case application properties has focused on instruction-level parallelism [3, 21, 23, 27] since, for several design generations, performance gains were achieved via wide-issue superscalar out-of-order processors that exploited parallelism among instructions. These studies showed the potential ILP that can be extracted from sequential applications when they are executed under ideal conditions, i.e., with no architectural constraints and all dependences, except *true dependences* imposed by the semantics of the program, removed. They also evaluated the effect of control and resource dependences on the potential for parallel execution at the instruction level [29]. In all cases, these studies presented the *average* limit-case ILP over the execution of an application, equivalent to an analysis of the whole dataflow graph based on *span* and *work* analysis [9, 13]. As is demonstrated in Section 5, the *distribution* of ILP over a program's execution is such that, in some cases, upwards of 80% of a program's dynamic execution stream has available ILP that is an order of magnitude or more *smaller* than the mean value. Even the consideration of refinements of the average ILP, such as considering its *smoothability* [26], do not provide the same insights as the distributions presented in this paper, as they are still aggregate values. Thus, even though the implementation of wide ILP-exploiting superscalar out-of-order architectures is an important limiter to exploiting ILP, the amount of "usable" ILP in many applications may be smaller than previously commonly believed.

As new hardware architectures started enabling multithreading, either as statically identified by a programmer, at compile time [20], via simultaneous multithreading and thread-level speculation [4, 18], or with extensions to the sequential programming model to expose additional parallelism [5], growing interest in coarser forms of parallelism arose. The software threads in question may be considered conceptually at the level of functions, loops within functions, or down to individual basic blocks that may execute concurrently. A number of studies [18, 19] explored how to extract parallelism from sequential instruction streams by analyzing control-independent threads at the basic-block level, and showed the potential of thread-level speculation in upper-bound TLP. Other studies [15] estimated limit-case TLP through the use of dynamic instruction number versus ready-time (DIN versus RDY) plots. More recently, tools that automatically estimate upper bounds on available TLP, based on the analysis of data dependences between parallel threads, have been proposed [13]. These tools have however required programmer involvement in the specification of coarse-grained threads, via code annotations such as Cilk++ keywords.

Limit studies of task-level partitioning and ideal-case data-level parallelism have been paid less attention, due to a prevailing notion that these coarser levels of parallelism will typically be extracted by manual restructuring of programs using abstractions such as the message passing interface (MPI). *Data-level parallelism (DLP)* may be exploited at a range of granularities, from *single instruction multiple data (SIMD)* architectures at the instruction level, to data-parallel tasks processing stream datasets. Limit studies on SIMD DLP have employed a variety of approaches to discover SIMD DLP, based, for example, on packing algorithms that group dynamic instructions that implement the same operation code over related data [24]. Contemporary examples of exploiting coarse-grained DLP include the idioms usually employed in applications implemented using the MapReduce [10] runtime system. The term *task-level parallelism* can be used to refer to the granularity of parallelism often involving instances of code regions, e.g., functions. These are typically manually instantiated in programs, and communicate either through shared memory or explicit message passing; examples include MPI tasks. Such task-level parallelism is typically exploited in hardware through the use of multiple cores on a die, or multiple processors.

Harnessing parallelism at different granularities impacts data movement properties, due to the need for communication between parallel partitions to satisfy data dependences. For example, the exploitation of ILP in a speculative wide-issue superscalar processor may increase the memory accesses due to mispredicted branches [8]. Architectural approaches for exploiting thread-level parallelism, such as those facilitating dynamic thread migration [6], also lead to the implicit requirement for data movement within an architecture. At a coarser level, the explicit communication characteristics of large-scale scientific applications, such as point-to-point and collective communication, have previously been studied by Vetter *et al.* [28].

3. LIMIT-CASE PARALLELISM

There are many important motivators for estimating parallelism that can be extracted from applications. First, parallelism characterization across classes of application and kernel types (i.e., dwarfs) provides quantitative insight into the degree of variation of parallelism across algorithms and their corresponding implementations. Second, the methodology presented in this work may be applied when, e.g., a decision must be made to invest time in modifying applications to better take advantage of the particular mix of parallelism in future hardware platforms. As is shown in Section 5,

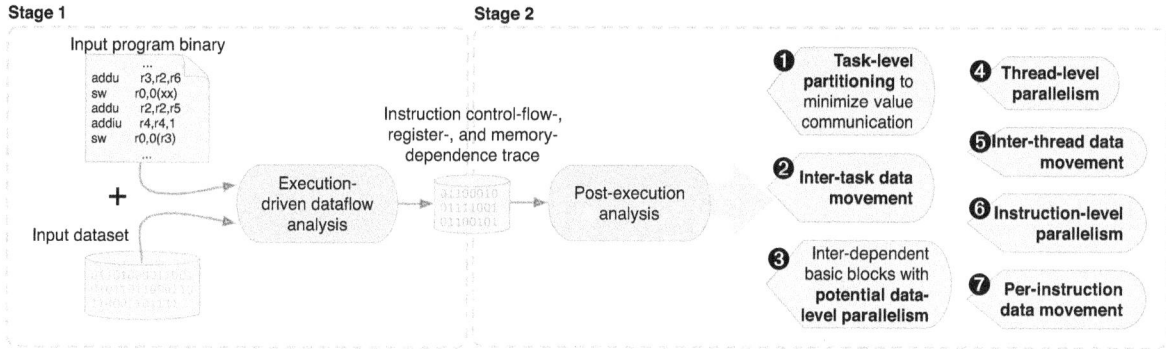

Figure 1: Overview of methodology for characterizing ideal-case parallelism and data movement properties.

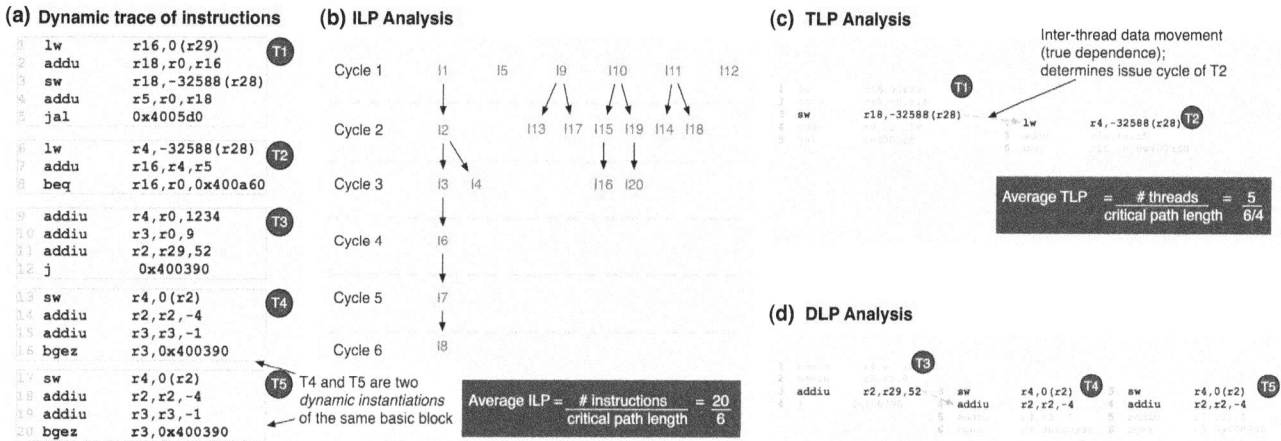

Figure 2: Illustration of ILP, TLP, and DLP estimation, from execution-driven instruction trace.

applications with low ideal-case ILP in practice experience low actual realized ILP, when run on a variety of narrow- to wide-issue machines.

In studying bounds on available parallelism within applications, an idealized or *oracle* machine model is typically employed. In such a machine, parallelism is limited only by true data dependences—i.e., the dependences determined by the semantics of the program. Such an idealized machine, and its embodiment, typically in a microarchitectural simulator, was also used in previous limit studies [23, 26]. The machine has unlimited instruction issue and scheduling windows, an unlimited number of functional units to overcome structural hazards, perfect caches, perfect branch prediction to remove control dependences, and employs register renaming and memory disambiguation techniques to eliminate output and anti-dependences.

Figure 1 depicts an overview of the parallelism estimation techniques employed in this work. The analysis is divided into two stages: a dataflow runtime analysis (stage 1 in Figure 1), and an offline processing of the data collected in the previous phase (stage 2). Applications are cross-compiled for execution on a MIPS-IV ISA simulator [7] that emulates the microarchitecture of the oracle machine. During the runtime analysis of the dynamic instruction trace, inter-instruction and inter-basic-block true data dependences are determined by monitoring all memory and register reads and writes, and this information is captured and used in the subsequent analysis to determine instruction- and basic-block-level parallelism, data movement, and task-level partitioning, as detailed in the following sections.

3.1 Instruction-level parallelism

Contemporary VLIW implementations (e.g., the TI TMS320C6-7x) are currently limited to an issue width of 8 [25], while the widest superscalar out-of-order architectures, e.g., the IBM Power7 [16], can issue up to 8 instructions per cycle but may have up to 12 instructions executing simultaneously. Thus, applications containing *less* available ILP, even under idealized execution assumptions, will be inherently unable to take advantage of such architectures. If, however, such applications have available coarser-grained (thread-, task-, data-level) parallelism, they might be better suited by narrow-issue architectures with many cores. Therefore, the characterization of the available *instruction-level parallelism (ILP)* in applications is relevant because it provides a view of the most a particular application would benefit from hardware that harnesses ILP.

ILP is limited by data, control and resource dependences [14]. Those dependences in which there is no value being transmitted between instructions can be removed with techniques such as *register* and *memory renaming*, in the case of data dependences, or *prediction techniques* and speculative execution for control dependences. Resource dependences are caused by limitations in, e.g., the number of functional units, or the instruction window size. By emulating a machine in which these resources are unlimited, these "false" dependences can be eliminated.

Figure 2 illustrates how ideal ILP is estimated from a dynamic trace of instructions (shown in Figure 2(a)). This approach of analyzing the dynamic serial instruction stream of applications and tracking the usage of each register and memory location to determine the earliest cycle in which an instruction or basic-block can be scheduled, is equivalent to building a *control and data de-*

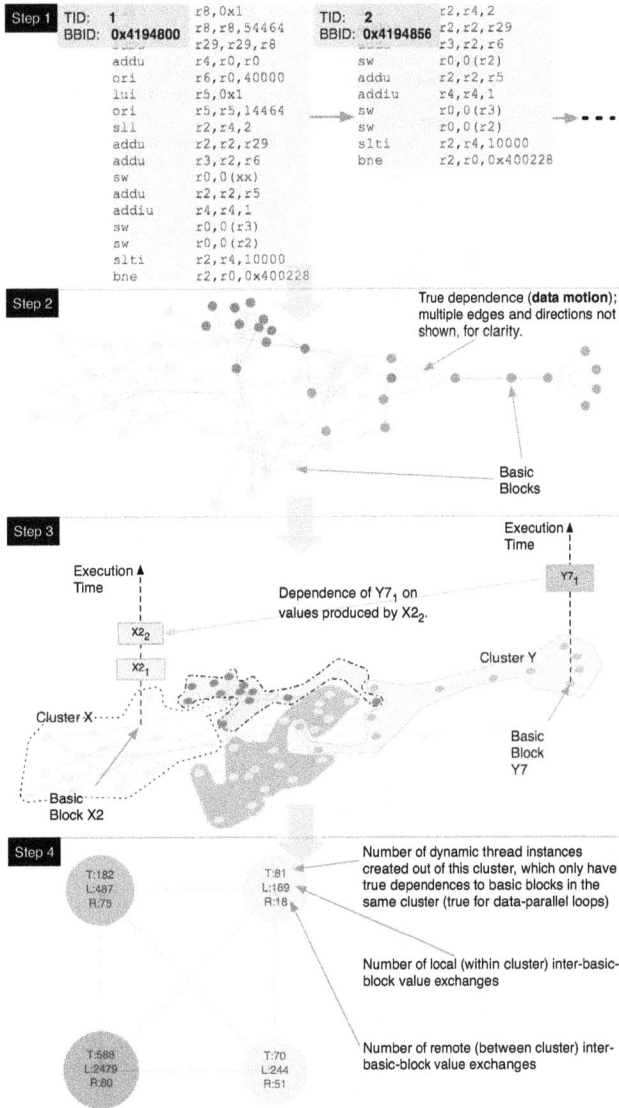

Figure 3: Methodology for analyzing task partitioning and data-level parallelism. The dynamic thread instance ID (TID) denotes the number of basic blocks executed up to a given point. The basic block ID (BBID) is the program counter value corresponding to the code entry point of a given static basic block.

pendence graph (DDG), and determining the *span* and *work* [9], while taking into account the dynamic control flow resulting from a program's input. Performing the analysis for each execution cycle (Figure 2(b)) enables the complete distribution of ILP over a program's execution to be obtained, as opposed to a single average value that would be obtained by applying span and work analysis to the whole program's dataflow graph. As demonstrated in Section 5, the former approach provides new insights into the available parallelism in applications.

3.2 Thread-level parallelism

While instruction-level parallelism relates to parallelism between instructions along a single execution path, it is often possible to identify paths in a program's execution that have neither true data dependences nor control dependences on each other. Such independent paths of control—*threads*—may be identified with analysis similar to that employed for ILP (Figure 2(c)).

```
void calc_cov(int **mat, int *mean, int **cov) {
  for (i = 0; i < num_rows; i++) {
    for (j = i; j < num_rows; j++) {
      sum = 0;
      for (k = 0; k < num_cols; k++) {
        sum += ((mat[i][k] - mean[i])*
                (mat[j][k] - mean[j]));
      }
      cov[i][j] = cov[j][i] = sum/(num_cols-1);
    }
  }
}

int main(void) {
  < ... Initialization, and computation of mean ...>
  calc_cov(mat, mean, cov);
  return 0;
}
```

Figure 4: PCA kernel adapted from the Phoenix MapReduce benchmark suite [22], with potential for task- and data-level parallelism.

The segments of the instruction stream that constitute a thread are usually *control structures*, such as functions, loops or basic blocks [18]. The benefits of performing analyses at different granularities depend on the difficulty of automatically identifying independent threads from the sequential execution stream, and the trade-off between speedup and overhead in exploiting parallelism at these levels. Basic blocks can be considered as the minimum indivisible units across which it makes sense to exploit parallelism. In what follows, basic blocks are used as the units from which threads are constructed to estimate the upper bound on available TLP. Analysis at the basic-block level implicitly captures higher-level control structures, while removing much of the complexity from attempting to precisely identify, e.g., loops, which is often complicated by compile-time transformations. As with the ILP analysis, thread IDs that are scheduled in every execution cycle are stored for determining the distribution of thread-level parallelism.

3.3 Task-level partitioning

Available instruction- and thread-level parallelism in applications is typically exploited by hardware resources within a single processor core or processor package. In many applications however, the available parallelism may be at a coarser grain. Applications may be partitioned into a collection of communicating processes, or may comprise a single body of code that is applied, in a *single program multiple data (SPMD)* [11] manner, over multiple independent data streams. Automatic partitioning of applications to exploit inter-task concurrency and SPMD parallelism is a difficult problem with much prior and ongoing research [13]. Estimating the *potential SPMD parallelism*, or the *ideal task-level partitioning*, based on the data movement patterns due to true data dependences between portions of an application, is however tractable. This is because such estimations purposefully sidestep the thorny issues pertaining to actual implementation, such as the necessary synchronization between tasks, coherence between their memory spaces, and so on.

To illustrate, consider the example shown in Figure 4. It corresponds to an application that computes the mean vector and covariance matrix, two steps in performing *principal component analysis (PCA)*. The actual parallelization of the program, for execution on, say, a multiprocessor system, is not a trivial task, even though casual inspection of the code leads one to believe that some portions of the computation could execute concurrently. Furthermore, successive iterations of the loops may be independent, and may be executed in parallel, such available parallelism increasing with the size of the input dataset.

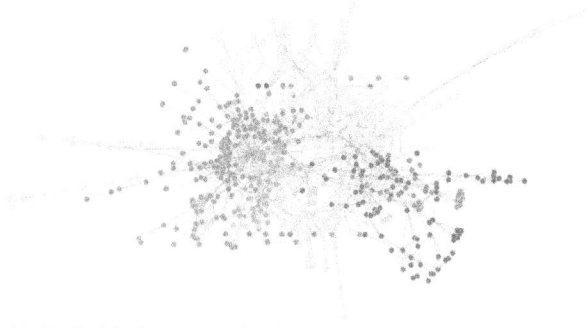

(a) Basic block communication graph, representing the static basic blocks, and the dynamic data movement through registers and memory, between basic blocks.

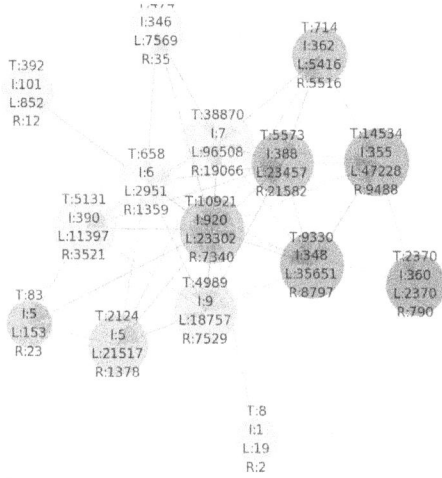

(b) Clustered basic block communication graph, with clusters having more intra- than inter-cluster data movement.

Figure 5: Communication-minimizing task partitioning and potential data-level parallelism from analysis of the program execution of the example in Figure 4.

3.3.1 Task partitioning algorithm

Estimates of the ideal task partitioning and data-level parallelism can be obtained by analyzing the true dependences between basic blocks over the course of an application's execution. For that purpose, a list of basic blocks that are *creators* of register/memory values, and basic blocks that are *consumers* of such values is maintained over the course of the execution-driven analysis. This removes the need to continually check for dependences between all pairs of basic blocks.

The approach employed is illustrated in Figure 3. Over the course of program execution, information is kept on the identity of each unique basic block executed, identified by its entry program counter (referred to as the BBID in Figure 3). The dynamic instantiations of the same basic block are referred to as the TIDs in Figure 3. TIDs, memory and register values used during execution (true data dependences), and the instantiations of which basic blocks produce the values used are also maintained (step 1). This information, which constitutes the dynamic control and dataflow between basic blocks, is used to build a basic block dependence graph, in which the vertices are unique basic blocks, and the edges correspond to data values exchanged between two basic blocks (step 2). In Figure 3 and in what follows, the multiple directional edges that may exists between two basic blocks are shown as a single undirected edge, for clarity. A clustering algorithm is then

```
1    ▷ BBdeps[N] is a data structure representing inter basic
2    ▷ block dependences. FINDCLUSTERS(V) returns the
3    ▷ communication-minimizing clustering. CLUSTERID(B)
4    ▷ returns the ID of the cluster to which B belongs.
5    for i ← 0 to N
6        do
7            for j ← 0 to |BBdeps[i]|
8                do
9                    adjcy[BBdeps[i][1]][BBdeps[i][j]] + +
10   codePartitions ← FINDCLUSTERS(adjcy + adjcy^T)
11
12   for i ← 0 to N
13       do
14           for j ← 0 to |BBdeps[i]|
15               do
16                   if CLUSTERID(i) == CLUSTERID(j)
17                       then lcomm[CLUSTERID(i)] + +
18                   else
19                       rcomm[CLUSTERID(i)] + +
20                       rcomm[CLUSTERID(j)] + +
21
22   ▷ Tdeps[M] is a data structure representing inter-thread,
23   ▷ dependences. WEAKCOMPONENTS(V) returns the
24   ▷ number of groups of threads with no interdependence.
25   for i ← 0 to |codePartitions|
26       do
27           for j ← 0 to M
28               do
29                   if CLUSTERID(Tdeps[j]) == i   &&
30                       Tdeps[j] ≥ threshold
31                   then for k ← 1 to |Tdeps[j]|
32                       do
33                           if Tdeps[k] ≥ threshold
34                               then adjcy[j][k] + +
35   dataPartitions[i] ← WEAKCOMPONENTS(adjcy)
```

Figure 6: Algorithm for estimating the code partitioning and automatic detection of DLP.

used to color the basic block dependence graph, such that groups of basic blocks which have more edge weight *within* the group than *across* groups are given the same color (step 3); each such cluster corresponds to the clustering of basic blocks into a task, that would reduce the communication between tasks[2].

Such clusters however hide the amount of communication that occurs *within* a cluster, e.g., due to a large number of cross-iteration true dependences in a long-running loop. The number of intra-cluster data value exchanges due to true dependences can be characterized by analyzing the number of dynamic basic block instantiations which consume all their values from other dynamic basic block instantiations created from blocks within the same cluster (step 4).

3.3.2 DLP estimation

By construction, the code clusters in the foregoing discussion contain potential sources of data parallelism such as loops. An analysis of the dependences between dynamic instantiations of basic blocks in a given cluster (e.g., $X2_1$ and $X2_2$ from cluster X2 in Figure 3, step 3) can thus be used as a starting point for estimating potential data-level parallelism.

If a given cluster does indeed represent a data-parallel loop, then the dynamic instances (TIDs) of basic blocks, e.g., $X2_1$ and $X2_2$ from cluster X2 in Figure 3, will have no true dependences across

---

[2]Some clusters may sometimes present slightly more remote communication than local because this is the partitioning that minimizes the *overall* remote communication.

Table 1: Applications from SPEC CPU2000[a], MiBench[b] and Phoenix MapReduce[c] benchmark suites used for parallelism and data movement analysis, and mapping into dwarf classes.

Dwarf 1: Dense Linear Algebra (DLA)	JPEG[b](encode, decode), kmeans[c](KME), pca[c]
Dwarf 2: Sparse Linear Algebra (SLA)	basicmath[b](BM), bitcount[b] (BC), matrix_multiply[c](MM)
Dwarf 3: Spectral Methods (SM)	lame[b], FFT[b], IFFT[b]
Dwarf 4: N-Body Methods (NB)	ammp[a]
Dwarf 5: Structured Grids (SG)	JPEG[b](encode, decode)
Dwarf 6: Unstructured Grids (UG)	equake[a](EQK)
Dwarf 7: MapReduce (MR)	mesa[a]
Dwarf 8: Combinational Logic (CL)	rijndael[b](encode (RIJNe), decode (RIJNd)), sha[b]
Dwarf 9: Graph Traversal (GT)	qsort[b](QSRT), dijkstra[b] (DIJKS)
Dwarf 10: Dynamic Programming (DP)	None
Dwarf 11: Backtrack / Branch+Bound (BT)	vpr[a], mcf[a], art[a], susan[b](SUS)
Dwarf 12: Graphical Models (GM)	None
Dwarf 13: Finite State Machine (FSM)	gzip[a], gcc[a], parser[a](PARS), stringsearch[b](SS)

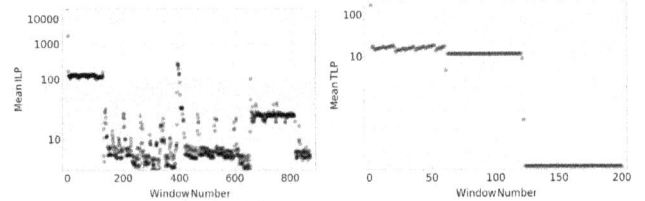

(a) Example ILP distribution.   (b) Example TLP distribution.

Figure 7: ILP and TLP distributions over execution cycles. To ease visualization, execution is split into windows of 25K cycles.

loop iterations. Clustering these TIDs spawned off a given code cluster into groups of *weakly-connected components* (i.e., groups of TIDs with *any* dependence path between them) would thus lead to a cluster of dynamic basic block instances per data-parallel loop iteration. Thus, in contrast to the code clustering of basic blocks to minimize the amount of communication (dependence edge weight) between clusters, which we refer to as *BBID clusters*, these *TID clusters* are simply clusters of dynamic instances that do not depend on each other *in any way*; there are therefore no edges between TID clusters.

The combined algorithm for task-partitioning and DLP cluster identification is shown in Figure 6. In processing the dynamic basic block instances that constitute a loop, however, it was necessary to elide dependences on initializers prior to the loop—with all loop iterations having true dependences on such initializers, the TID clustering would always yield a single dependence cluster. It was however observed that employing a heuristic of culling the first few (e.g., 10%) TIDs instantiated from a given code cluster, such dependences could be effectively removed, while not affecting the estimative power of the approach. Figure 5 illustrates the results from applying this analysis to the example from Figure 4. In the figure, the number of data-independent TID clusters is labeled as I:*number*.

4. DATA MOTION PROPERTIES

When available parallelism, at any granularity, is harnessed in practice, it results in the need to communicate values, as true data dependences that existed in the non-parallel execution may now need to be satisfied across the parallel partitions. Analyzing data movement properties thus sheds light on potential obstacles (or opportunities) to harnessing various forms of parallelism.

4.1 Memory references

Application memory access patterns impact the suitability of pipelined, wide-issue out-of-order architectures, since instructions whose dependences must be resolved through a memory access may cause stalls that inhibit potential gains in performance from the exploitation of instruction-level parallelism. The analysis of memory access patterns also provides insight into memory bandwidth requirements and limitations. In the simulation framework presented in the previous section, memory data movement is analyzed by tracking the number of loads from, and stores to, an idealized cache hierarchy (perfect hit rate).

4.2 Inter-thread data flow

In the analysis presented in this paper, inter-thread data flow is defined as the number of data exchanges between threads (per thread), where a data exchange occurs when a thread reads a value (from a register or memory) that was generated by another thread. To enable quantitative characterization of inter-thread data movement properties, the dynamic instruction stream of the serial application is treated as a composition of basic-block-granularity threads, as described in Section 3.2. The usage of every register and memory location is monitored such that the simulation infrastructure not only provides information about *when* the corresponding data is first available, but also the TID of the thread that generated the value. Hence, when a thread reads a value from a register or memory location, it is determined whether that value was written by a previously scheduled thread and, therefore, whether it will produce flow of data between threads.

Section 5.2 presents a detailed characterization of both the number of memory references per instruction, and the per-thread communication requirements.

5. RESULTS OF PARALLELISM AND DATA MOTION CHARACTERIZATION

The following presents the ILP, TLP, and data motion characterization for a suite of applications. Communication-minimizing task partitioning and DLP estimation are not presented in detail, but results for the former are briefly summarized for the suite of applications, in Section 6.

Applications from SPEC2000, MiBench [12], and the Phoenix MapReduce runtime [22] were used to quantitatively characterize the available ILP, TLP, and data movement across contemporary application classes. Table 1 lists the applications, classified according to the computational motifs/dwarfs they are dominated by. Two of the 26 applications studied (JPEG encode and JPEG decode) can be classified into both the Dense Linear Algebra (DLA) and Structured Grids (SG) dwarfs. In the remainder of the analysis therefore, there will be 28 applications listed, 26 of which will be unique applications. They will be referenced using the dwarf abbreviations in Table 1, and a subscript that corresponds to their ordinal position in the associated row of the table. All the applications were compiled with optimization flags -O3 -funroll-loops, and executed with large/reference input data sets. Figure 8 shows the instruction mix for the applications investigated. From the instruction breakdown, it can be seen that the compute characteristics span a broad range, from floating-point intensive applications (ammp (NB)) to memory-intensive (parser (FSM_3)) and integer-intensive applications (susan (BT_4)).

5.1 Instruction- and thread-level parallelism

Prior limit studies of ILP and TLP reported mean values thereof. Due to the amount of information generated during execution-

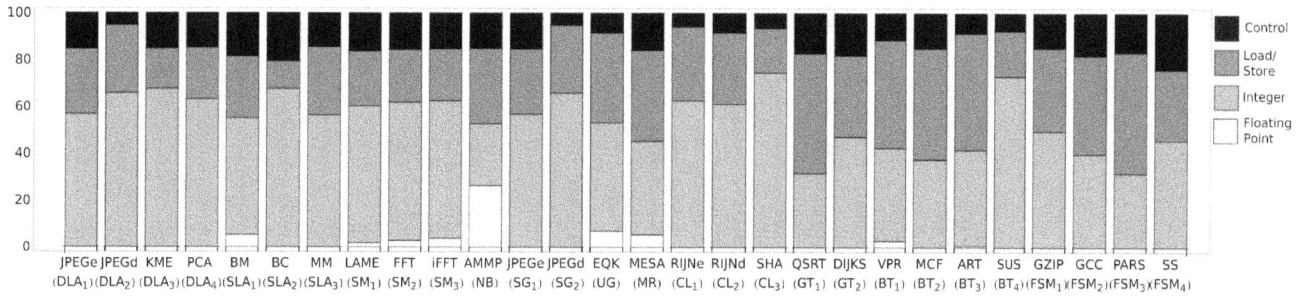

Figure 8: Instruction-execution profile of applications listed in Table 1.

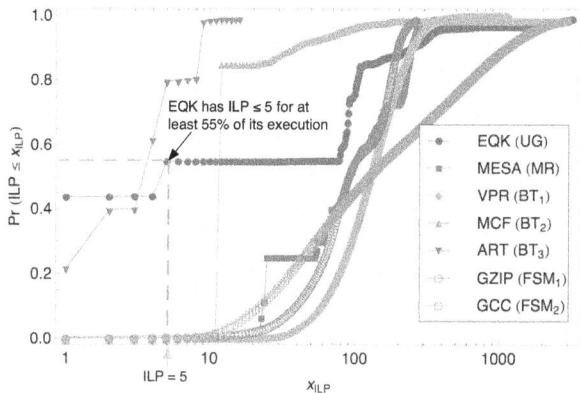

Figure 9: Cumulative distribution function (CDF) over the duration of execution of the available ideal ILP. (From the minimum ILP (always one) to the value of the maximum ILP in 99% of the execution (4000).) Flat curves which reach high CDF values on the left side of the plot, (e.g., `art`), indicate most cycles have low ILP. For most applications, more than 50% of the cycles have ILP less than 100.

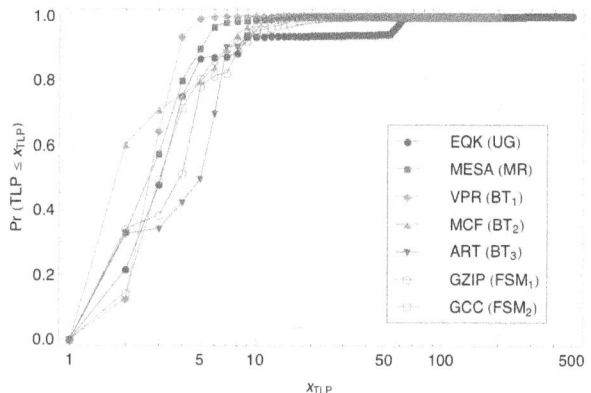

Figure 10: Cumulative Distribution Function (CDF) of the available TLP. TLP values range from the minimum (one) to 500, which is the maximum TLP during 99% of the execution.

driven analysis, it was only feasible to compute mean values *in situ* during simulation, as opposed to obtaining a full trace of limit ILP and TLP per cycle. Analyzing only mean values however does not provide an accurate portrayal of the amount of *usable* ILP and TLP in applications. To illustrate, Figure 7 shows two examples of a complete ILP trace and a TLP trace. If the available parallelism in regions where it is high is however *smoothable* [26], the parallel work from these regions can be *spread* over regions with low parallelism, counteracting the Amdahl bottleneck [1].

In all applications, a large number of instructions, typically NOPs, immediate loads, unconditional jumps, arithmetic operations with register zero or constants, and instructions that involve operations with the stack pointer[3], can be scheduled in the first few cycles. After this initial phase, ILP and TLP still vary significantly, both across windows, as well as within windows (as captured by the standard deviations). Thus, simply looking at mean values over an application's complete duration does not provide a complete picture of the "usable" ILP/TLP. A more meaningful characterization is however to observe the cumulative distribution function (CDF) of the ILP and TLP over the complete set of execution cycles. Examples of the ILP and TLP CDFs of some of the applications studied are shown in Figures 9 and 10. In the figures, the horizontal axis denotes values of ILP/TLP, from the minimum (one for all the applications), to the maximum ILP/TLP observed in 99% of the execution, while the vertical axis denotes the cumulative fraction of

cycles having the corresponding ILP or TLP values. For example, in Figure 9, it is observed that `equake`, while having mean ILP upward of 100, has an ILP of less than 10 for more than half of its execution.

Based on the information in the CDF analysis of ILP and TLP for each application, Figures 11 and 12 show the amounts of available ILP and TLP in applications for 50%, 60%, 70%, and 80% of the execution time, in comparison to the mean values over the entire execution. Thus, for example, while `susan` (BT_4) has ILP close to 1 for up to 70% of its execution, an additional 10% of its execution contributes almost an order of magnitude more to it, and the average across the entire execution is three orders of magnitude greater than that. Other applications, such as `bitcount`, `rijndael` or `stringsearch`, however, have average ILP that is smaller than the ILP at 80% of the execution. Simply considering the mean ILP over execution would not capture these particular behaviors, and in some cases would obviously be misleading.

By looking at the cumulative distribution of instruction-level parallelism (ILP), it can be observed that previously reported limit studies on ILP were overly optimistic, since the cumulative proportion of execution cycles with a given level of available ILP paints a different picture—less available parallelism, in some cases, up to a factor of 1000. Although the ideal maximum parallelism exposed by many applications is higher than that provided by modern processors, some applications expose low instruction-level parallelism during most of their execution. Applications that present this behavior will not benefit from complex wide-issue cores; however, they might exhibit parallelism at other levels that can be exploited with alternative architectures such as multithreading, multi-core, or multiple processors. So, e.g., while `sha` (CL_3) presents an ILP significantly lower than the mean ILP across applications, it exhibits a high TLP that is above the average for 50% of the execution cycles.

---

[3]For the ILP and TLP analysis, dependences through the stack pointer and return address register have been excluded as they are not a direct result of program semantics.

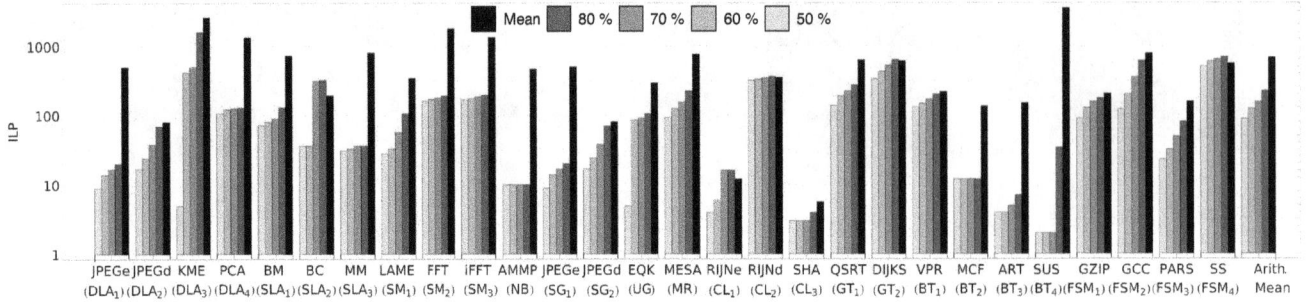

Figure 11: Cumulative ILP for 50%, 60%, 70%, and 80% of the execution time, versus mean ILP (last bar per group).

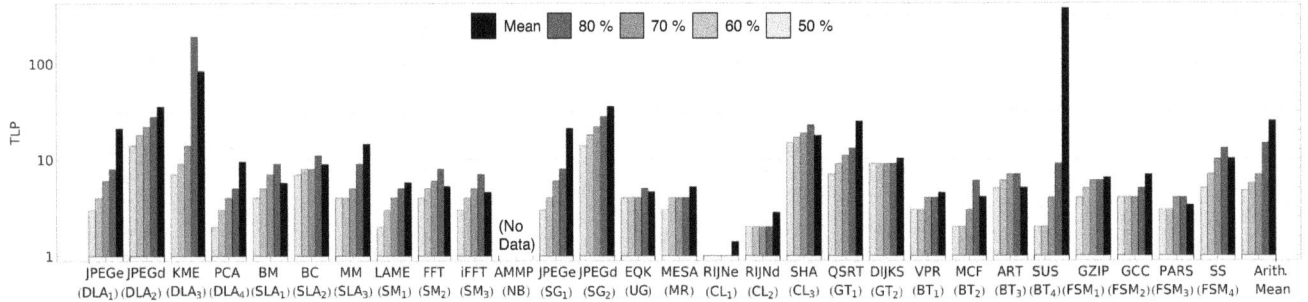

Figure 12: Cumulative TLP for 50%, 60%, 70%, and 80% of the execution time, versus mean TLP (last bar per group).

Similarly, even though applications that are dominated by dwarf 13 (FSM) are postulated to have little coarse-grained parallelism [2], all examples examined have high available ILP. This implies they would be well served by *ILP processors* versus multi-core.

5.2 Memory access and communication

Figure 13 presents the data movement properties described in Section 4, for the applications of Table 1. For each application, the left bar represents the normalized average number of *memory references per instruction*. Although, on average, one out of three instructions are memory references, the memory accesses per instruction vary significantly across the set of applications analyzed. For example, while `bitcount` issues, on average, one memory access every ten instructions, other applications such as `parser` or `quicksort`, require one memory reference every second instruction. The right bar represents the normalized number of inter-basic-block *data exchanges per basic block*. It may be interpreted as inter-thread communication requirements, if the applications were executed on a hardware platform (e.g., a speculative multi-threading processor) that speculated on threads at the basic block granularity.

5.3 ILP and TLP across dwarf classes

Similarity within dwarf classes can be measured by the range of ILP and TLP values exhibited by the applications categorized in a given dwarf. Although applications that belong to some dwarf classes, like the ones of the dwarf SG, present a similar ILP during 50% of their execution (the ILP difference between the maximum and the minimum value is just 4), they do not show a similar behavior in terms of TLP. Some other application classes, like GT, however, are very similar in terms of their thread-level parallelism, but they have an ILP span of 198. A similar analysis across all the dwarfs demonstrates that no application class presents a well-defined instruction- or thread-level parallelism pattern.

Dwarf classes, therefore, although believed to have similar coarse-grained computation and communication characteristics—

Table 2: Architectural parameters of ideal machine and contemporary processors used for evaluation of IPC.

Processor/ Core Architecture	Max. Instructions issued per Cycle	Cache Hierarchy	GCC Architecture-Specific Flags
Ideal Machine	Unlimited	Perfect memory hierarchy	
Atom D510/ x86-64	2	32 K/24 K L1 I/D (per core) and 1 M L2	-march=atom
P2020/ Power e500	5	32 K/32 K L1 I/D (per core), 512 K shared L2	-mcpu=8540, -mfloat-gprs= double
Power7	8	32 K/32 K L1 I/D, 256 K L2 (per core), 32 M shared L3	-mcpu=power7, -mtune=power7

and thus similar implied opportunities for coarse-grained parallelism—exhibit insignificant similarity in terms of ILP, TLP, per-instruction memory accesses and data movement between basic-block-level threads. Since future parallel systems will need to exploit parallelism at all levels of granularity, from the instruction level, to communicating coarse-grained tasks, it might be ill-advised to assume applications fit into a given class of characteristics, when their similarities may hold only at one level of granularity. This raises the question of whether it is possible to define an application taxonomy that properly groups applications according to those properties that are relevant to system design at a given abstraction level or granularity. Given the broad range of ILP and TLP exhibited by applications (the total ILP span, measured across all the applications regardless the dwarf they belong to, is 538, and the TLP span is 6, for 50% of execution cycles), it will be challenging to find hardware architectures that will efficiently accommodate such a diversity of application demands.

5.4 Validation of ideal ILP trends

The trends in ideal ILP across the applications studied were compared against actual achieved instructions per cycle (IPC), on a set of contemporary processors whose properties are listed in Table 2.

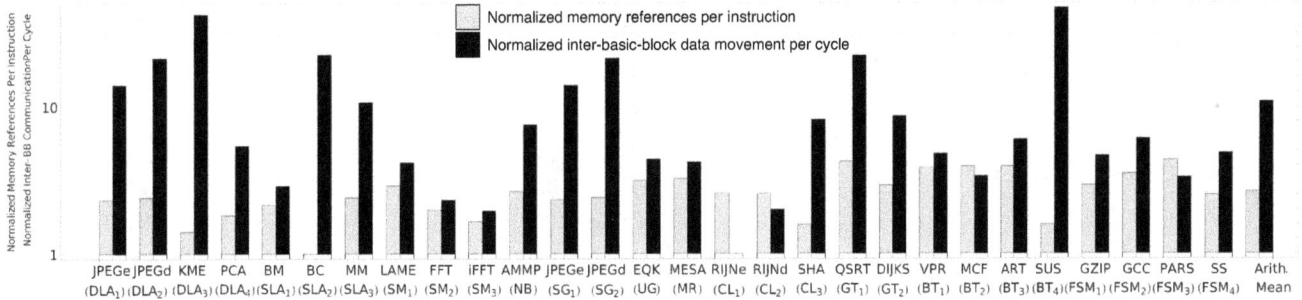

Figure 13: Memory references per instruction (left bar) normalized to the lowest value (0.12) and inter-basic-block communication (right bar), again normalized to the smallest value (0.64).

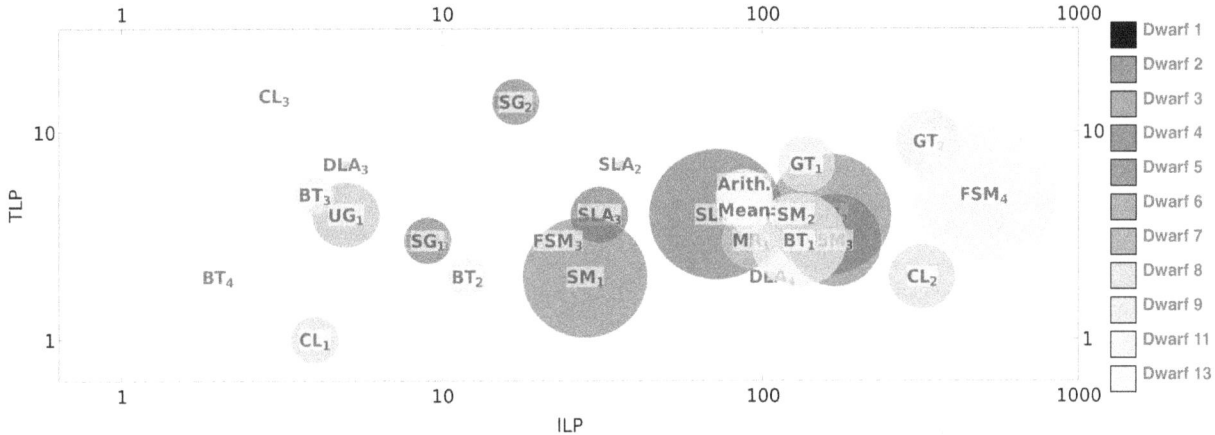

Figure 14: Summary of the ILP and TLP (for 50% of execution), and MPMD task partitions, across the investigated applications. The radii of the disks are proportional to the average number of communication-minimizing code partitions over execution time. Labels of the disks denote the dwarfs that dominate the corresponding applications, with dwarfs in the same class having the same shading.

The processors range from a high-performance wide-issue RISC (Power7), to a more conservative Power e500 (Freescale P2020), and a top-of-the-line Intel Atom, and the IPC values were measured by monitoring hardware performance counter registers. All the applications were executed on Linux 2.6.32-based systems and were all compiled with optimization flags `-O3 -fpeel-loops -funroll-loops -ftree-vectorize`, and the additional architecture-specific flags listed in Table 2.

IPC values follow the general trend of the ideal ILP values shown previously in Figure 11. `Art` exhibits the minimum IPC in all the platforms (0.27, 0.16 and 0.52 on Atom D510, Power e500 and Power7, respectively), and is one of the applications with lower ideal ILP (four for at least 50% of its execution). Similarly, applications that show high values of ILP in the ideal case, like `rijndael decode` (with an ideal ILP of 319), exhibit high relative IPC—0.8 for Atom D510, 1.36 in Power e500, and 1.06 in Power7. Achievable IPC for a given application, in contrast to the ideal ILP, depends on the target microarchitecture, mix of functional units, cache and TLB miss rates, etc. The IPC results from our performance counter measurements could be scaled to account for the application instruction mix, the mix of hardware functional units, and cache/TLB miss rates, to obtain values that account for these hardware restrictions. This is a direction of ongoing work.

6. SUMMARY AND DISCUSSION

This work presented a framework for characterizing the distributions of fine-grained machine-extractable parallelism, data movement, potential data-level parallelism, and communication-minimizing code partitions, over complete program executions. The framework was applied to a suite of 26 applications covering most of the Berkeley "dwarf" or "computational motif" classes. Figure 14 summarizes the ILP (disk x-coordinate), TLP (y-coordinate), and number of communication-minimizing code partitions (disk sizes), valid for 50% of the execution of each application. In terms of these quantitative metrics, applications containing or dominated by a given dwarf do not exhibit significant similarity—i.e., disks corresponding to a given dwarf are neither always clustered together, nor always of similar size.

The analysis also highlights the variation in the amount of ideal-case parallelism of different granularities present in individual applications. For example, while `sha` (CL_3) presents an ILP significantly lower than the mean ILP across applications, it exhibits a high TLP that is above the average. Similarly, even though dwarf 13 is postulated to have little coarse-grained parallelism, all examples examined that belong to this dwarf have high available ILP. This implies they would be well served by *ILP processors*, as opposed to multi-core or multi-threaded processors. Data movement requirements can also be used to support architectural design decisions. For example, although `susan` is the application with the least memory references per instruction, its inter-thread communication requirements (between basic-block-granularity threads) are significantly higher than the average for most of the application classes. So, although the application exhibits high levels of coarse-grain parallelism, exploiting such parallelism may have high communication bandwidth requirements that might limit performance scaling.

Acknowledgments

This work was supported by the Department of Defense (DoD) and used resources at the Extreme Scale Systems Center, located at Oak Ridge National Laboratory (ORNL), and the National Center for Computational Sciences at ORNL, supported by the U.S. Department of Energy Office of Science under Contract No. DE-AC05-00OR22725.

7. REFERENCES

[1] G. M. Amdahl. Validity of the single processor approach to achieving large scale computing capabilities. In *Proceedings of the April 18-20, 1967, spring joint computer conference*, AFIPS '67 (Spring), pages 483–485. ACM, 1967.

[2] K. Asanovic, R. Bodik, B. C. Catanzaro, J. J. Gebis, P. Husbands, K. Keutzer, D. A. Patterson, W. L. Plishker, J. Shalf, S. W. Williams, and K. A. Yelick. The landscape of parallel computing research: a view from berkeley. Technical report, University of California at Berkeley, December 2006.

[3] T. M. Austin and G. S. Sohi. Dynamic dependency analysis of ordinary programs. *SIGARCH Comput. Archit. News*, 20(2):342–351, 1992.

[4] S. E. Breach, T. N. Vijaykumar, and G. S. Sohi. Multiscalar processors. In *ISCA '95: Proceedings of the 22nd Annual International Symposium on Computer Architecture*, pages 414–425, Los Alamitos, CA, USA, 1995.

[5] M. Bridges, N. Vachharajani, Y. Zhang, T. Jablin, and D. August. Revisiting the sequential programming model for multi-core. In *MICRO 40: Proceedings of the 40th Annual IEEE/ACM International Symposium on Microarchitecture*, pages 69–84, Washington, DC, USA, 2007.

[6] J. A. Brown and D. M. Tullsen. The shared-thread multiprocessor. In *ICS '08: Proceedings of the 22nd annual international conference on Supercomputing*, pages 73–82. ACM, 2008.

[7] D. Burger and T. M. Austin. The simplescalar tool set, version 2.0. *SIGARCH Comput. Archit. News*, 25(3):13–25, 1997.

[8] D. Burger, J. R. Goodman, and A. Kägi. Memory bandwidth limitations of future microprocessors. In *Proceedings of the 23rd annual international symposium on Computer architecture*, ISCA '96, pages 78–89. ACM, 1996.

[9] T. H. Cormen, C. E. Leiserson, R. L. Rivest, and C. Stein. Introduction to algorithms, third edition, 2009.

[10] J. Dean and S. Ghemawat. Mapreduce: simplified data processing on large clusters. *Commun. ACM*, 51(1):107–113, 2008.

[11] M. J. Flynn. Toward more efficient computer organizations. In *AFIPS '72 (Spring): Proceedings of the May 16-18, 1972, spring joint computer conference*, pages 1211–1217. ACM, 1972.

[12] M. R. Guthaus, J. S. Ringenberg, D. Ernst, T. M. Austin, T. Mudge, and R. B. Brown. Mibench: A free, commercially representative embedded benchmark suite. In *WWC '01: Proceedings of the IEEE International Workshop on Workload Characterization*, pages 3–14, Washington, DC, USA, 2001. IEEE Computer Society.

[13] Y. He, C. E. Leiserson, and W. M. Leiserson. The cilkview scalability analyzer. In *Proceedings of the 22nd ACM symposium on Parallelism in algorithms and architectures*, SPAA '10, pages 145–156. ACM, 2010.

[14] J. L. Hennessy and D. A. Patterson. *Computer architecture: a quantitative approach*. Morgan Kaufmann Publishers Inc., 2002.

[15] M. Iyer, C. Ashok, J. Stone, N. Vachharajani, D. A. Connors, and M. Vachharajani. Finding parallelism for future epic machines. In *Proceedings of the 4th Workshop on Explicitly Parallel Instruction Computing Techniques*, 2005.

[16] R. Kalla, B. Sinharoy, W. J. Starke, and M. Floyd. Power7: IBM's next-generation server processor. *IEEE Micro*, 30:7–15, 2010.

[17] K. Kennedy and U. Kremer. Automatic data layout for distributed-memory machines. *ACM Trans. Program. Lang. Syst.*, 20(4):869–916, 1998.

[18] M. S. Lam and R. P. Wilson. Limits of control flow on parallelism. *SIGARCH Comput. Archit. News*, 20(2):46–57, 1992.

[19] A. Nakajima, R. Kobayashi, H. Ando, and T. Shimada. Limits of thread-level parallelism in non-numerical programs. In *IPSJ Transactions on Advanced Computing Systems*, pages 12–20, 2006.

[20] G. Ottoni, R. Rangan, A. Stoler, and D. I. August. Automatic thread extraction with decoupled software pipelining. In *MICRO 38: Proceedings of the 38th annual IEEE/ACM International Symposium on Microarchitecture*, pages 105–118, Washington, DC, USA, 2005.

[21] M. A. Postiff, D. A. Greene, G. S. Tyson, and T. N. Mudge. The limits of instruction level parallelism in SPEC95 applications. *SIGARCH Comput. Archit. News*, 27(1):31–34, 1999.

[22] C. Ranger, R. Raghuraman, A. Penmetsa, G. Bradski, and C. Kozyrakis. Evaluating mapreduce for multi-core and multiprocessor systems. In *HPCA '07: Proceedings of the 13th International Symposium on High-Performance Computer Architecture*, pages 13–24, 2007.

[23] E. Riseman and C. Foster. The inhibition of potential parallelism by conditional jumps. *IEEE Transactions on Computers*, 21:1405–1411, 1972.

[24] K. Scott and J. Davidson. Exploring the limits of sub-word level parallelism. In *PACT '00: Proceedings of the 2000 International Conference on Parallel Architectures and Compilation Techniques*, page 81, Washington, DC, USA, 2000. IEEE Computer Society.

[25] R. Simar and R. Tatge. How TI adopted VLIW in digital signal processors. *Solid-State Circuits Magazine, IEEE*, 1(3):10–14, summer 2009.

[26] K. B. Theobald, G. R. Gao, and L. J. Hendren. On the limits of program parallelism and its smoothability. In *Proceedings of the 25th annual international symposium on Microarchitecture*, MICRO 25, pages 10–19, Los Alamitos, CA, USA, 1992. IEEE Computer Society Press.

[27] G. S. Tjaden and M. J. Flynn. Detection and parallel execution of independent instructions. *IEEE Trans. Comput.*, 19(10):889–895, 1970.

[28] J. S. Vetter and F. Mueller. Communication characteristics of large-scale scientific applications for contemporary cluster architectures. *J. Parallel Distrib. Comput.*, 63(9):853–865, 2003.

[29] D. Wall. Limits of instruction-level parallelism. In *ASPLOS-IV: Proceedings of the fourth international conference on Architectural support for programming languages and operating systems*, pages 176–188. ACM, 1991.

Work-stealing for Mixed-mode Parallelism by Deterministic Team-building*

Martin Wimmer
Faculty of Computer Science
University of Vienna
Nordbergstrasse 15/C/3
A-1090 Vienna/Wien, Austria
wimmer@par.univie.ac.at

Jesper Larsson Träff
Faculty of Computer Science
University of Vienna
Nordbergstrasse 15/C/3
A-1090 Vienna/Wien, Austria
traff@par.univie.ac.at

ABSTRACT

We show how to extend classical work-stealing to deal with *tightly coupled data parallel tasks* that can *require* any number of threads $r \geq 1$ for their execution, and term this extension *work-stealing with deterministic team-building*. As threads become idle they attempt to join a *team of threads* designated for a task requiring $r > 1$ threads for its execution, alternatively to steal a task, requiring no central coordination. Team building and stealing are done according to a deterministic hierarchy and involve at most a logarithmic number of possibly randomized steal attempts. Threads attempting to join the team for a task requiring a large number of threads may help smaller teams while waiting for the large team to form. Once a team has been formed the threads can in close coordination execute the data parallel task. Implementation can be done with standard lock-free data structures, and takes only a single extra compare-and-swap (CAS) operation per thread to build a team. In the degenerate case where all tasks require only a single thread, the implementation coincides with a locality aware work-stealing implementation. Using a prototype C++ implementation of our extended work-stealing algorithm, a *mixed-mode parallel* Quicksort algorithm with a data parallel partitioning step has been implemented. We compare our (improved) implementation of this algorithm on top of our extended work-stealing scheduler to a standard task-parallel implementation with this scheduler, and with Intel Cilk Plus and Threading Building Blocks. In addition, we also compare to the optimized parallel MCSTL Quicksort. Results are shown for a 32-core Intel Nehalem EX system and a 16-core Sun T2+ system supporting up to 128 hardware threads. The mixed-mode parallel algorithm performs consistently better than the fork-join implementation, often significantly.

*The research leading to these results has received funding from the European Union Seventh Framework Programme (FP7/2007-2013) under grant agreement no. 248481 (PEP-PHER Project, www.peppher.eu).

Categories and Subject Descriptors

D.4.1 [**Operating Systems**]: Process Management—*Scheduling*; D.3.2 [**Programming Languages**]: Language Classifications—*concurrent, distributed, and parallel languages*

General Terms

Algorithms

Keywords

Work-stealing, mixed-mode parallelism, deterministic team-building, Quicksort

1. INTRODUCTION

Work-stealing is a classical, efficient strategy for dynamically scheduling parallel work-loads of independent, sequential tasks on shared-memory systems with possibly varying number of available processing resources [1, 3]. With work-stealing, the sequential tasks of a DAG-structured computation are executed by the available independent hardware threads. Ready (and newly spawned) tasks are kept in local queues, and only when a thread locally runs out of tasks does it attempt to steal work (tasks) from other threads. Despite its localized nature with no global synchronization, it is nevertheless often possible to prove good time bounds and thread and memory/cache utilization for work-stealing based schedulers. Work-stealing is used in Cilk [2], Intel's TBB [12], and many other task-parallel programming systems. Efficient work-stealing implementations rely heavily on lock- and/or wait-free data structures [11].

In the dynamic, task-based programming models that fit well with work-stealing, data-parallel loops are typically handled by recursively breaking the loop into chunks that are then handled sequentially by the available hardware threads. Work-stealing provides no means of ensuring simultaneous scheduling of the tasks responsible for such pieces, and no control over when (and where) the pieces are eventually executed. Thus, tightly coupled data-parallel tasks with dependencies and synchronization are not well suited to work-stealing, and algorithms and applications that are naturally expressed by a mixture of task and data parallelism are not easily executed by work-stealing schedulers: a concrete example is the *mixed-mode parallel* Quicksort implementation that will be explained in Section 4. This limitation has often been addressed and frameworks that allow communicating tasks have been proposed, see e.g. [8]. Phasers as known from Habanero [16] that allow loose synchronization of single-threaded tasks are another approach for overcoming this shortcoming. The benefits of *mixed-mode parallelism* are discussed in [5, 21]. Centralized scheduling methods for handling mixed-mode parallel applications were likewise often described, see for instance [4, 5, 6, 7, 9, 13, 14, 15].

We address the problem differently by extending work-stealing to directly support parallel tasks that may require more than a single thread for their execution. The model we consider is DAG-structured computations with dynamically spawned, *non-malleable tasks with fixed thread requirements*, that is, each new task must be executed by some number of threads determined at spawn time. The problem here is how to gather the threads that will eventually execute a tightly coupled data-parallel task that needs more than a single thread, avoid unnecessary idle times in the process, make sure that such gathered threads can be activated together, and that a convenient virtual numbering of the threads is available, such that the co-scheduled tasks have a means of identifying and communicating with each other.

As will be shown, the dynamic, greedy, decentralized work-stealing approach can be extended to address these problems, and still provide efficient utilization of resources. As far as we are aware, such a generalization of work-stealing has not been given before. We term our work-stealing extension *deterministic team-building*. Whenever a thread runs out of tasks in its local queue, it tries to help other threads to execute a data-parallel task requiring more than a single thread for its execution thereby forming a *team*. Coordination is thus, like in work-stealing, done by the *thieves* and not coordinated from "the top" by the threads having the data-parallel tasks in their local queues. The overhead for forming a new team is a single extra atomic compare-and-swap (CAS) instruction per thread joining the team. In order to avoid idle times of threads waiting for large teams to form, threads wanting to join a large team can help threads with tasks requiring fewer threads. Work-stealing and team-building are done relative to a fixed hierarchy. Each thread becoming idle has $\log p$ possible partners (p being the number of hardware threads) corresponding to the levels in the hierarchy from which it attempts to steal work respectively build teams. At each level randomization can be applied among 2^i possible partners for $i = 0, \ldots \log p - 1$.

This paper presents the algorithmic idea behind work-stealing with deterministic team-building. An implementation has been given in C++, and we use this to give a very natural implementation of the mixed-mode parallel Quicksort algorithm in [19]. Other mixed-mode parallel applications have been considered in the companion paper [21].

The work described here was partly motivated by the European FP7 project PEPPHER (for "PErformance Portability and Programmability for HEterogeneous many-core aRchitectures", see www.peppher.eu) that develops a framework for enhancing performance portability of applications that consist of component-tasks that may already have been parallelized and make explicit requirements for specific (processor) resources (with complimentary guarantees of staying within the requested limits). Among other issues, PEPPHER investigates scheduling strategies and software for such situations.

2. WORK-STEALING WITH DETERMINISTIC TEAM-BUILDING

We extend work-stealing to cater for mixed-mode parallelism, where tasks requiring a certain, determined number of processors or threads for their execution can be dynamically spawned. This thread requirement is denoted by r. In the standard task-parallel work-stealing setting $r = 1$ for all tasks, whereas we want to allow for any $1 \leq r \leq p$ number of required threads (requirements $r > p$ are of course infeasible). Thread requirements are fulfilled by building *teams* of threads for tasks with $r > 1$. When a team of r threads has been formed for some task, the task can be executed. For applications it is most often important that the threads of the team are numbered consecutively, such that a thread can identify the other threads of the team and communicate with them. Since each thread of the scheduler is normally bound to a processor in the system, we use the terms *thread* and *processor* interchangeably.

The basic prerequisite behind *deterministic team-building* is to structure the processors of the systems hierarchically into disjoint groups of consecutively numbered processors. In the simplest case, which we will use for convenience for most of the paper, we assume that p is a power of two and the structure imposed by a binary tree. The levels of the tree are numbered starting from the leaves. At level 0 there are p groups and each processor is its own group, at level 1, there are $p/2$ groups of 2 processors per group, and so on. At the topmost level $\log p - 1$ the root node of the binary tree forms a single group containing all p processors.

To execute a task with a thread requirement r, a thread tries to build up a team of $t \geq r$ processors. A team always consists of all processors in a single group at a certain level in the processor hierarchy. The team that will eventually be built therefore consists of consecutively numbered threads. If we assume that all processor groups at a single level ℓ are of the same size, the ids of the threads in the team will be $kt, kt+1, \ldots, i, \ldots, (k+1)t - 1$ for some k in the range $0 \leq k < p/t$. From this a virtual numbering of the threads in the team from 0 to $r - 1$ can easily be computed. As described here, the actual team sizes are restricted to the sizes of the processor groups in the system. We show later how this restriction can be relieved. For correctness, we require a thread to first process all tasks in its queue with smaller thread requirements, before building a team at a certain size.

When a thread starts to build a team for the execution of a task, it is assigned to be the *coordinator* for the team. This thread is responsible for managing the task execution, and providing information to the other team-members, and only this thread is allowed to disband a team. Typically, a coordinator will try to execute as many tasks with the same thread requirement as possible, before disbanding the team in order to amortize the team-building overhead.

Each thread has a local data-structure containing all relevant information for the thread. Each thread has a fixed (integer) id I, $0 \leq I < p$, that is used to determine the partner for work-stealing and team-building attempts and later compute the local thread ids in a team. We assume that the data-structure for each thread can be accessed directly through its id (technically, a mapping from ids to thread references would be needed). The data-structure for each thread has the following components, which may be accessed by other threads during the stealing and coordination phases:

- The unique thread id I, $0 \leq I < p$.

- A double ended queue Q of spawned tasks. Local accesses always happen at the bottom, while stealing is done from the top of the queue. The queue needs to be able to only return tasks for certain levels in the processor hierarchy. A simple way to do this is to provide a queue for each level in the hierarchy.

- The id c of the coordinator of the thread. If the thread is itself a coordinator $c = I$. This is the case when scheduling tasks with $r = 1$, or when the thread has run out of work. An invariant of the team-building work-stealer is that a coordinator is always set.

- An integer r storing the number of threads that are required by the next task to be executed.

- A reference to a ready task that can be executed by the current team. This is accessed by the task field. When the coordinator task becomes nonempty, all threads in the team can start execution of the task.

- A countdown G for the ready task that is initialized to $r - 1$ before task is set (r is the number of threads required for this task). Each non-coordinator thread must atomically decrement this field when it starts executing the task. When $G = 0$, the coordinator can be sure that execution has started by all threads in the team, and can then reset the task field.

The following methods are needed for team-building. In Section 3 we show how to implement them in a lock-free manner.

- registerThread(I) is called by threads trying to join a team. It takes the id of the calling thread as parameter. The method first checks whether the given thread is eligible for the team, and if this is the case registers the thread for the team.

- When a thread wants to drop out of a team to start working on something else, it must call dropThread(I). This tries to remove the thread from the team, and returns true on success. A call to this method is only successful if the team is not yet built. If a team has been built, only the coordinator can free threads from it.

- The coordinator can check if the team-building process has finished by teamBuilt(). No thread may by its own leave a team after it has been built. The coordinator can reuse and if needed downsize an already built team.

- The coordinator (only) can disband an already built team by disbandTeam().

- inTeam(I) is used by threads to check whether they are still members of a team. This may not be the case if the coordinator has disbanded the team, or if the team has been resized.

Algorithm 1 stealTasks()

1: $\ell \leftarrow 1$
2: **while** $2^\ell \leq p$ **do**
3:     $x \leftarrow$ getPartnerForLevel(ℓ) {Partner thread at level ℓ; random or deterministic depending on policy}
4:     $xc \leftarrow x.c$ {The partner's coordinator}
5:     $xcr \leftarrow xc.r$ {The thread requirement of the team being built}
6:     **if** $xcr \geq 2^\ell$ **then** {Partner's coordinator requires this thread for execution of its task}
7:         xc.registerThread(I) {Join this team}
8:         $c \leftarrow xc$ {and set coordinator}
9:         **return**
10:     **else**
11:         {Steal from partner instead}
12:         **if** Q.popappend($x.Q, 2^{\ell-1}$) > 0 **then**
13:             {At least one task stolen}
14:             **return**
15:         **end if**
16:         {Nothing to steal, next level in the hierarchy}
17:         $\ell \leftarrow \ell + 1$
18:     **end if**
19: **end while**
20: {No success in stealing procedure}
21: backoff()

A key property of work-stealing is that threads do local work as long as work is available, and only resort to stealing when they run out of work. Deterministic team-building preserves this property, as each team will work on its local queue of tasks for the current level in the processor hierarchy. Only when a team runs out of work, it is disbanded, and the modified stealing procedure starts. The stealing procedure can now be shown as Algorithm 1.

Stealing occurs when the current thread is not being coordinated by another thread, and it has run out of tasks to process, including tasks requiring teams. The stealing procedure iterates through the levels of the processor hierarchy. At each level, a unique partner is selected, either randomly or deterministically by the getPartnerForLevel() function. Which policy to use is a decision to be made in the implementation. The chosen partner must be in the same group of processors at level ℓ as the stealing processor, but not in the same group at level $\ell - 1$. When the partner is selected, the stealing thread checks whether this partner is trying to build a team at this level or higher in the hierarchy. If this is the case, the thread joins the team and exits the stealing procedure. Otherwise it tries to steal at least one task. This is done with the popappend(q, maxTeam) method of the queue structure. It tries to pop a number of tasks from the queue q and append them to its own queue. The exact amount of work to steal is a tuning parameter left to the actual implementation. However, this call is only allowed to steal tasks with a thread requirement that is at most maxTeam, which is $2^{\ell-1}$ in the stealing procedure. This ensures that only tasks get stolen that do not require both the stealing thread and the thread stolen from in their team. If the popappend() procedure fails to steal any work, stealing continues at the next level in the hierarchy.

Each thread actively checks whether its partner thread is building a team that requires this thread and joins the team-building process if this is the case. Threads are not

Algorithm 2 pollPartners(r)

```
1: ℓ ← 1
2: while 2^ℓ ≤ r do
3:     x ← getPartnerForLevel(ℓ) {Partner thread at level
       ℓ; random or deterministic depending on policy}
4:     xc ← x.c {The partner's coordinator}
5:     xcr ← xc.r {The thread requirement of the team be-
       ing built}
6:     if xc ≠ c then {Partner has a different coordinator}
7:         if xcr ≥ 2^ℓ then {Partner's coordinator requires
           this thread for execution of its task}
8:             {Conflicting teams being built, choose}
9:             if chooseTeam(c, xc) = xc then
10:                {Other team wins, switch}
11:                if c.dropThread(I) then
12:                    xc.registerThread(I) {Join this team}
13:                    c ← xc
14:                    return
15:                end if
16:            end if
17:            {Our team wins, other threads will eventually
               switch}
18:        else
19:            {Steal from partner instead}
20:            if Q.popappend(x.Q, 2^(ℓ-1)) > 0 then
21:                {At least one task stolen}
22:                if c.dropThread(I) then
23:                    {Try to drop from team being built}
24:                    c ← I {Thread becomes coordinator}
25:                end if
26:                return
27:            end if
28:            {Nothing to steal, next level in the hierarchy}
29:        end if
30:    end if
31:    ℓ ← ℓ + 1
32: end while
33: if ¬ c.taskIsReady(I) then
34:    backoff()
35: end if
```

Algorithm 3 getTask()

```
1: task ← ⊥
2: repeat
3:     if c ≠ I then
4:         {Thread is in team coordinated by another thread}
5:         if c.task ≠ ⊥ then
6:             {The coordinators task is ready, and thread is in
               team}
7:             return c.task
8:         else if c.inTeam(I) then
9:             pollPartners(c.r)
10:        else
11:            c ← I
12:        end if
13:    else if Q.isEmpty() then
14:        if teamBuilt() then
15:            {Out of work, so team is not needed anymore}
16:            disbandTeam()
17:        end if
18:        stealTasks()
19:    else
20:        {Thread is coordinator}
21:        if teamBuilt() then
22:            task ← Q.popBottom(r)
23:            return task
24:        else
25:            pollPartners(r)
26:        end if
27:    end if
28: until task ≠ ⊥
```

notified about the team-building process, so as long as a thread/team has enough work to process, it will not find out about a team being built. This fits well with the philosophy of work-stealing, where a thread only communicates when it has nothing better to do, and no extra coordination overhead is introduced. A team will only be built when each thread required for the team has finished processing its local work. To speed up this process, a helping scheme is introduced, where threads that enter the team-building process steal tasks from threads that still have local work. This is shown in Algorithm 2, which is part of the team-building procedure and is being repeatedly executed by threads trying to build a team.

The pollPartners() procedure in Algorithm 2 is similar to the stealTask() procedure from Algorithm 1. It is called during team-building by threads that have already joined the team. It iterates through the levels of the processor hierarchy, and checks whether teams are being built. If another team is found that conflicts with the team currently being built, this is resolved by a tie-breaking scheme. Thus, sooner or later all threads in the conflicting team will join

the other team. For correctness the tie-breaking scheme in chooseTeam(I, J) must be deterministic, commutative and transitive. Another requirement is that teams with smaller thread requirements must be chosen over teams with larger requirements. If no conflicting team is found, the thread tries to steal at least one task, and continues at the next level of the hierarchy if this fails. The polling procedure only visits the levels of the processor hierarchy up to the level of the team being built to ensure that the team tasks are executed before tasks from outside the team are stolen.

We now put the pieces together in the getTask() procedure shown as Algorithm 3. This procedure is called when a thread is ready to process the next task. It distinguishes three different situations. If the thread is coordinated by another thread, it calls the pollPartners() procedure, until the team is ready, a task has been stolen, or the team-building canceled due to a conflict. Otherwise the thread is a coordinator itself. Either it is out of work, which means that the team can be disbanded and stealing can start using the stealTasks procedure, or team-building is still in progress, which means that the pollPartners() procedure is called, or the team is ready. In case the team is ready, the next task with thread requirement r is retrieved from the queue using the popBottom(r) method and then prepared for execution by the team.

2.1 Basic properties

Teams are always built out of consecutive threads. The threads that are allowed to join a team of a certain size at a certain coordinator are static and deterministic as they have to be members of the same group of processors at a certain level in the processor hierarchy. Due to the requirement that threads in a single group in the processor hierarchy are numbered consecutively, the threads in a team are numbered consecutively as well. By subtracting the (known) lowest id of a thread in the group from the thread ids, team-local thread ids in the range $[0, r-1]$ can easily be computed. With a binary tree processor hierarchy finding the id of the first thread in the team is particularly easy and requires finding only the most significant bit in the team size t. This can often be done by a hardware instruction, or in $O(\log \log t)$ steps.

Teams stay together as long as the coordinator's next task is the same size as the team. If the next task is smaller, it is also possible for the coordinator to shrink the team. If the next task is larger, the coordinator breaks up the team as soon as execution of the previous task has finished. The team for the larger task then has to be rebuilt from scratch.

Stealing follows a deterministic pattern with possibly randomized individual steps. We contact $\log p$ partner threads, before backing off. This was necessary in order for the teams to build properly, and may furthermore be advantageous to ensure memory-locality. If the processor hierarchy in the scheduler is constructed such that it reflects the system memory hierarchy, deterministic team-building will ensure that teams are formed by threads that are close in the memory hierarchy. Such locality optimizations by deterministic stealing have often been considered, see for instance the BubbleSched framework [18].

An important property of work-stealing is that as long as a thread can execute tasks it does not have to communicate with other threads. We can extend this property to teams of arbitrary sizes, with the restriction that this only holds as long as the next task requires the same (or smaller) number of threads as the previous task. Of course, communication cannot be completely omitted with tasks requiring more than one thread, as threads in a team have to poll the coordinator for the next task, and have to notify it when execution starts, but this overhead is small.

2.2 Correctness

LEMMA 1. *Assume the computation is finite. A thread I has spawned a task requiring $r \geq 1$ threads. This task will eventually be executed.*

PROOF. For $r = 1$ the case is clear. Tasks requiring a single thread will be popped or stolen and executed before tasks using more threads. No coordination is required before execution, so the task will eventually be executed, as in standard work-stealing.

Let $r > 1$ and assume the task is coordinated by I (it might have been stolen from some other thread). Eventually the other threads will join the team for the task as they run out of tasks requiring less than r threads. These will be executed because threads waiting for the formation of the large team help smaller teams to empty their task queues. Threads joining the team set their coordinator to I such that other threads that have to join the team eventually see that the team is coordinated by I. When all threads have joined the team the task will be executed. □

LEMMA 2. *If two or more threads trying to build teams compete for threads to join their team, the conflict is resolved deterministically.*

PROOF. Assume that thread x and thread y both try to build a team and compete for the same threads to join the team. Over time each of the threads will join one of the teams. As soon as a thread has joined a team, it will poll the other threads required for the team, and eventually see the other team. In this case, the `chooseTeam(I, J)` function is called to resolve the conflict. It is required to be deterministic and commutative. Assume the team of thread x is deterministically chosen over the team for thread y. Each thread in team y will then switch to team x as soon as it meets a thread in team x. Over time all threads will have joined team x. As `chooseTeam(I, J)` is also required to be be transitive, the argument extends to more than two conflicting teams. □

In our current implementation, `chooseTeam` selects the team with the smaller thread requirement, and selects the team with the smaller coordinator id on a tie. This fulfills both the transitivity and commutativity requirements.

LEMMA 3. *Each task is executed exactly once by each of the threads in a team.*

PROOF. A task is always managed by only one thread (the coordinator) and cannot occur in two queues at the same time. When a task is stolen, it is first removed from one queue, before being added to the other one. The start of task execution is managed by the coordinator by providing a pointer to the current task. Each thread stores a pointer to the last task it executed for the team, which is a null-pointer if no task has been executed in this team yet. A task may only be executed by a thread if the pointer to it differs from the pointer to the previous task. Therefore a task cannot be executed more than once.

Before starting to execute a task, each thread atomically decrements the countdown variable G at the coordinator. The coordinator is only allowed to modify the task pointer when $G = 0$, which is only the case when all threads in the team have started execution of the task, since each thread will decrement it exactly once. Also, the coordinator may only disband a team when the countdown reached zero. This shows that the task will eventually be executed by the threads of the team. □

The last lemma shows that depth-first execution order is preserved for tasks of the same size as long as they are in the queue of a single thread.

LEMMA 4. *Assume, we have two tasks x and y with the same thread requirement ($r_x = r_y$) with $n \geq 0$ tasks in-between them. Further assume that no task reordering scheme is employed inside the queue. In this case, x and y cannot change relative position inside a local queue.*

PROOF. Assume that x is nearer to the top of the queue than y. Therefore, x would be stolen first. If both x and y get stolen by the same thread at the same time, then the order of both tasks in the target queue will stay the same. The only case when x and y could switch order would be if a thread had y in its queue, and then stole x. A task can only be stolen in two cases: If the stealing thread is out of work, or during coordination. If the stealing thread is out of work, y cannot be in its queue. If stealing occured during coordination, coordination would happen for a task with thread requirement r_y or smaller due to the requirement that coordination is always done for the task that requires the least amount of threads. During coordination, only tasks can be stolen that require less threads than the thread requirement of the team. For x to be stolen this means that $r_x < r_y$ which contradicts $r_x = r_y$. $\square$

3. IMPLEMENTATION

A number of technical details and policy choices need to be fixed when implementing work-stealing with deterministic team-building as described in Section 2. We structure the processor hierarchy as a binary tree, which allows us to generate all information about teams and partner threads on the fly. Determining the partner at level ℓ can, for instance, be done simply by an exclusive or of the id of the thread and some x with $2^{\ell-1} \leq x < 2^{\ell}$. For deterministic schemes all threads should at each level use the same x so that different threads choose different partners. Randomized schemes choose x randomly. In this scheme we assume that p is a power of two and later describe how to cope with an arbitrary number of processors.

For the algorithm to work correctly, the double-ended queue that stores the work for a thread must, as explained, return only tasks with certain thread requirements during stealing. If tasks are ordered with respect to their thread requirement, the overhead of building teams can be better amortized since already built teams can be reused for the next task. In our current implementation, we solve this by using $\log p$ local queues to store the work for a thread. The queue for level ℓ contains tasks with thread requirements 2^{ℓ}. We additionally store information about the highest and lowest-level queues containing work, to ensure that not all queues have to be checked during stealing. Nonetheless, in the worst case, up to $\log p$ queues have to be checked during a single stealing attempt. This may be improved using a different data-structure for storing tasks. The queues themselves are implemented as well-known lock-free deques [1, 11].

When starting execution of a task every thread atomically decrements a countdown variable. The countdown for started tasks is relevant for the coordinator to check whether all threads have started execution of a previous task before scheduling the next one. An extra, similar countdown for the end of task execution can be used for synchronization constructs that check whether execution of a task has been completed. Neither of the countdowns have to be decremented atomically by the coordinator, so that for single processor tasks no atomic operations are necessary as in standard work-stealing.

3.1 Lock-free implementation of the registration mechanism

A central aspect of the deterministic team-building algorithm is the registration mechanism which we now show how to implement in a lock-free fashion. Each thread maintains a registration structure R that is modified by a *compare-and-swap* (CAS) operation when a thread registers or deregisters from a team. The coordinating thread does not need to use compare-and-swap operations. The registration structure is used for keeping track of a team being built for a task currently at the bottom of the threads queue, and contains the following fields:

- The number of *required* threads r for the task at the

bottom of the queue. This is modified every time a new task is added to the bottom of the local queue.

- The number of *acquired* (or *registered*) threads a, which is the number of threads currently registered for the team. Only threads that are required for a team of size r can be registered. If a new task is added to bottom that requires more threads, this number can stay. If it requires less threads, we have to reset it to the number of teamed threads and increment the new counter N (see below) to ensure that no invalid thread has registered.

- The number of *teamed* threads t is set to the size of the team by the coordinator after all threads have registered, therefore fixing the team. By default t is set to 1, which means that the team consists of a single thread (the coordinator). Teams can be shrunk by setting t to the new team-size. Disbanding a team means shrinking a team to size 1.

- A *new counter* N which is incremented every time the coordinator decides to reset the number of acquired threads to the current team size t, in order to signal to all acquired threads that team-building has to start over again. This happens every time the coordinator calls the `disbandTeam()` method. It is also incremented in some cases where teams are resized, but as team resizing is an optimization not required for the basic algorithm, we do not cover it here.

The full registration structure can be packed into a 64-bit integer, and thus all fields updated by a single 64-bit CAS instruction by assigning 16 bits to each field. For smaller numbers of hardware threads a 32-bit CAS suffices. In theory N would have to be unbounded, but in practice a finite N with wrap around suffices.

Now we describe how the registration structure is accessed and updated:

- `registerThread(I)` atomically increments the number of acquired threads a using a *compare-and-swap* operation. The thread that registers for the team locally stores the current value of N at the time of incrementing a.

- `dropThread(I)` tries to decrement a, therefore reversing the registration. If N has changed since the last call to `registerThread(I)`, the thread has already been dropped by the coordinator, and therefore decrementing is not required. If $a = r$, or the given thread id is part of the already built team of size t, dropping out is forbidden, and therefore fails.

- `teamBuilt()` first checks whether the thread requirement changed since the last call. If this is the case, the team is disbanded as described below, and team-building restarted by setting r to the new thread requirement. (In our actual implementation teams are resized when possible to reduce team-building overhead.) Otherwise, the algorithm checks whether $a = r$. If this is the case, the team is fixed by setting $t = r$. This does not require atomic operations, as the registration structure may not be modified by other threads after all threads have registered for a team.

- `disbandTeam()` atomically overwrites the registration structure with a new version. In the new version $r = 1$, $t = 1$, $a = 1$ and N is incremented. This does not require a compare-and-swap, but only an atomic write to the integer containing the registration structure.

As currently implemented we estimate the extra overheads in deterministic team-building as follows: an extra CAS used when a thread registers to or deregisters from a team. If all tasks require $r = 1$ the algorithm coincides with a locality-aware work-stealing scheduler where $\log p$ partners are tried before the `backoff()`. The additional CAS is never executed in this case.

3.2 Technical details

We have implemented a prototype work-stealing scheduler with deterministic team-building as described above in C++ using Pthreads to start the p hardware threads. The atomic operations used in the implementation are *compare-and-swap* and *fetch-and-decrement*, which are all available as atomic builtins in `gcc`, the Intel compilers and *Solaris*. The *compare-and-swap* primitive is required for modifications on the registration structure, and for accesses to the work-stealing deque. We use *fetch-and-decrement* for counting down started tasks. To retrieve the most significant bit of an integer, we use the `bsrl` assembly instruction available on Intel architectures, as this operation is not provided as a library call under Linux. Under BSD, the `fls` library function can be used instead. Retrieving the most significant bit is necessary for calculating the boundaries of a team as explained in Section 2.1, and for choosing in which queue to store a task.

3.3 Design decisions

The following design decisions have been made for the implementation:

- Tasks are implemented as objects derived from a base task class, quite similar to TBB [12].

- For simplicity, we only provide one linear runtime stack per thread in our implementation. A cactus-stack as used in Cilk [2] might be more efficient.

- When stealing tasks, the last stolen task is not appended to the deque but instead returned immediately from the `stealTasks()` function. This is necessary to prevent situations where a task is stolen back and forth with no thread being able to execute it.

- The scheduler terminates as soon as all threads have registered as idle. They can register as idle if their stack and all queues are empty and stealing has failed multiple times. Registration is canceled before a thread starts to steal again.

- We have noticed that we can often achieve better scheduling if we steal the largest allowed tasks. This comes from the fact that a thread only steals from a thread at a certain level if all partner threads at lower levels had empty queues. Therefore, the chances are high that the stealing thread will be able to build up a team soon.

- For the processing order of tasks, our decision was to generally prioritize tasks that require a team of the same size as the current team-size. If no such tasks are available, the queues at lower levels are checked for tasks to be processed, starting at level $\ell - 1$. Only if no tasks are found in this process, we check the higher-level queues. This means that a task at level ℓ will only be processed as soon as none of the threads in the team has a task at lower levels to be executed. We have to enforce the prioritization of lower-level tasks, as we only guarantee that a thread will check for a team of size ℓ being built if it has processed all lower-level tasks. A different execution order, where higher-level tasks are executed before lower-level tasks, might also lead to threads stealing tasks at a certain level during team-building although its queue at the given level is not empty.

Some tunable parameters of the implementation are given below. Performance of the implementation might be improved by choosing the right values, and the optimal values might differ depending on the hardware the scheduler is run on.

- Backoff intervals - For our backoff function, we used exponential backoff, starting at 1 microsecond, and going up to 10 milliseconds.

- Number of tasks to steal - We decided to steal $2^{\ell-1}$ tasks from a partner, where ℓ is the partner's level in the hierarchy. This comes from the assumption that, if we reached the ℓth partner during stealing, it is likely that all $2^{\ell-1}$ threads in the same group as the stealing thread on level $\ell - 1$ are running out of tasks as well. Therefore it makes sense to steal enough tasks for all of them.

3.4 Arbitrary thread requirements

We now indicate how to cope with the case where each new task can require an arbitrary number of threads $r \leq p$, instead of only numbers of threads coinciding with the levels in the processor hierarchy

The easiest way to do this would be to just allocate a team with a size equal to the number of threads supported by the next-higher level in the processor hierarchy, and to let some threads sit idle during execution. (Either the first or the last $t - r$ threads.) This is of course far from ideal, and it would be preferable if the threads that would otherwise be idle worked on smaller tasks. Nonetheless, we cannot completely ignore those threads, as they might be the first partners visited by a thread which is required for the team.

We propose that during coordination such threads that will not actually work on a task silently register at the coordinator. This means that the thread's coordination is set, but that the registration counter of the coordinator is not incremented. As soon as execution of the task starts, the thread can exit coordination.

We note that it is still necessary to help silently registered tasks empty their queues, even if they might not always interfere in coordination and might later run out of work. Some such threads might be coordinating other tasks that require a team that does not intersect with the team being built. We do not need to steal from those threads as they will not interfere with our task.

Although it is thus possible to support arbitrary task sizes, we can only provide weak guarantees concerning the hardware thread utilization. In the worst case, nearly half of the threads may sit idle. In a processor hierarchy represented as a binary tree this would happen if we have tasks with thread requirement $r = 2^k + 1$ to execute, and all smaller tasks on silently registered threads have already been executed before forming the team. Therefore the application programmer should preferably use tasks that are aligned to the processor hierarchy.

3.5 Arbitrary number of hardware threads

We finally extend to the general situation where an arbitrary (finite, fixed) number of threads is given from the outset, and each newly spawned task can require an arbitrary number of threads. In our description of the algorithm, we assumed that the number of processors in the system is a power of two, and that we use a binary tree to represent the processor hierarchy. Here we just have to remark that the algorithms will work with any other processor hierarchy, as long as groups are disjoint and consecutively numbered. Of course, in such cases it may not be possible to compute the needed information about group sizes on the fly, so preprocessing will be necessary. Also, it may be necessary to perform more than a single, deterministic stealing/polling attempt within each group, in order to make sure that all threads are eventually visited. The solution of course has to be combined with the scheme of the previous section for tasks requiring a number of threads that do not fit with the size of a group to which the thread belongs. The best hierarchy will furthermore depend on the properties of the (memory) architecture of the system.

4. A MIXED-MODE PARALLEL APPLICATION WITH EXPERIMENTAL RESULTS

The Quicksort algorithm lends itself naturally to task-parallel implementation using work-stealing. A standard implementation is shown as Algorithm 4. The **async** statement we use here creates a task out of the following function call. The **sync** statement waits for all spawned tasks in the same scope to complete. As is common, we provide a CUT-OFF value at which we switch to sequential sorting when the task-creation overhead is higher than the gains. To get all threads busy at least p tasks must be spawned, which takes at least $\log_2 p$ parallel steps.

Algorithm 4 Qsort(data, n)

1: **if** $n \leq$ CUTOFF **then**
2:    **return** sequentialSort(data, n)
3: **else**
4:    pivot $\leftarrow$ **partition**(data, n)
5:    **async** Qsort(data, pivot)
6:    **async** Qsort(data + pivot + 1, pivot − n − 1)
7:    **sync**
8: **end if**

The problem with Algorithm 4 is that the partitioning (and pivot selection) is done sequentially, takes linear time, and therefore introduces at least a linear time bottleneck before all threads can be active.

This problem is solved in [19] with a tightly coupled, data-parallel partitioning step. This Quicksort implementation starts off with all processors partitioning a single array. Then, after partitioning is complete, the processors are split into two groups, where each group gets a single subsequence

to work on. In the final phase, each processor has a single subsequence that it can sort locally. To achieve better load-balancing, a helping scheme similar to work-stealing is used. The last phase can be seen as similar to the task-based Quicksort algorithm in Algorithm 4.

As classic work-stealing is not able to handle data-parallel tasks, the implementation of Quicksort with data-parallel partitioning has to rely on manual scheduling and a manually implemented helping scheme as explained in [19]. A better, more convenient way of implementing this algorithm would be to formulate it instead as a mixed-mode parallel algorithm. This is shown in Algorithm 5.

This mixed-mode parallel Quicksort incorporates the data-parallel partitioning step developed in [19]. It is implemented as a data-parallel task started with a *team* of np threads, $np \geq 1$. After partitioning is done, two subtasks are launched by the thread with local team id 0. The *async* statement now spawns a potentially parallel task with the number of threads given in brackets. For Quicksort a good number of threads is determined by the call to getBestNp(n). How it is actually implemented may have a major influence on performance as the overhead for data-parallel partitioning is higher than for sequential partitioning, so it should only be used when either the data is large enough so that the overhead is negligible or there is too little work to do for sequential tasks. In our implementation we decided on a policy that each thread attempting partitioning in parallel should at least have 128 blocks to work on. If the number of threads required by a newly launched task np equals 1, we switch to the standard task-based implementation from Algorithm 4.

Algorithm 5 mmQsort(data, n)

1: {np is the number of threads for this task}
2: **if** $np = 1$ **then**
3:    **return** Qsort(data, n)
4: **else**
5:    pivot $\leftarrow$ **parallelPartition**(data, n)
6:    **if** localId = 0 **then**
7:       **async**(getBestNp(pivot)) mmQsort(data, pivot)
8:       **async**(getBestNp((n−pivot−1))) mmQsort(data+ pivot + 1, n − pivot − 1)
9:       **sync**
10:    **end if**
11: **end if**

We now explain how the data-parallel partitioning step works. During partitioning, the array is split into equally sized, cache-aligned blocks (the pivot itself is removed from the array). Each thread takes one block from each side of the array to be partitioned, and tries to *neutralize* (see [19] for details on this concept) blocks by swapping elements in the left block that are larger than the pivot with elements in the right block that are smaller than the pivot. As soon as one of the blocks has been neutralized, the thread tries to acquire another block from the same side of the array, until it runs out of free blocks.

After this [19] proposes that a single thread then collects the remaining blocks from all other threads, and neutralizes them sequentially. We can improve this slightly. In our implementation, any thread that needs to acquire a block decides whether it wants to be a producer or a consumer, depending on its current id and the number of blocks on this

Size	Seq/STL	SeqQS	Qsort	SU	Cilk	SU	TBB	SU	MCSTL	SU	mmQsort	SU
Random												
10000000	1.240	1.312	0.362	3.4	0.311	4.0	0.173	7.2	0.163	7.6	0.230	5.4
100000000	13.355	13.212	2.782	4.8	2.394	5.6	1.840	7.3	1.714	7.8	1.130	11.8
1000000000	131.144	139.687	22.016	6.0	22.837	5.7	18.090	7.2	17.597	7.5	14.464	9.1
8388607	1.030	1.089	0.322	3.2	0.287	3.6	0.142	7.3	0.150	6.9	0.187	5.5
33554431	4.464	4.642	0.795	5.6	0.751	5.9	0.543	8.2	0.510	8.7	0.528	8.4
134217727	17.615	17.907	3.241	5.4	2.686	6.6	2.179	8.1	2.473	7.1	1.463	12.0
Gauss												
10000000	1.234	1.308	0.310	4.0	0.281	4.4	0.166	7.4	0.160	7.7	0.169	7.3
100000000	11.735	12.597	2.724	4.3	2.575	4.6	1.927	6.1	1.641	7.2	1.413	8.3
1000000000	119.289	126.611	20.732	5.8	22.294	5.4	18.446	6.5	18.915	6.3	13.399	8.9
8388607	1.028	1.083	0.313	3.3	0.287	3.6	0.160	6.4	0.143	7.2	0.213	4.8
33554431	4.374	4.073	0.897	4.9	0.835	5.2	0.588	7.4	0.586	7.5	0.535	8.2
134217727	15.738	16.682	2.747	5.7	2.452	6.4	2.117	7.4	2.219	7.1	1.375	11.4
Bucket												
10000000	1.096	1.175	0.278	3.9	0.230	4.8	0.102	10.7	0.153	7.2	0.209	5.2
100000000	11.953	11.901	1.362	8.8	1.110	10.8	0.858	13.9	1.572	7.6	1.020	11.7
1000000000	118.501	127.512	15.906	7.5	13.395	8.8	13.689	8.7	16.576	7.1	12.666	9.4
8388607	0.895	0.973	0.227	3.9	0.178	5.0	0.072	12.4	0.132	6.8	0.160	5.6
33554431	4.007	4.177	0.738	5.4	0.655	6.1	0.439	9.1	0.497	8.1	0.588	6.8
134217727	15.771	16.411	2.093	7.5	1.932	8.2	1.501	10.5	2.219	7.1	1.458	10.8
Staggered												
10000000	1.111	1.275	0.432	2.6	0.503	2.2	0.318	3.5	0.161	6.9	0.283	3.9
100000000	11.611	12.307	2.536	4.6	4.212	2.8	3.812	3.0	1.602	7.2	1.284	9.0
1000000000	112.151	138.031	39.629	2.8	73.558	1.5	71.466	1.6	17.887	6.3	30.633	3.7
8388607	0.939	1.151	0.502	1.9	0.476	2.0	0.296	3.2	0.129	7.3	0.367	2.6
33554431	3.983	4.390	0.962	4.1	1.097	3.6	0.972	4.1	0.536	7.4	0.686	5.8
134217727	15.730	16.164	2.234	7.0	2.128	7.4	1.684	9.3	2.362	6.7	1.702	9.2

Table 1: Quicksort on the 32-core Intel Nehalem EX system. Average running times over 10 repetitions in seconds. Speedups are calculated relative to the (best) sequential STL implementation.

side that have to be processed. Producing threads put their remaining block, and the current processing position into an exchanger data-structure, and then exit the computation. Consuming threads retrieve blocks from the exchanger data-structure and continue to neutralize blocks. During this execution more and more threads switch from being a consumer to being a producer, until only thread 0 remains. Finally, only thread 0 has blocks from one side remaining. A variation of the sequential partitioner is now used for the remaining blocks.

For the number of threads assigned for each subtask, we select the largest power of two such that each thread can process at least 128 blocks on average during the partitioning step, and of course upper bounded by the number of started hardware threads. If only one thread would process the array, we switch to the classic task parallel Quicksort implementation with a sequential partitioning step given as Algorithm 4.

Tunable parameters of the mixed-mode parallel Quicksort implementation are the following:

- Blocksize for parallel partitioning. This should be at least as large as the cacheline size. We decided on a blocksize of 4096 (We sorted 4-byte integer values).

- Number of threads for the data-parallel partitioning step. A thread should be able to process at least 128 blocks on average. We only allow powers of two for

the number of threads. The concrete choice is encapsulated in the getBestNp function.

- Cutoff for task-based Quicksort: we decided to let all subsequences with less than 512 elements be sorted by STL sort.

We did not concentrate on finding the best values for these parameters (or the tuning parameters of the work-stealing scheduler), therefore performance might be improved using different values.

4.1 Experimental results

To investigate the advantage of mixed-mode parallelism, and the capabilities and overheads of our new scheduler we compare the mixed-mode parallel Quicksort (Algorithm 5) to a standard task-based Quicksort (Algorithm 4) implementation. Both are run on our scheduler.

Speedup is in all cases computed relative to the best available sequential sort implementation which we take to be the STL sort function. This is also used in our implementation for subsequences shorter than 512 elements. In the current version of the STL delivered with gcc, the Introsort algorithm is used that is based on Quicksort, but has a better worst-case complexity. For each variant, we report the average of 10 measurements. We sorted differently generated sequences of 4-Byte integers distributed as in [10, 19], namely uniformly random, random Gaussian, Buckets and Staggered.

Type	Size	Seq/STL	SeqQS	Qsort	SU	mmQsort	SU
Random	10000000	4.541	5.449	2.128	2.1	1.464	3.1
	100000000	54.208	64.659	14.672	3.7	6.385	8.5
	8388607	3.718	4.441	1.509	2.5	1.094	3.4
	33554431	16.427	20.167	5.189	3.2	3.502	4.7
	134217727	75.126	86.858	16.198	4.6	10.849	6.9
Gauss	10000000	4.474	5.237	1.766	2.5	1.267	3.5
	100000000	52.630	62.650	13.144	4.0	5.235	10.1
	8388607	3.552	4.545	1.578	2.3	1.149	3.1
	33554431	16.590	19.514	5.481	3.0	3.344	5.0
	134217727	72.759	90.817	23.120	3.1	9.452	7.7
Buckets	10000000	4.787	5.728	2.288	2.1	1.412	3.4
	100000000	56.710	67.763	16.825	3.4	7.653	7.4
	8388607	3.807	4.516	1.439	2.6	1.220	3.1
	33554431	17.371	20.607	5.487	3.2	3.335	5.2
	134217727	76.133	91.296	21.056	3.6	11.717	6.5
Staggered	10000000	4.315	7.052	3.538	1.2	2.021	2.1
	100000000	52.795	79.495	27.864	1.9	8.334	6.3
	8388607	3.570	5.376	2.037	1.8	1.438	2.5
	33554431	16.762	21.383	5.872	2.9	3.488	4.8
	134217727	71.398	102.328	31.826	2.2	8.327	8.6

Table 2: Quicksort on the 16-core Sun T2+ system running with 32 threads. Average running times over 10 repetitions in seconds. Speedups are calculated relative to the (best) sequential STL implementation.

Experiments were performed on two different systems:

- a 4-socket Intel Xeon X7560 system, where each CPU has 8 cores (Intel Xeon X7560 2.26 GHz, 24MB cache)

- a 2-socket Sun UltraSPARC T2+ system, where each CPU has 8 cores and up 64 hardware threads

Results of the experiments are shown in Tables 1 and 2. Here, colums Seq/STL list the running times for the "best" sequential implementation available (STL), while columns SeqQS give the running times for the handwritten reference Quicksort implementation that uses the same CUTOFF value to switch to STL sort as the parallel implementations. Columns Qsort list the running times with Algorithm 4 on our work-stealer (here all tasks have thread requirement 1). Finally, columns mmQsort are our mixed-mode parallel algorithm shown as Algorithm 5. On the Intel Xeon system, we also performed comparisons to other parallel Quicksort implementations. Column Cilk gives the running times using Intel Cilk Plus. TBB denotes Quicksort implemented using Intel Threading Building Blocks. Both the Cilk and the TBB Quicksort have been manually implemented and follow the pattern of Algorithm 4 including a CUTOFF value. Column MCSTL gives the running times of the Quicksort provided as part of the MCSTL library [17].

On the Intel Xeon system, all implementations were compiled using the Intel Parallel Studio XE 2011 compilers, with the exception of MCSTL, which is a gcc-builtin and therefore had to be compiled using gcc. On the Sun UltraSPARC T2+ system, the Sun Studio 12 compilers were used.

Compared to the task-based Quicksort, our mixed mode implementation on top to the new work-stealing scheduler improves speedup often by a significant fraction, sometimes by more than a factor of 2. On the 32-core Nehalem system we achieve better results for larger problem sizes than with TBB, except for the Buckets distribution where TBB is better. The Intel Cilk Plus implementation is constantly out-

performed by our implementation. (It is worth noting that previous experiments done with CilkArts Cilk++ yielded better performance than with Intel Cilk Plus. Nonetheless it is still outperformed by TBB. The results of those measurements can be found in [20].) The MCSTL Quicksort implementation stands out as the Quicksort implementation that can provide the most stable speedup, but our mixed-mode parallel implementation is still able to outperform it on large problem sizes.

On the Sun T2+ system speedup is very competitive for 32 threads as shown in Table 2. Here, more than a factor 3 speedup improvement is sometimes achieved over the standard fork-join implementation.

Further, more detailed results on other systems showing similar behaviors are available in [20]. Other mixed-mode parallel applications were implemented and experimentally evaluated in [21].

5. CONCLUSION

We showed how to extend standard work-stealing to deal with mixed-mode task and data parallel programs, in which dynamically spawned tasks can make (fixed) requirements for a number (larger than one) of threads for their execution. We concentrated on explaining the basic algorithm, which we termed *work-stealing with deterministic team-building*, and outlined a number of variations and tunable parameters. We have implemented such a work-stealer in C++, and used it to give a natural application of the mixed-mode parallel Quicksort algorithm described in [19]. On two different many-core systems with 32 cores (Intel Nehalem), and 16 cores (Sun T2+) respectively, we showed that speedup could be improved significantly compared to a standard, task-parallel Quicksort algorithm. Other mixed-mode parallel applications were considered in [21], where either a more natural implementation and/or better performance could be achieved.

In future work we will investigate further mixed-mode parallel applications, and continue to improve the work-stealing with deterministic team-building implementation, including additional ways of improving processor utilization in cases where the number of threads per task does not fit well with the processor hierarchy. One way to do this might be to allow tasks that are malleable within certain limits. We also plan to explore the theoretical properties of work-stealing with deterministic team-building and to provide bounds on the time that threads may be idle compared to other mixed-mode scheduling approaches. Eventually we would like to experiment with the approach within the overall PEPPHER framework.

6. REFERENCES

[1] N. S. Arora, R. D. Blumofe, and C. G. Plaxton. Thread scheduling for multiprogrammed multiprocessors. *Theory of Computing Systems*, 34(2):115–144, 2001.

[2] R. D. Blumofe, C. F. Joerg, B. C. Kuszmaul, C. E. Leiserson, K. H. Randall, and Y. Zhou. Cilk: An efficient multithreaded runtime system. *Journal of Parallel and Distributed Computing*, 37(1):55–69, 1996.

[3] R. D. Blumofe and C. E. Leiserson. Scheduling multithreaded computations by work stealing. *Journal of the ACM*, 46(5):720–748, 1999.

[4] V. Boudet, F. Desprez, and F. Suter. One-step algorithm for mixed data and task parallel scheduling without data replication. In *17th International Parallel and Distributed Processing Symposium (IPDPS)*, page 41, 2003.

[5] S. Chakrabarti, J. Demmel, and K. A. Yelick. Models and scheduling algorithms for mixed data and task parallel programs. *Journal of Parallel and Distributed Computing*, 47(2):168–184, 1997.

[6] L. A. Crowl, M. Crovella, T. J. LeBlanc, and M. L. Scott. The advantages of multiple parallelizations in combinatorial search. *Journal of Parallel and Distributed Computing*, 21(1):110–123, 1994.

[7] F. Desprez and F. Suter. Impact of mixed-parallelism on parallel implementations of the Strassen and Winograd matrix multiplication algorithms. *Concurrency - Practice and Experience*, 16(8):771–797, 2004.

[8] J. Dümmler, T. Rauber, and G. Rünger. Communicating multiprocessor-tasks. In *Languages and Compilers for Parallel Computing (LCPC)*, volume 5234 of *Lecture Notes in Computer Science*, pages 292–307, 2007.

[9] P.-F. Dutot, T. N'Takpé, F. Suter, and H. Casanova. Scheduling parallel task graphs on (almost) homogeneous multicluster platforms. *IEEE Transactions on Parallel and Distributed Systems*, 20(7):940–952, 2009.

[10] D. R. Helman, D. A. Bader, and J. JáJá. A randomized parallel sorting algorithm with an experimental study. *Journal of Parallel and Distributed Computing*, 52(1):1–23, 1998.

[11] M. Herlihy and N. Shavit. *The Art of Multiprocessor Programming*. Morgan Kaufmann Publishers, 2008.

[12] A. Kukanov and M. J. Voss. The foundations for scalable multi-core software in Intel Threading Building Blocks. *Intel Technology Journal*, 11(4), 2007.

[13] A. Radulescu and A. J. C. van Gemund. A low-cost approach towards mixed task and data parallel scheduling. In *Proceedings of the 2001 International Conference on Parallel Processing (ICPP)*, pages 69–76, 2001.

[14] T. Rauber and G. Rünger. A coordination language for mixed task and and data parallel programs. In *Proceedings of the 1999 ACM Symposium on Applied Computing (SAC)*, pages 146–155, 1999.

[15] T. Rauber and G. Rünger. Mixed task and data parallel executions in general linear methods. *Scientific Programming*, 15(3):137–155, 2007.

[16] J. Shirako, D. M. Peixotto, V. Sarkar, and W. N. S. III. Phasers: a unified deadlock-free construct for collective and point-to-point synchronization. In *Proceedings of the 22nd Annual International Conference on Supercomputing (ICS)*, pages 277–288. ACM, 2008.

[17] J. Singler, P. Sanders, and F. Putze. MCSTL: The Multi-core Standard Template Library. In *13th International Euro-Par Conference*, volume 4641 of *LNCS*, pages 682–694. Springer, 2007.

[18] S. Thibault, R. Namyst, and P.-A. Wacrenier. Building portable thread schedulers for hierarchical multiprocessors: The BubbleSched framework. In *Euro-Par, Parallel Processing*, volume 4641 of *Lecture Notes in Computer Science*, pages 42–51, 2007.

[19] P. Tsigas and Y. Zhang. A simple, fast parallel implementation of quicksort and its performance evaluation on SUN Enterprise 10000. In *Eleventh Euromicro Conference on Parallel, Distributed and Network-Based Processing (PDP)*, pages 372–381, 2003.

[20] M. Wimmer and J. L. Träff. Work-stealing for mixed-mode parallelism by deterministic team-building. *CoRR*, abs/1012.5030, 2010.

[21] M. Wimmer and J. L. Träff. A work-stealing framework for mixed-mode parallel applications. In *Workshop on Multi-threaded Architectures and Applications (MTAAP 2011) at International Parallel and Distributed Processing Symposium (IPDPS 2011)*, 2011.

The Pochoir Stencil Compiler

Yuan Tang   Rezaul Chowdhury   Bradley C. Kuszmaul

Chi-Keung Luk   Charles E. Leiserson

MIT Computer Science and Artificial Intelligence Laboratory
Cambridge, MA 02139, USA

ABSTRACT

A stencil computation repeatedly updates each point of a d-dimensional grid as a function of itself and its near neighbors. Parallel cache-efficient stencil algorithms based on "trapezoidal decompositions" are known, but most programmers find them difficult to write. The Pochoir stencil compiler allows a programmer to write a simple specification of a stencil in a domain-specific stencil language embedded in C++ which the Pochoir compiler then translates into high-performing Cilk code that employs an efficient parallel cache-oblivious algorithm. Pochoir supports general d-dimensional stencils and handles both periodic and aperiodic boundary conditions in one unified algorithm. The Pochoir system provides a C++ template library that allows the user's stencil specification to be executed directly in C++ without the Pochoir compiler (albeit more slowly), which simplifies user debugging and greatly simplified the implementation of the Pochoir compiler itself. A host of stencil benchmarks run on a modern multicore machine demonstrates that Pochoir outperforms standard parallel-loop implementations, typically running 2–10 times faster. The algorithm behind Pochoir improves on prior cache-efficient algorithms on multidimensional grids by making "hyperspace" cuts, which yield asymptotically more parallelism for the same cache efficiency.

Categories and Subject Descriptors

D.1.3 [**Programming Techniques**]: Concurrent Programming—
Parallel programming; D.3.2 [**Programming Languages**]: Language Classifications—*Specialized application languages*; G.4 [**Mathematical Software**]: *Algorithm design and analysis*.

This work was supported in part by a grant from Intel Corporation and in part by the National Science Foundation under Grants CCF-0937860 and CNS-1017058.

Yuan Tang is Assistant Professor of Computer Science at Fudan University in China and a Visiting Scientist at MIT CSAIL. Bradley C. Kuszmaul is Research Scientist at MIT CSAIL and Chief Architect at Tokutek, Inc. Chi-Keung Luk is Senior Staff Engineer at Intel Corporation and a Research Affiliate at MIT CSAIL. Rezaul Chowdhury is Research Scientist at Boston University and Research Affiliate at MIT CSAIL. Charles E. Leiserson is Professor of Computer Science and Engineering at MIT CSAIL.

General Terms

Algorithms, Languages, Performance.

Keywords

C++, cache-oblivious algorithm, Cilk, compiler, embedded domain-specific language, multicore, parallel computation, stencil, trapezoidal decomposition.

1. INTRODUCTION

Pochoir (pronounced "PO-shwar") is a compiler and runtime system for implementing stencil computations on multicore processors. A *stencil* defines the value of a grid point in a d-dimensional spatial grid at time t as a function of neighboring grid points at recent times before t. A *stencil computation* [2, 9, 11, 12, 16, 17, 26–28, 33, 34, 36, 40, 41] computes the stencil for each grid point over many time steps.

Stencil computations are conceptually simple to implement using nested loops, but looping implementations suffer from poor cache performance. Cache-oblivious [15, 38] divide-and-conquer stencil codes [16, 17] are much more efficient, but they are difficult to write, and when parallelism is factored into the mix, most application programmers do not have the programming skills or patience to produce efficient multithreaded codes.

As an example, consider how the 2D *heat equation* [13]

$$\frac{\partial u_t(x,y)}{\partial t} = \alpha \left(\frac{\partial^2 u_t(x,y)}{\partial x^2} + \frac{\partial^2 u_t(x,y)}{\partial y^2} \right)$$

on an $X \times Y$ grid, where $u_t(x,y)$ is the heat at a point (x,y) at time t and α is the thermal diffusivity, might be solved using a stencil computation. By discretizing space and time, this partial differential equation can be solved approximately by using the following Jacobi-style update equation:

$$\begin{aligned}
u_{t+1}(x,y) &= u_t(x,y) \\
&+ \frac{\alpha \Delta t}{\Delta x^2} \left(u_t(x-1,y) + u_t(x+1,y) - 2u_t(x,y) \right) \\
&+ \frac{\alpha \Delta t}{\Delta y^2} \left(u_t(x,y-1) + u_t(x,y+1) - 2u_t(x,y) \right).
\end{aligned}$$

One simple parallel program to implement a stencil computation based on this update equation is with a triply nested loop, as shown in Figure 1. The code is invoked as $\text{LOOPS}(u;0,T;0,X;0,Y)$ to perform the stencil computation over T time steps. Although the loop indexing the time dimension is serial, the loops indexing the spatial dimensions can be parallelized, although as a practical matter, only the outer loop needs to be parallelized. There is generally no need to store the entire space-time grid, and so the code uses two

LOOPS(u; ta, tb; xa, xb; ya, yb)

```
1   for t = ta to tb − 1
2       parallel for x = xa to xb − 1
3           for y = ya to ya − 1
4               u((t + 1) mod 2, x, y) = u(t mod 2, x, y)
                    + CX · (u(t mod 2, (x − 1) mod X, y)
                    + u(t mod 2, (x + 1) mod X, y) − 2u(t mod 2, x, y))
                    + CY · (u(t mod 2, x, (y − 1) mod Y)
                    + u(t mod 2, x, (y + 1) mod Y) − 2u(t mod 2, x, y))
```

Figure 1: A parallel looping implementation of a stencil computation for the 2D heat equation with periodic boundary conditions. The array u keeps two copies of an $X \times Y$ array of grid points, one for time t and one for time $t + 1$. The parameters ta and tb are the beginning and ending time steps, and xa, xb, ya, and yb are the coordinates defining the region of the array u on which to perform the stencil computation. The constants $CX = \alpha\Delta t/\Delta x^2$ and $CY = \alpha\Delta t/\Delta y^2$ are precomputed. The call LOOPS(u; 0, T; 0, X; 0, Y) performs the stencil computation over the whole 2D array for T time steps.

copies of the spatial grid, swapping their roles on alternate time steps. This code assumes that the boundary conditions are ***periodic***, meaning that the spatial grid wraps around to form a torus, and hence the index calculations for x and y are performed modulo X and Y, respectively.

This loop nest is simple and fairly easy to understand, but its performance may suffer from poor cache locality. Let $\mathcal{M}$ be the number of grid points that fit in cache, and let $\mathcal{B}$ be the number of grid points that fit on a cache line. If the space grid does not fit in cache — that is, $XY \gg \mathcal{M}$ — then this simple computation incurs $\Theta(TXY/\mathcal{B})$ cache misses in the ideal-cache model [15].

Figure 2 shows the pseudocode for a more efficient cache-oblivious algorithm called TRAP, which is the basis of the algorithm used by the Pochoir compiler. We shall explain this algorithm in Section 3. It achieves $\Theta(TXY/\mathcal{B}\sqrt{\mathcal{M}})$ cache misses, assuming that $X \approx Y$ and $T = \Omega(X)$. TRAP easily outperforms LOOPS on large data sets. For example, we ran both algorithms on a 5000×5000 spatial grid iterated for 5000 time steps using the Intel C++ version 12.0.0 compiler with Intel Cilk Plus [23] on a 12-core Intel Core i7 (Nehalem) machine with a private 32-KB L1-data-cache, a private 256-KB L2-cache, and a shared 12-MB L3-cache. The code based on LOOPS ran in 248 seconds, whereas the Pochoir-generated code based on TRAP required about 24 seconds, more than a factor of 10 performance advantage.

Figure 3 shows Pochoir's performance on a wider range of benchmarks, including heat equation (Heat) [13] on a 2D grid, a 2D torus, and a 4D grid; Conway's game of Life (Life) [18]; 3D finite-difference wave equation (Wave) [32]; lattice Boltzmann method (LBM) [30]; RNA secondary structure prediction (RNA) [1, 6]; pairwise sequence alignment (PSA) [19]; longest common subsequence (LCS) [7]; and American put stock option pricing (APOP) [24]. Pochoir achieves a substantial performance improvement over a straightforward loop parallelization for typical stencil applications, such as Heat and Life. Even LBM, which is a complex stencil having many states, achieves good speedup. When Pochoir does not achieve as much speedup over the loop code, it is often due to the space-time grid being too small to yield good parallelism, the innermost loop containing many branch conditionals, or the benchmark containing a high ratio of floating-point operations to memory accesses. For example, RNA's small grid size of 300^2 yields a parallelism of just over 5 for both Pochoir and parallel loops, and its innermost loop contains many branch conditionals. PSA operates over a diamond-shaped domain, and so the application employs many conditional branches in the kernel in order to distinguish interior points from exterior points. These overheads

TRAP(u; ta, tb; xa, xb, dxa, dxb; ya, yb, dya, dyb)

```
1   Δt = tb − ta
2   Δx = max {xb − xa, (xb + dxbΔt) − (xa + dxaΔt)}  // Longer x-base
3   Δy = max {yb − ya, (yb + dybΔt) − (ya + dyaΔt)}  // Longer y-base
4   k = 0 // Try hyperspace cut
5   if Δx ≥ 2σ_x Δt
6       Trisect the zoid with x-cuts
7       k += 1
8   if Δy ≥ 2σ_y Δt
9       Trisect the zoid with y-cuts
10      k += 1
11  if k > 0
12      Assign dependency levels 0, 1, . . . , k to subzoids
13      for i = 0 to k // for each dependency level i
14          parallel for all subzoids
                (ta, tb; xa', xb', dxa', dxb'; ya', yb', dya', dyb')
                with dependency level i
15              TRAP(ta, tb; xa', xb', dxa', dxb'; ya', yb', dya', dyb')
16  elseif Δt > 1 // time cut
17      // Recursively walk the lower zoid and then the upper
18      TRAP(ta, ta + Δt/2; xa, xb, dxa, dxb; ya, yb, dya, dyb)
19      TRAP(ta + Δt/2, tb; xa + dxaΔt/2, xb + dxbΔt/2, dxa, dxb;
            ya + dyaΔt/2, yb + dybΔt/2, dya, dyb)
20  else // base case
21      for t = ta to tb − 1
22          for x = xa to xb − 1
23              for y = ya to yb − 1
24                  u((t + 1) mod 2, x, y) = u(t mod 2, x, y)
                        + CX · (u(t mod 2, (x − 1) mod X, y)
                        + u(t mod 2, (x + 1) mod X, y) − 2u(t mod 2, x, y))
                        + CY · (u(t mod 2, x, (y − 1) mod Y)
                        + u(t mod 2, x, (y + 1) mod Y) − 2u(t mod 2, x, y))
25      xa += dxa
26      xb += dxb
27      ya += dya
28      yb += dyb
```

Figure 2: The Pochoir cache-oblivious algorithm that implements a 2D stencil computation to solve the 2D heat equation using a trapezoidal decomposition with hyperspace cuts. The parameter u is an $X \times Y$ array of grid points. The remaining variables describe the hypertrapezoid, or "zoid," embedded in space-time that is being processed: ta and tb are the beginning and ending time steps; xa, xb, ya, and yb are the coordinates defining the base of the zoid; dxa, dxb, dya, and dyb are the slopes (actually inverse slopes) of the sides of the zoid. The values σ_x and σ_y are the slopes of the stencil in the x- and y-dimensions, respectively, which are both 1 for the heat equation.

can sometimes significantly mitigate a cache-efficient algorithm's advantage in incurring fewer cache misses.

The Berkeley autotuner [8, 26, 41] focuses on optimizing the performance of stencil kernels by automatically selecting tuning parameters. Their work serves as a good benchmark for the maximum possible speedup one can get on a stencil. K. Datta and S. Williams graciously gave us their code for computing a 7-point stencil and a 27-point stencil on a 258^3 grid with "ghost cells" (see Section 4) using their system. Unfortunately, we were unable to reproduce the reported results from [8] — presumably because there were too many differences in hardware, compilers, and operating system — and thus we are unable to offer a direct side-by-side comparison. Instead, we present in Figure 5 a comparison of our results to their reported results.

We tried to make the operating conditions of the Pochoir tests as similar as possible to the Berkeley environment reported in [8]. We compared Pochoir running 8 worker threads on a 12-core system to the reported numbers for the Berkeley autotuner running 8 threads on 8 cores. The comparison may result in a disadvantage to the Berkeley autotuner, because their reported numbers involve

Benchmark	Dims	Grid size	Time steps	Pochoir			Serial loops		12-core loops	
				1 core	12 cores	speedup	time	ratio	time	ratio
Heat	2	$16,000^2$	500	277s	24s	11.5	612s	25.5	149s	6.2
Heat	2p	$16,000^2$	500	281s	24s	11.7	1,647s	68.6	248s	10.3
Heat	4	150^4	100	154s	54s	2.9	433s	8.0	104s	1.9
Life	2p	$16,000^2$	500	345s	28s	12.3	2,419s	86.4	332s	11.9
Wave	3	$1,000^3$	500	3,082s	447s	6.9	3,170s	7.1	1,071s	2.4
LBM	3	$100^2 \times 130$	3,000	345s	68s	5.1	304s	4.5	220s	3.2
RNA	2	300^2	900	90s	20s	4.5	121s	6.1	26s	1.3
PSA	1	100,000	200,000	105s	18s	5.8	432s	24.0	77s	4.3
LCS	1	100,000	200,000	57s	9s	6.3	105s	11.7	27s	3.0
APOP	1	2,000.000	10,000	43s	4s	10.7	515s	128.8	48s	12.0

Figure 3: Pochoir performance on an Intel Core i7 (Nehalem) machine. The stencils are nonperiodic unless the *Dims* column contains a "p." The header *Serial loops* means a serial `for` loop implementation running on one core, whereas *12-core loops* means a parallel `cilk_for` loop implementation running on 12 cores. The header *ratio* indicates how much slower the looping implementation is than the 12-core Pochoir implementation. For nonperiodic stencils, the looping implementations employ ghost cells [8] to avoid boundary processing.

only a single time step, whereas the Pochoir code runs for 200 time steps. (It does not make sense to run Pochoir for only 1 time step, since its efficiency is in large measure due to the temporal locality of cache use.) Likewise, the Pochoir figures may exhibit a disadvantage compared with the Berkeley ones, because Pochoir had to cope with load imbalances due to the scheduling of 8 threads on 12 cores. Notwithstanding these issues, as can be seen from the figure, Pochoir's performance is generally comparable to that of the Berkeley autotuner on these two benchmarks.

The Pochoir-generated TRAP code is a cache-oblivious [15, 38] divide-and-conquer algorithm based on the notion of *trapezoidal decompositions* introduced by Frigo and Strumpen [16, 17]. We improve on their code by using *hyperspace* cuts, which produce an asymptotic improvement in parallelism while attaining essentially the same cache efficiency. As can be seen from Figure 2, however, this divide-and-conquer parallel code is far more complex than LOOPS, involving recursion over irregular geometric regions. Moreover, TRAP presents many opportunities for optimization, including coarsening the base case of the recursion and handling boundary conditions. We contend that one cannot expect average application programmers to be able to write such complex high-performing code for each stencil computation they wish to perform.

The Pochoir stencil compiler allows programmers to write simple functional specification for arbitrary d-dimensional stencils, and then it automatically produces a highly optimized, cache-efficient, parallel implementation. The Pochoir language can be viewed as a domain-specific language [10, 21, 31] embedded in the base language C++ with the Cilk multithreading extensions [23].

As shown in Figure 4, the Pochoir system operates in two phases, only the second of which involves the Pochoir compiler itself. For the first phase, the programmer compiles the source program with the ordinary Intel C++ compiler using the Pochoir template library, which implements Pochoir's linguistic constructs using unoptimized but functionally correct algorithms. This phase ensures that the source program is *Pochoir-compliant*. For the second phase, the programmer runs the source through the Pochoir compiler, which acts as a preprocessor to the Intel C++ compiler, performing a source-to-source translation into a postsource C++ program that employs the Cilk extensions. The postsource is then compiled with the Intel compiler to produce the optimized binary executable. The Pochoir compiler makes the following promise:

The Pochoir Guarantee: If the stencil program compiles and runs with the Pochoir template library during Phase 1, no errors will occur during Phase 2 when it

	Berkeley	Pochoir
CPU	Xeon X5550	Xeon X5650
Clock	2.66GHz	2.66 GHz
cores/socket	4	6
Total # cores	8	12
Hyperthreading	Enabled	Disabled
L1 data cache/core	32KB	32KB
L2 cache/core	256KB	256KB
L3 cache/socket	8MB	12 MB
Peak computation	85 GFLOPS	120 GFLOPS
Compiler	icc 10.0.0	icc 12.0.0
Linux kernel		2.6.32
Threading model	Pthreads	Cilk Plus
3D 7-point	2.0 GStencil/s	2.49 GStencil/s
8 cores	15.8 GFLOPS	19.92 GFLOPS
3D 27-point	0.95 GStencil/s	0.88 GStencil/s
8 cores	28.5 GFLOPS	26.4 GFLOPS

Figure 5: A comparison of Pochoir to the reported results from [8]. The 7-point stencil requires 8 floating-point operations per grid point, whereas the 27-point stencil requires 30 floating-point operations per grid point.

is compiled with the Pochoir compiler or during the subsequent running of the optimized binary.

Pochoir's novel two-phase compilation strategy allowed us to build significant domain-specific optimizations into the Pochoir compiler without taking on the massive job of parsing and typechecking the full C++ language. Knowing that the source program compiles error-free with the Pochoir template library during Phase 1 allows the Pochoir compiler in Phase 2 to treat portions of the source as uninterpreted text, confident that the Intel compiler will compile it correctly in the optimized postsource. Moreover, the Pochoir template library allows the programmer to debug his or her code using a comfortable native C++ tool chain without the complications of the Pochoir compiler.

Figure 6 shows the Pochoir source code for the periodic 2D heat equation. We leave the specification of the Pochoir language to Section 2, but outline the salient features of the language using this code as an example.

Line 6 declares the *Pochoir shape* of the stencil, and line 7 creates the 2-dimensional *Pochoir object* `heat` having that shape. The Pochoir object will contain all the state necessary to perform the computation. Each triple in the array `2D_five_pt` corresponds to a relative offset from the space-time grid point (t,x,y) that the stencil kernel (declared in lines 11–13) will access. The compiler cannot infer the stencil shape from the kernel, because the kernel can be arbitrary code, and accesses to the grid points can be hidden in subroutines. The Pochoir template library complains during Phase 1, however, if an access to a grid point during the kernel computation falls outside the region specified by the shape declaration.

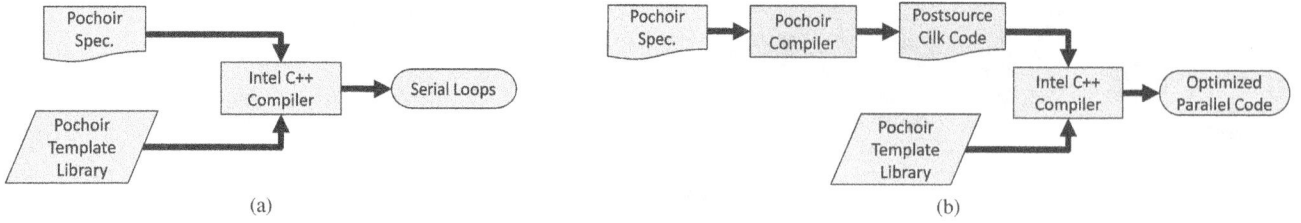

(a)   (b)

Figure 4: Pochoir's two-phase compilation strategy. (a) During Phase 1 the programmer uses the normal Intel C++ compiler to compile his or her code with the Pochoir template library. Phase 1 verifies that the programmer's stencil specification is Pochoir compliant. (b) During Phase 2 the programmer uses the Pochoir compiler, which acts as a preprocessor to the Intel C++ compiler, to generate optimized multithreaded Cilk code.

```
1    #define mod(r,m)  ((r)%(m) + ((r)<0)? (m):0)

2    Pochoir_Boundary_2D(heat_bv, a, t, x, y)
3      return a.get(t,mod(x,a.size(1)),mod(y,a.size(0)));
4    Pochoir_Boundary_End

5    int main(void) {

6      Pochoir_Shape_2D 2D_five_pt[] = {{1,0,0}, {0,1,0},
          {0,-1,0}, {0,-1,-1}, {0,0,-1}, {0,0,1}};
7      Pochoir_2D heat(2D_five_pt);

8      Pochoir_Array_2D(double) u(X, Y);
9      u.Register_Boundary(heat_bv);
10     heat.Register_Array(u);

11     Pochoir_Kernel_2D(heat_fn, t, x, y)
12       u(t+1, x, y) = CX * (u(t, x+1, y) - 2 * u(t, x,
            y) + u(t, x-1, y)) + CY * (u(t, x, y+1) - 2
            * u(t, x, y) + u(t, x, y-1)) + u(t, x, y);
13     Pochoir_Kernel_End

14     for (int x = 0; x < X; ++x)
15       for (int y = 0; y < Y; ++y)
16         u(0, x, y) = rand();

17     heat.Run(T, heat_fn);

18     for (int x = 0; x < X; ++x)
19       for (int y = 0; y < Y; ++y)
20         cout << u(T, x, y);

22     return 0;
23   }
```

Figure 6: The Pochoir stencil source code for a periodic 2D heat equation. Pochoir keywords are boldfaced.

Line 8 declares u as an X×Y **Pochoir array** of double-precision floating-point numbers representing the spatial grid. Lines 2–4 define a **boundary function** that will be called when the kernel function accesses grid points outside the computing domain, that is, if it tries to access u(t, x, y) with $x < 0$, $x \geq X$, $y < 0$, or $y \geq Y$. The boundary function for this periodic stencil performs calculations modulo the dimensions of the spatial grid. (Section 2 shows how nonperiodic stencils can be specified, including how to specify Dirichlet and Neumann boundary conditions [14].) Line 9 associates the boundary function heat_bv with the Pochoir array u. Each Pochoir array has exactly one boundary function to supply a value when the computation accesses grid points outside of the computing domain. Line 10 registers the Pochoir array u with the heat Pochoir object. A Pochoir array can be registered with more than one Pochoir object, and a Pochoir object can have multiple Pochoir arrays registered.

Lines 11–13 define a **kernel function** heat_fn, which specifies how the stencil is computed for every grid point. This kernel can be an arbitrary piece of code, but accesses to the registered Pochoir arrays must respect the declared shape(s).

Lines 14–16 initialize the Pochoir array u with values for time step 0. If a stencil depends on more than one prior step as indicated by the Pochoir shape, multiple time steps may need to be initialized. Line 17 executes the stencil object heat for T time steps using ker-

nel function heat_fn. Lines 18–20 prints the result of the computation by reading the elements u(T, x, y) of the Pochoir array. In fact, Pochoir overloads the "<<" operator so that the Pochoir array can be pretty-printed by simply writing "cout << u;".

The remainder of this paper is organized as follows. Section 2 provides a full specification of the Pochoir embedded language. Section 3 describes the cache-oblivious parallel algorithm used by the compiled code and analyzes its theoretical performance. Section 4 describes four important optimizations employed by the Pochoir compiler. Section 5 describes related work, and Section 6 offers some concluding remarks.

2. THE POCHOIR SPECIFICATION LANGUAGE

This section describes the formal syntax and semantics of the Pochoir language, which was designed with a view to offer as much expressiveness as possible without violating the Pochoir Guarantee. Since we wanted to allow third-party developers to implement their own stencil compilers that could use the Pochoir specification language, we avoided to the extent possible making the language too specific to the Pochoir compiler, the Intel C++ compiler, and the multicore machines we used for benchmarking.

The static information about a Pochoir stencil computation, such as the computing kernel, the boundary conditions, and the stencil shape, is stored in a **Pochoir object**, which is declared as follows:

- **Pochoir_**_dim_**D** _name_ (_shape_);

This statement declares _name_ as a Pochoir object with _dim_ spatial dimensions and computing shape _shape_, where _dim_ is a small positive integer and _shape_ is an array of arrays which describes the shape of the stencil as elaborated below.

We now itemize the remaining Pochoir constructs and explain the semantics of each.

- **Pochoir_Shape_**_dim_**D** _name_ [] = {_cells_}

This statement declares _name_ as a **Pochoir shape** that can hold shape information for _dim_ spatial dimensions. The Pochoir shape is equivalent to an array of arrays, each of which contains $dim + 1$ integer numbers. These numbers represent the offset of each memory footprint in the stencil kernel relative to the space-time grid point $\langle t, x, y, \cdots \rangle$. For example, suppose that the computing kernel employs the following update equation:

$$
\begin{aligned}
u_t(x,y) = {} & u_{t-1}(x,y) \\
& + \frac{\alpha \Delta t}{\Delta x^2}\left(u_{t-1}(x-1,y) + u_{t-1}(x+1,y) - 2u_{t-1}(x,y)\right) \\
& + \frac{\alpha \Delta t}{\Delta y^2}\left(u_{t-1}(x,y-1) + u_{t-1}(x,y+1) - 2u_{t-1}(x,y)\right).
\end{aligned}
$$

The shape of this stencil is {{0,0,0}, {−1,1,0}, {−1,0,0}, {−1,−1,0}, {−1,0,1}, {−1,0,−1}}.

The first cell in the shape is the **home** cell, whose spatial coordinates must all be 0. During the computation, this cell corresponds to the grid point being updated. The remaining cells must have time offsets that are smaller than the time coordinate of the home cell, and the corresponding grid points during the computation are read-only.

The **depth** of a shape is the time coordinate of the home cell minus the minimum time coordinate of any cell in the shape. The depth corresponds to the number of time steps on which a grid point depends. For our example stencil, the depth of the shape is 1, since a point at time t depends on points at time $t-1$.. If a stencil shape has depth k, the programmer must initialize all Pochoir arrays for time steps $0, 1, \ldots, k-1$ before running the computation.

- **Pochoir_Array_**dim**D** $(type, depth)$ $name$ $(size_{dim-1}, \ldots, size_1, size_0)$

This statement declares $name$ as a **Pochoir array** of type $type$ with dim spatial dimensions and a temporal dimension. The size of the ith spatial dimension, where $i \in \{0, 1, \ldots, dim\}$, is given by $size_i$. The temporal dimension has size $k+1$, where k is the depth of the Pochoir shape, and are reused modulo $k+1$ as the computation proceeds. The user may not obtain an alias to the Pochoir array or its elements.

- **Pochoir_Boundary_**dim**D**$(name, array, idx_t, idx_{dim-1}, \ldots, idx_1, idx_0)$
    $\langle definition \rangle$
  Pochoir_Boundary_End

This construct defines a **boundary function** called $name$ that will be invokeda to supply a value when the stencil computation accesses a point outside the domain of the Pochoir array $array$. The Pochoir array $array$ has dim spatial dimensions, and $\langle idx_{dim-1}, \ldots, idx_1, idx_0 \rangle$ are the spatial coordinates of the given point outside the domain of $array$. The coordinate in the time dimension is given by idx_t. The function body $\langle definition \rangle$) is C++ code that defines the values of $array$ on its boundary. A current restriction is that this construct must be declared outside of any function, that is, the boundary function is declared global.

- **Pochoir_Kernel_**dim**D**$(name, array, idx_t, idx_{dim-1}, \ldots, idx_1, idx_0)$
    $\langle definition \rangle$
  Pochoir_Kernel_End

This construct defines a **kernel function** named $name$ for updating a stencil on a spatial grid with dim spatial dimensions. The spatial coordinates of the point to update are $\langle idx_{dim-1}, \ldots, idx_1, idx_0 \rangle$, and idx_t is the coordinate in time dimension. The function body $\langle definition \rangle$ may contain arbitrary C++ code to compute the stencil. Unlike boundary functions, this construct can be defined in any context.

- $name.$**Register_Array**$(array)$

A call to this member function of a Pochoir object $name$ informs $name$ that the Pochoir array $array$ will participate in its stencil computation.

- $name.$**Register_Boundary**$(bdry)$

A call to this member function of a Pochoir array $name$ associates the declared boundary function $bdry$ with $name$. The boundary function is invoked to supply a value whenever an off-domain memory access occurs. Each Pochoir array is associated with exactly one boundary function at any given time, but the programmer can change boundary functions by registering a new one.

- $name.$**Run**$(T, kern)$

This function call runs the stencil computation on the Pochoir object $name$ for T time steps using computing kernel function $kern$.

After running the computation for T steps, the results of the computation can be accessed by indexing its Pochoir arrays at time $T + k - 1$, where k is the depth of the stencil shape. The programmer may resume the running of the stencil after examining the result of the computation by calling $name.$Run$(T', kern)$, where T' is the number of additional steps to execute. The result of the computation is then in the computation's Pochoir arrays indexed by time $T + T' + k - 1$.

Rationale

The Pochoir language is a product of many design decisions, some of which were influenced by the current capabilities of the Intel 12.0.0 C++ compiler. We now discuss some of the more important design decisions.

Although we chose to pass a kernel function to the Run method of a Pochoir object, we would have preferred to simply store the kernel function with the Pochoir object. The kernel function is a C++ lambda function [5], however, whose type is not available to us. Thus, although we can pass the lambda function as a template type, we cannot store it unless we create a `std::function` to capture its type. Since the Intel compiler does not yet support `std::function`, this avenue was lost to us. There is only one kernel function per Pochoir object, however, and so we decided as a second-best alternative that it would be most convenient for users if they could declare a kernel function in any context and we just pass it as an argument to the Run member function.

The lack of support for function objects also had an impact on the declaration of boundary functions. We wanted to store each boundary function with a Pochoir array so that whenever an access to the array falls outside the computing domain, we can call the boundary function to supply a value. The only way to create a function that can be stored is to use an ordinary function, which must be declared in a global scope. We hope to improve Pochoir's linguistic design when function objects are fully supported by the compiler.

We chose to specify the kernel function imperatively rather than as a pure function or as an expression that returns a value for the grid point being updated. This approach allows a user to write multiple statements in a kernel function and provides flexibility on how to specify a stencil formula. For example, the user can choose to specify a stencil formula as `a(t, i, j) = ...` or `a(t+1, i, j) = ...`, whichever is more convenient.

We chose to make the user copy data in and out of Pochoir internal data structures, rather than operate directly on the user's arrays. Since the user is typically running the stencil computation for many time steps, we decided that the copy-in/copy-out approach would not cause much overhead. Moreover, the layout of data is now under the control of the compiler, allowing it to optimize the storage for cache efficiency.

3. POCHOIR'S CACHE-OBLIVIOUS PARALLEL ALGORITHM

This section describes the parallel algorithm at the core of Pochoir's efficiency. TRAP is a cache-oblivious algorithm based on "trapezoidal decompositions" [16, 17], but which employs a novel "hyperspace-cut" strategy to improve parallelism without sacrificing cache-efficiency. On a d-dimensional spatial grid with all "normalized" spatial dimensions equal to w and the time dimension a power-of-2 multiple of w, TRAP achieves $\Theta(w^{d-\lg(d+2)+1}/d^2)$ parallelism, whereas Frigo and Strumpen's original parallel trapezoidal decomposition algorithm [17] achieves $\Theta(w^{d-\lg(2^d+1)+1}/2^d) = O(w)$ parallelism. Both algorithms exhibit the same asymptotic cache complexity of $\Theta(hw^d/\mathcal{M}^{1/d}\mathcal{B})$ proved by Frigo and Strumpen, where h is the height of the time dimension, $\mathcal{M}$ is the cache size, and $\mathcal{B}$ is the cache-block size.

TRAP uses a cache-oblivious [15] divide-and-conquer strategy based on a recursive trapezoidal decomposition of the space-time grid, which was introduced by Frigo and Strumpen [16]. They originally used the technique for serial stencil computations, but later extended it to parallel stencil computations [17]. Whereas Frigo and Strumpen's parallel algorithm cuts the spatial dimensions of a hypertrapezoid, or "zoid," one at a time with "parallel space cuts," TRAP performs a **hyperspace cut** where it applies parallel space cuts simultaneously to as many dimensions as possible, yielding asymptotically more parallelism when the number of spatial dimensions is 2 or greater. As we will argue later in this section, TRAP achieves this improvement in parallelism while attaining the same cache complexity as Frigo and Strumpen's original parallel algorithm.

TRAP operates as follows. Line 5 of Figure 2 determines whether the x-dimension of the zoid can be cut with a parallel space cut, and if so, line 6 trisects the zoid, as we shall describe later in this section and in Figure 7, but it does not immediately spawn recursive tasks to process the subzoids, as Frigo and Strumpen's algorithm would. Instead, the code attempts to make a "hyperspace cut" by proceeding to the y-dimension, and if there were more dimensions, to those, cutting as many dimensions as possible before spawning recursive tasks to handle the subzoids. The counter k keeps track of how many spatial dimensions are cut. If $k > 0$ spatial dimensions are trisected, as tested for in line 11, then line 12 assigns each subzoid to one of $k + 1$ dependency levels such that the subzoids assigned to the same level are independent and can be processed in parallel, as we describe later in this section and in Figure 8. Lines 13–15 recursively walk all subzoids level by level in parallel. Lines 17–19 perform a time cut if no space cut can be performed. Lines 20–28 perform the base-case computation if the zoid is sufficiently small that no space or time cut is productive.

We first introduce some notations and definitions, many of which have been borrowed or adapted from [16, 17]. A $(d + 1)$-dimensional **space-time hypertrapezoid**, or $(d + 1)$-**zoid**, $\mathcal{Z} = (ta, tb;\ xa_0, xb_0, dxa_0, dxb_0;\ xa_1, xb_1, dxa_1, dxb_1;\ \dots;\ xa_{d-1}, xb_{d-1}, dxa_{d-1}, dxb_{d-1})$, where all variables are integers, is the set of integer grid points $\langle t, x_0, x_1, \dots, x_{d-1} \rangle$ such that $ta \leq t < tb$ and $xa_i + dxa_i(t - ta) \leq x_i < xb_i + dxb_i(t - ta)$ for all $i \in \{0, 1, \dots, d-1\}$. The **height** of $\mathcal{Z}$ is $\Delta t = ta - tb$. Define the **projection trapezoid** $\mathcal{Z}_i$ of $\mathcal{Z}$ along spatial dimension i to be the 2D trapezoid that results from projecting the zoid $\mathcal{Z}$ onto the dimensions x_i and t. The projection trapezoid $\mathcal{Z}_i$ has two **bases** (sides parallel to the x_i axis) of lengths $\Delta x_i = xb_i - xa_i$ and $\nabla x_i = (xa_i + dxa_i\Delta t) - (xb_i + dxb_i\Delta t)$. We define the **width**[1] w_i of $\mathcal{Z}_i$ to be the length of the longer of the two bases (parallel sides) of $\mathcal{Z}_i$, that is $w_i = \max\{\Delta x_i, \nabla x_i\}$. The value w_i is also called the **width** of $\mathcal{Z}$ along spatial dimension i. We say that $\mathcal{Z}_i$ is **upright** if $w_i = \Delta x_i$ — the longer base corresponds to time ta — and **inverted** otherwise. A zoid $\mathcal{Z}$ is **well-defined** if its height is positive, its widths along all spatial dimensions are positive, and the lengths of its bases along all spatial dimensions are nonnegative. A projection trapezoid $\mathcal{Z}_i$ is **minimal** if $\mathcal{Z}_i$ is upright and $\nabla x_i = 0$, or $\mathcal{Z}_i$ is inverted and $\Delta x_i = 0$. A zoid $\mathcal{Z}$ is **minimal** if all its $\mathcal{Z}_i$'s are minimal.

Given the shape S of a d-dimensional stencil (as described in

(a)

(b)

(c)

Figure 7: Cutting projection trapezoids. The spatial dimension increases to the right, and the time runs upward. (a) Trisecting an upright trapezoid using a parallel space cut produces two black trapezoids that can be processed in parallel and a gray trapezoid that must be processed after the black ones. (b) Trisecting an inverted trapezoid using a parallel space cut produces two black trapezoids that can be processed in parallel and a gray trapezoid that must be processed before the black ones. (c) A time cut produces a lower and an upper trapezoid where the lower trapezoid must be processed before the upper.

Section 2), define t_{home} be the time index of the home cell. We define the **slope**[2] of a cell $c = (t, x_0, x_1, \dots, x_{d-1}) \in S$ along dimension $i \in \{0, 1, \dots, d-1\}$ as $\sigma_i(c) = |x_i/(t_{\text{home}} - t)|$, and we define the **slope** of the stencil along spatial dimension i as $\sigma_i = \max_{c \in S} \lceil \sigma_i(c) \rceil$. (Pochoir assumes for simplicity that the stencil is symmetric in each dimension.) We define the **normalized width** of a zoid $\mathcal{Z}$ along dimension i by $\widehat{w}_i = w_i/2\sigma_i$.

Parallel space cuts

Our trapezoidal decomposition differs from that of Strumpen and Frigo in the way we do parallel space cuts. A **parallel space cut** can be applied along a given spatial dimension i of a well-defined zoid $\mathcal{Z}$ provided that the projection trapezoid $\mathcal{Z}_i$ can be trisected into 3 well-defined subtrapezoids, as shown in Figures 7(a) and 7(b). The triangle-shaped gray subtrapezoid that lies in the middle is a minimal trapezoid. The larger base of $\mathcal{Z}_i$ is split in half with each half forming the larger base of a black subtrapezoid. These three subtrapezoids of $\mathcal{Z}_i$ correspond to three subzoids of $\mathcal{Z}$. Since the two black subzoids have no interdependencies, they can be processed in parallel. As shown in Figure 7(a), for an upright projection trapezoid, the subzoids corresponding to the black trapezoids are processed first, after which the subzoid corresponding to the gray subtrapezoid can be processed. For an inverted projection trape-

---

[1]Frigo and Strumpen [16, 17] define width as the average of the two bases.

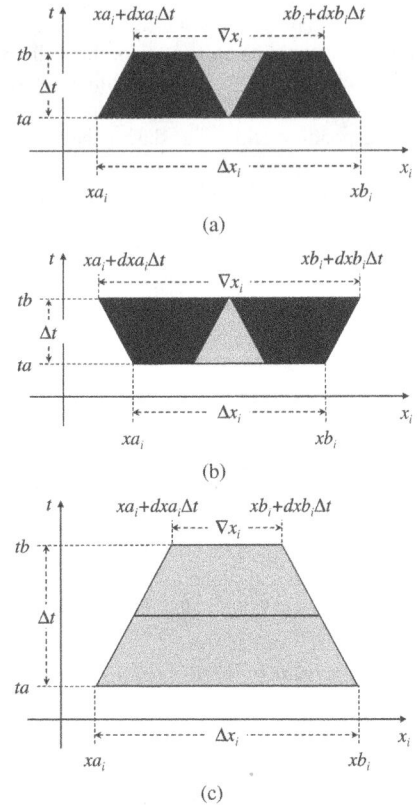

[2]Actually, the reciprocal of slope, but we follow Frigo and Strumpen's terminology.

(a)

(b)

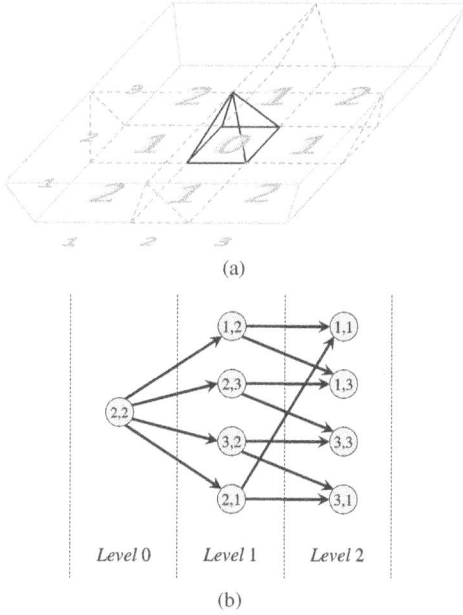

Figure 8: Dependency levels of subzoids resulting from a hyperspace cut along both spatial dimensions of a 3-zoid. (a) Labeling of coordinates of subzoids and their dependency levels. (b) The corresponding dependency graph.

zoid, as shown in Figure 7(b), the opposite is done. In either case, the 3 subzoids can be processed in parallel in the time to process 2 of them, what we shall call 2 *parallel steps*. The following lemma describes the general case.

LEMMA 1. *All 3^k subzoids created by a hyperspace cut on $k \geq 1$ of the $d \geq k$ spatial dimensions of a $(d+1)$-zoid $\mathcal{Z}$ can be processed in $k+1$ parallel steps.*

PROOF. Assume without loss of generality that the hyperspace cut is applied to the first k spatial dimensions of $\mathcal{Z}$. For each such dimension i, label the projection subtrapezoids in 2D space-time resulting from the parallel space cut (see Figures 7(a) and 7(b)) with the numbers 1, 2, and 3, where the black trapezoids are labeled 1 and 3 and the gray trapezoid is labeled 2. When the hyperspace cut consisting of all k parallel space cuts is applied, it creates a set S of 3^k subzoids in $(k+1)$-dimensional space-time. Each subzoid can be identified by a unique k-tuple $\langle u_0, u_1, \ldots, u_{k-1} \rangle$, where $u_i \in \{1,2,3\}$ for $i = 0, 1, \ldots, k-1$. Let $I_i = 1$ if the projection trapezoid $\mathcal{Z}_i$ along the ith dimension is upright and $I_i = 0$ if $\mathcal{Z}_i$ is inverted. The *dependency level* of a zoid $\langle u_0, u_1, \ldots, u_{k-1} \rangle \in S$ is given by

$$dep(\langle u_0, u_1, \ldots, u_{k-1} \rangle) = \sum_{i=0}^{k-1} ((u_i + I_i) \bmod 2) .$$

Observe that this equation implies exactly $k+1$ dependency levels, since each term of the summation may be either 0 or 1. Figure 8(a) shows the dependency levels for the subzoids of a 3-zoid, both of whose projection trapezoids are inverted, generated by a hyperspace cut with $k = 2$.

We claim that all zoids in S with the same dependency level are independent, and thus all of S can be processed in $k+1$ parallel steps. As illustrated in Figure 8(b), we can construct a directed graph $G = (S, E)$ that captures the dependency relationships among the subzoids of S as follows. Given any pair of zoids $\langle u_0, u_1, \ldots, u_{k-1} \rangle, \langle u'_0, u'_1, \ldots, u'_{k-1} \rangle \in S$, we include an edge $(\langle u_0, u_1, \ldots, u_{k-1} \rangle, \langle u'_0, u'_1, \ldots, u'_{k-1} \rangle) \in E$, meaning that a grid point in $\langle u'_0, u'_1, \ldots, u'_{k-1} \rangle$ directly depends on a grid point in

$\langle u_0, u_1, \ldots, u_{k-1} \rangle$, if there exists a dimension $i \in \{0, 1, \ldots, k-1\}$ such that the following conditions hold:

- $u_j = u'_j$ for all $j \in \{0, 1, \ldots, i-1, i+1, \ldots, k-1\}$,
- $(I_i + u_i) \bmod 2 = 0$,
- $(I_i + u'_i) \bmod 2 = 1$.

Under these conditions, we have $dep(\langle u'_0, u'_1, \ldots, u'_{k-1} \rangle) = dep(\langle u_0, u_1, \ldots, u_{k-1} \rangle) + 1$. Thus, along any path in G, the dependency levels are strictly increasing, and no two nodes with the same dependency level can lie on the same path. As a result, all zoids in S with the same dependency level form an antichain and can be processed simultaneously. Thus, all zoids in S can be processed in $k+1$ parallel steps with step $s \in \{0, 1, \ldots, k\}$ processing all zoids having dependency level s. $\square$

Pochoir's cache-oblivious parallel algorithm

Given a well-defined zoid $\mathcal{Z}$, the algorithm TRAP from Figure 2 works by recursively decomposing $\mathcal{Z}$ into smaller well-defined zoids as follows.

Hyperspace cut. Lines 4–10 in Figure 2 apply a hyperspace cut involving all dimensions on which a parallel space cut can be applied, as shown in Figures 7(a) and 7(b). If the number k of dimensions of $\mathcal{Z}$ on which a space cut can be applied is at least 1, as tested for in line 11 of Figure 2, then dependency levels are computed for all resulting subzoids in line 12, and then lines 13–15 recursively process them in order according to dependency level as described in the proof of Lemma 1.

Time cut. If a hyperspace cut is not applicable and $\mathcal{Z}$ has height greater than 1, as tested for in line 16, then lines 17–19 cut $\mathcal{Z}$ in the middle of its time dimension and recursively process the lower subzoid followed by the upper subzoid, as shown in Figure 7(c).

Base case. If neither a hyperspace cut nor a time cut can be applied, lines 20–28 processes $\mathcal{Z}$ directly by invoking the stencil-specific kernel function. In practice, the base case is *coarsened* (see Section 4) by choosing a suitable threshold larger than 1 for Δt in line 16, which cuts down on overhead due to the recursion.

Analysis

We can analyze the parallelism using a work/span analysis [7, Ch. 27]. The *work* T_1 of a computation is its serial running time, and the *span* T_∞ is the longest path of dependencies, or equivalently, the running time on an infinite number of processors assuming no overheads for scheduling. The *parallelism* of a computation is the ratio T_1/T_∞ of work to span.

The next lemma provides a tight bound on the span of TRAP algorithm on a minimal zoid.

LEMMA 2. *Consider a minimal $(d+1)$-zoid $\mathcal{Z}$ with height h and normalized widths $\widehat{w}_i = h$ for $i \in \{0, 1, \ldots, d-1\}$. Then the span of TRAP when processing $\mathcal{Z}$ is $\Theta(dh^{\lg(d+2)})$.*

PROOF. For simplicity we assume that a call to the kernel function costs $O(1)$, as in [17]. As TRAP processes $\mathcal{Z}$, some of the subzoids generated recursively have normalized widths equal to their heights and some have twice that amount. Let us denote by $T_\infty(h, k, d-k)$ the span of TRAP processing a $(d+1)$-zoid with height h where $k \geq 0$ of the d spatial dimensions have normalized width $2h$ and $d-k$ spatial dimensions have normalized width h. Using Lemma 1, the span of TRAP processing a zoid $\mathcal{Z}$ when it undergoes a hyperspace cut can be described by the recurrence

$$T_\infty(h, k, d-k) = (k+1)T_\infty(h, 0, d) + \Theta\left(\sum_{i=0}^{k} \lg(3^k)\right)$$

$$= (k+1)T_\infty(h, 0, d) + \Theta(k^2) ,$$

where $T(1,0,d) = \Theta(1)$ is the base case. The summation in this derivation represents the span due to spawning. A parallel **for** with r iterations adds $\Theta(\lg r)$ to the span, and since the number of zoids at all levels is 3^k, this value upper-bounds the number of iterations at any given level. Moreover, the lower bound on the number of zoids on a given level is at least the average $3^k/(k+1)$, whose logarithm is asymptotically the same as $\lg(3^k)$, and hence the bound is asymptotically tight.

A time cut can be applied when the zoid $\mathcal{Z}$ is minimal. Assume that $k \geq 0$ projection trapezoids $\mathcal{Z}_i$'s are upright and the rest are inverted. Then for each upright projection trapezoid $\mathcal{Z}_i$, the normalized width of the lower zoid generated by the hyperspace cut is $\widehat{w}_i = h$, the same as for $\mathcal{Z}$, and for each inverted projection trapezoid $\mathcal{Z}_i$, the lower zoid has normalized width $\widehat{w}_i - h/2 = h/2$. Similarly, for each upright projection trapezoid $\mathcal{Z}_i$, the normalized width of the upper zoid is $\widehat{w}_i - h/2 = h/2$, and for each inverted projection trapezoid $\mathcal{Z}_i$, the upper zoid has normalized width $\widehat{w}_i$. Thus, the recurrence for the span of TRAP when a minimal $\mathcal{Z}$ undergoes a time cut can be written as follows:

$$T_\infty(h,0,d) = T_\infty(h/2,k,d-k) + T_\infty(h/2,d-k,k) + \Theta(1) .$$

Applying hyperspace cuts to the subzoids on the right-hand side of this recurrence yields

$$
\begin{aligned}
T_\infty(h,0,d) &= (d+2)T_\infty(h/2,0,d) + \Theta(k^2) + \Theta((d-k)^2) \\
&= (d+2)T_\infty(h/2,0,d) + \Theta(d^2) \\
&= \Theta(d^2(d+2)^{\lg h - 1}) + \Theta((d+2)^{\lg h}) \\
&= \Theta(dh^{\lg(d+2)}) . \quad \square
\end{aligned}
$$

THEOREM 3. *Consider a $(d+1)$-dimensional grid $\mathcal{Z}$ with $\widehat{w}_i = w$ for $i \in \{0,1,\ldots,d-1\}$ and height $h = 2^r w$. Then the parallelism of* TRAP *when processing $\mathcal{Z}$ using a stencil with constant slopes is $\Theta(w^{d-\lg(d+2)+1}/d^2)$.*

PROOF. Assume without loss of generality that the stencil is periodic. (As will be discussed in Section 4, Pochoir implements TRAP so that the control structure for nonperiodic stencils is the same as that for periodic.) The algorithm first applies a series of r time cuts, dividing the original time dimension into $h/w = 2^r$ subgrids with $\widehat{w}_i = w$ with height w. These grids are processed serially. The next action of TRAP applies a hyperspace cut to all d spatial dimensions of $\mathcal{Z}$, dividing the grid into $d+1$ minimal zoids which are then processed serially. Applying Lemma 2 yields a span of

$$
\begin{aligned}
T_\infty &= (h/w)(d+1) \cdot \Theta(dw^{\lg(d+2)}) \\
&= \Theta((d^2 h)w^{\lg(d+2)-1}) .
\end{aligned}
$$

The work is the volume of $\mathcal{Z}$, which is $T_1 = \Theta(hw^d)$, since the stencil has constant slopes. Thus, the parallelism is

$$T_1/T_\infty = \Theta(w^{d-\lg(d+2)+1}/d^2) . \quad \square$$

We can compare TRAP with a version of Frigo and Strumpen's parallel stencil algorithm [17] we call STRAP, which performs the space cuts serially as in Figures 7(a) and 7(b). Each space cut results in one synchronization point, and hence a sequence of k space cuts applied by STRAP introduces 2^k parallel steps compared to the $k+1$ parallel steps generated by TRAP (see Lemma 1). Thus, each space cut virtually doubles STRAP's span. Figure 8(a) shows a simple example where STRAP produces $2^2 - 1 = 3$ synchronization points while TRAP introduces only 2. The next lemma and theorem analyze STRAP, mimicking Lemma 2 and Theorem 3. Their proofs are omitted.

LEMMA 4. *Consider a minimal $(d+1)$-zoid $\mathcal{Z}$ with height h and normalized widths $\widehat{w}_i = h$ for $i \in \{0,1,\ldots,d-1\}$. Then the span of* STRAP *when processing $\mathcal{Z}$ is $\Theta(h^{\lg(2^d+1)})$.* $\square$

THEOREM 5. *Consider a $(d+1)$-dimensional grid $\mathcal{Z}$ with $\widehat{w}_i = w$ for $i \in \{0,1,\ldots,d-1\}$ and height $h = 2^r w$. Then the parallelism of* STRAP *when processing $\mathcal{Z}$ using a stencil with constant slopes is $\Theta(w^{d-\lg(2^d+1)+1}/2^d)$.* $\square$

Discussion

As can be seen from Theorems 3 and 5, both TRAP and STRAP have the same asymptotic parallelism $\Theta(w^{2-\lg 3})$ for $d = 1$, but for $d = 2$, TRAP has $\Theta(w^2)$ while STRAP has $\Theta(w^{3-\lg 5})$, and the difference grows with the number of dimensions.

The cache complexities of TRAP and STRAP are the same, which follows from the observation that both algorithms apply exactly the same time cuts in exactly the same order, and immediately before each time cut, both are in exactly the same state in terms of the spatial cuts applied. Thus, they arrive at exactly the same configuration — number, shape, and size — of subzoids before each time cut.

Frigo and Strumpen's parallel stencil algorithm is actually slightly different from STRAP. For any fixed integer $r > 1$, a space cut in their algorithm produces r black zoids and between $r - 1$ and $r + 1$ gray zoids. STRAP is a special case of that algorithm with $r = 2$ for upright projection trapezoids and $r = 1$ for inverted projection trapezoids. For larger values of r, Frigo and Strumpen's algorithm achieves more parallelism but the cache efficiency drops. It is straightforward to extend TRAP to perform r multiple cuts along each dimension to match the cache complexity of Frigo and Strumpen's algorithm while providing asymptotically more parallelism.

Empirical results

Figure 9 shows the results of using the Cilkview scalability analyzer [20] to compare the parallelism of TRAP and STRAP on two typical benchmarks. We measured the two algorithms with uncoarsened base cases. As can be seen from the figure, TRAP's asymptotic advantage in parallelism is borne out in practice for these benchmarks.

We used the Linux perf tool [29] to verify that TRAP does not suffer any loss in cache efficiency compared to the STRAP algorithm. Figure 10 also plots the cache-miss ratio of the straightforward parallel loop algorithm, showing that it exhibits poorer cache performance than the two cache-oblivious algorithms.

4. COMPILER OPTIMIZATIONS

The Pochoir compiler transforms code written in the Pochoir specification language into optimized C++ code that employs the Intel Cilk multithreading extensions [23]. The Pochoir compiler is written in Haskell [37], and it performs numerous optimizations, the most important of which are code cloning, loop-index calculations, unifying periodic and nonperiodic boundary conditions, and coarsening the base case of recursion. This section describes how the Pochoir compiler implements these optimizations.

Before a programmer compiles a stencil code with the Pochoir compiler, he or she is expected to perform Phase 1 of Pochoir's two-phase methodology which requires that it be compiled using the Pochoir template library and debugged. This C++ template library is employed by both Phases 1 and 2 and includes both loop-based and trapezoidal algorithms. Differences between stencils, such as dimensionality or data structure, are incorporated into these generic algorithms at compile-time via C++ template metaprogramming.

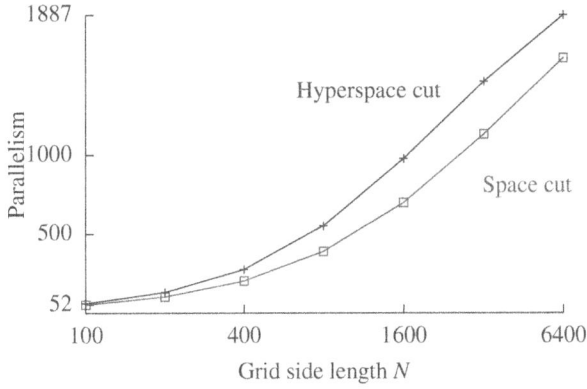

(a)

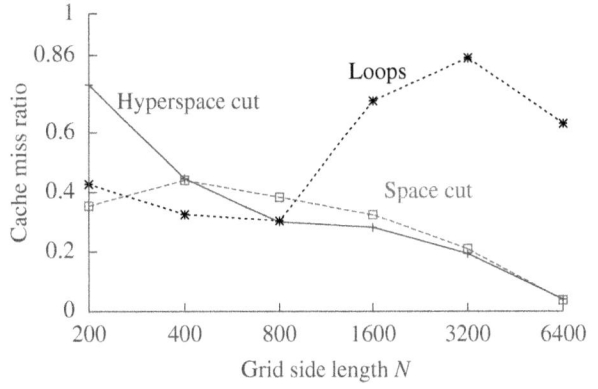

(b)

Figure 9: Parallelism comparison on two benchmarks between TRAP, which employs hyperspace cuts, and STRAP, which uses serial space cuts. Measurements are of code without base-case coarsening. (a) 2D nonperiodic heat equation. Space-time size is $1000N^2$. (b) 3D nonperiodic wave equation. Space-time size is $1000N^3$.

Handling boundary conditions by code cloning

The handling of boundary conditions can easily dominate the runtime of a stencil computation. For example, we coded the 2D heat equation on a periodic torus using Pochoir, and we compared it to a comparable code that simply employs a modulo operation on every array index. For a 5000^2 spatial grid over 5000 time steps, the runtime of the modular-indexing implementation degraded by a factor of 2.3.

For nonperiodic stencil computations, where a value must be provided on the boundary, performance can degrade even more if a test is made at every point to determine whether the index falls off the grid. Stencil implementers often handle constant nonperiodic boundary conditions with the simple trick of introducing *ghost cells* [8] that form a *halo* around the periphery of the grid. Ghost cells are read but never written. The stencil computation can apply the kernel function to the grid points on the real grid, and accesses that "fall off" the edge into the halo obtain their values from the ghost cells without any need to check boundary conditions.

In practice, however, nonperiodic boundary conditions can be more complicated than simple constants, and we wanted to allow Pochoir users flexibility in the kinds of boundary conditions they could specify. For example, Dirichlet boundary conditions may specify boundary values that change with time, and Neumann boundary conditions may specify the value the derivative should

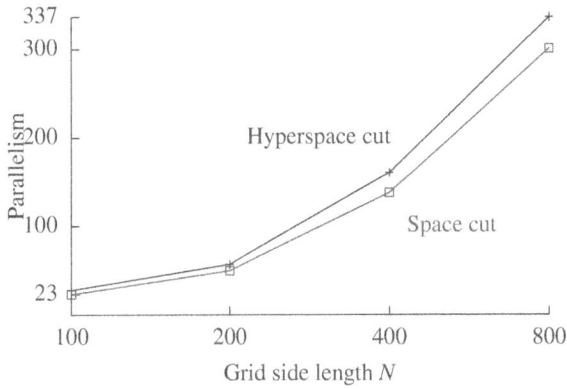

(a)

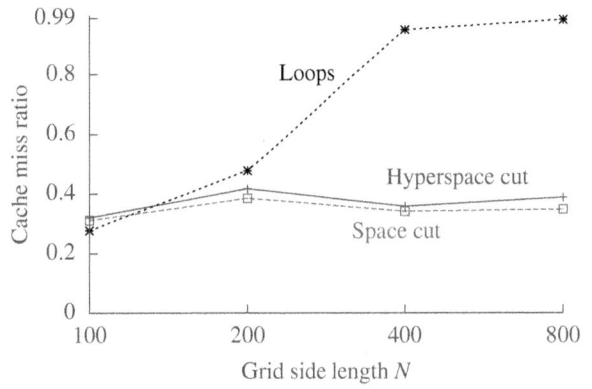

(b)

Figure 10: Cache-miss ratios for two benchmarks using TRAP, STRAP, and a parallel-loop algorithm. The cache-miss ratio is the ratio of the cache misses to the number of memory references. Measurements are of code without base-case coarsening. (a) 2D nonperiodic heat equation. Space-time is $1000N^2$. (b) 3D nonperiodic wave equation. Space-time is $1000N^3$.

```
1   Pochoir_Boundary_2D(dirichlet, arr, t, x, y)
2       return 100 + 0.2*t;
3   Pochoir_Boundary_End
                        (a)

1   Pochoir_Boundary_2D(neumann, arr, t, x, y)
2       int newx = x;
3       if (x < 0) newx = 0;
4       if (x >= arr.size(1)) newx = arr.size(1);
5       int newy = y;
6       if (y < 0) newy = 0;
7       if (y >= arr.size(0)) newy = arr.size(0);
8       return arr.get(t, newx, newy);
9   Pochoir_Boundary_End
                        (b)
```

Figure 11: Pochoir code for specifying nonperiodic boundary conditions. (a) A Dirichlet condition with constrained boundary value (set equal to a function of t). (b) A Neumann condition with constrained derivative at the boundary (set equal to 0).

take on the boundary [14]. Figure 11(a) shows a Pochoir specification of a Dirichlet boundary condition, and Figure 11(b) shows the Pochoir specification of a Neumann boundary condition.

To handle boundaries efficiently, the Pochoir compiler generates two code clones of the kernel function: a slower *boundary* clone and a faster *interior* clone. The boundary clone is used for *boundary* zoids: those that contain at least one point whose computation requires an off-grid access. The interior clone is used for *interior* zoids: those all of whose points can be updated without indexing

```
1   Pochoir_Kernel_1D(heat_1D_fn, t, i)
2       a(t+1, i) = 0.125 * (a(t, i-1) + 2 * a(t, i) +
                  a(t, i+1));
3   Pochoir_Kernel_End
```

(a)

```
1   /* a.interior() is a function to dereference the
          value without checking boundary conditions */
2   #define a(t, i) a.interior(t, i)
3   Pochoir_Kernel_1D(heat_1D_fn, t, i)
4       a(t + 1, i) = 0.125 * (a(t, i - 1) + 2 * a(t, i
                  ) + a(t, i + 1));
5   Pochoir_Kernel_End
6   #undef a(t, i)
```

(b)

```
1    Pochoir_Kernel_1D(heat_1D_fn, t, i)
2    /* The base address of the Pochoir array 'a' */
3    double *a_base = a.data();
4    /* Pointers to be used in the innermost loop */
5    double *iter0, *iter1, *iter2, *iter3;
6    /* Total size of the Pochoir array 'a' */
7    const int l_a_total_size = a.total_size();
8    int gap_a_0;
9    const int l_stride_a_0 = a.stride(0);
10   for (int t = ta; t < tb; ++t) {
11       double * baseIter_1;
12       double * baseIter_0;
13       baseIter_0 = a_base + ((t + 1) & 0xb) *
                  l_a_total_size + (l_grid.xa[0]) *
                  l_stride_a_0;
14       baseIter_1 = a_base + ((t) & 0xb) *
                  l_a_total_size + (l_grid.xa[0]) *
                  l_stride_a_0;
15       iter0 = baseIter_0 + (0) * l_stride_a_0;
16       iter1 = baseIter_1 + (-1) * l_stride_a_0;
17       iter2 = baseIter_1 + (0) * l_stride_a_0;
18       iter3 = baseIter_1 + (1) * l_stride_a_0;
19       for (int i = l_grid.xa[0]; i < l_grid.xb[0];
                  ++i, ++iter0, ++iter1, ++iter2, ++iter3) {
20          (*iter0) = 0.125 * ((*iter1) + 2 * (*iter2) +
                  (*iter3));   }
21   }
22   Pochoir_Kernel_End
```

(c)

Figure 12: Pochoir's loop-indexing optimizations illustrated on a 1D heat equation. (a) The original Pochoir code for the kernel function. (b) The code as transformed by -split-macro-shadow. (c) The code as transformed by -split-pointer.

off the edge of the grid. Whether a zoid is interior or boundary is determined at runtime.

In the base case of the recursive trapezoidal decomposition, the boundary clone invokes the user-supplied boundary function to perform the relatively expensive checks on the coordinates of each point in the zoid to see whether they fall outside the boundary. If so, the user-supplied boundary function determines what value to use. The base case of the interior clone avoids this calculation, since it knows that no such test is necessary, and it simply accesses the necessary grid points.

The trapezoidal-decomposition algorithm exploits the fact that all subzoids of an interior zoid remain interior. If all the dimensions of the grid are approximately the same size, the boundary of the grid is much smaller than its (hyper)volume. Consequently, the faster interior clones dominate the running time, and the slower boundary clones contribute little.

Loop indexing

Because the interior zoids asymptotically dominate the computing time, most of the optimizations performed by Pochoir compiler focus on the interior clone. Two important optimizations relate to loop indexing. The particular optimization is chosen automatically by the Pochoir compiler, or it can be mandated by user as a command-line option. Consistent with their command-line names, the optimizations are called -split-macro-shadow and -split-pointer.

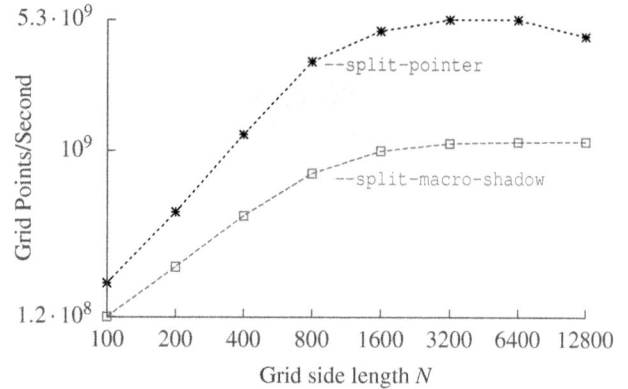

Figure 13: The performance of different loop-index optimizations on a 2D heat equation on torus. The grid is N^2 with 1000 time steps.

The -split-macro-shadow option causes the Pochoir compiler to employ macro tricks on the interior clone to eliminate the boundary-checking overhead. Consider the code snippet in Figure 12(a) which defines the kernel function for a 1D heat equation. Figure 12(b) shows the postsource code generated by the Pochoir compiler using -split-macro-shadow. Line 2 defines a macro that replaces the original accessing function a, which also does boundary checking, with one that performs the address calculation but without boundary checking.

The -split-pointer command-line option causes the Pochoir compiler to transform the indexing of Pochoir arrays in the interior clone into C-style pointer manipulation, as illustrated in Figure 12(c). A C-style pointer represents each term in the stencil formula. The resulting array indexing appears on line 20. For each consecutive iteration, the code increments each pointer. When iterating outer loops, the code adds a precomputed constant to each pointer as shown in lines 15–18.

The Pochoir compiler tries to use the -split-pointer optimization if possible. It can do so if it can parse and "understand" the C++ syntax of the user's specification. Because our prototype Haskell compiler does not contain a complete C++ front end, however, it sometimes may not understand unusually complex C++ code written by the user, in which case, it employs the -split-macro-shadow optimization, relying on Phase 1 to ensure that the code is Pochoir-compliant.

Figure 13 compares the performances of the two optimizing options for a 2D heat equation on a torus. Other benchmarks show similar relative performances.

Unifying periodic and nonperiodic boundary conditions

Typical stencil codes discriminate between periodic and nonperiodic stencils, implementing them in different ways. To make the specification of boundary functions as flexible as possible, we investigated how periodic and nonperiodic stencils could be implemented using the same algorithmic framework, leaving the choice of boundary function up to the user. Our unified algorithm allows the user to program boundary functions with arbitrary periodic/nonperiodic behavior, providing support, for example, for a 2D cylindrical domain, where one dimension is periodic and the other is nonperiodic.

The key idea is to treat the entire computation as if it were periodic in all dimensions and handle nonperiodicity and other boundary conditions in the base case of the boundary clone where the kernel function is invoked. When a zoid wraps around the grid in a given dimension i, meaning that $xa_i > xb_i$, we represent the lower-

and upper-bound coordinates of the zoid in dimension i by ***virtual*** coordinates $(xa_i, N_i + xb_i)$, where N_i is the size of the periodic grid in dimension i. In the base of the recursion of the boundary clone, Pochoir calls the kernel function and supplies it with the true coordinates of the grid point being updated by performing a modulo computation on each coordinate. Within the kernel function, accesses to the Pochoir arrays now call the boundary function, which provides the correct value for grid points that are outside the true grid. Of course, no such checking is required for interior zoids, which are always represented by true coordinates.

Coarsening of base cases

Previous work [9, 26, 27, 34] has found that although trapezoidal decomposition dramatically reduces cache-miss rates, overall performance can suffer from function-call overhead unless the base case of the recursion is coarsened. For example, proper coarsening of the base case of the 2D heat-equation stencil (running for 5000 time steps on a 5000×5000 toroidal grid) improves the performance by a factor of 36 over running the recursion down to a single grid point.

Since choosing the optimal size of the base case can be difficult, we integrated the ISAT autotuner [22] into Pochoir. Despite the advantage of finding the optimal coarsening factor on any specific platform, this autotuning process can take hours to find the optimal value, which may be unacceptable for some users.

In practice, Pochoir employs some heuristics to choose a reasonable coarsening. One principle is that to maximize data reuse, we want to make the spatial dimensions all about the same size. Another principle is that to exploit hardware prefetching, we want to avoid cutting the unit-stride spatial dimension and avoid odd-shaped base cases. For example, for 2D problems, a square-shaped computing domain often offers the best performance. We have found that for 3D problems, the effect of hardware prefetching can often be more important than cache efficiency for reasonably sized base cases. Consequently, for 3 or more dimensions, Pochoir adopts the strategy of never cutting the unit-stride spatial dimension, and it cuts the rest of the spatial dimensions into small hypercubes to ensure that the entire base case stays in cache. Given all that potential complexity, the compiler's heuristic is actually fairly simple. For 2D problems, Pochoir stops the recursion at 100×100 space chunks with 5 time steps. For 3D problems, the recursion stops at $1000 \times 3 \times 3$ with 3 time steps.

5. RELATED WORK

Attempts to compile stencils into highly optimized code are not new. This section briefly reviews the history of stencil compilers and discusses some of the more recent innovative strategies for optimizing stencil codes.

Special-purpose stencil compilers for distributed-memory machines first came into existence at least two decades ago [3, 4, 39]. The goal of these researchers was generally to reduce interprocessor data transfer and improve the performance of loop-based stencil computations through loop-level optimizations. The compilers expected the stencils to be expressed in some normalized form.

More recently, Krishnamoorthy *et al.* [28] have considered automatic parallelization of loop-based stencil codes through loop tiling, focusing on load-balancing the execution of the tiles. Kamil *et al.* [25] have explored automatic parallelization and tuning of stencil computations for chip multiprocessors. The stencils are specified using a domain-specific language which is a subset of Fortran 95. An abstract syntax tree is built from the stencil specified in the input language, from which multiple formats of output can be generated, including Fortran, C, and CUDA. The parallelization is based on blocked loops.

We have discussed Frigo and Strumpen's seminal trapezoidal-decomposition algorithms [16, 17] at length, since they form the foundation of the Pochoir algorithm. Nitsure [34] has studied how to use Frigo and Strumpen's parallel algorithm to implement 2D and 3D lattice Boltzmann methods. In addition to several other optimizations, Nitsure employs two code clones for the kernel to reduce the overhead of boundary checking, which Pochoir does as well. Nitsure's stencil code is parallelized with OpenMP [35], and data dependencies among subdomains are maintained by locking.

Cache-aware techniques have been used extensively to improve the stencil performance. Datta *et al.* [9] and Kamil *et al.* [26, 27] have applied both algorithmic and coding optimizations to loop-based stencil computations. Their algorithmic optimizations include an explicitly blocked time-skewing algorithm which overlaps subregions to improve parallelism at the cost of redundant memory storage and computation. Their coding optimizations include processor-affinity binding, kernel inlining, an explicit user stack, early cutoff, indirection instead of modulo, and autotuning.

Researchers at the University of Southern California [11, 12, 36] have performed extensive studies on how to improve the performance of high-order stencil computations though parallelization and optimization. Their techniques, which apply variously to multicore and cluster machines, include intranode, internode, and data-parallel optimizations, such as cache blocking, register blocking, manual SIMD-izing, and software prefetching.

6. CONCLUDING REMARKS

It is remarkable how complex a simple computation can be when performance is at stake. Parallelism and caching make stencil computations interesting. As discussed in Section 5, many researchers have investigated how various other features of modern machines — such as prefetching units, graphical processing units, and clustering — can be exploited to provide even more performance. We see many ways to improve Pochoir by taking advantage of these machine capabilities.

In addition, we see ample opportunity to enhance the linguistic features of the Pochoir specification language to provide more generality and flexibility to the user. For example, we are considering how to allow the user to specify irregularly shaped domains. As long as the boundary of a region, however irregular, is small compared to the region's interior, special-case code to handle the boundary should not adversely impact the overall performance. Even more challenging is coping with boundaries that change with time. We believe that such capabilities will dramatically speed up the PSA, RNA, and LCS benchmarks which operate on diamond-shaped space-time domains.

Pochoir's two-phase compilation strategy introduces a new method for building domain-specific languages embedded in C++. Historically, the complexity of parsing and type-checking C++ has impeded such separately compiled domain-specific languages. C++'s template programming does provide a good measure of expressiveness for describing special-purpose computations, but it provides no ability to perform the domain-specific optimizations such as those that Pochoir employs. Pochoir's compilation strategy offers a new way to build optimizing compilers for domain-specific languages embedded in C++ where the compiler can parse and "understand" only as much of the programmer's C++ code as it is able, confident that code it does not understand is nevertheless correct.

The Pochoir compiler can be downloaded from http://supertech.csail.mit.edu/pochoir.

7. ACKNOWLEDGMENTS

Thanks to Matteo Frigo of Axis Semiconductor and Volker Strumpen of the University of Linz, Austria, for providing us with their code for trapezoidal decomposition of the 2D heat equation which served as a model and inspiration for Pochoir. Thanks to Kaushik Datta of Reservoir Labs and Sam Williams of Lawrence Berkeley National Laboratory for providing us with the Berkeley autotuner code and help with running it. Thanks to Geoff Lowney of Intel for his support and critical appraisal of the system and to Robert Geva of Intel for an enormously helpful discussion that led to a great simplification of the Pochoir specification language. Many thanks to the Intel Cilk team for support during the development of Pochoir, and especially Will Leiserson for his responsiveness as the SPAA submission deadline approached. Thanks to Will Hasenplaugh of Intel and to members of the MIT Supertech Research Group for helpful discussions.

8. REFERENCES

[1] T. Akutsu. Dynamic programming algorithms for RNA secondary structure prediction with pseudoknots. *Discrete Applied Mathematics*, 104:45–62, 2000.

[2] R. Bleck, C. Rooth, D. Hu, and L. T. Smith. Salinity-driven thermocline transients in a wind- and thermohaline-forced isopycnic coordinate model of the North Atlantic. *Journal of Physical Oceanography*, 22(12):1486–1505, 1992.

[3] R. G. Brickner, W. George, S. L. Johnsson, and A. Ruttenberg. A stencil compiler for the Connection Machine models CM-2/200. In *Workshop on Compilers for Parallel Computers*, 1993.

[4] M. Bromley, S. Heller, T. McNerney, and G. L. Steele Jr. Fortran at ten Gigaflops: The Connection Machine convolution compiler. In *PLDI*, pages 145–156, Toronto, Ontario, Canada, June 26–28 1991.

[5] C++ Standards Committee. Working draft, standard for programming language C++. available from http://www.open-std.org/jtc1/sc22/wg21/docs/papers/2011/n3242.pdf, 2011. ISO/IEC Document Number N3242=11-0012.

[6] R. A. Chowdhury, H.-S. Le, and V. Ramachandran. Cache-oblivious dynamic programming for bioinformatics. *TCBB*, 7(3):495–510, July-Sept. 2010.

[7] T. H. Cormen, C. E. Leiserson, R. L. Rivest, and C. Stein. *Introduction to Algorithms*. The MIT Press, third edition, 2009.

[8] K. Datta. *Auto-tuning Stencil Codes for Cache-Based Multicore Platforms*. PhD thesis, EECS Department, University of California, Berkeley, Dec 2009.

[9] K. Datta, M. Murphy, V. Volkov, S. Williams, J. Carter, L. Oliker, D. Patterson, J. Shalf, and K. Yelick. Stencil computation optimization and auto-tuning on state-of-the-art multicore architectures. In *SC*, pages 4:1–4:12, Austin, TX, Nov. 15–18 2008.

[10] A. van Deursen, P. Klint, and J. Visser. Domain-specific languages: An annotated bibliography. *SIGPLAN Not.*, 35(6):26–36, June 2000.

[11] H. Dursun, K.-i. Nomura, L. Peng, R. Seymour, W. Wang, R. K. Kalia, A. Nakano, and P. Vashishta. A multilevel parallelization framework for high-order stencil computations. In *Euro-Par*, pages 642–653, Delft, The Netherlands, Aug. 25–28 2009.

[12] H. Dursun, K.-i. Nomura, W. Wang, M. Kunaseth, L. Peng, R. Seymour, R. K. Kalia, A. Nakano, and P. Vashishta. In-core optimization of high-order stencil computations. In *PDPTA*, pages 533–538, Las Vegas, NV, July13–16 2009.

[13] J. F. Epperson. *An Introduction to Numerical Methods and Analysis*. Wiley-Interscience, 2007.

[14] H. Feshbach and P. Morse. *Methods of Theoretical Physics*. Feshbach Publishing, 1981.

[15] M. Frigo, C. E. Leiserson, H. Prokop, and S. Ramachandran. Cache-oblivious algorithms. In *FOCS*, pages 285–297, New York, NY, Oct. 17–19 1999.

[16] M. Frigo and V. Strumpen. Cache oblivious stencil computations. In *ICS*, pages 361–366, Cambridge, MA, June 20–22 2005.

[17] M. Frigo and V. Strumpen. The cache complexity of multithreaded cache oblivious algorithms. *Theory of Computing Systems*, 45(2):203–233, 2009.

[18] M. Gardner. Mathematical Games. *Scientific American*, 223(4):120–123, 1970.

[19] O. Gotoh. An improved algorithm for matching biological sequences. *Journal of Molecular Biology*, 162:705–708, 1982.

[20] Y. He, C. E. Leiserson, and W. M. Leiserson. The Cilkview scalability analyzer. In *SPAA*, pages 145–156, Santorini, Greece, June 13–15 2010.

[21] P. Hudak. Building domain-specific embedded languages. *ACM Computing Surveys*, 28(4), December 1996.

[22] Intel software autotuning tool. http://software.intel.com/en-us/articles/intel-software-autotuning-tool/, 2010.

[23] Intel Corporation. *Intel Cilk Plus Language Specification*, 2010. Document Number: 324396-001US. Available from http://software.intel.com/sites/products/cilk-plus/cilk_plus_language_specification.pdf.

[24] C. John. *Options, Futures, and Other Derivatives*. Prentice Hall, 2006.

[25] S. Kamil, C. Chan, L. Oliker, J. Shalf, and S. Williams. An auto-tuning framework for parallel multicore stencil computations. In *IPDPS*, pages 1–12, 2010.

[26] S. Kamil, K. Datta, S. Williams, L. Oliker, J. Shalf, and K. Yelick. Implicit and explicit optimizations for stencil computations. In *MSPC*, pages 51–60, San Jose, CA, 2006.

[27] S. Kamil, P. Husbands, L. Oliker, J. Shalf, and K. Yelick. Impact of modern memory subsystems on cache optimizations for stencil computations. In *MSP*, pages 36–43, Chicago, IL, June 12 2005.

[28] S. Krishnamoorthy, M. Baskaran, U. Bondhugula, J. Ramanujam, A. Rountev, and P. Sadayappan. Effective automatic parallelization of stencil computations. In *PLDI*, San Diego, CA, June 10–13 2007.

[29] https://perf.wiki.kernel.org/index.php/Main_Page.

[30] R. Mei, W. Shyy, D. Yu, and L. Luo. Lattice Boltzmann method for 3-D flows with curved boundary. *J. of Comput. Phys*, 161(2):680–699, 2000.

[31] M. Mernik, J. Heering, and A. M. Sloane. When and how to develop domain-specific languages. *ACM Computing Surveys*, 37:316–344, December 2005.

[32] P. Micikevicius. 3D finite difference computation on GPUs using CUDA. In *GPPGPU*, pages 79–84, Washington, DC, Mar. 8 2009.

[33] A. Nakano, R. Kalia, and P. Vashishta. Multiresolution molecular dynamics algorithm for realistic materials modeling on parallel computers. *Computer Physics Communications*, 83(2-3):197–214, 1994.

[34] A. Nitsure. Implementation and optimization of a cache oblivious lattice Boltzmann algorithm. Master's thesis, Institut für Informatic, Friedrich-Alexander-Universität Erlangen-Nürnberg, July 2006.

[35] OpenMP application program interface, version 2.5. OpenMP specification, May 2005.

[36] L. Peng, R. Seymour, K.-i. Nomura, R. K. Kalia, A. Nakano, P. Vashishta, A. Loddoch, M. Netzband, W. R. Volz, and C. C. Wong. High-order stencil computations on multicore clusters. In *IPDPS*, pages 1–11, Rome, Italy, May 23–29 2009.

[37] S. Peyton Jones. *Haskell 98 Language and Libraries: The Revised Report*. Cambridge University Press, 1998.

[38] H. Prokop. Cache-oblivious algorithms. Master's thesis, Department of Electrical Engineering and Computer Science, Massachusetts Institute of Technology, June 1999.

[39] G. Roth, J. Mellor-Crummey, K. Kennedy, and R. G. Brickner. Compiling stencils in High Performance Fortran. In *SC*, pages 1–20, San Jose, CA, Nov. 16–20 1997. ACM.

[40] A. Taflove and S. Hagness. *Computational Electrodynamics: The Finite-Difference Time-Domain Method*. Artech House, Norwood, MA, 2000.

[41] S. Williams, J. Carter, L. Oliker, J. Shalf, and K. Yelick. Lattice Boltzmann simulation optimization on leading multicore platforms. In *IPDPS*, pages 1–14, Miami, FL, Apr. 2008.

Brief Announcement: Full Reversal Routing as a Linear Dynamical System *

Bernadette Charron-Bost
Ecole polytechnique
charron@lix.polytechnique.fr

Matthias Függer[†]
TU Wien
fuegger@ecs.tuwien.ac.at

Jennifer L. Welch[‡]
Texas A&M University
welch@cse.tamu.edu

Josef Widder[§]
Texas A&M University
widder@cse.tamu.edu

ABSTRACT

Although substantial analysis has been done on the Full Reversal (FR) routing algorithm since its introduction by Gafni and Bertsekas in 1981, a complete understanding of its functioning—especially its time complexity—has been missing until now. In this paper, we derive the first exact formula for the time complexity of FR: given any (acyclic) graph the formula provides the exact time complexity of any node in terms of some simple properties of the graph. Our major technical insight is to describe executions of FR as a dynamical system, and to observe that this system is linear in the min-plus algebra.

As a consequence of the insight provided by the new formula, we are able to prove that FR is time-efficient when executed on tree networks. This result exposes an unstable aspect of the time complexity of FR that has not previously been reported. Finally, our results for FR are instrumental in providing an exact formula for the time complexity of a generalization of FR, as we show in a companion paper that the generalization can be reduced to FR.

Categories and Subject Descriptors: C.2.4 [Computer-Communication Networks]: Distributed Systems; F.2.m [Analysis of Algorithms and Problem Complexity]: Misc ellaneous; G.2.2 [Discrete Mathematics]: Graph Theory.

General Terms: Algorithms, Theory.

Keywords: routing, link reversal, time complexity, linear dynamical systems, min-plus algebra.

Introduction. Link reversal is a versatile algorithm design paradigm, originally proposed by Gafni and Bertsekas [6] for the problem of routing to a destination node in a wireless network subject to link failures. It has been used in solu-

tions to resource allocation, distributed queuing, and various problems in mobile ad-hoc networks as routing, mutual exclusion, and leader election.

Link reversal is a way to change the orientation of links in a directed graph in order to accomplish some goal. In this paper, we focus on the problem of routing to a destination node; the goal is to ensure that, starting from some initial directed graph, ultimately every node in the graph has a (directed) path to the destination. Nodes that are *sinks* (that is, have no outgoing links) reverse the direction of a subset of their incident links. Different link reversal algorithms correspond to different choices of which incident links to reverse. The original paper [6] focused on two schemes, one called *Full Reversal (FR)*, in which all links incident on a sink are reversed, and the other called *Partial Reversal (PR)*, in which, roughly speaking, sinks only reverse those incident links that have not been reversed since the last time this node was a sink. The mechanism employed in [6] was to assign to each node a unique value called a *height*, to consider the link between two nodes as directed from the node with larger height to the node with smaller, and to reverse the direction of a link by increasing the height of a sink.

Surprisingly, there was no systematic study of the complexity of these algorithms until that of Busch et al. [2, 3]. In these papers, the authors considered the height-based implementations of FR and PR, and analyzed the *work* complexity, which is the total number of reversals done by all the nodes. For FR, an exact formula was derived for the work complexity of any node in any graph, implying that the total work complexity in the worst case is at most quadratic in the number of nodes; a family of graphs was presented to show that this worst-case quadratic bound is tight. Similar results were given for PR with asymptotically tight bounds.

The other natural complexity measure for link reversal algorithms is *time*, which is the number of iterations required until termination in "greedy" executions [1], where, in each iteration, all sinks take steps. Greedy executions are those with the highest possible parallelism. Clearly, global work complexity is the number of iterations in completely sequential executions, and so is at least equal to global time complexity. For both FR and PR, this implies a quadratic upper bound on global time complexity. Concerning time complexity, Busch et al. [2, 3] only obtained limited results: for each of FR and PR, they described a family of graphs on which the algorithm achieves quadratic global time com-

---

*A longer version of this paper is available as *TU Wien, Institut für Technische Informatik, Research Report 7/2011.*

[†]Supported in part by the FATAL project (P21694) of the Austrian Science Fund (FWF)

[‡]Supported in part by NSF grant 0964696

[§]Supported in part by NSF grant 0964696

plexity. However, no more precise results were given, and in particular no insights into the local time complexity of individual nodes in arbitrary graphs were provided.

Time complexity analysis. To address the open problem of the time complexity of FR, we start by observing the interleaving of steps: between two consecutive steps by a node i, each neighbor of i takes exactly one step. Moreover, the initial direction of links determines which of two neighboring nodes, if any, takes its first step. This observation allows us to establish a recurrence relation where the number of steps some node has taken by time $t+1$ is a function of the number of steps its neigbors have taken by time t. This recurrence relation corresponds to a discrete dynamical system that turns out to be *linear* in the min-plus algebra.

The dynamical system can be represented as a matrix which in turn can be interpreted as the adjacency matrix of a graph that is very closely related to the initial directed graph. This insight allows us to characterize exactly the FR time complexity of an arbitrary node in an arbitrary acyclic graph, solely via properties of the initial directed graph.

In more detail, we define a chain potential $r(c)$ to be the number of the links in a chain c that are directed towards the end of the chain. (A *chain* is a sequence of nodes $v_0, v_1, \ldots, v_k$ such that either (v_i, v_{i+1}) or (v_{i+1}, v_i) is a link for all i.) We recall that the work w_i of a node i is the minimum potential of all the chains connecting i to the destination; although this result has been shown previously in [2, 3, 5], we also give a new, more conceptual, proof based on viewing the behavior of LR as a dynamical system. Next we define the notion of a *time-critical chain* of node i as a chain c of maximal length λ among all chains ending at i with $r(c) = w_i - 1$. Denoting by $\mathcal{C}(\to i, G)$ the set of all chains ending at node i, we prove:

THEOREM 1. *The termination time θ_i of any node i in the greedy FR execution from an initial connected acyclic graph G is equal to 0 if $w_i = 0$, and is equal to one plus the length of any time-critical chain of i if $w_i > 0$, i.e.,*
$$\theta_i = \max\{\lambda(c) \colon c \in \mathcal{C}(\to i, G) \wedge r(c) = w_i - 1\} + 1.$$

In sharp contrast to all previous results on the time complexity, this theorem provides an *exact* formula that can be applied to any node in any graph. Previous results [2, 3] were primarily based on immediate relationships between work and time complexity: the time complexity cannot be larger than the work complexity, which provides a trivial (quadratic) upper bound on the time complexity. For the lower bound, Busch *et al.* constructed, for each N, an N-node graph containing a clique of size $N/2$ such that each node in the clique has work complexity $N/2$. As in a clique only one node may take a step in each iteration, the greedy execution on this graph is basically sequential, leading to an asymptotic N^2 matching lower bound for graphs of this form. This time complexity lower bound is consequently heavily based on the work complexity results paired with the sequential execution of cliques.

From Theorem 1, however, we observe that even nodes with small work may have large termination time provided that there are certain chains in the graph. It is this property which constituted the technical difficulty in coming up with a more precise result, and which is the major finding that we were able to develop.

Using our formula, we can prove that in trees of N nodes, the time complexity is at most $2N - 1$. To the best of our understanding, this result cannot be obtained by any previous approach in the literature. Moreover, this result shows an unstable aspect of FR with respect to time complexity: for each N, we can construct an N-node tree, which has linear time complexity, but if one particular link is added to the tree, the result is a (non-tree) graph which has quadratic time complexity. That is, a small change in the input graph may lead to a considerable change in time complexity.

In a companion paper [4], we demonstrate how to reduce the general LR algorithm to FR, thus showing FR is actually the fundamental algorithm. In that paper, we extend Theorem 1 in order to get a simple formula for the time complexity of the LR algorithm introduced in [5] which generalizes both FR and PR.

Conclusion. The idea to model executions of distributed algorithms as dynamical systems and to consider tropical algebra is not new. For instance, Malka and Rajsbaum [7] applied max-plus algebra and recurrence relations to analyze the time behavior of distributed algorithms, including the link-reversal-based algorithm for distributed scheduling by Barbosa and Gafni [1]. Unfortunately, the recurrence relations in [7] are not linear, and they only obtained upper bounds on time behaviors.

Compared to this work, our major contribution is the analysis of of FR using work and min-plus algebra, instead of time and max-plus, which notably produces *linear* recurrences for FR. This linearity allows us to represent the recurrences as a matrix that is very similar to the adjacency matrix of the initial graph, and consequently to obtain exact expressions for work and time complexity of FR as simple properties of the initial graph.

1. REFERENCES

[1] V. C. Barbosa and E. Gafni. Concurrency in heavily loaded neighborhood-constrained systems. *ACM Trans. Program. Lang. Syst.*, 11(4):562–584, 1989.

[2] C. Busch, S. Surapaneni, and S. Tirthapura. Analysis of link reversal routing algorithms for mobile ad hoc networks. In *Proceedings of the 15th ACM Symposium on Parallelism in Algorithms and Architectures (SPAA)*, pages 210–219, 2003.

[3] C. Busch and S. Tirthapura. Analysis of link reversal routing algorithms. *SIAM Journal on Computing*, 35(2):305–326, 2005.

[4] B. Charron-Bost, M. Függer, J. L. Welch, and J. Widder. Partial is Full, 2011. Manuscript.

[5] B. Charron-Bost, A. Gaillard, J. L. Welch, and J. Widder. Routing without ordering. In *Proceedings of the 21st ACM Symposium on Parallelism in Algorithms and Architectures (SPAA)*, pages 145–153, 2009.

[6] E. Gafni and D. P. Bertsekas. Distributed algorithms for generating loop-free routes in networks with frequently changing topology. *IEEE Transactions on Communications*, 29(1):11–18, January 1981.

[7] Y. Malka and S. Rajsbaum. Analysis of distributed algorithms based on recurrence relations (preliminary version). In *5th International Workshop on Distributed Algorithms (WDAG)*, pages 242–253, 1991.

Brief Announcement: Better Speedups for Parallel Max-Flow

George C. Caragea
Dept. of Computer Science
University of Maryland, College Park
george@cs.umd.edu

Uzi Vishkin
Institute for Advanced Computer Studies
University of Maryland, College Park
vishkin@umiacs.umd.edu

ABSTRACT

We present a parallel solution to the Maximum-Flow (Max-Flow) problem, suitable for a modern many-core architecture. We show that by starting from a PRAM algorithm, following an established "programmer's workflow" and targeting XMT, a PRAM-inspired many-core architecture, we achieve significantly higher speed-ups than previous approaches. Comparison with the fastest known serial max-flow implementation on a modern CPU demonstrates for the first time potential for orders-of-magnitude performance improvement for Max-Flow. Using XMT, the PRAM Max-Flow algorithm is also much easier to program than for other parallel platforms, contributing a powerful example toward dual validation of both PRAM algorithmics and XMT.

Categories and Subject Descriptors: C.1.4 Parallel Architectures C.4 Performance of Systems

General Terms: Algorithms, Performance

1. INTRODUCTION

The maximum flow (Max-Flow) problem is a fundamental graph theory problem, with applications in numerous domains. Given a graph G with arc capacities, a source s, and a sink t, the problem is to find a flow of maximum value from s to t. A flow is a function on arcs that satisfies *capacity constraints* for all arcs and *conservation constraints* for all vertices except the source and the sink (see e.g. [8]).

In the serial realm, efficient algorithms and implementations exist (e.g. [2]). In the parallel area, several PRAM algorithms have been proposed [12, 7]. However, even though implementations of the parallel algorithms abound (e.g. [1, 3, 9]), the speedups are quite low considering the parallel machines used (e.g. less than 2.5x speedup for a GPU [9]). This suggests that the Max-Flow algorithm is "difficult to parallelize" on existing parallel platforms.

In this paper we evaluate an efficient, scalable implementation of a PRAM Max-Flow algorithm for explicit multi-threading (XMT), a many-core architecture designed from the ground up to support PRAM-like programming. Using XMT, the algorithm is both easier to program and achieves higher speedups than prior work when compared to the best serial implementation. This supports the argument that the previous low speedups are not caused by inefficient algorithms or implementations, but by the mismatch between the algorithm and the underlying platform. It also strengthens the case for XMT as an efficient, general-purpose, easy-to-program many-core.

2. MAX-FLOW ALGORITHMS

Numerous **serial Max-Flow algorithms** have been developed over the years which proposed improving complexity bounds. Some early Max-Flow algorithms worked by finding augmenting paths, using the layered network approach of Dinic. Using Karzanov's concept of preflow, Shiloach and Vishkin [12] contributed an alternative method that also introduced parallelism to Max-Flow. Goldberg and Tarjan replaced the layered network approach by introducing the concept of distance labels into the Shiloach-Vishkin (SV) algorithm. Distance labels were easier to manipulate than layered networks and led to asymptotic improvements [8]. In practice however, the Goldberg-Tarjan algorithm had poor performance. Apparently distance labels were more helpful for improving asymptotic results than implementation runtime. Indeed, Goldberg's PhD thesis noted the advantage of *global relabels* (in effect, layered networks) making the implementation closer to the original SV algorithm. The fastest serial implementation that we are aware of (Goldberg, [6]), includes other heuristics and optimizations, such as *gap relabeling* and *highest-level node selection* [5].

There have been fewer improvements when it comes to **parallel algorithms** for Max-Flow. Shiloach and Vishkin [12] proposed a first $O(n^2 \log n)$ time and $O(nm)$ space parallel algorithm for directed graphs. Goldberg and Tarjan [7] introduced an algorithm for acyclic graphs that runs in $O(n \log n)$ time and $O(nm)$ space. Vishkin [14] extended [12] to acyclic graphs and showed that an improved $O(n^2)$ space bound applies to both [12, 14]. By incorporating distance labels into the SV algorithm, Goldberg and Tarjan reduced the space requirement down to $O(m)$ [8]. The resulting algorithm, called Push-Relabel, is the one used as basis for most subsequent implementations.

As was the case for the sequential version, implementations of the basic parallel Push-Relabel algorithm were observed to be slow in practice. All existing parallel implementations are enhanced with global relabeling, which is effectively a periodical breadth-first search (BFS) on the residual graph. Anderson and Setubal [1] evaluated an implementation for a 14-processor SMP, and observed performance improvements of *up to two orders of magnitude due only to global relabeling*. Bader and Sachdeva [3] designed a cache-friendly version of the parallel algorithm for a multiprocessor, adding a parallel gap-relabel heuristic implementation. Both [1, 3] use locks to handle concurrent updates.

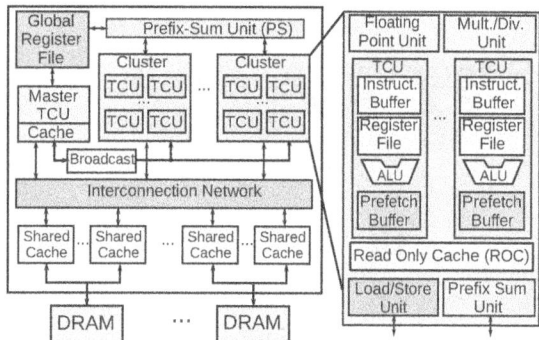

Figure 1: Block diagram of the XMT architecture

Name	Nodes/Edges	Type
AD-1K	1K/500K	acyclic-dense
Random-10K	10K/30K	uniform random
Random-64K	64K/200K	uniform random
RLG-Long	64K/195K	long layered
RLG-Wide	64K/196K	wide layered
RMF-Long	8K/45K	long, parallel grids
RMF-Wide	8K/46K	wide, parallel grids
Rome-99	3.3K/9K	road network

Table 1: Input datasets used.

Several GPU MaxFlow implementations have also been proposed. [10, 13] present restriced MaxFlow solutions applicable only for grids. He and Hong [9] evaluate a lock-free, hybrid CPU-GPU implementation designed for general graphs, reporting speedups of up to 2.5x over the fastest sequential code. With GPU-like peak computing capacity and bandwidth, better speedups seem possible.

The XMT Max-Flow Space limitations allow very limited review of our XMT Max-Flow implementation. Its PRAM description of the Push-Relabel Max-Flow algorithm starts with a Work-Depth description (introduced in [12]) per the "XMT programmer's workflow" [15] for advancing from a high level abstraction to a program in XMTC, a modest extension of C. Our implementation is completely lock-free, allowing it to scale to many more cores; both the push and relabel operations are split into two phases, one to compute and one to propagate results. The atomic prefix-sum operation is used to coordinate accumulation of flow from multiple sources. We drastically reduced the amount of work by maintaining a list of all active nodes and using only one thread per active node. A parallel BFS is run periodically on the residual graph to perform global relabeling.

3. XMT – AN EASY TO PROGRAM MANY-CORE PLATFORM

The primary goal of the XMT on-chip general-purpose computer architecture (e.g. [15]) has been improving single-task performance through parallelism, a goal orthogonal and complementary to throughput oriented architectures such as some multi-cores. XMT was designed to capitalize on the huge on-chip resources becoming available in order to support the formidable body of knowledge, known as Parallel Random Access Model (PRAM) algorithmics, and the latent, though not widespread, familiarity with it.

The XMT architecture, depicted in Fig. 1, includes an array of lightweight cores or Thread Control Units (TCUs) and a serial core with its own cache (Master TCU). The architecture includes several clusters of TCUs connected by a high-bandwidth low-latency interconnection network. The underlying programming model of the XMT framework is arbitrary CRCW (concurrent read/write) reduced-synchrony PRAM-like model [15], with serial and parallel execution modes. Each thread progresses at its own speed without ever having to busy-wait for other threads, a methodology called "independence of order semantics (IOS)." XMT also incorporates hardware implementation of a powerful atomic prefix-sum primitive that provides constant, low overhead inter-thread coordination. The high-bandwidth interconnection network, the low-overhead creation of many threads

and the low-cost synchronization primitives facilitate efficient support for fine-grained, irregular parallelism.

We have prototyped the XMT architecture using FPGA technology. *Paraleap*, a 64-core configuration running at 75MHz, has been in use since 2007 at UMD. It showed the feasibility of a PRAM-On-Chip architecture, and served to run initial performance comparisons with existing CPUs [16]. In addition to Paraleap, we used XMTSim, the XMT cycle-accurate software simulator. Cycle-accuracy of XMT-Sim is achieved by modeling timing after after both the FPGA and synthesized Verilog code, and it can be customized to realistically simulate larger configurations, beyond the limitations of the prototype. The XMT compiler and simulator are publicly available [11].

4. EXPERIMENTAL RESULTS

We evaluated the speedups of our parallel Max-Flow implementation by comparing to the running time of the fastest known serial code **hi_pr** [6] that incorporated an insight from [5]. To collect the serial running time, we ran **hi_pr** on two platforms: (i) a modern 64-bit x86 CPU: a quadcore AMD Phenom 9600B at 2.3GHz, and (ii) the Master TCU of the Paraleap 64-core XMT prototype. Each input was ran 100 times, and the average cycle count was read and recorded. On the x86 platform, the *rdtsc* instruction was used to get accurate timing information.

The parallel implementation ran on two different embodiments of the XMT architecture: (i) the 64-core Paraleap prototype, built using FPGA technology, whose cycle count has been shown to reflect a much faster ASIC; e.g. 800MHz per [16] and (ii) a forward-looking 1024-core configuration simulated using XMTSim. Previous work [4] has shown that this configuration, if built using same technology as today's GPUs, would use approximately the same area as an NVIDIA GTX280 chip, and could run at similar clock speed.

The input datasets we used are listed in Table 1. We used input graphs that represent a broad variety: the acyclic-dense (AD), Random-Level Graph (RLG) and RMF were proposed in the DIMACS challenge (e.g. [2]), and have been widely used to evaluate Max-Flow; in the Random graphs, edges are added between pairs of nodes uniformly at random, resulting in a graph with relatively small diameter; and Rome-99 is a city road network.

Fig. 2 shows our performance results. The figure shows the running times of the implementations, measured in cycles, and normalized to the running time of the x86 serial time (hi_pr.x86). The hi_pr.MTCU shows the running time of the same serial implementation on the Paraleap Master TCU, the serial processor included in the XMT architecture. Since the XMT MTCU is not as optimized as an industry-grade CPU, slow-down was observed compared to the x86 version. We see no reason why, given the same amount of engineering

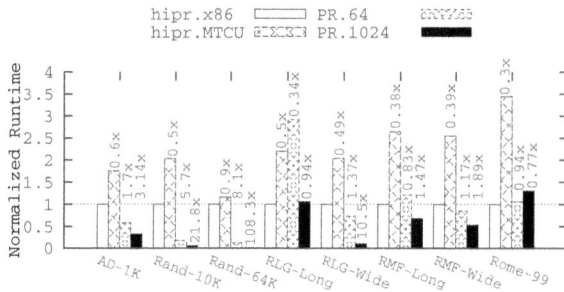

Figure 2: Performance of XMT Parallel Max-Flow. Numbers on bars represent speed-up relative to hipr.x86

effort, the performance of the MTCU would not match a same-generation CPU.

The PR.64 and PR.1024 results show the run time of our parallel implementation on the 64-TCU FPGA XMT, and on the 1024-TCU XMTSim simulator respectively. We observe large performance improvements for the AD and Random graphs, especially the larger Rand-64K. In these graphs, the degree of parallelism is high, keeping the hardware occupancy high, resulting in good performance: speedups range from 3.14x to 108.3x relative to the hi_pr.x86 running time, or 5.53x to 125.73x when compared to hi_pr.MTCU. The RLG-Wide has a large degree of parallelism as well, resulting in good speedups. There is less parallelism in RLG-Long, causing performance to be lower. The 1024-configuration is still significantly faster than the 64-TCU one, since some parts of the algorithm (e.g. the BFS pass) can take take advantage of the more TCUs. The level of parallelism in the Rome99 graph is lower, causing a small slowdown. Note that the speedups reported in [9] were in the [0.59 . . . 1.65] range for a CUDA-only implementation and [1.0 . . . 2.5] for a hybrid CPU-GPU solution; these exhibit the same large variability between input graph types that we observed, albeit with lower overall performance.

The speedups reported above are already much higher than the ones reported for GPUs [9]. Moreover, there is potential for even higher speedups, if we assume that the XMT architecture undergoes industry-grade optimizations: if the running time of the hi_pr.MTCU is brought down to match hi_pr.x86, it is reasonable to infer that the execution time of the parallel code will also be reduced, although by a smaller factor. In this case, it is likely that speedups will be accomplished on all inputs, since the upgraded MTCU will ensure that there will never be a slow-down.

5. CONCLUSION

We reviewed an XMT many-core implementation of the Max-Flow algorithm and its evaluation. Although other implementations could not achieve speedups in excess of 2.5x versus a best serial algorithm (**hi_pr**) on current many-cores, we demonstrated a potential for much better performance on XMT. This example provides powerful new evidence that XMT is better suited to handle general-purpose, irregular applications. It provides performance and increased programmer's productivity by directly relying on a simple and well-established algorithmic model coupled with a programmer's workflow.

Voiding PRAM criticism and addressing asymptotic analysis criticism. Criticism of the PRAM model has

sometime been confused with criticism of constant factors suppressed by asymptotic analysis. In our opinion the XMT platform and the performance it facilitated have voided much of the criticism on the PRAM model. However, one has to be a bit more careful with understanding the issue of constant factors. In the same way that theoretical papers on serial algorithms and their asymptotic analysis were often followed by separate efforts minimizing constant factors, the current work complements the original theory PRAM papers by reducing them to practice with respect to XMT, accounting for constant factors and concrete speedups. This often amounts to first modifying a published PRAM algorithm to another PRAM algorithm, or using alternative data structures with better constant factors, and only then program it for the XMT platform. The former is where the intellectual merit of this work lies. The good news is that the latter turns out to be a rather simple task.

6. REFERENCES

[1] R. J. Anderson and J. Setubal. On the parallel implementation of goldberg's maximum flow algorithm. In *Proc. 4th ACM SPAA*, 168–177, 1992.

[2] R. J. Anderson and J. Setubal. Goldberg's algorithm for maximum flow in perspective: a computational study. *In D. Johnson and C. McGeoch, eds., Network Flows and Matching: First DIMACS Implementation Challenge*, 1993.

[3] D. Bader and V. Sachdeva. A cache-aware parallel implementation of the push-relabel network flow algorithm and experimental evaluation of the gap relabeling heuristic. In *Proc. of the 18th ISCA International Conference on Parallel and Distributed Computing Systems*, 2005.

[4] G. C. Caragea, F. Keceli, A. Tzannes, and U. Vishkin. General-purpose vs. gpu: Comparison of many-cores on irregular workloads. In *HotPar '10: Proceedings of the 2nd Workshop on Hot Topics in Parallelism*. USENIX,2010.

[5] J. Cheriyan and K. Mehlhorn. An analysis of the highest-level selection rule in the preflow-push max-flow algorithm. *Information Processing Letters*, 69:69–239, 1998.

[6] A. Goldberg. Network optimization library. http://www.avglab.com/andrew/soft.html, 2006.

[7] A. Goldberg and R. Tarjan. A parallel algorithm for finding a blocking flow in an acyclic network. *Information Processing Letters*, 31:265–271, 1989.

[8] A. V. Goldberg and R. E. Tarjan. A new approach to the maximum-flow problem. *J. ACM*, 35(4):921–940, 1988.

[9] Z. He and B. Hong. Dynamically tuned push-relabel algorithm for the maximum flow problem on cpu-gpu-hybrid platforms. In *The 24th IEEE International Parallel and Distributed Processing Symposium*, 2010.

[10] M. Hussein, A. Varshney, and L. Davis. On implementing graph cuts on cuda. In *First Workshop on General Purpose Processing on Graphics Processing Units (GPGPU)*, 2007.

[11] F. Keceli, A. Tzannes, G. C. Caragea, R. Barua, and U. Vishkin. Toolchain for programming, simulating and studying the xmt many-core architecture. In *Proc. International Workshop on High-Level Parallel Programming Models and Supportive Environments*, 2011.

[12] Y. Shiloach and U. Vishkin. An $O(n^2 \log n)$ parallel max-flow algorithm. *J. Algorithms*, 3(2):128–146, 1982.

[13] V. Vineet and P. Narayanan. Cuda cuts: Fast graph cuts on the gpu. In *Computer Vision and Pattern Recognition Workshops (CVPR)*, 2008.

[14] U. Vishkin. A parallel blocking flow algorithm for acyclic networks. *J. Algorithms*, 13(3):489–501, 1992.

[15] U. Vishkin. Using simple abstraction to reinvent computing for parallelism. *Comm. ACM*, 54:75–85, Jan. 2011.

[16] X. Wen and U. Vishkin. Fpga-based prototype of a pram-on-chip processor. In *CF '08: Proc. of the Conference on Computing frontiers*, 2008. ACM.

Brief Announcement: Reclaiming the Energy of a Schedule, Models and Algorithms [*]

Guillaume Aupy, Anne Benoit, Fanny Dufossé and Yves Robert

LIP, École Normale Supérieure de Lyon, France

{Guillaume.Aupy|Anne.Benoit|Fanny.Dufosse|Yves.Robert}@ens-lyon.fr

ABSTRACT

We consider a task graph to be executed on a set of processors. We assume that the mapping is given, say by an ordered list of tasks to execute on each processor, and we aim at optimizing the energy consumption while enforcing a prescribed bound on the execution time. While it is not possible to change the allocation of a task, it is possible to change its speed. We study the complexity of the problem for different models: continuous speeds, discrete modes, distributed either arbitrarily or regularly, and VDD-hopping.

Categories and Subject Descriptors

F.2.2 [**Analysis of algorithms and problem complexity**]: Nonnumerical Algorithms and Problems—*Sequencing and scheduling*

General Terms

Performance, Theory, Algorithms.

Keywords

Energy models, complexity, bi-criteria optimization, algorithms, scheduling.

1. INTRODUCTION

The *energy consumption* of computational platforms has recently become a critical problem, both for economic and environmental reasons. Their power consumption is the sum of a static part (the cost for a processor to be turned on) and a dynamic part, which is a strictly convex function of the processor speed. More precisely, a processor running at speed s dissipates s^3 watts [4, 5] per time-unit, hence consumes $s^3 \times t$ joules when operated during t units of time.

Energy-aware scheduling aims at minimizing the energy consumed during the execution of the target application. Obviously, it makes sense only if it is coupled with some performance bound to achieve, otherwise, the optimal solution always is to run each processor at the slowest possible speed. In this paper, we investigate energy-aware scheduling strategies for executing a task graph on a set of processors.

[*]The authors are with Université de Lyon, France. A. Benoit and Y. Robert are with the Institut Universitaire de France. This work was supported in part by the ANR *StochaGrid* and *RESCUE* projects.

The main originality is that we assume that the mapping of the task graph is given, say by an ordered list of tasks to execute on each processor. There are many situations in which this problem is important, such as optimizing for legacy applications, or accounting for affinities between tasks and resources, or even when tasks are pre-allocated, for example for security reasons.

Optimization problem. Consider an application task graph $\mathcal{G} = (V, \mathcal{E})$, with $n = |V|$ tasks, $V = \{T_1, T_2, \ldots, T_n\}$: $\mathcal{E}$ denotes the precedence edges between tasks. Task T_i has a cost w_i for $1 \leq i \leq n$. We assume that the tasks in $\mathcal{G}$ have been allocated onto a parallel platform made up of identical processors. The *execution graph* generated by this allocation is $G = (V, E)$, with an augmented set of edges E: $\mathcal{E} \subseteq E$, and if T_1 and T_2 are executed successively, in this order, on the same processor, then $(T_1, T_2) \in E$. The goal is to minimize the energy consumed during the execution while enforcing a deadline D on the execution time. We formalize this MinEnergy(G,D) optimization problem in the simpler case where each task is executed at constant speed (valid for all models but the VDD-hopping one). Let d_i be the duration of the execution of task T_i, t_i its completion time, and s_i the speed at which it is executed.

$$
\begin{aligned}
\text{Minimize} \quad & \textstyle\sum_{i=1}^n s_i^3 \times d_i \\
\text{subject to (i)} \quad & w_i = s_i \times d_i \text{ for each } T_i \in V \\
\text{(ii)} \quad & t_i + d_j \leq t_j \text{ for each } (T_i, T_j) \in E \\
\text{(iii)} \quad & t_i \leq D \text{ for each } T_i \in V
\end{aligned}
\tag{1}
$$

We have $d_i = w_i/s_i$, hence a geometric problem in the non-negative variables t_i and $1/s_i$, with linear constraints and objective function rewritten as $\sum_{i=1}^n (1/s_i)^{-2} \times w_i$.

Energy models. In all models, when a processor operates at speed s during d time-units, the corresponding consumed energy is $s^3 \times d$, which is the dynamic part of the energy consumption [4, 5]. We do not take static energy into account, because all processors are up and alive during the whole execution. We now detail the possible speed values in each energy model, which should be added as a constraint in Equation (1).

CONTINUOUS: processors can have arbitrary speeds, from 0 to a maximum value s_{max}, and a processor can change its speed at any time during execution. This model is unrealistic but theoretically appealing [2].

DISCRETE: processors have a set of possible speed values, or modes, denoted as $s_1, \ldots, s_m$. There is no assumption on the range and distribution of these modes. The speed of a processor cannot change during the computation of a task, but it can change from task to task [7].

VDD-HOPPING: a processor can run at different speeds as in the previous model $(s_1, ..., s_m)$, but it can also change its speed during a computation. Any rational speed can be simulated [6]. The energy consumed during the execution of one task is the sum, on each time interval with constant speed s, of the energy consumed during this interval at speed s.

INCREMENTAL: we introduce a value δ that corresponds to the minimum permissible speed (i.e., voltage) increment. Possible speed values are obtained as $s = s_{min} + i \times \delta$, where i is an integer such that $0 \leq i \leq \frac{s_{max} - s_{min}}{\delta}$. Admissible speeds lie in the interval $[s_{min}, s_{max}]$. The different modes are spread regularly between $s_1 = s_{min}$ and $s_m = s_{max}$, instead of being arbitrarily chosen. This is intended as the modern counterpart of a potentiometer knob!

2. RESULTS

All proofs, algorithms, and related work can be found in the companion research report [1].

2.1 The CONTINUOUS model

THEOREM 1. When G is a fork graph with $n + 1$ tasks $T_0, T_1, \ldots, T_n$, where T_0 is the source, the optimal solution to MINENERGY(G,D) is to execute T_0 at speed

$$s_0 = \frac{\left(\sum_{i=1}^n w_i^3\right)^{\frac{1}{3}} + w_0}{D},$$

and T_i (for $1 \leq i \leq n$) at speed

$$s_i = s_0 \times \frac{w_i}{\left(\sum_{i=1}^n w_i^3\right)^{\frac{1}{3}}}, \qquad if \quad s_0 \leq s_{max}.$$

Otherwise, T_0 should be executed at speed $s_0 = s_{max}$, and the other speeds are $s_i = \frac{w_i}{D'}$, with $D' = D - \frac{w_0}{s_{max}}$, if they do not exceed s_{max}, otherwise there is no solution.

THEOREM 2. MINENERGY(G,D) can be solved in polynomial time when G is a tree, or a series-parallel graph (in the latter case, assuming $s_{max} = +\infty$).

For arbitrary execution graphs, we have a geometric programming problem (see [3, Section 4.5]) for which efficient numerical schemes exist. However, as illustrated on simple fork graphs, the optimal speeds are not expected to be rational numbers but instead arbitrarily complex expressions (we have the cubic root of the sum of cubes for forks, and nested expressions of this form for trees). We do not know how to encode such numbers in polynomial size of the input (the rational task weights and the execution deadline). Still, we can always solve the problem numerically and get fixed-size numbers which are good approximations of the optimal values.

2.2 Discrete models

THEOREM 3. With the VDD-HOPPING model, MINENERGY(G,D) can be solved in polynomial time (via linear programming).

THEOREM 4. With the INCREMENTAL model (and hence the DISCRETE model), MINENERGY(G,D) is NP-complete.

THEOREM 5. With the INCREMENTAL model, for any integer $K > 0$, the MINENERGY(G,D) problem can be approximated within a factor $(1 + \frac{\delta}{s_{min}})^2 \times (1 + \frac{1}{K})^2$, in a time polynomial in the size of the instance and in K.

PROPOSITION 1.
- For any integer $\delta > 0$, any instance of MINENERGY(G,D) with the CONTINUOUS model can be approximated within a factor $(1 + \frac{\delta}{s_{min}})^2$ in the INCREMENTAL model with speed increment δ.
- For any integer $K > 0$, any instance of MINENERGY(G,D) with the DISCRETE model can be approximated within a factor $(1 + \frac{\alpha}{s_1})^2 \times (1 + \frac{1}{K})^2$, with $\alpha = \max_{1 \leq i < m}\{s_{i+1} - s_i\}$, in a time polynomial in the size of the instance and in K.

3. CONCLUSION

We have assessed the tractability of a classical scheduling problem, with task preallocation, under various energy models. We have given several results related to CONTINUOUS speeds. However, while these are of conceptual importance, they cannot be achieved with physical devices, and we have analyzed several models enforcing a bounded number of achievable speeds, a.k.a. modes. In the classical DISCRETE model, admissible speeds can be irregularly distributed, which motivates the VDD-HOPPING approach that mixes two consecutive modes optimally. While computing optimal speeds is NP-hard with discrete modes, it has polynomial complexity when mixing speeds. Intuitively, the VDD-HOPPING approach allows for smoothing out the discrete nature of the modes. An alternate (and simpler in practice) solution to VDD-HOPPING is the INCREMENTAL model, where one sticks with unique speeds during task execution as in the DISCRETE model, but where consecutive modes are regularly spaced. Such a model can be made arbitrarily efficient, according to our approximation results. Altogether, this paper has laid the theoretical foundations for a comparative study of energy models.

4. REFERENCES

[1] G. Aupy, A. Benoit, F. Dufossé, and Y. Robert. Reclaiming the energy of a schedule: models and algorithms. Research report, INRIA, Lyon, France, Apr. 2011. Available at http://graal.ens-lyon.fr/~abenoit.

[2] N. Bansal, T. Kimbrel, and K. Pruhs. Speed scaling to manage energy and temperature. *Journal of the ACM*, 54(1):1 – 39, 2007.

[3] S. Boyd and L. Vandenberghe. *Convex Optimization*. Cambridge University Press, 2004.

[4] A. P. Chandrakasan and A. Sinha. JouleTrack: A Web Based Tool for Software Energy Profiling. In *Design Automation Conference*, pages 220–225, 2001.

[5] T. Ishihara and H. Yasuura. Voltage scheduling problem for dynamically variable voltage processors. In *ISLPED*, pages 197–202. ACM Press, 1998.

[6] S. Miermont, P. Vivet, and M. Renaudin. A Power Supply Selector for Energy- and Area-Efficient Local Dynamic Voltage Scaling. In *Integrated Circuit and System Design*, LNCS 4644, pages 556–565, 2007.

[7] T. Okuma, H. Yasuura, and T. Ishihara. Software energy reduction techniques for variable-voltage processors. *IEEE Design Test of Computers*, 18(2):31–41, 2001.

Brief Announcement: Paging for Multicore Processors

Alejandro López-Ortiz
David R. Cheriton School of Computer Science
University of Waterloo
Waterloo, Ontario, Canada
alopez-o@uwaterloo.ca

Alejandro Salinger
David R. Cheriton School of Computer Science
University of Waterloo
Waterloo, Ontario, Canada
ajsalinger@uwaterloo.ca

ABSTRACT

Paging for multicore processors extends the classical paging problem to a setting in which several processes simultaneously share the cache. Recently, Hassidim [6] studied cache eviction policies for multicores under the traditional competitive analysis metric, showing that LRU is not competitive against an offline policy that has the power of arbitrarily delaying request sequences to its advantage. In this paper we study caching under the more conservative model in which requests must be served as they arrive. We derive bounds on the competitive ratios of natural strategies to manage the cache, and we show that the offline problem is NP-complete, but that it admits an algorithm that runs in polynomial time in the length of the request sequences.

Categories and Subject Descriptors

F.1.2 [**Computation by Abstract Devices**]: Modes of Computation—*Parallelism and concurrency, Online computation*; F.2.m [**Analysis of Algorithms and Problem Complexity**]: Miscellaneous

General Terms

Algorithms, Theory

Keywords

multicore, chip multiprocessor, cache, paging, online algorithms

1. INTRODUCTION

In the last few years, multicore processors have become the dominant processor architecture. While cache eviction policies have been widely studied both in theory and practice for sequential processors, in the case in which various simultaneous processes share a common cache, the performance of even the most common eviction policies is not yet fully understood. In particular, there is almost no theoretical backing for the use of current eviction policies in multicore processors. Recently, a work by Hassidim [6] presented a theoretical study of paging strategies for shared caches in multicores or Chip Multiprocessors (CMPs). In a CMP system with p cores, a shared cache might receive up to p page requests simultaneously. Hassidim proposes a somewhat unconventional model in which the paging strategy can schedule the execution of threads. While in principle there is no reason why this cannot be so, historically the scheduler within the operating system concentrates in fairness and throughput considerations to determine which task should be executed while the paging algorithm focuses on which of the pages currently in cache should be evicted upon a fault.

In this work we assume a more conservative model, in which cache algorithms are not allowed to make any scheduling decisions but must serve all active requests. In this model, a paging strategy serves a set of p request sequences $\mathcal{R} = \{R_1, \ldots, R_p\}$ of total length n with a shared cache of size K. Requests can be served in parallel, thus various pages can be read from cache or fetched from memory simultaneously, and a fault delays the remaining requests of the sequence involved by τ units of time. We define as **FINAL-TOTAL-FAULTS (FTF)** the problem of minimizing the total number of faults, and as **PARTIAL-INDIVIDUAL-FAULTS (PIF)** the problem of deciding, given a request sequence $\mathcal{R}$ and bound vector $\vec{b} \in \mathbb{N}^p$, whether $\mathcal{R}$ can be served such that at time t the number of faults on each sequence R_i is at most b_i.

Without loss of generality we define a cache strategy as a combination of a possible partition policy, and an eviction policy, and compare the performance of natural strategies for FTF within this framework. We then study properties of the offline cache problem, both for FTF and PIF. We show that the latter is NP-complete, and give algorithms for both problems that run in polynomial time in the length of the sequences (and exponential in the number of sequences).

The performance of the cache in the presence of multiple threads has been extensively studied. From a theoretical perspective, researchers have studied schedulers and algorithms with good theoretical cache performance (See e.g. [3, 2, 4] and references therein). More directly concerned with cache replacement policies, *multiapplication caching* is studied in [1] in the competitive analysis framework. In this model sequences are not delayed upon faults, hence the problem is substantially different from ours. The work in [5] proposes an analytical model which predicts the performance of cache replacement policies in an application-by-application basis. Our work is concerned with arbitrary input sequences. Hassidim [6] considers minimizing completion time and shows that the competitive ratio of LRU is $\Omega(\tau)$. He also shows that computing the optimal offline schedule is NP-complete, and presents a PTAS for constant p and τ.

2. ONLINE PAGING BOUNDS

In a shared cache strategy, any cache cell can hold a page corresponding to any processor. In a partition strategy, the cache is partitioned in p parts, with each part destined exclusively to store pages of requests from one processor. We denote by S_A the shared strategy with eviction policy A, and by sP_A^B and dP_A^D the static and dynamic partition strategies with eviction policy A in each part and partition function B and D, respectively. For strategies with dynamic partitions, evictions resulting from reductions in the size of a part are determined by the eviction policy. For example, S_{LRU} evicts the least recently used page in the entire cache and sP_{LRU}^{OPT} performs LRU on each part of the partition, which is determined offline so as to minimize the total number of faults.

The following list shows a comparison of strategies. $Alg(\mathcal{R})$ denotes the number of faults of Alg on $\mathcal{R}$, A denotes any online marking algorithm, $B = \{k_1, ..., k_p\}$ is any online static partition strategy, D is a dynamic partition strategy, and D' is any online dynamic partition strategy that changes the sizes of the parts $o(n)$ times.

1. $\exists \mathcal{R}$ s.t. $sP_A^B(\mathcal{R})/sP_{OPT}^B(\mathcal{R}) = \Omega(\max_j\{k_j\})$

2. $\forall \mathcal{R}$ $sP_A^B(\mathcal{R})/sP_{OPT}^B(\mathcal{R}) \leq \max_j\{k_j\}$

3. $\exists \mathcal{R}$ s.t. $sP_A^B(\mathcal{R})/sP_{LRU}^{OPT}(\mathcal{R}) \geq \frac{n}{K^2 p} = \Omega(n)$

4. $\exists \mathcal{R}$ s.t. $sP_{OPT}^{OPT}(\mathcal{R})/S_{LRU}(\mathcal{R}) = \Omega(n)$

5. $\forall \mathcal{R}$ $S_{LRU}(\mathcal{R})/sP_{OPT}^{OPT}(\mathcal{R}) \leq K$

6. $\exists \mathcal{R}$ s.t. $dP_A^{D'}(\mathcal{R})/S_{LRU}(\mathcal{R}) = \omega(1)$

7. $\exists D$ s.t. $\forall$ (disjoint) $\mathcal{R}, dP_{LRU}^D(\mathcal{R}) = S_{LRU}(\mathcal{R})$

8. $\exists \mathcal{R}$ s.t. $S_A(\mathcal{R})/S_{OPT}(\mathcal{R}) = \Omega(p(\tau + 1))$

For static partition strategies the choice of a good partition is more important than the choice of the eviction policy. If we consider the competitiveness of the eviction policy alone we observe that with equal partitions, both lower bounds (1 above) and upper bounds (2 above) on the competitive ratio of an online eviction policy are close to the size of the cache, as in the sequential setting. In contrast, no online partition strategy is competitive against offline partitions (3).

These bounds also imply that shared strategies are preferable over static partition strategies. While this is perhaps to be expected for non-disjoint sequences, surprisingly this holds even for disjoint sequences (4). Although a static partition can perform better than an online shared strategy, the ratio between their number of faults is bounded, even for offline static partition strategies (5). Hence we focus on dynamic partition strategies, noting that dynamic partitions that do not change the partition frequently enough are also not competitive against shared strategies (6). We should therefore require dynamic partitions to change often. Although a dynamic partition strategy executes an eviction policy in each part separately, if the variation in the partition can be determined globally, then any shared strategy can be simulated by a dynamic partition on disjoint sequences (7).

Finally, unlike classical paging, S_{LRU} (or any online cache eviction policy) can have an unbounded competitive ratio for large τ (8). Although OPT cannot schedule requests, it can choose to delay one sequence while serving the rest of the sequences with enough cache.

3. THE OFFLINE PROBLEM

Even if the set of request sequences is known in advance, the multicore cache problem is hard. This is in contrast to classical paging of a single sequence, for which Furthest-In-The-Future (FITF) is known to be optimal.

THEOREM 1. *PIF is NP-complete.*

Multicore paging differs from classical paging mainly due to the effect of faults on the alignment of future requests. Offline algorithms can benefit from properly aligning the demand periods of sequences. Even without explicit scheduling, a strategy can try to schedule sequences to its convenience by means of faults and their corresponding delays. For this purpose, an algorithm could evict a page voluntarily before it is requested in order to force a fault. We show, however, that forcing faults in this way is not beneficial.

THEOREM 2. *Let Alg be an offline optimal algorithm that is capable of forcing faults. $\exists$ an offline algorithm Alg' that does not force faults s.t. $\forall$ disjoint $\mathcal{R}$, $Alg'(\mathcal{R}) = Alg(\mathcal{R})$.*

Although FITF is not optimal, Hassidim shows that there is an optimal solution for minimizing the makespan that on each fault evicts the page that is furthest in the future for some sequence. The result holds in our model as well, which implies an $O(p^n)$ time optimal algorithm that upon each fault chooses the sequence to evict from by trying all possibilities. However, both FTF and PIF can be solved in polynomial time in n (but exponential in p) via dynamic programming, hence if the number of sequences is constant, both problems admit polynomial time algorithms. For FTF, the idea is that given a request $\mathcal{R}$ we compute, for each possible cache configuration C and indices $\vec{x} = (x_1, \ldots, x_p)$ in $\mathcal{R}$ (including fetching periods), the minimum number of faults required to serve $\mathcal{R}$ up to $\vec{x}$, arriving at a cache configuration C. We compute and store these values in a $(p + 1)$-dimensional table in a bottom up fashion. This algorithm can be extended to decide a PIF instance by keeping track of feasible solutions (faults in each sequences and time) for each cache configuration and position within the sequences. Please refer to the full paper [7] for details and proofs.

THEOREM 3. *Let p, K be constants. FTF and PIF can be solved in $O(n^{K+p}(\tau + 1)^p)$ and $O(n^{K+2p+1}(\tau + 1)^p)$ time, respectively.*

Acknowledgments. We wish to thank Reza Dorrigiv, Robert Fraser, and Patrick Nicholson for insightful discussions.

4. REFERENCES

[1] R. D. Barve, E. F. Grove, and J. S. Vitter. Application-controlled paging for a shared cache. *SIAM J. Comput.*, 29, 2000.

[2] G. E. Blelloch and P. B. Gibbons. Effectively sharing a cache among threads. In *ACM SPAA'04*, 2004.

[3] G. E. Blelloch, P. B. Gibbons, and H. V. Simhadri. Low depth cache-oblivious algorithms. In *ACM SPAA'10*, 2010.

[4] R. A. Chowdhury, F. Silvestri, B. Blakeley, and V. Ramachandran. Oblivious algorithms for multicores and network of processors. In *IPDPS'10*, 2010.

[5] F. Guo and Y. Solihin. An analytical model for cache replacement policy performance. In *ACM SIGMETRICS/Performance'06*, 2006.

[6] A. Hassidim. Cache replacement policies for multicore processors. In *ICS'10*, 2010.

[7] A. López-Ortiz and A. Salinger. Paging for multicore processors. Tech. Report CS-2011-12, U. of Waterloo, 2011.

A Tight Runtime Bound for Synchronous Gathering of Autonomous Robots with Limited Visibility*

Bastian Degener
Heinz Nixdorf Institute &
Department of Computer
Science
University of Paderborn
bastian.degener@upb.de

Barbara Kempkes
Heinz Nixdorf Institute &
Department of Computer
Science
University of Paderborn
barbaras@upb.de

Tobias Langner
Computer Engineering and
Networks Lab (TIK)
ETH Zurich
langnert@tik.ee.ethz.ch

Friedhelm Meyer
auf der Heide
Heinz Nixdorf Institute &
Department of Computer
Science
University of Paderborn
fmadh@upb.de

Peter Pietrzyk
Heinz Nixdorf Institute &
Department of Computer
Science
University of Paderborn
toon@upb.de

Roger Wattenhofer
Computer Engineering and
Networks Lab (TIK)
ETH Zurich
wattenhofer@tik.ee.ethz.ch

ABSTRACT

The problem of gathering n autonomous robots in the Euclidean plane at one (not predefined) point is well-studied under various restrictions on the capabilities of the robots and in several time models. However, only very few runtime bounds are known. We consider the scenario of *local algorithms* in which the robots can only observe their environment within a fixed viewing range and have to base their decision where to move in the next step solely on the relative positions of the robots within their viewing range. Such local algorithms have to guarantee that the (initially connected) unit disk graph defined by the viewing range of the robots stays connected at all times.

In this paper, we focus on the synchronous setting in which all robots are activated concurrently. Ando et al. [2] presented an algorithm where a robot essentially moves to the center of the smallest enclosing circle of the robots in its viewing range and showed that this strategy performs gathering of the robots in finite time. However, no bounds on the number of rounds needed by the algorithm are known. We present a lower bound of $\Omega(n^2)$ for the number of rounds as well as a matching upper bound of $\mathcal{O}(n^2)$ and thereby obtain a tight runtime analysis of the algorithm of $\Theta(n^2)$.

Categories and Subject Descriptors

F.1.2 [**Theory of Computation**]: Modes of Computation; F.2.2 [**Analysis of Algorithms and Problem Complexity**]: Nonnumerical Algorithms and Problems—*geometrical problems and computations*; I.2.9 [**Artificial Intelligence**]: Robotics—*autonomous vehicles*; I.2.11 [**Artificial Intelligence**]: Distributed Artificial Intelligence—*multiagent systems, intelligent agents*

General Terms

Algorithms, Performance, Theory

Keywords

local algorithms, distributed algorithms, robot gathering, mobile robots, multiagent systems

1. INTRODUCTION

In the future, large groups of small and cheap mobile robots can potentially replace few and expensive robots for many tasks. Thus, there is a growing interest in figuring out which kinds of tasks can be solved by such robotic teams. For mobile robots, it is especially interesting whether they can build a given formation and which sensoric and actoric capabilities are needed to do so. Naturally, the goal is to require as few capabilities as possible in order to be able to use robots that are as cheap as possible.

In this paper we study a classic mobile network problem, the robot-gathering problem. As we discuss in more detail in the related work section, robot-gathering has received considerable attention in the past few years, and there exist various model variants. We are particularly interested in the concurrent version of the problem: We are given n robots, modeled as points in the two-dimensional Euclidean plane, and these robots want to gather at a single point. In each synchronous round, every robot observes the plane and the other robots, decides where to move, and moves there, concurrently with all other robots. The next round does not

*Partially supported by the EU within FP7-ICT-2007-1 under contract no. 215270 (FRONTS) and DFG-project "Smart Teams" within the SPP 1183 "Organic Computing"

start before the last movement has finished. If robots have full visibility, the problem is trivial as all robots can compute the unique center of the smallest enclosing circle (SEC) of all robots, and then concurrently move there, finishing in one single round. Hence, we study the distributed version of the problem where each robot has a limited viewing range and can only observe other robots that are within unit distance of its position. This notion implies that the visibility graph of the robots is a unit disk graph (UDG). Clearly, the UDG of the robots must be connected initially, meaning that there is a path from any robot to any other robot just following the visibility neighborhoods. Additionally we assume that robots are anonymous, in the sense that they do not have unique IDs. Again, if robots have unique IDs, the problem becomes much simpler, as the robots just have to agree on meeting at the location of the robot with the minimum ID.

The most important question in the aforementioned model is whether the robots are able to meet at a single point and how long it takes to do so. The answer to the first question is known for 15 years. In their seminal paper, Ando, Suzuki, and Yamashita [2] presented an algorithm that gathers the robots. In each round, every robot simply moves to the center of the SEC of the robots in its viewing range, only constrained by the condition that robots must not lose visibility to their neighboring robots. As Ando et al. proved, this approach works, and the robots eventually meet.

More recently, Chazelle [6] showed that similar processes may have an exponential behavior. It is therefore an interesting task to examine runtime bounds of the original SEC algorithm by Ando et al. In this paper we show that the algorithm gathers all robots at a single point in a number of rounds polynomial in the number of nodes n, in particular $\mathcal{O}(n^2)$. Furthermore, we give a matching lower bound of $\Omega(n^2)$ and altogether present a tight analysis of the SEC algorithm, showing that the algorithm needs $\Theta(n^2)$ rounds to gather all robots.

2. RELATED WORK

The problem of gathering a set of robots has gained a lot of interest during the last 15 years. In early work, all robots had a global view of the positions of the other robots [24, 25]. Several articles have been published for the fully asynchronous and continuous setting, where the robots do not have a common notion of time, and hence may also observe each other while moving. A promising approach seems to let all robots move to the *Weber* point that – unlike the center of gravity or the center of the SEC – is invariant to movements of robots towards it. However, Bajaj [4] showed that the Weber point cannot be computed because it involves calculating roots of high-order polynomials. Cieliebak et al. [8] gave an algorithm that solves the gathering problem if the robots are able to detect whether there is more than one robot at a given point (multiplicity detection). Cohen et al. showed that moving to the center of gravity of the robots leads to convergence, even in highly asynchronous models [9, 10]. Furthermore, Izumi et al. [19] showed exponential lower bounds for the convergence of a certain class of randomized algorithms.

We are mainly interested in the local model with limited visibility, where the robots have to base their decisions only on the positions of the neighboring robots within a given range. This setting is more difficult, because a robot does not know the system as a whole, often not even the total

number of robots. Furthermore, it is essential to always guarantee the connectivity of the neighborhood graph, given that it is connected in the beginning. Otherwise it cannot be ensured that the connectivity will ever be regained. This is especially an issue in a synchronous and discrete round model, which is common in the literature [2, 15, 24] and which we also consider in this paper. As the robots move at the same time (possibly based on different information), it is difficult to keep the connectivity.

The gathering problem in the local setting was already tackled some time ago by Ando et al. [2]. Similar to other local algorithms for the gathering problem, their robots move to the center of the smallest enclosing circle of their neighbors' locations. This target point definition guarantees that connectivity is maintained if no two robots are activated at the same time. But it can be easily seen that connectivity is not necessarily maintained in the synchronous setting. To overcome this problem, the authors restrict the distance that a robot moves towards its target point in a clever way, such that connectivity is guaranteed even under worst-case movement of the other robots performing the same algorithm. Furthermore, Ando et al. showed that their algorithm allows the robots to gather in a finite number of rounds. Beyond this result, no runtime bounds were given. A follow-up article [3] evaluated the quality of their algorithm in a more realistic environment, where sensor data is not perfectly accurate, and suggested that the algorithm is robust against measurement errors of the sensors.

The same algorithm, but in an asynchronous setting, was used by Meyer auf der Heide et al. [22]. Here, the robots only move one at a time, and so no connectivity maintenance is required. It is shown that the robots also gather in this setting, but again, no runtime bounds are given.

Flocchini et al. [17] showed that having a common orientation among the robots is sufficient to solve the gathering problem in finite time in the fully asynchronous model. The work by Degener et al. [13] is closest to our new contribution. It is shown that gathering can be achieved in expected $\mathcal{O}(n^3 \log n)$ rounds if the robots move sequentially: in each step only one robot (chosen uniformly at random) is activated. Moreover, when active, robots do not only move themselves, but they need the additional capability to assign new target points to neighbors, which may then move as well. This is a very powerful assumption, since it enables a robot to move several robots to the same position and let them act like one single robot from then on.

Apart from this result, there are no runtime bounds known for other algorithms for the local gathering problem so far.

Other researchers have analyzed how the algorithms can cope with failure or inaccuracies of sensor readings. Among others, Souissi et al. [23] and Izumi et al. [18] presented algorithms that are able to deal with erroneous readings from a compass. Agmon et al. [1] studied algorithms that tolerate the crash of a single robot, and still are able to achieve gathering of the remaining robots.

The more general problem of constructing geometrical formations with a set of autonomous robots has also attracted a lot of research. Current work shows how these robots can form lines between fixed stations [12, 15, 16, 20, 21] or circles [5, 11].

In this paper, we provide a lower bound of $\Omega(n^2)$ and, as our main result, a matching upper bound of $\mathcal{O}(n^2)$ for the number of rounds required to gather the robots using the local algorithm for the synchronous setting presented by Ando et al. [2]. The robots used here are considerably weaker than those discussed in the work of Degener et al. [13], as they they cannot instruct any robots to move and are not allowed to view any further than their communication range.

Note, that the needed capabilities are quite restrictive compared to related work from robot formation problems. Other capabilities that are considered are for instance compasses [18, 23] and other time models such as the semi-synchronous model, where arbitrary subgroups of robots move synchronously [14].

3. MODEL DEFINITION

Problem description and notation.

Our model is essentially the one defined by Ando et al. [2]. Given a set $\mathcal{R}$ of n robots $r_1, \ldots, r_n$ in the Euclidean plane, the goal is to gather all robots in one point. A robot is represented as a singular point in the plane, which means that robots cannot block each other's views or paths. We use a discrete, synchronous time model: In each round t, $t \in \mathbb{N}_0$, all robots act synchronously at the same time. We call the positions $p_1(t), \ldots, p_n(t)$ of the robots at the beginning of round t the *configuration* at time t. When the round t under consideration is clear from the context, we will sometimes identify a robot r_i with its position $p_i(t)$. We further call the configuration at time 0 the *start configuration*. When we say *time t*, we refer to the beginning of round t. The (Euclidean) distance between two robots r_i and r_j is indicated by $d(p_i(t), p_j(t))$ or also by $d(r_i, r_j)$. Two robots r_i and r_j can see each other, if $d(r_i, r_j) \leq 1$, where we call r_i and r_j *neighbors* and the distance 1 the *viewing range* of the robots. The set of all neighbors of a robot r_i – its *neighborhood* – at time t is denoted as $N_t(r_i)$ or just $N(r_i)$ if the time is clear from the context. The notion of limited visibility induces a unit disk graph, the *visibility graph* $UDG_t = (\mathcal{R}, E_t)$, where $(r_i, r_j) \in E_t$ iff r_i and r_j are mutually visible at time t, i.e. $\text{dist}(r_i(t), r_j(t)) \leq 1$. We will furthermore use the convex hull of a set of robot positions to which we will also refer by the convex hull of these robots.

We measure the quality of the algorithm by counting the number of synchronous rounds until the robots have gathered in one point. During each round, the robots act according to the *Look-Compute-Move* (*LCM*) model: First all robots synchronously observe their environment and determine the positions of their neighbors relative to their own position (Look-operation). During the Compute-operation, they use the observed positions as input for the algorithm described in Section 4. The algorithm outputs the point to which the robots move during the following Move-operation.

The algorithm is based on the smallest enclosing circle (*SEC*) of a point set $\mathcal{P}$ (which are robot positions in our context). Its center is the point that minimizes the maximum distance to any point in $\mathcal{P}$.

Robot model.

Our robots have a limited viewing range, they are oblivious, which means that they do not have a memory, they do not communicate and they do not use a common coordinate system. Moreover, they cannot be distinguished from each other – they are anonymous. On the other hand, we abstract from technical issues. In particular, we assume the robots to be able to measure positions of neighbors relative to their own position accurately, they can compute geometric properties and they can occupy the same position as other robots.

4. THE ALGORITHM

Algorithm 1 Algorithm of robot r_i in round t

1: {*compute target point*}
2: $\mathcal{R}_i(t) := \{$all robots visible from r_i including r_i itself$\}$
3: $\mathcal{C}_i(t) :=$ smallest enclosing circle of $\mathcal{R}_i(t)$
4: $c_i(t) :=$ center of $\mathcal{C}_i(t)$
5: {*keep connectivity*}
6: $\forall r_j \in \mathcal{R}_i(t) : m_j :=$ midpoint between $p_i(t)$ and $p_j(t)$
7: $\forall r_j \in \mathcal{R}_i(t) : \mathcal{D}_j :=$ circle with radius $\frac{1}{2}$ around m_j
8: $\text{seg} :=$ line segment $\overline{p_i(t), c_i(t)}$
9: $\mathcal{A} := \bigcap_{r_j \in \mathcal{R}} \mathcal{D}_j \cap \text{seg}$
10: $x :=$ point in A that minimizes $d(x, c_i(t))$
11: {*Note that $\mathcal{A} \neq \emptyset$, since $p_i(t) \in \mathcal{A}$*}
12: $p_i(t+1) := x$

The algorithm, which was introduced in [2], works as follows. First, r_i computes its *target point* $c_i(t)$, which is the center of the smallest enclosing circle around itself and its neighbors. Because the connectivity of the unit disk graph could break if all robots would move to their target point, a second phase is used to compute a point x on the line segment between $p_i(t)$ and $c_i(t)$ to which r_i finally moves. For each neighbor r_j, r_i computes the midpoint m_j between their positions and the *limit circle* D_j with center m_j and radius $1/2$. As long as both r_i and r_j do not leave this circle, they will be in distance 1 of each other and therefore neighbors at the beginning of the next round. Finally, x is the point on the line segment between $p_i(t)$ and $c_i(t)$ that maximizes the distance that r_i moves under the constraint that r_i does not leave the circle D_j for any neighbor r_j. Since all robots execute this algorithm, this procedure makes sure that two neighboring robots never lose their connection.

LEMMA 4.1 (ANDO ET AL. [2]). *If two robots are neighbors in UDG_t at time t, then they are still neighbors in UDG_{t+1}. In particular, if UDG_0 is connected, then UDG_t is connected for all $t \geq 0$.*

Because of the procedure to keep connectivity, it is possible that a robot does not move far in direction towards its target point. We say that a robot r_j *hinders* another robot r_i from reaching some point p on the line segment between $p_i(t)$ and $c_i(t)$, if r_i would leave D_j when moving to p. If in any round, two robots move to the exact same point, they will stay at a common point for the rest of the execution of the algorithm, because they see the same neighborhood and hence behave exactly the same. We call such robots to have *merged*.

In [2], the authors have already shown that this algorithm gathers the robots in one point within finite time, but so far no runtime bounds were known. We will now first show a lower bound $\Omega(n^2)$, and then our main result, namely the upper runtime bound of $\mathcal{O}(n^2)$ rounds.

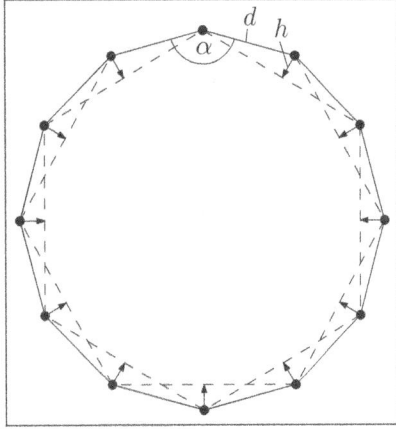

Figure 1: A robot configuration on the vertices of a regular convex polygon yields a worst-case running time of the algorithm.

5. THE LOWER BOUND

For a lower bound on the number of rounds until gathering when using the algorithm described in Section 4, consider a configuration with the robots positioned on the boundary of a circle, such that each robot has only two neighbors and the distance between two neighbors on the circle is the same for all robots. In this configuration, all robots have the same local view and so all robots do the same. The robots will therefore still be positioned on the boundary of a circle in the next round. We will use this observation to prove the following result.

THEOREM 5.1. *There is a start configuration such that the algorithm takes $\Omega(n^2)$ rounds to gather the robots in one point.*

PROOF. Let the robots be positioned on a circle with an initial distance of 1 between two neighboring robots (see Figure 1 for an illustration). This means that the initial circumference of the circle is $\approx n$, and its radius is $\approx \frac{n}{2\pi}$. We will show that it takes $\Omega(n^2)$ rounds until the circumference of the circle is reduced to $\frac{2}{3}n$.

If the circumference of the circle is greater than $\frac{2}{3}n$, each robot r has only two neighbors, which are in equal distance d, $\frac{1}{2} < d \leq 1$, from r. The center of the SEC of r's neighborhood is the midpoint between its neighbors. We can therefore compute the distance that r moves as the height h of the equilateral triangle formed by r and its two neighbors. To compute h, let α be the internal angle of the triangle at robot r. Due to the definition of the cosine, $h = \cos(\frac{\alpha}{2}) \cdot d$. In the interval between 0 and $\frac{\pi}{2}$, the cosine can be upper bounded by $\cos(x) \leq -x + \frac{\pi}{2}$. As $0 < \frac{\alpha}{2} < \frac{\pi}{2}$, we can apply this bound and thus $\cos(\frac{\alpha}{2}) \leq -\frac{\alpha}{2} + \frac{\pi}{2}$, resulting in $h \leq \left(-\frac{\alpha}{2} + \frac{\pi}{2}\right) \cdot d$. Moreover, since the robots form a regular polygon with n vertices and the sum of the internal angles of such a polygon is $\pi n - 2\pi$, we get that $\alpha = \pi - \frac{2\pi}{n}$ for all robots. Thus,

$$
\begin{aligned}
h &\leq \left(-\frac{\alpha}{2} + \frac{\pi}{2}\right) \cdot d \\
&\leq \left(-\left(\frac{\pi}{2} - \frac{\pi}{n}\right) + \frac{\pi}{2}\right) \cdot d \\
&= \frac{\pi}{n} \cdot d \leq \frac{\pi}{n}
\end{aligned}
$$

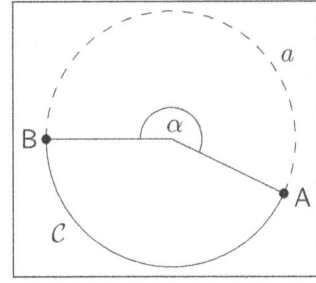

Figure 2: The central angle α of an arc a of the circle $\mathcal{C}$ is the angle subtended at the center of $\mathcal{C}$ by the two points A and B delimiting the arc.

and the robots move at most a distance of $\frac{\pi}{n}$ in each round. Therefore, it takes at least $\frac{1}{3\pi}n^2$ rounds until the radius is decreased by at least $\frac{1}{3}n$. As the circumference is 2π times the radius of a circle, decreasing the radius by $\frac{1}{3}n$ also decreases the circumference by $\frac{1}{3}n$. Thus, it takes at least $\frac{1}{3\pi}n^2$ rounds until the circumference is decreased to $\frac{2}{3}n$. □

6. THE UPPER BOUND

In this section we will show that the robots gather in $\mathcal{O}(n^2)$ rounds. But before we start with the analysis, we state some well-known facts about smallest enclosing circles, on which our analysis will rely heavily.

PROPOSITION 6.1 (CHRYSTAL [7]). *Let $\mathcal{C}$ be the smallest enclosing circle (SEC) of a point set $\mathcal{S}$. Then either*

1. *there are two points $P, Q \in \mathcal{S}$ on the circumference of $\mathcal{C}$ such that the line segment $\overline{PQ}$ is a diameter of $\mathcal{C}$, or*

2. *there are three points $P, Q, R \in \mathcal{S}$ on the circumference of $\mathcal{C}$ such that the center c of $\mathcal{C}$ is inside $\triangle PQR$, which means that $\triangle PQR$ is acute-angled.*

Furthermore, the SEC of a set of points is unique.

From this proposition follows directly that the SEC of a point set P is always within the convex hull of P.

The following definition is illustrated in Figure 2.

DEFINITION 6.2. *Let $\mathcal{C}$ be the SEC of a set of points $\mathcal{S}$. An arc of $\mathcal{C}$ that contains no points is called a point-free arc. The length of this arc is defined as the central angle of the arc.*

Note that the central angle of an arc is greater than π if the arc extends over more than half the circumference of the circle.

PROPOSITION 6.3 (CHRYSTAL [7]). *Let $\mathcal{C}$ be the SEC of a set of $n \geq 2$ points. Then there is no point-free arc with length greater than π.*

With these basics, we can now define how we measure progress. We will use two progress measures.

- As a first progress measure, we will count the number of rounds in which robots merge. As we have n robots in the beginning, there can be at most $n-1$ such rounds.

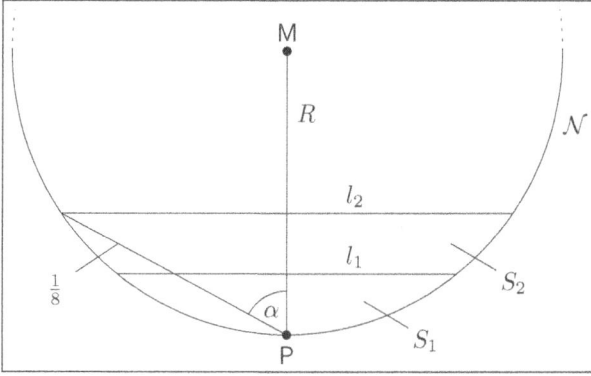

Figure 3: The segments S_1 and $S_1 \cup S_2$ of the global SEC are later used to measure the progress of the algorithm.

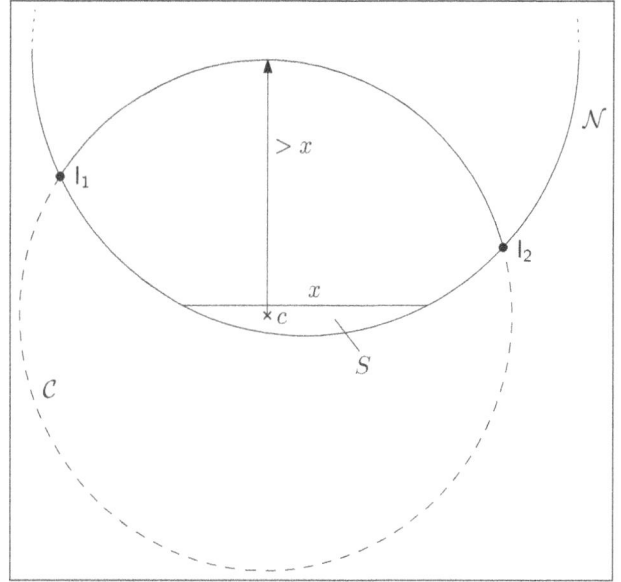

Figure 4: A circle with center in S and a radius exceeding the chord length of S intersects with $\mathcal{N}$ outside of S.

- Since the algorithm is deterministic and it was already proven in Ando et al.'s original paper [2] that the robots gather in finite time, we know that, for a given start configuration, the point where the robots gather is fixed. We will call this point the *gathering point* M. We define a circle $\mathcal{N}_t$ with center M and radius R_t for a round t, such that $\mathcal{N}_t$ contains all robots in round t and its radius is minimal. Due to the definition of the algorithm and because the center of the SEC of a point set is always within the convex hull of the point set, the robots never leave the convex hull of their neighbors as well as the global convex hull. R_t can therefore only decrease. We will use R_t as a second progress measure.

As the robots gather at a point inside the convex hull of the robot positions in any round t, M is inside the convex hull of the robot positions of the start configuration. Moreover, since UDG_0 is connected, the diameter of the convex hull of the robots in round 0 can be at most $n-1$ and therefore also $R_0 \leq n-1$. The idea of the proof is to show that in a constant number of rounds in which no robots merge, R_t decreases by at least $\Omega(\frac{1}{n})$.

Using these two progress measures, with $R_0 \leq n-1$ and at most $n-1$ rounds in which robots merge, it follows directly that the robots gather in $\mathcal{O}(n^2)$ rounds.

From now on, we will consider an arbitrary but fixed round t_0. Let $\mathcal{N} := \mathcal{N}_{t_0}$ and $R := R_{t_0}$. For this round, we introduce some further notions (see Figure 3): first, fix an arbitrary point P on the boundary of $\mathcal{N}$ and draw a line between P and M. A line l_2 that is perpendicular to this line defines a circular segment of $\mathcal{N}$. The intersection points of l_2 and the circle $\mathcal{N}$ are in distance $\frac{1}{8}$ from P. Observe that the length of l_2 is bounded by $\frac{1}{4}$. We call S_1 the circular segment with half the height of the segment defined by l_2, such that a line l_1 that is parallel to l_2 is its chord. Moreover, we define S_2 to be the area of the segment defined by l_2 minus the area of S_1. The main idea of the analysis is to show that in round t_0 and t_0+1, either two robots merge or all robots leave S_1. We will conclude that this leads to the desired number of rounds.

The following analysis is divided into geometric prerequi-

sites regarding S_1 and S_2 (Section 6.1) and the actual analysis of the algorithm (Section 6.2).

6.1 Geometric Prerequisites

In this section we want to give prerequisites regarding S_1 and S_2 and smallest enclosing circles with centers in these segments. These will be used later to make a statement about which robots can compute target points inside one of the segments.

LEMMA 6.4. *Let x be the length of a chord defining a circular segment S of $\mathcal{N}$. Then any circle $\mathcal{C}$ with its center c in S and radius $r > x$ has an arc outside of $\mathcal{N}$ with a central angle larger than π and thus cannot be the SEC of points only from $\mathcal{N}$.*

PROOF. See Figure 4 for an illustration of the setting described by the lemma. Since r is larger than the length of the maximum distance between two points in S, both intersection points l_1 and l_2 of the circle $\mathcal{N}$ with any circle with center in S and radius $r > x$ lie outside of S. Because the center c lies in S, it follows that the (longer) arc of $\mathcal{C}$ from l_1 to l_2 outside of $\mathcal{N}$ has a central angle larger than π (the dashed part of the circumference in Figure 4). $\square$

Since the chord length of $S_1 \cup S_2$ is bounded by $\frac{1}{4}$, the following corollary is immediate.

COROLLARY 6.5. *The radius of a SEC of a point set $\mathcal{S} \subseteq \mathcal{N}$ with its center in $S_1 \cup S_2$ is at most $\frac{1}{4}$.*

In the following, we will show two geometrical lemmas for the position of the center of a SEC, if the configuration of the underlying points adheres to a few restrictions. The first lemma follows from Corollary 6.5 and will be used to show that if a robot can see a robot that is far away from $S_1 \cup S_2$, it cannot compute a target point inside this circular segment.

LEMMA 6.6. *Let $S \subseteq \mathcal{N}$ be a set of points. Now let* A *be a point in $S_1 \cup S_2$ and* B $\in S$ *be a point in distance at least 1 from* A. *Then the center of the SEC of S cannot lie in the segment $S_1 \cup S_2$.*

Note that A does not need to be in S.

PROOF. Assume that the SEC $\mathcal{C}$ has its center c inside $S_1 \cup S_2$. We know from Corollary 6.5 that $\mathcal{C}$ can have at most radius $\frac{1}{4}$. Since the maximum distance of two points in $S_1 \cup S_2$ is bounded by $\frac{1}{4}$, B must have a distance of at least $\frac{3}{4}$ from $S_1 \cup S_2$ in order to be in distance at least 1 from A. Hence, B cannot lie in $\mathcal{C}$. □

The next lemma is similar to the last one in the sense that it makes a statement about configurations, for which robots cannot compute a target point in S_1. In particular, it will be used for robots that can only see one single robot in $S_1 \cup S_2$. These robots cannot compute a target point in S_1.

LEMMA 6.7. *The center of the SEC of a non-empty point set $S \subseteq \mathcal{N} \setminus (S_1 \cup S_2)$ and a point* A $\in S_1 \cup S_2$ *cannot lie in the segment S_1.*

PROOF. Assume that the SEC $\mathcal{C}$ has its center c inside S_1. We distinguish two cases as given by Proposition 1.

1. $\mathcal{C}$ is defined by two points P_1 and P_2. A must be one of these points, say P_2, otherwise c cannot lie in S_1. Since P_1 cannot lie in S_1 or S_2 by assumption and because the height of S_1 is equal to the height of S_2, the midpoint c of $\overline{AP_1}$ cannot lie in S_1.

2. $\mathcal{C}$ is defined by three points P_1, P_1 and P_3. A must be one of these points, say P_3, otherwise c cannot lie in S_1. Since $\mathcal{C}$ is the circumcircle of $\triangle P_1 P_2 A$, it lies on the intersection of the perpendicular bisectors of $\overline{AP_1}$ and $\overline{AP_2}$. The centers of these two segments lie outside S_1 and since the perpendicular bisectors intersect in the interior of $\triangle P_1 P_2 A$ and this triangle is acute, their intersection point also cannot lie in S_1.

This completes the proof. □

Finally, as the main idea of the analysis is to show that if no robots merge, S_1 is empty after two rounds, we will need the height of S_1 to compute the progress with respect to R_t within two rounds.

LEMMA 6.8. *The segment S_1 has a height h of at least $\frac{1}{128\pi \cdot R} \in \Omega\left(\frac{1}{n}\right)$.*

PROOF. We start by computing the angle α (see Figure 3 for a definition of α). The circumference of $\mathcal{N}$ is $2\pi R$. Thus, we can position at most $16\pi R$ points on the boundary of $\mathcal{N}$ that are in distance $\frac{1}{8}$ from the points closest to them and that form a regular convex polygon. The internal angle of each of the points of this polygon is equal to 2α. To compute such an internal angle, we use that the sum of the internal angles of a convex polygon is $(m - 2) \cdot \pi$, where m is the number of vertices of the polygon. In our case, this is at most $(16\pi R - 2) \cdot \pi$. It follows that each angle is at most $\frac{(16\pi R - 2) \cdot \pi}{16\pi R} = \pi - \frac{1}{8R}$, and thus $\alpha \leq \frac{\pi}{2} - \frac{1}{16R}$.

Now we can use α and the fact that $\cos(x) \geq -\frac{2}{\pi} x + 1$ in

the interval $x \in [0, \frac{\pi}{2}]$ to compute the height h of S_1:

$$
\begin{aligned}
h = \frac{\cos \alpha}{16} &\geq \frac{\cos\left(\frac{\pi}{2} - \frac{1}{16R}\right)}{16} \\
&\geq \frac{1}{16} \cdot \left(-\frac{2}{\pi} \cdot \left(\frac{\pi}{2} - \frac{1}{16R}\right) + 1\right) \\
&= \frac{1}{128\pi R}
\end{aligned}
$$

Because $R \leq n$, we have shown $h \in \Omega(\frac{1}{n})$. □

6.2 Gathering Algorithm Analysis

Now we can proceed to the actual analysis of the algorithm. We can use the lemmas from Section 6.1 to determine robots that cannot compute a target point in S_1 or $S_1 \cup S_2$. Nevertheless, according to the algorithm, robots do not always reach their target point; it is also possible that they are hindered by other robots. So knowing that a target point is outside S_1 or $S_1 \cup S_2$ does not necessarily mean that the robot actually leaves the respective segment. The following two lemmas show that robots always reach their target point, if it is in $S_1 \cup S_2$, and that they cannot be hindered from leaving S_1 and S_2.

LEMMA 6.9. *Robots that compute a target point in $S_1 \cup S_2$ cannot be hindered from reaching it by the limit circle of any other robot.*

PROOF. Let r_i be a robot that computes a target point c (which is the center of the SEC $\mathcal{C}$) inside $S_1 \cup S_2$. Then, according to Corollary 6.5, the radius of $\mathcal{C}$ cannot exceed $\frac{1}{4}$ and thus the distance between r_i and c is also upper bounded by $\frac{1}{4}$. Now assume that there is a robot r_e that hinders r_i from reaching c. Since r_e must be a neighbor of r_i, it must also be included in $\mathcal{C}$ and therefore, r_e can have at most distance $\frac{1}{2}$ from r_i. Now let m_e be the midpoint between r_i and r_e and therefore the center of the limit circle that hinders r_i from reaching c. m_e can be at most in distance $\frac{1}{4}$ from r_i. But that means that r_i can move freely in any direction a distance of $\frac{1}{2} - \frac{1}{4} = \frac{1}{4}$ and hence it can reach its target point without being hindered by r_e. □

LEMMA 6.10. *Robots cannot be hindered from leaving $S_1 \cup S_2$ by the limit circle of any other robot.*

PROOF. Let r_i be a robot that computes a target point outside $S_1 \cup S_2$ in round t_0. Now assume for the sake of contradiction that there is one robot r_j that hinders r_i from leaving $S_1 \cup S_2$. This is only possible if r_j is a neighbor of r_i and thus r_j must be within distance 1 of r_i (see the circle C_1 in Figure 5 with center r_i and radius 1: r_j must be in C_1). Now let m be the point where r_i would leave $S_1 \cup S_2$ if moving to its target point. According to the algorithm it is only possible that r_i is hindered by r_j to leave $S_1 \cup S_2$, if m is not within distance $\frac{1}{2}$ from the midpoint m_j between r_i and r_j (line 6 – 10 of the algorithm). It follows that m_j cannot be inside the circle C_2 (Figure 5) with center m and radius $\frac{1}{2}$. Based on C_2 we can define a circle C_3 which may not contain r_j, if m_j is not in C_2: C_3's center is p'_i, which is p_i reflected with respect to the point m, and its radius is 1 (see Figure 5). Summing up, r_j must be inside of C_1, but outside of C_3. Moreover, the smallest enclosing circle computed by the algorithm has at most radius 1, and so r_i's target point is at most in distance 1 of r_j. It follows that r_i's target point must be on the line between m and p'_i, because

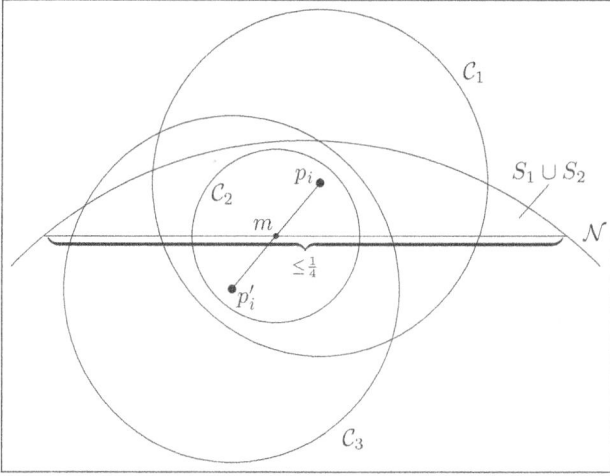

Figure 5: Illustration of the proof of Lemma 6.10. The circles indicate where r_j can be positioned: $\mathcal{C}_1$ is a circle with center p_i and radius 1 and must contain r_j. $\mathcal{C}_2$ has center m and radius $\frac{1}{2}$, and $\mathcal{C}_3$'s center is p_i' with radius 1. r_j must not be in $\mathcal{C}_3$.

each point on the straight line through p_i and m beyond p_i' is in distance more than 1 from any point that is in $\mathcal{C}_1$, but not in $\mathcal{C}_3$.

Case 1: r_j is in $S_1 \cup S_2$. Then, because the chord length of $S_1 \cup S_2$ is at most $\frac{1}{4}$, the distance between r_i and r_j is also at most $\frac{1}{4}$. But that means that r_i is at most in distance $\frac{1}{8}$ from the midpoint between r_i and r_j and thus it can move at least distance $\frac{1}{2} - \frac{1}{8} = \frac{3}{8} > \frac{1}{4}$ freely in any direction without being hindered by r_j. But after r_i has moved a distance of $\frac{1}{4}$, it has left $S_1 \cup S_2$ leading to a contradiction.

Case 2: r_j is not in $S_1 \cup S_2$. Since a SEC is defined by two or three points with at least one point on each half of the boundary of the SEC (Proposition 6.3), there must be a robot r_k that is in $S_1 \cup S_2$ and on the boundary of the SEC defining r_i's target point. It follows that r_k can be at most in distance $\frac{1}{4}$ from m. As p_i is also at most in distance $\frac{1}{4}$ from m, so is p_i' and also p_i's target point, which is between m and p_i' (see above). Thus, r_k is at most in distance $\frac{1}{2}$ from r_i's target point. Since r_k is on the boundary of the SEC that defines r_i's target point, it follows that the SEC can have at most a radius of $\frac{1}{2}$. Now, since r_j is outside of $\mathcal{C}_3$ and because the distance between m and p_i' is at most $\frac{1}{4}$ (see above), r_j must be in distance greater than $\frac{1}{2}$ from r_i's target point. Thus, r_j cannot be in the SEC that defines r_i's target point, which is a contradiction to r_i and r_j being neighbors. It follows that r_j cannot hinder r_i from leaving $S_1 \cup S_2$. $\square$

With all these prerequisites, we can now show that if no robots merge, S_1 is empty after two rounds. We first analyze the behavior of some robots in round t_0 in Lemma 6.11, before we plug things together in Lemma 6.12.

LEMMA 6.11. *Let $\mathcal{S}$ be a set of robots in round t_0 that are all positioned in or compute a target point in $S_1 \cup S_2$ and that all have a pairwise different neighborhood. Then at most one of those robots is in $S_1 \cup S_2$ at the beginning of the next round.*

PROOF. Since all robots from $\mathcal{S}$ have different neighbors,

there exists a robot $r_i \in \mathcal{S}$ for which no robot from $\mathcal{S}$ has a set of neighbors that is a subset of the neighbors of r_i. Thus, all robots $r_j \in \mathcal{S} \setminus \{r_i\}$ have a neighbor that is not visible from r_i and therefore in distance more than 1 from r_i. If r_i is positioned in $S_1 \cup S_2$, all robots $r_j \in \mathcal{S} \setminus \{r_i\}$ see a point B in $\mathcal{N}$ (namely the position of the neighbor that r_i cannot see) that is in distance 1 from a point A in $S_1 \cup S_2$ (namely the position of r_i). Lemma 6.6 therefore guarantees that all neighbors of r_i compute a target point outside of $S_1 \cup S_2$. According to Lemma 6.10, no robot is hindered from leaving $S_1 \cup S_2$. Thus, only r_i can stay in $S_1 \cup S_2$.

If r_i is positioned outside $S_1 \cup S_2$, it has its target point in $S_1 \cup S_2$ according to the definition of $\mathcal{S}$. Corollary 6.5 now gives that the radius of r_i's SEC cannot exceed $\frac{1}{4}$ and thus r_i is in distance at most $\frac{1}{4}$ from $S_1 \cup S_2$. Using that the distance between two points in $S_1 \cup S_2$ is at most $\frac{1}{4}$, it follows that all points within $S_1 \cup S_2$ are in distance at most $\frac{1}{2}$ from r_i. Now consider a robot $r_j \in \mathcal{S} \setminus \{r_i\}$ and a neighbor r_k of r_j that is in distance more than 1 from r_i. This robot r_k must then be in distance more than $\frac{1}{2}$ from $S_1 \cup S_2$. Since r_k is r_j's neighbor, we know from Corollary 6.5, that the center of r_j's SEC – its target point – cannot be in $S_1 \cup S_2$ and according to Lemma 6.10 r_j is not hindered from leaving $S_1 \cup S_2$. Since this holds for all robots $r_j \in \mathcal{S} \setminus \{r_i\}$, r_i is the only robot that can be in $S_1 \cup S_2$ in round $t + 1$. $\square$

LEMMA 6.12. *If $R_t \geq \frac{1}{2}$, either there are robots that merge in round t or after two rounds, the segment S_1 does not contain any robots.*

PROOF. We consider all robots that are positioned in $S_1 \cup S_2$ or compute a target point in $S_1 \cup S_2$ in round t. We divide this set of robots into two subsets and analyze them separately.

- First, we consider all robots that have a neighbor with the same neighborhood. Thus, for all these robots there is another robot that computes the same target point. Then there are two possibilities: Either one of these target points is in $S_1 \cup S_2$. According to Lemma 6.9, the robots with this target point are not hindered from reaching it and therefore they merge. If all target points are outside $S_1 \cup S_2$, Lemma 6.10 guarantees that all these robots leave $S_1 \cup S_2$.

- Now consider the robots that have a pairwise different neighborhood. According to Lemma 6.11, at most one of those robots stays in $S_1 \cup S_2$ during this round.

Thus, if r_i is positioned outside S_1 at the end of round t, we are done. Otherwise, since apart from r_i no robot is still in $S_1 \cup S_2$, we know from Lemma 6.7, that neither r_i nor a neighbor of r_i can compute a target point in S_1 in round $t + 1$. Thus, r_i leaves S_1 in round $t + 1$ (Lemma 6.10) and none of its neighbors enters S_1. All other robots that are not neighbors of r_i do not see a robot in S_1 and thus they cannot enter S_1. $\square$

Lemma 6.12 will be used to show that if no robots merge, R_t decreases by $\Omega\left(\frac{1}{n}\right)$ every two rounds. According to the following Lemma, this procedure stops as soon as $R_t < \frac{1}{2}$.

LEMMA 6.13 (ANDO ET AL. [2]). *If $R_t < \frac{1}{2}$, the robots have gathered at one point in round $t + 1$.*

This lemma holds because if $R_t < \frac{1}{2}$, all robots can see each other and thus all robots compute the same target point. It is shown Ando et al.'s original work [2] that the robots do not hinder each other from reaching this point.

Putting everything together, we are now able to prove the final result.

THEOREM 6.14. *The robots gather within $\mathcal{O}(n^2)$ rounds.*

PROOF. Fix an arbitrary round $t_0 \geq 0$. Since Lemma 6.12 holds for any point on the boundary of N_{t_0}, after two rounds either two robots have merged or all robots must be in distance greater than the height of S_1 from the boundary of N_{t_0}. According to Lemma 6.8, the height of S_1 is at least $\frac{1}{128 \cdot R_t}$ and thus if the robots do not merge, the radius decreases by at least $\frac{1}{128 \cdot R_t}$, giving that $R_{t+2} \leq R_t - \frac{1}{128 \cdot R_t} \leq R_t - \frac{1}{128 \cdot R_0}$. It follows that after $2 \cdot 128 \cdot (R_0)^2 = 256 \cdot (R_0)^2$ rounds without merging robots, the radius must be less than $\frac{1}{2}$. Now it takes one round to gather the robots (Lemma 6.13). Moreover, since UDG_0 is connected, $R_0 \leq n$. There are at most $n - 1$ rounds in which robots merge. The total number of rounds is therefore at most $256 \cdot n^2 + n$. □

7. CONCLUSION AND OUTLOOK

In this paper we have shown that mobile robots can gather at a single point in $\mathcal{O}(n^2)$ rounds, when they execute the classic synchronous algorithm by Ando et al. [2]. Furthermore we showed that this bound is asymptotically tight for the algorithm by providing a matching lower bound. This raises the question whether there are more efficient algorithms.

On the other hand there are no nontrivial lower bounds known for classes of local algorithms for gathering or other formation problems. One would need a clean definition of asynchronous or synchronous local gathering strategies. A crucial property restricting such strategies is that connectivity has to be maintained. Just looking at the start configuration of the lower bound instance from Section 5, for example, and only demanding connectivity for this specific start configuration is not sufficient: consider the synchronous algorithm in which each point moves in the direction of the target point of our algorithm, but goes beyond this point until the distance to its neighbors is 1. This algorithm maintains connectivity for our specific start configuration, but needs only a linear number of rounds, if the start configuration positions neighboring robots in distance $\frac{2}{3}$ on the cycle. Similar results can be shown for asynchronous strategies with specific activation policies. Such examples demonstrate that the connectivity constraint has to be reflected much more severely in lower-bound models for local gathering strategies.

References

[1] Noa Agmon and David Peleg. Fault-tolerant gathering algorithms for autonomous mobile robots. In *Proceedings of the Fifteenth Annual ACM-SIAM Symposium on Discrete Algorithms, SODA 2004*, pages 1070–1078, January 2004.

[2] Hideki Ando, Yoshinobu Suzuki, and Masafumi Yamashita. Formation and agreement problems for synchronous mobile robots with limited visibility. In *Proceedings of the 1995 IEEE International Symposium on Intelligent Control, ISIC 1995*, pages 453–460, August 1995.

[3] Hideki Ando, Yoshinobu Oasa, Ichiro Suzuki, and Masafumi Yamashita. Distributed memoryless point convergence algorithm for mobile robots with limited visibility. *IEEE Transactions on Robotics and Automation*, 15(5):818–828, 1999.

[4] Chanderjit Bajaj. The algebraic degree of geometric optimization problems. *Discrete & Computational Geometry*, 3:177–191, 1988.

[5] I. Chatzigiannakis, M. Markou, and S. Nikoletseas. Distributed circle formation for anonymous oblivious robots. In *Proceedings of the Third International Workshop on Experimental and Efficient Algorithms, WEA 2004*, pages 159–174, May 2004.

[6] Bernard Chazelle. Natural algorithms. In *Proceedings of the Twentieth Annual ACM-SIAM Symposium on Discrete Algorithms, SODA 2009*, pages 422–431, January 2009.

[7] George Chrystal. On the problem to construct the minimum circle enclosing n given points in a plane. In *Proceedings of the Edinburgh Mathematical Society, Third Meeting*, pages 30–35, 1885.

[8] M. Cieliebak, P. Flocchini, G. Prencipe, and N. Santoro. Solving the robots gathering problem. In *Proceedings of the Thirtieth International Colloquium on Automata, Languages and Programming, ICALP 2003*, pages 1181–1196, June 2003.

[9] Reuven Cohen and David Peleg. Robot convergence via center-of-gravity algorithms. In *Proceedings of the 11th International Colloquium on Structural Information and Communication Complexity, SIROCCO 2004*, pages 79–88, June 2004.

[10] Reuven Cohen and David Peleg. Convergence properties of the gravitational algorithm in asynchronous robot systems. *SIAM Journal on Computing*, 34(6): 1516–1528, 2005.

[11] X. Défago and A. Konagaya. Circle formation for oblivious anonymous mobile robots with no common sense of orientation. In *Proceedings of the 2nd ACM International Workshop on Principles of Mobile Computing, POMC 2002*, pages 97–104, October 2002.

[12] Bastian Degener, Barbara Kempkes, Peter Kling, and Friedhelm Meyer auf der Heide. A continuous, local strategy for constructing a short chain of mobile robots. In *Proceedings of the 17th International Colloquium on Structural Information and Communication Complexity, SIROCCO 2010*, pages 168–182, June 2010.

[13] Bastian Degener, Barbara Kempkes, and Friedhelm Meyer auf der Heide. A local $O(n^2)$ gathering algorithm. In *Proceedings of the 22nd Annual ACM Symposium on Parallelism in Algorithms and Architectures, SPAA 2010*, pages 217–223, June 2010.

[14] Yoann Dieudonné and Franck Petit. Self-stabilizing deterministic gathering. In *Proceedings of the 5th International Workshop on Algorithmic Aspects of Wireless Sensor Networks, ALGOSENSORS 2009*, pages 230–241, July 2009.

[15] Miroslaw Dynia, Jarosław Kutyłowski, Paweł Lorek, and Friedhelm Meyer auf der Heide. Maintaining communication between an explorer and a base station. In *Proceedings of the 1st IFIP International Conference on Biologically Inspired Collaborative Computing, BICC 2006*, pages 137–146, August 2006.

[16] Miroslaw Dynia, Jarosław Kutyłowski, Friedhelm Meyer auf der Heide, and Jonas Schrieb. Local strategies for maintaining a chain of relay stations between an explorer and a base station. In *Proceedings of the nineteenth annual ACM symposium on Parallel algorithms and architectures, SPAA 2007*, pages 260–269, January 2007.

[17] Paola Flocchini, Giuseppe Prencipe, Nicola Santoro, and Peter Widmayer. Gathering of asynchronous robots with limited visibility. *Theoretical Computer Science*, 337(1–3):147–168, 2005.

[18] Taisuke Izumi, Yoshiaki Katayama, Nobuhiro Inuzuka, and Koichi Wada. Gathering autonomous mobile robots with dynamic compasses: An optimal result. In *Proceedings of the 21st International Symposium on Distributed Computing, DISC 2007*, pages 298–312, September 2007.

[19] Taisuke Izumi, Tomoko Izumi, Sayaka Kamei, and Fukuhito Ooshita. Randomized gathering of mobile robots with local-multiplicity detection. In *Proceedings of the 11th International Symposium on Stabilization, Safety, and Security of Distributed Systems, SSS 2009*, pages 384–398, November 2009.

[20] Peter Kling and Friedhelm Meyer auf der Heide. Convergence of local communication chain strategies via linear transformations. this conference.

[21] Jaroslaw Kutylowski and Friedhelm Meyer auf der Heide. Optimal strategies for maintaining a chain of relays between an explorer and a base camp. *Theoretical Computer Science*, 410(36):3391–3405, 2009.

[22] Friedhelm Meyer auf der Heide and Barbara Schneider. Local strategies for connecting stations by small robotic networks. In *Proceedings of the 2nd IFIP International Conference on Biologically Inspired Collaborative Computing, BICC 2008*, pages 95–104, September 2008.

[23] Samia Souissi, Xavier Défago, and Masafumi Yamashita. Gathering asynchronous mobile robots with inaccurate compasses. In *Proceedings of the 25th Annual ACM Symposium on Principles of Distributed Systems, PODC 2006*, pages 333–349, July 2006.

[24] I. Suzuki and M. Yamashita. Distributed anonymous mobile robots: Formation of geometric patterns. *SIAM Journal on Computing*, 28(4):1347–1363, 1999.

[25] Ichiro Suzuki and Masafumi Yamashita. Formation and agreement problems for anonymous mobile robots. In *Proceedings of the 31st Annual Allerton Conference on Communication, Control, and Computing*, pages 93–102, September 1993.

Stabilizing Consensus With the Power of Two Choices

Benjamin Doerr
Max Planck Institute for
Informatics
Saarbrücken, Germany

Leslie Ann Goldberg[*]
Dept. of Computer Science
University of Liverpool
Liverpool, UK

Lorenz Minder
Computer Science Division
University of California
Berkeley, USA

Thomas Sauerwald[†]
Max Planck Institute for
Informatics
Saarbrücken, Germany

Christian Scheideler[‡]
Dept. of Computer Science
University of Paderborn
Paderborn, Germany

ABSTRACT

In the standard consensus problem there are n processes with possibly different input values and the goal is to eventually reach a point at which all processes commit to exactly one of these values. We are studying a slight variant of the consensus problem called the *stabilizing consensus problem* [2]. In this problem, we do not require that each process commits to a final value at some point, but that eventually they arrive at a common, stable value without necessarily being aware of that. This should work irrespective of the states in which the processes are starting. Our main result is a simple randomized algorithm called *median rule* that, with high probability, just needs $\mathcal{O}(\log m \log \log n + \log n)$ time and work per process to arrive at an almost stable consensus for any set of m legal values as long as an adversary can corrupt the states of at most $\sqrt{n}$ processes at any time. Without adversarial involvement, just $O(\log n)$ time and work is needed for a stable consensus, with high probability. As a by-product, we obtain a simple distributed algorithm for approximating the median of n numbers in time $\mathcal{O}(\log m \log \log n + \log n)$ under adversarial presence.

Categories and Subject Descriptors

F.2 [**Theory of Computation**]: Analysis of Algorithms and Problem Complexity

---

[*]Partially supported by EPSRC grant EP/I011528/1

[†]Email: sauerwal@mpi-inf.mpg.de

[‡]Email: scheideler@upb.de. Partially supported by DFG grant SCHE 1592/1-1.

General Terms

Algorithms, Theory

Keywords

distributed consensus, self-stabilization, randomized algorithms

1. INTRODUCTION

Consensus problems occur in many contexts and have therefore been extensively studied in the past (e.g., [8, 32]). Interesting applications are the consolidation of replicated states or information and the synchronization of processes and devices. In the original consensus problem, every process proposes a value, and the goal is to decide on a single value from all those proposed. If all processes are working in a correct and timely manner, the consensus problem is easy to solve by performing a leader election, for example. However, if there are faulty or adversarial processes, the consensus problem becomes much harder. In fact, Fischer, Lynch and Paterson have shown that in an asynchronous message passing system, where processes have no common clock and run at arbitrarily varying speeds, the problem is impossible to solve if one process may crash at any time [21]. Also in a synchronous message passing system, where all processes run at the same speed, consensus is impossible if at least a third of the processes can experience Byzantine failures [20]. However, these two results only apply to deterministic algorithms and only to the case where processes need to commit to a value and this commitment can only be done once.

We are studying a slight variant of the consensus problem called the *stabilizing consensus problem* [2]. In this problem, we do not require that each process irrevocably commits to a final value but that eventually they arrive at a common, stable value without necessarily being aware of that. This should work irrespective of the states in which the processes are starting. In other words, we are searching for a *self-stabilizing* algorithm for the consensus problem. Coming up with such an algorithm is easy without adversarial involvement, but we allow some adversary to continuously corrupt the state of some processes. Despite these corruptions, we would like most of the processes to arrive quickly at a common value that will be preserved for any polynomial in n

many steps. Interestingly, we will demonstrate that there is a simple randomized algorithm for this problem that essentially needs logarithmic time and work with high probability to arrive at such a stable value.

1.1 Our approach

We will focus on synchronous message-passing systems with adversarial state corruptions. The time proceeds in synchronized *rounds*. In each round, every process can send out one or more requests, receive replies to its requests, and perform some local computation based on these replies.

We assume that we have a fixed set of n processes that faithfully follow the protocol (based on their current state, which might be corrupted), and every process knows all the other processes in the system (i.e., there are no connectivity constraints). As usual in the literature, the *state* of a process contains all of its variables but does not include its contact information about the other processes and the protocol (which are fixed throughout the lifetime of the processes). The *system state* includes all of the processes' local states. In general, a system is called *self-stabilizing* if in the absence of state corruptions (caused by faults or adversarial behavior) it holds that (1) when started in an arbitrary state, the system eventually reaches a legal state (*convergence*) and (2) given that the system is in a legal state, it will stay in a legal state (*closure*). In the *stabilizing consensus problem* we are more strict as we do not just demand that a consensus is reached and from that point on a consensus is maintained but that we have a *stable* consensus. That is, the n processes may initially have arbitrary states with values $v_1, \ldots, v_n$ out of some set S of legal values and the goal is to arrive at a single, stable value among these values. A system state S is called *stable* if in all possible executions starting from S, the values of the processes do not change. If every process has the same value x in a stable system state S, we say that the values *stabilize* to x. A *self-stabilizing consensus protocol* must satisfy the following properties (given that there are no state corruptions):

- **Stabilization**: the protocol eventually reaches a stable state.

- **Validity**: if a process has some value v, then some process must have had v in the previous round.

- **Agreement**: for every reachable stable state, all processes have the same value.

Note that the validity rule prevents the processes from just changing to a default value. Otherwise, the consensus problem would be trivial.

The *runtime* of a self-stabilizing consensus protocol is the number of communication rounds it takes until a stable state is reached. Besides the runtime, we will also consider the *work* of such a protocol, which is the maximum number of messages (i.e., requests and replies) a process has to handle until a stable state is reached. This disqualifies simple strategies like "everybody contacts process 1" as its work would be n while its runtime is 1. For a distributed system to be scalable, both the runtime and the work has to be as low as possible, therefore we are focussing on protocols with low runtime *and* work.

The adversary

We assume that adversarial state corruptions can continuously happen during the self-stabilizing process. Most of the self-stabilizing algorithms proposed in the literature are not guaranteed any more to reach a legal state in this case, so finding algorithms that still converge to a legal state is a non-trivial problem. We assume that there is a *T-bounded adversary* that knows the entire state of the system at the end of each communication round. Based on that information, it may corrupt the state of up to T processes in an arbitrary way before the next round starts.

Of course, under a T-bounded adversary we cannot reach a stable state any more. Therefore, we will only require the system to reach a state S so that for any $\text{poly}(n)$ many time steps following S, all but at most $\mathcal{O}(T)$ processes agree on some stable value v (note that these $\mathcal{O}(T)$ processes can be different from round to round). We will call this an *almost stable state*. The goal is to come up with an efficient protocol so that for values of T that are as large as possible, an almost stable state can be reached with a runtime and work that is as low as possible.

1.2 Our contributions

We are focussing on stabilizing consensus problems based on an arbitrary (finite or countably infinite) set S of *legal* values with a total order. Classical examples are $S = \{0, 1\}$ and $S = \mathbb{N}$. All initial values of the processes must be from S and also the adversary is restricted to choosing only values in S. (If the adversary chooses a value outside of S in some process p, we may assume that p instantly recognizes that and then switches over to some default value in S.)

If no process is ever corrupted, we can restrict S to be the set of initial values as no new values will ever be introduced by a protocol satisfying the validity rule. In this case, the stabilizing consensus problem could easily be solved with the following *minimum rule*: Suppose that the current value of process i is v_i. In each round, every process i contacts some random process j in the system and updates its value to $v_i := \min\{v_i, v_j\}$. It is easy to see that this rule needs just $\mathcal{O}(\log n)$ time and work with high probability (or short, w.h.p.)[1] until all processes have the same value, namely the minimum of the initial values $v_1, \ldots, v_n$. Since they will not deviate from that value any more, we have reached a stable state. However, if some processes can be corrupted, then even for $S = \{0, 1\}$ *no runtime bound* can be given for the minimum rule to reach an (almost) stable state: if all processes start with 1, then the adversary could inject 0 at any time later to cause a change in the consensus. In fact, a 1-bounded adversary would be sufficient for that. Therefore, we are proposing a different rule called the *median rule*:

In each round, every process i picks two processes j and k uniformly and independently at random among all processes (including itself) and requests their values. It then updates v_i to the *median* of v_i, v_j and v_k. Any request sent to process i will be answered with the value that i had *at the beginning* of the current round.

For example, if $v_i = 10$, $v_j = 12$ and $v_k = 130$, then the new value of v_i is 12. When taking the *mean* of a selected group of values instead of the median, the convergence properties towards a single number have already been formally analyzed [16]. However, with the mean rule we are no longer

---

[1] We write w.h.p. to refer to an event that holds with probability at least $1 - n^{-c}$ for any constant $c > 1$.

guaranteed to solve the stabilizing consensus problem as the validity rule may be violated. Moreover, the approach in [16] is quite different from our approach (as it is based on a repeated all-to-all exchange of values and some filtering mechanism before computing means), so its analysis cannot be adapted to the median rule.

The median rule works surprisingly well. We prove the following results that are also summarized in Figure 1.

THEOREM 1.1. *For any initial state it holds that if no process is ever corrupted, then the median rule needs just $\mathcal{O}(\log n)$ time and work to reach a stable consensus w.h.p.*

Hence, the median rule is as effective as the minimum rule in the non-adversarial case. Contrary to the minimum rule, the median rule also works for the adversarial case. Let $m = |S|$ be the number of legal values. Then it holds:

THEOREM 1.2. *For any $\sqrt{n}$-bounded adversary, the median rule needs just $\mathcal{O}(\log m \cdot \log \log n + \log n)$ time and work to reach an almost stable consensus w.h.p.*

Of course, $|S|$ may not be finite. In this case, Theorem 1.2 still holds if we define m as the number of legal values between v_ℓ and v_r, where v_ℓ is the $(n/2 - c\sqrt{n \log n})$-smallest and v_r is the $(n/2 + c\sqrt{n \log n})$-smallest value of the initial values for some sufficiently large constant c. As a byproduct, the median rule computes a good approximation of the median, even under the presence of an adversary.

COROLLARY 1.3. *For any $\sqrt{n}$-bounded adversary, the median rule needs just $\mathcal{O}(\log m \cdot \log \log n + \log n)$ time and work to compute an almost stable value that is between the $(n/2 - c\sqrt{n \log n})$-largest value and the $(n/2 + c\sqrt{n \log n})$-largest value of the initial values w.h.p.*

The bound on T is essentially tight as $T = \Omega(\sqrt{n \log n})$ would not allow the median rule to stabilize any more w.h.p. because the adversary could keep two groups of processes with equal values in perfect balance for at least a polynomially long time. A further improvement of Theorem 1.2 can be obtained in an average-case setting:

THEOREM 1.4. *Let $m \leq n^{1/2-\epsilon}$. If initially each process chooses one out of m legal values uniformly at random, then for any $\sqrt{n}$-bounded adversary, the median rule needs $\Theta(\log n)$ time and work w.h.p., if m is even, and $\mathcal{O}(\log m + \log \log n)$ time and work w.h.p., if m is odd, to reach an almost stable consensus.*

Finally, if the T-bounded adversary is *static* in a sense that there is a *fixed* set of T faulty processes throughout the execution, then we present a simple extension of the median rule to a so-called *careful median rule* that reaches, within the time bound given in Theorem 1.2, a consensus that is stable for poly(n) many rounds for *all non-faulty processes* w.h.p. This is not possible with the original median rule as with $T = \sqrt{n}$ there is a constant probability that some process contacts two corrupted processes and therefore changes its value to a value selected by the adversary.

With these results, the median rule is yet another demonstration of the *power of two choices* as the time needed by the minimum rule (as well as the maximum rule) can be unbounded even for $S = \{0, 1\}$ and 1-bounded adversaries. This power of two choices has also been demonstrated in

many other contexts [26, 15, 9, 13, 14, 18] (mostly in the balls into bins model, which is why we will use that notation later), but we are not aware of any result using it in the context of consensus.

1.3 Model discussion

Theorem 1.2 also holds for other adversarial models. We just consider two of them:

Adversarial processes: Suppose that we have a $\sqrt{n}/4$-bounded adversary that can pick any $\sqrt{n}/4$ processes at the beginning of a round that behave in an arbitrary adversarial manner throughout that round. Since these processes will only be contacted by at most $3\sqrt{n}/4$ other processes w.h.p. when using the median rule, we can emulate the effect of $\sqrt{n}/4$ adversarial processes on the system by $\sqrt{n}$ adversarial state corruptions, which is our original model. So our results extend to adversarial processes.

Sleep scheduling: Suppose that we have a $\sqrt{n}/4$-bounded adversary that can just put any $\sqrt{n}/4$ processes to sleep in a round. Also this model can be simulated by our original $\sqrt{n}$-bounded adversary using the same arguments as for adversarial processes. More interestingly, one can already show for the sleep scheduling model that if the adversary can put $\Omega(\sqrt{n \log n})$ processes to sleep in each round, a consensus cannot be reached any more for polynomially many steps w.h.p. even if $|S| = 2$. (The proof as well as the strategy achieving this is simple: given an imbalance of Δ, put 2Δ processes of the majority value to sleep. This increases the presence of the minority value which reduces the imbalance.) This implies that even a slight asynchrony that is under the control of an *adaptive* adversary can lead to a failure of the median rule. However, we note that the protocol by Angluin et al. [1] would suffer from the same problem, so adaptive asynchrony seems to be hard to handle for simple distributed algorithms.

1.4 Related work

Randomized algorithms are known that can solve the consensus problem with probability approaching one in many different cases ranging from asynchronous message passing models to shared memory models (see, e.g., [34, 12, 19, 10, 17, 11, 30, 25, 4, 5, 27] or [3] for a survey). Most of these algorithms can tolerate a constant fraction of Byzantine fail/stop failures or nodes but at the cost of spending $\Omega(n)$ expected individual work. Also several lower bounds are known. Ben-Or and Bar-Joseph [10] have shown that any consensus protocol that tolerates $\Theta(n)$ adaptive fail-stop faults runs for $\tilde{\Omega}(\sqrt{n})$ rounds. Attiya and Censor [7] proved that $\Omega(n^2)$ is a lower bound on the total work under adaptive adversaries in the shared memory model. The same authors [6] also showed for message passing as well as shared memory systems that for every integer k, the probability that an f-resilient randomized consensus algorithm for n processes does not terminate with agreement within $k(n - f)$ steps is at least $1/c^k$ for some constant c.

Recently, Gilbert and Kowalski [22] presented a randomized consensus algorithm that runs in $\mathcal{O}(\log n)$ time and uses only $\mathcal{O}(n)$ bits in total for all messages. However, the adversary is not fully adaptive; it has to specify the set of faulty processes in advance. In addition, there are some processes which have to send $\Omega(n/\log n)$ bits during the execution of the algorithm. Very recently, King and Saia [29] presented a randomized algorithm for Byzantine agreement that runs in

	with adversary	without adversary
worst-case, $m = 2$	$\mathcal{O}(\log n)$	$\mathcal{O}(\log n)$
worst-case, arb. m	$\mathcal{O}(\log m \log \log n + \log n)$	$\mathcal{O}(\log n)$
average-case, arb. m	$\mathcal{O}(\log m + \log \log n)$ if m is odd $\Theta(\log n)$ if m is even	$\mathcal{O}(\log m + \log \log n)$ if m is odd $\Theta(\log n)$ if m is even

Figure 1: Our results on the time and work required to reach an almost stable consensus (with adversary) or stable consensus (without adversary). m is the number of legal values. By average-case we refer to the case where every initial value is chosen independently and uniformly at random among the m legal values. The results for the average case with adversary require that $m \leq n^{1/2-\epsilon}$ for some constant $\epsilon > 0$.

polylogarithmic time and only needs $\tilde{\mathcal{O}}(\sqrt{n})$ bits per process against an adaptive adversary.

The consensus problem has also been studied in the context of population protocols, which are protocols for extremely simple, passively mobile systems. Angluin et al. [1] show that with high probability, n agents that meet at random reach consensus in $O(n \log n)$ pairwise interactions and the value chosen is the majority provided that its initial margin is at least $\omega(\sqrt{n \log n})$. This protocol has the additional property of tolerating Byzantine behavior in $o(\sqrt{n})$ of the agents. We can also show these properties for the median rule, but we are more general than Angluin et al. as we allow a set of legal values of arbitrary cardinality whereas Angluin et al. only consider two different values. The result by Angluin et al. can be extended to m different values, but their analysis would only allow one to conclude a runtime of $O(\log m \log n)$ for the non-adversarial as well as the adversarial situation whereas our runtime bounds are $O(\log n)$ and $O(\log m \log \log n + \log n)$ respectively.

Due to the fact that even in the adversarial setting, the median rule stabilizes to a value that is the k-smallest of the initial values for some $k \in [n/2 - c\sqrt{n \log n}, n/2 + c\sqrt{n \log n}]$ w.h.p. and therefore gives a good approximation of the median of the initial values, it is also interesting to compare the median rule with other distributed algorithms for finding the median. Kempe et al. [28] proposed a gossip-based algorithm that computes the median within $O(\log^2 n)$ communication rounds in a complete graph w.h.p. Patt-Shamir [33] showed that the median can be approximated to within ϵn distance from the median with just $O((\log \log n)^3)$ bit transmissions per node if each element can be encoded with $O(\log n)$ bits. Kuhn et al. [31] showed that in networks of diameter D, the median can be found in $O(D \log_D n)$ communication rounds w.h.p. and also prove a matching lower bound holding for a general class of distributed algorithms. The median problem has also been studied in the context of sensors networks (e.g., [35]), but mostly experimentally. However, none of these previous results consider the adversarial case.

2. TWO VALUES WITH ADVERSARY

In this section, we focus on the case that there are only two legal values, x_0 and x_1 with $x_0 < x_1$. Before we analyze the median rule for that case, we propose an alternative notation for our consensus problem based on balls into bins. We have n balls representing the processes and 2 bins representing the two legal values. In that notation, the state of the system at the beginning of a round is represented by a distribution of the balls among the bins, and a T-bounded adversary may pick up any T balls at the end of each round and throw them into any of the two bins. Even though the two-bin

case sounds fairly restrictive, this case turns out to be of general interest, as our analysis for more than two bins will use some results of this section. For the two-bin case, the median rule is equivalent to the *majority rule*, where a ball's next bin is chosen to be the bin that is used by the majority of itself and the two random balls.

THEOREM 2.1. *For* $|S| = 2$ *and any initial distribution of the balls,* $\mathcal{O}(\log n)$ *rounds of the median (majority) rule suffice for any* $\sqrt{n}$-*bounded adversary to reach an almost stable consensus, w.h.p.*

In this theorem as well as the other theorems below, we will just focus on providing time bounds as the work bounds in Section 1.2 immediately follow from the time bounds with the help of standard Chernoff bounds when using the median rule:

LEMMA 2.2 (CHERNOFF BOUNDS). *Let* $X_1, \ldots, X_n$ *be independent binary random variables, let* $X = \sum_{i=1}^n X_i$ *and* $\mu = \mathrm{E}[X]$. *Then it holds for all* $\delta > 0$ *that*

$$\Pr[X \geq (1+\delta)\mu] \leq \left(\frac{e^\delta}{(1+\delta)^{1+\delta}} \right)^\mu \leq e^{-\min[\delta^2, \, \delta] \cdot \mu/3} .$$

Furthermore, it holds for all $0 < \delta < 1$ *that*

$$\Pr[X \leq (1-\delta)\mu] \leq \left(\frac{e^{-\delta}}{(1-\delta)^{1-\delta}} \right)^\mu \leq e^{-\delta^2 \mu/2} .$$

The rest of this section is dedicated to the proof of this theorem. In the following, let L_t be the number of balls in the left bin at (the end of) step t and let R_t be the number of balls in the right bin at step t. Let $X_t = \min(L_t, R_t)$ and let $Y_t = \max(L_t, R_t)$. For simplicity, we focus on the case with even n, since the proof for odd n follows along the same lines. The *imbalance* at a step t is given by $\Delta_t = (Y_t - X_t)/2$ (which is a non-negative integer). We will use $\tilde{X}_t, \tilde{\Delta}_t$ to denote the corresponding numbers before the adversary is allowed to change the location of up to T balls at the end of round t. Based on the imbalance Δ_t we distinguish between three cases.

Case 1: $\Delta_t \geq n/4$

We will show the following lemma whose proof uses standard Chernoff bounds (see Lemma 2.2).

LEMMA 2.3. *If there is a step* t_0 *with* $\Delta_{t_0} \geq n/4$, *then there is a step* $t_1 = t_0 + \mathcal{O}(\log \log n)$ *at which we reach a stable consensus (if there is no adversary) or an almost stable consensus (for any* $\sqrt{n}$-*bounded adversary) w.h.p.*

PROOF. Note that initially $X_t \leq n/4$ (as by assumption, $\Delta_t \geq n/4$). Assume without loss of generality that the left bin initially has fewer balls, so $L_{t_0} = X_{t_0}$ and $R_{t_0} = Y_{t_0}$, and for simplicity we may assume that $t_0 = 0$. For any step t, set $p_t := L_t/n$.

Without adversary: For any ball i let the binary random variable $L_{t,i}$ be 1 if and only if ball i is in the left bin after t rounds, and 0 otherwise. If ball i was in the left bin in round $t-1$, then writing $p_{t-1} = L_{t-1}/n$, we have $\mathrm{E}[L_{t,i}] = \Pr[L_{t,i} = 1] = 1 - (1 - p_{t-1})^2$. Similarly, if the ball i was in the right bin, we have $\mathrm{E}[L_{t,i}] = p_{t-1}^2$. As $L_t = \sum_i L_{t,i}$ is the total number of balls in the left bin after r rounds, we have

$$\mathrm{E}[L_t] = L_{t-1} \cdot (1 - (1 - p_{t-1})^2) + (n - L_{t-1}) \cdot p_{t-1}^2$$
$$= L_{t-1}p_{t-1} \cdot (3 - 2p_{t-1}) \leq L_{t-1}^2/n \cdot 3.$$

Hence, again by using a Chernoff bound argument, we get

$$\Pr\left[L_t \geq \frac{9L_{t-1}^2}{2n}\right] \leq \exp\left(-\frac{9L_{t-1}^2}{4n}\right),$$

which, if $L_{t-1} \geq \sqrt{\epsilon n \log(n)}$, is polynomially small in n (depending on the constant ϵ). To see that this needs $\mathcal{O}(\log \log n)$ steps, note the successive squaring in the mapping $x \mapsto 9x^2/(2n)$. Once we are at a step t with $L_t \leq \sqrt{\epsilon n \log n}$, we get

$$\Pr[L_{t+1} \geq 2C \cdot \log n]$$
$$\leq \binom{\sqrt{\epsilon n \log n}}{C \log n} \cdot \left(1 - \left(1 - \frac{\sqrt{\epsilon n \log n}}{n}\right)^2\right)^{C \log n}$$
$$+ \binom{n}{C \log n} \cdot \left(\frac{\sqrt{\epsilon n \log n}}{n}\right)^{2C \log n}$$
$$\leq \left(\frac{e\sqrt{\epsilon n}}{C\sqrt{\log n}}\right)^{C \log n} \cdot \left(\frac{2\sqrt{\epsilon n \log n}}{n}\right)^{C \log n}$$
$$+ \left(\frac{en}{C \log n}\right)^{C \log n} \cdot \left(\frac{\sqrt{\epsilon n \log n}}{n}\right)^{2C \log n},$$

which is smaller than n^{-2} for sufficiently large C. If $L_t \leq 2C \cdot \log n$ for some step t, then $\mathrm{E}[L_{t+1}] = \mathcal{O}((\log n)^2/n)$ and by Markov's inequality $\Pr[L_{t+1} \geq 1] \leq \mathrm{E}[L_{t+1}] = \mathcal{O}((\log n)^2/n)$.

With adversary: As observed earlier, the adversary can only change the location of $T = \sqrt{n}$ balls at the end of each round. Hence we obtain as above that after $\mathcal{O}(\log \log n)$ steps we reach a step t with $L_t \leq \sqrt{\epsilon n \log n}$. Then we know from the analysis above, that in the next step we have $L_t \leq 2C \cdot \log n + \sqrt{n}$ with high probability and this will hold for polynomially many time steps with high probability. $\square$

Case 2: $c\sqrt{n \ln n} \leq \Delta_t < n/4$ for a sufficiently large constant c

Here, we will show the following lemma. Again, the proof is elementary and uses standard Chernoff bounds.

LEMMA 2.4. *If there is a step t_0 with $c\sqrt{n \ln n} \leq \Delta_{t_0} \leq n/4$ for a sufficiently large constant c, then for any $\sqrt{n}$-bounded adversary there is a step $t_1 = t_0 + \mathcal{O}(\log n)$ with $\Delta_{t_1} \geq n/4$ w.h.p.*

PROOF. Recall that $X_t = n/2 - \Delta_t$ is the number of balls in the smaller bin at step t. Furthermore, we define $\delta_t := \Delta_t/n$ and recall that by assumption, $\delta_t \in [c\sqrt{\ln n}/\sqrt{n}, 1/4]$.

The probability that a ball that is in the smaller bin at step t chooses its new median also in the same bin at step

$t+1$ is $1 - (1/2 + \delta_t)^2 = 3/4 - \delta_t - \delta_t^2$. Similarly the probability that a ball in the larger bin at step t chooses its new median in the other bin is $(1/2 - \delta_t)^2 = 1/4 - \delta_t + \delta_t^2$. Recall that $\tilde{X}_{t+1}$ is the number of balls in the smaller bin before the action of the adversary at the end of step $t+1$. Linearity of expectation gives

$$\mathrm{E}[\tilde{X}_{t+1}] = (1/2 - \delta_t)n \cdot (3/4 - \delta_t - \delta_t^2)$$
$$+ (1/2 + \delta_t)n \cdot (1/4 - \delta_t + \delta_t^2)$$
$$= (1/2 - (3/2)\delta_t + 2\delta_t^3)n \qquad (1)$$
$$= n/2 - \Delta_t - ((1/2)\delta_t - 2\delta_t^3)n$$
$$\leq n/2 - \Delta_t - (1/4)\delta_t n \qquad \text{(using } \delta_t \leq 1/4)$$
$$\leq X_t - (\delta_t/2)X_t \qquad \text{(using } X_t \leq n/2)$$
$$= (1 - \delta_t/2)X_t.$$

Since the choices of the balls are independent, it follows from the Chernoff bounds that for $\epsilon = \delta_t/4$,

$$\Pr[\tilde{X}_{t+1} \geq (1 - \delta_t/4)X_t] \leq \Pr[\tilde{X}_{t+1} \geq (1 + \epsilon)\mathrm{E}[\tilde{X}_{t+1}]]$$
$$\leq e^{-\epsilon^2 \mathrm{E}[\tilde{X}_{t+1}]/3}$$
$$\leq e^{-(\delta_t/4)^2(1 - \delta_t/2)(n/2)/3}$$
$$\leq e^{-(c^2 \ln n/n)n/96} = n^{-c^2/96}.$$

This implies that $\tilde{X}_{t+1} \leq (1 - \delta/4)X_t$ w.h.p. Since the adversary can only change the location of at most $T = \sqrt{n}$ balls at the end of round $t+1$, we have w.h.p. that X_{t+1} is at most $(1 - \delta_t/4)X_t + \sqrt{n}$. Hence, w.h.p., $n/2 - \Delta_{t+1} \leq (1 - \delta_t/4) \cdot (n/2 - \Delta_t) + \sqrt{n}$, and further rearranging gives that, w.h.p.,

$$\Delta_{t+1} \geq \Delta_t + \delta_t n/8 - \delta_t \Delta_t/4 - \sqrt{n}$$
$$\geq \Delta_t + \Delta_t/8 - \Delta_t/16 - \Delta_t/32$$
$$\geq (1 + 1/32)\Delta_t.$$

Hence, taking the union bound over $\mathcal{O}(\log n)$ rounds, we reach a step with an imbalance of at least $n/4$ w.h.p. $\square$

Case 3: $\Delta_t < c\sqrt{n \ln n}$

In contrast to the previous cases, the imbalance is now rather small which requires a more careful analysis.

In the next lemma, we use the Central Limit Theorem to prove that with constant probability, we have a sufficiently large imbalance regardless of the previous imbalance.

LEMMA 2.5. *Assume no adversary is present. Let $\gamma > 0$ be any constant. Then for any $\Delta_t \geq 0$, $\Pr[\Delta_{t+1} \geq \gamma\sqrt{n}] \geq \frac{1}{\sqrt{4\pi}(1 + 4\gamma/\sqrt{3})}e^{-8\gamma^2/3}$, provided n is large enough.*

PROOF. For the proof of Lemma 2.5, we need the following notation. We say that a random variable Y *stochastically dominates* a random variable Z, and write $Y \succeq Z$, if $\Pr[Y \geq x] \geq \Pr[Z \geq x]$ for any x. Finally, we define the *labeled imbalance* by $\Psi_t = (R_t - L_t)/2$.

CLAIM 2.6. *For any two labeled imbalances Ψ_t and Ψ_t' with $\Psi_t \geq \Psi_t' \geq 0$ it holds that $\Psi_{t+1} \succeq \Psi_{t+1}'$.*

PROOF. We show stochastic domination for any two labeled imbalances Ψ_t and $\Psi_t' = \Psi_t - 1$. The rest follows by induction. Let $z = n/2 - \Psi_t'$. Without loss of generality, we assume that balls 1 to $z - 1$ are in the left bin in both Ψ_t and Ψ_t', and balls $z + 1, \ldots, n$ are in the right bin in both

Ψ_t and Ψ'_t. Ball z is in the right bin in Ψ_t and in the left bin in Ψ'_t.

Let Ω be the space of all possible outcomes of the random experiment in which every ball chooses two balls independently and uniformly at random. Consider any such outcome $w \in \Omega$.

Any ball $b \neq z$ that does not choose ball z in w goes to the same bin in both scenarios. If ball z goes to the right bin in the Ψ'_t scenario (in which it started in the left bin) then it will also go the right bin in the Ψ_t scenario (in which it started in the right bin). Finally, consider a ball $b \neq z$ that chooses ball z as one (or both) of its choices in w. If it goes to the right bin in the Ψ'_t scenario (in which the z ball is dragging it left) it will also go to the right bin in the Ψ_t scenario.

So R_{t+1} dominates R'_{t+1} and L'_{t+1} dominates L_{t+1}, and therefore, $R_{t+1} - L_{t+1}$ dominates $R'_{t+1} - L'_{t+1}$, which proves the claim. $\square$

We now return to the proof of Lemma 2.5. We only need to prove it for $\Psi_t = 0$ because the general case follows from stochastic domination (see Claim 2.6). Assume that at step t balls 1 to $n/2$ reside in the left bin and balls $n/2+1$ to n reside in the right bin. Let $Z_1, \ldots, Z_{n/2} \in \{0,1\}$ be random variables defined as follows:

$$Z_i = \begin{cases} 1 & \text{if ball } i \text{ moves to the right bin,} \\ 0 & \text{otherwise.} \end{cases}$$

Then the Z_i are independent Bernoulli variables with $\Pr[Z_i = 1] = 1/4$. Analogously, for balls $n/2+1$ to n, we define the random variables $Z_{n/2+1}$ to Z_n to be 1 if the corresponding ball moves from the right bin to the left bin. We again have $\Pr[Z_i = 1] = 1/4$ for these variables. Then

$$\Psi_{t+1} = \sum_{i=1}^{n/2} Z_i - \sum_{i=n/2+1}^{n} Z_i.$$

Let $\Psi_{t+1}^{(1)} = \sum_{i=1}^{n/2} Z_i$ and $\Psi_{t+1}^{(2)} = \sum_{i=n/2+1}^{n} Z_i$. Each $\Psi_{t+1}^{(j)}$ is binomially distributed with parameters $n/2$ and $p = 1/4$. Thus, $\mathrm{E}[\Psi_{t+1}^{(j)}] = p \cdot n/2 = n/8$ and $\mathrm{V}[\Psi_{t+1}^{(j)}] = p(1-p) \cdot n/2 = (3/4) \cdot n/8$. Since $\Psi_{t+1}^{(1)}$ and $\Psi_{t+1}^{(2)}$ are stochastically independent, it holds that $\mathrm{E}[\Psi_{t+1}] = \mathrm{E}[\Psi_{t+1}^{(1)}] - \mathrm{E}[\Psi_{t+1}^{(2)}] = 0$ and $\mathrm{V}[\Psi_{t+1}] = \mathrm{V}[\Psi_{t+1}^{(1)}] - \mathrm{V}[\Psi_{t+1}^{(2)}] = 3n/16$. Let $\Phi(x) = \frac{1}{\sqrt{2\pi}} \int_{-\infty}^{x} e^{-u^2/2} du$ and let $X = \sum_{i=1}^{n} X_i$ be a sum of independent random variables X_i with finite $\mu = \mathrm{E}[X]$ and $\nu = \mathrm{V}[X]$. From the Central Limit Theorem it follows for $n \to \infty$ that for any $a < b$,

$$\lim_{n \to \infty} \Pr\left[a < \frac{X - \mu}{\sqrt{\nu}} < b \right] = \Phi(b) - \Phi(a).$$

Thus, it holds for any $\gamma > 0$ that

$$\Pr[\Psi_{t+1} \geq \gamma\sqrt{n}] \geq 1 - \Phi(\sqrt{16/3}\gamma) - \varepsilon$$

where $\varepsilon \to 0$ as $n \to \infty$. For $x \geq 0$, the value of $\Phi(x)$ can be bounded as follows (see e.g., [23] p. 17 and [24] p. 505):

$$\frac{1}{\sqrt{2\pi}(1+x)} \cdot e^{-x^2/2} \leq 1 - \Phi(x) \leq \frac{1}{\sqrt{\pi}(1+x)} \cdot e^{-x^2/2}.$$

Therefore, we can lower bound the above probability by

$$\frac{1}{\sqrt{2\pi}(1+4\gamma/\sqrt{3})} e^{-\frac{8\gamma^2}{3}} - \varepsilon \geq \frac{1}{\sqrt{4\pi}(1+4\gamma/\sqrt{3})} e^{-\frac{8\gamma^2}{3}}$$

if n is sufficiently large, which finishes the proof. $\square$

Finally, we prove via standard Chernoff bounds that beyond an imbalance of about $\sqrt{n}$ there is a strong drift to increase the imbalance by a constant factor.

LEMMA 2.7. *If $6\sqrt{n} \leq \Delta_t \leq c\sqrt{n \log n}$, then for any $\sqrt{n}$-bounded adversary,*

$$\Pr[\Delta_{t+1} \geq (7/6)\Delta_t] \geq 1 - \exp\left(-\Theta(\Delta_t^2/n)\right).$$

PROOF. In the proof of Lemma 2.4 (Equation 1) we showed that $\mathrm{E}[\tilde{X}_{t+1}] = n/2 - (3/2)\Delta_t + 2\delta^2\Delta_t$ which implies that $\mathrm{E}[\tilde{\Delta}_{t+1}] = (3/2 - 2\delta^2)\Delta_t$. As $\delta = \Delta_t/n = o(1)$ by our upper bound on Δ_t, it follows from the Chernoff bounds that

$$\Pr[\tilde{\Delta}_{t+1} \leq (4/3)\Delta_t] \leq \exp(-\Theta(\Delta_t)^2/n).$$

As $\Delta_{t+1} \geq \tilde{\Delta}_{t+1} - \sqrt{n}$, we note that $\tilde{\Delta}_{t+1} \geq (4/3)\Delta_t$ implies that $\Delta_{t+1} \geq (4/3)\Delta_t - \sqrt{n} \geq (4/3)\Delta_t - (1/6)\Delta_t \geq (7/6)\Delta_t$. $\square$

Now we can finish the case 3.

LEMMA 2.8. *If at a round t_0 we have $\Delta_{t_0} < c\sqrt{n \ln n}$ for the value of c needed by Lemma 2.4, then for any $\sqrt{n}$-bounded adversary there is a round $t_1 = t_0 + \mathcal{O}(\log n)$ with $\Delta_{t_1} \geq c\sqrt{n \ln n}$ w.h.p.*

PROOF. Lemma 2.5 implies that the expected number of steps until we are in the hypothesis of Lemma 2.7 is $\mathcal{O}(1)$. That is, $\Delta_t \geq c\sqrt{n}$. Now let $\Upsilon_\tau = \lfloor \Delta_{t+\tau-1}/(c\sqrt{n}) \rfloor$ and let $q = \lfloor (n/2)/(c\sqrt{n}) \rfloor$ denote maximum value of Υ_τ, that is, the possible values of Υ_τ are in $\{0, \ldots, q\}$. To continue, we need the following technical result. Its proof is omitted due to space constraints.

CLAIM 2.9. *Let $(X_t)_{t=1}^{\infty}$ be a Markov Chain with state space $\{0, \ldots, q\}$ that has the following properties:*

- *there are constants $c_1 > 1$ and $c_2 > 0$, such that for any $t \in \mathbb{N}$, $\Pr[X_{t+1} \geq \min\{c_1 X_t, q\}] \geq 1 - e^{-c_2 X_t}$,*

- *$X_t = 0 \Rightarrow X_{t+1} \geq 1$ with probability c_3 which is a constant greater than 0,*

Let $c_4 > 0$ be an arbitrary constant and $T := \min\{t \in \mathbb{N} : X_t \geq c_4 \log q\}$. Then for every constant $c_6 > 0$ there is a constant $c_5 = c_5(c_4, c_6) > 0$ such that

$$\Pr[T \leq c_5 \cdot \log q + \log_{c_1}(c_4 \log q)] \geq 1 - q^{-c_6}.$$

By this claim, $O(\log q)$ rounds suffice to achieve $\Upsilon_\tau \geq c_4 \log q$, or $\Delta_{t+\tau-1} \geq c\sqrt{n} \cdot c_4 \log q$, w.h.p. for any constant $c_4 > 0$, which finishes the proof. $\square$

3. MORE THAN TWO VALUES

In this section we consider the more challenging case that $|S| > 2$. We analyze the models with and without adversary separately.

3.1 Convergence without Adversary

In this section, we prove Theorem 1.1. Our proof proceeds as follows. Initially, we may have up to n non-empty bins as there can be up to n different initial values, but after just $\mathcal{O}(\log n)$ rounds, we end up with at most 2 non-empty bins. Then we can directly use our result for two bins to conclude that after additional $\mathcal{O}(\log n)$ rounds, the median rule stabilizes.

Assume that the bins and balls are numbered from 1 to n such that all balls with higher numbers are in higher bins and balls in the same bin form consecutive numbers. As an example, $(1, 2, 3 \mid 4, 5 \mid \mid 6 \mid 7, 8)$ describes a distribution of 8 balls into 5 bins, where the first bin holds 3 balls with numbers 1, 2 and 3, the second bin 2 balls, the third bin none and so on.

We associate with each ball $i \in [n]$ a value $g(i)$ called *gravity*, which is the expected number of balls that choose i as their median for the next step (when considering the ball ordering). The gravity $g(i)$ can be computed as follows. Ball i may either be chosen twice by a ball, or ball $j \in \{i+1, \ldots, n\}$ chooses ball i and a ball $i' \in \{1, \ldots, i-1\}$, or ball $j \in \{1, \ldots, i-1\}$ chooses ball i and a ball $i' \in \{i+1, \ldots, n\}$, or ball i chooses one ball out of $\{1, \ldots, i-1\}$ and the other out of $\{i+1, \ldots, n\}$, or ball i chooses itself and some ball $j \neq i$. This gives

$$g(i) = n \cdot \frac{1}{n^2} + (n-i) \cdot \frac{2(i-1)}{n^2} + (i-1) \cdot \frac{2(n-i)}{n^2} +$$
$$1 \cdot \frac{2(n-i)(i-1)}{n^2} + 1 \cdot \frac{2(n-1)}{n^2}$$

Simplifying this expression gives

$$g(i) = 6\frac{(n-i)(i-1)}{n^2} + \frac{3n-2}{n^2}. \qquad (2)$$

Note that the gravity of a ball i is maximized for the median-ball, which has number $\lceil n/2 \rceil$ according to our ordering. Fix a bin j. By linearity of the expectation and the definition of gravity, the expected load of j at a time $t+1$ is equal to the sum of gravities of the balls in bin j at time t.

For each bin $j \in [n]$ at step t, we define a set of heavy balls $\mathcal{H}_{t,j}$ which is defined as the subset of the $\Phi = C\sqrt{n \log n}$ balls in bin j with largest gravity. $C > 0$ is a sufficiently large constant. Note that by definition, $0 \leq |\mathcal{H}_{t,j}| \leq \Phi$. We first prove the following:

LEMMA 3.1. *If there is a ball $i \in \mathcal{H}_{t,j}$ with $g(i) < 4/3$, then at step $t+1$ either there is a ball $l \in \mathcal{H}_{t+1,j}$ with $g(l) < 4/3$ or bin j is empty w.h.p.*

PROOF. Assume w.l.o.g. that $j \leq m_t$ (the case $j \geq m_t$ follows with identical arguments), where m_t is the median ball at round t. Let i be the number of a ball in $\mathcal{H}_{t,j}$ with gravity $g(i) < 4/3$. When plugging $g(i) < 4/3$ into Equation (2), we get

$$\frac{4}{3} > 6\frac{(n-i)(i-1)}{n^2} + \mathcal{O}\left(\frac{1}{n}\right),$$

which readily implies that $i \leq n/3 + \mathcal{O}(1)$. Hence, there are at most $n/3 + \Phi + \mathcal{O}(1)$ balls in the bins 1 to j. Then consolidate all bins from 1 to j into a superbin A, and all other bins into a superbin B. Let $L_{t,A}$ be the load of superbin A in step t, so $L_{t,A} \leq n/3 + \Phi + \mathcal{O}(1)$. Using the arguments from the two-bin case (Lemmas 2.3 and 2.4) we conclude that ,w.h.p., $L_{t+1,A} \leq n/(3+\epsilon)$, for a constant $\epsilon > 0$. Hence by (2), every ball $l \in \mathcal{H}_{t+1,j}$ in bin j satisfies $g(l) < 4/3$ w.h.p. (provided that $\mathcal{H}_{t+1,j} \neq \emptyset$). $\square$

On the other hand, it holds:

LEMMA 3.2. *If $|\mathcal{H}_{t,j}| = \Phi$ and there is no ball in $\mathcal{H}_{t,j}$ with $g(i) < 4/3$, then $|\mathcal{H}_{t+1,j}| = \Phi$ w.h.p.*

PROOF. Suppose that $\mathcal{H}_{t,j} \geq \Phi$ and there is no ball $l \in \mathcal{H}_{t+1,j}$ with $g(l) < 4/3$. Then it follows from the definition of the gravity that the expected number of balls in bin j at step $t+1$ is at least $(4/3) \cdot \Phi$. Thus, the Chernoff bounds imply that the number of balls in bin j at step $t+1$ is at least Φ w.h.p., and therefore, $\mathcal{H}_{t+1,j} \geq \Phi$. $\square$

Using Lemma 3.1 and Lemma 3.2, we can now prove the following.

LEMMA 3.3. *For any initial configuration it takes at most $\mathcal{O}(\log n)$ rounds until at least one of the following two cases holds for all bins j w.h.p.:*

1. *at least one ball $i \in \mathcal{H}_{t,j}$ satisfies $g(i) < 4/3$ (or $\mathcal{H}_{t,j}$ is empty), or*

2. *$|\mathcal{H}_{t,j}| = \Phi$.*

PROOF. Consider an arbitrary but fixed round t. Our goal is to apply the following technical result. Its proof is similar to Claim 2.9 and omitted due to space constraints.

CLAIM 3.4. *Let $(X_t)_{t=1}^\infty$ be a Markov Chain with state space $\{0, \ldots, q\}$ that has the following properties,*

- *there are constants $c_1 > 1$ and $c_2 > 0$, such that for any $t \in \mathbb{N}$, $\Pr[X_{t+1} \geq \min\{c_1 X_t, q\}] \geq 1 - e^{-c_2 X_t}$,*

- *$X_t = 0 \Rightarrow X_{t+1} = 0$ with probability 1,*

- *$X_t = q \Rightarrow X_{t+1} = q$ with probability 1.*

Let $c_4 > 0$ be an arbitrary constant and $T := \min\{t \in \mathbb{N}: X_t \in \{0\} \cup \{q\}\}$. Then for every constant $c_6 > 0$ there is a constant $c_5 > 0$ such that $\Pr[T \leq c_5 \log q] \geq 1 - q^{-c_6}$.

We first identify two absorbing states concerning $\mathcal{H}_{t,j}$:

1. There is a ball $i \in \mathcal{H}_{t,j}$ with $g(i) < 4/3$. Then Lemma 3.1 implies that $\mathcal{H}_{t+1,j}$ contains at least one ball l with $g(l) < 4/3$, or $\mathcal{H}_{t+1,j}$ is empty, w.h.p.

2. $|\mathcal{H}_{t,j}| = \Phi$ and all balls $i \in \mathcal{H}_{t,j}$ satisfy $g(i) \geq 4/3$. Then it follows from Lemma 3.2 that $|\mathcal{H}_{t+1,j}| = \Phi$ w.h.p.

If $\mathcal{H}_{t,j}$ does not fulfill one of these conditions, all balls in $\mathcal{H}_{t,j}$ have a gravity of at least $4/3$. In this case, the expected number of balls in bin j at step $t+1$ would be at least $(4/3)|\mathcal{H}_{t,j}|$. Since the median rule is applied independently at random to each ball, the Chernoff bounds imply

$$\Pr\left[|\mathcal{H}_{t+1,j}| \geq \min\{\Phi, \frac{5}{4}|\mathcal{H}_{t,j}|\}\right] \geq 1 - \exp(-\Theta(|\mathcal{H}_{t,j}|)).$$

Thus, applying Claim 3.4, we conclude that one of the two absorbing states is reached within $t_1 = \mathcal{O}(\log n)$ rounds w.h.p. $\square$

We are now ready to prove the main result of this section.

Proof of Theorem 1.1: Let $t_1 = \mathcal{O}(\log n)$ be the round that satisfies Lemma 3.3. For this t_1 let $j_{\min}$ and $j_{\max}$ be the positions (w.r.t. our unique ball ordering) of the leftmost and rightmost balls in bin b_t, where bin b_t is the one containing the median ball. Note that by Lemma 3.3, the load of bin b_t is at least Φ. We proceed by a case distinction on the positions of $j_{\min}$ and $j_{\max}$.

1. $n/2 - j_{\min} \le \Phi/2$. Let $b_t - 1$ be the left bin of bin b_t. Equation 2 implies that all heavy balls in bin $b_t - 1$ have gravity at least $4/3$. So, Lemma 3.3 implies that the load of bin $b_t - 1$ is at least Φ. Consolidate all bins from $1, \ldots, b_t - 2$ and all bins from $b_t + 1, \ldots, n$ into two superbins A and B, respectively. By our arguments above, both superbins have a load of at most $n/2 - \Phi/2$. Therefore for C large enough, Lemmas 2.3 and 2.4 imply that both superbins will die out within the next $\mathcal{O}(\log n)$ steps w.h.p. After this has happened, we only end up with two bins, $b_t - 1$ and b_t. A final application of our two-bin analysis (Theorem 2.1) reduces the number of bins from 2 to 1 within additional $\mathcal{O}(\log n)$ rounds, and our theorem follows.

2. $j_{max} - n/2 \le \Phi/2$. This case is handled in the same way as before.

3. $n/2 - j_{\min} > \Phi/2$ and $j_{max} - n/2 > \Phi/2$: In this case, it follows as in the previous cases that by Lemmas 2.3 and 2.4, all bins except bin b_t will vanish after the next $\mathcal{O}(\log n)$ rounds.

□

3.2 Convergence with Adversary

In this section we prove Theorem 1.2. First, let $m = |S|$ and assume that m is finite.

THEOREM 3.5. *For any $\sqrt{n}$-bounded adversary, it will take at most $\mathcal{O}(\log m \log \log n + \log n)$ time w.h.p. until the median rule reaches an almost stable consensus.*

PROOF. We shall use the following Chernoff bound which can be easily derived from the standard Chernoff bound for binomial random variables.

LEMMA 3.6. *Consider some fixed $0 < \delta < 1$. Suppose that $X_1, \ldots, X_n$ are independent geometric random variables on $\mathbb{N}$ with $\Pr[X_i = k] = (1 - \delta)^{k-1}\delta$ for every $k \in \mathbb{N}$. Let $X = \sum_{i=1}^{n} X_i$, $\mu = \mathrm{E}[X]$. Then it holds for all $\epsilon > 0$ that*

$$\Pr[X \ge (1 + \epsilon)\mu] \le e^{-\epsilon^2/(2(1+\epsilon))\cdot n}.$$

Let the set of non-empty bins be $\{1, \ldots, m\}$ at the beginning. We divide the time into $\log m + 1$ phases, numbered from 1 to $\log m + 1$. Each phase i, $1 \le i \le \log m$ takes only $\mathcal{O}(\log \log n)$ steps in expectation, while the last phase will take $\mathcal{O}(\log n)$ steps. For each phase i with $1 \le i \le \log m$, we shall prove by induction that at the end of the phase, there is a set $S_i \subseteq \{1, \ldots, m\}$ of consecutive bins of size $|S_i| \le m/2^i + 1$ that satisfies

$$\min\{R(S_i), L(S_i)\} \ge \frac{n}{2} + C\sqrt{n \log n}, \qquad (3)$$

where $R(S_i)$ (resp. $L(S_i)$) denotes the total load of all bins that are in the set S_i or located right (resp. left) from S_i, respectively. The idea behind the definition is that at the end of each phase i, we know that the bin that gets all balls at the end (up to $\mathcal{O}(\sqrt{n})$ balls due to the adversary) is located in S_i (which follows from applying the two-bin analysis to the sets $R(S_i)$ and $\{1, \ldots, m\} \setminus R(S_i)$ as well as $L(S_i)$ and $\{1, \ldots, m\} \setminus L(S_i)$).

Let us now prove (3) by induction. For the induction base, cut the set of all bins into two equally-sized, consecutive sets of bins $S_1^{\text{left}} := \{1, \ldots, \lfloor m/2 \rfloor\}$ and $S_1^{\text{right}} := \{\lfloor m/2 \rfloor + 1, \ldots, m\}$. Now regard S_1^{left} and S_1^{right} as two bins. Our aim is to prove that after $\mathcal{O}(\log \log n)$ steps, one of the two bins will have at least $\frac{n}{2} + C\sqrt{n \log n}$ balls. To show this, we apply the Lemma 2.5 and Lemma 2.7 from the two-bin analysis. Let t be the first time step of phase i and recall that Δ_t is the imbalance at time t.

First we apply Lemma 2.5 to get that with constant probability > 0, $\Delta_{t+1} \ge 5\sqrt{n}$ holds (if there is no adversary). Since the adversary can influence at most $4\sqrt{n}$ balls (w.h.p.), we have $\Delta_{t+1} \ge \sqrt{n}$ with constant probability. Then we apply Lemma 2.7 to obtain

$$\Pr[\Delta_{t+\mathcal{O}(\log \log n)} \ge C\sqrt{n \log n}]$$
$$\ge \prod_{k=1}^{\mathcal{O}(\log \log n)} \left(1 - \exp(-\Theta((4/3)^k)) \right),$$

which is at least a constant greater than zero. As this holds for any imbalance Δ_t, the expected time to reach a step t_0 with $\Delta_{t_0} \ge C\sqrt{n \log n}$ is $\mathcal{O}(\log \log n)$, which completes the induction base.

Assume now more generally, that at the end of phase i, a set S_i of size at most $m/2^i + 1$ exists with

$$\min\{R(S_i), L(S_i)\} \ge \frac{n}{2} + C\sqrt{n \log n}.$$

Again, we divide S_i into two consecutive sets of bins S_i^{left} and S_i^{right}, each of size at most $m/2^{i+1} + 1$. Now regard S_i^{left} together with all bins left from it and S_i^{right} together will all bins right from it as two separate bins, $L(S_i^{\text{left}})$ and $R(S_i^{\text{right}})$. Applying the same arguments as from the induction base, we obtain that after expected $\mathcal{O}(\log \log n)$ steps, the imbalance between $L(S_i^{\text{left}})$ and $R(S_i^{\text{right}})$ is at least $C\sqrt{n \log n}$. Assume w.l.o.g. that $L(S_i^{\text{left}}) \ge \frac{n}{2} + C\sqrt{n \log n}$. Then we set $S_{i+1} := S_i^{\text{left}}$ and note that by assumption,

$$L(S_{i+1}) = L(S_i^{\text{left}}) \ge \frac{n}{2} + C\sqrt{n \log n}.$$

Moreover, we know from the induction hypothesis, that at the end of the previous phase, $R(S_i) \ge \frac{n}{2} + C\sqrt{n \log n}$. Also, the proof of Lemma 2.4 implies that if the load of any set of balls is above $n/2 + C\sqrt{n \log n}$, it never decreases in any following round with high probability. Hence using that the leftmost bin in S_i^{left} is also the leftmost bin in S_i,

$$R(S_{i+1}) = R(S_i^{\text{left}}) \ge R(S_i) \ge \frac{n}{2} + C\sqrt{n \log n}.$$

This completes the induction and proves (3).

So we have shown that the time to reach the end of phase $\log m$ can be bounded by the sum of $\log m$ independent geometric random variables, each with mean $\mathcal{O}(\log \log n)$. Hence Lemma 3.6 implies that after $\mathcal{O}(\log m \log \log n + \log n)$ steps, we have completed phase $\log m$ with high probability.

Now at the end phase of $\log m$, there is a set of two bins $S = S_{\log m} = \{j, j + 1\}$ with

$$\min\{R(S), L(S)\} \ge \frac{n}{2} + C\sqrt{n \log n}.$$

Applying Lemma 2.3 and Lemma 2.4 to $R(S)$ and $L(S)$, we obtain that $R(S)$ and $L(S)$ are both larger than $n - (C/2)\sqrt{n \log n}$ after additional $\mathcal{O}(\log n)$ rounds with high probability. Since the intersection of bins in $R(S)$ and $L(S)$ is at most two, we conclude that there is a set of at most two bins that contains $n - C\sqrt{n \log n}$ balls with high probability. Applying Theorem 2.1, we conclude that after additional $\mathcal{O}(\log n)$ rounds, we will have reached an almost stable consensus. $\square$

As an alternative definition of m, we can also define m to be the number of legal values between v_ℓ and v_r, where v_ℓ is the $(n/2 - c\sqrt{n \log n})$-smallest and v_r is the $(n/2 + c\sqrt{n \log n})$-smallest value of the initial values for some sufficiently large constant c. Let us throw all values $v < v_\ell$ into one superbin A and all values $v > v_r$ into one superbin B. Then it follows from Lemmas 2.3 and 2.4 that after $\mathcal{O}(\log n)$ rounds, the superbins A and B run empty except for $\mathcal{O}(\sqrt{n})$ many balls, w.h.p., which implies the following lemma.

LEMMA 3.7. *For any $\sqrt{n}$-bounded adversary it holds that after $\mathcal{O}(\log n)$ rounds, all processes apart from $\mathcal{O}(\sqrt{n})$ have values between v_ℓ and v_r w.h.p.*

Using the outcome of this lemma as the starting point in the analysis of Theorem 3.5, one can easily check that Theorem 3.5 is still valid when defining m to be the number of legal values between v_ℓ and v_r.

3.3 Static Adversary

Suppose that the adversary has to choose a fixed set of $\sqrt{n}$ corrupted balls throughout the execution. Since this is a special case of our T-bounded adversary, Theorem 3.5 still holds. However, the expected number of non-corrupted balls leaving the stable bin is at least $(n - \sqrt{n}) \cdot (1/\sqrt{n})^2 = 1 - o(1)$ in each round, and it can be up to $\Theta(\log n)$ with probability at least $1/n$. Thus, they still have to do some update work. To prevent any update work (i.e., *all* non-corrupted balls stay at the stable bin for at least a polynomial number of rounds w.h.p.), a simple extension of the median rule, called the *careful median rule*, suffices:

Each process i executes the median rule as before but in addition to this maintains a *stable value* sv_i and keeps track of the last k outcomes of the median rule for some constant $k \geq 3$. Whenever the majority of the last k outcomes agrees on a single value, say v, sv_i is set to v.

Our goal is to reach a consensus for the sv_i values that holds as long as possible.

THEOREM 3.8. *For any static $\sqrt{n}$-bounded adversary, the careful median rule needs at most $\mathcal{O}(\log m \log \log n + \log n)$ rounds to reach a stable consensus for all non-corrupted processes that holds for poly(n) many steps w.h.p.*

PROOF. Theorem 3.5 implies that after $\mathcal{O}(\log m \log \log n + \log n)$ rounds the (standard median rule) values v_i of the honest processes form an almost stable consensus w.h.p., say, on value v. Now, focus on any honest process i. Once an almost stable consensus is reached, the probability that v_i deviates from v at the end of round t is bounded by $\mathcal{O}(T/n)$, which is the probability that i contacts one of the at most $\mathcal{O}(T)$ processes that deviate from the consensus, even if i itself deviates from the consensus at the beginning of t. Since this upper bound on the probability holds independently for each round, it follows that the probability that at least $k/2$ of the k last values of i deviate from v is at most

$$\binom{k}{k/2} \mathcal{O}\left(\frac{1}{\sqrt{n}}\right)^{k/2} = 2^k \cdot \mathcal{O}\left(\frac{1}{n}\right)^{k/4} = \mathcal{O}\left(\frac{1}{n}\right)^{k/4}$$

for a constant k which implies the theorem. $\square$

4. AVERAGE CASE ANALYSIS

In this section, we investigate the case where all n balls are initially put independently and uniformly at random into m bins. Without the adversary, we get the following result.

THEOREM 4.1. *Assume that each of the n balls is initially assigned uniformly at random to one of the m bins. Then the median rule reaches a stable consensus w.h.p. after the following time:*

$$\begin{array}{ll} \mathcal{O}(\log m + \log \log n) & \text{if } m \text{ is odd,} \\ \Theta(\log n) & \text{if } m \text{ is even.} \end{array}$$

Intuitively, the reason for this dichotomy is that for odd m there is already a large imbalance at the beginning when we consider all balls that are in bins left to the middle bin versus all the remaining balls. Hence we reach in just $\mathcal{O}(\log m)$ an imbalance of $\Omega(n)$, for which we have shown in Lemma 2.3 that already $\mathcal{O}(\log \log n)$ further steps are enough reach a stable consensus. However, if m is even, then there is only a relatively small imbalance at the beginning and it takes $\Omega(\log n)$ rounds to reach a sufficiently large imbalance.

Let us now analyze the adversarial model.

THEOREM 4.2. *Consider any $\sqrt{n}$-bounded adversary and suppose that $m \leq n^{1/2 - \epsilon}$ for some constant $\epsilon > 0$. Then the median rule reaches an almost stable consensus w.h.p. after the following time:*

$$\begin{array}{ll} \mathcal{O}(\log m + \log \log n) & \text{if } m \text{ is odd and} \\ \Theta(\log n) & \text{if } m \text{ is even.} \end{array}$$

5. CONCLUSIONS

In this paper we presented a surprisingly simple, efficient and robust consensus mechanism demonstrating the power of two choices. While we were able to prove a tight time bound for this algorithm in the non-adversarial case, the time bound for the adversarial case is not optimal yet (it is $\mathcal{O}(\log n \log \log n)$ instead of the suspected $\mathcal{O}(\log n)$), so further work is needed. Also, it is open whether lightweight self-stabilizing consensus mechanisms exist beyond $\mathcal{O}(\sqrt{n \log n})$ adversarial processes.

Acknowledgments

We would like to thank Michael Bender for suggesting a related problem that initiated this research.

6. REFERENCES

[1] D. Angluin, J. Aspnes, and D. Eisenstat. A simple population protocol for fast robust approximate majority. In *Proc. of the 21st Int. Symposium on Distributed Computing (DISC)*, pages 20–32, 2007.

[2] D. Angluin, M. Fischer, and H. Jiang. Stabilizing consensus in mobile networks. In *Proc. of the Intl. Conference on Distributed Computing in Sensor Networks (DCOSS)*, pages 37–50, 2006.

[3] J. Aspnes. Randomized protocols for aynchronous consensus. *Distributed Computing*, 16(2-3):165–176, 2003.

[4] J. Aspnes, H. Attiya, and K. Censor. Randomized consensus in expected $o(n \log n)$ individual work. In *Proc. of the 27th ACM Symp. on Principles of Distributed Computing (PODC)*, pages 325–333, 2008.

[5] J. Aspnes and K. Censor. Approximate shared-memory counting despite a strong adversary. In *Proc. of the 20th ACM Symp. on Discrete Algorithms (SODA)*, pages 441–450, 2009.

[6] H. Attiya and K. Censor. Lower bounds for randomized consensus under a weak adversary. In *Proc. of the 27th ACM Symp. on Principles of Distributed Computing (PODC)*, pages 315–324, 2008.

[7] H. Attiya and K. Censor. Tight bounds for asynchronous randomized consensus. *Journal of the ACM*, 55(5):1–26, 2008.

[8] H. Attiya and J. Welch. *Distributed Computing: Fundamentals, Simulations, and Advanced Topics (2nd Edition)*. John Wiley and Sons, 2004.

[9] Y. Azar, A. Broder, A. Karlin, and E. Upfal. Balanced allocations. *SIAM Journal on Computing*, 29(1):180–200, 1999.

[10] Z. Bar Joseph and M. Ben-Or. A tight lower bound for randomized synchronous consensus. In *Proc. of the 17th ACM Symp. on Principles of Distributed Computing (PODC)*, pages 193–199, 1998.

[11] M. Ben-Or, E. Pavlov, and V. Vaikuntanathan. Byzantine agreement in the full-information model in $\mathcal{O}(\log n)$ rounds. In *Proc. of the 38th ACM Symp. on Theory of Computing (STOC)*, pages 179–186, 2006.

[12] R. Canetti and T. Rabin. Fast asynchronous Byzantine agreement with optimal resilience. In *Proc. of the 25th ACM Symp. on Theory of Computing (STOC)*, pages 42–51, 1993.

[13] R. Cole, A. Frieze, B.M. Maggs, M. Mitzenmacher, A.W. Richa, R.K. Sitaraman, and E. Upfal. On balls and bins with deletions. In *Proc. of the 2nd Intl. Workshop on Randomization and Approximation Techniques in Computer Science (RANDOM)*, 1998.

[14] R. Cole, B.M. Maggs, F. Meyer auf der Heide, M. Mitzenmacher, A.W. Richa, K. Schröder, R.K. Sitaraman, and B. Vöcking. Randomized protocols for low-congestion circuit routing in multistage interconnection networks. In *Proc. of the 29th ACM Symp. on Theory of Computing (STOC)*, pages 378–388, 1998.

[15] M. Dietzfelbinger and F. Meyer auf der Heide. Simple, efficient shared memory simulations. In *Proc. of the 10th ACM Symp. on Parallel Algorithms and Architectures (SPAA)*, pages 110–119, 1993.

[16] D. Dolev, N. Lynch, S. Pinter, E. Stark, and W. Weihl. Reaching approximate agreement in the presence of faults. *Journal of the ACM*, 33(3):499–516, 1986.

[17] S. Dolev, R. Kat, and E. Schiller. When consensus meets self-stabilization. In *Proc. of the 10th International Conference on Principle of Distributed Systems (OPODIS)*, pages 45–63, 2006.

[18] R. Elsässer and T. Sauerwald. The power of memory in randomized broadcasting. In *Proc. of the 19th ACM Symp. on Discrete Algorithms (SODA)*, pages 773–781, 2008.

[19] P. Feldman and S. Micali. An optimal probabilistic protocol for synchronous Byzantine agreement. *SIAM Journal on Computing*, 26(4):873–933, 1997.

[20] M. Fischer, N. Lynch, and M. Merritt. Easy impossibility proofs for distributed consensus problems. *Distributed Computing*, 1(1):26–39, 1986.

[21] M. Fischer, N. Lynch, and M. Paterson. Impossibility of distributed consensus with one faulty process. *Journal of the ACM*, 32(2):374–382, 1985.

[22] S. Gilbert and D. Kowalski. Distributed agreement with optimal communication complexity. In *Proc. of the 21st ACM Symp. on Discrete Algorithms (SODA)*, pages 965–977, 2010.

[23] K. Ito and H.P. McKean. *Diffusion Processes and their Sample Paths*. Springer Verlag, Heidelberg, 1974.

[24] N.L. Johnson and S. Kotz. *Encyclopedia of Statistical Sciences*. John Wiley, New York, 1982.

[25] B. Kapron, D. Kempe, V. King, J. Saia, and V. Sanwalani. Fast asynchronous Byzantine agreement and leader election with full information. In *Proc. of the 19th ACM Symp. on Discrete Algorithms (SODA)*, pages 1038–1047, 2008.

[26] R. Karp, M. Luby, and F. Meyer auf der Heide. Efficient PRAM simulation on a distributed memory machine. In *Proc. of the 24th ACM Symp. on Theory of Computing (STOC)*, pages 318–326, 1992.

[27] J. Katz and C.-Y. Koo. On expected constant-round protocols for Byzantine agreement. *Journal of Computer and System Sciences*, 75(2):91–112, 2009.

[28] D. Kempe, A. Dobra, and J. Gehrke. Gossip-based computation of aggregate information. In *Proc. of the 44 IEEE Symp. on Foundations of Computer Science (FOCS)*, pages 482–491, 2003.

[29] V. King and J. Saia. Breaking the $O(n^2)$ bit barrier: Scalable Byzantine agreement with an adaptive adversary. In *Proc. of the 29th ACM Symp. on Principles of Distributed Computing (PODC)*, pages 420–429, 2010.

[30] V. King, J. Saia, V. Sanwalani, and E. Vee. Towards secure and scalable computation in peer-to-peer networks. In *Proc. of the 47th IEEE Symp. on Foundations of Computer Science (FOCS)*, pages 87–98, 2006.

[31] F. Kuhn, T. Locher, and R. Wattenhofer. Tight bounds for distributed selection. In *Proc. of the 19th ACM Symp. on Parallel Algorithms and Architectures (SPAA)*, pages 145–153, 2007.

[32] N. Lynch. *Distributed Algorithms*. Morgan Kaufmann Publishers, 1996.

[33] B. Patt-Shamir. A note on efficient aggregate queries in sensor networks. *Theoretical Computer Science*, 370(1–3):254–264, 2007.

[34] M. Rabin. Randomized Byzantine generals. In *Proc. of the 24th IEEE Symp. on Foundations of Computer Science (FOCS)*, pages 403–409, 1983.

[35] N. Shrivastava, C. Buragohain, D. Agrawal, and S. Suri. Medians and beyond: new aggregation techniques for sensor networks. In *Proc. of the 2nd Intl. Conference on Embedded Networked Sensor Systems (SenSys)*, pages 239–249, 2004.

Convergence of Local Communication Chain Strategies via Linear Transformations[*]

or how to trade locality for speed

Peter Kling
Heinz Nixdorf Institute &
Department of Computer Science
University of Paderborn
peter.kling@uni-paderborn.de

Friedhelm Meyer auf der Heide
Heinz Nixdorf Institute &
Department of Computer Science
University of Paderborn
fmadh@uni-paderborn.de

ABSTRACT

Consider two far apart base stations connected by an arbitrarily winding chain of n relay robots to transfer messages between them. Each relay acts autonomously, has a limited communication range, and knows only a small, local part of its environment. We seek a strategy for the relays to minimize the chain's length. We describe a large strategy class in form of linear transformations of the spatial vectors connecting neighboring robots. This yields surprising correlations between several strategy properties and characteristics of these transformations (e.g., "reasonable" strategies correspond to transformations given by doubly stochastic matrices). Based on these results, we give almost tight bounds on the strategies' convergence speed by applying and extending results about the mixing time of Markov chains. Eventually, our framework enables us to define strategies where each relay bases its decision where to move only on the positions of its k next left and right neighbors, and to prove a convergence speed of $\Theta\left(\frac{n^2}{k^2} \log n\right)$ for these strategies. This not only closes a gap between upper and lower runtime bounds of a known strategy (Go-To-The-Middle), but also allows for a trade-off between convergence properties and locality.

Categories and Subject Descriptors

F.1.2 [**Computation by Abstract Devices**]: Modes of Computation—*Parallelism and concurrency*; F.2.2 [**Analysis of Algorithms and Problem Complexity**]: Nonnumerical Algorithms and Problems; G.3 [**Probability and Statistics**]: *Markov processes*

General Terms

Algorithms, Performance, Theory

---

[*]Partially supported by the EU within FP7-ICT-2007-1 under contract no. 215270 (FRONTS), DFG-project "Smart Teams" within the SPP 1183 "Organic Computing", and the Paderborn Institute for Scientific Computation (PaSCo).

Keywords

swarm robotics, local algorithms, distributed algorithms, gathering, Markov chains, mixing time

1. INTRODUCTION

Envision a scenario where two far apart robotic devices (*base stations*) want to communicate. They are assumed to have a limited communication range. Thus, in order to establish a communication link between them, the signal has to be relayed. For this purpose, we consider a chain of autonomous, mobile, and simple devices (*relays*), which are to forward the signal along this chain. Each relay has a limited communication range and a unique predecessor and successor in the chain. Initially, the communication chain may be arbitrarily long and winding, causing an increased energy usage compared to a straight chain. Such a winding chain may be the result of an explorer that left the first base station, moved around, and eventually stopped and became itself a base station. To reduce energy consumption (and possibly the number of relays needed), the relays should try to minimize the total length of the chain — if possible, they should form a straight line. However, each single relay knows only a small, local part of its environment. Thus, we seek a distributed movement strategy to be applied by the relays, with the goal of eventually achieving a (nearly) optimal communication chain. In doing so, the robots must not break the connection between the base stations (e.g., by exceeding the communication range to one of its neighbors).

Problem Classification.

This *communication chain problem* falls into the class of robotic formation problems. Such problems have gained much attention by biologists, engineers, and computer scientists. Autonomous robots have become an essential part in the exploration of difficult to access areas (e.g., enemy territory, deep sea, or outer space). Additionally, there is a shift from a few complex and expensive robots to a larger number of simple and cheap devices. Such solutions seem to be more robust (e.g., in the case that some devices fail) and may allow to exploit some underlying parallelizability of the task at hand. However, these approaches pose the problem of coordination: How to coordinate such a large number of autonomous devices with rather limited capabilities? This question has been the concern of many researchers, both in applied (e.g., [2, 17]) and theoretical computer science. From the perspective of theoretical computer science, research has concentrated on several fundamental problem variants, such as gathering multiple robots at a single position or forming simple geometric shapes [20, 21]. In the course of this research, a central, guiding principle has been to pinpoint the capabilities needed to achieve certain goals. Abilities to be considered include identification of other robots (unique IDs vs. anonymity), amount of needed memory (non-oblivious vs. oblivious), common orientation, communication, and locality constraints. For example, Dieudonné and Petit [7] show that, using a very weak robot model (anonymous, disoriented, oblivious, and no communication), gathering is possible if and only if the number of robots is odd. Besides the question whether gathering can be achieved in finite time, recent research has focused on providing runtime bounds. Izumi et al. [10] show that, in a very restrictive robot model, randomized gathering for n robots needs $\Omega(e^n)$ rounds. In the presence of locality constraints, where robots can perceive their environment only within a certain distance, Degener et al. [5] suggest an algorithm that gathers the robots in (expected) $O(n^2)$ asynchronous rounds. A recent result of Degener et al. [6] studies a deterministic algorithm in a synchronous time model and a very weak robot model. This algorithm is shown to require $O(n^4)$ rounds.

1.1 Known Results & Our Contribution

Known Results.

The communication chain problem has been the subject of several prior studies. A simple and very intuitive strategy was first suggested by Dynia et al. [8]: the GO-TO-THE-MIDDLE strategy. Here, robots compute and move to the midpoint of the line segment connecting their direct neighbors. It is shown that it takes $O\left(n^2 \log \frac{n}{\varepsilon}\right)$ time steps to let all relays reach an ε-approximation of their optimal positions. Kutyłowski [13] gives a lower bound of $\Omega(n^2 - \varepsilon n)$. A seemingly better strategy, called CHASE-EXPLORER, has been suggested by Dynia et al. [9]. It considers a variant of the communication chain problem where one of the base stations (the explorer) is mobile. CHASE-EXPLORER is shown to be nearly optimal, while GO-TO-THE-MIDDLE has severe performance drawbacks in this situation. However, CHASE-EXPLORER sacrifices locality: the relays need (at least partial) global knowledge. Another strategy considered is the HOPPER strategy, introduced by Kutyłowski and Meyer auf der Heide [14]. Although it features a linear running time, a direct comparison with GO-TO-THE-MIDDLE is difficult: HOPPER does not converge to the optimal chain, uses a different robot model, and allows for deletions of relays during execution. Recently, Degener et al. [4] proposed a strategy in a continuous time model achieving an optimal time bound of $O(n)$.

Our Contribution.

We propose a general class of communication chain strategies, which we call *linear strategies*. Such a strategy can be represented by a linear transformation of the spatial vectors connecting neighboring robots. Moreover, we prove a one-to-one correspondence between natural properties of these transformations and the corresponding strategies. For example, such a strategy will not break the communication link and preserves the optimal chain if and only if the matrix corresponding to the linear transformation is doubly stochastic. Similarly, convergence properties can be characterized by irreducible and aperiodic matrices. Our main result is a surprising correlation between these communication chain strategies and time-homogeneous Markov processes over finite state spaces. Our results not only allow us to identify "good" strategies, but also to easily provide nearly tight upper and lower bounds on quality measures (such as the number of steps needed by the strategy or the maximum distance traveled by the relays). As an application, we provide nontrivial bounds for a generalization of the GO-TO-THE-MIDDLE strategy. The resulting strategies allow for a trade-off between the degree of locality and the different quality measures. For example, if the relays have access to their k next left and right neighbors, a chain of n relays needs at most $\Theta\left(\frac{n^2}{k^2} \log n\right)$ time steps to become nearly optimal. For $k = 1$ (GO-TO-THE-MIDDLE), this closes the logarithmic gap between upper and lower runtime bounds.

1.2 Model & Problem Description

Let us consider $n + 2$ robots $r_0, r_1, \ldots, r_{n+1}$ in the Euclidean plane $\mathbb{R}^2$. The robots r_0 and r_{n+1} are called *base stations* and are assumed to be stationary. The remaining n robots $r_1, r_2, \ldots, r_n$, called *relays*, are mobile and used to establish a communication link between the base stations. Given a robot r_i, the robots r_{i-1} and r_{i+1} are called its left and right *neighbors*, respectively. Time is modeled using discrete steps, starting at time $t = 0$. By $p_i(t) \in \mathbb{R}^2$ we denote the (global) position of robot r_i at time $t \in \mathbb{N}_0$. The vector pointing from base station r_0 to r_{n+1} is denoted by $\mathcal{D} = (\mathcal{D}_X, \mathcal{D}_Y)^T \in \mathbb{R}^2$.

Robot Capabilities.

The robots (especially the relays) are assumed to have very limited abilities. They have no global knowledge and are oblivious (i.e., have no memory). Furthermore, they have a limited communication range $\mathcal{C} > 0$. At any time, the relays have to ensure that the distance between any two neighbors does not exceed the communication range because this would break the communication link between the base stations. Each single relay knows only a limited, local part of its environment, namely the positions of its k next left and right neighbors (i.e., $r_{i-k}, \ldots, r_{i-1}, r_{i+1}, \ldots, r_{i+k}$). Thus, the relays are called k-local ($k \in \mathbb{N}$). At a given time $t \in \mathbb{N}_0$, a relay observes these positions, uses them to compute its next position, and finally moves there. The robots do not need to have identities, but a relay r_i must be able to distinguish its k next left and right neighbors from the remaining robots. Moreover, the robots are not required to have a common coordinate system.

Configurations.

A given placement of the robots is called a *configuration*. Given the position of the first base station r_0, a configuration is uniquely determined by the sequence of (spatial) vectors pointing from each robot to its right neighbor. Thus, defining $\vec{v_i}(t) := p_i(t) - p_{i-1}(t)$ for $i \in \{1, 2, \ldots, n+1\}$ and fixing the first base station, a configuration can be written as $v(t) := (\vec{v_1}(t), \vec{v_2}(t), \ldots, \vec{v_{n+1}}(t))^T$. We consider $v(t)$ as a column vector of $n + 1$ components, each from $\mathbb{R}^2$. In the remainder, we will (w.l.o.g.) assume the first base station to be positioned at the origin. This way, a configuration at time $t \in \mathbb{N}_0$ is uniquely determined by $v(t)$. Note that we can write $\mathcal{D} = \sum_{i=1}^{n+1} \vec{v_i}(t)$ and that this sum is independent of the current time t. If not needed or evident from the context, we omit the time parameter t. We call a configuration v *valid* if $\|\vec{v_i}\|_2 \leq \mathcal{C}$ for all $i \in \{1, 2, \ldots, n+1\}$ (i.e., the communication link is not broken). The number of relays n is called a configuration's *size* and $\sum_{i=1}^{n+1} \|\vec{v_i}\|_2$ its *length*. In the *optimal configuration* $v(\infty) := (\vec{v_1}(\infty), \vec{v_2}(\infty), \ldots, \vec{v_{n+1}}(\infty))^T$, the relays form a straight line between the base stations and are distributed uniformly on this line. More exactly, we have $\vec{v_i}(\infty) = \frac{\mathcal{D}}{n+1}$ for all $i \in \{1, 2, \ldots, n+1\}$. See Figure 1 for an illustration of these notions.

Communication Chain Strategies.

A *communication chain strategy* is an algorithm performed by each single relay. Its goal is to shorten the configuration and eventually reach (or at least converge to) the optimal configuration, while

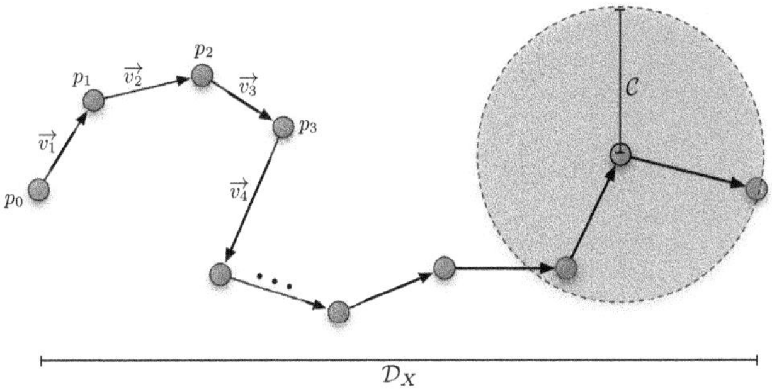

Figure 1: A configuration of size 8 formed by the relays $r_1, r_2, \ldots, r_8$ and base stations r_0 and r_9. The coordinate system is aligned such that $\mathcal{D}_Y = 0$ and $\mathcal{D}_X \geq 0$.

minimizing the number of steps needed and/or the maximum distance traveled by the relays. A strategy is called *valid* if, when applied by relays in a valid configuration, it ends in a valid configuration. It is called *k-local* if it can be applied by k-local relays. Finally, we call a strategy *correct* if it is valid and converges to the optimal configuration for any valid initial configuration $v(0)$ (i.e., $\lim_{t \to \infty} v(t) = v(\infty)$ component-wise).

One of the most simple and intuitive strategies is GO-TO-THE-MIDDLE: each relay moves to the midpoint of the line segment connecting its two neighbors. This strategy is correct, 1-local, and has been shown to need at most $\mathrm{O}\left(n^2 \log n\right)$ and in the worst-case $\Omega\left(n^2\right)$ time steps to reach a nearly optimal configuration [8, 13]. In the following, we define a more general class of communication chain strategies.

Definition 1. A communication chain strategy $\mathfrak{S}$ is said to be *k-linear*, if the new position of a relay is computed as a linear combination of the positions of its k next left and right neighbors.

The GO-TO-THE-MIDDLE strategy is an example for a 1-linear strategy. Note that, since the same algorithm is performed by each single relay and the relays have no identities, the linear combination used for the computation is the same for all relays. The only exception are the *border relays* $r_1, \ldots, r_{k-1}$ and $r_{n+1-(k-1)}, \ldots, r_n$: these can determine their position in the communication chain by counting the number of left/right neighbors. Using global coordinates, the general form of a linear strategy for a non-border relay r_i is given by:

$$p_i(t+1) = p_i(t) + \sum_{\substack{j=-k \\ j \neq 0}}^{k} \alpha_j \cdot \left(p_{i+j}(t) - p_i(t)\right) , \quad (1)$$

with coefficients $\alpha_j \in \mathbb{R}$. This form ensures that the relays can compute their new position in their *local* coordinate systems. In the case of border relays r_i, we have distinct coefficients $\alpha_{i,j}$. For formal reasons, we define additional coefficients $\alpha_{0,j} := 0$, $\alpha_{k,j} := \alpha_j$, and $\alpha_{n+1-k} := \alpha_j$. Note that, for arbitrary coefficients, such a strategy is not necessarily valid or even correct. We will deal with this issue in the course of the next section.

1.3 Structure of the Paper

We start by establishing a connection between linear strategies and matrices representing linear transformations on the spatial vectors connecting neighboring robots in Section 2.1. The correlation is deepened by proving several one-to-one relations between strategies and Markov processes (corresponding to the related linear transformation's matrix) in Section 2.2. This part culminates in

Section 2.3, which proves general bounds on quality measures for linear strategies by means of the mixing time of Markov processes. Section 3 applies the developed framework to analyze a generalization of the GO-TO-THE-MIDDLE strategy, yielding an interesting trade-off between locality and convergence speed.

2. LINEAR STRATEGIES

This section introduces the representation of linear strategies by linear transformations in form of *strategy matrices*. We formulate some basic properties connecting such a representation with the corresponding strategy and show how to use it to derive upper and lower bounds on the number of time steps and the maximal distance traveled by the relays.

2.1 Strategy Matrices

Consider a linear strategy $\mathfrak{S}$ given by the coefficients α_j for non-border relays and $\alpha_{i,j}$ for border relays r_i (cf. Equation (1)). Given a configuration $v := (\vec{v_1}, \vec{v_2}, \ldots, \overrightarrow{v_{n+1}})^T$ and applying one step of the strategy, how does the resulting configuration $v' := (\vec{v_1}', \vec{v_2}', \ldots, \overrightarrow{v_{n+1}}')^T$ look like? Easy computations (using the relation $\vec{v_i} = p_i - p_{i-1}$) lead to the following equation for vectors of non-border relays:

$$\vec{v_i}' = \sum_{\substack{j=-k \\ j \neq 0}}^{k} \alpha_j \cdot \overrightarrow{v_{i+j}} + \vec{v_i} \cdot \left(1 - \sum_{\substack{j=-k \\ j \neq 0}}^{k} \alpha_j\right) . \quad (2)$$

Similar relations can be shown for border relays. For example, in the case of vectors for left border relays (i.e., $i \in \{1, 2, \ldots, k\}$) we get:

$$\begin{aligned}
\vec{v_i}' = & \sum_{l=1}^{i-1} \vec{v_l} \cdot \left(-\sum_{j=-i}^{l-1-i} \alpha_{i,j} + \sum_{j=-i+1}^{l-i} \alpha_{i-1,j}\right) \\
& + \vec{v_i} \cdot \left(1 - \sum_{j=-i}^{-1} \alpha_{i,j} - \sum_{j=1}^{k} \alpha_{i-1,j}\right) \\
& + \sum_{l=i+1}^{i+k} \vec{v_l} \cdot \left(\sum_{j=l-i}^{k} \alpha_{i,j} - \sum_{j=l-i+1}^{k} \alpha_{i-1,j}\right) .
\end{aligned} \quad (3)$$

Thus, v' is a linear expression in the components of configuration v. Letting $\beta_{i,l}$ denote the coefficients for left border relays, $\gamma_{i,l}$ the corresponding coefficients for right border relays, and setting $\delta := 1 - \sum_{j=-k}^{-1} \alpha_j - \sum_{j=1}^{k} \alpha_j$, the linear transformation $\mathbb{R}^{n+1} \to \mathbb{R}^{n+1}$ implied by Equations (2) and (3) (and the corresponding equations for right border relays) can be written as a k-band matrix:

$$S := \begin{pmatrix} \boxed{\beta_{i,l}} \\ \begin{smallmatrix} \alpha_{-k} & \alpha_{-k+1} & \cdots & \alpha_{-1} & \delta & \alpha_1 & \cdots & \alpha_{k-1} & \alpha_k \\ & \alpha_{-k} & \alpha_{k-1} & \cdots & \alpha_{-1} & \delta & \alpha_1 & \cdots & \alpha_{k-1} & \alpha_k \\ & & \ddots & & & & & & & \ddots \\ & & & \alpha_{-k} & \alpha_{k-1} & \cdots & \alpha_{-1} & \delta & \alpha_1 & \cdots & \alpha_{k-1} & \alpha_k \end{smallmatrix} \\ \boxed{\gamma_{i,l}} \end{pmatrix} . \quad (4)$$

We call $S \in \mathbb{R}^{n+1 \times n+1}$ the *strategy matrix* for the linear strategy $\mathfrak{S}$. One step of the linear strategy on a configuration $v(t)$ can now be written as a matrix-vector product: $v(t+1) = S \cdot v(t)$. Thus, starting in a configuration $v(0)$, the relays end in configuration $v(t) = S^t \cdot v(0)$ when applying strategy $\mathfrak{S}$ for t time steps.

It is not too hard to see that the system of linear equations for the $k(3k+1)/2$ coefficients $\beta_{i,l}$ with the $k(3k+1)/2$ variables $\alpha_{i,j}$ defined by Equation (3) is linearly independent. Thus, essentially any matrix of the form given in Equation (4) yields a (kind of) linear strategy. The next subsection provides means to choose the entries such that the resulting strategy is reasonable.

2.2 Strategy Matrices and Markov Chains

So far, we did not consider restrictions on the coefficients α_j and $\alpha_{i,j}$ of a linear strategy $\mathfrak{S}$. For arbitrary real values, the resulting "strategy" needs not to be reasonable: it may be invalid or not even converge to the optimal configuration. Using the strategy matrix $S \in \mathbb{R}^{n+1 \times n+1}$ of $\mathfrak{S}$, we can characterize strategy properties such as validity and convergence by means of natural matrix properties. Especially, as we will see shortly, strategy matrices of correct linear strategies are always doubly stochastic[1]. This allows us to interpret such matrices as the transition matrix of a time-homogeneous, finite Markov chain. The convergence of this Markov chain is directly related to the convergence of the strategy, which will enable us to make use of the rich theory that has been developed for Markov chains. In the remainder, we assume the reader is aware of Markov chain notions such as transition matrix, irreducibility, aperiodicity, or mixing time[2]. A good overview can be found in [15]. The main result of this subsection is the following theorem.

THEOREM 1. *A linear strategy $\mathfrak{S}$ is correct if and only if its strategy matrix is doubly stochastic, irreducible, and aperiodic.*

To prove this result, let us first gather some basic properties of an arbitrary strategy matrix $S \in \mathbb{R}^{n+1 \times n+1}$. For the moment, we will ignore the rather explicit but unhandy characterization given in Equation (4).

PROPOSITION 1. *Consider an arbitrary strategy matrix $S \in \mathbb{R}^{n+1 \times n+1}$ for a linear strategy $\mathfrak{S}$.*

(a) *$\mathfrak{S}$ is valid if and only if $\sum_{j=1}^{n+1} |S_{i,j}| \leq 1$ holds for all i.*

(b) *The optimal configuration is preserved by $\mathfrak{S}$ if and only if $\sum_{j=1}^{n+1} S_{i,j} = 1$ holds for all i.*

(c) *$\mathfrak{S}$ respects the positions of the base stations if and only if $\sum_{i=1}^{n+1} S_{i,j} = 1$ holds for all j.*

(d) *$\mathfrak{S}$ is valid, preserves the optimal configuration, and respects the positions of the base stations if and only if S is doubly stochastic.*

PROOF. (a) If the absolute row sums sum up to at most one and we have a valid configuration v, applying the triangle inequality easily yields $\|(S \cdot v)_i\|_2 \leq \mathcal{C}$ for all $i \in \{1, 2, \ldots, n+1\}$. That is, $\mathfrak{S}$ is valid. For the other direction, assume that there is a row i of S such that its absolute row sum is larger than one. Define configuration v by setting the Y-coordinates of all vectors to zero and the X-coordinate of the j-th vector to $\text{sign}(S_{i,j})\mathcal{C}$. Then, v is valid and one can easily check that $\|(S \cdot v)_i\|_2 > \mathcal{C}$. Thus, $\mathfrak{S}$ is not valid.

(b) Follows immediately from the fact that each component of the optimal configuration $v(\infty)$ equals $\frac{\mathcal{D}}{n+1}$.

----

[1] That is, they contain only non-negative entries and each row *and* column sums up to one.

[2] We give a short, intuitive explanation for the mixing time in Section 2.3

(c) If the column sums of S equal one, an easy computation using $p_{n+1}(t) - p_0(t) = \sum_{i=1}^{n+1} \overrightarrow{v_i}(t)$ yields that $p_{n+1}(t) - p_0(t)$ is independent of t. For the other direction, fix a $k \in \{1, 2, \ldots, n+1\}$ and define configuration $v(0)$ by setting the i-th vector $\overrightarrow{v_i}(0) := (\mathcal{C}, 0)^T$ and all others to $0 \in \mathbb{R}^2$. Now,

$$\overrightarrow{v_k}(0) = \sum_{i=1}^{n+1} \overrightarrow{v_i}(0) = \sum_{i=1}^{n+1} \overrightarrow{v_i}(1)$$

$$= \sum_{i=1}^{n+1} \sum_{j=1}^{n+1} S_{i,j} \overrightarrow{v_j}(0) = \sum_{i=1}^{n+1} S_{i,k} \overrightarrow{v_k}(0)$$

yields $\sum_{i=1}^{n+1} S_{i,k} = 1$.

(d) This follows immediately from (a), (b), and (c). □

The following known results establish a connection between the component-wise limit of matrix powers and Markov chain properties.

LEMMA 1 (OLDENBURGER [18]). *For any complex matrix $A \in \mathbb{C}^{n \times n}$, the component-wise limit $\lim_{t \to \infty} A^t$ exists if and only if the following holds: if λ is an eigenvalue of A, then $\lambda = 1$ or $|\lambda| < 1$; and if 1 is an eigenvalue of A, then its algebraic and geometric multiplicities match.*

LEMMA 2 (ÇINLAR [3, COROLLARY 4.15]). *Given an irreducible transition matrix $P \in \mathbb{R}^{n \times n}$, 1 is a simple eigenvalue of P and any other eigenvalue has absolute value at most one. Furthermore, P is aperiodic if and only if 1 is the only eigenvalue of absolute value one.*

PROOF OF THEOREM 1. Let us first assume $\mathfrak{S}$ to be correct. Then, by definition, it is valid and converges for any valid initial configuration $v(0)$ to the optimal configuration $v(\infty) = (\frac{\mathcal{D}}{n+1})_{i=1}^{n+1}$. More formally, we have $\lim_{t \to \infty} v(t) = \lim_{t \to \infty} (S^t \cdot v(0)) = v(\infty)$. Choosing the (valid) configuration $\overrightarrow{v_i}(0) = (\mathcal{C}, 0)^T$ for a fixed $i \in \{1, 2, \ldots, n+1\}$ and $\overrightarrow{v_j}(0) = 0$ for $j \neq i$, the above equation implies $\lim_{t \to \infty} (S^t)_{i,j} = \frac{1}{n+1}$. We denote the resulting matrix by $S^\infty := \lim_{t \to \infty} S^t$. Note that, for *any* valid initial configuration $v(0)$, we have $S^\infty \cdot v(0) = v(\infty)$. Thus, any correct linear strategy preserves the optimal configuration: $S \cdot v(\infty) = S \cdot (S^\infty \cdot v(0)) = S^\infty \cdot v(0) = v(\infty)$. Now, Proposition 1.(d) implies that S is doubly stochastic. Moreover, S is irreducible (since $\lim_{t \to \infty} S^t = S^\infty > 0$ component-wise). Combining Lemma 1 and Lemma 2, we see that S must be aperiodic (since the component-wise limit $\lim_{t \to \infty} S^t$ exists, $\lambda = 1$ is the only eigenvalue of absolute value one).

For the other direction, assume S to be doubly stochastic, irreducible, and aperiodic. Then, by Proposition 1.(a), S is valid. Let us define $\pi := (\frac{1}{n+1})_1^{n+1} \in \mathbb{R}^{n+1}$. Since S is doubly stochastic, we have $\pi^T \cdot S = \pi$. That is, π is a stationary distribution of S. Because S is furthermore irreducible and aperiodic, the Convergence Theorem (see, e.g., [15, 16]) guarantees that π is unique and that the limit $\lim_{t \to \infty} (S^t)_{i,j}$ exists, is independent of i, and equals $\pi_j = \frac{1}{n+1}$. It is now easy to verify that $\lim_{t \to \infty} v(t) = (\lim_{t \to \infty} S^t) \cdot v(0) = v(\infty)$ for any valid initial configuration $v(0)$. Thus, $\mathfrak{S}$ is correct. □

2.3 General Bounds for Linear Strategies

Given a correct linear strategy $\mathfrak{S}$ and its strategy matrix $S \in \mathbb{R}^{n+1}$, we want to know how fast the configuration $v(t) = S^t \cdot v(0)$

converges to the optimal configuration $v(\infty)$. We investigate two types of convergence: how long it takes until each single vector $\vec{v_i}(t)$ is nearly optimal ($\|\vec{v_i}(t) - \vec{v_i}(\infty)\|_\infty \leq \varepsilon$), and how long it takes until each single relay r_i has nearly reached its optimal position ($\|p_i(t) - p_i(\infty)\|_\infty \leq \varepsilon$). We call the first notion an ε-approximation of the optimal configuration and the second notion an ε-approximation of the optimal positions.

Preliminaries.

In the following, we use $\|\cdot\|_\infty$ to refer to the maximum norm of a vector and to the maximum row sum norm of a matrix. Furthermore, let $\|\mu - \nu\|_{\mathrm{TV}} := \frac{1}{2}\sum_{i=1}^n |\mu_i - \nu_i|$ denote the *total variation distance* of two probability distributions μ and ν over a finite state space of size n. We can interpret any row $P_{i,\cdot}$ of a stochastic matrix $P \in \mathbb{R}^{n\times n}$ as a probability distribution. Given an irreducible and aperiodic stochastic matrix $P \in \mathbb{R}^{n\times n}$ with stationary distribution $\pi \in \mathbb{R}^n$ (i.e., $\pi \cdot P = \pi$), its *distance from stationarity* after t steps is defined as $d(t) := \max_{1\leq i\leq n}\|P^t_{i,\cdot} - \pi\|_{\mathrm{TV}}$. The *mixing time* of a stochastic matrix (or the corresponding Markov chain) is defined as $t_{\mathrm{mix}}(\varepsilon) := \min\{t \in \mathbb{N}_0 \mid d(t) \leq \varepsilon\}$. Intuitively, this formalizes the number of steps it takes until a Markov chain has nearly reached its stationary distribution. See [11] or [15] for a more detailed introduction of these concepts.

THEOREM 2 (UPPER BOUND). *Let $\mathfrak{S}$ denote a correct linear strategy. Then, the strategy $\mathfrak{S}$ needs at most $t_{\mathrm{mix}}\left(\frac{\varepsilon}{2\mathcal{C}}\right)$ time steps to achieve an ε-approximation of the optimal configuration.*

PROOF. Let $S \in \mathbb{R}^{n+1\times n+1}$ denote the strategy matrix of $\mathfrak{S}$ and consider the situation after $t \geq t_{\mathrm{mix}}\left(\frac{\varepsilon}{2\mathcal{C}}\right)$ time steps. Then, we have $d(t) \leq \frac{\varepsilon}{2\mathcal{C}}$. Let $v_X(t)$ denote the restriction of configuration $v(t)$ to the X-coordinates of all vectors $\vec{v_i}(t)$. Furthermore, remember that $S^\infty := \lim_{t\to\infty} S^t$ exists and that all its elements equal $\frac{1}{n+1}$ (see proof of Theorem 1). Exploiting the consistency of the maximum (vector) norm and maximum row sum norm, we get

$$\|v_X(t) - v_X(\infty)\|_\infty = \|(S^t - S^\infty) \cdot v_X(0)\|_\infty$$
$$\leq \|S^t - S^\infty\|_\infty \cdot \|v_X(0)\|_\infty$$
$$= 2d(t) \cdot \|v_X(0)\|_\infty \leq \varepsilon \ .$$

$\square$

THEOREM 3 (LOWER BOUND). *Let $\mathfrak{S}$ denote a correct linear strategy. Then, there exists an initial configuration such that $\mathfrak{S}$ needs at least $t_{\mathrm{mix}}\left(\frac{\varepsilon}{2\mathcal{C}}\right)$ time steps to achieve an ε-approximation of the optimal configuration.*

PROOF. Let $S \in \mathbb{R}^{n+1\times n+1}$ denote the strategy matrix of $\mathfrak{S}$ and consider the situation after $t < t_{\mathrm{mix}}\left(\frac{\varepsilon}{2\mathcal{C}}\right)$ time steps. Then, we have $\|S^t - S^\infty\|_\infty = 2d(t) > \frac{\varepsilon}{\mathcal{C}}$. This implies the existence of an $i \in \{1, 2, \ldots, n+1\}$ such that $\sum_{j=1}^{n+1}|(S^t - S^\infty)_{i,j}| > \frac{\varepsilon}{\mathcal{C}}$. Define the initial configuration $v(0)$ by setting the Y-coordinates of all vectors to zero and the X-coordinates of the j-th vector to $\mathcal{C} \cdot \mathrm{sign}\left(S^t - S^\infty\right)_{i,j}$. One can easily check that this is a valid configuration and $\|\vec{v_i}(t) - \vec{v_i}(\infty)\|_\infty = \sum_{j=1}^{n+1}\mathcal{C} \cdot |(S^t - S^\infty)_{i,j}| > \varepsilon$. $\square$

Applying these theorems for $\frac{\varepsilon}{n}$ and 2ε, respectively, we get:

COROLLARY 1. *Let $\mathfrak{S}$ denote a correct linear strategy. Then:*

(a) To achieve an ε-approximation of the optimal positions, strategy $\mathfrak{S}$ needs at most $t_{\mathrm{mix}}\left(\frac{\varepsilon}{2\mathcal{C}n}\right)$ time steps.

(b) There is an initial configuration such that $\mathfrak{S}$ needs at least $t_{\mathrm{mix}}\left(\frac{\varepsilon}{\mathcal{C}}\right)$ time steps to achieve an ε-approximation of the optimal positions.

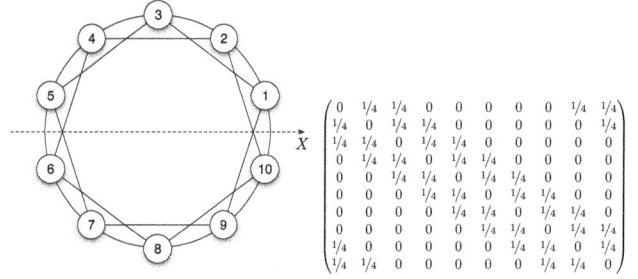

Figure 2: A circular random walk on 10 states with range 2 and its transition matrix $R_{10,2}$.

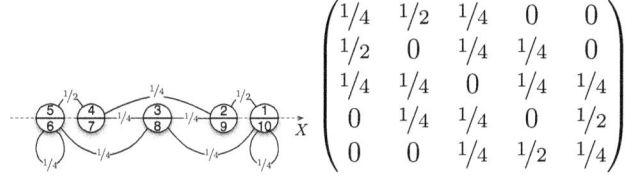

Figure 3: A reflecting random walk on a line of 5 states with range 2 and its transition matrix $S_{4,3}$.

These results give rather general time bounds for any linear communication chain strategy, provided that we know its strategy matrix and can compute or at least bound its mixing time. Section 3 uses this framework to show how a certain class of k-local linear strategies scales with k.

3. TRADING LOCALITY FOR SPEED

Let us use the developed framework to analyze a concrete class of k-linear communication chain strategies $\mathfrak{S}_{n,k}$ for n relays. We define these strategies by their strategy matrices $S_{n,k} \in \mathbb{R}^{n+1\times n+1}$. For this purpose, let us first define a helper matrix $R_{n,k} \in \mathbb{R}^{n\times n}$ ($n, k \in \mathbb{N}$ and $k \leq n$). It is defined as the transition matrix of a circular random walk over n states with range k. See Figure 2 for a more explicit illustration. The strategy matrix $S_{n,k} \in \mathbb{R}^{n+1\times n+1}$ is defined as

$$(S_{n,k})_{i,j} := (R_{2(n+1),k})_{i,j} + (R_{2(n+1),k})_{i,2(n+1)+1-j} \ .$$

This definition corresponds to the random walk on the projection of the graph for $R_{2(n+1),k}$ onto the X-axis (cf. Figures 2 and 3). Note that this projection cuts the number of states from $2(n+1)$ down to $n+1$ by identifying states with the same X-coordinate. It furthermore enable us to give concrete formulas for the eigenvalues of $S_{n,k}$ (Lemma 3). The strategy $\mathfrak{S}_{n,1}$ is GO-TO-THE-MIDDLE. For general k, we get a k-linear strategy. In order to apply the developed framework we have to compute or at least bound the mixing time of $S_{n,k}$. To do so, we use results from [15] to relate the mixing time of certain Markov chains to its spectral gap.

THEOREM 4 ([15, THEOREMS 12.3 AND 12.4]). *Let P denote the transition matrix of a reversible, irreducible, and aperiodic Markov chain over a state space of size n. Furthermore, let $\pi_{\min}$ be the smallest entry of its stationary distribution and $\lambda_* := \max\{|\lambda| \mid 1 \neq \lambda$ eigenvalue of $P\}$ its spectral gap. Then, we have $\left(\frac{1}{1-\lambda_*} - 1\right) \cdot \log\frac{1}{2\varepsilon} \leq t_{\mathrm{mix}}(\varepsilon) \leq \frac{1}{1-\lambda_*} \cdot \ln\frac{1}{\varepsilon \cdot \pi_{\min}}.$*

To obtain bounds for the asymptotic behavior of $\mathfrak{S}_{n,k}$, it remains to bound λ_* of $S_{n,k}$. We first provide formulas for the eigenvalues of $S_{n,k}$ and use these to bound λ_* afterwards.

LEMMA 3. *The eigenvalues λ_j ($j \in \{0, 1, \ldots, n\}$) of $S_{n,k}$ are given by $\lambda_j = \frac{1}{k} \sum_{r=1}^{k} \cos \frac{j \cdot r \cdot \pi}{n+1}$.*

PROOF. We first show how the eigenvalues of $S_{n,k}$ relate to the eigenvalues of $R_{2(n+1),k}$. Let $m := 2(n+1)$ and number the states of the Markov chain corresponding to $R_{m,k}$ from 1 to m. Consider the equivalence relation $\sim$ on $\{1, 2, \ldots, m\}^2$ defined as $i \sim j$ if and only if $i = j$ or $i = m + 1 - j$. This is a projection from m to $n + 1$ states that identifies the i-th state with the i-th state from behind. If $[i]$ denotes the equivalence class of $i \in \{1, 2, \ldots, n + 1\}$, $R_{m,k}$ and this projection induce a Markov chain on $\{[1], [2], \ldots, [n + 1]\}$ in the natural way. Let λ_j for $j \in \{0, 1, \ldots, m - 1\}$ denote the eigenvalues of $R_{m,k}$. The projection described above does preserve the eigenvalues. More exactly, the eigenvalues of $S_{n,k}$ are given by $\lambda_0, \lambda_1, \ldots, \lambda_n$ (see, e.g., [15, Lemma 12.8] for more details). Thus, it is sufficient to show that the lemma's statement holds for all eigenvalues λ_j of $R_{m,k}$. To this end, note that $R_{m,k}$ is a circulant matrix: any row is a right shift of the preceding row. Formulas for eigenvalues of circulant matrices are well known (see, e.g., [1]). We get:

$$\lambda_j = \sum_{r=0}^{m-1} (R_{m,k})_{1,r+1} \cdot e^{\frac{j \cdot r \cdot 2\pi i}{m}}$$

$$= \sum_{r=1}^{k} \frac{1}{2k} e^{\frac{j \cdot r \cdot 2\pi i}{m}} + \sum_{r=1}^{k} \frac{1}{2k} e^{\frac{j \cdot (m-r) \cdot 2\pi i}{m}} \frac{1}{k} \sum_{r=1}^{k} \cos \frac{j \cdot r \cdot \pi}{n+1}$$

for $j \in \{0, 1, \ldots, m - 1\}$. Note that $\lambda_j = \lambda_{m-j}$. $\square$

THEOREM 5. *For $n \geq 8$, the spectral gap λ_* of $S_{n,k}$ fulfills the following inequalities:*

$$1 - \frac{5(k+1)(2k+1)}{6(n+1)^2} \leq \lambda_* \leq 1 - \frac{(k+1)(2k+1)}{3(n+1)^2} \ .$$

PROOF. Let λ_j for $j \in \{0, 1, \ldots, n\}$ denote the eigenvalues of $S_{n,k}$ and consider the equation from Lemma 3. Obviously, $\lambda_0 = 1$ and $|\lambda_j| < 1$ for $j \in \{1, 2, \ldots, n\}$. Moreover, for $1 \leq j \leq \frac{n+1}{2k}$, all cosine arguments lie in the interval $\left(0, \frac{\pi}{2}\right]$. Thus, for these j we have $0 < \lambda_j \leq \lambda_1$. Now, let us consider $j > \frac{n+1}{2k}$. Using the trigonometric identity $\sum_{i=0}^{n-1} \cos(a + i \cdot b) = \frac{\sin nb/2}{\sin b/2} \sin \left(a + \frac{(n-1)b}{2}\right)$ (see, e.g., [12]), we can write

$$\lambda_j = \frac{1}{k} \cdot \sum_{r=1}^{k} \cos \frac{j \cdot r \cdot \pi}{n+1}$$

$$= \frac{1}{k} \frac{\sin \frac{k \cdot j \cdot \pi}{2(n+1)}}{\sin \frac{j \cdot \pi}{2(n+1)}} \cdot \cos \frac{(k+1) \cdot j \cdot \pi}{2(n+1)} \ . \quad (5)$$

In the following, let us assume k to be a power of 2: $k = 2^l$ for some $l \in \mathbb{N}_0$[3]. Applying the trigonometric identity $\sin x = 2 \sin \frac{x}{2} \cos \frac{x}{2}$ l times to the numerator of the fraction of sines in Equation (5), we get

$$\lambda_j = \cos \frac{(k+1) \cdot j \cdot \pi}{2(n+1)} \cdot \prod_{s=1}^{l} \cos \frac{2^{-s} \cdot k \cdot j \cdot \pi}{2(n+1)} \ . \quad (6)$$

For $s \in \{2, 3, \ldots, l\}$, define intervals $I_s := \left[2^{s-3} \frac{n+1}{k}, 2^s \frac{n+1}{k}\right]$. We have $j \in \left(\frac{n+1}{2k}, n\right] \subseteq \left[\frac{n+1}{2k}, n+1\right] = \bigcup_{s=2}^{l} I_s$. This implies the existence of an index $s \in \{2, 3, \ldots, l\}$ such that $j \in I_s$. This is equivalent to $\frac{2^{-s} \cdot k \cdot j \cdot \pi}{2(n+1)} \in \left[\frac{\pi}{16}, \frac{\pi}{2}\right]$. Thus, in the product of cosines

---

[3]Otherwise, choose $l \in \mathbb{N}$ such that $2^{l-1} < k < 2^l$ and adjust the proof accordingly.

in Equation (6), there is one term of the form $\cos x \cdot \cos 2x$ with $x \in \left[\frac{\pi}{16}, \frac{\pi}{2}\right]$. The function $x \mapsto |\cos x \cdot \cos 2x|$ is maximal for $x = \frac{\pi}{16}$. This yields $|\lambda_j| \leq \cos \frac{\pi}{16} \cdot \cos \frac{\pi}{8} =: \alpha \approx 0.906$. Together, we have $|\lambda_j| \leq \max \{\lambda_1, \alpha\}$ for all $j \in \{1, 2, \ldots, n\}$.

Using the inequalities $\cos x \leq 1 - \frac{2}{\pi^2} x^2$ and $\cos x \geq 1 - \frac{5}{\pi^2} x^2$ (both holding for $x \in [0, \pi]$) and the relation $1 \leq k \leq n$, we can bound λ_1 as follows:

$$\lambda_1 = \frac{1}{k} \cdot \sum_{r=1}^{k} \cos \frac{r \cdot \pi}{n+1} \leq \frac{1}{k} \cdot \sum_{r=1}^{k} \left(1 - \frac{2r^2}{(n+1)^2}\right)$$

$$= 1 - \frac{2}{k \cdot (n+1)^2} \sum_{r=1}^{k} r^2 = 1 - \frac{(k+1)(2k+1)}{3(n+1)^2}$$

and

$$\lambda_1 = \frac{1}{k} \cdot \sum_{r=1}^{k} \cos \frac{r \cdot \pi}{n+1} \geq \frac{1}{k} \sum_{r=1}^{k} \left(1 - \frac{5r^2}{(n+1)^2}\right)$$

$$= 1 - \frac{5}{k(n+1)^2} \sum_{r=1}^{k} r^2 = 1 - \frac{5(k+1)(2k+1)}{6(n+1)^2} \ .$$

The lower bound is larger than α for $n \geq 8$. For these n, we get $\lambda_1 = \max \{|\lambda_j| \mid j = 1, 2, \ldots, n\} = \lambda_*$. $\square$

Together, Theorems 4 and 5 yield the following inequalities for the mixing time of $S_{n,k}$ (for $n \geq 8$):

$$t_{\text{mix}}(\varepsilon) \geq \left(\frac{6(n+1)^2}{5(k+1)(2k+1)} - 1\right) \cdot \log \frac{1}{2\varepsilon}$$

and

$$t_{\text{mix}}(\varepsilon) \leq \frac{3(n+1)^2}{(k+1)(2k+1)} \ln \frac{n}{\varepsilon} \ .$$

Combined with Theorems 2 and 3 and Corollary 1, we get the following result:

COROLLARY 2. $\mathfrak{S}_{n,k}$ *needs worst-case time* $O\left(\frac{n^2}{k^2} \log \frac{n}{\varepsilon}\right)$ *and* $\Omega\left(\frac{n^2}{k^2} \log \frac{1}{\varepsilon}\right)$ *to achieve (a) an ε-approximation of the optimal configuration and (b) an ε-approximation of the optimal positions.*

We conjecture that $\Theta\left(\frac{n^2}{k^2} \log \frac{1}{\varepsilon}\right)$ is the tight runtime bound in case (a). For $k = 1$ (GO-TO-THE-MIDDLE), this can be proven by use of more sophisticated bounds on the mixing time of $S_{n,1}$ [11]. The tight bound for case (b) is $\Theta\left(\frac{n^2}{k^2} \log \frac{n}{\varepsilon}\right)$, as stated in the following theorem. In the special case of $k = 1$, this closes the logarithmic gap between upper and lower runtime bound of GO-TO-THE-MIDDLE left in its original analysis [8, 13]. Note that even for $k = \Theta(n)$, $\mathfrak{S}_{n,k}$ needs logarithmic time to achieve nearly optimal positions.

THEOREM 6. $\mathfrak{S}_{n,k}$ *needs time* $\Theta\left(\frac{n^2}{k^2} \log \frac{n}{\varepsilon}\right)$ *to achieve an ε-approximation of the optimal positions. The lower bound holds for $k = k(n)$, where $1 \leq k(n) \leq \frac{n+1}{4}$ grows monotonically.*

PROOF SKETCH. It remains to prove the lower bound. To do so, place both base stations at the origin and distribute the n relays such that all robots together form a circle. We assume the circle's midpoint to lie on the positive Y-axis and the robots to be uniformly distributed along the circle's circumference. Moreover, we can choose these positions such that the circle's radius is linear in n. Now assume for a moment that we replace the base stations with *one* relay having r_1 and r_n as neighbors. In this case, all these $n + 1$ relays would behave *exactly* identical, moving towards the center of the circle. Thus, one step of $\mathfrak{S}_{n,k}$ would simply shrink the circle's radius. Let $r(t)$ denote this radius at time t and observe that, in the case of an ordinary communication chain, a gathering to the origin happens. If we restrict our view to the X-coordinates of all robots, the communication chain behaves *exactly* as the circular chain. Thus, the maximum X-distance of a relay to the origin at time t is given by $r(t)$. We now show that it takes $\Theta\left(\frac{n^2}{k^2}\right)$ time steps to halve $r(t)$. An easy geometric argument yields $r(t+1) = r(t)/k \sum_{j=1}^{k} \cos \frac{j \cdot 2\pi}{n+1}$, and thus (cf. the proof of Theorem 5):

$$r(t+1) = \frac{r(t)}{k} \cdot \frac{\sin \frac{k \cdot \pi}{n+1}}{\sin \frac{\pi}{n+1}} \cdot \cos \frac{(k+1) \cdot \pi}{n+1} =: r(t) \cdot \gamma(n,k) \ .$$

The restriction $k(n) \leq \frac{n+1}{4}$ guarantees that this expression is positive. Considering a time t with $r(t) = r^{(0)}/2$ yields $t = -\frac{1}{\log \gamma(n,k)}$. One can compute

$$\lim_{n \to \infty} t^{-1} \cdot \frac{n^2}{k^2} = \frac{2k^2\pi^2 + 3\pi^2 k + \pi^2}{3k^2} \in \left[\frac{2}{3}\pi^2, 2\pi^2\right] \ ,$$

which yields $t = \Theta\left(\frac{n^2}{k^2}\right)$ for constant k. A more elaborate argument yields the Theorem. $\square$

4. CONCLUSION & FUTURE WORK

We presented a correlation between properties of communication chain strategies and Markov processes. This correlation not only allows for a rather general analysis of the class of linear communication chain strategies, but also enabled us to prove a trade-off between locality constraints (how many of its neighbors does a robot know) and convergence speed for certain strategies. Note that the original analysis of GO-TO-THE-MIDDLE [8] was based on similar techniques, involving convergence properties of *sub*stochastic matrices. However, the authors used a problem representation that did not allow such a direct connection to the well-studied area of Markov chain theory, and did not facilitate such an easy generalization as in our case.

It seems difficult to transfer our approach to other robotic formation problems, as for example gathering. However, if we consider a circular connection of n mobile relays instead of a chain with fixed end points, our techniques yield gathering strategies and similar convergence results as for communication chains [11]. Another interesting question is whether and to what extent adaptive linear strategies, which allow the relays to change the linear transformations during runtime, may help to improve convergence speed. Given the connection between non-adaptive linear strategies and time-homogeneous Markov chains, such adaptive strategies may yield interesting correlations to the theory of time-inhomogeneous Markov chains. The general convergence properties of this kind of Markov processes seem to be much less understood than for time-homogeneous processes. However, under some (strong) assumptions (see, e.g., [19]) convergence results are possible.

References

[1] Albrecht Böttcher and Sergei M. Grudsky. *Spectral Properties of Banded Toeplitz Matrices*. Society for Industrial and Applied Mathematics, Philadelphia, PA, USA, 2005. ISBN 0898715997.

[2] Oleg Burdakov, Patrick Doherty, Kaj Holmberg, Jonas Kvarnström, and Per-Magnus Olsson. Positioning unmanned aerial vehicles as communication relays for surveillance tasks. *The International Journal of Robotics Research*, 29(8), April 2010. doi: 10.1177/0278364910369463.

[3] Erhan Çinlar. *Introduction to Stochastic Processes*. Prentice-Halll, Inc., 1975.

[4] Bastian Degener, Barbara Kempkes, Peter Kling, and Friedhelm Meyer auf der Heide. A continuous, local strategy for constructing a short chain of mobile robots. In *Proceedings of the 17th International Colloquium on Structural Information and Communication Complexity (SIROCCO)*, 2010.

[5] Bastian Degener, Barbara Kempkes, and Friedhelm Meyer auf der Heide. A local O(n^2) gathering algorithm. In *Proceedings of the 22th Annual ACM Symposium on Parallel Algorithms and Architectures (SPAA)*, New York, USA, 2010. ACM Press.

[6] Bastian Degener, Barbara Kempkes, Friedhelm Meyer auf der Heide, Peter Pietrzyk, Tobias Langner, and Roger Wattenhofer. A tight runtime bound for synchronous gathering of autonomous robots with limited visibility. In *this conference*, 2011.

[7] Yoann Dieudonné and Franck Petit. Self-stabilizing deterministic gathering. In Shlomi Dolev, editor, *Proceedings of the 5th International Workshop on Algorithmic Aspects of Wireless Sensor Networks (ALGOSENSORS)*, volume 5804, pages 230–241, 2009. doi: 10.1007/978-3-642-05434-1_23.

[8] Miroslaw Dynia, Jarosław Kutyłowski, Paweł Lorek, and Friedhelm Meyer auf der Heide. Maintaining communication between an explorer and a base station. In Yi Pan, Franz Rammig, Hartmut Schmeck, and Mauricio Solar, editors, *Biologically Inspired Cooperative Computing*, volume 216 of *IFIP International Federation for Information Processing*, pages 137–146. Springer Boston, 2006. ISBN 978-0-387-34632-8. doi: 10.1007/978-0-387-34733-2_14.

[9] Miroslaw Dynia, Jarosław Kutyłowski, Friedhelm Meyer auf der Heide, and Jonas Schrieb. Local strategies for maintaining a chain of relay stations between an explorer and a base station. In *Proceedings of the 19th Annual ACM Symposium on Parallel Algorithms and Architectures (SPAA)*, pages 260–269, New York, USA, January 2007. ACM Press. ISBN 978-1-59593-667-7. doi: 10.1145/1248377.1248420.

[10] Taisuke Izumi, Tomoko Izumi, Sayaka Kamei, and Fukuhito Ooshita. Randomized gathering of mobile robots with local-multiplicity detection. In *Proceedings of the 11th International Symposium on Stabilization, Safety, and Security of Distributed Systems (SSS)*, pages 384–398, Berlin, Heidelberg, 2009. Springer-Verlag. ISBN 978-3-642-05117-3. doi: 10.1007/978-3-642-05118-0_27.

[11] Peter Kling. Unifying the analysis of communication chain strategies. Master's thesis, University of Paderborn, May 2010.

[12] Michael P. Knapp. Sines and cosines of angles in arithmetic progression. *Mathematics Magazine*, 82(5):371–372(2), December 2009. doi: 10.4169/193009809X468724.

[13] Jarosław Kutyłowski. *Using Mobile Relays for Ensuring Connectivity in Sparse Networks*. PhD thesis, International Graduate School of Dynamic Intelligent Systems, December 2007.

[14] Jarosław Kutyłowski and Friedhelm Meyer auf der Heide. Optimal strategies for maintaining a chain of relays between an explorer and a base camp. *Theoretical Computer Science*, 410 (36):3391–3405, 2009. ISSN 0304-3975.

[15] David A. Levin, Yuval Perres, and Elizabeth L. Wilmer. *Markov Chains and Mixing Times*. American Mathematical Society, December 2008. ISBN 978-0-8218-4739-8.

[16] Michael Mitzenmacher and Eli Upfal. *Probability and Computing*. Cambridge University Press, 2005. ISBN 0-521-83540-2.

[17] H. G. Nguyen, N. Pezeshkian, A. Gupta, and N. Farrington. Maintaining communication link for a robot operating in a hazardous environment. In *Proceedings of the 10th International Conference on Robotics and Remote Systems for Hazardous Environments*, pages 28–31, 2004.

[18] Rufus Oldenburger. Infinite powers of matrices and characteristic roots. *Duke Mathematical Journal*, 6(2):357–361, 1940. doi: 10.1215/S0012-7094-40-00627-5.

[19] L. Saloff-Coste and J. Zúñiga. Convergence of some time inhomogeneous markov chains via spectral techniques. *Stochastic Processes and their Applications*, 117(8):961–979, 2007. ISSN 0304-4149. doi: 10.1016/j.spa.2006.11.004.

[20] Kazuo Sugihara and Ichiro Suzuki. Distributed motion coordination of multiple mobile robots. In *Proceedings of the 5th IEEE International Symposium on Intelligent Control (ISIC)*, volume 1, pages 138–143, September 1990.

[21] Ichiro Suzuki and Masafumi Yamashita. Distributed anonymous mobile robots: Formation of geometric patterns. *SIAM Journal on Computing*, 28(4):1347–1363, 1999.

The Car Sharing Problem

Patrick Briest
Heinz Nixdorf Institute
& Dept. of Computer Science
University of Paderborn
Fürstenallee 11
Paderborn, Germany
patrick.briest@upb.de

Christoph Raupach[*]
Heinz Nixdorf Institute
& Dept. of Computer Science
University of Paderborn
Fürstenallee 11
Paderborn, Germany
craupach@gmail.com

ABSTRACT

We consider a novel type of metric task system, termed the
car sharing problem, in which the operator of a car sharing
program aims to serve the requests of customers occurring
at different locations. Requests are modeled as a stochastic
process with known parameters and a request is served if a
car is located at the position of its occurrence at this time.
Customers pay the service provider according to the distance
they travel and similarly the service provider incurs cost
proportional to the distance traveled when relocating a car
from one position to another between requests.

We derive an efficient algorithm to compute a redistribution policy that yields average long-term revenue within a
factor of 2 of optimal and provide a complementing proof
of APX-hardness. Considering a variation of the problem
in which requests occur simultaneously in all locations, we
arrive at an interesting repeated balls-into-bins process, for
which we prove bounds on the average number of occupied
bins.

Categories and Subject Descriptors

F.2.0 [**Theory of Computation**]: Analysis of Algorithms
and Problem Complexity: General

General Terms

Algorithms, Theory

Keywords

Metric Task Systems, Queuing Networks, Approximation
Algorithms

1. INTRODUCTION

In a world of limited natural resources and an ever increasing demand for individual mobility, car sharing schemes have

---

[*]Currently affiliated with Google Germany.

been gaining importance as an urban means of transportation. Recently, both car manufacturers and independent
companies have started to install car sharing programs in
many major cities worldwide.

Most of these programs work roughly like this: Once registered, customers can call a hotline or use a web based
service to locate available cars, which they can access using
their member card. Upon arriving at their destination, they
leave the car at a designated parking spot or just park it
anywhere on the road. In the latter case, GPS based systems can be used to keep track of a car's location and route
customers to their closest vehicle. Billing happens automatically based on the distance traveled.

A major concern in the operation of such a car sharing
scheme consists of keeping the fleet of cars well distributed
within the city limits. It might, for example, be the case
that on an average Saturday morning, customers tend to
take the bus to get to the shopping mall and, a few hours
later, would like to have car in order to take their purchases
home. Thus, in general we expect the occurring customer
requests to be quite asymmetric and eventually lead to a
somewhat unfavorable (i.e., unbalanced) distribution of the
cars. Consequently, one needs a means of redistributing cars
(e.g., taking them out to the mall around noon on a Saturday) to avoid this kind of scenario.

To this end, companies can employ staff to relocate cars
based on the expected future customer requests. Of course,
this redistribution process does come at a cost, and so from
a company's point of view it is desirable to find the right
balance between relocating a car and waiting for a customer
to appear and take care of it instead.

In this paper, we initiate the investigation of this type of
problem from an algorithmic point of view. We model customer requests as a random process with known parameters
and assume that the cost of relocating a car is proportional
to the distance it is moved. For this setting, we devise an
efficient 2-approximation algorithm for maximizing the car
sharing scheme's long term average revenue. Before we describe our contribution in more detail, let us define the problem formally.

1.1 Model and Preliminaries

(**Metric**) **Continuous-Time Car Sharing.** A *continuous-time instance* of the *car sharing problem* is a tuple
$(n, m, d, R, \alpha, (\mu_i)_{i \in [n]})$, where $[n]$ is the set of locations
(*nodes*), $[m]$ is the set of cars, $d : [n] \times [n] \to \mathbb{R}^{>0}$ is a
distance function on $[n]$, $R \in \mathbb{R}^{n \times n}$ is a stochastic matrix

describing the probability of a request occurring between any two nodes (*request matrix*), $\alpha \in \mathbb{R}^+$ is the *reward factor* and μ_i is the mean time between two requests at node $i \in [n]$ (*request time*). A continuous-time instance is called *metric* if the distance function defines a metric on $[n]$.

We model the occurrence of requests for a node $i \in [n]$ by a Poisson process with rate $\frac{1}{\mu_i}$, where μ_i is the mean time between two requests occurring. Whenever a request occurs at node u, its target node v is a random variable distributed according to R_u (the u-th row of the request matrix). Since the requests are generated by Poisson processes the mean time between two requests is distributed exponentially for each node of an instance I.

States. For a given instance $I = (n, m, d, R, \alpha, (\mu_i)_{i \in [n]})$, a *state* p is a function $p : [m] \to [n]$, which associates cars with their location $i \in [n]$. The state at the beginning of time-step t is denoted by p_t. The set of all states is denoted by $\mathcal{S}(I) = \{p \mid p : [m] \to [n]\}$ with $|\mathcal{S}(I)| = n^m$.

Policies. A redistribution policy defines a target state $t \in \mathcal{S}(I)$ for each possible state $p \in \mathcal{S}(I)$ to be established via relocation of some of the cars. Formally, a *policy* π for an instance I is a function $\pi : \mathcal{S}(I) \to \mathcal{S}(I)$. The set of all possible policies for an instance I is denoted as $\mathcal{P}(I)$, or simply as $\mathcal{P}$ if there is no danger of confusion.

In the continuous-time car sharing process, whenever a request occurs, the policy is applied and cars are relocated accordingly. If a car serves a request between nodes $u, v \in [n]$, we receive a reward of $(1 + \alpha) \cdot d(u, v)$. If the policy relocates a car from node u to v we incur a cost of $d(u, v)$. For a given policy π we define the *gain* of the policy as the time-average of the reward minus its cost. Our goal is to find a policy with maximum gain[1].

1.2 Related Work

We are not aware of any existing literature addressing the problem considered in this paper as such. However, general metrical task systems, i.e., the problem of servicing various kinds of customer requests occurring in a metric space via a number of vehicles or similar devices, are of course well studied from several perspectives.

In the simplest case, requests can be served *in place*, i.e. without causing additional movement of the service device. When requests are modeled in an adversarial fashion and service devices can be moved to the location of the request *after* it occurs, this corresponds to the classic k-server-problem [9, 10], a paradigmatic problem in the competitive analysis of online algorithms.

In the *taxi problem*, which has received considerable attention in the operations research community, service devices are taxis and, contrary to the k-server scenario, servicing a customer request causes the service to move to a different location. In the existing literature [5, 13], requests are generally modeled as stochastic processes. We are not aware of any rigorous analytical results addressing the existence of efficient approximation algorithms for this kind of problem.

Other papers in this area address similar questions regarding the positioning and dispatching of ambulances or fire engines [5, 11].

As we point out in more detail below and in Section 4, the discrete-time version of our problem, in which requests occur simultaneously at discrete points in time, is intimately related to questions of load balancing [1, 4] and, in particular, balls-into-bins processes [12, 14]. Our problem leads to the investigation of statistics of a repeated version of these processes, which to the best of our knowledge has not been addressed before in this form.

1.3 Our Contributions

In this paper, we initiate the investigation of the car sharing problem defined above, which differs from other previously investigated servicing problems in the fact that we are not allowed to react to customer requests after they occur by moving a car to the place of occurrence. This is in contrast to both the k-sever problem in online algorithms and taxi or ambulance dispatch problems considered in the OR community. We note that due to this characteristic of the problem, modeling customer requests adversarially does seem to be a somewhat problematic approach and, thus, we adopt a stochastic model as commonly used in OR.

In Section 2, we present an efficient approximation algorithm for the car sharing problem that achieves an approximation guarantee of 2 for the average long term revenue. The algorithm returns a simple probabilistic policy which redistributes cars from each node according to a fixed (node-specific) probability distribution. This is obtained by first solving a linear program that returns an upper bound on the optimal *flow rates* between nodes, i.e., the average number of cars traveling along a certain edge per time unit under an optimal redistribution policy, either due to customer requests or because of a relocation. We then interpret the (normalized) resulting relocation flow rates as probabilities for the random relocation process described above and use results from the theory of closed queuing networks to analyze the resulting congestion, which then allows us to lower bound the average gain in terms of the flow rates found by the LP.

In Section 3 we show that the problem of computing an optimal redistribution policy, or in fact even its value, is APX-hard and, thus, does not allow approximation within arbitrary constant factors. The result is based on a reduction from the set packing problem. From a technical perspective, the main difficulty here lies in the fact that we need to encode the problem using a stochastic process generating the customer requests and that we have to argue about arbitrary redistribution policies, which might not even be encodable in polynomial space.

In Section 4 we discuss a variation of the problem, in which we assume that requests occur simultaneously at all nodes at equal time intervals. In this *discrete-time* version, our general analysis cannot be applied, because the (P)ASTA ((Poisson) arrivals see time average) property, on which our analysis heavily relies, is not satisfied for discrete-time queuing networks. However, we analyze the special case of uniform requests, which corresponds to the following balls-into-bins process: In the first round, place each of n balls independently uniformly at random in one of n bins. In each step thereafter, take one ball out of every non-empty bin and place it independently uniformly at random in one of the

---

[1] Note, that in general the gain of a policy π may depend on the starting state. However, it is not difficult to argue that this is not the case for optimal policies and, thus, the optimal gain achievable on a given instance is well defined independently of the initial configuration of the system.

bins. We prove a lower bound on the fraction of non-empty bins, which approaches $2 - \sqrt{2}$ as $n \to \infty$. Experiments we performed suggest that this bound, which is slightly below the value of $1 - 1/e$ one obtains in a single round, is tight. This is somewhat surprising, as even in the repeated process the location of each individual ball remains uniformly distributed at all times. This result might be of interest independently from its application in the car sharing problem.

2. A 2-APPROXIMATION ALGORITHM

Let $I = (n, m, d, R, \alpha, (\mu_i)_{i \in [n]})$ be a continuous-time instance of the car sharing problem and assume for now that $\mu_i = 1$ for all $i \in [n]$, i.e., requests at all nodes appear with rate 1. We will define a policy LP-Flow based on the following linear program (LP 1), non-negativity constraints omitted:

$$\text{max.} \sum_{u,v \in [n]} (1 + \alpha)d(u,v)r_{uv} - \sum_{u,v \in [n]} d(u,v)m_{uv} \quad (1)$$

$$\text{s.t.} \sum_{u \in [n]} m_{vu} \le y_v \qquad \forall v \in [n] \quad (2)$$

$$r_{vu} \le R[v,u] \qquad \forall u,v \in [n] \quad (3)$$

$$r_{vu} \le R[v,u]x_v \qquad \forall u,v \in [n] \quad (4)$$

$$\sum_{u \in [n]} r_{vu} \le x_v \qquad \forall v \in [n] \quad (5)$$

$$y_v = x_v + \sum_{u \in [n]} r_{uv} - \sum_{u \in [n]} r_{vu} \qquad \forall v \in [n] \quad (6)$$

$$x_v = y_v + \sum_{u \in [n]} m_{uv} - \sum_{u \in [n]} m_{vu} \qquad \forall v \in [n] \quad (7)$$

$$\sum_{v \in [n]} x_v \le m \quad (8)$$

We interpret the r_{uv} and m_{uv} variables of LP1 as describing the average number of cars moving between nodes u and v per time unit due to customer requests or the redistribution policy in place, respectively. Variable x_v and y_v correspond to the average number of cars at node v when a request occurs in any location and after a request has been served. It is straightforward to argue that these quantities as resulting from any feasible policy satisfy constraints (2) - (8) and, thus, the optimal solution to LP1 defines an upper bound on the optimal gain achievable on instance I.

PROPOSITION 2.1. *The optimal solution to LP1 is an upper bound on the gain of any redistribution policy for continuous-time car sharing instance I.*

The LP-Flow Policy. Policy LP-Flow is a randomized policy based on the solution to LP1. Every time a request moves a car from a node u to a node v, we immediately relocate the car to a random target node w sampled from distribution $p_{vw} = m_{vw}/y_v$. Note, that this may include some probability for not relocating the car at all, if $m_{vv} > 0$ in the optimal LP solution. The LP-Flow policy has the special property, that cars are relocated independently from every node. We refer to this kind of policy as *node oblivious*.

The key to the analysis of the LP-Flow policy's gain lies in the observation that the resulting dynamics are intimately related to the behavior of closed queuing networks.

Corresponding Queuing Networks. Consider a randomized node oblivious policy π for a car sharing instance I. Let $\pi(i, j)$ be the move probability from $i \in [n]$ to $j \in [n]$ The *corresponding queuing network* $Q_{I,\pi} = \{q_1, \ldots, q_n\}$ for I under π is a closed queuing network with n queues. We call q_i the *corresponding queue* to node $i \in [n]$ in I. Each queue q_i has exponentially distributed service time with mean μ_i. The transition probability between queues $q_i, q_j \in Q_{I,\pi}$ is p_{ij} where p_{ij} is defined as $p_{ij} = \sum_{w \in [n]} R[i, w] \cdot \pi(w, j)$.

Clearly, for a randomized node oblivious policy π like LP-Flow, the distribution of cars on the nodes of an instance I equals the distribution of jobs in the queues of its corresponding queuing network. A car that gets a request in I moves from its node i to a node w according to request matrix R and is then immediately moved to a node j according to π. Consequently, the probability that a car located at node i moves to node j is exactly p_{ij}.

Closed queuing networks with exponentially distributed service times are very well researched. In [8] and [6], *product form* queuing networks are introduced for both open and closed systems. An important result for these networks is the Arrival Theorem shown in [15], which will be of use when proving bounds for the car sharing problem.

THEOREM 2.2 (ARRIVAL THEOREM [15]). *Consider a closed queuing network $Q = \{q_1, \ldots, q_n\}$ with m jobs and transition probabilities p_{ij} between queues q_i, q_j. For each queue q_i let the service time be distributed exponentially with mean μ_i. Let $\overline{R}_i(m)$ be the mean response time of a fixed job at queue q_i if m jobs are in the system. Let $\overline{L}_i(m)$ be the mean number of jobs at queue q_i if m jobs are in the system. Then it holds for all $i \in [n]$ that $\overline{R}_i(m) = \mu_i \cdot \left(1 + \overline{L}_i(m-1)\right)$.*

Informally, Theorem 2.2 states that in a system with m jobs, when arriving at queue j each job sees an average queue length equal to the average length of queue j in a system with $m-1$ jobs. This property is guaranteed by the fact that service times (and, thus, arrival times) are determined by Poisson processes. In other words, *Poisson arrivals see time averages* or PASTA, for short. Finally, another important definition in the context of queuing networks are *visit ratios*, which we introduce next.

Visit Ratios [3]. Consider a closed connected queuing network $Q = \{q_1, \ldots, q_n\}$. Let λ_i be the *arrival rate* (the average number of jobs arriving per time unit) of queue $q_i \in Q$, and let λ be the *throughput* of the queuing network, i.e., the average number of jobs served per time unit. Then the *visit ratio* e_i of queue q_i is defined by $e_i = \lambda_i/\lambda$. In a closed queuing network the visit ratio can also be computed directly from the transition probabilities p_{ij} by solving the equation system defined by $e_i = \sum_{j=1}^n e_j p_{ji}$ for all $i \in [n]$, $\sum_{i=1}^n e_i = 1$.

2.1 Analysis

This section analyzes the dynamics of the LP-Flow policy on continuous-time instances with $\mu_i = 1$ for all $i \in [n]$. As a technicality we will usually assume that the corresponding queuing network for an instance is connected. However, extending the proofs to non-connected networks is straightforward, as the individual connected components can be treated separately.

The central theorem of this section is Theorem 2.7, which states that the mean response time for the queuing network corresponding to a continuous-time instance I with m cars and n nodes is at most $1 + (m-1)/m$. This immediately yields a bound of 2 on the approximation guarantee obtained by our randomized policy LP-Flow, as stated formally in Theorem 2.3 below.

THEOREM 2.3. *Let $I = (n, m, d, R, \alpha, (\mu_i)_{i\in[n]})$ be a metric car sharing instance. Then policy LP-Flow yields a gain within a factor of 2 of the optimal policy's gain.*

As already mentioned above, in this section we will only prove Theorem 2.3 for the special case that for all $i \in [n]$ it holds that $\mu_i = 1$. This case can be extended to cover general mean waiting times as described in Section 2.2.

The following Lemmas 2.4, 2.5, and 2.6 establish that the visit ratio of any node in a queuing network corresponding to an instance of the car sharing problem with $m \leq n$ cars is $1/m$. This will be enough to prove Theorem 2.7 for the case that $m \leq n$. For $m > n$, it is easy to check that the value of an optimal solution to LP1 is not larger than for $m = n$, which implies Theorem 2.3 for values $m > n$, as well.

LEMMA 2.4. *Consider a metric car sharing instance $I = (n, m, d, R, \alpha, (\mu_i)_{i\in[n]})$, such that $m \leq n$. Then there exists an optimal solution of LP1, such that $x_v \leq 1$ for all $v \in [n]$.*

PROOF. Intuitively, as on average only a single request occurs at each node per time unit, the objective function value of any solution to LP1 cannot be improved by keeping more than a single car at any node.

More formally, consider an optimal solution to LP1 for car sharing instance I and assume that there exists a node $v \in [n]$ such that $x_v = 1 + \varepsilon$ for some $\varepsilon > 0$. We claim that we can reduce both x_v and y_v by ε without violating any constraint. We first note that, for $x_v \geq 1$, Constraints (4) are dominated by (3). Also, Constraints (3) imply $\sum_{u \in [n]} r_{vu} \leq 1$, because R is a stochastic matrix, and so the claim follows easily for Constraints (3) through (8).

It remains to show that Constraint (2) is not violated. If $m_{vu} > 0$ for any $u \neq v$, then it holds w.l.o.g. that $m_{wv} = 0$ for all $w \neq v$. If this was not the case and $\delta = \min\{m_{wv}, m_{vu}\} > 0$ for some $u, w \neq v$, we could decrease m_{wv} and m_{vu} by δ and increase m_{wu} by the same amount. Since $d(w, u) \leq d(w, v) + d(v, u)$ by the triangle inequality, this would only decrease the objective function value of the solution.

Fix node v. If $m_{uv} = 0$ for all $u \in [n]$, then Constraint (2) is trivially satisfied. As argued above, if $m_{uv} > 0$ for some $u \neq v$, then Constraint (7) guarantees that

$$x_v = y_v - \sum_{u \in [n]} m_{vu},$$

and, thus, decreasing y_v by $\varepsilon < x_v$ cannot violate Constraint (2), which finishes the proof. $\square$

Lemma 2.5 establishes the distribution of target nodes v for a car serving a request from a fixed node u under a policy π. This will help us proving the visit ratios for the corresponding queuing network.

LEMMA 2.5. *Consider a metric car-sharing instance $I = (n, m, d, R, \alpha, (\mu_i)_{i\in[n]})$, and let π be the LP-Flow policy for*

I. If a node $u \in [n]$ is selected randomly with probability $x_u/(\sum_{k\in[n]} x_k)$ and a car is placed at this node, then the probability that the car reaches node v after serving the first occurring request at u and being relocated according to π is $x_v/(\sum_{k\in[n]} x_k)$.

PROOF. Consider the random experiment described above, where the car is initially placed at each node u with probability $x_u/(\sum_{k\in[n]} x_k)$. The probability to reach node $w \in [n]$ with the first occurring request is

$$\sum_{u \in [n]} \frac{x_u}{\sum_{k\in[n]} x_k} \cdot R[u, w].$$

Note, that in an optimal solution to LP1 it holds w.l.o.g. that $r_{uw} = R[u, w] \cdot x_u$. Hence, we may rewrite the above as

$$\sum_{u \in [n]} \frac{r_{uw}}{\sum_{k\in[n]} x_k} = \frac{\sum_{u\in[n]} r_{uw}}{\sum_{k\in[n]} x_k}.$$

Now, recall that policy LP-Flow relocates a car from node w to node v with probability $\pi(w, v) = m_{wv}/y_w$ upon its arrival at w. To simplify notation, we assume that $m_{ww} = y_w - \sum_{v \neq w} m_{wv}$. Now, the probability $\Pr[v]$ to reach v after serving a request and invoking π can be written as

$$\Pr[v] = \sum_{w \in [n]} \frac{\sum_{u\in[n]} r_{uw}}{\sum_{k\in[n]} x_k} \cdot \frac{m_{wv}}{y_w}.$$

Since $y_w = x_w + \sum_{u\in[n]} r_{uw} - \sum_{u\in[n]} r_{wu}$ by Constraint (6), we obtain

$$\Pr[v] = \frac{1}{\sum_{k\in[n]} x_k} \sum_{w \in [n]} m_{wv} \frac{\sum_{u\in[n]} r_{uw}}{x_w + \sum_{u\in[n]} r_{uw} - \sum_{u\in[n]} r_{wu}}.$$

It is not difficult to see that in an optimal solution to LP1 it holds w.l.o.g. that $x_w = \sum_{u\in[n]} r_{wu}$. Thus, we can simplify to

$$\Pr[v] = \frac{1}{\sum_{k\in[n]} x_k} \sum_{w \in [n]} m_{wv}.$$

Case 1: $\exists w \neq v : m_{wv} > 0$. By the triangle inequality, if there exists $w \neq v$ with $m_{wv} > 0$, all m_{vw} are equal to 0 for $v \neq w$ in a optimal solution to LP1 as argued in the proof of Lemma 2.4. In this case, it holds that $x_v = y_v + \sum_{w \neq v} m_{wv}$. Now recall that we defined $m_{vv} = y_v - \sum_{w\neq v} m_{vw}$, which simplifies to $m_{vv} = y_v$. It follows that $\sum_{w\in[n]} m_{wv} = x_v$ and we obtain $\Pr[v] = x_v/(\sum_{k\in[n]} x_k)$.

Case 2: $\forall w \neq v : m_{wv} = 0$: If there is no $w \neq v$ with $m_{wv} > 0$, it holds that $x_v = y_v - \sum_{w\neq v} m_{vw}$. Again, we have $m_{vv} = y_v - \sum_{w\neq v} m_{vw}$ by definition. Thus,

$$\sum_{w\in[n]} m_{wv} = m_{vv} + \sum_{w\neq v} m_{wv} = x_v,$$

and it follows that $\Pr[v] = x_v/(\sum_{k\in[n]} x_k)$. $\square$

Applying Lemma 2.5 and using the fact that transition probabilities in the corresponding queuing network are determined by the probabilities of moving between nodes via a single request and a subsequent invocation of the random relocation policy in the car sharing instance, we can now bound the visit ratios in the queuing network.

LEMMA 2.6. *Consider the corresponding queuing network $Q = \{q_1, \ldots, q_n\}$ of a car sharing instance $I =*

$(n, m, d, R, \alpha, (\mu_i)_{i\in[n]})$ with $m \le n$ and $\mu_i = 1$ for all $i \in [n]$. For the visit ratio e_i of each queue q_i, it holds that

$$e_i = \frac{x_i}{\sum_{k\in[n]} x_k} \le \frac{1}{m}.$$

PROOF. Recall that we can compute visit ratios of queues in a closed queuing network by solving the system

$$e_v = \sum_{u\in[n]} e_u \cdot p_{uv} \quad \forall v \in [n] \tag{9}$$

$$\sum_{v\in[n]} e_v = 1 \tag{10}$$

of linear equalities, where p_{uv} is the transition probability between queues u and v. Alternatively, we can think of p_{uv} as the probability that a car located at node u reaches node v after serving the first occurring request at u and being relocated according to policy π subsequently.

Thus, by Lemma 2.5, (9) and (10) are satisfied by choosing $e_v = x_v/(\sum_{k\in[n]} x_k)$. Using that w.l.o.g. $\sum_{k\in[n]} x_k = m$ yields the claim. $\square$

With the visit ratios established, we can now use the Arrival Theorem 2.2 to show that the mean response times in a queuing network corresponding to a car sharing instance with $m \le n$ cars are bounded by $1 + (m-1)/m$.

THEOREM 2.7. *Consider a closed connected queuing network $Q = \{q_1, \ldots, q_n\}$ with $m \le n$ jobs corresponding to a car sharing instance $I = (n, m, d, R, \alpha, (\mu_i)_{i\in[n]})$ with $\mu_i = 1$ for all $i \in [n]$. Let p_{ij} be the transition probabilities between queues $q_i, q_j \in Q$. Then the mean response time of any fixed job in the queuing network is at most*

$$1 + \frac{m-1}{m}.$$

PROOF. Fix some job and let $\overline{R}_i(m)$ be the mean response time of this job at queue q_i, $\overline{L}_i(m)$ the mean number of jobs at queue q_i when there is a total of m jobs in the system. By the Arrival Theorem 2.2 and using that $\mu_i = 1$ for all $i \in [n]$, it holds that

$$\overline{R}_i(m) = 1 + \overline{L}_i(m-1).$$

By Lemma 2.6, we have $e_i \le 1/m$ for the visit ratio of each queue q_i. Thus, we can write the mean response time of the job as

$$
\begin{aligned}
\overline{R}(m) &= \sum_{i=1}^{n} e_i \overline{R}_i(m) \\
&= \sum_{i=1}^{n} e_i \left(1 + \overline{L}_i(m-1)\right) \\
&\le 1 + \frac{1}{m} \sum_{i=1}^{n} \overline{L}_i(m-1) \\
&= 1 + \frac{m-1}{m},
\end{aligned}
$$

where the final equality uses the fact that the sum of mean queue lengths equals the number of jobs in the system. $\square$

Finally, we can apply Theorem 2.7 to the corresponding queuing networks of car sharing instances with mean request intervals $\mu_i = 1$ for all $i \in [n]$ to prove Theorem 2.3 for this special case.

PROOF OF THEOREM 2.3. Given a car sharing instance $I = (n, m, d, R, \alpha, (\mu_i)_{i\in[n]})$, let $(x_v), (y_v), (r_{uv}), (m_{uv})$ be an optimal solution to LP1 and let opt denote its objective function value. Let π be the associated LP-Flow policy and $Q_{I,\pi}$ the corresponding queuing network.

Fix a car and its corresponding job in $Q_{I,\pi}$. Recall that w.l.o.g. $\sum_{k\in[n]} x_k = m$. By the definition of π, the car alternates between serving requests and being relocated according to π (we count leaving the car at the destination of a request as relocating it). By the visit ratios established in Lemma 2.6, an x_u/m fraction of requests served by the car originate at node u. Thus, requests between any two nodes u and v account for a

$$\frac{x_u}{m} \cdot R[u, v] = \frac{r_{uv}}{m}$$

fraction of the requests served by the car. Consequently, the frequency of arrivals at any node u after serving a request is y_u/m and, thus, relocations from node u to a node v account for a

$$\frac{y_u}{m} \cdot \frac{m_{uv}}{y_u} = \frac{m_{uv}}{m}$$

fraction of relocations of the car.

Finally, by Theorem 2.7, on average a car waits at most 2 time units for its next request after being relocated, and so each car achieves a gain of

$$
\begin{aligned}
&\frac{1}{2}\left(\sum_{u,v\in[n]} (1+\alpha) d(u,v) \frac{r_{uv}}{m} - \sum_{u,v\in[n]} d(u,v) \frac{m_{uv}}{m} \right) \\
&= \frac{1}{2m} \text{opt}.
\end{aligned}
$$

Summing over all cars yields the claim. $\square$

2.2 Extension of Theorem 2.3 to General Mean Waiting Times

We proceed by presenting the main ideas required to extend Theorem 2.3 to car sharing instances with arbitrary mean waiting times μ_i. One key ingredient is the following well known fact regarding Poisson processes:

LEMMA 2.8. *Consider a Poisson process $(N(t))$ with rate λ. Assume that each event is accepted with probability p and rejected otherwise, and let $(N'(t))$ be the resulting process of accepted events. Then $(N'(t))$ defines a Poisson process with rate $p\lambda$.*

Lemma 2.8 immediately suggests a way to reduce car sharing with arbitrary mean waiting times to the uniform case analyzed in the previous section. We simply replace a request generating Poisson process with mean waiting time μ_i with a process with mean waiting time 1 and probability $p_i = \mu_i$ of *accepting* a request. This can be achieved by introducing an (additional) probability of μ_i for a request from the node *to itself* (a *self-loop*), which has length 0 and, thus, can be safely ignored as it does not yield any revenue or modifies the distribution of cars.

The problem with this approach is that it allows the LP-Flow policy to relocate cars every time they serve one of the self-loop requests. In the original instance with arbitrary mean waiting times, this would be equivalent to allowing the policy to relocate a car without a request if it has been waiting too long at some node.

To avoid this problem, we apply the following trick. Instead of simply introducing self-loops, we replace the original

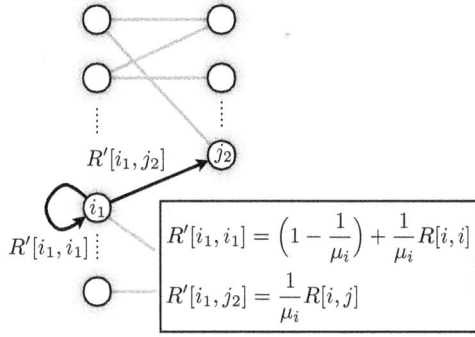

Figure 1: Bipartite counterpart to an instance with arbitrary mean waiting times μ_i.

instance I with a bipartite instance I', in which each node $i \in [n]$ is replaced by two nodes i_1, i_2 on opposite sides of the bipartition. We define a modified request matrix R' by

$$R'[i_1, i_1] = \left(1 - \frac{1}{\mu_i}\right) + \frac{1}{\mu_i}R[i, i],$$

$$R'[i_1, j_2] = \frac{1}{\mu_i}R[i, j] \text{ for } i \neq j,$$

and all other entries equal to zero. This construction is illustrated in Fig. 1.

In the resulting bipartite instance, all requests occur, say, on the left side of the bipartition, and all except the self-loop requests have a target node on the opposite site. By a careful analysis of linear program LP1 for this type of bipartite instance, one can show that the `LP-Flow` policy induced by the optimal solution only relocates cars from the right side of the bipartition back to the left. Thus, it has a natural interpretation as a feasible `LP-Flow` policy on the original instance resulting in identical gain. We leave the detailed proofs of this construction for the full version of the paper.

3. HARDNESS OF APPROXIMATION

In this section we will prove that the car sharing problem is APX-hard and, thus, under standard complexity theoretic assumptions cannot be approximated within better than some constant factor. We will establish APX-hardness via a reduction from the Set Packing problem.

The Set Packing Problem. Given a universe U of elements, $|U| = n$, and sets $S_1, \ldots, S_m \subseteq U$, find a maximum collection of pairwise disjoint subsets.

THEOREM 3.1 (COMPLEXITY OF SET PACKING [7]).
It is NP-hard to approximate Set Packing to within $O(d/\ln(d))$, if all sets have size $|S_i| = d$.

THEOREM 3.2. *The metric car sharing problem is APX-hard.*

PROOF. We reduce the gap-version of Set Packing. Given an instance with universe U, sets $S_1, \ldots, S_m$ with $|S_j| = d$ and $k \in \mathbb{N}$, we want to decide whether the maximum set packing has size at least k or at most ck, where $c = \Omega(\ln(d)/d)$.

We construct a car sharing instance $I = (n + m + 1, k, d, R, 0, (1))$ as follows. For each element $i \in U$ and each subset $S_j \subseteq U$ we introduce a node. Let v_i be the node corresponding to element $i \in U$ for $1 \leq i \leq n$ (*element nodes*). Similarly, let u_j be the node corresponding to subset $S_j \subseteq U$ for $1 \leq j \leq m$ (*set nodes*). We also introduce a special node w. We now define the distance function such that $d(v_i, w) = 1$ for all v_i, $d(u_j, v_i) = 1$ for all u_j, v_i and $d(w, u_j) = \varepsilon$ for all u_j. All other distances are derived from the shortest-path metric. It remains to define the request matrix R. For all v_i we define $R[v_i, w] = 1$. If $i \in S_j$ we define $R[u_j, v_i] = 1/d$. All other entries in the request matrix are zero. Intuitively, requests originating at set nodes are uniformly distributed among the element nodes corresponding to elements in the respective set, requests originating at element nodes take the cars back to special vertex w. Note, that the number of cars in the instance is k. The construction is depicted in Fig. 2.

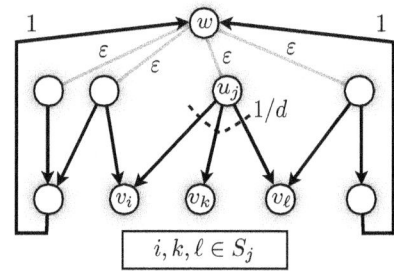

Figure 2: Car sharing instance from the proof of Theorem 3.2. Requests occurring at set node u_j corresponding to set S_j, $|S_j| = d$, have a destination uniformly distributed among element nodes v_i corresponding to elements $i \in S_j$.

Completeness: Consider a Set Packing instance which contains a set packing of size k. The optimal policy π for the constructed car sharing instance can always distribute cars arriving at w on the set nodes belonging to the set packing. This ensures that no car ever meets another car at any node. The gain of π is therefore $(1 - \frac{\varepsilon}{2})k$. This is also the maximal gain achievable on such an instance since all cars must be relocated along an edge of length ε after reaching w.

Soundness: Let us assume that the optimal policy achieves a gain of ck for some constant $0 < c \leq 1$. Then at least $(c/2)k$ many cars achieve a gain of $c/2$ each. We make the following observation about the distribution of these cars in the network:

FACT. *A car with gain $c/2$ spends at least a $c/4$-fraction of time waiting at set nodes.*

To see this, note that a car can only serve requests from an element node to w (*element requests*) or from a set to an element node (*set requests*). Consider a car serving an element request. If the car is moved back to an element node after serving the request, this causes cost 1 and so the contribution to the overall gain is 0. Thus, all gain the car achieves stems from serving alternating set and element requests. As the average waiting time for a request at any node is 1, a car with gain $c/2$ spends a $c/2$-fraction of time waiting for requests, and half of this at set nodes.

Using linearity of expectation and a straightforward Markov type argument, we get that for an overall gain of ck, $(c/8)k$ many cars have to spend a $c/8$-fraction of time servicing set requests. (This is counting the time a car is located at a set node *and* is the car that will be serving the next occurring request.)

Now assume that the maximum cardinality set packing has size $c'k \leq (c/16)k$, which we can guarantee by choosing parameter d sufficiently large. We consider a point T in time at which $(c/8)k$ cars sit on set nodes and note that these points occur with frequency at least $c/8$ by our previous arguments. Compute a maximal packing of sets associated with nodes occupied by the cars and call the corresponding nodes P. Note, that $|P| \leq (c/16)k$.

We say that a car sitting on a set node outside P has a *collision*, if it is moved to the same element node as a car from a set node in P after this car has been moved there, but before it has left the element node again due to another request. Note, that every collision can have one of two possible effects: either the first car moved to the respective element node is repositioned at cost 1 before a request arrives, or the the second car arriving has to wait an expected 2 time units before it can serve a request.

As every set node outside P corresponds to a set that has at least one element in common with some set associated with a set node in P and all nodes in P are occupied by cars, we get that

$$\Pr(\text{car from outside } P \text{ collides}) \geq \frac{1}{4}\left(\frac{1}{d}\right)^2,$$

since we only need that two set requests go to the same element node and these two plus the following element request occur in the right order. Thus, we have that the expected number of collisions is at least $c/(64d^2)k$.

Consequently, the expected overall revenue in the time interval $[T, T+3]$ is at most $3k - (c/(64d^2))k$, because an expected number of $c/(64d^2)k$ cars can only serve 2 requests during this time without being moved away from an element node at cost 1. This results in gain $(1 - c/(192d^2))k$ for this time interval. Using that time points with sufficiently many cars at set nodes occur with frequency at least $c/8$, we may finally conclude that the gain of any policy is bounded by $(1 - c'')k$ for some constant c'' depending only on d. □

4. A DISCRETE-TIME MODEL

In the *discrete-time* version of the car sharing problem, the occurrence of requests is not controlled by Poisson processes, but requests occur simultaneously at all nodes in regular intervals. In each such *round*, a request from node i to node j occurs with probability p_{ij}. After each round of requests, a policy π may relocate all cars independently of whether they were moved by a request. Rewards for served requests and the cost of relocating cars are defined as in the continuous-time case.

We can define the LP-Flow policy based on LP1 similar to the continuous-time case, except that now at each invocation of the policy, *all* cars are moved according to the node-specific distributions. Just as before, the behavior of the resulting system can be described in terms of a corresponding queuing network. However, as no discrete-time analogue of the aforementioned PASTA property is known for discrete-time queuing networks, there is no obvious way in which the analysis from the continuous-time case can be

applied here. Nevertheless, we present some partial progress and prove a result for simple *clique instances*, in which all nodes are at equal distances and requests are distributed uniformly.

Clique Instances. An instance $I = (n, m, d, R, \alpha)$ of the discrete-time car sharing problem is called *clique instance*, if for all $i, j \in [n]$ with $i \neq j$ it holds that $d(i, j) = 1$ and $R[i, j] = \frac{1}{n}$.

On clique instances, policy LP-Flow is particularly simple: it never relocates a car. This follows by observing that in LP1, we can now set all variables m_{uv} to 0 and all variables r_{uv} to $1/n$, resulting in an optimal LP solution. In Theorem 4.1 below, we will consider the corresponding discrete-time queuing network with uniform transition probabilities between its queues and prove a lower bound on the average number of non-empty queues in its steady state distribution. As the number of occupied queues corresponds to the number of nodes with a car on them and, thus, the average number of requests served per round, this also yields a bound on the approximation guarantee of LP-Flow on clique instances.

For the special case that $k = n$, i.e., the number of queues and jobs coincide, the lower bound approaches $2 - \sqrt{2}$ as $n \to \infty$, which experiments suggest to be tight.

Discrete-Time Queuing. A *closed discrete-time queuing network* is a closed queuing network $Q = \{q_1, \ldots, q_n\}$ with n queues in which the first jobs in all queues are served (and then moved) simultaneously in rounds. Jobs arriving at a queue in the same round are enqueued in uniformly random order.

THEOREM 4.1. *Consider a discrete-time closed queuing network $Q = \{q_1, \ldots, q_n\}$ with uniform transition probabilities $p_{ij} = \frac{1}{n}$ for all $q_i, q_j \in Q$. If there are k jobs in the network, then in the steady state distribution the average fraction of non-empty queues is*

$$\phi \geq \frac{n + k - \frac{1}{2} - \sqrt{\left(n + k - \frac{1}{2}\right)^2 - 2nk}}{n}.$$

In particular, for the case that $k = n$, we have $\lim_{n \to \infty} \phi \geq 2 - \sqrt{2}$.

PROOF. Consider a state $s = (s_1, \ldots, s_n)$ of the system where s_i equals the number of jobs in queue i. Then the number of jobs being served in this time-step is $b(s) = |\{s_i \mid s_i > 0\}|$. Now for each queue $i \in [n]$, define h_i as the length of the queue after the jobs have been served in state s but before any new jobs arrive for the next round. Clearly, $h_i = 0$, if $s_i = 0$, $h_i = s_i - 1$, else, and it holds that $\sum_{i \in [n]} h_i = k - b(s)$.

Now consider the experiment of picking one of the jobs that are served uniformly at random and let T denote its *waiting time*, i.e., the total number of rounds it has to wait before it is served again by one of the queues. Let X_i denote the event that the randomly selected job is moved to queue i. Since a total of $b(s)$ jobs are moved, the expected number of other jobs moved to a queue i is $(b(s)-1)/n$, and since jobs arriving at a queue are enqueued in random order, the conditional expectation of newly arriving jobs enqueued in front of a job arriving at any queue is $(b(s)-1)/(2n)$.

Observing that a job is moved to each queue with probability $1/n$ and waits one additional round for its service after reaching the front of a queue, we get

$$
\begin{aligned}
\mathrm{E}[T \mid s] &= 1 + \sum_{i \in [n]} \Pr[X_i] \cdot \left(h_i + \frac{b(s) - 1}{2n} \right) \\
&= 1 + \frac{b(s) - 1}{2n} + \frac{1}{n} \sum_{i \in [n]} h_i \\
&= 1 + \frac{b(s) - 1 + 2k - 2b(s)}{2n} \\
&= 1 + \frac{2k - b(s) - 1}{2n}.
\end{aligned}
$$

Since the queuing system defines an ergodic Markov chain, there exists a steady state distribution. We denote by $\pi(s)$ the steady state probability of state s and define

$$
\bar{b} = \sum_s \pi(s) b(s)
$$

as the average number of occupied queues in the steady state distribution.

We are interested in the expected waiting time of a job leaving any queue when the system is in its steady state distribution. The probability that a job is served in state s is $\pi(s)b(s)/\bar{b}$. The crucial observation for the proof is that this distribution is biased towards states with large $b(s)$-values compared to distribution π, and these are the states with smallest expected waiting times for jobs leaving a queue. Formally, applying Jensen's inequality yields

$$
\bar{b}^2 = \left(\sum_s \pi(s) b(s) \right)^2 \le \sum_s \pi(s) b(s)^2,
$$

and we may write,

$$
\begin{aligned}
\mathrm{E}[T] &= \sum_s \frac{\pi(s) b(s)}{\bar{b}} \mathrm{E}[T \mid s] \\
&= \frac{1}{\bar{b}} \sum_s \pi(s) b(s) \left(1 + \frac{2k - 2b(s) - 1}{2n} \right) \\
&= 1 + \frac{2k - 1}{2n} - \frac{1}{2n} \frac{1}{\bar{b}} \sum_s \pi(s) b(s)^2 \\
&\le 1 + \frac{2k - \bar{b} - 1}{2n}.
\end{aligned}
$$

Now observe that since the frequency with which a job is moved in the steady state is $\mathrm{E}[T]^{-1}$, the expected number of jobs moving per time step under the steady state distribution is $k\mathrm{E}[T]^{-1}$. However, the expected number of moves also coincides with the expected number $\bar{b}$ of occupied queues, and so we have that

$$
\bar{b} = \frac{k}{E[T]} = k \frac{1}{1 + \frac{2k - \bar{b} - 1}{2n}},
$$

and, finally, solving for $\bar{b}$ results in

$$
\bar{b} = n + k - \frac{1}{2} - \sqrt{\left(n + k - \frac{1}{2} \right)^2 - 2nk},
$$

which concludes the proof. $\square$

5. CONCLUSIONS AND OPEN PROBLEMS

We have presented a a 2-approximation algorithm for the continuous-time car sharing problem, together with a proof of APX-hardness. In our opinion, it would be very interesting to obtain similar results for the discrete-time model introduced in Section 4. While our proof of APX-hardness carries over easily to the discrete-time setting, algorithmic results appear to be more of a problem. In particular, analyzing our node-oblivious randomized policy in this setting poses the challenge of analyzing discrete-time closed queuing networks, which seems to be a tough nut to crack in general. However, we were able to make some partial progress by analyzing these networks in the case of uniform transition probabilities and, thus, are somewhat hopeful that similar results for the general case might be within reach.

6. ACKNOWLEDGMENTS

We are very grateful to Bobby Kleinberg, Yogi Sharma, and David Williamson for numerous insightful discussions in the initial stages of the research leading up to this paper.

7. REFERENCES

[1] Y. Azar. *On-line Load Balancing*. Theoretical Computer Science, 1992.

[2] F. Baskett, K. Chandy, R. Muntz, and F. Palacios. *Open, closed, and mixed networks of queues with different classes of customers*. Journal of the ACM, 22, 1975.

[3] G. Bolch, S. Greiner, H. Meer, and K. Trivedi. *Queuing Networks and Markov Chains*. John Wiley & Sons, 2006.

[4] M. Englert, D. Özmen, and M. Westermann. *The Power of Reordering for Online Minimum Makespan Scheduling*. In Proc. of the 49th Symposium on Foundations of Computer Science (FOCS), 2008.

[5] M. Gendreaub, G. Laportea, and R. Seguin. *Stochastic Vehicle Routing*. European Journal of Operational Research, 88(1), 1996.

[6] W. Gordon and G. Newell. *Closed Queuing Systems With Exponential Servers*. Operations Research, 15, 1967.

[7] E. Hazan, S. Safra, and O. Schwartz. *On the Complexity of Approximating k−Set Packing*. In Computational Complexity, 15, 2006.

[8] J. Jackson. *Jobshop-Like Queuing Systems*. Management Science, 50, 2004.

[9] E. Koutsoupias and C. Papadimitriou. *On the k-Server Conjecture*. Journal of the ACM, 42, 1995.

[10] M. Manasse, L. McGeoch, and D. Sleator. *Competitive Algorithms for Server Problems*. Journal of Algorithms, 11(2), 1990.

[11] M. Maxwell, M. Restrepo, S. Henderson, and H. Topaloglu. *Approximate Dynamic Programming for Ambulance Redeployment*. INFORMS Journal on Computing, 22(2), 2010.

[12] Y. Peres, K. Talwar, and U. Wieder. *The (1+β)-Choice Process and Weighted Balls-into-Bins*. In Proc. of the 21st Symposium on Discrete Algorithms (SODA), 2010.

[13] W. Powell. *A Stochastic Formulation of the Dynamic Assignment Problem, with an Application to Truckload Motor Carriers.* Transportation Science, 30(3), 1996.

[14] M. Raab and A. Steger. *"Balls into Bins" - A Simple and Tight Analysis.* In Proc. of the 2nd Workshop on Randomization and Approximation Techniques in Computer Science, 1998.

[15] M. Reiser and S. Lavenberg. *Mean Value Analysis of Closed Multichain Queuing Networks.* Journal of the ACM, 27, 1980.

Approximation Algorithms for Secondary Spectrum Auctions[*]

Martin Hoefer   Thomas Kesselheim   Berthold Vöcking

RWTH Aachen University
Department of Computer Science
52056 Aachen, Germany
{mhoefer, kesselheim, voecking}@cs.rwth-aachen.de

ABSTRACT

We study combinatorial auctions for the secondary spectrum market. In this market, short-term licenses shall be given to wireless nodes for communication in their local neighborhood. In contrast to the primary market, channels can be assigned to multiple bidders, provided that the corresponding devices are well separated such that the interference is sufficiently low. Interference conflicts are described in terms of a conflict graph in which the nodes represent the bidders and the edges represent conflicts such that the feasible allocations for a channel correspond to the independent sets in the conflict graph.

In this paper, we suggest a novel LP formulation for combinatorial auctions with conflict graph using a non-standard graph parameter, the so-called *inductive independence number*. Taking into account this parameter enables us to bypass the well-known lower bound of $\Omega(n^{1-\varepsilon})$ on the approximability of independent set in general graphs with n nodes (bidders). We achieve significantly better approximation results by showing that interference constraints for wireless networks yield conflict graphs with bounded inductive independence number.

Our framework covers various established models of wireless communication, e.g., the protocol or the physical model. For the protocol model, we achieve an $O(\sqrt{k})$-approximation, where k is the number of available channels. For the more realistic physical model, we achieve an $O(\sqrt{k}\log^2 n)$ approximation based on edge-weighted conflict graphs. Combining our approach with the LP-based framework of Lavi and Swamy, we obtain incentive compatible mechanisms for general bidders with arbitrary valuations on bundles of channels specified in terms of demand oracles.

[*]This work has been supported by DFG through UMIC Research Centre, RWTH Aachen University, and grant Ho 3831/3-1.

Categories and Subject Descriptors

C.2.1 [**Computer-Communication Networks**]: Network Architecture and Design—*Wireless Communication, Distributed Networks*; F.2.2 [**Analysis of Algorithms and Problem Complexity**]: Non Numerical Algorithms and Problems

General Terms

Algorithms, Theory

Keywords

Physical Interference Model, Combinatorial Auctions, Inductive Independence Number, SINR, Independent Set Problem

1. INTRODUCTION

A major challenge of today's wireless networks and mobile communication is spectrum management, as devices use common frequency bands that are subject to interference between multiple transmitters in the same area. In fact, spectrum allocation has become one of the key problems that currently limits the growth and evolution of wireless networks. The reason is that, traditionally, frequencies were given away to large service providers in a static way by regulators for entire countries. Examples include FCC auctions in the US or the auctions for UMTS and LTE that took place in Europe. However, demands for services vary at different times and in different areas. Depending on time and place this causes frequency bands licensed for one application to become overloaded. On the other hand, different bands are idle at the same time. A promising solution to this problem is to use market approaches that result in a flexible and thus more efficient redistribution of access rights – thereby overcoming the artificial shortage of available spectrum. In this case, parts of the spectrum that are currently unused by so-called *primary users* for the originally intended purpose (such as TV or telecommunication) can be offered to so-called *secondary users*. Licenses for such secondary usage are valid only for a local area.

A sustainable approach (concisely termed "eBay in the Sky" in [30]) to automatically run such a secondary spectrum market is to auction licenses for secondary users on a regular basis. In this paper, we propose a general framework and efficient algorithms to implement such a secondary spectrum auction. In our model, there are n secondary users who can bid for bundles of the k wireless channels. Depending on the scenario a user can correspond to a base station that strives to cover a specific area or a pair of devices that want to exchange data (e.g., a base station and a mobile device). In order to account for channel aggregation capabilities of modern devices, users should be able to acquire multiple channels. We allow each user v to have an arbitrary valuation $b_{v,T}$ for each subset T of channels. This level of generality is necessary because of different needs, applications, and hardware abilities of the users, but also because of different locations, spectrum availability, and interference conditions. For instance, the presence of a primary user might allow access to a channel only for a subset of mobile devices located in selected areas. We assume no restrictions on the valuation functions, not even monotonicity.

In this paper, we devise approximation algorithms for spectrum allocation on the secondary market with the objective of maximizing social welfare. We focus on the underlying combinatorial problems and describe interference conflicts by an edge-weighted conflict graph. In unweighted graphs, the vertices represent the bidders and the edges represent conflicts such that the feasible allocations for a channel correspond to the independent sets in the conflict graph. For edge-weighted graphs, we extend the definition of independent set to weighted edges by requiring the sum of all incoming weights to be less than 1. We address the following problem.

Problem 1 (Combinatorial Auction with Conflict Graph). *Given a graph $G = (V, E)$, a natural number k, and a valuation function $b \colon V \times 2^{[k]} \to \mathbb{N}$, find a feasible allocation $S \colon V \to 2^{[k]}$ that maximizes the social welfare $b(S) := \sum_{v \in V} b_{v,S(v)}$.*
An allocation S is called feasible if for all channels $j \in [k]$, the set of vertices that are assigned to this channel, i.e. $\{v \in V \mid j \in S(v)\}$, is an independent set.

Observe that this problem generalizes combinatorial auctions (where the conflict graph is a clique) and maximum weight independent set (where $k = 1$). This formulation covers a large number of binary interference models (such as the protocol model). As we will see, edge weights allow to express even more realistic models like the physical model. Here, we can even take the effects of power control into account.

1.1 Our contribution

We devise the first approximation algorithms for the combinatorial auction problem with conflict graph. Our approach is based on a novel LP formulation for the independent set problem using a non-standard graph parameter.

Definition 1 (inductive independence number ρ). *For a graph $G = (V, E)$, the inductive independence number ρ is the smallest number such that there is an ordering π of the vertices satisfying: For all $v \in V$ and all independent sets $M \subseteq V$, we have $|M \cap \{u \in V \mid \{u, v\} \in E, \pi(u) < \pi(v)\}| \le \rho$.*

In words, for every vertex $v \in V$, the size of an independent set in the *backward neighborhood* of v, i.e., the set of neighbors u of v with $\pi(u) < \pi(v)$, is at most ρ. Conflict graphs derived from various simple models of wireless communication with binary conflicts like, e.g., the protocol model, distance-2 matchings, or disk graphs, have $\rho = O(1)$,

see, e.g., [28]. The corresponding ordering π is efficiently computable in these cases. We exploit this property in our algorithms.

Our main results concern the so-called physical model which is common in the engineering community and was only recently subject to theoretical work. In binary models of wireless communication usually studied in theoretical computer science, we make the oversimplifying assumption that interference caused by a signal stops at some boundary around the sender, and receivers beyond this boundary are not disturbed by this signal. In contrast, the physical model takes into account realistic propagation effects and additivity of signals. Feasibility of simultaneous transmissions is modeled in terms of signal to interference plus noise ratio (SINR) constraints. We study two variants of this model, one in which signals are sent at given powers (e.g., uniform) and one where the powers are subject to optimization themselves. We show how to represent SINR constraints for both of these variants in terms of an edge-weighted conflict graph and introduce appropriate notions of "independent set" and "inductive independence number" for edge-weighted graphs. Note that the combinatorial auctions with edge-weighted conflict graphs can be defined in the same way as stated in Problem 1 given an appropriate definition of "independent set".

At first, we prove that the inductive independence number ρ for edge-weighted graphs obtained from the physical model (in both variants) is bounded by $O(\log n)$ and the corresponding ordering is efficiently computable. This enables us to bypass the well-known lower bound of $\Omega(n^{1-\varepsilon})$ on the approximability of independent set in general graphs. In particular, we present an LP relaxation capturing both interference constraints and valuations of users for subsets of channels. Similar to regular combinatorial auctions, the LP might require an exponential number of valuations $b_{v,T}$ to be written down explicitly. However, we show how to solve the LP using only oracle access to bidder valuations. Our LP based framework is able to handle edge-weighted conflict graphs resulting from the physical model. By rounding the LP optimum, our algorithm achieves an $O(\rho \cdot \sqrt{k} \log n)$ approximation guarantee. Combining this with the bound on ρ gives an $O(\sqrt{k} \log^2 n)$-approximation of the social welfare for spectrum auctions in the physical model (in both variants).

For more simple binary models of wireless communication such as the protocol model, our approach yields an $\mathcal{O}(\rho \cdot \sqrt{k})$-approximation. Using the bounds on ρ mentioned above, this yields an $\mathcal{O}(\sqrt{k})$ approximation guarantee. In this case, we also provide some complementing hardness results. In general, it is hard to approximate the combinatorial auction problem with conflict graphs to a factor of $\mathcal{O}(\rho^{1-\epsilon})$ and to a factor of $O(k^{\frac{1}{2}-\epsilon})$ for any constant $\epsilon > 0$. While for some specific models better approximations exist, in general the bounds provided by our algorithms for binary models cannot be improved in terms of a single parameter ρ or k. In addition, we provide stronger lower bounds for the case of asymmetric channels, in which the conflict graph can be different for each channel. In this case, our algorithm guarantees a factor of $O(\rho \cdot k)$, which is best possible in general.

Our approach can be used to derive incentive compatible mechanisms using the LP-based framework of Lavi and Swamy [24] for general bidders with demand oracles. In fact, we slightly extend this framework by starting with an infeasible rather than feasible ILP formulation. The approximation algorithm computes a linear combination of feasible solutions approximating the optimal solution of the corresponding LP and then chooses one of these solutions at random. The obtained mechanism is truthful in expectation.

Outline. For technical reasons, we present our results in a different order than stated above. We first introduce the basic approach in the context of unweighted conflict graphs in Section 2. The extensions to edge-weighted graphs including formal definitions of independent sets and inductive independence number are given in Section 3. The aforementioned wireless models (especially the variants of the physical model) are formally introduced in Section 4, where we also show the bounds on the inductive independence number. The application of the framework by Lavi and Swamy is discussed in Section 5. Finally, the results on asymmetric channels are presented in Section 6.

1.2 Related Work

The idea of establishing secondary spectrum markets has attracted much attention among researchers in applied networking and engineering communities [30, 14, 5, 21]. There are many different fundamental regulatory questions that need to be addressed when implementing such a market. For example it has to be clarified who runs the market and who is allowed to sell and buy spectrum there. Possible actors could be network providers, brokers, regulators and end-users. In addition, it has to be guaranteed that existing services are not harmed. In most of the literature on spectrum markets the technological aspects dominate. Many results in this area are only of qualitative nature, only a few examples (such as [30, 31]) do explicitly consider truthfulness. We believe that our combinatorial models based on (edge-weighted) conflict graphs taking into account the bounded inductive independence number allows us to neglect technological aspects and to focus on the underlying combinatorial and algorithmic questions. To the best of our knowledge there is no previous work on auctions using the general framework of conflict graphs, or, in general, nontrivial provable worst-case guarantees on the efficiency of the allocation.

In contrast, combinatorial auctions have been a prominent research area in algorithmic game theory over the last decade. A variety of works treats auctions with special valuation functions, such as submodular valuations or ones expressible by specific bidding languages. For an introduction see, e.g., [25, Chapters 11 and 12] or [7]. In addition, designing (non-truthful) approximation algorithms for the allocation problems has found interest, most notably for submodular valuations (e.g., [27, 12]). More relevant to our work, however, are results that deal with truthful mechanisms for general valuations. Most notably, Lavi and Swamy [24] and Dobzinski et al. [8] derive mechanisms using only demand oracles that achieve an $\sqrt{k}$-approximation with truthfulness in expectation and universal truthfulness, respectively. A deterministic truthful $(k/\sqrt{\log k})$-approximation is obtained by Holzman et al. [20].

Over the last decades, there has been much research on finding maximum independent sets in the context of interference models for wireless networks. One of the simplest models in this area are disk graphs, which are mostly analyzed using geometric arguments. See [13, 16] for a summary on the results and typical techniques. Recently and independently from our work, Christodoulou et al. [6] study combinatorial auctions for geometric objects. Similar to our approach, they present an LP formulation based on a property in terms of an ordering, the fatness of geometric objects.

Akcoglu et al. [1] and Ye and Borodin [29] also use the inductive independence number to approximate independent sets. However, their motivation is stemming from cordal graphs, and they do not consider wireless communication, multiple channels or truthful auctions.

Algorithmic aspects of the physical model have become popular in theoretical research recently, particularly the problem of scheduling, i.e., partitioning a given set of requests in a small number of classes such that all requests are successful. New challenges arise since graph-theoretic coloring methods cannot be directly applied. For example, there have been a number of results on how to choose powers for short schedule lengths [11, 10, 18]. A popular method is fixing powers according to some distance-based scheme. For uniform power assignments, a constant-factor approximation algorithm for the problem of finding an independent set (i.e., a maximum set that may share a single channel) is presented in [15]. An online version of the problem has been studied in [9] presenting tight bounds depending on the difference in lengths of the requests. Most recently, a constant-factor approximation algorithm for arbitrary power schemes has been obtained by Kesselheim [22].

2. UNWEIGHTED CONFLICT GRAPHS

2.1 Our LP relaxation

In contrast to the regular, edge-based LP formulation, we here present a different LP based on the *inductive indepence number* ρ (recall Definition 1). As we will see later, in typical conflict graphs the inductive independence number is constant and the corresponding ordering π can be efficiently calculated. Here we use $\Gamma_\pi(v) = \{u \in V \mid \{u,v\} \in E, \pi(u) < \pi(v)\}$ to denote the backward neighborhood of v. This allows to use the following LP relaxation that has one constraint for each combination of a vertex and a channel and another one for each vertex.

$$\text{Max.} \sum_{v \in V} \sum_{T \subseteq [k]} b_{v,T} x_{v,T} \tag{1a}$$

$$\text{s.t.} \sum_{u \in \Gamma_\pi(v)} \sum_{\substack{T \subseteq [k] \\ j \in T}} x_{u,T} \leq \rho \quad \text{for all } v \in V, j \in [k] \tag{1b}$$

$$\sum_{T \subseteq [k]} x_{v,T} \leq 1 \quad \text{for all } v \in V \tag{1c}$$

$$x_{v,T} \geq 0 \quad \text{for all } v \in V, T \subseteq [k] \tag{1d}$$

This LP works as follows. For each vertex v and each possible set $T \subseteq [k]$ of channels assigned to this vertex, there is one variable $x_{v,T}$. Due to the bounded inductive independence number all feasible allocations correspond to solutions of the LP. However, not all integer solutions of the LP necessarily correspond to feasible channel allocations. Nevertheless, we will show how to compute a feasible allocation from each solution.

Lemma 1. *Let S be a feasible allocation and x be defined by $x_{v,T} = 1$ if $S(v) = T$ and 0 otherwise, then x is a feasible LP solution.*

As all coefficients are non-negative, this LP has a packing structure. In particular, we can observe the following decomposition property.

Observation 2. *Let x be a feasible solution to the LP, and $x^{(1)}$ be a vector such that $0 \leq x^{(1)}_{v,T} \leq x_{v,T}$ for all $v \in V$, $T \subseteq [k]$. Then $x^{(1)}$ and $x^{(2)} := x - x^{(1)}$ are feasible LP solutions as well.*

If there are only $\mathcal{O}(\log n)$ valuations $b_{v,T}$ non-zero, this LP is solvable in polynomial time. In general, the elementary representation of the $b_{v,T}$ values is exponential in k. We can still solve the LP optimally if bidders can be represented by demand oracles.

2.2 Demand Oracles

If there is an arbitrary number of channels, we must define an appropriate way to query the valuation functions of the requests, as an elementary description becomes prohibitively large. A standard way to deal with this issue in the auction literature is the representation by so-called *demand oracles*. To query the demand oracle of bidder v, we assign each channel i a price p_i. Then the oracle delivers his "demand" $S = \arg\max_{T \subseteq [k]} b_{v,T} - \sum_{i \in T} p_i$, i.e., a bundle that maximizes the utility of v given that he pays the sum of prices of channels in the bundle. In ordinary combinatorial auctions such demand oracles can be used to separate the dual of the underlying LP. We here show that such demand oracles can also be used for the solution of our LP (1). Consider the dual given by

$$\text{Min.} \quad \sum_{v \in V} \sum_{j \in [k]} \rho y_{v,j} + \sum_{v \in V} z_v \tag{2a}$$

$$\text{s.t.} \quad \sum_{\substack{u \in V \\ v \in \Gamma_\pi(u)}} \sum_{j \in T} y_{u,j} + z_v \geq b_{v,T} \quad \text{for all } v \in V, T \subseteq [k] \tag{2b}$$

$$y_{v,j} \geq 0 \qquad\qquad \text{for all } v \in V, j \in T \tag{2c}$$

In contrast to ordinary combinatorial auctions, we cannot use the solution (y, z) directly as the channel prices. Instead, we choose *bidder-specific* channel prices by

$$p_{v,j} = \sum_{\substack{u \in V \\ v \in \Gamma_\pi(u)}} y_{u,j} \ .$$

Using this idea we see that the constraints of the dual are indeed equivalent to upper bounds on the utility with bidder-specific channel prices. By obtaining the demand bundle with highest utility for each player, we find a violated constraint or verify that none exists. This allows to separate the dual LP and to solve it efficiently using the ellipsoid method. This way, we get an equivalent primal LP with only polynomially constraints. The corresponding primal solution has only polynomially many variables with $x^*_{v,T} > 0$.

2.3 Rounding LP Solutions

Having described the LP relaxation, we now analyze Algorithm 1 computing feasible allocations from LP solutions as follows. First, it decomposes the given LP solution to two solutions $x^{(1)}$ and $x^{(2)}$ (line 1). In $x^{(1)}$ all fractional variables $x_{v,T}$ for sets T with $|T| \geq \sqrt{k}$ are set to zero. To get $x^{(2)}$

the exact opposite is performed. From each one, a feasible allocating is computed and the better one is selected at the end. This means, the algorithm either allocates only sets of size at most $\sqrt{k}$ or only of size at least $\sqrt{k}$. The actual computation of the allocation works the same way for both LP solutions. It consists of two major parts: a rounding stage and a conflict resolution stage. In the rounding stage (lines 3–4), a tentative allocation is generated as follows. For each vertex v the set of allocated channels $S^{(l)}(v)$ is determined independently at random. Each set $T \neq \emptyset$ is taken with probability $x^{(l)}_{v,T}/2\sqrt{k}\rho$ and with the remaining probability the empty set is allocated.

Conflicts can occur when two adjacent vertices share the same channel. In this case, the conflict is resolved (lines 5–8) by allocating the channel to the vertex with smaller index in the π ordering. The other vertex is removed from the solution by being allocated the empty set.

Algorithm 1: LP rounding algorithm for the combinatorial auction problem with unweighted conflict graphs

---

1   decompose x into two solutions $x^{(1)}$ and $x^{(2)}$ by $x^{(1)}_{v,T} = x_{v,T}$ if $|T| \leq \sqrt{k}$ and $x^{(1)}_{v,T} = 0$ otherwise. $x^{(2)} = x - x^{(1)}$;

2   **for** $l \in \{1, 2\}$ **do**

3   **for** $v \in V$ **do**   /* Rounding Stage */

4   with probability $\frac{x^{(l)}_{v,T}}{2\sqrt{k}\rho}$ set $S^{(l)}(v) := T$;

5   **for** $v \in V$ **do** /* Conflict-Resolution Stage */

6   **for** $u \in V$ with $\pi(u) < \pi(v)$ and $\{u, v\} \in E$ **do**

7   **if** $S^{(l)}(u) \cap S^{(l)}(v) \neq \emptyset$ **then**

8              $S^{(l)}(v) := \emptyset$;

9   return the better one of the solutions $S^{(1)}$ and $S^{(2)}$;

Theorem 3. *For any feasible LP solution x^* with value b^*, Algorithm 1 calculates a feasible allocation S of value at least $b^*/8\sqrt{k}\rho$ in expectation.*

PROOF. The allocations $S^{(1)}$ and $S^{(2)}$ are obviously feasible allocations because if $\{u, v\} \in E$, then $S^{(1)}(u) \cap S^{(1)}(v) = \emptyset$ and $S^{(2)}(u) \cap S^{(2)}(v) = \emptyset$. Therefore, the output is also a feasible allocation.

Let us now bound the expected values of solutions $S^{(1)}$ and $S^{(2)}$. Let $l \in \{1, 2\}$ be fixed. Let $X_{v,T}$ be a 0/1 random variable indicating if $S^{(l)}(v)$ is set to T after the rounding stage. Clearly, we have

$$\mathbf{E}[X_{v,T}] = \frac{x^{(l)}_{v,T}}{2\sqrt{k}\rho} \ . \tag{3}$$

Let $X'_{v,T}$ be a 0/1 random variable indicating if $S^{(l)}(v)$ is set to T after the conflict-resolution stage. We consider the event that $X'_{v,T} = 0$, given that $X_{v,T} = 1$, i.e. that v is removed in the conflict-resolution stage after having survived the rounding stage.

Lemma 4. *The probability of being removed in the conflict-resolution stage after having survived the rounding stage is at most $1/2$.*

PROOF. The event can only occur if $X_{u,T'} = 1$ for some $u \in V$ with $\pi(u) < \pi(v)$, $\{u, v\} \in E$, and $T \cap T' \neq \emptyset$. In terms of the random variables $X_{u,T}$ this is

$$\sum_{u \in \Gamma_\pi(v)} \sum_{\substack{T' \subseteq [k] \\ T \cap T' \neq \emptyset}} X_{u,T'} \geq 1 \; .$$

Using this notation we can bound the probability of the event by using the Markov inequality

$$\mathbf{Pr}\left[X'_{v,T} = 0 \mid X_{v,T} = 1\right] \leq \mathbf{Pr}\left[\sum_{u \in \Gamma_\pi(v)} \sum_{\substack{T' \subseteq [k] \\ T \cap T' \neq \emptyset}} X_{u,T'} \geq 1\right]$$

$$\leq \mathbf{E}\left[\sum_{u \in \Gamma_\pi(v)} \sum_{\substack{T' \subseteq [k] \\ T \cap T' \neq \emptyset}} X_{u,T'}\right] \; .$$

We will now show separately that this expectation is at most $1/2$ for each of the two possible values of l ($l = 1$ or $l = 2$).

Case 1 ($l = 1$): We have:

$$\mathbf{E}\left[\sum_{u \in \Gamma_\pi(v)} \sum_{\substack{T' \subseteq [k] \\ T \cap T' \neq \emptyset}} X_{u,T'}\right] \leq \mathbf{E}\left[\sum_{j \in T} \sum_{u \in \Gamma_\pi(v)} \sum_{\substack{T' \subseteq [k] \\ j \in T'}} X_{u,T'}\right] \; .$$

Due to linearity of expectation this is equal to

$$\sum_{j \in T} \sum_{u \in \Gamma_\pi(v)} \sum_{\substack{T' \subseteq [k] \\ j \in T'}} \mathbf{E}\left[X_{u,T'}\right] \; .$$

Using Equation (3) and the fact that $x^{(1)}$ is an LP solution, this is

$$\sum_{j \in T} \sum_{u \in \Gamma_\pi(v)} \sum_{\substack{T' \subseteq [k] \\ j \in T'}} \frac{x^{(1)}_{u,T'}}{2\sqrt{k}\rho} \leq \sum_{j \in T} \frac{1}{2\sqrt{k}} \; .$$

Recall that we only have to deal with sets T for which $|T| \leq \sqrt{k}$ in this case. Hence, the expectation is at most $1/2$, and so is the probability that v is removed in the conflict-resolution stage.

Case 2 ($l = 2$): In this case, we have $X_{u,T'} > 0$ only for sets T' with $|T'| \geq \sqrt{k}$. This yields for all $u \in V$

$$\sum_{\substack{T' \subseteq [k] \\ T \cap T' \neq \emptyset}} X_{u,T'} \leq \sum_{\substack{T' \subseteq [k] \\ T' \neq \emptyset}} X_{u,T'} = \sum_{\substack{T' \subseteq [k] \\ T' \neq \emptyset}} \sum_{j \in T'} \frac{X_{u,T'}}{|T'|}$$

$$= \sum_{j \in [k]} \sum_{\substack{T' \subseteq [k] \\ j \in T'}} \frac{X_{u,T'}}{|T'|} \leq \frac{1}{\sqrt{k}} \sum_{j \in [k]} \sum_{\substack{T' \subseteq [k] \\ j \in T'}} X_{u,T'} \; .$$

So, we get

$$\mathbf{E}\left[\sum_{u \in \Gamma_\pi(v)} \sum_{\substack{T' \subseteq [k] \\ T \cap T' \neq \emptyset}} X_{u,T'}\right] \leq \mathbf{E}\left[\frac{1}{\sqrt{k}} \sum_{j \in [k]} \sum_{u \in \Gamma_\pi(v)} \sum_{\substack{T' \subseteq [k] \\ j \in T'}} X_{u,T'}\right] \; .$$

Again, we use linearity of expectation, Equation (3) and the fact that $x^{(2)}$ is an LP solution. This gives us

$$\frac{1}{\sqrt{k}} \sum_{j \in [k]} \sum_{u \in \Gamma_\pi(v)} \sum_{\substack{T' \subseteq [k] \\ j \in T'}} \frac{x^{(2)}_{u,T'}}{2\sqrt{k}\rho} \leq \frac{1}{\sqrt{k}} \sum_{j \in [k]} \frac{1}{2\sqrt{k}} \leq \frac{1}{2} \; .$$

This bounds the probability for the second case.

In both cases we have $\mathbf{Pr}\left[X'_{v,T} = 0 \mid X_{v,T} = 1\right] \leq 1/2$. $\square$

Using Lemma 4 and Equation (3) we get for all $v \in V$ and $T \subseteq [k]$

$$\mathbf{E}\left[X'_{v,T}\right] \geq \frac{x^{(l)}_{v,T}}{4\sqrt{k}\rho} \; .$$

This yields that both calculated solutions $S^{(l)}$ for $l \in \{1, 2\}$ have expected value

$$\mathbf{E}\left[b(S^{(l)})\right] = \mathbf{E}\left[\sum_{v \in V} \sum_{T \subseteq [k]} b_{v,T} \cdot X'_{v,T}\right]$$

$$= \sum_{v \in V} \sum_{T \subseteq [k]} b_{v,T} \cdot \mathbf{E}\left[X'_{v,T}\right] \geq \frac{1}{4\sqrt{k}\rho} \sum_{v \in V} \sum_{T \subseteq [k]} b_{v,T} x^{(l)}_{v,T} \; .$$

So, the better ones of the two solutions has expected value

$$\mathbf{E}\left[\max\{b(S^{(1)}), b(S^{(2)})\}\right] \geq \frac{1}{2}\left(\mathbf{E}\left[b(S^{(1)})\right] + \mathbf{E}\left[b(S^{(2)})\right]\right)$$

$$\geq \frac{1}{8\sqrt{k}\rho} \sum_{v \in V} \sum_{S \subseteq [k]} b_{v,S}\left(x^{(1)}_{v,S} + x^{(2)}_{v,S}\right)$$

$$= \frac{1}{8\sqrt{k}\rho} \sum_{v \in V} \sum_{S \subseteq [k]} b_{v,S} x_{v,S} = \frac{b^*}{8\sqrt{k}\rho} \; . \qquad \square$$

2.4 Hardness Results

In this section we provide matching lower bounds for the approximation ratios of our algorithms. This shows that the above results cannot be vitally improved without further restricting the model. Our results are based on the hardness of approximating independent set in bounded-degree graphs [26] or general graphs [19]. A first result is that the $\mathcal{O}(\rho)$ algorithm for the case $k = 1$ is almost optimal.

Theorem 5. *For $k = 1$ and for each $\rho = \mathcal{O}(\log n)$ there is no $\rho/2^{\mathcal{O}(\sqrt{\log \rho})}$ approximation algorithm unless* P = NP.

PROOF. Such an algorithm could be used to approximate Independent Set in bounded-degree graphs. Given a graph with maximum degree d its inductive independence number ρ is also at most d. Trevisan [26] shows that there is no $d/2^{\mathcal{O}(\sqrt{\log d})}$-approximation algorithm for all $d = \mathcal{O}(\log n)$ unless P = NP. This directly yields the claim. $\square$

As a second result we can also prove the impact of the number of channels k has to be as large as $\sqrt{k}$.

Theorem 6. *Even for $\rho = 1$ there is no $k^{\frac{1}{2} - \varepsilon}$-approximation algorithm unless* ZPP = NP.

Our framework extends general combinatorial auctions with k items, and this is a standard result in the area [25, Chapter 9] derived from the hardness of independent set in general graphs.

In conclusion, our algorithmic results are supported by almost matching lower bounds in each parameter. Without further restricting the graph properties (which means to use additional properties of an interference model) no vitally better approximation guarantees can be achieved in terms of ρ resp. k. However, this does not prove no $O(\rho + \sqrt{k})$ approximation can exist.

3. EDGE-WEIGHTED CONFLICT GRAPHS

In this section we extend conflicts over binary relations (conflict/no-conflict). In wireless communication, we encounter situations that a radio transmission is exposed to interference by a number of devices relatively far away. If there was only a single one of them, interference would be acceptable but their overall interference is too high. For such aggregation aspects we introduce edge-weighted conflict graphs, in which there is a non-negative weight $w(u, v)$ between any pair of vertices $u, v \in V$. An *independent set* is defined as a set $M \subseteq V$ such that $\sum_{u \in M} w(u, v) < 1$ for all $v \in M$.

The definition of the inductive independence number can be generalized in a straightforward way. Since edge weights need not be symmetric, it turns out to be convenient to use the following symmetric edge weights $\bar{w}(u, v) = w(u, v) + w(v, u)$.

Definition 2. *The* inductive independence number *of an edge-weighted graph G is the minimum number ρ such that there is a total ordering $\pi \colon V \to [n]$ (bijective function) which fulfills for all vertices v and all independent sets $M \subseteq \{u \in V \mid \pi(u) < \pi(v)\}$ the following condition:*

$$\sum_{u \in M} \bar{w}(u, v) \leq \rho \ .$$

In the same way as in the unweighted case, we can use the definition to formulate the LP relaxation.

$$\text{Max.} \quad \sum_{v \in V} \sum_{T \subseteq [k]} b_{v,T} x_{v,T} \tag{4a}$$

$$\text{s.t.} \quad \sum_{\substack{u \in V \\ \pi(u) < \pi(v)}} \sum_{\substack{T \subseteq [k] \\ j \in T}} \bar{w}(u, v) \cdot x_{u,T} \leq \rho$$
$$\text{for all } v \in V,\ j \in [k] \tag{4b}$$

$$\sum_{T \subseteq [k]} x_{v,T} \leq 1 \qquad \text{for all } v \in V \tag{4c}$$

$$x_{v,T} \geq 0 \qquad \text{for all } v \in V,\ T \subseteq [k] \tag{4d}$$

In weighted graphs we lose an important property we made use of in unweighted graphs. In particular, resolving conflicts in one direction only does not suffice. To cope with this issue, we increase the scaling by another factor of 2. We use rounding and conflict resolution as previously to ensure that for each vertex v the sum of edge weights to neighboring vertices that have smaller indices and share a channel with v is at most $1/2$. Formally, a *partly-feasible allocation* is an allocation $S \colon V \to 2^{[k]}$ such that

$$\sum_{\substack{u \in V \\ \pi(u) < \pi(v) \\ S(v) \cap S(u) \neq \emptyset}} \bar{w}(u, v) < \frac{1}{2} \ . \tag{5}$$

Rounding LP solutions to such partly-feasible allocations can be carried out in a similar way as Algorithm 1. Algorithm 2 decomposes the given LP solution the same way as

Algorithm 1. Afterwards, it also performs two stages. In the rounding stage (lines 2–4), again a tentative allocation is determined randomly by considering the LP solution as a probability distribution.

Afterwards, only a partial conflict resolution (lines 5–8) is performed: If for some vertex v the sum of edge weights to neighbors that have lower π values and share a channel exceeds $1/2$, it is removed from the solution (i.e. it is allocated the empty set). Such a partly-feasible solution satisfies Equation (5).

Algorithm 2: LP rounding algorithm for the combinatorial auction problem with weighted conflict graphs

1   decompose x into two solutions $x^{(1)}$ and $x^{(2)}$ by
   $x_{v,T}^{(1)} = x_{v,T}$ if $|T| \leq \sqrt{k}$ and $x_{v,S}^{(1)} = 0$ otherwise.
   $x^{(2)} = x - x^{(1)}$;

2   **for** $l \in \{1, 2\}$ **do**

3   **for** $v \in V$ **do**   /* Rounding Stage */

4   with probability $\frac{x_{v,T}}{4\sqrt{k}\rho}$ set $S^{(l)}(v) := T$

5   **for** $v \in V$ **do**   /* Partial Conf.-Res. Stage */

6   set $U(v) := \{u \in V \mid \pi(u) < \pi(v),$
       $S^{(l)}(v) \cap S^{(l)}(u) \neq \emptyset\}$;

7   **if** $\sum_{u \in U(v)} \bar{w}(u, v) \geq \frac{1}{2}$ **then**

8       $S^{(l)}(v) := \emptyset$

9   **return** the better one of the allocations $S^{(1)}$ and $S^{(2)}$

Due to space limitations, the analysis of the algorithm can only be found in the full version.

Lemma 7. *For any feasible LP solution x^* with value b^*, Algorithm 2 calculates a partly-feasible allocation S of value at least $b^*/16\sqrt{k}\rho$ in expectation.*

Given a partly-feasible allocation S, Algorithm 3 implements the necessary additional conflict resolution to derive a fully-feasible one. The algorithm decomposes the partly-feasible allocation to a number of feasible candidate allocations $S_1, S_2, \ldots$. Each allocation S_i is initialized such that $S_i(v) = S(v)$ if vertex v has been removed from all previous allocations $S_1, \ldots, S_{i-1}$. Otherwise $S_i(v) = \emptyset$. Then a conflict resolution is performed on S_i: The vertices are considered by decreasing indices in the π ordering. If the weight bound is violated for some vertex v in the current allocation S_i, it is removed from the allocation by allocating the empty set. At the end, the best one of the candidate allocations is returned. We will see that each candidate allocation allocates at least half of the remaining vertices a non-empty set. Therefore at most $\log n$ candidates are computed and the best one has value at least $b(S)/\log n$.

Lemma 8. *Given a (not necessarily feasible) allocation S in which Condition 5 is fulfilled for all $v \in V$, Algorithm 3 calculates a feasible allocation of value at least $b(S)/\log n$.*

PROOF. Obviously, by construction all candidates are feasible and so is the output allocation.

Next, we prove that we need at most $\log n$ iterations of the while loop by showing that in each iteration at most half of the remaining vertices are removed from the allocation. This means the cardinality of V' is at least halved in each iteration. Let V_i' be the set V' after the ith iteration of the *while* loop; $V_0' = V$.

Algorithm 3: Making a partly-feasible allocation fully feasible

---
1 $i := 1$;
2 $V' := V$;
3 **while** $V' \neq \emptyset$ **do**
4   initialize S_i by $S_i(v) := S(v)$ for $v \in V'$ and $S_i(v) := \emptyset$ otherwise ;
5   **for** $v \in V'$ *in order of decreasing π values* **do**
6   **if** $\sum_{u \in V', \, S_i(v) \cap S_i(u) \neq \emptyset} \bar{w}(u,v) < 1$ **then**
7   delete v from V' /* v stays in S_i */;
8   **else**
9 $S_i(v) := \emptyset$ /* v is removed from S_i */;
10 $i := i + 1$;
11 return the best one of the allocations $S_1, S_2, \ldots$

Let us fix $i \in \mathbb{N}$, and $v \in V'_{i+1}$. We know that v has been removed from S_i by the algorithm. This only happens if

$$\sum_{\substack{u \in V'_i \\ S'_i(v) \cap S'_i(u) \neq \emptyset}} \bar{w}(u,v) \geq 1$$

where S'_i is the current state of S_i while the algorithm considers v. Since Equation 5 is obviously also satisfied for S'_i, it has to be

$$\sum_{\substack{u \in V'_i \\ \pi(u) > \pi(v) \\ S'_i(v) \cap S'_i(u) \neq \emptyset}} \bar{w}(u,v) \geq \frac{1}{2} \ .$$

For a vertex $u \in V'_i$ with $\pi(u) > \pi(v)$ we know that the vertex has either been removed from the allocation before (then $u \in V'_{i+1}$) or it stays in S_i (i.e. $S'_i(u) = S_i(u) = S(u)$ and $u \notin V'_{i+1}$). Hence

$$S'_i(u) = \begin{cases} \emptyset & \text{if } u \in V'_{i+1} \\ S(u) & \text{else} \end{cases} \ .$$

Combining these two insights, we get a necessary condition: if $v \in V'_{i+1}$ then

$$\sum_{u \in U_i(v) \setminus U_{i+1}(v)} \bar{w}(u,v) \geq \frac{1}{2} \ ,$$

where $U_i(v) = \{u \in V'_i \mid \pi(u) > \pi(v), S(v) \cap S(u) \neq \emptyset\}$. Summing up all $v \in V'_{i+1}$ we get

$$\sum_{v \in V'_{i+1}} \sum_{u \in U_i(v) \setminus U_{i+1}(v)} \bar{w}(u,v) \geq \frac{1}{2} |V'_{i+1}| \ .$$

On the other hand, we can change the ordering of the sums and use the symmetry of the weights $\bar{w}$ to get

$$\sum_{v \in V'_{i+1}} \sum_{u \in U_i(v) \setminus U_{i+1}(v)} \bar{w}(u,v) = \sum_{u \in V'_i \setminus V'_{i+1}} \sum_{\substack{v \in V'_{i+1} \\ \pi(u) > \pi(v) \\ S(v) \cap S(u) \neq \emptyset}} \bar{w}(u,v)$$

$$= \sum_{u \in V'_i \setminus V'_{i+1}} \sum_{\substack{u \in V'_{i+1} \\ \pi(u) < \pi(v) \\ S(v) \cap S(u) \neq \emptyset}} \bar{w}(u,v) < \frac{1}{2} |V'_i \setminus V'_{i+1}|$$

where the last bound is due to Condition (5).

In combination this yields

$$|V'_{i+1}| < |V'_i \setminus V'_{i+1}| \ ,$$

which implies

$$|V'_{i+1}| < \frac{1}{2} |V'_i| \ ,$$

meaning less than half of the remaining vertices are removed in each iteration.

So, since $|V'_0| = n$, we can conclude that

$$|V'_i| < \frac{1}{2^i} \cdot n \ .$$

Therefore, we get $|V'_{\log n}| < 1$. Thus the algorithm terminates within $\log n$ steps.

By definition, for all vertices $S_i(v) = S(v)$ for exactly one $i \in [\log n]$ and $S_i(v) = \emptyset$ else. So $\sum_{i \in [\log n]} b(S_i) = b(S)$. This yields for the value of the output

$$\max_{i \in [\log n]} b(S_i) \geq \frac{1}{\log n} \sum_{i \in [\log n]} b(S_i) = \frac{b(S)}{\log n} \ .$$

$\square$

As a consequence, the computed feasible allocation has a value that in expectation is at most an $\mathcal{O}(\sqrt{k}\rho \log n)$ factor smaller than that of the optimal LP solution.

4. APPLICATIONS

In the previous sections we have described a general algorithmic approach to channel allocation problems when the underlying conflict graph has bounded inductive independence number. Here we will show that this property is particularly wide-spread among models for interference in wireless communication. The concept of conflict graphs can be applied in two basic scenarios. On the one hand, the task could be to allocate channels to *transmitters*. Each transmitter intends to cover a certain area, e.g., a base station in a cellular network. The interference model defines which transmitters can be assigned the same channels. On the other hand, instead of single transmitters one can consider pairs of network nodes (*links*) that act as sender and receiver. In such a scenario, "users" are no single network nodes but links. Therefore, the vertices of the conflict graph are links, and edges define which links can be assigned the same channels.

Simple transmitter scenarios such as disk graphs models have been studied extensively in theoretical computer science. While our framework applies in this case and can be used to obtain $O(\sqrt{k})$-approximations (see the full version), there are existing algorithmic approaches that provide better guarantees for this special case. In addition, disk graphs are known to be an inadequate model for many aspects of realistic wireless communication. Instead, we here focus on models for link-based scenarios with different level of detail. Our aim is not to prove optimal bounds in each case but to show why we believe a bounded inductive independence number to be a key insight for understanding algorithmic problems in wireless networking.

4.1 Unweighted Link-Based Scenarios

There are a number of different interference models for link-based scenarios that can be described by some unweighted

183

conflict graph. They are often called graph-based interference models, but to avoid ambiguities we refer to them as *binary interference models*. Due to the large variety, we have to confine ourselves to some selected examples.

Probably the best known binary model is the *Protocol Model* [17]. Network nodes are modeled by points located in the plane. A link consisting of sender s and receiver r may be allocated to a channel if and only if for all other senders s' on this channel $d(s', r) \geq (1 + \Delta)d(s, r)$ for some constant $\Delta > 0$.

Proposition 9 (Wan [28]). *For the protocol model, the resulting conflict graph has an inductive independence number of*

$$\rho \leq \left\lceil \pi / \arcsin \frac{\Delta}{2(\Delta + 1)} \right\rceil - 1 \ . \ .$$

The *IEEE 802.11 Model* by Alicherry et al. [2] is a bidirectional variant of this model, and in this case $\rho \leq 23$ [28].

A more graph-theoretical approach is *distance-2 matching* [3]. In this case, two edges $e \neq e'$ may be allocated to the same channel if there are at least two edges on any connecting path. Typically, results are restricted to certain graph classes, because in general approximating maximum distance-2 matchings is hard. For disk graphs, we can also show that the corresponding conflict graph has $\rho = \mathcal{O}(1)$. Interestingly, for distance-2 matching there is already an algorithm and analysis based on the observation that the inductive independence number is bounded, but the concepts are termed differently. Barrett et al. [4] analyze a greedy approach to find a maximum independent set. For a link $e = (u, v)$, they define $r(e) = r(u) + r(v)$, where $r(u)$ and $r(v)$ are the radius of the disk surrounding u resp. v. The algorithm orders the links by increasing values of $r(e)$. The key observation is now that for all links e the maximum number of links of higher index that collide with e but not with each other is $\mathcal{O}(1)$. This immediately yields $\rho = \mathcal{O}(1)$.

Corollary 10. *For distance-2 matching in disk graphs the associated conflict graph has an inductive independence number $\rho = \mathcal{O}(1)$.*

Analyses of greedy algorithms are often carried out in a similar manner. Such arguments already suffice to bound the inductive independence number. There is plenty of opportunity to further extend our results by similar observations.

4.2 Physical Model

The models mentioned above go well with graph-theoretic concepts. However, radio transmissions typically decrease asymptotically with increasing distance. The *physical model* captures this property much more accurately and is particularly wide-spread among engineers. Even though the physical model does not fit in the traditional binary graph-theoretic context, it has similar properties allowing it to be expressed using edge-weighted conflict graphs.

In this model, network nodes are located in a metric space. The received signal strength decreases as the distance increases. If a node transmits at a power level p, the signal strength at a distance of d is p/d^α, for a constant α. A transmission is received successfully if the signal strength by concurrent transmissions plus ambient noise is below some constant threshold $\beta > 0$. More formally, given pairs of senders s_i and receivers r_i that transmit at power level p_i, receiver r_i can decode the signal from sender s_i successfully if the SINR constraint

$$\frac{p_i}{d(s_i, r_i)^\alpha} \geq \beta \left(\sum_{j \in M \setminus \{i\}} \frac{p_j}{d(s_j, r_i)^\alpha} + \nu \right)$$

is fulfilled. Here M is the set of links transmitting at the same time on the same channel and $\nu \geq 0$ is a constant expressing ambient noise.

Note that we can easily reduce the model to a conflict graph if transmission powers are fixed. Prominent and simple classes of power assignments $p: V \to \mathbb{R}_{>0}$ are uniform ($p(v) = 1$) or linear ($p(v) = d(s_v, r_v)^\alpha$) assignments. More generally, we can consider assignments satisfying the following monotonicity constraints. If $d(\ell) \leq d(\ell')$ for two links ℓ, ℓ' then

$$p(\ell) \leq p(\ell') \quad \text{and} \quad \frac{p(\ell)}{d(\ell)^\alpha} \geq \frac{p(\ell')}{d(\ell')^\alpha} \ .$$

We furthermore assume the noise to play a minor role (cf. [23]).

Proposition 11. *The interference constraints in the physical model with fixed transmission power can be represented by a weighted conflict graph. If the power assignment satisfies the above constraints, the resulting inductive independence number is at most $\mathcal{O}(\log n)$.*

Interestingly, we can also use our approach if transmission powers are not given upfront. In this case, our algorithm has to decide about the assignment of links to channels and which transmission powers to use for each link. The first part is solved by LP rounding as above. In the LP we use edge weights ensuring that there is a feasible power assignment for the computed set of links. The second task of power assignment can then by done using a power control procedure by Kesselheim [22].

Note that, in contrast to the interference models mentioned above, in this case not all feasible solutions (i.e., feasibly scheduled sets of links) correspond to independent sets in the weighted graph. However, for our argument it suffices to observe that each set of feasible links corresponds to an LP solution for some ρ and that integral LP solutions with $\rho = 1$ also correspond to feasible sets of links. Combining these insights with the bounds in [22] and the ones we proved above, we obtain the following result.

Theorem 12. *There is a choice of edge weights such that our algorithm in combination with the power control procedure in [22] achieves an $\mathcal{O}(\sqrt{k} \log n)$ approximation in fading metrics and an $\mathcal{O}(\sqrt{k} \log^2 n)$ approximation in general metrics.*

5. MECHANISM DESIGN

In this section we show how to apply the framework proposed by Lavi and Swamy [24] to obtain a truthful mechanism for the problem, in which the valuations for the allocations are private information. We only highlight the main ideas of this technique and the most important observations that allow the use for our problem.

The main idea of the approach is to decompose an optimal LP solution x^* into a set of polynomially many integral solutions with the following property. For each integral solution we determine a probability, and the expected cost of a randomly chosen solution according to the probabilities is exactly b^*/α, where in our case $\alpha \leq 8 \cdot \sqrt{k} \cdot \rho$. Given such a decomposition, we can use scaled VCG payments to implement a randomized mechanism that is truthful in expectation. For an accessible presentation of the complete technique, see [25, Chapter 12] or [24].

In particular, for simplicity let us first consider only a constant number of channels; the adjustment to arbitrary many channels is treated below. We ask the vertices to obtain all valuations for all channel bundles and solve the corresponding LP (interference information is assumed to be publicly available). Note that at this point we are given the optimal solution to an *infeasible* LP. We set up a decomposition LP with exponentially many variables – one for each *feasible* integral solution – that represent our desired probabilities. This LP has exponentially many constraints but polynomially many variables. We can construct the dual with polynomially many variables and exponentially many constraints. The variables can be interpreted as valuations in an adjusted combinatorial auction problem. If this problem has an algorithm that verifies an integrality gap, we obtain a separation oracle and can solve the dual decomposition LP in polynomial time. In particular, it allows us to construct an equivalent LP with a polynomial number of constraints, i. e., the ones corresponding to the solutions obtained by our algorithm. For this polynomial-sized dual we construct the primal and determine the polynomially many probabilities of the solutions found by our algorithm, which completes the decomposition.

It remains to verify that our algorithms provide integral solutions within the desired integrality gap of α for the adjusted combinatorial auction problems using dual variables as valuations. We note here that our algorithms bound the integrality gap of LP (1) and (4), and they can be derandomized using the technique of pairwise independence. In this way, given an optimal LP solution x^* we can obtain an integral solution of value at least b^*/α. Note that our LP describe, in fact, relaxations of the combinatorial auction problem with conflict graphs, because Conditions (1b) and (4b) allow each vertex to have multiple neighbors on the same channel. An arbitrary integral solution to the LP might thus be infeasible for the original problem. This is even more severe in the case of the physical model with power control, where even the interpretation of edge weights is significantly disconnected from the actual interference that is received. However, our algorithms produce feasible integral solutions with the desired gap to the infeasible fractional optimum. Thus, they also prove the gap for a potential fractional optimum to the LP describing the (more constrained) exact combinatorial auction problem with conflict graphs in the respective cases. The remaining arguments can be adapted from [24] almost without adjustment.

In case of an arbitrary number of channels, we can use demand oracles to solve the LPs. This results in only a polynomial number of (non-zero) variables for the LP and for the dual of the decomposition LP. Note that the procedure to separate the dual of the decomposition LP does not require demand oracles. In fact, the complete decomposition procedure can be carried out without accessing the original bidder valuations.

6. ASYMMETRIC CHANNELS

Up to now, channels were symmetric in terms of interfer-

ence, which means the same interference model is applied to each channel. In a more general setting, for each of the k channels a different edge set E_j resp. a different edge-weight function w_j for the interference graph is given.

In this case, we have an edge weight function $\bar{w}_j$ for each channel $j \in [k]$. The above LP relaxation be easily adapted by exchanging $\bar{w}$ by $\bar{w}_j$ in the constraints (1b). In contrast, the analysis of the rounding algorithms internally depends on the assumption of symmetric channels. In particular, the proof of Lemma 4 uses the symmetry.

However, when exchanging the probability for a vertex v to choose set T by $x_{v,T}^{(l)}/2k\rho$ resp. $x_{v,T}^{(l)}/4k\rho$, the proof of Lemma 4 can be carried out the same way without using the symmetry.

Hence, for the asymmetric case, we lose a factor of $\mathcal{O}(k \cdot \rho)$ resp. $\mathcal{O}(k \cdot \rho \cdot \log n)$ in the LP rounding step. This represents our approximation ratio. The result may seem like a trivial generalization of the $k = 1$ case. However, this is not true as multiple graphs make the problem much harder. We can justify the approximation factor by a hardness bound, which is proven in the full version.

Theorem 13. *For each ρ, k with $\rho \cdot k = \mathcal{O}(\log n)$ there is no $\rho \cdot k/2^{\mathcal{O}(\sqrt{\log(\rho \cdot k)})}$ approximation algorithm for asymmetric channels unless $\mathsf{P} = \mathsf{NP}$.*

As we see, for asymmetric channels our algorithms are close to optimal without making further assumptions about the interference model.

7. OPEN PROBLEMS

In this paper we present a general framework for secondary spectrum auctions that works with a large number of interference models. Our approach can easily be extended to even more models by proving bounds on the inductive independence number in the associated graphs. To improve the results in this paper, it would, e.g., be interesting to know if for the physical model it also holds that $\rho = \mathcal{O}(1)$ in general metrics or for distance-based power assignments.

For obtaining a truthful mechanism we use decomposition and rounding of LP solutions, and we heavily rely on the ellipsoid method. It is an interesting question if this could be avoided to make the algorithm more applicable in practice.

8. REFERENCES

[1] Karhan Akcoglu, James Aspnes, Bhaskar DasGupta, and Ming-Yang Kao. Opportunity cost algorithms for combinatorial auctions. *CoRR*, cs.CE/0010031, 2000.

[2] Mansoor Alicherry, Randeep Bhatia, and Li (Erran) Li. Joint channel assignment and routing for throughput optimization in multi-radio wireless mesh networks. In *Proceedings of the 11th International Conference on Mobile Computing and Networking (MobiCom)*, pages 58–72, 2005.

[3] H. Balakrishnan, C.L. Barrett, V.S.A. Kumar, M.V. Marathe, and S. Thite. The distance-2 matching problem and its relationship to the mac-layer capacity of ad hoc wireless networks. *Selected Areas in Communications, IEEE Journal on*, 22(6):1069 – 1079, aug. 2004.

[4] Christopher L. Barrett, V. S. Anil Kumar, Madhav V. Marathe, Shripad Thite, and Gabriel Istrate. Strong edge coloring for channel assignment in wireless radio

networks. In *Proceedings of the 4th annual IEEE international conference on Pervasive Computing and Communications Workshops (PERCOMW)*, page 106, 2006.

[5] Milind M. Buddhikot, Paul Kolodzy, Scott Miller, Kevin Ryan, and Jason Evans. Dimsumnet: New directions in wireless networking using coordinated dynamic spectrum access. In *Proceedings of the IEEE WoWMoM*, pages 78–85, 2005.

[6] George Christodoulou, Khaled Elbassioni, and Mahmoud Fouz. Truthful mechanisms for exhibitions. In *Proceedings of the 6th Workshop on Internet & Network Economics (WINE)*, pages 170–181, 2010.

[7] Peter Cramton, Yoav Shoham, and Richard Steinberg, editors. *Combinatorial Auctions*. MIT Press, 2006.

[8] Shahar Dobzinski, Noam Nisan, and Michael Schapira. Truthful randomized mechanisms for combinatorial auctions. In *Proceedings of the 38th ACM Symposium on Theory of Computing (STOC)*, pages 644–652, 2006.

[9] Alexander Fanghänel, Sascha Geulen, Martin Hoefer, and Berthold Vöcking. Online capacity maximization in wireless networks. In *Proceedings of the 22nd ACM Symposium on Parallelism in Algorithms and Architectures (SPAA)*, pages 92–99, 2010.

[10] Alexander Fanghänel, Thomas Kesselheim, Harald Räcke, and Berthold Vöcking. Oblivious interference scheduling. In *Proceedings of the 28th ACM Symposium on Principles of Distributed Computing (PODC)*, pages 220–229, 2009.

[11] Alexander Fanghänel, Thomas Kesselheim, and Berthold Vöcking. Improved algorithms for latency minimization in wireless networks. In *Proceedings of the 36th International EATCS Colloquium on Automata, Languages and Programming (ICALP)*, volume 2, pages 208–219, 2009.

[12] Uriel Feige and Jan Vondrák. Approximation algorithms for allocation problems: Improving the factor of 1-1/e. In *Proceedings of the 47th IEEE Symposium on Foundations of Computer Science (FOCS)*, pages 667–676, 2006.

[13] Aleksei V. Fishkin. Disk graphs: A short survey. In *Proceedings of the First Workshop on Approximation and Online Algorithms (WAOA)*, pages 260–264, 2003.

[14] S. Gandhi, C. Buragohain, Lili Cao, Haitao Zheng, and S. Suri. A general framework for wireless spectrum auctions. In *Proceedings of the 2nd IEEE International Symposium on New Frontiers in Dynamic Spectrum Access Networks (DySPAN)*, pages 22–33, April 2007.

[15] Olga Goussevskaia, Roger Wattenhofer, Magnús M. Halldórsson, and Emo Welzl. Capacity of arbitrary wireless networks. In *Proceedings of the 28th Conference of the IEEE Communications Society (INFOCOM)*, pages 1872–1880, 2009.

[16] Albert Gräf, Martin Stumpf, and Gerhard Weißenfels. On coloring unit disk graphs. *Algorithmica*, 20:277–293, 1994.

[17] Piyush Gupta and P. R. Kumar. The capacity of wireless networks. *IEEE Transactions on Information Theory*, 46:388–404, 2000.

[18] Magnús M. Halldórsson. Wireless scheduling with power control. In *Proceedings of the 17th European Symposium on Algorithms (ESA)*, pages 361–372, 2009.

[19] J. Håstad. Clique is hard to approximate within $n^{1-\varepsilon}$. *Acta Mathematica*, 182(1):105–142, 1999.

[20] Ron Holzman, Noa Kfir-Dahav, Dov Monderer, and Moshe Tennenholtz. Bundling equilibrium in combinatorial auctions. *Games and Economic Behavior*, 47(1):104–123, 2004.

[21] Omer Ileri, Dragan Samardzija, Theodore Sizer, and Narayan B. Mandayam. Demand responsive pricing and competitive spectrum allocation via a spectrum server. In *Proceedings of the 1st IEEE International Symposium on New Frontiers in Dynamic Spectrum Access Networks (DySPAN)*, pages 194–202, 2005.

[22] Thomas Kesselheim. A constant-factor approximation for wireless capacity maximization with power control in the SINR model. In *Proceedings of the 22nd ACM-SIAM Symposium on Discrete Algorithms (SODA)*, pages 1549–1559, 2011.

[23] Thomas Kesselheim and Berthold Vöcking. Distributed contention resolution in wireless networks. In *Proceedings of the 24th Symposium on Distributed Computing (DISC)*, pages 149–163, 2010.

[24] Ron Lavi and Chaitanya Swamy. Truthful and near-optimal mechanism design via linear programming. In *Proceedings of the 46th IEEE Symposium on Foundations of Computer Science (FOCS)*, pages 595–604, 2005.

[25] Noam Nisan, Éva Tardos, Tim Roughgarden, and Vijay Vazirani, editors. *Algorithmic Game Theory*. Cambridge University Press, 2007.

[26] Luca Trevisan. Non-approximability results for optimization problems on bounded degree instances. In *Proceedings of the 33rd ACM Symposium on Theory of Computing (STOC)*, pages 453–461, 2001.

[27] Jan Vondrák. Optimal approximation for the submodular welfare problem in the value oracle model. In *Proceedings of the 40th ACM Symposium on Theory of Computing (STOC)*, pages 67–74, 2008.

[28] Peng-Jun Wan. Multiflows in multihop wireless networks. In *Proceedings of the 10th ACM International Symposium Mobile Ad-Hoc Networking and Computing (MOBIHOC)*, pages 85–94, 2009.

[29] Yuli Ye and Allan Borodin. Elimination graphs. In *Proceedings of the 36th International EATCS Colloquium on Automata, Languages and Programming (ICALP)*, pages 774–785, 2009.

[30] Xia Zhou, Sorabh Gandhi, Subhash Suri, and Haitao Zheng. eBay in the Sky: Strategy-proof wireless spectrum auctions. In *Proceedings of the 14th International Conference on Mobile Computing and Networking (MobiCom)*, pages 2–13, 2008.

[31] Xia Zhou and Haitao Zheng. TRUST: A general framework for truthful double spectrum auctions. In *Proceedings of the 28th Conference of the IEEE Communications Society (INFOCOM)*, pages 999–1007, 2009.

Maximising Lifetime for Fault-Tolerant Target Coverage in Sensor Networks

Thomas Erlebach
Dept. of Computer Science,
University of Leicester,
England
t.erlebach@mcs.le.ac.uk

Tom Grant
Dept. of Computer Science,
University of Leicester,
England
tg53@mcs.le.ac.uk

Frank Kammer
Institut für Informatik,
Universität Augsburg,
Germany
kammer@informatik.uni-augsburg.de

ABSTRACT

We study the problem of maximising the lifetime of a sensor network for fault-tolerant target coverage in a setting with composite events. Here, a composite event is the simultaneous occurrence of a combination of atomic events, such as the detection of smoke and high temperature. We are given sensor nodes that have an initial battery level and can monitor certain event types, and a set of points at which composite events need to be detected. The points and sensor nodes are located in the Euclidean plane, and all nodes have the same sensing radius. The goal is to compute a longest activity schedule with the property that at any point in time, each event point is monitored by at least two active sensor nodes. We present a $(6 + \varepsilon)$-approximation algorithm for this problem by devising an approximation algorithm with the same ratio for the dual problem of minimising the weight of a fault-tolerant sensor cover and applying the Garg-Könemann algorithm. Our algorithm for the minimum-weight fault-tolerant sensor cover problem generalises previous approximation algorithms for geometric set cover with weighted unit disks and is obtained by enumerating properties of the optimal solution that guide a dynamic programming approach.

Categories and Subject Descriptors

F.2.2 [**Analysis of Algorithms and Problem Complexity**]: Nonnumerical Algorithms and Problems—*Geometrical problems and computations*

General Terms

Algorithms, Theory

Keywords

Approximation algorithm, unit disk graph, set multi-cover, dynamic programming

1. INTRODUCTION

Consider a sensor network whose task is to detect the occurrence of events at a given set of event points. Since sensors often have a limited battery supply, it is important to address the problem of maximising the lifetime of the network, i.e., the length of time during which the network can carry out its monitoring task successfully. The lifetime of the network can be prolonged by calculating an activity schedule in which only a subset of the sensor nodes is active at any point in time, and the remaining sensors are in a sleep mode that saves energy. The active nodes must be sufficient for performing the required monitoring task. Following [17, 14], we consider the setting where the events to be detected are *composite events*, i.e., events comprised of several simultaneous *atomic events* at the same location detected by different sensor types (e.g., detecting a fire by observing the atomic events of high temperature and smoke), and the sensor coverage is required to be *fault-tolerant*, i.e., the failure of any one sensor does not affect the sensing task. We assume that the sensor nodes and event points are located in the Euclidean plane, and all sensor nodes have the same sensing radius. Each sensor node can monitor a certain set of event types, and the composite event to be detected at each event point is a combination of atomic events corresponding to different event types.

A common approach to lifetime maximisation is to formulate the problem as a linear program and obtain an approximate solution by approximating the dual problem of computing a sensor cover of minimum weight (see, e.g., [2, 3, 8]). We follow the same approach and hence mainly consider the dual problem of minimising the weight of a fault-tolerant sensor cover. We model the latter problem as a weighted multi-cover problem with unit disks and a set of event types.

In the special case of atomic events of just one event type and no fault-tolerance requirements, the minimum weight sensor cover problem is a standard geometric set cover problem where the aim is to cover a given set of points using unit disks of minimum total weight. The best known approximation ratio for that problem is $4 + \varepsilon$ [9, 20]. Our setting poses the additional challenges of having to cover every point twice (turning the problem into a *multi-cover* problem) while avoiding the loss of a factor of two in the approximation ratio, and of dealing with different event types and composite events. Addressing these challenges requires us to refine the techniques that have been developed for the standard geometric set cover problem with unit disks.

1.1 Related Work

Sensor cover problems have been studied in several variants, including target coverage problems where a discrete set of points that need to be monitored is specified in the input, and region coverage problems where the area to be monitored is specified as a (typically convex) region in the plane. We refer to the survey by Thai et al. [16] for an overview. Berman et al. [2, 3] show that the region coverage problem can be reduced to the target coverage problem and present an algorithm with logarithmic approximation ratio. They also show that a minimum cost sensor cover algorithm with approximation ratio ρ implies an approximation algorithm with ratio $\rho(1 + \varepsilon)$ for the lifetime maximisation problem using the Garg-Könemann algorithm [11]. Zhao and Gurusamy [18] study the target coverage problem with the additional requirement that the sensors that are active at any time are connected. They obtain an algorithm with logarithmic approximation ratio and also present a performance evaluation based on simulation experiments. Sanders and Schieferdecker [15] show that the target coverage problem for sensors represented by unit disks with the objective of lifetime maximisation is $\mathcal{NP}$-hard. They provide a $(1 + \varepsilon)$-approximation algorithm using resource augmentation, i.e., their algorithm needs to increase the sensing range of every sensor node by a factor of $1 + \delta$, for some fixed $\delta > 0$. Vu et al. [17] and Marta et al. [14] consider fault-tolerant sensor cover problems with composite events. They present centralised and distributed heuristics and evaluate them in simulations. In this paper, we aim at designing approximation algorithms with provable performance guarantees for fault-tolerant sensor cover problems with composite events.

A special case of the minimum cost sensor cover problem is the weighted geometric set cover problem with unit disks. This problem has received considerable attention as it includes the weighted dominating set problem for unit disk graphs, which is relevant for routing backbone construction in wireless networks. This relationship also shows that the problem is $\mathcal{NP}$-hard [6]. A series of papers has presented approximation algorithms with smaller and smaller constant approximation ratios for weighted set cover with unit disks [1, 13, 7, 9, 20]. The currently best known ratio is $4 + \varepsilon$ [9, 20]. These results apply also to the minimum-weight dominating set problem in unit disk graphs. If one is interested in a minimum-weight *connected* dominating set, a standard approach is to first compute a cheap dominating set and then solve a node-weighted Steiner tree problem to connect it [1, 7, 9, 13, 20]. The node-weighted Steiner tree problem admits a 2.5α-approximation algorithm in unit disk graphs [10, 19], where α is the approximation ratio of the best known approximation algorithm for edge-weighted Steiner trees. Since $\alpha < 1.39$ [4], this gives approximation ratio less than 3.475. Together with the $(4 + \varepsilon)$-approximation from [9, 20], this yields a 7.475-approximation algorithm for minimum-weight connected dominating sets in unit disk graphs.

The unweighted set multi-cover problem has been studied in geometric settings by Chekuri et al. [5]. They present an $O(\log \text{OPT})$-approximation algorithm for set systems of bounded VC dimension, where OPT is the size of an optimal cover, and constant-factor approximation algorithms for covering points by half-spaces in three dimensions or for covering points with pseudo-disks in the Euclidean plane. Their results only apply to the unweighted case.

1.2 Our Results

We model the fault-tolerant target coverage problem with composite events as a generalised geometric multi-cover problem with unit disks and present a $(6 + \varepsilon)$-approximation algorithm, both for the lifetime maximisation variant and for the minimum cost sensor cover variant of the problem. On a high level, we solve the minimum cost sensor cover problem by providing a 6-approximation algorithm for the case where all event points are located in a square of bounded size (which we refer to as a *block*) and employing the geometric shifting strategy [12, 13]. To obtain the 6-approximation algorithm for a block, we 'guess' a number of properties of an optimal solution by enumeration, and then apply dynamic programming along horizontal and vertical strips of smaller squares. Because of the results of the 'guessing' step, we only need to handle the case where disks with centre outside a strip are used to cover points inside the strip, which makes a dynamic programming approach feasible. Our algorithm requires significant adaptations compared to previous work because of the multi-cover aspect and because there is more than one sensor type. Firstly, we need a considerably more involved 'guessing' step that allows us to classify the points in terms of the location of the disk which provides the covering. In particular, we need a non-trivial generalisation of the sandglass concept and we need to find a solution for the problem such that we do not count the same disk twice (once in a horizontal and once in a vertical strip) in order to ensure a feasible solution. In addition, we have to extend the dynamic programming algorithm such that we can find a 2-covering for the points and such that the algorithm can handle different event types. Using our approximation algorithm for minimum cost sensor cover as a subroutine in the Garg-Könemann algorithm [11], we also obtain approximation ratio $6 + \varepsilon$ for lifetime maximisation. Furthermore, provided that the communication radius of a sensor node is at least twice its sensing radius, we can use the known approximation algorithm for node-weighted Steiner trees in unit disk graphs and obtain approximation ratio 9.475 for the problem variants where the sets of active sensors are required to form a connected communication network.

The remainder of the paper is structured as follows. Section 2 covers preliminaries. In Section 3, we present the details of our dynamic programming approach to solve the minimum cost fault-tolerant sensor cover problem in a block. In Section 4, we describe the enumeration procedure that 'guesses' the properties of a fixed optimal solution that the dynamic program requires as input. Section 5 concludes the paper.

2. PRELIMINARIES

Consider the two-dimensional Euclidean plane. The x-coordinate and y-coordinate of a point p is denoted by x_p and y_p, respectively. The Euclidean distance between two points p and q is denoted by $\delta(p, q)$. If d is a disk, we also use d to refer to the centre of d, so that we can write $\delta(d, p)$ for the Euclidean distance between the centre of d and a point p. The power set of a set S is denoted by $\mathcal{P}(S)$. An algorithm for a maximisation, or minimisation, problem is a ρ-approximation algorithm if it runs in polynomial time and always outputs a solution with objective value at least OPT/ρ, or at most $\rho \cdot \text{OPT}$, where OPT denotes the objective value of an optimal solution.

2.1 Problem Definitions

Let T be a (constant-size) set of different event types (e.g., smoke, temperature, etc.). Consider a set P of points in the two-dimensional Euclidean plane and a set D of weighted unit disks. All disks have the same radius r, and without loss of generality we assume $r = 2$ throughout this paper. In the context of the target coverage problem, the disks in D correspond to sensor nodes (with r representing the sensing radius) and the points in P correspond to targets (event points) that need to be monitored. The weight of a disk $d \in D$ is non-negative and denoted by $w(d)$ or w_d. The total weight of a set $D' \subseteq D$ of disks is denoted by $w(D') = \sum_{d \in D'} w(d)$. Every disk (sensor) $d \in D$ has sensing components for a subset $T_d \subseteq T$ of event types. Every target $p \in P$ specifies a positive integer k_p as its coverage requirement and an event type $t_p \in T$ that needs to be monitored at p. (A target p at which composite events composed of the event types in some $T' \subseteq T$ need to be monitored is represented by $|T'|$ copies of p, with each copy p' associated with a different event type $t_{p'} \in T'$.)

We say that a disk $d \in D$ *covers* a point $p \in P$ if p is in d and $t_p \in T_d$. A set $D' \subseteq D$ of disks *meets the coverage requirements* of a point $p \in P$ if p is covered by at least k_p distinct disks in D', and D' is a *feasible multi-T-cover* if it meets the coverage requirements of all points $p \in P$. The objective of the *weighted multi-T-cover problem with unit disks*, denoted by WMCUD-T, is to compute a feasible multi-T-cover of minimum total weight. We mostly assume that $k_p \leq 2$ for all $p \in P$ and refer to this restriction of WMCUD-T as W2CUD-T.

The lifetime maximisation variant is defined as follows: We are given points and disks as in an instance of WMCUD-T, but additionally each disk $d \in D$ specifies an initial battery level b_d, expressed in suitable units so that b_d is the total duration during which d can be active before its battery runs out. A schedule is a set of pairs (D_i, x_i), where $D_i \subseteq D$ is a feasible multi-T-cover and $x_i \geq 0$. A schedule is feasible if for each $d \in D$, the sum of the x_i values of all pairs (D_i, x_i) with $d \in D_i$ does not exceed b_d. The lifetime of a schedule is the sum of the x_i values of all its pairs (D_i, x_i). The goal is to compute a feasible schedule of maximum lifetime. We refer to this problem as the *maximum lifetime multi-T-cover problem with unit disks* (MLMCUD-T), and the restricted version where $k_p \leq 2$ for all $p \in P$ as ML2CUD-T.

2.2 Lifetime Maximisation and the Algorithm by Garg and Könemann

A linear program Π of the form $\{\max c^T x \mid Ax \leq b, x \geq 0\}$, where A, b and c are non-negative, is called a *packing problem*. The linear program may be given implicitly, and the number of variables x_j may be exponential. For a given vector w, the problem of finding a column j of A such that $\sum_i A_{i,j} w_i / c_j$ is minimised is called the problem of *computing a column of minimum length* with respect to Π. It is known [2] that, if a packing problem Π' admits a ρ-approximation algorithm for the problem of computing a column of minimum length with respect to Π' for any given vector w, then the algorithm by Garg and Könemann [11] can be used to compute a $(1 + \varepsilon)\rho$-approximate solution to Π'.

The lifetime maximisation problem can be written as a linear program with a variable $x_{D'}$ for every feasible sensor cover $D' \subseteq D$, representing the length of the part of the schedule during which the set of active sensors is D'. A linear constraint for every node ensures that the total time during which the node is active does not exceed the battery life of that node. The linear program does not have polynomial size, as the number of variables $x_{D'}$ can be exponential, but it is a packing problem, and the algorithm by Garg and Könemann [11] can be applied. The problem of computing a column of minimum length is simply the problem of computing a feasible sensor cover D' of minimum cost, where the cost of a node $d \in D$ is given by some weight w_d. In our case, the latter problem is W2CUD-T. As we present a $(6 + \varepsilon)$-approximation algorithm for W2CUD-T in the remainder of the paper (Theorem 1), we obtain that, for every fixed $\varepsilon > 0$, there is a $(6 + \varepsilon)$-approximation algorithm for ML2CUD-T.

2.3 Plane Partition

As in previous work (e.g., [13]), our algorithms employ a partition of the plane. Imagine an infinite grid that partitions the plane into squares of side length 1.4 (any number sufficiently close to, but strictly less than, $\sqrt{2}$ would do). Consider an arbitrary such square S_{ij}. Note that any disk of radius 2 with centre in S_{ij} contains the whole square. Let $P_{ij} \subseteq P$ be the set of points from P that lie in S_{ij}. We can assume without loss of generality that no point or disk centre lies exactly on the boundary between two adjacent squares. The neighbouring infinite regions of a square S_{ij} are referenced as shown in Figure 1, with UL standing for 'upper left,' CR for 'centre right,' LM for 'lower middle', etc. Furthermore, let UPPER be the union of the regions UL, UM, UL, let LOWER be the union of LL, LM, LR, let LEFT be the union of UL, CL, LL, and let RIGHT be the union of UR, CR, LR.

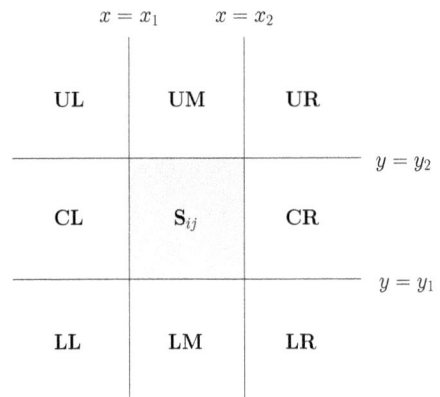

Figure 1: Square S_{ij} and neighbouring regions

For an integer constant $K > 0$ (which determines the ε term in the final approximation ratio), consider a partition of the plane into *blocks* so that each block B consists of $K \times K$ squares S_{ij}. If we have a ρ-approximation for W2CUD-T instances whose points lie in one block, we can obtain a $\rho(1 + O(1/K))$-approximation for general instances of W2CUD-T using the standard geometric shifting strategy [12]. (We omit further details of this process.) Consequently, the key to obtaining a good approximation algorithm for W2CUD-T is to achieve a good approximation ratio for instances where the points are located in one block.

3. 6-APPROXIMATION FOR W2CUD-T IN A BLOCK

Our approach to solve W2CUD-T in a $K \times K$ block consists of two stages: In the first stage, using enumeration we 'guess' properties of a fixed optimal solution. (Here and in the following, any reference to 'the optimal solution' refers to that fixed optimal solution.) In the second stage, we approximate the best solution with these properties using dynamic programming. We defer the details of the enumeration stage to Section 4. The outcome of the enumeration stage is that we can assume that we know for every point p in a square S_{ij} how often (zero times, once, or at least twice) it is to be covered by disks with centre in S_{ij} (and what up to two of those disks are), how often by disks with centre in UPPER or LOWER, and how often by disks with centre in LEFT or RIGHT. Moreover, for points that are to be covered once by a disk in UPPER or LOWER and once by a disk in LEFT or RIGHT, for one of the two cases we know that the point is to be covered by a disk from UM $\cup$ LM, or by a disk from CL $\cup$ CR. (This ensures that the two disks computed by the two different dynamic programs dealing with the point are distinct.) Dynamic programming is applied to each horizontal and each vertical strip of squares contained in the block B. In the following, we describe the dynamic program for a horizontal strip. Vertical strips are dealt with analogously.

3.1 Strip problem

Consider a horizontal strip H of squares, consisting of K squares S_{ij}. We are given a set P_H of points in the strip, and a set $D_{\bar{H}}$ of disks with centre above or below the strip (i.e., all the disks have centres in the union of the regions UPPER $\cup$ LOWER for all squares S_{ij} in the strip H). Each disk $d \in D_{\bar{H}}$ is associated with a weight $w(d)$ and a set T_d of event types. Each point $p \in P$ has an event type t_p and a coverage requirement $k_p \in \{1, 2\}$. If $k_p = 1$, the point may additionally specify that it must be covered by a disk with centre in UM $\cup$ LM (as opposed to being covered by any disk from UPPER $\cup$ LOWER). We let n_H denote the number of points in P_H. Let the points in $P_H = \{p_1, p_2, \ldots, p_{n_H}\}$ be ordered by non-decreasing x-coordinates, breaking ties arbitrarily.

A set $D' \subseteq D_{\bar{H}}$ of disks *meets the coverage requirement* of $p \in P_H$ if the following holds: If $k_p = 2$, then D' contains two distinct disks that cover p. If $k_p = 1$, then D' contains a disk that covers p, and if p requires to be covered by a disk from UM $\cup$ LM, then D' contains a disk that covers p and lies in that pair of regions. (Note that regions are specified with respect to the square S_{ij} that contains p.) It is easy to detect infeasible instances, so we only consider the case that there is a feasible solution, i.e., a set of disks $D' \subseteq D_{\bar{H}}$ that meets the coverage requirements of all points in P_H. The goal is to compute a feasible solution of minimum weight. We refer to this problem as the *strip problem*.

3.2 Outer and Inner Envelopes

For every $T' \in \mathcal{P}(T) \setminus \{\emptyset\}$, i.e., for every non-empty combination of event types in T, we consider twelve *envelopes*. Consider an arbitrary set $D_{T'}$ of disks that intersect a square S_{ij} and monitor exactly all the event types in T', i.e., $T_d = T'$ for all $d \in D_{T'}$. We consider an *outer T' envelope* and an *inner T' envelope* (with respect to $D_{T'}$) for each of the regions UL, UM, UR, LL, LM and LR. The purpose of

envelopes is to represent the disks lying in that region that cover points in P_H in a solution, in the sense that any point in P_H that is covered once or twice by disks from that region is also covered at least the same number of times by disks that are on the two envelopes of that region. The algorithm then aims at computing envelopes corresponding to a solution of minimum cost.

We next define the outer and inner T' envelope for the region UM (with respect to $D_{T'}$). (Envelopes for the remaining five regions can be defined analogously.) The *outer T' envelope* for the region UM represents the boundary of the union of all disks in $D_{T'}$ that have centre in the region UM. More specifically, the envelope is the segment of the boundary that lies in the square S_{ij}. (If at some x-coordinate there is no disk from UM that overlaps S_{ij}, we let the upper boundary of the square form a part of the envelope.) The *inner T' envelope for* UM is the envelope formed by the set of disks in $D_{T'}$ with centre in UM that remain after discarding the set of disks that form the outer T' envelope for UM. We view the set of disks in an envelope as ordered by non-decreasing x coordinates of their centres. Note that this is the order in which the disks appear on the envelope if we trace the envelope from left to right.

3.3 Dynamic Programming

We create a table W_{p_i} for every point $p_i \in P_H$. For every $T' \in \mathcal{P}(T) \setminus \{\emptyset\}$, we have the following indexes for the table W_{p_i}: For each of the six regions UL, UM, UR, LL, LM and LR, we have a set of up to three disks that are candidates for the disk d that is on the outer T' envelope of that region at position $x = x_{p_i}$, for the disk just before d on that envelope, and for the disk just after d on that envelope. For the inner T' envelope of each of the six regions, we have one disk that is a candidate for being the disk on that envelope at position $x = x_{p_i}$. Hence, an entry of the table W_{p_i} is indexed by $24 \cdot (2^{|T|} - 1)$ disks (three disks for each of the six outer envelopes, and one disk for each of the six inner envelopes, for each choice $T' \subseteq T$). For ease of presentation, we write the indexes for the table W_{p_i} as two sets of disks D_{U} and D_{L}, where D_{U} contains all the disks from inner and outer T' envelopes for any T' and regions UL, UM and UR, and D_{L} contains all the disks from inner and outer T' envelopes for any T' and regions LL, LM and LR.

Consider the case that the indexes for the table W_{p_i} for each T' are chosen as the disks that actually form the envelopes under consideration in the optimal solution. We can observe that, if p_i is covered once or twice by the optimal solution, then it is also covered once or twice, respectively, by the disks constituting the indexes for the table.

The value of an entry of table W_{p_i} is infinity if the disks indexing the table entry do not meet the coverage requirement for p_i, and otherwise the minimum cost of a set of disks that includes all the disks indexing the table entry of W_{p_i} and that also meets the coverage requirements of all points preceding p_i in P_H. Once all the tables W_{p_i} have been computed, the set of disks corresponding to the minimum value of any entry of $W_{p_{n_H}}$ is output as the solution.

The table entries for the leftmost point $p_1 \in P_H$ are initialised as follows. For every choice of indexes D_{U} and D_{L}, the table entry $W_{p_1}(D_{\text{U}}, D_{\text{L}})$ is set to $w(D_{\text{U}}) + w(D_{\text{L}})$ if $D_{\text{U}} \cup D_{\text{L}}$ meets the coverage requirement of point p_1, and to ∞ otherwise. For subsequent points $p_i \in P_H$, the value of an entry of W_{p_i} is calculated as the cost for the set of disks specified as indexes of the entry plus the cost of a cheapest set of disks covering all points up to p_{i-1}, which can be found in the table $W_{p_{i-1}}$, while ensuring that the costs of disks contained in both sets are counted only once:

$$W_{p_i}(D_U, D_L) =$$

$$\begin{cases} \infty, & \text{if } D_U \cup D_L \text{ does not meet} \\ & \quad \text{the coverage requirement for } p_i \\ \min_{D_U', D_L'} \left\{ \begin{array}{l} W_{p_{i-1}}(D_U', D_L') + \\ w(D_U - D_U') + w(D_L - D_L') \end{array} \right\}, & \text{otherwise} \end{cases}$$

Consider the last point $p_{n_H} \in P_H$. The minimum value in the table $W_{p_{n_H}}$ is the cost of the minimum weight solution that covers all points in P_H. The proof of correctness is omitted due to space limitations.

3.4 Solving W2CUD-T in a Block

Consider an instance of W2CUD-T in a block B of $K \times K$ squares, and assume that we know from the enumeration stage how often each point is to be covered by disks from different regions. We apply the dynamic program to the strip problem for each of the K horizontal strips in B and (by rotating the plane by $90°$) each of the K vertical strips. The union of the $2K$ solutions together with the set of disks that has been determined to be in the solution by the enumeration stage is then output as the solution for the entire block B. This gives a 6-approximation algorithm for instances of W2CUD-T where all points lie in one $K \times K$ block. (Details are deferred to the full version.) As remarked in Section 2, this implies the following.

THEOREM 1. *For every fixed $\varepsilon > 0$, there is a $(6 + \varepsilon)$-approximation algorithm for* W2CUD-T.

3.5 Connected Sensor Cover

Up to now we have considered only the condition that the selected sensors meet the coverage requirement of each point in P. In many applications, such as the settings described in [14, 17], it is additionally required that the selected sensors form a connected network. For this, it is assumed that each sensor node is equipped with a wireless radio that allows it to transmit messages to any other node that is located within a certain communication radius r_c from it. (This corresponds to a communication graph where the sensor nodes are represented by disks of radius $r_c/2$ and two nodes are adjacent if their disks intersect.) It is natural to expect that r_c is larger than the sensing radius r. Under the assumption that $r_c \geq 2r$, we can extend our approximation algorithms for W2CUD-T and ML2CUD-T to the problem variants with connectivity requirement.

For W2CUD-T with connectivity requirement, we first compute a $(6 + \varepsilon)$-approximate solution D' to the problem without the connectivity requirement, by using the algorithm from Theorem 1. Then, viewing the given disks as disks of radius $r_c/2$, we solve the minimum node-weighted Steiner tree problem in the corresponding unit-disk graph for the disks in D' as terminals, using the algorithm with approximation ratio less than 3.475 for node-weighted Steiner trees in unit disk graphs [10, 19, 4]. Let S be the set of Steiner nodes output by the algorithm. The set $D' \cup S$ is then output as a solution to W2CUD-T with connectivity

requirement. Let OPT_c be an optimal solution to W2CUD-T with connectivity requirement. Observe that OPT_c is a (superset of a) feasible solution to the Steiner tree problem considered above: OPT_c is connected and contains disks covering every point in P. Every disk in D' covers a point in P, and hence the centre of any disk in D' is within distance $r + r \leq r_c$ of the centre of some disk in OPT_c. Consequently, $\text{OPT}_c \cup D'$ is connected. This shows that the Steiner tree approximation algorithm produces a set S of cost less than 3.475 times the cost of OPT_c. As the cost of D' is within a factor of $6 + \varepsilon$ of the optimal solution to W2CUD-T without connectivity requirement, and thus within the same factor of the cost of OPT_c, the overall approximation ratio is bounded by 9.475 if ε is chosen sufficiently small.

THEOREM 2. *There is a 9.475-approximation algorithm for the variants of* W2CUD-T *and* ML2CUD-T *where the active disks need to be connected and $r_c \geq 2r$.*

4. GUESSING PROPERTIES OF THE OPTIMAL SOLUTION BY ENUMERATION

In this section, we describe how the knowledge of properties of the optimal solution that is required by the dynamic programming algorithm in Section 3 can be obtained using enumeration techniques. Fix an arbitrary optimal solution OPT_B to the given instance of W2CUD-T in a block B. We present the enumeration technique using the notion of 'guessing'. When we write that the algorithm 'guesses' a property of OPT_B, this means that the algorithm enumerates all possibilities for that property in such a way that one of the possibilities is guaranteed to be the desired property of the optimal solution. The enumeration is done for each of the K^2 squares S_{ij} contained in B. Consider one such square S_{ij}. Let the left and right boundary of S_{ij} lie on the line $x = x_1$ and $x = x_2$, respectively, and the bottom and top boundary on the line $y = y_1$ and $y = y_2$, respectively (cf. Figure 1).

First, for every event type t_l in T, we guess whether OPT_B contains 0, 1 or at least 2 disks with centre in S_{ij} that monitor event type t_l. Furthermore, in the second and third case we also guess the one disk or two of those disks, respectively. Note that a disk with centre in S_{ij} must contain the whole square S_{ij}, as the disk has radius $r = 2$ and the square has side length less than $\sqrt{2}$. Furthermore, two disks with centre in S_{ij} that cover event type t_l are sufficient to meet the coverage requirements of all points $p \in P_{ij}$ with $t_p = t_l$, so it is not necessary to guess more than two such disks.

Next, we aim at guessing a partition of the square S_{ij} into areas such that for the points p in the same area, we know whether they are covered by UPPER $\cup$ LOWER, by LEFT $\cup$ RIGHT, or once by UPPER $\cup$ LOWER (possibly restricted to UM $\cup$ LM) and once by LEFT $\cup$ RIGHT (possibly restricted to CL $\cup$ CR). Moreover, we guess a separate such partition for each event type $t_l \in T$. For each $t_l \in T$, the steps involved in guessing the partition are as follows. First, we determine areas called *2-watching t_l sandglasses* (the terminology is motivated by a similar sandglass concept in [13]) for the four regions UM, LM, CL and CR. For each of these areas, we can require that points are covered only by UPPER $\cup$ LOWER, or only by LEFT $\cup$ RIGHT. Second, we consider *1-watching envelopes*, i.e., envelopes of the disks in OPT_B with centre in one of the regions UM, LM, CL and CR, and guess the four points where adjacent envelopes intersect. Based on the locations of these intersection points, we can segment the square into smaller areas and deduce for each of the smaller areas whether the points located in the area are to be covered from UPPER ∪ LOWER or from LEFT ∪ RIGHT (or from both). The details of the partition of the square into areas for one specific event type t_l are presented in the following.

4.1 2-Watching Sandglasses

We define the 2-watching t_l sandglass for the region LM. The sandglasses for the regions UM, CR and CL are defined similarly (by rotation). Let P'_{ij} be the set of points in P_{ij} that have event type t_l, i.e., the set of points p with $t_p = t_l$. Consider the set $P^2_{LM} \subseteq P'_{ij}$ of all points in P'_{ij} that are covered by two distinct disks from LM in OPT$_B$, but not covered by any disk in OPT$_B$ that does not have centre in LM. For each $p \in P^2_{LM}$, consider the line l_p through p with slope 1, and let p' be the point where l_p intersects the line $y = y_1$. Let p_l be the point in P^2_{LM} for which p' is leftmost. Similarly, let l'_p be the line through p with slope -1, and let p'' be the intersection point of l'_p and $y = y_1$. Let p_r be the point in P^2_{LM} for which p'' is rightmost. The 2-watching t_l sandglass for LM is now defined as the area that is obtained as the intersection of the halfplane below l_{p_l}, the halfplane below l'_{p_r}, and the square S_{ij}. See Figure 2 for an illustration.[1] Note that this sandglass is uniquely determined by p_l and p_r and there are $O(|P_{ij}|^2)$ possibilities for guessing p_l and p_r.

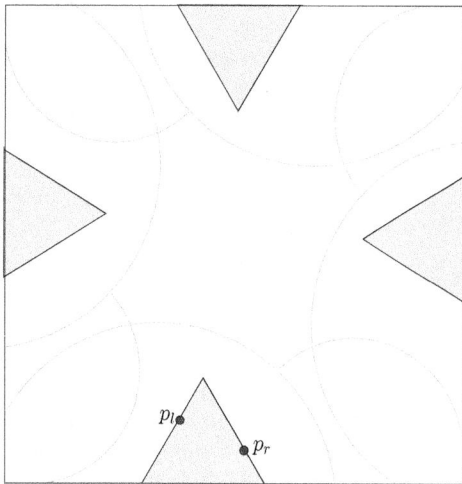

Figure 2: 2-watching sandglasses

We show that the coverage requirements of any point of P'_{ij} located in the 2-watching t_l sandglass for LM are met by disks from UPPER ∪ LOWER. Let the *lower-shadow* of a point p be the region that is the intersection of the halfplane below the line with slope 1 through p, the halfplane below the line with slope -1 through p, and the square S_{ij}. The left-shadow, up-shadow, and right-shadow of a point are defined analogously.

We state the following lemma due to Huang et al. [13].

LEMMA 1. [13] *If a point $p \in P'_{ij}$ is covered by a disk d from LM, then any point in the lower-shadow of p is also covered by the same disk from LM.*

---
[1]Figure 2 and subsequent figures are not drawn to scale as they serve only illustrative purposes.

The lemma directly implies the following corollary.

COROLLARY 1. *If a point $p \in P'_{ij}$ is covered by two disks d_1, d_2 from LM, then any point in the lower-shadow of p is also covered by the same two disks d_1, d_2 from LM.*

We also require the following lemma, which we prove by application of Lemma 1.

LEMMA 2. *The coverage requirement for any point $p \in P'_{ij}$ that lies inside the 2-watching t_l sandglass for LM is met by disks in OPT$_B$ from UPPER ∪ LOWER.*

PROOF. Consider the points p_l and p_r defining the 2-watching t_l sandglass for LM. For points in the lower-shadow of p_l or in the lower-shadow of p_r, the lemma follows from Corollary 1. Let p be a point that lies in the 2-watching t_l sandglass for LM, but not in the lower-shadows of p_l or p_r. Assume that p is covered by a disk d with centre in CL or CR by OPT$_B$. Then, by Lemma 1 applied to the left-shadow or right-shadow of p, respectively, we find that p_l or p_r is also covered by d, a contradiction to the choice of p_l and p_r. □

It follows that the coverage requirements of all points in the 2-watching t_l sandglasses for LM and for UM are satisfied by disks in OPT$_B$ from UPPER ∪ LOWER, and the coverage requirements of all points in the 2-watching t_l sandglasses for CL and for CR are satisfied by disks in OPT$_B$ from LEFT ∪ RIGHT. Hence, all the points from P'_{ij} that lie in 2-watching t_l sandglasses can be classified accordingly. These points are ignored for the classifications of points described in the following sections, i.e., their classification is not changed if they are contained in one of the areas under consideration there.

4.2 1-Watching Envelopes

It remains to deal with points from P'_{ij} that do not lie in one of the 2-watching t_l sandglasses. For each of the four regions UM, LM, CL and CR, we consider a *1-watching t_l envelope* that represents the boundary of disks in OPT$_B$ that monitor event type t_l and have centre in that region. More precisely, the 1-watching t_l envelope is formed by the intersection of that boundary with the square S_{ij}. See Figure 3a, where the 1-watching UM and LM envelopes are drawn in bold, for an illustration. The boundary of the square is used to fill in parts of the envelope where no disk from the respective region intersects the square. We have separate envelopes for each $t_l \in T$.

We call the 1-watching envelopes of CL and UM *adjacent*, and similarly those of UM and CR, etc. Allow us to define *intersection points* of adjacent 1-watching envelopes and describe how they are used to partition the remainder of square S_{ij} into areas such that we can specify for the points in each region whether they are covered by OPT$_B$ using disks in UPPER ∪ LOWER or in LEFT ∪ RIGHT.

LEMMA 3. *Adjacent 1-watching t_l envelopes intersect in exactly one intersection point.*

PROOF. By the dimension of the square S_{ij} and the radius of the disks, it follows that the direction of any tangent to the 1-watching t_l envelope for UM or LM is in the open interval $(-\pi/4, \pi/4)$, and the direction of any tangent to the 1-watching t_l envelope for CL or CR is in the open interval

$(\pi/4, 3\pi/4)$. Therefore, it is impossible that two adjacent 1-watching t_l envelopes have more than one intersection point. As each envelope is a curve connecting points on opposite sides of the square, it follows that two adjacent envelopes always intersect. □

Hence, there are four intersection points between adjacent 1-watching t_l envelopes. Note that each of these intersection points is uniquely specified by the two disks whose boundaries intersect at that point. Therefore, it suffices to guess 8 disks in order to determine the four intersection points.

Let the intersection point of the 1-watching t_l envelopes for CL and UM be denoted by $i_{\mathrm{CL}}^{\mathrm{UM}}$. Similarly, let $i_{\mathrm{CR}}^{\mathrm{UM}}$ be the intersection point of the 1-watching t_l envelopes of UM and CR, $i_{\mathrm{CR}}^{\mathrm{LM}}$ the intersection point of the 1-watching t_l envelopes for CR and LM, and $i_{\mathrm{CL}}^{\mathrm{LM}}$ the intersection point of the 1-watching t_l envelopes for LM and CL.

4.3 Areas in a Square

Assume that $i_{\mathrm{CL}}^{\mathrm{UM}}$ is to the left of $i_{\mathrm{CR}}^{\mathrm{UM}}$ (i.e., has smaller x-coordinate), $i_{\mathrm{CR}}^{\mathrm{UM}}$ is above $i_{\mathrm{CR}}^{\mathrm{LM}}$ (i.e., has larger y-coordinate), $i_{\mathrm{CR}}^{\mathrm{LM}}$ is to the right of $i_{\mathrm{CL}}^{\mathrm{LM}}$, and $i_{\mathrm{CL}}^{\mathrm{LM}}$ is below $i_{\mathrm{CL}}^{\mathrm{UM}}$. We call this the *standard configuration*. The treatment of other alternative configurations is deferred to subsequent sections. For the standard configuration, define i_1 to be $i_{\mathrm{CL}}^{\mathrm{UM}}$, i_2 to be $i_{\mathrm{CR}}^{\mathrm{UM}}$, i_3 to be $i_{\mathrm{CR}}^{\mathrm{LM}}$, and i_4 to be $i_{\mathrm{CL}}^{\mathrm{LM}}$, as shown in Figure 3a. For an arbitrary intersection point i_s, let l_s and l_s' be the two lines through i_s with slope 1 and -1, respectively. As illustrated in Figure 3b, define MIDDLE to be the region that is the intersection of the halfplanes below l_1 and l_2' and the halfplanes above l_3 and l_4'. Let MIDDLE-L be the region that is the intersection of the halfplanes below l_1 and l_1' and the halfplanes above l_4 and l_4', and similarly let MIDDLE-R be the region that is the intersection of the halfplanes below l_2 and l_2' and the halfplanes above l_3 and l_3', as shown in Figure 3b. We claim that the coverage requirements of all points in the regions MIDDLE-L and MIDDLE-R are met in OPT_B by disks with centre in LEFT $\cup$ RIGHT. We state the arguments for points within the region MIDDLE-L, and identical arguments apply to MIDDLE-R. Observe that the region MIDDLE-L lies entirely below the 1-watching t_l envelope for UM. This is because MIDDLE-L is contained in the 90 degree cone below i_1 that lies between l_1 and l_1', while the 1-watching t_l envelope for UM lies in the union of the halfplanes above l_1 and above l_1' (this is because the tangent to any point in the 1-watching t_l envelope for UM has direction between $-\pi/4$ and $\pi/4$, which follows because S_{ij} has side length less than $\sqrt{2}$ and the disks have radius 2). Similarly, MIDDLE-L lies entirely above the 1-watching t_l envelope for LM. Therefore, it is not possible that a point in MIDDLE-L is covered by a disk with centre in UM or LM in OPT_B, and so the coverage requirements of all points in MIDDLE-L are indeed met in OPT_B by disks from LEFT $\cup$ RIGHT. Thus, we can classify the points in MIDDLE-L and MIDDLE-R accordingly.

The regions MIDDLE-U and MIDDLE-D are defined analogously to MIDDLE-L and MIDDLE-R, with MIDDLE-U enclosed by lines l_1, l_1', l_2, l_2' and MIDDLE-D enclosed by lines l_3, l_3', l_4, l_4', see Figure 3b. Furthermore, the region obtained by removing MIDDLE-L, MIDDLE-U, MIDDLE-R and MIDDLE-D from MIDDLE (which may be empty) is denoted by MIDDLE-M. By arguments analogous to those given above, the coverage requirements of points in regions MIDDLE-U and MIDDLE-D are met in OPT_B by disks from UPPER $\cup$ LOWER. Hence, the points in these regions can be classified accordingly. Fi-

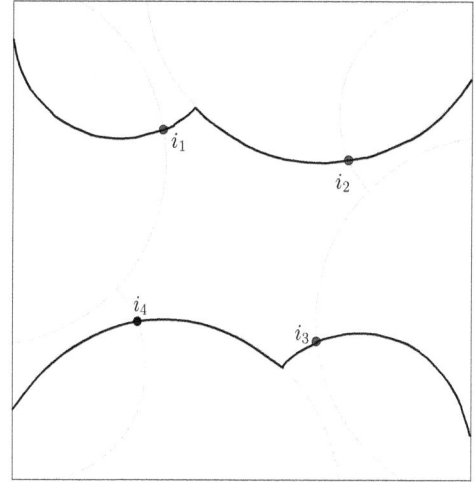

(a) Intersection points

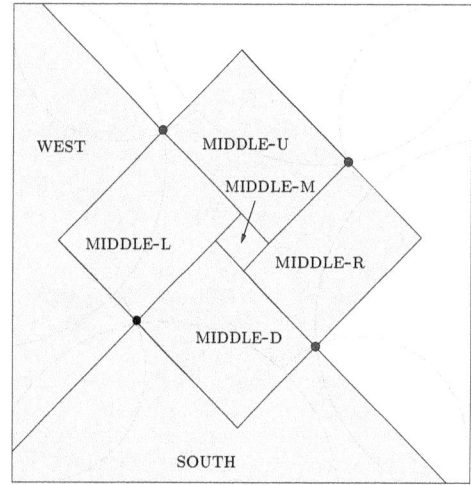

(b) Regions

Figure 3: Intersection points of 1-watching envelopes, and resulting central and peripheral regions

nally, the region MIDDLE-M lies outside all four 1-watching t_l envelopes, and so the points in that region can only be covered in OPT_B by disks from regions UL, UR, LL or LR. These regions are in UPPER $\cup$ LOWER and in LEFT $\cup$ RIGHT, so we can (arbitrarily giving preference to the former) classify these points as points that have to be covered by disks in UPPER $\cup$ LOWER.

We refer to the part of S_{ij} that is not in MIDDLE as the *peripheral part*. Consider the peripheral area SOUTH shown in Figure 3b. This is the area that is the union of the lower-shadow of i_3 and the lower-shadow of i_4. Recall that points in SOUTH that are also in a 2-watching sandglass have already been classified and are not considered further. For any remaining point p located in SOUTH we know that p is covered by a disk from LM (as SOUTH lies below the 1-watching t_l envelope for LM). Furthermore, if p has to be covered by a second disk, we know that p is covered by at least one disk whose centre is not in LM, because otherwise p would lie in the 2-watching t_l envelope for LM and would have been classified already. Hence, if $k_p = 1$, we specify that p must be covered by UPPER $\cup$ LOWER, and if $k_p = 2$, we specify that p must be covered once by LEFT∪RIGHT and once by LM ∪ UM. The areas WEST, NORTH and EAST are defined and handled analogously.

As each point in P'_{ij} is contained in one of the areas defined above, all these points are classified, i.e, we have determined for each point how often it must be covered by LEFT∪RIGHT (or CL∪CR) and how often by UPPER∪LOWER (or UM∪LM).

4.4 Areas in a Square – Other Configurations

Recall that $i_{\mathrm{CL}}^{\mathrm{UM}}$ is the intersection point between the 1-watching t_l envelopes for UM and CL, and $i_{\mathrm{CL}}^{\mathrm{LM}}$, $i_{\mathrm{CR}}^{\mathrm{LM}}$ and $i_{\mathrm{CR}}^{\mathrm{UM}}$ are defined analogously. In the standard configuration shown in Figure 3a, we have that $i_{\mathrm{CL}}^{\mathrm{UM}}$ is to the left of $i_{\mathrm{CR}}^{\mathrm{UM}}$, $i_{\mathrm{CR}}^{\mathrm{UM}}$ above $i_{\mathrm{CR}}^{\mathrm{LM}}$, $i_{\mathrm{CL}}^{\mathrm{UM}}$ above $i_{\mathrm{CL}}^{\mathrm{LM}}$, and $i_{\mathrm{CL}}^{\mathrm{LM}}$ to the left of $i_{\mathrm{CR}}^{\mathrm{LM}}$. In the following, we discuss how to handle all other possible configurations.

The definition of 2-watching t_l sandglasses does not depend on the configuration of intersection points, this means 2-watching sandglasses can be handled as before. The definition of the peripheral areas is adapted as follows. The area SOUTH is the union of the lower-shadow of the lower of the two points $i_{\mathrm{CL}}^{\mathrm{UM}}$, $i_{\mathrm{CL}}^{\mathrm{LM}}$ and the lower-shadow of the lower of the two points $i_{\mathrm{CR}}^{\mathrm{UM}}$, $i_{\mathrm{CR}}^{\mathrm{LM}}$. The area WEST is the union of the left-shadow of the point that is further left among the two points $i_{\mathrm{CL}}^{\mathrm{UM}}$, $i_{\mathrm{CR}}^{\mathrm{UM}}$ and the left-shadow of the point that is further left among the two points $i_{\mathrm{CL}}^{\mathrm{LM}}$, $i_{\mathrm{CR}}^{\mathrm{LM}}$. The definitions of EAST and NORTH are analogous. We observe that each of the four peripheral regions can be handled in the same way as before. For example, we still have that every point in SOUTH is covered by a disk with centre in LM, and if the point has to be covered by a second disk, there is a disk covering it with centre in LEFT ∪ RIGHT.

Let us introduce some terminology. We say that the 1-watching t_l envelopes for CL and CR are *opposite*, and so are the envelopes for UM and LM. Furthermore, we say that the 1-watching t_l envelopes for CL and CR *overlap* if $i_{\mathrm{CL}}^{\mathrm{UM}}$ is to the right of $i_{\mathrm{CR}}^{\mathrm{UM}}$ and $i_{\mathrm{CL}}^{\mathrm{LM}}$ is to the right of $i_{\mathrm{CR}}^{\mathrm{LM}}$. In other words, the relations between $i_{\mathrm{CL}}^{\mathrm{UM}}$ and $i_{\mathrm{CR}}^{\mathrm{UM}}$ and between $i_{\mathrm{CL}}^{\mathrm{LM}}$ and $i_{\mathrm{CR}}^{\mathrm{LM}}$ are both reversed compared to the standard configuration. Similarly, we say that the 1-watching t_l envelopes for CL and CR *cross* if only one of the two relations is reversed compared to the standard configuration. For the 1-watching t_l envelopes for UM and LM, the notions of overlapping and crossing are defined analogously by considering the relations between $i_{\mathrm{CL}}^{\mathrm{UM}}$ and $i_{\mathrm{CL}}^{\mathrm{LM}}$ and between $i_{\mathrm{CR}}^{\mathrm{UM}}$ and $i_{\mathrm{CR}}^{\mathrm{LM}}$.

One Pair of Opposite Envelopes Overlap. The first alternative configuration that we consider is the case where one pair of opposite envelopes overlap, and the other pair of opposite envelopes neither overlap nor cross. Without loss of generality, assume that the 1-watching t_l envelopes for UM and LM overlap, as illustrated in Figure 4a. (The other case is symmetric.) Note that $i_{\mathrm{CL}}^{\mathrm{LM}}$ is above $i_{\mathrm{CL}}^{\mathrm{UM}}$, and $i_{\mathrm{CR}}^{\mathrm{LM}}$ is above $i_{\mathrm{CR}}^{\mathrm{UM}}$.

Let $i_1 = i_{\mathrm{CL}}^{\mathrm{LM}}$, $i_2 = i_{\mathrm{CR}}^{\mathrm{LM}}$, $i_3 = i_{\mathrm{CR}}^{\mathrm{UM}}$, $i_4 = i_{\mathrm{CL}}^{\mathrm{UM}}$. Now let the regions MIDDLE, MIDDLE-L, etc. be defined in terms of i_1, i_2, i_3, i_4 as in the standard configuration. Consider the regions MIDDLE-L, MIDDLE-M and MIDDLE-R. These regions are always enclosed within both the UM envelope and the LM envelope. Therefore, points within those regions can be classified as requiring to be covered by disks from UPPER∪LOWER. The regions MIDDLE-U and MIDDLE-D are always outside the 1-watching t_l envelopes for CL and CR, and therefore the points in these regions can also be classified as requiring to

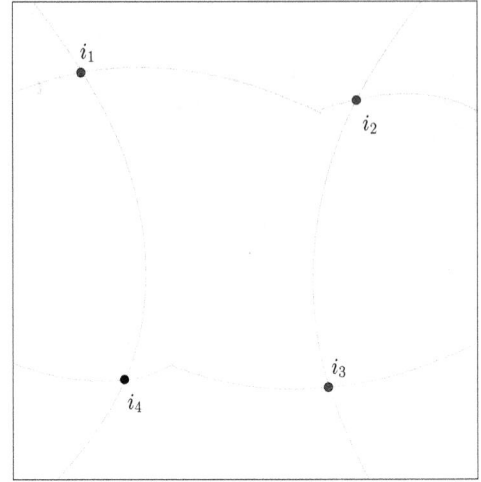

(a) The UM envelope and the LM envelope overlap

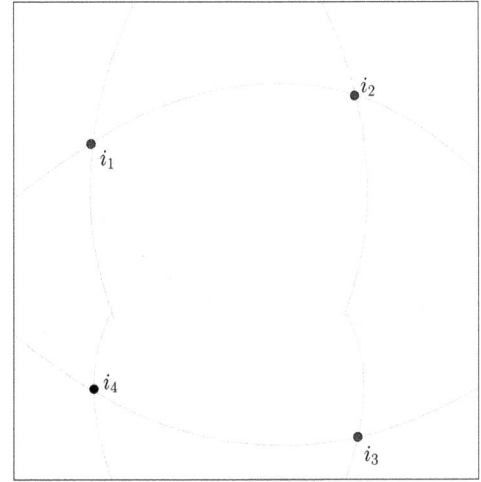

(b) UM envelope overlaps LM envelope, and CL envelope overlaps CR envelope

Figure 4: Configurations with overlapping envelopes

be covered only by disks in UPPER ∪ LOWER—for the same reason as in the standard configuration.

Both Pairs of Opposite Envelopes Overlap. Now consider the configuration shown in Figure 4b where the CL and CR envelopes overlap, and the UM and LM envelopes also overlap. For the definition of the MIDDLE regions, let $i_1 = i_{\mathrm{CR}}^{\mathrm{LM}}$, $i_2 = i_{\mathrm{CL}}^{\mathrm{LM}}$, $i_3 = i_{\mathrm{CL}}^{\mathrm{UM}}$, $i_4 = i_{\mathrm{CR}}^{\mathrm{UM}}$.

Points within the regions MIDDLE-U and MIDDLE-D are covered twice by disks in LEFT ∪ RIGHT as those regions are enclosed within both the CL envelope and the CR envelope. Similarly, the regions MIDDLE-L and MIDDLE-R are contained entirely inside the UM envelope and the LM envelope and as such all points within these regions can be classified as requiring to be covered by disks from UPPER∪LOWER. Points within the region MIDDLE-M can be classified as requiring to be covered by disks from UPPER∪LOWER.

One Pair of Opposite Envelopes Cross. Now consider a configuration where one pair of opposite envelopes cross, and the other pair of opposite envelopes neither cross nor overlap. Without loss of generality, assume that the 1-watching

t_l envelopes for CL and CR cross, and that $i_{\mathrm{CL}}^{\mathrm{UM}}$ is to the left of $i_{\mathrm{CR}}^{\mathrm{UM}}$ and $i_{\mathrm{CL}}^{\mathrm{LM}}$ is to the right of $i_{\mathrm{CR}}^{\mathrm{LM}}$, as shown in Figure 5a. (The other cases are symmetric.)

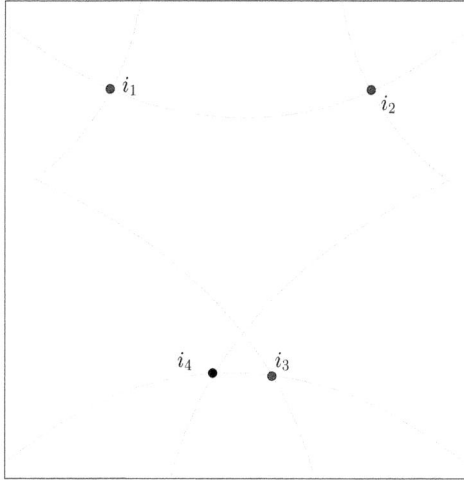

(a) CL envelope crosses CR envelope

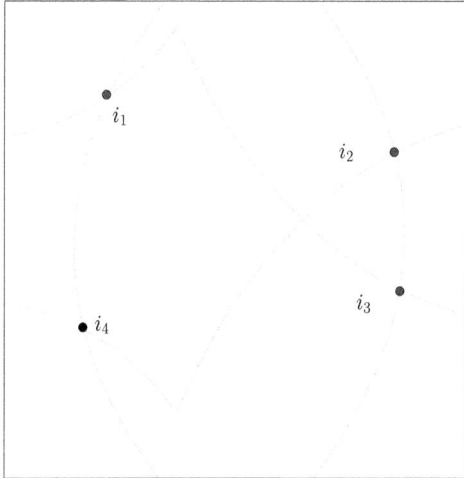

(b) UM envelope crosses LM envelope, CR and CL envelopes overlap

Figure 5: Configurations with crossing envelopes

Let $i_1 = i_{\mathrm{CL}}^{\mathrm{UM}}$, $i_2 = i_{\mathrm{CR}}^{\mathrm{UM}}$, $i_3 = i_{\mathrm{CL}}^{\mathrm{LM}}$, and $i_4 = i_{\mathrm{CR}}^{\mathrm{LM}}$, and define the MIDDLE regions accordingly. The areas MIDDLE-L, MIDDLE-R and MIDDLE-M are outside the 1-watching t_l envelopes for UM and LM, and thus the points in these regions can be classified as requiring to be covered by disks from LEFT ∪ RIGHT. The area MIDDLE-U is outside the 1-watching t_l envelopes for CL and CR, and thus the points in MIDDLE-U can be classified as requiring to be covered by disks from UPPER ∪ LOWER. The area MIDDLE-D is inside the 1-watching envelopes for both UM and LM, and thus the points in MIDDLE-D can be classified as requiring to be covered by disks from LEFT ∪ RIGHT.

One Pair of Envelopes Overlap, One Pair of Envelopes Cross. Consider now the case where two opposite envelopes overlap and the two other opposite envelopes cross. Without loss of generality, consider the case where the UM envelope crosses the LM envelope and the CL enve-

lope overlaps the CR envelope, and assume that $i_{\mathrm{CR}}^{\mathrm{UM}}$ is above $i_{\mathrm{CR}}^{\mathrm{LM}}$ and $i_{\mathrm{CL}}^{\mathrm{UM}}$ is below $i_{\mathrm{CL}}^{\mathrm{LM}}$, as illustrated in Figure 5b.

The area MIDDLE-L is outside the envelopes for UM and LM, and the points in MIDDLE-L can be classified as requiring to be covered by disks in LEFT ∪ RIGHT. The area MIDDLE-R is within both the UM and the LM envelope, and the points in MIDDLE-R are classified as requiring to be covered by disks in UPPER ∪ LOWER. The regions MIDDLE-U, MIDDLE-M and MIDDLE-D are contained in the envelopes for both CL and CR, and all points in these regions are classified as requiring to be covered by disks in LEFT ∪ RIGHT.

Both Pairs of Opposite Envelopes Cross. The only configuration that has not yet been considered is the case where both pairs of opposite envelopes cross. One such configuration would have $i_{\mathrm{CL}}^{\mathrm{UM}}$ strictly to the the left of $i_{\mathrm{CR}}^{\mathrm{UM}}$, $i_{\mathrm{CL}}^{\mathrm{LM}}$ strictly to the right of $i_{\mathrm{CR}}^{\mathrm{LM}}$, $i_{\mathrm{CL}}^{\mathrm{UM}}$ strictly above $i_{\mathrm{CL}}^{\mathrm{LM}}$, and $i_{\mathrm{CR}}^{\mathrm{UM}}$ strictly below $i_{\mathrm{CR}}^{\mathrm{LM}}$. (We can assume strict relationships since if two points coincide, we are free to choose the relation and arrive at a previously considered configuration where it is not the case that both pairs of envelopes cross.) To show that this is impossible, consider the line l of slope -1 through $i_{\mathrm{CL}}^{\mathrm{UM}}$. Since $i_{\mathrm{CL}}^{\mathrm{UM}}$ is above $i_{\mathrm{CL}}^{\mathrm{LM}}$ and both points lie on the CL envelope, we get that $i_{\mathrm{CL}}^{\mathrm{LM}}$ is strictly below the line l. Since $i_{\mathrm{CR}}^{\mathrm{UM}}$ is on the line l and $i_{\mathrm{CR}}^{\mathrm{UM}}$ is to the right of $i_{\mathrm{CL}}^{\mathrm{UM}}$ and also lies on the UM envelope, we get that $i_{\mathrm{CR}}^{\mathrm{UM}}$ is above l. Since $i_{\mathrm{CR}}^{\mathrm{UM}}$ is below $i_{\mathrm{CR}}^{\mathrm{LM}}$ and both points are on the CR envelope, it follows that $i_{\mathrm{CR}}^{\mathrm{LM}}$ is above l. Since $i_{\mathrm{CL}}^{\mathrm{LM}}$ is to the right of $i_{\mathrm{CR}}^{\mathrm{LM}}$ and both points are on the LM envelope, we obtain that $i_{\mathrm{CL}}^{\mathrm{LM}}$ is strictly above the line l. This is a contradiction to the conclusion that $i_{\mathrm{CL}}^{\mathrm{LM}}$ is strictly below l that we derived above. Hence, this configuration is not possible. The other configurations where both envelopes cross can be excluded similarly.

Complexity of Enumeration. For each of the K^2 squares S_{ij} in a block, and for each event type t_l in T, we enumerate up to two disks with centre in S_{ij} (these form the set OPT'_B of disks that are determined to be in the solution by the guessing stage), eight points defining the 2-watching sandglasses, and four intersection points (each identified by two disks) of the 1-watching envelopes. Hence, if there are m_B disks and n_B points in the given instance of W2CUD-T in a block B, there are $O((m_B^2 n_B^8 m_B^8)^{|T|}) = (m_B + n_B)^{O(|T|)}$ choices per square, and thus $(m_B + n_B)^{O(K^2|T|)}$ choices for the whole block B. Since K and $|T|$ are constants, this is a polynomial number of choices. For each of these choices, the resulting classification of points and candidate set of disks for OPT'_B are passed to the second stage of the algorithm from Section 3. (For some choices, the algorithm may find that there is no feasible solution.) The algorithm outputs the cheapest solution among the feasible solutions obtained for any of the $(m_B + n_B)^{O(K^2|T|)}$ different guesses of the properties of the optimal solution. For the choice in which the guessed properties are indeed those of OPT_B, the algorithm is guaranteed to produce a 6-approximation. Hence, the solution output by the algorithm is a 6-approximation for instances of W2CUD-T where all points lie in one $K \times K$ block.

5. CONCLUSION

We have presented a $(6 + \varepsilon)$-approximation algorithm for the target coverage problem with composite events and fault-tolerance requirements, both for the lifetime maximisation variant and for the problem of covering all event points by sensors of minimum total cost. Our approach is based on guessing properties of the optimal solution (by enumeration) and then using these properties to guide a dynamic programming algorithm. This is a generalisation of the approach employed by Huang et al. [13] to obtain a $(6+\varepsilon)$-approximation for weighted set cover with unit disks. For the latter problem, subsequent work has improved the approximation ratio to $5+\varepsilon$ [7] and then to $4+\varepsilon$ [9, 20]. The main idea of these improvements is to perform the dynamic programming in several strips simultaneously. One possible direction for future work would be to see whether these improvements can also be adapted to the fault-tolerant target coverage problem with composite events.

Another question of interest is whether our approach can be adapted to arbitrary coverage requirements k_p, i.e., without the restriction $k_p \leq 2$ for all $p \in P$. For W2CUD-T and also for the special case of weighted geometric set cover with unit disks, it is an interesting open problem whether a polynomial-time approximation scheme (PTAS) can be obtained. Finally, the study of settings where the sensors and targets are located in three-dimensional space would be interesting.

6. REFERENCES

[1] C. Ambühl, T. Erlebach, M. Mihalák, and M. Nunkesser. Constant-factor approximation for minimum-weight (connected) dominating sets in unit disk graphs. In *Proceedings of the 9th International Workshop on Approximation Algorithms for Combinatorial Optimization Problems (APPROX 2006)*, LNCS 4110, pages 3–14. Springer, 2006.

[2] P. Berman, G. Calinescu, C. Shah, and A. Zelikovsky. Power efficient monitoring schedules in sensor networks. In *IEEE Wireless Communication and Networking Conference (WCNC 2004)*, pages 2329–2334, 2004.

[3] P. Berman, G. Calinescu, C. Shah, and A. Zelikovsky. Efficient energy management in sensor networks. In Y. Xiao and Y. Pan, editors, *Ad Hoc and Sensor Networks, Wireless Networks and Mobile Computing*, volume 2, pages 71–90. Nova Science Publishers, 2005.

[4] J. Byrka, F. Grandoni, T. Rothvoß, and L. Sanità. An improved LP-based approximation for Steiner tree. In *Proceedings of the 42nd ACM Symposium on Theory of Computing (STOC 2010)*, pages 583–592. ACM, 2010.

[5] C. Chekuri, K. L. Clarkson, and S. Har-Peled. On the set multi-cover problem in geometric settings. In *Proceedings of the 25th Annual Symposium on Computational Geometry (SCG'09)*, pages 341–350. ACM, 2009.

[6] B. N. Clark, C. J. Colbourn, and D. S. Johnson. Unit disk graphs. *Discrete Mathematics*, 86:165–177, 1990.

[7] D. Dai and C. Yu. A $(5 + \epsilon)$-approximation algorithm for minimum weighted dominating set in unit disk graph. *Theoretical Computer Science*, 410(8-10):756–765, 2009.

[8] A. Dhawan, C. T. Vu, A. Zelikovsky, Y. Li, and S. K. Prasad. Maximum lifetime of sensor networks with adjustable sensing range. In *Proceedings of the 7th International Conference on Software Engineering, Artificial Intelligence, Networking and*

Parallel/Distributed Computing & International Workshop on Self-Assembling Wireless Networks (SNPD-SAWN 2006)*, pages 285–289, 2006.

[9] T. Erlebach and M. Mihalák. A $(4 + \epsilon)$-approximation for the minimum-weight dominating set problem in unit disk graphs. In *Proceedings of the 7th International Workshop on Approximation and Online Algorithms (WAOA 2009)*, LNCS 5893, pages 135–146. Springer, 2009.

[10] T. Erlebach and A. Shahnaz. Approximating node-weighted multicast trees in wireless ad-hoc networks. In *Proceedings of the 2009 International Conference on Wireless Communications and Mobile Computing: Connecting the World Wirelessly (IWCMC 2009)*, pages 639–643. ACM, 2009.

[11] N. Garg and J. Könemann. Faster and simpler algorithms for multicommodity flow and other fractional packing problems. *SIAM Journal on Computing*, 37(2):630–652, 2007.

[12] D. S. Hochbaum and W. Maass. Approximation schemes for covering and packing problems in image processing and VLSI. *Journal of the ACM*, 32(1):130–136, 1985.

[13] Y. Huang, X. Gao, Z. Zhang, and W. Wu. A better constant-factor approximation for weighted dominating set in unit disk graph. *Journal of Combinatorial Optimization*, 18(2):179–194, 2009.

[14] M. Marta, Y. Yang, and M. Cardei. Energy-efficient composite event detection in wireless sensor networks. In *Proceedings of the 4th International Conference on Wireless Algorithms, Systems, and Applications (WASA 2009)*, LNCS 5682, pages 94–103. Springer, 2009.

[15] P. Sanders and D. Schieferdecker. Lifetime maximization of monitoring sensor networks. In *Proceedings of the 6th International Workshop on Algorithms for Sensor Systems, Wireless Ad Hoc Networks, and Autonomous Mobile Entities (ALGOSENSORS 2010)*, LNCS 6541, pages 134–147. Springer, 2010.

[16] M. T. Thai, F. Wang, D. H. Du, and X. Jia. Coverage problems in wireless sensor networks: designs and analysis. *International Journal of Sensor Networks*, 3:191–200, May 2008.

[17] C. Vu, R. Beyah, and Y. Li. Composite event detection in wireless sensor networks. In *IEEE International Performance, Computing, and Communications Conference (IPCCC 2007)*, pages 264–271, 2007.

[18] Q. Zhao and M. Gurusamy. Lifetime maximization for connected target coverage in wireless sensor networks. *IEEE/ACM Transactions on Networking*, 16:1378–1391, December 2008.

[19] F. Zou, X. Li, S. Gao, and W. Wu. Node-weighted Steiner tree approximation in unit disk graphs. *Journal of Combinatorial Optimization*, 18(4):342–349, 2009.

[20] F. Zou, Y. Wang, X. Xu, X. Li, H. Du, P. Wan, and W. Wu. New approximations for minimum-weighted dominating sets and minimum-weighted connected dominating sets on unit disk graphs. *Theoretical Computer Science*, 412:198–208, January 2011.

Convergence to Equilibrium of Logit Dynamics for Strategic Games[*]

Vincenzo Auletta
Dipartimento di Informatica
Università di Salerno
84084 - Fisciano (SA), Italy
auletta@dia.unisa.it

Diodato Ferraioli
Dipartimento di Informatica
Università di Salerno
84084 - Fisciano (SA), Italy
ferraioli@dia.unisa.it

Francesco Pasquale
Dipartimento di Informatica
Università di Salerno
84084 - Fisciano (SA), Italy
pasquale@dia.unisa.it

Paolo Penna
Dipartimento di Informatica
Università di Salerno
84084 - Fisciano (SA), Italy
penna@dia.unisa.it

Giuseppe Persiano
Dipartimento di Informatica
Università di Salerno
84084 - Fisciano (SA), Italy
giuper@dia.unisa.it

ABSTRACT

We present the first general bounds on the mixing time of logit dynamics for wide classes of strategic games. The logit dynamics describes the behaviour of a complex system whose individual components act *selfishly* and keep responding according to some partial ("noisy") knowledge of the system. In particular, we prove nearly tight bounds for potential games and games with dominant strategies. Our results show that, for potential games, the mixing time is upper and lower bounded by an *exponential* in the inverse of the noise and in the maximum potential difference. Instead, for games with dominant strategies, the mixing time cannot grow arbitrarily with the inverse of the noise. Finally, we refine our analysis for a subclass of potential games called *graphical* coordination games and we give evidence that the mixing time strongly depends on the structure of the underlying graph. Games in this class have been previously studied in Physics and, more recently, in Computer Science in the context of diffusion of new technologies.

Categories and Subject Descriptors

G.3 [**Probability and Statistics**]: Markov processes; J.4 [**Social and Behavioral Sciences**]: Economics

General Terms

Algorithms, Theory

Keywords

Game Theory, Markov Chains, Mixing Time

[*]Partially supported by MIUR PRIN project COGENT.

1. INTRODUCTION

Complex systems are often studied by looking at their dynamics and the equilibria induced by these dynamics. In this paper we concentrate on specific complex systems arising from *strategic games*. Here we have a set of selfish agents or *players*, each with a set of possible actions or *strategies*. An agent continuously evaluates her utility or *payoff*, that depends on her own strategy and on the strategies played by the other agents. A dynamics specifies the rule used by the players to update their strategies. In its most general form an equilibrium is a distribution over the set of states that has the property of being invariant with respect to the dynamics. For example, a very well-studied dynamics for strategic games is the *best response dynamics* whose associated equilibria are the Nash equilibria.

There are several characteristics of a dynamics and of the associated equilibrium concept that concur to make the dynamics descriptive of a system. First of all, it is desirable that the dynamics gives only one equilibrium state or, in case a system admits more than one equilibrium for a given dynamics, that the equilibria look similar. For example, this is not the case for Nash equilibria as a game can admit more than one Nash equilibrium and sometimes the equilibria have strikingly different characteristics. In addition, the dynamics must be descriptive of the way individual agents behave. For example, the best response dynamics is well-tailored for modeling players that have a complete knowledge of the global state of the system and of their payoffs. Finally, if a dynamics takes very long time to reach an equilibrium then the system spends most of its life outside of the equilibrium and thus knowledge gained from the study of the equilibrium is not very relevant.

In this work we study a specific *noisy* best-response dynamics, the *logit dynamics* (defined in [4]) in which, at each time step, a player is randomly selected for strategy update and the update is performed with respect to a "noisy" knowledge of the game and of the state of the system, that is, the strategies currently played by the players. Intuitively, "high noise" represents the situation where players choose their strategies "nearly at random" because they have a limited knowledge of the system; instead, "low noise" represents the situation where players "almost surely" play the best response; that is, they pick the strategies yielding high payoff with "much higher" probability. After a sufficiently large number of steps, the probability that the system is found in a specific profile remains essentially unchanged and we say that the logit dynamics has converged to a *stationary distribution*, that is unique and independent of the starting state. We believe that this makes the logit dynamics the elective choice of a dynamics for large and complex systems in which agents have limited knowledge. However, one more step is needed to complete the picture. How long does the logit dynamics take to converge to the stationary distribution? This is the main technical focus of this paper. Specifically, we study the *mixing time* of the logit dynamics, that is, the time needed to get close to the stationary distribution. This depends on the underlying game and on the noise of the system (roughly speaking, the payoffs and how much players care about them). Since previous work has shown that the mixing time can vary a lot (from linear to exponential [2]) it is natural to ask the following questions: (1) How do the *noise* level and the *structure* of the game affect the mixing time? (2) Can the mixing time grow *arbitrarily*? We give general bounds on the mixing time for wide classes of games, including potential games and games with dominant strategies, and coordination games played between neighboring nodes of a given network.

We prove that, for all potential games, the mixing time of the logit dynamics is upper-bounded by a *polynomial* in the number of players and by an *exponential* in the inverse of the noise and in the maximum potential difference, an important structural property of the game.

We complement the upper bound with a lower bound showing that there exist potential games with mixing time exponential in the inverse of the noise and in the maximum potential difference. Thus the mixing time can grow indefinitely in potential games as noise decreases. We also study a special class of potential games, the *graphical coordination games*, in which players are connected by a network and adjacent players play a two-player coordination game. By looking at two extreme cases, we give evidence that the mixing time depends on the connectedness of the underlying network. Specifically, we prove that, as a function of the number of players, the mixing time is exponential on the clique and polynomial on the ring, for a class of coordination games.

Going to the second question, we show that for games with dominant strategies (not necessarily potential games) the mixing time cannot exceed some *absolute bound* T which depends uniquely on the number of players n and on the number of strategies m. Though $T = T(n, m)$ is of the form $\mathcal{O}(m^n)$, it is independent of the noise and we show that, in general, such an exponential growth is the best possible.

Our results suggest that the structural properties of the game are important for the mixing time. For small noise, players tend to play best response and for those games that have more than one pure Nash equilibrium (PNE) with similar potential the system is likely to remain in a PNE for a long time, whereas the stationary distribution gives each PNE approximately the same weight. This happens for (certain) potential games, whence the exponential growth of mixing time with respect to the noise. On the contrary, for games with dominant strategies there is a PNE (a dominant profile) with high stationary probability *and* players

are guaranteed to play that profile with non-vanishing probability (regardless of the noise).

Related works. The logit dynamics was first studied by Blume [4] who showed that, for 2×2 coordination games, the long-term behavior of the system is concentrated in the risk dominant equilibrium (see [6]). The study of the mixing time of the logit dynamics for strategic games has been initiated in [2], where, among others, bounds were given for the class of 2×2 coordination games studied in [4]. Before the work reported in [2], the rate of convergence was studied only for the hitting time of specific profiles; see for example the work by Asadpour and Saberi [1] who studied the hitting time of the Nash equilibrium for a class of congestion games.

Graphical coordination games are often used to model the spread of a new technology in a social network [14] with the strategy of maximum potential corresponding to adopting the new technology; players prefer to choose the same technology as their neighbors and the new technology is at least as preferable as the old one. Ellison [5] studied the logit dynamics for graphical coordination games on rings and showed that some large fraction of the players will eventually choose the strategy with maximum potential. Similar results were obtained by Peyton Young [14] for the logit dynamics and for more general families of graphs. Montanari and Saberi [11] gave bounds on the hitting time of the highest potential equilibrium for the logit dynamics in terms of some graph theoretic properties of the underlying interaction network. We notice that none of [4, 5, 14] gave bounds on the convergence rate of the dynamics, while Montanari and Saberi [11] studied the convergence time of a specific configuration, namely the hitting time of the highest potential equilibrium.

Our work is also strictly related to the well-studied Glauber dynamics on the Ising model (see, for example, [9] and Chapter 15 of [7]). Indeed, the Ising model can be seen as a special graphical coordination game without risk dominant equilibria, and the Glauber dynamics on the Ising model is equivalent to the logit dynamics. In particular, we note that Berger et al. [3] relate the mixing time of the Ising model to the cutwidth of the underlying graph. Their results can be specialized to derive upper bounds on the mixing time of graphical coordination games without risk dominant equilibria. However the bounds we present in Section 5 are tighter.

Even if the logit dynamics has attracted a lot of attention in different scientific communities, many other promising dynamics that deal with partial or noise-corrupted knowledge of the game have been proposed (see, for example, the recent work of Marden et al. [8] and of Mertikopoulos and Moustakas [10] and references in [13]).

Paper organization. We give formal definitions of logit dynamics and some of the used techniques in Section 2. The upper bounds for potential games, for games with dominant strategies, and for graphical coordination games are given in Section 3, Section 4, and Section 5, respectively. For the sake of completeness, in Appendix A we present some known facts about Markov chains that we use throughout the paper.

2. PRELIMINARIES

In this section we review the background on strategic games, introduce the logit dynamics and describe the proof techniques for deriving our bounds.

Games. In a *strategic game* we are given a finite set of players $\{1, \dots, n\}$, with each player i having a finite set of *strategies* S_i and a *utility* function $u_i : S_1 \times \dots \times S_n \to \mathbb{R}$. Each player can choose a strategy $x_i \in S_i$ and the resulting strategy *profile* is the vector $\mathbf{x} = (x_1, \dots, x_n)$. Given a profile $\mathbf{x}$, the utility (or payoff) for player i is $u_i(\mathbf{x})$. Throughout the paper we adopt the standard game theoretic notation and write $(a, \mathbf{x}_{-i})$ to denote the vector $(x_1, \dots, x_{i-1}, a, x_{i+1}, \dots, x_n)$. We also let $S := S_1 \times \dots \times S_n$ denote the set of all strategy profiles.

Logit dynamics. In this paper we consider the logit dynamics (see [4]). In the *logit dynamics with inverse noise* $\beta \geqslant 0$ for an n-player strategic game $\mathcal{G} = (S_1, \dots, S_n, u_1, \dots, u_n)$ at every time step a player i is selected uniformly at random and her strategy is updated to strategy $y \in S_i$ with probability $\sigma_i(y \mid \mathbf{x})$ defined as

$$\sigma_i(y \mid \mathbf{x}) := \frac{1}{T_i(\mathbf{x})} e^{\beta u_i(y, \mathbf{x}_{-i})} \tag{1}$$

where $\mathbf{x} \in S$ is the current strategy profile and $T_i(\mathbf{x}) = \sum_{z \in S_i} e^{\beta u_i(z, \mathbf{x}_{-i})}$ is the normalizing factor.

The logit dynamics for $\mathcal{G}$ naturally defines a Markov chain $\mathcal{M}_\beta^{\mathcal{G}} = \{X_t : t \in \mathbb{N}\}$ with state space $\Omega = S$ and transition probabilities

$$P(\mathbf{x}, \mathbf{y}) = \begin{cases} \frac{1}{n} \cdot \sigma_i(y_i \mid \mathbf{x}), & \text{if } \mathbf{x} \neq \mathbf{y} \text{ and } \mathbf{x}_{-i} = \mathbf{y}_{-i}; \\ \frac{1}{n} \cdot \sum_{i=1}^n \sigma_i(y_i \mid \mathbf{x}), & \text{if } \mathbf{x} = \mathbf{y}; \\ 0, & \text{otherwise.} \end{cases} \tag{2}$$

We will find convenient to identify the logit dynamics for $\mathcal{G}$ with the Markov chain $\mathcal{M}_\beta^{\mathcal{G}}$. It is easy to see that $\mathcal{M}_\beta^{\mathcal{G}}$ is irreducible and aperiodic. Therefore, there exists a unique *stationary distribution* π, such that, for every initial profile $\mathbf{x}$, the distribution $P^t(\mathbf{x}, \cdot)$ of the position of the chain after t steps converges to π as t tends to infinity. We are interested in the *mixing time* of the chain; i.e., the time needed for $P^t(\mathbf{x}, \cdot)$ to be close to π for every initial configuration $\mathbf{x}$:

$$t_{\text{mix}}(\varepsilon) = \min \left\{ t \in \mathbb{N} : \|P^t(\mathbf{x}, \cdot) - \pi\|_{\text{TV}} \leqslant \varepsilon \text{ for all } \mathbf{x} \in \Omega \right\}$$

where $\|P^t(\mathbf{x}, \cdot) - \pi\|_{\text{TV}} = \frac{1}{2} \sum_{\mathbf{y} \in \Omega} |P^t(\mathbf{x}, \mathbf{y}) - \pi(\mathbf{y})|$ is the *total variation distance*. We will use the standard convention of setting $t_{\text{mix}} = t_{\text{mix}}(1/4)$ and observe that $t_{\text{mix}}(\varepsilon) \leqslant t_{\text{mix}}(1/4) \cdot \log 1/\varepsilon$.

For an irreducible and aperiodic Markov chain over finite state space Ω with transition matrix P and stationary distribution π, we will call *edge stationary distribution* the probability distribution Q over the set $\Omega \times \Omega$ given by $Q(\mathbf{x}, \mathbf{y}) = \pi(\mathbf{x}) P(\mathbf{x}, \mathbf{y})$.

Potential games. A strategic game is a *potential game* if there exists a function $\Phi : S \to \mathbb{R}$ such that for every player i, every profile $\mathbf{x} \in S$, and every pair of strategies $a, b \in S_i$, it holds that

$$u_i(a, \mathbf{x}_{-i}) - u_i(b, \mathbf{x}_{-i}) = \Phi(a, \mathbf{x}_{-i}) - \Phi(b, \mathbf{x}_{-i}).$$

For every potential game $\mathcal{G}$ with potential function Φ, let π be the so-called Gibbs measure

$$\pi(\mathbf{x}) = \frac{1}{Z} e^{\beta \Phi(\mathbf{x})} \tag{3}$$

where $Z = \sum_{\mathbf{y} \in S} e^{\beta \Phi(\mathbf{y})}$ is the normalizing constant, also called the *partition function*. We write Z_β and π_β when we want to stress the dependence on the inverse noise β.

It is easy to see that $\mathcal{M}_\beta^{\mathcal{G}}$ is reversible (i.e., $Q(\mathbf{x}, \mathbf{y}) = Q(\mathbf{y}, \mathbf{x})$ for all states $\mathbf{x}, \mathbf{y}$) and the Gibbs measure π in (3) is its stationary distribution.

Further notation. We use bold symbols for vectors. We write $|\mathbf{x}|_a$ for the number of occurrences of a in $\mathbf{x}$, i.e., $|\mathbf{x}|_a = |\{i \in [n] : x_i = a\}|$. We write $\mathbf{x} \sim \mathbf{y}$ to denote the fact that $\mathbf{x}$ differs from $\mathbf{y}$ in exactly one coordinate.

2.1 Proof techniques for the upper bounds

To derive our upper bounds, we employ two techniques: Markov chain coupling and Markov chain comparison. Coupling is a well-established technique for bounding the mixing time and it is summarized in Theorems 17 and 18 in Appendix A. We next review the comparison technique.

Let P be the transition matrix of a Markov chain with finite state space Ω and let us label the eigenvalues of P in non-increasing order

$$\lambda_1 \geqslant \lambda_2 \geqslant \dots \geqslant \lambda_{|\Omega|}.$$

It is well-known (see, for example, Lemma 12.1 in [7]) that, if P is irreducible and aperiodic, then $\lambda_2 < 1$ and $\lambda_{|\Omega|} > -1$. For irreducible and aperiodic chains the *relaxation time* t_{rel} is defined as

$$t_{\text{rel}} = \max \left\{ \frac{1}{1 - \lambda_2}, \frac{1}{1 + \lambda_{|\Omega|}} \right\},$$

and for reversible Markov chains (and thus also for the logit dynamics of potential games) it is related to the mixing time by the following theorem (see, for example, Theorem 12.3 in [7]).

THEOREM 1. *Let P the transition matrix of a reversible, irreducible, and aperiodic Markov chain with state space Ω and stationary distribution π. Then it holds that*

$$t_{\text{mix}} \leqslant \log \left(\frac{1}{\pi_{\text{min}}} \right) t_{\text{rel}}$$

where $\pi_{\text{min}} = \min_{\mathbf{x} \in \Omega} \pi(\mathbf{x})$.

The following theorem allows us to relate the relaxation times of two chains by comparing their stationary and edge-stationary distributions. We will use it in Theorem 5 to relate the logit dynamics with a random walk on a generalized hypercube whose relaxation time is known.

THEOREM 2 (COMPARISON THEOREM). *Let P and $\hat{P}$ be the transition matrices of two reversible, irreducible, and aperiodic Markov chains with the same state space Ω, stationary distributions π and $\hat{\pi}$ respectively, and edge stationary distributions Q and $\hat{Q}$ respectively. Suppose that two constants α, γ exist such that, for all $x, y \in \Omega$,*

$$\hat{Q}(x, y) \leqslant \alpha \cdot Q(x, y) \tag{4}$$
$$\pi(x) \leqslant \gamma \cdot \hat{\pi}(x). \tag{5}$$

Then the relaxation time t_{rel} of P and the relaxation time $\hat{t}_{\text{rel}}$ of $\hat{P}$ satisfy $t_{\text{rel}} \leqslant \alpha \cdot \gamma \cdot \hat{t}_{\text{rel}}$.

When $t_{\text{rel}} = \frac{1}{1 - \lambda_2}$ Theorem 2 can be derived from Lemma 13.22 in [7]. For completeness sake, we give a full proof for the general case in Appendix B.

2.2 Proof technique for lower bounds

To derive our lower bounds we will use the the Bottleneck Ratio Theorem (see Theorem 19 in Appendix A) and a refinement of it for the logit dynamics of potential games (see Theorem 3 below).

Let $\mathbf{x} \in S$ be a profile of a potential game and let $M \subseteq S \setminus \{\mathbf{x}\}$ be a set of profiles different from $\mathbf{x}$. We define $R_{\mathbf{x},M}$ as the set of profiles in the connected component of the Hamming graph[1] with vertex set $S \setminus M$ that contains $\mathbf{x}$ and define

$$\partial R_{\mathbf{x},M} := \{\mathbf{y} \in R_{\mathbf{x},M} : \mathbf{y} \sim \mathbf{z} \text{ for some } \mathbf{z} \in M\}.$$

In other words, $\partial R_{\mathbf{x},M}$ consists exactly of those profiles in $R_{\mathbf{x},M}$ that have a neighbor in M. We have the following theorem.

THEOREM 3. *For any potential game $\mathcal{G}$ in which each player has exactly 2 strategies, for any profile $\mathbf{x} \in S$ and for any $M \subset S \setminus \{\mathbf{x}\}$, if $R = R_{\mathbf{x},M}$ satisfies $\pi(R) \leqslant 1/2$ then the mixing time of the logit dynamics with inverse noise β for $\mathcal{G}$ satisfies*

$$t_{\mathrm{mix}} = \Omega\left(\frac{e^{\beta(\Phi^R - \Phi^M)}}{|\partial R|}\right),$$

where Φ^R and Φ^M are the maximum potential among profiles in R and M, respectively.

PROOF. Observe that for every pair $\mathbf{y}, \mathbf{z}$ of adjacent profiles it holds that

$$\pi(\mathbf{y})P(\mathbf{y},\mathbf{z}) = \frac{e^{\beta\Phi(\mathbf{y})}}{Z} \cdot \frac{1}{n} \cdot \frac{e^{\beta\Phi(\mathbf{z})}}{e^{\beta\Phi(\mathbf{y})} + e^{\beta\Phi(\mathbf{z})}} \leqslant \frac{e^{\beta\Phi(\mathbf{z})}}{nZ}.$$

Note that for every $\mathbf{y} \in \partial R$ there are at most n neighbors outside R and all of them belong to M by definition, thus

$$\begin{aligned} Q\left(R, \overline{R}\right) &= \sum_{\substack{\mathbf{y} \in R \\ \mathbf{z} \in \overline{R}}} \pi(\mathbf{y})P(\mathbf{y},\mathbf{z}) = \sum_{\substack{\mathbf{y} \in \partial R \\ \mathbf{z} \in M}} \pi(\mathbf{y})P(\mathbf{y},\mathbf{z}) \\ &\leqslant \sum_{\substack{\mathbf{y} \in \partial R \\ \mathbf{z} \in M}} \frac{e^{\beta\Phi(\mathbf{z})}}{nZ} \leqslant |\partial R| \frac{e^{\beta\Phi^M}}{Z}. \end{aligned}$$

Let $\mathbf{x}^+ \in R$ be a profile with the highest potential in R; that is, $\Phi(\mathbf{x}^+) = \Phi^R$. Obviously

$$\pi(R) \geqslant \pi(\mathbf{x}^+) = \frac{e^{\beta\Phi^R}}{Z}.$$

These two inequalities yield

$$\frac{Q\left(R, \overline{R}\right)}{\pi(R)} \leqslant \frac{|\partial R|}{e^{\beta(\Phi^R - \Phi^M)}}$$

and since $\pi(R) \leqslant 1/2$ the thesis follows from the Bottleneck Ratio Theorem (Theorem 19 in the appendix). □

The above theorem gives good lower bounds when we choose $\mathbf{x}$ and M such that all profiles in M have low potential, the resulting set $R = R_{\mathbf{x},M}$ contains at least one profile of high potential (and thus $\Phi^R - \Phi^M$ is large) and the boundary ∂R is small.

---

[1] In the Hamming graph with vertex set $S' \subseteq S$, two profiles $\mathbf{x}$ and $\mathbf{y}$ are adjacent if and only if they differ in exactly one component.

3. POTENTIAL GAMES

For a function $\Phi : S \to \mathbb{R}$ over a finite set S, let us name $\Delta\Phi$ the difference between the maximum and minimum values of Φ and L its Lipschitz constant, i.e.

$$\begin{aligned} \Delta\Phi &= \Phi_{\max} - \Phi_{\min} = \max\{\Phi(\mathbf{x}) - \Phi(\mathbf{y}) : \mathbf{x}, \mathbf{y} \in S\} \\ L &= \max\{\Phi(\mathbf{x}) - \Phi(\mathbf{y}) : \mathbf{x}, \mathbf{y} \in S, \mathbf{x} \sim \mathbf{y}\}. \end{aligned}$$

In this section we shall see that it is possible to give upper bounds on the mixing time of the logit dynamics for potential games depending only on those two quantities. Moreover we will show that such bounds are nearly tight by providing examples of games whose logit dynamics mixing time is close to the given upper bound.

Upper bound. In order to give the upper bound on the mixing time, we first give an upper bound on the relaxation time and then use Theorem 1.

In the proof of Theorem 5 we obtain the upper bound on the relaxation time by comparing the logit dynamics with inverse noise β for a potential game $\mathcal{G}$ and the logit dynamics with inverse noise 0 for the same game. When the inverse noise is zero, the logit dynamics is a random walk on a generalized hypercube. Next lemma evaluates the relaxation time of such a chain. The proof is a simple generalization of the proof for the relaxation time of the lazy random walk on the hypercube and is omitted.

LEMMA 4. *For every n-player game the relaxation time of the logit dynamics with inverse noise $\beta = 0$ is $t_{\mathrm{rel}} = n$.*

The following theorem is the main result of this section.

THEOREM 5. *Let $\mathcal{G}$ be a n-player potential game with potential function Φ. The relaxation time of the logit dynamics for $\mathcal{G}$ with inverse noise β is $t_{\mathrm{rel}} = \mathcal{O}\left(n \cdot e^{\beta(\Delta\Phi + L)}\right)$.*

PROOF. Remember that the stationary distribution is

$$\pi_\beta(\mathbf{x}) = \frac{e^{\beta\Phi(\mathbf{x})}}{Z_\beta} \leqslant \frac{e^{\beta\Phi_{\max}}}{Z_\beta} \qquad \text{for all profiles } \mathbf{x} \in S$$

where $Z_\beta = \sum_{\mathbf{y} \in S} e^{\beta\Phi(\mathbf{y})}$ is the partition function. As for the edge-stationary distribution, for two adjacent profiles $\mathbf{x} \sim \mathbf{y}$ that differ at player $i \in [n]$ we have

$$Q_\beta(\mathbf{x},\mathbf{y}) = \frac{e^{\beta\Phi(\mathbf{x})}}{Z_\beta} \frac{1}{n} \frac{e^{\beta\Phi(\mathbf{y})}}{T_i(\mathbf{x})} \geqslant \frac{e^{\beta\Phi_{\min}}}{Z_\beta} \frac{1}{n} \frac{1}{|S_i| \cdot e^{\beta L}}, \quad (6)$$

where we used that

$$\begin{aligned} \frac{e^{\beta\Phi(\mathbf{y})}}{T_i(\mathbf{x})} &= \frac{e^{\beta\Phi(\mathbf{y})}}{\sum_{z \in S_i} e^{\beta\Phi(\mathbf{x}_{-i},z)}} \\ &= \frac{1}{\sum_{z \in S_i} e^{\beta\left[\Phi(\mathbf{x}_{-i},z) - \Phi(\mathbf{y})\right]}} \geqslant \frac{1}{|S_i| \cdot e^{\beta L}}. \end{aligned}$$

Moreover, for any profile $\mathbf{x}$ we have

$$Q_\beta(\mathbf{x},\mathbf{x}) = \frac{e^{\beta\Phi(\mathbf{x})}}{Z_\beta} \frac{1}{n} \sum_{i=1}^{n} \frac{e^{\beta\Phi(\mathbf{x})}}{T_i(\mathbf{x})} \geqslant \frac{e^{\beta\Phi_{\min}}}{Z_\beta} \frac{1}{n} \frac{1}{e^{\beta L}} \sum_{i=1}^{n} \frac{1}{|S_i|}.$$

Hence, for all $\mathbf{x}, \mathbf{y} \in S$ it holds that

$$\begin{aligned} \pi_\beta(\mathbf{x}) &\leqslant \frac{Z_0}{Z_\beta} e^{\beta\Phi_{\max}} \pi_0(\mathbf{x}) \\ Q_\beta(\mathbf{x},\mathbf{y}) &\geqslant \frac{Z_0}{Z_\beta} \frac{e^{\beta\Phi_{\min}}}{e^{\beta L}} Q_0(\mathbf{x},\mathbf{y}). \end{aligned}$$

Since from Lemma 4 it holds that for $\beta = 0$ the relaxation time is $\mathcal{O}(n)$, the thesis follows by applying the comparison theorem (Theorem 2) with

$$\alpha = \frac{Z_\beta}{Z_0} \frac{e^{\beta L}}{e^{\beta \Phi_{\min}}} \qquad \text{and} \qquad \gamma = \frac{Z_0}{Z_\beta} e^{\beta \Phi_{\max}}.$$

$\square$

A slightly better upper bound holds when the players have two strategies.

COROLLARY 6. *If every player has only two strategies then the relaxation time is $t_{rel} = \mathcal{O}\left(n \cdot e^{\beta \Delta \Phi}\right)$.*

PROOF. Observe that, when every player has two strategies, in Equation (6) we have that

$$\frac{e^{\beta \Phi(\mathbf{x})} e^{\beta \Phi(\mathbf{y})}}{T_i(\mathbf{x})} = \frac{e^{\beta \Phi(\mathbf{x})} e^{\beta \Phi(\mathbf{y})}}{e^{\beta \Phi(\mathbf{x})} + e^{\beta \Phi(\mathbf{y})}} \geq \frac{e^{\beta \min\{\Phi(\mathbf{x}), \Phi(\mathbf{y})\}}}{2}.$$

Hence, we obtain

$$Q_\beta(\mathbf{x}, \mathbf{y}) \geq \frac{e^{\beta \Phi_{\min}}}{Z_\beta} \frac{1}{2n} \qquad \text{and} \qquad Q_\beta(\mathbf{x}, \mathbf{x}) \geq \frac{e^{\beta \Phi_{\min}}}{Z_\beta} \frac{1}{2}$$

and we can apply the comparison theorem with

$$\alpha = \frac{Z_\beta}{Z_0} \frac{1}{e^{\beta \Phi_{\min}}} \qquad \text{and} \qquad \gamma = \frac{Z_0}{Z_\beta} e^{\beta \Phi_{\max}}.$$

$\square$

Finally, we can obtain the bounds on the mixing time by using Theorem 1 and the fact that $\pi_{\min} \geq 1/\left(e^{\beta \Delta \Phi} |S|\right)$.

COROLLARY 7. *For every potential game the mixing time of the logit dynamics is*

$$t_{\mathrm{mix}} = \mathcal{O}\left(n \cdot e^{\beta(\Delta \Phi + L)} \left(\beta \Delta \Phi + \log |S|\right)\right),$$

where S is the set of strategy profiles.
For potential games with two strategies per player the mixing time is $\mathcal{O}\left(n \cdot e^{\beta \Delta \Phi} (\beta \Delta \Phi + \log |S|)\right)$.

Lower bound. It is easy to find potential games whose logit dynamics mixing time is $\Omega(e^{\beta \Delta \Phi})$ when $\Delta \Phi = L$; e.g., games whose potential function Φ has only two values and at least two non-adjacent maxima (see, for example, 2-player coordination games studied in [2]). One naturally wonders whether a similar lower bound can be achieved for games where the Lipschitz constant L is small compared to $\Delta \Phi$. The following theorem shows that the term $e^{\beta \Delta \Phi}$ in the upper bound in Corollary 7 cannot be essentially improved for L smaller than $\Delta \Phi$.

THEOREM 8. *For every $0 < \delta < 1$ and for every $L = \omega(\log n)$ a family of potential games with two strategies per player exists such that the potential function Φ has Lipschitz constant L, it satisfies $\Delta \Phi / L > n^\delta$ and the mixing time of the logit dynamics is $\Omega\left(e^{(\beta - o(1))\Delta \Phi}\right)$.*

PROOF. Consider the game with n players in which every player has strategies 0 and 1, and whose potential function is

$$\Phi(\mathbf{x}) = \Phi(|\mathbf{x}|_1) = \min \left\{c; \; \left|c - |\mathbf{x}|_1\right|\right\} \cdot L$$

where $c = \lceil n^\delta \rceil$. Note that the maximum of the potential is $\Phi(\mathbf{0}) = \Delta \Phi = cL$, while the minimum is zero and is attained at all states in the set $M = \left\{\mathbf{x} \in S : |\mathbf{x}|_1 = c\right\}$.
Consider the set $R_{\mathbf{0}, M}$ (see Section 2) and observe that

$$\begin{aligned} R_{\mathbf{0}, M} &= \left\{\mathbf{x} \in S : |\mathbf{x}|_1 < c\right\} \\ \partial R_{\mathbf{0}, M} &= \left\{\mathbf{x} \in S : |\mathbf{x}|_1 = c - 1\right\}. \end{aligned}$$

By the symmetry of the potential function, the stationary probability of $R_{\mathbf{0}, M}$ is $\pi(R_{\mathbf{0}, M}) \leq \frac{1}{2}$ and the size of its boundary is

$$|\partial R_{\mathbf{0}, M}| \leq \binom{n}{c} \leq e^{c \log n} = e^{(\Delta \Phi / L) \log n}.$$

Thus, from Theorem 3 we have that the mixing time of the logit dynamics is

$$t_{\mathrm{mix}} = \Omega\left(e^{\beta \Delta \Phi - (\Delta \Phi / L) \log n}\right)$$

and since $L = \omega(\log n)$ the thesis follows. $\square$

4. DOMINANT STRATEGIES GAMES

In the previous section, we analyzed potential games and derived upper and lower bounds on the mixing time for the logit dynamics that are exponential in β. In this section we prove that, for the class of games with *dominant strategies*, it is possible to give upper bounds that are independent of β. In other words, the mixing time of the logit dynamics for games with dominant strategies does not grow arbitrarily as β tends to infinity.

A strategy $z \in S_i$ is *dominant* for player i if it yields the maximum payoff regardless of the strategies of the other players; that is, $u_i(z, \mathbf{x}_{-i}) \geq u_i(z', \mathbf{x}_{-i})$ for every $z' \in S_i$ and every $\mathbf{x}_{-i} \in S_{-i}$. In a *game with dominant strategies* every player has a dominant strategy. Let us name 0 a dominant strategy for all players and consider the profile $\mathbf{0} = (0, \dots, 0)$. It is easy to see that the following observation holds for the logit dynamics of a game with dominant strategies.

OBSERVATION 9. *In every profile and for every β, if player i is selected then her strategy is updated to the dominant strategy with probability at least $1/|S_i|$. That is, for all $\mathbf{x}$, β and i, $\sigma_i(0 \mid \mathbf{x}) \geq 1/|S_i|$.*

We are now ready to derive an upper bound on the mixing time of the logit dynamics for dominant strategy games.

THEOREM 10. *For n-player games with dominant strategies where each player has at most m strategies, the mixing time is $t_{\mathrm{mix}} = \mathcal{O}\left(m^n n \log n\right)$.*

PROOF. We apply the coupling technique (see Theorem 17 in Appendix A). Let $\{X_t\}$ and $\{Y_t\}$ be two instances of the logit dynamics starting at $\mathbf{x}$ and $\mathbf{y}$ respectively, and consider a coupling with the following properties: at every step the same player in both chains is chosen for the update, the probability that the strategy of the chosen player is updated to 0 in both chains is at least $1/|S_i| \geq 1/m$ (notice that this is possible because of Observation 9), and once the two chains coalesce they stay coupled for all the following time steps. An example of such a coupling can be found in Appendix C.

Let τ be the first time such that all the players have been selected at least once and let $t^* = 2n \log n$. Observe that for all starting profiles $\mathbf{z}$ and $\mathbf{w}$, it holds that

$$\mathbf{P}_{\mathbf{z},\mathbf{w}} \left(X_{t^*} = \mathbf{0} \text{ and } Y_{t^*} = \mathbf{0} \mid \tau \leqslant t^* \right) \geqslant \frac{1}{m^n}. \qquad (7)$$

Indeed, given that all players have been selected at least once within time t^*, both chains are in profile $\mathbf{0}$ at time t^* if and only if every player chose strategy 0 in both chains the last time she played before time t^*. From the construction of the coupling it follows that such event holds with probability at least $1/m^n$.

Hence, for all starting profiles $\mathbf{z}$ and $\mathbf{w}$, we have that

$$\mathbf{P}_{\mathbf{z},\mathbf{w}} \left(X_{t^*} = Y_{t^*} \right) \geqslant \mathbf{P}_{\mathbf{z},\mathbf{w}} \left(X_{t^*} = \mathbf{0} \text{ and } Y_{t^*} = \mathbf{0} \right)$$

$$\geqslant \mathbf{P}_{\mathbf{z},\mathbf{w}} \left(X_{t^*} = \mathbf{0} \text{ and } Y_{t^*} = \mathbf{0} \mid \tau \leqslant t^* \right) \mathbf{P}_{\mathbf{z},\mathbf{w}} \left(\tau \leqslant t^* \right)$$

$$\geqslant \frac{1}{m^n} \cdot \frac{1}{2} \qquad (8)$$

where in the last inequality we used (7) and the Coupon Collector's argument.

Therefore, by considering k phases each one lasting t^* time steps, since the bound in (8) holds for every starting states of the Markov chain, we have that the probability that the two chains have not yet coupled after kt^* time steps is

$$\mathbf{P}_{\mathbf{x},\mathbf{y}} \left(X_{kt^*} \neq Y_{kt^*} \right) \leqslant \left(1 - \frac{1}{2m^n} \right)^k \leqslant e^{-k/2m^n}$$

which is less than $1/4$, for $k = \mathcal{O}(m^n)$. By applying the Coupling Theorem (see Theorem 17 in the Appendix) we have that $t_{\text{mix}} = \mathcal{O}\left(m^n n \log n \right)$. $\square$

In [2] a n-player game with two strategies per player is shown whose logit dynamics mixing time is $\Omega(2^n)$ for large values of β. We next prove that, for every $m \geqslant 2$, there are n-player games with m strategies per player whose logit dynamics mixing time is $\Omega\left(m^{n-1}\right)$. Thus the m^n factor in the upper bound given by Theorem 10 cannot be essentially improved.

THEOREM 11. *For every $m \geqslant 2$ and $n \geqslant 2$, there exists a n-player potential game with dominant strategies where each player has m strategies and such that, for sufficiently large β, $t_{\text{mix}} = \Omega\left(m^{n-1}\right)$.*

PROOF. Consider the game with n players, each of them having strategies $\{0, \ldots, m-1\}$, such that for every player i:

$$u_i(\mathbf{x}) = \begin{cases} 0, & \text{if } \mathbf{x} = \mathbf{0}; \\ -1, & \text{otherwise.} \end{cases}$$

Note that 0 is a dominant strategy. This is a potential game with potential $\Phi(\mathbf{x}) = u_i(\mathbf{x})$ and thus the stationary distribution is given by the Gibbs measure. We apply the bottleneck ratio (see Theorem 19 in Appendix A) with $R = \{0, \ldots, m-1\}^n \setminus \{\mathbf{0}\}$, for which we have

$$\pi(R) = \frac{e^{-\beta}}{Z}(m^n - 1)$$

with $Z = 1 + e^{-\beta}(m^n - 1)$. It is easy to see that $\pi(R) < 1/2$ for $\beta > \log(m^n - 1)$ and furthermore

$$Q(R, \overline{R}) = \sum_{\mathbf{x} \in R} \pi(\mathbf{x}) P(\mathbf{x}, \mathbf{0})$$

$$= \frac{e^{-\beta}}{Z} \sum_{\mathbf{x} \in R} P(\mathbf{x}, \mathbf{0}) = \frac{e^{-\beta}}{Z} \sum_{\mathbf{x} \in R_1} P(\mathbf{x}, \mathbf{0}),$$

where R_1 is the subset of R containing all states with exactly one non-zero entry. Notice that, for every $\mathbf{x} \in R_1$, we have

$$P(\mathbf{x}, \mathbf{0}) = \frac{1}{n} \cdot \frac{1}{1 + (m-1)e^{-\beta}}.$$

As $|R_1| = n(m-1)$, we have

$$Q(R, \overline{R}) = \frac{e^{-\beta}}{Z} |R_1| \frac{1}{n} \cdot \frac{1}{1 + (m-1)e^{-\beta}}$$

$$= \frac{e^{-\beta}}{Z} \cdot \frac{m-1}{1 + (m-1)e^{-\beta}}$$

whence

$$t_{\text{mix}} \geqslant \frac{1}{4} \cdot \frac{\pi(R)}{Q(R, \overline{R})}$$

$$\geqslant \frac{1}{4} \cdot (m^n - 1) \cdot \frac{1 + (m-1)e^{-\beta}}{m-1} > \frac{1}{4} \cdot \frac{m^n - 1}{m - 1}.$$

$\square$

Extensions. Observe that, by using the same techniques exploited in this section, it is possible to prove an upper bound *independent of β* for *max-solvable* games [12], a class which contains games with dominant strategies as a special case, albeit with an upper bound that is much larger than $\mathcal{O}(m^n n \log n)$.

5. GRAPHICAL COORDINATION GAMES

Consider the following basic two-player coordination game

	0	1
0	a, a	c, d
1	d, c	b, b

$$(9)$$

We assume that $a > d$ and $b > c$ which implies that players have an advantage in selecting the same strategy and that $(0,0)$ and $(1,1)$ are Nash equilibria. If $a - d > b - c$ then equilibrium $(0,0)$ is said to be *risk dominant* and, analogously, if $a - d < b - c$ then equilibrium $(1,1)$ is said to be *risk dominant* [6]. Tight bounds for the mixing time of the basic coordination games have been given in [2].

In this section we consider *graphical coordination games* in which n players are connected by a network G (encoding, for example, social relationships) and every player plays the basic coordination game (9) with each of the adjacent players. Specifically, when a player selects her strategy, such a strategy is played against each one of her adjacent players. The payoff of a player is given by the sum of the payoffs gained from each instance of the basic coordination game. We focus on two network topologies: the clique (Section 5.1), where the mixing time dependence on $e^{\beta \Delta \Phi}$ showed in Corollary 7 cannot be improved, and the ring (Section 5.2), where a more local interaction implies a faster convergence to the stationary distribution.

In the rest of this section we will assume w.l.o.g. that $a - d \geqslant b - c$.

5.1 Coordination games on the clique

We study the mixing time of graphical coordination games on the clique; that is, every player plays the basic coordination game (9) with every other player. We give upper and lower bounds on the mixing time. As we shall see, both such bounds turn out to be exponential in n, even for $\beta = \Theta(1)$.

We first observe that the game is a potential game. This will allow us to use Corollary 7 to derive an upper bound on the mixing time and to use Theorem 3 to get a lower bound.

It is not difficult to see that $\Phi(\mathbf{x}) = \phi(|\mathbf{x}|_0)$ is a potential function for the graphical coordination game on the clique, where

$$\phi(k) := (k^\star - k)\left(\frac{2n - k^\star - k - 1}{2}(b-c) - \frac{k^\star + k - 1}{2}(a-d)\right)$$

and $k^\star = \left\lceil (n-1)\frac{b-c}{(a-d)+(b-c)}\right\rceil$. Notice that the minimum of the potential is attained when $k^\star$ players are playing 0 and, since $\phi(k^\star) = 0$, we have that $\Delta\Phi = \max_k \phi(k)$. Moreover, it is easy to check that $\phi(k)$ monotonically decreases as k goes from 0 to $k^\star$ and then monotonically increases as k goes from $k^\star$ to n. Therefore, $\Delta\Phi = \max\{\phi(0), \phi(n)\}$.

Notice that, since $a - d \geqslant b - c$, then $\phi(k) \leqslant \phi(n-k)$ for $k < k^\star$, $\Delta\Phi = \phi(n)$ and

$$\sum_{k=0}^{k^\star} \Phi(k) \leqslant \sum_{k=n-k^\star}^{n} \Phi(k). \tag{10}$$

Since $\Delta\Phi = \phi(n)$, by applying our general result on the mixing time of the logit dynamics of potential games (see Corollary 7) we get $t_{\mathrm{mix}} = \mathcal{O}\left(n \cdot e^{\beta\phi(n)} \cdot (\beta\phi(n) + n)\right)$. We next state a lower bound on the mixing time for coordination games on a clique.

LEMMA 12. *For coordination games on a clique the mixing time is* $t_{\mathrm{mix}} = \Omega\left(e^{(\beta - o(1))\phi(0)}\right)$.

PROOF. We obtain our lower bound by applying Theorem 3 with configuration $\mathbf{x}^\star = (1, \ldots, 1)$ and set $M = \{\mathbf{x} \in S : |\mathbf{x}|_0 = k^\star\}$.

The connected component R of $S \setminus M$ that contains $\mathbf{x}^\star$ is

$$R = \left\{\mathbf{x} \in S \colon |\mathbf{x}|_0 < k^\star\right\}$$

From (10) it follows that $\pi(R) \leqslant \frac{1}{2}$. Finally, notice that

$$\begin{aligned}|\partial R| &\leqslant |\{\mathbf{x} \in \Omega \colon |\mathbf{x}|_0 = k^\star - 1\}| \\ &= \binom{n}{k^\star - 1} \leqslant n^{k^\star} \leqslant n^{\frac{2}{b-c}\frac{\phi(0)}{n-1}}.\end{aligned}$$

The lemma follows by applying Theorem 3 and by observing that the maximum potential among profiles in R and M are $\Phi^R = \phi(0)$ and $\Phi^M = 0$, respectively. $\square$

We stress that when the basic coordination game has no risk dominant strategy (that is the case $a - d = b - c$), $\phi(0) = \phi(n)$ and thus the exponents of the upper and lower bound coincide up to a $o(1)$ term. In general, by observing that $\phi(0), \phi(n) = \Theta(n^2)$, we can say that the mixing time is exponential in n^2 and β. More precisely, we obtain the following theorem.

THEOREM 13. *For every graphical coordination game on a clique there exist two constants C and D such that $C^{\beta n^2} \leqslant t_{\mathrm{mix}} \leqslant D^{\beta n^2}$.*

5.2 Coordination games on the ring

In this section we give upper and lower bounds on the mixing time for graphical coordination games on the ring when there is no risk dominant strategy. Unlike the clique, the ring encodes a very local type of interaction between the players which is more likely to occur in a social context. Our results show that the mixing time is polynomial in the number of players n and e^β.

Let us name $\delta := a - d = b - c$. It is not difficult to see that $\Phi(\mathbf{x}) = \sum_{i=1}^{n} \Phi_i(\mathbf{x})$ is a potential for the coordination game on the ring, where

$$\Phi_i(\mathbf{x}) = \begin{cases} \delta, & \text{if } x_{i-1} = x_i = x_{i+1}; \\ \frac{\delta}{2}, & \text{if } x_{i-1} \neq x_{i+1}; \\ 0, & \text{if } x_i \neq x_{i-1} = x_{i+1}. \end{cases}$$

Observe that $\Phi(\mathbf{1}) = \Phi(\mathbf{0}) = n\delta$. Moreover, if n is even, the configuration $\mathbf{x}$ where every player selects a strategy different from the one selected by her neighbors has potential $\Phi(\mathbf{x}) = 0$: thus, there are graphical coordination games on the ring where $\Delta\Phi = n\delta$. If we used Corollary 7, we would get an upper bound exponential in n. Instead we here show a upper bound that is polynomial in n.

The proof of the upper bound uses the path coupling technique (see Theorem 18) and can be seen as a generalization of the upper bound on the mixing time for the Ising model on the ring (see Chapter 15 of [7]).

THEOREM 14. *For graphical coordination games with no risk-dominant strategy ($a - d = b - c = \delta$) on a ring with n players the mixing time is $t_{\mathrm{mix}} = \mathcal{O}\left(n \log n \cdot e^{2\beta\delta}\right)$.*

PROOF. We identify the n players with the integers in $\{0, \ldots, n-1\}$ and assume that every player i plays the basic coordination game with her two adjacent players, $(i-1) \bmod n$ and $(i+1) \bmod n$. Let $S = \{0, 1\}^n$ be the set of profiles for n players playing the graphical coordination game on the ring and consider the Hamming graph G over S where profiles $\mathbf{x}$ and $\mathbf{y}$ are adjacent if and only if they differ in exactly one position.

Let us consider two adjacent configurations $\mathbf{x}$ and $\mathbf{y}$. Denote by j the position in which they differ and assume, without loss of generality, that $x_j = 1$ and $y_j = 0$. We consider the following coupling for two chains X and Y starting respectively from $X_0 = \mathbf{x}$ and $Y_0 = \mathbf{y}$: Pick $i \in \{0, \ldots, n-1\}$ and $U \in [0, 1]$ independently and uniformly at random and update position i of $\mathbf{x}$ and $\mathbf{y}$ by setting

$$x_i = \begin{cases} 0, & \text{if } U \leqslant \sigma_i(0 \mid \mathbf{x}); \\ 1, & \text{if } U > \sigma_i(0 \mid \mathbf{x}); \end{cases} \quad y_i = \begin{cases} 0, & \text{if } U \leqslant \sigma_i(0 \mid \mathbf{y}); \\ 1, & \text{if } U > \sigma_i(0 \mid \mathbf{y}). \end{cases}$$

We next compute the expected distance between X_1 and Y_1 after one step of the coupling. Notice that $\sigma_i(0 \mid \mathbf{x})$ only depends on x_{i-1} and x_{i+1} and $\sigma_i(0 \mid \mathbf{y})$ only on y_{i-1} and y_{i+1}. Therefore, since $\mathbf{x}$ and $\mathbf{y}$ only differ at position j, $\sigma_i(0 \mid \mathbf{x}) = \sigma_i(0 \mid \mathbf{y})$ for $i \neq j - 1, j + 1$.

We start by observing that if position j is chosen for update (this happens with probability $1/n$) then, by the observation above, both chains perform the same update. Since $\mathbf{x}$ and $\mathbf{y}$ differ only for player j, we have that the two chains are coupled (and thus at distance 0). Similarly, if $i \neq j - 1, j, j + 1$ (which happens with probability $(n-3)/n$) we have that both chains perform the same update and thus remain at distance 1. Finally, let us consider the case in which $i \in \{j-1, j+1\}$. In this case, since $x_j = 1$ and $y_j = 0$, we have that $\sigma_i(0|\mathbf{x}) \leqslant \sigma_i(0|\mathbf{y})$. Therefore, with probability $\sigma_i(0\,|\,\mathbf{x})$ both chains update position i to 0 and thus remain at distance 1; with probability $1 - \sigma_i(0\,|\,\mathbf{y})$ both chains update position i to 1 and thus remain at distance 1; and with probability $\sigma_i(0\,|\,\mathbf{y}) - \sigma_i(0\,|\,\mathbf{x})$ chain X updates position i to 1 and chain Y updates position i to 0 and thus the two chains go to distance 2. By summing up, we have that the expected distance $E[\rho(X_1, Y_1)]$ after one step of coupling of the two chains is

$$E[\rho(X_1, Y_1)] =$$

$$= \frac{n-3}{n} + \frac{1}{n} \sum_{i \in \{j-1, j+1\}} [\sigma_i(0\,|\,\mathbf{x}) + 1 - \sigma_i(0\,|\,\mathbf{y})$$
$$+ 2 \cdot (\sigma_i(0\,|\,\mathbf{y}) - \sigma_i(0\,|\,\mathbf{x}))]$$

$$= \frac{n-3}{n} + \frac{1}{n} \cdot \sum_{i \in \{j-1, j+1\}} (1 + \sigma_i(0\,|\,\mathbf{y}) - \sigma_i(0\,|\,\mathbf{x}))$$

$$= \frac{n-1}{n} + \frac{1}{n} \cdot \sum_{i \in \{j-1, j+1\}} (\sigma_i(0\,|\,\mathbf{y}) - \sigma_i(0\,|\,\mathbf{x}))$$

Let us now evaluate the difference $\sigma_i(0\,|\,\mathbf{y}) - \sigma_i(0\,|\,\mathbf{x})$ for $i = j - 1$ (the same computation holds for $i = j + 1$). We distinguish two cases depending on the strategies of player $j - 2$ and start with the case $x_{j-2} = y_{j-2} = 1$. In this case we have that

$$\sigma_{j-1}(0\,|\,\mathbf{x}) = \frac{1}{1 + e^{2\beta\delta}} \text{ and } \sigma_{j-1}(0\,|\,\mathbf{y}) = \frac{1}{2}.$$

Thus,

$$\sigma_{j-1}(0\,|\,\mathbf{y}) - \sigma_{j-1}(0\,|\,\mathbf{x}) = \frac{1}{2} - \frac{1}{1 + e^{2\beta\delta}}.$$

If instead $x_{j-2} = y_{j-2} = 0$, we have

$$\sigma_{j-1}(0\,|\,\mathbf{x}) = \frac{1}{2} \text{ and } \sigma_{j-1}(0\,|\,\mathbf{y}) = \frac{1}{1 + e^{-2\beta\delta}}.$$

Thus

$$\sigma_{j-1}(0\,|\,\mathbf{y}) - \sigma_{j-1}(0|\mathbf{x}) = \frac{1}{1 + e^{-2\beta\delta}} - \frac{1}{2}$$

$$= 1 - \frac{1}{1 + e^{2\beta\delta}} - \frac{1}{2} = \frac{1}{2} - \frac{1}{1 + e^{2\beta\delta}}.$$

We can conclude that the expected distance after one step of the chain is

$$E[\rho(X_1, Y_1)] = \frac{n-1}{n} + \frac{1}{n} \left(1 - \frac{2}{1 + e^{2\beta\delta}}\right)$$

$$= 1 - \frac{2}{n(1 + e^{2\beta\delta})} \leqslant e^{-\frac{2}{n(1 + e^{2\beta\delta})}}.$$

Since the diameter of G is $\mathrm{diam}(G) = n$, by applying Theorem 18 with $\alpha = \frac{2}{n(1 + e^{2\beta\delta})}$, we obtain the theorem. $\square$

The upper bound in Theorem 14 is nearly tight (up to the $n \log n$ factor). Indeed, a lower bound can be obtained by applying the Bottleneck Ratio technique (see Theorem 19 in Appendix A) to the set $R = \{\mathbf{1}\}$. Notice that $\pi(R) \leqslant \frac{1}{2}$ since profile $\mathbf{0}$ has the same potential as $\mathbf{1}$. Thus set R satisfies

the hypothesis of Theorem 19. Simple computations show that the bottleneck ratio is

$$B(R) = \sum_{\mathbf{y} \neq \mathbf{1}} P(\mathbf{1}, \mathbf{y}) = \frac{1}{1 + e^{2\beta\delta}}.$$

Thus, by applying Theorem 19, we obtain the following bound.

THEOREM 15. *For graphical coordination games with no risk-dominant strategy on a ring with n players the mixing time is $t_{\mathrm{mix}} = \Omega\left(e^{2\beta\delta}\right)$.*

6. CONCLUSIONS AND OPEN PROBLEMS

In this work we give bounds on the mixing time of the logit dynamics for wide classes of games, highlighting how the noise level of the logit dynamics and the structural properties of the game affect the convergence rate to stationarity. In fact, we show that the mixing time for potential games depends polynomially on the number of players and exponentially on the inverse noise and the maximum potential difference $\Delta\Phi$: this dependence shows both in the upper and the lower bound, even if they are not completely matching; thus, it is natural to ask if it is possible to close the gap.

On the other hand, we show that there exists a class of games, namely dominant strategy games, such that the mixing time of the logit dynamics does not grow indefinitely with the inverse noise.

Finally, we consider coordination games on the clique and the ring, a subset of potential games, where we give evidence that the mixing time is affected also by other structural properties as the connectedness of the network: it might be interesting to investigate other graph structures to highlight other properties influencing the mixing time (e.g., degree of the graph, expansion, etc.)

The main goal of this line of research is to give general bounds on the logit dynamics mixing time for any game, highlighting the features of the game that distinguish between polynomial and exponential mixing time. We stress that, when the game is not a potential game, in general there is not a simple closed form for the stationary distribution like Equation (3).

At every step of the logit dynamics one single player is selected to update her strategy. It would be interesting to consider variations of such dynamics where players are allowed to update their strategies simultaneously. The special case of parallel best response (that is $\beta = \infty$) has been studied in [12]. Another interesting variant of the logit dynamics is the one in which the value of β is not fixed, but varies according to some *learning process* by which players acquire more information on the game as time progresses.

When the mixing time of the logit dynamics is polynomial, we know that the stationary distribution gives good predictions of the state of the system after a polynomial number of time steps. When the mixing time is exponential, it would be interesting to analyze the *transient* phase of the logit dynamics, in order to investigate what kind of predictions can be made about the state of the system in such a phase.

7. REFERENCES

[1] Arash Asadpour and Amin Saberi. On the inefficiency ratio of stable equilibria in congestion games. In *Proc. of the 5th International Workshop on Internet and*

Network Economics (WINE'09), volume 5929 of *LNCS*, pages 545–552. Springer, 2009.

[2] Vincenzo Auletta, Diodato Ferraioli, Francesco Pasquale, and Giuseppe Persiano. Mixing time and stationary expected social welfare of logit dynamics. In *3rd Int. Symp. on Algorithmic Game Theory (SAGT)*, volume 6386 of *LNCS*, pages 54–65. Springer, 2010.

[3] Noam Berger, Claire Kenyon, Elchanan Mossel, and Yuval Peres. Glauber dynamics on trees and hyperbolic graphs. *Probability Theory and Related Fields*, 131:311–340, 2005.

[4] Lawrence E. Blume. The statistical mechanics of strategic interaction. *Games and Economic Behavior*, 5:387–424, 1993.

[5] Glenn Ellison. Learning, local interaction, and coordination. *Econometrica*, 61(5):1047–1071, 1993.

[6] John C. Harsanyi and Reinhard Selten. *A General Theory of Equilibrium Selection in Games*. MIT Press, 1988.

[7] David Levin, Yuval Peres, and Elizabeth L. Wilmer. *Markov Chains and Mixing Times*. American Mathematical Society, 2008.

[8] Jason R. Marden, H. Peyton Young, Gürdal Arslan, and Jeff S. Shamma. Payoff-based dynamics for multiplayer weakly acyclic games. *SIAM Journal on Control and Optimization*, 48(1):373–396, 2009.

[9] Fabio Martinelli. Lectures on Glauber dynamics for discrete spin models. In *Lectures on Probability Theory and Statistics (Saint-Flour, 1997)*, volume 1717 of *Lecture Notes in Math.*, pages 93–191. Springer, 1999.

[10] Panayotis Mertikopoulos and Aris L. Moustakas. The emergence of rational behavior in the presence of stochastic perturbations. *The Annals of Applied Probability*, 20(4):1359–1388, 2010.

[11] Andrea Montanari and Amin Saberi. Convergence to equilibrium in local interaction games. In *Proc. of the 50th Annual Symposium on Foundations of Computer Science (FOCS)*, pages 303–312. IEEE, 2009.

[12] Noam Nisan, Michael Schapira, and Aviv Zohar. Asynchronous best-reply dynamics. In *4th International Workshop on Internet and Network Economics (WINE)*, volume 5385 of *LNCS*, pages 531–538. Springer, 2008.

[13] H. Peyton Young. Adaptive learning in systems of interacting agents. In *Internet and Network Economics*, volume 5929 of *LNCS*, pages 13–16. Springer Berlin / Heidelberg, 2009.

[14] H. Peyton Young. *The diffusion of innovations in social networks*, chapter in "The Economy as a Complex Evolving System", vol. III, Lawrence E. Blume and Steven N. Durlauf, eds. Oxford University Press, 2003.

APPENDIX

A. MARKOV CHAINS' SUMMARY

We summarize the main tools we use to bound the mixing time of Markov chains (for a complete description of such tools see, for example, Chapters 4.2, 5.2, 7.2 and 14.2 in [7]).

Definition 16. A *coupling* of two probability distributions μ and ν is a pair of random variables (X, Y) defined on the same probability space such that the marginal distribution of X is μ and the marginal distribution of Y is ν. That is, a coupling (X, Y) of μ and ν satisfies $\mathbf{P}(X = x) = \mu(x)$ and $\mathbf{P}(Y = y) = \nu(y)$.

THEOREM 17 (COUPLING). *Let $\mathcal{M}$ be an irreducible and aperiodic Markov chain with finite state space Ω and transition matrix P. For two states x and y, let (X_t, Y_t) be a coupling of $P^t(x, \cdot)$ and $P^t(y, \cdot)$ such that $X_s = Y_s$ implies $X_t = Y_t$ for $t \geqslant s$. Let τ_{couple} be the first time the chains meet, $\tau_{couple} := \min\{t : X_t = Y_t\}$. Then, the mixing time is*

$$t_{\mathrm{mix}}(\varepsilon) \leqslant \min\left\{t \in \mathbb{N} \ : \ \max_{x,y \in \Omega} \mathbf{P}_{x,y}(\tau_{couple} > t) \leqslant \epsilon\right\}.$$

THEOREM 18 (PATH COUPLING). *Let $\mathcal{M} = \{X_t : t \in \mathbb{N}\}$ be an irreducible and aperiodic Markov chain with finite state space Ω and transition matrix P. Let $G = (\Omega, E)$ be a connected graph, let $\ell : E \to \mathbb{R}$ be a function assigning weights to edges such that $\ell(e) \geqslant 1$ for every edge $e \in E$, and let $\rho : \Omega \times \Omega \to \mathbb{R}$ be the corresponding path distance, i.e. $\rho(x, y)$ is the length of the (weighted) shortest path in G between x and y.*
Suppose that for every edge $\{x, y\} \in E$ a coupling (X, Y) of distributions $P(x, \cdot)$ and $P(y, \cdot)$ exists such that

$$\mathbf{E}_{x,y}[\rho(X, Y)] \leqslant \ell(\{x, y\})e^{-\alpha}$$

for some $\alpha > 0$, then the mixing time of $\mathcal{M}$ is

$$t_{\mathrm{mix}}(\varepsilon) \leqslant \frac{\log(diam(G)) + \log(1/\varepsilon)}{\alpha}$$

where $diam(G)$ is the (weighted) diameter of G.

THEOREM 19 (BOTTLENECK RATIO). *Let $\mathcal{M} = \{X_t : t \in \mathbb{N}\}$ be an irreducible and aperiodic Markov chain with finite state space Ω, transition matrix P and stationary distribution π. Let $R \subseteq \Omega$ be any set with $\pi(R) \leqslant 1/2$. Then the mixing time is*

$$t_{\mathrm{mix}}(\varepsilon) \geqslant \frac{1 - 2\epsilon}{2B(R)}$$

where

$$B(R) = \frac{Q(R, \overline{R})}{\pi(R)} \quad and \quad Q(R, \overline{R}) = \sum_{x \in R, y \in \overline{R}} \pi(x)P(x, y).$$

B. PROOF OF COMPARISON THEOREM

Let P be the transition matrix of an irreducible, aperiodic, and reversible Markov chain with finite state space Ω and stationary distribution π.

For a function $f : \Omega \to \mathbb{R}$ let $\mathcal{E}_\pi(f)$ be its Dirichlet form, i.e. $\mathcal{E}_\pi(f) = \langle(I - P)f, f\rangle_\pi$, where I is the identity matrix of size $|\Omega|$ and $\langle \cdot, \cdot \rangle_\pi$ is the inner product defined by

$$\langle f, g \rangle_\pi = \sum_{x \in \Omega} \pi(x)f(x)g(x) \qquad \text{for } f, g : \Omega \to \mathbb{R}$$

The Dirichlet form of a function f can be written as (see Lemma 13.11 in [7])

$$\mathcal{E}_\pi(f) = \frac{1}{2} \sum_{x,y \in \Omega} Q(x, y)(f(x) - f(y))^2 \qquad (11)$$

The following lemma states that by comparing the Dirichlet forms and the stationary distributions of two chains over the same state space it is possible to compare their spectral gaps.

LEMMA 20 (SEE LEMMA 13.22 IN [7]). *Let P and $\hat{P}$ be irreducible and reversible transition matrices over the same state space Ω and stationary distributions π and $\hat{\pi}$, respectively. If $\mathcal{E}_{\hat{\pi}}(f) \leqslant \alpha \mathcal{E}_{\pi}(f)$ for any function f, then*

$$1 - \hat{\lambda}_2 \leqslant \left[\max_{x \in \Omega} \frac{\pi(x)}{\hat{\pi}(x)} \right] \alpha(1 - \lambda_2)$$

In order to compare the relaxation times of two chains, we still need to compare their last eigenvalues. To this aim, consider the form $\mathcal{E}_{\pi}^{+}(f) = \langle (I + P)f, f \rangle_{\pi}$.

OBSERVATION 21.

$$\mathcal{E}_{\pi}^{+}(f) = \frac{1}{2} \sum_{x,y \in \Omega} Q(x,y) (f(x) + f(y))^2 \qquad (12)$$

PROOF.

$$\sum_{x,y \in \Omega} Q(x,y)(f(x) + f(y))^2 =$$

$$= 2 \sum_{x \in \Omega} \pi(x) f(x)^2 + 2 \sum_{x \in \Omega} \pi(x) f(x) (Pf)(x)$$

$$= 2\langle f, f \rangle_{\pi} + 2\langle Pf, f \rangle_{\pi} = 2\langle (I+P)f, f \rangle_{\pi}$$

□

The next observation shows that, just like the Dirichlet form is related to the spectral gap, $\mathcal{E}^+$ is related to the smallest eigenvalue of the transition matrix.

OBSERVATION 22.

$$1 + \lambda_{|\Omega|} = \min_{f \neq 0} \frac{\mathcal{E}_{\pi}^{+}(f)}{\langle f, f \rangle_{\pi}}$$

PROOF. Since P is irreducible, aperiodic, and reversible there is a basis of $\mathbb{R}^{\Omega}$ formed by eigenvectors of P that are orthonormal w.r.t. the inner product $\langle \cdot, \cdot \rangle_{\pi}$ (see e.g. Lemma 12.2 in [7]). Let $f_1, \ldots, f_{|\Omega|}$ be such a basis where f_i is the eigenvector with eigenvalue λ_i. Let f be any function, then it can be written as a linear combination of eigenvectors $f = \sum_{i=1}^{|\Omega|} \alpha_i f_i$. Hence $Pf = \sum_{i=1}^{|\Omega|} \alpha_i P f_i = \sum_{i=1}^{|\Omega|} \alpha_i \lambda_i f_i$. Since $f_1, \ldots, f_{|\Omega|}$ are orthonormal w.r.t. $\langle \cdot, \cdot \rangle_{\pi}$ it holds that

$$\langle f, f \rangle_{\pi} = \sum_i \alpha_i^2$$

$$\langle Pf, f \rangle_{\pi} = \sum_{i=1}^{|\Omega|} \sum_{j=1}^{|\Omega|} \lambda_i \alpha_i \alpha_j \langle f_i, f_j \rangle_{\pi}$$

$$= \sum_{i=1}^{|\Omega|} \lambda_i \alpha_i^2 \geqslant \lambda_{|\Omega|} \langle f, f \rangle_{\pi}$$

Thus, for every function $f \neq 0$ we have that

$$\frac{\mathcal{E}_{\pi}^{+}(f)}{\langle f, f \rangle_{\pi}} = \frac{\langle f, f \rangle_{\pi} + \langle Pf, f \rangle_{\pi}}{\langle f, f \rangle_{\pi}} \geqslant 1 + \lambda_{|\Omega|}$$

And by taking the eigenvector $f_{|\Omega|}$ we have

$$\mathcal{E}_{\pi}^{+}\left(f_{|\Omega|}\right) / \langle f_{|\Omega|}, f_{|\Omega|} \rangle_{\pi} = 1 + \lambda_{|\Omega|}.$$

□

By using the form $\mathcal{E}^+$ an analogous of Lemma 20 can be shown for the last eigenvalue.

LEMMA 23. *Let P and $\hat{P}$ be irreducible and reversible transition matrices over the same state space Ω and stationary distributions π and $\hat{\pi}$, respectively. If $\mathcal{E}_{\hat{\pi}}^{+}(f) \leqslant \alpha \mathcal{E}_{\pi}^{+}(f)$, then*

$$1 + \hat{\lambda}_{|\Omega|} \leqslant \left[\max_{x \in \Omega} \frac{\pi(x)}{\hat{\pi}(x)} \right] \alpha(1 + \lambda_{|\Omega|})$$

PROOF. Let $c(\pi, \hat{\pi}) = \max\{\pi(x)/\hat{\pi}(x) : x \in \Omega\}$ be the maximum ratio between π and $\hat{\pi}$, then for every function f, the π-norm squared is at most $c(\pi, \hat{\pi})$ times the $\hat{\pi}$-norm squared, i.e.

$$\langle f, f \rangle_{\pi} = \sum_{x \in \Omega} f(x)^2 \pi(x) = \sum_{x \in \Omega} f(x)^2 \frac{\pi(x)}{\hat{\pi}(x)} \hat{\pi}(x) \leqslant c(\pi, \hat{\pi}) \langle f, f \rangle_{\hat{\pi}}$$

Hence, by using the hypothesis $\mathcal{E}_{\hat{\pi}}^{+}(f) \leqslant \alpha \mathcal{E}_{\pi}^{+}(f)$, for every function $f \neq 0$ we have that

$$\frac{\mathcal{E}_{\hat{\pi}}^{+}(f)}{\langle f, f \rangle_{\hat{\pi}}} \leqslant \alpha c(\pi, \hat{\pi}) \frac{\mathcal{E}_{\pi}^{+}(f)}{\langle f, f \rangle_{\pi}} \qquad (13)$$

And the thesis follows from Observation 22 by taking the minimum over all $f \neq 0$ on both sides of (13). □

Finally, we can prove the Comparison Theorem as stated in Section 2.

Proof of Theorem 2. Since $\hat{Q}(x,y) \leqslant \alpha Q(x,y)$ for all $x, y \in \Omega$, from (11) and (12) it follows that $\mathcal{E}_{\hat{\pi}}(f) \leqslant \alpha \mathcal{E}_{\pi}(f)$ and $\mathcal{E}_{\hat{\pi}}^{+}(f) \leqslant \alpha \mathcal{E}_{\pi}^{+}(f)$ for every function f. Since $\pi(x) \leqslant \gamma \hat{\pi}(x)$, from Lemmas 20 and 23 it follows that

$$1 - \hat{\lambda}_2 \leqslant \alpha \gamma (1 - \lambda_2) \quad \text{and} \quad 1 + \hat{\lambda}_{|\Omega|} \leqslant \alpha \gamma (1 + \lambda_{|\Omega|})$$

The thesis follows from the definition of relaxation time. □

C. THE COUPLING

In this section, we describe, for each $\mathbf{x}, \mathbf{y} \in S$, a coupling of $P(\mathbf{x}, \cdot)$ and $P(\mathbf{y}, \cdot)$ for the Markov chain $\mathcal{M}_{\beta}^{\mathcal{G}}$ whose transition matrix P is given by Equation (2). We will then show that the coupling described has the properties required by the proof of Theorem 10.

For each player i, we partition two copies of the interval $[0,1]$, called $I_{X,i}$ and $I_{Y,i}$, in sub-intervals each labeled with a strategy from the set $S_i = \{z_1, \ldots, z_{|S_i|}\}$ of strategies of player i. The sub-intervals are constructed as follows. For $k = 1, \ldots, |S_i|$, we take the leftmost not yet labeled interval of length $l_k = \min\{\sigma_i(z_k \mid \mathbf{x}), \sigma_i(z_k \mid \mathbf{y})\}$ of both $I_{X,i}$ and $I_{Y,i}$ and label it with strategy z_k. In addition, we take the rightmost non yet labeled interval of length $\sigma_i(z_k \mid \mathbf{x}) - l_k$ of I_X and the rightmost non yet labeled interval of length $\sigma_i(z_k \mid \mathbf{y}) - l_k$ of I_Y and label both with z_k. Notice that at least one of these two intervals has length 0. Define functions $h_{X,i} \colon I_{X,i} \to S_i$ and $h_{Y,i} \colon I_{Y,i} \to S_i$ that for $s \in [0,1]$ return the labels $h_{X,i}(s)$ and $h_{Y,i}(s)$ of the sub-intervals containing s.

Given the above partitions of $I_{X,i}$ and $I_{Y,i}$ for each i, the coupling can be described as follows: pick $i \in [n]$ and $U \in [0,1]$ uniformly at random and update X and Y by setting $X_i = h_{X,i}(U)$ and $Y_i = h_{Y,i}(U)$). By construction we have that (X, Y) is a coupling of $P(\mathbf{x}, \cdot)$ and $P(\mathbf{y}, \cdot)$.

We finish by observing that, if player i is selected, the probability that both chains choose strategy z for player i is exactly $\min\{\sigma_i(z \mid \mathbf{x}), \sigma_i(z \mid \mathbf{y})\}$. If z is dominant for player i, we have that $\sigma_i(z \mid \mathbf{x}), \sigma_i(z \mid \mathbf{y}) \geqslant 1/|S_i|$ and thus the probability that the coupling updates to z is at least $1/|S_i|$.

On a Bounded Budget Network Creation Game

Shayan Ehsan, MohammadAmin Fazli, Sina Sadeghian Sadeghabad, MohammadAli Safari[*], Morteza Saghafian and Saber ShokatFadaei
Dept. of Computer Engineering, Sharif University of Technology
Tehran, Iran
ehsani@ce.sharif.edu, fazli@ce.sharif.edu, s_sadeghian@ce.sharif.edu,
msafari@sharif.edu, saghafian@ce.sharif.edu, shokat@ce.sharif.edu

Abbas Mehrabian[†]
Department of Combinatorics and Optimization
University of Waterloo
Waterloo, Canada
amehrabi@uwaterloo.ca

ABSTRACT

We consider a network creation game in which, each player (vertex) has a limited budget to establish links to other players. In our model, each link has a unit cost and each agent tries to minimize its cost which is its local diameter or its total distance to other players in the (undirected) underlying graph of the created network. Two variants of the game are studied: in the MAX version, the cost incurred to a vertex is the maximum distance between that vertex and other vertices, and in the SUM version, the cost incurred to a vertex is the sum of distances between that vertex and other vertices. We prove that in both versions pure Nash equilibria exist, but the problem of finding the best response of a vertex is NP-hard. Next, we study the maximum possible diameter of an equilibrium graph with n vertices in various cases. For infinite numbers of n, we construct an equilibrium tree with diameter $\Theta(n)$ in the MAX version. Also, we prove that the diameter of any equilibrium tree is $O(\log n)$ in the SUM version and this bound is tight. When all vertices have unit budgets (i.e. can establish link to just one vertex), the diameter in both versions is $O(1)$. We give an example of equilibrium graph in MAX version, such that all vertices have positive budgets and yet the diameter is as large as $\Omega(\sqrt{\log n})$. This interesting result shows that the diameter does not decrease necessarily and may increase as the budgets are increased. For the SUM version, we prove that every equilibrium graph has diameter $2^{O(\sqrt{\log n})}$ when all vertices have positive budgets. Moreover, if the budget

of every players is at least k, then every equilibrium graph with diameter more than 3 is k-connected.

Categories and Subject Descriptors

F.2.2 [**Theory of Computation**]: Analysis of Algorithms and Problem Complexity-Nonnumerical Algorithms and Problems; G.2.2 [**Mathematics of Computing**]: Discrete Mathematics-graph theory , network problems

General Terms

Performance, Design, Economics

Keywords

Network Design, Game Theory, Nash Equilibrium

1. INTRODUCTION

In recent years, a lot of research has been conducted on network design problems, because of their importance in computer science and operations research. The aim in this line of research is usually to build a minimum cost network that satisfies certain properties. The most well studied problem in this area is, perhaps, the problem of finding the minimum cost spanning tree. The network structure is usually determined by a central authority. This is, however, in contrast to many real world situations such as social networks, where networks are formed in a distributed manner by selfish agents. Therefore, a novel game theoretic approach has also been proposed (see [6, 1, 5]), in which it is assumed that each agent has its own objective, and attempts to minimize the cost it incurs in the network, regardless of how its actions affect other agents.

Fabrikant et al. [6] first introduced this approach and took into account both the creation and the usage cost of the network. In their model, the players correspond to the vertices of the network graph, and every player aims at minimizing the sum of its shortest-path distances to other vertices plus the price she pays for building links (edges) to other players. After that, various network creation games were proposed (see [1, 5, 4, 3, 7]), which vary in the way players participate in network creation. In most of these games,

[*]The work is partially supported by Grant no. CS1389-4-09 from IPM (Institute for Research in Fundamental Sciences)
[†]Department of Combinatorics and Optimization, University of Waterloo, Waterloo, Canada

there is a certain cost for building links, and the goal of each player is to minimize its maximum distance or total distance to other vertices.

Our work is motivated by the work of Laoutaris et al.[10]. In their model, every player has a specific budget for purchasing links. The objective of every player is to use its budget to establish some links to other vertices so as to minimize its maximum distance or total distance to other vertices in the resulting network. They focused on the case where all players have the same budget and all links cost are the same, so each player can establish a fixed number of links. In their model, links are directed and properties of the created directed graph is studied.

In this paper, we have considered an undirected variant of their model. In our model, once a link is established, both its endpoints can use it equally. This is a natural model in applications where the direction of links does not matter, for example, in computer networks. Although in our model links are undirected, each edge has just one owner and only one of its endpoints can be changed during the game. We also allow the players to have non-equal budgets.

1.1 The model and notation

Let n be a positive integer and $d_1, d_2, \ldots, d_n$ be nonnegative integers. A *bounded budget network creation game* with parameters $d_1, d_2, \ldots, d_n$, denoted by $(d_1, d_2, \cdots, d_n)$-BG, is the following game. There are n players and the strategy of player i is a subset $S_i \subseteq \{1, 2, \ldots, n\} \backslash \{i\}$ with $|S_i| = d_i$. We may build a directed graph G for every strategy profile $(S_1, \ldots, S_n)$ of this game, which has vertex set $V(G) = \{u_1, \ldots, u_n\}$, and for all i, j, (u_i, u_j) is an arc in G if $j \in S_i$. If (u_i, u_j) is an arc, then we say the arc (u_i, u_j) is *owned by* player i. As there is clear correspondence between the players and the vertices, we may sometime abuse notation and write statements like "vertex u_i owns the arc (u_i, u_j)," or "player i has an arc to vertex u_j." We think of the d_i as the *budget* available to player i. The *underlying graph* of G, which is an undirected graph obtained by ignoring the edge directions in G, is denoted by $U(G)$. If both arcs (u_i, u_j) and (u_j, u_i) are in G, then there is only one edge $u_i u_j$ in $U(G)$ (see Fig. 1). In this case, the edge $u_i u_j$ is called a *double edge*. In the following, whenever we refer to the distance between two vertices, we mean their distance in $U(G)$. The distance between two vertices u, v is denoted by $dist(u, v)$. For a directed or undirected graph G, the *diameter* of G is the maximum distance between any two vertices of G.

We define two models for the bounded budget network creation game, which differ in the definition of the cost function. In the *SUM* model, the cost of each player is the sum of its distances to other vertices, that is, for each vertex $u \in V(G)$,

$$c_{SUM}(u) = \sum_{v \in V(G)} dist(u, v)$$

while in the *MAX* model, the cost of each player is the maximum of its distances to other vertices, that is, for each vertex $u \in V(G)$,

$$c_{MAX}(u) = \max\{dist(u, v) : v \in V(G)\}$$

The value $c_{MAX}(u)$ is sometimes called the *local diameter* of u.

We say a player is playing its *best response* if it cannot

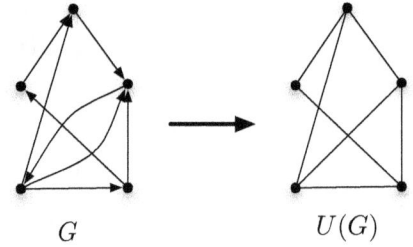

Figure 1: The illustration of $U(G)$

decrease its cost by changing its strategy (while the other players' strategies are fixed), and we say a strategy profile is a *Nash Equilibrium (NE)* if all players are playing their best responses. If this happens, then the graph G is also said to be a *Nash Equilibrium graph*, or simply an *equilibrium graph* for $(d_1, d_2, \ldots, d_n)$-BG.

We have also studied the *Price of Anarchy (PoA)* and the *Price of Stability (PoS)* where the social utility function is the diameter of the graph. Price of Anarchy, introduced by Papadimitriou et al.[9], measures the effect of selfish agents on social utility, i.e. computes the worst ratio of the value of social utility function on every (pure) equilibrium to the optimal value. The best such ratio is called the Price of Stability. In this paper, the social utility function is the diameter of the created network.

1.2 Our results

In this paper, we study various properties of equilibrium graphs for bounded budget network creation game. First, in the next section, we prove that for every nonnegative sequence $d_1, \ldots, d_n$, $(d_1, d_2, \cdots, d_n)$-BG has a Nash equilibrium in both models. Next, we turn our attention to the diameter of equilibrium graphs. Our focus in this part are equilibria that have maximum diameters, which is related to the concept of price of anarchy when the social utility is the diameter of the created graph. We consider two special cases in Section 3, and find tight bounds for the maximum diameter. The two cases are unit budgets (in which $d_i = 1$, for every i) and trees (in which $d_1 + d_2 + \cdots + d_n = n - 1$). For the former, we prove that the diameter is always bounded above by a constant, and for the latter, we prove a $\Theta(n)$ bound for the MAX version and a $\Theta(\log n)$ bound for the SUM version. Then, in Section 4, we consider a more general case in which $d_i \geq 1$ for all $1 \leq i \leq n$, and obtain an upper bound $2^{O(\sqrt{\log n})}$ for the SUM version, and a lower bound $\Omega(\sqrt{\log n})$ for the MAX version.

The latter result disproves an intuitive guess that increasing the budgets, i.e the d_i's, decreases the diameter of equilibrium graphs: while the diameter is $O(1)$ for the unit degree case it could be as large as $\Omega(\sqrt{\log n})$ for larger values of d_i's in the MAX version. We also prove that in the SUM version, if $d_i \geq k$ for all i, then every equilibrium graph with diameter more than 3, is k-connected. We conclude with discussion of our results and suggesting some interesting open problems.

Table 1: **The results of this paper on diameter of the equilibrium graphs**

	MAX	SUM
Tree	$\Omega(n)$	$\Theta(\log(n))$
Unit Budget	$O(1)$	$O(1)$
General	$\Omega(\sqrt{\log(n)})$	$2^{O(\sqrt{\log n})}$

2. EXISTENCE OF EQUILIBRIA

Before proving the main result of this section, we show that computing best response is an intractable problem.

THEOREM 1. *The problem of finding the best response in both MAX and SUM models of $(d_1, \cdots, d_n)$-BG is NP-Hard.*

PROOF. We can reduce the k-center problem [8] to the problem of finding the best response in the MAX version of the game. In the k-center problem, a graph G is given and the aim is to find a subset C of k vertices of G so as to minimize the maximum distance from a vertex to its nearest neighbor in C, i.e. $\max_{v \in V(G)} \min_{c \in C} dist(c, v)$. Assume that we are given an undirected graph H, and we are supposed to find its k-center. Add a vertex $n+1$ to H and define $d_{n+1} = k$. Consider a directed graph G such that $U(G) = H$. Now compute the best response for the $(n+1)$'th player in MAX version in response to G. This essentially finds a subset of k vertices of G whose maximum distance to the remaining vertices of G is minimized, which is clearly a k-center for G.

Similarly, we can reduce the k-median problem [11] to find the best response in the SUM version of the game. □

In this section, we prove that for every nonnegative $d_1, d_2, \cdots, d_n$, Nash equilibria exist for both MAX and SUM versions. First, we prove a sufficient condition for each vertex to play its best response, and then prove the main theorem by considering several cases. The diameter of the equilibrium constructed in this theorem is $O(1)$ which proves that the price of stability is $O(1)$.

LEMMA 1. *Let u be a vertex. If $c_{MAX}(u) \leq 2$ and u is not an endpoint of any double edge or $c_{MAX}(u) = 1$ then u plays its best response in both MAX and SUM models.*

PROOF. If $c_{MAX}(u) = 1$, then we are done. Otherwise, let V^- be the set of vertices that have an arc to u and V^+ be the set of vertices that have an arc from u. Since u is not an endpoint of any double edge, $V^+ \cap V^- = \emptyset$. It is easy to verify that no matter how u plays, it always has distance one to at most $|V^+| + |V^-|$ vertices, and distance at least two to the rest of the vertices. Therefore, regardless of how u plays, its cost in MAX model will be at least 2, and its cost in SUM model will be at least $2(n - 1 - |V^-| - |V^+|) + |V^+| + |V^-|$. Therefore, u is already playing its best response. □

We are now ready to prove the main theorem of this section.

THEOREM 2. *For every nonnegative $d_1, d_2, \cdots, d_n$, Nash equilibria exists for both MAX and SUM versions of $(d_1, \ldots, d_n)$-BG.*

PROOF. The proof is constructive. We consider several cases, and prove it separately for each case. Without loss of generality, assume that $d_1 \leq d_2 \leq \cdots \leq d_n$.

Let $D = d_1 + d_2 + \cdots + d_n$. If $D < n - 1$ then the obtained graph, $U(G)$, is always disconnected and both MAX and SUM costs of every vertex are ∞. Therefore, for all vertices, every strategy is a best response. So, assume that $D \geq n - 1$. Let z be the number of players with zero budget, so we have $d_1 = \cdots = d_z = 0 < d_{z+1}$. There are two cases to consider:

Case 1: $d_n \geq z$

We provide an algorithm to build a graph G, such that all of its vertices satisfy the conditions of Lemma 1. G has vertex set $\{u_1, \ldots, u_n\}$ and is initially empty. We add the arcs (u_n, u_1), (u_n, u_2), $\ldots, (u_n, u_{d_n})$ and then the arcs $(u_{d_n+1}, u_n), (u_{d_n+2}, u_n), \cdots, (u_{n-1}, u_n)$ to G. Note that G has diameter 2 at this point, but there might be vertices whose outdegrees are less than their budgets. If u_i is such a vertex, add arcs from u_i to arbitrary vertices until its budget is consumed. This operation clearly does not increase the diameter, but this may result in double edges. For every double edge uv such that u has local diameter two and there exists a vertex w not adjacent to u, replace the arc (u, v) by (u, w). This can be done only a finite number of times, since after every replacement the number of double edges decreases. It is easy to see that the vertices of the obtained graph have the properties of Lemma 1 and thus this graph is a NE.

Case 2: $d_n < z$

As in Case 1, we build a graph G that is a Nash equilibrium, but the proof is more involved in this case. Let $t > z$ be the largest index with $d_n + d_{n-1} + \cdots + d_t \geq z + n - t$. Such value of t exists, as for $t = z + 1$, we have $d_n + d_{n-1} + \cdots + d_{z+1} = D \geq n - 1 = z + n - t$. Let $A = \{v_1, v_2, \cdots, v_z\}$, $B = \{v_{z+1}, v_{z+2}, \cdots, v_t\}$ and $C = \{v_{t+1}, v_{t+2}, \cdots, v_{n-1}\}$.

We start with an empty graph G and add arcs in four steps until the budgets of vertices are consumed (See Fig. 2)

1. An arc from every vertex in $B \cup C$ to v_n (dotted arcs in Fig. 2).

2. Arcs from $\{v_t\} \cup C \cup \{v_n\}$ to A. First, d_n arcs from v_n to the first d_n vertices of A then $d_{n-1} - 1$ arcs from v_{n-1} to the next $d_{n-1} - 1$ vertices of A and so on, until every vertex in A receives *exactly one* arc (dashed arcs in Fig. 2).

3. Arcs from B to C. For every vertex u in B that has remaining budget, we add arcs from u to vertices in C in reverse order, i.e. $v_{n-1}, v_{n-2}, \cdots$ (gray arcs in Fig. 2).

4. Arcs from B to A. For every vertex u in B that still has remaining budget, we add arcs from u to vertices in A in order, i.e. $v_1, v_2, \cdots$. So, every vertex in B is only adjacent to neighboring vertices of v_n in A because for every $z < i \leq t$, we have $d_i \leq d_n$.(black arcs in Fig. 2).

We now prove that every vertex is playing its best response in this graph. Vertices in A are obviously playing their best strategies as their budgets are zero. It is easy to verify that we are not creating a double edge in our construction. Since v_n has local diameter two, it plays its best response by Lemma 1. Every arc from a vertex $u \in C$ is either connected to v_n or to some vertex in $v \in A$. The latter cannot be changed, as changing it would disconnect v from G and increases the cost of u. It is also easy to verify that u is better off staying connected to v_n.

209

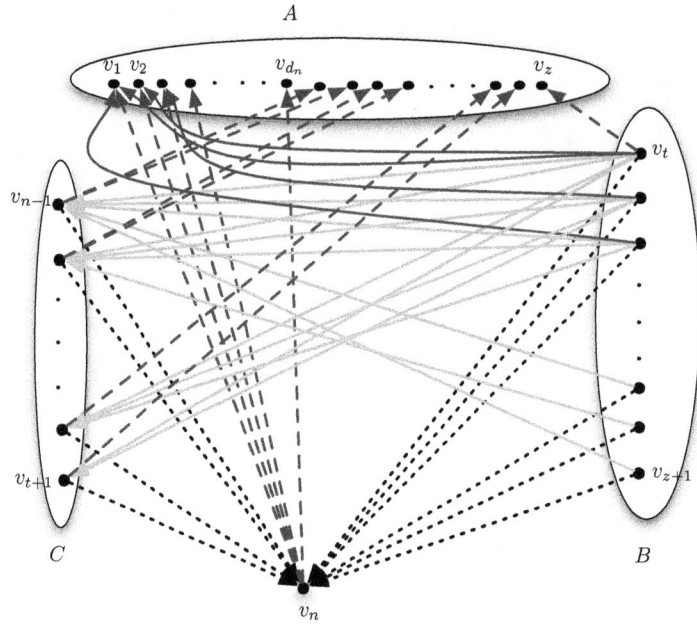

Figure 2: Case 2 of theorem 2

At last, consider a vertex u in B. If u creates arcs in step 4, then it has arcs to all vertices in C (step 3) and therefore, it has diameter two, since every vertex in A is a neighbour of v_n or one vertex in C. Thus in this case, vertex u satisfies the conditions of Lemma 1 and it plays its best response. Otherwise, u has local diameter three. The vertex u must have $K < |C|$ available budget in step 3. First, it is clear that u does not change its arc to v_n. Furthermore, since for any vertex $w \in C$ there is a vertex $w' \in A$ such that w' is only adjacent to w in $U(G)$, vertex u can not make its local diameter less than 3. Thus in this case, it plays its best response in the MAX version. Also, in the SUM version, it is easy to verify that its best strategy is to connect to the most influential vertices, i.e. $v_n, v_{n-1}, \cdots, v_{n-K}$. □

3. SPECIAL CASES

In this section, we find tight bounds for price of anarchy in two special cases. First we consider a situation where every player has unit budget and prove that the diameter of equilibrium graphs is bounded by a constant. Next, we consider the case where the equilibrium graphs are always trees, and find different bounds for MAX and SUM variants.

Note: we only consider connected equilibrium graphs. Any graph with more than d components, where $d = \max\{d_1, d_2, \cdots, d_n\}$, is a Nash equilibrium as no vertex can make the graph connected and the maximum and total distance of every player is always infinity. One way to solve this is to take the number of connected components into account for cost functions and, therefore, encourage players to reduce the number of connected components even though that may not reduce their local diameter.

3.1 Unit Budget Case

One special case of the problem is when all d_i's are one. In this case, we prove that all equilibrium graphs have diameter

$O(1)$. The proof is left to the journal version due to space shortage.

THEOREM 3. In $(1, 1, \cdots, 1)$-BG all the equilibrium graphs in both MAX and SUM versions have $O(1)$ diameters.

3.2 Trees

If $d_1 + d_2 + \cdots + d_n = n - 1$, then it can be easily seen that every equilibrium graph is a tree. From now on, we use the notion Tree-BG to indicate the instances of bounded budget network creation games that have $\sum_{i=1}^{n} d_i = n - 1$. In this section, we study the diameter of connected equilibrium graphs of Tree-BG in both MAX and SUM models. We prove that in the MAX model, there exists equilibrium graphs with diameter $\Omega(n)$, while in the SUM model, equilibrium graphs always have diameter $O(\log n)$, and this bound is tight.

THEOREM 4. In the MAX model, there are Tree-BG instances that have equilibrium graphs with diameter $\Omega(n)$.

PROOF. Let k be a positive integer, and let $n = 3k + 1$, $X = \{x_1, x_2, \cdots, x_k\}$, $Y = \{y_1, y_2, \cdots, y_k\}$, and $Z = \{z_1, z_2, \cdots, z_k\}$. Also, let $d_1 = \cdots = d_4 = 0$, $d_5 = d_6 = d_7 = 2$, and $d_8 = d_9 = \cdots = d_n = 1$. Let G be a graph with vertex set $X \cup Y \cup Z \cup \{w\}$ and with set of arcs $\{(x_1, x_2), \ldots, (x_{k-1}, x_k)\} \cup \{(y_1, y_2), \ldots, (y_{k-1}, y_k)\} \cup \{(z_1, z_2), \ldots, (z_{k-1}, z_k)\} \cup \{(x_1, w), (y_1, w), (z_1, w)\}$

We claim that for all $1 \leq i \leq k$, x_i is playing its best response. The proof for y_i's and z_i's are similar. If $i > 1$, then x_i has unit budget and currently has an arc to x_{i+1}. If it changes its arc to (x_i, x_j) for some $j > i+1$, then its local diameter doesn't decrease. If it changes to any other arc, then the graph gets disconnected, and x_i will have infinite local diameter.

If $i = 1$, then x_1 should choose a vertex from each of the two disjoint paths $x_2x_3\cdots x_k$ and $z_kz_{k-1}z_1wy_1y_2\cdots y_k$, and establish links to these two vertices otherwise the graph will be disconnected. Its best response is obviously to choose the middle of the second path (which is w) and an arbitrary vertex in the first path.

$\square$

In the next theorem, we will show that the diameters of equilibrium graphs in the SUM model are much smaller.

THEOREM 5. *In SUM model, all equilibrium graphs of Tree-BG have diameter $O(\log(n))$.*

PROOF. Let G be an equilibrium graph with diameter d, and let $P = v_0v_1\cdots v_d$ be its longest path. Trivially at least half of the arcs of P are in the same direction along P. By symmetry, we may assume that these are the arcs $(v_{i_1}, v_{i_1+1}), (v_{i_2}, v_{i_2+1}), \ldots, (v_{i_{\lceil d/2\rceil}}, v_{i_{\lceil d/2\rceil}+1})$. Let A_i be the set of vertices that are connected to P through v_i (including v_i), and let $a_i = |A_i|$. Notice that $a_0 = a_d = 1$ as P is the longest path in G. See Fig. 3 for an example.

For $1 \le j < \lceil d/2 \rceil$, if v_{i_j} changes its arc from (v_{i_j}, v_{i_j+1}) to (v_{i_j}, v_{i_j+2}), then its distance to vertices in A_{i_j+1} increases by one, and its distance to vertices in A_k, $k > i_j + 1$, decreases by one. Since v_{i_j} is playing its best response,

$$a_{i_j+1} \ge \sum_{k=i_j+2}^{d} a_k \ge \sum_{k=j+1}^{\lceil \frac{d}{2}\rceil} a_{i_k+1}$$

Since $v_j \in A_j$, we have $a_j \ge 1$.

$$
\begin{aligned}
a_{(i_{\lceil \frac{d}{2}\rceil}+1)} &\ge 1 \\
a_{(i_{\lceil \frac{d}{2}\rceil-1}+1)} &\ge a_{(i_{\lceil \frac{d}{2}\rceil}+1)} \\
a_{(i_{\lceil \frac{d}{2}\rceil-2}+1)} &\ge a_{(i_{\lceil \frac{d}{2}\rceil-1}+1)} + a_{(i_{\lceil \frac{d}{2}\rceil}+1)} \\
&\cdots \\
a_{(i_2+1)} &\ge a_{i_3+1} + \cdots + a_{(i_{\lceil \frac{d}{2}\rceil}+1)} \\
a_{(i_1+1)} &\ge a_{i_2+1} + a_{i_3+1} + \cdots + a_{(i_{\lceil \frac{d}{2}\rceil}+1)}
\end{aligned}
$$

We can prove by induction that $a_{i_j+1} \ge 2^{\lceil \frac{d}{2}\rceil - j - 1}$ for $1 \le j < \lceil \frac{d}{2}\rceil$. Therefore,

$$
\begin{aligned}
a_{(i_1+1)} + a_{(i_2+1)} + \cdots + a_{(i_{\lceil \frac{d}{2}\rceil}+1)} &\ge \\
2^{\lceil \frac{d}{2}\rceil-2} + 2^{\lceil \frac{d}{2}\rceil-3} + \cdots + 2^1 + 2^0 + 2^0 &= \\
2^{\lceil \frac{d}{2}\rceil-1}
\end{aligned}
$$

On the other hand, since all vertices appear in one of the sets A_i, we have $a_1 + a_2 + \cdots + a_d = n - 1$. Thus,

$$n - 1 = a_1 + a_2 + \cdots + a_d \ge \sum_{j=1}^{\lceil \frac{d}{2}\rceil} a_{(i_j+1)} \ge 2^{\lceil \frac{d}{2}\rceil-1},$$

Therefore, $d = O(\log n)$. $\square$

The bound $O(\log n)$ is tight as there exist instances with diameter $\Omega(\log n)$.

THEOREM 6. *For infinitely many n, there exists an equilibrium graph for Tree-BG in the SUM model with diameter $\Omega(\log(n))$.*

PROOF. Let k be a positive integer, and let $n = 2^{k+1} - 1$, $d_1 = d_2 = \cdots = d_{2^k-1} = 2, d_{2^k} = d_{2^k+1} = \cdots = d_n = 0$, Consider a balanced binary tree on n vertices in which vertex i $(1 \le i < n/2)$ has arcs to vertices $2i$ and $2i + 1$. For each i, let T_i be the tree rooted at vertex i. For each $i < 2^k$, vertex i must have an arc to a vertex in T_{2i} and to a vertex in T_{2i+1} in order to keep the graph connected. Observe that for every j, vertex j has less total distance to vertices in T_j than any other vertex in T_j, and so all vertices are playing their best responses. The diameter of this equilibrium graph is $2(\log(n + 1) - 1) = \Theta(\log(n))$. $\square$

4. GENERAL CASE

In this section, we assume that all players have positive budgets i.e. for each $1 \le i \le n$, $d_i \ge 1$. It appears intuitive that increasing the budgets (i.e. d_i's) would decrease the diameter. This is, however, not true and we prove an $\Omega(\sqrt{\log(n)})$ lower bound for the price of anarchy in the MAX version. We also prove that the diameter of an equilibrium graph in the SUM version is $2^{O(\sqrt{\log n})}$.

4.1 Upper bound for SUM

In this subsection we consider the SUM model only, and prove that for any NE graph the diameter is $2^{O(\sqrt{\log n})}$. The proof follows the line of proof of Theorem 9 of [2], but the first step is more involved. Specifically, the proof of the following proposition, which is somewhat easy in the model defined in [2], is much harder in our model.

PROPOSITION 1. *Let u be a vertex of an NE graph G and r be a positive integer. Assume that the subgraph of $U(G)$ induced by the set of vertices whose distance from u is at most r, is a tree. Then we have $r = O(\log |V(G)|)$.*

We will work with weighted graphs in this subsection. Let G be a weighted graph, that is, every vertex u has a weight $w(u)$, which is a positive integer. For every vertex u, the cost of u is defined as

$$c(u) = \sum_{v \in V} w(v)dist(u, v).$$

Note that if all vertices have unit weight, then this reduces to our unweighted model. We say that G is a *weak Nash equilibrium* (abbreviated wNE) if for every arc $(u, v) \in E$ and $x \in V$ with $(u, x) \notin E$, the cost of u does not decrease if we replace the arc (u, v) with (u, x). For a vertex u and a nonnegative integer r, define

$$B_r(u) = \{v : dist(u, v) \le r\}.$$

For $A \subseteq V$ define

$$w(A) = w_A = w(G[A]) = w_{G[A]} = \sum_{a \in A} w(a),$$

where $G[A]$ denotes the directed subgraph of G induced by A.

Clearly a Nash equilibrium graph is also a weak Nash equilibrium graph, and thus it is enough to show that the diameter of any wNE graph is $2^{O(\sqrt{\log n})}$.

Using the defined notation, we will prove the following generalization of Proposition 1:

LEMMA 2. *Let G be wNE, $u \in V$ and $r > 0$. Assume that $U(G[B_r(u)])$ is a tree T. Then we have $r = O(\log |w_G|)$.*

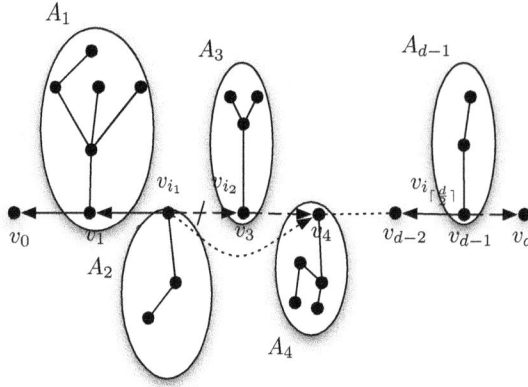

Figure 3: The proof of theorem 5

Note that if every vertex $v \in V(T)$ has at least two children then $r = O(\log |V(T)|) = O(\log |w_T|)$. Hence the problematic vertices are those with zero or one child. A vertex with degree 1 is called a *leaf*. Thus every vertex in T with no child is a leaf. It turns out that one should distinguish between two types of leaves: a *poor* leaf is a leaf with out-degree zero, and a *rich* leaf is a leaf with out-degree one. The poor leaves cause the most trouble and they are the reason for introducing the weights.

Let $l \in V$ be a poor leaf in G and $(u, l) \in E$. Let $G_0 = (V_0, E_0, w_0)$ be a weighted graph with $V_0 = V - \{l\}$, $E_0 = E - \{(u, l)\}$, $w_0(v) = w(v)$ for $v \neq u$ and $w_0(u) = w(u) + w(l)$. Then it can be verified that if G is a wNE then so is G_0. We say that G_0 is obtained by *folding* the poor leaf l. The proof of the following lemma is left to the journal version of this paper due to space shortage.

LEMMA 3. *Let G be a wNE and T be an induced subtree of $U(G)$. Let $r \in V(T)$ be such that if we choose r as the root of T, then every edge of T is oriented away from r. In other words, if u, v are vertices in T and (u, v) is an arc in G then u is the parent of v in T. Then the depth of T is at most $\log w_T + 1$.*

Remark. Note that if the conditions of the above lemma hold, then one can fold the whole subtree T into the vertex r. Moreover, folding this subtree does not decrease the diameter of G significantly. That is, if G is wNE and we perform a sequence of subtree folds on it until we reach a new digraph G' with no poor leaves, then G' is also wNE and $\mathrm{diam}(G) = \mathrm{diam}(G') + O(\log w(G))$.

From now on, we will assume that the weak Nash equilibrium we are studying has no poor leaves (the diameter would be the same, modulo an $O(\log w(G))$ term). Handling rich leaves is easy, as shown by the following lemma (whose proof can be found in the journal version of this paper).

LEMMA 4. *Let G be wNE. Then the distance between any two rich leaves is at most 2.*

To handle the vertices of degree 2 (which have one child) we use the following lemma, whose proof can be found in the journal version as well.

LEMMA 5. *Let G be wNE and P be a path in $U(G)$ such that for every two vertices $u, v \in V(P)$, the shortest (u, v)-path in P is the unique shortest (u, v)-path (which implies, in particular, that P is an induced subgraph). Then the number of edges $\{u, v\} \in E(P)$ such that both u, v have degree 2 is $O(\log w_P)$.*

PROOF OF LEMMA 2. By the remark after Lemma 3 we may assume that G has no poor leaves. For each edge $\{u, v\} \in E(P)$ such that both u and v have degree 2, we contract that edge, and repeat until no such edge exists. By Lemma 5, the depth changes by at most $O(\log w_G)$. By Lemma 4, there is at most one vertex that has children who are leaves. Hence the depth of the tree is $O(\log |V(T)|)$. Consequently, the depth of T is $O(\log w_G)$. □

The rest of the proof is almost identical to the proof of Theorem 9 of [2]. In the following we will assume that the graphs are unweighted (equivalently, all vertices have unit weights). Note that in this case $w_G = n$.

LEMMA 6. *Let G be wNE. Given any vertex u, there is an arc (x, y) with $dist(x, u) = O(\log n)$ and whose removal increases the cost of x by at most $O(n \log n)$.*

Hence for some constants $a, b > 0$, if G is an wNE then for any $u \in V$, there is an arc (x, y) with $dist(x, u) \leq a \log n$ and whose removal increases the cost of x by at most $bn \log n$. The proof of the following can be found in the journal version of this paper.

COROLLARY 1. *In any wNE the addition of any arc (u, v) decreases the cost of u by at most $(a + b + 1)n \log n$.*

THEOREM 7. *The diameter of any wNE is $2^{O(\sqrt{\log n})}$.*

4.2 Lower bound for MAX

In this section, we prove that for some positive d_i's there exist equilibrium graphs for MAX model with diameter $\Omega(\sqrt{\log n})$.

For an undirected graph U, vertex $u \in V(U)$ and subset $A \subseteq V(U)$, the distance between u and A is defined as $dist(u, A) = \min\{dist(u, a) : a \in A\}$.

LEMMA 7. *Let U be an undirected graph with diameter k and maximum degree Δ with the following properties:*

1. All vertices have local diameter k.

2. $\Delta^k - 1 < n(\Delta - 1)$.

Then every G with no double edge, with $U = U(G)$ is a Nash equilibrium for the MAX model.

PROOF. Assume for the sake of contradiction that v is a vertex that is not playing its best response. Let A be the set of neighbors of v if it had changed its strategy and played its best response. As v has degree at most Δ, we have $|A| \leq \Delta$. By property (1) the local diameter of v is exactly k before changing its strategy.

Claim. There exists a vertex u, different from v, with $dist(u, A) > k - 2$.

PROOF. There are at most $|A|\Delta$ vertices whose distance from A is exactly 1. Similarly, there are at most $|A|\Delta^2$ vertices with distance exactly 2 from A. Continuing in the same way, we find that there are at most $|A|\Delta^{k-2}$ vertices with distance exactly $k-2$ from A. If there is no $u \neq v$ with $dist(u, A) > k - 2$, then we must have

$$
\begin{aligned}
n &\leq 1 + |A| + |A|\Delta + \cdots + |A|\Delta^{k-2} &\leq \\
&\quad 1 + \Delta + \Delta^2 + \cdots + \Delta^{k-1} &= \\
&\quad \tfrac{\Delta^k - 1}{\Delta - 1},
\end{aligned}
$$

which contradicts the property (2). □

After v changes its strategy so that its neighborhood becomes A, its distance to u becomes at least k, which is a contradiction.

LEMMA 8. *For every integers $t, k > 3$ satisfying $1 + 2^k < 2t$, there exists an undirected graph U with t^k vertices, minimum degree at least 2, and diameter k, such that every G with no double edge and $U = U(G)$ is a Nash equilibrium for the MAX model.*

PROOF. Let $V(U) = \{1, 2, \ldots, t\}^k$ with $(a_1, a_2, \ldots, a_k)$ adjacent to $(b_1, b_2, \ldots, b_k)$ if at least one of the following happens:

1. $a_i = b_{i+1}$ for all $1 \leq i \leq k - 1$,

2. $b_i = a_{i+1}$ for all $1 \leq i \leq k - 1$.

Then U has minimum degree $2t - 2$, maximum degree $2t$ and t^k vertices. The local diameter of every vertex is k: for an arbitrary $(a_1, \ldots, a_k) \in V(U)$ choose $b_1, \ldots, b_k \notin \{a_1, \ldots, a_k\}$. Then it is easy to check that the distance between $(a_1, \ldots, a_k)$ and $(b_1, \ldots, b_k)$ is k. The condition $\Delta^k - 1 < n(\Delta - 1)$ of the previous Lemma follows from $1 + 2^k < 2t$ and a little calculation. □

THEOREM 8. *For infinitely many n, there exists an equilibrium graph with positive d_i's for the MAX model with diameter $\sqrt{\log_2 n}$.*

PROOF. Let $k > 3$ and $t = 2^k$. Using the previous theorem, we find an undirected graph U with $n = (2^k)^k = 2^{k^2}$ vertices and diameter $k = \sqrt{\log_2 n}$. Now, let G be a directed graph with $U(G) = U$ and such that the outgoing degree of all vertices of G is at least 1. Such a G can always be found as the minimum degree of U is larger than 1. Then G satisfies the conditions of the theorem. □

4.3 κ-Connectivity

One of the most important issues in designing stable networks is the connectivity of the built network. In this section, we find a direct connection between the budget limits and the connectivity of the equilibrium graph, which shows that we can guarantee stronger connectivity for our network when all players have enough budgets. The proof is left to the journal version due to space shortage.

THEOREM 9. *Suppose that G is an equilibrium graph for $(d_1, d_2, \ldots, d_n)$-BG in SUM version and $d_i \geq k$ for all $1 \leq i \leq n$. If G has diameter greater than 3, then it is k-vertex connected.*

5. CONCLUSION

In this paper, we analyzed the diameter of equilibrium graphs in network creation games where every player has a specific budget for the number of vertices that it can establish links to. We found tight bounds for two special cases, trees and unit budget. For the case where all players have positive budget, we proved a non-trivial lower bound for the MAX version and upper bound for SUM version.

Improving these bounds for both versions are interesting problems to work on. Considering other special cases (e.g. the case where $d_i = c$ for some constant $c \geq 2$) is also a good problem to work on. We have tried several examples and it appears that in the positive budgets case, the diameter of every SUM equilibrium is bounded by a constant. Either proving that this is correct, or finding a counter-example is another interesting open problem. Last but not least, the convergence rate of the game is another interesting parameter to study. That is, to determine how quickly the game converges to an equilibrium, if at each step, one player is chosen and plays its best response.

6. ACKNOWLEDGMENTS

The authors are thankful to Nastaran Nikparto for her useful comments throughout the preparation of this paper.

7. REFERENCES

[1] S. Albers, S. Eilts, E. Even-Dar, Y. Mansour, and L. Roditty, On Nash equilibria for a network creation game, in Proceedings of the 17th Annual ACM-SIAM Symposium on Discrete Algorithms (SODA), Miami, Florida, 2006, pp. 89-98.

[2] N.Alon, E.D.Demaine, M.Hajiaghayi, T.Leighton, Basic Network Creation Games, in Proceeding of the 22rd ACM Symposium on Parallelism in Algorithms and Architectures(SPAA),2010, pp. 106–113.

[3] N. Andelman, M. Feldman, and Y. Mansour, Strong price of anarchy, in Proceedings of the 18th Annual ACM-SIAM Symposium on Discrete Algorithms (SODA), 2007, pp. 189-198.

[4] J. Corbo and D. Parkes, The price of selfish behavior in bilateral network formation, in Proceedings of the 24th Annual ACM Symposium on Principles of Distributed Computing (PODC), Las Vegas, Nevada, 2005, pp. 99-107.

[5] E.D. Demaine, M.Hajiaghayi, H.Mahini, and M.Zadimoghaddam. The Price of Anarchy in Network Creation Games. In Proceedings of the 26th

Annual ACM Symposium on Principles of
Distributed Computing (PODC), Portland, Oregon,
2007, pp. 292-298.

[6] A. Fabrikant, A. Luthra, E. Maneva, C. H.
Papadimitriou, and S. Shenker, On a network
creation game, in Proceedings of the 22nd Annual
Symposium on Principles of Distributed Computing
(PODC), Boston, Massachusetts, 2003, pp. 347-351.

[7] Y. Halevi and Y. Mansour, A network creation game
with nonuniform interests, in Proceedings of the 3rd
International Workshop on Internet and Network
Economics (WINE), vol. 4858 of Lecture Notes in
Computer Science, San Diego, CA, 2007, pp. 287-292.

[8] W. L.Hsu and G.L.Nemhauser, Easy and hard
bottleneck location problems, Disc. Appl. Math. 1,
209-216,1979.

[9] E.Koutsoupias and C.H. Papadimitriou, Worst-case
equilibria, Computer Science Review, 1999, pp.
65-69.

[10] N. Laoutaris, L. J. Poplawski, R. Rajaraman, R.
Sundaram, and S.-H. Teng, Bounded budget
connection (BBC) games or how to make friends and
influence people, on a budget, in Proceedings of the
27th ACM Symposium on Principles of Distributed
Computing (PODC), 2008, pp. 165-174.

[11] J.H.Lin and J.S.Vitter, ε-approximations with
minimum packing constraint violation, Proc. 24th
Ann. ACM Symp. on Theory of Comp., ACM,
771-782, 1992.

Online Packet-Routing in Grids with Bounded Buffers

[Extended Abstract] *

Guy Even
School of Electrical Engineering
Tel-Aviv Univ.
Tel-Aviv 69978, Israel
guy@eng.tau.ac.il

Moti Medina
School of Electrical Engineering
Tel-Aviv Univ.
Tel-Aviv 69978, Israel
medinamo@eng.tau.ac.il

ABSTRACT

We present the first online algorithm with a polylogarithmic competitive ratio for the problem of online routing of packets in unidirectional grids. The goal is to maximize the throughput, i.e., the number of delivered packets. Our online algorithm is deterministic, centralized, handles packets with deadlines, allows bounded buffers, uses adaptive routing, and may drop packets before they reach their destination.

All previous online algorithms for packet routing on a unidirectional line with polylogarithmic competitive ratios are randomized [AZ05, AKK09, EM10]. Our algorithm is the first *deterministic* online algorithm with a polylogarithmic competitive ratio.

Categories and Subject Descriptors

C.2.1 [**Computer-Communication Networks**]: Network Architecture and Design—*Packet-switching networks, Store and forward networks*; F.2.2 [**Analysis of Algorithms and Problem Complexity**]: Nonnumerical Algorithms and Problems—*Routing and layout, Sequencing and scheduling*; G.2.2 [**Discrete-Mathematics**]: Graph Theory—*Network problems*

General Terms

Algorithms, Theory

Keywords

Online Algorithms, Packet Routing, Bounded Buffers, Admission Control

1. INTRODUCTION

We study the Competitive Network Throughput Model introduced by [AKOR03] for dynamic routing on networks

---

*A full version of this paper is available at http://www.eng.tau.ac.il/~medinamo

with bounded buffers. The goal is to route packets (i.e., constant length formatted data) in a network of n nodes. Nodes in this model are switches with local memories, called buffers. An incoming packet is either forwarded to a neighbor switch, stored in the buffer, or erased. The resources of a packet network are specified by two parameters: c - the capacity of links and B - the size of buffers. The capacity of a link is an upper bound on the number of packets that can be transmitted in one time step along the link. The buffer size is the maximum number of packets that can be stored in a switch.

Previous Work.

Algorithms for dynamic routing on networks with bounded buffers have been studied both in theory and in practice. Angelov et al. [AKK09] showed that the competitive ratio of greedy algorithms in unidirectional 2-dimensional grids is $\Omega(\sqrt{n})$ and that Nearest-to-Go achieves a competitive ratio of $\tilde{\Theta}(n^{2/3})$. Offline algorithms for trees and meshes were studied in [AKRR03] . They obtained a logarithmic approximation ratio for unbounded buffers and a constant approximation ratio for bufferless networks. Routing in optical mesh networks was studied in [BL97]. They showed both upper and lower bounds of $O(\log n)$ on the competitiveness of online algorithms. Kleinberg and Tardos [KT95] studied the disjoint path problem in undirected grids and presented both offline and online randomized algorithms for this problem. The networks we study are unidirectional grids of d dimensions. Such 2-dimensional grids with or without buffers serve as crossbars in networks (see [ARSU02, AKRR03, Tur09] for many references from the networking community). Thus, even centralized algorithms for this task are of interest since they can be used to control a crossbar. For a detailed list of previous work on lines see [EM10]. See the full version of this paper for a comparison between the results presented in this paper and in [EM10].

The seminal work of Leighton et al. [LMR94] and subsequent works [LMR99, RT96, ST97] deal with routing all the packets. The latency of each packet is $O(C + D)$, where C denotes the maximum congestion and D denotes the length of a longest path. Clearly, D can be $\Omega(n)$, and C is unbounded in terms of n. Apart from having large constants, these works require unbounded input queues, and therefore do not apply to our setting.

Our result.

We present a centralized deterministic online algorithm for packet routing in unidirectional grids with n nodes. Our algorithm is preemptive, i.e., it may drop packets before they reach their destination, uses adaptive routing, deals with deadlines, and achieves a polylogarithmic competitive ratio for the following combinations of parameters:

(i) For $B, c \in [3..\log n]$ the competitive ratio of the algorithm is $O(\log^{d+4} n)$ for unidirectional grids of dimension d.

(ii) For $B = 0$ and $c \geq 3$ the competitive ratio of the algorithm is $O(\log^{d+2} n)$ for unidirectional grids of d dimensions.

(iii) For $B, c \geq \log n$ and $B/c = n^{O(1)}$ the competitive ratio of the algorithm is $O(\log n)$ for unidirectional grids, independent of the dimension d.

Techniques.

Packet routing is reduced to a circuit switching problem [KT95, AAP93], by applying a *space-time transformation* [AAF96, ARSU02, AZ05, RR09, EM10]. We extend the space-time transformation of [AZ05] so that it also supports deadlines.

The reduction of packet routing to circuit switching relies on a lemma [AZ05] that *bounds the maximum path length* while incurring a constant loss to the throughput. We extend the lemma of [AZ05] to d-dimensional grids and to general values of c and B.

A *sketch graph* with logarithmic capacities is obtained by coalescing groups of nodes [KT95, BL97]. The groups are disjoint subgrids with logarithmic side-lengths. Now, we pack paths in an online fashion in the sketch graph. For ease of presentation we use the framework of Buchbinder and Naor [BN06, BN09] for *online path packing*. In this stage some of the packets might be rejected. Injected packets are assigned paths in the sketch graph.

The paths in the sketch graph must be translated to paths in the space-time graph. This translation, called *detailed routing*, is adaptive. Namely, the detailed path of injected packet is not determined when the packet is injected. The detailed path respects the sketch path in the sense that it traverses the same tiles. Detailed routing may fail, causing the injected packet to be dropped. Detailed routing has been addressed before in *undirected* graphs [KT95, BL97]. There is a significant difference in the execution of detailed routing between *directed* and *undirected* graphs [RR09] (note that a unidirectional grid is a *directed* graph).

Our detailed routing technique partitions each path in the sketch graph into three parts, and *reserves* a unit of capacity for each part. This is the reason why the algorithm requires $B, c \geq 3$.

In some parts of the detailed routing, we reduce the problem of detailed routing to *online interval packing*. This reduction uses an online procedure for packing intervals on a line. We apply an online distributed simulation of the optimal interval packing algorithm [GLL82]. This simulation works since we allow preemptions.

2. PROBLEM DEFINITION

Store-and-Forward Packet Routing Networks.

We consider a synchronous store-and-forward packet routing network [AKOR03, AKK09, AZ05].

Each packet is specified by a 4-tuple $r_i = (a_i, b_i, t_i, d_i)$, where $a_i \in V$ is the source node of the packet, $b_i \in V$ is the destination node, and $t_i \in \mathbb{N}$ is the time step in which the packet is input to a_i and d_i is the deadline. Since we consider an online setting, no information is known about a packet r_i before time t_i. We consider packet routing with deadlines, namely, the algorithm is credited for each packet r_i that arrives to its destination b_i before time d_i.

The network is a directed graph $G = (V, E)$. Each edge has a capacity c that specifies the number of packets that can be transmitted along the edge in one time step. Each node has a local buffer of size B that can store at most B packets. Each node has a local input through which multiple packets may be input in each time step. The network operates in a synchronous fashion with a delay of one time step for communication. This means that a single time step is needed for a packet to traverse a single link.

In each time step, a node v considers the packets arriving via the local input, the packets arriving from incoming edges, and the packets stored in the buffer. Packets destined to node v (i.e., $b_i = v$) are removed from the network (this is considered a success and no further routing of the packet is required). As for the other packets, the node determines which packets are sent along outgoing edges (i.e., forwarded), which packets are stored in the buffer. The remaining packets are *deleted*.

The literature contains two different models of node functionality. We use the model used by [ARSU02, RR09, EM10]. The reader is referred to Appendix A for a comparison between two different models of node functionality.

We use the following terminology. A packet is *rejected* if it is locally input to a node and the node deletes it. A packet is *injected* if it is not rejected. A packet is *preempted* or *dropped* if it was injected and deleted before it reached its destination.

Grid Networks.

A two dimensional $\ell_1 \times \ell_2$ unidirectional grid network is a directed graph $G = (V, E)$ defined as follows (see Fig. 1), a d-dimensional grid is defined analogously. The set of vertices is $V \triangleq [0..\ell_1 - 1] \times [0..\ell_2 - 1]$, where $[0..\ell]$ denotes the set of integers $\{0, \ldots, \ell\}$. We denote the number of vertices by n (i.e., $n = \ell_1 \cdot \ell_2$). There are two types of edges: horizontal edges $(i, j) \to (i + 1, j)$ and vertical edges $(i, j) \to (i, j + 1)$. For each packet, the source node $a_i = (a_i(x), a_i(y))$ and the destination node $b_i = (b_i(x), b_i(y))$ satisfy $a_i \leq b_i$ (i.e., $a_i(x) \leq b_i(x)$ and $a_i(y) \leq b_i(y)$). We refer to an $\ell_1 \times \ell_2$ two dimensional directed grid network simply as a grid.

Capacities and Buffers.

We assume uniform capacities and buffer sizes. Namely, (i) all edges in the grid have the same capacity, denoted by c; and (ii) all nodes have the same buffer size, denoted by B.

Online Maximum Throughput in Networks.

The *throughput* of a packet routing algorithm is the number of packets that are delivered to their destination *before their deadline*. We consider the problem of maximizing the throughput of an online centralized deterministic packet-routing algorithm.

Let $|Alg|$ denote the throughput obtained by Algorithm

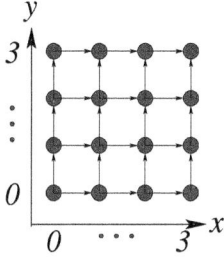

Figure 1: A 4×4 grid network.

Alg. An online deterministic *Alg* is *ρ-competitive* if for every input sequence σ, $|Alg(\sigma)| \geq \frac{1}{\rho} \cdot |OPT(\sigma)|$.

3. PRELIMINARIES

3.1 Space-Time Transformation

A *space-time transformation* is a method to map traffic in a directed graph over time into a directed acyclic graph [AAF96, ARSU02, AZ05, RR09, EM10]. Consider a directed $G = (V, E)$ with edge capacities c and buffer size B. The space-time transformation of G is the acyclic directed graph $G^{st} = (V^{st}, E^{st})$ with edge capacities $c^{st}(e)$ for $e \in E^{st}$, where: (i) $V^{st} \triangleq V \times \mathbb{N}$. (ii) $E^{st} \triangleq E_0 \cup E_1$ where $E_0 \triangleq \{(u,t) \to (v, t+1) : (u,v) \in E, t \in \mathbb{N}\}$ and $E_1 \triangleq \{(u,t) \to (u, t+1) : u \in V, t \in \mathbb{N}\}$. (iii) The capacity of all edges in E_0 is c, and all edges in E_1 have capacity B. Note that the space-time graph corresponding to a d-dimensional grid is a $(d+1)$-dimensional grid.

3.2 Tiling

The term *tiling* refers to a partitioning of the nodes of the space-time graph G^{st} into finite sets with identical geometric "shape". A standard drawing[1] of the space-time graph of a grid is a lattice generated by non-orthogonal vectors. This drawing is hard to depict and deal with, hence we apply untilting defined as follows (see [RR09] for untilting in two dimensions).

Untilting.
We rectify the drawing of the space-time graph of a grid by applying an automorphism $q : \mathbb{Z}^{d+1} \to \mathbb{Z}^{d+1}$ defined by $q(x_1, \ldots, x_d, t) \triangleq (x_1, \ldots, x_d, t - \sum_{i=1}^{d} x_i)$. We refer to this transformation as *untilting*. The sole purpose of applying untilting is to obtain a drawing of the space-time graph of a grid in which the edges are axis parallel. Such an axis parallel drawing simplifies the definition of tiles. Note that the image of some of the vertices in G^{st} is outside the positive quadrant.

Tiling is obtained by a partitioning of $\mathbb{Z}^{d+1}$ by disjoint $(d + 1)$-dimensional cubes with side-length k. A tile s is a subset of V^{st} such that its image $q(s)$ (after untilting) is contained in a cube.

Formally, given a cube side-length k, a tile is defined by its *lower corner* $p \in \mathbb{Z}^{d+1}$, where the coordinates of p are integral multiple of k. The lower corner p defines the tile

$s_p \triangleq \{v \in V^{st} : p \leq q(v) < p + k \cdot \vec{1}\}$, where $\vec{1}$ is the all ones vector. Note that some of the tiles outside the positive quadrant are *partial*, namely contain less than k^d vertices.

3.3 The Sketch Graph

The sketch graph is the graph obtained from the space-time graph after coalescing each tile into a single node. There is a directed edge (s_1, s_2) between two tiles s_1, s_2 in the sketch graph if there is a directed edge $(\alpha, \beta) \in G^{st}$ such that $\alpha \in s_1$ and $\beta \in s_2$. The capacity $c(s_1, s_2)$ of an edge (s_1, s_2) in the sketch graph is simply the sum of the capacities of the edges in G^{st} from vertices in s_1 to vertices in s_2.

Notation.
We denote the sketch graph by $S = (V(S), E(S))$. Note that each node of S is a tile. Sketch edges are denoted by $\hat{e}$ and their capacity is denoted by $c(\hat{e})$.

3.4 Online Packing of Paths

A reduction of packet routing to packing of paths is presented in Section 5.1. We briefly overview the topic of online packing of paths (see also [EM10]).

Consider a graph $G = (V, E)$ with edge capacities $c(e)$. Edges have soft capacity constraints (i.e., the capacity constraint may be violated, and one goal is to minimize the violation). The adversary introduces a sequence of connection requests $\{r_i\}_i$, where each request is a source-destination pair (a_i, b_i). The online packing algorithm must either return a path p_i from a_i to b_i or reject the request.

Consider a sequence $R = \{r_i\}_{i \in I}$ of requests. A sequence $P = \{p_i\}_{i \in J}$ is a (partial) *routing* with respect to R if $J \subseteq I$ and each path p_i (for $i \in J$) connects the source-destination pair r_i. The *load* of an edge e induced by a routing P is the ratio $|\{p_j : j \in J, e \in p_j\}|/c(e)$. A routing P with respect to R is called a *β-packing* if the load of each edge is at most β. The *throughput* of a packing $P = \{p_i\}_{i \in J}$ is simply $|J|$.

An online path packing algorithm is *(α, β)-competitive* if it computes a β-packing P whose throughput is at least α times the maximum throughput over all 1-packings.

A *fractional* packing is a multi-commodity flow. Each demand can be served by a combination of fractions of flows along paths. An optimal offline fractional packing can be computed by solving a linear program. Obviously, the throughput of an optimal fractional packing is an upper bound on the throughput of an optimal integral packing.

The proof of the following theorem appears in the full version. The proof is based on techniques from [AAP93, BN06]. We refer to the online algorithm for online integral path packing by IPP.

THEOREM 1. *Consider an infinite graph with edge capacities such that $\min_e c(e) \geq 1$. Consider an online path packing problem in which a path is legal if it contains at most $p_{\max}$ edges. Assume that there is an oracle, that given edge weights and a connection request, finds a lightest legal path from the source to the destination. Then, there exists a $(2, \log(1 + 3 \cdot p_{\max}))$-competitive online integral path packing algorithm. Moreover, the throughput is a 2-approximation of the maximum throughput over all fractional packings.*

---

[1] For $d = 2$, the G^{st} has a 3-dimensional standard drawing in which: (i) a node $(i, j, t) \in V^{st}$ is mapped to the point (i, j, t), and (ii) edges are mapped to straight segments between their endpoints.

Notation.

Given a set R of packet requests, let $\text{OPT}(R)$ denote the maximum (offline) throughput. Let $\text{OPT}_f(R)$ denote the maximum fractional throughput.

3.5 Polynomial Path Lengths

Consider a $(d+1)$-dimensional unidirectional grid $\mathcal{G}$, where one of the dimensions corresponding to *time* is unbounded. Formally, for $\ell \in \mathbb{N}$ let $[\ell] \triangleq \{1, \ldots, \ell\}$, then: (I) $\mathcal{G} = (V \times \mathbb{N}, E)$, (II) $V = [\ell_1] \times [\ell_2] \times \ldots \times [\ell_d]$, where $\prod_i \ell_i = n$, (III) $E_1 \triangleq \{(v,t) \to (u, t+1) \; : \; v, u \in V, \; t \in \mathbb{N}, \; v - u = e_i \; , i \in [d]\}$, where e_i is the ith unit vector, (IV) $E_2 \triangleq \{(v,t) \to (v, t+1) \; : \; v \in V, \; t \in \mathbb{N}\}$, (V) $E \triangleq E_1 \cup E_2$. (VI) Every $e \in E_1$ has capacity $c(e) = c$ and every $e \in E_2$ has capacity $c(e) = B$.

Consider a sequence $\{r_i\}_i$ of routing requests over grid $\mathcal{G}$, where $r_i = (a_i, b_i, t_i)$; $a_i, \; b_i \in V, \; t_i \in \mathbb{N}$. Our goal is to route a path from $(a_i, t_i) \to (b_i, t)$ for $t \geq t_i$.

The maximum throughput for routing $\{r_i\}_i$ is upper bounded by the throughput of an optimal fractional path packing with respect to $\{r_i\}_i$. Our goal is to prove that the throughput of an optimal fractional path packing does not decrease by much if path lengths are bounded.

Formally, let $\text{OPT}_f(R \mid p_{\max})$ denote the throughput of an optimal fractional path packing in $\mathcal{G}$ with respect to $R = \{r_i\}_i$ under the constraint that path lengths are at most $p_{\max}$. The following lemma shows that bounding path lengths by $O(n \cdot (\sum_i \ell_i) \cdot (B/c))$ decreases the fractional throughput by at most a constant factor. The lemma generalizes the lemma from [AZ05] that deals with the line network with unit capacities. The proof of the following lemma appears in the full version.

LEMMA 2. *Let* $\gamma \triangleq (B + d \cdot c)/c$. *Let* $p_{\max} \geq (\sum_i \ell_i) \cdot (1 + 2\gamma n)$. *Then,* $\text{OPT}_f(R \mid p_{\max}) \geq \frac{1}{2} \cdot (1 - \frac{1}{e}) \cdot \text{OPT}_f(R)$.

Remarks.

(I) If $\mathcal{G}$ is the sketch graph of a unidirectional line then, $d = 1$, $\ell_1 = \lceil n/k \rceil$, hence $p_{\max} \triangleq \lceil \frac{n}{k} \rceil \cdot (1 + 2\gamma n)$. (II) Using the same technique, one can prove that $\text{OPT}_f(R \mid p_{\max}) \geq (1 - \varepsilon) \cdot \text{OPT}_f(R)$ for $p_{\max} \geq (\sum_i \ell_i) \cdot (1 + 2\gamma n \cdot \ln \frac{1}{\varepsilon})$.

4. ALGORITHM OUTLINE

We outline the algorithm below. To simplify the description, we present a detailed description and proof for the one-dimensional case in Sec. 5. The required modifications for d dimensions are described in Sec. 6.

Upon arrival of a request r_i, the algorithm executes the following steps (if r_i is rejected in any step, then the algorithm does not continue to the next steps):

1. Reduce the packet requests to an online integral path packing over the sketch graph with bounded paths. Execute the IPP algorithm with respect to these path requests. If the path request is rejected by the IPP algorithm, then **reject** r_i. Otherwise, let $\hat{p}_i$ denote the sketch path assigned to the request r_i.

2. **Inject** the request r_i with its sketch path $\hat{p}_i$ and perform detailed routing in the space-time graph G^{st}. Detailed routing in G^{st} may fail. In case of failure, **preempt** r_i.

5. THE ONE DIMENSIONAL CASE

In this section we present the details of the algorithm for $d = 1$. For simplicity, we assume all deadlines are unbounded, hence each packet is specified by a 3-tuple $r_i = (a_i, b_i, t_i)$; we reintroduce deadlines in Section 5.4.

Parameters.

The parameters of the unidirectional line network G are: n nodes, buffer size B in each node, and link capacity c in each direction. We assume that $B, c \in [3 .. \log n]$. Let $\gamma \triangleq (B + 2c)/c$. Let $p_{\max} \geq n \cdot (1 + 2\gamma n)$. Let $k \triangleq \lceil \log(1 + 3p_{\max}) \rceil$. The length of a tile's side is k.

PROPOSITION 3. *If* $B, c \leq \log n$, *then (i)* $k = O(\log n)$, *and (ii) the capacity of each edge in the sketch graph is at most* $k \cdot \max\{B, c\} = O(\log^2 n)$.

The sketch graph is obtained by tiling of the space-time graph G^{st} of the unidirectional line G. Without loss of generality, we may assume that the tile side-length k divides the line length n. Otherwise, simply augment the line by adding extra nodes. This augmentation does not help routing of packets since the grid is unidirectional.

5.1 Reduction to Online Integral Path Packing

The reduction to path packing has to deal with these issues: (i) Handling requests *inside* a tile. (ii) Assign unit capacities to guarantee light loads on the sketch edges. (iii) Determine a specific destination node per request. To deal with these issues, we augment the sketch graph as follows.

Adding Sink Nodes.

Following [AZ05], we add sink nodes to define a specific destination node for each request. For every vertex v in the line, we define a sink node $\hat{v}$. Each tile s that contains a node (v, t) (for some t) is connected to the sink node $\hat{v}$ by an edge with infinite capacity.

Handling Requests Inside a Tile.

We introduce node capacities by splitting every sketch node $s \in V_S$ to two "halves" s_{in} and s_{out}. The incoming edges of s enter s_{in} and the outgoing edges of s emanate from s_{out}. We add an additional edge called an *interior edge* between s_{in} and s_{out}. Let E_S^{int} denote the set of interior edges.

To summarize, the sketch graph is augmented by sink nodes, infinite capacity edges entering the sinks, and a splitting of sketch edges. Note that, since nodes are split, we use $2 \cdot p_{\max}$ as a bound on the maximum path.

Assigning Capacities.

We assign unit capacities $c(\hat{e}) = 1$ to all sketch edges $\hat{e} \in E_S$ and $c(\hat{e}) = 2$ to every interior edge $\hat{e} \in E_S^{int}$. We refer to the augmented sketch graph with these capacities as the $\{1, 2, \infty\}$-*sketch graph*. We denote the $\{1, 2, \infty\}$-sketch graph by $\hat{S}$.

The Reduction.

A request $r_i = (a_i, b_i, t_i)$ to deliver a packet is reduced to a path request in the $\{1, 2, \infty\}$-sketch graph $\hat{S}$. The source of the path request is the half tile s_{in} where the tile s contains the vertex (a_i, t_i). The destination of the path request is simply the sink $\hat{b}_i$.

The sole purpose of the sink node is for a clean reduction to path packing. Once the IPP algorithm returns the sketch path $\hat{p}_i$, the sink is removed from $\hat{p}_i$, and the last tile in the sketch path is regraded as its destination.

Theorem 1 implies that the IPP algorithm returns an integral packing of paths in the $\hat{S}$ that is $(2, k)$-competitive with respect to the optimal fractional path packing in $\hat{S}$.

5.2 Detailed Routing

Our goal in detailed routing is to compute a (detailed) path p_i in the space-time graph G^{st} given a (sketch) path $\hat{p}_i$ in the $\{1, 2, \infty\}$-sketch graph $\hat{S}$. The term "detailed routing" is justified by the fact that the detailed path p_i traverses the same tiles that are traversed by the sketch path $\hat{p}_i$. Namely, the projection of p_i to $\hat{S}$ equals $\hat{p}_i$. Our detailed routing algorithm has the additional property that, except for the last tile, the detailed path p_i and the sketch path $\hat{p}_i$ contain bends in the same tiles.

Each path $\hat{p}_i$ in $\hat{S}$ is a concatenation of straight segments where each segment is parallel to one of the two axes. Each segment is directed, so we may refer to the first and second endpoints of a segment. A segment is *special* if it is the first or the last segment of a sketch path.

Detailed Routing is Partitioned into Three Parts:.

(I) Special segments. (II) Nonspecial segments. (III) Last tile - this part takes care of routing the request from the point that it enters the last tile till a destination of the path.

Reservation of Capacities.

The algorithm reserves one unit of capacity in each edge $e \in E^{st}$ for each part of detailed routing. This is the reason for the requirement that $B, c \geq 3$.

Preemptions may occur in parts (I) and (III) of the detailed routing. Preemptions occur only between detailed routing of the same kind. Namely, a special segment can only preempt another special segment. Similarly, detailed routing in the last tile preempts only routes that end in the same tile.

Entry and Exit Sides.

For each tile traversed by the sketch path $\hat{p}_i$, the sketch path specifies through which side of the tile the detailed path should enter and exit the tile. We refer to the side through which the detailed path should exit a tile as the *exit side*. Similarly, we refer to the side through which the detailed path enters a tile as the *entry side*.

Special Segments.

Detailed routing in the first segment is simply a straight path from the source to the entry side of the tile that is the end of the segment (see Fig. 2a).

This straight path might be already saturated. Hence the detailed routing of the first segment is reduced to the problem of packing intervals in a line (see Definition 1). For simplicity, consider a first segment that is parallel to the time axis (the other case is similar). Consider a first segment that starts in tile s_1 and ends in s_2, where $(a_i, t_i) \in s_1$. The reduction to interval packing reduces this first segment to the interval $[t_i, t_{\max}]$, where $t_{\max} \triangleq \max\{t : (a_i, t) \in s_2\}$. The

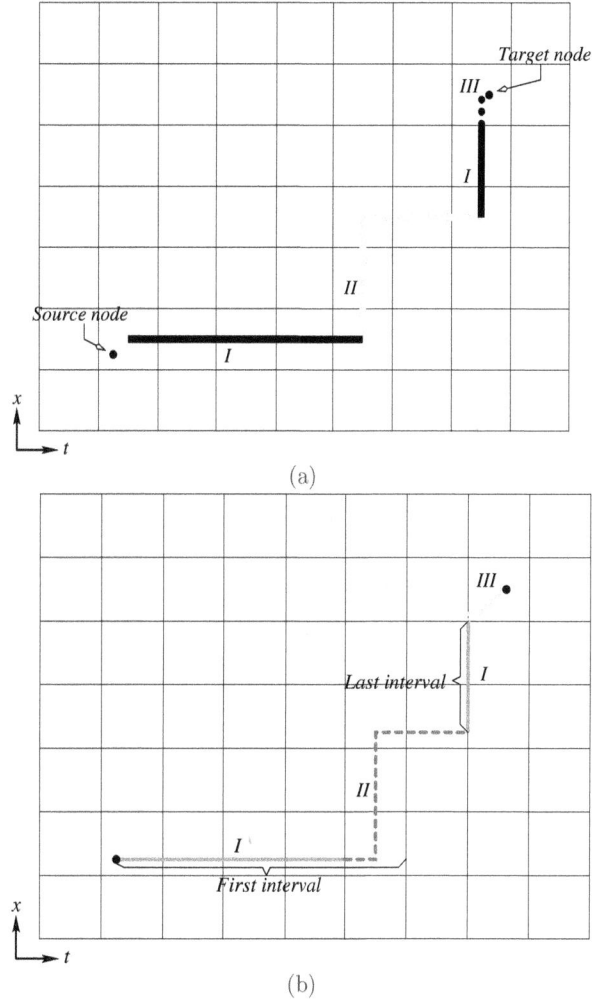

(a)

(b)

Figure 2: (a) The sketch path is depicted by a thick line. Detailed routing is partitioned into three parts, e.g, (I)-(III). Part (I) consists of first and last segments, depicted by thick segments. Part (II) is depicted by dashed segments. Part (III) is routing in the last tile, which is depicted by a dotted line. The source node of the packet request in the first tile of the sketch path, the target node of the packet request is in the last tile of the sketch path. (b) The detailed path induced by the sketch path. The detailed path is depicted by a thin line, that traverses the same tiles as the sketch path. The detailed routing of the first segment is depicted by the line emanating from the source node. The dashed line depicts the detailed routing after the first segment. The detailed routing of the last segment turns on the entry side of the tile that contains the last bend. The detailed routing in the last tile is depicted by a dotted thin line. The intervals that are input to the interval packing algorithm are depicted by braces.

algorithm executes a separate reduction to interval packing for each row and column of the untilted space-time grid.

Detailed routing in the last segment is simply a straight path from the entry side of the tile that contains the last bend of the sketch path, till the entry side of the last tile (see Fig. 2a). This straight path might be already saturated. Again, the detailed routing of the last segment is reduced to the problem of packing intervals in a line (see Definition 1). For simplicity, consider a last segment that is parallel to the vertices axis (the other case is similar). Consider a last segment that starts in tile s_1 and ends in s_2, where the last bend occurs in s_1. Let $(x, t) \in s_1$ be the node on the entry side of s_1 where the previous detailed routing ended. The reduction to interval packing reduces this last segment to the interval $[x, x_{\min}]$, where $x_{\min} \triangleq \min\{x : (x, t) \in s_2\}$. The algorithm executes a separate reduction to interval packing for each row and column of the space-time grid (see last interval in Figure 2b).

DEFINITION 1. *The problem of packing intervals in a line is defined as follows.*

1. *Input: G and I, where: (1) G is a line consisting of n vertices. Namely, G is a graph (V, E), where $V = \{v_0, \ldots, v_{n-1}\}$ and $E = \{(v_j, v_{j+1}) : 0 \le j < n - 1\}$. (2) I is a sequence of paths in G.*

2. *Output: A subset $I' \subseteq I$ with maximum cardinality such that, for each edge e, there is at most one path p in I' that contains e.*

In the context of special segments, we solve the online variant of interval packing, where the left endpoints of the requests are input in ascending order. This variant is solved by simulating an optimal algorithm for maximum independent sets in interval graphs [GLL82]. For the purpose of describing the algorithm, we assume that the line is from left to right. The algorithm is as follows. Each node v along the line is input a set of accepted intervals from its left neighbor and the intervals that start is v. Among these intervals, the node v simply "forwards" an interval with the leftmost right endpoint. The other incoming intervals are preempted. See Proposition 7 for an analysis of the interval packing algorithm.

Nonspecial Segments.

We begin by describing how detailed routing of nonspecial segments takes place in a tile s. Assume first that this routing needs to handle sketch paths that enter and exit the tile along nonspecial segments. there are two cases: (i) paths that contain a bend in s, and (ii) paths that traverse s without a bend.

A sketch path $\hat{p}_i$ that does not contain a bend in s simply traverses s in a straight line. Thus, a row or a column is reserved for it.

A bend is performed as follows. Assume that a sketch path $\hat{p}_i$ enters s in the t-direction and exits s in the x direction (the other case is handled similarly). Detailed routing routes $\hat{p}_i$ in s along the t-direction (continuing in straight line) until the first free edge in the x-direction is found. A turn at this free edge is taken, and the detailed path continues in the x-direction until the exit side of s.

We need to show that such a free edge always exists. Let ρ denote the row in s from the entry point of $\hat{p}_i$ in the t-direction. Suppose that occupied edges in the x-direction incident to ρ serve only nonspecial segments of sketch paths with the same exit side as $\hat{p}_i$. Since there are at most k such sketch paths (includes $\hat{p}_i$), there must be a free edge in the x-direction.

We deal with occupied edges in the x-direction that serve sketch paths whose exit side is different from $\hat{p}_i$ by introducing *knock-knee* bends. Namely, the detailed route of $\hat{p}_i$ makes a turn in the x-direction, thus freeing the suffix of the row ρ. The conflicting detailed route takes a turn in t-direction, thus freeing the suffix of the column in the x-direction.

We now deal with transitions from part (I) to part (II) of detailed routing. This transition is based on the reservation made for p_i in part (I) for the whole row ρ. Thus, the portion of p_i before the bend in s is accounted for by part (I).

Finally, we deal with the case where tile is not in the positive quadrant and it is partial. For such a partial tile the side-length in the direction of entry is k. This implies that a free edge to make a turn at always exists. Thus, as the description above holds for this case as well. We conclude that detailed routing is always successful in this part.

Detailed Routing in the Last Tile.

Detailed routing in the last tile is straightforward greedy routing from the entry point to a destination node in the tile. Note that any node (b_i, t) in the tile may serve as destinations for the request r_i. Conflicts are resolved by preempting all but one path (see Proposition 8). We refer to requests whose sketch path is a single tile as *near* requests. Note that detailed routing of a near request consists only of part (III).

5.3 Analysis of the Algorithm for $d = 1$

THEOREM 4. *The competitive ratio of the algorithm for unidirectional line networks is $O(\log^5 n)$ provided that $B, c \in [3 .. \log n]$.*

PROOF. We begin by a sketch of the proof. The algorithm uses the path packing algorithm IPP over the $\{1, 2, \infty\}$-sketch graph. This means that capacities are reduced by a factor of at most $k^2 \cdot \max\{B, c\} = O(k^3)$. The fact that path lengths are bounded by $p_{\max}$ reduces the throughput only by a constant factor. The throughput of algorithm IPP is $O(1)$-competitive.

Detailed routing succeeds in routing a polylogarithmic fraction of the sketch paths. There are two causes for loss of packets: routing of special segments and routing in the last tile. Routing of special segments succeeds for a fraction of $1/2k$ for each special segment. In fact, it succeeds for $1/4k$ for all special segments (i.e., the success rate is not multiplied). Routing in the last tile succeeds for a fraction of $1/2k$ per tile. Putting things together we get a competitive ratio of $O(k^5)$, as required. We now present a detailed proof.

Notation.

Let R be a fixed sequence of packet requests. Let IPP denote the set of requests in R that IPP injected. Recall that the IPP algorithm routes the requests over the $\{1, 2, \infty\}$-sketch graph, and that we removed the sink nodes from the sketch paths.

Let ALG denote the set of requests in R such that ALG succeeded in routing them to their destination. Let ALG_s denote the set of requests in ALG such that ALG succeeded in routing them to a node in s.

Let ALG' denote the set of requests in R such that ALG succeeded in routing them to the entry side the last tile.

Let ALG$'_s$ denote the set of requests in ALG$'$ that their sketch path ends in s.

Let f^* denote the optimal fractional flow with respect to R over the sketch graph. Let $f^*_{\{1,2,\infty\}}$ denote the optimal fractional flow with respect to R over the $\{1,2,\infty\}$-sketch graph. Let $f^*_{\{1,2,\infty\}}(R \mid p_{\max})$ denote the throughput of an optimal fractional path packing in the $\{1,2,\infty\}$-sketch graph with respect to R under the constraint that sketch path lengths are at most $p_{\max}$.

PROPOSITION 5. $k^2 \cdot \max\{B,c\} \cdot f^*_{\{1,2,\infty\}} \geq f^* \geq f^*_{\{1,2,\infty\}}$

PROOF. By Proposition 3, the capacity of every sketch edge is at most $k \cdot \max\{B,c\}$. The number of near requests that can be served in a tile is at most $k^2 \cdot \max\{B,c\}$. Hence, the capacities in $f^*_{\{1,2,\infty\}}$ are scaled down by a factor of at most $k^2 \cdot \max\{B,c\}$. The first inequality follows since capacity scaling reduces the optimal fractional path packing by at most the scaling factor. The second inequality follows since every feasible flow with respect to the $\{1,2,\infty\}$-sketch graph is feasible with respect to the sketch graph. $\square$

PROPOSITION 6. IPP $\geq \Omega\left(\frac{1}{k^2 \cdot \max\{B,c\}}\right) \cdot f^*$

PROOF. Theorem 1, Lemma 2 and Proposition 5 imply the following.

$$
\begin{aligned}
\text{IPP} &\geq \frac{1}{2} \cdot f^*_{\{1,2,\infty\}}(R \mid p_{\max}) \\
&\geq \frac{1}{2} \cdot \frac{1}{2} \cdot \left(1 - \frac{1}{e}\right) \cdot f^*_{\{1,2,\infty\}} \\
&\geq \Omega\left(\frac{1}{k^2 \cdot \max\{B,c\}}\right) \cdot f^* .
\end{aligned}
$$

$\square$

PROPOSITION 7. ALG$' \geq \frac{1}{4k} \cdot$ IPP

PROOF. Consider a row or a column L of nodes in G^{st}. Let R' denote the set of requests that contain special segments that compete over edges in L. From the point of view of L, each request $r_i \in R'$ is a request for an interval $I_i \subseteq L$. The detailed routing of the requests R' along L simulates an optimal interval packing algorithm [GLL82]. In particular, the simulation has the property that if an interval $I_i = [a_i, b_i]$ preempts an interval $I_j = [a_j, b_j]$, then $a_j \leq a_i < b_i \leq b_j$. Consider the "forest of preemptions" over the intervals, where the set of intervals that were preempted by I_i are children of I_i. Hence, if interval I_j is a descendant of I_i in this forest, then $I_i \subseteq I_j$. The load induced by IPP on each $\{1,2,\infty\}$-sketch edge is at most $2k$ (i.e., the load on a side is at most k, and the load on an interior edge is at most $2k$). Therefore, the maximum number of proper descendants of I_i in the forest is $(2k-1)$ (not including I_i).

Consider a bipartite graph of preemptions over ALG$' \cup$ (IPP $\setminus$ ALG$'$). There is an edge (r_i, r_j) if the request $r_i \in$ ALG$'$ is an ancestor of the request $r_j \in$ (IPP $\setminus$ ALG$'$) in the forest of preemptions corresponding to detailed routing. Since a preempted request is preempted only once, the degree of the nodes in IPP $\setminus$ ALG$'$ is one. By the discussion above, the degree of a node in ALG$'$ is bounded by $2 \cdot (2k-1)$; at most $(2k-1)$ per each special segment. Recall that each sketch path contains at most 2 special segments. By counting edges in the bipartite graph, we conclude that $|$ALG$'| \cdot 2 \cdot (2k-1) \geq |$IPP $\setminus$ ALG$'|$, and the proposition follows. $\square$

PROPOSITION 8. ALG $\geq \frac{1}{2k} \cdot$ ALG$'$

PROOF. Let R_s denote the set of requests in R whose sketch paths (computed by algorithm IPP) end in tile s. Recall that we removed the sink nodes from the sketch paths. Note that, for near requests, the sketch path belongs to a single tile; near requests in s trivially belong to R_s.

Every sketch path of a request in R_s traverses the interior edge of s whose capacity is 2. Theorem 1 implies that this capacity is violated by at most a factor of k, hence $R_s \leq 2k$.

Since a unit of capacity is reserved for the last cube and since a greedy algorithm is applied in the detailed routing in the last cube, at least one request from ALG$'_s$ is successfully routed if ALG$'_s \neq \emptyset$. Since $\{R_s\}_{s \in V(S)}$ is a partition of R the proposition follows. $\square$

We now put things together to complete the proof of Theorem 4.

$$
\begin{aligned}
\text{ALG} &\geq \frac{1}{2k} \cdot \text{ALG}' \geq \frac{1}{2k} \cdot \frac{1}{4k} \cdot \text{IPP} \\
&= \Omega\left(\frac{1}{k^4 \cdot \max\{B,c\}}\right) \cdot f^* \\
&\geq \Omega\left(\frac{1}{k^4 \cdot \max\{B,c\}}\right) \cdot \text{OPT}_f .
\end{aligned}
$$

The first inequality is justified by Proposition 8. The second inequality is justified by Proposition 7. The third inequality is justified by to Proposition 6. The last inequality follows since every feasible flow with respect to G^{st} is feasible with respect to the sketch graph, and the theorem follows.

5.4 Requests With Deadlines

In this section we present the modification needed to deal with packet requests with deadlines. The change to the algorithm is in the reduction to online integral path packing (see Section 5.1), i.e., we need to change the sink node in the reduction as follows.

Adding Sink Nodes for Requests with Deadlines.
A request to deliver a packet is of the form $r_i = (a_i, b_i, t_i, d_i)$, where d_i is the deadline. In terms of a path request in the space-time graph G^{st}, this means that we need to assign a path from (a_i, t_i) to a vertex (b_i, t'), where $t_i \leq t' \leq d_i$. Thus, the destination is a set of vertices rather than one specific vertex. We add a sink node for each request as follows. For every request r_i, introduce a new vertex $sink_i$. Connect every vertex in $\{(b_i, t')\}_{t'=t_i}^{d_i}$ to $sink_i$ with an edge of infinite capacity.

Now, a packet request $r_i = (a_i, b_i, t_i, d_i)$ is reduced to a path request in the $\{1,2,\infty\}$-sketch graph from the half-tile s_{in} (where the tile s contains (a_i, t_i)) to $sink_i$. A path from (a_i, t_i) to $sink_i$ contains at most $d_i - t_i + 1$ edges. We still bound the path length by $p_{\max}$, as before, to obtain an $O(\log p_{\max})$ capacity augmentation by IPP.

6. GENERALIZATIONS

In this section we present a generalization of the algorithm to the d-dimensional case and extensions to special cases, such as: bufferless grids, and grids with large buffers and large link capacities.

The d-Dimensional Case.

Two modifications are needed to extend the algorithm to d-dimensional grids. (1) The capacity assigned to internal edges within each tile is $d+1$. (2) A segment of the sketch path is *special* if it is the first segment or if it is the last segment in its direction. This implies that there are at most $d+1$ special segments in each sketch path. (3) Detailed routing of a segment followed by a special segment proceeds as in the one dimensional case. Namely, a turn is taken upon entry to the face of the tile that contains the bend. The detailed route of a special segment reserves a straight path till the end of the tile that contains the end of the special segment. (4) Partial tiles are more complicated to describe, but retain the property that the side-length in the direction entry from the point of entry equals the tile's side-length. In the full version , partial tiles for $d = 2$ are discussed. The following theorem bounds the competitive ratio of the algorithm for general dimensionality d. The proof of Theorem 13 is outlined as follows.

The proof of the propositions below follows the analogous proofs in Section 5.3.

PROPOSITION 9.

$$k^{d+1} \cdot \frac{\max\{B,c\}}{d+1} \cdot f^*_{\{1,d+1,\infty\}} \geq f^* \geq f^*_{\{1,d+1,\infty\}}$$

PROPOSITION 10. $\text{IPP} \geq \Omega\left(\frac{d+1}{k^{d+1} \cdot \max\{B,c\}}\right) \cdot f^*$

PROPOSITION 11. $\text{ALG}' \geq \frac{1}{(d+1)^2 \cdot k} \cdot \text{IPP}$

PROPOSITION 12. $\text{ALG} \geq \frac{1}{(d+1) \cdot k} \cdot \text{ALG}'$

The proof of Theorem 13 follows the proof of Theorem 4.

THEOREM 13. *The competitive ratio of the algorithm for d-dimensional grid networks is $O\left(d^2 \cdot \log^{d+4} n\right)$ provided that $B, c \in [3 .. \log n]$.*

Proof sketch of Theorem 13: Bounding path lengths incurs a constant loss to the competitive ratio. Algorithm IPP incurs an additional constant loss to the competitive ratio. The capacity assignment of $\{1, d+1\}$ reduces the throughput by a factor of $k^{d+1} \cdot \frac{\max\{B,c\}}{d+1}$. Finally, preemptions and detailed routing in the last tile incur a $(d+1)^3 \cdot k^2$ loss to the competitive ratio. The theorem follows since $B, c \in [3 .. \log n]$. $\square$

Bufferless Grids.

For the case $B = 0$ and $c \geq 3$ (no upper bound on c), we obtain the following result.

THEOREM 14. *There exists an online deterministic preemptive algorithm for packet routing in bufferless d-dimensional grids with a competitive ratio of $O(d^2 \cdot \log^{d+2} n)$.*

Proof sketch of Theorem 14: Since $B = 0$, the space-time graph G^{st} after untilting consists of unconnected d-dimensional planes. A plane with a t-coordinate that equals t' deals with the routing of the subset of requests for which $t_i - \|a_i\|_1 = t'$. Within each such plane, we apply a version of our algorithm over a space-time grid with dimension d. Note that since $B = 0$, $p_{\max} \leq \sum_i \ell_i$ (i.e., the diameter of the grid) and does not depend on c. Note also that the destination is a single node (b_i, t'), where $t' = t_i + \|a_i - b_i\|_1$. Thus we

need not introduce sink nodes, The edge capacities are not changed, hence we assign capacity $d \cdot c$ to every interior edge (instead of $(d+1)$). Hence, the capacity assignment reduces the throughput by a factor of $\frac{k^d}{d}$ (instead of $k^{d+1} \cdot \frac{\max\{B,c\}}{d+1}$). $\square$

Large Buffers & Large Link Capacities.

Recall that $\gamma \triangleq (B + d \cdot c)/c$, $p_{\max} \geq (\sum_i \ell_i) \cdot (1 + 2\gamma n)$, and $k \triangleq \lceil \log(1 + 3p_{\max}) \rceil$. For the case $B, c \geq k$, we obtain the following result.

THEOREM 15. *There exists an online deterministic preemptive algorithm for packet routing in d-dimensional grids with a competitive ratio of $O(k)$ if $B, c \geq k$.*

Proof sketch of Theorem 15: Scale B and c by setting $B' \leftarrow \frac{B}{k}$ and $c' \leftarrow \frac{c}{k}$. Use G^{st} with the scaled capacities as the input to algorithm IPP so that it computes detailed paths. Hence, we get an $(O(k), 1)$-competitive algorithm, as required. $\square$

Note that if $B/c = n^{O(1)}$, then $k = O(\log n)$, hence Theorem 15 yields a logarithmic competitive ratio in case $B, c \geq k$.

7. DISCUSSION

Two main problems that remain open are: (i) Does there exist a *distributed* algorithm for packet routing on grids with a polylogarithmic competitive ratio? (Our algorithm is centralized) (ii) Design an online algorithm for packet routing with a constant competitive ratio or prove a non-constant lower bound. These questions remain open even for unidirectional lines.

We do not know how to obtain a polylogarithmic competitive ratio without using adaptive routing and preemptions. On the positive side, by appending the sketch path to each packet, detailed routing can take place in a distributed fashion (i.e., each node of the network makes the decisions locally). Thus, only the online path packing subroutine over the sketch graph requires a centralized algorithm.

Acknowledgments

We thank Boaz Patt-Shamir and Adi Rosen for useful discussions.

8. REFERENCES

[AAF96] Baruch Awerbuch, Yossi Azar, and Amos Fiat. Packet routing via min-cost circuit routing. In *ISTCS*, pages 37–42, 1996.

[AAP93] Baruch Awerbuch, Yossi Azar, and Serge A. Plotkin. Throughput-competitive on-line routing. In *FOCS '93: Proceedings of the 1993 IEEE 34th Annual Foundations of Computer Science*, pages 32–40, Washington, DC, USA, 1993. IEEE Computer Society.

[AKK09] Stanislav Angelov, Sanjeev Khanna, and Keshav Kunal. The network as a storage device: Dynamic routing with bounded buffers. *Algorithmica*, 55(1):71–94, 2009. (Appeared in APPROX-05).

[AKOR03] William Aiello, Eyal Kushilevitz, Rafail Ostrovsky, and Adi Rosén. Dynamic routing on networks with fixed-size buffers. In *SODA*, pages 771–780, 2003.

[AKRR03] Micah Adler, Sanjeev Khanna, Rajmohan Rajaraman, and Adi Rosén. Time-constrained scheduling of weighted packets on trees and meshes. *Algorithmica*, 36(2):123–152, 2003.

[ARSU02] Micah Adler, Arnold L. Rosenberg, Ramesh K. Sitaraman, and Walter Unger. Scheduling time-constrained communication in linear networks. *Theory Comput. Syst.*, 35(6):599–623, 2002.

[AZ05] Yossi Azar and Rafi Zachut. Packet routing and information gathering in lines, rings and trees. In *ESA*, pages 484–495, 2005. (See also manuscript in `http://www.cs.tau.ac.il/~azar/`).

[BL97] Yair Bartal and Stefano Leonardi. On-line routing in all-optical networks. In *ICALP*, pages 516–526, 1997.

[BN06] Niv Buchbinder and Joseph (Seffi) Naor. Improved bounds for online routing and packing via a primal-dual approach. In *FOCS*, pages 293–304, 2006.

[BN09] Niv Buchbinder and Joseph (Seffi) Naor. The design of competitive online algorithms via a primal-dual approach. *Foundations and Trends in Theoretical Computer Science*, 3(2-3):99–263, 2009.

[EM10] Guy Even and Moti Medina. An $O(\log n)$-Competitive Online Centralized Randomized Packet-Routing Algorithm for Lines. 2010. Accepted to ICALP 2010. (Manuscript available in `http://www.eng.tau.ac.il/~medinamo/`).

[GLL82] U. I. Gupta, D. T. Lee, and J. Y.-T. Leung. Efficient algorithms for interval graphs and circular-arc graphs. *Networks*, 12(4):459–467, 1982.

[KT95] Jon M. Kleinberg and Éva Tardos. Disjoint paths in densely embedded graphs. In *FOCS*, pages 52–61, 1995. (See also manuscript in `http://www.cs.cornell.edu/home/kleinber/`).

[LMR94] FT Leighton, B.M. Maggs, and S.B. Rao. Packet routing and job-shop scheduling in $O(congestion + dilation)$ steps. *Combinatorica*, 14(2):167–186, 1994.

[LMR99] T. Leighton, B. Maggs, and A.W. Richa. Fast algorithms for finding $O(congestion + dilation)$ packet routing schedules. *Combinatorica*, 19(3):375–401, 1999.

[RR09] Harald Räcke and Adi Rosén. Approximation algorithms for time-constrained scheduling on line networks. In *SPAA*, pages 337–346, 2009.

[RT96] Yuval Rabani and Éva Tardos. Distributed packet switching in arbitrary networks. In *STOC '96: Proceedings of the twenty-eighth annual ACM symposium on Theory of computing*, pages 366–375, New York, NY, USA, 1996. ACM.

[ST97] A. Srinivasan and C.P. Teo. A constant-factor approximation algorithm for packet routing, and balancing local vs. global criteria. In *Proceedings of the twenty-ninth annual ACM symposium on Theory of computing*, pages 636–643. ACM, 1997.

[Tur09] Jonathan S. Turner. Strong performance guarantees for asynchronous buffered crossbar scheduler. *IEEE/ACM Trans. Netw.*, 17(4):1017–1028, 2009.

APPENDIX

A. TWO MODELS FOR NODES IN STORE-AND-FORWARD NETWORKS

The literature contains two different models of node functionality. In an effort to make the comparison concrete and perhaps clearer, we present schematic implementations of the nodes in each model.

To simplify the discussion, we use two type of packets: regular packets and ghost packets. A regular packets has a unit utility (if delivered) and a ghost packet has zero utility (i.e., it acts as a "place holder"). This means, for example, that a buffer always holds B packets. In case the buffer is empty, all the packets in the buffer are simply ghost packets.

Model 1.

This model is used by [ARSU02, RR09, EM10]. Figure 3a depicts a block diagram of a node. A node contains a combinational circuit *comb*, a buffer consisting of B flip-flops, and c flip-flops on each link that emanates the node.

In each clock cycle, the combinational circuit *comb* receives c packets from each incoming link, B packets from its buffer, and $B + c$ packets from its local inputs. It outputs B packets to the buffer and c packets along each outgoing link. Packets that were input but not output are considered dropped packets unless the node is their destination.

Model 2.

This model is used by [AKK09, AZ05]. Figure 3b depicts a block diagram of a node. A node contains two combinational circuits $comb_0$ and $comb_1$, two sets of B latches each, and one latch on each link that emanates the node. Note that this implementation uses a two-phase clock. The phases are denoted by ϕ_0 and ϕ_1.

In the first phase of each clock cycle, the combinational circuit $comb_0$ receives one packet from each incoming link, B packets from its buffer, and B packets from its local inputs. It outputs B packets. The input packets that it could not output are dropped (unless they reached their destination). In the second clock phase of each clock cycle, the combinational circuit $comb_1$ outputs one packet along each outgoing link and B packets to back to $comb_0$.

Remarks.

(i) We could also allow for more injected packets in each node. In this case, the node must drop some of them. Of course, the online algorithm has to decide which packets should be dropped. (ii) The linear lower bounds for $B = 1$ in [AZ05, AKK09] hold only with respect to Model 2. (iii) It is not clear how to extend Model 2 for the case that $c > 1$ or $B = 0$. (iv) Under the common assumption that the cost of a flip-flop is roughly twice the cost of a latch, the hardware needed for the latches of a node in Model 2 is roughly the same as the cost of flip-flops of a node in Model 1 (with $c = 1$).

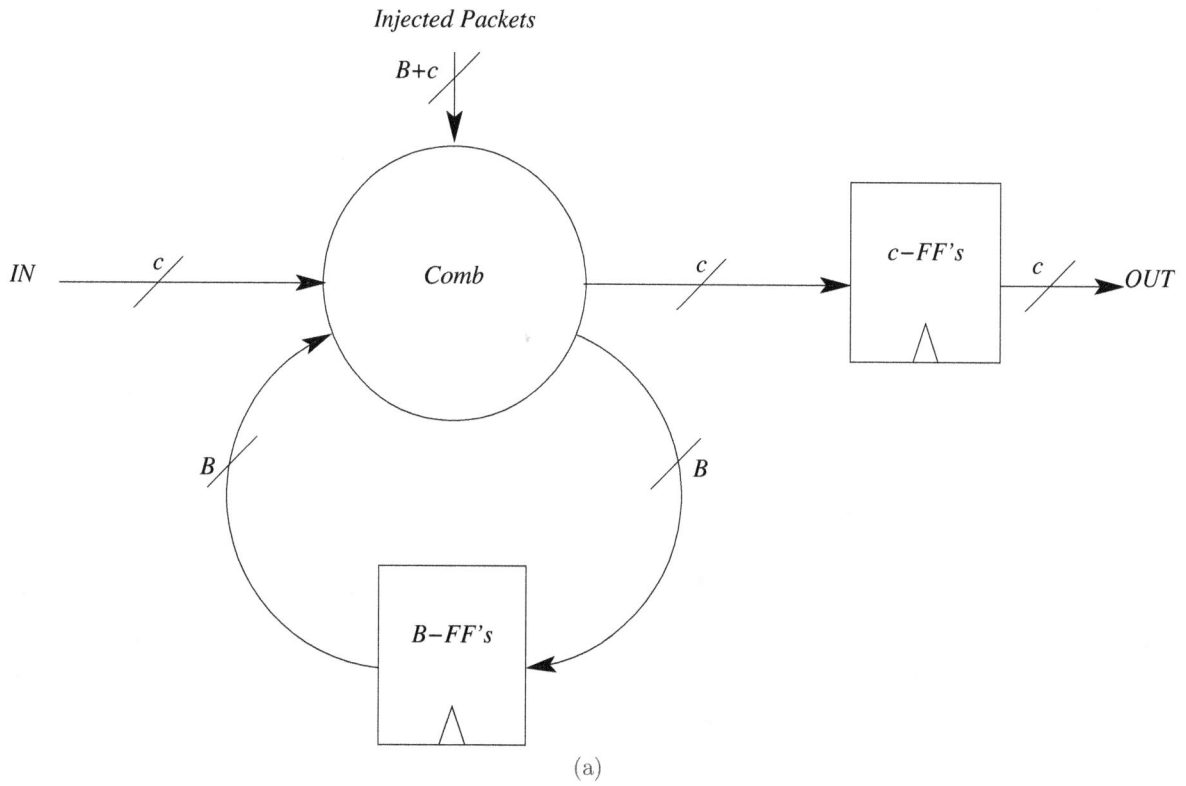

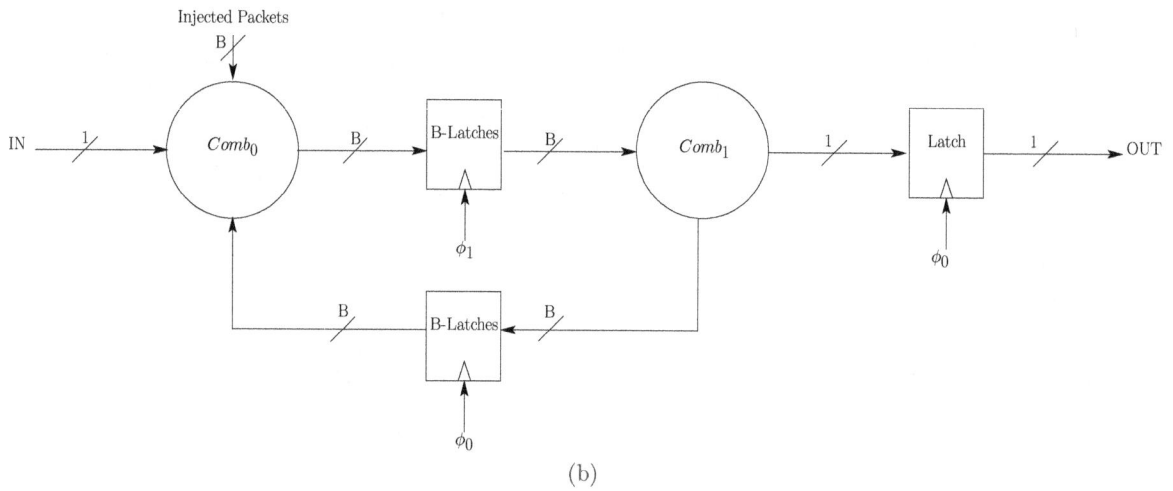

Figure 3: (a) A schematic of a node in Model-1. (b) A schematic of a node in Model-2.

Sparse Spanners vs. Compact Routing

Cyril Gavoille[*]
LaBRI - Université de Bordeaux
351, cours de la Libération
33405 Talence cedex, France
gavoille@labri.fr

Christian Sommer[†]
Massachusetts Institute of Technology
77 Massachusetts Avenue
Cambridge, MA 02139-4307
csom@mit.edu

ABSTRACT

Routing with *multiplicative* stretch 3 (which means that the path used by the routing scheme can be up to three times longer than a shortest path) can be done with routing tables of $\tilde{\Theta}(\sqrt{n})$ bits[1] per node. The space lower bound is due to the existence of dense graphs with large girth. Dense graphs can be sparsified to subgraphs, called *spanners*, with various stretch guarantees. There are spanners with *additive* stretch guarantees (some even have constant additive stretch) but only very few additive routing schemes are known.

In this paper, we give reasons why routing in unweighted graphs with *additive* stretch is difficult in the form of space lower bounds for general graphs and for planar graphs. We prove that any routing scheme using routing tables of size μ bits per node and addresses of poly-logarithmic length has additive stretch $\tilde{\Omega}(\sqrt{n/\mu})$ for general graphs, and $\tilde{\Omega}(\sqrt[4]{n/\mu})$ for planar graphs, respectively. Routing with tables of size $\tilde{O}(n^{1/3})$ thus requires a polynomial additive stretch of $\tilde{\Omega}(n^{1/3})$, whereas spanners with average degree $O(n^{1/3})$ and *constant* additive stretch exist for all graphs. Spanners, however sparse they are, do not tell us how to route. These bounds provide the first separation of sparse spanner problems and compact routing problems.

On the positive side, we give an almost tight upper bound: we present the first non-trivial compact routing scheme with $o(\lg^2 n)$-bit addresses, *additive* stretch $\tilde{O}(n^{1/3})$, and table size $\tilde{O}(n^{1/3})$ bits for all graphs with linear local tree-width such as planar, bounded-genus, and apex-minor-free graphs.

---

[*]C.G. is also member of "l'Institut Universitaire de France". He is also supported by ANR projects "ALADDIN", and the équipe-projet INRIA Sud-Ouest "CÉPAGE".

[†]Part of this work was done at the University of Tokyo and while C.S. visited LaBRI.

[1]Tilde-big-O notation is similar to big-O notation up to factors poly-logarithmic in n.

Categories and Subject Descriptors

C.2.2 [**Network Protocols**]: Network Architecture and Design—*Routing protocols*; F.2.2 [**Nonnumerical Algorithms and Problems**]: [Routing and layout]; G.2.2 [**Discrete Mathematics**]: Graph Theory—*Network problems, Graph labeling, Graph algorithms*.

General Terms

Algorithms, Theory.

Keywords

compact routing, shortest paths

1. INTRODUCTION

Routing is essential for communication in networks. For a network with n devices, we deem a routing scheme to be *compact*, if the maximum amount of memory used per routing table grows asymptotically slower than n. Research on *compact routing* [8, 20, 34, 35, 52] is concerned with the tradeoff between the space requirements and the quality of the routes, where the quality is measured with respect to the best possible route. The (multiplicative) *stretch* of a routing scheme is defined as the worst-case ratio for any pair of nodes of the route length divided by the shortest-path distance. A routing scheme that uses linear space per node may store information on all shortest routes. If the memory available per node (the *table size*) is $o(n \lg n)$, packets can not always be sent along shortest paths [41].

The fundamental tradeoff between stretch and routing table size has been investigated broadly and both upper and lower bounds for general graphs [4, 7, 20, 55] and for graphs stemming from specific classes such as trees [31, 32, 47, 48, 55], planar graphs [37, 49, 54], minor-free graphs [1, 3], non-positively curved plane graphs [18], graphs with bounded genus [37], with low doubling dimension [2, 45], chordal graphs [23, 24], "flat" networks [43], random graphs [28], power-law graphs [13, 16], permutation graphs, interval graphs and related classes [11, 25, 26], and others are known (see Table 1 for an overview).

The space lower bounds known for general graphs [36, 55] are based on dense graphs with given *girth*.[2] To overcome difficulties with dense graphs, sparse *spanners* [6, 19, 51] have been devised. Spanners are subgraphs with fewer edges that satisfy certain distance inequalities — spanners

---

[2]The girth of a graph is the length of its shortest cycle.

Graph	Stretch	Tables	Addresses	Ref.
General	1	$n \lg_2 n$	$O(\lg n)$	Folkl.
General	2	$(n - \sqrt{n}) \lg_2 n$	$O(\lg n)$	[42]
General	3	$\tilde{O}(n^{1/2})$	$O(\lg n)$	[55]
General	$4k - 5$	$\tilde{O}(n^{1/k})$	$o(k \lg^2 n)$	[55]
Trees	1	none	$o(\lg^2 n)$	[31, 55]
Tree-width τ	1	none	$O(\tau \lg^2 n)$	[50]
Planar	1	$7.18n + o(n)$	$O(\lg n)$	[49]
Genus γ	1	$n \lg_2 \gamma + O(n)$	$O(\lg n)$	[37]
Planar	$1 + \epsilon$	none	$o(\epsilon^{-1} \lg^2 n)$	[54]
Minor-free	$1 + \epsilon$	none	$o(\epsilon^{-1} \lg^2 n)$	[1]
Doubling dim. α	$1 + \epsilon$	$\epsilon^{-O(\alpha)} \lg^3 n$	$O(\lg n)$	[45]
$G_{n,p}$ $(p = 1/2)$	1	$n + O(\lg^4 n)$	$O(\lg n)$	[39]
$G_{n,p}$ $(np \in (\lg n, \sqrt[9]{n}))$	2	$\tilde{O}(n^{3/4})$	$O(\lg n)$	[28]
Random PL	5	$\tilde{O}(n^{1/3})$	$o(\lg^2 n)$	[16]

Table 1: Best results known on labeled (name-dependent) compact routing schemes for connected graphs on n nodes. The stretch is *multiplicative*, meaning the worst-case ratio between the path used by the routing scheme and the distance between source and target. For labeled schemes, the designer may choose arbitrary node names (also termed *addresses*), including, for example, names that depend on the topology and the edge weights of the graph.

ought to maintain distances up to small *stretch* factors. Recently, instead of spanners with multiplicative stretch, *additive spanners* [10, 12, 27, 53, 57, 58, 59] have been investigated as well. Spanners could potentially be used for routing — in fact, their usefulness for routing is often one of the (main) reasons stated in the introduction and motivation section of articles on spanners. However, the trade-off between routing table space requirements and worst-case stretch is not yet completely understood for sparse graphs. Indeed, sparse spanners do not tell the designer of the routing scheme how to find and encode short routes.

The *additive* stretch of a routing scheme (and, analogously, of a spanner) is defined as the worst-case difference for any pair of nodes of the route length minus the shortest-path distance (the graphs considered are assumed to be *unweighted* whenever we consider additive stretch). Instead of routing with multiplicative stretch, researchers have also started to investigate routing schemes with additive stretch guarantees. However, only very little is known (see Table 2 for an overview).

For general graphs, the following straightforward approach guarantees additive stretch β using routing tables of size $\tilde{O}(n/\beta)$, for any integral parameter β. The routing scheme routes along shortest-path spanning trees rooted at each node of a small $\frac{1}{2}\beta$-dominating set, that is a subset C of nodes such that every node u is at distance at most $\frac{1}{2}\beta$ from some *center* $c_u \in C$. It is well-known that every connected graph has a $\frac{1}{2}\beta$-dominating set of size $< 2n/(\beta + 1)$, computable efficiently [46]. By the triangle inequality, routes are stretched by an additive factor of at most β. The address of each node u consists of the node identifier of its closest center c_u, telling the source which tree to use. Since each tree contributes $o(\lg^2 n)$ bits per node to the routing tables [31, 55], the tables are of size $o(|C| \lg^2 n) = \tilde{O}(n/\beta)$.

A non-trivial compact routing scheme with additive stretch β should thus have table size $o(n/\beta)$. Schemes

with small tables and small additive stretch have been devised for restricted graph classes such as chordal graphs [24], graphs with bounded tree-length [23], and, more generally[3] graphs of bounded hyperbolicity [17]. Furthermore, Brady and Cowen [14] construct a routing scheme with additive stretch 6 given an *exact* distance labeling scheme [38, 40, 50]. Their approach yields sublinear table sizes for all graphs that allow for a distance labeling scheme with labels of length $o(\sqrt{n})$. Unfortunately, any exact distance labeling scheme in unweighted graphs requires at least $\Omega(n)$-bit labels in general, $\Omega(\sqrt{n})$-bit labels for bounded-degree graphs and $\Omega(n^{1/3})$-bit labels for planar graphs [40].

Other compact routing schemes have been proposed for internet-like topologies, with small multiplicative stretch and poly-logarithmic additive stretch [13, 33].

Graph	Stretch	Table	Addresses	Ref.
General	β	$\tilde{O}(n/\beta)$	$o(\lg^2 n)$	Folkl.
Diameter Δ	2Δ	none	$o(\lg^2 n)$	Folkl.
$\ell(n)$-Labels	6	$O(\sqrt{n}(\ell(n) + \lg^2 n))$	$O(\ell(n) + \lg^2 n)$	[14]
Interval	1	$O(\lg n)$	$O(\lg n)$	[14]
Circular-arc	1	$O(\lg n)$	$o(\lg^2 n)$	[14]
Chordal	2	$o(\lg^3 n)$	$o(\lg^3 n)$	[24]
Tree-length δ	$6\delta - 2$	$O(\delta \lg^2 n)$	$O(\delta \lg^2 n)$	[23]
δ-Hyperbolic	$O(\delta \lg n)$	$O(\delta \lg^2 n)$	$O(\delta \lg^2 n)$	[17]

Table 2: Best results known on compact routing schemes with *additive* stretch for unweighted connected graphs on n nodes. The scheme by Brady and Cowen [14] uses exact *distance labels* of length $\ell(n)$ to devise a routing scheme with additive stretch.

Although there are some routing schemes that guarantee additive stretch for restricted classes of graphs, the results on routing somehow cannot catch up with the results on spanners. While there are rather sparse additive spanners, additive routing schemes for (more) general graphs have not been found.

1.1 Contributions

In the current work, we investigate tradeoffs between the size of routing tables and the additive stretch. We give both upper and lower bounds. Our lower bounds explain why, unfortunately, sparse additive spanners cannot be converted into compact routing schemes. Routing with additive stretch requires large tables — even for planar graphs. We thus give the first separation of spanner problems and routing problems. On the positive side, we also give an almost tight upper bound for routing with additive stretch on graphs with linear local tree-width (a class of graphs that includes planar, bounded-genus, and apex-minor-free graphs).

Lower Bounds.

For general graphs on n nodes, we prove that any routing scheme using addresses of poly-logarithmic length and routing tables of size μ bits per node has additive stretch at least $\tilde{\Omega}(\sqrt{n/\mu})$ (Theorem 1). For planar graphs, we prove that the lower bound on the additive stretch is at least $\tilde{\Omega}(\sqrt[4]{n}/\mu)$ (Theorem 2).

---

[3]Chordal graphs have tree-length 1, graphs of tree-length δ are $O(\delta)$-hyperbolic, δ-hyperbolic graphs have tree-length $O(\delta \lg n)$.

Upper Bound.

We provide a rather general approach for compact routing with additive stretch. For planar graphs on n nodes (and actually for graphs of linear local tree-width, which includes all bounded-genus graphs), this general approach yields a compact routing scheme with poly-logarithmic addresses, table size $\tilde{O}(n^{1/3})$, and additive stretch $\tilde{O}(n^{1/3})$ (Theorem 3). Our upper bound is almost tight with respect to the lower bound of Theorem 2, which says that table size $\tilde{O}(n^{1/4})$ requires additive stretch $\tilde{\Omega}(n^{1/4})$. Actually, our scheme works for general graphs but with weaker bounds on the memory consumption.

2. LOWER BOUNDS

We first state and prove the general lower bound (Theorem 1). Second, we state and prove the lower bound for planar graphs (Theorem 2) as a special case of the general lower bound.

THEOREM 1. *For connected, unweighted graphs on n nodes, any labeled routing scheme using addresses of poly-logarithmic length and routing tables of size μ bits per node has worst-case additive stretch at least $\beta = \tilde{\Omega}(\sqrt{n/\mu})$.*

Before presenting our proof, let us observe that one cannot derive a lower bound on the additive stretch from multiplicative-stretch lower bounds for the following reason. It is known [36, 55] that there are worst-case dense graphs on k nodes for which any routing scheme with $o(k)$-bit routing tables cannot achieve shortest-path routing between all pairs of adjacent nodes (and so provide routes of length at least 2 for some edge uv). We may believe that by uniformly subdivising each edge of these dense graphs into k new edges we are done. Choosing $k \sim n^{1/3}$, we may obtain a graph with $O(k^2)$ edges and $O(k^3) = O(n)$ nodes in which any routing scheme between some distance-k nodes requires a route of length $\geq 2k$, and thus an additive stretch of $\geq 2k - k = n^{1/3}$. The argument is flawed since the route from u to v in the new graph can first make a short loop to collect routing information, before going straight to v. And, unfortunately, the degree of u is large by construction, and thus the routing information about u's neighbors could be efficiently distributed around u (e.g., by the use of some hash tables).

This reduction might work if worst-case graphs of bounded degree were known. Unfortunately, compact routing with small (multiplicative) stretch in bounded degree graphs is widely open. No upper and lower bounds (other than the ones for general graphs) are known for this problem.

PROOF. Our worst-case graphs (see Fig. 1) consist of a set of p sources $S = \{s_1, \dots s_p\}$, a set of q targets $T = \{t_1, \dots t_q\}$, and two graphs L (for left) and R (for right), both lying between the sources and the targets. Each source s_i is connected to a representative node s_i^L in L and a node s_i^R in R, on a path of length ρ, respectively. L and R connect these representative sources to the targets t_j. Both L and R are built from the same base graph (or *gadget*) but different shortcuts are added. For each pair (s_i, t_j) there is exactly one shortcut, *either* in L *or* in R. Except for these shortcuts, L and R thus look almost identical. For each pair (s_i, t_j), *independent of all other pairs*, there is only one shortest path, going *either* through L *or* through R (depending on whether

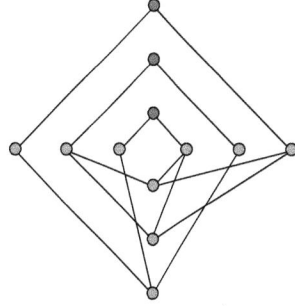

Figure 1: An example of the lower bound construction for general graphs. Each target (red, lower part) is connected to either the left part or the right part (independently for different targets). Intuitively speaking, to route from any source we need to know for all targets whether to send a message using the edge on the left or the edge on the right. If the number of sources is sufficiently large, the information cannot be encoded in the address.

the shortcut is in L or in R). The graphs are constructed such that any alternative path is much longer.

Let K be the $p \times q$ matrix with entries in $\{0, 1\}$, where $k_{i,j}$ is 0 if the shortcut for (s_i, t_j) is in L and 1 otherwise (i.e., the shortcut is in R). Since each shortcut (i, j) can be added either to L or to R independently, there are 2^{pq} different combinations and thus 2^{pq} different matrices K. An encoding of K thus requires at least $\lg_2 2^{pq} = pq$ bits. In the following, we argue that the addresses of the targets and the routing tables "around" the sources must *encode* K.

Intuitively speaking, to route from s_i, we need to know for all t_j whether to send a message using L or R. For any source s_i, a routing scheme that has additive stretch at most 2ρ may explore the routing tables of all the nodes at distance at most ρ from s_i to decide whether to use L or R. Recall that, in our construction, each source is connected to only two long paths of length ρ and thus the number of nodes within distance ρ is 2ρ. The collective information of all the nodes (including s_i) within distance ρ around source s_i is bounded by $(2\rho + 1)\mu$ bits. The collective information of all the nodes within distance ρ around all the p sources is bounded by $p(2\rho + 1)\mu$ bits. The addresses of the p sources and the q targets may also contribute to the encoding of K, adding another $(p + q)\alpha$ bits, where α is the maximum address length. We thus have

$$p(2\rho + 1)\mu + (p + q)\mu \geq pq. \qquad (1)$$

For the case of general graphs, the base graph (gadget) is very simple (Fig. 1 provides an illustration): it consists of p nodes $s_i^{\{L,R\}}$ (one for each source) and no edges. A "shortcut" for a pair of source and target (s_i, t_j) is a path of length ρ from $s_i^{\{L,R\}}$ to t_j. The graph uses $\Theta(p\rho)$ nodes and edges to connect S to L and R and $\Theta(pq\rho)$ nodes and edges to connect L and R to T. The shortest path from s_i to t_j has length 2ρ. Suppose that the shortcut (i, j) was in L. Any path from s_i to t_j in R has length at least $\rho + 3\rho$. To achieve additive stretch less than 2ρ, the routing scheme must know after ρ steps whether to use L or R.

Let us now fix the parameters p, q, ρ, with respect to α

(the address length), μ and n. The number of sources p is chosen such that the address of a target t_j cannot encode the L vs. R decision for each source s_i:

$$p = \omega(\alpha).$$

For poly-logarithmic address length α, we may choose p to be poly-logarithmic in n as well. Using $n = \Theta(pq\rho)$, Eq. (1) yields

$$p(2\rho+1)M + (p+q)\alpha \;\geq\; pq \qquad (2)$$
$$\rho M \;=\; \tilde{\Omega}(q) \qquad (3)$$
$$\rho \;=\; \tilde{\Omega}(\sqrt{n/\mu}). \qquad (4)$$

Since the additive stretch is at least ρ, the claim follows. $\square$

We observe that the worst-case graphs used in the our proof have less than $2n$ edges. The graphs itself are sparse spanners (trivial stretch). However, we prove that no additive compact routing scheme with small tables exists. Note that the optimal $\tilde{O}(n^{1/k})$-space routing scheme of Thorup and Zwick [55] also requires additive stretch no better than $n^{1/2-O(1/k)}$ for these graphs. However, the sampling technique used to design this optimal routing scheme has also been used [57] to produce spanners for unweighted graphs with stretch much smaller than $O(k)$, namely $1+\epsilon$ for any $\epsilon > 0$.

Note.

Techniques for compact routing schemes and for distance oracles [56] are often applicable to both problems. The graph (and the query pairs) we use in this lower bound, however, admits a straightforward, exact distance (and shortest-path) oracle using linear space. Our proof shows that the routing problem is much harder.

The lower-bound graph construction for general graphs can be combined with lower bounds for exact compact routing schemes [2]. Note that the upper part of the general construction is a planar graph. We thus need a planar gadget for the lower part. The general construction, combined with [2], yields a lower bound for additive stretch routing in planar graphs, and also bounded-doubling-dimension graphs (details and proof in Appendix A).

THEOREM 2. *For connected, unweighted bounded degree planar graphs on n nodes, any labeled routing scheme using addresses of poly-logarithmic length and routing tables of size μ bits per node has worst-case additive stretch at least $\beta = \tilde{\Omega}(\sqrt{n/\mu})$.*

3. UPPER BOUND

In this section, we provide a routing scheme with table sizes and additive stretch both $\tilde{O}(n^{1/3})$ for planar graphs. The tradeoff between table size and stretch almost matches the lower bound in Theorem 2. Actually, this trade-off applies to every graph having *linear local tree-width*, a much larger class of graphs including for instance all bounded-genus graphs.

A graph G with n nodes has *local tree-width* $\tau(r)$ if the subgraph induced by nodes within distance r of any node has tree-width at most $\tau(r)$. The local tree-with is *linear* if $\tau(r) = O(r)$. Planar graphs of radius[4] r have tree-width $\leq$

---

[4] A graph has radius r if it has a spanning tree of depth r.

$3r$, and for graphs of genus γ the tree-width is $O(\gamma r)$ [29], so all these graphs have linear local tree-width. More generally, all *apex-minor-free* graphs[5] have linear local tree-width [21]. These latter graphs can be recognized in linear time [44], and play an important role in Graph Minor Theory with important algorithmic applications [22]. The class of graphs with local tree-width is however not restricted to minor-closed families: bounded degree-d graphs have local tree-with $\tau(r) = O(d^r)$, and d-dimensional meshes have local tree-width $\tau(r) = O(r^d)$.

THEOREM 3. *Every connected, unweighted graph of linear local tree-width on n nodes has a labeled routing scheme constructible in polynomial time with $o(\lg^2 n)$-bit addresses, table size $\tilde{O}(n^{1/3})$, and additive stretch $\tilde{O}(n^{1/3})$.*

Our routing scheme is actually more general and it works for any graph G (with worse guarantees on the table size). The additive stretch and the table size bounds rely on a node partition of G and a clustering of it. An (r, σ)-*cell partition* of $G = (V, E)$ is a partition $\{V_i\}$ of its node-set V into σ parts such that each V_i, called *cell*, contains at least $r/2$ nodes and induces a subgraph of radius at most r. By definition, every (r, σ)-cell partition requires $\sigma \leq 2n/r$. A (δ, τ)-*clustering* of a cell partition $\{V_i\}$ is a collection $\{C_i\}$ of connected subgraphs of G, called *clusters*, such that:

1. every node of G belongs to at most δ clusters;
2. the tree-width of any cluster is at most τ; and
3. for every cell V_i there is a cluster C_i containing all shortest paths in G between nodes of V_i.

Thus, every shortest path in the subgraph C_i between two nodes of V_i is a shortest path in G.

The features of our general scheme are summarized as follows:

THEOREM 4. *Given an (r, σ)-cell partition with (δ, τ)-clustering of a connected unweighted graph with n nodes, one can construct in polynomial time a labeled routing scheme time with $o(\lg^2 n)$-bit addresses, table size $\tilde{O}(\sigma/r + \delta\tau)$, and additive stretch $O(r \lg \sigma)$.*

Let us first show that Theorem 3 is a direct corollary of Theorem 4.

It is not difficult to see that every connected graph G has an $(r, 2n/r)$-cell partition constructible efficiently (see Lemma 2 in Appendix B). Then, if G has linear local tree-width, we can construct a $(O(\lg n), O(r \lg n))$-clustering based on a *sparse cover* of G, a notion introduced by Awerbuch and Peleg [9], closely related to the (δ, τ)-clustering definition.

A (ρ, d, s)-*sparse cover* is a collection of connected subgraphs $\{G_i\}$ of G such that:

1. every node of G belongs to at most d subgraphs;
2. the radius of each G_i is at most $s\rho$; and
3. for each node of G at least one G_i contains all neighbors within distance ρ;

---

[5] That is the graphs excluding some apices as minor. An apex is a graph with one vertex whose removal leaves a planar graph. K_5 and $K_{3,3}$ are apices, so planar graphs are apex-minor-free.

For general graphs and for any k, ρ there are polynomial-time constructions of $(\rho, O(kn^{1/k}), 2k-1)$-sparse covers. This leads to the construction of $(\rho, O(\lg n), O(\lg n))$-sparse covers by taking $k = \lg n$. Sparse covers can be refined for planar graphs [15], minor-free graphs [5], and graphs of bounded doubling dimension [2]. All these graphs support $(\rho, O(1), O(1))$-sparse covers.

An important observation is that, if G has local tree-width $\tau(r)$, then a $(2r, d, s)$-sparse cover is also a $(d, \tau(2rs))$-clustering (see Lemma 3 in Appendix C). Choosing $d = s = O(\lg n)$, it follows that G has an $(O(\lg n), \tau(O(r \lg n)))$-clustering, which, by linearity of τ, is a $(O(\lg n), O(r \lg n))$-clustering.

In particular, plugging $r = n^{1/3}$ in Theorem 4, wet get $\sigma = O(n^{2/3})$, $\tau = O(n^{1/3} \lg n)$, and $\delta = O(\lg n)$. The additive stretch is $O(r \lg \sigma) = \tilde{O}(n^{1/3})$ and the routing tables have length $\tilde{O}(\sigma/r + \delta\tau) = \tilde{O}(n^{1/3})$, as claimed.

The remainder of this section is dedicated to prove Theorem 4.

3.1 Overview of the Scheme

We start with any (r, σ)-cell partition $\{V_i\}$ and a (δ, τ)-clustering $\{G_i\}$ of G. With each cell V_i, we associate a rooted spanning tree of $G[V_i]$, denoted by T_i, and of depth no more than r. The root of T_i, denoted by c_i, is called the *center* of V_i.

The address of any node u of G is a pair (i, ℓ_u) composed of the unique index i such that $u \in V_i$, and a label ℓ_u allowing shortest-path routing in the tree T_i. According to [31, 55], given the labels ℓ_u, ℓ_v of nodes $u, v \in T_i$, it is possible to compute the next hop on the unique path from u to v in T_i, i.e., the port number leading to a neighbor of u on the path towards v. The length of ℓ_u is $O(\lg^2 |V_i| / \lg\lg |V_i|)$ bits, and thus the length of the address (i, ℓ_u) is $o(\lg^2 n)$ bits.[6]

As one component of our scheme, each node uses a *local* shortest-path routing scheme for all targets in its cluster. A node thus stores the routing information for this local scheme for each cluster C_i it belongs to. Recall that, by definition of the clustering, each node is in at most δ clusters. Tables for these local routing schemes require $o(\tau \lg^2 n)$ bits. Routing between nodes in the same cell is achieved by these local routing schemes as we guarantee that any shortest path between two nodes in the same cell is totally contained in at least one cluster. Note that the shortest paths between nodes of a cell (as opposed to a cluster) may leave and re-enter the cell multiple times.

Routing between different cells (say between two cell centers) is achieved by encoding (in the message header) a summary — which we call *trail* — of a "cell path." As paths within cells are handled by the local routing schemes, trails only encode the inter-cell edges of the cell path. A source center has $\sigma - 1$ potential target centers, and each trail may contain $\Omega(\sigma)$ edges. Remembering all these trails potentially requires $\Omega(\sigma^2)$ bits. Since this quantity is too much for one source center, we use a specific collection of trails

---

[6]In this paper, we assume that port numbers of all the edges are fixed (by some adversary) before the labeling of the tree. The label length can be reduced to $(1 + o(1)) \lg_2 |V_i|$ if the designer of the scheme is allowed to permute the port numbers of T_i. In this model, and since all the trees are disjoint, the address length is only $(1 + o(1)) \lg_2 n$ bits by ordering cells according to their number of nodes, so that (i, ℓ_u) has length $\lg_2 (i) + (1 + o(1)) \lg_2 (n/i)$.

(simultaneously for all target centers) that can collectively be encoded within $\tilde{O}(\sigma)$ bits. This is done at the price of increasing the additive stretch of the trails.

Tables of each node are restricted to roughly $\tilde{O}(\sigma/r)$ bits, which is r times less than the information required to store all the trails originating at a given source center. As a first step, a particular routing scheme is in charge of *collecting* the routing information, distributed to $\Omega(r)$ nodes within the cell. Since cells have $\geq r/2$ nodes, and radius $O(r)$, the scheme can use a walk of length $O(r)$ to collect all the information.

Then, the trail leading to the target is extracted form this routing information, and the message is sent along the trail. The message is routed between the trail edges using the local routing scheme (inside the clusters).

Summary.

When sending a message from $s \in V_i$ to $t \in V_j$, the following steps are performed (see also Figure 2):

1. from s we route to its center c_i using tree T_i;

2. the routing table of node c_i contains the encoding of a walk of length $O(r)$, which we follow to collect the $\tilde{O}(\sigma)$ bits of routing information on trails (Section 3.3);

3. from the address of t we extract its center c_j, to which we compute the trail from the information collected at c_i (Section 3.2);

4. we route the message along the trail from c_i to c_j by alternatively using edges of the trail and the local routing schemes; and

5. we route to the final destination t using tree T_j.

3.2 Trail Routing

We assume that the routing task is to send messages between centers only, i.e., we skip Step 1 and 5 of the general routing scheme. The routing between arbitrary nodes reduces to this problem, up to additive stretch $O(r)$ using the trees within the cell.

We consider a source center $c_s \in V_s$. Let T be any tree rooted at c_s spanning all the centers of the partition. For a tree T we define two parameters important for the analysis of our scheme: its *distortion*, and its number of *gates*. Tree T has distortion d if for every center c, $d_T(c_s, c) \leq d_G(c_s, c) + d$. A node u in cell V_i is a *gate* if $u = c_i$, or u has neither a proper ancestor nor a proper descendant in V_i. In other words, on the path from c_s to u in T, u is either the first node entering V_i or the last node leaving V_i.

Routing from c_s to any destination center $c_t \in V_t$ can be done using the subpath from c_s to c_t in T, denoted by $T[c_t]$. The *trail* of $T[c_t]$ is the sequence of gates encountered from c_s to c_t.

Consider two consecutive gates of the trail of $T[c_t]$. If u, v belong to the same cluster V_i, then the routing from u to v is performed using the local routing scheme in cluster C_i (see Lemma 4 in Appendix D). It uses shortest paths, and tables of $\tilde{O}(\tau)$ bits per node in C_i, and requires a piece of *advice* of $o(\lg^2 n)$ bits about u, v. This advice is attached to the trail collected at c_s. If u, v belong to different cells, then they must be adjacent, and the port number of this edge is also attached to the trail. Therefore, the information required at c_s only depends on the number of gates in $T[c_t]$.

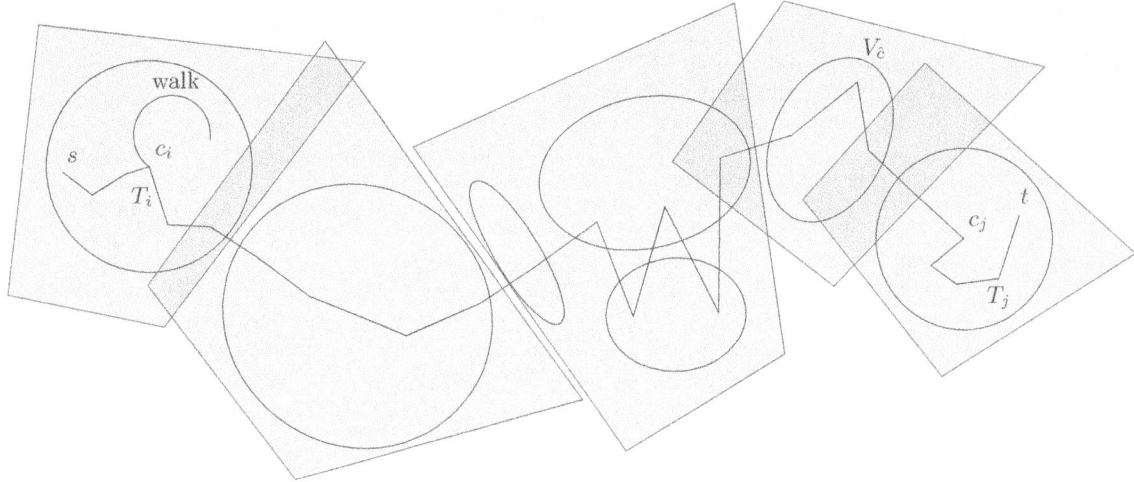

Figure 2: Trail Routing Example: from source s to center c_i on tree T_i, on walk to collect routing information, on *trail* to c_j using the internal scheme within cells and gates between cells, and then on T_j to t.

If T is constructed as a shortest-path tree (without any distortion), it may occur that $T[c_s]$ contains $\Omega(\sigma)$ gates. The number of gates for T can also be as large as $\Theta(\sigma^2)$. This is due to the fact that many paths of T can cross the same cell using different gates. For our purposes, this would be too large. Clearly, there are trees with only $O(\sigma)$ gates, based on spanning trees of the cell graph (nodes correspond to cells, nodes corresponding to neighboring cells are connected by an edge). However, such trees with $O(\sigma)$ gates may have a very large distortion.

The goal of this section is to show that there are trees with both small distortion and only few gates. More precisely, we prove the following.

LEMMA 1. *For every center c, there is a tree rooted at c spanning all the centers with distortion $O(r \lg \sigma)$ and with $O(\sigma \lg \sigma)$ gates.*

PROOF. We fix a center $c \in C$, we run a breadth-first search in G from c and we cut all subtrees that do not contain any center $c' \in C$. Let B denote this tree (spanning C). Although the number of clusters is $|C| = \sigma$, the number of gates may be $\Omega(n)$. For each center $c' \in C$ there is a unique path $T_{c,c'}$ in B from c to c'.

Intuition: to reduce the number of gates, we *merge* some paths at each cluster such that

- each path gets merged with another path at most $\lceil \lg_2 \sigma \rceil$ times, and

- the number of gates from any cluster towards the root is at most $\lceil \lg_2 \sigma \rceil$.

The *merge* operation works as follows: given two paths $T_{c,c'}, T_{c,c''}$ to be merged at a cluster $V_{\hat{c}}$, we keep $T_{c,c'}$ and we replace $T_{c,c''}$ by the concatenation of three paths:

1. the first part of the path $T_{c,c'}$ before it enters $V_{\hat{c}}$ at gate g',

2. the second part of the path $T_{c,c''}$ after it leaves $V_{\hat{c}}$ at gate g'', and

3. any path of length $\le 2r$ in $V_{\hat{c}}$ (not necessarily in B) connecting g' to g''.

We use the best gate g'' to leave $V_{\hat{c}}$ but we may use a suboptimal gate g' to enter $V_{\hat{c}}$ since the first part of $T_{c,c'}$ is not necessarily optimal for c''. Using the wrong edge to enter $V_{\hat{c}}$ adds a detour of length at most $2r + 2r$, where $2r$ is the diameter of $V_{\hat{c}}$ and another $2r$ is from the potential detour going through g' (using the triangle inequality).

Note that all the gates of $T_{c,c''}$ above $V_{\hat{c}}$ are not needed anymore (as long as they do not appear in other paths) since $T_{c,c''}$ has been merged with $T_{c,c'}$.

We now describe *which paths* to merge. We assign a weight to each path T, corresponding to the number of centers reached through T. At the beginning, all the weights are set to 1. Throughout the merge process, all the weights are powers of two. We start at all the leafs of B (the centers) and merge while proceeding towards the root. Whenever we are at a cluster $V_{\hat{c}}$ where two paths T_1, T_2 with the same weight 2^i meet, we merge them. In this merge, path T_1 is assigned weight $2^i + 2^i = 2^{i+1}$ (and T_2 is not considered anymore). This merging process might continue recursively until all the paths going out of $V_{\hat{c}}$ towards the root have distinct weights. Consequently, at most $\lceil \lg_2 \sigma \rceil$ trails can proceed towards the root, providing a bound on the number of gates towards the root. Since each cell has at most $\lceil \lg_2 \sigma \rceil$ gates towards the root, the total number of gates is at most $O(\sigma \lg \sigma)$.

Since each path is merged at most $\lceil \lg_2 \sigma \rceil$ times (at most once for each i), the length of the path has distortion at most $O(r \lg \sigma)$, as claimed. $\square$

3.3 Collecting the Routing Information

By definition of the (r, σ)-cell partition, each cell contains at least $r/2$ nodes and induces a subgraph of radius at most r. We distribute the routing information evenly among $r/2$ nodes on a walk of length r from the center (using an Euler tour of a tree spanning the $r/2$ closest nodes of the center).

230

4. CONCLUSION

We prove that routing with additive stretch requires large table sizes — even for graphs as restricted as planar graphs. Routing thus requires a lot of information stored in large tables even for sparse graphs. The existence of dense graphs with large girth was not the only reason for the "hardness" of compact routing. Our lower bounds separate spanner problems from routing problems and give a reason why not more additive routing schemes have been found yet.

Despite these negative results we also provide a new additive compact routing scheme that almost matches the lower bound for planar graphs. Our scheme is also the first additive routing scheme for planar graphs (and, more generally, graphs with linear local tree-width), for which there are compact routing schemes with multiplicative stretch $1 + \epsilon$ and table sizes $\tilde{O}(\epsilon^{-1})$ bits. By our new lower bound we now know that tables of this size imply additive stretch $\tilde{\Omega}(\sqrt{\epsilon n})$.

Although the stretch-space tradeoff of our new scheme almost matches the lower bound, there is also room for improvement: our scheme is rather complicated and the header length is not yet satisfactory (also, headers may require updates on the way). Our lower bound currently does not incorporate headers. The upper bound almost matches the bound on all the parameters involved. Modeling and giving lower bounds on headers remains an open problem.

5. REFERENCES

[1] I. Abraham and C. Gavoille. Object location using path separators. In *Proceedings of the Twenty-Fifth Annual ACM Symposium on Principles of Distributed Computing, PODC 2006, Denver, CO, USA, July 23-26, 2006*, pages 188–197, 2006.

[2] I. Abraham, C. Gavoille, A. V. Goldberg, and D. Malkhi. Routing in networks with low doubling dimension. In *26th IEEE International Conference on Distributed Computing Systems (ICDCS 2006), 4-7 July 2006, Lisboa, Portugal*, page 75, 2006.

[3] I. Abraham, C. Gavoille, and D. Malkhi. Compact routing for graphs excluding a fixed minor. In *DISC*, pages 442–456, 2005.

[4] I. Abraham, C. Gavoille, D. Malkhi, N. Nisan, and M. Thorup. Compact name-independent routing with minimum stretch. *ACM Transactions on Algorithms*, 4(3), 2008. Announced at SPAA 2004.

[5] I. Abraham, C. Gavoille, D. Malkhi, and U. Wieder. Strong-diameter decompositions of minor free graphs. In *SPAA 2007: Proceedings of the 19th Annual ACM Symposium on Parallel Algorithms and Architectures, San Diego, California, USA, June 9-11, 2007*, pages 16–24, 2007.

[6] I. Althöfer, G. Das, D. P. Dobkin, D. Joseph, and J. Soares. On sparse spanners of weighted graphs. *Discrete & Computational Geometry*, 9:81–100, 1993.

[7] M. Arias, L. Cowen, K. A. Laing, R. Rajaraman, and O. Taka. Compact routing with name independence. *SIAM J. Discrete Math.*, 20(3):705–726, 2006. Announced at SPAA 2003.

[8] B. Awerbuch, A. B. Noy, N. Linial, and D. Peleg. Improved routing strategies with succinct tables. *Journal of Algorithms*, 11(3):307–341, 1990.

[9] B. Awerbuch and D. Peleg. Sparse partitions (extended abstract). In *31st Annual Symposium on Foundations of Computer Science, 22-24 October 1990, St. Louis, Missouri, USA*, pages 503–513, 1990.

[10] S. Baswana, T. Kavitha, K. Mehlhorn, and S. Pettie. Additive spanners and (α, β)-spanners. *ACM Transactions on Algorithms*, 7(1), Nov. 2010.

[11] F. Bazzaro and C. Gavoille. Localized and compact data-structure for comparability graphs. *Discrete Mathematics*, 309(11):3465–3484, June 2009.

[12] B. Bollobás, D. Coppersmith, and M. L. Elkin. Sparse distance preservers and additive spanners. In *Symposium on Discrete Algorithms (SODA)*, 2003.

[13] A. Brady and L. J. Cowen. Compact routing on power law graphs with additive stretch. In 8th *Workshop on Algorithm Engineering and Experiments (ALENEX)*, pages 119–128, Jan. 2006.

[14] A. Brady and L. J. Cowen. Exact distance labelings yield additive-stretch compact routing schemes. In 20th *International Symposium on Distributed Computing (DISC)*, volume 4167 of Lecture Notes in Computer Science, pages 339–354. Springer, Sept. 2006.

[15] C. Busch, R. LaFortune, and S. Tirthapura. Improved sparse covers for graphs excluding a fixed minor. In *Proceedings of the Twenty-Sixth Annual ACM Symposium on Principles of Distributed Computing,*

PODC 2007, Portland, Oregon, USA, August 12-15, 2007, pages 61–70, 2007.

[16] W. Chen, C. Sommer, S.-H. Teng, and Y. Wang. Compact routing in power-law graphs. In *Distributed Computing, 23rd International Symposium, DISC 2009, Elche, Spain, September 23-25, 2009. Proceedings*, pages 379–391, 2009.

[17] V. D. Chepoi, F. F. Dragan, B. Estellon, M. Habib, and Y. Vaxès. Additive spanners and distance and routing labeling schemes for hyperbolic graphs, 2009. preprint.

[18] V. D. Chepoi, F. F. Dragan, and Y. Vaxès. Distance and routing labeling schemes for non-positively curved plane graphs. *Journal of Algorithms*, 61(2):60–88, 2006.

[19] E. Cohen. Fast algorithms for constructing t-spanners and paths with stretch t. *SIAM Journal on Computing*, 28(1):210–236, 1998. Announced at FOCS 1993.

[20] L. Cowen. Compact routing with minimum stretch. *Journal of Algorithms*, 38(1):170–183, 2001. Announced at SODA 1999.

[21] E. D. Demaine and M. Hajiaghayi. Equivalence of local treewidth and linear local treewidth and its algorithmic applications. In 14th *Symposium on Discrete Algorithms (SODA)*, pages 840–849. ACM-SIAM, Jan. 2004.

[22] E. D. Demaine, M. Hajiaghayi, and K. Kawarabayashi. Approximation algorithms via structural results for apex-minor-free graphs. In 36th *International Colloquium on Automata, Languages and Programming (ICALP)*, volume 5555 of Lecture Notes in Computer Science, pages 316–327. Springer, July 2009.

[23] Y. Dourisboure. Compact routing schemes for bounded tree-length graphs and for k-chordal graphs. In *Distributed Computing, 18th International Conference, DISC 2004, Amsterdam, The Netherlands, October 4-7, 2004, Proceedings*, pages 365–378, 2004.

[24] Y. Dourisboure and C. Gavoille. Improved compact routing scheme for chordal graphs. In *Distributed Computing, 16th International Conference, DISC 2002, Toulouse, France, October 28-30, 2002 Proceedings*, pages 252–264, 2002.

[25] F. F. Dragan and I. Lomonosov. On compact and efficient routing in certain graph classes. *Discrete Applied Mathematics*, 155(11):1458–1470, 2007.

[26] F. F. Dragan, C. Yan, and D. G. Corneil. Collective tree spanners and routing in AT-free related graphs. In 30th *International Workshop on Graph-Theoretic Concepts in Computer Science (WG)*, volume 3353 of Lecture Notes in Computer Science. Springer, June 2004. 68-80.

[27] M. L. Elkin and D. Peleg. $(1 + \epsilon, \beta)$-spanner constructions for general graphs. *SIAM Journal on Computing*, 33(3):608–631, 2004.

[28] M. Enachescu, M. Wang, and A. Goel. Reducing maximum stretch in compact routing. In *INFOCOM 2008. 27th IEEE International Conference on Computer Communications, Joint Conference of the IEEE Computer and Communications Societies, 13-18 April 2008, Phoenix, AZ, USA*, pages 336–340, 2008.

[29] D. Eppstein. Diameter and treewidth in minor-closed graph families. *Algorithmica*, 27(3):275–291, 2000.

[30] U. Feige, M. T. Hajiaghayi, and J. R. Lee. Improved approximation algorithms for minimum weight vertex separators. *SIAM J. Comput.*, 38(2):629–657, 2008. Announced at STOC 2005.

[31] P. Fraigniaud and C. Gavoille. Routing in trees. In *Automata, Languages and Programming, 28th International Colloquium, ICALP 2001, Crete, Greece, July 8-12, 2001, Proceedings*, pages 757–772, 2001.

[32] P. Fraigniaud and C. Gavoille. A space lower bound for routing in trees. In *STACS 2002, 19th Annual Symposium on Theoretical Aspects of Computer Science, Antibes - Juan les Pins, France, March 14-16, 2002, Proceedings*, pages 65–75, 2002.

[33] P. Fraigniaud, E. Lebhar, and L. Viennot. The inframetric model for the internet. In 27th *Annual IEEE Conference on Computer Communications (INFOCOM)*, pages 1085–1093, Apr. 2008.

[34] G. N. Frederickson and R. Janardan. Designing networks with compact routing tables. *Algorithmica*, 3:171–190, 1988.

[35] C. Gavoille. Routing in distributed networks: overview and open problems. *SIGACT News*, 32(1):36–52, 2001.

[36] C. Gavoille and M. Gengler. Space-efficiency of routing schemes of stretch factor three. *Journal of Parallel and Distributed Computing*, 61(5):679–687, 2001.

[37] C. Gavoille and N. Hanusse. Compact routing tables for graphs of bounded genus. In *Automata, Languages and Programming, 26th International Colloquium, ICALP'99, Prague, Czech Republic, July 11-15, 1999, Proceedings*, pages 351–360, 1999.

[38] C. Gavoille, M. Katz, N. A. Katz, C. Paul, and D. Peleg. Approximate distance labeling schemes. In *Algorithms - ESA 2001, 9th Annual European Symposium, Aarhus, Denmark, August 28-31, 2001, Proceedings*, pages 476–487, 2001.

[39] C. Gavoille and D. Peleg. The compactness of interval routing for almost all graphs. *SIAM Journal on Computing*, 31(3):706–721, 2001.

[40] C. Gavoille, D. Peleg, S. Pérennes, and R. Raz. Distance labeling in graphs. *J. Algorithms*, 53(1):85–112, 2004. Announced at SODA 2001.

[41] C. Gavoille and S. Pérennès. Memory requirement for routing in distributed networks. In 15th *Annual ACM Symposium on Principles of Distributed Computing (PODC)*, pages 125–133. ACM Press, May 1996.

[42] K. Iwama and A. Kawachi. Compact routing with stretch factor of less than three. *IEICE Transactions*, 88-D(1):47–52, 2005. Announced at PODC 2000.

[43] K. Iwama and M. Okita. Compact routing for flat networks. In *Distributed Computing, 17th International Conference, DISC 2003, Sorrento, Italy, October 1-3, 2003, Proceedings*, pages 196–210, 2003.

[44] K. Kawarabayashi. Planarity allowing few error vertices in linear time. In 50st *Annual IEEE Symposium on Foundations of Computer Science (FOCS)*, pages 639–648. IEEE Computer Society Press, Oct. 2009.

[45] G. Konjevod, A. W. Richa, and D. Xia. Optimal scale-free compact routing schemes in networks of low

doubling dimension. In *Proceedings of the Eighteenth Annual ACM-SIAM Symposium on Discrete Algorithms, SODA 2007, New Orleans, Louisiana, USA, January 7-9, 2007*, pages 939–948, 2007.

[46] S. Kutten and D. Peleg. Fast distributed construction of small *k*-dominating sets and applications. *Journal of Algorithms*, 28(1):40–66, 1998. Announced at PODC 1995.

[47] K. A. Laing. Name-independent compact routing in trees. *Inf. Process. Lett.*, 103(2):57–60, 2007. Announced at PODC 2004.

[48] K. A. Laing and R. Rajaraman. A space lower bound for name-independent compact routing in trees. *Journal of Interconnection Networks*, 8(3):229–251, 2007. Announced at SPAA 2005.

[49] H.-I. Lu. Improved compact routing tables for planar networks via orderly spanning trees. *SIAM J. Discrete Math.*, 23(4):2079–2092, 2010. Announced at COCOON 2002.

[50] D. Peleg. Proximity-preserving labeling schemes. *J. Graph Theory*, 33(3):167–176, 2000. Announced at WG 1999.

[51] D. Peleg and A. A. Schäffer. Graph spanners. *Journal of Graph Theory*, 13(1):99–116, 1989.

[52] D. Peleg and E. Upfal. A trade-off between space and efficiency for routing tables. *Journal of the ACM*, 36(3):510–530, July 1989. Announced at STOC 1988.

[53] S. Pettie. Low distortion spanners. In *Automata, Languages and Programming, 34th International Colloquium, ICALP 2007, Wroclaw, Poland, July 9-13, 2007, Proceedings*, pages 78–89, 2007.

[54] M. Thorup. Compact oracles for reachability and approximate distances in planar digraphs. *J. ACM*, 51(6):993–1024, 2004. Announced at FOCS 2001.

[55] M. Thorup and U. Zwick. Compact routing schemes. In *SPAA*, pages 1–10, 2001.

[56] M. Thorup and U. Zwick. Approximate distance oracles. *Journal of the ACM*, 52(1):1–24, 2005. Announced at STOC 2001.

[57] M. Thorup and U. Zwick. Spanners and emulators with sublinear distance errors. In *Proceedings of the Seventeenth Annual ACM-SIAM Symposium on Discrete Algorithms, SODA 2006, Miami, Florida, USA, January 22-26, 2006*, pages 802–809, 2006.

[58] D. P. Woodruff. Lower bounds for additive spanners, emulators, and more. In *47th Annual IEEE Symposium on Foundations of Computer Science (FOCS 2006), 21-24 October 2006, Berkeley, California, USA, Proceedings*, pages 389–398, 2006.

[59] D. P. Woodruff. Additive spanners in nearly quadratic time. In *37th International Colloquium on Automata, Languages and Programming (ICALP)*, volume 6198 of Lecture Notes in Computer Science (ARCoSS), pages 463–474. Springer, July 2010.

APPENDIX

A. PLANAR LOWER BOUND

Theorem 2.

For connected, unweighted bounded degree planar graphs on n nodes, any labeled routing scheme using addresses of poly-logarithmic length and routing tables of size μ bits per node has worst-case additive stretch at least $\beta = \tilde{\Omega}(\sqrt{n}/\mu)$.

PROOF. Our family of worst-case graphs is a combination of the construction for general graphs (Theorem 1, see also Fig. 1) and techniques by Abraham et al. [2]. For each pair of source s_i and target t_j there is a shortcut in the "skew mesh" *either* on the left-hand-side *or* on the right-hand-side.

"Skew mesh" construction(s).

We closely follow the exposition in [2, Theorem 7]. The final graph will be unweighted. To simplify the exposition, we begin our description with a weighted graph. Let p, q, ρ be positive integers. Let M be a $(p+1) \times (q+1)$ weighted mesh. Each edge in row i has weight $2i$ and each edge in row j has weight $2j$. Due to these weights, the unique shortest path from $(i, q+1)$ to $(p+1, j)$ consists of edges from column i and row j *only*. The shortest path length from $(i, q+1)$ to $(p+1, j)$ is $2i(q+1-j) + 2j(p+1-i)$. Let L be a mesh based on M with some "half-diagonals" (i, j) added as follows. First, each weighted edge is subdivided into two edges of length 1 and $2i-1$, respectively, where the shorter edge is assigned to the part closer to the origin $(1, 1)$. Second, independent of all other half-diagnolas, the non-identical endpoints of these adjacent edges with weight 1 (the two newly added nodes) can be connected by a new edge with weight 1. If diagonal (i, j) is included, the shortest path length from $(i, q+1)$ to $(p+1, j)$ is reduced by 1. Let R be the mesh built from M containing the half-diagonals that were not added to L. Each half-diagonal (i, j) is thus *either* in L *or* in R. The weighted graphs L, R have $\Theta(pq)$ nodes and $\Theta(pq)$ edges. In their unweighted form (by replacing each edge with integral weight w by w edges), the graphs have $\Theta(pq(p+q))$ nodes and edges. We further subdivide each edge into ρ edges — the resulting graphs have $\Theta(pq(p+q)\rho)$ nodes and edges.

In the final step, we combine these skew meshes with the construction for general graphs (proof of Theorem 1). We add p sources s_i and q targets t_j; we connect each s_i to $l_{i,q+1}$ and $r_{i,q+1}$ using a path with ρ edges and each t_j to $l_{p+1,j}$ and $r_{p+1,j}$ (also using a path with ρ edges[7]). This construction adds another $\Theta((p+q)\rho)$ nodes and edges. Now, for any source s_i and target t_j, if a message is routed using the mesh that does not contain the diagonal (i, j), the route length increases by at least ρ.

In the construction for planar graphs, we have that the number of nodes is $n = \Theta(pq \max\{p, q\}\rho)$. The lower bound changes accordingly. For poly-logarithmic α, we have $p = o(q)$ and thus $n = \Theta(pq^2\rho)$. We obtain (using Eq. (3))

$$
\begin{aligned}
p(2\rho + 1)\mu + (p+q)\alpha &\geq pq \\
\rho\mu &= \tilde{\Omega}(q) \\
\rho &= \tilde{\Omega}(\sqrt{n}/\mu).
\end{aligned}
$$

---

[7]In the construction for planar graphs, a single edge would be enough.

The statement follows since the additive stretch is at least ρ. $\square$

B. CELL PARTITION

LEMMA 2. *Every connected graph with $n \geq r/2$ nodes has a $(r, 2n/r)$-cell partition computable in polynomial time.*

PROOF. The number of parts of any (r, σ)-partition is no more $2n/r$. Consider any spanning tree T_0 of the graph and rooted at some node u_0. We greedily construct the cells of the partition as follows. Initially, we set $T := T_0$, and $i := 1$. We iteratively select a node $u \in T$ such that T_u (the subtree of T rooted at u) has depth $\leq r$ and contains $\geq r/2$ nodes. If u is found, we let $V_i := T_u$, we update T by removing T_u, and we repeat for the next cell V_{i+1}.

Clearly, all cells constructed as above satisfy the constraints on the radius and on the number of nodes. So, if T is empty at the end of the loop, then we are done. If T is not empty, we then consider the last cell created, say V_i, and u the last node selected such that $V_i = T_u$, and we update $V_i := T_u \cup T$.

Note that u is well-defined. Indeed, if no node u has been selected in T_0, then every proper subtree has $< r/2$ nodes. It follows that T_0 has depth $\leq r$ (actually depth $\leq r/2$). Since $n \geq r/2$, node u_0 could have been selected in T_0: contradiction.

Cell V_i contains T_u, so it has at least $r/2$ nodes. We need to check that the radius of V_i is $\leq r$. If the depth of T of depth is $\geq r/2$, then T must contains a node w such that T_w has depth $\leq r$ and contains $\geq r/2$ nodes (in particular a node at distance $r/2$ from a leaf of maximum depth in T). So, the depth of T is $< r/2$, and so the distance from u to u_0 is $\leq r/2$. It follows that the distance in T_0 from u to any node $w \in T$ is $\leq r$. Therefore, the radius of V_i is $\leq r$, as claimed. $\square$

C. SPARSE COVERS

LEMMA 3. *If G has local tree-width $\tau(r)$, then any $(2r, d, s)$-sparse cover is also a $(d, \tau(2rs))$-clustering of a (r, σ)-cell partition.*

PROOF. Consider a $(2r, d, s)$-sparse cover $\{G_j\}$ and $(d, \tau(2rs))$-clustering $\{C_i\}$ of G for some (r, σ)-cell partition $\{V_i\}$. It is enough to let for C_i the subgraph G_j covering the $2r$-radius ball around center $c_i \in V_i$.

Clearly, each node belongs to at most d cluster C_i. The radius of G_j is no more than $2rs$, so the tree-with of C_i is bounded by $\tau(2rs)$.

Consider any shortest path P in G between $x, y \in V_i$, and let $u \in P$. Using a path from u to c_i going thru x, we get

$$d_G(u, c_i) \leq d_P(u, x) + d_{G[V_i]}(x, c_i) \leq d_G(u, x) + r$$

since P is a shortest path in G and $G[V_i]$ has radius at most r. Similarly, using a path from u to c_i going thru y, we get $d_G(u, c_i) \leq d_G(u, y) + r$. It follows that:

$$d_G(u, c_i) \leq \min\{d_G(u, x), d_G(u, y)\} + r \leq \frac{1}{2}(d_G(u, x) + d_G(u, y)) + r.$$

We observe that $d_G(u, x) + d_G(u, y) = d_G(x, y) \leq 2r$. If follows that $d_G(u, c_i) \leq 2r$, and thus $u \in C_i$, and so path P is wholly included in C_i as required. $\square$

D. LOCAL ROUTING

LEMMA 4. *Let G be a connected (weighted) graph with n nodes and tree-with τ. There is a routing scheme for G, constructible in polynomial time, with $O(\lg n)$-bit addresses and routing tables of $\tilde{O}(\tau)$ bits such that routing from any source s to any target t can be done along a shortest path provided an advice $A(s, t)$ given at s of $O(\lg^2 n)$ bits.*

This result is based on the classical shortest path routing in tree-width τ graphs. However, the classical solution requires addresses of $\tilde{O}(\tau)$. This is too much, since we need to store target addresses for each gates of our trails. Items of only $\tilde{O}(1)$ are allowed to specify a gate.

PROOF. We first compute a decomposition of G into small pieces using balanced separators (sets of nodes separating the graph into components of size roughly half). If G has tree-width τ, then a decomposition with separators of size $O(\tau\sqrt{\lg \tau})$ can be done in polynomial time [30].

Each node u stores a hierarchy H_u of $O(\lg n)$ separators, and for each node in these separators, it stores the port number leading to it along a shortest path. In total, the routing table for u has length $O(\tau\sqrt{\lg \tau}\lg^2 n) = \tilde{O}(\tau)$ bits. The hierarchy of $O(\lg n)$ separators is chosen such that any two nodes u, v share at least one separator of the hierarchy, i.e., $H_u \cap H_v \neq \emptyset$.

Consider a shortest path P from s to t. Similarly to the cell partition (cf. Section 3), we consider each separator in the set $H_s \cup H_t$ as a cell. And, analogously, we call the first node of P entering and the last one leaving a separator a *gate*. (Note however that separators may not be disjoint.) The number of gates is at most $|H_s \cup H_t| = O(\lg n)$. Because the hierarchy is shared by all the nodes of P, it follows that a trail specifying the gates of P suffices to route, provided that every node in the graph has a routing table for all the nodes of its hierarchy of separators. Each gate can be specified with a $O(\lg n)$ identifier, so an advice $A(s, t)$ of $O(\lg^2 n)$ bits allows shortest-path routing in G from s to t along P. $\square$

Re-Chord: A Self-stabilizing Chord Overlay Network*

Sebastian Kniesburges, Andreas Koutsopoulos, Christian Scheideler
University of Paderborn
Paderborn, Germany
seppel@upb.de, koutsopo@mail.upb.de, scheideler@mail.upb.de

ABSTRACT

The Chord peer-to-peer system is considered, together with CAN, Tapestry and Pastry, as one of the pioneering works on peer-to-peer distributed hash tables (DHT) that inspired a large volume of papers and projects on DHTs as well as peer-to-peer systems in general. Chord, in particular, has been studied thoroughly, and many variants of Chord have been presented that optimize various criteria. Also, several implementations of Chord are available on various platforms. Though Chord is known to be very efficient and scalable and it can handle churn quite well, no protocol is known yet that guarantees that Chord is self-stabilizing, i.e., the Chord network can be recovered from any initial state in which the network is still weakly connected. This is not too surprising since it is known that in the Chord network it is not locally checkable whether its current topology matches the correct topology. We present a slight extension of the Chord network, called Re-Chord (reactive Chord), that turns out to be locally checkable, and we present a self-stabilizing distributed protocol for it that can recover the Re-Chord network from any initial state, in which the n peers are weakly connected, in $\mathcal{O}(n \log n)$ communication rounds. We also show that our protocol allows a new peer to join or an old peer to leave an already stable Re-Chord network so that within $\mathcal{O}((\log n)^2)$ communication rounds the Re-Chord network is stable again.

Categories and Subject Descriptors

G.2.2 [**Discrete Mathematics**]: Graph Theory—*graph algorithms, network problems*; E.1 [**Data**]: Data Structures—*Distributed Data Structures*; C.2.1 [**Computer Communication Networks**]: Network Architecture and Design—*Distributed networks*

General Terms

Algorithms, Theory, Reliability

Keywords

Chord, peer-to-peer networks, self-stabilizing protocols

*Partially supported by DFG grant SCHE 1592/1-1.

1. INTRODUCTION

Peer-to-peer systems have received a lot of attention in the past years as they have many interesting applications including social networks, file sharing, streaming, instant messaging or VoIP. In research, the pioneering and most influential systems are usually considered to be Chord [28], CAN [24], Pastry [25] and Tapestry [30]. The networks of these systems have in common that they have a low diameter and degree while being quite robust to churn. However, no self-stabilizing protocol is known for any of these four, i.e., no distributed protocol is known for these that can recover the desired topology from any weakly connected state. Self-stabilization is important as unusually high churn, network partitions or adversarial behavior may push these networks into a state from which they cannot recover using the known protocols. In this paper we present Re-Chord, a self-stabilizing variant of the Chord network [28]. We will show that efficient self-stabilization is possible for Re-Chord while maintaining the advantages of the Chord network.

1.1 The Chord network and its variants

The Chord system was introduced in an influential paper by Stoica, Morris, Karger, Kaashoek and Balakrishnan [28]. Chord is basically a combination of a hypercubic network with an indexing method called consistent hashing [16]. The Chord overlay network is defined as follows. Let U be the space of all peer addresses and $V \subseteq U$ be the current set of peers (also called *nodes* in the following) with $n = |V|$. There is a (pseudo-)random hash function $h : U \to [0, 1)$ (in Chord, SHA-1) that assigns to each node v an *identifier* $h(v)$ uniformly at random from the $[0, 1)$-interval. The basic structure of Chord is formed by a directed cycle, the so-called *Chord ring*, in which each node connects to its closest successor in the identifier space, where the $[0, 1)$-interval is considered to form a ring. In addition to this, every node v has edges to nodes $p_i(v)$, called *fingers*, with

$$p_i(v) = \text{argmin}\{w \in V \mid h(w) \geq h(v) + 1/2^i (\text{mod } 1)\}$$

for every $1 \leq i \leq m$, so that $h(v) + 1/2^m (\text{mod } 1) \leq h(succe-ssor(v)) \leq h(v) + 1/2^{m-1} (\text{mod } 1)$. If there is no node $w \in V$ with $h(w) \geq h(v) + 1/2^i (\text{mod } 1)$, then the node $w \in V$ with smallest identifier is chosen. In order to route a message from node u to node w, the Chord overlay network uses a path $p(u, v)$ consisting of a sequence of nodes $v_0, v_1, v_2, \ldots, v_\ell$ with the property that $v_0 = u$, for all $j \in \{0, \ldots, \ell-1\}$, $v_{j+1} = p_{i_j}(v_j)$ where i_j is the smallest integer so that $h(v_{j+1}) \leq h(w)$, and $v_{\ell-1}$ is the first node that has a successor pointer to w. Hence, the path basically represents a binary search strategy and can be shown to be of length at most $\mathcal{O}(\log n)$ with high probability (given that the nodes have random identifiers).

Several variants of Chord have already been studied since the presentation of the Chord network. In [18] a variant called EPI Chord is presented that allows the system to do parallel searches for the best route to the node storing the data for a certain search key. This does not improve the asymptotical worst-case cost of $\mathcal{O}(\log n)$ messages of Chord but it can achieve $\mathcal{O}(1)$ hop lookup performance under lookup intensive workloads due to caching. In [20] another modification of Chord is presented. In this approach Chord is extended by symmetric fingers, hence one can search in both directions of the circle. A similar idea is given in [15] and [29], where links to the predecessors are stored instead of only links to the successors of a node. In [29] also the physical distance is taken into account to estimate the shortest route. All these variants only care about the lookup cost, but present no self-stabilizing process to maintain the Chord structure. In [21] an algorithm is presented to build a Chord network from scratch in $\mathcal{O}(\log n)$ rounds, but still this algorithm is not self-stabilizing.

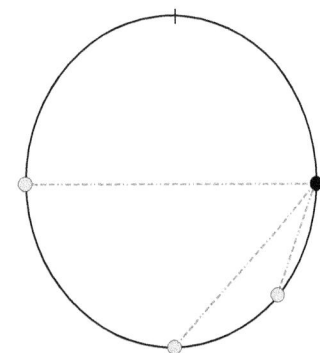

Figure 1: A real node (black) has its virtual nodes (fingers) at distance $1/2^k$ away from itself, at the clockwise direction.

1.2 Other related work

There is a large body of literature on how to maintain peer-to-peer networks efficiently, e.g., [1, 2, 4, 25, 11, 17, 19, 22, 24, 28, 26]. While many results are already known on how to keep an overlay network in a legal state, not much is known about self-stabilizing overlay networks. In the field of self-stabilization, researchers are interested in algorithms that are guaranteed to eventually converge to a desirable system state from any initial configuration. The idea of self-stabilization in distributed computing first appeared in a classical paper by E.W. Dijkstra in 1974 [8] in which he looked at the problem of self-stabilization in a token ring. Since Dijkstra's paper, self-stabilization has been studied in many contexts, including communication protocols, graph theory problems, termination detection, clock synchronization, and fault containment. For a survey see, e.g., [5, 9, 12].

Interestingly, though self-stabilizing distributed computing has received a lot of attention for many years, the problem of designing self-stabilizing networks has attracted much less attention. The universal techniques known for distributed computing in static networks (like logging) are not applicable here as they have not been designed to actively perform local topology changes (network changes are only considered as faults or dynamics not under the control of the algorithm). In order to recover scalable overlays from any initial graph, researchers have started with simple non-scalable line and ring networks. The Iterative Successor Pointer Rewiring Protocol [7] and the Ring Network [27] organize the nodes in a sorted

ring. In [23], Onus et al. present a local-control strategy called linearization for converting an arbitrary connected graph into a sorted list. Clouser et al. [6] formulate a variant of the linearization technique for asynchronous systems in order to design a self-stabilizing skip list. Gall et al. [10] discuss models that capture the parallel time complexity of locally self-stabilizing networks that avoids bottlenecks and contention. Jacob et al. [14] generalize insights gained from graph linearization to two dimensions and present a self-stabilizing construction for Delaunay graphs. In another paper, Jacob et al. [13] present a self-stabilizing variant of the skip graph and show that it can recover its network topology from any weakly connected state in $\mathcal{O}(\log^2 n)$ communication rounds with high probability. In [3] the authors present a general framework for the self-stabilizing construction of any overlay network. However, the algorithm requires the knowledge of the 2-hop neighborhood for each node and involves the construction of a clique. In that way, failures at the structure of the overlay network can easily be detected and repaired.

1.3 Our contributions

In this paper we present Re-Chord, a self-stabilizing variant of Chord. The self-stabilization mechanism is purely local in that a node only has to inspect its local state in order for the algorithm to work. No global knowledge of the network is needed. Our main result is the following.

THEOREM 1.1. *Re-Chord stabilizes after $O(n \log n)$ rounds from any weakly connected state w.h.p. The final state of Re-Chord contains Chord as a subgraph, so it can faithfully emulate any applications on top of Chord.*

Moreover, isolated join and leave requests can be handled in $\mathcal{O}(\log^2 n)$ resp. $\mathcal{O}(\log n)$ rounds with the self-stabilization mechanism of Re-Chord.

1.4 Organization of the Paper

The paper is organized as follows: In Section 2 a formal presentation of the self-stabilization rules is given. In Section 3 we prove that our rules indeed lead the network into a stable state, and in Section 4 we analyze the steps needed for the network to recover after a peer joins or leaves the network. In Section 5 we present our simulation results and, finally, in Section 6 we derive our conclusions.

2. THE RE-CHORD NETWORK

2.1 Our model

We model the overlay network as a directed graph $G = (V, E)$ where $|V| = n$. Each node is assumed to have a unique identifier, a real number in $[0, 1)$ that is immutable. For simplicity, we assume that time proceeds in synchronous rounds, and all messages generated in round i are delivered simultaneously at the end of round i. So we are using the standard synchronous message-passing model. In each round, each node can only inspect its own state. Beyond that, a node does not know anything, including the current size of the overlay network. Only local topology changes are allowed, i.e., a node may decide to cut a link to a neighbor or ask two of its neighbors to establish a link. The decisions to cut or establish links are controlled through actions (which we will also call rules) that we define more precisely later in this section.

When using the synchronous message-passing model, the global state of the system at the beginning of each round is well-defined. A computation is a sequence of states such that for each state s_i

at the beginning of round i, the next state s_{i+1} is obtained after executing all actions that were fired in round i and receiving all messages that they generated. We call a distributed algorithm *self-stabilizing* if from any initial state in which the overlay network is weakly connected, i.e. it forms a weakly connected directed graph (so that a legal state is still reachable), it eventually reaches a legal state in which no more state changes are taking place in the nodes. In our context, a legal state corresponds to the desired Re-Chord topology.

2.2 State of Re-Chord

In the Re-Chord network each node u representing a peer has an identifier $u_{id} \in [0, 1)$ that defines its position in the $[0, 1)$-interval. In the following $u = u_{id}$. For the *self-stabiliza-tion* process every *real* node simulates a number of *virtual nodes*. A simulated virtual node u_i belonging to a real node u has the identifier $u_i = u + \frac{1}{2^i}$ mod 1. We further define $u_0 = u$. The virtual nodes belonging to the same real node are called siblings. Given a node u, we define $m \in \mathbb{N}$ to be the maximal value such that u has no outgoing edge to a real node that is in the interval $\left[u_0, u + \frac{1}{2^m}\right]$. Then u_m is the virtual node with the smallest distance to u. In the stable Re-Chord network each node (virtual or real) has a connection to its closest left (smaller) and closest right (larger) node, as well as to closest left and closest right *real* node among all nodes in the system.

To describe the Re-Chord network and the corresponding self-stabilizing algorithm we need the following notation:

- The graph consists of three different kinds of edges: E_u denotes the set of *unmarked edges*, E_c the set of *connection edges* and E_r the set of *ring edges*. Let $E = E_u \cup E_c \cup E_r$. The graph can be a multi-graph, i.e. an edge (u, v) can be in E more than once due to different markings u, c, r.

- The graph consists of two different kinds of nodes V_r and V_v, where V_r denotes all real nodes and V_v denotes all virtual nodes. Let $V = V_r \cup V_v$.

- Let $[u, v]$ be the interval from u to v that contains all nodes w with identifiers $u < w < v$, for the case $u < v$, and identifiers w for which $w < v$ or $u < w$ for the case $u > v$. E.g. $0, 2 \in [0.8, 0.3]$, but $0.2 \notin [0.3, 0.8]$.

- Let $N_u(u_i) = \{v \in V | (u_i, v) \in E_u\}$ be the unmarked neighborhood of a node u_i (virtual or real). Let $N_r(u_i)$ and $N_c(u_i)$ be the neighborhoods given by the outgoing ring or connection edges of u_i.

- Let $S(u_i) = \{u_0, u_1, \cdots u_m\}$ be the set of siblings of a node u_i.

- Let $N(u_i) = S(u_i) \cup \left(\bigcup_{0 \leq j \leq m} N_u(u_j)\right)$ be the known neighborhood of node u_i, due to the unmarked edges only.

Note that $V_r \cap N(u_0) \neq \varnothing$ at any point in time since $u_0 \in N(u_0)$. The virtual nodes and edge sets E_u, E_r and E_c are needed for the self-stabilization process and are computed internally by every real node (peer). The final Re-Chord network is built on top of this internal graph. The Re-Chord network is a network on the real nodes. The edges in the Re-Chord network are defined by

$$E_{Re-Chord} = \left\{(u, v) \in V_r^2 : \exists i, (u_i, v) \in E_u \cup E_r\right\}$$

Chord has two kinds of edges, successor-predecessor edges that form the Chord ring, as well as fingers. In the stable state each real node in Re-Chord has an edge to its closest right and closest left real neighbor (which would be the successor and predecessor of that

node in Chord), so these edges simulate the successor-predecessor edges. In Chord, each node u has a finger edge, which connects the node with the node being the closest successor of $u + \frac{1}{2^i}$ (mod 1) (formally described in section 1.1), in a clockwise direction along a $[0, 1)$ circle, for different values of i. Re-Chord achieves the same as each real node u creates a virtual node having value $u + \frac{1}{2^i}$ (mod 1). Since this particular virtual node will be connected to the real node being the closest successor to $u + \frac{1}{2^i}$ (mod 1), this leads to the same connection as in the Chord network. Therefore, each edge of Chord is included in Re-Chord, which implies the following fact.

FACT 2.1. *In the stable state, Chord is a subgraph of Re-Chord.*

So, for each connection in Chord there is a virtual node in Re-Chord. Since each node in Re-Chord (virtual or real) has at most 4 outgoing unmarked edges (two to their closest left and right neighbors, as well as two edges to their closest left and right real neighbors) it holds that $|E_u \cup E_r| \leq 4|E_{Chord}|$, where E_{Chord} is the set of edges of Chord. We also use connection edges, which do not participate in the routing, but only serve for the self-stabilization process. As we will see, each virtual node generates $\Theta(\log(n))$ connection edges in expectation, and since the number of nodes in Re-Chord are $O(n \log(n))$ w.h.p., the expected number of connection edges is $O(n \log^2(n))$.

2.3 Self-Stabilization Rules

In the following we will define the distributed algorithm by formulating the rules carried out by every node. For each rule we will give a short informal description. and a formal definition as a set of actions. An action has the form:

$$< name >:< guard > \rightarrow < commands >$$

The $< name >$ is the label of the action, $< guard >$ is a Boolean predicate over variables of the node and the term $< commands >$ is a sequence of commands that may involve any of the variables of the executing node or its neighbors [10]. A *command* can be a direct assignment. In addition, we introduce the notion $A \leftarrow B$, where A and B are sets and $\leftarrow$ can be interpreted as a "delayed" := (assignment). That means that this assignment will only be executed right before the next round.

Note that these rules are all applied for all combinations of parameters in one round and in the order in which they are presented below, in each node (although a parallel application will not violate the correctness). In addition, if node v inserts an edge (u, w) between its neighbors $u, w \in N(v)$, then u is only aware of that edge in the next round. On the other hand, if a node v deletes an edge (v, w) the edge will not be considered in the rules for v for the rest of the same round. Note also that the rules are based on local knowledge.

Before a node applies the set of rules, it updates its variables by computing a new m, as defined above, and the new neighborhoods.

1. Virtual Nodes: Create all virtual nodes u_i, $i \leq m$ (if not existing). Delete all virtual nodes u_j, $j > m$ (if existing) as they are needless. In case a virtual node u_i is deleted, the virtual node u_m is informed about u_i's neighborhood.

   - $create - virtualnodes(u) : u_i \notin S(u) \land i \leq m \rightarrow S(u) := S(u) \cup \{u_i\}$

   - $delete - virtualnodes(u) : u_i \in S(u) \land i > m \rightarrow S(u) := S(u)/\{u_i\}, N_u(u_m) := N_u(u_m) \cup N_u(u_i) \cup N_r(u_i) \cup N_c(u_i)$

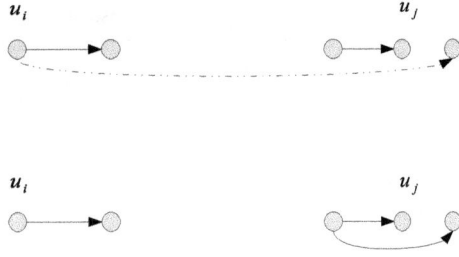

Figure 2: Nodes before and after the application of the overlapping neighborhood rule. The dotted line is an overlapping edge. After the rule the node is reassigned to another neighborhood

2. Overlapping Neighborhood: Let u be a real node. For each u_i check the neighborhood $N_u(u_i)$. If there is a $w \in N_u(u_i)$ and a $u_j \in S(u_i)$ such that $w < u_j < u_i$ or $w > u_j > u_i$, then replace (u_i, w) by (u_j, w). This is done, because u_j is closer to w and u_i is aware of this fact as u_i and u_j belong to the same real node (See Fig 2).

- $check - all - neighborhoods(u) : u_i \in S(u) \rightarrow check - neighborhood(u_i)$

- $check - neighborhood(u_i) : w \in N_u(u_i) \wedge u_j \in S(u_i) \wedge (w < u_j < u_i \vee w > u_j > u_i) \rightarrow N_u(u_j) := N_u(u_j) \cup \{w\}, N_u(u_i) := N_u(u_i)/\{w\}$

3. Closest Real Neighbor: For each u_i find the closest left and right real neighbor. Inform all neighbors in the interval between the closest real neighbors about the found closest real neighbors. We also define the closest left and right real nodes of u_i as
$r_l(u_i) = \max \{w \in N(u_i) : w \in V_r \wedge w < u_i\}$ and $r_r(u_i) = \min \{w \in N(u_i) : w \in V_r \wedge w > u_i\}$.

- $all - realneighbors(u) : u_i \in S(u) \rightarrow left - realneighbor(u_i), right - realneighbor(u_i)$

- $left - realneighbor(u_i) :$
$v = \max \{w \in N(u_i) : w \in V_r \wedge w < u_i\}, y \in N_u(u_i), y > u_i \vee v < y < u_i, v > r_l(y) \rightarrow N_u(u_i) := N_u(u_i) \cup \{v\}, N_u(y) \leftarrow N_u(y) \cup \{v\}, r_l(u_i) := v$

- $right - realneighbor(u_i) :$
$v = \min \{w \in N(u_i) : w \in V_r \wedge w > u_i\}, y \in N_u(u_i), y < u_i \vee v > y > u_i, v < r_r(y) \rightarrow N_u(u_i) := N_u(u_i) \cup \{v\}, N_u(y) \leftarrow N_u(y) \cup \{v\}, r_r(u_i) := v$

4. Linearization: For each u_i do: Sort all $w \in N_u(u_i), w < u_i$ in descending order and create edges (w_l, w_{l+1}). Sort all $w \in N_u(u_i), w > u_i$ in ascending order and create edges (w_l, w_{l+1}). We call this forwarding of an edge, because the starting point of an edge is moved to a node closer to its endpoint. Create backward edges from the closest neighbors to u_i. We call this mirroring of an edge. Note: When the mirroring rule is executed, u_i has only its two closest (left and right) neighbors, by rule 3.

- $linearize - all(u) : u_i \in S(u) \rightarrow lin - left(u_i), lin - right(u_i), mirroring(u_i)$

- $lin - left(u_i) : w, v \in N_u(u_i) \wedge v, w < u_i \wedge v = \max \{y \in N_u(u_i) : y < w\}) \rightarrow N_u(w) \leftarrow N_u(w) \cup \{v\}, N_u(u_i) := N_u(u_i)/\{v\}$

- $lin - right(u_i) : w, v \in N_u(u_i) \wedge v, w > u_i \wedge v = \min \{y \in N_u(u_i) : y > w\} \rightarrow N_u(w) \leftarrow N_u(w) \cup \{v\}, N_u(u_i) := N_u(u_i)/\{v\}$

- $mirroring(u_i) : v \in N(u_i) \rightarrow N_u(v) \leftarrow N_u(v) \cup \{u_i\}, N_u(u_i) := N_u(u_i) \cup \{r_l(u_i)\}, N_u(u_i) := N_u(u_i) \cup \{r_r(u_i)\}$

5. Ring Edge: By the linearization rule only a sorted list can be achieved. We need further rules to close the ring. We establish special marked ring edges E_r to do so. These edges are created if a node misses a right or left neighbor and assumes to be the node of maximal or minimal identifier in $[0, 1)$. The edges are directed to the node missing a neighbor, so are outgoing edges and can be forwarded by the nodes assumed to be the minimal/maximal node. For each u_i do: if the node has no right (resp. left) neighbor create a special ring edge from the smallest (resp. largest) known node $x \in N(u_i)$ to u_i. If u_i has such an outgoing ring edge, say to node w, and $w > u_i$ (resp. $w < u_i$) then create an unmarked edge (x, w) with $x \in N(u_i) \cup N_r(u_i), u_i < w < x$ (resp. $x < w < u_i$). If there is no such x create the ring edge (v, w) to the smallest (resp. largest) known $v \in N(u)$. If a x or v can be found, delete the ring edge (u_i, w).

- $create - all - ring - edges(u) : u_i \in S(u) \rightarrow create - ring - edge - left(u_i), create - ring - edge - right(u_i)$

- $create - ring - edge - left(u_i) :$
$v = \max \{x \in N(u)\} \wedge \nexists w \in N_u(u_i) : w < u_i \rightarrow N_r(v) \leftarrow \{u_i\} \cup N_r(v)$

- $create - ring - edge - right(u_i) :$
$v = \min \{x \in N(u)\} \wedge \nexists w \in N_u(u_i) : w > u_i \rightarrow N_r(v) \leftarrow \{u_i\} \cup N_r(v)$

- $forward - all - ring - edges(u) : u_i \in S(u) \rightarrow forward - ring - edge - l1(u_i), forward - ring - edge - l2(u_i), forward - ring - edge - r1(u_i), forward - ring - edge - r2(u_i)$

- $forward - ring - edge - l1(u_i) : w \in N_r(u_i) \wedge w > u_i \wedge v = \min \{x \in N(u_i)\} \wedge v \neq u_i \wedge \nexists x \in N(u_i) \cup N_r(u_i) : x > w \rightarrow N_r(v) \leftarrow \{w\} \cup N_r(v), N_r(u_i) := N_r(u_i)/\{w\}$

- $forward - ring - edge - l2(u_i) : w \in N_r(u_i) \wedge w > u_i \wedge \exists x \in N(u_i) \cup N_r(u_i) : x > w \rightarrow N_u(x) \leftarrow \{w\} \cup N_u(x), N_r(u_i) := N_r(u_i)/\{w\}$

- $forward - ring - edge - r1(u_i) : w \in N_r(u_i) \wedge w < u_i \wedge v = \max \{x \in N(u_i)\} \wedge v \neq u_i \wedge \nexists x \in N(u_i) \cup N_r(u_i) \wedge x < w \rightarrow N_r(v) \leftarrow \{w\} \cup N_r(v), N_r(u_i) := N_r(u_i)/\{w\}$

- $forward - ring - edge - r2(u_i) : w \in N_r(u_i) \wedge w < u_i \wedge \exists x \in N(u_i) \cup N_r(u_i) \wedge x < w \rightarrow N_u(x) \leftarrow \{w\} \cup N_u(x), N_r(u_i) := N_r(u_i)/\{w\}$

6. Connection Edges: We introduce another set of edges, the connection edges, which are used to ensure that all nodes are in one connected component closing possible gaps between

contiguous virtual siblings. For all neighbored virtual nodes u_i, u_j, i.e. $u_i < u_j = \min\{u_l : u_l > u_i\}$, connection edge between u_i, u_j is created. If a node u_i has an outgoing connection edge (u_i, x) it creates a new connection edge (w, x) with $w = \max\{v \in N_u(u_i) \cup S(u_i)\}$. If such an w does not exist, u_i creates a (unmarked) backward edge (x, u_i).

- $connect-virtual-nodes(u) : u_i, u_j \in S(u) \wedge u_j = \min\{u_l \in S(u), u_l > u_i\} \rightarrow N_c(u_i) := N_c(u_i) \cup \{u_j\}$

- $forward-all-cedges(u) : u_i \in S(u) \rightarrow forward-cedges-1(u_i), forward-cedges-2(u_i)$

- $forward-cedges-1(u_i) : v \in N_c(u_i) \wedge w = \max\{x \in N_u(u_i) \cup S(u_i) : x < v\} \wedge w \neq u_i \rightarrow N_c(w) \leftarrow N_c(w) \cup \{v\}, N_c(u_i) := N_c(u_i)/\{v\}$

- $forward-cedges-2(u_i) : v \in N_c(u_i) \wedge u_i = \max\{x \in N_u(u_i) \cup S(u_i) : x < v\} \wedge w = u_i \rightarrow N_u(v) \leftarrow N_u(v) \cup \{u_i\}, N_c(u_i) := N_c(u_i)/\{v\}$

3. ANALYSIS

We will frequently need the following result, which follows from standard techniques.

LEMMA 3.1. *The number of virtual nodes between two real nodes are no more than $c \log n$, where c is a constant, w.h.p.. The total number of nodes in the network is $\Theta(n \log n)$ w.h.p.*

3.1 Correctness

We will show the correctness of the algorithm given by the rules by proving our main theorem. For this we will divide the self-stabilization process into different phases and determine the correctness and running time of each phase. In our proof we will assume that the phases finish one after the other, though this does not restrict the general case, as the resulting properties of this phase hold forever once established.

3.1.1 Phase 1:Connection

First we want to ensure that all virtual and real nodes belong to the same connected component formed by unmarked edges. In the initial state the graph formed by the real nodes is weakly connected , i.e. there is an edge (u, v) in the graph given by the real nodes, if there is an edge $(u_i, v_j) \in E_r \cup E_u \cup E_c$. However the initial graph given by the virtual (including the real) nodes does not have to be weakly connected as there might be nodes u_i, u_j that are not connected. Note that this is the only case that the graph of virtual nodes is not weakly connected. We will show:

LEMMA 3.2. *After $\mathcal{O}(n \log n)$ rounds all nodes are weakly connected by unmarked edges, i.e. there is path of unmarked edges, which can be traversed in both directions, for each pair of nodes connecting them. Two contiguous virtual siblings u_i, u_j are connected by unmarked edges over nodes w with $u_i < w < u_j$.*

We will prove the lemma by proving three claims, that show that the graph becomes weakly connected by connecting all u_i, u_j and if it is weakly connected it will become weakly connected by unmarked edges.

CLAIM 3.3. *After $\mathcal{O}(n \log n)$ rounds two contiguous virtual siblings u_i, u_j are connected by unmarked edges over nodes w with $u_i < w < u_j$ w.h.p. and the graph is weakly connected.*

PROOF. The proof is given by induction over the number of pairs of contiguous virtual siblings v_i, v_j in $[u_i, u_j]$:
Basis: Let u_i, u_j be a pair of contiguous virtual siblings with either $u_j = u_{i-1}$ or $u_i = u_0, u_j = u_m$, such that there is no pair of virtual siblings $v_{i'}, v_{j'}$ in the interval $[u_i, u_j]$. According to rule 6 u_i forms a connection edge to u_j and creates a new connection edge (w_1, u_j) from $w_1 = \max\{w' \in N_u(u_i) : u_i < w' < u_j\}$ to u_j if w_1 exists. Otherwise u_i creates an unmarked backwards edge from u_j to u_i and the claim is fulfilled. Again, based on rule 6, each w_l creates a new connection edge (w_{l+1}, u_j) as long as a $w_{l+1} = \max\{w' \in N_u(w_l) : w_l < w' < u_j\}$ exists. Because there is no pair of virtual siblings $v_{i'}, v_{j'}$ in $[u_i, u_j]$, this is the only command with a true guard and all w_l and w_{l+1} are connected by unmarked edges. If for w_l $w_l + 1$ does not exist, an unmarked backward edge from u_j to w_l is created. Obviously $l \in \mathcal{O}(n \log n)$ w.h.p. Unmarked edges are never converted to ring or connection edges. Thus, either w_{l+1} remains in $N_u(w_l)$ or the edge (w_l, w_{l+1}) is substituted by a path of unmarked edges by the linearization rule.

Inductive step: Let u_i, u_j be defined as above. For all pairs v_i, v_j of contiguous virtual siblings in $[u_i, u_j]$ we know that the induction hypothesis holds. Obviously it takes at most $\mathcal{O}(n \log n)$ rounds until a backwards edge from u_j is created as this is the number of nodes w.h.p.. Let $w_1, \cdots w_l$ be defined as above. We will show that there is a connection between every pair w_l, w_{l+1}. Either $w_{l+1} \in N_u(w_l)$ or $w_{l+1} \in S(w_l)$. In the first case w_l and w_{l+1} are connected with unmarked edges over nodes w with $w_l < w < w_{l+1}$, as w_l and w_{l+1} are neighbors or the edge (w_l, w_{l+1}) is substituted by a path due to linearization. In the second case w_{l+1} is a sibling of w_l and w_l and $w_l + 1$ will be connected via unmarked edges over nodes w with $w_l < w < w_{l+1}$ by the induction hypothesis. Thus in the end all consecutive virtual nodes u_i, u_j are connected by unmarked edges over nodes w $u_i < w < u_j$. □

It might happen that for a real node u new virtual nodes are created in the self-stabilization process. Imagine that after some rounds u is informed about a closest real neighbor that is smaller than its current closest virtual node u_m. Note that this is the only case new virtual nodes are created. All other virtual nodes u_i, $i < m$ do already exist before due to rule 1 and these are eventually connected by unmarked edges by the claim above. Let u and u_m be the existing nodes and $u_{m'}$ the new created closest virtual node with $u < u_{m'} < u_m$. Initially the neighborhood $N_u(u_{m''})$ is empty for all $m' \geq m'' > m$ and so a sequence of unmarked backward edges from u_m to $u_{m'}$ over the $u_{m''}$s is formed by rule 6. The same holds for the pair $u, u_{m'}$ as u is always $u_{m'}$'s closest real neighbor according to rule 3.

CLAIM 3.4. *If a pair of nodes u_i, v_j is weakly connected only by a connection edge $(u_i, v_j) \in E_c$, after $\mathcal{O}(n \log n)$ rounds u_i, v_j are weakly connected by unmarked edges.*

The proof follows from the same arguments as the proof of 3.3.

CLAIM 3.5. *If a pair of nodes u_i, v_j is weakly connected only by a ring edge $(u_i, v_j) \in E_r$, after $\mathcal{O}(n \log n)$ rounds u_i, v_j are weakly connected by unmarked edges.*

PROOF. W.l.o.g we assume $v_j < u_i$, i.e. u_i assumes v_j is missing a left neighbor $< v_j$. From 3.4 we can assume that all nodes are weakly connected by unmarked edges or ring edges. Now there can be four cases: (1) There is a node $w_l \in N(u_i)$ with $w_l < v_j$, (2) there is a node $w_l \in N_r(u_i)$ with $w_l < u_i$ and w_l, u_i are weakly connected by unmarked edges, (3) there is a node $w_l \in N_r(u_i)$

with $w_l < u_i$ and w_l, u_i are not weakly connected by unmarked edges and (4) otherwise.

In case 1 and 2 u_i and v_j are weakly connected by unmarked edges afterwards by the rule 5. In case 3 also by rule 5 one ring edge $(u_i, v_j), (u_i, w_l)$ remains and u_i and v_j are only weakly connected by the remaining ring edge, which will be forwarded to the node $y = \max\{x \in N(u_i)\}$, i.e. $(y, v_j) \in E_r$ in the next round. In case 4 by the same rule the ring edge (u_i, v_j) will be forwarded to the node $y = \max\{x \in N(u_i)\}$. This means that in each round the ring edge is forwarded or u_i, v_j become connected by unmarked edges. If u_i, v_j do not become connected by unmarked edges after $\mathcal{O}(n \log n)$ rounds the connecting ring edge is forwarded to the largest node weakly connected to u by unmarked edges. Note that also the smallest node that is weakly connected to u_i by unmarked edges creates a ring edge. Also this ring edge will be forwarded to the largest and thus after $\mathcal{O}(n \log n)$ rounds case 2 is fulfilled and u_i, v_j are weakly connected by unmarked edges. $\square$

From the Claims 3.3, 3.4 and 3.5 follows Lemma 3.2.

3.1.2 Phase 2: Linearization

After phase 1 each pair of nodes $v, w \in V$ is connected by a not necessarily directed path of unmarked edges. We call such an path a connecting path of v and w. In this phase only the order of a node in $[0, 1)$ is relevant and not its identifier (position). We define the range of an edge to be the difference of the orders of its endpoints and the range of a path to be the difference of the maximal and minimal order of nodes in the path. Considering a pair of consecutive nodes v, w and its connecting path we will show that the range of the path can be decreased to 1 in $\mathcal{O}(n \log n)$ expected rounds, which means that at the end v and w are direct neighbors.

LEMMA 3.6. *After $\mathcal{O}(n \log n)$ rounds a pair of consecutive (in the sorted order) nodes v, w are connected by unmarked edges (v, w) and (w, v) w.h.p..*

We will show this lemma by proving two claims. We firstly look on the node of the smallest order min on the connecting path, assuming $min \neq v$ and $min \neq w$. If min has two outgoing edges $(min, x), (min, y) \in p$, (w.l.o.g. $x < y$), on the path, we will show that the path can be contracted and the range of the path is decreased. In the second claim we will show that after i rounds it takes at most $cn \log n - i$ further rounds until the minimal node on the path has two outgoing edges.

CLAIM 3.7. *Let p be a connecting path of two consecutive nodes v and w, and let min be the minimal node on the path. If min has two outgoing edges $(min, x), (min, y) \in p$, there exists another path p' that connects v, w with a minimal node $min' > min$.*

PROOF. Due to the edges (min, x) and (min, y) either the linearization rule or the overlapping neighborhood rule is applied. See Figure 3. If only the linearization rule is applied, x, y stay connected by a path of unmarked edges with nodes $> min$. Therefore, a new path can be selected connecting v, w with a new node of the smallest order $min' = x > min$. If due to the two edges (min, x) and (min, y) only the overlapping neighborhood rule is applied, (min, x) is forwarded to some min_i and (min, y) to min_j, $min_i \leq min_j$. Lemma 3.2 shows that min_i, min_j are connected by a path of unmarked edges and the path is in the interval of $[min_i, min_j]$. Then also x, y are connected by unmarked edges over nodes u with $min_i < u < min_j$. Therefore a new path connecting v, w via the nodes x, y can be constructed with a

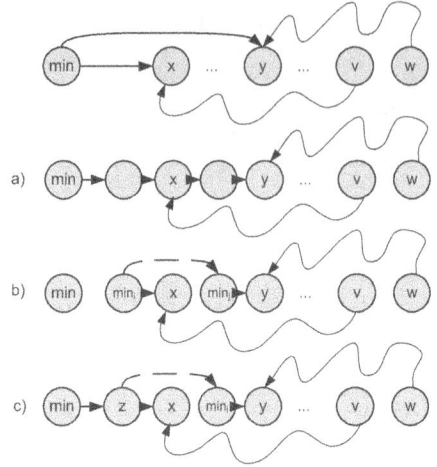

Figure 3: The three cases to increase min on the path from v to w: a)Only the linearization rule, b)only the overlapping neighborhood rule, c) linearization and the overlapping neighborhood rule

new node of minimal order $min' = min_i > min$. If the linearization and the overlapping neighborhood rule are applied, then for x the linearization rule is applied and x is connected with min over min's closest neighbor $z > min$ or x is directly connected as its closest neighbor, then $z = x$. The edge (min, y) is forwarded to min_i and y stays connected with min by Lemma 3.2. This path from min to min_i has to go over min's closest real neighbor. Therefore x, y are connected over z and a path connecting v, w can be constructed with a new minimum $min' \geq z > min$. $\square$

To show the second claim we firstly give a construction scheme for the new connecting path. Let p be the old path connecting v, w over min and let p' be the new one. The new connecting path p' is similar to p except that each edge that is forwarded due to the linearization rule can be substituted by a directed path of unmarked edges within the range of the edge due to the linearization. And each edge (u_i, x) that is forwarded to u_j in the overlapping rule can be substituted by a path within the range of the edge between the virtual siblings u_i, u_j, that exists after phase 1 due to Lemma 3.2 and an edge (u_j, x) from the virtual node u_j to x. If an edge (x, y), $x < y$ is mirrored, it is substituted by (y, x). Once min has two outgoing edges on the path the first claim holds and the formerly incoming edges of min are substituted by paths over a new min' according to the proof of Claim 3.7.

CLAIM 3.8. *After i rounds it can take at most $\max\{1, cn \log n - i\}$ rounds till an incoming edge $(x, v) \in p$ with $x > v$ results in an outgoing edge (v, x') for each node $v \in p$.*

PROOF. Proof by induction over the number of rounds i:

Basis($i=0$): The longest distance (in number of nodes on a connecting path) between two nodes on p is the total number of nodes $cn \log n$. Thus an edge can be forwarded up to $\mathcal{O}(n \log n)$ times before it is mirrored.

Inductive step($i \to i + 1$): For all edges on the connecting path p it holds (induction hypothesis) that each incoming edge will be mirrored after at most $cn \log n - i$ rounds. Let $(x, y) \in p$ be such an edge. According to rule 4 the edge is either forwarded or mirrored. An edge that is forwarded, is replaced by a subpath from x to y with all nodes in the interval (x, y) in the connecting path.

This means for all the edges (x', y') on the subpath that the range of (x', y') is less than the range of (x, y), so at most $cn \log n - i - 1$. Thus after at most $cn \log n - (i + 1)$ rounds these edges are mirrored. $\square$

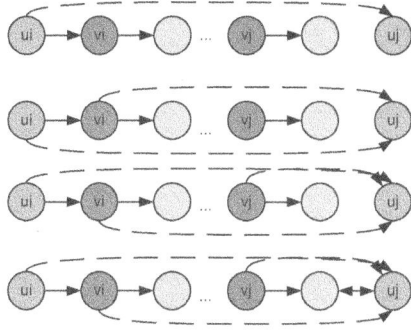

Figure 4: A sequence of connection edges to create a connection between v_i and v_j

Note that outgoing edges are only replaced by outgoing edges constructing the new connecting path p'. Obviously it follows that after i rounds the actual min can be replaced by a $min' > min$ after at most $cn \log n - i$ further rounds. Thus, after $\mathcal{O}(n \log n)$ rounds $min = v$ w.h.p. The same arguments hold for max. Thus, after $\mathcal{O}(n \log n)$ further rounds $max = w$ w.h.p. and v, w are directly connected. Notice that all other rules do not lead to a deletion of unmarked edges, so the described process is valid and two neighbored nodes that are connected will never be disconnected.

3.1.3 Phase 3: Ring

After phase 1 and phase 2 the nodes are ordered in a sorted list. To establish the Re-Chord network the nodes need to form a ring. After phase 2 each node except the minimum and the maximum nodes has a left and right neighbor. Therefore after phase 2 only these two nodes establish marked ring edges.

LEMMA 3.9. *After $\mathcal{O}(n \log n)$ rounds the nodes establish a ring sorted in clockwise order w.h.p..*

PROOF. Let max be the maximum node and min be the minimum node of all nodes. As after phase 2 we already have a sorted list max has no right neighbor and therefore establishes a marked backward edge from the smallest known node. This node is either the minimum node or has a left neighbor, and informs max about it, which will establish a new ring edge from this node to itself. After at most $\mathcal{O}(n \log n)$ rounds max is informed about min w.h.p. and creates the edge (min, max). And analogue min will create the edge (max, min). So after phase 3 all nodes form a sorted ring. $\square$

3.1.4 Phase 4: Closest Real Neighbor

After phase 1, 2 and 3 the nodes are ordered in a sorted ring, i.e. each node has its left and right closest neighbor. However what might be still wrong are the closest real neighbors of some nodes.

LEMMA 3.10. *After $\mathcal{O}(\log n)$ rounds w.h.p. every node knows its closest real neighbors.*

PROOF. Assume that between two neighbored real nodes u, v $u < v$ one node has a missing or wrong closest real neighbor instead of u or v. At least the closest neighbor of u (v) knows v and informs its neighbors (closest neighbor rule). Then after 1 round

at least two nodes know u (resp. v) as their closest real neighbor and again inform their neighbors. After $c \log n$ rounds w.h.p. all $c \log n$ (w.h.p.) nodes between u and v are informed about their correct closest real neighbors. $\square$

3.1.5 Phase 5: Finish

After the phases 1-4 the Re-Chord network is finished except some for unnecessary edges. These edges are forwarded up to $\mathcal{O}(n \log n)$ times. Unnecessary edges are edges that might be created during the self-stabilization process but are not part of the desired chord like network. E.g. a edge (u, v) is unnecessary if the edge is unmarked and u and v are no next (real) neighbors. We will show that the length of the longest unnecessary edge decreases with each round.

LEMMA 3.11. *After $\mathcal{O}(n \log n)$ rounds w.h.p. all unnecessary edges are gone.*

PROOF. Let (x, y) be one of the longest unnecessary edges. We know x and y can not be neighbored and so x forwards the edge either to one of its neighbors which exists or to one of its virtual siblings u_i. In the first case the edge is substituted by a directed path $x, x_1, x_2 \cdots, x_n, y$ over the edge to x's closest real neighbor x_1 and a path from the closest real neighbor to y. On this path could be unnecessary edges, but with length $< |(x, y)|$ as $x_i < x_i + 1$ if $y > x$ and $x_i > x_i + 1$ if $y < x$. In the second case the edge (x, y) is substituted by a path $x, x_1, x_2, \cdots, x_l = u_i, y$. The subpath $x, \cdots x_l$ consists of edges $|(x_i, x_i + 1)| = 1$, because every node knows its closest neighbor on the way to x_l. The edge (x_l, y) could be unnecessary, but with a length $< |(x, y)|$.

Assuming that an edge (x', y') with length $|(x, y)|$ is created in this round. Then there can only be three cases. There has been an edge (y', x') which is now mirrored. This can not be the case, because we already showed that every node knows its final closest neighbor. Or it could be that an edge (z', y') is forwarded to x' in the lineariziation rule or the overlapping neighborhood rule. This also can not be the case, because then $|(z', y')| > |(x, y)|$, which would be contradictory to our assumption of the longest unnecessary edge. Therefore after at most $\mathcal{O}(n \log n)$ rounds all unnecessary edges are vanished w.h.p.. $\square$

Proving the Lemmas 3.2, 3.6, 3.9, 3.10 and 3.11 we have shown that at the end of phase 5 a stable Re-Chord structure is reached and as every phase takes at most $\mathcal{O}(n \log n)$ rounds, the complete running time to reach this stable structure is $\mathcal{O}(n \log n)$ rounds.

3.1.6 Stability of Re-Chord

Once a stable Re-Chord structure is reached no further changes will take place. Each node u will perform the stabilization rules. It will not create any new virtual nodes, since in the stable state there is always a node u_m between u and its closest real neighbor. Each u_i, for $0 \le i \le m$ already has one left and one right real neighbor and will create (the already existing edges) to these neighbors. If there does not exist a right/left neighbor (in the case of the largest and smallest node of all nodes) a circle edge is created to the smallest/largest known node, which already existed. Each u_i will sort its neighborhood. At each side u_i has at most two neighbors, as we know. Lets say that at the right/left side u_i/u_{i-1} has edges to v_1/v_2 and r_1/r_2, the closest right/left node and right/left real node. As these neighborhoods are sorted, no overlapping occurs. So after the linearization, in the interval $(id_{u_i}, id_{u_{i-1}})$ edges (u_i, v_1), (v_1, r_1), (u_{i-1}, v_2) and (v_2, r_2) are created. These edges obviously existed before. A connection edge is created between the largest neighbor of u_i and u_{i-1}. Also, another connection edge could be present starting u_i, which is a propagated connection edge originally created by another neighborhood. In Re-Chord the same connection edges already existed.Similarly we can show that our network structure is preserved in the case where u_i or u_{i-1} would have only one neighbor , an even more trivial case. We showed the preservation of the stable state for the larger neighbors of u_i. The state is also preserved for its smaller neighbors (if there are any). As u_i is an arbitrary node the above results hold for all u_i, $0 \leq i \leq m$.

4. JOINING OR LEAVING OF A NODE IN THE NETWORK

4.1 Join

We now examine the number of steps needed to successfully integrate a new node to the stable network, which means that the network is again in a stable state. In order to join the network, a peer connects to one peer in the network. Let u be the corresponding new node, which is inserted into the network, i.e. it is connected to an arbitrary real node (of the peer in the network) of the network. We will distinguish two possible cases. Either the node is inserted (connected) to a node smaller than itself, or the opposite. For both cases we will show the following theorem.

THEOREM 4.1. *After at most $\mathcal{O}(\log^2 n)$ rounds, a joining node u is integrated in the Chord network, i.e. every node has stable next and next real neighbors and all virtual nodes are created.*

PROOF. The new node u is initially connected to a real node v. In the first round after the joining u creates its virtual nodes. Then v is the neighbor of one u_i, $v < u_i \leq u$ after performing the overlapping neighborhood rule. As no other (real) node of the network is known to u and its virtual nodes, v is assumed to be u_i's next neighbor and the edge (v, u_i) is created. If $v < u_i$ and u_i's position is between $1/2^{i+1}$ and $1/2^i$ away from v, the edge will be propagated to the virtual node v_j at position $v + 1/2^{i+1}$ and the distance will be at least halved. If there is no such virtual node v_j, u_i falls in the interval between v and the next greater real node. Thus v is its next real neighbor. After the propagation of the edge u_i is not connected to a real node $< u_i$, but a virtual node $v_j < u_i$. Then a real node $v_j < v' < u_i$ will be found in one round if such a node exists. If v_j's next greater real neighbor has a smaller id than u_i the edge (v', u_i) will be created by the linearization rule. If the next greater real neighbor of v_j is greater than u_i, v_j and u_i fall in the same interval of real nodes and v_j next real neighbor is u_i's next real neighbor. Thus in every second round the distance to u_i is halved and it takes at most $\mathcal{O}(\log n)$ rounds until it is connected to one of its next real neighbors. From that point on the procedure is trivial. In $\mathcal{O}(\log n)$ rounds u_i will be connected to its stable-state neighbors, since we showed that between two consecutive real nodes there are no more than $\mathcal{O}(\log n)$ virtual nodes w.h.p.. If $v < u_i$, v is the right neighbor of one u_i, $v > u_i \geq u$. If there is another $u_{i-1} > u_i$ a connection edge (v, u_{i-1}) will be created to connect u_{i-1}, u_i. With the same arguments as above u_{i-1} will be connected to its stable-state neighbors after $\mathcal{O}(\log n)$ rounds. But if there is no $u_{i-1} > u_i$, v will not be the left neighbor of any of the u_is. In this case the smallest virtual node of u (or u itself), lets call this node y, will create a circle edge from the largest known node to u to y. The largest known node so far is v so a circle edge (v, y) is created. This edge is also propagated according to the circle edge rules, and for the propagation procedure the same arguments hold as for the former case and y will reach its stable-state neighbors in $\mathcal{O}(\log n)$ steps.

As soon as the first virtual node is fully integrated in the ring structure by case 1 or 2 it knows its next real neighbors and will connect them by a connection edge with its next virtual sibling u_j. This will also be integrated following the argument of case 1 or case 2. So, until the last virtual sibling of u is integrated, $\mathcal{O}(\log n)\Theta(\log(n)) = \mathcal{O}((\log n)^2)$ rounds will be needed. After the integration of u and its virtual nodes the routing and search mechanisms of Chord can be applied again, because all the information of the old nodes of the former ring are updated during the joining process. An old real node v creates only a new smallest virtual node v_m if the joining node u is its new next real neighbor, Thus this new virtual node v_m is integrated in at most $\mathcal{O}(\log n)$ rounds. Also all virtual nodes in the corresponding interval are informed about their new next real neighbor u in at most $\mathcal{O}(\log n)$ rounds after u is connected to its next neighbors. Note that there still might be unnecessary edges created during the joining process, that will be eliminated after at most $\mathcal{O}(n \log n)$ rounds. $\square$

4.2 Leave

This case is simpler than the insertion. A node can either leave the network, or a fault can occur and the node, as well as its connections, fail. When a node leaves the network, it and all of its virtual nodes will be deleted. Before a node is deleted it informs its neighbors about each other and so the ring structure is maintained. When a node fails, the network is also able to recover to its ring structure.

THEOREM 4.2. *After at most $\mathcal{O}(\log n)$ rounds the Chord network is stabilized again after the leaving or failure of a node.*

PROOF. If a node fails it can not inform the neighbored nodes about its failure. When a virtual node fails a "gap" between two consecutive nodes exists that is filled with an edge at most after 2 rounds. These nodes realize their next neighbor is now their next real neighbor, an edge from that real neighbor to the node is created and after at most $\mathcal{O}(\log n)$ rounds the desired edge is created due to the linearization rule. When a real neighbor fails, a similar gap is created, but now the next real neighbor of the neighbored nodes is missing. But the nodes at the gap create new connection or ring edges according to rule 5 and 6, which will close the gap after at most $\mathcal{O}(\log n)$ rounds with the same arguments as for the joining process, as the rest of the ring is maintained. $\square$

5. SIMULATIONS

As a simulation environment for our algorithm we use Matlab 7.8.0. We simulate a random undirected weakly connected graph. Each vertex represents a node of the chord network and has a real number (id) assigned to it, which is chosen uniformly at random from $(0,1)$. This number also indicates the position of the node in the chord network circle. The vertices present at initialization represent the real nodes. The self-stabilization rules are applied repeatedly to the nodes of the graph. After some steps the graph has reached the desired stable state of the chord network.

The metrics that are measured are the number of steps it takes for the network to stabilize, the number of edges that exist at the stabilization state (normal edges as well as connection edges) and the total number of nodes that exist in the network (the real nodes of the initialized state, as well as the virtual nodes produced). By number of steps we mean the number of times a real node applies to itself (and to its virtual nodes) the self-stabilization rules. Note that nodes work in parallel.

The simulations are run for various numbers of (real) nodes: 5, 15, 25, 35, 45, 65, 85, 105. For each of these scenarios we run the simulation for 30 different graphs and compute then the mean value of the values of the metrics we get.

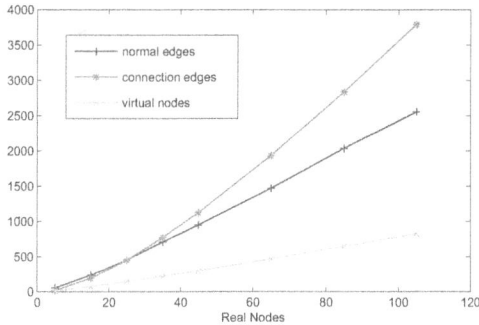

Figure 5: Edges and nodes measured from various simulation runs of the algorithm

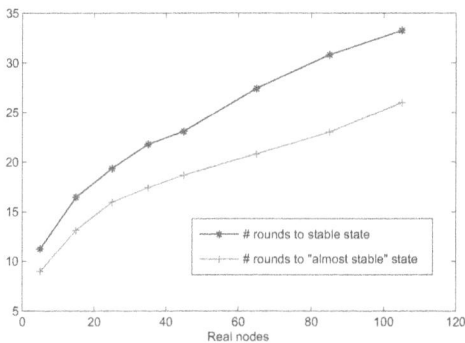

Figure 6: Number of steps needed to reach the stable state and "Almost stable" state

As we derived from our simulations, the network indeed stabilizes after a number of rounds, and the stabilization state is indeed the chord network state. This shows that our algorithm works correctly.

We also can see from Fig. 6 that the number of steps needed in order to reach the stabilization state is relatively small. In particular, the steps needed at low numbers of nodes are from 10 to 25 (for 30 nodes) and don't get much more for higher numbers. They seem to increase sublinear, or at most linear. Here, a gap between the experimental results and the results from the analysis seems to exist, where we showed that the convergence to the Chord structure takes $\mathcal{O}(n \log n)$, whereas the simulations show that the steps needed are (at most) linear. This implies that our upper bound may not be a tight one. We can also see in the figure that the network converges relatively early to an "almost stable" state, before it gets its final stable state. The "almost stable" state describes a network, where all the desired edges of the Re-Chord network exist, but also some extra edges exist. In Fig. 5 we consider the number of edges and nodes. In particular, we measure the amount of connection edges, which are the ones created due to rule 6 of our algorithm. By normal edges we mean all the other edges that exist and are created due to the algorithm except the connection edges. We can see a remarkable smoothness in Figure 5, which also indicates the small variation of the metrics that was observed during the experiments. The normal edges seem to increase a bit faster than linear, as expected. It is notable that the connection edges increase faster than the normal edges, as the number of real nodes gets higher. This is no surprise, as described in Section 2.2. The curve seems

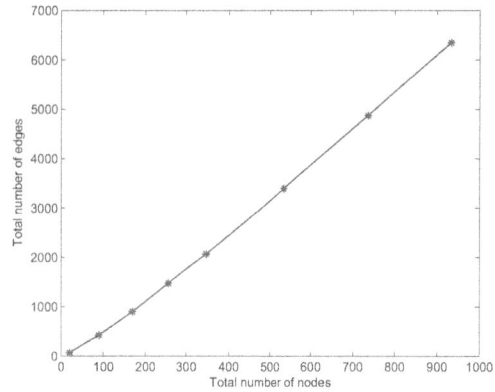

Figure 7: The total number of edges to the total number of nodes in the final graph

to be almost identical to a $cn(\log n)^2$ curve that follows from the theory. If we add the edges and take into account the number of total edges, we can see that it increases with a rate compared to to the total number of nodes, which seems to support the theory, as described in Section 2.2. The virtual nodes increase at least linear, which supports the theoretical result, as there are $\mathcal{O}(n \log n)$ virtual nodes. By number of total edges we mean the sum of the connection and normal edges, and by number of total nodes we mean the sum of the real and virtual nodes.

6. CONCLUSIONS

We showed that it is possible for a network to reach a Chord-network state in a distributed manner, i.e. using only local actions, from any arbitrary structure and remain at that state. In fact these local actions are a set of rules, based on the principle of the linearization technique, which basically consists of sorting all neighbors of each node into a line. We extended this technique by expanding the rules in a way, in order to deal with the problems occurred by trying to self-stabilize the graph into a Chord state. This convergence was shown through rigorous analysis, but also by the simulation experiments we conducted. We also saw through simulations that this self-stabilization happens in a relatively small number of steps and by creating not too many edges. By analyzing the algorithm we proved that this convergence to the stable Chord structure takes always at most $cn \log n$ steps, where n is the size of the network, i.e. the number of peers. We also showed that once a network is in the stable state, and a peer joins or leaves the network, the network will recover to the stable state at most at $\mathcal{O}((\log n)^2)$ steps at the case of joining and at most $\mathcal{O}(\log n)$ at the case of leaving. It would be interesting to further investigate if there could be even more efficient rules that lead to self-stabilization, or study other types of graphs that could be formed in a self-stabilization process, from an arbitrary weakly connected network.

7. REFERENCES

[1] J. Aspnes and G. Shah. Skip graphs. In *SODA*, pages 384–393, 2003.

[2] B. Awerbuch and C. Scheideler. The hyperring: a low-congestion deterministic data structure for distributed environments. In *SODA*, pages 318–327, 2004.

[3] A. Berns, S. Ghosh, and S. V. Pemmaraju. Brief announcement: a framework for building self-stabilizing overlay networks. In *PODC*, pages 398–399, 2010.

[4] A. Bhargava, K. Kothapalli, C. Riley, C. Scheideler, and M. Thober. Pagoda: A dynamic overlay network for routing, data management, and multicasting. In *SPAA*, pages 170–179, 2004.

[5] J. Brzezinski, M. Szychowiak, and D. Wawrzyniak. Self-stabilization in distributed systems - a short survey, 2000.

[6] T. Clouser, M. Nesterenko, and C. Scheideler. Tiara: A self-stabilizing deterministic skip list. In *SSS*, pages 124–140, Berlin, Heidelberg, 2008. Springer-Verlag.

[7] C. Cramer and T. Fuhrmann. Self-stabilizing ring networks on connected graphs. Technical report, University of Karlsruhe (TH), Technical Report 2005-5, 2005.

[8] E. W. Dijkstra. Self-stabilizing systems in spite of distributed control. *Commun. ACM*, 17:643–644, November 1974.

[9] S. Dolev. *Self-Stabilization*. MIT Press, 2000.

[10] D. Gall, R. Jacob, A. W. Richa, C. Scheideler, S. Schmid, and H. Täubig. Time complexity of distributed topological self-stabilization: The case of graph linearization. In *LATIN*, pages 294–305, 2010.

[11] N. J. A. Harvey, M. B. Jones, S. Saroiu, M. Theimer, and A. Wolman. Skipnet: a scalable overlay network with practical locality properties. In *USITS*, pages 9–9, 2003.

[12] T. Herman. Self-stabilization bibliography: Access guide, December 2002.

[13] R. Jacob, A. W. Richa, C. Scheideler, S. Schmid, and H. Täubig. A distributed polylogarithmic time algorithm for self-stabilizing skip graphs. In *PODC*, pages 131–140, 2009.

[14] R. Jacob, S. Ritscher, C. Scheideler, and S. Schmid. A self-stabilizing and local delaunay graph construction. In *Algorithms and Computation*, volume 5878 of *Lecture Notes in Computer Science*, pages 771–780. Springer Berlin / Heidelberg, 2009.

[15] J. Jiang, R. Pan, C. Liang, and W. Wang. Bichord: An improved approach for lookup routing in chord. In *ADBIS*, pages 338–348, 2005.

[16] D. Karger, E. Lehman, T. Leighton, R. Panigrahy, M. Levine, and D. Lewin. Consistent hashing and random trees: distributed caching protocols for relieving hot spots on the world wide web. In *STOC*, pages 654–663, 1997. ACM.

[17] F. Kuhn, S. Schmid, and R. Wattenhofer. A self-repairing peer-to-peer system resilient to dynamic adversarial churn. In *IPTPS*, pages 13–23, 2005.

[18] B. Leong, B. Liskov, and E. D. Demaine. Epichord: Parallelizing the chord lookup algorithm with reactive routing state management. In *ICON*, pages 1243–1259, 2004.

[19] D. Malkhi, M. Naor, and D. Ratajczak. Viceroy: a scalable and dynamic emulation of the butterfly. In *PODC*, pages 183–192, 2002. ACM.

[20] V. A. Mesaros, B. Carton, P. V. Roy, and P. S. Barbe. S-chord: Using symmetry to improve lookup efficiency in chord. In *PDPTA03*, pages 23–26, 2003.

[21] A. Montresor, M. Jelasity, and Ö. Babaoglu. Chord on demand. In *Peer-to-Peer Computing*, pages 87–94, 2005.

[22] M. Naor and U. Wieder. Novel architectures for p2p applications: The continuous-discrete approach. *ACM Transactions on Algorithms*, 3(3), 2007.

[23] M. Onus, A. W. Richa, and C. Scheideler. Linearization: Locally self-stabilizing sorting in graphs. In *ALENEX*, 2007.

[24] S. Ratnasamy, P. Francis, M. Handley, R. Karp, and S. Shenker. A scalable content-addressable network. In *SIGCOMM*, pages 161–172, 2001.

[25] A. I. T. Rowstron and P. Druschel. Pastry: Scalable, decentralized object location, and routing for large-scale peer-to-peer systems. In *Middleware '01*, pages 329–350, 2001. Springer-Verlag.

[26] C. Scheideler and S. Schmid. A distributed and oblivious heap. In *ICALP*, pages 571–582, 2009.

[27] A. Shaker and D. S. Reeves. Self-stabilizing structured ring topology p2p systems. In *Peer-to-Peer Computing*, pages 39–46, 2005.

[28] I. Stoica, R. Morris, D. Liben-nowell, D. Karger, M. Frans, K. F. Dabek, and H. Balakrishnan. Chord: A scalable peer-to-peer lookup service for internet applications. In *SIGCOMM*, pages 149–160, 2001.

[29] J. Wang and Z. Yu. A new variation of chord with novel improvement on lookup locality. In *GCA*, pages 18–24, 2006.

[30] B. Zhao, L. Huang, J. Stribling, S. Rhea, A. Joseph, and J. Kubiatowicz. Tapestry: a resilient global-scale overlay for service deployment. *Selected Areas in Communications, IEEE Journal on*, 22(1):41 – 53, Jan. 2004.

Recommender Systems With Non-Binary Grades

Yossi Azar[*]
School of Computer Science
Tel Aviv University
Tel Aviv 69978
Israel
azar@tau.ac.il

Aviv Nisgav
School of Electrical
Engineering
Tel Aviv University
Tel Aviv 69978, Israel
avivns@eng.tau.ac.il

Boaz Patt-Shamir[†]
School of Electrical
Engineering
Tel Aviv University
Tel Aviv 69978, Israel
boaz@eng.tau.ac.il

ABSTRACT

We consider the interactive model of recommender systems, in which users are asked about just a few of their preferences, and in return the system outputs an approximation of all their preferences. The measure of performance is the *probe complexity* of the algorithm, defined to be the maximal number of answers any user should provide (probe complexity typically depends inversely on the number of users with similar preferences and on the quality of the desired approximation). Previous interactive recommendation algorithms assume that user preferences are binary, meaning that each object is either "liked" or "disliked" by each user. In this paper we consider the general case in which users may have a more refined scale of preference, namely more than two possible grades. We show how to reduce the non-binary case to the binary one, proving the following results. For discrete grades with s possible values, we give a simple deterministic reduction that preserves the approximation properties of the binary algorithm at the cost of increasing probe complexity by factor s. Our main result is for the general case, where we assume that user grades are arbitrary real numbers. For this case we present an algorithm that preserves the approximation properties of the binary algorithm while incurring only polylogarithmic overhead.

Keywords

recommendation systems, collaborative filtering.

General Terms

Algorithms, Theory.

[*]Supported in part by the Israel Science Foundation (grant No. 1404/10).

[†]Supported in part by the Israel Science Foundation (grant 1372/09) and by Israel Ministry of Science and Technology. Research partly done while visiting MIT CSAIL.

Categories and Subject Descriptors

F.2.2 [**Analysis of Algorithms and Problem Complexity**]: Nonnumerical Algorithms and Problems

1. INTRODUCTION

Arguably, helping people identify objects they may desire has always been a central part of civilization, but recently, with the advent of the so-called "information age" it has taken new forms. On one hand, many more objects are available (because many objects are digital and can be obtained by a click of a button), and on the other hand, sophisticated algorithms can provide the users with relatively-intelligent advices when seeking something, where typical goals may be movies to watch, articles to read, authoritative web pages, restaurants, similar users in a social network etc.

One of the main ways to find such objects is a *recommender system*, such as *collaborative filtering* (see, e.g., [14, 15] for some early work). The basic idea in collaborative filtering is that the system collects data about user preferences, and makes recommendation to each user based past choices of that user and the choices of other users.

Much of the current research in collaborative filtering considers the following model. There is a large dataset that contains all past choices of users (be it purchase history, or, say, movie grades), and the goal is to predict the way a user would grade an object she did not examine yet.[1] The problem with this approach is that it ignores the existence of feedback in the model: Assuming that the recommender system indeed affects user choices, the dataset is biased toward objects recommended by the system, and does not reflect the "true" preference of the users. It follows that analytically, such a system makes sense only for a single recommendation to each user (this way there's no feedback), or under the implicit assumption that users actually choose objects based on some external recommendations (making the feedback effect weak enough to ignore). Obviously, these assumptions are unsatisfactory in most cases.

This gap is bridged by the *interactive recommender system* model [7, 4]. In this model, it is assumed that the system can observe the user's reaction to recommendations and act on it. More specifically, the model is that the system

---

[1]It may be interesting to note that in the Netflix Challenge [6], the algorithm is asked to predict the grade users have already gave to some objects.

proposes an object to the user, and the user, in response, informs the system (perhaps implicitly) of her grade for that object. The system uses this input when making future recommendations. It is usually assumed that the system starts out with no knowledge at all about user grades. (Note that in this case, the system is more likely to propose controversial objects to the user at the beginning, because the way users grade them conveys more information.)

The model. There is a set of n users and a set of m objects, and each user has a grade for each object. The grades are initially unknown, and the goal is to find them, by means of asking users for their grades for certain objects (a.k.a. "probing"). The performance measure we are interested in is the *probe complexity*, defined as the maximal number of grades any user is asked to report. The strongest possible goal for a recommender algorithm is to reconstruct all user preferences. Obviously, reconstructing preferences of an esoteric user may require many more probes than reconstructing the preferences shared by many users. We therefore introduce two parameters, $0 < \alpha \leq 1$ and $D \geq 0$ and assume that the following holds: For each user u there is a set of αn other users whose preferences are at most distance D away from the preferences of u, under some appropriate metric. It is not hard to see that in order to reconstruct user preferences to within distance D, users need to examine $\Omega(m/\alpha n)$ objects on average: Intuitively, the αn similar users need to examine all m objects between them.

Previous work. The goal of the algorithms presented in [7, 4] is to find a single "good object" for the users. Since being a "good" object is a binary predicate, these algorithms effectively assume binary grades. In [2], full preference reconstruction algorithms are presented for arbitrary grades, but the algorithms are applicable only under the assumption that $D = 0$, namely reconstruction is guaranteed to work only if αn users share *exactly* the same preferences. A general reconstruction result is presented in [1], where any $0 \leq D \leq n/\log n$ is allowed. However, the latter algorithm relies strongly on the assumption that preference grades are binary. The metric used in [1] is the Hamming distance, namely the distance between two users is the number of objects on which their grades differ. An improved reconstruction algorithm is presented [8], where the presence of some Byzantine users can be tolerated.

Our Contribution. In this paper we extend this line of work by considering real-valued grades (normalized to the range $[0, 1]$). The metric we use to measure distance between preference vectors is L_1, i.e., the distance between two users is the sum, over all objects, of difference in their grades.

Our algorithms use algorithms for the binary model as a black box, so the main contribution of the paper is showing how to reduce the continuous-scale grades recommendation model to the binary one. Let us note upfront that simple discretization approaches do not work. For example, suppose we round each grade to 0 or 1 (i.e., round$(x) = \lfloor x + \frac{1}{2} \rfloor$), and apply a binary algorithm to the rounded grades. Such a rounding performs miserably in the case of a cluster of αn users whose preferences have small diameter D, but all their grades are uniformly distributed around $\frac{1}{2}$. Intuitively, the

rounding splits this tight cluster into many sets, and places them very far from each other. More precisely, consider the possible parameters α and D to be supplied to the binary algorithm: If we insist on keeping all αn users as a cluster, then the binary algorithm must use distance parameter $\Omega(m)$, and if we insist on keeping D as the distance parameter, the binary algorithm must use $\alpha/2^{m-D}$ as the number of neighbors. Both alternatives give us trivial parameters, because the distance can never be greater than m, and $\alpha \geq 1/n$ always. It is easy to see that *any* rounding threshold will suffer from the same problem.

Thus, the main technique we introduce in this paper is a way to do the rounding while increasing D and decreasing α by only a constant factor, and increasing the probe complexity of the underlying binary algorithm by only polylogarithmic factor. Roughly speaking, we show the following result. Suppose that for each user there are at least αn users whose preferences are at most D away, where $D > \epsilon$ for some constant $\epsilon > 0$ (the case of $D = 0$ is simpler [2]). Then the preferences of all users can be reconstructed, with high probability, to within $O(D)$, using $O(\frac{m}{\alpha n} \log^{9/2} n)$ probes per user. (Note that the $\frac{m}{\alpha n}$ factor is unavoidable: if αn users agree on $m - D$ objects, then each of the $m - D$ objects must be probed by at least one of the αn similar users.) The precise statement is slightly more involved: See Theorem 4.1.

As an intermediate output, our algorithm produces estimates of "inter-user distances," i.e., each user can identify (approximately) what is her distance from any other user (Theorem 4.7). We believe that this result may be of independent interest, say in the context of social networks [12].

Another result we present is a linear-reduction algorithm for multiple evenly-spaced discrete grades (Theorem 3.1). In this case, to handle $s + 1$ possible grades, the cost of the algorithm grows by a factor s, compared to the cost of a binary algorithm. From the theoretical viewpoint the linear reduction is very simple. However, we include it here because in many practical situations the grades are discrete and there are only a few of them, in which case the linear reduction is more efficient than the algorithm for the general case. More formally, assuming $m = \Theta(n)$, the linear reduction has better probe complexity than the general algorithm if the number of grades s satisfies $s \leq \log n/D$.

Related Work. Our model is closely related to models of recommender systems [5, 7, 4], in which the users grades are structured as a user-product matrix where each entry is a user opinion on an object and the goal is to produce an estimate of this matrix. Some variants of recommender systems assume partial information about the matrix, which is presented as known entries, and the task of the algorithm is to predict unknown entries based on the given data. Other variants assume that all entries are unknown, and the task of the algorithm is to instruct the users which products to try (thereby revealing some entries of the matrix) so that the algorithm can recommend a good product more effectively.

In the model where a partial matrix is given, it is common to assume a linear generative model for user's opinion vectors and apply algebraic techniques such as principal component analysis [9] or singular value decomposition [16]. Papadimitriou et al. [13] and Azar et al. [5] prove conditions

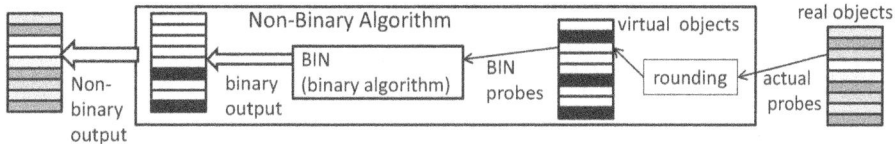

Figure 1: Framework for reducing real value algorithms to binary value algorithms

under which SVD is effective. Other generative user models that were considered include simple Markov chain models [10, 11], where users randomly select their "type," and each type is a probability distribution over the objects.

Drineas et al. [7] were the first to propose a competitive model, where the algorithm directs the users which products to try and the results of the tries are fed back to the algorithm. In [4] it was shown that in this model, a user sharing its preference with at least α fraction of the users ($D = 0$ in our terms), can find a product he likes in $O\left(\lceil \frac{m}{n} \rceil \log n / \alpha\right)$ tries. Later, in the same model Awerbuch et al. [2] reconstruct the users preference for all objects with similar probe complexity and show this is a lower bound.

In case users grade objects in a binary fashion (e.g. "like" or "dislike") Alon et al. [1] present an algorithm where user preference vectors are computed approximately using similar users in a competitive way. In that algorithm, if for every user there is a set of αn other users whose preferences are at most Hamming-distance $\log(n)$ away, then the number of queries by each user is $O\left(\lceil \frac{m}{n} \rceil \log^{3.5} n / \alpha\right)$.

Awerbuch et al. [3] study recommendations algorithms in a model where an adversarial (oblivious) schedule determines which user will make the next probe, and the algorithm may only say which object should that user probe.

Organization. In Section 2 we formalize the model, define some notation and present the overall framework. In Section 3 we consider the discrete model. In Section 4 we present our main result, an algorithm for the continuous model.

2. PRELIMINARIES

Basic concepts and notation. There are n *users* and m *objects*. Each user has a *grade* for each object (the grades are initially unknown). In the *discrete* case, there are $s + 1$ grades, assumed to be the set $\left\{0, \frac{1}{s}, \frac{2}{s}, \ldots, 1\right\}$. In the *continuous* case, grades are real numbers in the interval $[0, 1]$. We sometimes refer to the complete set of user grades as the *preference matrix* A, of dimension $n \times m$. A_{ij} is the grade of user i to object j, and row i, denoted A_i, is called user i's *preference vector*. The *distance* between two preference vectors A_i and $A_{i'}$ is the L_1 norm of their difference, i.e., $\text{dist}(A_i, A_{i'}) \overset{\text{def}}{=} \sum_{j=1}^{m} |A_{ij} - A_{i'j}|$. A matrix $A_{n \times m}$ is called (α, D)-*similar* if for each row A_i it holds that $|\{i' : \text{dist}(A_i, A_{i'}) \leq D\}| \geq \alpha n$, i.e., there are at least αn row vectors whose distance from A_i is at most D.

The recommendation problem statement. The input is an (α, D)-similar matrix $A_{n \times m}$, of which only α, D, and the dimensions n and m are initially known. The output is a matrix $\hat{A}_{n \times m}$, which is an estimate of A. The *approximation factor* of the output is $\max\left\{\frac{\text{dist}(A_i, \hat{A}_i)}{D} : 1 \leq i \leq n\right\}$.

Computational model. Algorithms proceed in synchronous *rounds*. In each round, each user is asked to reveal its grade for at most one object (a "probe"). (In a distributed model, the results of probes are published on a public "billboard," i.e., they are available to all users.) The maximal number of grades any user provides is the *probe complexity* of the algorithm. Trivially, the recommendation problem can be solved without errors in probe complexity m. It is also not difficult to see that $\Omega(m/\alpha n)$ probe complexity is necessary to produce $O(1)$-approximation of (α, D)-similar matrix.

Binary Algorithms. We shall assume that we have at our disposal an algorithm denoted BIN that solves the recommendation problem when all grades are binary. More precisely, when run on an (α, D)-similar binary matrix of dimension $n \times m$, BIN produces, at the cost of $T_{\text{BIN}}(n, m, \alpha, D)$ probe complexity, a γ_{BIN}-approximation, for some constant $\gamma_{\text{BIN}} \geq 0$. The binary algorithms we use are typically randomized; we assume that they are high-probability Monte Carlo algorithms, namely they succeed with probability $1 - n^{-c}$ for any desired constant c. Since in our algorithms, the number of invocations of BIN is always polynomial in n, we may apply the Union Bound to deduce that w.h.p., all invocations of BIN are successful.

Let us now explain how invocations of BIN are carried out. The problem is that we cannot apply BIN directly when preferences are not binary. We use the following natural on-line reduction framework (see Figure 1). The binary algorithm is presented with the same set of users, but with different set of objects which we call *virtual objects*, where each virtual object corresponds to exactly one real object (but one real object may correspond to none or several virtual objects). Whenever BIN asks user i to probe virtual object j, the non-binary algorithm asks user i to probe the real object corresponding to j, and presents BIN with a binary value derived from the real grade by applying some rounding function that depends on the non-binary algorithm.

Our algorithms solve the continuous-scale problem using a black-box implementation of a binary algorithm. For concreteness, we use the following result from [1].

THEOREM 2.1. *Given an $(\alpha, \log n)$-similar $n \times m$ binary matrix B, algorithm Small_Radius from [1] reconstructs B with probe complexity $O\left(\frac{1}{\alpha} \lceil \frac{m}{n} \rceil \log^{7/2} n\right)$ and approximation factor $O(1)$.*

3. THE DISCRETE CASE: A LINEAR REDUCTION

In this section we present an algorithm for the discrete preference case, where there are $s + 1$ possible grades. This

---

Algorithm 1 DISCRETE_RECONST($A_{n \times m}, \alpha, D$)

(1) Define matrix $B_{n \times sm}$ for $i \in [1, n]$, $j \in [1, m]$ and
$k \in [1, s]$ by $B_{i,(j-1)s+k} = \begin{cases} 1 & \text{If } A_{i,j} > \frac{k-1}{s} \\ 0 & \text{Otherwise} \end{cases}$

(2) Invoke BIN(B, α, sD), and let $\hat{B}$ denote its output.

(3) Find $l_{i,j} \in [0, s]$ that minimizes

$$\sum_{l=1}^{l_{i,j}} \left(1 - \hat{B}_{i,(j-1)s+l} \right) + \sum_{l=l_{i,j}+1}^{s} \hat{B}_{i,(j-1)s+l}$$

for $i \in [1, n]$ and $j \in [1, m]$.

(4) Let $L_{n \times m}$ be the matrix over S defined by $L_{i,j} = \frac{l_{i,j}}{s}$.
Output L.

---

reduction is very simple, but it might be practical for small values of s, and it serves as a gentle warm-up to our main result for the continuous model.

We assume that the grades are the set $S = \left\{ 0, \frac{1}{s}, \frac{2}{s}, \ldots, 1 \right\}$, where $s = |S| - 1$. The algorithm works as follows (pseudocode is provided in Algorithm 1). For each real object j define s binary virtual objects $j_1, \ldots, j_s$. Whenever BIN asks user i to probe some virtual object j_ℓ, we apply the following rounding procedure. If none of the virtual objects corresponding to j was probed by user i so far, then we ask i to probe (real) object j, and obtain the value of A_{ij}. Suppose the value is such that $\frac{k-1}{s} < A_{ij} \leq \frac{k}{s}$ for some $1 \leq k \leq s$. Then we set the values (for user i) of virtual objects $j_1, \ldots j_k$ to 1, and the values of $j_{k+1}, \ldots, j_s$ to 0 (intuitively, the grades are coded in unary). Finally, if j was already probed in the past by i, we can use the known A_{ij} value to return a virtual probe value to BIN. This concludes the description of the rounding procedure.

Note that the output of BIN is a binary matrix, which does not necessarily represent valid encoding of grades the way the input was encoded, because it is only an approximation. In the algorithm, we choose the closest (under Hamming distance) valid encoding of a preference vector.

We have the following result, assuming that BIN succeeds with probability $1 - n^{-\Omega(1)}$.

THEOREM 3.1. *With probability* $1 - n^{-\Omega(1)}$, *for any user* i, *Algorithm* DISCRETE_RECONST *reconstructs the preference vector of user* i *with probe complexity* $T_{\text{BIN}}(n, sm, \alpha, sD)$ *and approximation factor* $O(\gamma_{\text{BIN}})$.

Proof: Let i, i' be any two users. Then by Step 1 of the algorithm,

$$\text{dist}(B_i, B_{i'}) = \sum_{j=1}^{m} \sum_{k=1}^{s} \left| B_{i,(j-1)s+k} - B_{i',(j-1)s+k} \right|$$

$$= \sum_{j=1}^{m} s \left| A_{i,j} - A_{i',j} \right|$$

$$= s \cdot \text{dist}(A_i, A_{i'}),$$

and therefore, by the properties of BIN, we get that its invo-

cation in Step 2 yields $\hat{B}$ such that $\text{dist}(B_i, \hat{B}_i) \leq \gamma_{\text{BIN}} \cdot sD$ for any user i.

Next, for any i, j, let $l_{i,j}^* = sA_{i,j}$. Let $\hat{B}^{i,j}$ denote the vector $\hat{B}_{i,(j-1)s+1}, \ldots, \hat{B}_{i,js}$, and let U_l denote the binary vector of s bits with the first $l-1$ bits set to 1. By Step 3 of the algorithm, $\text{dist}(U_{l_{i,j}}, \hat{B}^{i,j}) \leq \text{dist}(U_{l_{i,j}^*}, \hat{B}^{i,j})$. Using the triangle inequality we obtain

$$\|L_i - A_i\| = \sum_{j=1}^{m} \left| S_{l_{i,j}} - S_{l_{i,j}^*} \right|$$

$$= \frac{1}{s} \sum_{j=1}^{m} \left\| U_{l_{i,j}} - U_{l_{i,j}^*} \right\|$$

$$\leq \frac{2}{s} \sum_{j=1}^{m} \left\| U_{l_{i,j}^*} - \hat{B}^{i,j} \right\|$$

$$= \frac{2}{s} \left\| B_i - \hat{B}_i \right\|$$

$$= 2\gamma D.$$

which proves the approximation claim. The probe complexity follows directly from the fact that in Algorithm 1 probes are done only while evaluating BIN(B, α, sD) in Step 2. ∎

We note that the probe complexity of BIN is typically linear in the number of objects, and hence Algorithm DISCRETE_RECONST guarantees no degradation in approximation, but the cost grows linearly with the number of discrete grades. In particular, when compared with the general construction presented in the following section, Algorithm DISCRETE_RECONST is superior in terms of probe complexity when the number of grades $s + 1$ satisfies $s = O(\log n/D)$.

4. THE CONTINUOUS CASE

In this section we present our main result: an algorithm for the case grades are arbitrary bounded real numbers. W.l.o.g., we may assume in this case that the grades are in the unit interval $[0, 1]$.

The most natural idea is to reduce the continuous case to the discrete case. But similarly to the argument mentioned in the introduction, simplistic discretization approaches fail. If we use resolution of $1/s$, then discretization may end up in adding an overall m/s error. In other words, there are inputs where users are nicely concentrated in the continuous model, but after discretization they will end up with linear distance between them (if we use resolution of $O(1/m)$, then Algorithm DISCRETE_RECONST results in increasing the probe complexity by a factor of m, which is trivial to achieve).

The intuition behind our algorithm is as follows. While any discretization has bad instances in which clusters are split along discretization borders, a random discretization is likely to avoid many of these bad events. If we use many discretizations, many of them should not split many clusters. It turns out that this intuition is roughly correct, but it is not readily clear how to use this random discretizations. Our solution is to construct a metric embedding from L_1-norm in $[0, 1]^m$ to Hamming distance in $\{0, 1\}^{\Theta(\frac{m \log n}{D})}$ in order to use BIN to estimate the distance between users preference vectors. Specifically, we propose to use the concept of *friends detector*, defined as follows.

DEFINITION 4.1. *Given a set of users with preference vectors $A_1, \ldots, A_n$ and $0 \leq D_1 \leq D_2$, a (D_1, D_2)-friends detector is a predicate that takes any two users i, i', whose value is true if $dist(A_i, A_{i'}) \leq D_1$ and false if $dist(A_i, A_{i'}) > D_2$.*

The result of a friends detector may be arbitrary for users whose distance is between D_1 and D_2.[2]

High-level algorithm. Conceptually, our algorithm works as follows.

(1) Invoke Procedure DISTANCE_EST(A, α, D), and obtain a good friends detector. (This step uses a reduction to BIN.)

(2) Using the friends detector and additional probes, obtain a good approximation of A.

In Step 2, users probe random real objects directly, so that each object has sufficiently large coverage by all users types, and then, each user collects the results of probes obtained in the second stage by users close to him (as identified by the friends detector computed in Step 1), and outputs their average as an estimate of his grade vector. We elaborate on the implementation of each step later in this section, but state the following corollary, which summarizes the algorithm performance for α, D-similar preference matrix. It follows from Theorem 4.9, applied with Theorem 2.1.

THEOREM 4.1. *There is a distributed algorithm that, with overwhelming probability, reconstructs for each user its preference vectors with $O(D)$ L_1-distance error. This algorithm has a probe complexity $O\left(\frac{1}{\alpha} \left\lceil \frac{m}{n} \right\rceil \cdot \left\lceil \frac{\log n}{D} \right\rceil \log^{3.5}(m+n)\right)$.*

4.1 Estimating L_1-distances between users

The core of the first stage is carried out by Algorithm DISTANCE_EST, which uses a reduction to BIN. The idea is as follows. First we choose $\Theta(\frac{m \log n}{D})$ objects at random as virtual objects. This has the consequence that the expected distance between users whose distance over all m objects is D, is reduced to distance $\Theta(\log n)$ when considering only the virtual objects. Now, for each such virtual object a *random threshold* is selected independently and uniformly from $[0, 1]$: the results of probes will be rounded according to these random thresholds.

More specifically, the algorithm works as follows (see Algorithm 2 for pseudo-code). Let $K = \lceil 3cm \log n / D \rceil$ for some constant $c > 4$. The algorithm chooses K tuples $\langle t_k, j_k \rangle_{k=1}^K$ where t_k are i.i.d. uniform random variable from $[0, 1]$, and j_k are objects chosen independently, uniformly at random from $\{1, \ldots, m\}$. (Note that K, the number of virtual objects, might be larger or smaller than the number of real objects, m.) We define a binary matrix $B_{n \times K}$, where each row i corresponds to user i (whose real preference vector is A_i), and each column k corresponds to object j_k (i.e. to column j_k in A). B is defined as follows: Entry $B_{i,k}$ is the grade of user i for object j_k, rounded using t_k as a threshold. Algorithm BIN is invoked on B using the reduction framework of Figure 1, yielding reconstructed matrix $\hat{B}$. The output $W(i, i')$, the distance estimate between users i, i', is simply the adjusted Hamming distance between rows i, i' in $\hat{B}$.

---

[2]We note that [12] presents an implementation of a friends detector for the much simpler case where $D_1 = 0$.

Algorithm 2 DISTANCE_EST(A, α, D)

(1) Let $K = \lceil 3cm \log n / D \rceil$.

(2) For each $k \in \{1, \ldots, K\}$ let $\langle t_k, j_k \rangle$ be such that t_k is chosen independently uniformly at random from $[0, 1]$ and j_k independently uniformly at random from $\{1, \ldots, m\}$ (with repetitions).

(3) Let B be a binary matrix of size $n \times K$ defined by
$$B_{i,k} = \begin{cases} 1 & \text{If } A_{i,j_k} > t_k \\ 0 & \text{Otherwise}. \end{cases}$$

(4) Let $\hat{B}$ be the output of BIN($B, \alpha/2, 4KD/m$). (Note that $4KD/m = \Theta(\log n)$.)

(5) Let $W(i, i') = \frac{m}{K} dist(\hat{B}_i, \hat{B}_{i'})$. Output W.

We now turn to analyze Algorithm DISTANCE_EST. We first bound the errors due to the random choices of j_k and t_k values, and then consider the errors introduced by the imperfection of BIN.

Below, we maintain the following naming convention. We consider users i_1, i_2, i_3 such that $dist(A_{i_1}, A_{i_2}) \leq D$ and $dist(A_{i_1}, A_{i_3}) > 5\beta$ where $\beta \stackrel{\text{def}}{=} 4D \cdot \max(\gamma_{\text{BIN}}, 1)$. We will prove that the algorithm estimates the distances between users preferences with error bounded by $O(D\gamma_{\text{BIN}})$.

LEMMA 4.2. *If $dist(A_{i_1}, A_{i_2}) \leq D$ then $dist(B_{i_1}, B_{i_2}) \leq \frac{\beta}{2} \cdot \frac{K}{m}$ with probability at least $1 - n^{-c/4}$.*

Proof: Let χ_k be a random variable taking the value 1 if t_k falls in between A_{i_1, j_k} and A_{i_2, j_k} and 0 otherwise. Clearly $dist(B_{i_1}, B_{i_2}) = \sum_{k=1}^K \chi_k$. Since t_k is chosen uniformly from $[0, 1]$ we have

$$\begin{aligned} \Pr(\chi_k = 1) &= \sum_{j=1}^m \Pr(j_k = j) \Pr(\chi_k = 1 \mid j_k = j) \\ &= \sum_{j=1}^m \frac{1}{m} |A_{i_1, j} - A_{i_2, j}| \\ &\leq D/m, \end{aligned}$$

and hence $E[dist(B_{i_1}, B_{i_2})] = E\left[\sum_{k=1}^K \chi_k\right] \leq KD/m = 3c \log n$. Therefore, since χ_k are independent Bernoulli random variables, Chernoff Bound implies that

$$\begin{aligned} \Pr(dist(B_{i_1}, B_{i_2}) > 2KD/m) &= \Pr\left(\sum_{k=1}^K \chi_k > 2KD/m\right) \\ &< \exp\left(-\frac{1}{4} c \log n\right) \\ &= n^{-c/4}. \end{aligned}$$

The lemma follows, because $\beta \geq 4D$. ∎

LEMMA 4.3. *For all users i_1, $dist(\hat{B}_{i_1}, B_{i_1}) \leq \beta \cdot \frac{K}{m}$ with probability at least $1 - n^{-c/4-1}$.*

Proof: The lemma holds due to fulfillment of the conditions required for the success of BIN in Step 4 of Algorithm DISTANCE_EST. Let I be the αn preference vectors in A closest to A_{i_1}. By assumption, their distance from A_{i_1} is at most D. For any $i \in I$ and $k \in \{1 \ldots K\}$, let $\chi_{i,k}$ be random variable taking the value 1 iff t_k is between A_{i_1,j_k} and A_{i,j_k}. By definition of I, $E[\chi_{i,k}] \leq D/m$ for any $i \in I$. By linearity of expectation, $E[\sum_{i \in I} \text{dist}(B_{i_1}, B_i)] = \sum_{i \in I} \sum_{k=1}^{K} E[\chi_{i,k}] \leq \alpha n D K/m$.

For each k, consider the random variable $\frac{1}{\alpha n} \sum_{i \in I} \chi_{i,k}$. This is a set of independent random variables in $[0,1]$, so by the Chernoff Bound we have

$$\Pr\left(\sum_{i \in I} \text{dist}(B_{i_1}, B_i) > 2\alpha n D K/m\right)$$
$$= \Pr\left(\sum_{k=1}^{K}\left(\frac{1}{\alpha n}\sum_{i \in I}\chi_{i,k}\right) > 2DK/m\right)$$
$$< \exp(-c/4 \log n) = n^{-c/4}.$$

It follows from the Markov Inequality that there is a subset $I_B \subseteq I$ such that $|I_B| \geq \frac{1}{2}|I|$ and $\text{dist}(B_{i_1}, B_i) \leq 4KD/m$ for any $i \in I_B$. Finally, we apply the Union Bound and deduce that the probability such I_B exists for all n users is at least $1 - n^{-c/4-1}$. The result now follows from the fact that $\hat{B}$ is obtained by applying BIN with parameters $\alpha/2$ and $4KD/m$. ∎

Combining the above two bounds yields the first property of the algorithm

LEMMA 4.4. *For any* i_1, i_2 *satisfying* $\text{dist}(A_{i_1}, A_{i_2}) \leq D$ *we have* $W(i_1, i_2) \leq \frac{5}{2}\beta$, *with probability* $1 - n^{-\Omega(1)}$.

Proof: Summing over objects and using the triangle inequality with Lemmas 4.2 and 4.3, we obtain: with probability $1 - n^{-\Omega(1)}$, if $\text{dist}(A_{i_1}, A_{i_2}) \leq D$ then

$$W(i_1, i_2) = \frac{m}{K}\text{dist}(\hat{B}_{i_1}, \hat{B}_{i_2})$$
$$= \frac{m}{K}\sum_{j=1}^{K}\left|\hat{B}_{i_1,j} - \hat{B}_{i_2,j}\right|$$
$$\leq \frac{m}{K}\left(\sum_{j=1}^{K}\left|\hat{B}_{i_1,j} - B_{i_1,j}\right|\right.$$
$$+ \sum_{j=1}^{K}\left|B_{i_1,j} - B_{i_2,j}\right|$$
$$\left.+ \sum_{j=1}^{K}\left|\hat{B}_{i_2,j} - B_{i_2,j}\right|\right)$$
$$\leq \frac{5}{2}\beta.$$ ∎

Applying similar analysis, we can bound from below the distance estimates of users whose preference vectors are far away from each other.

LEMMA 4.5. *If* $\text{dist}(A_{i_1}, A_{i_3}) > 5\beta$ *then* $\text{dist}(B_{i_1}, B_{i_3}) > \frac{9}{2}\beta \cdot \frac{K}{m}$ *with probability at least* $1 - n^{-\frac{3c}{10}}$.

Proof: For any k, define χ_k be a random variable taking the value 1 if t_k falls in between A_{i_1,j_k} and $A_{i_3 j_k}$ and 0 otherwise. Clearly $\text{dist}(B_{i_1}, B_{i_3}) = \sum_{k=1}^{K}\chi_k$. Since t_k is

chosen uniformly from $[0,1]$ we have

$$\Pr(\chi_k = 1) = \sum_{j=1}^{m}\Pr(j_k = j)\Pr(\chi_k = 1 \mid j_k = j)$$
$$= \sum_{j=1}^{m}\frac{1}{m}\left|A_{i_1,j} - A_{i_3,j}\right|$$
$$> \frac{5\beta}{m},$$

and hence $E[\text{dist}(B_{i_1}, B_{i_3})] = E\left[\sum_{k=1}^{K}\chi_k\right] > \frac{5K}{m}\beta$. Therefore, since χ_k are independent Bernoulli random variables, we can apply the Chernoff Bound to obtain

$$\Pr\left(\text{dist}(B_{i_1}, B_{i_3}) \leq \frac{9K}{2m}\beta\right) = \Pr\left(\sum_{k=1}^{K}\chi_k \leq \frac{9K}{2m}\beta\right)$$
$$\leq \exp\left(-\frac{K\beta}{40m}\right)$$
$$\leq n^{-\frac{3c}{10}}.$$

The last inequality follows from the fact $\beta \geq 4D$. ∎

LEMMA 4.6. *If* $\text{dist}(A_{i_1}, A_{i_3}) > 5\beta$ *then* $W(i_1, i_3) > \frac{5}{2}\beta$ *with probability* $1 - n^{-\Omega(1)}$.

Proof: Similarly to the proof of Lemma 4.4, summing over columns and using the triangle inequality with Lemmas 4.5 and 4.3, we get that if $\text{dist}(A_{i_1}, A_{i_3}) > 5\beta$ then with probability $1 - n^{-\Omega(1)}$

$$W(i_1, i_3) = \frac{m}{K}\text{dist}(\hat{B}_{i_1}, \hat{B}_{i_3})$$
$$= \frac{m}{K}\sum_{j=1}^{K}\left|\hat{B}_{i_1,j} - \hat{B}_{i_3,j}\right|$$
$$\geq \frac{m}{K}\left(\sum_{j=1}^{K}\left|B_{i_1,j} - B_{i_1,j}\right|\right.$$
$$- \sum_{j=1}^{K}\left|\hat{B}_{i_1,j} - B_{i_3,j}\right|$$
$$\left.- \sum_{j=1}^{K}\left|\hat{B}_{i_3,j} - B_{i_3,j}\right|\right)$$
$$> \frac{5}{2}\beta.$$ ∎

Finally, we claim that DISTANCE_EST can be used to obtain a good implementation of a friends detector (cf. Def. 4.1). The following theorem is implied by Lemmas 4.4 and 4.6

THEOREM 4.7. *Let* $A_{n \times m}$ *be a* (α, D)-*similar matrix with real values from* $[0,1]$. *Then, given a binary reconstruction algorithm* BIN, *a* $(D, 20\lceil\gamma_{\text{BIN}}\rceil D)$-*friends detector can be implemented, with probe complexity* $T_{\text{BIN}}(n, K, \alpha/2, c_1 \cdot \log n)$ *for some constant* c_1, *and with success probability* $1 - n^{-\Omega(1)}$.

Proof: Compute W by algorithm DISTANCE_EST and output "true" iff $W(i, i') \leq \frac{5}{2}\beta$. ∎

Algorithm 3 BUILD_PREFS(A, α, D, β) By user i

(1) Invoke Algorithm DISTANCE_EST(A, α, D) to compute a $(D, 5\beta)$-friends detector.

    Let $I = \left\{ i' : W(i', i) \leq \frac{5}{2}\beta \right\}$ be the set of users detected as "friends". (Recall that $\beta = 4\lceil\gamma\rceil D$.)

(2) Let $\mathcal{C} = \emptyset$. Repeat $r \log n$ times:

    (2a) Probe each object j, independently with probability $\frac{\log(m+n)}{\alpha n}$ and post probe results on the billboard.

        Let S_i be the set of objects probed by user i.

        For each object j, let $I^j = \{i' \in I : j \in S_{i'}\}$, i.e., members of I that probed j.

    (2b) For each object j do:

        (2bi) If $j \in S_i$ then set C_j to $A_{i,j}$ as probed in Step 2a.

        (2bii) If $j \notin S_i$ then set $C_j = \frac{1}{|I_i^j|} \sum_{i' \in I_i^j} A_{i',j}$. If $I_i^j = \emptyset$ set $C_j = 1/2$ (this will happen with negligible probability).

    (2c) $\mathcal{C} \leftarrow \mathcal{C} \cup \{C\}$.

(3) Return $C_l \in \mathcal{C}$ which maximizes
$$|\{C_{l'} \in \mathcal{C} : \mathrm{dist}(C_l, C_{l'}) \leq 30\beta\}|.$$

4.2   Reconstructing the preference vectors

We now describe the complete algorithm, assuming that we are given a good friends detector (Definition 4.1), and our task is to reconstruct an approximation of the preference vectors.

The idea is as follows (see pseudo-code in Algorithm 3). First, the users probe an appropriately large random sample of the objects: intuitively, this is to get sufficient coverage. Next, each user looks at the results of probes of users who are deemed "close," as determined by the friends detector; for each object, the user computes the averages of the friends' grades as a candidate output, thereby obtaining a candidate vector. We prove that in expectation, the candidate vector is close to the true preference vector. However, its variance is unknown, and therefore, to get a usable approximation, we repeat the procedure: we construct many candidate vectors independently, and output the one with many close neighbors (this is akin to picking the median of single-dimension samples). For that output, we prove that with high probability, the result is a good approximation.

We now analyze the algorithm. We start by considering a single candidate.

LEMMA 4.8. *Let A be (α, D)-similar, and suppose that Algorithm BUILD_PREFS uses a $(D, 4\lceil\gamma_{\text{BIN}}\rceil D)$-friends detector over A. Then for any candidate vector C computed by user i in Step 2b of Algorithm BUILD_PREFS, $E[dist(C, A_i)] \leq 20\lceil\gamma_{\text{BIN}}\rceil D$.*

Proof: Since there are at least αn users with $\mathrm{dist}(A_i, A_{i'}) \leq D$, Theorem 4.7 ensures that $|I| \geq \alpha n$, and hence $E[I^j] \geq \log(m+n)$. By the Chernoff Bound $|I^j| \geq 1$ with overwhelming probability. We apply the Union Bound and deduce that, with overwhelming probability, $|I^j| \geq 1$ for all

j. Theorem 4.7 also ensures that I includes only users with preference vectors at distance at most $5\beta \leq 20\lceil\gamma_{\text{BIN}}\rceil D$ from user i preference vector.

Fix i. For any $i' \in I$ and any $j \in S_{i'}$ let $\eta_{i'}^j$ be the random variable $\eta_{i'}^j = |A_{i,j} - A_{i',j}|$ with expectation (over the choices by user i') $E[\eta_{i'}^j] \leq \frac{5\beta}{m}$. As the objects probed by each user are chosen independently of the values in the matrix A we may conclude that the random variables $\eta_{i'}^j = |A_{i,j} - A_{i',j}|$ are independent from the random variables I^j. By the triangle inequality,

$$
\begin{aligned}
E[\mathrm{dist}(C, A_i)] &= E\left[\sum_{j=1}^{m} |C_j - A_{i,j}|\right] \\
&\leq E\left[\sum_{j=1}^{m} \frac{1}{|I^j|} \sum_{i' \in I^j} \eta_{i'}^j\right] \\
&= \sum_{j=1}^{m} \frac{1}{|I^j|} \sum_{i' \in I^j} E[\eta_{i'}^j] \\
&\leq 5\beta.
\end{aligned}
$$
∎

Lemma 4.8 bounded the expected error of the reconstruction done by BUILD_PREFS. We now summarize the overall algorithm.

THEOREM 4.9. *Let $A_{n \times m}$ be (α, D)-similar matrix with entries in $[0, 1]$, and let BIN be a binary reconstruction algorithm with approximation ratio γ_{BIN} and probe complexity T_{BIN}. Then with probability $1 - n^{-\Omega(1)}$, Algorithm BUILD_PREFS reconstructs A with approximation ratio $O(\gamma_{\text{BIN}})$ and probe complexity $T_{\text{BIN}}\left(n, K, \frac{\alpha}{2}, \frac{4KD}{m}\right) + O\left(\frac{m}{n} \cdot \frac{\log^2(m+n)}{\alpha}\right)$, where $K = \lceil 3cm\log n/D\rceil = O(\frac{m}{D}\log n)$.*

Proof: For each candidate $C \in \mathcal{C}$ let y be the random variable equal to the distance of the candidate from the user's preference vector, i.e. $y = |C - A_i|$. As the distances are non-negative random variables, Markov's Inequality implies that the probability of each distance to be larger than 3 times its expectation is less than $\frac{1}{3}$. By the Chernoff Bound, the probability that at least half of the distances are higher than 3 times their expectation is at most $n^{-r/36}$. Hence, with probability $1 - n^{-r/36}$, there is a subset $\mathcal{C}^*$ with $|\mathcal{C}^*| > \frac{1}{2}|\mathcal{C}|$ such that for each candidate $C \in \mathcal{C}^*$ we have that $\mathrm{dist}(C, A_i) \leq 3E[y]$. It follows there is at least one candidate with at least $\frac{1}{2}|\mathcal{C}|$ neighbors at distance at most $6E[y]$ from it. Every candidate with at least $\frac{1}{2}|\mathcal{C}|$ neighbors has at least one neighbor at distance at most $3E[y]$ from A_i. Hence, the output vector is at distance at most $3E[y] + 30\beta$ from A_i. The Theorem follows, because $E[y] \leq 5\beta$ by Lemma 4.8.

The complexity bound follows from Theorem 4.7 and the fact that only $O\left(\frac{m}{n} \cdot \frac{\log n \cdot \log(m+n)}{\alpha}\right)$ probes are added by Step 2a of Algorithm BUILD_PREFS. ∎

5. REFERENCES

[1] N. Alon, B. Awerbuch, Y. Azar, and B. Patt-Shamir. Tell me who I am: an interactive recommendation system. In *Proc. 18th Ann. ACM Symp. on Parallelism in Algorithms and Architectures (SPAA)*, pages 1–10, 2006.

[2] B. Awerbuch, Y. Azar, Z. Lotker, B. Patt-Shamir, and M. Tuttle. Collaborate with strangers to find own preferences. In *Proc. 17th ACM Symp. on Parallelism in Algorithms and Architectures (SPAA)*, pages 263–269, 2005.

[3] B. Awerbuch, A. Nisgav, and B. Patt-Shamir. Asynchronous active recommendation systems. In *Principles of distributed systems : 11th international conference (OPODIS 2007)*, volume 4878 of *LNCS*, pages 48–61, 2007.

[4] B. Awerbuch, B. Patt-Shamir, D. Peleg, and M. Tuttle. Improved recommendation systems. In *Proc. 16th Ann. ACM-SIAM Symp. on Discrete Algorithms (SODA)*, pages 1174–1183, 2005.

[5] Y. Azar, A. Fiat, A. Karlin, F. McSherry, and J. Saia. Spectral analysis of data. In *Proc. 33rd ACM Symp. on Theory of Computing (STOC)*, pages 619–626, 2001.

[6] R. M. Bell and Y. Koren. Lessons from the netflix prize challenge. *SIGKDD Explor. Newsl.*, 9(2):75–79, 2007.

[7] P. Drineas, I. Kerenidis, and P. Raghavan. Competitive recommendation systems. In *Proc. 34th ACM Symp. on Theory of Computing (STOC)*, pages 82–90, 2002.

[8] S. Gilbert, R. Guerraoui, F. M. Rad, and M. Zadimoghaddam. Collaborative scoring with dishonest participants. In *Proc. 22nd Ann. ACM Symp. on Parallel Algorithms and Architectures (SPAA)*, pages 41–49, 2010.

[9] K. Goldberg, T. Roeder, D. Gupta, , and C. Perkins. Eigentaste: A constant time collaborative filtering algorithm. *Information Retrieval Journal*, 4(2):133–151, July 2001.

[10] J. Kleinberg and M. Sandler. Convergent algorithms for collaborative filtering. In *Proc. 4th ACM Conf. on Electronic Commerce (EC)*, pages 1–10, 2003.

[11] R. Kumar, P. Raghavan, S. Rajagopalan, and A. Tomkins. Recommendation systems: A probabilistic analysis. In *Proc. 39th IEEE Symp. on Foundations of Computer Science (FOCS)*, pages 664–673, 1998.

[12] A. Nisgav and B. Patt-Shamir. Finding similar users in social networks: extended abstract. In *Proc. 21st Ann. ACM Symp. on Parallelism in Algorithms and Architectures (SPAA)*, pages 169–177, 2009.

[13] C. H. Papadimitriou, P. Raghavan, H. Tamaki, and S. Vempala. Latent semantic indexing: A probabilistic analysis. In *Proc. 17th ACM Symp. on Principles of Database Systems (PODS)*, pages 159–168. ACM Press, 1998.

[14] P. Resnick, N. Iacovou, M. Suchak, P. Bergstrom, and J. Riedl. Grouplens: an open architecture for collaborative filtering of netnews. In *Proc. 1994 ACM Conf. on Computer Supported Cooperative Work*, pages 175–186, Oct. 1994.

[15] P. Resnick and H. R. Varian. Recommender systems. *Commun. ACM*, 40(3):56–58, 1997.

[16] B. Sarwar, G. Karypis, J. Konstan, and J. Riedl. Analysis of recommendation algorithms for e-commerce. In *Proc. 2nd ACM Conf. on Electronic Commerce (EC)*, pages 158–167. ACM Press, 2000.

Brief Announcement: Distributed Shared Memory based on Computation Migration

Mieszko Lis   Keun Sup Shim   Myong Hyon Cho   Christopher W. Fletcher
Michel Kinsy   Ilia Lebedev   Omer Khan   Srinivas Devadas

Computer Science and Artificial Intelligence Laboratory
Massachusetts Institute of Technology
Cambridge, MA, USA

{mieszko,ksshim,mhcho,cwfletcher,mkinsy,ilebedev,okhan,devadas}@csail.mit.edu

Categories and Subject Descriptors: B.3.2 [Memory Structures]: Design Styles: Shared Memory; C.1.4 [Processor Architectures]: Parallel Architectures.

General Terms: Design, Performance.

1. BACKGROUND

Driven by increasingly unbalanced technology scaling and power dissipation limits, microprocessor designers have resorted to increasing the number of cores on a single chip, and pundits expect 1000-core designs to materialize in the next few years [1]. But how will memory architectures scale and how will these next-generation multicores be programmed?

One barrier to scaling current memory architectures is the *off-chip memory bandwidth wall* [1,2]: off-chip bandwidth grows with package pin density, which scales much more slowly than on-die transistor density [3]. To reduce reliance on external memories and keep data on-chip, today's multicores integrate very large shared last-level caches on chip [4]; interconnects used with such shared caches, however, do not scale beyond relatively few cores, and the power requirements and access latencies of large caches exclude their use in chips on a 1000-core scale. For massive-scale multicores, then, we are left with relatively small per-core caches.

Per-core caches on a 1000-core scale, in turn, raise the question of memory coherence. On the one hand, a shared memory abstraction is a practical necessity for general-purpose programming, and most programmers prefer a shared memory model [5]. On the other hand, ensuring coherence among private caches is an expensive proposition: bus-based and snoopy protocols don't scale beyond relatively few cores, and directory sizes needed in cache-coherence protocols must equal a significant portion of the *combined* size of the per-core caches as otherwise directory evictions will limit performance [6]. Moreover, directory-based coherence protocols are notoriously difficult to implement and verify [7].

2. EXECUTION MIGRATION MACHINE

The Execution Migration Machine (EM^2) [8,9] maintains memory coherence by allowing each address to be cached in only one core cache (the *home*), and efficiently migrating execution to the

home core whenever another core wishes to access that address. A hardware-level thread migration protocol ensures that execution transfer is efficient: the architectural context (program counter, register file, and possibly other state like the TLB) is unloaded onto the interconnect network, travels to the destination core, and is loaded into the architectural state elements there [8]. Because each thread always accesses a given address from the same core, threads never disagree about the contents of memory locations so sequential consistency is trivially ensured.

The flow of a memory access under EM^2 is shown in Figure 1. Depending on the implementation, each core may be capable of multiplexing execution among several contexts at instruction granularity; when all contexts are occupied, an incoming migration causes one of them to be evicted. For deadlock-free migrations, each core has one *native* context for each of the threads that originated on that core in addition for the *guest* contexts for threads originally started on other cores: an evicted thread travels to its dedicated native context on a separate virtual network to avoid dependency loops and deadlock [10].

EM^2 can potentially outperform traditional directory-based cache coherence (CC) by avoiding the data replication and loss of effective cache capacity of CC [8,9] and by enabling data access through a one-way migration protocol. However, migrations can negatively affect performance because of the delays involved in stopping, migrating, and restarting threads; moreover, each migration must transfer the entire execution context (1–2 KBits in a 32-bit Atom-like processor [8]) over the on-chip network, causing significant power consumption.

Optimizing performance and power, therefore, requires either (a) reducing the migration rate, or (b) reducing the amount of data transferred in each migration (and so making migrations faster and more power-efficient). Since migrations depend on the assignment

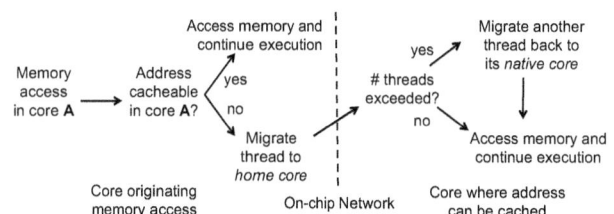

Figure 1: The life of a memory access under EM^2

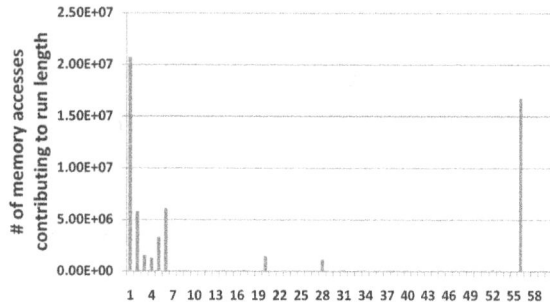

Figure 2: The number of accesses to memory cached at non-native cores for a SPLASH-2 [13] OCEAN benchmark run, binned by the number of consequent accesses to the same core (the *run length*). About half of the accesses migrate after one memory reference, while the other half keep accessing memory at the core where they have migrated. 64-core/64-thread EM^2 simulation using Graphite [14], with 16KB L1 + 64KB L2 data caches and first-touch data placement.

of addresses to per-core caches, a good data placement method (one which keeps a thread's private data assigned to that thread's native core, and allocates shared data among the sharers) is critical. Since data placement has been investigated in the context of CC-NUMA architectures (e.g., [11]) and EM^2-specific program-level replication techniques have also been explored [12], the remainder of this paper focuses on part (b), and outlines two approaches to reducing the average migration cost.

3. EM² WITH REMOTE CACHE ACCESS

One scenario where EM^2 performance and power efficiency can be improved is evident from Figure 2: in about half of the non-local cache accesses (which cause the accessing thread to migrate), the thread migrates to another core after just one memory access (and possibly other non-memory instructions), usually back to the core from which the first migration originated (data not shown). In each case, a full execution context (including the entire register file) traverses the on-chip interconnect only to bring back one word of data (or, for writes, no data), clearly a suboptimal scenario.

To address this, we propose to extend EM^2 with a remote cache access capability: for some memory accesses, a thread will contact the remote cache and retrieve (or write) the necessary word instead of migrating back and forth. Although memory coherence approaches based entirely on remote cache access have been proposed [15], they must make a separate access for each word to ensure memory coherence; the combination with EM^2 is therefore uniquely poised to address both the one-off remote cache accesses and the runs of consequent accesses shown in Figure 2.

Figure 3 illustrates the memory access process under this hybrid architecture (EM^2-RA). To avoid interconnect deadlock, the remote-access virtual subnetwork must be separate from the subnetworks used for migrations and (cf. [10]), requiring six virtual channels in total. Clearly, the migration-vs.-remote-access decision is crucial to EM^2-RA performance; we therefore outline a simplified analytical model that establishes an upper bound on performance of decision schemes and thus allows us to quickly evaluate how close to optimal a given hardware-implementable scheme is.

The simplified model considers one thread at a time (and so ignores evictions caused by migrations to a core with no free guest

contexts), ignores local memory access delays (since the migration-vs.-RA decision mainly affects network delays), and assumes knowledge of the full memory trace of the application as well as the address-to-core data placement. Under these assumptions, the solution can be obtained efficiently via the following dynamic program:

Given a thread memory trace $m_1, \cdots, m_N$, the data placement implies a corresponding sequence of cores $d(m_1), \cdots, d(m_N)$. Suppose we have the optimal solution to the sub-trace $m_1, \cdots, m_k$ when the thread starts at core c_0 and ends at core c_i; call this $OPT(m_1, m_k, c_i)$. The solution for the longer memory sub-trace $m_1, \cdots, m_k, m_{k+1}$, with the thread ending at a particular core c_j, can be broken into two cases:

- Core miss for m_{k+1}: $c_j \neq d(m_{k+1})$. The thread stays at c_j and performs a remote access, so we return:
  $$OPT(m_1, m_k, c_j) + cost_{remote\_access}(c_j, d(m_{k+1})).$$

- Core hit for m_{k+1}: $c_j = d(m_{k+1})$. The thread either stays at c_j and accesses the *local* cache (for free) or migrates from another core and then accesses the local cache, so we return:
  $$\min \big(OPT(m_1, m_k, c_j),$$
  $$\min_{c_i : c_i \neq c_j} OPT(m_1, m_k, c_i) + cost_{migration}(c_i, c_j) \big).$$

This optimal solution can be computed in time $O(NP^2)$, where N is the length of the trace and P is the number of processor cores. Computing the equivalent cost of a specific decision requires applying the decision procedure to each memory access in the trace, and so is $O(N)$.

4. STACK-BASED EM² ARCHITECTURE

While the EM^2-RA hybrid effectively reduces the migrated context size on average by replacing some migrations with round-trip remote cache accesses, optimal performance requires potentially complex logic in each core to make the migration vs. remote access decision.

But how can we reduce the migrated context size for *all* migrations? The minimum migration context comprises the program counter (necessary to retrieve the next instructions) and the entire register file (necessary to execute the instructions). Although one could imagine sending only a portion of the register file (based, for example, on the operands of the next few instructions), the register file is a random-access data structure and the next few instructions could refer to any subset of registers, necessitating complex muxing in and out of the register file block. Clearly, to drastically reduce migration context size we must dramatically reduce or entirely give up the register file.

Stack architectures, which do not have a random-access register file, offer a natural solution. In a stack-based ISA, most instructions do not specify their operands but instead access the top of the stack: for example, an ADD instruction would replace the top two entries on the stack with one entry containing their sum. Most often, there are two stacks (the expression stack, used for evaluation, and the return stack, used for procedure return addresses and loop counters); the top few entries of each stack are typically cached in registers and backed by a region of main memory with overflows and underflows of the stack cache automatically and transparently handled in hardware.

The stack-machine approach has been used to ensure fast procedure calls in early computers (e.g., the Burroughs B5000), simplify embedded and resilient controller architectures (see [16] for a review), and to reduce code footprint in virtual machines (e.g.,

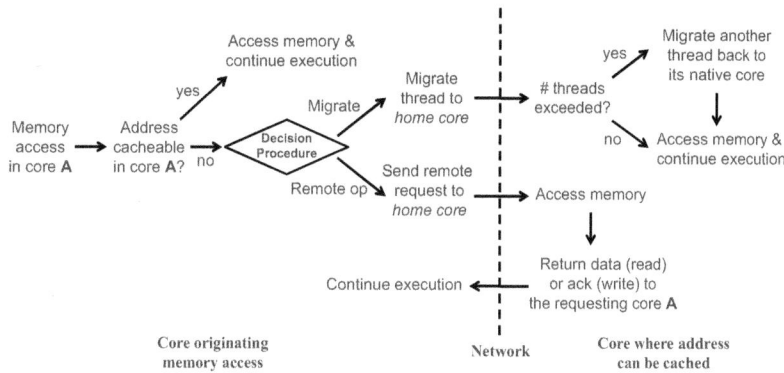

Figure 3: The life of a memory access under EM^2-RA.

the JVM). For EM^2, a stack machine dramatically reduces the required context size: because instructions can only access the top of the stack, only the top few entries must be sent over to a remote core when a memory access causes a migration. Since stack overflows and underflows are handled by loads and stores to memory, the offending thread will automatically migrate back to its native core (where its stack memory is assigned) when the migrated stack overflows or underflows.

A stack-based EM^2 architecture can choose to migrate only a portion of the stack cache—with enough data to continue execution on the remote core while data accesses are being made there, and enough space to carry back any results without overflows—and flush the rest to the stack memory prior to migration. Since the migrated depth can be different for every access, determining the best per-migration depth requires a decision algorithm. Indeed, to evaluate such schemes, we can use the same analytical model described for the EM^2-RA case and a similar optimization formulation to compute the optimal stack depths (instead of the binary migrate-vs.-RA decision, the algorithm considers the various stack depths) and compares them against a given depth-decision scheme.

5. CONCLUSION

The Execution Migration Machine (EM^2) is a memory architecture that provides distributed shared memory using fast, hardware-level thread migrations. In this paper, we focus on reducing the size of execution context that is sent over the network in every migration, which improves both latency (especially on low-bandwidth interconnects) and power dissipation. To this end, we introduce two variant architectures which reduce average context size: (a) EM^2 with remote cache access that replaces some migrations with smaller round-trip remote accesses, and (b) a stack-machine EM^2 architecture where the migrated context size can vary from a few top-of-stack registers to a larger portion of the stack.

Both architectures require a fast core-local decision for every memory access: for EM^2-RA, whether to migrate or do a remote cache access, and for stack-EM^2, how much of the stack to migrate. We therefore introduce a simplified analytical model of EM^2 performance together with a dynamic-programming algorithm to compute the optimal decision sequence from an application's memory access trace, which will allow us to evaluate hardware-implementable decision schemes that will be a focus of our future research.

6. REFERENCES

[1] S. Borkar, "Thousand core chips: a technology perspective," in *DAC*, 2007.

[2] N. Hardavellas, M. Ferdman, B. Falsafi, and A. Ailamaki, "Reactive NUCA: near-optimal block placement and replication in distributed caches," in *ISCA*, 2009.

[3] I. T. R. for Semiconductors, "Assembly and packaging," 2007.

[4] S. Rusu, S. Tam, H. Muljono, D. Ayers, J. Chang, R. Varada, M. Ratta, and S. Vora, "A 45nm 8-core enterprise Xeon® processor," in *A-SSCC*, 2009.

[5] A. C. Sodan, "Message-Passing and Shared-Data Programming Models—Wish vs. Reality," in *HPCS*, 2005.

[6] A. Gupta, W. Weber, and T. Mowry, "Reducing memory and traffic requirements for scalable directory-based cache coherence schemes," in *International Conference on Parallel Processing*, 1990.

[7] D. Abts, S. Scott, and D. J. Lilja, "So Many States, So Little Time: Verifying Memory Coherence in the Cray X1," in *IPDPS*, 2003.

[8] O. Khan, M. Lis, and S. Devadas, "EM^2: A Scalable Shared-Memory Multicore Architecture," *MIT-CSAIL-TR-2010-030*, 2010.

[9] M. Lis, K. S. Shim, O. Khan, and S. Devadas, "Shared Memory via Execution Migration," in *ASPLOS I&P*, 2011.

[10] M. H. Cho, K. S. Shim, M. Lis, O. Khan, and S. Devadas, "Deadlock-Free Fine-Grained Thread Migration," in *NOCS*, 2011.

[11] B. Verghese, S. Devine, A. Gupta, and M. Rosenblum, "Operating system support for improving data locality on CC-NUMA compute servers," *SIGPLAN Not.*, vol. 31, no. 9, pp. 279–289, 1996.

[12] K. S. Shim, M. Lis, M. H. Cho, O. Khan, and S. Devadas, "System-level Optimizations for Memory Access in the Execution Migration Machine (EM^2)," in *CAOS*, 2011.

[13] S. Woo, M. Ohara, E. Torrie, J. Singh, and A. Gupta, "The SPLASH-2 programs: characterization and methodological considerations," in *ISCA*, 1995.

[14] J. E. Miller, H. Kasture, G. Kurian, C. Gruenwald, N. Beckmann, C. Celio, J. Eastep, and A. Agarwal, "Graphite: A distributed parallel simulator for multicores," in *HPCA*, 2010.

[15] C. Fensch and M. Cintra, "An OS-Based Alternative to Full Hardware Coherence on Tiled CMPs," in *HPCA*, 2008.

[16] P. Koopman, *Stack Computers: The New Wave.* Ellis Horwood, 1989.

Brief Announcement: Communication Bounds for Heterogeneous Architectures

Grey Ballard[*]
UC Berkeley
ballard@cs.berkeley.edu

James Demmel[*]
UC Berkeley
demmel@cs.berkeley.edu

Andrew Gearhart[*]
UC Berkeley
agearh@cs.berkeley.edu

ABSTRACT

As the gap between the cost of communication (i.e., data movement) and computation continues to grow, the importance of pursuing algorithms which minimize communication also increases. Toward this end, we seek asymptotic communication lower bounds for general memory models and classes of algorithms. Recent work [2] has established lower bounds for a wide set of linear algebra algorithms on a sequential machine and on a parallel machine with identical processors. This work extends these previous bounds to a heterogeneous model in which processors access data and perform floating point operations at differing speeds. We also present an algorithm for dense matrix multiplication which attains the lower bound.

Categories and Subject Descriptors: F.2.1 [Analysis of Algorithms and Problem Complexity]: Numerical Algorithms and Problems: Computations on matrices
ACM General Terms: algorithms
Keywords: communication-avoiding, heterogeneity

1. INTRODUCTION

Recently, existing lower bounds [4, 5] for any $O(n^3)$ matrix multiplication algorithm on a sequential architecture with two memory levels were generalized to most "direct" linear algebra algorithms [2]. These results present a lower bound on the number of words W transferred between fast and slow memory: $W \geq \frac{G}{8\sqrt{M}}$, where G is the number of floating point operations that fit the requirements of [2] and M is the size of fast memory (in words). In this memory model, words which are stored contiguously in slow memory may be read together in one "message." We represent the time cost of a single message between fast memory and slow memory as: $T_{\text{msg}} = \alpha + \beta w$, where w is the number of words transferred, α is the latency cost per message and β is the cost to transfer a word (inverse bandwidth). By noting that the size of the largest message is M, we obtain a similar lower bound on the number of messages L transferred between fast and slow memory: $L \geq \frac{G}{8M^{3/2}}$. Both of these lower bounds have been extended to parallel distributed-memory architectures with homogeneous processors [2, 5].

[*]Research supported by Microsoft (Award #024263) and Intel (Award #024894) funding and by matching funding by U.C. Discovery (Award #DIG07-10227).

2. COMMUNICATION LOWER BOUNDS

To capture the non-uniform nature of a heterogeneous computing environment, we model the machine as a set of compute elements proc_i $(1 \leq i \leq P)$ connected via independent links to a large shared global memory. Each proc_i has several element-specific parameters: β_i (inverse bandwidth), α_i (latency), M_i (local memory size), and γ_i (flops per second). We assume that the initial data for the problem is stored within global memory.

Suppose we run an algorithm which executes G flops on a heterogeneous machine, and suppose the algorithm assigns F_i flops to proc_i for $1 \leq i \leq P$, such that $\sum F_i = G$. Then we can focus our attention on one compute element proc_i and model the communication between the local memory of proc_i and global memory as two levels of a sequential machine. In this way, we can apply the inequalities from the previous section and obtain a lower bound on the number of words W_i transferred to/from proc_i and, similarly, a lower bound on the number of messages L_i. Although we can obtain separate lower bounds for each compute element, the bounds apply only to a particular partitioning of the total flops. We seek a lower bound which applies to any assignment of the G flops to the different compute elements.

Toward this end, we broaden our focus from the individual communication costs of each compute element to the total parallel runtime. By ignoring idle time, we lower bound proc_i's total runtime T_i by the sum of three terms: $T_i \geq \gamma_i F_i + \beta_i W_i + \alpha_i L_i$, where F_i, W_i, and L_i are the number of flops executed, words communicated, and messages communicated, respectively, by proc_i during the course of the algorithm. The parallel runtime is determined by the last compute element to finish its computation. Thus, given a partition $\{F_i\}$ of the G flops, we have

$$T(\{F_i\}) \geq \max_{1 \leq i \leq P} \left(\gamma_i F_i + \beta_i W_i + \alpha_i L_i \right).$$

In order to obtain a more general lower bound, we can find the minimum over all possible partitions. Assuming that sequential lower bounds hold for each compute element individually, we can apply them to obtain our heterogeneous lower bound on parallel runtime:

$$T \geq \min_{\sum F_i = G} \max_{1 \leq i \leq P} \left(\gamma_i F_i + \frac{\beta_i F_i}{8\sqrt{M_i}} + \frac{\alpha_i F_i}{8M_i^{3/2}} \right).$$

We can simplify the min-max expression by solving a linear program for the optimal partition $\{\hat{F}_i\}$, and we obtain

$$T \geq \max_{1 \leq i \leq P} \delta_i \hat{F}_i = \frac{G}{\sum_j \frac{1}{\delta_j}}, \qquad (1)$$

where $\delta_i = \gamma_i + \frac{\beta_i}{8\sqrt{M_i}} + \frac{\alpha_i}{8M_i^{3/2}}$ and

$$\hat{F}_i = \frac{\frac{1}{\delta_i}}{\sum_j \frac{1}{\delta_j}} G. \qquad (2)$$

In the next section we present an algorithm to compute square matrix multiplication that attains this lower bound.

3. MATRIX MULTIPLICATION

We base our algorithm, shown as Algorithm 1, on the square recursive general matrix multiplication algorithm, or rec-GEMM (see [3] for example). In this algorithm, each of the matrices is divided into four $\frac{n}{2} \times \frac{n}{2}$ submatrices and the blocked multiplication of these submatrices yields eight subproblems of $2(n/2)^3$ flops each, which can be solved recursively. We assume that n is a power of two in this section, and require that the $n \times n$ input matrices A and B are stored block-recursively [6] so that every subproblem will be associated with contiguous data. We assign a number of flops to each processor based on the optimal partition $\{\hat{F}_i\}$ given in equation (2), and our goal will be to organize the distribution of flops such that communication is minimized for each compute element. We will also assume that for a given heterogeneous machine, the problem size is large enough such that the number of flops assigned to proc_i satisfies

$$\hat{F}_i \geq (M_i/3)^{3/2} \qquad (3)$$

for each $1 \leq i \leq P$. Note that on a sequential machine, this degenerates to $3n^2 \geq M$, where the matrix multiplication problem (two input matrices and one output matrix) is too large to fit entirely in fast memory.

Algorithm 1 Heterogeneous matrix-matrix multiplication

Require: Matrices $A, B \in \mathbb{R}^{n \times n}$ are stored in block-recursive order, n is a power of two
1: Measure $a_i, \beta_j, \gamma_i, M_i$ for each $1 \leq i \leq P$
2: **for** $i = 1$ to P **do**
3:    Set F_i according to equation (2) where $G = n^3$
4:    Set k_i to be largest integer s.t. $3(n/2^{k_i})^2 \geq M_i$
5:    Round F_i/G to the k_i^{th} octal digit: $0.d_1^{(i)} d_2^{(i)} \cdots d_{k_i}^{(i)}$
6: **end for**
7: Initialize $S = \{A \cdot B\}$ as set of problems
8: **for** $j = 1$ to max k_i **do**
9:    Subdivide all problems in S into 8 subproblems
10:    **for** $i = 1$ to p **do**
11:       Assign $d_j^{(i)}$ problems to proc_i and remove from S
12:    **end for**
13: **end for**
14: **for all** proc_i parallel **do**
15:    Compute assigned subproblems using rec-GEMM
16: **end for**
Ensure: Matrix $C = AB$, stored in block-recursive order

While the optimal partition given in equation (2) specifies *how many* flops should be assigned to each compute element, it does not specify *which* flops should be assigned. The idea behind Algorithm 1 is to organize the computation on each compute element in order to minimize communication costs. Note that a subproblem of size b involves $O(b^2)$ (contiguous) data and $O(b^3)$ flops. In order to maximize the possible data re-use we wish to assign large subtrees (i.e., subproblems) of the global recursion tree of rec-GEMM to the same

compute element. By converting F_i/G to the octal digits $(0.d_1^{(i)} d_2^{(i)} \cdots)_8$ and assigning to proc_i $d_1^{(i)}$ subproblems at the first level of recursion, $d_2^{(i)}$ subproblems at the second level of recursion, and so on, we assign the desired amount of flops to a given compute element in a manner that assigns larger subproblems first. For example, if $F_1/G = (0.123)_8$, then proc_1 is assigned one $\frac{n}{2} \times \frac{n}{2}$ subproblem, two $\frac{n}{4} \times \frac{n}{4}$ subproblems, and three $\frac{n}{8} \times \frac{n}{8}$ subproblems.

However, in order to achieve optimal sequential communication costs on each compute element, we must ensure that no subproblem is assigned to a compute element which fits entirely in its local memory. Thus, we round the octal fractions to k_i digits as specified in line 4 (which varies by compute element). Lines 7-13 compose the static scheduling of subproblems to compute elements, and lines 14-16 constitute the actual computations which are all independent (we ignore the $O(n^2)$ work to sum the results of subproblems).

THEOREM 1. *Assuming the problem size is large enough such that inequality (3) is satisfied, Algorithm 1 attains the parallel run-time lower bound given in inequality (1) for dense matrix multiplication on any heterogeneous machine which fits the model specified in Section 2.*

PROOF. See [1] for a detailed proof. The argument hinges on the fact that rounding F_i/G to k_i octal digits does not cause more than a constant factor of deviation from the optimal partitioning of flops, and that no subproblem assigned to a compute element is small enough to fit in local memory which ensures that rec-GEMM attains asymptotically optimal sequential communication costs. ☐

4. REFERENCES

[1] G. Ballard, J. Demmel, and A. Gearhart. Communication bounds for heterogeneous architectures. Technical report, UC Berkeley EECS-2011-13, Feb. 2011.

[2] G. Ballard, J. Demmel, O. Holtz, and O. Schwartz. Minimizing communication in linear algebra. Technical report, UC Berkeley EECS-2011-15, Feb. 2011.

[3] R. Blumofe, M. Frigo, C. Joerg, C. Leiserson, and K. Randall. DAG-consistent distributed shared memory. In *IPPS '96: Proceedings of the 10th international parallel processing symposium*, pages 132–141, 1996.

[4] J. W. Hong and H. T. Kung. I/O complexity: The red-blue pebble game. In *STOC '81: Proceedings of the thirteenth annual ACM symposium on theory of computing*, pages 326–333, New York, NY, USA, 1981. ACM.

[5] D. Irony, S. Toledo, and A. Tiskin. Communication lower bounds for distributed-memory matrix multiplication. *J. Parallel Distrib. Comput.*, 64(9):1017–1026, 2004.

[6] D. Wise. Ahnentafel indexing into Morton-ordered arrays, or matrix locality for free. In A. Bode, T. Ludwig, W. Karl, and R. Wismüller, editors, *Euro-Par 2000 Parallel Processing*, volume 1900 of *Lecture Notes in Computer Science*, pages 774–783. Springer Berlin / Heidelberg, 2000.

Brief Announcement: Large-Scale Multimaps

Michael T. Goodrich
Dept. of Computer Science
University of California, Irvine
goodrich(at)acm.org

Michael Mitzenmacher
Dept. of Computer Science
Harvard University
michaelm(at)eecs.harvard.edu

ABSTRACT

Many data structures support dictionaries, also known as maps or associative arrays, which store and manage a set of key-value pairs. A *multimap* is generalization that allows multiple values to be associated with the same key. We study how multimaps can be implemented efficiently online in external memory frameworks, with constant expected I/O. The key technique used to achieve our results is a combination of cuckoo hashing using buckets that hold multiple items with a multiqueue implementation to cope with varying numbers of values per key.

Categories and Subject Descriptors

F.2.2 [**Analysis of Algorithms and Problem Complexity**]: Nonnumerical Algorithms and Problems

General Terms

Algorithms, Theory

Keywords

Multimap, inverted index, cuckoo hashing, multiqueue.

1. INTRODUCTION

A *multimap* is a simple abstract data type (ADT) that generalizes the the map ADT to support key-value associations in a way that allows multiple values to be associated with the same key. Specifically, it is a dynamic container, C, of key-value pairs, which we call *items*, supporting (at least) the following operations:

- insert(k, v): insert the key-value pair, (k, v). This operation allows for there to be existing key-value pairs having the same key as k, but we assume w.l.o.g. that the particular key-value pair (k, v) is itself not already present in C.

- isMember(k, v): return true if and only if the key-value pair, (k, v), is present in C.

- remove(k, v): remove the key-value pair, (k, v), from C. This operation returns an error condition if (k, v) is not currently in C.

- findAll(k): return the set of all key-value pairs in C having key equal to k.

- removeAll(k): remove from C all key-value pairs having key equal to k.

Surprisingly, we are not familiar with any previous discussion of this specific abstract data type in the theoretical algorithms and data structures literature. Nevertheless, abstract data types equivalent to the above ADT, as well as multimap implementations, are included in the C++ Standard Template Library (STL), Guava–the Google Java Collections Library, and the Apache Commons Collection 3.2.1 API. The existence of these implementations provides empirical evidence for the utility of this abstract data type.

One of the primary motivations for studying the multimap ADT is that associative data in the real world can exhibit significant non-uniformities with respect to the relationships between keys and values. For example, many real-world data sets follow a power law with respect to data frequencies indexed by rank. Specifically, in natural language documents, the frequency of the word of rank j is predicted to be roughly proportional to j^{-s} for some parameters s. Thus, if we wished to construct a data structure to retrieve all instances of any query word in such a corpus, subject to insertions and deletions of documents, then we could use a multimap, but would require one that could handle large skews in the number of values per key. In this case, the multimap could be viewed as providing a dynamic functionality for a classic static data structure, known as' an *inverted file* or *inverted index* (e.g., see Knuth [3]). Such data structures are often used in modern search engines (e.g., see Zobel and Moffat [9]). Dynamic inverted indexes have been studied in the past, but generally from a systems viewpoint rather than a theoretical one. (See, e.g., [4, 5], and references therein.)

Our work utilizes a variation on cuckoo hash tables. We assume the reader has some familiarity with such hash tables, as originally presented by Pagh and Rodler [6]. (A general description can be found on Wikipedia at `http://en.wikipedia.org/wiki/Cuckoo_hashing`.) We describe an external-memory implementation of the multimap ADT, based on the standard two-level I/O model (e.g., see [1, 8]). We also have a parallel algorithm abstracted using the bulk synchronous parallel (BSP) model [7], which we do not describe due to lack of space. We support an online implementation where each operation must be completely finished executing prior to our beginning execution of any subsequent operations. The bounds we achieve are shown in Table 1.

Our constructions are based on the combination of external-memory cuckoo hash tables and multiqueues. We show that external-memory cuckoo hashing supports a cuckoo-type method for insertions that can be implemented in a way that allows us to prove that only an expected constant num-

Method	Amortized I/O Performance
insert(k, v)	$\bar{O}(1)$
isMember(k, v)	$O(1)$
remove(k, v)	$O(1)$
findAll(k)	$O(1 + n_k/B)$
removeAll(k)	$O(1)$

Table 1: Performance bounds for our multimap implementation. We use $\bar{O}(*)$ to denote an expected bound; B to denote the block size; N to denote the number of key-value pairs; and n_k to denote the number of key-value pairs with key equal to k.

ber of I/Os are needed to find a place where each new item can be placed. We then show that this performance can be combined with amortized expected constant I/O complexity for multiqueues to design a multimap implementation that has constant amortized worst-case or expected I/O performance for most methods. Our methods imply that one can maintain an inverted file in external memory so as to support a constant amortized expected number of I/Os for insertions and worst-case constant amortized I/Os for lookups and item removal.

2. BRIEF SKETCH

For our external-memory cuckoo hash table, each bucket can store up to B items, where B defines our block size and is not necessarily a constant. Formally, let $\mathcal{T} = (T_0, T_1)$ be a cuckoo hash table such that each T_i consists of $\gamma n/2$ buckets, where each bucket stores a block of size B, with $n = N/B$. Of particular interest is when $\gamma = 1 + \epsilon$ for some (small) $\epsilon > 0$, so that space overhead of the hash table is only an ϵ factor over the minimum possible. The items in $\mathcal{T}$ are indexed by keys and stored in one of two locations, $T_0[h_0(k)]$ or $T_1[h_1(k)]$, where h_0 and h_1 are random hash functions.

We modify previous analyses of two-choice cuckoo hashing with multiple items per bucket from [2] by splitting the items into sub-buckets to show that we can stay within a $1 + \epsilon$ factor of the total space required for all elements while maintaining an expected $\log(1/\epsilon)^{O(\log \log(1/\epsilon))}$ insertion time, using a breadth first search approach. As noted in [2], a more practical approach is to use *random walk cuckoo hashing* in place of breadth first search cuckoo hashing, but it is not known if there is a random walk cuckoo hashing scheme using $(1 + \epsilon)N$ total space for N items, two bucket choices, and multiple items per bucket that similarly achieves expected constant insertion time and logarithmic insertion time with high probability.

To implement the multimap ADT, we begin with a primary structure that is an external-memory cuckoo hash table storing just the set of keys. In particular, each record $R(k)$ in $\mathcal{T}$ is associated with a specific key k and holds the following fields: the key k; the number n_k of key-value pairs in C with key equal to k; and a pointer p_k to a block X in a secondary table, $\mathcal{S}$, that stores items in C with key equal to k. If $n_k < B$, then X stores all the items with key equal to k (plus possibly some items with keys not equal to k). Otherwise, if $n_k \geq B$, then p_k points to a *first* block of items with key equal to k, with the other blocks of such items being stored elsewhere in $\mathcal{S}$.

This secondary storage is an external-memory data struc-

ture we call a *multiqueue*. It maintains a set $\mathcal{Q}$ of queues in external memory. The *header* pointers for these queues are stored in an array $\mathcal{T}$, which in our external-memory multimap construction is the external-memory cuckoo hash table described above. For any queue Q, we wish to support the following operations: enqueue(x, H) adds the element x to Q given a pointer to its header H; remove(x) removes x from Q; and isMember(x): determine whether x is in some queue Q. In addition, we wish to maintain all these queues in a space-efficient manner, so that the total storage is proportional to their total size. To enable this efficiency, we store all the blocks used for queue elements in a secondary table, $\mathcal{S}$, of blocks of size B each. Thus, each header record H in $\mathcal{T}$ points to a block in $\mathcal{S}$. In addition, we maintain a second cuckoo table, D, which uses entire key-value pairs as its keys. For each one, it provides a pointer to the block in $\mathcal{S}$ that stores this key-value pair (the data structure, D, is what allows us to perform fast removals).

Our intent is to store each queue Q as a doubly-linked list of blocks from $\mathcal{S}$. Unfortunately, some queues in $\mathcal{Q}$ are too small to deserve an entire block in S dedicated to storing their elements. So small queues must share their first block of storage with other small queues until they are large enough to deserve dedicated storage blocks. Managing the small and large queues with dynamic insertions and deletions is the further challenge in our construction, which we give in the full version of this paper[1].

3. REFERENCES

[1] A. Aggarwal and J. S. Vitter. The input/output complexity of sorting and related problems. *Commun. ACM*, 31:1116–1127, 1988.

[2] M. Dietzfelbinger and C. Weidling. Balanced allocation and dictionaries with tightly packed constant size bins. *Theoretical Computer Science*, 380:47–68, 2007.

[3] D. E. Knuth. *Sorting and Searching*, volume 3 of *The Art of Computer Programming*. Addison-Wesley, Reading, MA, 1973.

[4] N. Lester, A. Moffat, and J. Zobel. Efficient online index construction for text databases. *ACM Trans. Database Syst.*, 33:19:1–19:33, September 2008.

[5] N. Lester, J. Zobel, and H. Williams. Efficient online index maintenance for contiguous inverted lists. *Inf. Processing & Management*, 42(4):916–933, 2006.

[6] R. Pagh and F. Rodler. Cuckoo hashing. *Journal of Algorithms*, 52:122–144, 2004.

[7] L. G. Valiant. A bridging model for parallel computation. *Commun. ACM*, 33(8):103–111, 1990.

[8] J. S. Vitter. External sorting and permuting. In M.-Y. Kao, editor, *Encyclopedia of Algorithms*. Springer, 2008.

[9] J. Zobel and A. Moffat. Inverted files for text search engines. *ACM Comput. Surv.*, 38, July 2006.

[1]Goodrich was supported in part by the NSF under grants 0724806, 0713046, and 0847968, and by the ONR under MURI grant N00014-08-1-1015. Mitzenmacher was supported in part by the NSF under grants 0915922 and 0964473.

Brief Announcement: Processor Allocation for Optimistic Parallelization of Irregular Programs

Francesco Versaci[*]
Department of Information Engineering
University of Padova
versacif@dei.unipd.it

Keshav Pingali[†]
Department of Computer Science & Institute for
Computational Engineering and Sciences
The University of Texas at Austin
pingali@cs.utexas.edu

ABSTRACT

Optimistic parallelization is a promising approach for the parallelization of irregular algorithms: potentially interfering tasks are launched dynamically, and the runtime system detects conflicts between concurrent activities, aborting and rolling back conflicting tasks. However, parallelism in irregular algorithms can be a function of input parameters, and the amount of parallelism can vary dramatically during the execution. Therefore, determine how many processors should be allocated to execute (the *processor allocation* problem) for irregular algorithms is very difficult. In this work, we outline the first systematic strategy for addressing this problem.

Categories and Subject Descriptors

F.1.2 [**Modes of Computation**]: Parallelism and concurrency

General Terms

Algorithms, Performance, Theory.

Keywords

Irregular algorithms, Optimistic parallelization, Amorphous data-parallelism, Processor allocation, Turán's theorem.

1. INTRODUCTION

The advent of on-chip multiprocessors has made parallel programming a mainstream concern. Unfortunately writing correct and efficient parallel programs is a challenging task for the average programmer. Automation is more difficult when the algorithms are *irregular* and use pointer-based data structures such as graphs and sets. One promising approach is based on the concept of *amorphous data parallelism* [3]. Algorithms are formulated as iterative computations on *work-sets*, and each iteration is identified as a

[*]Supported by PAT-INFN Project *AuroraScience*, by MIUR-PRIN Project *AlgoDEEP*, and by the University of Padova Projects *STPD08JA32* and *CPDA099949*.

[†]This work is supported in part by NSF grants 0923907, 0833162, 0719966, and 0702353 and by grants from IBM, NEC and Intel.

quantum of work (task) that can potentially be executed in parallel with other iterations. The Galois project has shown that algorithms formulated in this way can be parallelized automatically using *optimistic parallelization* [2]: iterations are executed speculatively in parallel and, when an iteration conflicts with concurrently executing iterations, it is rolled-back.

In a regular algorithm like dense matrix multiplication, the amount of parallelism can usually be expressed as a function of the problem size, so it is reasonably straightforward to determine how many processors should be allocated to execute a regular algorithm of a certain size (this is called the *processor allocation* problem). In contrast, parallelism in irregular algorithms can be a function of input parameters. Optimistic parallelization complicates this problem even more: if there are too many processors and too little parallel work, not only might some processors be idle but speculative conflicts may actually retard the progress of even those processors that have useful work to do, increasing both program execution time and power consumption. In the following we give a simple graph-theoretic model for optimistic parallelization (Section 2), we identify a worst-case class of problems for an optimistic parallelizer (Section 3), and finally we propose an adaptive controller that dynamically solves the processor allocation problem for amorphous data-parallel programs (Section 4).

2. MODELING OPTIMISTIC PARALLELIZATION

Optimistic execution of amorphous data-parallel algorithms is modeled as follows. At any point during the execution, the work that needs to be done is represented as a computations/conflicts (CC) graph $G_t = (V_t, E_t)$ in which (i) nodes represent activities that must be performed atomically, and (ii) edges represent conflicts between activities (see Figure 1). Execution proceeds in rounds. In round t, a scheduler picks uniformly at random m_t nodes and tries to process them. In general, conflicts between activities become known only *during* the execution of these activities, which we model by assuming that the scheduler initially has no knowledge of the edges of graph G_t. When the system processes a node v, it figures out if there are conflict edges to other nodes: if a neighbor has already been processed at the current time step, the processing of node v aborts; otherwise, node v is considered processed, and at the end of the current round, it is removed from the graph and some op-

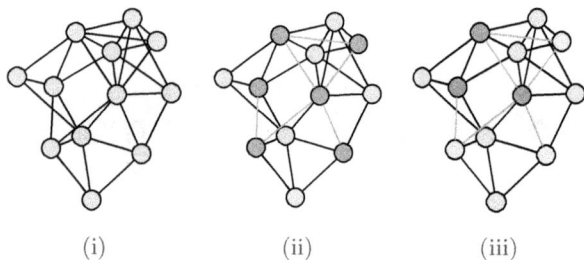

(i)   (ii)   (iii)

Figure 1: Optimistic parallelization. (i) Computations and conflicts between them. (ii) m nodes are chosen at random for execution in the current round. (iii) Conflicts are detected and some nodes abort, leaving a maximal independent set in the subgraph induced by the choice of the initial nodes.

erations may be performed such as adding new nodes with edges or altering the neighbors.

When we parallelize a program optimistically, we have two contrasting goals: we want to exploit a lot of parallelism to reduce the critical path through the program, but at the same time, we want to minimize conflicts to reduce lost work and wasted power. These two goals are not necessarily compatible: increasing the number of processors assigned to execute the program may reduce execution time but it may also increase the number of aborted activities, so there is a trade-off.

Let k_t be the number of tasks aborted at round t and let $r_t = k_t/m_t$ (i.e., the aborts fraction). We define the *conflict ratio* $\bar{r}_t(m)$ to be the expected aborts fraction at time t if the system is run with m processors. The control problem we want to solve is the following: *given r_τ and m_τ for $\tau < t$, choose $m_t = \mu_t$ such that $\bar{r}_t(\mu_t) \simeq \rho$, where ρ is a suitable parameter ($\rho = 20 \div 30\%$ is often reasonable).*

3. EXPLOITING PARALLELISM

A measure of the available parallelism for a given amorphous data-parallel algorithm has been identified in [3] considering, at each round, a maximal independent set of its CC graph. This gives a reasonable and computable estimate of the available parallelism. However, this is not enough to predict the actual amount of parallelism that a scheduler can exploit while keeping a low conflict ratio.

A more realistic estimate of the performance of a scheduler can be obtained analyzing the CC graph sparsity. The average degree of the CC graph is linked to the expected size of a maximal independent set of the graph by the following well known theorem: (in the variant shown in [1]):

THEOREM 1. *(Turán, strong formulation). Let $G = (V, E)$ be a graph, $n = |V|$ and let d be the average degree of G. Then the expected size of a maximal independent set, obtained choosing greedily the nodes from a random permutation, is at least $s = n/(d+1)$.*

The previous bound is existentially tight: let K_d^n be the graph made up of $s = n/(d+1)$ cliques of size $d+1$, then the average degree is d and the size of every maximal (and maximum) independent set is exactly s.

The properties of the graph K_d^n has suggested us the formulation of an extension of the Turán's theorem. We prove that the graphs K_d^n provide a worst case (for a given degree

d) for the generalization of this problem obtained by focusing on maximal independent set of induced subgraphs. This allows, when given a target conflict ratio ρ, the computation of a lower bound for the parallelism a scheduler can exploit.

THEOREM 2. *Let G be a graph with same nodes number and degree of K_d^n and let $\mathrm{EM}_m(G)$ be the expected size of a maximal independent set of the subgraph induced by a uniformly random choice of m nodes in G, then*

$$\mathrm{EM}_m(G) \geq \mathrm{EM}_m(K_d^n) \ . \tag{1}$$

Hence, the worst case for a scheduler among the graphs with the same number of nodes and edges is obtained for the graph K_d^n, for which we can analytically approximate the performance, providing the bound shown below.

THEOREM 3. *Let d be the average degree of $G = (V, E)$ with $n = |V|$. The conflict ratio is bounded from above as*

$$\bar{r}(m) \leq 1 - \frac{n}{m(d+1)} \left(1 - \prod_{i=1}^{m} \frac{n-d-i}{n+1-i} \right) \ . \tag{2}$$

4. PROPOSED CONTROLLER

The control strategy we propose is based on recurrence relations, i.e., we compute m_{t+1} as a function F of the target conflict ratio ρ and of the parameters which characterize the system at the previous timestep: $m_{t+1}^F = F(\rho, r_t, m_t)$. The initial value m_0 for a recurrence can be chosen to be 2 but, if we have an estimate of the CC graph average degree d, we can choose a better value. Our control heuristic is a hybridization of two simple recurrences:

$$m_{t+1}^A = (1 - r_t + \rho)m_t \ , \qquad m_{t+1}^B = \frac{\rho}{r_t} m_t \ . \tag{3}$$

The first recurrence is quite natural and increases m based on the distance between r and ρ, while the second recurrence exploits an initial linearity of the conflict ratio emerged from both theoretical and experimental facts. Since r_t can have a big variance the controller also integrates various techniques to smooth down the oscillations.

To validate our controller we have run the following simulation: a random CC graph of fixed average degree d is built and the controller runs on it, starting with $m_0 = 2$. We are interested in seeing how many temporal steps it takes to converge to $m_t \simeq \mu$. As can be seen in [3] the parallelism profile of many practical applications can vary quite abruptly, e.g., Delauney triangulation can go from no parallelism to one thousand possible parallel tasks in just 30 rounds. Therefore, an algorithm that wants to efficiently control the processor allocation for these kinds of problems must adapt very quickly to changes in the available parallelism. Our controller, which uses the very fast recurrence B in the initial phase, proves to do a fast enough job: in about 15 steps, it converges close to the desired μ value.

The proposed control heuristic is now being integrated in the Galois system, and it will be evaluated on more realistic workloads.

5. REFERENCES

[1] ALON, N., AND SPENCER, J. *The probabilistic method.* Wiley-Interscience, 2000.
[2] KULKARNI, M., ET AL. Optimistic parallelism requires abstractions. *Commun. ACM 52*, 9 (2009), 89–97.
[3] PINGALI, K., ET AL. The Tao of parallelism in algorithms. In *ACM PLDI* (2011).

Brief Announcement: Locality-enhancing Loop Transformations for Tree Traversal Algorithms

Youngjoon Jo and Milind Kulkarni
School of Electrical and Computer Engineering
Purdue University
{yjo, milind}@purdue.edu

ABSTRACT

In this paper, we discuss transformations that can be applied to irregular programs that perform tree traversals, which can be seen as analogs of the popular regular transformations of loop tiling. We demonstrate the utility of these transformations on two tree traversal algorithms, the Barnes-Hut algorithm and raytracing, achieving speedups of up to 237% over the baseline implementation.

Categories and Subject Descriptors

D.3.4 [**Software Engineering**]: Processors—*compilers,optimization*

General Terms

Languages

Keywords

locality transformations, irregular programs, n-body codes

1. INTRODUCTION

In this paper, we focus on enhancing and exploiting locality in *tree-traversal* applications. Such applications are widespread; examples include scientific algorithms such as Barnes-Hut [2], graphics algorithms such as bounding volume hierarchies [6] and Lightcuts [7], and data mining algorithms such as k-nearest neighbor [3].

The tree traversals performed by the aforementioned algorithms are highly irregular in nature. This is because the structure of the tree is determined primarily by the input data and because the actual layout of the tree in memory is unpredictable. Nevertheless, the trees constructed in these algorithms are traversed numerous times, leading to significant data reuse. Any time there is data reuse, there may be an opportunity to exploit temporal locality.

One of the motivating insights of this paper is that tree traversal algorithms exhibit similar locality properties to vector-vector outer product, a simple, regular algorithm. Moreover, loop transformations such as *loop interchange* and *tiling* have analogues that apply to tree traversals. By developing an abstract model of tree traversals based on outer products, we can reason about the locality effects of transformations on irregular tree traversals by appealing to their effects on the abstract model, and assess the relative impacts of various transformations proposed in the literature [5, 1]. Our model implies, and experimental results bear out, that these transformations lose their effectiveness as data sets increase. However, by leveraging the correspondence between loop transformations on regular programs and transformations for tree traversal codes, we

```
1  Set<Particle> particles = /* entities in algorithm */
2  Set<Particle> objects = particles;
3  OctTreeCell root = buildTreeAndComputeCofM(objects);
4  foreach (Particle p : particles) {
5    foreach (OctTreeCell c : traverse(root, p)) {
6      if (farEnough(p, c.cofm) || c.isLeaf) {
7        updateContribution(p, c.cofm);
8      }
9    }
10 }
```

Figure 1: Abstract algorithm for tree-traversal

```
1  Particle p[n] = /* particles */
2  OctTreeCell c[m] = /* traversal */
3  for (int i = 0; i < n; i++)
4    for (int j = 0; j < m; j++)
5      Update(i, j); //A[i][j] = p[i]*c[j]
6
7  void Update(Particle p, OctTreeCell c) {
8    if (farEnough(p, c.cofm || c.isLeaf))
9      updateContribution(p, c.cofm);
10 }
```

Figure 2: Tree traversal as outer product

develop a new transformation, based on loop tiling, that more thoroughly exploits locality for large data sets. We demonstrate the effectiveness of our transformation through two case studies of tree traversal algorithms, the Barnes-Hut n-body code (BH) and a raytracing benchmark based on bounding volume hierarchies (RT). We show that our transformation can yield performance improvements of up to 237% over an optimized sequential baseline, and that this advantage persists when running in parallel.

2. AN ABSTRACT MODEL

Rather than viewing a traversal as a recursive, pre-order walk of a tree, we can instead visualize the traversal in terms of the actual tree cells touched. Fundamentally, processing a single particle requires accessing some sequence of tree cells. The particular arrangement within the tree of those cells is irrelevant; all that matters is the ultimate sequence in which those cells are touched. If we imagine that there is an oracle function `traverse` that generates the sequence of cells accessed while processing a particular particle, we can rewrite the accelerated BH code as shown in Figure 1. In other words, we can view the algorithm as a simple, doubly-nested loop.

Sorting the particles according to their geometric position, so that adjacent particles in the sorted order are nearby geometrically [1, 5], is a common optimization to exploit locality in tree traversal codes. Consider the behavior of two consecutive particles, p_1 and p_2. Without sorting, there is little overlap between $traverse(p_1)$ and $traverse(p_2)$, and there will be little temporal locality between consecutive traversals. Sorting the particles such that consecutive points have similar traversals will result in cache hits.

When the points are sorted, the variability between consecutive traversals is often a fairly small second-order effect, so we can simply consider consecutive traversals in the sorted case to be the same. This approximation lets us further simplify the abstract algorithm. The outer loop iterates over a vector (of particles) and, for each particle, the inner loop iterates over a vector (containing the cells

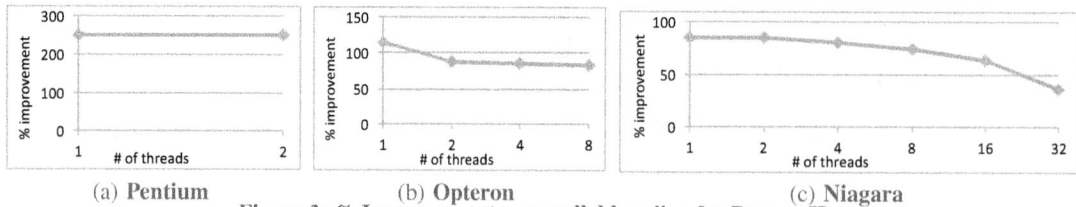

(a) Pentium   (b) Opteron   (c) Niagara

Figure 3: % Improvement vs parallel baseline for Barnes-Hut

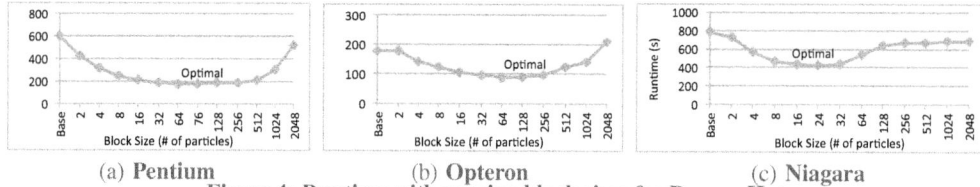

(a) Pentium   (b) Opteron   (c) Niagara

Figure 4: Runtime with varying block sizes for Barnes-Hut

of the traversal). Figure 2 demonstrates this correspondence, showing how a tree traversal is analogous to the outer product of a vector p and a vector c.

One insight we can glean from this model is that the efficacy of sorting points to improve locality diminishes as the tree, and hence traversals, get larger. Consider the behavior of outer product when the c vector is small enough to fit in cache. For an element from the p vector, every element from the c vector is touched. When the next element is drawn from the p vector, all of c will be in cache, and there will be no further cache misses. Unfortunately, once c is too large to fit in cache, an LRU replacement policy will lead to disastrous results: when the second iteration of the outer loop begins, although some of c is in cache, the first element(s) will not be. Bringing those elements into cache will kick the next elements out of cache, and no accesses to c will ever hit.

3. LOOP TRANSFORMATIONS

Loop tiling is a well known loop transformation, which can be used to exploit locality in the above case when both vectors are too large to fit in cache. For BH, while tiling the traversal loop is complex, tiling the particle loop is straightforward:

```
foreach (ParticleBlock b : particles)
  foreach (OctTreeCell c : traversal(b))
    foreach (Particle p : b)
      //do work
```

The outer loop chooses a block p_B (of size B) from p. It then iterates over c, processing every element from p_B for each element of c. If B is chosen appropriately, then the elements of p_B are never evicted from cache while the block is processed, and elements of c only incur misses the first time they are touched per block. This results in radically fewer cache misses.

4. EVALUATION

Figure 3 shows % improvement of the blocked implementation with an empirically determined optimal block size compared to the parallel baseline for BH. We attain improvements of up to 237%, 96% and 80% over the parallel baseline respectively for the **Pentium**, **Opteron** and **Niagara** systems. We emphasize that our baseline uses sorting to enhance locality of consecutive particles as in [5]. We also implemented sorting by space filling curves as in [1] and found little difference in performance to sorting as in [5].

Figure 4 shows the serial runtimes in seconds with varying block sizes for the three systems. We expect that a block size that is too small would perform poorly due both to the additional instruction overhead and to the fact that misses in the tree are incurred for every block (fewer blocks will result in fewer misses in the traversal). However, if the block becomes too large to fit in cache, then we will begin to incur misses on the particles instead. We thus expect

there to be a "sweet spot," where the blocks are large enough to avoid most misses in the tree, but small enough to fit in cache, an expectation borne out by the results. In each figure, the best block size is highlighted, and is surrounded by block sizes that perform worse. The optimal block sizes were found to be 24, 76 and 128 for the Niagara, Pentium and Opteron systems respectively. We note that the optimal block size is correlated with the L1 cache sizes of the systems. The relationship is not linear due to the irregularity of the application, and other locality effects (such as those from L2).

We attain improvements of up to 55%, 26% and 7% over the parallel baseline respectively for RT. We found that the improvements were less significant for RT compared to BH, because RT had a smaller average traversal size, resulting in a lower L1/L2 miss rate and less room for improvement with our transformations.

An extended version of this work can be found in [4] with further details on efficiently implement tiling in tree-traversal codes, more experimental results, and related work.

5. REFERENCES

[1] M. Amor, F. Argüello, J. López, O. G. Plata, and E. L. Zapata. A data parallel formulation of the barnes-hut method for n -body simulations. In *Proceedings of the 5th International Workshop on Applied Parallel Computing, New Paradigms for HPC in Industry and Academia*, PARA '00, pages 342–349, London, UK, 2001. Springer-Verlag.

[2] J. Barnes and P. Hut. A hierarchical $o(nlogn)$ force-calculation algorithm. *Nature*, 324(4):446–449, December 1986.

[3] A. G. Gray and A. W. Moore. N-Body Problems in Statistical Learning. In T. K. Leen, T. G. Dietterich, and V. Tresp, editors, *Advances in Neural Information Processing Systems (NIPS) 13 (Dec 2000)*. MIT Press, 2001.

[4] Y. Jo and M. Kulkarni. Locality-enhancing loop transformations for parallel tree traversal algorithms. Technical Report TR-ECE-11-03, School of Electrial and Computer Engineering, Purdue University, February 2011.

[5] J. P. Singh, C. Holt, T. Totsuka, A. Gupta, and J. Hennessy. Load balancing and data locality in adaptive hierarchical n-body methods: Barnes-hut, fast multipole, and radiosity. *J. Parallel Distrib. Comput.*, 27(2):118–141, 1995.

[6] I. Wald. On fast construction of sah-based bounding volume hierarchies. In *RT '07: Proceedings of the 2007 IEEE Symposium on Interactive Ray Tracing*, pages 33–40, Washington, DC, USA, 2007. IEEE Computer Society.

[7] B. Walter, S. Fernandez, A. Arbree, K. Bala, M. Donikian, and D. Greenberg. Lightcuts: a scalable approach to illumination. *ACM Transactions on Graphics (SIGGRAPH)*, 24(3):1098–1107, July 2005.

Brief Announcement: Program Regularization in Verifying Memory Consistency

Lei Li, Tianshi Chen, Yunji Chen, Ling Li, Cheng Qian, and Weiwu Hu
Institute of Computing Technology, Chinese Academy of Sciences, Beijing 100190, P. R. China
{lilei-cpu,chentianshi,cyj,liling,qiancheng,hww}@ict.ac.cn

ABSTRACT

Verifying memory consistency, which is to verify the executions of parallel test programs on a multiprocessor system against the given memory consistency model, is NP-hard. To accelerate verifying memory consistency in practice, we devise a technique called "*program regularization*". The key intuition behind program regularization is that a parallel program with some specific patterns can enable efficient verification. More specifically, for any original program, program regularization introduces some auxiliary memory locations, and periodically inserts store/load operations accessing these locations to the original program. With the regularized program, verifying memory consistency only requires a linear time complexity (with respect to the number of memory operations).

Categories and Subject Descriptors

B.3.2 [**Memory Structures**]: Design Styles

General Terms

Algorithms, Theory, Verification

Keywords

Verifying Memory Consistency, Frontier Graph

1. INTRODUCTION

A widely-used methodology for verifying memory subsystem is dynamic verification. To be specific, it first executes parallel test programs on the chip multiprocessor (CMP), and then verifies the executions against the memory consistency model given by the CMP. The latter step is called *verifying memory consistency* or *memory consistency verification* problem, which is NP-hard [4, 5, 6].

Concretely, verifying memory consistency needs to assign a sound total ordering among all n memory operations. Such a task needs to consider $O(n!)$ possible interleavings of all memory operations in the worst case. Some previous approaches seek the assistance of hardware (e.g., global clock [3]) for more execution information and have a time complexity of $O(n^2)$ [2] or even $O(n)$ [1]. From a novel perspective, we focus on efficient verification benefited from *specific*

programs. Technically, if some orders between memory operations have been restricted by the pattern of a program, a large number of infeasible memory operation interleavings can be excluded, leading to faster verification.

Based on the above idea, we propose a new technique called *program regularization*, which aims at converting an original program to a specific program that enables efficient memory consistency verification. More specifically, for any input program with p processes, program regularization introduces p auxiliary memory locations, say, $a_0, a_1, \ldots, a_{p-1}$. For each memory location a_i ($i \in \{0, \ldots, p-1\}$), program regularization inserts store operations to a_i on process $\mathcal{P}_i$ periodically. Each value stored to a_i by $\mathcal{P}_i$ is unique. Hence, through inserting load operations to a_i on all processes periodically, the approximate progress of $\mathcal{P}_i$ can be known by all processes in the regularized program. Any interleaving of memory operations inconsistent with the progresses can be excluded in verifying memory consistency. Using the frontier graph technique proposed by Gibbons and Korach [5], we find that verifying memory consistency with the regularized program has only a linear time complexity with respect to the number of memory operations.

2. PROGRAM REGULARIZATION

Generally speaking, program regularization is a mapping rule $\mathcal{R}$ which maps a parallel program G to another program $G^{(1)}$: $G \xrightarrow{\mathcal{R}} G^{(1)}$. As shown in Algorithm 1, for a p-process program G, p additional memory locations (denoted by $a_0, \ldots, a_{p-1}$) are required to regularize G. For each process $\mathcal{P}_i$ ($i \in \{0, \ldots, p-1\}$), the regularization inserts a sender and a receiver for every τ memory operations, where the parameter τ is a constant determined by verification engineers. The sender is responsible for broadcasting the progress of its host process, while the receiver is responsible for obtaining the progresses of all processes.

Concretely, in the regularized program $G^{(1)}$, $\mathcal{P}_i$'s k-th sender is a store operation ($s(a_i, k)$ in Algorithm 1), which stores k to memory location a_i. It is inserted between the $(k-1)\tau$-th and $k\tau$-th memory operations of process $\mathcal{P}_i$ in the original program G. $\mathcal{P}_i$'s k-th receiver consists of p load operations accessing $a_0, \ldots, a_{p-1}$ respectively, which are also inserted between the $(k-1)\tau$-th and $k\tau$-th memory operations of process $\mathcal{P}_i$ in the original program. Since different senders of $\mathcal{P}_i$ write distinct values to a_i, the receivers of other processes are ware of the *approximate* progress of $\mathcal{P}_i$ through loading the value of a_i (e.g., if some process loads value k from a_i, then it will know that $\mathcal{P}_i$'s progress is around the $k\tau$-th memory operation of $\mathcal{P}_i$). Considering that the

Algorithm 1 Program Regularization

```
/*u_x^y represents the y-th operation on process P_x in program G;
n_x represents the total number of operations on P_x in program
G.*/
int Program_Regularization(G);
G^(1) = G;
for(each P_i in G){
    for(k=1;kτ < n_i;k++){
        Insert s(a_i,k) between u_i^((k-1)τ) and u_i^kτ to P_i;
//P_i's k-th sender, s(a_i,k) refers to a store operation to
location a_i with value k.
        for(j=0;j < p;j++){
            Insert l(a_j) between u_i^((k-1)τ) and u_i^kτ to P_i;
        }
//P_i's k-th receiver, l(a_j) refers to a load operation to loca-
tion a_j.
    }
}
return(G^(1));
```

senders and receivers have been deployed to each process, the overall *approximate* progress of the whole system is periodically obtained by each process. Although the regularized program is a little longer than the original program, we will find in the next section that the additional memory operations can dramatically reduce the running time of verifying memory consistency.

3. ROUGH COMPLEXITY ANALYSIS

Gibbons and Korach proposed a frontier graph technique to investigate the time complexity of verifying memory consistency [5]. Each node of the frontier graph (called a frontier), which represents a possible snapshot of all processes, consists of a vector of operations $u_0, \ldots, u_{p-1}$, where u_i is the currently executing operation on process P_i ($i \in \{0, \ldots, p-1\}$). A directed edge, from one frontier $F = (u_0, \ldots, u_i, \ldots, u_{p-1})$ to another frontier $F' = (u_0, \ldots, u_i', \ldots, u_{p-1})$, implies that process P_i has finished the execution of u_i and begins the execution of u_i', where u_i' is the direct successor of u_i in program order. According to Gibbons and Korach, verifying sequential consistency is equivalent to finding a directed path from the starting frontier (which consists of p null operations) to the terminating frontier (which consists of the last operation on each process). Thus, the time complexity of verifying memory consistency is linear with the number of nodes and edges in the frontier graph.

For the execution of a regularized program, many frontiers and edges can be naturally excluded from the frontier graph with the progress information provided by the receivers in regularized programs. Figure 1 illustrates how to calculate a bound of the number of frontiers for a regularized program.

For each operation u executed on process P_i, let $recv\_i(j)$ (operation $l(a_j)$ in receivers of process P_i) be the last load on location a_j before u in program order, and $send\_i$ be the first store on location a_i after u in program order. There are at most 3τ memory operations between $send\_i$ and $recv\_i(j)$ according to Algorithm 1. $send\_j$ is the responsible store operation for $recv\_i(j)$ on process P_j, i.e., $recv\_(i,j)$ gets the value stored by $send\_j$. When u is executed on process P_i, process P_j must have finished $send\_j$ as $recv\_i(j)$ has loaded its stored value. As each frontier is a possible snapshot of all processes, only operations after $send\_j$ in program order on process P_j can be in a frontier containing u. Likewise, let $recv\_j(i)$, (operation $l(a_i)$ in receivers of process P_j) be the first load operation on a_i on process P_j which gets the value

written by $send\_i$ or some sender after $send\_i$ in program order. Only operations before $recv\_j(i)$ in program order on process P_j can be in a frontier containing u, since process P_i must have finished u before $recv\_j(i)$ is in execution.

Denote by B the maximal number of memory operations between $send\_j$ and $recv\_j$ for arbitrary i and j ($i, j \in \{0, \ldots, p-1\}$), the number of frontiers containing any given operation u is less than B^p (each process has at most B choices). Considering that we have n choices when specifying operation u, the number of frontiers is less than $B^p n$. As the out-degree of each frontier is no more than p, the number of edges is less than $pB^p n$. Since B and p are not related to n, verifying memory consistency with a regularized program can be solved with a time complexity of $O(pB^p n)$.

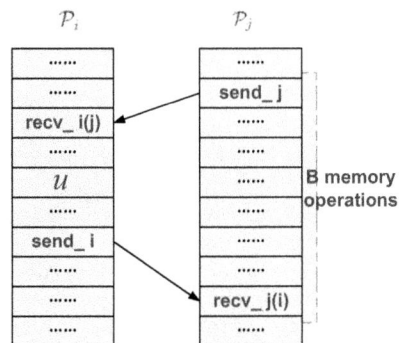

Figure 1: $send\_j$ **and** $recv\_j(i)$ **bound the number of frontiers containing** u, $(i, j \in \{0, \ldots, p-1\})$.

4. CONCLUSION

Verifying memory consistency is a crucial problem in validating the memory subsystem pf a CMP. To accelerate verifying memory consistency, we propose the program regularization technique. The regularized program can be efficiently verified against the given memory consistency model. To our best knowledge, it is the first time that verifying memory consistency is analyzed from the perspective of parallel programs. Moreover, our technique can be beneficial to both pre-silicon and post-silicon validation of CMP since it does not need any dedicated hardware support.

5. REFERENCES

[1] W. Hu, Y. Chen, T. Chen, C. Qian, and L. Li. Linear time memory consistency verification. *IEEE Transactions on Computers*, in press, 2011.

[2] Y. Chen, Y. Lv, W. Hu, T. Chen, H. Shen, P. Wang, and H. Pan. Fast complete memory consistency verification. In *Proceedings of HPCA-15*, 2009, pages 381-392.

[3] Y. Chen, T. Chen, and W. Hu. "Global Clock, Physical Time Order and Pending Period Analysis in Multiprocessor Systems". CoRR abs/0903.4961, 2009.

[4] P. Gibbons and E. Korach. The complexity of sequential consistency. In *Proceedings of SPDP'92*, 1992, pages 317-325.

[5] P. Gibbons and E. Korach. On testing cache-coherent shared memories. In *Proceedings of SPAA'94*, 1994, pages 177-188.

[6] P. Gibbons and E. Korach. Testing shared memories. *SIAM Journal on Computing* 26(4):1208-1244, 1997.

Brief Announcement: RedRem: A Parallel Redundancy Remover

H. B. Acharya
University of Texas at Austin
acharya@cs.utexas.edu

M. G. Gouda
University of Texas at Austin
National Science Foundation
mgouda@nsf.gov

ABSTRACT

Policies defined by a sequence of predicate-decision rules, with first-match semantics, are widely used; a notable example is their use in firewalls, where the rules are used to decide whether to accept or discard each packet. Owing to the critical importance of correctness of such policies, as well as the need for high performance, they have been the subject of considerable analysis. In earlier work, we have demonstrated that the problem of removing redundant rules from firewalls is theoretically equivalent to verifying that a firewall satisfies a property, and proposed that this theorem be used to build a high performance redundancy remover. In this paper, we realize this promise, and build a fast linear-space redundancy remover, one to three orders of magnitude faster than current approaches. Further, we show that our algorithm is easy to parallelize- there exists a natural way to partition a large instance of the problem into independent small ones.

Categories and Subject Descriptors

C.2.0 [**Computer Systems Organization**]: Computer-Communication Networks

General Terms

Performance

Keywords

Firewall optimization, Redundancy

1. INTRODUCTION

A firewall is a security system that acts as a protective boundary. In the context of computer networks, a firewall is a packet filter that is placed at the point where a private computer network connects to the "outside world", usually the rest of the Internet. The firewall intercepts each packet exchanged between the network and the Internet, examines the headers of the packet, and makes a decision: it may "accept" the packet (allow it to proceed), or it may "discard" the packet.

The decision that a firewall makes when it receives a packet depends on the values in the headers of the packet. A firewall is a sequence of rules; each rule matches certain packets,

with specific header values, and specifies the decision (accept or discard) to be made for that packet. When multiple rules match a packet, the first rule (according to the order of the rule sequence), that matches the packet, takes precedence.

Firewalls deal with large volumes of packets, and speed of processing is a serious concern as in the case of a denial-of-service attack a slow firewall will cause a server to fail. There exists an optimal solution to the problem of fast firewall execution: Ternary Content Addressable Memory (TCAM), which returns the decision for a packet in constant time. However, TCAMs have small capacity, and are large custom circuits (and thus very expensive). Thus, while used for extremely high-end routing, they are usually not suitable for firewalls (or packet classifiers in general).

In [3], the authors propose that a packet classifier can be optimized to fit on a TCAM, and develop an algorithm to restructure a given packet classifier and remove all redundant rules. However, applying their method to firewalls reveals a serious disadvantage: the algorithm requires the construction of an all-match tree. An all-match tree has a size at least as large as that of the corresponding Firewall Decision Diagram - which has a space complexity of $(2n)^d$ [4], where n is the number of rules in a firewall and d is the number of fields in a rule. The value of n may be less than a dozen, in small firewalls, but in complex cases it may be over a thousand. d is 4 to 6, with the usual value being 5 (the usual fields checked are source and destination port, source and destination IP address, and protocol).

In this paper, we use our result that firewall verification is equivalent to redundancy detection [1], and build upon the *probe* algorithm of firewall verification [2], to implement RedRem, a new system that detects and removes all redundant rules in a given firewall.

In contrast to prior approaches, RedRem runs in space $O(nd)$ (which is the size of the firewall and thus a lower bound on the space complexity). We also verify experimentally that, in practice, the algorithm requires very little memory to run (around 0.5 kB per rule for large firewalls). Our time complexity is still $O(n^d)$ (indeed, we conjecture that this may be a lower bound for a deterministic algorithm that completely removes redundancies). However, our algorithm runs very fast in practical cases; we show by extensive testing that we greatly outperform earlier redundancy detection algorithms. Furthermore, our algorithm can be used in conjunction with the techniques of projection and division to decompose a problem instance into many smaller, independent instances, so an additional advantage of our algorithm is that it can naturally take advantage of a parallel machine.

2. RESULTS

Our model of firewalls is that a firewall is a sequence of rules, which consist of predicates and decisions (accept/discard). In each predicate, there are d fields, for each of which there is an interval of natural numbers (a, b). A packet is represented by its header values, which the firewall examines to decide whether to accept or discard it. Hence our model of a packet is a d-tuple of integers, which is said to *match* a rule if every field of the packet is a member of the corresponding field of the predicate of the rule. The first rule in the sequence that is matched by a packet is said to *resolve* the packet, i.e. its decision is the decision of the firewall for the packet.

A rule in a firewall is redundant iff removing it from the firewall does not change the decision of the firewall for any packet. In our earlier paper [1], we demonstrate that the necessary and sufficient condition for a rule R_j in firewall F to be redundant is that it resolves no packet p that is resolved in firewall $F - R_j$ by a rule R_k, whose decision is opposite to the decision of R_j. Every packet that matches R_j is resolved by either R_j or some preceding rule R_i, so if we change the decisions of all rules R_i that precede R_j in firewall F to the decision of R_j, thereby creating firewall F', then in firewall $F' - R_j$ there is no packet matching R_j that is resolved by some rule R_k that conflicts with R_j (i.e. whose decision is opposite to that of R_j). In other words, $F' - R_j$ satisfies property R_j - a firewall verification problem.

Further, this algorithm can be speeded up by taking notice of the fact that if there is indeed even one conflicting R_k that resolves a packet matching R_j in $F' - R_j$, rule R_j is not redundant in F. Hence we can parallelize the search for such a packet (the *signature packet* of R_j) by dividing the firewall $F' - R_j$ into slices. Each slice consists of one conflicting rule R_k, preceded by the compliant (non-conflicting with R_j) rules that precede R_k in $F' - R_j$. We further optimize the search by projecting the slice over R_k, i.e. removing any portion of the predicate of any rule that does not belong to the predicate of R_k. Finally, we verify, using the probe algorithm of [2], that each slice satisfies the projection of R_j over the corresponding R_k. Such verification can be executed in parallel for all the conflicting rules R_k that are preceded by R_j in F. If there exists a slice which does not satisfy the property, R_j is non-redundant.

In this paper, we present a system, which we name RedRem, that uses the above algorithm to identify and remove all redundant rules from a large sample set of firewalls. As RedRem is faster for smaller firewalls, we were able to test a larger number of short firewalls. We tested $100,000$ firewalls of each length varying from 50 to 250 rules in steps of 50, and $10,000$ firewalls of each length from 300 to 1000 in steps of 50. In total, we tested our algorithm on $650,000$ firewalls, which vary in length from 50 to 1000. Our test firewalls have the number of fields $d = 5$.

Our results are presented in Figures 1(a) and 1(b), respectively. Our algorithm is clearly superior to the fastest previous algorithm, all-match trees [3], as we demonstrate in Table 1. (Unfortunately, the authors published their performance test with only three firewalls so we cannot provide a more comprehensive comparison.) In addition, our algorithm has several other important advantages. Firstly, as we have demonstrated, it can be naturally decomposed into subproblems that can be solved in parallel. Secondly, on

Length	RedRem	First-match tree	All-match tree
42	0.44	491	171
87	1.5	179	47
661	69	1105	750

Table 1: Running time (ms.)

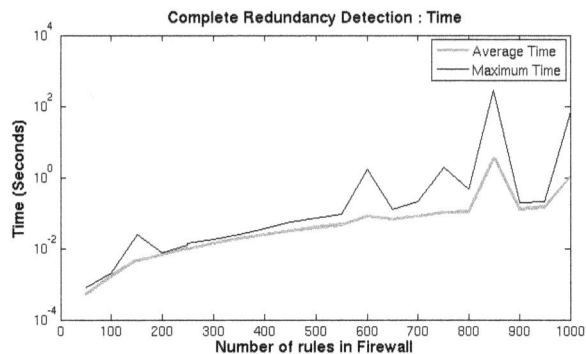

(a) Execution time of Algorithm.

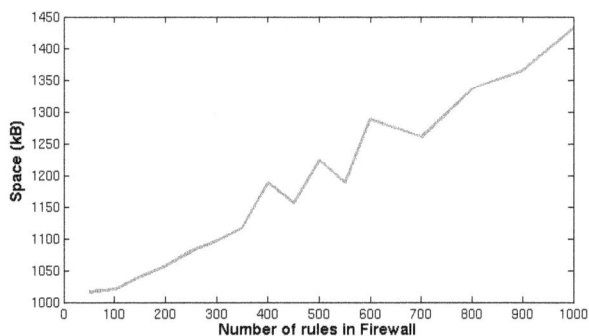

(b) Space required by Algorithm.

a sequential computer it uses $O(nd)$ space, as opposed to $O(n^d)$ for all-match trees.

3. REFERENCES

[1] H. B. Acharya and M. G. Gouda. Firewall Verification and Redundancy Checking are Equivalent. In *Proceedings of IEEE INFOCOM*, 2011.

[2] H. B. Acharya and M. G. Gouda. Projection and division: Linear-space verification of firewalls. In *Proceedings of ICDCS*, 2010.

[3] C. R. Meiners, A. X. Liu, and E. Torng. Tcam Razor: A systematic approach towards minimizing packet classifiers in tcams. In *Proceedings of the IEEE Conference on Network Protocols (ICNP)*, pages 266–275, 2007.

[4] A. X. Liu and M. G. Gouda. Diverse firewall design. *IEEE Transaction on Parallel and Distributed Systems*, 19(9):1237–1251, 2008.

On a Local Protocol for Concurrent File Transfers

MohammadTaghi
Hajiaghayi [*]
Dep. of Computer Science
University of Maryland
College Park, MD
hajiagha@cs.umd.edu

Rohit Khandekar
IBM T.J. Watson Research
Center
19 Skyline Drive
Hawthorne, NY
rohitk@us.ibm.com

Guy Kortsarz [†]
Dep. of Computer Science
Rutgers University-Camden
Camden, NJ
guyk@camden.rutgers.edu

Vahid Liaghat
Dep. of Computer Science
University of Maryland
College Park, MD
vliaghat@cs.umd.edu

ABSTRACT

We study a very natural *local* protocol for a file transfer problem. Consider a scenario where several files, which may have varied sizes and get created over a period of time, are to be transferred between pairs of hosts in a distributed environment. Our protocol assumes that while executing the file transfers, an individual host does not use any global knowledge; and simply subdivides its I/O resources *equally* among all the active file transfers at that host at any point in time. This protocol is motivated by its simplicity of use and its applications to scheduling map-reduce workloads.

Here we study the problem of deciding the start times of individual file transfers to optimize QoS metrics like average completion time or MakeSpan. To begin with, we show that these problems are NP-hard. We next argue that the ability of scheduling multiple concurrent file transfers at a host makes our protocol stronger than previously studied protocols that schedule a sequence of matchings, in which no two active file transfers share a host at any time. We then generalize the approach of Queyranne and Sviridenko (J. Scheduling, 2002) and Gandhi et al. (ACM T. Algorithms, 2008) that relates the MakeSpan and completion time objectives and present constant factor approximation algorithms.

Categories and Subject Descriptors

F.2.2 [**Theory of Computation**]: Analysis of Algorithms and Problem ComplexityNon-numerical Algorithms and Problems; G.2.2 [**Mathematics of Computing**]: Discrete Mathematics—*graph theory, network problems*

---

[*]Supported in part by NSF CAREER award 1053605 and Google Faculty Research Award.

[†]Supported in part by NSF grant number 0829959.

General Terms

Theory

Keywords

local protocol, scheduling, file transfer, average completion time, MakeSpan

1. INTRODUCTION

1.1 Motivation

Today's technologies have enabled resources for compiling enormous amounts of data, often beyond the capacity of individual disks, and too large for processing with a single CPU. Such data is then naturally stored across a cluster of compute hosts and is shared and processed using distributed computing environments. One distributed computing paradigm which has attracted a lot of interest recently is Map-Reduce [25]. A typical Map-Reduce job has three phases. The *Map phase* processes data, often available on local disks, block-by-block and for each such block produces (key, value)-pairs that are written to the local disk. In a typical implementation, these pairs are organized into multiple files where each file corresponds to a specific key. The *Shuffle phase* transfers these files containing the (key, value)-pairs from the hosts that run Map tasks to the hosts that run Reduce tasks. Finally, the *Reduce phase* applies some function on all the values corresponding to each individual key and computes an output. The Shuffle phase involves the transfer of several files across multiple machines and can be quite I/O intensive. This phase can be naturally modeled as a file transfer problem. Let us denote the set of hosts participating in a Map-Reduce computation by V. The Map tasks may be present on two or more of these hosts. As a Map task finishes, the data produced by it becomes available for the transfer. Note that the amount of data produced by different Map tasks to be consumed by different Reduce tasks can be quite different. Let edge $e = \{u, v\}$ represent the data or a file to be transferred from a host u running a Map task to a host v running a Reduce task. Since we do not distinguish between the overheads caused by incoming or outgoing transfers, we model the transfers by undirected edges. Let $r(e)$ denote the time at which file e becomes available for transfer, namely its *release time*. Let $\ell(e)$ denote the size of file e. Although the exact values of $r(e)$ and $\ell(e)$ are not known a-priori, we assume that they can be estimated by some profiling mechanism. Once a file transfer has started, it cannot be preempted and it continues till completion. This assumption is important to eliminate the necessity to keep state and ensure fault tolerance. We next try to model the rates at which multiple active file transfers that share a host can proceed concurrently. The active file transfers originating or terminating at a common host share the disk and other I/O resources of that host. Thus if the number active file transfers at a host goes up, the rate of an individual file transfer goes down. To keep the model simple while capturing the essence of this resource sharing, we assume that if there are n active file transfers at a host, each file transfer can take place at a rate no more than $1/n$ times the rate on a dedicated host. Suppose that at some point while file $e = \{u, v\}$ is being transferred, there are a total of n_u active file transfers at host u and a total of n_v active file transfers at host v. We assume that the effective rate at which e gets transferred is given by the minimum of the rates it can get at the two end hosts: $\min\{1/n_u, 1/n_v\}$. Of course, this rate may change over a period of time, since n_u or n_v may change with time. The scheduler for the Shuffle phase, thus has to decide the start times for the individual files. Once the start times are fixed, the files get transferred at rates given by the above model. There are several useful objective functions a scheduler may try to optimize. One such objective function is the average completion time. This MinSum objective gives an estimate on how soon the transfers finish so that the Reduce tasks can start. Another objective function is the MakeSpan. This MinMax objective captures the finish time of the last file transfer which, in turn, is a useful lower bound on the completion time of the overall Map-Reduce job.

1.2 Problem Formulation

A *file transfer model* is a triple (G, ℓ, r) where $G = (V, E)$ is an undirected multi-graph. The vertices V represent the hosts (or compute nodes) and the edges E denote the files to be transferred between the hosts. Assume that hosts are homogeneous and have identical processing capability of 1. Function $\ell : E \mapsto \mathbb{N}$ is the length function where for each edge $e = \{u, v\} \in E$, $\ell(e)$ corresponds to the size of file e to be transferred between u and v. Function $r : E \mapsto \mathbb{N}$ is the release time function; we cannot start transferring file e before its release time $r(e)$. A *uniform transfer model* is a transfer model where the length of all files are 1, i.e., $\forall e \in E, \ell(e) = 1$. A *zero-release transfer model* is a transfer model where all the files are available from the start, i.e., $\forall e \in E, r(e) = 0$. Any schedule S defines a function $s_S : E \mapsto \mathbb{R}^+ \cup \{0\}$, where $s_S(e)$ is the starting time for the edge e. Once a file e is started to be transferred, it cannot be preempted and continues until it completes at time $f_S(e)$. The rate at which the file is transferred however can vary over time and depends on how loaded the hosts u and v are at a particular time during its transfer. More precisely, consider a time t during the transfer. Let $n_u(t)$ and $n_v(t)$ denote the total number of file transfers active at time t involving hosts u and v respectively. Let E_v for any $v \in V$, denote the edges adjacent to v. The processing capability of each host gets divided equally among all the file transfers involving that host. The effective processing e gets at time t is the minimum of the two processing capabilities at the end-points: $\min\{1/n_u(t), 1/n_v(t)\}$. This denotes the units of file transferred per unit time at time t. The file e continues till it gets a total processing of $\ell(e)$. There are two different cost functions which we like to minimize. In the *MakeSpan* version of the problem, the cost of a schedule S is the finishing time of the last transfer (job), i.e., $\text{MAX}(S) = \max_{e \in E}\{f_S(e)\}$. In the *MinSum* version, the cost of a schedule S is the sum of finishing times for all the file transfers, i.e., $\text{SUM}(S) = \sum_{e \in E} f_S(e)$. Note that the MinSum criterion corresponds to minimizing the average finishing time of all edges.

For any instance of the problem, consider opt_{ms} as a schedule with the minimum MakeSpan cost of $\text{OPT}_{ms} = \text{MAX}(opt_{ms})$. Similarly, consider opt_{sum} as a schedule with the MinSum cost of $\text{OPT}_{sum} = \text{SUM}(opt_{sum})$. We may omit the ms and sum indexes if they are clear from the context.

1.3 Our Model vs. the Non-Concurrent Model

The distinguishing feature of our model is that it allows multiple active file transfers at a host. If at each round only a matching can be scheduled, the model is called a non-concurrent model. Here we give simple examples in which our concurrent file transfer model gives better values of MakeSpan or average completion time by a constant factor than the non-concurrent model. Let $G = K_3$ be a triangle and let $r(e) = 0$ and $\ell(e) = 1$ for all $e \in G$. If we start transferring all three files at time 0, each file receives a rate of $1/2$ and completes at time 2, giving MakeSpan of 2. If however we insist that no two active files can share a host, the best way to schedule these edges is one-by-one, giving a MakeSpan of 3. Moreover, the MakeSpan problem with uniform file sizes has a simple scheduling in the concurrent file transfer (see Section 4), in the Non-concurrent model it is equivalent to properly coloring the edges of a graph, which is an NP-Complete problem (see for example [8]). We can also give a simple example for the MinSum criteria. Let G be a path of length 2 with edges e and e'. Let $\ell(e) = M, \ell(e') = 1, r(e) = 0$ and $r(e') = M/2$. If we start transferring files right on their release times, the sum of completion times would be $f(e) + f(e') = (M + 1) + (M/2 + 2) = 1.5M + 3$. But if we are not able to transfer the files incident to a host concurrently we must transfer them in some order. If we start transferring e at time zero, then the total cost would be $M + (M + 1) = 2M + 1$. If we want to transfer e' before e, then the total cost would be $(M/2 + 1) + (M/2 + 1 + M) = 2M + 3$. Therefore the cost of the optimum solution is almost $2M$ in the Non-concurrent model but the cost of the optimum in concurrent model is almost $1.5M$.

1.4 Our Contributions

THEOREM 1. *The problem of computing schedules with minimum MakeSpan is NP-complete. The problem of computing minimum average completion time in the file transfer model is NP-complete even on trees, and even with file sizes 1 or 2.*

In Sections 3.2 and 3.1, we then present constant factor approximations for our problems.

THEOREM 2. *There exist polynomial-time algorithms that achieve the following approximation factors for various versions of the problems we study. Here $e \approx 2.718$ stands for the base of the natural logarithms.*

File sizes	Release Times	MakeSpan	Avg. Resp. Time
Non-Uniform	General	3 §3.2	6e §3.3
	Zero-Release	2 §3.2	4e §3.3
Uniform	General	3 §3.2	6e §3.3
	Zero-Release	1 §4	3.658 §4
			Bipartite: $\sqrt{2}$ §4

Our techniques. We generalize the technique given by Queyranne and Sviridenko [18] and Kortsarz et al. [3] for our framework in section 3.1. They use a method to reduce the MinSum criteria to MakeSpan criteria. Their basic idea is to divide the vertices into disjoint subsets according to a function and reduce the problem to a MakeSpan problem on every subgraph induced by the vertices.

They require a specific relation between the maximum weighted clique in the vertices of each subset and the partitioning function. They also need a similar relation between the maximum weighted clique and the MakeSpan scheduling algorithm. We generalize this technique to partition the edges (instead of vertices) using any partitioning function and scheduling algorithm with a simple, and much more general, relation between the function and the scheduling algorithm. This Meta-algorithm provides a very general tool for scheduling conflicting jobs under the MinSum criteria. Using this approach, we present constant approximation algorithms for the general file transfer problem with the MinSum criteria.

1.5 Related Work

A closely related problem to the file transfer problem is the "Data Migration" problem. The data migration problem arises in large storage systems, such as Storage allocation or Scheduling on dedicated processors [3], where a network of hosts is used to store multimedia data. As the data access pattern changes over time, the load across the hosts needs to be re-balanced. This is done by computing a new data layout and then "migrating" data to convert the initial data layout to the target data layout. Clearly it is important to compute a data migration schedule that converts the initial layout to the target layout quickly.

This problem can be modeled as a transfer graph, in which the vertices represent the hosts and an edge between two vertices u and v corresponds to a data object that must be transferred from u to v, or vice-versa. Each edge has a length that represents the transfer time of a data object between the hosts corresponding to the endpoints of the edge. In data migration problem we assume that any host can be involved in at most one transfer at any time. Several variations of the data migration problem have been studied. These variations arise either due to different objective functions or due to additional constraints.

There are usually three different objective functions to optimize. One common objective function is to minimize the MakeSpan of the migration schedule, i.e., the time by which all migrations complete. Coffman et al. [9] introduced this problem. They showed that when edges may have arbitrary lengths, a class of greedy algorithms yields a 2-approximation to the minimum MakeSpan. In the special case where the lengths are uniform, i.e., edges have equal (unit) lengths, the problem reduces to edge coloring of the transfer (multi)graph of the system for which an asymptotic approximation scheme is now known [13].

Another objective function is to minimize the average completion time over all hosts (vertices). In this version we usually consider the weighted sum of finishing times of vertices, i.e., each vertex v is associated with a weight $w(v)$ and the completion time of each vertex $C(v)$ is the last finishing time of edges adjacent to v and we want to minimize $\sum_v w(v)C(v)$. Kim [6] proved that the problem is NP-hard and showed that Graham's list scheduling algorithm [14], when guided by an optimal solution to a linear programming relaxation, gives an approximation ratio of 3. She also gave a 9-approximation algorithm for the case where edges have arbitrary lengths. Gandhi et al. [11] showed that the analysis of the 3-approximation algorithm is tight. They also gave a 5.06-approximation algorithm for a more general case when edges have release times and arbitrary lengths.

Bar-Noy et al. [10] studied the data migration problem with the objective to minimize the average completion time over all data migrations (edges). They showed that the problem is NP-hard and gave a simple 2-approximation algorithm for the uniform case (which is also known as *Min Sum Edge Coloring Problem*).

Halldórsson et al. [2] improved this ratio to 1.8298. For arbitrary edge lengths, the best known ratio is 7.682 by [3].

A problem related to the data migration problem is open shop scheduling. In this problem, we have a set of machines and a set of jobs with positive weights. Each job consists of a set of operations. Each operation has a processing time and must be processed on an specific machine. Each machine can process a single operation at any time, and two operations that belong to the same job cannot be processed simultaneously. The objective is to minimize the sum of weighted completion times of all jobs. This problem is a special case of the data migration problem [11]. Open shop scheduling problem has been studied in [11, 15, 16, 17, 18].

For different models of data migration, see [21, 20, 19].

2. NP-COMPLETE RESULTS

THEOREM 3. *The file transfer problem is NP-hard even in trees and even if the jobs have length 1 or 2.*

The reduction used is the same as used by Marx [22]. The problem Marx showed hardness for is *preemptive sum multicoloring of the edges of the a tree* (MEPS). In this problem we are given a tree and every edge has an integral length $\ell(e)$. We have to color the edges of the tree and the colors we use are positive integers $1, 2, 3 \ldots$. If e and e' share a vertex. then their color sets must be disjoint. To satisfy that, a solution must choose a matching at every round (and the edges in the matching get the color of the round number). Every edge e must belong to $\ell(e)$ matchings. Let Ψ be a proper coloring and $f_\Psi(e)$ be the largest color assigned to e by Ψ. The goal is to minimize $\sum_{e \in E} f_\Psi(e)$ In the non-preemptive case, every e must receive $\ell(e)$ *consecutive* integers. Consider MEPS. The solution of [22] for a yes instance happens to be *non-preemptive* as we shall see. Note that this implies a hardness for the non preemptive case as well. For us this fact is important as it fits our model which is non-preemptive. We now state some observations used by [22] (albeit, not made explicitly in [22]).

Definition Given an undirected graph $G(V, E)$ a *vertex cover* (of the edges) is a subset $A \subseteq V$ so that for every edge $e = uv \in E$ either $u \in A$ or $v \in A$. An *exact vertex cover* A, is a vertex cover A, so that for every $e = uv$ *exactly one of* u or v belongs to A.

Consider an exact vertex cover A of the edges of the graph. Say that $v, u \in A$. Let $E(v), E(u)$ be the edges of v and u in G.

CLAIM 1. $E(v) \cap E(u) = \emptyset$.

Proof. If $E(v) \cap E(u) \neq \emptyset$ then $E(v) \cap E(u) = uv$ as uv is the only edge that can appear both in $E(v)$ and in $E(u)$. But our assumption that $u \in A$ and $v \in A$ implies that A is not an exact cover (uv is covered twice). This is a contradiction. □

Hence the collection of edges $\{E(v) \mid v \in A\}$ is a collection of *edge-disjoint stars*, with v the center of $E(v)$. This collection includes all edges. Namely, every edge appears in exactly one of these stars.

Definition A perfect coloring of a star $E(v)$ of A is a coloring that takes the star, deletes the rest of the edges from the graph, and assigns this star its optimum coloring (disregarding conflicts that may occur with other stars). A perfect coloring, is a perfect coloring of all stars $E(v), v \in A$.

Clearly, it is not clear a-priori that a perfect coloring exists. However, we can prove the following.

CLAIM 2. *If we can find an exact cover A and it is possible to find perfect and legal (consistent) coloring of all stars, then the coloring is optimal.*

Proof. Since the stars are edge-disjoint we consider every star separately. Given a star collection of A, the perfect sum coloring corresponding to each star lower bounds the contribution of this star to the sum. This is because this coloring is locally optimal (disregarding all other stars). Thus the sum of the contribution of a perfect coloring over all stars of A is a lower bound on the optimum sum. Since we assume that a perfect coloring can be obtained in a consistent way, the coloring is optimal. □

Consider a general star with center v and let $E(v) = e_1, e_2, \ldots, e_k$. Assume without loss of generality that $\ell(e_1) \leq \ell(e_2) \leq \ldots \leq \ell(e_k)$.

CLAIM 3. **A perfect coloring of a star.** *A perfect coloring of the star, in the file transfer model first schedules e_1 for $\ell(e_1)$ time units, and then schedules e_2 for $\ell(e_2)$ minutes, and so on.*

Proof. Let $i < j$. The edges e_i and e_j share a vertex (namely, share v). This means that one of the edges will add to the delay of the other or wise versa. As $\ell(e_i) \leq \ell(e_j)$, then the contribution to the delay of this pair is at least $\min\{\ell(e_i), \ell(e_j)\} = \ell(e_i)$. For this e_i has to be scheduled in fully, before e_j starts scheduling. The option of scheduling edges together, which holds in the file transfer model does not produce a perfect coloring. It works in 'half speed'. More precisely, if we schedule e_i, e_j for $\epsilon > 0$ time units together, then e_i and e_j both get ϵ units of delay and $\epsilon/2$ units of their jobs were finished by now. Now, even if the $\epsilon/2$ time units of the mutual schedule were the last time units e_i needed, the rest of the job e_i delayed e_j by $\ell(e_i) - \epsilon/2$. Thus the total delay corresponding to these two edges is $\epsilon + (\ell(e_i) - \epsilon/2) = \ell(e_i) + \epsilon/2$ which is a non-perfect coloring. It is easy to see that after e_i and e_j were scheduled for $\epsilon > 0$ time units together, *no coloring completion* can derive a perfect coloring. Now, if we schedule e_1 fully first and then e_2 and so own, for every $i < j$, the delay caused by the pair e_i to e_j is the minimum possible $\ell(e_i)$. Hence all delays for all edge pairs is the minimum possible and the coloring is perfect. □

The following theorem is proved in [22]. We start with a $3-\text{SAT}$ instance so that every literal appears twice non-negated and twice negated. This problem is still NP-hard. See [24]. We denote this problem by $3-\text{SAT}-4$. In [22] a reduction from $3-\text{SAT}-4$ to MEPS is given. The instance of MEPS is called a *yes instance* if it corresponds to a satisfiable $3-\text{SAT}-4$ formula. Else it is called a no-instance.

THEOREM 4. [22] *In the yes instance of MEPS, there exists an exact vertex cover A and a legal perfect coloring of its stars. In addition, the coloring is* non-preemptive. *A no instance, does not admit a (consistent) perfect coloring of A and so the sum is larger than the one given by a perfect sum.*

In [22] it is shown that there exist an optimum solution for a MEPS instance such that the maximum color is at most $p \cdot (2\Delta - 1)$ with p the maximum demand and Δ the maximum degree in the graph. If p is exponential in n then a solution for MEPS is exponential (in the no instance, as the preemptive coloring is concerned, there may be no short description of the coloring). Therefore we assume that p is bounded by a polynomial in n.

COROLLARY 1. *If there exists a polynomial time algorithm for the file transfer problem, then $P = NP$. Clearly this means that that the file transfer problem is NP-hard as it is immediate to verify in polynomial time if a given coloring is optimum, as by the above remark every color given to an edge is polynomial in n.*

Proof. Given that the solution of [22] for a yes instance, happens to be non-preemptive, and given Claim 3 for the file transfer problem, in a yes instance the solutions of MEPS and the file transfer problem are *identical*. This is because every non-perfect coloring is suboptimal, as in the yes-instance a perfect coloring exists. The perfect coloring is optimum for both models. Moreover, an optimal solution for MEPS in a yes instance defines a satisfying assignment for the $3-\text{SAT}-4$ instance. So for a yes instance, by the assumed algorithm for MEPS we can find a legal perfect coloring (we use here the fact that the coloring in MEPS is non-preemptive and so, legal for the file transfer model). This is also a perfect coloring for MEPS. We will know if the coloring is perfect as we know A and we can check in polynomial time if that the coloring is perfect. Hence, we can recognize a yes-instance of MEPS. In a no instance, the optimum (preemptive) solution for MEPS and the optimum solution for the file transfer problem have nothing in common. However, the value of the no-instance for both models is larger than the value of a perfect coloring. Consider the optimum solution returned for the file transfer algorithm. Since A is known, we can check that the returned a non-perfect coloring. As a perfect coloring for the file transfer does not exists, we will know that this instance is a no-instance of MEPS, and so we can tell if the instance is a yes instance or a no instance and so $P = NP$. Further details are omitted for lack of space. □

2.1 NP-Complete for MakeSpan

We reduce the strongly NP-hard problem called *3-partition* to the problem of computing a schedule with minimum MakeSpan. An instance of the 3-partition problem is given by an integer $B > 0$ and $3n$ integers $s_1, \ldots, s_{3n}$ such that $B/4 < s_i < B/2$ for all $i \in [3n]$ and $\sum_{i=1}^{3n} s_i = nB$. Here $[k]$ stands for $\{1, \ldots, k\}$. An instance is called a YES instance if the $3n$ integers can be partitioned into subsets $G_1, \ldots, G_n$ such that each G_j has 3 elements adding up to exactly B. An instance that is not a YES instance is called a NO instance. It is well known that it is strongly NP-hard to distinguish between YES and NO instances [24].

We now give a polynomial-time procedure that, given an instance of the 3-partition problem, creates an instance of the MakeSpan minimization problem. The graph G of the MakeSpan minimization instance created is given in Figure 1. The release times and lengths of the various edges are also given in the adjacent table.

LEMMA 1. *An instance obtained from a YES instance of the 3-partition problem has optimum MakeSpan $(B + 1)n - 1$, while an instance obtained from a NO instance of the 3-partition problem has optimum MakeSpan strictly more than $(B + 1)n - 1$.*

Proof. Consider an instance obtained from a YES instance of the 3-partition problem. We create a non-concurrent schedule, i.e., a schedule which does not schedule multiple edges incident to a host at any point in time, with MakeSpan $(B + 1)n - 1$. First schedule all the edges of the form $\{v, b_j\}, \{b_j, a_j\}, \{b_j, c_j\}$ for $j \in [n - 1]$ starting at their respective release times. It is easy to note that no two adjacent edges among these will be active at any point in time. Now the only time windows that are open for scheduling edges of the form $\{v, u_i\}$ for $i \in [3n]$ are $W_j = [(B + 1)(j - 1), (B + 1)(j - 1) + B)$ for $j \in [n]$. Note that each of these windows is of length exactly B. Let $G_1, \ldots, G_n$ be the partition of the $3n$ integers into subsets of size 3 each adding up to B. Fix $j \in [n]$ and let $G_j = \{s_{j_1}, s_{j_2}, s_{j_3}\}$ so that $s_{j_1} + s_{j_2} + s_{j_3} = B$. Now schedule the edges $\{v, u_{j_1}\}, \{v, u_{j_2}\}, \{v, u_{j_3}\}$ in window W_j one after the other. It is easy to see that this in fact gives a non-current schedule with MakeSpan $(B + 1)n - 1$.

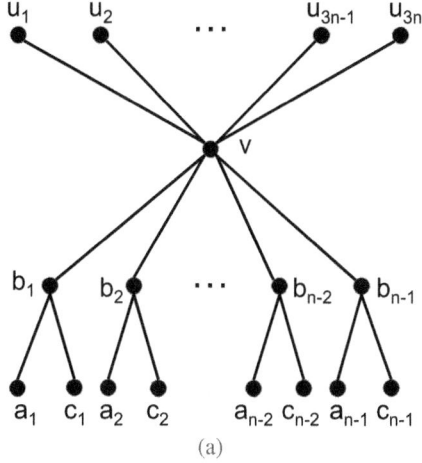

(a)

Edge e	Release time $r(e)$	Length $\ell(e)$
$\{v, u_i\}$ for $i \in [3n]$	0	s_i
$\{v, b_j\}$ for $j \in [n-1]$	$(B+1)j - 1$	1
$\{b_j, a_j\}$ for $j \in [n-1]$	0	$(B+1)j - 1$
$\{b_j, c_j\}$ for $j \in [n-1]$	$(B+1)j$	$(B+1)(n-j) - 1$

(b)

Figure 1: MakeSpan minimization instance in the reduction

Now it is enough to show that if there is a schedule (either concurrent or non-concurrent) with MakeSpan at most $(B+1)n - 1$, the instance must have been created from a YES instance of the 3-partition problem. Note that the edges incident to each b_j have total length exactly $(B+1)n - 1$. Considering their release times, it is clear that for the MakeSpan to be at most $(B+1)n - 1$, these edges must be schedules at their respective release times in a noonconcurrent manner. This again gives that the only time windows that are open for scheduling edges of the form $\{v, u_i\}$ for $i \in [3n]$ are W_j for $j \in [n]$ defined above. Furthermore no edge $\{v, u_i\}$ can be active in more than one window. Thus each edge $\{v, u_i\}$ maps to a unique window W_j. The edges mapping to any single window must have total length exactly B. This naturally induces a feasible solution to the 3-partition problem and hence gives that the starting instance of the 3-partition problem must have been a YES instance. □

3. NON-UNIFORM TRANSFER MODEL

In this section we present different algorithms for finding schedules under the non-uniform transfer model. In Section 3.1, we generalize the approach in [4] and [3] to give a meta-algorithm for solving the SUM problem by partitioning the jobs into different blocks and then using an algorithm with good MakeSpan time for each block.

In Section 3.2, we give constant competitive algorithms for the MakeSpan problem. Finally in Section 3.3, by providing different bucketing functions and using algorithms in Section 3.2, we give constant competitive algorithms for the MinSum problem.

3.1 Overview of the Approach for Solving the MinSum Problem

We use a meta-algorithm which provides a very general tool for scheduling conflicting jobs under the minimum sum criteria. The meta-algorithm uses a *bucketing function* f^* to divide the jobs into disjoint blocks such that each block has a "uniformity property" (e.g., in a near optimum scheduling these blocks end up roughly

having the same finishing time). Then we simply schedule each block using a MakeSpan algorithm $\mathcal{A}$. The trick is to find a bucketing function such that the sum of values assigned to jobs is in a small constant approximation of OPT_{sum} (this imposes an upper bound on *bucket values*), and the maximum bucket value should also be a constant approximation of OPT_{max} (this imposes a lower bound on bucket values).

Now we elaborate how to partition the job set E into different blocks $E^0, E^1, \ldots, E^k$. Assume for an instance (G, ℓ, r) of the problem a value $f^*(e)$ (which we call the *bucket value* of e) is associated with each job e. Let $a > 1$ be a constant real number and α be a value chosen uniformly at random from $[0, 1)$. Let $l_i = a^{\alpha + i}$, for $i = -1, 0, 1, \ldots, k$. Define the block $E^i = \{e \in E | l_{i-1} < f^*(e) \le l_i\}$, for $i = 0, \ldots, k$. So the edge set E, is divided into disjoint blocks of $E^0, \ldots, E^k$. Denote by b_e the block into which edge e belongs (which of course, is a function of α). The meta-algorithm $\mathbf{ALG}(\mathcal{A}, f^*)$ given in the figure, applies $\mathcal{A}$ (which will give us a near optimum MakeSpan time) on all the blocks separately. We may use the same notation $\mathbf{ALG}(\mathcal{A}, f^*)$ as the schedule given by this algorithm on an instance of the file transfer problem.

Algorithm 1 $\mathbf{ALG}(\mathcal{A}, f^*)$

1: Choose α uniformly at random from $[0, 1)$.
2: Using the bucket function f^*, partition the edges into blocks $E^0, \ldots, E^k$.
3: Schedule the blocks in sequence using algorithm $\mathcal{A}$.

We give sufficient properties for the bucket function (regarding the MakeSpan algorithm $\mathcal{A}$ and the optimum answer OPT_{sum}) in order for $\mathbf{ALG}$ to have a constant approximation ratio. Let f^* be a bucketing function and $\mathcal{A}$ be a scheduling algorithm such that for any instance of the transfer problem $\langle G, \ell, r \rangle$:

(P1) $\forall_{e \in E} \exists_{e' \in E} f_{\mathcal{A}}(e) \le \beta f^*(e')$

(P2) $\sum_{e \in E} f^*(e) \le \gamma \text{OPT}_{sum}$

where β and γ are constants. Lemma 2 gives an upper-bound on the expected value of finishing times of edges in $\mathbf{ALG}$.

LEMMA 2. *Let f^* and $\mathcal{A}$ have the property (P1) and let $\mathbf{ALG}(\mathcal{A}, f^*)$ be the corresponding schedule. For each edge $e \in E$, $\mathbf{E}[f_{\mathbf{ALG}}(e)] \le \beta \frac{a}{\ln a} f^*(e) \le \beta e f^*(e)$. Here $e \approx 2.718$ stands for the base of the natural logarithms.*

Proof. In $\mathbf{ALG}$ before scheduling the block i, we wait for blocks $0 \le j < i$ to finish transferring all their files, and then we schedule the edges in E^i, using $\mathcal{A}$. To bound the finishing time of edges we consider an arbitrary block i separately and then we consider the waiting time required for transferring previous blocks.

Let $f_{\mathcal{A}}(e)$ be the finishing time of edge e when the block E^{b_e} has been scheduled separately by $\mathcal{A}$. According to (P1) for $G = \langle V, E^{b_e} \rangle$ we have:

$$f_{\mathcal{A}}(e) \le \beta f^*(e') \le \beta l_{b_{e'}} = \beta l_{b_e}$$

in which the last equality follows from the fact that e and e' are in the same block. This shows that if we consider each block i separately, an edge e finishes at most on βl_{b_e}. Recall that $l_i = a^{\alpha+i}$. Considering the waiting time for blocks before b_e, we have:

$$f_{\mathbf{ALG}}(e) \le \sum_{i=0}^{b_e} \beta l_i = \beta \sum_{i=0}^{b_e} a^{\alpha+i} \le \frac{\beta a^{\alpha + b_e + 1}}{a - 1} = \beta \frac{a}{a-1} t_{b_e}$$

273

where $t_{b_e} = a^{\alpha + b_e}$. Since α is a random variable, then b_e and t_{b_e} are also random variables. We use the same method as in [3] to compute the expected value of t_{b_e}. Let $z = \log_a f^*(e)$, for $e \in E$. Define $y_e = \alpha + b_e - z$. Since b_e is the smallest integer such that $\alpha + b_e \geq z$, then y_e is uniformly distributed on $[0, 1)$. Therefore

$$
\begin{aligned}
\mathbf{E}[f_{\mathbf{ALG}}(e)] &\leq \beta \frac{a}{a-1} \mathbf{E}[a^{y_e + z}] = \beta \frac{a}{a-1} f^*(e) \int_0^1 a^t dt \\
&= \beta \frac{a}{a-1} f^*(e) \frac{a-1}{\ln a} = \beta \frac{a}{\ln a} f^*(e).
\end{aligned}
$$

The function $f(a) = \frac{a}{\ln a}$ is maximized when $a = e \approx 2.718$, therefore $\mathbf{E}[f_{\mathbf{ALG}}(e)] \leq \beta e f^*(e)$. $\square$

Considering Lemma 2 we would have the following.

THEOREM 5. *The sum cost of* $\mathbf{ALG}(\mathcal{A}, f^*)$ *is less than* $\beta \gamma e \mathrm{OPT}_{sum}$ *for any instance of transfer problem* (G, ℓ, r) *and bucketing function* f^* *and scheduling algorithm* $\mathcal{A}$ *with both properties (P1) and (P2).*

Proof. By Lemma 2, $\mathrm{SUM}(\mathbf{ALG}) = \sum_{e \in E} f_{\mathbf{ALG}}(e) \leq \beta e \sum_{e \in E} f^*(e)$. Thus by (P2) we have $\mathrm{SUM}(\mathbf{ALG}) \leq \beta \gamma e \mathrm{OPT}$. $\square$

3.2 MakeSpan Problem

We call a schedule $\mathcal{S}$, *non-concurrent schedule* if by applying that schedule no processor runs more than one transfer at any time, i.e., for any two adjacent edges e and e', we have either $s(e) \geq f(e')$ or $s(e') \geq f(e)$. Let deg_v for any $v \in V$ denote the degree of v in G. Next theorem shows that a greedy algorithm can guarantee a 3-factor of the optimum solution in the MakeSpan version.

THEOREM 6. *There is an algorithm* Greedy MakeSpan *(or* **GMS***) which for any instance of transfer problem* (G, ℓ, r) *gives a non-concurrent schedule with a MakeSpan cost at most* $3\mathrm{OPT}_{ms}$. *In addition for every edge* $e = \{u, v\} \in E$ *the finishing time is at most* $r(e) + \sum_{e' \in E_u} \ell(e') + \sum_{e' \in E_v} \ell(e') - \ell(e)$.

Proof. We use a sweep line method to make a non-concurrent schedule (thus $f(e)$ would be equal to $s(e) + \ell(e)$ for any edge $e \in E$). In each step of the algorithm given in the figure, we schedule the edge which can start sooner than all other edges which are not yet scheduled, breaking ties arbitrarily. Formally, consider U_i as the subset of edges which are scheduled by our algorithm before step i. Initially U_1 is empty and at each step of the algorithm we schedule a new edge. Recall that E_v for any $v \in V$, denotes the edges adjacent to v. In step i, for any edge $e = \{u, v\} \notin U_i$, consider $p_i(e)$ as the first *possible* starting time of e, i.e., the time after its release time and after transferring all currently scheduled edges which are adjacent to u and v. Let e_i be the edge with minimum possible starting time in step i. We set the starting time of e_i equal to $p_i(e)$, set $U_{i+1} = U_i \cup \{e_i\}$, and continue the algorithm in the next step. We observe that the resulting sequence of starting times $s(e_1), \ldots, s(e_{|E|})$ is non-decreasing.

Now we show that for each edge $e^* = \{u, v\}$, $s(e^*)$ is at most $r(e^*) + \sum_{e \in E_u} \ell(e) - \ell(e^*) + \sum_{e \in E_v} \ell(e) - \ell(e^*)$. To show this, we will prove by contradiction that u and v are never idle in the same time between $r(e^*)$ and $s(e^*)$. Let $r(e^*) \leq t < s(e^*)$ be the moment that both u and v are idle. Let k be the first step which we schedule an edge after t, i.e., $k = \min_{\{i | s(e_i) > t\}} i$. In step k, $p_k(e_k) > t$ and $s(e) \leq t$ for all edges $e \in U_k$. Since u and v are both idle on time t and no scheduled edge is started after that time, the minimum possible starting time of e^* at step k is $p_k(e^*) = t$.

Algorithm 2 Greedy MakeSpan (**GMS**)

Input: An instance of transfer problem $(G = (V, E), \ell, r)$.
Output: A schedule $\mathcal{S}$ with corresponding starting times for each edge in E.

1: Define $U_1 = \phi$.
2: **for** $i = 1$ to $|E|$ **do**
3:     For every edge $e' = \{u, v\} \notin U_i$, define $p_i(e) = \max\{r(e), \max_{e' \in U_i \cap (E_u \cup E_v)} f_{\mathcal{S}}(e')\}$.
4:     Let $e_i \in \operatorname{argmin}_{e \notin U_i} p_i(e)$.
5:     Set $s_{\mathcal{S}}(e_i) = p_i(e_i)$ and thus $f_{\mathcal{S}}(e_i) = s_{\mathcal{S}}(e_i) + \ell(e_i)$.
6:     Define $U_{i+1} = U_i \cup \{e_i\}$.

But the edge with minimum possible starting time at step k is e_k with $p_k(e_k) > t$, which is a contradiction.

Therefore the finishing time of each edge $e^* = \{u, v\}$ is at most

$$
\begin{aligned}
f(e^*) &= s(e^*) + \ell(e^*) \\
&\leq r(e^*) + \sum_{e \in E_u} \ell(e) + \sum_{e \in E_v} \ell(e) - \ell(e^*) \\
&\leq 3\mathrm{OPT} - \ell(e^*).
\end{aligned}
$$

The last inequality follows from the fact that $\mathrm{OPT} \geq \sum_{e \in E_v} \ell(e)$ for any vertex $v \in V$ and $\mathrm{OPT} \geq r(e) + \ell(e)$ for any edge $e \in E$. $\square$

We note that by Theorem 6, any edge $e = \{u, v\}$ with release time of zero finishes at most on $\sum_{e' \in E_u} \ell(e') + \sum_{e' \in E_v} \ell(e') - \ell(e) \leq 2\mathrm{OPT}$. Hence in a zero-release transfer problem **GMS** is always in 2-approximation of the optimum.

COROLLARY 2. *For any instance of zero-release transfer problem* (G, ℓ), **GMS** *gives a non-concurrent schedule with a MakeSpan cost at most* $2\mathrm{OPT}_{ms}$.

3.3 MinSum Problem

In this section we present a bucketing function with both properties (P1) and (P2) according to the MakeSpan algorithm **GMS** given in section 3.2. For an instance of the problem (G, ℓ, r), let $\pi_1, \ldots, \pi_{|E|}$ be the edges sorted by their length i.e for any $1 \leq i < j \leq |E|$, $\ell(\pi_i) \leq \ell(\pi_j)$. Let $S^i(v)$ for $v \in V$ and $1 \leq i \leq |E|$, be the sum of the lengths of all edges π_1 to π_i in E_v.

For any edge $e \in E$ let $bp(e)$ be $r(e) + \ell(e)$, i.e., the *best possible* finishing time for e. Now consider the edges sorted by their best possible finishing times. Formally, label the edges from e_1 to $e_{|E|}$ such that for any $1 \leq i < j \leq |E|$, $bp(e_i) \leq bp(e_j)$. For any edge $e_i = \{u, v\} \in E$, let the bucket value of e_i be $f^*(e_i) = \max\{bp(e_i), S^i(u), S^i(v)\}$. The following two lemmas show the existence of both properties P1 and P2 for the bucketing function f^* and algorithm **GMS**.

LEMMA 3. *For any edge* $e = \{u, v\} \in E$ *there exists an edge* e^* *such that* $f_{\mathbf{GMS}}(e) \leq 3f^*(e^*)$ *and thus satisfying property P1 with* $\beta = 3$. *In addition if* e *is released at time zero (i.e.* $r(e) = 0$*) then* $f_{\mathbf{GMS}}(e) \leq 2f^*(e^*)$ *for some edge* $e^* \in E$.

Proof. By Theorem 6 we have $f(e) \leq r(e) + \sum_{e' \in E_u} \ell(e') + \sum_{e' \in E_v} \ell(e') - \ell(e)$. Assume that e_x and e_y are the files with the largest best possible finishing time adjacent to u and v respectively. Thus $S^x(u)$ ($S^y(v)$) is actually the sum of the lengths of all edges in E_u (E_v). By the definition of the bucketing function f^* we have

- $f^*(e) \geq bp(e) = r(e) + \ell(e)$.

- $f^*(e_x) \geq S^x(u) = \sum_{e' \in E_u} \ell(e')$,

- $f^*(e_y) \geq S^y(v) = \sum_{e' \in E_v} \ell(e')$,

Therefore

$$
\begin{aligned}
f_{\mathbf{GMS}}(e) &\leq r(e) + \sum_{e' \in E_u} \ell(e') + \sum_{e' \in E_v} \ell(e') - \ell(e) \\
&\leq f^*(e) - \ell(e) + f^*(e_x) + f^*(e_y) - \ell(e) \\
&\leq 3f^*(e^*) - 2\ell(e)
\end{aligned}
$$

where e^* is the edge with the maximum bucket value among all edges in E. We note that if $r(e) = 0$ then the above inequality would be $f_{\mathbf{GMS}}(e) \leq 2f^*(e^*) - \ell(e)$. □

The number k in the following lemma is the number of buckets resulting by $\mathbf{ALG}(\mathcal{A}, f^*)$.

LEMMA 4. *The sum of the bucket values of all edges in E is at most* $2\mathrm{OPT}_{sum}$ *and thus satisfying property P2 with* $\gamma = 2$.

Proof. Let *opt* be the optimum schedule. Consider the finishing times of edges adjacent to an arbitrary vertex $v \in V$ in *opt* and let x_{vi} denote the ith smallest finishing time among them. Assume that among the sorted sequence of edges $e_1, \ldots, e_{|E|}$, the sequence $e_{i_1}, \ldots, e_{i_{deg_v}}$ are the edges in E_v. Vertex $v \in V$ should have finished transferring at least k files at time x_{vk}. Thus

(i) x_{vk} cannot be less than the sum of lengths of the smallest k edges in E_v, i.e., $x_{vk} \geq S^{i_k}(v)$.

(ii) x_{vk} cannot be less than the kth smallest best possible finishing time of edges in E_v, i.e., $x_{vk} \geq bp(e_{i_k})$.

Therefore $x_{vk} \geq \max\{bp(e_{i_k}), S^{i_k}(v)\}$. Now by summing x_{vk} for all edges adjacent to all vertices we obtain an upper bound on the sum of the bucket values.

$$
\begin{aligned}
2\mathrm{OPT} &= \sum_{v \in V} \sum_{k=1}^{deg_v} x_{vk} \\
&\geq \sum_{v \in V} \sum_{k=1}^{deg_v} \max\{bp(e_{i_k}), S^{i_k}(v)\} \\
&= \sum_{v \in V} \sum_{e_i \in E_v} \max\{bp(e_i), S^i(v)\} \\
&= \sum_{e_i = \{u,v\} \in E} [\max\{bp(e_i), S^i(u)\} \\
&\qquad\qquad + \max\{bp(e_i), S^i(v)\}] \\
&\geq \sum_{e_i = \{u,v\} \in E} \max\{bp(e_i), S^i(u), S^i(v)\} \\
&= \sum_{e_i \in E} f^*(e_i).
\end{aligned}
$$

□

Finally using the meta-algorithm provided in Section 3.1, we get a constant competitive algorithm for the general transfer problem.

THEOREM 7. *For an instance of transfer problem (G, ℓ, r), $\mathbf{ALG}(\mathbf{GMS}, f^*)$ is a $6\mathrm{e}$-approximation algorithm for the Min-Sum problem.*

Proof. By Lemma 3 the bucketing function f^* has (P1) property with $\beta = 3$ and by Lemma 4 has (P2) property with $\gamma = 2$. The claim follows directly from Theorem 5. □

We note that similar to Corollary 2, by Lemma 3 for a zero-release transfer problem we get property (P1) with $\beta = 2$ which improves the approximation ratio of the algorithm.

COROLLARY 3. *For an instance of zero-release transfer problem (G, ℓ), $\mathbf{ALG}(\mathbf{GMS}, f^*)$ is a $4\mathrm{e}$-approximation algorithm for the MinSum problem.*

4. UNIFORM ZERO-RELEASE TRANSFER MODEL

In this section we consider the uniform zero-release transfer model. First we show that by running all the file transfers simultaneously, we could obtain an exact solution for the MakeSpan version. We call this scheduling algorithm in which $\forall e \in E, s(e) = 0$ by *Simultaneous Start* or simply SS.

THEOREM 8. *For any graph $G = (V, E)$ with uniform length file transfers, $\mathrm{MAX}(SS) = \mathrm{OPT}_{ms}$.*

Proof. Let $\Delta(G)$ be the maximum degree of vertices of G and let u be one of the vertices with degree $\Delta(G)$. The vertex u needs to transfer $\Delta(G)$ units of file and transferring these files takes at least $\Delta(G)$ units of time. So we have $\mathrm{OPT} \geq \Delta(G)$. However, if we start all the jobs simultaneously, in each unit of time we run at least $\frac{1}{\Delta(G)}$ of each transfer. Therefore $\mathrm{MAX}(SS) = \Delta(G) = \mathrm{OPT}$. □

We note that if the files can have arbitrary lengths, SS may not have the optimum cost. We give an example for zero-release non-uniform file transfer model where the cost of SS can be almost two times the OPT. Consider the tree shown in Figure 4. Vertex v is adjacent to $n \geq 2$ vertices $u_1, \ldots, u_n$ through the edges $e_1, \ldots, e_n$. The length of all edges adjacent to v is an arbitrary integer M. For every $i \in [n]$ the vertex u_i is adjacent to $(n-1)M$ leaves through the edges of length 1. We can show that $\mathrm{OPT}_{ms} = nM$ but the MakeSpan cost of SS is $\mathrm{MAX}(SS) = 2nM - (M + n - 1)$.

The optimum schedule has n stages. In stage i vertex u_i starts transferring e_i and for every $j \neq i$ the vertex u_j starts transferring with M of its adjacent leaves. Therefore each stage takes exactly M units of time and OPT_{ms} would be equal to nM (the sum of edges adjacent to v is nM and thus OPT cannot be smaller).

The schedule SS starts all edges simultaneously at time zero. Since all edges are adjacent to a vertex with degree $(n-1)M + 1$, the edges adjacent to leaves finish at time $(n-1)M + 1$. After that the remaining $M - 1$ units of data on edges adjacent to v will be transferred with speed of $1/n$ and SS finishes all transfers at time $(n-1)M + 1 + (M-1)n$. Therefore by choosing $n = M$ the ratio between the optimum cost and the cost of SS would be

$$
\frac{\mathrm{MAX}(SS)}{\mathrm{OPT}_{ms}} \geq \frac{2n^2 - 2n}{n^2} = 2\frac{n-1}{n}.
$$

Now we show there is always a non-concurrent schedule with a cost less than twice the optimum solution in the MinSum problem. First we need to give a lower bound on the optimum cost.

LEMMA 5. *For any graph $G = (V, E)$ with uniform length file transfers, $\mathrm{OPT}_{sum} \geq \frac{1}{4} \sum_{v \in V} (deg_v^2 + deg_v)$.*

Proof. Let *opt* be the optimum schedule. Consider the finishing times of edges adjacent to an arbitrary vertex $v \in V$ in *opt* and let x_{vi} denote the ith smallest finishing time among them. Since $x_{vi} \geq i$ for all $1 \leq i \leq deg_v$, we have $\sum_{e \in E_v} f_{opt}(e) = \sum_{i=1}^{deg_v} x_{vi} \geq$

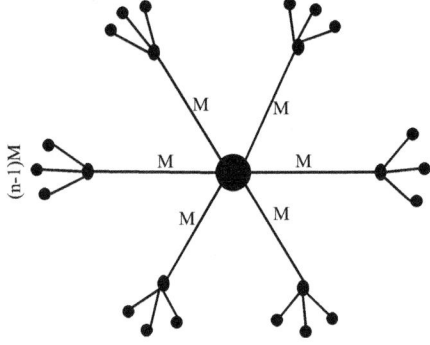

$\frac{deg_v(deg_v+1)}{2}$. Therefore

$$2\text{OPT} = 2\sum_{e \in E} f_{opt}(e)$$

$$= \sum_{v \in V}\sum_{e \in E_v} f_{opt}(e) \geq \sum_{v \in V} \frac{deg_v^2 + deg_v}{2}.$$

$\square$

THEOREM 9. *For any graph $G = (V, E)$ with uniform length file transfers, there is a non-concurrent schedule $\mathcal{S}$ with $\text{SUM}(\mathcal{S}) \leq 2\text{OPT}_{sum}$ with integral starting times.*

Proof omitted due to lack of space.

COROLLARY 4. *The uniform file transfer problem without release times on planar graphs admits a $2 + \epsilon$ approximation ratio.*

This follows from the non-concurrent PTAS of Marx [23] for coloring the edges of a planar graph.

In uniform transfer model, if all the starting times are integers in a non-concurrent schedule, the schedule is indeed a partition of the edges E, into k matchings $M_1, \ldots, M_k$ for some k, where M_i is the set of all edges starting on time $i - 1$ and therefore finishing at time i. The cost of this schedule would be $\sum_{1 \leq i \leq k} i|M_i|$. Halldórsson et. al. [2] give an approximation algorithm of ratio 1.8289 for finding the minimum sum cost edge coloring. By Theorem 9, the same algorithm gives us a 3.658-approximation algorithm for the zero-release uniform transfer model.

COROLLARY 5. *There is a polynomial time algorithm which gives a non-concurrent schedule with the cost less than 3.658-factor of OPT_{sum} for the zero-release uniform transfer model.*

5. FILE TRANSFER ON BIPARTITE GRAPHS

For certain classes of graphs we may get a smaller constant approximation. Consider a graph $G = (V, E)$ and a non-concurrent schedule of E into k matchings $M_1, \ldots, M_k$. If for every vertex $v \in V$ all edges adjacent to v are in the first deg_v matchings, then the sum of edges adjacent to v would be $\sum_{i=1}^{deg_v} i = deg_v(deg_v + 1)/2$. Therefore the sum of finishing times over all edges would be $\frac{1}{2}\sum_{v \in V} deg_v(deg_v + 1)/2$ which by Lemma 5 is equal to the optimum cost. For example, in r-regular bipartite graphs we can always find such a schedule by simply partitioning the edges into k perfect matchings, thus:

COROLLARY 6. *For any regular bipartite graph G we can find a schedule with the cost equal to OPT_{sum} in polynomial time.*

The nature of many transfer problems are transferring files between hosts and clients thus bipartite graphs are of separate interest. We present a 1.414-approximation algorithm for finding a schedule with minimum sum cost in bipartite graphs. We rely on the algorithm [5] in non-concurrent settings but we need to change it somewhat. We first argue a simple ratio 2 approximation MinSum file transfer of unit jobs on bipartite graphs (without release time). Then we show a $\sqrt{2}$ approximation based on [5] for the sum version.

Let $G = (V, E)$ be a graph. We say vertex v is *full* in G when $deg_v = \Delta(G)$[1]. A graph G is in *class 1* iff $\chi'(G) = \Delta(G)$ where $\chi'(G)$ is the edge-chromatic number of G. Theorem 17.2 of [1] shows any bipartite graph G is in *class 1* and can be partitioned into $\chi'(G)$ matchings in polynomial time. Assume an instance of the uniform zero-release file transfer problem with a bipartite graph $G = (V, E)$. Since $\chi'(G) = \Delta(G)$ we can partition the edge set E, into $\Delta(G)$ matchings. Consider M as one of these matchings. If we remove the edges of M from the graph, the resulting graph would have an edge chromatic number of $\Delta(G) - 1$ and thus the maximum degree of $\Delta(G) - 1$ (since the resulting graph is also in class 1). Therefore every full vertex v in G must have one edge in M. Let $E_{\Delta(G)}$ be the subset of the edges of M which are adjacent to at least one full vertex in G.

Let $G^{\Delta(G)-1} = (V, E \backslash E_{\Delta(G)})$. Since every full vertex in G has an edge in $E_{\Delta(G)}$ we have $\Delta(G^{\Delta(G)-1}) = \Delta(G) - 1$. With the same argument we can find a matching $E_{\Delta(G)-1}$ in $G^{\Delta(G)-1}$, such that every full vertex in $G^{\Delta(G)-1}$ has one adjacent edge in that matching, and each edge in that matching is adjacent to at least one full vertex in $G^{\Delta(G)-1}$.

Now the graph $G^{\Delta(G)-2} = (V, E \backslash (E_{\Delta(G)} \cup E_{\Delta(G)-1}))$ has the maximum degree of $\Delta(G) - 2$. By repeating this procedure we partition E into $\Delta(G)$ matchings $E_{\Delta(G)}, E_{\Delta(G)-1}, \ldots, E_1$.

Algorithm 3

Input: An instance of zero-release uniform file transfer problem $G = (V, E)$ where G is bipartite.

Output: A schedule $\mathcal{S}$ with corresponding starting times for each edge in E.

1: Define $G^{\Delta(G)} = G$.
2: **for** $i = \Delta(G)$ to 1 **do**
3:     Partition the edges of G^i into $\chi'(G^i) = \Delta(G^i)$ matchings and let M be one of the matchings.
4:     Let $V_{full}^i \subseteq V$ be the set full vertices in G^i.
5:     Let $E_i \subseteq M$ be the subset of edges in M which are adjacent to at least one of the vertices in V_{full}^i.
6:     For any edge e in E_i, set $s_{\mathcal{S}}(e) = i - 1$.
7:     Define $G^{i-1} = (V, E \backslash \bigcup_{j=i}^{\Delta(G)} E_j)$.

It can easily be shown that Algorithm 3 is a 2-approximation algorithm.

THEOREM 10. *Algorithm 3 is a 2-approximation algorithm for the MinSum cost in uniform zero-release file transfer problem in bipartite graphs.*

Proof. Consider the bipartite graph $G = (V, E)$. Running Algorithm 3 gives us a schedule $\mathcal{S}$. The schedule $\mathcal{S}$ partitions the edges into $\Delta(G)$ matchings $E_1, \ldots, E_{\Delta(G)}$ such that for any i,

---
[1]For a graph H, $\Delta(H)$ is the maximum degree in H

$1 \leq i \leq \Delta(G)$, any full vertex in G^i has an edge in E_i and any edge in E_i is adjacent to at least one full vertex in G^i (where $G^i = (V, E \setminus \bigcup_{j=i+1}^{\Delta(G)} E_j)$). Let $V_{full}^i \subseteq V$ be the set of full vertices in G^i. Since each edge in E_i is adjacent to at least one vertex in V_{full}^i we have $|E_i| \leq |V_{full}^i|$.

Let $n(i)$ denote the number of vertices in G with degree at least i, i.e., $n(i) = |\{v \in V | deg_v \geq i\}|$. Recall that a vertex is full in G^i iff the degree of v in G^i is equal to $\Delta(G^i)$. The maximum degree $\Delta(G^i)$ is equal to i since G^i is the union of i matchings and thus the degree of any full vertex in G^i would be at least i in G. Therefore $|V_{full}^i| \leq n(i)$. Considering the sum cost of the schedule we have

$$
\begin{aligned}
\text{SUM}(\mathcal{S}) &= \sum_{1 \leq i \leq \Delta(G)} i \, |E_i| \\
&\leq \sum_{1 \leq i \leq \Delta(G)} i \, |V_{full}^i| \leq \sum_{1 \leq i \leq \Delta(G)} i \, n(i) \\
&= \sum_{1 \leq i \leq \Delta(G)} i \sum_{\{v | deg_v \geq i\}} 1 = \sum_{v \in V} \sum_{1 \leq i \leq deg(v)} i \\
&= \sum_{v \in V} \frac{deg(v)(deg(v)+1)}{2} \leq 2\text{OPT}_{sum}.
\end{aligned}
$$

The last line is the result of Lemma 5. □

In [5] it is shown that the algorithm is $\sqrt{2}$-approximate and there analysis is almost tight. We can slightly change their proof to obtain the same approximation ratio. The proof is presented in Appendix.

COROLLARY 7. *There is a polynomial time algorithm which gives a non-concurrent schedule with the cost less than $\sqrt{2}$-factor of OPT_{sum} for the zero-release uniform transfer problem in bipartite graphs.*

6. APPROXIMATION RATIO OF ALGORITHM 3

With a slight change in the proof of Theorem 3 given in [5], one can prove that the same property in [5] is sufficient for a scheduling to be $\sqrt{2}$-approximate in the uniform zero-release file transfer model. Not all graphs have a scheduling with this property but in some classes of graphs such as bipartite graphs we can give polynomial time algorithms to find such scheduling. For the sake of completeness we present a slightly modified proof.

Let $G = (V, E)$ and let $\mathcal{S}$ be a non-concurrent schedule of E. Recall that $\mathcal{S}$ can be shown as the partition of E into matchings $M_1, \ldots, M_k$. For i, $1 \leq i \leq k$, let $G^i = \left(V, \bigcup_{j=1}^{i} M_j \right)$ (thus $G^k = G$). Let deg_v^i for a vertex $v \in V$ and $1 \leq i \leq k$ denote the degree of vertex v in G^i. By borrowing notations from [5], we say vertex v is *full* in G^i when $deg_v^i = \Delta(G^i)$.

We call $\mathcal{S}$ *strongly minimal* if for every i, $1 \leq i \leq k$:

- For every full vertex v in G^i, there is one edge adjacent to v in M_i.

- At least one of the endpoints of every edge of E_i is full in G^i.

Another way to look at this property is that G^i is a maximal i-matching w.r.t G for every $i \leq k$. We note that by definition of strongly minimal schedule the number of matchings k is indeed equal to $\Delta(G)$. Furthermore, since every full vertex in E^i has exactly one edge in M_i we have $\Delta(G^{i-1}) = \Delta(G^i) - 1$ and in general for every i, $1 \leq i \leq \Delta(G)$, $\Delta(G^i) = i$. Thus if v is full in G^i for some i, then it is full in G^j for every $j \leq i$.

THEOREM 11. *For $G = (V, E)$ in the uniform zero-release file transfer model any strongly minimal schedule $\mathcal{S}$ is $\sqrt{2}$-approximate.*

Proof. The idea is to make a full vertex in G^i responsible for paying the finishing time of its adjacent edge in E^i. Formally, for an edge $e = \{u, v\}$ assume that that e is in the matching M_i. By the definition of $\mathcal{S}$ at lease one of u or v is full in G^i. If both endpoints are full then each of u and v are *half-responsible* for e. If only one of the endpoints, say u, is full then u is *fully-responsible* for e.

Now consider an arbitrary vertex $v \in V$. Assume that v is fully-responsible and half-responsible for the set of edges R_v^1 and R_v^2 respectively. Define $C_{opt}(v) = \sum_{e \in R_v^1} f_{opt}(e) + \sum_{e \in R_v^2} \frac{f_{opt}(e)}{2}$ where opt is the optimum schedule for G. Similarly define $C_{\mathcal{S}}(v) = \sum_{e \in R_v^1} f_{\mathcal{S}}(e) + \sum_{e \in R_v^2} \frac{f_{\mathcal{S}}(e)}{2}$. In other words v always pays the finishing times of edges in R_v^1 and pays the half of the finishing times of edges in R_v^2. Thus $\text{SUM}(opt) = \sum_v C_{opt}(v)$ and $\text{SUM}(\mathcal{S}) = \sum_v C_{\mathcal{S}}(v)$.

To show that $\mathcal{S}$ is α-approximate it is sufficient to show that $\frac{C_{\mathcal{S}}(v)}{C_{opt}(v)} \leq \alpha$. Vertex v is full in $G^1, \ldots, G^{n_1+n_2}$ since each vertex gets at least a half responsibility when it is full in some G^i. Thus for an edge $e \in R_v^1 \cup R_v^2$ the finishing time of e in $\mathcal{S}$ is not greater than $n_1 + n_2$. More precisely, the set of finishing times of edges in $R_v^1 \cup R_v^2$ is exactly $\{1, \ldots, n_1 + n_2\}$. Therefore

$$
\begin{aligned}
C_{\mathcal{S}}(v) &= \sum_{e \in R_v^1} f_{\mathcal{S}}(e) + \sum_{e \in R_v^2} \frac{f_{\mathcal{S}}(e)}{2} \\
&= \sum_{e \in R_v^1 \cup R_v^2} \frac{f_{\mathcal{S}}(e)}{2} + \sum_{e \in R_v^1} \frac{f_{\mathcal{S}}(e)}{2} \\
&= \sum_{i=1}^{n_1+n_2} i + \sum_{e \in R_v^1} \frac{f_{\mathcal{S}}(e)}{2} \\
&\leq \sum_{i=1}^{n_1+n_2} i + \sum_{i=n_2+1}^{n_1+n_2} i \\
&= (n_1+n_2)(n_1+n_2+1) - (n_2)(n_2+1)/2 \\
&= (n_1^2 + n_1) + (n_2^2 + n_2)/2 + 2(n_1 n_2).
\end{aligned}
$$

Since the edges in R_v^1 and R_v^2 are all adjacent opt cannot finish transferring all of them sooner than $n_1 + n_2$, thus

$$
\begin{aligned}
C_{opt}(v) &= \sum_{e \in R_v^1} f_{opt}(e) + \sum_{e \in R_v^2} \frac{f_{opt}(e)}{2} \\
&= \sum_{e \in R_v^1 \cup R_v^2} \frac{f_{opt}(e)}{2} + \sum_{e \in R_v^1} \frac{f_{opt}(e)}{2} \\
&\geq \sum_{i=1}^{n_1+n_2} i + \sum_{e \in R_v^1} \frac{f_{opt}(e)}{2} \\
&\geq \sum_{i=1}^{n_1+n_2} i + \sum_{i=1}^{n_1} i \\
&= (n_1+n_2)(n_1+n_2+1)/2 + (n_1)(n_1+1)/2 \\
&= (n_1^2 + n_1) + (n_2^2 + n_2)/2 + (n_1 n_2).
\end{aligned}
$$

We need to determine the smallest α such that

$$
\alpha \geq \frac{(n_1^2+n_1) + (n_2^2+n_2)/2 + 2(n_1 n_2)}{(n_1^2+n_1) + (n_2^2+n_2)/2 + (n_1 n_2)} \geq \frac{2n_1^2 + n_2^2 + 4n_1 n_2}{2n_1^2 + n_2^2 + 2n_1 n_2}.
$$

By changing the variable to $x = \frac{n_1}{n_1 + n_2}$ we get

$$\alpha \geq \frac{1 + 2x - x^2}{1 + x^2}.$$

Finally the right hand side is maximized for $x = \sqrt{2} - 1$, which gives us $\alpha \geq \sqrt{2}$. $\square$

Running Algorithm 3 on a bipartite graph $G = (V, E)$ gives us a schedule $\mathcal{S}$. The schedule $\mathcal{S}$ partitions the edges into $\Delta(G)$ matchings $E_1, \ldots, E_{\Delta(G)}$ such that for any i, $1 \leq i \leq \Delta(G)$, any full vertex in G^i has an edge in E_i and any edge in E_i is adjacent to at least one full vertex in G^i (where $G^i = (V, E \backslash \bigcup_{j=i+1}^{\Delta(G)} E_j)$). This shows that the schedule given by Algorithm 3 is strongly minimal and thus proves Corollary 7. The reduction used is the same as used by Marx [22]. The problem Marx showed hardness for is *preemptive sum multicoloring of the edges of the a tree* (MEPS). In this problem we are given a tree and every edge has an integral length $\ell(e)$. We have to color the edges of the tree and the colors we use are positive integers $1, 2, 3 \ldots$. If e and e' share a vertex. then their color sets must be disjoint. To satisfy that, a solution must choose a matching at every round (and the edges in the matching get the color of the round number). Every edge e must belong to $\ell(e)$ matchings. Let Ψ be a proper coloring and $f_\Psi(e)$ be the largest color assigned to e by Ψ. The goal is to minimize $\sum_{e \in E} f_\Psi(e)$

In the non-preemptive case, every e must receive $\ell(e)$ *consecutive* integers.

7. CONCLUSION AND OPEN PROBLEMS

This paper studies a local protocol for file transfer problems which to the best of our knowledge, have not been studied before in theoretical computer science. Among the problems we consider, we highlight one open problem of primary concern: Is there a gap between the optimum concurrent schedule and optimum non-concurrent schedule when minimizing the average finishing time in the case of the zero-release file transfer model? In this paper most of our algorithms give non-concurrent solutions paying a constant factor compared to the optimum concurrent schedule. It would be instructive to see whether we can design concurrent algorithms with better approximation factors. This shows the importance of finding the gap between optimum concurrent and optimum non-concurrent schedules.

It would also be interesting to consider the online version of the problem, where the release times are revealed to the algorithm in an online fashion. Could we get constant approximations in non-preemptive model or do we need to add preemptive assumptions to the problem?

8. REFERENCES

[1] J.A. Bondy and U.S.R. Murty. *Graph Theory.* Graduate Texts in Mathematics, 244. Springer, New York, 2008.

[2] M.M. Halldórsson, G. Kortsarz and M. Sviridenko. *Min Sum Edge Coloring in Multigraphs Via Configuration LP.* In Proc. 13th Conf. Integer Prog. Combin. Optimiz. (IPCO), 2008.

[3] R. Gandhi, M. M. Halldórsson, G. Kortsarz and H. Shachnai. *Improved Bounds for Scheduling Conflicting Jobs with Minsum Criteria.* ACM Transactions on Algorithms. Vol. 4, No. 1, 2008.

[4] M.M. Halldórsson and G. Kortsarz. *Tools for multicoloring with applications to planar graphs and partial k-trees.* Journal of Algorithms 42, 2, 334-366, 2002.

[5] R. Gandhi and J. Mestre. *Combinatorial Algorithms for Data Migration to Minimize Average Completion Time.* Algorithmica 54, 1,pp 54-71, 2009.

[6] Y. Kim. *Data Migration to Minimize the Average Completion Time.* Journal of Algorithms,55:42-57, 2005.

[7] M.K. Goldberg, *Edge-coloring of multigraphs: recoloring technique.* J. Graph Theory, 8:121-137, 1984

[8] D.S. Hochbaum, T. Nishizeki, and D.B. Shmoys. *A better than "Best Possible" algorithm to edge color multigraphs.* Journal of Algorithm 7:79-104, 1986.

[9] E. G. Coffman, M. R. Garey, D. S. Johnson, and A. S. Lapaugh. *Scheduling file transfers.* SIAM Journal on Computing, 14(3):744-780, 1985.

[10] A. Bar-Noy, M. Bellare, M. M. Halldórsson, H. Shachnai, and T. Tamir. *On chromatic sums and distributed resource allocation.* Information and Computation, Vol. 140, pp. 183-202, 1998.

[11] R. Gandhi, M. M. Halldórsson, G. Kortsarz, and H. Shachnai. *Improved Results for Data Migration and Openshop Scheduling.* ACM Transactions on Algorithms, 2(1):116-129, 2006.

[12] M. M. Halldorsson, G. Kortsarz, and H. Shachnai. *Sum Coloring Interval Graphs and k-Claw Free Graphs with Applications for Scheduling Dependent Jobs.* Algorithmica, 37:187-209, 2003.

[13] P. Sanders and D. Steurer. *An Asymptotic Approximation Scheme for Multigraph Edge Coloring.* Proc. of the 16th ACM-SIAM Symposium on Discrete Algorithms, 2005.

[14] R. Graham. *Bounds for certain multiprocessing anomalies.* Bell System Technical Journal, 45:15631581, 1966.

[15] S. Chakrabarti, C. A. Phillips, A. S. Schulz, D. B. Shmoys, C. Stein, and J. Wein. *Improved Scheduling Problems For Minsum Criteria.* Proc. of the 23rd International Colloquium on Automata, Languages, and Programming, LNCS 1099, 646-657, 1996.

[16] H. Hoogeveen, P. Schuurman, and G. Woeginger. *Non-approximability Results For Scheduling Problems with Minsum Criteria.* Proc. of the 6th International Conference on Integer Programming and Combinatorial Optimization, LNCS 1412, 353-366, 1998.

[17] M. Queyranne and M. Sviridenko. *A $(2 + \epsilon)$-Approximation Algorithm for Generalized Preemptive Open Shop Problem with Minsum Objective.* Journal of Algorithms, 45:202-212, 2002.

[18] M. Queyranne and M. Sviridenko. *Approximation Algorithms for Shop Scheduling Problems with Minsum Objective.* Journal of Scheduling, 5:287-305, 2002.

[19] E. Anderson, J. Hall, J. Hartline, M. Hobbes, A. Karlin, J. Saia, R. Swaminathan, and J. Wilkes. *An Experimental Study of Data Migration Algorithms.* Workshop on Algorithm Engineering, pages 145-158, 2001.

[20] J. Hall, J. Hartline, A. Karlin, J. Saia, and J. Wilkes. *On Algorithms for Efficient Data Migration.* Proc. of the 12th ACM-SIAM Symposium on Discrete Algorithms, pages 620-629, 2001.

[21] S. Khuller, Y. Kim, and Y. C. Wan. *Algorithms for Data Migration with Cloning.* In Proc. of the 22nd ACM Symposium on Principles of Database Systems, pages 27-36, 2003.

[22] Dániel Marx, *Minimum sum multicoloring on the edges of trees.* Theor. Comput. Sci., volume 361, number 2-3, pages 133-149, 2006.

[23] Dániel Marx, *Minimum sum multicoloring on the edges of planar graphs.* WAOA, pages 9-22, 2004

[24] , M. Garey and D. Johnson. *Computer and intractability. A guide to the theory of NP-completeness* Freeman, 1979.

[25] J. Dean and S. Ghemawat. *MapReduce: Simplified Data Processing on Large Clusters.* In Proc. of the 6th Symposium on Operating System Design and Implementation, pages 137-150, 2004.

On Multi-Processor Speed Scaling with Migration

[Extended Abstract]

Susanne Albers [*]   Antonios Antoniadis
Dept. of Computer Science
Humboldt-Universität zu Berlin
Berlin, Germany
{albers,antoniad}@informatik.hu-berlin.de

Gero Greiner
Dept. of Computer Science
Technische Universität München
Garching, Germany
greiner@informatik.tu-muenchen.de

ABSTRACT

We investigate a very basic problem in dynamic speed scaling where a sequence of jobs, each specified by an arrival time, a deadline and a processing volume, has to be processed so as to minimize energy consumption. Previous work has focused mostly on the setting where a single variable-speed processor is available. In this paper we study multi-processor environments with m parallel variable-speed processors assuming that job migration is allowed, i.e. whenever a job is preempted it may be moved to a different processor.

We first study the offline problem and show that optimal schedules can be computed efficiently in polynomial time. In contrast to a previously known strategy, our algorithm does not resort to linear programming. We develop a fully combinatorial algorithm that relies on repeated maximum flow computations. The approach might be useful to solve other problems in dynamic speed scaling. For the online problem, we extend two algorithms *Optimal Available* and *Average Rate* proposed by Yao et al. [16] for the single processor setting. We prove that *Optimal Available* is α^α-competitive, as in the single processor case. Here $\alpha > 1$ is the exponent of the power consumption function. While it is straightforward to extend *Optimal Available* to parallel processing environments, the competitive analysis becomes considerably more involved. For *Average Rate* we show a competitiveness of $(3\alpha)^\alpha/2 + 2^\alpha$.

Categories and Subject Descriptors

F.2.2 [**Theory of Computation**]: Analysis of Algorithms and Problem Complexity—*sequencing and scheduling*; F.1.2 [**Theory of Computation**]: Computation by Abstract Devices—*online computation*

---

[*]Work supported by a Gottfried Wilhelm Leibniz Award of the Germany Research Foundation.

General Terms

Algorithms, Theory

Keywords

energy efficiency, offline algorithm, online algorithm, flow computation, competitive analysis

1. INTRODUCTION

Algorithmic techniques for energy savings in computing devices have received considerable research interest recently. A relatively new, effective approach is *dynamic speed scaling*. It relies on the fact that many modern microprocessors can operate at variable speed. Both Intel and AMD offer a range of such variable-speed processors. Obviously, high speed implies high performance. However, the higher the speed, the higher the energy consumption. The goal of dynamic speed scaling is to utilize the full speed/frequency spectrum of a processor and to use low speeds whenever possible.

In a seminal paper, initiating the algorithmic study of dynamic speed scaling, Yao, Demers and Shenker [16] introduced the following problem. Consider a sequence $\sigma = J_1, \ldots, J_n$ of n jobs that have to be scheduled on a variable-speed processor. Each job J_i is specified by a release time r_i, a deadline d_i and a processing volume w_i, $1 \le i \le n$. In a feasible schedule, J_i must be processed within the time interval $[r_i, d_i)$. The processing volume w_i is the amount of work that must be finished to complete J_i and, intuitively, can be viewed as the number of required CPU cycles. The processing time of a job depends on the processor speed. If J_i is processed at speed s, then it takes w_i/s time units to complete the job. Preemption of jobs is allowed, i.e. the execution of a job may be stopped and resumed later. The well-known cube-root rule for CMOS devices states that the speed s of a processor is proportional to the cube-root of the power or, equivalently, that power is proportional to s^3. We consider a generalization of this rule. If a processor runs at speed s, then the required power is $P(s) = s^\alpha$, where $\alpha > 1$ is a constant. Obviously, energy is power integrated over time. The goal is to find a feasible schedule for the given job instance $\sigma = J_1, \ldots, J_n$ minimizing energy consumption.

The scheduling problem defined above is by far the most extensively studied speed scaling problem in the algorithms literature. We will present the most important results below. Almost all of the previous work assumes that a single variable-speed processor is given. However, energy conservation and speed scaling techniques are equally interesting in multi-processor environments. Multi-core and many-core platforms will be the dominant processor architectures in the future. Nowadays many PCs and laptops are already equipped with dual-core and quad-core designs. Moreover, compute clusters and server farms, usually consisting of many high-speed processors, represent parallel multi-processor systems that have been used successfully in academia and enterprises for many years. Power dissipation has become a major concern in these environments. Finally, in research, multi-processor systems have always been investigated extensively, in particular as far as scheduling and resource management problems are concerned.

In this paper we study dynamic speed scaling in multi-processor environments. We adopt the framework by Yao et al. [16], as defined above, but assume that m parallel processors are given. Each processor can individually run at variable speed s; the associated power function is again $P(s) = s^\alpha$ where $\alpha > 1$. *Job migration* is allowed, i.e. whenever a job is preempted it may be moved to a different processor. Hence, over time, a job may be executed on various processors as long as the respective processing intervals do not overlap. Executing a job in parallel on two or more processors is not allowed. The goal is to construct a feasible schedule minimizing the total energy consumption incurred by all the processors.

Two scenarios are of interest. In the offline setting, all jobs and their characteristics are known in advance. We wish to construct optimal schedules minimizing energy consumption. In the online setting, jobs arrive over time. Whenever a new job J_i arrives at time r_i, its deadline d_i and processing volume w_i are known. However, future jobs J_k, with $k > i$, are unknown. We use competitive analysis to evaluate the performance of online strategies [15]. An online algorithm A is called c-competitive if, for any job sequence σ, the energy consumption of A is at most c times the consumption of an optimal offline schedule.

Previous work: We review results on dynamic speed scaling, focusing on deadline-based scheduling introduced by Yao et al. [16]. As mentioned above, almost all of the previous work addresses single-processor environments. In [16] Yao et al. first study the offline problem and present a polynomial time algorithm for computing optimal schedules. Refinements of the algorithm were given by Li et al. [12, 13]. Yao et al. also presented two elegant online algorithms called *Optimal Available* and *Average Rate*. They proved that *Average Rate* achieves a competitive ratio of $(2\alpha)^\alpha/2$. The analysis is essentially tight as Bansal et al. [2] showed a nearly matching lower bound of $((2-\delta)\alpha)^\alpha/2$, where δ goes to zero as α tends to infinity. Bansal, Kimbrel and Pruhs [5] analyzed *Optimal Available* and, using a clever potential function, proved a competitiveness of exactly α^α. They also proposed a new strategy that attains a competitive ratio of $2(\frac{\alpha}{\alpha-1})e^\alpha$. As for lower bounds, Bansal et al. [4] showed that the competitiveness of any deterministic strategy is at least $e^{\alpha-1}/\alpha$.

The framework by Yao et al. assumes that there is no upper bound on the allowed processor speed. Articles [3, 7, 14] study settings in which the processor has a maximum speed or only a finite set of discrete speed levels. Irani et al. [10] consider an extended problem where a variable-speed processor is equipped with an additional sleep state, assuming that even at speed zero a positive amount of energy is consumed.

The only previous work addressing deadline-based scheduling in multi-processor systems is [1, 6, 9, 11]. Bingham and Greenstreet [6] show that, if job migration is allowed, the offline problem can be solved in polynomial time using linear programming. Lam et al. [11] study a setting with two speed-bounded processors. They show online algorithms that are constant competitive w.r.t. energy minimization and throughput maximization. Papers [1, 9] assume that job migration is *not* allowed. In this case the offline problem is NP-hard, even if all jobs have the same processing volume [1]. A randomized B_α-approximation algorithm and a randomized $2(\frac{\alpha}{\alpha-1})e^\alpha B_\alpha$-competitive online algorithm are given in [9]. Here B_α is the α-th Bell number.

Our contribution: In this paper we investigate dynamic speed scaling in general multi-processor environments, assuming that job migration is allowed. Using migration, scheduling algorithms can take advantage of the parallelism given by a multi-processor system in an effective way. We present a comprehensive study addressing the offline and, for the first time, also the online scenario.

First in Section 2 we study the offline problem and develop an efficient polynomial time algorithm for computing optimal schedules. As mentioned above, Bingham and Greenstreet [6] showed that the offline problem can be solved using linear programming. However, the authors mention that the compexity of their algorithm is too high for most practical applications. Instead in this paper we develop a strongly combinatorial algorithm that relies on repeated maximum flow computations. The approach might be helpful to solve other problems in scheduling and speed scaling.

Our algorithm is completely different from the single-processor strategy by Yao et al. [16]. In a series of phases, the algorithm partitions the jobs $J_1, \ldots, J_n$ into job sets $\mathcal{J}_1, \ldots, \mathcal{J}_p$ such that all jobs $J_k \in \mathcal{J}_i$ are processed at the same uniform speed s_i, $1 \leq i \leq p$. Each such job set is computed using maximum flow calculations. In order to construct a flow network, we have to identify various properties of optimal schedules. A key property is that, knowing $\mathcal{J}_1, \ldots, \mathcal{J}_{i-1}$, one can exactly determine the number of processors to be allocated to $\mathcal{J}_i$. At the beginning of the phase computing $\mathcal{J}_i$, the algorithm conjectures that the set $S_i = \{J_1, \ldots, J_n\} \setminus (\mathcal{J}_1, \ldots, \mathcal{J}_{i-1})$ of all remaining jobs forms the next set $\mathcal{J}_i$. If this turns out not to be the case, the algorithm repeatedly removes jobs $J_k \in S_i$ that do not belong to $\mathcal{J}_i$. The crucial step in the correctness analysis is to show that each of these job removals is indeed correct so that, when the process terminates, the true set $\mathcal{J}_i$ is computed.

In Section 3 we study the online problem and adapt the two popular strategies *Optimal Available* and *Average Rate* to multi-processor environments. Algorithm *Optimal Available*, whenever a new job arrives, computes an optimal schedule for the remaining workload. This can be done using our new offline algorithm. We prove that *Optimal Available* is α^α-competitive. While the adaption of the algorithm is immediate, its competitive analysis becomes considerably more involved, compared to the single-processor case. We can extend the potential function analysis by Bansal et al. [5] but have to define a refined potential and have to prove several properties that specify how an optimal schedule changes in response to the arrival of a new job. As for the second algorithm *Average Rate*, we present a strategy that distributes jobs among the processors so that job densities $\delta_i = w_i/(d_i - r_i)$ are approximately balanced. To this end we apply the concept of *Sorted List Scheduling*. We prove that *Average Rate* achieves a competitiveness of $(3\alpha)^\alpha/2 + 2^\alpha$.

2. A COMBINATORIAL OFFLINE ALGORITHM

We develop a strongly combinatorial algorithm for constructing optimal offline schedules in polynomial time. Let $\mathcal{S}_{OPT}$ be an optimal schedule and $s_1 > s_2 > \ldots > s_p$ be the different speed levels used in $\mathcal{S}_{OPT}$. Lemma 1 below implies $p \leq n$. Our algorithm constructs an optimal schedule in p phases, starting from an initially empty schedule $\mathcal{S}_0$. Let $\mathcal{S}_{i-1}$ be the schedule obtained at the end of phase $i-1$, $1 \leq i \leq p$. In phase i the algorithm identifies the set $\mathcal{J}_i$ of jobs that are processed at speed s_i, $1 \leq i \leq p$. Schedule $\mathcal{S}_{i-1}$ is then extended by the jobs of $\mathcal{J}_i$ to form a new schedule $\mathcal{S}_i$. Our algorithm implies, in particular, that an optimal solution is unique in terms of the speed levels s_i, the associated job sets $\mathcal{J}_i$ and the times at which they are scheduled.

Consider any optimal schedule $\mathcal{S}_{OPT}$. The following lemma states that in an optimal schedule no job is ever processed at varying speed. This implies that the n jobs $J_1, \ldots, J_n$ can indeed be partitioned into sets $\mathcal{J}_1, \ldots, \mathcal{J}_p$ such that all the jobs of $\mathcal{J}_i$ are processed at the same speed s_i, $1 \leq i \leq p$. Each job belongs to exactly one of these sets. The proofs of the next two lemmas are presented in the full version of the paper.

LEMMA 1. *In any optimal schedule every job J_i, $1 \leq i \leq n$, is always processed at the same speed.*

The next lemma implies that any optimal schedule can be modified such that the processor speeds change only at the release times and deadlines of jobs. Let $\mathcal{I} = \{r_i, d_i \mid 1 \leq i \leq n\}$ be the set of all release times and deadlines. We consider the elements of $\mathcal{I}$ in sorted order $\tau_1 < \ldots < \tau_{|\mathcal{I}|}$, where $|\mathcal{I}| \leq 2n$. The time horizon in which jobs can be scheduled is $[\tau_1, \tau_{|\mathcal{I}|})$. We partition this time horizon along the job release times and deadlines into intervals $I_j = [\tau_j, \tau_{j+1})$, $1 \leq j < |\mathcal{I}|$. Let $|I_j| = \tau_{j+1} - \tau_j$ be the length of I_j.

LEMMA 2. *Given any optimal schedule $\mathcal{S}_{OPT}$, in each interval I_j we can rearrange the schedule such that every processor uses a fixed, non-varying speed in I_j, $1 \leq i < |\mathcal{I}|$. The modified schedule is feasible and incurs the same minimum energy as $\mathcal{S}_{OPT}$.*

In the remainder of this section we consider an optimal schedule $\mathcal{S}_{OPT}$ satisfying the property of Lemma 2. As described above, we construct $\mathcal{S}_{OPT}$ in phases. In phase i we identify the set $\mathcal{J}_i$ of jobs processed a speed s_i, $1 \leq i \leq p$. By Lemma 2, in each interval I_j, $1 \leq j < |\mathcal{I}|$, the sets $\mathcal{J}_1, \ldots, \mathcal{J}_p$ occupy different processors, i.e. there is no processor handling jobs of two different sets. Hence, in phase i, when determining $\mathcal{J}_i$ and extending the previous schedule $\mathcal{S}_{i-1}$, we only need to know the number of processors occupied by $\mathcal{J}_1, \ldots, \mathcal{J}_{i-1}$ in any interval I_j, $1 \leq j < |\mathcal{I}|$. The exact assignment of the corresponding jobs to the reserved processors is irrelevant though, as $\mathcal{J}_i$ does not share processors with the previous sets. In determining $\mathcal{J}_i$ a crucial question is, how many processors to allocate to the jobs of $\mathcal{J}_i$ in any interval I_j, $1 \leq j < |\mathcal{I}|$. Here the following lemma is essential.

A job J_k, $1 \leq k \leq n$, is called *active* in I_j if $I_j \subseteq [r_k, d_k)$, i.e. the time period in which J_k can be scheduled includes I_j. Given $\mathcal{S}_{OPT}$, let n_{ij} be the number of jobs of $\mathcal{J}_i$ that are active in I_j. Furthermore, let m_{ij} be the number of processors occupied by $\mathcal{J}_i$ in I_j.

LEMMA 3. *In $\mathcal{S}_{OPT}$ the jobs of $\mathcal{J}_i$ occupy $m_{ij} = \min\{n_{ij}, m - \sum_{l=1}^{i-1} m_{lj}\}$ processors in I_j, where $1 \leq i \leq p$ and $1 \leq j < |\mathcal{I}|$.*

PROOF. Consider a set $\mathcal{J}_i$ and interval I_j. Obviously, the n_{ij} jobs of $\mathcal{J}_i$ that are active in I_j cannot occupy more than n_{ij} processors using a positive speed s_i throughout I_j. Furthermore, the jobs can only occupy the $m - \sum_{l=1}^{i-1} m_{lj}$ processors not taken by $\mathcal{J}_1, \ldots, \mathcal{J}_{i-1}$. We show that in fact $m_{ij} = \min\{n_{ij}, m - \sum_{l=1}^{i-1} m_{lj}\}$ processors are used by $\mathcal{J}_i$

So suppose that $m'_{ij} < m_{ij}$ processors are used. Then, since $m'_{ij} < m - \sum_{l=1}^{i-1} m_{lj}$, there exists at least one processor P running at speed s with $s < s_i$ in I_j. Consider the schedule at the beginning of I_j. Choose a δ, $\delta > 0$, such that the m'_{ij} processors handling $\mathcal{J}_i$ and processor P do not preempt jobs in $[\tau_j, \tau_j + \delta)$, i.e. they each handle at most one job in that time window. In fact P might not handle a job if $s = 0$. As $m'_{ij} < n_{ij}$, there must exist one job $J_k \in \mathcal{J}_i$ that is active in I_j but not scheduled within $[\tau_j, \tau_j + \delta)$ on any of the m'_{ij} processors using speed s_i. This job is not scheduled on any other processor within $[\tau_j, \tau_j + \delta)$ either, because the other processors run at speeds higher or lower than s_i. Thus J_k is not executed on any processor within $[\tau_j, \tau_j + \delta)$. In the entire schedule, consider a processor and an associated time window W of length $\delta' \leq \delta$ handling J_k. We now modify the schedule by reducing the speed in W by ϵ, where $\epsilon < (s_i - s)/2$. At the same time we increase the speed in $[\tau_j, \tau_j + \delta')$ by ϵ and use the extra processing capacity to complete the missing portion of J_k not finished in W. The modified schedule is feasible and, by the convexity of the power function, has a strictly smaller energy consumption, which contradicts the fact that the original schedule was optimal. $\square$

Lemma 3 has an interesting implication: Suppose that job sets $\mathcal{J}_1, \ldots, \mathcal{J}_{i-1}$ along with the number of occupied processors $m_{1j}, \ldots, m_{i-1,j}$, for $1 \leq j < |\mathcal{I}|$, have been determined. Furthermore, suppose that the set $\mathcal{J}_i$ is known. Then, using Lemma 3, we can immediately determine the number m_{ij} of processors used by $\mathcal{J}_i$ in I_j, $1 \leq j < |\mathcal{I}|$. Moreover, we can compute the speed s_i by observing that s_i is the minimum average speed necessary to complete the jobs of $\mathcal{J}_i$ in the reserved processing intervals. More precisely, let $W_i = \sum_{J_k \in \mathcal{J}_i} w_k$ be the total processing volume of $\mathcal{J}_i$ and $P_i = \sum_{1 \leq j < |\mathcal{I}|} m_{ij}|I_j|$ be the total length of the reserved processing intervals. Then $s_i = W_i/P_i$. We will make use of this fact when identifying $\mathcal{J}_i$.

We next describe the algorithm for determining $\mathcal{J}_i$. Assume again that $\mathcal{J}_1, \ldots, \mathcal{J}_{i-1}$ along with processor numbers $m_{1j}, \ldots, m_{i-1,j}$, for $1 \leq j < |\mathcal{I}|$, are given. The algorithm operates in a series of rounds, maintaining a job set $\mathcal{J}$ that represents the current estimate for the true $\mathcal{J}_i$. At any time the invariant $\mathcal{J}_i \subseteq \mathcal{J}$ holds. Initially, prior to the first round, we set $\mathcal{J} := \{J_1, \ldots, J_n\} \setminus (\mathcal{J}_1 \cup \ldots \cup \mathcal{J}_{i-1})$, which is the set of all remaining jobs, and the invariant is obviously satisfied. In each round we check if the current $\mathcal{J}$ is the desired $\mathcal{J}_i$. This can be checked using a maximum flow computation. If $\mathcal{J}$ turns out to be $\mathcal{J}_i$, then the algorithm for computing $\mathcal{J}_i$ stops. Otherwise we determine a job $J_k \in \mathcal{J} \setminus \mathcal{J}_i$, remove that job from $\mathcal{J}$ and start the next round in which the updated set $\mathcal{J}$ is checked.

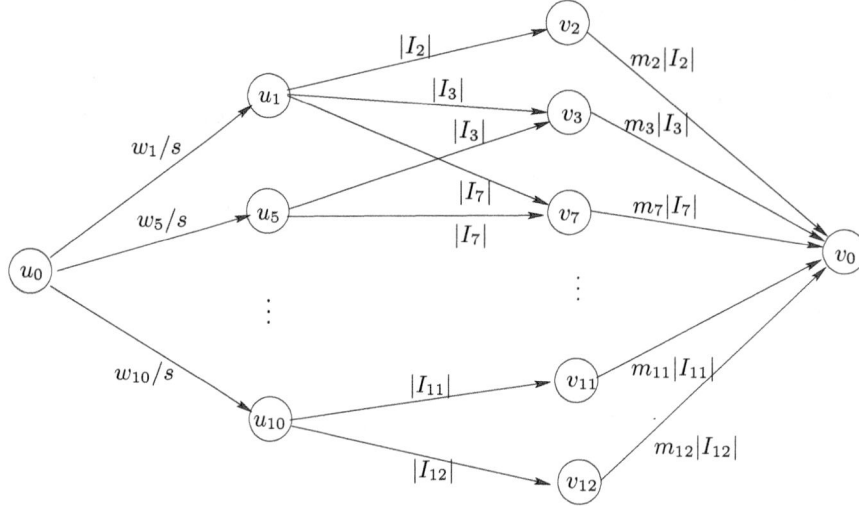

Figure 1: The basic structure of $G(\mathcal{J}, \vec{m}, s)$, assuming that set $\mathcal{J} = \{J_1, J_5, \ldots, J_{10}\}$ can be scheduled in intervals $I_2, I_3, I_7, \ldots, I_{11}, I_{12}$.

In the following we describe the maximum flow computation invoked for a given $\mathcal{J}$. First we determine the number of processors to be allocated to $\mathcal{J}$ in each interval. For any I_j, $1 \leq j < |\mathcal{I}|$, let n_j be the number of jobs in $\mathcal{J}$ that are active in $|I_j|$. According to Lemma 3 we reserve $m_j = \min\{n_j, m - \sum_{l=1}^{i-1} m_{lj}\}$ processors in I_j. These numbers form a vector $\vec{m} = (m_j)_{1 \leq j < |\mathcal{I}|}$. The speed is set to $s = W/P$, where $W = \sum_{J_k \in \mathcal{J}} w_k$ is the total processing volume and $P = \sum_{1 \leq j < |\mathcal{I}|} m_j |I_j|$ is the reserved processing time.

Next we define the graph $G(\mathcal{J}, \vec{m}, s)$ of our maximum flow computation. For each job $J_k \in \mathcal{J}$ we introduce a vertex u_k, and for each interval I_j with $m_j > 0$ we introduce a vertex v_j. For any u_k and v_j such that J_k is active in I_j we add a directed edge (u_k, v_j) of capacity $|I_j|$. Hence each u_k is connected to exactly those v_j such that J_k can be scheduled in I_j. The edge capacity of (u_k, v_j) is equal to $|I_j|$, i.e. the maximum time for which a job can be processed in I_j. Furthermore, we introduce a source vertex u_0 that is connected to every u_k on a directed edge (u_0, u_k). The edge capacity is set to w_k/s, which is the total processing time needed for J_k using speed s. Finally we introduce a sink v_0 and connect each v_j to v_0 via a directed edge (v_j, v_0) of capacity $m_j |I_j|$, which is the total processing time available on the reserved processors in I_j. The global structure of $G(\mathcal{J}, \vec{m}, s)$ is depicted in Figure 1. The value of a maximum flow in $G(\mathcal{J}, \vec{m}, s)$ is upper bounded by $F_G = \sum_{J_k \in \mathcal{J}} w_k/s$ because this is the total capacity of the edges leaving the source u_0. This is equal to the total capacity of the edges leading into the sink v_0 because that value is

$$\sum_{1 \leq j < |\mathcal{I}|} m_j |I_j| = P = W/s = \sum_{J_k \in \mathcal{J}} w_k/s = F_G.$$

We argue that job set $\mathcal{J}$ using a continuous speed of s can be feasibly scheduled on the reserved processors represented by $\vec{m}$ if and only if there exists a maximum flow of value F_G in $G(\mathcal{J}, \vec{m}, s)$. First suppose that there exists a feasible schedule using speed s. Then each $J_k \in \mathcal{J}$ is processed for w_k/s time units and we send w_k/s units of flow along edge

(u_0, u_k). The w_k/s processing units of J_k are scheduled in intervals I_j in which the job is active. If J_k is processed for t_{kj} time units in I_j, then we send t_{kj} units of flow along edge (u_k, v_j). The edge capacity is observed because $t_{kj} \leq |I_j|$. The total amount of flow entering and hence leaving any v_j is equal to the total processing time on the m_j reserved processor in I_j. This value is equal to $m_j |I_j|$ because, by the choice of s, all reserved processors are busy throughout the execution intervals. Hence the amount of flow sent along (v_j, v_0) is equal to the edge capacity.

On the other hand, assume that a flow of value F_G is given. If t_{kj} units of flow are routed along (u_k, v_j), we process J_k for t_{kj} time units in I_j. This is possible because J_k is active in I_j and $t_{kj} \leq |I_j|$. The capacity constraints on the edge (v_j, v_0) ensure that not more than $m_j I_j$ time units are assigned to I_j. Moreover, since the flow value is F_G, each edge (u_0, u_k) is saturated and hence J_k is fully processed for w_k/s time units at speed s. Within each I_j we can easily construct a feasible schedule by concatenating the processing intervals of length t_{kj} associated with the jobs J_k active in I_j. The resulting sequential schedule, say $\mathcal{T}$, of length $\sum_{J_k \in \mathcal{J}} t_{kj} = m_j |I_j|$ is split among the m_j reserved processors by assigning time range $[(\mu - 1)|I_j|, \mu|I_j|)$ of $\mathcal{T}$ to the μ-th reserved processor, $1 \leq \mu \leq m_j$.

We return to the description of the algorithm for determining $\mathcal{J}_i$, which operates in a series of rounds. In each round, for the current set $\mathcal{J}$, we invoke a maximum flow computation in the graph $G(\mathcal{J}, \vec{m}, s)$ defined in the previous paragraphs. If the flow value is equal to F_G, then we stop and set $\mathcal{J}_i := \mathcal{J}$. We will prove below that in this case the current $\mathcal{J}$ is indeed equal to $\mathcal{J}_i$. If the flow value is smaller than F_G, then there must exist an edge (v_j, v_0) into the sink carrying less than $m_j |I_j|$ units of flow. Hence there must exist an edge (u_k, v_j) carrying less than $|I_j|$ units of flow because at least m_j jobs of $\mathcal{J}$ are active in I_j. The corresponding job J_k is removed, i.e. $\mathcal{J} := \mathcal{J} \setminus \{J_k\}$. We will also prove below that this removal is correct, i.e. $\mathcal{J}_i$ does not contain J_k. For the new set $\mathcal{J}$ we start the next round, invoke a maximum flow computation in the updated graph

$G(\mathcal{J}, \vec{m}, s)$, where $\vec{m}$ and s are updated too. The sequence of rounds ends when finally a flow of value F_G in the current graph $G(\mathcal{J}, \vec{m}, s)$ is found. A formal description of the entire algorithm is given in Figure 2. The pseudo-code uses a boolean variable set_found that keeps track whether or not the desired $\mathcal{J}_i$ has been correctly determined.

Algorithm Optimal Schedule

1. $\mathcal{J} := \{J_1, \ldots, J_n\}$; $i := 0$; $\mathcal{S}_0 :=$ empty schedule;
2. **while** $\mathcal{J} \neq \emptyset$ **do**
3. $i := i + 1$; set_found := false;
4. **while** ¬set_found **do**
5. $n_j :=$ number of jobs of $\mathcal{J}$ that are active in I_j, for $1 \leq j < |\mathcal{I}|$;
6. $m_j := \min\{n_j, \sum_{l=1}^{i-1} m_{lj}\}$; $\vec{m} := (m_j)_{1 \leq j < |\mathcal{I}|}$;
7. $W := \sum_{J_k \in \mathcal{J}} w_k$; $P := \sum_{1 \leq j < |\mathcal{I}|} m_j |I_j|$; $s := W/P$;
8. Compute the value F of a maximum flow in $G(\mathcal{J}, \vec{m}, s)$;
9. **if** $F = W/s$ **then** set_found := true;
10. **else** Determine edge (v_j, v_0) carrying less than $m_j |I_j|$ units of flow and edge (u_k, v_j) carrying less than $|I_j|$ units; of flow; Set $\mathcal{J} := \mathcal{J} \setminus \{J_k\}$;
11. $\mathcal{J}_i := \mathcal{J}$; $s_i := s$; $m_{ij} := m_j$ for $1 \leq j < |\mathcal{I}|$;
12. Extend $\mathcal{S}_{i-1}$ by a feasible schedule for $\mathcal{J}_i$ using speed s_i and m_{ij} processors in I_j; Let $\mathcal{S}_i$ be the resulting schedule;
13. $\mathcal{J} := \{J_1, \ldots, J_n\} \setminus (\mathcal{J}_1 \cup \ldots \cup \mathcal{J}_i)$;

Figure 2: The entire offline algorithm for computing an optimal schedule.

It remains to prove correctness of our algorithm. We prove that in any phase i, $\mathcal{J}_i$ is correctly determined. Lemma 3 immediately implies that the number m_{ij} of reserved processors, for $1 \leq j < |\mathcal{I}|$, as specified in lines 6 and 11 of the algorithm is correct. A schedule for $\mathcal{J}_i$ on the reserved processors can be derived easily from the maximum flow computed in line 8. We described the construction of this schedule earlier when arguing that a flow of maximum value F_G in $G(\mathcal{J}, \vec{m}, s)$ implies a feasible schedule using speed s on the reserved processors $\vec{m}$. It remains to show that sets $\mathcal{J}_1, \ldots, \mathcal{J}_p$ are correct. Consider an i, $1 \leq i \leq p$, and suppose that $\mathcal{J}_1, \ldots, \mathcal{J}_{i-1}$ have been computed correctly. Correctness of $\mathcal{J}_i$ follows from Lemmas 4 and 5.

LEMMA 4. *In phase i, the set $\mathcal{J}$ maintained by the algorithm always satisfies the invariant $\mathcal{J}_i \subseteq \mathcal{J}$.*

PROOF. At the beginning of the phase $\mathcal{J} = \{J_1, \ldots, J_n\} \setminus (\mathcal{J}_1, \ldots, \mathcal{J}_{i-1})$ is the set of all remaining jobs and the invariant is satisfied. Consider a round, represented by lines 5 to 10 of the algorithm, where in the beginning $\mathcal{J}_i \subseteq \mathcal{J}$ holds and a job J_{k_0} is removed in line 10 at the end of the round. We prove that J_{k_0} does not belong to $\mathcal{J}_i$.

Consider the flow computed in line 8 of the round. We call a vertex v_j *saturated* if the amount of flow routed along the outgoing edge (v_j, v_0) is equal to the capacity $m_j |I_j|$. Otherwise v_j is *unsaturated*. Since the computed flow has value $F < F_G = W/s = P = \sum_{1 \leq j < |\mathcal{I}|} m_j |I_j|$, there exists at least one unsaturated vertex. We now modify the flow so as to increase the number of unsaturated vertices. For an edge e in the graph, let $f(e)$ be the amount of flow

routed along it. The modification is as follows: While there exists a vertex u_k with flow $f(u_k, v_j) < |I_j|$ into an unsaturated vertex v_j and positive flow $f(u_k, v_{j'}) > 0$ into a saturated vertex $v_{j'}$, change the flow as follows. Along (u_k, v_j) and (v_j, v_0) we increase the flow by ϵ and along $(u_k, v_{j'})$ and $(v_{j'}, v_0)$ we reduce the flow by ϵ, where $\epsilon = \frac{1}{2} \min\{f(u_k, v_{j'}), |I_j| - f(u_k, v_j), m_j |I_j| - f(v_j, v_0)\}$. At u_k, v_j and $v_{j'}$ the flow conservation law is observed. By the choice of ϵ, the new flow along $(u_k, v_{j'})$ and $(v_{j'}, v_0)$ is positive. Also, by the choice of ϵ, the capacity constraints on (u_k, v_j) and (v_j, v_0) are not violated. Hence the new flow is feasible. Moreover, the total value F of the flow does not changed. Vertex $v_{j'}$ is a new unsaturated vertex while v_j continues to be unsaturated because $\epsilon < m_j |I_j| - f(v_j, v_0)$ and hence the new flow along (v_j, v_0) is strictly smaller than the capacity. Also, since $\epsilon < |I_j| - f(u_k, v_j)$, the new flow along (u_k, v_j) remains strictly below $|I_j|$. The modifications stop when the required conditions are not satisfied anymore, which happens after less than $|\mathcal{I}|$ steps.

Given the modified flow, let $S = \{j \mid v_j \text{ is unsaturated}\}$ be the indices of the unsaturated vertices. Intuitively, these vertices correspond to the intervals in which less than $m_j |I_j|$ units of processing time would be scheduled. Let $\mathcal{J}'$, $\mathcal{J}' \subseteq \mathcal{J}$, be the set of jobs J_k such that $f(u_0, u_k) = w_k/s$ and the outgoing edges leaving u_k that carry positive flow all lead into unsaturated vertices. We argue that the job J_{k_0} removed from $\mathcal{J}$ in line 10 of the algorithm belongs to $\mathcal{J}'$: Prior to the flow modifications, there was an unsaturated vertex v_{j_0} having an incoming edge (u_{k_0}, v_{j_0}) with $f(u_{k_0}, v_{j_0}) < |I_{j_0}|$. Throughout the flow modifications, v_{j_0} remains a unsaturated vertex, and any flow update on (u_{k_0}, v_{j_0}) ensures that the amount of flow is strictly below $|I_{j_0}|$. Hence, if u_{k_0} had an outgoing edge with positive flow into a saturated vertex, the flow modifications would not have stopped. Moreover, if $f(u_0, u_{k_0}) < w_{k_0}/s$ held, we could increase the flow along edges (u_0, u_{k_0}), (u_{k_0}, v_{j_0}) and (v_{j_0}, v_0), thereby increasing the total value F of the flow.

Next let $\mathcal{J}''$, $\mathcal{J}'' \subseteq \mathcal{J} \setminus \mathcal{J}'$, be the set of jobs J_k such that u_k has at least one edge (u_k, v_j) into a unsaturated vertex v_j. Here we argue that for any such job, all the edges (u_k, v_j) into unsaturated vertices v_j carry a flow of exactly $|I_j|$ units: First observe that a job $J_k \in \mathcal{J}''$ does not belong to $\mathcal{J}'$ and hence (a) there is an edge (u_k, v_j) with positive flow into a saturated vertex v_j or (b) $f(u_0, u_k) < w_k/s$. In case (a), if there was an edge (u_k, v_j) carrying less than $|I_j|$ units of flow into a unsaturated vertex v_j, the flow modifications would not have stopped. In case (b), we could increase the flow along (u_0, u_k), (u_k, v_j) and (v_j, v_0), thereby raising the flow value F.

For any I_j, let $\mathcal{J}'(I_j)$, be the set of jobs of $\mathcal{J}'$ that are active in I_j. Set $\mathcal{J}''(I_j)$ is defined analogously. Given the modified flow, let t_{kj} be the amount of flow along (u_k, v_j). Note that for no job $J_k \in \mathcal{J} \setminus (\mathcal{J}' \cup \mathcal{J}'')$ there exists an edge (u_k, v_j) into a unsaturated vertex and hence J_k is not active in an I_j with $j \in S$. Hence, for any $j \in S$, since v_j is unsaturated, $\sum_{J_k \in \mathcal{J}'(I_j) \cup \mathcal{J}''(I_j)} t_{kj} < m_j |I_j|$. As $t_{kj} = |I_j|$, for $J_k \in \mathcal{J}''(I_j)$,

$$\sum_{J_k \in \mathcal{J}'(I_j)} t_{kj} < (m_j - |\mathcal{J}''(I_j)|)|I_j|. \qquad (1)$$

We next prove that the job J_{k_0} removed at the end of the round in line 10 of the algorithm does not belong to $\mathcal{J}' \cap \mathcal{J}_i$ and hence does not belong to $\mathcal{J}_i$. So suppose that $J_{k_0} \in \mathcal{J}' \cap$

$\mathcal{J}_i$. We show that in this case the total processing volume of $\mathcal{J}_i$ is not large enough to fill the reserved processing intervals using a continuous speed of s_i. We observe that s_i is at least as large as the speed s computed in the current round of the algorithm: If $s_i < s$, then in the optimal schedule, all jobs of $\mathcal{J}$ would be processed at a speed smaller than s. However, the total length of the available processing intervals for $\mathcal{J}$ is not more than $P = \sum_{1 \le j < |\mathcal{I}|} m_j |I_j|$ and total work to be completed is $W = \sum_{J_k \in \mathcal{J}} w_k$. Hence a speed of $s_i < s = W/P$ is not sufficient to finish the jobs in time.

Let m_{ij} be the number of processors used by $\mathcal{J}_i$ in interval I_j in an optimal solution. We prove that the jobs of $\mathcal{J}_i$ cannot fill all the reserved processors in intervals I_j with $j \in S$ using a speed of $s_i \ge s$. Recall that no job of $\mathcal{J} \setminus (\mathcal{J}' \cup \mathcal{J}'')$ is active in any interval I_j with $j \in S$. Only the jobs of $\mathcal{J}'(I_j) \cap \mathcal{J}_i$ and $\mathcal{J}''(I_j) \cap \mathcal{J}_i$ are active. The jobs of $\mathcal{J}'(I_j) \cap \mathcal{J}_i$ must fill at least $m_{ij} - |\mathcal{J}''(I_j) \cap \mathcal{J}_i|$ processors over a time window of length $|I_j|$ because each job of $\mathcal{J}''(I_j) \cap \mathcal{J}_i$ can fill at best one processor. Thus, over all intervals I_j with $j \in S$, the jobs of $\mathcal{J}' \cap \mathcal{J}_i$ have to provide a work of at least

$$\sum_{j \in S} (m_{ij} - |\mathcal{J}''(I_j) \cap \mathcal{J}_i|) |I_j| s_i.$$

We show that this is not the case. The total work of $\mathcal{J}' \cap \mathcal{J}_i$ is

$$\sum_{J_k \in \mathcal{J}' \cap \mathcal{J}_i} w_k = \sum_{J_k \in \mathcal{J}' \cap \mathcal{J}_i} f(u_0, u_k) s = \sum_{j \in S} \sum_{J_k \in \mathcal{J}' \cap \mathcal{J}_i} t_{kj} s, \tag{2}$$

where t_{kj} is the amount of flow along (u_k, v_j) in the modified flow. The first and second equalities hold because, for any $J_k \in \mathcal{J}'$, $f(u_0, u_k) = w_k/s$ and along edges (u_k, v_j) positive amounts of flow are routed only into unsaturated vertices v_j, $j \in S$. For any $j \in S$, we have

$$\sum_{J_k \in \mathcal{J}'(I_j) \cap \mathcal{J}_i} t_{kj} \le |\mathcal{J}'(I_j) \cap \mathcal{J}_i| |I_j|$$

because the edge capacity of (u_k, v_j) is $|I_j|$. For the unsaturated vertex v_{j_0} and the job J_{k_0}, determined in line 10 of the algorithm, the flow along (u_{k_0}, v_{j_0}) is strictly below $|I_{j_0}|$. Hence for $j_0 \in S$ the stronger relation

$$\sum_{J_k \in \mathcal{J}'(I_{j_0}) \cap \mathcal{J}_i} t_{kj_0} < |\mathcal{J}'(I_{j_0}) \cap \mathcal{J}_i| |I_{j_0}|$$

holds because by assumption $J_{k_0} \in \mathcal{J}' \cap \mathcal{J}_i$. Taking into account (1), we obtain that expression (2) is

$$\sum_{J_k \in \mathcal{J}' \cap \mathcal{J}_i} w_k < \sum_{j \in S} \min\{|\mathcal{J}'(I_j) \cap \mathcal{J}_i|, m_j - |\mathcal{J}''(I_j)|\} |I_j| s.$$

We will show that for any $j \in S$,

$$\min\{|\mathcal{J}'(I_j) \cap \mathcal{J}_i|, m_j - |\mathcal{J}''(I_j)|\} \le m_{ij} - |\mathcal{J}''(I_j) \cap \mathcal{J}_i|. \tag{3}$$

This implies that the total work of $\mathcal{J}' \cap \mathcal{J}_i$ is strictly smaller than $\sum_{j \in S}(m_{ij} - |\mathcal{J}''(I_j) \cap \mathcal{J}_i|) |I_j| s_i$ since $s_i \ge s$.

So suppose that (3) is violated for some $j \in S$. Then $|\mathcal{J}'(I_j) \cap \mathcal{J}_i| > m_{ij} - |\mathcal{J}''(I_j) \cap \mathcal{J}_i|$ and the number of jobs of $\mathcal{J}_i$ that are active in I_j is strictly larger than m_{ij}. Hence m_{ij} is the total number of processors not yet occupied by $\mathcal{J}_i \cup \ldots \cup \mathcal{J}_{i-1}$. As the number of jobs of $\mathcal{J}$ active in I_j is at least as large as the corresponding number of jobs of $\mathcal{J}_i$, we have $m_j = m_{ij}$. Since $|\mathcal{J}''(I_j)| \ge |\mathcal{J}''(I_j) \cap \mathcal{J}_i|$ we

have $m_j - |\mathcal{J}''(I_j)| \le m_{ij} - |\mathcal{J}''(I_j) \cap \mathcal{J}_i|$, contradicting the assumption that (3) was violated. □

LEMMA 5. *When phase i ends, $\mathcal{J} = \mathcal{J}_i$.*

PROOF. When phase i ends, consider set $\mathcal{J}$ and the flow in the current graph $G = (\mathcal{J}, \vec{m}, s)$. Again, for any edge e let $f(e)$ the amount of flow along e. Since the value of the computed flow is equal to F_G we have $f(u_0, u_k) = w_k/s$, for any $J_k \in \mathcal{J}$. By Lemma 4, $\mathcal{J}_i \subseteq \mathcal{J}$. So suppose $\mathcal{J}_i \ne \mathcal{J}$, which implies $\mathcal{J}_i \subset \mathcal{J}$. We prove that in this case the speed s_i used for $\mathcal{J}_i$ in an optimal schedule satisfies $s_i \le s$ and then derive a contradiction.

In the graph $G = (\mathcal{J}, \vec{m}, s)$ we remove the flow associated with any $J_k \in \mathcal{J} \setminus \mathcal{J}_i$. More specifically, for any such J_k, we remove $f(u_k, v_j)$ units of flow along the path (u_0, u_k), (u_k, v_j) and (v_j, v_0) until the flow along (u_0, u_k) is zero. Let $f'(v_j, v_0)$ be the new amount of flow along (v_j, v_0) after the modifications. Then for any interval I_j, at least $\lceil f'(v_j, v_0)/|I_j| \rceil$ jobs of $\mathcal{J}_i$ are active in I_j because for each J_k at most $|I_j|$ units of flow are routed into v_j. Also, at least $\lceil f'(v_j, v_0)/|I_j| \rceil$ processors are available because $m_j = f(v_j, v_0)/|I_j|$ processors are availble in I_j. Hence

$$s_i \le \sum_{J_k \in \mathcal{J}_i} w_k / \sum_{1 \le j < |\mathcal{I}|} \lceil f'(v_j, v_0)/|I_j| \rceil |I_j|.$$

The latter expression is upper bounded by s because

$$\begin{aligned}
\sum_{J_k \in \mathcal{J}_i} w_k &= s \sum_{J_k \in \mathcal{J}_i} w_k/s = s \sum_{J_k \in \mathcal{J}_i} f(u_0, u_k) \\
&= s \sum_{1 \le j < |\mathcal{I}|} f'(v_j, v_0) \\
&\le s \sum_{1 \le j < |\mathcal{I}|} \lceil f'(v_j, v_0)/|I_j| \rceil |I_j|.
\end{aligned}$$

Hence $\mathcal{J}_i$ is processed at speed $s_i \le s$ while jobs of $\mathcal{J} \setminus \mathcal{J}_i$ are processed at speed s' with $s' < s_i \le s$. However, this is impossible because the minimum average speed to process the jobs of $\mathcal{J}$ is $s = \sum_{J_k \in \mathcal{J}} w_k / \sum_{1 \le j < |\mathcal{I}|} m_j |I_j|$. □

We conclude with the following theorem.

THEOREM 1. *An optimal schedule can be computed in polynomial time using combinatorial techniques.*

3. ONLINE ALGORITHMS

We present adaptions and extensions of the single processor algorithms *Optimal Available* and *Average Rate* [16].

3.1 Algorithm Optimal Available

For single processor environments, *Optimal Available (OA)* works as follows: Whenever a new job arrives, *OA* computes an optimal schedule for the currently available, unfinished jobs. While it is straightforward to extend this strategy to parallel processing environments, the corresponding competitive analysis becomes considerably more involved. We have to prove a series of properties of the online algorithm's schedule and analyze how a schedule changes in response to the arrival of a new job. Our algorithm for parallel processors works as follows.

Algorithm OA(m): Whenever a new job arrives, compute

an optimal schedule for the currently available unfinished jobs. This can be done using the algorithm of Section 2.

At any given time t_0, let $\mathcal{S}_{OA(m)}$ denote the schedule of $OA(m)$ for the currently available unfinished jobs. Let $J_1, \ldots, J_n$ be the corresponding jobs, which have arrived by time t_0 but are still unfinished. Let w_i be the remaining processing volume of J_i, $1 \leq i \leq n$. Since $J_1, \ldots, J_n$ are available at time t_0 we can ignore release times and only have to consider the deadlines $d_1, \ldots, d_n$. Let $\mathcal{I} = \{t_0\} \cup \{d_i \mid 1 \leq i \leq n\}$ be the set of relevant time points and $\tau_1 < \ldots < \tau_{|\mathcal{I}|}$ be the sorted order of the elements of $\mathcal{I}$, where $|\mathcal{I}| \leq n+1$. In the time horizon $[\tau_1, \tau_{|\mathcal{I}|})$, the j-th interval is $I_j = [\tau_j, \tau_{j+1})$, where $1 \leq j < |\mathcal{I}|$.

Schedule $\mathcal{S}_{OA(m)}$ is an optimal schedule for the unfinished work currently available; otherwise when last computing a schedule, $OA(m)$ would have obtained a better solution for time horizon $[\tau_1, \tau_{|\mathcal{I}|})$. By Lemma 2, in each interval I_j of $\mathcal{S}_{OA(m)}$ we can rearrange the schedule such that each processor uses a fixed, non-varying speed in I_j, $1 \leq j < |\mathcal{I}|$. In the following we restrict ourselves to schedules $\mathcal{S}_{OA(m)}$ satisfying this property. Such schedules are feasible and incur a minimum energy. Let $s_{l,j}$ be the speed used by processor l in I_j, where $1 \leq l \leq m$ and $1 \leq j < |\mathcal{I}|$. The next Lemma 6 states that we can modify $\mathcal{S}_{OA(m)}$ even further so that on each processor the speed levels used form a non-increasing sequence. The modification is obtained by simply permuting within each interval I_j the schedules on the m processors, $1 \leq j < |\mathcal{I}|$. Hence feasibility and energy consumption of the overall schedule are not affected. Throughout the analysis we always consider schedules $\mathcal{S}_{OA(m)}$ that also fulfill this second property. The proof of Lemma 6 as well as those of Lemmas 8–11 are presented in the full version of the paper.

LEMMA 6. *Given $\mathcal{S}_{OA(m)}$, in each interval I_j, $1 \leq j < |\mathcal{I}|$, we can permute the schedules on the m processors such that finally the following property holds. For any processor l, $1 \leq l \leq m$, inequality $s_{l,j} \geq s_{l,j+1}$ is satisfied for $j = 1, \ldots, |\mathcal{I}| - 2$.*

We investigate the event that a new job J_{n+1} arrives at time t_0. As usual d_{n+1} and w_{n+1} are the deadline and the processing volume of J_{n+1}. Let $\mathcal{S}_{OA(m)}$ be the schedule of $OA(m)$ immediately before the arrival of J_{n+1}, and let $\mathcal{S}'_{OA(m)}$ be the schedule immediately after the arrival when $OA(m)$ has just computed a new schedule. We present two lemmas that relate the two schedules. Loosely speaking we prove that processor speeds can only increase. The speed at which a job J_k, $1 \leq k \leq n$, is processed in $\mathcal{S}'_{OA(m)}$ is at least as high as the corresponding speed in $\mathcal{S}_{OA(m)}$. Furthermore, at any time $t \geq t_0$, the minimum processor speed in $\mathcal{S}'_{OA(m)}$ is at least as high as that in $\mathcal{S}_{OA(m)}$.

Schedules $\mathcal{S}_{OA(m)}$ and $\mathcal{S}'_{OA(m)}$ are optimal schedules for the respective workloads. Recall that, by Lemma 1, they process jobs at fixed, non-varying speeds. Let $s(J_k)$ be the speed at which J_k is processed in $\mathcal{S}_{OA(m)}$, $1 \leq k \leq n$. Let $s'(J_k)$ be the speed used for J_k in $\mathcal{S}'_{OA(m)}$, $1 \leq k \leq n+1$.

LEMMA 7. *There holds $s'(J_k) \geq s(J_k)$, for any $1 \leq k \leq n$.*

PROOF. In $\mathcal{S}_{OA(m)}$ let $s_1 > s_2 > \ldots > s_p$ be the speeds used in the schedule and let $\mathcal{J}_1, \ldots, \mathcal{J}_p$ be the associated job sets, i.e. the jobs of $\mathcal{J}_i$ are processed at speed s_i, $1 \leq i \leq p$. In the following we assume that the statement of the lemma

does not hold and derive a contradiction. So let i be the smallest index such that $\mathcal{J}_i$ contains a job J_k with $s'(J_k) < s(J_k) = s_i$. We partition $\mathcal{J}_i$ into two sets $\mathcal{J}_{i1}$ and $\mathcal{J}_{i2}$ such that all $J_k \in \mathcal{J}_{i1}$ satisfy $s'(J_k) \geq s_i$, as desired. For each job $J_k \in \mathcal{J}_{i2}$ we have $s'(J_k) < s_i$. By the choice of i, any job $J_k \in \mathcal{J}_1 \cup \ldots \cup \mathcal{J}_{i-1}$ also fulfills the desired property $s'(J_k) \geq s(J_k)$.

Let t_1 be the first point of time when the processing of any job of $\mathcal{J}_{i2}$ starts in $\mathcal{S}'_{OA(m)}$. Let P be a processor executing such a job at time t_1. We first argue that any $J_k \in \mathcal{J}_1 \cup \ldots \cup \mathcal{J}_{i-1} \cup \mathcal{J}_{i1}$ that is active at time $t \geq t_1$, i.e. that satisfies $d_k > t_1$, is scheduled at all times throughout $[t_1, d_k)$: So suppose J_k were not executed on any of the processors in a time window $W \subseteq [t_1, d_k)$ and let $\delta > 0$ be the length of W. Determine a δ' with $0 < \delta' \leq \delta$ such that during the first δ' time units of W processor P does not change the job it executes. We set $\delta_k = \min\{\delta', w_k/s'(J_k)\}$. Here $w_k/s'(J_k)$ is the total time for which J_k is scheduled in $\mathcal{S}'_{OA(m)}$. Let $s(P, W)$ be the maximum speed used by processor P within W and set $\epsilon = (s'(J_k) - s(P, W))/2$. The value of ϵ is strictly positive because $s'(J_k) \geq s_i > s(P, W)$. The last inequality holds because at time t_1 processor P executes a job of $\mathcal{J}_{i2}$ at a speed that is strictly smaller than s_i and we consider schedules that satisfy the property of Lemma 6, i.e. on each processor the speed levels over time are non-increasing. We now modify $\mathcal{S}'_{OA(m)}$ as follows. During any δ_k time units where J_k is processed we reduce the speed by ϵ. During the first δ_k time units of W we increase the speed by ϵ and use the extra processing capacity of $\delta_k \epsilon$ units to execute $\delta_k \epsilon$ units of J_k. Hence we obtain a new feasible schedule. Since $s'(J_k) - \epsilon \geq s(P, W) + \epsilon$, by the convexity of the power function the schedule has a strictly smaller energy consumption, contradicting the fact that $\mathcal{S}'_{OA(m)}$ is an optimal schedule for the given workload.

Next consider any fixed time $t \geq t_1$. In $\mathcal{S}_{OA(m)}$ let m_{i2} be the number of processors that execute jobs of J_{i2} at time t. Similarly, in $\mathcal{S}'_{OA(m)}$ let m'_{i2} be the number of processors that execute jobs of J_{i2} at time t. We will prove $m_{i2} \geq m'_{i2}$. Let n_l, where $1 \leq l \leq i-1$, be the number of jobs J_k of $\mathcal{J}_l$ that are active at time t, i.e. that satisfy $d_k > t$. Furthermore, let n_{i1} and n_{i2} be the numer of jobs of $\mathcal{J}_{i1}$ and $\mathcal{J}_{i2}$, respectively, that are active at time t. As shown in the last paragraph, all job of $\mathcal{J}_1 \cup \ldots \cup \mathcal{J}_{i-1} \cup \mathcal{J}_{i1}$ that are active at time t are also processed at this time in $\mathcal{S}'_{OA(m)}$. Hence

$$m'_{i2} \leq m - \sum_{l=1}^{i-1} n_l - n_{i1}. \tag{4}$$

Strict inequality holds, for instance, if the new job J_{n+1} or a job of $\mathcal{J}_{i+1} \cup \ldots \cup \mathcal{J}_p$ is scheduled at time t. Let m_l be the number of processors executing jobs of $\mathcal{J}_l$ in $\mathcal{S}_{OA(m)}$, where $1 \leq l \leq i$. By Lemma 3, $m_i = \min\{n_i, m - \sum_{l=1}^{i-1} m_l\}$. We remark that Lemma 3 is formulated with respect to an interval I_j. We can apply the statement simply by considering the interval containing t. Since $m_l \leq n_l$, for $1 \leq l \leq i-1$, we obtain

$$m_i \geq \min\{n_i, m - \sum_{l=1}^{i-1} n_l\}. \tag{5}$$

If the latter minimum is given by the term $m - \sum_{l=1}^{i-1} n_l$, then in (4) we obtain $m'_{i2} \leq m - \sum_{l=1}^{i-1} n_l - n_{i1} \leq m_i - n_{i1} \leq m_{i2}$. The last inequality holds because m_{i2} cannot be smaller than m_i, the number of machines used by jobs of $\mathcal{J}_i$, minus the

285

number of jobs of $\mathcal{J}_{i1}$ active at time t. Hence $m'_{i2} \leq m_{i2}$, as desired. If the minimum in (5) is given by n_i, then since $m_{i2} \geq m_i - n_{i1}$, we have $m_{i2} \geq n_i - n_{i1}$. As $n_i - n_{i1} = n_{i2} \geq m'_{i2}$ we conclude again $m_{i2} \geq m'_{i2}$.

Finally let T' be the total processing time used for jobs of $\mathcal{J}_{i2}$ in $\mathcal{S}'_{OA(m)}$. This value can be determined as follows. The time horizon of $\mathcal{S}'_{OA(m)}$ is partitioned into maximal intervals such that the number of processors handling jobs of $\mathcal{J}_{i2}$ does not change within an interval. For each such interval, the length of the interval is multiplied by the number of processors executing jobs of $\mathcal{J}_{i2}$. Value T' is simply the sum of all these products. Similarly, let T be the total processing time used for jobs of $\mathcal{J}_{i2}$ in $\mathcal{S}_{OA(m)}$. At any time t we have $m_{i2} \geq m'_{i2}$. This was shown above for times $t \geq t_1$. It trivially holds for times t with $t_0 \leq t < t_1$ because no jobs of $\mathcal{J}_{i2}$ are processed in $\mathcal{S}'_{OA(m)}$ at that time. Hence the number of processors handling jobs of $\mathcal{J}_{i2}$ in $\mathcal{S}_{OA(m)}$ is always at least as high as the corresponding number in $\mathcal{S}'_{OA(m)}$. This implies $T \geq T'$. The total processing volume $\sum_{J_k \in \mathcal{J}_{i2}} w_k$ of jobs in $\mathcal{J}_{i2}$ fills T' time units using a speed or speeds of $s < s_i$ in $\mathcal{S}'_{OA(m)}$. Thus using a speed of s_i the processing volume is not sufficient to fill $T > T'$ time units in $\mathcal{S}_{OA(m)}$. We obtain a contradiction to the fact that job of $\mathcal{J}_i$ are processed at constant speed s_i in $\mathcal{S}_{OA(m)}$. $\square$

LEMMA 8. *At any time t, where $t \geq t_0$, the minimum speed used by the m processors at time t in $\mathcal{S}'_{OA(m)}$ is at least as high as the minimum speed used on the m processors at time t in $\mathcal{S}_{OA(m)}$.*

We finally need a lemma that specifies the minimum processor speed for a time window if a job finishes at some time strictly before its deadline.

LEMMA 9. *If in $\mathcal{S}_{OA(m)}$ a job J_k finishes at some time t with $t < d_k$, then throughout $[t, d_k)$ the minimum speed on the m processors is at least $s(J_k)$.*

We next turn to the competitive analysis of $OA(m)$. We use a potential function that is inspired by a potential used by Bansal et al. [5]. We first define our modified potential function. At any time t consider the schedule of $\mathcal{S}_{OA(m)}$. Let $s_1 > \ldots > s_p$ be the speeds used in the schedule and let $\mathcal{J}_1, \ldots, \mathcal{J}_p$ be the associated job sets, i.e. jobs of $\mathcal{J}_i$ are processed at speed s_i. Let $W_{OA(m)}(i)$ be the total remaining processing volume of jobs $J_k \in \mathcal{J}_i$ in $OA(m)$'s schedule $1 \leq i \leq p$. Similarly, let $W_{OPT}(i)$ be the total remaining processing volume that OPT has to finish for jobs $J_k \in \mathcal{J}_i$, $1 \leq i \leq p$. We remark that, for a job $J_k \in \mathcal{J}_i$, OPT's remaining work might be larger than that of $OA(m)$ if OPT has completed less work on J_k so far. Sets $\mathcal{J}_1, \ldots, \mathcal{J}_p$ represent the jobs that $OA(m)$ has not yet finished. Let $\mathcal{J}'$ be the set of jobs that are finished by $OA(m)$ but still unfinished by OPT. Obviously, these jobs have a deadline after the current time t. If $\mathcal{J}' \neq \emptyset$, then for any job of $\mathcal{J}'$ consider the speed $OA(m)$ used when last processing the job. Partition $\mathcal{J}'$ according to these speeds, i.e. $\mathcal{J}'_i$ consists of those jobs that $OA(m)$ executed last at speed s'_i, where $1 \leq i \leq p'$ for some positive p'. Let $W'_{OPT}(i)$ be the total remaining processing volume OPT has to finish on jobs of $\mathcal{J}'_i$, $1 \leq i \leq p'$. If $\mathcal{J}' = \emptyset$, we simply set $s'_1 = 0$ and $\mathcal{J}'_1 = \emptyset$. The potential

Φ is defined as follows.

$$\Phi = \alpha \sum_{i \geq 1} (s_i)^{\alpha-1} (W_{OA(m)}(i) - \alpha W_{OPT}(i))$$
$$- \alpha^2 \sum_{i \geq 1} (s'_i)^{\alpha-1} W'_{OPT}(i)$$

Compared to the potential function used to analyze OA in the single processor setting, our function here consists of a second term representing OPT's unfinished work. This second term is essential to establish the competitiveness of α^α and, in particular, is crucially used in the analysis of the working case (see below).

At any time t let $s_{OA(m),1}(t) \geq \ldots \geq s_{OA(m),m}(t)$ and $s_{OPT,1}(t) \geq \ldots \geq s_{OPT),m}(t)$ be the speeds used by $OA(m)$ and OPT on the m processors, respectively. In the remainder of this section we will prove the following properties.

(a) Whenever a new job arrives or a job is finished by $OA(m)$ or OPT, the potential does not increase.

(b) At all other times

$$\sum_{l=1}^{m} (s_{OA(m),l}(t))^\alpha - \alpha^\alpha \sum_{l=1}^{m} (s_{OPT,l}(t))^\alpha + \frac{d\Phi(t)}{dt} \leq 0.$$
(6)

Integrating over all times we obtain that $OA(m)$ is α^α-competitive.

Working case: We prove property (b). So let t be any time when the algorithms are working on jobs. In a first step we match the processors of $OA(m)$ to those of OPT. This matching is constructed as follows. First, processors handling the same jobs are paired. More specifically, if a job J_k is executed on a processor l in $OA(m)$'s schedule and on processor l' in OPT's schedule, then we match the two processors l and l'. All remaining processors of $OA(m)$ and OPT, handling disjoint job sets, are matched in an arbitrary way.

For each matched processor pair l, l', we consider its contribution in (6) and prove that the contribution is nonpositive. Summing over all pairs l, l', this establishes (6). If the speed of processor l' in OPT's schedule is 0, then the analysis is simple: If the speed on processor l in $OA(m)$ schedule is also 0, then the contribution of the processor pair l, l' in (6) is 0. If the speed on processor l is positive, then $OA(m)$ executes a job on the processor. Suppose that the job is contained in set $\mathcal{J}_i$. Then in Φ the value of $W_{OA(m)}(i)$ decreases at rate s_i and the contribution of the processor pair l, l' in (6) is $s_i^\alpha - \alpha(s_i)^{\alpha-1} s_i < 0$.

Hence in the following we assume that the speed of processor l' in OPT's schedule is positive. We show that $OA(m)$ also executes a job J_k on its processor l and that the contribution of the processor pair $l.l'$ is upper bounded by

$$(1-\alpha)s_i^\alpha + \alpha^2 s_i^{\alpha-1} s_{OPT,l'}(t) - \alpha^\alpha (s_{OPT,l'}(t))^\alpha, \quad (7)$$

where i is the index such that $J_k \in \mathcal{J}_i$. As in [5] one can then show the non-positivity of this expression. First consider the case that both processors l and l' handle the same job J_k. Let $\mathcal{J}_i$ be the set containing J_k. Then $W_{OA(m)}(i)$ decreases at rate s_i and $W_{OPT}(i)$ decreases at rate $s_{OPT,l'}(t)$. Hence the contribution of the processor pair in (6) is $s_i^\alpha - \alpha^\alpha (s_{OPT,l'}(t))^\alpha + (-\alpha(s_i)^{\alpha-1} s_i + \alpha^2 (s_i)^{\alpha-1} s_{OPT,l'}(t)) = (1-\alpha)s_i^\alpha + \alpha^2 (s_i)^{\alpha-1} s_{OPT,l'}(t) - \alpha^\alpha (s_{OPT,l'}(t))^\alpha$, as stated in (7).

Next consider the case that the job $J_{k'}$ executed on processor l' in OPT's schedule is not executed by $OA(m)$ on processor l and hence is not executed on any of its processors at time t. If $J_{k'}$ is still unfinished by $OA(m)$, then let $\mathcal{J}_{i'}$ be the set containing $J_{k'}$. Recall that $OA(m)$'s schedule is optimal. Hence, by Lemma 3, it always processes the jobs from the smallest indexed sets $\mathcal{J}_i$, which in turn use the highest speeds s_i. Thus, if $J_{k'}$ is not executed by $OA(m)$, then the schedule currently processes m jobs, each of which is contained in $\mathcal{J}_1 \cup \ldots \cup \mathcal{J}_{i'-1}$ or contained in $\mathcal{J}_{i'}$ but is different from $J_{k'}$. Let J_k be the job executed by $OA(m)$ on processor l and let $\mathcal{J}_i$ be the job set containing J_k. Then $i \leq i'$ and $s_i \geq s_{i'}$. In Φ the term $W_{OA(m)}(i)$ decreases at rate s_i while the term $W_{OPT}(i')$ decreases at rate $s_{OPT,l'}(t)$. Hence the contribution of the processor pair l, l' in (6) is $s_i^\alpha - \alpha^\alpha(s_{OPT,l'}(t))^\alpha + (-\alpha(s_i)^{\alpha-1}s_i + \alpha^2(s_{i'})^{\alpha-1}s_{OPT,l'}(t)) \leq (1-\alpha)s_i^\alpha + \alpha^2(s_i)^{\alpha-1}s_{OPT,l'}(t) - \alpha^\alpha(s_{OPT,l'}(t))^\alpha$, which is the bound of (7).

It remains to consider the case that $J_{k'}$ is already finished by $OA(m)$. Then $J_{k'}$ is contained in the set $\mathcal{J}'$ of jobs that are finished by $OA(m)$ but unfinished by OPT. Let $\mathcal{J}'_{i'}$ be the set containing $J_{k'}$. In Φ the term $W'_{OPT}(i')$ decreases at rate $s_{OPT,l'}(t)$. When $OA(m)$ finished $J_{k'}$ in its schedule, it used speed $s'_{i'}$. By Lemma 9, in the former schedule of $OA(m)$, the minimum processor speed throughout the time window until $d_{k'}$ was always at least $s'_{i'}$. This time window contains the current time, i.e. $t < d_{k'}$. Since the completion of $J_{k'}$ $OA(m)$ might have computed new schedules in response to the arrival of new jobs but, by Lemma 8, the minimum processor speed at any time can only increase. Hence in the current schedule of $OA(m)$ and at the current time t the minimum processor speed is at least $s'_{i'}$. Thus on its processor l $OA(m)$ uses a speed of at least $s'_{i'} > 0$. Hence $OA(m)$ executes a job J_k that belongs to, say, set $\mathcal{J}_i$. We have $s_i \geq s'_{i'}$. In Φ the term $W_{OA(m)}(i)$ decreases at rate s_i. We conclude again that the contribution of the processor pair l, l' is $s_i^\alpha - \alpha^\alpha(s_{OPT,l'}(t))^\alpha + (-\alpha(s_i)^\alpha + \alpha^2(s'_{i'})^{\alpha-1}s_{OPT,l'}(t)) \leq (1-\alpha)s_i^\alpha + \alpha^2(s_i)^{\alpha-1}s_{OPT,l'}(t) - \alpha^\alpha(s_{OPT,l'}(t))^\alpha$, which is again the bound of (7).

Completion/Arrival case: When OPT finishes a job J_k the potential does not change because in the terms $W_{OPT}(i)$ or $W_{OPT}(i')$ the remaining processing volume of J_k simply goes to 0. Similarly if $OA(m)$ completes a job already finished by OPT, the potential does not change. If $OA(m)$ completes a job J_k not yet finished by OPT, then let $\mathcal{J}_i$ be the set containing J_k immediately before completion. In the first term of Φ, $W_{OPT}(i)$ increases by $\alpha^2(s_i)^{\alpha-1}w_k$, where w_k is the remaining work of J_k to be done by OPT. However, at the same time, the second term of Φ decreases by exactly $\alpha^2(s_i)^{\alpha-1}w_k$ because J_k opens or joins a set $\mathcal{J}'_{i'}$ with $s'_{i'} = s_i$.

When a new job J_{n+1} arrives, the structure of the analysis is similar to that in the single processor case, see [5]. We imagine that a job J_{n+1} of processing volume 0 arrives. Then we increase the processing volume to its true size. However, in the multi-processor setting, we have to study how the schedule of $OA(m)$ changes if the processing volume of J_{n+1} increases from a value w_{n+1} to $w'_{n+1} = w_{n+1} + \epsilon$, for some $\epsilon > 0$. Let $\mathcal{S}_{OA(m)}$ and $\mathcal{S}'_{OA(m)}$ be the schedules of $OA(m)$ before and after the increase, respectively. For any job J_k, $1 \leq k \leq n+1$, let $s(J_k)$ and $s'(J_k)$ be the speeds used for J_k in $\mathcal{S}_{OA(m)}$ and $\mathcal{S}'_{OA(m)}$, respectively. The next lemma

states that the speeds at which jobs are processed does not decrease. The proof is identical to that of Lemma 7.

LEMMA 10. *There holds* $s'(J_k) \geq s(J_k)$, *for any* $1 \leq k \leq n+1$.

In $\mathcal{S}_{OA(m)}$, let $\mathcal{J}_{i_0}$ be the job set containing J_{n+1}, i.e. $J_{n+1} \in \mathcal{J}_{i_0}$, where $1 \leq i_0 \leq p$. The following lemma implies that the speeds of jobs $J_k \in \mathcal{J}_{i_0+1} \cup \ldots \cup \mathcal{J}_p$ do not change when increasing the processing volume of J_{n+1}.

LEMMA 11. *There holds* $s'(J_k) = s(J_k)$, *for any* $J_k \in \mathcal{J}_{i_0+1} \cup \ldots \cup J_p$.

In the remainder of this section we describe the change in potential arising in response to the arrival of a new job J_{n+1}. If the deadline d_{n+1} does not coincide with the deadline of a previous job J_i, $1 \leq i \leq n$, we have to update the set of intervals I_j, $1 \leq j < |\mathcal{I}|$. We add d_{n+1} to $\mathcal{I}$. If d_{n+1} is the last deadline of any of the jobs, we introduce a new interval $[\tau_{\max}, d_{n+1})$, where $\tau_{\max} = \max_{1 \leq i \leq n} d_i$; otherwise we split the interval $[\tau_j, \tau_{j+1})$ containing d_{n+1} into two intervals $[\tau_j, d_{n+1})$ and $[d_{n+1}, \tau_{j+1})$.

In a next step we add J_{n+1} to the current schedule $\mathcal{S}_{OA(m)}$ assuming that the processing volume of J_{n+1} is zero. Let I_j be the interval ending at time d_{n+1}. If $\mathcal{S}_{OA(m)}$ has an idle processor in I_j, then we open a new job set $\mathcal{J}_{p+1}$ with associated speed $s_{p+1} = 0$. Otherwise let s_i be the lowest speed used by any of the processors in I_j. We add J_{n+1} to $\mathcal{J}_i$. In the following we increase the processing volume of J_{n+1} from zero to its final size w_{n+1}. The increase proceeds in a series of phases such that, during a phase, the job sets $\mathcal{J}_i$, $i \geq 1$, do not change. However, at the beginning of a phase the job set $\mathcal{J}_{i_0}$ containing J_{n+1} might split into two sets. Moreover, at the end of a phase the set $\mathcal{J}_{i_0}$ might merge with the next set $\mathcal{J}_{i_0-1}$ executed at the next higher speed level. So suppose that during a phase the processing volume of J_{n+1} increases by ϵ. By Lemma 11, the speeds of the jobs in sets $\mathcal{J}_i$, $i > i_0$, do not change. Moreover, by Lemma 10, the speeds of the other jobs can only increase. Hence, by convexity of the power function, an optimal solution will increase the speed at the lowest possible level, which is s_{i_0}. In the current schedule of $OA(m)$, let T_{i_0} be the total time for which jobs of $\mathcal{J}_{i_0}$ are processed. The speed at which jobs of $\mathcal{J}_{i_0}$ are processed increases from $W_{OA(m)}(i_0)/T_{i_0}$ to $(W_{OA(m)}(i_0) + \epsilon)/T_{i_0}$. Hence the potential change is given by

$$\Delta\Phi = \alpha\left(\frac{W_{OA(m)}(i_0) + \epsilon}{T_{i_0}}\right)(W_{OA(m)}(i_0) + \epsilon - \alpha(W_{OPT}(i_0) + \epsilon))$$
$$-\alpha\left(\frac{W_{OA(m)}(i_0)}{T_{i_0}}\right)(W_{OA(m)}(i_0) - \alpha(W_{OPT}(i_0))).$$

As in [5] we can show the non-positivity of the last expression.

At the beginning of a phase $\mathcal{J}_{i_0}$ might split into two sets $\mathcal{J}'_{i_0}$ and $\mathcal{J}''_{i_0}$. Set $\mathcal{J}'_{i_0}$ contains those jobs that, in an optimal schedule, cannot be executed at an increased speed when raising the processing volume of J_{n+1}. Set $\mathcal{J}''_{i_0}$ contains the jobs for which the speed can be increased. This split into two sets does not change the value of the potential function. A job of $\mathcal{J}_{i_0}$ whose execution starts, say, in interval $I_j = [\tau_j, \tau_{j+1})$ belongs to $\mathcal{J}'_{i_0}$ iff in the current schedule (a) no job $J_k \in \mathcal{J}_{i_0}$ with $d_k > \tau_j$ is processed before τ_j or (b) any job $J_k \in \mathcal{J}_{i_0}$ with $d_k > \tau_j$ that is also processed before τ_j is scheduled continuously without interruption throughout $[\tau_j, d_k)$. When the processing volume of J_{n+1} increases as described above, the jobs of $\mathcal{J}'_{i_0}$ remain at their speed level s_{i_0} while the speed of the jobs in $\mathcal{J}''_{i_0}$ increases.

At the end of a phase $\mathcal{J}_{i_0}$ might be merged with the next set $\mathcal{J}_{i_0-1}$. This event occurs if speed value s_{i_0} reaches the next higher level s_{i_0-1}. We always choose ϵ such that $(W_{OA(m)}(i_0) + \epsilon)/T_{i_0}$ does not exceed s_{i_0-1}. Again the merge of two job set does not change the value of the potential function.

THEOREM 2. *Algorithm OA(m) is α^α-competitive.*

3.2 Algorithm Average Rate

The original *Average Rate* algorithm for a single processor considers job densities, where the density δ_i of a job J_i is defined as $\delta_i = w_i/(d_i - r_i)$. At time t the processor speed s_t is set to the sum of the densities of the jobs active at time t. Using these speeds s_t, *AVR* always processes the job having the earliest deadline among the active unfinished jobs.

In the following we describe our algorithm, called *AVR(m)*, for m parallel processors. We assume without loss of generality that all release times and deadlines are integers. Moreover, we assume that the earliest release time $\min_{1 \le i \le n} r_i$ is equal to 0. Let $T = \max_{1 \le i \le n} d_i$ be the last deadline. For any time interval $I_t = [t, t+1)$, $0 \le t < T$, let $\mathcal{J}_t$ be the set of jobs J_i that are active in I_t, i.e. that satisfy $I_t \subseteq [r_i, d_i)$. Algorithm *AVR(m)* makes scheduling decisions for the intervals I_t over time, $0 \le t < T$. In each I_t the algorithm assigns the jobs of $\mathcal{J}_t$ to the m processors so as to approximately balance the job densities among the processors. To this end *AVR(m)* uses the idea of *Sorted List Scheduling*, known for makespan minimization on parallel machines [8]. More specifically, in any interval I_t, *AVR(m)* first sorts the jobs of $\mathcal{J}_t$ in order of non-increasing densities δ_i. Given this list L_t, the jobs are assigned one by one to the processors. Each job is placed on the processor having the smallest current *load* in I_t. At any point the load of a processor is the sum of the densities of the jobs assigned to the processor so far in I_t. When the assignment is finished, let $\mathcal{J}_{t,l}$ be the set of jobs placed on processor l, $1 \le l \le m$. In I_t the speed of processor l is set to $s_{t,l} = \sum_{J_i \in \mathcal{J}_{t,l}} \delta_i$. Each job $J_i \in \mathcal{J}_{t,l}$ is executed for $\delta_i/s_{t,l}$ time units on processor l in I_t. A summary of *AVR(m)* is given below.

It is easy to see that *AVR(m)* computes feasible schedules. In any interval I_t where a job J_i is active, $s_{t,l} \cdot \delta_i/s_{t,l} = \delta_i$ processing units of J_i are finished. Summing over all intervals where J_i is active, we obtain that exactly $\delta_i(d_i - r_i) = w_i$ processing units, i.e. the total work of J_i, are completed.

Algorithm AVR(m): In each interval I_t, $0 \le t < T$, execute the following steps.

(1) Construct a list L_t in which the jobs of $\mathcal{J}_t$ are sorted according to non-increasing job densities.

(2) Assign each job of L_t to the processor currently having the smallest load in I_t.

(3) Process each $J_i \in \mathcal{J}_{t,l}$ for $\delta_i/s_{t,l}$ time units using speed $s_{t,l} = \sum_{J_i \in \mathcal{J}_{t,l}} \delta_i$ on processor l, $1 \le l \le m$.

THEOREM 3. *AVR(m) achieves a competitive ratio of $(3\alpha)^\alpha/2 + 2^\alpha$.*

The proof is given in the full version of the paper.

4. REFERENCES

[1] S. Albers, F. Müller and S. Schmelzer. Speed scaling on parallel processors. *Proc. 19th ACM Symposium on Parallelism in Algorithms and Architectures*, 289–298, 2007.

[2] N. Bansal, D.P. Bunde, H.-L. Chan and K. Pruhs. Average rate speed scaling. *Proc. 8th Latin American Symposium on Theoretical Informatics*, Springer LNCS 4957, 240–251, 2008.

[3] N. Bansal, H.-L. Chan, T.-W. Lam and L.-K. Lee. Scheduling for speed bounded processors. *Proc. 35th International Colloqium on Automata, Languages and Programming (ICALP)*, Springer LNCS 5125, 409–420, 2008.

[4] N. Bansal, H.-L. Chan, K. Pruhs and D. Katz. Improved bounds for speed scaling in devices obeying the cube-root rule. *Proc. 36th International Colloqium on Automata, Languages and Programming*, Springer LNCS 5555, 144–155, 2009.

[5] N. Bansal, T. Kimbrel and K. Pruhs. Speed scaling to manage energy and temperature. *Journal of the ACM*, 54, 2007.

[6] B.D. Bingham and M.R. Greenstreet. Energy optimal scheduling on multiprocessors with migration. *Proc. IEEE International Symp. on Parallel and Distributed Processing with Applications*, 143–152, 2008.

[7] H.-L. Chan, W.-T. Chan, T.-W. Lam, L.-K. Lee, K.-S. Mak and P.W.H. Wong. Energy efficient online deadline scheduling. *Proc. 18th Annual ACM-SIAM Symposium on Discrete Algorithms*, 795–804, 2007.

[8] R.L. Graham. Bounds on multi-processing timing anomalies. *SIAM Journal on Applied Mathematics*, 17:416–429, 1969.

[9] G. Greiner, T. Nonner and A. Souza. The bell is ringing in speed-scaled multiprocessor scheduling. *Proc. 21st Annual ACM Symposium on Parallel Algorithms and Architectures*, 11–18, 2009.

[10] S. Irani, S.K. Shukla and R. Gupta. Algorithms for power savings. *ACM Transactions on Algorithms*, 3, 2007.

[11] T.-W. Lam, L.-K. Lee, I.K.-K. To and P.W.H. Wong. Energy efficient deadline scheduling in two processor systems. *Proc. 18th International Symposium on Algorithms and Computation*, Springer LNCS 4835, 476–487, 2007.

[12] M. Li, B.J. Liu and F.F. Yao. Min-energy voltage allocation for tree-structured tasks. *J. Comb. Optim.*, 11:305–319, 2006.

[13] M. Li, A.C. Yao and F.F. Yao. Discrete and continuous min-energy schedules for variable voltage processors. *Proc. National Academy of Sciences USA*, 103:3983–3987, 2006.

[14] M. Li and F.F. Yao. An efficient algorithm for computing optimal discrete voltage schedules. *SIAM Journal on Computing*, 35:658–671, 2005.

[15] D.D. Sleator and R.E. Tarjan. Amortized efficiency of list update and paging rules. *Communications of the ACM*, 28:202–208, 1985.

[16] F.F. Yao, A.J. Demers and S. Shenker. A scheduling model for reduced CPU energy. *Proc. 36th IEEE Symposium on Foundations of Computer Science*, 374–382, 1995.

On Scheduling in Map-Reduce and Flow-Shops

Benjamin Moseley*
University of Illinois
Urbana, IL
bmosele2@illinois.edu

Anirban Dasgupta   Ravi Kumar   Tamás Sarlós
Yahoo! Research
Sunnyvale, CA
{anirban,ravikumar,stamas}@yahoo-inc.com

ABSTRACT

The map-reduce paradigm is now standard in industry and academia for processing large-scale data. In this work, we formalize job scheduling in map-reduce as a novel generalization of the two-stage classical *flexible* flow shop (FFS) problem: instead of a single task at each stage, a job now consists of a set of tasks per stage. For this generalization, we consider the problem of minimizing the total *flowtime* and give an efficient 12-approximation in the offline setting and an online $(1 + \epsilon)$-speed $O(\frac{1}{\epsilon^2})$-competitive algorithm.

Motivated by map-reduce, we revisit the two-stage flow shop problem, where we give a dynamic program for minimizing the total *flowtime* when all jobs arrive at the same time. If there are fixed number of job-types the dynamic program yields a PTAS; it is also a QPTAS when the processing times of jobs are polynomially bounded. This gives the first improvement in approximation of flowtime for the two-stage flow shop problem since the trivial 2-approximation algorithm of Gonzalez and Sahni [29] in 1978, and the first known approximation for the FFS problem. We then consider the generalization of the two-stage FFS problem to the unrelated machines case, where we give an offline 6-approximation and an online $(1 + \epsilon)$-speed $O(\frac{1}{\epsilon^4})$-competitive algorithm.

Categories and Subject Descriptors

F.2.2 [**Analysis of Algorithms and Problem Complexity**]: Non-numerical Algorithms and Problems

General Terms

Algorithms, Theory

Keywords

Scheduling and resource allocation, Algorithm analysis, Approximation algorithms, On-line problems, Map-reduce, Flow-shops

1. INTRODUCTION

Map-reduce [9] has already established itself as the computing paradigm of choice to process massive data. The underlying idea

---

*Work done while visiting Yahoo! Labs. Partially supported by NSF grants CCF-0728782 and CCF-1016684.

in map-reduce is elegant. The input data is viewed as a stream of records comprising of key-value pairs. A map-reduce computation consists of a map phase, consisting of map tasks, followed by a reduce phase, consisting of reduce tasks. Each map task runs on a map machine and processes a portion of the input, outputting (possibly new) key-value pairs en route; the map tasks can be run in parallel. In the reduce phase, the key-value pairs output by the map machines are processed in parallel by reduce tasks, which run on the reduce machines, under the guarantee that all the records with the same key will be available together in one reduce machine. The reduce phase of a job therefore cannot begin until the map phase ends, i.e., all the map machines complete their work. Google's MapReduce and Apache Hadoop (hadoop.apache.org) are two existing implementations of map-reduce; both these implementations have useful enhancements such as job priorities, queues, batch processing, etc. The success of map-reduce as a parallel programming model can be attributed to its simplicity and its ability to hide low-level issues such as scheduling, failures, data locality, network bandwidth, and machine availability, from the end user.

Although map-reduce is a distributed computational model, the task-scheduling decisions are coordinated by a *centralized* job-tracker process that runs in a "master node." Designing new scheduling policies has been one of the active research topics in map-reduce because of the need to balance often contradictory needs, e.g., system utilization, fairness, and response times. There has been a great deal of empirical work demonstrating the value of a well-designed job-scheduling scheme in finding a good trade-off point among these different objectives [19, 34, 28, 35]. On the other hand, there has been very little work from a theoretical point of view. Wolf et al. [33] formalize the problem of allocation of slots among jobs by the Hadoop Fair scheduler (which is the default in many implementations), and present heuristic allocation schemes designed to optimize several scheduling metrics — these heuristics come with theoretical guarantees only in an idealized model that assumes infinitesimal task times, linear relation of processing times and allocated resources, no map-reduce dependencies, and one-shot allocation of resources. Fischer, Su, and Yin [11] show hardness results and present algorithms for the task-assignment problem with costs that reflect data locality. None of these papers presents theoretical guarantees for the underlying job-scheduling problem in terms of the commonly studied metrics in scheduling theory.

In this paper we study a scheduling model that captures the core challenges in map-reduce scheduling. The problem here is to assign jobs consisting of several map and reduce tasks to the available map and reduce machines in the best possible manner. However, it is tricky to adapt existing scheduling techniques to this setting due to the following non-negotiable reasons: (i) there are multiple map and reduce tasks in a job and multiple machines to which they can be assigned, (ii) map tasks have to be assigned to map machines and reduce tasks have to be assigned to reduce machines[1], (iii) no reduce task can be run before all map tasks from this job finish[2], (iv) the schedule can be preemptive but non-migratory, i.e., a task should be run on a single machine since it is wasteful to ship around partially processed data. It is also preferable to take data locality into account during the assignment of tasks to machines. Furthermore, both online and offline scenarios are relevant since map-reduce implementations typically permit batch as well online processing of jobs. Given that large map-reduce clusters are usually shared among several users, the most natural metric is to minimize the time between the arrival and the completion of a job, i.e., the *flowtime* [27].

Problem formulation. We formulate the problem of map-reduce scheduling by abstracting the above requirements and desiderata in scheduling terms. In particular, we focus on multiple-task multiple-machine two-stage non-migratory scheduling with precedence constraints; these constraints exist between each map task and reduce task for a job. This essentially captures the properties (i)–(iv) outlined above. We allow preemption in all our settings, unless noted, and focus on the objective of minimizing the total (equivalently, average) flowtime.

At a high-level, we consider two job scenarios, namely, the *offline* arrival of jobs and the *online* arrival. In the offline case, jobs arrive together; the algorithmic focus is on optimizing the approximation ratio. In the online case, jobs arrive over time and the scheduler makes decisions without knowing the jobs that are yet to arrive; the algorithmic focus is on optimizing the competitive ratio. Orthogonally, we consider two processing-time configurations. First, in the *identical machines* setting, all map machines have the same speed and all reduce machines have the same speed. Second, in the *unrelated machines* setting, the processing time for each task is a vector, specifying the task's running time on each of the machines; this is aimed at capturing the data locality desideratum. The unrelated machines model can also be used when different map machines have different amounts of memory and each task carries a minimum memory requirement to run. There is a large amount of literature on the unrelated machines model in scheduling theory and this is perhaps the most general machine model (see [14, 15, 4, 18, 32]).

Our results. Our main contribution is to model map-reduce scheduling as a generalization of the two-stage flexible flow-shop problem (FFS)[3]. The map-reduce scheduling problem generalizes FFS by having a *set* of map tasks per job that need to be scheduled on the map machines and a *set* of reduce tasks that are to be scheduled on the reduce machines. Our aim is to design schedules that minimize the total flowtime. Our main results are in the identical machines setting, where we obtain a 12-approximation algorithm

---

[1]This requirement does not follow immediately from the map-reduce programming model. However map and reduce tasks have typically different resource requirements and dividing a physical machine into multiple virtual map and reduce machines helps balance the load; Hadoop follows this model. Our results also extend to the case when a machine can execute both map and reduce tasks; see Section 3.

[2]We ignore in our model the data-aggregation (*shuffle*) phase of reduce that precedes the running of the user-code in reduce tasks, and can start before maps finish.

[3]In FFS each job consists of two tasks and the first task can be scheduled on a set of identical machines (say, map machines) and the second task can be scheduled on a different set of identical machines (say, reduce machines); the first task must be completed before the second can be started.

	Offline	Online
Map-reduce, Identical machines	NP-hard, 12-approx. (Corollary 3)	$\Omega(\min\{\log P, \log n/N\})$ [25], $(1+\epsilon)$-speed $O(\frac{1}{\epsilon^2})$-comp. (Corollary 8)
FFS, Unrelated machines	NP-hard, 6-approx. (Corollary 15)	unbounded [14], $(1+\epsilon)$-speed $O(\frac{1}{\epsilon^4})$-comp. (Corollary 20)

Table 1: Summary of results on minimizing total flow-time. P is the ratio of the largest task size to the smallest, N is the total number of machines, and n is the number of jobs. For the FFS identical machines case, we obtain a QPTAS for polynomial job sizes (Theorem 11) and a PTAS for fixed processing times (Theorem 12).

for the offline case and a $(1 + \epsilon)$-speed $O(1/\epsilon^2)$-competitive algorithm for the online case where $0 < \epsilon \leq 1$; the online result assumes resource augmentation [21], which is necessary to circumvent lower bounds. It is important to note that in the offline setting, we consider the case where all jobs arrive simultaneously; otherwise, if jobs arrive over time, a constant approximation cannot be achieved without resource augmentation [14].

Using the ideas developed for the identical machine case, we consider the unrelated machines case. However, it seems difficult to find good schedulers when there are multiple map and reduce tasks per job. In an effort to find such algorithms, we consider a natural generalization of FFS to the unrelated machines case while each job still has one map and one reduce task. We obtain a 6-approximation algorithm for the offline case and a $(1 + \epsilon)$-speed $O(1/\epsilon^5)$-competitive algorithm for the online case where $0 < \epsilon \leq 1$; these results can be found in Section 5.

The two-stage flow (not flexible) shop problem F1S is an important special case of FFS, where there is only one map machine and one reduce machine. F1S is known to be strongly NP-hard [13]. We give the *first* non-trivial approximation algorithm for F1S and FFS offline. Specifically, we give a quasi-polynomial time approximation scheme (QPTAS) when the largest job is polynomial-sized. Our algorithm is also a polynomial time approximation scheme (PTAS) in the case that there are a fixed number of processing times for each job. This is the only approximation algorithm known for FFS or F1S problems besides the trivial 2-approximation for F1S shown in [29] over three decades ago.

Related work. The two stage flexible flow shop problem (FFS) has been studied extensively; see [30, 23, 31, 16] for pointers to recent work. In the map-reduce case, on the other hand, we have multiple tasks per job per stage. We feel that beyond being practically important, the map-reduce scheduling problem is also a novel generalization of FFS that has not been previously studied.

Almost all previous work on FFS has focused on the case where all jobs arrive at the same time and the objective is to minimize the *maximum* completion time of any job. For this problem a PTAS was given in [16] for a fixed number of machines per stage and extended in [31] to a variable number of machines. Johnson's well-known algorithm [20] is also optimal for F1S when minimizing the maximum completion time. As mentioned, throughout this paper we focus on minimizing the *total flowtime*. Little is known about this objective for the FFS and F1S problems; there are no approximation algorithms known for FFS, while a trivial 2-approximation was shown for F1S [29]. It was suggested by Schuurman and Woeginger in the survey [31] that improving the 2-approximation for F1S is an important open question.

Most of the algorithmic work on map-reduce that has been done so far falls into one of the following three categories. The first is the development of computational models that faithfully capture the power and limitations of map-reduce, e.g., the work of Feldman et al. [10] and Karloff et al. [24]. The second is the development of map-reduce algorithms for several basic problems [24, 7]; problems such as MST, maximum cover, connectivity were shown to have efficient map-reduce algorithms. The third is the development of practical map-reduce-based heuristics to solve large-scale data problems, especially in text processing, graph analysis, and machine learning; see, for example, [22, 26, 8].

A critique. Since our goal is to provide a simple formalization of the scheduling problem in the map-reduce framework, we have deliberately ignored many issues in real systems that often have a large effect on the performance. We discuss some of these issues here. In the real system, intermediate data is transferred from the map machines to the reduce machines and thus the network bandwidth forms a significant bottleneck. Data locality — running the map tasks in the machines where data is located — is another important issue, as we mentioned earlier. Instead of modeling processing times as function of the network topology, we chose to model the effect of locality by the rather stylized unrelated machine setting. We also do not model task and machine failures, another important topic. In the map-reduce setting the dependence between map and reduce-tasks is more subtle than what we have described here due to the presence of the intermediate shuffle phase, which happens in parallel with the map tasks. We assume preemption, which is not yet a feature in Hadoop; interestingly, it is not hard to show that an online algorithm will have a large competitive ratio if preemption is not allowed without resource augmentation. Finally, we assume that the scheduler is aware of the job sizes. These may not be immediately available in practice, but in nearly all circumstances approximate job sizes can be determined based on historical data [12, 33].

2. PRELIMINARIES

Job and task. A *job* consists of sets of *tasks*, where tasks in a set can be run in parallel, but the sets themselves have to be run sequentially. In the map-reduce setting, we assume that each job has two sets of tasks, namely, a set of *map* tasks and a set of *reduce* tasks, where no reduce task can be started until all map tasks for the job are completed. Thus, the scheduling problem is precedence-constrained.

Let $\mathcal{J}$ be the set of jobs and let $J \in \mathcal{J}$ denote a generic job. Let $\{J_i^m\}$ and $\{J_i^r\}$ be the set of map and reduce tasks of J, respectively. When both these sets are singletons, we call this the *single task* case; otherwise, it is the *multiple task* case. Let the function $p(\cdot)$ be the *processing time* of a job or a task. In the case where the processing time depends on the machine assignment, let $p_x(\cdot)$ be the processing time of a job or a task on machine x. If a machine runs a task J at speed s, then it needs $p(J)/s$ time to complete the task; unless otherwise noted, we assume all machines run at unit speed. We also assume that the processing times of the tasks are known to the algorithms.

To avoid being repetitive, throughout the paper, let $b \in \{m, r\}$; this will be used to capture both map- and reduce-related statements for both machines and tasks, i.e., when b is used, it is fixed to either m or r. Let $J^{b,*} = \arg\max_i p(J_i^b)$ be the task with the maximum processing time in a set of tasks and let $J^* = \arg\max\{p(J^{m,*}), p(J^{r,*})\}$ be the task with the maximum processing time. Let a_J be the arrival time of job J.

Schedule. Let σ be a schedule of jobs. Given σ, for any job or task, let the function $\mathsf{s}_\sigma(\cdot)$ denote its starting time and the function $\mathsf{f}_\sigma(\cdot)$ denote its completion time, both with respect to the schedule σ. We also define $\mathsf{s}_\sigma^b(J) = \min_i \mathsf{s}_\sigma(J_i^b)$ and $\mathsf{f}_\sigma^b(J) = \max_i \mathsf{f}(J_i^b)$, the starting and finishing times for a set of tasks; thus, $\mathsf{s}_\sigma(J) = \mathsf{s}_\sigma^m(J)$, $\mathsf{f}_\sigma(J) = \mathsf{f}_\sigma^r(J)$. Let N_m be the number of map machines, i.e., machines on which map tasks can be run and let N_r be the number of reduce machines, i.e., machines on which reduce tasks can be run. A schedule σ is called *viable* if for each job J: (i) all map tasks of J are scheduled only on the map machines, (ii) all reduce tasks of J are scheduled only on the reduce machines, (iii) every reduce task for job J is scheduled only after all map tasks for job J are completed, i.e., $\mathsf{f}_\sigma^m(J) \leq \mathsf{s}_\sigma^r(J)$. A schedule σ is called *non-migratory* if each task is run only on one machine.

The *flowtime* of a job J with respect to a schedule σ is $\mathtt{flow}_\sigma(J) = \mathsf{f}_\sigma(J) - a_J$; let $\mathtt{flow}_\sigma = \sum_J \mathtt{flow}_\sigma(J)$ be the total flowtime. The total *completion time* of a schedule σ is $\sum_J \mathsf{f}_\sigma(J)$. When all jobs arrive at time 0, completion time is the same as flowtime. We will consider two different scheduling metrics: minimizing the total flowtime (equivalently, the average flowtime) and minimizing the total completion time. For a time interval I, let $|I|$ denote its length.

3. MAP-REDUCE: IDENTICAL MACHINES CASE

Consider the map-reduce scheduling problem when all the map machines are identical, all the reduce machines are identical, and each job can have multiple map tasks and multiple reduce tasks. We will construct the map-reduce schedule out of two individual schedules for the map and the reduce tasks. Let σ_m denote some schedule on a single map machine of speed N_m for just the map tasks. Likewise, ignoring the precedence constraints between map and reduce, let σ_r denote some schedule for all the reduce tasks on a single reduce machine of speed N_r.

3.1 Offline scheduling

We first construct a non-migratory schedule σ for the offline setting where all jobs arrive at time 0. Our goal is to reduce the precedence constrained map-reduce scheduling problem to simpler scheduling problems. To do this, we will use σ_m and σ_r to assign priorities to tasks and construct the final schedule σ using these priorities.

THEOREM 1. *Given schedules σ_m and σ_r, there is a viable non-migratory schedule σ such that for all job J it holds that $\mathsf{f}_\sigma(J) \leq 4 \max\{\mathsf{f}_{\sigma_m}^m(J), \mathsf{f}_{\sigma_r}^r(J), p(J^*)\}$.*

PROOF. We now describe the algorithm to construct σ. Define w_J, the *width* of job J, as the maximum of map and reduce finish times of the job and the maximum task length, i.e., $w_J = \max\{\mathsf{f}_{\sigma_m}^m(J), \mathsf{f}_{\sigma_r}^r(J), p(J^*)\}$. Note that while width incorporates the maximum flowtime that J incurs in σ_r or σ_m, it also incorporates the processing time of the largest task of job J; this will later be used to ensure that a unit speed scheduler can finish the largest task of J in time w_J. The width of a job is its priority and a smaller width means higher priority.

We first show a generic bound on the finish time of the task in terms of when it is available for scheduling and its width. Let $\mathsf{a}_\sigma(J_i^b)$ be the earliest time that task J_i^b is available to schedule by our algorithm. As we will see later, if $b = m$, then $\mathsf{a}_\sigma(J_i^b) = 0$ and if $b = r$, then the task will be available at time $2w_J$.

```
Algorithm: Offline Schedule
Simulate the schedules σ_m on single N_m-speed and σ_r on a
single N_r-speed machine respectively
w_J ← max{f^m_{σ_m}(J), f^r_{σ_r}(J), p(J*)}
for each job J by w_J increasing do
    for each map task J^m_i of job J do
        Assign J^m_i to the least loaded map machine
    end for
    for each reduce task J^r_i of job J do
        Let x be the earliest available reduce machine
        if x is available before time w_J then
            Idle x till time 2w_J
        end if
        Assign J^r_i to x
    end for
end for
```

LEMMA 2. *For any task J^b_i, it is the case that $f_\sigma(J^b_i) \leq a_\sigma(J^b_i) + 2w_J$.*

PROOF. Assume that the statement is false and consider a task J^b_i where $f_\sigma(J^b_i) > a_\sigma(J^b_i) + 2w_J$. By definition, this task was available from time $a_\sigma(J^b_i)$ and the hence schedule σ must have been working on tasks with width at most w_J in the time interval $[a_\sigma(J^b_i), f_\sigma(J^b_i) - p(J*)]$. By definition of width and the assumption, we know $f_\sigma(J^b_i) - p(J*) - a_\sigma(J^b_i) > 2w_J - p(J*) \geq w_J$. Note that also by definition, σ uses N_b machines for this interval and is busy. Therefore, the above tasks that have width at most w_J represent strictly more than $N_b \cdot w_J$ volume of work. However, the width of a job is at least the completion time of the job in σ_b. This implies that σ_b must complete strictly more than a $N_b \cdot w_J$ volume of work by time w_J. But this is a contradiction since σ_b has a single machine of speed N_b. □

To schedule the map tasks, the algorithm runs the N_m map tasks with the smallest width across the identical machines, breaking ties arbitrarily but consistently. Notice that any map task is scheduled on a single machine since no task will be preempted. Furthermore, map tasks are scheduled only on map machines. By setting $a_\sigma(J^m_i) = 0$ for all tasks, Lemma 2 yields $f_\sigma(J^m_i) \leq 2w_J$. Scheduling reduce tasks is less obvious since we have to ensure that each reduce task is processed by only one machine. Consider a reduce task J^r_i. Our algorithm will not consider scheduling this task until time $2w_J$. The algorithm then runs the set of at most N_r reduce tasks that are available to schedule with minimum width. By Lemma 2, it must be the case that all map tasks for a job J are finished by time $2w_J$. Hence, the reduce tasks of a job are scheduled after the map tasks. Further, by definition of this algorithm, after time $2w_J$ the only reduce tasks that become available to schedule have width greater than w_J. This implies that the algorithm will never preempt a reduce task. Thus this schedule assigns each reduce task to only one machine. By once again appealing to Lemma 2 with $a_\sigma(J^r_i) = 2w_J$ yields $f_\sigma(J^r_i) \leq 4w_J$. Combining the bounds completes the proof.

We now show an application of the theorem.

COROLLARY 3. *There exists a non-migratory 12-approximation algorithm for flowtime (completion time) in the offline, identical machines, multiple task, map-reduce setting.*

PROOF. It is known that the algorithm Shortest Remaining Processing Time (SRPT) is optimal for average flowtime on a

single machine where there is one task per job and no precedence constraints. Knowing that on a single machine having more than one task per job is irrelevant, we can use SRPT to generate the two schedules σ_m and σ_r. Let $\texttt{flow}_{\sigma_m}$ denote SRPT's flowtime for the schedule σ_m and let $\texttt{flow}_{\sigma_r}$ denote SRPT's flowtime for the schedule σ_r. Let OPT be the optimal schedule. Notice that $\texttt{flow}_{\text{OPT}} \geq \max\{\texttt{flow}_{\sigma_m}, \texttt{flow}_{\sigma_r}\}$ and that $\texttt{flow}_{\text{OPT}} \geq \sum_J p(J*)$. Theorem 1 implies that $\texttt{flow}_\sigma \leq 4(\texttt{flow}_{\sigma_m} + \texttt{flow}_{\sigma_r} + \sum_J p(J*)) \leq 12\texttt{flow}_{\text{OPT}}$. □

This analysis can be extended to the case when map and reduce machines are indistinguishable.

COROLLARY 4. *There exists a non-migratory 12-approximation algorithm for total flowtime (completion time) in the offline, identical machines, multiple task, map-reduce setting when tasks can be assigned to any machine.*

3.2 Online scheduling

In this section, we consider a similar scheduling instance as in Section 3.1 except, now jobs can arrive over time and the scheduler must be online. Consider a fixed sequence of jobs. As before, our plan is to construct a schedule σ by using σ_m and σ_r, which are schedules of the map and reduce tasks on N_m and N_r machines respectively.

In the online scheduling case, when there are no precedence constraints (no map-reduce phases), there are N identical machines, each of the n jobs has only one task, and the ratio of the maximum job size to the minimum job size is P, it is known that there is an $\Omega(\min\{\log P, \log n/N\})$ lower bound on the competitive ratio for flowtime [25]. Our scheduling model strictly generalizes this setting, therefore this is also a lower bound on flowtime in our setting. Thus, for an algorithm to be $O(1)$-competitive, *resource augmentation* [21] is necessary. I.e., we assume that the schedule σ is given N_m map machines each of speed $(1 + \epsilon)$ and N_r reduce machine each of speed $(1 + \epsilon)$ where $0 < \epsilon \leq 1$.

THEOREM 5. *Given online schedules σ_r and σ_m, there is a viable online non-migratory $(1 + \epsilon)$-resource augmented schedule σ such that $f_\sigma(J) \leq a_J + \frac{128}{\epsilon^2} \max\{(\max\{f^m_{\sigma_m}(J), f^r_{\sigma_r}(J)\} - a_J), p(J*)\}$.*

To construct the schedule σ, we will use the following algorithm, which employs ideas from [3, 2, 6, 5]. The algorithm simulates the schedules σ_m and σ_r, but needs to be more sophisticated than the offline case, since online load balancing between the machines will be necessary. For a job J, we will define its *width* to be $w_J = \max\{(\max\{f^m_{\sigma_m}(J), f^r_{\sigma_r}(J)\} - a_J), p(J*)\}$. Our algorithm will group tasks according to their width. A job J together with its tasks is said to be in *class* k if $w_J \in [2^k, 2^{k+1})$. The algorithm will maintain the total processing time (volume) of map jobs assigned to a map machine x for each class k. Let $U^{m,x}_{=k}(t)$ denote the total processing time of tasks in class k assigned to map machine x by time t. Likewise, let $U^{r,x}_{=k}(t)$ denote the total processing time of tasks in class k assigned to reduce machine x by time t.

The idea behind the algorithm is to use the schedules σ_r and σ_m to give priorities to the jobs, where the priority of a job is captured by its width. We group tasks geometrically according to their width to balance the volume of work for a specific width across the machines. Notice that the assignment is not based on the current volume of unfinished work, but is based on the total volume of jobs that were assigned to machines up until now. This algorithm is online if σ_m and σ_r are online, since no task for some job J is scheduled by the algorithm unless all tasks for job J are

Algorithm: Online Schedule(t)

Simulate the schedules σ_m and σ_r

if time t is the first time all map tasks for job J are finished in σ_m and all reduce tasks for job J are finished in σ_r **then**

Let k be J's class

for each map task J_i^m of job J **do**

Assign J_i^m to the map machine x where $U_{=k}^{m,x}(t) = \min_y U_{=k}^{m,y}(t)$

$U_{=k}^{m,x}(t) \leftarrow U_{=k}^{m,x}(t) + p(J_i^m)$

end for

end if

if time t is the first time that all map tasks for job J are finished in the new schedule σ **then**

Let k be J's class

for each reduce task J_i^r of job J **do**

Assign J_i^r to the reduce machine x where $U_{=k}^{r,x}(t) = \min_y U_{=k}^{r,y}(t)$

$U_{=k}^{r,x}(t) \leftarrow U_{=k}^{r,x}(t) + p(J_i^r)$

end for

end if

On each map and reduce machine run the task assigned to that machine such that the job associated with the task has minimum width.

---

completed in σ_m and σ_r. It can also been seen that the algorithm is non-migratory, since each task is assigned to a single machine, and viable. Thus, we only need to show the guarantee on the job completion time.

Before we begin the analysis, we will introduce a fair bit of notation. As before, let $b \in \{m, r\}$. Since we deal with viable schedules, when we mean machine or task, it will be clear from the context if it is map-related or reduce-related. For each time t, a machine x, and class k we define several quantities. The notation "$\leq k$" will indicate classes 1 to k. Thus, $U_{\leq k}^{b,x}(t)$ is the total volume of tasks in classes 1 to k assigned to machine x. Let $R_{=k}^{b,x}(t)$ denote the remaining processing time of tasks in class k on machine x. Let $P_{=k}^{b,x}(t)$ denote the total volume of tasks in class k machine x has processed up to time t. It can be noted that $P_{=k}^{b,x}(t) = U_{=k}^{b,x}(t) - R_{=k}^{b,x}(t)$. Each of the previously discussed quantities refers to our algorithm. Let $V_{=k}^{*b}(t)$ be the total remaining volume of unsatisfied tasks in class k in the optimal solution's schedule at time t. Let $V_{=k}^{b}(t) = \sum_x R_{=k}^{b,x}(t)$ be the total remaining volume of tasks in class k in our algorithm solution's schedule at time t. We now state some basic facts about these quantities, which will be used to show that our algorithm properly load balanced jobs in each class; the proofs are an extension of those in [2, 6].

LEMMA 6. *At any time t and any two machines x and y, we have the following: (i) $|U_{=k}^{b,x}(t) - U_{=k}^{b,y}(t)| \leq 2^{k+1}$ and $|U_{\leq k}^{b,x}(t) - U_{\leq k}^{b,y}(t)| \leq 2^{k+2}$; (ii) $|P_{\leq k}^{b,x}(t) - P_{\leq k}^{b,y}(t)| \leq 2^{k+2}$; and (iii) $|R_{\leq k}^{b,x}(t) - R_{\leq k}^{b,y}(t)| \leq 2^{k+3}$.*

PROOF. (i) The first inequality is true because the size of a task that belongs to some job J has processing at most $w_J \leq 2^{k+1}$. The second inequality is immediate given the first.

(ii) For the sake of contradiction assume the statement is false. Let t_0 be the first time when $|P_{\leq k}^{m,x}(t_0) - P_{\leq k}^{m,y}(t_0)| = 2^{k+2}$ and a small constant δ such that $|P_{\leq k}^{m,x}(t_0+\delta) - P_{\leq k}^{m,y}(t_0+\delta)| > 2^{k+2}$. This can only occur if machine x processes a task of class $\leq k$ during $I = [t_0, t_0 + \delta]$ while y processes some task of class $> k$. Knowing that each machine always processes the task of minimum

width, the machine y must have no tasks in class $\leq k$ during I. This shows that $U_{\leq k}^{m,y}(t_0+\delta) = P^{m,y}(t_0+\delta)$. Thus we have,

$$U_{\leq k}^{m,y}(t_0+\delta) = P^{m,y}(t_0+\delta)$$
$$< P^{m,x}(t_0+\delta) - 2^{k+2} \leq U_{\leq k}^{m,x}(t_0+\delta) - 2^{k+2},$$

knowing that $P_{\leq k}^{m,x}(t_0+\delta) \leq U_{\leq k}^{m,x}(t_0+\delta)$. However, then we have that $U_{\leq k}^{m,y}(t_0+\delta) < U_{\leq k}^{m,x}(t_0+\delta) - 2^{k+2}$, but this is a contradiction to (i). The proof is similar for any two reduce machines. (iii) We know that $R(t) = U(t) - P(t)$. Combining this with (ii), we have that

$$|R_{\leq k}^{m,x}(t) - R_{\leq k}^{m,y}(t)|$$
$$\leq |U_{\leq k}^{m,x}(t) - U_{\leq k}^{m,y}(t)| + |P_{\leq k}^{m,x}(t) - P_{\leq k}^{m,y}(t)|$$
$$\leq 2 \cdot 2^{k+2} = 2^{k+3}.$$

The proof is similar for a reduce machine. □

The remainder of the analysis differs from [2, 6]. We first concentrate on showing that each task for each job J is not completed too long after $a_J + w_J$. To do this, our analysis will use the fact that our algorithm is given resource augmentation over the schedules σ_b. We now prove a generic bound on the time gap between the dispatching of a task by our algorithm and its completion. Fix k to be some class and fix $b \in \{m, r\}$. Let job J be the job in class k such that $f_\sigma^b(J) - a_J$ is maximized. Let task J_i^b be the task for job J that was finished last by our algorithm and let machine x be the machine to which the task J_i^b was assigned. Let the time t_b be the last time before time $f_\sigma^b(J)$ that our algorithm processed a task of class greater than k on machine x; this implies that machine x is busy processing tasks of class $\leq k$ during $[t_b, f_\sigma^b(J))$.

LEMMA 7. *For any job J that is in some class k and arrived after time $t_b - \beta_J$, it is the case that $f_\sigma^b(J) - t_b \leq (2^{k+4} + \beta_J)/\epsilon$ and therefore $(f_\sigma^b(J) - a_J) \leq (2^{k+4} + \beta_J)/\epsilon$, where $\beta_J > 0$.*

PROOF. By definition of our algorithm, machine x processes a total volume of $(1+\epsilon)(f_\sigma^b(J) - t_b)$ of work on tasks of class $\leq k$ during $[t_b, f_\sigma^b(J))$. This and Lemma 6(ii) show that any other machine y also processes a volume of $(1+\epsilon)(f_\sigma^b(J) - t_b) - 2^{k+3}$ on tasks of class $\leq k$ during $[t_b, f_\sigma^b(J))$. Further, by definition of time t_b and our algorithm, the machine x has no tasks of class $\leq k$ at time t_b. Thus by Lemma 6(iii) for any machine y we have that $R_{\leq k}^{b,y} \leq 2^{k+3}$. Together this shows that the total volume processed by our algorithm on machines during $[t_b, f_\sigma^b(J))$ of jobs of class $\leq k$ that were dispatched to machines *after* time t_b is at most $N_b(1+\epsilon)(f_\sigma^b(J) - t_b) - N_b 2^{k+4}$.

Note that our algorithm does not process any task until the schedule σ_b completes the task. Thus the schedule σ_b must process this volume of work during the interval $[t_b - \beta_J, f_\sigma^b(J)]$. This implies that $N_b(1+\epsilon)(f_\sigma^b(J) - t_b) - N_b 2^{k+4} \leq N_b(f_\sigma^b(J) - t_b + \beta_J)$, since the schedule σ_b has a single machine of speed N_b. However, this implies that $\epsilon(f_\sigma^b(J) - t_b) \leq 2^{k+4} + \beta_J$, completing the proof. □

Now we apply Lemma 7 to the map tasks and show that our algorithm completes all map tasks in a relatively short amount of time when compared to σ_m. To do this, recall that a map task associated with some job J is dispatched by our algorithm by time $a_J + w_J$. For this case, set $b = m$. The definition of t_m implies $a_J + w_J \geq t_m$. It must be the case that job J arrived after time $t_m - 2^{k+1}$ since the job is of class $\leq k$ and therefore has width $\leq 2^{k+1}$. Hence, Lemma 7 with $\beta_J = 2^{k+1}$ yields that $(f_\sigma^m(J) - a_J) \leq 2^{k+5}/\epsilon \leq (32/\epsilon)w_J$.

Next, we would like to to show the same thing about reduce tasks. First set $b = r$. Recall the reduce task is dispatched by our algorithm at time $f_\sigma^m(J)$, the time that all map tasks of J are completed. From the above argument we have $(f_\sigma^m(J) - a_J) \leq (32/\epsilon)w_J \leq 2^{k+6}/\epsilon$. Thus $a_J \geq f_\sigma^m(J) - 2^{k+6}/\epsilon \geq t_r - 2^{k+6}/\epsilon$. Appealing to Lemma 7 with $\beta_J = 2^{k+6}/\epsilon$ yields $(f_\sigma^r(J) - a_J) \leq \frac{2^{k+4} + 2^{k+6}/\epsilon}{\epsilon} \leq 2^{k+7}/\epsilon^2 \leq (128/\epsilon^2)w_J$. This completes the proof of Theorem 5.

3.2.1 An application of Theorem 5

Using SRPT to generate the schedules σ_m and σ_r we can show the following.

COROLLARY 8. *There exists a non-migratory $(1 + \epsilon)$-speed $O(\frac{1}{\epsilon^2})$-competitive algorithm for average flowtime in the online, identical machines, multiple task, map-reduce setting where $0 < \epsilon \leq 1$.*

PROOF. It is well know that the online algorithm SRPT is optimal for average flowtime in a standard scheduling instance when there is a single machine. We use SRPT to generate the two schedules σ_m and σ_r. The rest of the proof follows from Theorem 5 and the proof of Corollary 3. □

Considering a simple extension of the previous analysis gives a scheduler that is competitive with resource augmentation when there is no separation between map and reduce machines. When considering this setting, simple extensions of the previous analysis lose a factor of 2 in this speed. This is because it is difficult for the scheduler to decide how to prioritize between map and reduce tasks on a single machine.

REMARK 1. *There exists a non-migratory $(2 + \epsilon)$-speed $O(\frac{1}{\epsilon^2})$-competitive algorithm for average flowtime in the online, identical machines, multiple task, map-reduce setting when tasks can be scheduled on any machine where $0 < \epsilon \leq 1$.*

Chekuri et al. [5] introduce another model of resource augmentation where the online algorithm is provided with $(1 + \epsilon)$ as many 1-speed machines. It is not hard to see that section's results hold in this setting as well.

4. FLOW SHOP: PTAS AND QPTAS

In the section we describe our approximation scheme when each job consists of one map task and one reduce task. For the ease of presentation, we assume that there is only one map machine and only one reduce machine; later, we will show how to extend this to the multiple machine case. Our dynamic programming algorithm and proof follow the ideas presented in [1]. We begin by assuming that the processing time of a task is polynomially bounded and we give a quasi-PTAS in this case; this problem is NP-hard even under this assumption [13]. The analysis extends to the case where there is a fixed number of jobs types; our algorithm yields a PTAS in this case. Since there is only one map and one reduce task per job, we let J^b denote job J's map or reduce task, where $b \in \{m, r\}$. We assume preemption is not allowed and unlike the other offline settings we consider, we will allow jobs to arrive over time, but we focus on the objective of total *completion time*. Recall that this is the same as flowtime if jobs arrive at time 0.

The approximation schema that we present is a dynamic program. We first apply a number of structural modifications to the input — these are all inspired by [1], where they have shown to be useful in the problem instance before applying a dynamic program.

The core intuition in the design of the dynamic program is the use of Johnson's celebrated algorithm [20] that optimizes makespan as a subroutine to verify feasibility.

Structural modifications. In this section we give an informal description of the various structural modifications applied to the problem in preprocessing. Appendix A outlines the formal lemma statements and proofs corresponding to these modifications.

Let $0 < \epsilon \leq 1/2$. For an arbitrary integer x, define $R_x = (1+\epsilon)^x$. We partition the time interval $(0, \infty)$ into disjoint intervals of the form $I_x = [R_x, R_{x+1})$; we will use I_x to refer to both the interval and the size, $R_{x+1} - R_x$, of the interval. We will often use the fact that $I_x = \epsilon R_x$, i.e., the length of the interval is ϵ times its start time.

We apply the preprocessing in a number of steps, while causing only a $(1+\epsilon)$ factor loss to the optimal value for each step. Each arrival time is rounded to be of the form R_x for some x (Lemma 21). Each task processing time is also rounded to be a power of $(1 + \epsilon)$ (Lemma 21). With another $(1 + \epsilon)$ factor loss (Lemma 22), we ensure that the task J^m is not started before $a_J + \epsilon p(J^m)$, and task J^r before $\max(f^m(J^m), \epsilon p(J^r))$. As a result of these modifications, Lemma 24 shows that no task crosses too many intervals. We define time to be stretched by a factor of $1 + \epsilon$ when we multiply each interval endpoint by a factor of $1 + \epsilon$; this again causes the OPT to degrade by another factor of at most $1 + \epsilon$.

We say that a job with its map task running in interval I_J^m and reduce task in interval I_J^r is *small* if $p(J^m) \leq \epsilon I_J^m$ and $\max(p(J^m), p(J^r)) \leq \epsilon I_J^r$. Otherwise the task is large. If a task has a processing time $(1 + \epsilon)^x$ we say it is of type x. We call a job J to be of type (x, y) if J^m is of type x and J^r is of type y. Sets of jobs are denoted as vectors, e.g., a vector $\mathbf{s}$ of counts s_{xy} corresponding to each of the types (x, y). For any two sequences $\mathbf{a}$ and $\mathbf{b}$, define $\mathbf{a} \preceq \mathbf{b}$ if $a_{xy} \leq b_{xy}$ for all (x, y). All sequences $\mathbf{s}$ that we consider will satisfy $\mathbf{0} \preceq \mathbf{s}$.

Algorithm. Our algorithm is a dynamic program that creates the schedule interval-wise. The crucial observation is that given a set of map-reduce tasks, we can test the feasibility of scheduling these jobs in an interval by using Johnson's algorithm [20] for minimizing makespan in a two-stage two-machine flowshop. Our algorithm also guesses the last $\frac{25}{\epsilon^{10}}$ tasks that will be completed in the optimal schedule and does not consider these tasks in the dynamic program.

At time R_t, let $\mathbf{n}$ be the set of all jobs that have arrived up until now and let $\mathbf{c}$ denote the set of completed jobs. Define a job to be *partially done* if the map task is completed. Let $\mathbf{p}$ denote the set of partially done jobs at R_t. The dynamic program at iteration t will select a set of tasks to be scheduled in some interval I_{t+1}. This set could consist of both the tasks of a job, only the map task of a job, or a reduce task whose corresponding map task has been completed. If a reduce task is scheduled in an interval and the map task for this job was scheduled in an earlier interval, we will implicitly incorporate a map task of length zero to precede this reduce. We now describe the algorithm.

(1) Assume the arrival time of each job to be $\max(a_J, \frac{p(J^m)}{\epsilon^2})$. Also assume that the reduce task of J is not available before $p(J^r)/\epsilon^2$ (and of course, before completing the corresponding map task).

(2) If $\mathbf{n}$ jobs have arrived up until time interval I_t, define $C[\mathbf{c}, \mathbf{p}, \mathbf{n}, t]$ be the total completion time when scheduling all tasks in $\mathbf{c}$ completely and just the map tasks for jobs in $\mathbf{p} - \mathbf{c}$ during $[0, R_{t+1})$. Since the tasks in $\mathbf{p} - \mathbf{c}$ are not completed, we do not include their completion time in the total. If $\mathbf{n}$ does not correspond to the number of arrived jobs, or if $\mathbf{c} \preceq \mathbf{p} \preceq \mathbf{n}$ is not satisfied, then

$C[\mathbf{c}, \mathbf{p}, \mathbf{n}, t] = \infty$. We also define $C[\mathbf{0}, \mathbf{0}, \mathbf{0}, -1] = 0$. We use the following dynamic program for all but the last $\frac{25}{\epsilon^{10}}$ that we guessed.

(3) Suppose $I_{t+1} = [R_{t+1}, R_{t+2})$ be the current interval. Let $\mathbf{v}$ be the sequence of new jobs that arrive at the beginning of this interval. Let $\mathbf{q}, \mathbf{m}$, and $\mathbf{r}$ be such that $\mathbf{m} + \mathbf{q} \preceq \mathbf{n} + \mathbf{v} - \mathbf{p}$ and $\mathbf{r} \preceq \mathbf{p} - \mathbf{c}$. Intuitively, $\mathbf{q}$ denotes the set of jobs for which we are going to schedule both the map and reduce tasks in I_{t+1}, $\mathbf{m}$ the set of jobs for which we are going to schedule only the map task, and $\mathbf{r}$ the set of jobs for which we schedule only the reduce. Given these sets our algorithm would like to schedule the tasks in $\mathbf{q} + \mathbf{m} + \mathbf{r}$ during the interval I_{t+1}. We verify the feasibility of this schedule using Johnson's algorithm [20] for optimal makespan in two-stage two machine setting. Define the scheduling cost for this interval to be $Q(\mathbf{q}, \mathbf{m}, \mathbf{r}, I_{t+1}) = R_{t+2} \sum_{ij}(q_{ij} + r_{ij})$ if Johnson's algorithm returns a feasible schedule and $Q(\mathbf{q}, \mathbf{m}, \mathbf{r}, I_{t+1}) = \infty$ else. Notice that this cost function assumes that completion time of the jobs scheduled in interval I_{t+1} is R_{t+2}. This is because each task completed during I_{t+1} is finished before time R_{t+2}. We justify this in the analysis by showing that this increases the schedule's cost by at most a $(1 + \epsilon)$ factor. Thus, the dynamic program computes

$$C[\mathbf{c}, \mathbf{p}, \mathbf{n} + \mathbf{v}, t + 1] =$$
$$\min_{\mathbf{q}, \mathbf{m}, \mathbf{r}} C[\mathbf{c} - \mathbf{q} - \mathbf{r}, \mathbf{p} - \mathbf{m} - \mathbf{q} - \mathbf{r}, \mathbf{n}, t] + Q(\mathbf{q}, \mathbf{m}, \mathbf{r}, I_{t+1}).$$

(4) After all jobs are scheduled using the dynamic program, enumerate the possible ways to finish the final $\frac{25}{\epsilon^{10}}$ jobs that were guessed.

Let $P = \max_J p(J^*)$ be the processing time of the largest task and $T = \sum_J p(J^m) + p(J^r)$ be an upper-bound on the schedule length. The time taken by the above procedure is given by $n^{O(\log_{1+\epsilon}(P))} \log T$ for fixed ϵ. As a first step in establishing our claims, we motivate our algorithm with the following lemma whose proof follows the proof of Lemma 3.1 in [1].

LEMMA 9. *If in the optimal solution, all jobs are small, then the above algorithm gives a $(1 + 3\epsilon)$-approximate solution.*

PROOF. Let $R(I)$ denote the starting point of interval I. If the jobs are small in the optimal solution, then from Lemma 22 it follows that $s_*^m(J) \geq R(I_J^m) = \frac{I_J^m}{\epsilon} \geq p(J^m)/\epsilon^2$. Also, similarly, $s_*^r(J) \geq R(I_J^r) \geq p(J^r)/\epsilon^2$. Hence, changing the arrival times does not matter for the optimal solution. Also, since each job is small for the interval, by stretching each interval by a factor of $(1 + \epsilon)$ we ensure that all jobs finish completely inside their interval (Lemma 25). Given this condition, we first claim that the dynamic program computes a $(1 + \epsilon)$ approximation to the optimal solution. Consider the $C[\mathbf{c}, \mathbf{p}, \mathbf{m}, \mathbf{n}, t - 1]$ that corresponds to the optimal algorithm's choice of $\mathbf{c}, \mathbf{p}, \mathbf{m}$ up until interval I_{t-1} — by inductive hypothesis this is a $1 + \epsilon$ approximation. If the optimal solution chooses the task sets from the jobs in $\mathbf{q}^* + \mathbf{m}^* + \mathbf{r}^*$ to schedule in this interval $I_t = [R_t, R_{t+1})$, then it incurs at least $R_t \sum_{ij}(q_{ij}^* + r_{ij}^*)$. By looking at all possible assignments, our algorithm makes a choice such that the resulting minimum value of C is at most $(1 + \epsilon)$ of the value incurred by the OPT at the end of I_t. This is because Johnson's algorithm ensures that the tasks are scheduled within the interval I_t. Further, a task's completion time is at most R_{t+1} if the task was scheduled during I_t. Hence at the end of the dynamic program, we still have a $(1+\epsilon)$ approximation.

Since stretching the time by a factor of $(1 + \epsilon)$ increases the total completion time by the same factor, and we pay another $(1 + \epsilon)$ in the dynamic program. Overall we have a $(1 + 3\epsilon)$ factor approximation. $\square$

Let $t_h = 2\epsilon^{10}$OPT be a threshold time. Notice that in the optimal solution there are at most $\frac{1}{2\epsilon^{10}}$ jobs that are completed after time t_h. The goal of the next lemma is to show that large jobs can be postponed. To do this, we show that there is an approximate optimal solution where either a job is small or it is done after time t_h. To prove the lemma, we consider shifting large jobs in the optimal solution to intervals where the jobs are small. We create room for these jobs by expanding the interval lengths by a factor of $(1 + O(\epsilon))$. We also show that shifting the large jobs does not effect the value of the optimal solution by more than a factor of $(1 + O(\epsilon))$. The proof of the lemma is quite technical since we have to be careful on how map and reduce tasks for the same job are shifted.

LEMMA 10. *There exists a $(1 + 13\epsilon)$-approximate optimal schedule in which, for each job J, $s_*^m(J) \geq \min(\frac{p(J^m)}{\epsilon^2}, t_h)$ and $s_*^r(J) \geq \min(\max(f_*^m(J), p(J^r)/\epsilon^2), t_h)$.*

PROOF. The proof argument is similar to that of Lemma 3.2 in [1]. Fix some job J. Let $I^m = [R^m, S^m)$ be the interval the J^m is processed during and $I^r = [R^r, S^r)$ be the interval J^r is processed during. If J is small, then $p(J^m) \leq \epsilon I^m \leq \epsilon^2 R^m \leq \epsilon^2 s_*^m(J)$. Also, for the reduce job, $s_*^r(J) \geq f_*^m(J)$. Furthermore, by the smallness of J, $p(J^r) \leq \epsilon I^r \leq \epsilon^2 R^r \leq \epsilon^2 s_*^r(J)$. Hence, if J is small both the conditions are satisfied.

The two cases we need to worry about are i) $\max(p(J^r), p(J^m)) > \epsilon I^r$ and ii) $p(J^m) > \epsilon I^m$. To handle both of these cases, we will show how jobs in the optimal solution can be shifted to satisfy the lemma.

We handle case (i) first. The first subcase (i.A) is $p(J^r) > \epsilon I^r$. Let $s = \log_{1+\epsilon}(\frac{1}{\epsilon^6})$. We move the map and reduce task of J to the interval $I' = I^r + s = [R', R'')$. In this case, if $s^m(J)$ and $s^r(J)$ denotes the new starting point of the map and reduce tasks, then similar to the argument in Lemma 3.2 of [1], we have that $p(J^m) \leq s_*^m(J)/\epsilon \leq \epsilon^5 R' \leq \epsilon^5 s^m(J)$. We can show similarly $p(J^r) < \epsilon^5 s^r(J)$. We now need to show that we can fit the shifted jobs in this interval. Since $p(J^r) > \epsilon I_r$, there are at most $\frac{1}{\epsilon}$ such jobs from interval I_r that move into interval I', where each of then requires a total time of $p(J^m) + p(J^r) < 2\epsilon^4 I'$. Hence, the total time required by these shifted jobs in interval I' is $2\epsilon^3 I'$. By stretching time by a $(1 + 2\epsilon)$ factor, we can easily accommodate these jobs. Hence the condition is fulfilled.

The only case where the above construction will not work is when there is a single task (either in map or reduce machine) that spans the entire interval I'. Then, we use Lemma 25 to say that we could as well insert this $\epsilon I'$ space at the beginning of the crossing job. That is, shift the single crossing task and place the space before the task. If the new interval is I'', as at most $\log_{1+\epsilon} \frac{1}{\epsilon}$ intervals are crossed by the job, $I'' = \epsilon I$, and thus each of $p(J^m)$ and $p(J^r)$ are at most $\epsilon^2 I''$ and are small.

For the second subcase (i.B), $p(J^m) > \epsilon I^r$. We again move the entire job to $I' = I^r + s$. Now, we need to justify as before that there are small number of such jobs being shifted to I'. In this case, since both the map and reduce happen by the interval I^r and the interval lengths are geometrically increasing, the total time taken by such jobs is at most I^r/ϵ and thus there can be at most $\frac{1}{\epsilon^2}$ of such jobs. After shifting to the interval I', such jobs take up at most $\frac{1}{\epsilon^2} \cdot 2\epsilon^3 I' \leq 2\epsilon I'$. The case where there is a single task covering I' can be handled similar as before.

Next, we handle case (ii). The first subcase (ii.A) is when $I' = I^m + s \leq I^r$. In this case, only the map task is moved to interval I'.

In case (ii.B), $I' = I^m + s > I^r$. In this case, we move both the map and the reduce to the interval I'. The number of jobs shifted to interval I' can be bounded now by $\frac{1}{\epsilon}$ by the fact that $p(J^m) > \epsilon I^m$. Hence, again by stretching time by a $1 + 2\epsilon$ factor, we can accommodate all jobs.

Now we bound the cost of the solution after performing these shifting operations. We might need to expand by schedule twice by factors of $1 + 2\epsilon$ because of the two cases – this increases the cost by a factor of $1 + 2\epsilon$. By doing the shift, we increase the completion time of any job ending in R_x to most $R_{x+s+1} \leq \frac{(1+\epsilon)R_x}{\epsilon^6}$ factor, and there are at most $\frac{2}{\epsilon^2}$ jobs being shifted overall. The last interval from which jobs are being shifted ends at t_h. Thus, the total completion time of the shifted jobs is

$$
\begin{aligned}
\sum_{R_x < t_h} \frac{2}{\epsilon^2} \frac{(1+\epsilon)R_x}{\epsilon^6} &\leq \frac{2t_h}{\epsilon^8} \sum_{i \geq 0} \frac{1}{(1+\epsilon)^i} \\
&\leq \frac{2t_h}{\epsilon^8} \frac{(1+\epsilon)^2}{\epsilon} \\
&\leq \epsilon(1+\epsilon)^2 \text{OPT} < 2\epsilon\text{OPT},
\end{aligned}
$$

since $t_h = 2\epsilon^{10}\text{OPT}$. Since we stretched time by a $1 + \epsilon$ factor for rounding processing times, $1 + \epsilon$ factor for Lemma 22, and $1 + 2\epsilon$ factor for this lemma, and added a 2ϵ cost, we have a $1 + 13\epsilon$ factor approximation overall. $\square$

By combining the Lemmas 9 and 10, we now show how to get a $(1 + O(\epsilon))$ approximation. Note that if $\mathsf{s}_*^m(J) \geq \frac{p(J^m)}{\epsilon^2}$ and $\mathsf{s}_*^r(J) \geq \max(\mathsf{f}_*^m(J), p(J^r)/\epsilon^2)$, then the job J is small when run. By the Lemma 10, we have a $(1 + 13\epsilon)$ approximate solution for these jobs. Now suppose we fix the positions of the last $\frac{25}{\epsilon^{10}}$ tasks. Given the fixed position of these non-small tasks, the dynamic program will still find a $(1 + 3\epsilon)$ approximate solution to the current OPT, and hence a $(1 + 13\epsilon)(1 + 3\epsilon) \leq (1 + 50\epsilon)$ approximate solution overall assuming $\epsilon \leq 1/2$. Hence, if we run this dynamic program, at the end of time $t_h = 2\epsilon^{10}\text{OPT}$, the number of jobs left is at most $(1 + 50\epsilon)\frac{1}{2\epsilon^{10}} \leq \frac{25}{\epsilon^{10}}$. Hence, all tasks scheduled by the dynamic program finish by time t_h and the last jobs were enumerated.

THEOREM 11. *For the offline case with arrival times, and one map and one reduce task per job on identical machines, there exists a $1 + O(\epsilon)$ approximate algorithm that runs in time $n^{O(\frac{1}{\epsilon^{10}})}(n^{\log_{1+\epsilon}(P)}\log T + \frac{25}{\epsilon^{10}}!)$.*

Notice that this theorem gives a quasi-polynomial time algorithm when maximum processing time a task is polynomially bounded. Now consider the case where there are a constant δ number of tasks types. In this case, the dynamic program needs to enumerate over each of the task types. Thus, for this case we have the following theorem.

THEOREM 12. *For the offline case with arrival times, one map and one reduce task per job on identical machines and there are δ task types, there exists a $1 + O(\epsilon)$ approximate algorithm that runs in time $n^{O(\frac{1}{\epsilon^{10}})}(n^\delta \log T + \frac{25}{\epsilon^{10}}!)$.*

The final case we consider is when there are multiple map and reduce machines. Notice that in the dynamic program, Johnson's algorithm was used to actually schedule the tasks assigned to an interval. This is the only part of the analysis where we used the fact that there was a single machine at each stage. We can consider the case where there are multiple map and reduce machines by using the PTAS for maximum completion time in the two stage flexible flow shop problem to determine how to schedule tasks within an interval [31]. By stretching time by another factor of $(1 + \epsilon)$ it can be ensured that this PTAS is able to fit all jobs into an interval.

Lastly we remark that although the run-time of the (Q)PTAS might seem daunting at first sight, Hepner and Stein [17] have already demonstrated how a related algorithm can be implemented in practice.

5. FLEXIBLE FLOW SHOP: UNRELATED MACHINES CASE

In this section we consider the most general multiple machine scheduling model known as the *unrelated* machines model. In the unrelated machines model, the processing time of a task depends on the machine to which the task is assigned. In general, for $x \neq y$, $p_x(\cdot)$ and $p_y(\cdot)$ may be uncorrelated. In fact, the processing time of a task may be ∞ on some machines, capturing the case where a task cannot be assigned to a specific machine, e.g., when there is not enough memory on a machine to run a specific task.

Due to the generality of the unrelated machines model, it seems difficult to find an algorithm that performs well when there are multiple map and reduce tasks per job. Working towards the goal of finding good algorithms for multiple task instances, we consider the single task case in this section. This is the FFS problem generalized to unrelated machines.

Let σ_m be a non-migratory schedule on the unrelated map machines for only map jobs and let σ_r be a non-migratory schedule on the unrelated reduce machines for only reduce jobs. Unlike the identical machine cases, these two schedules are *not* on a single machine, but rather they are on the original set of machines.

We assign each job J width $w_J = \max\{\mathsf{f}_{\sigma_m}(J), \mathsf{f}_{\sigma_r}(J)\}$. Notice that in this case, the width of a job only depends on the simulated schedules and does not include the maximum processing time of task.

5.1 Offline scheduling

First we address the case where the scheduler is offline and all jobs arrive at time 0.

THEOREM 13. *Given σ_m and σ_r, there is a non-migratory viable schedule σ such that all tasks for job J are completed by time $2\max\{\mathsf{f}_{\sigma_m}(J), \mathsf{f}_{\sigma_r}(J)\}$.*

Our algorithm simulates the schedules σ_m and σ_r. The algorithm assigns each map (reduce) task to the same machine it was processed on in the schedule σ_m (σ_r). A map machine runs the task with shortest width assigned to it. At any time, a reduce machine only runs a reduce task whose corresponding map task is complete. The algorithm always runs the reduce task with smallest width amongst the reduce tasks which are available to schedule. It is easy to check that this schedule is non-migratory and viable. To bound the completion time of the tasks, first we consider the map tasks. Since there is only one map and one reduce task per job, we drop the index of the tasks. Thus, J^b denotes the task for job J and $\mathsf{f}_\sigma(J^b)$ denote the time the task of job J is completed in σ. Again, we give a generic bound on the completion times of tasks based on their earliest availability and width. Recall that for a task J^b, $b \in \{m, r\}$, $\mathsf{a}_\sigma(J^b)$ is the earliest time when the task is available to the schedule σ.

LEMMA 14. *For any task J^b, $\mathsf{f}_\sigma(J^b) \leq \mathsf{a}_\sigma(J^b) + w_J$.*

PROOF. For the sake of contradiction, assume that the lemma is false. Consider a task J^b where $\mathsf{f}_\sigma(J^b) > \mathsf{a}_\sigma(J^b) + w_J$. We know that this task has been available to schedule since time $\mathsf{a}_\sigma(J^b)$. By definition of our algorithm, this implies that the machine task J^b is assigned to has been busy processing jobs with width at most w_J during $[\mathsf{a}_\sigma(J^b), \mathsf{f}_\sigma(J^b)]$. By definition of our algorithm and width, the schedule σ_b must processes strictly more than a w_J volume of work on this machine by time w_J, a contradiction. $\square$

By using the fact $\mathsf{a}_\sigma(J^m) = 0$ for all map tasks, we have that for any map task J^m, $\mathsf{f}_\sigma(J^m) \leq w_J$. Similarly, the completion time of a reduce task is bounded by using the above lemma that $\mathsf{a}_\sigma(J^r) = \max_{J^m \in J} \mathsf{f}_\sigma(J^m) \leq w_J$. We have now bounded the completion times of the jobs. Using Theorem 13, we can construct an approximation algorithm for average flowtime in the scheduling setting.

COROLLARY 15. *There exists a non-migratory 6-approximation algorithm for flowtime (completion time) in the offline, unrelated machines, single task, map-reduce setting.*

PROOF. Skutella in [32] gave a $\frac{3}{2}$-approximation algorithm for minimizing the total completion time on unrelated machines where there is one task per job, no precedence constraints and all jobs arrive at time 0. Since there are only one map and one reduce task per job in our scheduling instance, in the scheduling instances the schedules σ_m and σ_r consider there is one task per job. Thus, the algorithm of Skutella can be used to construct the schedules σ_m and σ_r. Since $\mathtt{flow}_{\mathrm{OPT}} \geq \frac{2}{3}\max\{\mathtt{flow}_{\sigma_m}, \mathtt{flow}_{\sigma_r}\}$, Let F_σ denote the total flow Theorem 13 implies that $\mathtt{flow}_\sigma \leq 2(\mathtt{flow}_{\sigma_m} + \mathtt{flow}_{\sigma_r}) \leq 6\mathtt{flow}_{\mathrm{OPT}}$. $\square$

5.2 Online scheduling

We now consider the case when jobs arrive over time in an online fashion. In the online unrelated machines setting, even when there are no precedence constraints and all jobs consist of one task, it is known that no online algorithm has bounded competitive ratio for the objective of flowtime [14]. Thus, like in the identical machines setting, we resort to resource augmentation.

THEOREM 16. *Given online non-migratory schedules σ_m and σ_r, there is a viable online non-migratory $(1 + \epsilon)$-resource-augmented schedule σ such that all tasks for job J are completed by time $a_J + \frac{4}{\epsilon^2}(\max\{\mathsf{f}_{\sigma_m}(J), \mathsf{f}_{\sigma_r}(J)\} - a_J)$.*

Our algorithm simulates the schedules σ_m and σ_r similarly to the offline algorithm. It is easy to check that the scheduler is online, non-migratory, and viable.

We first present a common lemma that we will use in bounding both the map and the reduce finish times.

LEMMA 17. *Let $\alpha > 0$. Suppose that task J^b, $b \in \{m, r\}$, is available for scheduling by our schedule σ at time $a_J + \alpha w_J$. Then it is the case that $\mathsf{f}_\sigma(J^b) \leq a_J + \frac{2\alpha}{\epsilon} w_J$.*

PROOF. Let x be the machine (map or reduce) that the task J^b is assigned to. Let time t_b be the earliest time such that every task processed during $[t_b, \mathsf{f}_\sigma(J^b)]$ has width at most w_J on machine x. By the given condition, we know that task J^b is available to schedule at time $a_J + \alpha w_J$. Knowing that our algorithm always schedules the task with minimum width on each machine, we have that $t_b \leq a_J + \alpha w_J$.

We also claim that any task scheduled during $[t_b, \mathsf{f}_\sigma(J^b)]$ arrived at earliest $t_b - \alpha w_J$. This is because any task J' scheduled during $[t_b, \mathsf{f}_\sigma(J^b)]$ has width $w_{J'} \leq w_J$, and hence by given assumption has arrival time $a_{J'} \geq t_b - \alpha w_{J'} \geq t_b - \alpha w_J$.

Our algorithm has speed $1 + \epsilon$, thus the algorithm processes $(1 + \epsilon)(\mathsf{f}_\sigma(J^b) - t_b)$ volume of work in total during $[t_b, \mathsf{f}_\sigma(J^b)]$. All of the tasks processed by our algorithm during $[t_b, \mathsf{f}_\sigma(J^b)]$ must be processed on the interval $[t_b - \alpha w_J, \mathsf{f}_\sigma(J^b)]$ by the schedule σ_b on machine x itself. This is because all of the

tasks processed by σ during $[t_b, \mathsf{f}_\sigma(J^b)]$ arrived no earlier than $t_b - \alpha w_J$ by the previous argument. Further, our algorithm assigns any task to the same machine the schedule σ_b processed the task on. Therefore it must be the case that $(1 + \epsilon)(\mathsf{f}_\sigma(J^b) - t_b) \leq \mathsf{f}_\sigma(J^b) - t_b + \alpha w_J$. This implies that $\mathsf{f}_\sigma(J^b) \leq t_b + \frac{\alpha}{\epsilon} w_J \leq a_J + \alpha w_J + \frac{\alpha}{\epsilon} w_J \leq a_J + \frac{2\alpha}{\epsilon} w_J$ since $\epsilon < 1$. $\square$

We now use the above Lemma to deduct the following two corollaries. The first corollary is obtained from the above Lemma, combined with the fact that by construction of our algorithm, the map task J_m is available to σ at time $a_J + w_J$.

COROLLARY 18. *For any map task J^m it is the case that $\mathsf{f}_\sigma(J^m) \leq a_J + \frac{2}{\epsilon} w_J$.*

Similarly, using the above corollary, the reduce task J^r is available when all the corresponding maps are finished, and hence at time $a_J + \frac{2}{\epsilon} w_J$. Using this bound in Lemma 17, we have the following corollary.

COROLLARY 19. *For any reduce task J^r it is the case that $\mathsf{f}_\sigma(J^r) \leq a_J + \frac{4}{\epsilon^2} w_J$.*

5.2.1 Application of Theorem 16

First we consider the objective of total flowtime. As mentioned, it is known that no algorithm has bounded competitive ratio without resource augmentation [14]. Since our algorithm only uses ϵ resource augmentation, our algorithm is constant competitive when given the minimum advantage over the adversary.

COROLLARY 20. *There exists a non-migratory $(1 + \epsilon)$-speed $O(\frac{1}{\epsilon^4})$-competitive online algorithm for average flowtime in the online, unrelated machines, single task, map-reduce setting.*

PROOF. In a recent breakthrough result Chadha et al. showed a $(1 + \epsilon)$-speed $O(\frac{1}{\epsilon^2})$-competitive online non-migratory algorithm for average flowtime in the unrelated machine setting when there is one task per job and no precedence constraints [4]. Using this algorithm we can generate the schedules σ_m and σ_r. The result of Chadha et al. implies that $\mathrm{OPT} \geq \Omega(\epsilon^2)\max\{\mathtt{flow}_{\sigma_m}, \mathtt{flow}_{\sigma_r}\}$. Theorem 16 shows that $\mathtt{flow}_\sigma \leq \frac{4}{\epsilon^2}(\mathtt{flow}_{\sigma_m} + \mathtt{flow}_{\sigma_r})$. Thus, $\mathtt{flow}_\sigma \leq O(\frac{1}{\epsilon^4})\mathtt{flow}_{\mathrm{OPT}}$. $\square$

6. REFERENCES

[1] F. Afrati, E. Bampis, C. Chekuri, D. Karger, C. Kenyon, S. Khanna, I. Milis, M. Queyranne, M. Skutella, and C. Stein. Approximation schemes for minimizing average weighted completion time with release dates. In *Proc. 40th FOCS*, pages 32–44, 1999.

[2] N. Avrahami and Y. Azar. Minimizing total flow time and total completion time with immediate dispatching. *Algorithmica*, 47(3):253–268, 2007.

[3] N. Bansal, R. Krishnaswamy, and V. Nagarajan. Better scalable algorithms for broadcast scheduling. In *Proc. 37th ICALP*, pages 324–335, 2010.

[4] J. S. Chadha, N. Garg, A. Kumar, and V. N. Muralidhara. A competitive algorithm for minimizing weighted flow time on unrelated machines with speed augmentation. In *Proc. 41st STOC*, pages 679–684, 2009.

[5] C. Chekuri, A. Goel, S. Khanna, and A. Kumar. Multi-processor scheduling to minimize flow time with epsilon resource augmentation. In *Proc. 36th STOC*, pages 363–372, 2004.

[6] C. Chekuri and B. Moseley. Online scheduling to minimize the maximum delay factor. In *Proc. 19th SODA*, pages 1116–1125, 2009.

[7] F. Chierichetti, R. Kumar, and A. Tomkins. Max-cover in map-reduce. In *Proc. 19th WWW*, pages 231–240, 2010.

[8] C.-T. Chu, S. K. Kim, Y.-A. Lin, Y. Yu, G. R. Bradski, A. Y. Ng, and K. Olukotun. Map-reduce for machine learning on multicore. In *Proc. 20th NIPS*, pages 281–288, 2006.

[9] J. Dean and S. Ghemawat. Mapreduce: Simplified data processing on large clusters. *C. ACM*, 51:107–113, 2008.

[10] J. Feldman, S. Muthukrishnan, A. Sidiropoulos, C. Stein, and Z. Svitkina. On distributing symmetric streaming computations. In *Proc. 19th SODA*, pages 710–719, 2008.

[11] M. J. Fischer, X. Su, and Y. Yin. Assigning tasks for efficiency in hadoop: Extended abstract. In *Proc. 22nd SPAA*, pages 30–39, 2010.

[12] A. Ganapathi, Y. Chen, A. Fox, R. Katz, and D. Patterson. Statistics-driven workload modeling for the Cloud. In *Proc. Data Engineering Workshops at 26th ICDE*, pages 87–92, 2010.

[13] M. R. D. Garey, D. S. Johnson, and R. Sethi. The complexity of flowshop and jobshop scheduling. *Mathematics of Operations Research*, 1:1171–129, 1976.

[14] N. Garg and A. Kumar. Minimizing average flow-time : Upper and lower bounds. In *FOCS*, pages 603–613, 2007.

[15] N. Garg, A. Kumar, and V. N. Muralidhara. Minimizing total flow-time: The unrelated case. In *Proc. 19th ISAAC*, pages 424–435, 2008.

[16] L. A. Hall. Approximability of flow shop scheduling. In *Proc. 36th FOCS*, pages 82–91, 1995.

[17] C. Hepner and C. Stein. Implementation of a PTAS for scheduling with release dates. *Algorithm Engineering and Experimentation*, pages 202–215, 2001.

[18] S. Im and B. Moseley. An online scalable algorithm for minimizing ℓ_k-norms of weighted flow time on unrelated machines. In *Proc. 21st SODA*, pages 95–108, 2011.

[19] M. Isard, V. Prabhakaran, J. Currey, U. Wieder, K. Talwar, and A. Goldberg. Quincy: Fair scheduling for distributed computing clusters. In *Proc. 22nd SOSP*, pages 261–276, 2009.

[20] S. M. Johnson. Optimal two- and three-stage production schedules with setup times included. *Naval Research Logistics Quarterly*, 1:69–81, 1954.

[21] B. Kalyanasundaram and K. Pruhs. Speed is as powerful as clairvoyance. *J. ACM*, 47(4):617–643, 2000.

[22] U. Kang, C. E. Tsourakakis, A. Appel, C. Faloutsos, and J. Leskovec. HADI: Fast diameter estimation and mining in massive graphs with Hadoop. Technical Report CMU-ML-08-117, CMU, 2008.

[23] D. Karger, C. Stein, and J. Wein. Scheduling algorithms. In M. Atallah, editor, *Handbook on Algorithms and Theory of Computation*, chapter 34. Chapman and Hall/CRC, 1999.

[24] H. Karloff, S. Suri, and S. Vassilvitskii. A model of computation for MapReduce. In *Proc. 20th SODA*, pages 938–948, 2010.

[25] S. Leonardi and D. Raz. Approximating total flow time on parallel machines. *JCSS*, 73(6):875–891, 2007.

[26] J. Lin and C. Dyer. *Data-Intensive Text Processing with MapReduce*. Number 7 in Synthesis Lectures on Human Language Technologies. Morgan and Claypool, 2010.

[27] K. Pruhs, J. Sgall, and E. Torng. *Handbook of Scheduling: Algorithms, Models, and Performance Analysis*, chapter Online Scheduling. CRC Press, 2004.

[28] T. Sandholm and K. Lai. MapReduce optimization using regulated dynamic prioritization. In *Proc. 11th SIGMETRICS*, pages 299–310, 2009.

[29] P. Schuurman and G. J. Woeginger. Flowshop and jobshop schedules: Complexity and approximation. *Operations Research*, 26:136–152, 1978.

[30] P. Schuurman and G. J. Woeginger. Polynomial time approximation algorithms for machine scheduling: ten open problems. *Journal of Scheduling*, 2(5):203–213, 1999.

[31] P. Schuurman and G. J. Woeginger. A polynomial time approximation scheme for the two-stage multiprocessor flow shop problem. *TCS*, 237(1-2):105–122, 2000.

[32] M. Skutella. Convex quadratic and semidefinite programming relaxations in scheduling. *J. ACM*, 48(2):206–242, 2001.

[33] J. L. Wolf, D. Rajan, K. Hildrum, R. Khandekar, V. Kumar, S. Parekh, K.-L. Wu, and A. Balmin. FLEX: A slot allocation scheduling optimizer for MapReduce workloads. In *Middleware*, pages 1–20, 2010.

[34] M. Zaharia, D. Borthakur, J. Sen Sarma, K. Elmeleegy, S. Shenker, and I. Stoica. Delay scheduling: A simple technique for achieving locality and fairness in cluster scheduling. In *Proc. 5th EuroSys*, pages 265–278, 2010.

[35] M. Zaharia, A. Konwinski, A. Joseph, R. Katz, and I. Stoica. Improving MapReduce performance in heterogeneous environments. In *Proc. USENIX OSDI*, 2008.

APPENDIX

A. FLOW SHOP: PTAS AND QPTAS STRUCTURAL LEMMAS

In this section we state a few structural lemmas for our PTAS. These lemmas are adopted from [1] and the proofs are almost identical.

LEMMA 21   ([1]). *With $1 + \epsilon$ loss we can assume that all processing and arrival times are integer powers of $1 + \epsilon$.*

LEMMA 22   ([1]). *With $1 + O(\epsilon)$ loss, we can ensure that a job arrives after $\epsilon p(J^m)$ and a reduce task starts later than $p(J^m) + \epsilon p(J^r)$. Further, the arrival of jobs occur only at R_x for some x.*

PROOF. The same as in [1]. The second part follows by the $1 + \epsilon$ stretch and since the reduce task cannot start earlier than map completion.   □

DEFINITION 23. *We say that a task crosses an interval I_x if its execution overlaps with I_x but it is not contained in I_x completely.*

LEMMA 24   ([1]). *Each task crosses at most $s = \lceil \log_{1+\epsilon} \left(1 + \frac{1}{\epsilon}\right) \rceil$ intervals.*

PROOF. The proof follows the same idea as in [1]. Suppose that a task of job J starts in interval $I_x = [R_x, R_{x+1})$. Since $R_x \geq s^b(J)$ for both $b = \{m, r\}$, i.e., both map and reduce tasks and $s^b(J) \geq \epsilon p^b(J)$ by Lemma 22, we have $I_x = \epsilon R_x \geq \epsilon^2 p^b(J)$. The s intervals following x sum in size to $I_x / \epsilon^2 \geq p^b(J)$.   □

LEMMA 25   ([1]). *With $1 + \epsilon$ loss we can restrict our attention to schedules in which no small task crosses an interval.*

Finding Heavy Distinct Hitters in Data Streams

Thomas Locher
IBM Research – Zurich
thl@zurich.ibm.com

ABSTRACT

A simple indicator for an anomaly in a network is a rapid increase in the total number of distinct network connections. While it is fairly easy to maintain an accurate estimate of the current total number of distinct connections using streaming algorithms that exhibit both a low space and computational complexity, identifying the network entities that are involved in the largest number of distinct connections efficiently is considerably harder. In this paper, we study the problem of finding all entities whose number of distinct (outgoing or incoming) network connections is at least a specific fraction of the total number of distinct connections. These entities are referred to as heavy distinct hitters. Since this problem is hard in general, we focus on randomized approximation techniques and propose a sampling-based and a sketch-based streaming algorithm. Both algorithms output a list of the potential heavy distinct hitters including the estimated counts of the corresponding number of distinct connections. We prove that, depending on the required level of accuracy of the output list, the space complexities of the presented algorithms are asymptotically optimal up to small logarithmic factors. Additionally, the algorithms are evaluated and compared using real network data in order to determine their usefulness in practice.

Categories and Subject Descriptors

F.2.2 [**Analysis of Algorithms and Problem Complexity**]: Nonnumerical Algorithms and Problems—*computations on discrete structures*

General Terms

Algorithms, Theory

Keywords

Network Monitoring, Anomaly Detection, Streaming Algorithms, Heavy Distinct Hitter, Space Complexity

1. INTRODUCTION

Today's networks carry more and more data at increasing bitrates, which makes it progressively harder to monitor them and react to exceptional or undesirable situations in a timely fashion. An exceptional situation may be, e.g., some sort of attack on a machine in the network, a worm that propagates inside the network, or a suspicious activity that may precede an attack, such as a port scan. In particular the timeliness of detection is crucial in order to contain such incidents and limit the caused damage. In practice, intrusion prevention and detection systems such as Snort[1] are deployed, which typically store information about each network flow. Due to the increasing amount of traffic data, such simple approaches become insufficient as it becomes impractical or even infeasible to constantly sift through massive log files to spot unusual activity. Thus, there is a growing need for stream processing techniques that require little space and processing cost.

A simple and straightforward indicator for an anomaly is a substantial change in the number of distinct network connections. It is well known that this metric can be approximated accurately using little space. For example, during the spreading phase of a worm, infected machines try to establish connections to as many other entities in the network as possible. The opposite situation occurs in the case of a distributed denial of service (DDoS) attack, where many distinct entities target one or a small number of specific destinations. Note that, while such an attack often results in a significant increase in network traffic volume, there are certain DDoS attacks, e.g., *TCP SYN flooding attacks*, that do not necessarily cause a noticeable increase in bandwidth usage. In both scenarios, monitoring the number of distinct network connections allows a network administrator to quickly detect the anomaly. However, this simple approach has a major shortcoming: If an anomaly is detected, the entities that provoked it or, in case of an attack, that are targeted are not revealed, implying that log data would still have to be parsed in order to identify them. Thus, the main question is whether and how these entities can be found efficiently. Naturally, one would also like to know the number of distinct (incoming or outgoing) connections for each of those entities to quantify the severity of the situation.

In this paper, we study the following general problem, which encompasses the network security problems outlined above. Given a data stream, we consider two features of each flow, such as the source and the destination IP address. In other words, we abstract away all other features and as-

---
[1]See http://www.snort.org/.

sume that each flow consists of a pair of features, referred to as *element* and *value*. An element that occurs with a large number of *distinct* values in the data stream is called a *heavy distinct hitter*. The goal is to find the heavy distinct hitters and, for each heavy distinct hitter, the corresponding number of distinct values, using as little space as possible. The precise definition of the model and the considered problem is given in the following section.

It is easy to see that by using the IP source address as the element and the IP destination address as the value, each heavy distinct hitter may correspond to an infected machine that is spreading a worm, and, by using the reverse assignment, the heavy distinct hitters may be the victims of a DDoS attack. As many other important network monitoring problems can potentially be mapped to this general problem, space-efficient solutions could be highly useful for numerous practical applications. Moreover, given the connection to the fundamental problem of computing the number of distinct items for some feature, the considered problem is also interesting from a theoretical perspective. Thus, it comes as no surprise that many variations of this problem have already been studied. The most important related work is discussed in Section 4.

As we will see, finding heavy distinct hitters is hard in general, and we therefore have to settle for randomized approximation algorithms. Section 3 presents two simple and parallelizable approximation algorithms for this problem, including their analyses. The results in this section are the main contributions of this paper as they show that there are indeed efficient solutions for the given model. Furthermore, we prove that the achieved space bounds are close to optimal, depending on the required accuracy of the approximation. Additionally, the effectiveness of the proposed algorithms is validated using traces of real network data.

2. MODEL

A data stream $\mathcal{S}$ is modeled as a sequence of n element-value pairs $(e_1, v_1), \ldots, (e_n, v_n)$. The elements and values are taken from the domains E and V, respectively. Let $m \leq n$ denote the number of *distinct* element-value pairs, where two pairs (e_i, v_i) and (e_j, v_j) are considered distinct if $e_i \neq e_j$ or $v_i \neq v_j$ (or both). Furthermore, we define that $E_{\mathcal{S}} \subseteq E$ is the set of all elements that occur as part of an element-value pair in the stream $\mathcal{S}$. The cardinality of this set, which is upper bounded by m, is denoted by $\ell := |E_{\mathcal{S}}|$.

Simply speaking, an element is called a *heavy distinct hitter* if its contribution to the total number m of distinct pairs is large.[2] The contribution of an element is quantified by means of a function $w_{\mathcal{S}} : E \to \mathbb{N}$ mapping each element e to the number of distinct values that form an element-value pair with e in $\mathcal{S}$. Formally, the function $w_{\mathcal{S}}$ is defined as $w_{\mathcal{S}}(e) := |\{v \in V \mid (e, v) \in \mathcal{S}\}|$. We say that $w_{\mathcal{S}}(e)$ is the *weight* of element e in stream $\mathcal{S}$. Note that this definition implies that $\sum_{e \in E_{\mathcal{S}}} w_{\mathcal{S}}(e) = m$. Since we always consider a specific stream $\mathcal{S}$, we simply write $w(e)$ instead of $w_{\mathcal{S}}(e)$ in the following. It remains to specify what constitutes a sufficiently large weight: An element e is a heavy distinct hitter if its weight $w(e)$ is at least a certain threshold value

T, i.e., the parameter T establishes the boundary between heavy distinct hitters and the remaining elements.

Given a specific threshold T, the general goal is to compute the set $\Pi := \{(e, w(e)) \mid w(e) \geq T\}$. As argued in the previous section, it is desirable to use algorithms that require as little space as possible. The *space complexity* of an algorithm is defined as the number of words of memory that are stored during the computation of the (approximate) solution in the worst case for any data stream. We count the number of words instead of the number of bits in order to simplify the notation as we assume that all quantities, including elements, values, and also auxiliary data such as hash values etc., can be stored in one word of memory.

However, once we start to throw away information about the stream, an algorithm can no longer determine the exact weight of each element. In particular, deciding whether a weight reaches the threshold T becomes hard. This intuitive argument can be formalized using a simple reduction from the *set disjointness problem* [19, 22, 25], which yields that any *randomized* algorithm that computes Π with reasonable probability must store at least $\Omega(m)$ bits for any threshold T. This fundamental limitation forces us to resort to randomized approximation algorithms. Hence, instead of trying to compute the correct solution Π, we focus on algorithms that approximate Π in the sense that the computed weights may deviate from the true weights, but the deviation is bounded with a tunable probability. Consequently, the elements in the output set may not be identical to those in Π. The relaxed version of the heavy distinct hitter problem has two additional parameters and is defined as follows.

DEFINITION 2.1. ***Approximate Heavy Distinct Hitter Problem.*** *Given a stream $\mathcal{S}$, parameters $\varepsilon, \delta \in (0, 1)$, and a threshold value $T > 0$, output a set $\mathcal{L}$ of pairs $(e, \tilde{w}(e))$ for which it holds that*

(1) if element e is in $\mathcal{L}$, then $w(e) \geq (1 - \varepsilon)T$

(2) if element e is not in $\mathcal{L}$, then $w(e) < (1 + \varepsilon)T$

(3) for all $(e, \tilde{w}(e)) \in \mathcal{L}$ we have that $|w(e) - \tilde{w}(e)| \leq \varepsilon T$

with probability at least $1 - \delta$.

The parameter ε specifies that any element e for which $w(e) \in [(1 - \varepsilon)T, (1 + \varepsilon)T)$ may or may not be added to $\mathcal{L}$, whereas the decision must be correct for all other elements (Condition (1) and Condition (2)). Condition (3) upper bounds the error in the estimated weights, i.e., it imposes a constraint on the accuracy. It is convenient to take εT as the upper bound on the error for the following reason. If the error in each estimated weight $\tilde{w}(e)$ is at most εT (with a certain probability), then we can simply add exactly those elements e to $\mathcal{L}$ for which $\tilde{w}(e) \geq T$, and both Condition (1) and Condition (2) hold as well. The second parameter δ is the error probability of the algorithm, i.e., we consider *Monte Carlo* algorithms. We say that an algorithm (ε, δ)-*approximates* the correct solution Π if its output $\mathcal{L}$ meets all the requirements of Definition 2.1.

It may suffice to guarantee a bound on the error that is proportional to the true weight. In this case, we substitute the *strong accuracy* condition (Condition (3)) with the following *weak accuracy* condition:

(3') for all $(e, \tilde{w}(e)) \in \mathcal{L}$ we have that $|w(e) - \tilde{w}(e)| \leq \varepsilon w(e)$.

---

[2]In contrast, an element e is considered a *heavy hitter* (see, e.g., [9]) if the sum of values that occur together with e as a pair in the stream is large.

As we will see, there is a fundamental difference between strong and weak accuracy in that weak accuracy can be achieved using less space. The disadvantage of the weak accuracy condition is that it gives weaker guarantees on the correctness of an output list sorted according to the estimated weights, i.e., it is more likely that $w(e) > w(e')$ but $\tilde{w}(e) < \tilde{w}(e')$ for some elements $e, e' \in E_{\mathcal{S}}$. Note that strong accuracy implies that Condition (3') holds for $\varepsilon' := \frac{\varepsilon}{1-\varepsilon}$: Since all elements in $\mathcal{L}$ have a weight of at least $(1-\varepsilon)T$ and the error in the estimated weights is upper bounded by εT, we immediately get that $|w(e) - \tilde{w}(e)| \leq \frac{\varepsilon}{1-\varepsilon} w(e) = \varepsilon' w(e)$ for all $e \in \mathcal{L}$. Therefore, we focus on strong accuracy and discuss potential space optimizations for weak accuracy along the way.

In the traditional heavy hitter problem, the threshold T is simply a fraction of the length n of the data stream. This definition has also been used in the context of the heavy distinct hitter problem [26]. However, since we are interested in finding the elements that contribute the most to the "total weight" m, it is more natural to define T as a fraction of m. Another motivation for this definition is that in the case of applications where n constitutes the size of the considered window, no element may have a weight that is a significant fraction of n, yet some elements may have a large weight with respect to m if the number of duplicates in the data stream is large. Hence, we strive to identify the elements whose weight is at least $T = \phi m$ for a parameter $\phi \in (0, 1)$.[3]

3. ALGORITHMS

An essential ingredient for both algorithms discussed in this section are pseudo-random hash functions mapping elements or element-value pairs to a particular image uniformly at random. We assume that all hash functions are independent. In the first part of this section, a simple sampling-based algorithm is presented, followed by a discussion of a sketch-based algorithm in Section 3.2.

3.1 Sampling-Based Heavy Distinct Hitter Algorithm

A straightforward approach to reducing the space complexity is to randomly drop element-value pairs in the stream, i.e., merely a small, random sample of the entire stream is stored. The basic idea is that any element e that ends up in the sample together with many different values probably occurs in the stream with a large number of distinct values if each element-value pair has a small probability of being sampled. While this simple trick suffices to detect heavy distinct hitters with reasonable probability, the errors in the estimated weights may still be large. This problem is addressed by generating several samples in parallel and extracting a more accurate estimator from them.

3.1.1 Description

The most crucial parameter of the presented sampling algorithm, referred to as $\mathcal{A}^{sample}$, is the *sampling probability* $p \in (0, 1)$ as it must be large enough to ensure that all heavy distinct hitters are sampled frequently, but small enough to make sure that the space complexity remains low. As mentioned above, several samples are required in order to bound

---
[3]It is worth noting that, since $m \leq n$, a solution for $T = \phi m$ also contains all heavy distinct hitters for $T = \phi n$.

Algorithm 1 $\mathcal{A}^{sample}$: Process element-value pair (e, v).

> **for** $i := 1, \ldots, r$ **do**
>   **if** $h_i((e, v)) < p$ **and** $(e, v) \notin \mathcal{R}_i$ **then**
> $\mathcal{R}_i := \mathcal{R}_i \cup \{(e, v)\}$;
> $\tilde{w}_i(e) := |\{(e', v') \in \mathcal{R}_i \mid e = e'\}|/p$;
>   **end if**
> **end for**
> $\tilde{w}(e) := \text{median}(\tilde{w}_1(e), \ldots, \tilde{w}_r(e))$;
> **if** $\tilde{w}(e) \geq T$ **then**
> $\mathcal{L} := (\mathcal{L} \setminus \{(e, \cdot)\}) \cup \{(e, \tilde{w}(e))\}$;
> **end if**

---

the error in the estimated weights. Thus, the second parameter of $\mathcal{A}^{sample}$ is the number r of independent samples used by the algorithm.

For all $i \in \{1, \ldots, r\}$, a pseudo-random hash function $h_i : (E \times V) \rightarrow [0, 1]$, mapping element-value pairs to a value in the range $[0, 1]$ uniformly at random, is associated with the ith sample $\mathcal{R}_i$. These hash functions are used to determine whether an element-value pair is added to the sample as follows. When processing an element-value pair (e, v) in the stream, it is added independently to each sample $\mathcal{R}_i$ if $h_i((e, v)) < p$ and it has not been added before.[4] An estimate $\tilde{w}_i(e)$ of element e's weight is computed for each $i \in \{1, \ldots, r\}$, which is simply the number of distinct values that occur together with e in the sample divided by the sampling probability p. The final estimate $\tilde{w}(e)$ is the median of these r estimates. An element, together with its estimated weight, is added to the output set $\mathcal{L}$ if the estimated weight is at least $T = \phi m$. The issue that m, and hence T, is not known a priori will be discussed later. The algorithm is summarized in Algorithm 1.

3.1.2 Analysis

In order to simplify the analysis, we assume in the following that $\varepsilon \leq 1/2$. Moreover, the parameters of $\mathcal{A}^{sample}$ are set to $p := \frac{4e}{(\varepsilon\phi)^2 m}$ and $r := 2\lceil \log(\frac{4}{\phi\delta}) \rceil - 1$. As a first step, Lemma 3.1 shows that each estimate $\tilde{w}_i(e)$ is statistically unbiased, i.e., each estimate is $w(e)$ in expectation. In addition, the lemma upper bounds the variance of $\tilde{w}_i(e)$.

LEMMA 3.1. *For all $i \in \{1, \ldots, r\}$ and $e \in E_{\mathcal{S}}$, it holds that $\mathbb{E}[\tilde{w}_i(e)] = w(e)$ and $Var(\tilde{w}_i(e)) < w(e)\frac{(\varepsilon\phi)^2 m}{4e}$.*

PROOF. Consider any sampled element e and an arbitrary $i \in \{1, \ldots, r\}$. Let D_i denote the number of distinct values stored in $\mathcal{R}_i$ that form an element-value pair with e. We have that $\mathbb{E}[D_i] = p \cdot w(e)$ and thus $\mathbb{E}[\tilde{w}_i(e)] = \mathbb{E}[D_i/p] = w(e)$. The variance is $Var(\tilde{w}_i(e)) = Var(D_i/p) = Var(D_i)/p^2 = w(e)(1-p)/p < w(e)\frac{(\varepsilon\phi)^2 m}{4e}$. □

While the estimated weights of the heavy distinct hitters must be fairly accurate, the error for the remaining elements merely has to be small enough to ensure that they are not mistakenly considered heavy distinct hitters. In order to formalize this rule, we partition the set $E_{\mathcal{S}}$ of elements into disjoint classes $\mathcal{C}_j$, $j \in \{0, \ldots, \lceil \log(\phi m) \rceil - 1\}$, as follows. An element belongs to class $\mathcal{C}_0$ if $w(e) \geq \frac{\phi m}{2}$. For each element

---
[4]Note that the pseudo-randomness of the hash functions implies that an element-value pair (e, v) that is not added to some sample $\mathcal{R}_i$ will not be added to $\mathcal{R}_i$ at any later point in time.

$e \in C_0$ an upper bound of $b_0 := \varepsilon\phi m$ is imposed on the error of its estimated weight. We define that $e \in C_j$ for any $j \geq 1$ if $w(e) \in \left[\frac{\phi m}{2^{j+1}}, \frac{\phi m}{2^j}\right)$. For each element in any such class, we require that the error in the estimated weight is bounded by $b_1 := b_2 := \ldots := \frac{\phi m}{2}$. The following lemma reveals that the probability that $\tilde{w}(e)$ deviates from $w(e)$ by b_j or more is small for any element $e \in C_j$, and also that this probability becomes exponentially smaller as j increases.

LEMMA 3.2. *For each element e in any class C_j it holds that $\mathbb{P}[|\tilde{w}(e) - w(e)| \geq b_j] < \left(\frac{\phi\delta}{4}\right)^{j+1}$.*

PROOF. First, consider the case $j = 0$. According to Lemma 3.1, the variance of each estimate $\tilde{w}_i(e)$ is bounded by $Var(\tilde{w}_i(e)) < w(e)\frac{(\varepsilon\phi)^2 m}{4e} \leq \frac{(\varepsilon\phi m)^2}{4e}$ for all $i \in \{1, \ldots, r\}$. By applying Chebychev's inequality, we immediately get that $\mathbb{P}[|\tilde{w}_i(e) - w(e)| \geq \varepsilon\phi m] < \frac{1}{4e} = \frac{1}{2^{j+2}e}$. For $j > 0$, we have that $Var(\tilde{w}_i(e)) \leq w(e)\frac{(\varepsilon\phi)^2 m}{4e} < \frac{(\varepsilon\phi m)^2}{2^{j+2}e}$ and thus $\mathbb{P}[|\tilde{w}_i(e) - w(e)| \geq (\phi m)/2] < \frac{4\varepsilon^2}{2^{j+2}e} \leq \frac{1}{2^{j+2}e}$, using the assumption that $\varepsilon \leq 1/2$. Hence, we can conclude that

$$p_j := \mathbb{P}[|\tilde{w}_i(e) - w(e)| \geq b_j] < \frac{1}{2^{j+2}e} \qquad (1)$$

for any element $e \in C_j$, $j \in \{0, \ldots, \lceil \log(\phi m) \rceil - 1\}$.

Since the final estimate $\tilde{w}(e)$ is the median of r estimates, it is only possible that $|\tilde{w}(e) - w(e)| \geq b_j$ if more than $(r-1)/2$ estimates deviate from $w(e)$ by at least b_j. This probability is upper bounded by

$$
\begin{aligned}
\mathbb{P}[|\tilde{w}(e) - w(e)| \geq b_j] &\leq \sum_{k=(r+1)/2}^{r} \binom{r}{k} p_j^k (1-p_j)^{r-k} \\
&\leq \binom{r}{(r+1)/2} p_j^{(r+1)/2} \\
&< (2e)^{(r+1)/2} p_j^{(r+1)/2} \\
&\overset{(1)}{<} \left(\frac{1}{2^{j+1}}\right)^{\log(4/(\phi\delta))} = \left(\frac{\phi\delta}{4}\right)^{j+1}.
\end{aligned}
$$

□

Given this lemma, we are in the position to prove the main result in this section, which states that $\mathcal{A}^{sample}$ indeed computes an (ε, δ)-approximation. In addition, Theorem 3.3 gives a bound on the space complexity of $\mathcal{A}^{sample}$ that holds *with high probability*.[5]

THEOREM 3.3. *If $p := \frac{4e}{(\varepsilon\phi)^2 m}$ and $r := 2\lceil \log(\frac{4}{\phi\delta}) \rceil - 1$, $\mathcal{A}^{sample}$ (ε, δ)-approximates the correct solution $\Pi = \{(e, w(e)) \mid w(e) \geq T\}$. The space complexity is*

$$\mathcal{O}\left(\left(1 + \varepsilon\phi\sqrt{\log m}\right)\frac{\log(\frac{1}{\phi\delta})}{(\varepsilon\phi)^2}\right)$$

with high probability.

PROOF. As there are at most $\frac{2^{j+1}}{\phi}$ elements in class C_j, it follows from Lemma 3.2 that the probability that *any* element in this class does not satisfy the required bound is $\frac{2^{j+1}}{\phi}\left(\frac{\phi\delta}{4}\right)^{j+1} \leq \left(\frac{1}{2}\right)^{j+1}\delta$. Hence, by a union bound, the

probability that *any* element in *any* class does not satisfy the required bound is upper bounded by δ. Since the error in $\tilde{w}(e)$ for all $e \in C_0$ is upper bounded by $\varepsilon\phi m = \varepsilon T$ and the estimated weight is smaller than T for all other elements, $\mathcal{A}^{sample}$ (ε, δ)-approximates Π as claimed.

At most $\frac{1}{(1-\varepsilon)\phi}$ element-weight pairs are added to $\mathcal{L}$, i.e., the space complexity for storing $\mathcal{L}$ is $\mathcal{O}(1/\phi)$ provided that ε is bounded away from 1. Let R denote the total number of sampled element-value pairs.[6] The simple bound $2\lceil \log(\frac{4}{\phi\delta}) \rceil - 1 \geq 3$ implies that $\mathbb{E}[R] = rpm \geq \frac{12e}{(\varepsilon\phi)^2}$. Using a Chernoff bound, we get that

$$
\begin{aligned}
\mathbb{P}\left[R > \left(1 + \frac{\varepsilon\phi}{\sqrt{3e}}\sqrt{\lambda \ln m}\right)\mathbb{E}[R]\right] &\leq e^{-\frac{(\varepsilon\phi)^2}{12e}(\lambda \ln m)\mathbb{E}[R]} \\
&\leq e^{-\lambda \ln m} = \frac{1}{m^\lambda}.
\end{aligned}
$$

Since $\mathbb{E}[R] = rpm < \frac{8e}{(\varepsilon\phi)^2}\lceil \log(\frac{4}{\phi\delta}) \rceil$, the claimed bound on the space complexity follows. □

A nice property of $\mathcal{A}^{sample}$ is that it can be adapted to guarantee only weak accuracy at a lower space complexity. Not suprisingly, this reduction of the space complexity is achieved by reducing the sampling probability p, which yields the following result.

THEOREM 3.4. *If $p := \frac{4e}{(1-\varepsilon)\varepsilon^2\phi m}$ and $r := 2\lceil \log(\frac{4}{\phi\delta}) \rceil - 1$, $\mathcal{A}^{sample}$ (ε, δ)-approximates the correct solution $\Pi = \{(e, w(e)) \mid w(e) \geq T\}$ guaranteeing weak accuracy. The space complexity is*

$$\mathcal{O}\left(\left(1 + \varepsilon\sqrt{(1-\varepsilon)\phi\log m}\right)\frac{\log(\frac{1}{\phi\delta})}{(1-\varepsilon)\varepsilon^2\phi}\right)$$

with high probability.

PROOF. Due to the smaller sampling probability p, the variance increases slightly, i.e., we have that $Var(\tilde{w}_i(e)) < w(e)\frac{(1-\varepsilon)\phi\varepsilon^2 m}{4e}$ for all $i \in \{1, \ldots, r\}$ and $e \in E_S$. We will now show that Lemma 3.2 still holds if we split the class C_0 into two disjoint classes C_0^* and C_0 and define $b_0^*(e) := \varepsilon w(e)$ for all $e \in C_0^*$. An element belongs to class C_0^* if its weight is at least $(1-\varepsilon)\phi m$, i.e., exactly those elements are in C_0^* that are allowed to occur in $\mathcal{L}$. Each other element e, whose weight is in the range $[\frac{\phi m}{2}, (1-\varepsilon)\phi m)$, remains in class C_0 for which $b_0 := \varepsilon\phi m$.

Consider any element $e \in C_0^*$. It holds that $Var(\tilde{w}_i(e)) < w(e)\frac{(1-\varepsilon)\phi\varepsilon^2 m}{4e} \leq \frac{(\varepsilon w(e))^2}{4e}$. Thus, the probability that $\tilde{w}_i(e)$ deviates from $w(e)$ by at least $b_0^*(e) = \varepsilon w(e)$ is lower than $1/(4e)$. For each element $e \in C_0$ we have that $Var(\tilde{w}_i(e)) < w(e)\frac{(1-\varepsilon)\phi\varepsilon^2 m}{4e} < \frac{(\varepsilon\phi m)^2}{4e}$ and thus $\mathbb{P}[|\tilde{w}_i(e) - w(e)| \geq b_0] < 1/(4e)$. Hence, for each element in either C_0^* or C_0 the failure probability is lower than $1/(4e) = 1/(2^{j+2}e)$. For all $e \in C_j$, $j > 0$, and $i \in \{1, \ldots, r\}$, it holds that $Var(\tilde{w}_i(e)) < w(e)\frac{(1-\varepsilon)\phi\varepsilon^2 m}{4e} < \frac{(\varepsilon\phi m)^2}{2^{j+2}e}$, and thus $\mathbb{P}[|\tilde{w}_i(e) - w(e)| \geq b_j = \phi m/2] < 1/(2^{j+2}e)$, as $\varepsilon \leq 1/2$ by assumption. Using the same techniques as in Lemma 3.2, we again get that $\mathbb{P}[|\tilde{w}(e) - w(e)| \geq b_j] < \left(\frac{\phi\delta}{4}\right)^{j+1}$ for all j.

The proof of correctness is now identical to the proof of Theorem 3.3, and the space complexity is derived analogously. □

[5]For an input parameter m, an event holds *with high probability* if the probability that it occurs is at least $1 - 1/m^\lambda$, where $\lambda \geq 1$ is a parameter of the algorithm or the analysis.

[6]Note that the same stream element-value pair may occur in more than one sample $\mathcal{R}_i$. Given that p is small, this does not increase the space complexity substantially.

We see that the space complexity can be improved roughly by a factor of $(1 - \varepsilon)/\phi$ if weak accuracy suffices.

3.1.3 Discussion

It is easy to show that the bounds on the space complexity in Theorem 3.3 and Theorem 3.4 are asymptotically optimal up to logarithmic factors.

THEOREM 3.5. *Any algorithm $\mathcal{A}$ that (ε, δ)-approximates $\Pi = \{(e, w(e)) \mid w(e) \geq T\}$ guaranteeing weak accuracy must store $\Omega\big(\frac{1}{\varepsilon^2 \phi}\big)$ bits. If strong accuracy is required, any algorithm $\mathcal{A}$ that (ε, δ)-approximates Π must store $\Omega\big(\frac{1}{(\varepsilon\phi)^2}\big)$ bits.*

PROOF. Both bounds follow from simple reduction arguments. First, we consider the space required to guarantee weak accuracy. Assume that the heavy distinct hitters are *given*, i.e., it remains for algorithm $\mathcal{A}$ to estimate their weights. Without loss of generality, it is further assumed that the approximation of the weight of each heavy distinct hitter is independent. As there may be $\Omega(1/\phi)$ heavy distinct hitters, algorithm $\mathcal{A}$ must compute the number of distinct values for $\Omega(1/\phi)$ elements independently, implying that algorithm $\mathcal{A}$ must store $\Omega(1/\phi)$ times as many bits as are required to compute an accurate estimate of the weight of a single heavy distinct hitter. Since any algorithm computing an (ε, δ)-approximation of the number of distinct elements must store $\Omega(1/\varepsilon^2)$ bits if m is sufficiently large [17], $\Omega(1/\varepsilon^2)$ bits are also needed to get an accurate estimate of the weight of each heavy distinct hitter, which proves the claimed bound.

An algorithm $\mathcal{A}$ that (ε, δ)-approximates Π guaranteeing strong accuracy can be used to (ε', δ)-approximate m, where $\varepsilon' := \varepsilon\phi$, as follows. Each item x in the stream is converted into the element-value pair (e, x) and then processed by algorithm $\mathcal{A}$. In the end, $\mathcal{L}$ will contain $(e, \tilde{w}(e))$ for which it holds that $|\tilde{w}(e) - w(e)| = |\tilde{w}(e) - m| \leq \varepsilon(\phi m) = \varepsilon' m$ with probability at least $1 - \delta$. Again using the result that $\Omega(1/\varepsilon'^2)$ bits are required to (ε', δ)-approximate the number of distinct elements, we conclude that algorithm $\mathcal{A}$ must store at least $\Omega(1/(\varepsilon\phi)^2)$ bits. $\square$

A minor shortcoming of $\mathcal{A}^{sample}$ is that the bound on the space complexity is probabilistic. This issue can be overcome by fixing the maximum number of sampled elements, e.g., by setting it to a small multiple of the expected number, which slightly increases the failure probability of the algorithm. A more critical problem is that m is unknown. As mentioned earlier, m can be approximated fairly efficiently. Given an estimate $\tilde{m}$ that lies in the range $[(1-\rho)m, (1+\rho)m]$ with reasonable probability, p is computed using the estimate $\tilde{m}/(1 + \rho)$. This estimate is appropriate because the claimed error bounds on the weights with respect to the true m may be violated if m is overestimated. Thus, p may be too large by a factor of $(1 + \rho)/(1 - \rho)$, and the space complexity increases by the same factor. Naturally, the estimate $\tilde{m}$ and consequently the sampling probability p changes as elements are processed, i.e., it is necessary to iterate over the sampled elements and drop all the elements from each sample $\mathcal{R}_i$ if $h_i(e) < p$ does not hold anymore [23], in particular if intermediate results are required. In order to minimize the number of iterations, the estimate for m may only be increased if, e.g., $\tilde{m}$ reaches the next power of 2, which also leads to an increase in the space complexity.

Apparently, all these actions have a negative impact on the space complexity or the failure probability of the entire procedure. An obvious question is whether there are other approaches that are not affected by these problems. This issue is addressed in the following section, where an algorithm is presented whose parameters do no not depend linearly on m, which appears to be inherent to sampling-based approaches.

3.2 Sketch-Based Heavy Distinct Hitter Algorithm

A common technique for solving stream processing problems is to compute a so-called *sketch*, or *synopsis*, which is a space-efficient summary of a stream. The main difference to sampling is that typically the entire stream is added to the sketch (i.e., no input is simply dropped). Finding a suitable sketch for the heavy distinct hitter problem is challenging because only *distinct* values must be counted, which means that a heavy hitter approach cannot be used. The sketch introduced in this section solves this problem by employing pairs of distinct counting primitives capable of computing an estimate of the number of distinct items inserted. An element-value pair is processed by randomly inserting it into one of each pair of distinct counting primitives. The intuition is that updating the same counting primitive of each pair when processing $(e, \cdot)$ produces an imbalance between the estimates of the primitives, which can be exploited to estimate $w(e)$.

3.2.1 Description

The basic building block of our sketch is a distinct counting primitive C, which offers two functions: (1) $insert(x)$ processes the data item x and (2) $getNumberDistinct()$ returns an estimate of the (current) number of distinct inserted items. Any distinct counting primitive that satisfies the following criteria can be used: It can be stored using a constant number of words, and if m distinct items are inserted, $getNumberDistinct()$ returns the correct number m in expectation and the variance is αm^2 for some constant $\alpha > 0$. It can be shown that this bound on the variance is asymptotically optimal if the space complexity of C is constant [17]. Furthermore, we require that the estimate does not change when some item is inserted repeatedly. Several distinct counting algorithms described in the literature meet these requirements. We will discuss such algorithms in more detail later.

The algorithm, called $\mathcal{A}^{sketch}$, is similar to $\mathcal{A}^{sample}$ in that it also computes r estimates and returns the median as the final estimate. The second parameter s of $\mathcal{A}^{sketch}$ determines how many pairs of distinct counting primitives are used to compute each estimate. For a certain $i \in \{1, \ldots, r\}$ and $j \in \{1, \ldots, s\}$, the two distinct counting primitives that form the jth pair used for the ith estimate are denoted by C_{ij}^0 and C_{ij}^1. Each stream item (e, v) is processed by inserting it into one distinct counting primitive of each pair. A pseudo-random hash function $h_{ij} : E \to \{0, 1\}$, hashing each element e to 0 or 1 with equal probability, determines whether (e, v) is inserted into C_{ij}^0 or C_{ij}^1 irrespective of $v \in V$. After this insertion process, the updated estimate $\tilde{w}(e)$ can be computed and, as in $\mathcal{A}^{sample}$, $(e, \tilde{w}(e))$ is added to the output set $\mathcal{L}$ if $\tilde{w}(e) \geq T$ (i.e., T must again be approximated). The steps of $\mathcal{A}^{sketch}$ are given in Algorithm 2.

It remains to specify how $\tilde{w}(e)$ is determined. As men-

Algorithm 2 $\mathcal{A}^{sketch}$: Process element-value pair (e, v).

> **for** $i = 1, \dots, r$ **do**
>   **for** $j = 1, \dots, s$ **do**
> $C_{ij}^{h_{ij}(e)}$.insert$((e, v))$;
>   **end for**
> **end for**
> $\mathcal{L} := \mathcal{L} \setminus \{(e, \cdot)\}$;
> $\tilde{w}(e) := $ getEstimate(e);
> **if** $\tilde{w}(e) \geq T$ **then**
> $\mathcal{L} := \mathcal{L} \cup \{(e, \tilde{w}(e))\}$;
> **end if**

Algorithm 3 getEstimate(e): Compute the estimated weight of element e.

> **for** $i = 1, \dots, r$ **do**
> $\tilde{w}_i := 0$;
>   **for** $j = 1, \dots, s$ **do**
> $\tilde{w}_i := \tilde{w}_i + C_{ij}^{h_{ij}(e)}$.getNumberDistinct$()$
> $- C_{ij}^{1-h_{ij}(e)}$.getNumberDistinct$()$;
>   **end for**
> $\tilde{w}_i := \tilde{w}_i / s$;
> **end for**
> **return** median$(\{\tilde{w}_1, \dots, \tilde{w}_r\})$;

tioned before, it is the median of estimates $\tilde{w}_1(e), \dots, \tilde{w}_r(e)$. Each estimate $\tilde{w}_i(e)$, $i \in \{1, \dots, r\}$, is computed as follows. For all s pairs of distinct counting primitives, the difference between the estimated number of distinct insertions into $C_{ij}^{h_{ij}(e)}$ and $C_{ij}^{1-h_{ij}(e)}$ is computed, and $\tilde{w}_i(e)$ is simply set to the average of these differences. This procedure, called *getEstimate(e)*, is summarized in Algorithm 3.

3.2.2 Analysis

The analysis of algorithm $\mathcal{A}^{sketch}$ basically follows the same lines as the analysis of $\mathcal{A}^{sample}$. For the sake of simplicity, we assume in this section that $\varepsilon \leq 1/2 - c$ for some constant $c > 0$ (this assumption is used in the proof of Theorem 3.7). In the following, we will slightly abuse our notation and consider $C_{ij}^{h_{ij}(e)}$ a random variable whose value is the corresponding distinct counting primitive's estimate of the number of distinct inserted items. The key result, which is proved in the following lemma, is that $C_{ij}^{h_{ij}(e)} - C_{ij}^{1-h_{ij}(e)}$ is an unbiased estimator of the weight $w(e)$ of element e, and its variance is in the order of m^2.

LEMMA 3.6. *For all $i \in \{1, \dots, r\}$, $j \in \{1, \dots, s\}$, and $e \in E_{\mathcal{S}}$, it holds that $\mathbb{E}[C_{ij}^{h_{ij}(e)} - C_{ij}^{1-h_{ij}(e)}] = w(e)$ and $Var(C_{ij}^{h_{ij}(e)} - C_{ij}^{1-h_{ij}(e)}) \leq (1+\alpha)m^2 - mw(e)$.*

PROOF. For all $i \in \{1, \dots, r\}$, $j \in \{1, \dots, s\}$, and $q \in \{0, 1\}$, let the random variable $C_{ij}^q(t)$ denote the return value of C_{ij}^q.getNumberDistinct$()$ after t distinct items have been inserted. Recall that $\mathbb{E}[C_{ij}^q(t)] = t$ and $Var(C_{ij}^q(t)) = \alpha t^2$ according to our requirements of distinct counting primitives given in Section 3.2. For any two elements e and e', we define

$$s(e, e') := \begin{cases} 1 & \text{if } h_{ij}(e) = h_{ij}(e'), \\ 0 & \text{else.} \end{cases}$$

It holds that

$$\mathbb{E}\left[C_{ij}^{h_{ij}(e)}\right] = \mathbb{E}\left[C_{ij}^{h_{ij}(e)}\left(w(e) + \sum_{e' \in E_{\mathcal{S}} \setminus \{e\}} s(e, e')w(e')\right)\right]$$
$$= w(e) + \frac{m - w(e)}{2} = \frac{m + w(e)}{2}.$$

Similarly, we get that $\mathbb{E}[C_{ij}^{1-h_{ij}(e)}] = \frac{m - w(e)}{2}$, and thus $\mathbb{E}[C_{ij}^{h_{ij}(e)} - C_{ij}^{1-h_{ij}(e)}] = w(e)$ as claimed.

$\mathbb{E}[C_{ij}^q(t)] = t$ and $Var(C_{ij}^q(t)) = \alpha t^2$ together imply that $\mathbb{E}[(C_{ij}^q(t))^2] = (1+\alpha)t^2$. Let p_t denote the probability that the total number of distinct elements hashed to $C_{ij}^{h_{ij}(e)}$ is t.

We have that

$$\mathbb{E}\left[\left(C_{ij}^{h_{ij}(e)}\right)^2\right] = \sum_{t=w(e)}^{m} \mathbb{E}\left[\left(C_{ij}^{h_{ij}(e)}(t)\right)^2\right] p_t$$
$$= (1+\alpha) \sum_{t=w(e)}^{m} t^2 p_t$$
$$\leq \frac{1+\alpha}{2}\left(m^2 + w(e)^2\right). \quad (2)$$

The last inequality can be explained as follows. Due to the quadradic dependency on t, the sum is maximized if the probability that $t = m$ is maximized, i.e., the number of different elements is minimized. Assume that there is just one other element e' whose weight is $w(e') = m - w(e)$. In this case, $p_{w(e)} = p_m = 1/2$ and we get exactly $\mathbb{E}[(C_{ij}^{h_{ij}(e)})^2] = \frac{1+\alpha}{2}(m^2 + w(e)^2)$. Note that this bound also holds if e is the only element, which implies that $\mathbb{E}[(C_{ij}^{h_{ij}(e)})^2] = (1+\alpha)m^2$. If there are more elements, p_m is reduced, and $\mathbb{E}[(C_{ij}^{h_{ij}(e)})^2]$ becomes smaller as a result. The same argument also applies to $C_{ij}^{1-h_{ij}(e)}$ for which it holds that

$$\mathbb{E}\left[\left(C_{ij}^{1-h_{ij}(e)}\right)^2\right] \leq \frac{1+\alpha}{2}(m - w(e))^2. \quad (3)$$

In order to bound the variance, we need a lower bound on the covariance:

$$Cov\left(C_{ij}^{h_{ij}(e)}, C_{ij}^{1-h_{ij}(e)}\right) \geq -\mathbb{E}\left[C_{ij}^{h_{ij}(e)}\right]\mathbb{E}\left[C_{ij}^{1-h_{ij}(e)}\right]$$
$$= -\frac{m^2 - w(e)^2}{4}. \quad (4)$$

Given these bounds, we get the claimed bound on the variance of $\Delta C_{ij}(e) := C_{ij}^{h_{ij}(e)} - C_{ij}^{1-h_{ij}(e)}$ as follows.

$$Var(\Delta C_{ij}(e)) = Var\left(C_{ij}^{h_{ij}(e)}\right) + Var\left(C_{ij}^{1-h_{ij}(e)}\right)$$
$$\quad\quad -2Cov\left(C_{ij}^{h_{ij}(e)}, C_{ij}^{1-h_{ij}(e)}\right)$$
$$\overset{(2,3,4)}{\leq} \frac{1+\alpha}{2}\left(m^2 + w(e)^2\right) - \left(\frac{m + w(e)}{2}\right)^2$$
$$\quad\quad +\frac{1+\alpha}{2}(m - w(e))^2 - \left(\frac{m - w(e)}{2}\right)^2$$
$$\quad\quad +\frac{m^2 - w(e)^2}{2}$$
$$= (1+\alpha)m^2 + \alpha w(e)^2 - (1+\alpha)mw(e)$$
$$\leq (1+\alpha)m^2 - mw(e).$$
$\qquad\qquad\qquad\qquad\qquad\qquad\qquad\qquad\qquad\qquad\square$

Considering that $\mathcal{O}(m)$ distinct element-value pairs are inserted into each distinct counting primitive, it is not surprising that the variance of the difference between two distinct counting primitives is in the order of m^2. The fact that the variance is not bounded by $\mathcal{O}(mw(e))$ (as in algorithm $\mathcal{A}^{sample}$) entails that the space complexity depends logarithmically on the number ℓ of distinct elements in the stream as Theorem 3.7 reveals.

THEOREM 3.7. If $r := 2\lceil\max\{\ln(\frac{4}{\phi\delta}), \frac{1}{2}\log_{1/(2\varepsilon)}(\frac{\phi\ell}{2})\}\rceil -$ 1 and $s := \lceil\frac{(1+\alpha)2e^2}{(\phi\varepsilon)^2}\rceil$, $\mathcal{A}^{sketch}$ (ε,δ)-approximates the correct solution $\Pi = \{(e, w(e)) \mid w(e) \geq T\}$. The space complexity is

$$\mathcal{O}\left(\frac{\log(\frac{1}{\phi\delta}) + \log_{1/\varepsilon}(\phi\ell)}{(\phi\varepsilon)^2}\right).$$

PROOF. By assumption, repeated insertions of the same element-value pair do not have any effect on the distinct counting primitives. Therefore, we can assume without loss of generality that each element-value pair occurs only once in the stream.

Consider the time when a specific element e whose weight is at least $\frac{\phi m}{2}$ occurs the last time. At this point in time, e has been processed exactly $w(e)$ times. Each $\tilde{w}_i(e)$ is the average of s trials, which means that $\mathbb{E}[\tilde{w}_i(e)] = w(e)$ and $Var(\tilde{w}_i(e)) \leq \frac{(1+\alpha)m^2}{s} \leq \frac{(\varepsilon\phi m)^2}{2e^2}$ since at most m (distinct) element-value pairs have been processed. Consequently, using Chebychev's inequality, we get that $p' := \mathbb{P}[|\tilde{w}_i(e) - w(e)| > \varepsilon\phi m] \leq \frac{1}{2e^2}$. As in the analysis of algorithm $\mathcal{A}^{sample}$, the probability that the error of the final estimate $\tilde{w}(e)$ is at least $\varepsilon(\phi m)$ is upper bounded by the probability that more than $(r-1)/2$ estimates are off by at least $\varepsilon(\phi m)$, i.e.,

$$\mathbb{P}[|\tilde{w}(e) - w(e)| > \varepsilon\phi m] \leq \binom{r}{(r+1)/2} p'^{(r+1)/2}$$
$$\leq (2e)^{(r+1)/2} p'^{(r+1)/2} \leq \frac{\phi\delta}{4},$$

where we used that $r \geq 2\lceil\ln(4/(\phi\delta))\rceil - 1$. By means of a union-bound argument, we see that the probability that $\tilde{w}(e)$ deviates form $w(e)$ by more than $\varepsilon(\phi m)$ for any element whose weight is at least $\frac{\phi m}{2}$ is upper bounded by $\delta/2$ because there are at most $2/\phi$ such elements. Thus, all elements whose weight is at least $\frac{\phi m}{2}$ satisfy the requirements with probability at least $1 - \delta/2$.

For the remaining elements it suffices to show that the error does not exceed $\frac{\phi m}{2}$, which ensures that none of these elements is erroneously considered a heavy distinct hitter. Since $p'' := \mathbb{P}[|\tilde{w}_i(e) - w(e)| > \phi m/2] \leq \frac{2\varepsilon^2}{e^2}$, the probability that $\tilde{w}(e)$ of any such element e is larger than $\frac{\phi m}{2}$ is

$$\mathbb{P}\left[|\tilde{w}(e) - w(e)| > \frac{\phi m}{2}\right] \leq \binom{r}{(r+1)/2} p''^{(r+1)/2}$$
$$\leq (2e)^{(r+1)/2} p''^{(r+1)/2}$$
$$\leq \left(\frac{1}{e}\right)^{(r+1)/2} (4\varepsilon^2)^{(r+1)/2}$$
$$\leq \frac{\phi\delta}{4} (2\varepsilon)^{\log_{1/(2\varepsilon)}(\phi\ell/2)} \quad (5)$$
$$= \frac{\delta}{2\ell}.$$

In Inequality (5) we used that $r \geq 2\ln(4/(\phi\delta)) - 1$ and $r \geq \log_{1/(2\varepsilon)}(\phi\ell/2) - 1$. Again, using a union-bound argument, the probability that the estimated weight of any element exceeds $\frac{\phi m}{2}$ is upper bounded by $\delta/2$. Hence it follows that the estimates of all elements are as accurate as required with probability at least $1 - \delta$ as claimed.

The space complexity is $rs \cdot 2d + |\mathcal{L}|$ with d being the constant size of a distinct counting primitive. At most $\frac{1}{(1-\varepsilon)\phi}$ element-value pairs are added to $\mathcal{L}$, implying that $|\mathcal{L}| \in \mathcal{O}(1/\phi)$. Since $r := 2\lceil\max\{\ln(\frac{4}{\phi\delta}), \frac{1}{2}\log_{1/(2\varepsilon)}(\frac{\phi\ell}{2})\}\rceil - 1$, $s := \lceil\frac{(1+\alpha)2e^2}{(\phi\varepsilon)^2}\rceil$, and $\log_{1/(2\varepsilon)} x \leq \frac{1}{c}\log_{1/\varepsilon} x$ for any $x \geq 1$ due to the assumption that $\varepsilon \leq 1/2 - c$, the bound on the space complexity follows. $\square$

It is worth noting that (the less important case of) $\varepsilon \in [1/2, 1)$ can be handled by setting $r := 2\lceil\ln(\frac{\ell}{\delta})\rceil - 1$, which results in a space complexity of $\mathcal{O}\left(\frac{\log(\ell/\delta)}{(\phi\varepsilon)^2}\right)$.

3.2.3 Discussion

While the space complexity of $\mathcal{A}^{sample}$ is essentially constant, the space complexity of $\mathcal{A}^{sketch}$ depends logarithmically on ℓ. However, when taking a closer look at the parameter r in Theorem 3.7, it becomes apparent that $r = 2\lceil\ln(\frac{4}{\phi\delta})\rceil - 1$ unless ℓ is exceedingly large. For example, if $\phi = \delta = \varepsilon = 1/10$, r must be set to a larger value only if $\ell > 10^9$. Thus, the space complexity is constant for most practical purposes. What is more, if the space required for each distinct counting primitive is small—one possible implementation using little space is presented in Section 3.3—, the space complexities of the two algorithms are identical up to a small constant factor.

The advantage of $\mathcal{A}^{sketch}$ is that it does not rely on an accurate estimate of m. However, this increased robustness comes at a certain price: Due to the larger variance, algorithm $\mathcal{A}^{sketch}$ cannot be adapted for the weak accuracy constraint. Moreover, the computational cost is higher as many hash values have to be computed when processing an element-value pair. This processing cost can be reduced by caching the hash values of heavy or recently encountered elements, i.e., there is a trade-off between computational and space complexity.

3.3 Practical Evaluation

So far, we have discussed bounds on the space complexity and the accuracy of the proposed algorithms that hold regardless of the distribution of the input stream. Since worst-case distributions rarely occur in practice, it is worthwhile to investigate the performance of the algorithms when processing real network data. For this purpose, the algorithms have been implemented and tested using undirectional flow data captured at the edge between the IBM Research campus network and the Internet. The considered trace is a collection of more than 12 million flows recorded in five days in May 2009. Our focus is on finding the sources that connect to many distinct destination IP addresses. In total, there are more than 725,000 distinct source-destination pairs in the trace. Luckily, the trace is an ideal test candidate: Five machines scanned almost an entire 16-bit subnetwork during this time, which means that each of these machines is responsible for 8.8% of all distinct connections. The sum of distinct connections of the top 10 sources amounts to 64% of the total sum. The number of distinct connections of the other approximately 12,000 sources follows a heavy-tail distribution.

Before discussing the main results, we briefly describe the distinct counting primitive used in the implementation of $\mathcal{A}^{sketch}$. Each inserted item is hashed uniformly at random to a value in the range $(0, 1)$ and the k smallest hash values ever encountered are stored. If h_k is the kth smallest hash value (i.e., the largest stored value), the estimated number of distinct items is $(k-1)/h_k$ [16]. When inserting m distinct items, it can be shown that $\mathbb{E}[(k-1)/h_k] = m$ and $Var((k-1)/h_k) = \frac{k-1}{k-2}(m^2-m) - m^2 < \frac{m^2}{k-2}$. Thus, a variance of (at most) αm^2 is achieved by storing $\frac{1}{\alpha} + 2$ hash values. Given the factor $1 + \alpha$ in the parameter s, $k = 4$ minimizes the space requirements and is used in the implementation.[7]

After processing the data stream, both algorithms output the 10 elements with the largest estimated weights. We evaluate how many top 5 and top 10 sources are identified correctly, and also the error in the estimates. As the parameter r mainly helps to keep *all* errors bounded, it does not affect the *median error* significantly. For the sake of simplicity, we focus on this measure and state only average median errors over several runs using different hash functions and different $r \in \{1, 3, 5, 7, 9\}$. In order to compare the performance of $\mathcal{A}^{sample}$ and $\mathcal{A}^{sketch}$, they are both allowed to store a certain fraction of the total number of distinct connections. This constraint simplifies the sampling algorithm because maintaining an accurate estimate of m, as discussed in Section 3.1.3, is not required, which also means that $\mathcal{A}^{sample}$ is slightly favored. Since $\mathcal{A}^{sample}$ has the additional advantage that it must only store element-value pairs, instead of pairs of distinct counting primitives, we can expect $\mathcal{A}^{sample}$ to achieve more accurate results. By setting the memory budget to 10% of the total sum of distinct connections, $\mathcal{A}^{sketch}$ correctly finds all top 5 and top 10 sources, and the median error in the estimates of the top 5 and the top 10 sources is roughly 5% and 8%, respectively. The median error is still reasonably small when reducing the budget to 1% (19% for the top 5 and 27% for the top 10 sources), and all top 5 sources are identified correctly, but often only 6 or 7 of the correct top 10 sources are found. Given a memory budget of 1%, the median error of $\mathcal{A}^{sample}$ is around 5-6% for both the top 5 and top 10 sources, and all top 10 sources are in the output list, i.e., due to the lower variance, $\mathcal{A}^{sample}$ achieves a better accuracy particularly for the sources outside the top 5. Even a budget of 0.1% suffices for $\mathcal{A}^{sample}$ to identify at least 4 of the top 5 and 9 of the top 10 sources with a median error of about 20%. We conclude that both algorithms are capable of finding the heavy distinct hitters in the top 5 using little space; however, in this setting $\mathcal{A}^{sample}$ achieves a greater accuracy in the estimates, which is in accord with the theoretical analysis.

4. RELATED WORK

There is a large body of work on *streaming* (or *one-pass*) algorithms, which process data streams exactly once and in order. For a nice introduction to streaming algorithms, the interested reader is referred to [24]. As mentioned before, one of the most well-known and well-studied problems in the streaming model is computing the number m of distinct elements in a data stream. An elegant approach to approximate m is to map each element to a pseudo-random bit

---
[7]Note that $k = 3$ could have been used as well.

string and to store the largest index i where the first 1 occurs. Since we can expect that roughly $m/2^k$ elements have the first 1 at position k, i is approximately $\log m$ [13] (see also [4, 10, 12, 21] and references therein). The alternative technique outlined in the previous section is proposed and analyzed in [16]. It has been shown that any algorithm that outputs an estimate whose error is bounded by εm with reasonable probability must store $\Omega(\log m + \frac{1}{\varepsilon^2})$ bits [1, 17]. An algorithm that matches this bound has been proposed recently [21].

Alon et al. introduced the more general problem of approximating the *frequency moments* $F_k := \sum_{e_i \in E_S} m_i^k$, where m_i denotes the frequency of element e_i, of a data stream for any $k \geq 0$ [1]. Note that the number of distinct elements is the 0th frequency moment. In a series of papers, tight bounds (up to polylogarithmic factors) on the space requirements have been proved for all k [1, 3, 5, 8, 18].

The elements that occur frequently in a data stream may also be of interest. It has been shown that elements whose frequencies exceed a certain threshold can be found efficiently [23] using the "sample and hold" technique [15]. The basic idea is to sample each element with a certain probability. Once an element is sampled, its frequency is maintained correctly from this point on by updating it whenever the same element occurs again in the stream. This technique can also be used to find flows in a network that use up at least a certain fraction of the bandwidth by randomly sampling bytes [11]. While "sample and hold" is an elegant and efficient technique to count frequencies, it is not as useful for detecting heavy distinct hitters. The problem is that the frequencies of sampled elements cannot be updated easily, i.e., a distinct counting primitive must be used for each element, and the sampling rate must be $\Omega\left(\frac{1}{m\varepsilon\phi}\right)$, otherwise too many distinct values may be missed before sampling an element for the first time. Since the error must be bounded by $\varepsilon(\phi m)$ and some elements may have a weight in the order of m, the space requirement for such a distinct counting primitive is $\Omega\left(\frac{1}{(\varepsilon\phi)^2}\right)$ bits. Therefore, the resulting (expected) space requirement is $\Omega\left(\frac{1}{(\varepsilon\phi)^3}\right)$ bits, which is worse than the bounds in Section 3.

The problem of finding heavy distinct hitters has also been studied in the literature, although the considered models and the problem definitions are not identical. The most relevant related work focuses on finding *superspreaders* [26], which are entities in a network that connect to many distinct destinations, i.e., superspreaders are heavy distinct hitters. The authors show that straightforward sampling can be used to identify superspreaders using little space. In contrast to this work, the threshold is defined as $T = \phi n$, i.e., the number of distinct destinations must be a fraction of the length of the entire data stream. Moreover, their goal is primarily to *detect* superspreaders without considering how many distinct destinations are contacted. In particular, for a parameter b, their sampling algorithm detects each superspreader with probability at least $1 - \delta$, and a source that contacts at most T/b destinations is erroneously considered a superspreader with probability at most δ. By setting the sampling probability to an appropriate value, the space complexity of their algorithm is $\mathcal{O}\left(\frac{\log(1/\delta)}{\phi}\left(1 + \frac{1}{(b-1)^2}\right)\right)$ in expectation. If we apply our model and require that Condition (1) and Condition (2) hold, and also that *all* superspreaders are found with probability $1 - \delta$, the space complexity becomes

$\mathcal{O}\left(\frac{\log(1/(\phi\delta))}{\phi\varepsilon^2}\right)$. Note that algorithm $\mathcal{A}^{sample}$ achieves the same expected space complexity while additionally guaranteeing weak accuracy.

Numerous other techniques that are based on sampling have been proposed [7, 20, 27]. Cao et al. [7] focus on identifying heavy distinct hitters for a "moderately large" threshold T. They propose a two-phase filtering method using Bloom filters [6] whose purpose is to remove the majority of elements with small weights. The weight of the remaining elements is estimated using a thresholded bitmap. Since the computed weights are biased, the authors further introduce a simple technique for bias correction using unbiased weight estimates of a small random sample of elements. Zhao et al. [27] address the problem that some of the sampled element-value pairs may occur frequently, which entails that the data structure used to store the sampled pairs must process the same pairs again and again. As the arrival rate of element-value pairs may be significantly higher than the processing rate of this data structure, the sampling rate has to be small in order to ensure that the data structure is not overwhelmed. However, a small sampling rate results in low accuracy. The authors propose to use a Bloom filter to filter out element-value pairs that have been encountered before. Due to the possibility of hash collisions, the update procedure of the data structure must be modified to obtain unbiased weight estimates. Additionally, a more sophisticated approach is presented using a two-dimensional bitmap, which achieves more accurate results according to experiments using traces of real-world network traffic. A different approach to boost the performance of algorithms for the heavy distinct hitter problem is to use special associative memories [2].

In another work, the space complexity of finding the top-k heavy distinct hitters, i.e., the k elements with the largest weights, is studied. The authors consider SYN flooding attacks, where the weight of an element is defined as the number of half-open TCP connections [14]. Their model is somewhat more general in the sense that they can handle deletions, i.e., once a TCP connections is fully established, it no longer contributes to the weight of the (destination) element. The space complexity of their algorithm is $\mathcal{O}\left(\frac{m\log^2(n/\delta)\log^2 m}{w(e_k)\varepsilon^2}\right)$, where $w(e_k)$ denotes the kth largest weight.[8] If $w(e_k) \in \Omega(\phi m)$, the space complexity becomes $\mathcal{O}\left(\frac{\log^2(n/\delta)\log^2 m}{\phi\varepsilon^2}\right)$, i.e., if n, m, and the weight of the top-k elements are large, the space complexities of the algorithms presented in Section 3 are significantly lower.

5. CONCLUSION

As we have seen, while there is no space-efficient solution that finds the *correct* set of heavy distinct hitters and the corresponding weights, there are approximation techniques that yield accurate results with high probability and that have a small memory footprint. In particular, we have studied two classic approaches in stream processing, sampling and computing a sketch of the data stream. Both techniques achieve a space complexity that is asymptotically optimal up to small logarithmic factors given a *strong accuracy* con-

straint. The proposed sampling-based algorithm is further (almost) optimal if a weaker accuracy constraint suffices, whereas the sketch-based algorithm has the advantage that it does not rely on an accurate estimate of the number of distinct items in the data stream. The practical study shows that the sampling-based algorithm slightly outperforms the sketch-based counterpart in that its returned estimates are more accurate given the same memory budget. However, both algorithms are able to detect the heavy distinct hitters even when given considerably less space than the theoretical upper bounds demand. Another strong point of the proposed algorithms is that they are intrinsically parallelizable as they compute sets of independent estimates. These results suggest that the proposed algorithms may indeed be valuable for various stream processing applications.

6. REFERENCES

[1] N. Alon, Y. Matias, and M. Szegedy. The Space Complexity of Approximating the Frequency Moments. *Journal of Computer and System Sciences*, 58(1):137–147, 1999.

[2] N. Bandi, D. Agrawal, and A. El Abbadi. Fast Algorithms for Heavy Distinct Hitters using Associative Memories. In *Proc. 27th International Conference on Distributed Computing Systems (ICDCS)*, 2007.

[3] Z. Bar-Yossef, T. S. Jayram, R. Kumar, and D. Sivakumar. An Information Statistics Approach to Data Stream and Communication Complexity. *Journal of Computer and System Sciences*, 68(4):702–732, 2004.

[4] Z. Bar-Yossef, T. S. Jayram, R. Kumar, D. Sivakumar, and L. Trevisan. Counting Distinct Elements in a Data Stream. In *Proc. 6th International Workshop on Randomization and Approximation Techniques (RANDOM)*, pages 1–10, 2002.

[5] L. Bhuvanagiri, S. Ganguly, D. Kesh, and C. Saha. Simpler Algorithm for Estimating Frequency Moments of Data Streams. In *Proc. 17th Annual ACM-SIAM Symposium on Discrete Algorithms (SODA)*, pages 708–713, 2006.

[6] B. Bloom. Space/Time Trade-offs in Hash Coding with Allowable Errors. *Communications of the ACM (CACM)*, 13:422–426, 1970.

[7] J. Cao, Y. Jin, A. Chen, T. Bu, and Z.-L. Zhang. Identifying High Cardinality Internet Hosts. In *Proc. 28th IEEE Conference on Computer Communications (INFOCOM)*, pages 810–818, 2009.

[8] A. Chakrabarti, S. Khot, and X. Sun. Near-Optimal Lower Bounds on the Multi-Party Communication Complexity of Set Disjointness. In *In Proc. 18th IEEE Conference on Computational Complexity (CCC)*, pages 107–117, 2003.

[9] M. Charikar, K. Chen, and M. Farach-Colton. Finding Frequent Items in Data Streams. *Theoretical Computer Science*, 312(1):3–15, 2004.

[10] M. Durand and P. Flajolet. LogLog Counting of Large Cardinalities. In *Proc. 11th Annual European Symposium on Algorithms (ESA)*, pages 605–617, 2003.

---

[8]The space complexity given in their paper depends on the size of the domains E and V. Their bound can be reduced to the stated bound by hashing each pair to a value in a domain of size polynomial in m.

[11] C. Estan and G. Varghese. New Directions in Traffic Measurement and Accounting: Focusing on the Elephants, Ignoring the Mice. *ACM Transactions on Computer Systems*, 21(3):270–313, 2003.

[12] C. Estan, G. Varghese, and M. Fisk. Bitmap Algorithms for Counting Active Flows on High Speed Links. In *Proc. 3rd ACM SIGCOMM Conference on Internet Measurement (IMC)*, pages 153–166, 2003.

[13] P. Flajolet and G. N. Martin. Probabilistic Counting Algorithms for Data Base Applications. *Journal of Computer and System Sciences*, 31(2):182–209, 1985.

[14] S. Ganguly, M. Garofalakis, R. Rastogi, and K. Sabnani. Streaming Algorithms for Robust, Real-Time Detection of DDoS Attacks. In *Proc. 27th International Conference on Distributed Computing Systems (ICDCS)*, 2007.

[15] P. B. Gibbons and Y. Matias. New Sampling-Based Summary Statistics for Improving Approximate Query Answers. In *Proc. ACM SIGMOD International Conference on Management of Data*, pages 331–342, 1998.

[16] F. Giroire. Order Statistics and Estimating Cardinalities of Massive Data Sets. *Discrete Applied Mathematics*, 157(2):406–427, 2009.

[17] P. Indyk and D. Woodruff. Tight Lower Bounds for the Distinct Elements Problem. In *Proc. 44th Annual IEEE Symposium on Foundations of Computer Science (FOCS)*, 2003.

[18] P. Indyk and D. Woodruff. Optimal Approximations of the Frequency Moments of Data Streams. In *Proc. 37th Annual ACM Symposium on Theory of Computing (STOC)*, pages 202–208, 2005.

[19] B. Kalyanasundaram and G. Schnitger. The Probabilistic Communication Complexity of Set Intersection. *SIAM Journal on Discrete Mathematics*, 5(2):545–557, 1992.

[20] N. Kamiyama, T. Mori, and R. Kawahara. Simple and Adaptive Identification of Superspreaders by Flow Sampling. In *Proc. 26th IEEE Conference on Computer Communications (INFOCOM)*, pages 2481–2485, 2007.

[21] D. M. Kane, J. Nelson, and D. Woodruff. An Optimal Algorithm for the Distinct Elements Problem. In *Proc. 29th ACM SIGMOD Symposium on Principles of Database Systems (PODS)*, pages 41–52, 2010.

[22] E. Kushilevitz and N. Nisan. *Communication Complexity*. Cambridge University Press, 1997.

[23] G. Manku and R. Motwani. Approximate Frequency Counts Over Data Streams. In *Proc. 28th International Conference on Very Large Data Bases (VLDB)*, pages 346–357, 2002.

[24] S. Muthukrishnan. *Data Streams: Algorithms and Applications*. Foundations and Trends in Theoretical Computer Science, 2005.

[25] A. A. Razborov. On the Distributional Complexity of Disjointness. *Theoretical Computer Science*, 106(2):385–390, 1992.

[26] S. Venkatamaran, D. Song, P. B. Gibbons, and A. Blum. New Streaming Algorithms for Fast Detection of Superspreaders. In *Proc. 12th ISOC Symposium on Network and Distributed Systems Security (NDSS)*, pages 149–166, 2005.

[27] Q. Zhao, A. Kumar, and J. Xu. Joint Data Streaming and Sampling Techniques for Detection of Super Sources and Destinations. In *Proc. 5th ACM SIGCOMM Conference on Internet Measurement (IMC)*, pages 77–90, 2005.

Brief Announcement : A Partitioned Ticket Lock

Dave Dice
Oracle Labs
dave.dice@oracle.com

ABSTRACT

We introduce the *partitioned ticket lock*, a first-in-first-enabled FIFO lock with semi-local spinning. Our lock has fixed memory overhead, is extremely simple, and exhibits performance competitive with other local spinning locks.

Categories and Subject Descriptors

D.4.1 [**Operating Systems**]: Mutual Exclusion

General Terms

Performance, experiments, algorithms

Keywords

Concurrency, threads, locks, ticket locks, mutual exclusion

1. INTRODUCTION

Locks, which provide *mutual exclusion* remain an important and common structuring mechanism for thread-safe concurrent programming. The literature provides a rich variety of lock implementations. Broadly, when a lock is not available a thread can either spin (busy wait) or deschedule itself, voluntarily making itself ineligible to be dispatched by the operating system's scheduler. The latter is useful if other threads might be eligible to run or if power management is a concern. We are interested in the class of spin locks, however. An extremely simple "test-and-set" spin lock implementation will simply loop, attempting to use an atomic instruction to change a memory word from unlocked to locked state. Since all contending threads spin (loop, busy waiting) on the same lock variable, we say this technique uses *global spinning*. Other more "polite" forms of global spinning, such as "test-and-test-and-set" (TATAS) are possible. While simple, such locks, when contended, generate significant coherence traffic and may impair the performance of a system by saturating the interconnect from write coherence cache misses. In addition these forms do not provide FIFO ordering.

A *ticket lock* [4] is another example of simple global spinning lock. Briefly, the ticket lock consists of two words, a `ticket` variable and a `grant` variable. Arriving threads atomically fetch-and-increment the `ticket` and then spin, waiting for `grant` variable to match the value returned by the fetch-and-increment primitive. At that point the thread is said to own the lock and may safely enter the critical section. Upon exiting the critical section the thread

releases the lock by advancing the `grant` field. This can be accomplished with a simple store operation, although on some platforms with weak memory models, memory fences may be required. Advancing the grant field passes lock to the next entering thread, if any. Unlike the test-and-set lock, the ticket lock provides FIFO ordering.

To avoid the performance issues inherent in global spinning it may be useful to employ local spinning, where at most one threads spins on a given variable at any one time. This can reduce coherence traffic and coherence hot spots. When a thread releases a lock it marks the location upon which the next thread to take the lock is spinning, handing off ownership. MCS [4] and CLH [2] locks use local spinning but require memory management for nodes that are added and removed from a queue, where each node represents a contending thread that is spinning on a field within that node or a node adjacent in the queue. Anderson's array-based queue lock [1] avoids the use of such nodes but each lock instance must contain an array provisioned with at least one slot for each possible thread that might contend concurrently for that lock. In a system with a large number of threads the array, conservatively sized, could prove impractical.

A partitioned ticket lock consists of a `ticket` variable and an array of `grant` variables. Thread arriving to acquire the lock will atomically fetch-and-increment the `ticket` variable, obtaining a ticket value, use that ticket value to identify an index into the array of `grant` variables, and then spin on the specified `grant` variable, waiting for it match the ticket value, at which point the thread has acquired the lock and may enter the critical section. To release the lock, the thread computes the next value after the original ticket value, identifies the index into the `grant` array associated with that next value, and finally stores that next value into the index. Our approach provides semi-local spinning in that multiple threads may be spinning on the same `grant` field at a given time, but there will be fewer threads spinning on a given `grant` field than would be the case with a naive ticket lock. Our mechanism also provides strict FIFO ordering. Note that a degenerate partitioned ticket lock with an array of just one slot is just a classic ticket lock. Like a classic ticket lock, the partitioned ticket lock has a central `ticket` variable, but unlike the classic ticket lock, our approach has multiple `grant` variables.

A duality exists between our partitioned ticket locks and MCS and CLH locks in that during the acquisition phase a thread spins on one node (slot) and to release a lock a thread writes to *next* node (slot) in the local queue of threads contending for the lock.

Our technique is most similar to Anderson's array-based queue lock but it differs from that lock (a) by reducing the number of writes to shared data, which in turn further reduces coherence traffic and (b) eliminating the constraint in Anderson's lock to preallocate at least one slot per thread, making our lock both more flexible and more memory efficient. In our scheme threads can share slots, however, allowing for a smaller fixed-size array. The size of the array in our scheme impacts performance, not correctness. This allows the developer to strike an appropriate balance between memory contention and space (the number of slots in the grant array).

Composite abortable locks [3] are related to CLH and embed or associate an array of queue nodes directly into the lock. Arriving threads first spin, trying to acquire a randomly selected node, and then use that node to acquire the lock in the manner of CLH.

2. PERFORMANCE

In Figure 1 we report performance of a microbenchmark that iterates for 10 seconds. Each iteration acquires a lock, looks up a value in a small red-black tree of 10 elements, releases the lock, and then executes the non-critical section which has approximately 10 times the path length of the uncontended critical section. Only one lock and red-black tree are used. There are no writes in the critical section. Results are reported in the graph in terms of millions of iterations completed by all the threads collectively during the 10 second measurement interval. Data was collected on a 128-way 2-socket Sun T5240 system populated with UltraSPARC-T2™"Niagara" processors and running the Solaris™operating system. We report the performance of a simple ticket lock, the composite abortable lock configured with 16 internal nodes (labeled "CAL" in the graph), MCS locks, CLH locks, and our partitioned ticket lock configured with 16 slots (labeled "PTL"). As can be seen in the graph, all the lock implementations allow reasonable scaling up to 16 threads. Beyond that, however, the simple ticket lock starts to fade. Interestingly, the partitioned ticket lock manages to yield results fairly close to the MCS and CLH locks, making it competitive in many circumstances.

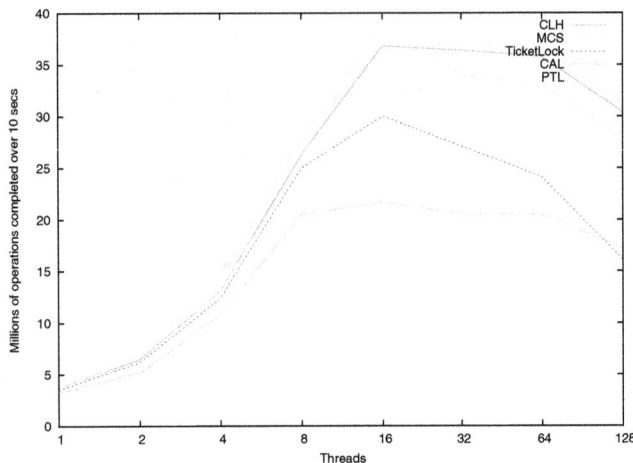

Figure 1: Lock Scalability

3. REFERENCES

[1] T. E. Anderson. The performance of spin lock alternatives for shared-memory multiprocessors. *IEEE Trans. Parallel Distrib. Syst.*, 1:6–16, January 1990.

[2] P. S. Magnusson, A. Landin, and E. Hagersten. Queue locks on cache coherent multiprocessors. In *Proceedings of the 8th International Symposium on Parallel Processing*, pages 165–171, Washington, DC, USA, 1994. IEEE Computer Society.

[3] V. J. Marathe, M. Moir, and N. Shavit. Composite abortable locks. In *Proceedings of the 20th international conference on Parallel and distributed processing*, IPDPS'06, pages 132–132, Washington, DC, USA, 2006. IEEE Computer Society.

[4] J. M. Mellor-Crummey and M. L. Scott. Algorithms for scalable synchronization on shared-memory multiprocessors. *ACM Trans. Comput. Syst.*, 9:21–65, February 1991.

APPENDIX

Listing 1: Partitioned Ticket-Lock Algorithm

```
 1  typedef struct {
 2      // Pad so that _Grant is sole occupant of the cache line
 3      // GrantLine length should be a power-of-two for fast indexing
 4      __CacheLinePad__ ;
 5      volatile int _Grant ;
 6  } GrantLine ;
 7
 8  typedef enum {
 9      GRANTSLOTS = 4, // Must be a power-of-two >= 1
10  } ManifestConstants ;
11
12  // TicketLock: Contains a single ticket and multiple grant fields
13  // All fields are initially 0
14
15  typedef struct {
16      volatile int Request ; // Ticket value
17      // Multiple grant fields -- divided into lanes
18      // Striped to reduce contention
19      GrantLine Grants [GRANTSLOTS] ;
20  } TicketLock ;
21
22  int TicketAcquire (TicketLock * L) {
23      // First-in-First-enabled doorway protocol
24      // Note that integer overflow and wrap-around of the
25      // Request variable is benign.
26      // Crucially, the trajectory of indices followed by
27      // the lock and unlock operations must be the same,
28      // but we do not require that the stream of indices
29      // be consecutive.
30      // The only constraint is that the number of contending
31      // threads be less than the range of an "int", which
32      // is not a concern in practice.
33      const int T = FetchIncrement (&L->Request) ; // Atomic fetch-and-add
34      while (L->Grants[T & (GRANTSLOTS-1)]._Grant != T) Delay() ;
35      return T ;
36  }
37
38  void TicketRelease (TicketLock * L, int T) {
39      // Advance -- increment to hand off the lock to successor
40      L->Grants[(T+1) & (GRANTSLOTS-1)]._Grant = T+1 ;
41  }
42
43  // Usage is:
44  // int t = TicketAcquire(L) ;
45  // <criticalsection>
46  // TicketRelease (L, t) ;
```

Brief Announcement: Transaction Polymorphism

Vincent Gramoli
EPFL
Switzerland
vincent.gramoli@epfl.ch

Rachid Guerraoui
EPFL
Switzerland
rachid.guerraoui@epfl.ch

ABSTRACT

In this work, we present *transaction polymorphism*, a synchronization technique that provides more control to the programmer than traditional (i.e., *monomorphic*) transactions to achieve comparable performance to generic lock-based and lock-free solutions.

We prove the following results: (i) Lock-based synchronization enables strictly higher concurrency than monomophic transactions. (ii) Polymorphic transactions enable strictly higher concurrency than monomorphic transactions. The former result indicates that there exist some transactional programs that will never perform as well as their lock-based counterparts, whatever improvement could be made at the hardware level to diminish the overhead associated with transactional accesses. The latter result shows, however, that transaction polymorphism is a promising solution to cope with this issue.

Categories and Subject Descriptors

D.1.3 [**Programming Techniques**]: Concurrent Programming—*Parallel programming*; D.3.3 [**Programming Languages**]: Language Constructs and Features—*Abstract data types, Concurrent programming structures*; D.3.2 [**Software Engineering**]: Reusable Software—*Reusable libraries*

General Terms

Algorithms, Theory, Languages, Performance

Keywords

Concurrency, Library

1. TRANSACTIONS FOR EXPERTS

Lock-based and lock-free concurrent implementations of abstract data types are often highly tuned to support a fixed set of efficient features, however, it is difficult to adapt them as they are not generic. For example, a hash table synchronizes efficiently concurrent insert, remove, and contains operations, as long as the number of elements remains proportional to the number of buckets [3]. Unfortunately, this data structure does not support a resize, therefore it is preferable to use a split ordered linked list [4] if one expect the structure to be unbalanced or overloaded.

The transaction paradigm is an appealing programming idiom for it guarantees to execute in isolation from the other existing transactions. Provided that every operation of an abstract data type is implemented as a transaction, any new operation encapsulated within a transaction will also be atomic. Hence, a novice programmer could reuse such a concurrent library straightforwardly to write other transaction-based concurrent programs. Concurrent programming with transactions is simple in part for this reason and because it consists in delimiting regions of sequential code (e.g., starting with a *start* delimiter). As a drawback, transactions limits concurrency by preventing the programmer from giving hints on the semantics of any transaction. Instead, all transactions execute the same safest semantics—we refer to them as *monomorphic*.

We propose *transaction polymorphism* a novel synchronization technique that allows multiple transactions, with distinct semantics, to run concurrently. To support polymorphism, a transactional memory has simply to accept a semantic parameter p when each transaction starts, e.g., $start(p)$. The application programmer can either set p to the desired semantics or omit it and the default semantics def will be used for the corresponding transaction. Transactional polymorphism has various applications in concurrent programming ranging from providing one liveness guarantee per transaction to distinguishing k-read-modify-write operations from operations whose read-write conflicts do not all impact their linearizability. We illustrate how to use transaction polymorphism to enable greater concurrency.

2. EVALUATING CONCURRENCY

We consider a shared memory partitioned into shared registers, supporting atomic reads/writes, and metadata used for synchronization of set of shared register accesses. A *read* of shared register x that returns value v is denoted by $r(x):v$ or more simply $r(x)$; a write of v on x is denoted by $w(x,v)$ or more simply $w(x)$. An *operation* π is a sequence of read and write accesses to shared registers and a *critical step* γ is a subsequence of an operation.

The *semantics s* of an operation π is an assignment of its accesses to critical steps. For example, the semantics s of a sorted linked list contains operation, $\pi = r(x), r(y), r(z)$, (Figure 1) assigns accesses to two critical steps γ_1 and γ_2 such that $r(x) \mapsto \gamma_1$, $r(y) \mapsto \gamma_1$ and $r(y) \mapsto \gamma_2$, $r(z) \mapsto \gamma_2$ indicating that there should exist a point in the execution where the value returned by $r(x)$ and $r(y)$ where both present, and another point where the values returned by $r(y)$ and $r(z)$ were both present, but not necessarily a point

p_1	p_2	p_3		p_1	p_2	p_3
lock(x)				start(weak)		
r(x)				r(x)		
lock(y)		lock(z)				start(def)
		w(z)				w(z)
		unlock(z)				commit
r(y)				r(y)		
unlock(x)					start(def)	
	lock(x)				w(x)	
	w(x)				commit	
lock(z)	unlock(x)			r(z)		
r(z)				commit		
unlock(y)						
unlock(z)						

Figure 1: Schedule that is accepted by lock-based and polymorphic transactions but not by monomorphic transactions.

at which both values from $r(x)$ and $r(z)$ were present. Intuitively, the semantics of an operation restricts the set of possible schedules comprising its inner accesses by defining its indivisible critical steps.

We consider three operation *synchronizations*: (i) *lock-based synchronization* with $lock(x)$ and $unlock(x)$ functions taking a shared register as a parameter, (ii) *monomorphic synchronization* with $start(\perp)$ and *commit* events delimiting monomorphic transactions, and (iii) *polymorphic synchronization* with $start(p)$ and *commit* events, where p is the semantic hint. A *transactional operation* (resp. *lock-based operation*) is an operation whose set of accesses is extended with the events $start(*)$ and *commit* (resp. $lock(x)$ and $unlock(x)$). (i) A lock-based operation is *well-formed* if for each shared register x every $lock(x)_i$ has a following $unlock(x)_i$ event. (ii) A transactional operation is *well-formed* if it starts with a *start* event and ends by a matching *commit* event. A lock-based (resp. transactional) *schedule* $\mathcal{I}$ is a sequence of events of well-formed lock-based (resp. transactional) operations. Two critical steps γ_1 and γ_2 are concurrent in schedule $\mathcal{I}$ if an event of γ_1 is ordered in $\mathcal{I}$ after the first event of γ_2 but before the last event of γ_2.

Intuitively, a history H is the result of the execution of a schedule $\mathcal{I}$ by synchronization $\mathcal{S}$. More formally, a *transactional history* H_{tx} is the result of the execution of the transactional schedule $\mathcal{I}_{tx}$ by a transactional memory where: (i) $start(*)_i$ events in $\mathcal{I}_{tx}$ are $start(\mathsf{def})_i$ in H_{tx} if $\mathcal{S}$ is the monomorphic synchronization or unchanged otherwise, (ii) one non-*start* event of π_i in $\mathcal{I}_{tx}$ may produce an abort and in this case the schedule is consider *invalid*; and for the remaining events, (iii) for any object x, $r(x)_i$ in $\mathcal{I}_{tx}$ is replaced by its corresponding execution $r(x) : v$ in H_{tx} that returns value v, and for any object x, $w(x)$ in $\mathcal{I}_{tx}$ is unchanged in H_{tx}. A *lock-based history* H_ℓ is the result of the execution of the lock-based schedule $\mathcal{I}_\ell$ where for any object x, (i) $r(x)$ in $\mathcal{I}_\ell$ is replaced by its corresponding execution $r(x) : v$ that returns value v in H_ℓ, (ii) $w(x)$ and $unlock(x)$ in $\mathcal{I}_\ell$ are unchanged in H_ℓ. Note that the ordering of an input schedule $\mathcal{I}$ is preserved in the resulting history H.

A *sequential history* is a history where no two critical steps are concurrent. A transactional history is *valid* with respect to synchronization $\mathcal{S}$ if it is equivalent to a sequential history and if it does not result from the execution by $\mathcal{S}$ of an invalid schedule (with abort events). (This notion generalizes the input acceptance [2] to $\mathcal{S}$.) A lock-based history is *valid* with respect to synchronization $\mathcal{S}$ if it is equivalent to a sequential history and for each object x, no $lock(x)_i$ occurs between a $lock(x)_j$ and an $unlock(x)_j$ where $i \neq i$.

A schedule is *accepted* by synchronization $\mathcal{S}$ if its execution results in a valid history.

DEFINITION 1 (CONCURRENCY RELATION). *A synchronization* $\mathcal{S}_1$ *enables higher concurrency* than *synchronization* $\mathcal{S}_2$, *denoted by* $\mathcal{S}_1 \rightrightarrows \mathcal{S}_2$, *if there exists a schedule accepted by* $\mathcal{S}_1$ *that is not accepted by* $\mathcal{S}_2$.

Using this definition, we can strictly compare the concurrency of two synchronizations: $\mathcal{S}_1$ enables *strictly higher concurrency* than another synchronization $\mathcal{S}_2$ if the following properties are satisfied: $\mathcal{S}_1 \rightrightarrows \mathcal{S}_2$ and $\mathcal{S}_2 \not\rightrightarrows \mathcal{S}_1$.

THEOREM 1. *Lock-based synchronization enables strictly higher concurrency than monomorphic synchronization.*

The first part of the proof ($\rightrightarrows$) relies on the fact that, unlike lock and unlock events, well-formed transactions are open-close blocks that cannot overlap as depicted by the schedule of Figure 1. The second part ($\not\rightrightarrows$) relies on the fact that fine-grained locks can implement 2-phase-locking.

Transaction polymorphism accepts the schedule of Figure 1 by simply using elastic transaction [1] each time a transaction is parameterized with the **weak** keyword. Next theorem relies on the fact that monomorphic transactions cannot distinguish between semantics $r(x), r(y), r(z) \mapsto \gamma_1$ and semantics $r(x)', r(y)' \mapsto \gamma_{1'}$ and $r(y)', r(z)' \mapsto \gamma_{2'}$ for the operation of p_1 in Figure 1 implying the existence of inconsistent operations or unaccepted schedules.

THEOREM 2. *Polymorphic synchronization enables strictly higher concurrency than monomorphic synchronization.*

3. CONCLUDING REMARKS

Transaction polymorphism allows the programmer to control the semantics of transactional operations to avoid concurrency limitations.

Transaction polymorphism raises important questions on the composition of transaction semantics in a common TM implementation. First, how to ensure that two transactions with different semantics could run concurrently without impacting each other semantics? For example, a multi versioned transaction could not return stale data if a singly versioned transaction does not backup data when overwriting it. Second, what should be the semantics of a nested transaction? the semantics indicated by its parameter as if it was not nested, the parent transaction semantics, or the strongest of the two?

4. ACKNOWLEDGMENTS

We are grateful to the anonymous reviewers and Petr Kuznetsov for their helpful comments. This work is supported in part by FP7 EU projects 216852 and 248465.

5. REFERENCES

[1] P. Felber, V. Gramoli, and R. Guerraoui. Elastic transactions. In *DISC*, 2009.
[2] V. Gramoli, D. Harmanci, and P. Felber. On the input acceptance of transactional memory. *Parallel Processing Letters*, 20(1), 2010.
[3] M. M. Michael. High performance dynamic lock-free hash tables and list-based sets. In *SPAA*, 2002.
[4] O. Shalev and N. Shavit. Split-ordered lists: Lock-free extensible hash tables. *J. ACM*, 53(3), 2006.

Brief Announcement: MultiLane - A Concurrent Blocking Multiset

Dave Dice
Oracle Labs
dave.dice@oracle.com

Oleksandr Otenko
Oracle Corporation
oleksandr.otenko@oracle.com

ABSTRACT

We introduce an extremely simple transformation that allows composition of a more scalable concurrent blocking multiset, or *bag*, from multiple "lanes" of a potentially less scalable underlying multiset. Our design disperses accesses over the various lanes, reducing contention and memory coherence hot spots. Implemented in Java, for instance, we construct a multiset from multiple lanes of *java.util.concurrent.SynchronousQueue* [9] that yields more than 8 times the aggregate throughput of a single instance of *SynchronousQueue* when run on a 64-way Sun Niagara-2 system with 16 producer threads and 16 consumer threads. We experimented with various queues from *java.util.conconcurrent* and found that in general a MultiLane form will outperform its underlying counterpart.

Categories and Subject Descriptors

D.4.1 [**Operating Systems**]: Concurrency

General Terms

Performance, experiments, algorithms

Keywords

Concurrency, queues, bags, concurrent multisets, resource pools, producer-consumer, message passing

1. INTRODUCTION

Concurrent multisets allowing multiple producers and multiple consumers can implement message passing mechanisms or when provisioned with elements representing resources they can be used as concurrent resource pools. They are found with increasing frequency in modern software. Our construct exposes blocking *non-total* take and put accessor methods. Take waits for an element to become available and then removes and returns that element to caller, while put inserts a new element, respecting the collection's capacity bound, if any, by first stalling until the collection is not at full capacity before adding the element. All of the JDK packages mentioned above expose blocking take and put operators except *ConcurrentLinkedQueue*, which is based on Michael and Scott's classic non-blocking queue [8]. For that specific construct we emulate take and put by spinning on offer and poll.

A MultiLane collection has a *put cursor* and a *take cursor*, which reflect the lanes to which arriving put and take operations will be dispatched, and an array of lanes. Each lane, in turn, consists of an instance of an underlying blocking sub-collection. Put and take operations on a MultiLane collection will first increment the appropriate cursor. These are the only centralized read-write variables in our algorithm and are accessed with a simple atomic fetch-and-add primitive. Both cursors are initially 0. After advancing a cursor the operation uses the cursor value to select a lane index and then invokes put or take, respectively on the underlying sub-collection. Because of the disjunct between advancing the cursor and then accessing the sub-collection identified by the cursor value, our collection are not FIFO even if the sub-collections happen to be. In practice, however, many applications do not require FIFO ordering. MultiLane multisets can be either unbounded or bounded depending on the underlying sub-collection. The progress properties of the constituent lanes are not necessarily reflected in the aggregate multilane collection.

A MultiLane collection is work-conserving if the underlying collections are work-conserving. Specifically, we say a collection has a surplus of takes when the number of take invocations on that collection exceeds the number of put operations. If we have a surplus of take operations on a MultiLane collection then the put cursor will select a lane that itself has a surplus of take operations, facilitating the expeditious pairing of put and take operations. Complementary statements hold for the take cursor. The general approach is similar to that of a ring buffer, except that there are no locks at the top level but only atomically updated cursors, and the ring elements are themselves blocking concurrent collections instead of storage locations.

The key benefits to our approach, as compared to existing collections, are (a) reduced coherence traffic as we distribute operations over the lanes, and (b) by dispersing operations we lessen the impact of critical sections or optimistic concurrent windows that might exist within those underlying collections. Relatively simple and less-scalable thread-safe collections can be easily composed into scalable MultiLane collections. The atomically-accessed cursor fields certainly constitute a coherence hot-spot and impediment to ultimate scalability, but they appear to admit more scaling than the centralized data in the underlying collections. Furthermore, atomic fetch-and-add may confer performance advantages relative to compare-and-swap [3].

We note too that a multilane semaphore can be readily constructed from multiple lanes of potentially less scalable underlying semaphores.

2. RELATED WORK

The literature is rich with scalable concurrent queue algorithms. Of late and of particular interest, Hendler et al. [5][6] show to use *flat combining* to construct scalable synchronous queues. Afek et al. [2] introduce the concept of *Quasi-linearizable* data structures and use the concept to construct relaxed and highly scalable queues. Most relevant to our work are the Elimination-Diffraction trees (*ED-Trees*) of Afek et al. [1] that, like our approach, uses multiple sub-collections. Mellor-Crummey [7] and others [4][10] used atomic fetch-and-ϕ to implement non-blocking queues but their algorithms are more complex and require additional read-write accesses to central variables.

3. PERFORMANCE

In Figure 1 we report the performance of a microbenchmark that runs a number of concurrent producer and consumer threads and measures aggregate message throughput rates with varying multiset implementations. Data was collected on a single-socket T5120 UltraSPARC-T2™"Niagara" system having 64 logical processors and 8 cores. The UltraSPARC-T2 has only two pipelines per core, so scaling above 16 threads is modest and arises only from memory-level parallelism. The MultiLane forms were configured with 8 lanes. Interestingly, we see that *LinkedTransferQueue* is faster than its MultiLane counterpart with 16 producer threads and 4 consumer threads. Further investigation showed that many messages were simultaneously in-flight under the MultiLane form, and that garbage collection activity dominated the measurement interval. This behavior arises because the underlying collection is unbounded and the underlying implementation allocates "container" nodes for each message, illustrating a potential confounding factor if we have unbounded collections and producer-consumer rate imbalance. (Augmenting the *LinkedTransferQueue* instances with semaphores to create bounded sub-collections provided relief, and, despite the overhead of the semaphores actually improved performance). Garbage collection overhead was negligible in all the other reported runs. To enable fair comparison, if the underlying form was bounded, as in the case of *ArrayBlockingQueue*, we reduced the bound by a factor of 8 for the MultiLane variation thereof, so the aggregate MultiLane would have the same effective bound at 8 lanes.

Implementation	4P : 16C		16P : 4C		16P : 16C	
	Base	MultiLane	Base	MultiLane	Base	MultiLane
ArrayBlockingQueue	509	653	1002	881	1017	11338
LinkedBlockingQueue	1312	4245	1183	4008	1123	10604
LinkedTransferQueue	6288	6737	6601	4425	5424	11376
ConcurrentLinkedQueue	2061	6404	3066	6326	1542	12134
SynchronousQueue	783	4945	671	5137	1177	9747

Table 1: Aggregate message throughput results shown in transfers completed per millisecond with varying implementations and producer:consumer ratios

4. REFERENCES

[1] Y. Afek, G. Korland, M. Natanzon, and N. Shavit. Scalable producer-consumer pools based on elimination-diffraction trees. Euro-Par'10. http://dx.doi.org/10.1007/978-3-642-15291-7_16.

[2] Y. Afek, G. Korland, and E. Yanovsky. Quasi-linearizability: Relaxed consistency for improved concurrency. PODC 2010.

[3] D. Dice. *Dave Dice's blog*, 2011 (accessed Feb 15, 2011). http://blogs.sun.com/dave/entry/atomic_fetch_and_add_vs.

[4] A. Gottlieb, B. D. Lubachevsky, and L. Rudolph. Basic techniques for the efficient coordination of very large numbers of cooperating sequential processors. *ACM Trans. Program. Lang. Syst.*, 5:164–189, April 1983.

[5] D. Hendler, I. Incze, N. Shavit, and M. Tzafrir. Flat combining and the synchronization-parallelism tradeoff. SPAA '10. http://doi.acm.org/10.1145/1810479.1810540.

[6] D. Hendler, I. Incze, N. Shavit, and M. Tzafrir. Scalable flat-combining based synchronous queues. In *Distributed Computing*. 2010. http://dx.doi.org/10.1007/978-3-642-15763-9_8.

[7] J. M. Mellor-Crummey. Concurrent queues: Practical fetch-and-ϕ algorithms. 1987. University of Rochester Computer Science Technical Report # 229.

[8] M. M. Michael and M. L. Scott. Simple, fast, and practical non-blocking and blocking concurrent queue algorithms. PODC '96. http://doi.acm.org/10.1145/248052.248106.

[9] W. N. Scherer, III, D. Lea, and M. L. Scott. Scalable synchronous queues. *Commun. ACM*, 52:100–111, May 2009.

[10] J. Wilson. *Operating System Data structures for Shared-Memory MIMD Machines with Fetch-and-Add*, 1988. PhD Dissertation, New York University.

APPENDIX

Listing 1: MultiLane Algorithm

```
1   public class MultiLane< T > {
2       // Implements a concurrent blocking multiset — — bag
3       // Transforms existing blocking multisets into multilane forms
4       // Exposes take() and put() accessor methods.
5
6       // Lanes: Array of underlying blocking concurrent collections ...
7       // Possible examples of sub−collection types include :
8       // ArrayBlockingQueue, LinkedBlockingQueue, LinkedTransferQueue,
9       // SynchronousQueue etc
10      // This particular example employs SynchronousQueue.
11      private final SynchronousQueue<T> [] Lanes;
12
13      // PutCursor and TakeCursor are write and read "cursors" that chase
14      // each other.
15      // These are the only central read−write variables in our algorithm.
16      // Invariant: the generated indices must follow the same trajectory
17      // The stream of indexes generated by PutCursor and TakeCursor does _not_
18      // need to be strictly cyclic, and in fact will not be when the PutCursor
19      // and TakeCursor overflow and change sign. That's benign.
20      // Progress property : obstruction within a lane impacts only that lane.
21      // Invariant: if there are any "written" lanes in the MultiLane collection then
22      // the lane identified by TakeCursor is written. "Written" means that the
23      // sub−collection at that specified lane has at least one available element,
24      // or that some arriving put() has advanced PutCursor and is poised to put()
25      // into that lane. Take() may thus pair−up promptly if put messages are
26      // available. Complementary invariants exist for readers.
27      // The general approach is similar to that of a ring buffer, except that
28      // there are no locks at the top level but only atomically updated cursors, and
29      // the ring elements are themselves blocking concurrent collections
30      private final AtomicInteger PutCursor = new AtomicInteger();
31      private final AtomicInteger TakeCursor = new AtomicInteger();
32
33      public MultiLane (int Width) {
34          // For brevity of explication require power−of−two Width value
35          // That allows efficient indexing of the form : Lanes[i & (Lanes.length−1)]
36          assert (Width & (Width−1)) == 0 && Width > 0 ;
37          Lanes = (SynchronousQueue< T >[]) new SynchronousQueue[Width];
38          for (int i = 0; i < Width; i++ ) {
39              Lanes[i] = new SynchronousQueue<T>();
40          }
41      }
42
43      public void put (T v) {
44          final int curs = PutCursor.getAndIncrement() ; // atomic fetch−and−add
45          Lanes [curs & (Lanes.length−1)].put(v) ; // put() is blocking
46      }
47
48      public T take() {
49          final int curs = TakeCursor.getAndIncrement(); // atomic fetch−and−add
50          return Lanes[curs & (Lanes.length−1)].take() ; // take() is blocking
51      }
52  }
```

Brief Announcement: Read Invisibility, Virtual World Consistency and Permissiveness are Compatible

Tyler Crain
IRISA
Campus de Beaulieu
35042 Rennes Cedex, France
tyler.crain@irisa.fr

Damien Imbs
IRISA
Campus de Beaulieu
35042 Rennes Cedex, France
damien.imbs@irisa.fr

Michel Raynal
IUF, IRISA
Campus de Beaulieu
35042 Rennes Cedex, France
raynal@irisa.fr

ABSTRACT

This brief announcement studies the relation between two STM properties (read invisibility and permissiveness) and two consistency conditions for STM systems, namely, opacity and virtual world consistency. A read operation issued by a transaction is invisible if it does not entail shared memory modifications. An STM system is permissive with respect to a consistency condition if it accepts every history that satisfies the condition. The brief announcement first shows that read invisibility, permissiveness and opacity are incompatible. It then shows that invisibility, permissiveness and virtual world consistency are compatible.

Category and Subject Descriptors:
D.1.3 [**Programming Techniques**]: Concurrent Programming ; D.2.4 [**Software Engineering**]: Software/Program Verification ; D.4.1 [**Operating Systems**]: Process Management, Concurrency

General Terms: Theory.

Keywords: Asynchronous shared memory system, Commit/abort, Concurrent object, Consistency condition, Opacity, Permissiveness, Software transactional memory, Transaction, Virtual world consistency.

1. SOFTWARE TRANSACTIONAL MEMORY (STM) SYSTEMS

The aim of an STM system is to simplify the design and the writing of concurrent programs by discharging the programmer from the explicit management of synchronization entailed by concurrent accesses to shared objects. What this means is that, when faced to synchronization, a programmer has to concentrate on where atomicity is required and not on the way it is realized.

More explicitly, an STM is a middleware approach that provides the programmers with the *transaction* concept. A process is designed as (or decomposed into) a sequence of transactions, each transaction being a piece of code that, while accessing any number of shared objects, always appears as being executed atomically. The job of the programmer is only to define the units of computation that are the transactions. He does not have to worry about the fact that the objects can be concurrently accessed by transactions. Except when he defines the beginning and the end of a transaction, the programmer is not concerned by syn-

chronization. It is the job of the STM system to ensure that transactions execute as if they were atomic.

Of course, a solution in which a single transaction executes at a time trivially implements transaction atomicity but is irrelevant from an efficiency point of view. So, a STM system has to do "its best" to execute and commit as many transactions per time unit as possible. Similarly to a scheduler, a STM system is an on-line algorithm that does not know the future. If the STM is not trivial (i.e., it allows several transactions that access the same objects in a conflicting manner to run concurrently), this intrinsic limitation can direct it to abort some transactions in order to ensure both transaction atomicity and object consistency. From a programming point of view, an aborted transaction has no effect (it is up to the process that issued an aborted transaction to re-issue it or not; usually, a transaction that is restarted is considered a new transaction). Abort is the price that has to be paid by transactional systems to cope with concurrency in absence of explicit synchronization mechanisms (such as locks or event queues).

2. TWO CONSISTENCY CONDITIONS FOR STM SYSTEMS

The opacity consistency condition. In contrast to database transactions that are usually produced by SQL queries, in a STM system the code encapsulated in a transaction is not restricted to particular patterns. Consequently a transaction always has to operate on a consistent state. To be more explicit, let us consider the following example where a transaction contains the statement $x \leftarrow a/(b - c)$ (where a, b and c are integer data), and let us assume that $b - c$ is different from 0 in all consistent states (intuitively, a consistent state is a global state that, considering only the committed transactions, could have existed at some real time instant). If the values of b and c read by a transaction come from different states, it is possible that the transaction obtains values such as $b = c$ (and $b = c$ defines an inconsistent state). If this occurs, the transaction throws an exception that has to be handled by the process that invoked the corresponding transaction. Even worse undesirable behaviors can be obtained when reading values from inconsistent states. This occurs for example when an inconsistent state provides a transaction with values that generate infinite loops. Such bad behaviors have to be prevented in STM systems: whatever its fate (commit or abort) a transaction always has to see a consistent state of the data it accesses. The aborted transactions have to be harmless.

Formally introduced and investigated in [3], the *opacity* consistency condition requires that no transaction reads values from an inconsistent global state where, considering only the committed transactions, a *consistent global state* is defined as the state of the shared memory at some real time instant. Let us associate with each aborted transaction T its execution prefix (called *read prefix*) that contains all its read operations until T aborts (if the abort is entailed by a read, this read is not included in the prefix). An execution of a set of transactions satisfies the *opacity* condition if (i) all committed transactions plus each aborted transaction reduced to its read prefix appear as if they have been executed sequentially and (ii) this sequence respects the transaction real-time occurrence order.

Virtual world consistency. This consistency condition, introduced in [4], is weaker than opacity while keeping its spirit. It states that (1) no transaction (committed or aborted) reads values from an inconsistent global state, (2) the consistent global states read by the committed transactions are mutually consistent (in the sense that they can be totally ordered) but (3) while the global state read by each aborted transaction is consistent from its individual point of view, the global states read by any two aborted transactions are not required to be mutually consistent. Said differently, virtual world consistency requires that (1) all the committed transactions be serializable (so they all have the same "witness sequential execution") or linearizable (if we want this witness execution to also respect real time) and (2) each aborted transaction (reduced to a read prefix as explained previously) reads values that are consistent with respect to its causal past only.

Because two aborted transactions can have different causal pasts, each can read from a global state that is consistent from its causal past point of view, but these two global states may be mutually inconsistent as aborted transactions have not necessarily the same causal past (hence the name *virtual world* consistency). This consistency condition can benefit many STM applications as, from its local point of view, a transaction cannot differentiate it from opacity.

In addition to the fact that it can allow more transactions to commit than opacity, one of the main advantages of virtual world consistency lies in the fact that, as opacity, it prevents bad phenomena (as described previously) from occurring without requiring all the transactions (committed or aborted) to agree on the very same witness execution. Let us assume that each transaction behaves correctly (e.g. it does not entail a division by 0, does not enter an infinite loop, etc.) when, executed alone, it reads values from a consistent global state. As, due to the virtual world consistency condition, no transaction (committed or aborted) reads from an inconsistent state, it cannot behave incorrectly despite concurrency, it can only be aborted. This is a first class requirement for transactional memories.

3. DESIRABLE PROPERTIES FOR STMS

Invisible read operation. A read operation issued by a transaction is *invisible* if it does not entail the modification of base shared objects used to implement the STM system. This is a desirable property for both efficiency and privacy.

Disjoint access parallelism. Ideally, an STM system should allow transactions that are on distinct objects to execute without interference, i.e., without accessing the same base shared variables. This is important for efficiency and restricts the number or unnecessary aborts.

Permissiveness. The notion of permissiveness has been introduced in [2]. It is on transaction abort. Intuitively, an STM system is *permissive* "if it never aborts a transaction unless necessary for correctness" (otherwise it is *non-permissive*). More precisely, an STM system is permissive with respect to a consistency condition (e.g., opacity) if it accepts every history that satisfies the condition.

Some STM systems are randomized in the sense that the commit/abort point of a transaction depends on a random coin toss. Probabilistic permissiveness is suited to such systems. A randomized STM system is *probabilistically permissive* with respect to a consistency condition if every history that satisfies the condition is accepted with positive probability [2].

As indicated in [2], an STM system that checks at commit time that the values of the objects read by a transaction have not been modified (and aborts the transaction if true) cannot be permissive with respect to opacity.

4. CONTENT OF THE PAPER

The full paper [1] is on permissive STM systems with invisible reads. It has several contributions.
- It first shows that an STM system that satisfies read invisibility and opacity cannot be permissive.
- The paper then presents an STM system (called IR_VWC_P) that satisfies read invisibility, virtual world consistency and probabilistic permissiveness. The IR_VWC_P protocol presents additional noteworthy properties.

  - It uses only base read/write operations and locks, each associated with a shared object. Moreover, a lock is used at most once by a transaction at the end of a transaction (when it executes an operation called try_to_commit()).

  - It satisfies the disjoint access parallelism property.

5. REFERENCES

[1] Crain T., Imbs D. and Raynal M., Read invisibility, virtual world consistency and permissiveness are compatible. *Tech Report #1958*, IRISA, Univ. de Rennes 1, France, November 2010.
[2] Guerraoui R., Henzinger T.A., Singh V., Permissiveness in Transactional Memories. *Proc. 22th Int'l Symposium on Distributed Computing (DISC'08)*, Springer-Verlag, LNCS #5218, pp. 305-318, 2008.
[3] Guerraoui R. and Kapałka M., On the Correctness of Transactional Memory. *Proc. 13th ACM SIGPLAN Symposium on Principles and Practice of Parallel Programming (PPoPP'08)*, pp. 175-184, 2008.
[4] Imbs D. and Raynal M., A versatile STM protocol with Invisible Read Operations that Satisfies the Virtual World Consistency Condition. *16th Colloquium on Structural Information and Communication Complexity (SIROCCO'09)*, Springer Verlag LNCS, #5869, pp. 266-280, 2009.

Tight Bounds for Anonymous Adopt-Commit Objects

James Aspnes [*]
Department of Computer Science
Yale University
New Haven, Connecticut, USA
aspnes@cs.yale.edu

Faith Ellen [†]
Department of Computer Science
University of Toronto
Toronto, Ontario, Canada
faith@cs.toronto.edu

ABSTRACT

We give matching upper and lower bounds of $\Theta\left(\min\left(\frac{\log m}{\log\log m}, n\right)\right)$ for the space and individual step complexity of a wait-free m-valued adopt-commit object implemented using multi-writer registers for n anonymous processes. While the upper bound is deterministic, the lower bound holds for randomized adopt-commit objects as well. Our results are based on showing that adopt-commit objects are equivalent, up to small additive constants, to a simpler class of objects that we call **weak conflict-detectors**.

It follows that the same lower bound holds on the individual step complexity of m-valued wait-free anonymous consensus, even for randomized algorithms with global coins against an oblivious adversary. The upper bound can also be used to slightly improve the cost of randomized consensus in the probabilistic-write model.

Categories and Subject Descriptors

F.1.2 [**Modes of Computation**]: Parallelism and concurrency

General Terms

Algorithms, Theory

Keywords

distributed computing, shared memory, anonymity, adopt-commit objects, conflict detectors, consensus

1. INTRODUCTION

An **adopt-commit object** [2] or **ratifier** [3] is a one-shot shared-memory object that represents the **adopt-commit**

[*]Supported in part by NSF grant CCF-0916389.

[†]Supported in part by the Natural Science and Engineering Research Council of Canada.

protocols of [14] and can be used to implement round-based protocols for set-agreement and consensus. An m-valued adopt-commit object supports a single operation, adopt-Commit (u), where u is an input from a set of m values. The result of this operation is an output of the form (commit, v) or (adopt, v), where the first component is a **decision bit** that indicates whether the process should decide value v immediately or adopt it as its preferred value in later rounds of the protocol. Improving the performance of adopt-commit objects can improve the performance of consensus protocols that use them. In addition, as observed in [3], lower bounds on adopt-commit objects also yield immediate lower bounds on consensus.

The requirements for an adopt-commit object are:

1. **Validity.** Every operation's output equals some operation's input.

2. **Termination.** Every operation finishes its operation in a finite number of steps with probability 1, where the probability is taken over the coin tosses performed by the algorithm.

3. **Coherence.**[1] If some operation returns (commit, v), every operation returns either (adopt, v) or (commit, v).

4. **Convergence.** If all inputs are v, all operations return (commit, v).

These requirements are closely related to the validity, termination, and agreement requirements for consensus. The difference is that agreement (which requires that all processes obtain the same output) is replaced by the weaker requirements of coherence and convergence. As observed in [3], this means that consensus objects satisfy the requirements of adopt-commit objects. It follows that lower bounds on adopt-commit objects immediately give lower bounds on consensus objects.

Until now, the best implementations of m-valued adopt-commit objects had $\Theta(n)$ individual step complexity, for n processes [14] or $\Theta(\log m)$ individual step complexity, for any number of processes [3]. Both these implementations are deterministic, but the latter is also **anonymous**. This means that all processes run the same code. Differences between the behaviour of two different processes can arise only as a result of different input values, (different supplies of random bits, in the case of a randomized protocol), and when

---

[1]The definition of adopt-commit objects in [2] uses the term *agreement* for this property. We use *agreement* instead for the stronger unconditional agreement property of consensus objects. The term *coherence* is from [3].

they are scheduled. A number of advantages of anonymity are are discussed in [5].

Here, we consider how much further we can improve the complexity of an implementation of an adopt-commit object without losing anonymity. We give two simple, deterministic, anonymous protocols for detecting multiple input values, from which we obtain implementations of m-valued adopt-commit objects. One of these has $O(n)$ individual step complexity, given an upper bound, n, on the number of processes. The other has $O\left(\frac{\log m}{\log\log m}\right)$ individual step complexity, for any number of processes. While this is only a small improvement in complexity, we show a matching lower bound on the individual step complexity of any anonymous implementation (including randomized implementations against an oblivious adversary) of an m-valued adopt-commit object that supports at least $\Omega\left(\frac{\log m}{\log\log m}\right)$ processes.

Our lower bound also implies a lower bound of $\Omega\left(\frac{\log m}{\log\log m}\right)$ on the individual step complexity for anonymous randomized consensus with sufficiently many processes, even against an oblivious adversary.

2. CONFLICT DETECTORS

The implementation of an adopt-commit object in [3] relies on a quorum-based conflict detection mechanism, where each process with value v writes to a set of registers W_v and detects conflicting values by reading a set of registers R_v, with the property that $W_v \cap R_{v'} \neq \emptyset$ when $v \neq v'$. It is shown there that the smallest possible size for these quorums is $\Theta(\log m)$, using tools from extremal combinatorics. The quorum-based mechanism generalizes a similar mechanism in [14], where a process detects conflicting values by performing a collect over single-writer registers, which requires individual step complexity linear in the number of processes.

If we set aside the quorum structure, we can define an abstract conflict-detector object as a generalization of these mechanisms. We begin with a linearizable version that can be used as a drop-in replacement for existing conflict detection mechanisms. Then we further reduce it to a weaker (and, thus, easier to implement) version that does not satisfy linearizability.

Formally, an m-**valued strong conflict-detector** supports two operations, write(v), for inputs v from a set of m values, and read(), where read() returns **true** (conflict) if two or more different values have previously been written and returns **false** (no conflict), otherwise. These operations must appear to be atomic to the user of the strong conflict-detector. Specifically, we require that any strong conflict-detector implementation be **linearizable** [15], meaning that, for any concurrent execution of strong conflict-detector operations, we can construct a sequential execution with the same operations such that each operation returns the same response in both executions and non-concurrent operations in the original execution occur in the same order as in the sequential execution.

Linearizability is sometimes difficult to prove. To make things simpler, we show that strong conflict-detectors can be built from even weaker objects, which we call **weak conflict-detectors**. An m-valued weak conflict-detector supports only a single operation check(v), with input v from a set of m values. It returns **true** (to indicate a conflict) or

false (to indicate no conflicts), and has the following two properties: In any execution that contains a check(v) operation and a check(v') operation with $v \neq v'$, at least one of these two operations returns **true**. In any execution in which all check operations have the same argument, they all return **false**. For weak conflict-detectors, we do not require linearizability: it is fine for one check operation to return **true** while subsequent check operations return false.

2.1 Equivalence of adopt-commit objects, strong conflict-detectors, and weak conflict-detectors

We show that the individual step complexities of adopt-commit objects, strong conflict-detectors, and weak conflict-detectors differ by small additive constants. Because our reductions are anonymous, this also holds for anonymous implementations. We use $T_{\texttt{adoptCommit}}$, $T_{\texttt{write}}$, $T_{\texttt{read}}$, and $T_{\texttt{check}}$ to denote the worst case step complexities of the adoptCommit, write, read, and check operations.

We give implementations of a weak conflict-detector from an adopt-commit object, a strong conflict-detector from a weak conflict-detector, and finally an adopt-commit object from a strong conflict-detector. We begin by showing how to implement a weak conflict-detector from an adopt-commit object. This is is the simplest case, since neither of these objects is required to satisfy linearizability. The code is presented in Figure 1.

---

shared data:
    adopt-commit object r;
1 **procedure** check(v)
2 **begin**
3     $(d, v') \leftarrow r.\texttt{adoptCommit}(v)$
4   **if** $(d, v') \neq (\textsf{commit}, v)$ **then**
5   **return** true
6   **else**
7   **return** false
8   **end**
9 **end**

Algorithm 1: A weak conflict-detector using an adopt-commit object.

LEMMA 1. *Algorithm 1 implements a weak conflict-detector with* $T_{\texttt{check}} = T_{\texttt{adoptCommit}}$.

PROOF. If all check operations have the same input v, then, they all call $r.\texttt{adoptCommit}(v)$, which, by the convergence property, all return (commit, v). In this case, all the check(v) operations return **false**. If there are two operations, check(v) and check(v'), with $v \neq v'$, then, they call $r.\texttt{adoptCommit}(v)$ and $r.\texttt{adoptCommit}(v')$, respectively. By coherence, it is not possible for (commit, v) to be the result of $r.\texttt{adoptCommit}(v)$ and for (commit, v') to be the result of $r.\texttt{adoptCommit}(v')$ in the same execution. It follows that **true** is returned by at least one of the two check operations. Thus, Algorithm 1 implements a weak conflict-detector.

The step complexity of check is the same as the step complexity of adoptCommit, since only Line 3 contains a nonlocal operation. □

To extend a weak conflict-detector to a strong conflict-detector, we add a one-bit register, conflict, which is set to true whenever a write operation detects a conflict. The code for read and write is presented in Algorithm 2. To carry out a read operation, a process simply reads the conflict bit and returns its value. We show, in Lemma 2, that this does, in fact, give a strong (i.e., linearizable) conflict-detector.

---

shared data:
    weak conflict-detector d;
    1-bit atomic register conflict, initially **false**.

```
1  procedure write(v)
2  begin
3      if d.check(v) then
4          conflict ← true
5      end
6  end
7  procedure read()
8  begin
9      return conflict
10 end
```

Algorithm 2: A strong conflict-detector using a weak conflict-detector.

LEMMA 2. *Algorithm 2 implements a strong conflict-detector with $T_{\texttt{write}} \leq T_{\texttt{check}} + 1$ and $T_{\texttt{read}} = 1$.*

PROOF. The running time is immediate from the code.

To show that Algorithm 2 implements a strong conflict-detector, we give an explicit linearization of the read and write operations in any execution. The linearization point, t_r, of a read operation, r, is the time at which it reads register conflict. Let τ be the first time during the execution at which some process sets conflict to true, or $+\infty$, if there is no such time. For each write operation w, let s_w be the time at which the write operation starts. The linearization point, t_w, of operation w is defined to be $\max(s_w, \tau)$, if w sets conflict to true, and s_w, otherwise.

We show that these assigned times (with ties broken arbitrarily) gives a correct linearization. A write operation that sets conflict to true is linearized when it starts or at the first time in the execution that some process sets conflict to true, whichever is later. Note that this occurs at or before the end of the operation. All other operations are linearized when they start. This linearization order is consistent with the observable execution order.

Recall that τ is the time at which conflict is set to true. Any read that is linearized before τ reads **false** from conflict. Similarly, any read that is linearized after τ reads **true** from conflict. We satisfy the specification of the strong conflict-detector if (a) at most one distinct value appears as an argument to any write operation linearized strictly before τ and (b) if $\tau \neq +\infty$, then at least two different values appear as arguments to write operations linearized at or before time τ.

To be linearized before τ, a write(v) operation must not set conflict to true and, hence, its call to d.check(v) must return **false**. But the specification of a weak conflict-detector implies that all d.check operations which return **false** must have the same input value. It follows that all write operations linearized before τ have the same input value. This proves (a).

If $\tau \neq +\infty$, then some write operation, w, sets conflict to true at time τ and $t_w = \max(s_w, \tau) = \tau$. This write oper-

ation previously completed a call to d.check that returned **true**. If all calls to d.check that started before τ have the same input value, then we can truncate the execution at time τ and allow all check operations to run to completion. This results in an execution of the weak conflict-detector d in which all calls to d.check have the same input value, but some call to d.check returns **true**, which violates the specification of a weak conflict-detector. Hence, there are two calls to d.check with different input values that started before τ. Thus, there must be two corresponding write operations w and w' with different input values that also started before τ. These are assigned linearization points $\max(s_w, \tau) = \max(s_{w'}, \tau) = \tau$. This proves (b). □

Finally, Algorithm 3 completes the cycle by showing how to turn an anonymous strong conflict-detector into an adopt-commit object, with the addition of an extra register for holding proposed values. The mechanism is essentially the same as in the adopt-commit implementation given in [3], with a generic strong conflict-detector taking the place of the quorum-based mechanism used there.

---

shared data:
    register proposal, initially $\perp$;
    strong conflict-detector c.

```
1   procedure adoptCommit(v)
2   begin
3       c.write(v)
4       u ← proposal
5       if u ≠ ⊥ then
6           v ← u
7       else
8           proposal ← v
9       end
10      if c.read() = true then
11          return (adopt, v)
12      else
13          return (commit, v)
14      end
15  end
```

Algorithm 3: An adopt-commit object using a strong conflict-detector.

LEMMA 3. *Algorithm 3 implements an adopt-commit object with $T_{\texttt{adoptCommit}} \leq T_{\texttt{write}} + T_{\texttt{read}} + 2$.*

PROOF. The proof of coherence relies on the following key observation: If an adoptCommit operation returns (commit, v), then proposal was set to v before any adoptCommit(v') operation with $v' \neq v$ finished its call to c.write. It follows that all adoptCommit(v') operations with $v' \neq v$ read v from proposal and return (adopt, v). The other properties of the adopt-commit object are easily verified. □

Since the specification of a weak conflict-detector is simpler than those of strong conflict-detectors or adopt-commit objects, it will be easiest to obtain bounds on their complexity by concentrating on weak conflict-detectors.

3. UPPER BOUNDS ON ANONYMOUS WEAK CONFLICT-DETECTORS

In this section, we give two complementary implementations of anonymous m-valued weak conflict-detectors. The first uses $O\left(\frac{\log m}{\log \log m}\right)$ steps for any number of processes, while the second uses $O(n)$ steps, for any value of m, where n is an upper bound on the number of processes. By choosing the first implementation when m is small and the second when m is large, we obtain a weak conflict-detector that runs in $O\left(\min\left(\frac{\log m}{\log \log m}, n\right)\right)$ steps, which we show to be optimal in Section 4.

3.1 Permutation-based weak conflict-detector

Algorithm 4 implements an anonymous, deterministic weak conflict-detector for $m \leq k!$ values using at most $2k$ operations for check(v). As a function of m, this gives a worst-case individual step complexity of $2\,\text{fact}^{-1}(m) = O\left(\frac{\log m}{\log \log m}\right)$, where $\text{fact}(k) = k!$ is the factorial function.

---

shared data:
    registers $R[1..k]$, initially $\perp$.
1 **procedure** check(v)
2 **begin**
3   **for** $i \leftarrow 1..k$ **do**
4     $r \leftarrow R[\pi_v(i)]$
5   **if** $r = \perp$ **then**
6       $R[\pi_v(i)] \leftarrow v$
7   **else if** $r \neq v$ **then**
8   **return true**
9   **end**
10   **end**
11   **return false**
12 **end**

Algorithm 4: Permutation-based weak conflict-detector for m values.

In the natural algorithm for two values, a process performing check(b), for $b \in \{0,1\}$, writes to $R[b]$ and then checks $R[1-b]$. Then, whichever of $R[0]$ or $R[1]$ is written first will later be seen to have a non-$\perp$ value by any process that writes to the other register, detecting the conflict.

Algorithm 4 is a generalization of this algorithm from $m = 2$ values to $m = k!$ values. Each of the $k!$ possible input values v is mapped to a distinct permutation $\pi_v : \{1, \ldots, k\} \rightarrow \{1, \ldots, k\}$. Then, for any two different input values, there exist two registers which function as in the natural two-value algorithm.

LEMMA 4. *Algorithm 4 implements a weak conflict-detector.*

PROOF. If all calls to check have the same input value v, then only v will be written to each register $R[i]$ and no process ever observes any value other than v or $\perp$. In this case, all operations correctly return **false**.

Now suppose there is an execution E in which two processes, p_u and $p_{u'}$, with different input values, u and u', both return **false**. Then both processes read from all of the registers $R[1], \ldots, R[k]$ and the values u and u' will both be written to all of the registers. Let $j, j' \in \{1, \ldots, k\}$ be two indexes such that j occurs before j' in π_u, but j' occurs before j in $\pi_{u'}$. If u is written to $R[j]$ before u' is written to

$R[j']$ in E, then, when $p_{u'}$ or any other process with value u' reads $R[j]$, it will not see $\perp$. This is because, before it reads $R[j]$, it either writes u' to $R[j']$ or reads u' from $R[j']$. This implies that no process writes u' to $R[j]$, which is a contradiction.

Therefore u' is written to $R[j']$ before u is written to $R[j]$. But, then, no process writes u to $R[j']$, which is also a contradiction. $\square$

3.2 Collect-based weak conflict-detector

Algorithm 5 is another implementation of a weak conflict-detector. It places no limit on the number of distinct values m, but it works only when an upper bound, n, on the number of processes is known. The worst-case individual step complexity of a check(v) operation in Algorithm 5 is $3n+1$.

---

shared data:
    registers $R[1..n]$, initially $\perp$;
    1-bit atomic register done, initially **false**.
1 **procedure** check(v)
2 **begin**
3   **for** $i \leftarrow 1..n$ **do**
4   **if** done **then**
5   **break**
6   **else**
7       $R[i] \leftarrow v$
8   **end**
9   **end**
10   done $\leftarrow$ **true**
11   **for** $i \leftarrow 1..n$ **do**
12   **if** $R[i] \neq v$ **then**
13   **return true**
14   **end**
15   **end**
16   **return false**
17 **end**

Algorithm 5: A collect-based weak conflict-detector for n processes.

The essential idea is that once some process finishes the first loop in check(v) and sets done to **true**, each of the at most $n-1$ other processes can write to at most one location in R before seeing done $=$ **true** and leaving the loop. Because no process executes the collect in the second loop until done $=$ **true**, any views obtained by two different processes in this loop can differ in at most $n-1$ places. It follows that no two processes with different inputs can both see their own input in all n positions during the collect. Therefore, at least one of them will return **true**. If all calls to check have the same input, then only this input will appear in R, so all the calls will return **false**.

More formally, we have shown:

LEMMA 5. *Algorithm 5 implements a weak conflict-detector.*

4. LOWER BOUND ON ANONYMOUS WEAK CONFLICT-DETECTORS

In this section, we show that any m-valued weak conflict-detector for n anonymous processes has $\Omega\left(\min\left(\frac{\log m}{\log\log m}, n\right)\right)$ worst-case solo step complexity. Fix some anonymous, deterministic implementation of an m-valued weak conflict-detector. For each input value v, we consider the solo execution E_v in which a process executes check(v) starting from the initial configuration. Note that, because processes are deterministic and anonymous, the sequence of operations in E_v is fully determined by v.

Let k_v be the step complexity of E_v. Let W_v be the set of registers that a process writes to in E_v and let X_v be the set of registers that it reads from but does not write to. Let A_v be the permutation of $W_v \cup X_v$ arranged in the order in which the registers in W_v are first written and the registers in X_v are last read in E_v.

LEMMA 6. *For all distinct input values u and v, if $k_u + k_v \leq n$, then there exist two registers $R_i, R_j \in (W_u \cup X_u) \cap (W_v \cup X_v)$ that occur in different orders in A_u and A_v.*

PROOF. Suppose there are two input values $u \neq v$ such that $k_u + k_v \leq n$ and all registers $R_i, R_j \in (W_u \cup X_u) \cap (W_v \cup X_v)$ occur in the same order in A_u and A_v. We show that an adversary can construct an execution E involving $k_u + k_v \leq n$ processes that is indistinguishable from E_u to some process p_u performing check(u) and indistinguishable from E_v to some other process p_v performing check(v). In this execution, both p_u and p_v return **false**, violating the specification of a weak conflict-detector.

For each $R_i \in W_u \cap (W_v \cup X_v)$, let $\sigma_{i,u}$ be the first write to R_i in E_u and, for each $R_i \in X_u \cap (W_v \cup X_v)$, let $\sigma_{i,u}$ be the last read from R_i in E_u. Let $S_u = \{\sigma_{i,u} \mid R_i \in (W_u \cup X_u) \cap (W_v \cup X_v)\}$. Define $\sigma_{i,v}$ and S_v analogously.

The adversary starts by constructing an interleaving E' of the operations in E_u and E_v. The operations in E' appear in the same order as in E_u. Hence $E'|p_u = E_u$. The adversary schedules each read operation $\sigma_{i,v} \in S_v$ immediately before $\sigma_{i,u}$ and schedules each write operation $\sigma_{i,v} \in S_v$ immediately after $\sigma_{i,u}$. Note that, by assumption, the operations in S_v appear in the same order in E' as they do in E_v, namely, in the order the registers $R_i \in (W_u \cup X_u) \cap (W_v \cup X_v)$ they access occur in A_u and A_v.

If no operations in S_v occur between $\sigma_{i,v}$ and $\sigma_{j,v}$, then, in E', the adversary arbitrarily interleaves the operations in E_v that occur strictly between $\sigma_{i,v}$ and $\sigma_{j,v}$ with the operations in E_u that occur strictly between $\sigma_{i,u}$ and $\sigma_{j,u}$. Likewise, the adversary arbitrarily interleaves the operations in E_v that occur before the first operation in S_v with the operations in E_u that occur before the first operation in S_u and the operations in E_v that occur after the last operation in S_v with the operations in E_u that occur after the last operation in S_u. Hence $E'|p_v = E_v$.

The sequence of operations in E' is not necessarily a valid execution, because p_u may read a value written by p_v or p_v may read a value written by p_u. To prevent this, we add **clones**, as used in [13]. A **clone** of a process p is a process with the same input and code as p, which proceeds in lockstep with p, reading and writing the same values as p, until immediately before some write to a register. The adversary has the clone perform that write at some later point in the execution to ensure that the value p reads from that register

is the same as the value p last wrote there. After performing its delayed write, a clone performs no further steps.

For each register $R_i \in W_u \cap W_v$, the adversary adds one clone of p_u to E' for each read of R_i by p_u after $\sigma_{i,v}$ and one clone of p_v to E' for each read of R_i by p_v after $\sigma_{i,v}$. Let E be the resulting execution.

If $R_i \in W_u \cap W_v$, then, by construction, any read of R_i by p_u in E after $\sigma_{i,v}$ sees the same value it saw in E_u, namely, the value it last wrote to R_i. Any read of R_i prior to $\sigma_{i,u}$ sees the initial value of R_i, since $\sigma_{i,u}$ and $\sigma_{i,v}$ are, by definition, the first writes to R_i by p_u and p_v in E' and, hence, E.

If $R_i \in X_u \cap W_v$, then all reads of R_i by p_u in E occur at or before $\sigma_{i,u}$ and, hence, see the initial value of R_i, as they do in E_u. This is because, in E, all writes to R_i by p_v occur at or after $\sigma_{i,v}$, which is after $\sigma_{i,u}$.

If $R_i \in (W_u \cup X_u) - W_v$, then p_v does not write to R_i in E, so all reads of R_i by p_u are the same as in E_u. Finally, if $R_i \notin W_u \cup X_u$, then p_u does not read R_i in E. Thus E_u and E are indistinguishable to p_u.

Similarly, E_v and E are indistinguishable to p_v. □

The following combinatorial lemma allows us to bound m as a function of the step complexities, k_v, of the solo executions E_v. The proof is similar to Lubell's proof of Sperner's Lemma [16].

LEMMA 7. *Let $\{A_1, \ldots, A_m\}$ be a set of finite sequences without repetition such that, for any two sequences A_i and A_j, there exist elements $x_{i,j}$ and $y_{i,j}$ that appear in different orders in A_i and A_j. Then $\sum_{i=1}^{m} \frac{1}{|A_i|!} \leq 1$.*

PROOF. Let $A = \bigcup_{i=1}^{m} A_i$ be the set of all elements appearing in any of the sequences $A_1, \ldots, A_m$. Choose an ordering of A uniformly at random. Let X_i be the indicator variable that has value 1, if the ordering of the elements in A_i is consistent with this ordering, and has value 0, otherwise. Let $X = \sum_{i=1}^{m} X_i$.

Note that $X_i = 1$ implies that $X_j = 0$ for all $j \neq i$. This is because $x_{i,j}$ and $y_{i,j}$ appear in different orders in A_i and A_j. It follows that $X \leq 1$.

For each sequence A_i, the probability that it is consistent with the chosen ordering is exactly $\frac{1}{|A_i|!}$, so $E[X_i] = \frac{1}{|A_i|!}$. Hence $\sum_{i=1}^{m} \frac{1}{|A_i|!} = \sum_{i=1}^{m} E[X_i] = E[X] \leq 1$. □

THEOREM 8. *The worst-case solo step complexity of any anonymous deterministic implementation of an m-valued weak conflict detector for n processes is at least $\min(\text{fact}^{-1}(m), n/2)$, where $\text{fact}(\ell) = \ell!$ is the factorial function.*

PROOF. Fix any anonymous deterministic implementation of an m-valued weak conflict-detector for n processes and let k be its worst-case solo step complexity. Then, for every input value v, $|A_v| \leq k_v \leq k$.

If $k > n/2$, then the claim is true, so suppose that $k \leq n/2$. Then, for all distinct inputs u and v, $k_u + k_v \leq n$ and, hence, by Lemma 6, there are two registers that occur in different orders in A_u and A_v. It follows from Lemma 7 that $\sum_v \frac{1}{|A_v|!} \leq 1$. Since there m different input values, $\sum_v \frac{1}{|A_v|!} \geq \sum_v \frac{1}{k!} = m/k!$. Thus $k \geq \text{fact}^{-1}(m)$. □

Theorem 8 implies that $T_{\text{check}} \geq \min(\text{fact}^{-1}(m), n/2)$. This matches the upper bound from Section 3 to within a small constant factor.

From Lemma 1, it follows that $T_{\text{adoptCommit}} \geq T_{\text{check}}$ and, from Lemma 3, it follows that $T_{\text{write}} + T_{\text{read}} \geq T_{\text{adoptCommit}} - 2$. Thus, we get lower bounds for the individual step complexities of adopt-commit objects and strong conflict-detectors.

Lemma 2 says that Algorithm 2 implements a strong conflict-detector with $T_{\text{write}} \leq T_{\text{check}} + 1$ and $T_{\text{read}} = 1$, so $T_{\text{write}} + T_{\text{read}} \leq T_{\text{adoptCommit}} + 2$. It is also possible to construct a strong conflict-detector with $T_{\text{write}} = 1$ using one Boolean register R_v for each input value v. The idea is to have write(v) set R_v to **true** and have read() return **true** if at least two of these m registers are **true**. Note that, for this algorithm, $T_{\text{write}} + T_{\text{read}} = m + 1$, which is much larger than the lower bound. It is still open whether an algorithm with constant T_{write} and smaller T_{read} is possible.

Because the requirements for weak conflict-detectors are safety properties, we can show that the lower bound applies to randomized anonymous implementations of weak conflict-detectors as well.

COROLLARY 9. *Given any anonymous randomized implementation of an m-valued weak conflict detector for n processes, there is an input v such that any solo execution of* check(v) *has step complexity at least* $\min(\text{fact}^{-1}(m), n/2)$ *with probability 1 against an oblivious adversary.*

PROOF. Suppose not. Then, for any input v, there is some sequence of coin-flip outcomes that causes a process p_v with input v to complete a solo execution of check(v) in less than $\min(\text{fact}^{-1}(m), n/2)$ steps. For each v, let E_v be the execution of the deterministic protocol obtained by fixing the coin-flips to have these outcomes. The proof of Theorem 8 constructs a combined execution E in which two processes p_u and p_v with different inputs both return **false**. Such an execution occurs with nonzero probability in the randomized algorithm, because p_u, p_v, and all of their respective clones can generate these fixed sequences of coin-flip outcomes. This violates the correctness of the implementation. □

The corresponding bounds also hold for anonymous randomized implementations of adopt-commit objects and strong conflict-detectors.

5. CONSEQUENCES FOR CONSENSUS

Here we consider the effect of our improved bounds for adopt-commit objects on the consensus problem. In the consensus problem, n processes must agree on a value, which must be equal to some process's input. A protocol is randomized wait-free if, in addition, any process can complete it in a finite expected number of steps, regardless of the timing of the other's processes' steps or the occurrence up to $n - 1$ crash failures.

The cost of consensus depends strongly on the power of the adversary scheduler that controls timing and process failures and, to a lesser extent, on the number of possible values. For an **adaptive adversary**, which can observe the internal states of the processes, there is a tight bound of $\Theta(n)$ on the individual step complexity of binary (two-valued) consensus [4, 6]. The high cost of consensus in this model has led to examination of models with weaker adversaries, particularly adversaries that are prevented from changing the schedule based on coin-flip values known only to one process.

One approach is to limit the adversary's ability to observe the state of the system. A **value-oblivious adversary** [8–10] cannot observe the internal states of processes, the contents of registers, or pending operations. It bases its choice of schedule only on the history of which operations the processes have applied to which registers. The best currently known protocol in this model, due to Aumann [8], achieves consensus with $O(\log n)$ expected individual step complexity for any number of input values.

An alternative is to give extra power to the algorithm by allowing **probabilistic writes** [1, 11, 12], where a process can flip a coin and choose to execute a write operation or not based on the outcome of the coin-flip, without affecting the scheduling done by the adversary. In this model, a protocol of Aspnes [3], based on combining adopt-commit objects and a class of randomized objects called **conciliators**, gives an anonymous protocol for m-valued consensus with expected $O(\log m + \log n)$ individual step complexity, where $O(\log m)$ is the cost of the adopt-commit and $O(\log n)$ is the cost of the conciliator using implementations given in [3].

An **oblivious adversary** that must fix the schedule in advance, without seeing the actions of the processes, gives an even stronger model than both the value-oblivious and probabilistic-write models. (As observed in [3], a process in an oblivious-adversary model can simulate a probabilistic write by choosing randomly between carrying out a write and a dummy operation.) In this model, Attiya and Censor-Hillel [7] have shown that any protocol with two input values runs for at least k steps with probability c^{-k} for some constant c, a bound that translates into constant expected individual step complexity.

Our results improve the previous upper bound for the probabilistic-write model and give a non-trivial lower bound on expected individual step complexity for the oblivious-adversary model when the number of input values m is $\omega(1)$. For the probabilistic-write model, substituting our improved adopt-commit implementation for the adopt-commit object in [3] reduces the expected individual step complexity from $O(\log m + \log n)$ to $O\left(\min\left(\frac{\log m}{\log \log m}, n\right) + \log n\right)$. For the oblivious-adversary model, our lower bound on anonymous adopt-commit objects gives an immediate $\Omega\left(\min\left(\frac{\log m}{\log \log m}, n\right)\right)$ lower bound with probability 1 on the worst-case individual step complexity of anonymous m-valued consensus implementations, because consensus objects satisfy the specification of adopt-commit objects. This is the first lower bound for consensus for which the number of values m is significant.

6. CONCLUSIONS

We have shown how to reduce adopt-commit objects to a much simpler class of weak conflict-detectors, and used this reduction to get tight bounds on the individual step complexity of anonymous m-valued adopt-commit objects. These bounds also translate into improved bounds on anonymous m-valued consensus. The natural question is what happens when the assumption of anonymity is removed. We conjecture that for unboundedly many processes, Ramsey-theoretic techniques may be used to show that similar bounds hold. However, the complexity of non-anonymous adopt-commit objects is still unknown.

7. REFERENCES

[1] Karl Abrahamson. On achieving consensus using a shared memory. In *Proceedings of the 7th Annual ACM Symposium on Principles of Distributed Computing (PODC)*, pages 291–302, 1988.

[2] Dan Alistarh, Seth Gilbert, Rachid Guerraoui, and Corentin Travers. Of choices, failures and asynchrony: The many faces of set agreement. In Yingfei Dong, Ding-Zhu Du, and Oscar H. Ibarra, editors, *ISAAC*, volume 5878 of *Lecture Notes in Computer Science*, pages 943–953. Springer, 2009.

[3] James Aspnes. A modular approach to shared-memory consensus, with applications to the probabilistic-write model. In *Proceedings of the Twenty-Ninth Annual ACM SIGACT-SIGOPS Symposium on Principles of Distributed Computing*, pages 460–467, July 2010.

[4] James Aspnes and Keren Censor. Approximate shared-memory counting despite a strong adversary. In Claire Mathieu, editor, *Proceedings of the Twentieth Annual ACM-SIAM Symposium on Discrete Algorithms, SODA 2009, New York, NY, USA, January 4-6, 2009*, pages 441–450. SIAM, 2009.

[5] James Aspnes, Faith Ellen Fich, and Eric Ruppert. Relationships between broadcast and shared memory in reliable anonymous distributed systems. *Distributed Computing*, 18(3):209–219, February 2006.

[6] Hagit Attiya and Keren Censor. Tight bounds for asynchronous randomized consensus. *J. ACM*, 55(5):20, 2008.

[7] Hagit Attiya and Keren Censor-Hillel. Lower bounds for randomized consensus under a weak adversary. *SIAM J. Comput.*, 39(8):3885–3904, 2010.

[8] Yonatan Aumann. Efficient asynchronous consensus with the weak adversary scheduler. In *PODC '97: Proceedings of the Sixteenth Annual ACM Symposium on Principles of Distributed Computing*, pages 209–218, New York, NY, USA, 1997. ACM.

[9] Yonatan Aumann and Michael A. Bender. Efficient low-contention asynchronous consensus with the value-oblivious adversary scheduler. *Distributed Computing*, 17(3):191–207, 2005.

[10] Tushar Deepak Chandra. Polylog randomized wait-free consensus. In *Proceedings of the Fifteenth Annual ACM Symposium on Principles of Distributed Computing*, pages 166–175, Philadelphia, Pennsylvania, USA, 23–26 May 1996.

[11] Ling Cheung. Randomized wait-free consensus using an atomicity assumption. In *Principles of Distributed Systems, 9th International Conference, OPODIS 2005, Pisa, Italy, December 12-14, 2005, Revised Selected Papers*, volume 3974 of *Lecture Notes in Computer Science*, pages 47–60. Springer, 2006.

[12] Benny Chor, Amos Israeli, and Ming Li. Wait-free consensus using asynchronous hardware. *SIAM J. Comput.*, 23(4):701–712, 1994.

[13] Faith Fich, Maurice Herlihy, and Nir Shavit. On the space complexity of randomized synchronization. *J. ACM*, 45:843–862, September 1998.

[14] Eli Gafni. Round-by-round fault detectors: Unifying synchrony and asynchrony (extended abstract). In *Proceedings of the Seventeenth Annual ACM Symposium on Principles of Distributed Computing*, pages 143–152, 1998.

[15] Maurice Herlihy and Jeannette M. Wing. Linearizability: A correctness condition for concurrent objects. *ACM Trans. Program. Lang. Syst.*, 12(3):463–492, 1990.

[16] D. A. Lubell. A short proof of Sperner's lemma. *Journal of Combinatorial Theory A*, 1(2):402, 1966.

A Highly-Efficient Wait-Free Universal Construction

Panagiota Fatourou
Department of Computer Science
University of Crete
& FORTH ICS
faturu@csd.uoc.gr

Nikolaos D. Kallimanis
Department of Computer Science
University of Ioannina
nkallima@cs.uoi.gr

ABSTRACT

We present a new simple wait-free universal construction, called Sim, that uses just a `Fetch&Add` and an LL/SC object and performs a constant number of shared memory accesses. We have implemented Sim in a real shared-memory machine. In theory terms, our practical version of Sim, called P-Sim, has worse complexity than its theoretical analog; in practice though, we experimentally show that P-Sim outperforms several state-of-the-art lock-based and lock-free techniques, and this given that it is *wait-free*, i.e., that it satisfies a stronger progress condition than all the algorithms it outperforms.

We have used P-Sim to get highly-efficient *wait-free* implementations of stacks and queues. Our experiments show that our implementations outperform the currently state-of-the-art shared stack and queue implementations which ensure only weaker progress properties than wait-freedom.

Categories and Subject Descriptors

E.1 [**Data**]: Data Structures—*distributed data structures, lists, stacks, queues*

General Terms

Algorithms, Experimentation, Theory

Keywords

Concurrent data structures, queues, stacks, universal constructions, wait free

1. INTRODUCTION

Designing efficient shared data structures has become ever so urgent due to the proliferation of multicore machines and the strong necessity of exploiting their computational power by developing parallel software; shared data structures, like stacks and queues, are the most widely used inter-thread communication structures, and therefore they

are major building blocks of such software. A *universal construction* is a generic mechanism to implement any shared data structure; it supports an operation, called APPLYOP, that takes as a parameter the sequential implementation of any operation of the simulated object, and simulates its execution in a concurrent environment.

Herlihy [18] introduced the *consensus hierarchy* which characterizes the power of a shared object to simulate (together with read-write registers) other objects in a wait-free manner; *wait-freedom* [18] ensures that each process should finish the execution of its operation within a finite number of its own steps independently of the speed or the failure of other processes. A shared object with *consensus number* n can be used to simulate (with the help of read-write registers) any other object in a system of n processes. The strongest types of objects are `CAS` and LL/SC which have infinite consensus number. A `CAS` object O supports the operations (1) `read`(O) which returns the current value of O, and (2) `CAS`(O, u, v) which checks if the current value of O is u, and if so, it changes the value of O to v and returns `TRUE`; otherwise, the status of O remains unchanged and `FALSE` is returned. An LL/SC *object* O supports the atomic operations (1) `LL`(O) which returns the current value of O and (2) `SC`(O, v); the execution of `SC`(O, v) by a process p must follow the execution of `LL`(O) by p, and it is successful only if no process has performed a successful `SC` on O since the execution of p's latest `LL` on O; if `SC`(O, v) is successful, the value of O changes to v and `TRUE` is returned. Otherwise, the value of O does not change and `FALSE` is returned. Although `CAS` (or LL/SC) are currently provided by several systems, it is highly desirable to perform as few such operations as possible since their current implementation is much slower than that of simpler types of objects.

A `Fetch&Add` object O is a weaker type of object (with consensus number 2), which supports in addition to `read`, the operation `Fetch&Add`(O, x) which adds some (positive or negative) value x to O and returns its previous value. `Fetch&Add` has performance advantages [14] compared to other synchronization primitives (like `CAS`, or LL/SC); in brief, a `Fetch&Add` requires only one memory access which minimizes serialization delays, it is combinable [13], and excessive contention for `Fetch&Add` objects can be reduced or eliminated by using appropriate software techniques [30]. In some architectures, a `Fetch&Add` is implemented in-memory (bypassing the cache and its coherence protocol) which was proved to be faster under contention than the integrated to the coherence protocol implementation of LL/SC [25].

In this paper, we investigate how to use `Fetch&Add` (in

addition to `LL/SC`) to design a highly-efficient wait-free universal construction. Jayanti [22] has proved a lower bound of $\Omega(\log n)$ on the shared memory accesses performed by any oblivious universal construction (an *oblivious* universal construction does not exploit the semantics of the object being simulated) using `LL/SC` objects. This lower bound holds even if shared-memory has an infinite number of words and each word is of unbounded size. One of the open problems mentioned in that paper is the following: *"If shared-memory supports all of* `read`, `write`, `LL/SC`, `swap`, `CAS`, `move`, `Fetch&Add`, `Fetch&Multiply`, *would the* $\Omega(\log n)$ *lower bound still hold?"* We present a simple oblivious universal construction, called Sim, that performs a constant number of shared memory accesses. It uses a single `Fetch&Add` object in addition to an `LL/SC` object, thus proving that the lower bound in [22] can be beaten, if we use just a single `Fetch&Add` object in addition to an `LL/SC` object.

Sim exploits the well-known technique [16, 26, 27, 30] of having a thread executing an operation helping other already announced operations. The high-level idea of the algorithm is as simple as follows. A process p that wants to execute an operation first announces it by applying `Fetch&Add` to a word of size linear to the number n of processes, it finds out which other operations are active by reading this word, and applies these operations to a local copy of the simulated object; finally, it tries to change the shared pointer to the simulated object's state to point to this local copy. Following the standard theoretical model of shared memory computation which allows each word to be arbitrarily large (or unbounded), the number of shared memory accesses performed by Sim is constant. However, Sim is not practical since it employs a large `Fetch&Add` object.

We have implemented a practical version of Sim, called P-Sim, and we have experimentally tested P-Sim on a real shared-memory machine. From a theoretical point of view, P-Sim performs more shared memory accesses than Sim, its theoretical analog. More specifically, P-Sim employs $O(n/b)$ `Fetch&Add` objects (where b is the actual size in bits of a memory word), and performs $O(n + s)$ shared memory accesses (where s is the number of memory words needed to store the state of the simulated object). Our experiments show however that achieving synchronization using P-Sim outperforms several state-of-the-art synchronization techniques, both lock-based (like local spinning) and lock-free (Figures 1, 3 and 4). We found this very interesting given that P-Sim is a *wait-free* algorithm whereas all these other techniques ensure only weaker progress properties. P-Sim proves that the common belief that ensuring wait-freedom is too expensive to be practical is in many cases wrong.

Flat-combining introduced by Hendler, Incze, Shavit, and Tzafrir [16] also employs the simple idea of having a thread executing sequentially all announced operations; in flat-combining, this is the thread that manages to acquire a global lock protecting the entire data structure. Apparently, the algorithm is blocking and therefore it is not robust (a thread holding the lock could be preempted causing all other threads to wait or it may fail causing the entire system to block). We experimentally study the performance of P-Sim and compare it to that of flat-combining (and other state-of-the-art algorithms). For up to 96 processes and when most of them are active, P-Sim has similar performance to flat-combining and sometimes outperforms it (Figures 1, 3 and 4); this is so, given that P-Sim ensures the strongest progress condi-

tion of wait-freedom. In systems with more than 96 active processes, the performance of flat-combining degrades significantly since the thread holding the lock is preempted which usually causes a serious performance degradation. However, in cases where the number of active threads is low, flat-combining outperforms P-Sim (Figure 2). Moreover, P-Sim requires knowledge of n (or of an upper bound of it), and its space complexity is higher than that of flat-combining.

We have used P-Sim to design new highly-efficient *wait-free* implementations of simple shared data structures like queues and stacks. We experimentally prove that our stack implementation, called SimStack, outperforms most well-known previous shared stack algorithms, like the lock-free stack implementation of Treiber [29], the elimination back-off stack [17], a stack implementation based on a CLH spin lock [9, 23], and a linked stack implementation based on flat-combining [16]. Similarly, our queue implementation, called SimQueue significantly outperforms the following previous implementations: a lock-based algorithm (using two CLH locks) and the lock-free algorithm presented in [24], as well as the implementation using flat-combining provided by Hendler *et. al* [16].

While designing Sim, we noticed that by using a single `Fetch&Add` we could get simple implementations of an active set, a collect object and a snapshot object that perform just one cache miss in cache-coherent machines with up to as many threads as the length c of the system's cache line, and $\lceil n/c \rceil$ cache misses in case $c < n$. Using these implementations, one could get improved performance for several previously presented algorithms [2, 5, 21, 28] in case $\lceil n/c \rceil$ is a small constant.

Fatourou and Kallimanis have presented in [10] a family of wait-free, adaptive, universal constructions, called RedBlue. The first algorithm (F-RedBlue) performed $O(min\{k, \log n\})$ shared memory accesses, where k is the *interval contention*, i.e., the maximum number of processes that are active during the execution interval of any operation; the second (S-RedBlue) used smaller objects than F-RedBlue and performed $O(k)$ shared memory accesses. Sim is much simpler than F-RedBlue and S-RedBlue, uses significantly less objects and performs much less shared memory accesses. Two additional adaptive RedBlue universal constructions [10] (LS-RedBlue and BLS-RedBlue) coped with large objects (i.e., objects that need a large amount of storage to maintain their state). These algorithms combined some of the techniques described by Anderson and Moir [4] with the techniques of the Red-Blue family to get the best of both worlds. Using Sim we can obtain much simpler versions of these algorithms which although perform the same number of shared memory accesses as LS-RedBlue and BLS-RedBlue, they employ $\Omega(n)$ less `LL/SC` objects and reduce the number of `LL/SC` instructions performed in any execution by a factor of $\Omega(\log k)$ per operation.

A summary of known wait-free universal algorithms is presented in Table 1. Most of these algorithms, like that presented in [18], GroupUpdate [1], F-RedBlue[10], S-RedBlue [10], Sim, and P-Sim copy the entire state of the object locally and perform any updates on the local copy. In all these algorithms (other than P-Sim), we follow the common convention that the entire state is stored in a single object, and reading or writing this object costs just a single shared memory access. In P-Sim we count a cost of $O(s)$ shared memory accesses to read the state of the object. The al-

Algorithm	Primitives	Shared Memory Accesses	Required Space
Herlihy [18]	consensus objects, r/w regs	$O(n)$	$O(n^3 s)$
GroupUpdate [1]	LL/SC, consensus objects, r/w regs	$O(\min\{n, k \log k\})$	$O(n^2 s \log n)$
IndividualUpdate [1]	$LL/VL/SC$	$O(kw \log w)$	$O(nw + s)$
F-RedBlue [10]	LL/SC	$O(\min\{k, \log n\})$	$O(n^2 + s)$
S-RedBlue [10]	$LL/VL/SC$, r/w regs	$O(k + s)$	$O(n^2 + ns)$
Anderson & Moir [3]	$LL/VL/SC$	$O((n/\min\{k, M/T\})(B + ML + nw))$	$O(n^2 + n(B + ML))$
LS-RedBlue [10]	$LL/VL/SC$, r/w regs	$O(B + k(w + TL))$	$O(n^2 + n(B + kTL))$
BLS-RedBlue [10]	$LL/VL/SC$, r/w regs	$O((k/\min\{k, M/T\})(B + ML + k + \min\{k, M/T\}w))$	$O(n^2 + n(B + ML))$
Chuong, et. al [7]	CAS, r/w regs	$O(nw)$	$O(n + s)$
Sim (this paper)	LL/SC or CAS, Fetch&Add	$O(1)$	$O(n + s)$
P-Sim (this paper)	LL/SC or CAS, Fetch&Add	$O(n + s)$	$O(n^2 + ns)$

Table 1: **Wait-free universal algorithms and their complexities**; w is the maximum number of different memory words accessed by an operation on the sequential data structure. In [3, 10], B is the number of blocks, each of size L, required to store the object's state, and each process is allowed to modify at most T blocks and help at most M/T other processes, where $M \geq 2T$ is some integer.

gorithms in [3], LS-RedBlue [10] and BLS-RedBlue [10] cope with large objects by assuming that the state of the object is stored in a sequence of consecutive blocks of size B each; each process copies and updates locally only the blocks that are required to perform its operation (and the operations of the processes that it helps). IndividualUpdate copes with large objects by ensuring that processes agree on the updates they will perform on the data structure; then, they all apply the same operations directly on the shared data structure. Finally, the algorithm in [7] operates by having processes to access directly the shared data structure by copying some of its words locally, performing updates on them, and writing back the updated versions of these words to the shared data structure. The algorithm uses $O(n + s)$ registers, each of which stores sequence numbers that take unbounded values. The space required by all other algorithms is measured in terms of memory words. All algorithms presented in Table 1 are oblivious.

The universality result [18] has motivated major hardware manufacturers to include strong instructions, like LL/SC or CAS, in the instruction set of most modern processors. Weaker instructions, like Fetch&Add, can possibly be implemented in hardware more easily than LL/SC or CAS. However, this is currently performed on top of LL/SC (or CAS) in some architectures, sometimes with uncertain progress guarantees. We believe that the results of this paper provide some motivation for seeing primitives such as Fetch&Add provided in the instruction set of more architectures in the future.

This paper is organized as follows. Section 2 presents a brief model. Sim is presented in Section 3. P-Sim and some experimental results on its performance are described in Section 4. The new wait-free stack and queue implementations, as well as their experimental analysis are presented in Section 5. Finally, Section 6 discusses some limitations of Sim and open problems.

2. MODEL

We consider an *asynchronous* system of n processes, $p_1, \ldots, p_n$, each of which may fail by *crashing*. An *active set* is a shared object that identifies a set of processes participating

in some computation; it supports the operations (1) JOIN which is called by a process to identify its participation to the computation, (2) LEAVE to request removal from the set of participating processes, and (3) GETSET which returns the set of the currently participating processes. A *collect* object consists of n components $A_1, ..., A_n$, one for each process, each of which stores a value from a set $D = \{0, ..., 2^d - 1\}$; it supports the operations (1) UPDATE(v) which, when executed by p_i, it stores the value v in A_i, and (2) COLLECT which returns a vector of n values, one for each component. An *implementation* of a (high-level) object from base objects provides an algorithm for each process to simulate each operation of the simulated object using the base objects. A *configuration* C is a vector containing the states of the processes and the values of the base objects at some point in time. At an *initial* configuration, registers contain initial values and processes are at initial states. A process completes the execution of a *step* each time it accesses a shared register (i.e., a step consists of a single access to the shared memory and may also contain some local computation). An *execution* is a sequence of steps by processes. A process is *active* at some configuration C, if it has executed the invocation of an operation op at C but it has not yet executed the response of op. The *execution interval* of op is the part of the execution that starts with op's invocation and ends with op's response.

Let α be any execution of an implementation of a (high-level) object from base objects. *Linearizability* [20] ensures that for each operation op on the simulated object in α, there is some point within its execution interval, called *linearization point*, such that the response returned by op in α is the same as the response op would return if all operations in α were executing serially in the order determined by their linearization points; when this holds, we say that the response of op is *consistent*. An implementation is *linearizable* if all its executions are linearizable.

We remark that implementations of active set and collect objects do not have to be linearizable. An implementation of an active set should rather satisfy the following: (1) the set returned by a GETSET GS must contain any process p that has finished the execution of a JOIN J before the invocation of GS, and it has not started the execution of a LEAVE in the interval between the end of J and the end of GS, and (2) the set returned by GS must not contain any process p that has finished the execution of a LEAVE L before the invocation of GS, and it has not invoked a JOIN in the interval between the end of L and the end of GS. Similarly, in an implementation of a collect object the vector returned by each COLLECT Col must contain, for each component A_i, the value written by the last UPDATE U on A_i by p_i that has finished its execution before the invocation of Col (or the initial value if such an UPDATE does not exist), given that p_i has not started the execution of a new UPDATE U' in the interval between the end of U and the end of Col. If p_i has started the execution of a new update U', then Col may return either the value of U' or that of U (or the initial value, if U does not exist) for A_i. A *snapshot* object is a collect object that satisfies the extra property of being linearizable (we then use the term SCAN instead of COLLECT).

3. A NEW UNIVERSAL CONSTRUCTION

We start with the presentation of a (single-writer) collect object, called SimCollect, which is a major constructing module of Sim. Recall that a collect object is comprised of n components, each of which capable of storing a value from a set D, and that d is the number of bits that are needed for the representation of any value in D. The implementation uses a Fetch&Add object O of nd bits. O is partitioned into n chunks of d bits each, one for each process. Process p_i owns the i-th chunk of d bits, and stores there the value of the component that has been assigned to it. An UPDATE U with value v by p_i first performs a Fetch&Add to ensure that v is written into the i-th chunk of O, and then keeps a copy of v into a local variable *prev*; this copy is maintained by p_i to discover the appropriate value that should be added to the i-th chunk of O during its next UPDATE (which will be the new value minus v). Whenever p_i executes a COLLECT operation, it simply reads the value stored in O and returns, for each component, the value stored in the corresponding chunk. Apparently, the number of shared memory accesses performed by SimCollect is 1.

If the size b of a Fetch&Add object is less than nd bits, then we can employ $\lceil nd/b \rceil$ Fetch&Add objects, $O_1, \ldots, O_{\lceil nd/b \rceil}$. In this case, the value last written by p_i is represented by the $(id \bmod b)$-th chunk of $O_{\lceil id/b \rceil}$[1]. An UPDATE by p_i adds an appropriate value to $O_{\lceil id/b \rceil}$, and COLLECT reads every Fetch&Add object once and returns the set of values written in the chunks. This version of the algorithm has step complexity 1 for UPDATE, and $O(nd/b)$ for COLLECT. Notice that in this version COLLECT is not linearizable (but recall that linearizability is not necessary for COLLECT). In case $b \geq nd$, COLLECT is linearizable, so then SimCollect can serve as a single-writer snapshot implementation. We remark that the same techniques as in SimCollect, can be used to get an implementation of an active set, called SimActSet, by a Fetch&Add object of n bits (one for each process) with step complexity 1 if $b < n$, or $\lceil n/b \rceil$ if $b > n$.

We continue to present Sim (Algorithm 1). Sim uses an LL/SC object S and an instance Col of the collect implemen-

---

Algorithm 1 Pseudocode for Sim.

```
type Pindex {1, ..., n};
typedef struct State{
    boolean applied[1..n];
    RetVal rvals[1..n];
    state st;
} State;

shared SimCollect Col;
shared State S = ⟨⟨ FALSE,..., FALSE⟩, ⟨⊥,...,⊥⟩,⊥⟩;

// Code for process p_i
RetVal APPLYOP(operation op){
1.   UPDATE(Col, i, op);
2.   Attempt();
3.   UPDATE(Col, i, ⊥);
4.   Attempt();
5.   return S.rvals[i];
}

void Attempt(){
    State ls;        Pindex i, j;
    BitVector act;  operation ops[1..n];

6.   for j=1 to 2 do{
7.      ls = LL(S);
8.      ops = COLLECT(Col);
9.      for i=1 to n do { // local loop
10.         if(ops[i] ≠ ⊥ AND ls.applied[i] == FALSE)
11.            apply ops[i] to ls.st and store
               into ls.rvals[i] the return value;
12.         if(ops[i] ≠ ⊥) ls.applied[i] = TRUE;
13.         else ls.applied[i] = FALSE;
        }
    }
14.  SC(S, ls);
}
```

---

tation discussed above. The LL/SC object stores the state st of the simulated object, a vector *applied* of n bits identifying whether the current operation (if any) of each process has been applied to the simulated object, and an array *rvals* of return values, one for each process; notice that the size of S could be reduced to just a single pointer using indirection. (In later sections, we present how we can get a practical version of Sim that outperforms most of the state of the art lock-based and lock-free algorithms.)

Whenever a process p_i wants to apply some operation op to the simulated object, it first announces op by updating its component in Col (line 1). Then, p_i executes a routine, called Attempt (line 2), to ensure that its operation has been applied to the object. Next, p_i updates its component with the special value $\perp$ (line 3) to inform the other processes that op has been completed. Then, p executes Attempt once more to eliminate any evidence of op (line 4).

We now discuss the details of Attempt. First, p executes an LL to S (line 7), and then a COLLECT to discover other active operations (line 8). Next, p applies all these operations (in addition to its own) to a local copy ls of the state of the simulated object, and calculates the return value for each applied operation (lines 9-13). Finally, p tries to update S to ls by executing an SC (line 14). We prove that it is enough for p to execute lines 7-14 twice to guarantee that

---

[1] For simplicity, we assume that d is a divisor of b, so that the d bits allocated to each process are not split across two Fetch&Add objects.

its operation *op* has been applied to the simulated object (or that the evidence of its last operation has been eliminated).

THEOREM 3.1. Sim *is a linearizable, wait-free implementation of a universal object using a* Fetch&Add *object of size b equal to nd bits and one* LL/SC *object.* Sim *performs* $O(1)$ *shared memory accesses. In case* $b < nd$, Sim *uses* $O(nd/b)$ Fetch&Add *objects and one* LL/SC *object; it performs* $O(nd/b)$ *shared memory accesses.*

SKETCH OF PROOF: Let α be any execution. We start by proving that at least two successful SC are executed in the execution interval of each instance of Attempt. We also prove that $S.applied[i] = $ TRUE at the end of the execution of the first instance of Attempt performed by any operation by p_i, and $S.applied[i] = $ FALSE at the end of the execution of the second such instance performed by the same operation.

Let op_i and op'_i be two consecutive operations executed by the same process p_i in α. By the pseudocode, op_i (op'_i) executes two instances of Attempt; let them be π_1 and π_2 (π'_1 and π'_2, respectively). We prove that there is a unique SC that changes the value of $S.applied[i]$ to TRUE after the execution of code line 1 by op_i (op'_i) and before the end of π_1 (π'_1, respectively); denote this SC by SC_1 (SC'_1). Similarly, there is a unique SC that changes the value of $S.applied[i]$ to FALSE after the execution of code line 3 by op_i (op'_i) and before the end of π_2 (π'_2); denote this SC by SC_2 (SC'_2). We prove that no other successful SC can change the value of $S.applied[i]$ between SC_1 (SC'_1) and SC_2 (SC'_2). So, $S.applied[i]$ equals to TRUE between SC_1 (SC'_1) and SC_2 (SC'_2). Similarly, we prove that no other successful SC can change the value of $S.applied[i]$ between SC_2 and SC'_1. So, $S.applied[i]$ equals to FALSE between SC_2 and SC'_1. Based on these facts, we prove that op_i is applied on the simulated object exactly once.

We assign the linearization point of op_i at SC_1; ties are broken by the order imposed by process identifiers. It is easy to argue that op_i is linearized within its execution interval. We consider appropriate prefixes of α and we prove inductively, on the length of these prefixes, that the responses of the operations executed in them are consistent. □

We finally discuss some implications of our universal construction. Jayanti [22] has proved that any oblivious implementation of a universal object from LL/SC objects has step complexity $\Omega(\log n)$. This lower bound holds even if shared-memory has an infinite number of words and each word has an unbounded size. Sim is oblivious, so the lower bound can be beaten if just one Fetch&Add object (or a collect object) is used in addition to an LL/SC object. Thus, our universal construction implies a lower bound of $\Omega(\log n)$ on the step complexity of any implementation of (1) a collect object, (2) a single-writer snapshot object, or (3) a Fetch&Add object, from LL/SC objects.

4. FROM THEORY TO PRACTICE

Implementation. We discuss the techniques applied to Sim to port it to a real-world machine architecture, like x86_64. This gives a practical version of Sim, called P-Sim. A simplified version of P-Sim is shown in Algorithms 2, 3.

The information stored in struct *State* is now maintained using indirection. Each process p_i maintains a pool of a constant number C of structs of (an enhanced version of) type *State*. These pools are implemented by allocating an array *Pool* of nC records of type *State*. Process p_i's pool is comprised by the $Pool[(i-1)C..iC-1]$ part of the array. We remark that using a pool of just $n+1$ records would be enough for correctness; we have chosen to use nC records for performance reasons. Variable S has now been replaced by a shared variable P which is an index in *Pool*. i.e., a "reference" to a record of type *State* which stores, in addition to other useful information, the current state of the simulated object. The use of sequence numbers ensure that, despite the recycling of these records, consistency is not violated.

A shared bit vector *Act* of size n is employed containing one bit for each process; when a process p_i initiates a new operation, it toggles $Act[i]$ by performing a Fetch&Add (lines 2-3). An operation by p_i is applied only if the i-th bit of *Act* differs from the i-th bit of *applied* read in the record pointed to by P (lines 10, 12, 15-19). In more detail, when a process p_i wants to execute its first operation op_i, it sets $Act[i]$ to TRUE (lines 2-3). Each process p that sees $Act[i] = $ TRUE and reads $applied[i] = $ FALSE in the record pointed to by P, will apply op_i to its local copy of the object's state. However, only one of them will succeed in updating P on line 25. This update changes $applied[i]$ in the record pointed to by P to TRUE. When p_i discovers that op_i has been simulated, it will find op_i's return value stored in the record of *Pool* pointed to by P. Only when p_i initiates its second operation, it will change $Act[i]$ to FALSE, thus storing in it a different value than that of the $applied[i]$ field of the record pointed to by P indicating that a new operation by p_i has been announced. Using this technique, there is no need for eliminating the evidence of an executed operation. This reduces the total number of cache misses to almost half giving a noticeable speed gain.

The collect object is replaced by a set of n single-writer read-write registers (the *Announce* array). When p_i wants to apply an operation *op*, announces it by writing *op* (and its parameters) in *Announce*[i] (line 1). Process p_i discovers the operations that other active processes want to perform by reading the appropriate entries of *Announce* (lines 15-19) . This increases the time complexity of Sim by a factor of $O(k)$ (where k is the interval contention) but it decreases the size of the Fetch&Add object.

Several modern shared memory machines (like those using the x86_64 architecture) support a Fetch&Add instruction on up to 64 bit words. In order to cope efficiently with more than 64 threads, the multi-word bit vector *Act* is implemented by storing its words to the minimum possible number of cache lines. Notice that a typical cache line is usually of 64 bytes; thus, it can be used to store one bit for each of up to 512 processes (so, more than one cache line may be needed only if the number of processes is more than 512; otherwise, we read *Act* with just one cache miss).

The majority of the commercially available shared memory machines support CAS rather than LL/SC. We simulate an LL on P with a read(P), and an SC with a CAS on a timestamped version of P to avoid the ABA problem. (This problem occurs when a process p reads some value A from a shared variable and then some other process p' modifies the variable to the value B and back to A; when p begins execution again, it sees that the variable has not changed and continues executing normally which might be incorrect.) Since P stores just an index to *Pool* (and not a full 64 bit pointer), there are enough bits (in our experiments 48) in a word to

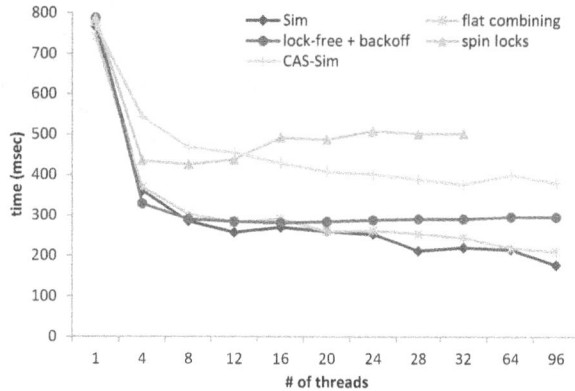

Figure 1: Performance of P-Sim.

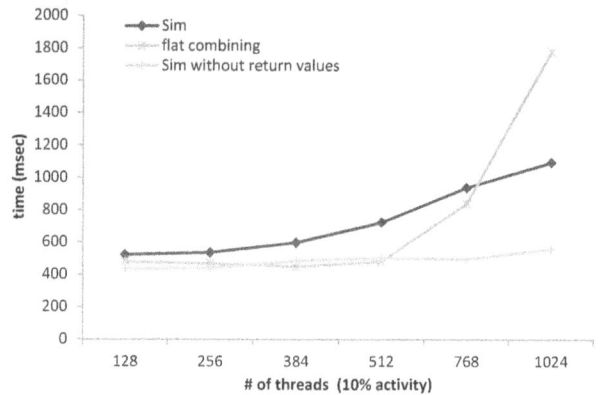

Figure 2: Performance of P-Sim in low contention.

store the timestamp (in systems with more processes, we could use 128 bit words, supported, e.g., in x86_64).

We remark that the performance of P-Sim gets enhanced when processes manage to help a large number of other processes while performing their operations. For exploring this property, we use an adaptive exponential backoff scheme which has some similarities to that used in [17]. A process p_i backoffs, after it has announced its operation and has indicated in Act that it is active. This results in increasing the number of operations that p_i will help while executing the current instance of its operation. However, it is worth pointing out that P-Sim achieves good performance even if no backoff is employed.

P-Sim performs $O(n + s)$ shared memory accesses. More specifically, reading a record of type $State$, performed on line 7, results in reading an array $rvals$ of n return values, a bit vector $applied$ stored in $O(n/b)$ memory words, and the entire state of the object, i.e., s memory words. Moreover, the read of Act on line 9 requires $O(n/b)$ additional memory accesses. The algorithm performs $O(k)$ memory accesses to read the appropriate elements of $Announce$. Thus, the shared memory accesses performed by P-Sim is $O(n + s)$. P-Sim uses a pool of $O(n)$ records of type $State$, each of size $O(n + s)$. The algorithm also employs a bit vector of size n and an array of n values. Thus, the space complexity of P-Sim is $O(n^2 + ns)$. A proof of correctness for P-Sim will be provided in the full version of the paper. The full code is provided at http://code.google.com/p/sim-universal-construction/.

Performance Evaluation. We run most of our experiments on a 32-core machine consisting of four AMD opteron 6134 processors (Magny Cours). Each processor consists of two dies and each of them contains four processing cores and an L3 cache shared by its cores. Dies and thus processors are connected to each other with Hyper Transport Links creating a topology with an average diameter of 1.25 [8]. All codes were compiled with gcc 4.3.4, and the Hoard memory allocator [6] was used to eliminate bottlenecks in memory allocation.

We first focus on a synthetic benchmark which shows the performance advantages of P-Sim over well-known blocking and lock-free techniques. More specifically, we have chosen a simple Fetch&Multiply instruction as a case study and used P-Sim to implement it; we measure the time needed to complete the execution of 10^6 Fetch&Multiply instructions

(with each thread executing $10^6/n$ such instructions) for different values of n. For each value of n, the experiment has been performed 10 times and averages have been taken. A random number (up to 512) of dummy loop iterations have been inserted between the execution of two Fetch&Multiply by the same process; in this way, we simulate a random work load large enough to avoid unrealistically low cache miss ratios (but not too big to reduce contention). A similar technique was employed by Michael and Scott in [24] for the same reasons.

We have performed the same experiment using the following mechanisms: CLH spin locks [9, 23], a simple lock-free algorithm with exponential back-off using a single CAS object, and flat-combining [15, 16]. We also implemented a version of P-Sim, called CAS-Sim, where Fetch&Add is simulated in a lock-free way using CAS. We carefully optimized these algorithms to achieve best performance in our computing environment. For those that use backoff schemes, we performed a large number of experiments to select the best backoff parameters in each case. CLH spin locks have been evaluated for only up to 32 threads (so that each thread runs on a distinct core), since otherwise they result in very poor performance. We used the flat-combining implementation provided by its inventors [15, 16] but we carefully chose its parameters (i.e., polling level, number of combining rounds) to optimize its performance in our computing environment. The simple lock-free algorithm uses a single CAS object O, and executes a CAS instruction on O repeatedly, until it successfully stores the new value there; the algorithm employs an exponential back-off scheme to reduce contention in accessing O. Given that this seems to be the simplest lock-free implementation, we expect that it performs well.

In our experiment, P-Sim has been proved to be up to 2.36 times faster than spin-locks, and up to 1.67 times faster than the simple lock-free algorithm (Figure 1). Since both P-Sim and flat-combining are based on the simple idea of having each process that performs an operation helping other active operations, it would be very interesting to see P-Sim (which is a wait-free algorithm) to perform the same well as flat-combining (which is blocking). As Figure 1 shows, this is indeed the case.

As illustrated in Figure 1, all algorithms scale well for up to 4 cores. For larger values of n, the performance of spin-locks and the simple lock free algorithm degrade as the number of threads increases. A major reason for this is that

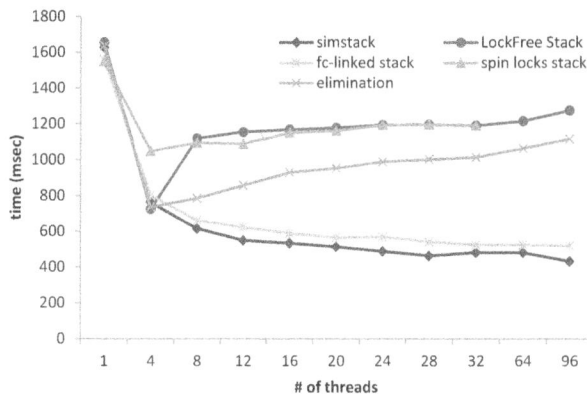

Figure 3: Performance of SimStack.

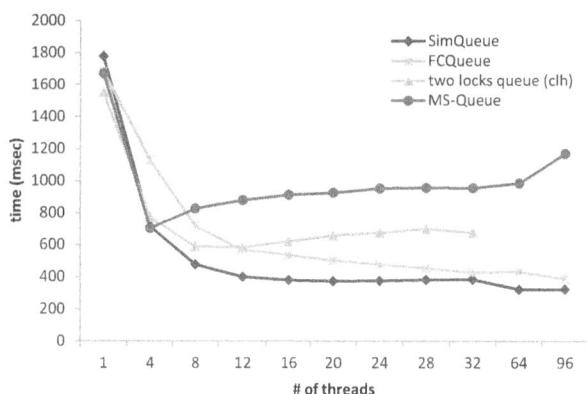

Figure 4: Performance of SimQueue.

the (intra)communication cost between dies is much higher than the (inter)communication cost between the four cores of the same die; additionally, the lock-free algorithm causes more contention as n increases. It is worth-pointing out that, up to some number of threads, the performance of P-Sim and flat-combining is being enhanced as the number of n increases (even for values of $n > 4$). This is so since the average degree of helping (where P-Sim and flat-combining owe their good performance) increases with the number of active operations in the system. We remark that this enhancement in performance is noticed even for values of $n > 32$ where the processing cores are oversubscribed. It is worth-pointing out that P-Sim is at least 2 times faster than CAS-Sim indicating that P-Sim performs better in machines that provide Fetch&Add in their instruction set.

Our next experiment studies how P-Sim performs in cases where a program has been written for a large number of threads but at any given time only a small number of them are active. Due to limitations on the number of threads that

---

Algorithm 2 Data structures used in P-Sim algorithm.

```
typedef struct State {
    int seq1, seq2;
    BitVector applied;
    state st;
    RetVal rvals[1..n];
} State;
typedef struct TimedPoolIndex {
    int index;   // 16 bit array index
    int tm;      // 48 bit timestamp
} TimedPoolIndex;

// Each element of pool is initialized
// as follows < 0, 0, < 0, ..., 0 >, ⊥, < ⊥, ..., ⊥ >>
shared State Pool[0..n*C];   // C > 1 is a small constant
shared TimedPoolIndex P = {n*C, 0};
shared BitVector Act = 0;
shared OpType Announce[1..n];

// private persistent variables of process p_i
// operator << implements a left bit shift
BitVector mask_i = 1 << i;
BitVector offset_i = -mask_i;
int pool_index_i = 0;
```

we were allowed to run on the Magny Cours machine, these experiments have been conducted in a 16-core machine consisting of 4 Quad core Opteron 8350 HE processors. In this experiment (Figure 2), we consider systems where the total number of threads ranges from 128 to 1024 but we let only 10% of the threads be active. The active threads execute 10^6 Fetch&Multiply instructions in a similar way as in the experiment of Figure 1. In order to discover the main overheads of P-Sim, we have implemented an additional version of it where no return values are calculated. Our experiment shows that the calculation of the return values is indeed the most expensive part of P-Sim's computation. When the total number of threads is up to 512, the version of P-Sim that does not calculate return values, has about the same performance as flat-combining, despite the fact that this experiment is the most favorable to the second. Thus, reading Act, which is a bit vector of size n, and the corresponding elements of $Announce$ does not cause any serious performance degradation. When return values are calculated, the performance of P-Sim degrades as n increases; in this case, flat-combining performs better than P-Sim. For larger numbers of total threads in the system, the performance of flat-combining degrades drastically since then the thread that owns the lock may be swapped out, due to oversubscribing, by the scheduler, which is very expensive. Apparently, P-Sim is a better solution in these cases since its execution time is unrelated to the scheduler decisions. When the percentage of active threads is larger than 10%, the performance of flat-combining starts degrading significantly from smaller values of n.

5. A STACK AND A QUEUE IMPLEMENTATION BASED ON P-SIM

In this section, we present new *wait-free* implementations of a stack and a queue based on P-Sim and we experimentally prove that these implementations have performance competitive to currently state-of-the-art implementations of stacks and queues.

A Wait-Free Implementation of a Shared Stack. We first present SimStack, the wait-free stack implementation. Implementing a stack object based on P-Sim is an easy task. The stack is implemented as a linked list of nodes and a pointer *top* points to the topmost element of this list. P-Sim is employed to atomically manipulate *top* (i.e., the state

Algorithm 3 Pseudocode for P-Sim algorithm.

```
RetVal ApplyOp(function sfunc, ArgVal arg) {  // Code for process p_i
    TimedPoolIndex lp, mp;
    ObjectState *lst;
    ArgVal tmp_arg;
    int j, k;
    BitVector Act;

1.  Announce[i] = arg;                      // announce the operation
2.  offset_i = -offset_i;                   // offset_i is added to Act to toggle p_i's bit
3.  FAA(Act, offset_i);                     // toggle p_i's bit in Act, Fetch&Add acts as a full write-barrier
4.  backoff();
5.  for j=0 to 1 do {                       // code of Attempt
6.    lp = P;                               // read reference to struct State
7.    lst = &Pool[i*n+pool_index_i];
8.    *lst = Pool[lp.index];                // read struct State in a local variable lst
9.    active = Act;                         // read Act
10.   diffs = lst → applied XOR active;          // determine the set of active processes
11.   if (lst → seq1 ≠ lst → seq2) continue;     // consistency check
12.   if (diffs AND mask_i == 0) return lst → rvals[p_i];   // if the operation has already been applied return
13.   if (j == 0) compute_backoff();
14.   lst → seq1 = lst → seq1 + 1;
15.   while (diffs != 0) {                  // as long as there are still processes to help
16.     k = bitSearchFirst(diffs);         // find the next such process
17.     tmp_arg = Announce[k];             // discover its operation
18.     lst → rvals[k] = sfunc(lst, tmp_arg);      // apply the operation to a local copy of the object's state
19.     diffs = diffs XOR (1 << k);        // extract this process from the set
      }
20.   lst → applied = active;              // change applied to be equal to what was read in Act
21.   lst→seq2 = lst→seq2 + 1;
      // compute a new reference mp to store in P
22.   mp.tm = lp.tm + 1;                    // increase P's timestamp
23.   mp.index = i*n + pool_index_i;        // store in mp.index the index in Pool where lst will be stored
24.   Pool[i*n+pool_index_i] = lst;         // store the new state in position mp.index of Pool
25.   if (CAS(P, lp, mp)) {                 // try to change P to the value mp
26.     pool_index_i = (pool_index_i + 1) mod C;  //if this happens successfully,use next item in p_i's pool next time
27.     return lst → rvals[i];             // return;
      }
    }
28. lp = P;                                 // after two unsuccessful efforts, read current value of P
29. lst = &Pool[lp.index];                  // read the element of Pool indicated by the index field of P
30. return lst → rvals[i];                  // return the value found in the record stored there
}
```

---

of the simulated object is just this pointer and not the entire stack state). During the execution of an operation, a thread uses a set of nodes allocated by itself, one for each of the PUSH operations it will perform (on behalf of others or itself). The thread creates a linked list containing these newly inserted nodes, makes the last element of the list to point to the currently topmost element of the stack, and tries to update *top* to point to the first element in this list.

We compare the experimental performance of SimStack with that of state-of-the-art concurrent stack implementations, like the lock free stack implementation presented by Treiber in [29], the elimination back-off stack [17], a stack implementation based on CLH spin lock [9, 23], and a linked stack implementation based on flat combining [15, 16].

Our experiment is similar to that performed by Michael and Scott for queues in [24]. More specifically, we measure the time needed to complete the execution of 10^6 pairs of a PUSH and a POP as the number of threads increases (Figure 3). Again, for each value of n, the experiments have been performed 10 times and averages have been taken; we have simulated a random workload by executing a random number of iterations of a dummy loop after each operation.

As shown in Figure 3, all algorithms scale well up to 4 threads but SimStack outperforms all other implementations

for $n > 4$. More specifically, SimStack is up to 2.94 times faster than the lock-free stack, up to 2.58 times faster than the spin-lock based stack, up to 2.57 times faster than the elimination back-off stack, and up to 1.17 times faster than flat-combining.

As expected the elimination backoff stack achieves better performance than the lock-free and the spin-locks based implementations in almost all experiments. Again, the performance of the spin-lock based and the lock free implementations, as well as that of the elimination back-off stack degrade as the number of threads increases once n becomes more than four. SimStack and flat combining significantly outperform the other stack implementations. A possible reason that SimStack exhibits better performance than flat-combining could be that executing the algorithm instead of performing local spinning may result in better cache locality.

A Wait-Free Implementation of a Shared Queue. The queue is implemented as a linked list of nodes and pointers *head* and *tail* point to the first and the last elements of the queue, respectively. To allow the enqueuers and dequeuers to run independently, we employed two instances of P-Sim. Whenever a process p performs an ENQUEUE, it helps only other enqueuers (ignoring currently active dequeuers). Process p creates a local list of nodes, one for each enqueuer it helps. These nodes are eventually inserted to the shared queue by changing the next field of the tail node to point to the first node of the list, and the queue's tail pointer to point to the last node of this list. To do so, the tail of the queue and pointers to the first and last nodes of this list are stored in the *EnqState* struct of the enqueuer's instance of P-Sim. If process p manages to successfully update *EnqP* (i.e., the pointer pointed to the *EnqState* struct), it also tries to update (using CAS) the next field of the tail node of the queue to point to the first node of its local list. To avoid situations where p crashes before doing this change but after it has written a new value in *EnqP*, any subsequent ENQUEUE also tries to connect (using CAS) the tail of the shared queue with the first node of the list (recorded in the *EnqP*). Similarly, a DEQUEUE helps only active dequeuers. The *DeqState* struct stores a pointer to the first element of the queue. To ensure consistency, each DEQUEUE also executes a CAS to connect the two parts of the queue in a similar way to what ENQUEUE operations do.

Each process maintains three pools of structs, one containing structs of type *EnqState*, one containing structs of type *DeqState* and one containing nodes of the queue. Each time a process wants to allocate a new struct, it simply uses one of the structs in the appropriate local pool. Due to lack of space, the pseudocode of the implementation and its proof of correctness will be provided in the full paper.

We compare the experimental performance of SimQueue with that of state-of-the-art concurrent queue implementations, like the lock-based implementation (using two CLH locks) and the lock-free algorithm presented in [24], and the implementation using flat combining [15, 16]. Similarly to the experiment performed in [24], we measure the time needed to complete the execution of 10^6 pairs of an ENQUEUE and a DEQUEUE operation as the number of threads increases (Figure 4). As in previous experiments, we simulate a random workload after each operation.

As shown in Figure 4, SimQueue significantly outperforms all other implementations for $n > 4$. More specifically, SimQueue is up to 3.06 times faster than the lock-free implementation, up to 1.82 times faster than the spin-lock based implementation, and up to 1.5 times faster than flat combining. As expected, flat combining outperforms all queue implementations other than SimQueue. However, SimQueue achieves much better performance than flat combining for almost any number of threads. This performance advantage of SimQueue over flat-combining is basically due to the fact that we used two instances of SimQueue for our queue implementation, thus achieving increased parallelism by having enqueuers and dequeuers run concurrently.

6. DISCUSSION

One limitation of Sim is that it cannot efficiently cope with large objects since it copies the object's state locally. To overcome this limitation, the main techniques of the universal construction presented by Chuong, Ellen and Ramachandran [7] can be combined with Sim to get a universal construction that operates directly on the shared data structure (and not on a local copy of the entire state). The resulted algorithm [12] exhibits all the advantages of the universal construction in [7] and improves upon it by being adaptive, i.e., it performs $O(kw)$ shared memory accesses instead of $O(nw)$ that does the algorithm in [7]; in cases where $k < n$, the new algorithm is superior to that in [7].

Since one of the goals of Sim is wait-freedom, each active thread executes all pending operations; this might be inefficient in terms of energy consumption. In contrast, in flat-combining, threads perform spinning until their operations have been applied (which seems to be less expensive in terms of resource usage). Measuring energy consumption is an interesting but not easy task since several parameters (e.g., the time it is required to perform the computation, the resource usage, the way the thread library is implemented, etc.) should be considered. So, we leave this as future work.

It is worth-pointing out that Sim has similar applicability limitations to flat-combining [16]; efficient implementations of data structures like search trees, where m lookups can be executed in parallel performing just a logarithmic number of shared memory accesses each, are expected to outperform Sim (since Sim applies each operation sequentially like most previous universal constructions [7, 10, 16, 18, 19]). This limitation can possibly be overcome by using multiple instances of Sim (as done in our queue implementation of Section 5); for more complicated data structures this will be part of our future work.

As indicated in Section 4, the main overhead of P-Sim in systems with a large number of threads comes from the calculation of the return values. We believe that in such systems, this calculation can be performed more efficiently as follows. The algorithm must keep track of which processes have not yet read their response values by using an additional instance of SimActSet, and copies the response values just for these processes. The experimental evaluation of this technique will be performed in the full paper.

Acknowledgments. We thank Dimitris Nikolopoulos, Angelos Bilas, and Manolis Katevenis for several useful discussions. We especially thank Dimitris Nikolopoulos for arranging the provision of access to some of the multi-core machines of the Department of Computer Science at Virginia Tech where we ran our experiments. Many thanks to Nir Shavit and Danny Hendler for providing the code of flat-combining. We would like to especially thank Nir Shavit for several fruitful discussions and for his valuable feedback on the paper. Thanks also to Faith Ellen for several useful comments on a preliminary version of this paper [11], and for suggesting to combine techniques from Sim and the algorithm in [7] to get the best of both worlds.

Nikolaos Kallimanis is supported by a PhD scholarship from Empirikion Foundation, Athens, Greece. The work of Panagiota Fatourou was supported by the European Commission under the 6th and 7th Framework Programs through the SARC (FP6-ICT-027648), ENCORE (FP7-ICT-248647), STREAM (FP7- ICT- 216181), HiPEAC (NoE-004408), HiPEAC2 (FP7-ICT-217068), and TransForm (FP7-MCITN-238639) projects.

References

[1] Yehuda Afek, Dalia Dauber, and Dan Touitou. Wait-free made fast. In *Proceedings of the 27th ACM Symposium on Theory of Computing*, pages 538–547, 1995.

[2] Yehuda Afek, Gideon Stupp, and Dan Touitou. Long-lived adaptive collect with applications. In *Proceedings of the 40th Symposium on Foundations of Computer Science*, pages 262–272, 1999.

[3] James H. Anderson and Mark Moir. Universal constructions for multi-object operations. In *Proceedings of*

the *14th ACM Symposium on Principles of Distributed Computing*, pages 184–193, 1995.

[4] James H. Anderson and Mark Moir. Universal constructions for large objects. *IEEE Transactions on Parallel and Distributed Systems*, 10(12):1317–1332, dec 1999.

[5] Hagit Attiya, Rachid Guerraoui, and Eric Ruppert. Partial snapshot objects. In *Proceedings of the 20th Annual ACM Symposium on Parallel Algorithms and Architectures*, pages 336–343, 2008.

[6] Emery D. Berger, Kathryn S. McKinley, Robert D. Blumofe, and Paul R. Wilson. Hoard: A scalable memory allocator for multithreaded applications. In *Proceedings of the 9th International Conference on Architectural Support for Programming Languages and Operating Systems*, pages 117–128, 2000.

[7] Phong Chuong, Faith Ellen, and Vijaya Ramachandran. A universal construction for wait-free transaction friendly data structures. In *Proceedings of the 22nd Annual ACM Symposium on Parallel Algorithms and Architectures*, pages 335–344, 2010.

[8] Pat Conway, Nathan Kalyanasundharam, Gregg Donley, Kevin Lepak, and Bill Hughes. Blade computing with the amd opteron processor (magny-cours). *Hot chips 21*, August 2009.

[9] T. S. Craig. Building fifo and priority-queueing spin locks from atomic swap. Technical Report TR 93-02-02, Department of Computer Science, University of Washington, February 1993.

[10] Panagiota Fatourou and Nikolaos D. Kallimanis. The RedBlue adaptive universal constractions. In *Proceedings of the 23rd International Symposium on Distributed Computing*, pages 127–141, 2009.

[11] Panagiota Fatourou and Nikolaos D. Kallimanis. Fast implementations of shared objects using fetch&add. Technical Report TR 02-2010, Department of Computer Science, University of Ioannina, February 2010.

[12] Panagiota Fatourou and Nikolaos D. Kallimanis. A highly-efficient wait-free universal costruction. Technical Report TR 01-2011, Department of Computer Science, University of Ioannina, January 2011.

[13] D. George S. Harvey W. Kleinfelder K. McAuliffe E. Melton V. Norton G. Pfister, W. Brantley and J. Weiss. The ibm research parallel processor prototype (rp3): Introduction and architecture. pages 764–771, 1985.

[14] P. Heidelberger, A. Norton, and John T. Robinson. Parallel quicksort using fetch-and-add. *IEEE Transactions on Computers.*, 39(1):133–138, 1990.

[15] Danny Hendler, Itai Incze, Nir Shavit, and Moran Tzafrir. The code for flat combining. http://github.com/mit-carbon/flat-combining.

[16] Danny Hendler, Itai Incze, Nir Shavit, and Moran Tzafrir. Flat combining and the synchronization-parallelism tradeoff. In *Proceedings of the 22nd Annual ACM Symposium on Parallel Algorithms and Architectures*, pages 355–364, 2010.

[17] Danny Hendler, Nir Shavit, and Lena Yerushalmi. A scalable lock-free stack algorithm. In *Proceedings of the 16th ACM Symposium on Parallel Algorithms and Architectures*, pages 206–215, 2004.

[18] Maurice Herlihy. Wait-free synchronization. *ACM Transactions on Programming Languages and Systems (TOPLAS)*, 13:124–149, jan 1991.

[19] Maurice Herlihy. A methodology for implementing highly concurrent data objects. *ACM Transactions on Programming Languages and Systems (TOPLAS)*, 15(5):745–770, nov 1993.

[20] Maurice P. Herlihy and Jeannette M. Wing. Linearizability: A correctness condition for concurrent objects. *ACM Transactions on Programming Languages and Systems (TOPLAS)*, 12:463–492, 1990.

[21] Damien Imbs and Michel Raynal. Help when needed, but no more: Efficient read/write partial snapshot. In *Proceedings of the 23rd International Symposium on Distributed Computing*, pages 142–156. Springer, 2009.

[22] Prasad Jayanti. A time complexity lower bound for randomized implementations of some shared objects. In *Proceedings of the 17th ACM Symposium on Principles of Distributed Computing*, pages 201–210, 1998.

[23] Peter S. Magnusson, Anders Landin, and Erik Hagersten. Queue locks on cache coherent multiprocessors. In *Proceedings of the 8th International Parallel Processing Symposium*, pages 165–171, 1994.

[24] Maged M. Michael and Michael L. Scott. Simple, fast, and practical non-blocking and blocking concurrent queue algorithms. In *Proceedings of the 15th ACM Symposium on Principles of Distributed Computing*, pages 267–275, 1996.

[25] Dimitrios S. Nikolopoulos and Theodore S. Papatheodorou. A quantitative architectural evaluation of synchronization algorithms and disciplines on ccnuma systems: the case of the sgi origin2000. In *Proceedings of the 13th international conference on Supercomputing (ICS '99)*, pages 319–328, New York, NY, USA, 1999. ACM.

[26] Ori Shalev and Nir Shavit. Predictive log-synchronization. In *EuroSys*, pages 305–315, 2006.

[27] Nir Shavit and Asaph Zemach. Combining funnels: A dynamic approach to software combining. *Journal of Parallel and Distributed Computing*, 60(11):1355–1387, 2000.

[28] Gadi Taubenfeld. *Synchronization Algorithms and Concurrent Programming.* Prentice-Hall, Inc., Upper Saddle River, NJ, USA, 2006.

[29] R. K. Treiber. Systems programming: Coping with parallelism. Technical Report RJ 5118, IBM Almaden Research Center, April 1986.

[30] Pen-Chung Yew, Nian-Feng Tzeng, and D.H. Lawrie. Distributing hot-spot addressing in large-scale multiprocessors. *IEEE Transactions on Computers*, C-36(4):388 –395, April 1987.

A Lock-Free Algorithm for Concurrent Bags

Håkan Sundell
School of Business and Informatics
University of Borås
501 90 Borås, Sweden
Hakan.Sundell@hb.se

Anders Gidenstam
School of Business and Informatics
University of Borås
501 90 Borås, Sweden
Anders.Gidenstam@hb.se

Marina Papatriantafilou
Department of Computer Science and
Engineering
Chalmers University of Technology
412 96 Göteborg, Sweden
ptrianta@chalmers.se

Philippas Tsigas
Department of Computer Science and
Engineering
Chalmers University of Technology
412 96 Göteborg, Sweden
tsigas@chalmers.se

ABSTRACT

A lock-free bag data structure supporting unordered buffering is presented in this paper. The algorithm supports multiple producers and multiple consumers, as well as dynamic collection sizes. To handle concurrency efficiently, the algorithm was designed to thrive for disjoint-access-parallelism for the supported semantics. Therefore, the algorithm exploits a distributed design combined with novel techniques for handling concurrent modifications of linked lists using double marks, detection of total emptiness, and efficient memory management with hazard pointer handover. Experiments on a 24-way multi-core platform show significantly better performance for the new algorithm compared to previous algorithms of relevance.

Categories and Subject Descriptors

D.1.3 [**Programming Techniques**]: Concurrent Programming— *Parallel programming*; E.1 [**Data Structures**]: Lists, stacks, and queues

General Terms

Algorithms, Performance, Reliability, Experimentation

Keywords

concurrent, data structure, non-blocking, shared memory

1. INTRODUCTION

Concurrent producer/consumer collections (e.g. set, bag, pool) are fundamental data structures that are key components in applications, algorithms, run-time and operating systems. This paper presents an efficient lock-free and linearizable bag data structure implementation for multiple producers and consumers, supporting the *Add* and the *TryRemoveAny* operations. The *Add* operation adds an item to the collection and the *TryRemoveAny* operation removes an item from the collection unless it is empty. The collection allows any number of occurrences of an item and keeps no information about the order in which items were inserted. A common use of this kind of collection is to communicate data items between producers and consumers in the task of parallelizing applications. Speedup is a major goal in these scenarios where both data and task parallelism are heavily exploited and the collection merely constitutes the "glue" in the application design. Because of this, it is essential that the collection implementation have as high scalability and low overhead as possible. The new algorithm for implementing a lock-free and linearizable bag is designed as a connected set of local data structures in order to maximize parallelism for disjoint accesses.

Non-blocking synchronization is often advocated for the emerging multicore architectures thanks to both its possible advantages in performance and its progress properties. With respect to the latter, the two most important non-blocking methods proposed in the literature are *lock-free* and *wait-free* [1]. Lock-free implementations of shared data structures guarantee that at any point in time in any possible execution some operation will complete in a finite number of steps. In cases with overlapping accesses by concurrent operations, some of them might have to repeat steps in order to complete the operation. However, real-time systems might have stronger requirements on progress, and thus in wait-free implementations each operation is guaranteed to complete in a bounded number of its own steps, regardless of possible concurrent overlaps of the individual steps and the relative execution speeds.

Producer/consumer collections are common means for implementing pipelined design patterns in parallel applications, whereas the proposed bag data structure fits directly when insertion-order are of no importance. Also directly applicable for this kind of parallel design are concurrent LIFO stack, FIFO queue, and "pool" data structures. Solutions for the load-balancing problem such as work-stealing deques [2] have many resemblances to the producer-consumer problem. However, due to different semantics, in order to use these deque data structures as a producer-consumer collection, a new overall connecting algorithm is needed, and the required and linearizable [3] overall semantics cannot be established without significant modifications to the deque algorithms.

Most contemporary programming language frameworks support multi-thread programming and their corresponding framework libraries include an increasing number of concurrent collection data structures. For example, .NET 4.0 has defined the `IProducer-ConsumerCollection` interface with semantics that guarantees no insertion-order of items removed, as well as a concrete implementation with the `ConcurrentBag` class. These data structure implementations, in the .NET and other frameworks, are using various synchronization techniques that are primarily aiming for efficiency. In this paper though, we focus exclusively on strictly non-blocking collection algorithms as implementations being just "concurrent" (while possibly efficient as e.g. "lock-less") are still prone to problems as e.g. deadlocks. Absence of explicit locks does not imply any non-blocking properties, unless the latter are proven to be fulfilled.

A large number of lock-free stack and queue implementations have appeared in the literature, e.g. [4][5][6][7][8][9] being the most influential or most efficient results. These results all have a number of specialties or drawbacks as e.g. static in size, requiring atomic primitives not available on contemporary architectures, and having a high overhead. Moreover, all stacks and queues are inherently limiting the level of disjoint-access-parallelism [10] due to the strict LIFO or FIFO ordering. Afek et al. [11] recently presented a concurrent "pool" implementation with semantics similar to our proposed bag algorithm. Its design aims at allowing high scalability and is also apparently lock-free (although not explicitly stated in the paper), but not linearizable (e.g. it lacks a global state indicating emptiness).

This paper improves on previous results by combining the underlying approaches and designing the new algorithm to maximize efficiency on contemporary multi-core platforms. Also very importantly, the paper aims to provide semantics that conform to a natural intuition of programmers, namely that a concurrent execution's outcome is as if the operations executed sequentially and consistently with their actual time order. Consequently, the new lock-free algorithm is fully linearizable, has no limitations on concurrency, supports a high degree of disjoint-access-parallelism, has a cache-aware design, is fully dynamic in size with efficient memory utilization, and only requires atomic primitives available on contemporary platforms. Experiments on a 24-way multi-core platform shows significantly better performance for the new algorithm compared to all previous semantically compatible lock-free implementations.

The rest of the paper is organized as follows. Section 2 presents the new algorithm together with intuitive arguments for linearizability. In Section 3, related works with lock-free producer/consumer collections are discussed. In Section 4, some benchmark and application experiments are shown. Finally, Section 5 concludes this paper. The detailed implementation description are provided in Appendix A. Corresponding proofs are outlined in more detail in [12].

2. THE NEW LOCK-FREE ALGORITHM

A common and efficient [13, 4] approach for implementing non-blocking collection data structures is to use a continuous (e.g. cyclic) array, where each array element holds a pointer to the stored items. In a concurrent environment, modifications (i.e., insertions and deletions of items) to the array elements are handled by using the CAS^1 atomic synchronization primitive. In ordered (e.g. stack and queue) collections, concurrent insertions or deletions have to compete on

[1]The Compare-And-Swap (CAS) atomic primitive will update a given memory word, if and only if the word still matches a given value (e.g. the one previously read). CAS is generally available in contemporary systems with shared memory, supported mostly directly by hardware and in other cases in combination with system software.

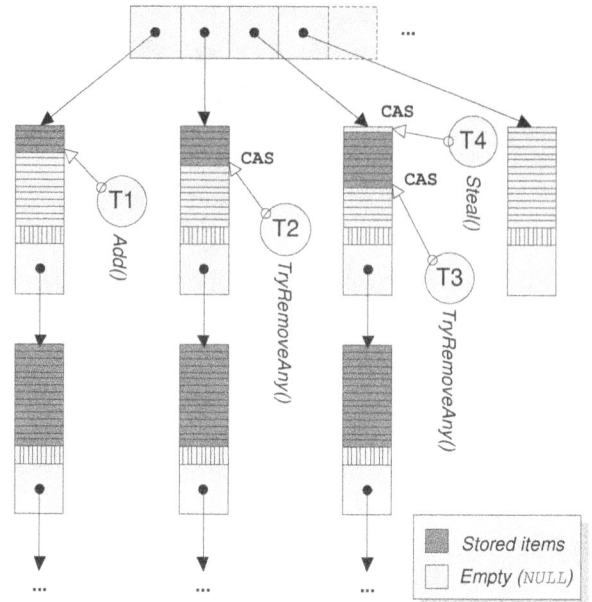

Figure 1: A lock-free bag implemented using a linked list of arrays, where each thread is normally working on its own array block.

modifying the same array element (e.g. at the head or tail array index) due to the required ordering semantics, thus limiting the parallelism[2]. However, in the case of the bag data structure there is no enforced ordering, and hence concurrent insertions and deletions can chose to modify any arbitrary array element, anytime. Therefore we propose to distribute the bag data structure by splitting the array, such that each thread normally only operates on its own array part. To enable dynamic growing and shrinking of the bag without any limitations except system memory, each thread maintains a linked list of fixed-size array blocks, where new array blocks are added or removed as needed. Thus, the bag data structure is constructed out of a shared array of linked lists of array blocks, as depicted in Figure 1.

The main algorithm steps of the *Add* and *TryRemoveAny* operations are shown in Algorithms 1 and 2 respectively. Each thread is using thread-local storage (TLS), for storing the current active position (threadHead) for adding or removing items and a pointer to the first block (threadBlock) in the thread's linked list. In case this list should be empty, the *TryRemoveAny* operation resorts to trying to steal any item from any other linked list in the bag, as shown in Algorithm 3. Each thread stores in TLS the last tried position (stealHead) and the last tried block (stealBlock).

However, as presented, this simple algorithm has a number of issues that need to be addressed:

- **Dynamic capacity.** As new array blocks are dynamically allocated, old and empty blocks also need to be freed. See section 2.1.

- **Stealing should stop when bag is empty.** As the bag is using a distributed design there is no single shared variable indicating emptiness. See section 2.2.

[2]Some optimizations are possible thanks to the definition of the linearizability property, although the parallelism is only achieved after observing contention on a certain array element.

- **Memory.** Lock-free and dynamic algorithms need lock-free and efficient memory management to avoid dangling pointers. See section 2.3.

Algorithm 1 $Add(item)$

1: **if** $threadHead$ has reached end of array **then**
2:    Allocate new block and add it in the linked list before $threadBlock$ and set $threadBlock$ to it
3:    $threadHead \leftarrow 0$
4: **end if**
5: $threadBlock[threadHead] \leftarrow item$
6: $threadHead \leftarrow threadHead + 1$

Algorithm 2 $TryRemoveAny()$

1: **loop**
2:   **if** $threadHead < 0$ **then**
3:     **if** $threadBlock$ is last block in linked list **then**
4:       **return** $Steal()$
5:     **end if**
6:     $threadBlock \leftarrow$ next array block in list
7:     $threadHead \leftarrow$ last array position
8:   **end if**
9:   $item \leftarrow threadBlock[threadHead]$
10:   **if** $item \neq NULL$ **and** $CAS(threadBlock[threadHead], item, NULL)$ **then**
11:     **return** $item$
12:   **else**
13:     $threadHead \leftarrow threadHead - 1$
14:   **end if**
15: **end loop**

Algorithm 3 $Steal()$

1: **loop**
2:   **if** $stealHead$ has reached end of array **then**
3:     $stealBlock \leftarrow$ next block in linked list or next list
4:     $stealHead \leftarrow 0$
5:   **end if**
6:   $item \leftarrow stealBlock[stealHead]$
7:   **if** $item \neq NULL$ **and** $CAS(stealBlock[stealHead], item, NULL)$ **then**
8:     **return** $item$
9:   **else**
10:     $stealHead \leftarrow stealHead + 1$
11:   **end if**
12: **end loop**

2.1 Linked list handling

Whenever any of the array blocks becomes empty (due to own *TryRemoveAny* or concurrent *Steal* operations), its memory should be freed. To handle concurrent deletions of linked list, the same main strategy as used by Harris [14] could be used where next pointers are augmented with a special mark (mark1) that indicates logical deletion. The logical deletion is done using *CAS* and any operation (current or concurrent) that observes this mark should try to perform the actual removal from the linked list of the block using *CAS*.

The *Steal* operations cannot safely (i.e., ensuring emptiness) delete the array blocks on the first position in a linked list, as concurrent *Add* operations would invalidate the performed scan of the array elements. Therefore, the first block should only be deleted by the owning *TryRemoveAny* operation. However, even blocks on the second or further position might be unsafe for *Steal* operations

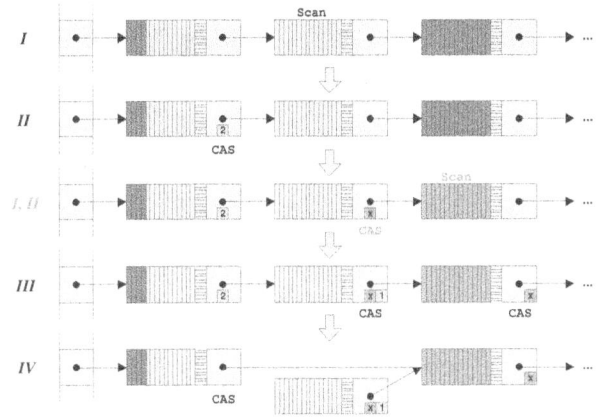

Figure 2: Multiple-step process for marking and deleting blocks (e.g. the middle block) noted to be empty. Another block (in red) might also concurrently be going through the same procedure.

to delete, as these blocks might have become the first block due to concurrent deletions of previous blocks. Our solution is to add an additional mark (mark2) that is set on the next pointer of the previous block using *CAS*, then indicating that the referenced block is logically deleted. Any operation (current or concurrent) that observes this mark should try to set mark1 on the referenced block using *CAS*, as seen in Figure 2. Note that between steps II and III a concurrent operation might succeed with its own steps I and II, and therefore causes an extra step between step III and IV where the current operation needs to propagate the observed mark further on to the next block before proceeding with step IV.

Algorithm 4 $DeleteBlock()$

1: **if** $stealPrev \neq NULL$ **then**
2:   **if** $CAS(stealPrev.next, stealBlock, stealBlock + mark2)$ **then**
3:     Set $mark1$ on $stealBlock.next$ using CAS
4:     **if** $stealBlock.next$ has $mark2$ **then**
5:       Set $mark1$ on $stealBlock.next.next$ using CAS
6:     **end if**
7:     **repeat**
8:       **if** $stealPrev.next$ is not referencing $stealBlock$ **then**
9:         $UpdateStealPrev()$
10:       **end if**
11:     **until** $stealPrev = NULL$ **or** $CAS(stealPrev.next, stealBlock + mark2, stealBlock.next - mark1)$
12:     $stealBlock \leftarrow$ next block in linked list or next list
13:   **end if**
14:   $UpdateStealPrev()$
15: **else**
16:   $stealPrev \leftarrow stealBlock$
17:   $stealBlock \leftarrow$ next block in linked list or next list
18: **end if**

To keep track of the previous block, the additional TLS-variable stealPrev is used and should be continuously set to reference the block preceding stealBlock. Whenever stealBlock is on a new list, stealPrev should be reset to NULL. The steps for conditionally deleting a block whenever a *Steal* operation has scanned all array elements to be empty, is described in Algorithm 4. Line 3 of Algorithm 3 should be replaced to a call to *DeleteBlock*. The pur-

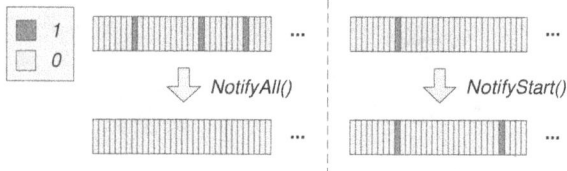

Figure 3: An atomic notification structure for registration of concurrent Add operations.

pose of the *UpdateStealPrev* procedure is to update stealPrev such that it references the block preceding stealBlock. To achieve this, it might have to search from the start of the linked list, and also apply helping of steps III-IV of concurrent operations whenever mark1 or mark2 is noticed on the traversed blocks. If the search fails, steal-Prev is set to NULL. Similar helping should also be performed during the deletion (using only mark1) that should take place in Line 6 of Algorithm 2.

2.2 Linearizability and global emptiness detection

To be correct, the algorithm should implement full semantics and for the caller, concurrent operations should appear to take effect atomically, i.e., the algorithm should be linearizable [3]. If the bag is totally empty, the *TryRemoveAny* should terminate and return failure (e.g. NULL). For ensuring total emptiness, the *Steal* operation needs to continuously scan the whole data structure, in combination with some ability to detect concurrent changes due to *Add* operations. Figure 3 illustrates how each individual thread can "subscribe" on pending *Add* operations on a particular block[3] by setting the corresponding bit in a bit array using *CAS*. If an *Add* operation is initiated on this block, it clears the whole bit array by simply writing zero to the memory words, before line 5 of Algorithm 1. By doing so, it notifies all subscribed threads on the pending insert (which will be done in line 6). However, there can be pending inserts that actually have taken place during the scanning, but were initiated before the scanning thread started subscribing. Therefore, we can only ensure total emptiness after having scanned the whole bag (while continuously ensuring no pending inserts and that all array elements are NULL) for as many repetitions as there are threads. The intuition behind this is that each thread can only have up to one pending insert, and thus the bag must have been empty during one of the repetitions. The extension steps to the *Steal* operation are shown in Algorithm 5.

We can now define the specific statements in the algorithm where the operations appear to take effect, i.e., the linearizability points:

- The *Add* operation, takes effect at the write statement in line 6 of Algorithm 1. This follows by the definition how array elements represent items belonging to the bag.

- The *TryRemoveAny* operation returning an item, takes effect at the successful *CAS* statement in line 10 of Algorithm 2 or line 7 of Algorithm 3. This follows by the definition how array elements represent items belonging to the bag.

---

[3]We chose to place this notification structure per block instead of per linked list, in order to reduce the number of cache lines invalidated by an *Add* operation. As a consequence of this choice, the last block in a linked list is never deleted, and notification state is propagated downwards whenever blocks are removed.

Algorithm 5 $Steal()$ − $Extension$

```
1:  for i = 0 to NR_THREADS + 1 do
2:      repeat
3:          Perform the steps of the Steal algorithm for one block at a time
4:          if i = 1 then
5:              Set the corresponding bit for this thread in the notification ar-
                ray of the block using CAS
6:          else if i > 1 then
7:              if The bit for this thread in the notification array is clear or a
                non-empty array element has been found then
8:                  i ← 0
9:              end if
10:         end if
11:     until All lists in the bag have been scanned
12: end for
13: return NULL
```

- The *TryRemoveAny* operation returning NULL, takes effect at the read statement of the set notification bit in line 7 of Algorithm 5 during one of the repetitions. This follows by the previous reasoning about detecting total emptiness.

2.3 Memory management

Whenever an empty array block has been fully removed (e.g. after the successful *CAS* in line 11 of Algorithm 4) from the linked list, its memory should be freed and be made available for system allocation. However, other threads are concurrently traversing the linked list, and might consequently have TLS or local variables that reference the deleted block. For handling this problem, we build on the efficient and lock-free memory management scheme proposed by Michael [9] which makes use of shared "hazard" pointers. Throughout the whole bag algorithm, whenever a new block is visited and its memory address stored in a variable, a corresponding hazard pointer must be set. The memory management system will then make sure that a block of memory is not reused until no hazard pointers are referencing it. Note that memory of a deleted block might be reused even though there are next pointers from other blocks pointing to it.

However, this becomes a problem when trying to dereference a next pointer with mark1. As the next pointer belongs to a block that is being deleted, it is not possible to acquire a safe pointer to the block referenced by the next pointer. On the other hand, this is something that the bag algorithm needs to do, e.g. line 5 of Algorithm 4. To meet this requirement, our solution is to extend the memory management scheme [9] such that it can handle a "handover" of a hazard pointer between two or more threads. This works in the way that before removing the block from the linked list with *CAS*, the current thread sets a hazard pointer to the block referenced by the next pointer. After having performed the full removal of the block containing the marked next pointer, the next pointer is set to NULL. Before clearing the hazard pointer (holding a reference to the block after the deleted one), it signals to the memory management system to perform another scan of hazard pointers, as another thread might now have set a hazard pointer to the same block. In this way, any other thread may now safely dereference also next pointers with mark1.

3. RELATED WORK DISCUSSION

Treiber presented a lock-free stack (a.k.a. IBM Freelist), which was later efficiently fixed from the ABA[4] problem by Michael [9].

---

[4]The ABA problem is due to the inability of *CAS* to detect concurrent changes of a memory word from a value (A) to something else (B) and then again back to the first value (A).

Hendler et al. [8] presented an extension where randomized elimination[5] is used as a back-off strategy and for increasing scalability when contention on the stack's head is noticed via failed *CAS* attempts.

Tsigas and Zhang [4] presented a lock-free queue that is an extension of [13] for multiple producers and consumers, where synchronization is done both directly on the array elements and the shared head and tail indices using *CAS*. In order to avoid the ABA problem when updating the array elements, the algorithm exploits using two (or more) null values. Moreover, for lowering the memory contention the algorithm alternates every other operation between scanning and updating the shared head and tail indices. Michael and Scott [5] presented a lock-free queue based on a linked list. Synchronization is done via shared pointers indicating the current head and tail node as well via the next pointer of the last node, all updated using *CAS*. The queue is fully dynamic as more nodes are allocated as needed when new items are added. The original presentation used unbounded version counters, and therefore required double-width *CAS* which is not supported on all contemporary platforms. The problem with the version counters can easily be avoided by using some memory management scheme as e.g. [9]. Moir et al. [6] presented an extension where randomized elimination is used as a back-off strategy and for increasing scalability when contention on the queue's head or tail is noticed via failed *CAS* attempts. However, elimination is only possible when the queue is close to be empty during the operation's invocation. Hoffman et al. [7] takes another approach to increase scalability by allowing concurrent *Enqueue* operations to insert the new node at adjacent positions in the linked list if contention is noticed during the attempted insert at the very end of the linked list. To enable these "baskets" of concurrently inserted nodes, removed nodes are logically deleted before the actual removal from the linked list, and as the algorithm traverses through the linked list it requires stronger memory management than [9] and a strategy to avoid long chains of logically deleted nodes.

In resemblance to [4] the new algorithm uses *CAS* and arrays to store (pointers to) the items. Moreover, shared indices are avoided and scanning [4] is always used for finding empty or occupied array elements. In contrast to [4] the array is not static or cyclic, but instead more arrays are dynamically allocated as needed when new items are added, making our bag fully dynamic. In resemblance to [5][6][7] the new algorithm is dynamic, and in resemblance to [7] removed blocks are logically deleted and blocks are being traversed. In contrast to [7], the new algorithm suffice with a slightly modified version of [9] for memory management purposes.

Afek et al. [11] presented a pool data structure, where the collection is consisting of several lock-free queues on which the load is distributed. The pool is using randomized elimination combined with diffraction in a tree-like manner, where elimination is used for increasing disjoint-access-parallelism. In resemblance to [11] the new algorithm uses several underlying data structures, but instead of randomization it is improving disjoint-access-parallelism inherently by its algorithmic design and avoiding global synchronization. In addition, the new algorithm is linearizable.

Fomitchev and Ruppert [15] extended the linked list structure by Harris [14] with having an additional mark on pointers, where the new mark was used on the node preceding the node to be marked ordinarily, in order to earlier inform concurrent operations traversing the linked list about the ongoing node removal. In contrast to [15], the new algorithm are using the additional mark in order to distinguish between logical deletions done by the owner thread and the stealing threads respectively.

Arora et al. [2] presented an efficient and lock-free work-stealing deque based on arrays. It was later improved to handle dynamic sizes by Hendler et al. [16] that used a doubly-linked list of arrays, where each array can be dynamically allocated. In resemblance to [2][16], the new algorithm assign each thread its own data structure, uses arrays as the basic representation for storing items, and *CAS* is only used for updates that can be concurrently updated by several threads. In resemblance to [16], additional array blocks are dynamically allocated when needed, although the new algorithm only maintains a single-linked list. In contrast to [2][16], the new algorithm provides linearizable bag semantics; e.g. provides a global state indicating emptiness.

Cache-aware algorithms for non-blocking data structures have attended an increasing interest, with several recent results in the literature, e.g. [17].

4. EXPERIMENTAL STUDY

We have evaluated the performance of our new lock-free bag implementation by the means of some custom micro-benchmarks. The purpose is to estimate how well the implementation compares with other known lock-free compatible implementations under high contention and increasing concurrency. The benchmarks are the following:

1. Random 50%/50%. Each thread is randomly (the sequence is decided beforehand) executing either an *Add* or *TryRemoveAny* operation.

2. 1 Producer / N-1 Consumers. Each thread (out of N) is either a producer or consumer, throughout the whole experiment. The producer is repeatedly executing *Add* operations, whereas the consumers are executing *TryRemoveAny*.

3. N-1 Producers / 1 Consumer. Performed as the previous benchmark, except with another distribution of producers and consumers.

4. N/2 Producers / N/2 Consumers. Performed as the previous benchmark, except with another distribution of producers and consumers.

We have also evaluated the performance of our new implementation in the scope of real applications. For this purpose we chose to compute and render an image of the Mandelbrot set [18] in parallel using the producer/consumer pattern. The program uses a shared collection data structure that is used for communication between the program's two major phases:

- Phase 1 consists of computing the number (with a maximum of 255) of iterations for a given set of points within a chosen region of the image. The results for each region together with its coordinates are then put in the collection data structure.

- Phase 2 consists of, for each computed region stored in the collection, computing the RGB values for each contained point and draw these pixels to the resulting image. The colors for the corresponding number of iterations are chosen according to a rainbow scheme, where low numbers are rendered within the red and high numbers are rendered within the violet spectrum.

Phase 1 is performed in parallel with phase 2, i.e., like a pipeline. Half of the threads perform phase 1 and the rest perform phase

---

[5]If not conflicting with linearizability, two concurrent and matching operations might be eliminated by exchanging data directly without passing through the main data structure.

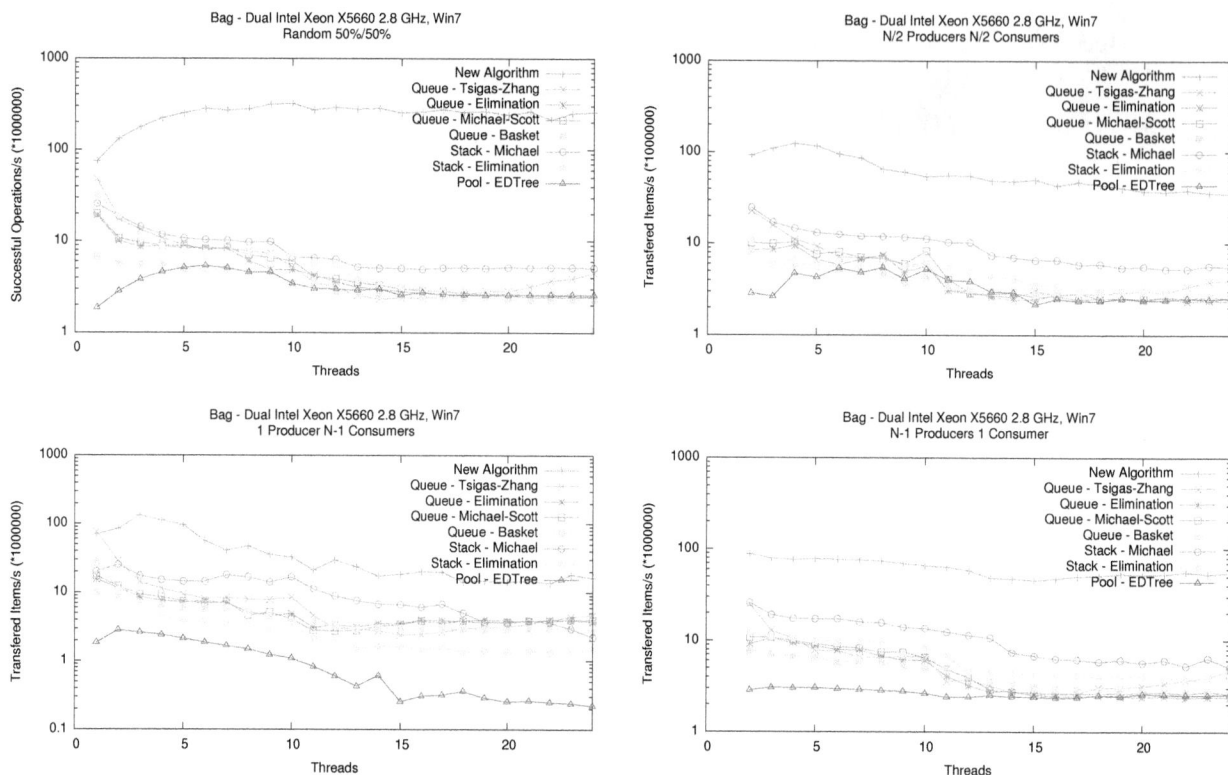

Figure 4: Benchmark experiments on a 24-way Dual Intel Xeon processor system.

2. We have implemented this application in C, for the purpose of rendering a 32-bit color image of 2048 times 2048 pixels. The size of each square-shaped region is chosen to be one of 16x16 (i.e., 16 by 16), 8x8, 4x4, or 2x2 pixels. The whole image is divided into a number (equal to the number of threads) of larger parts[6], where each producer thread (i.e., phase 1) work sequentially on the regions contained within its own part. The consumer threads (i.e., phase 2) render the regions got from the collection in the order that they were obtained, until the producer threads have finished and the collection is empty.

For comparison we have implemented the dynamic lock-free queue by Michael and Scott [5], the same with elimination [6], the baskets queue [7], and the static cyclic array lock-free queue presented in [4]. For comparison, we also implemented the lock-free stack by Michael [9], and the same with elimination by Hendler et al. [8]. Moreover, we implemented the ED-tree based lock-free (although not linearizable) pool by Afek et al. [11].

All dynamic stacks, queues and pools (as well as the new bag algorithm) have been implemented to support collection sizes only limited by the system's memory, i.e., using lock-free management schemes [9] or [19] and lock-free free-lists where appropriate. For the new implementation, the size of the array block (`BLOCK_SIZE`) is chosen to fit within one cache line. All implementations are written in C and compiled with the highest optimization level. For all implementations, synchronization hotspots were padded with

dummy bytes in order to avoid false sharing. In our benchmark experiments, each concurrent thread is started at the very same time and each benchmark runs for one second for each implementation. Exactly the same sequence of operations was performed per thread for all different implementations compared. A clean-cache operation was also performed just before each run, and final results are taken as an average over 10 runs. All benchmark and application experiments have been executed on a dual Intel Xeon X5660 2.8 GHz with 12 GB DDR3 1333 MHz system running Windows 7 64-bit. Each of the two processors has 6 cores, each core being capable of executing 2 threads each, making up to 24 hardware threads in total.

The results from the benchmark experiments with up to 24 threads are shown in Figure 4. Note that the results are shown in logarithmic scale, due to the very large difference in performance for the different implementations. The results of benchmarks 1 show the number of successful (failed *TryRemoveAny*s, *Pop*s or *Dequeue*s are not counted) operations executed per second in the system in total. The results of benchmarks 2-4 show the number of items per second that have passed through the collection (i.e., the number of successful *TryRemoveAny*, *Pop* or *Dequeue* operations). Interestingly, the new algorithm performs significantly, often with a magnitude, better than all the other implementations. The superior performance and scalability can be explained by the distributed design and the low synchronization overhead. The declining scalability with increasing number of threads (a behavior shared with the pool implementation) can be explained being in major due to memory bandwidth saturation.

The results from the application experiments with up to 24 threads are shown in Figure 5. As the Mandelbrot set is known as being an

---

[6]Due to the nature of the Mandelbrot set, this way of deciding each part might not be fair in respect of workload per thread. As can be seen in the experimental results, this partition pattern causes that 3 parts take longer time than 2 parts in parallel, because the total execution time depends on the slowest part.

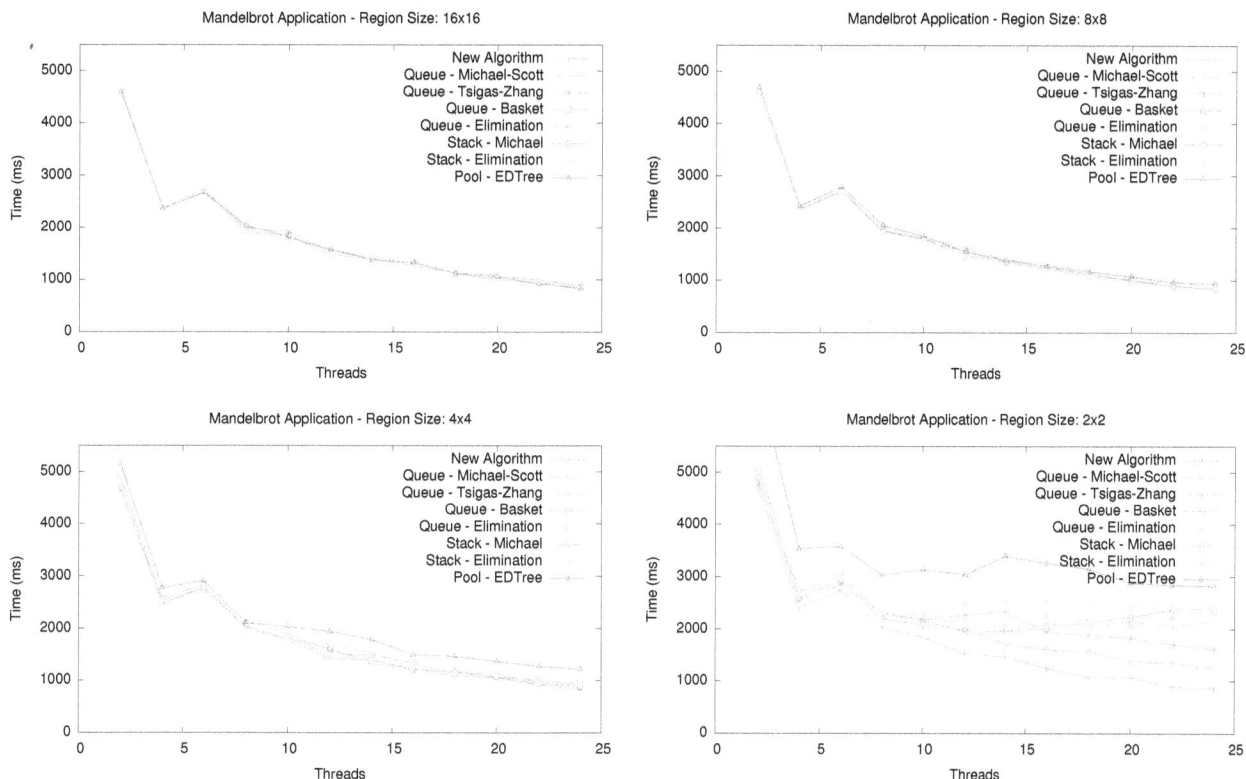

Figure 5: Application experiments on a 24-way Dual Intel Xeon processor system.

embarrassingly parallel problem, the amount of communication is relatively low, and therefore the impact of the choice of collection implementation is expected to be of minor importance. For example, this behavior is apparent with the experiment using 16x16-sized regions. However, as regions get smaller the amount of communication increases, and the performance of the collection will have a bigger impact on the overall performance. Consequently, as can be started to be seen with 4x4 and then with the 2x2 region size, the new algorithm is fast even in cases where there is no significant contention, and as contention becomes higher in more communication intensive instances the new algorithm shows its good parallel behavior.

5. CONCLUSIONS

We have presented a new algorithm for implementing a lock-free producer/consumer collection data structure. To the best of our knowledge, this is the first lock-free bag algorithm with all of the following properties:

- Distributed design, allowing disjoint-access-parallelism.

- Exploiting thread-local static storage.

- Dynamic in size via lock-free memory management.

- Only requires atomic primitives available in contemporary systems.

The algorithm has been shown to be lock-free and linearizable. Experiments on a contemporary multi-core platform shows significantly better performance for the new algorithm compared to previous state-of-the-art lock-free implementations of data structures

that can serve as producer/consumer platforms. We believe that our implementation should be of highly practical interest to contemporary and emerging multi-core and multi-processor system thanks to both its high performance and its strong progress and consistency guarantees.

6. REFERENCES

[1] M. Herlihy, "Wait-free synchronization," *ACM Transactions on Programming Languages and Systems*, vol. 11, no. 1, pp. 124–149, Jan. 1991.

[2] N. S. Arora, R. D. Blumofe, and C. G. Plaxton, "Thread scheduling for multiprogrammed multiprocessors," in *ACM Symposium on Parallel Algorithms and Architectures*, 1998, pp. 119–129.

[3] M. Herlihy and J. Wing, "Linearizability: a correctness condition for concurrent objects," *ACM Transactions on Programming Languages and Systems*, vol. 12, no. 3, pp. 463–492, 1990.

[4] P. Tsigas and Y. Zhang, "A simple, fast and scalable non-blocking concurrent FIFO queue for shared memory multiprocessor systems," in *Proceedings of the 13th annual ACM Symposium on Parallel Algorithms and Architectures*, 2001, pp. 134–143.

[5] M. M. Michael and M. L. Scott, "Simple, fast, and practical non-blocking and blocking concurrent queue algorithms," in *Proceedings of the 15th annual ACM Symposium on Principles of Distributed Computing*, 1996, pp. 267–275.

[6] M. Moir, D. Nussbaum, O. Shalev, and N. Shavit, "Using elimination to implement scalable and lock-free fifo queues,"

in *Proceedings of the 17th annual ACM Symposium on Parallelism in Algorithms and Architectures*, 2005, pp. 253–262.

[7] M. Hoffman, O. Shalev, and N. Shavit, "The baskets queue," in *Proceedings of the 11th International Conference on Principles of Distributed Systems*, ser. Lecture Notes in Computer Science, vol. 4878. Springer, 2007, pp. 401–414.

[8] D. Hendler, N. Shavit, and L. Yerushalmi, "A scalable lock-free stack algorithm," *Journal of Parallel and Distributed Computing*, vol. 70, no. 1, pp. 1–12, 2010.

[9] M. M. Michael, "Hazard pointers: Safe memory reclamation for lock-free objects," *IEEE Transactions on Parallel and Distributed Systems*, vol. 15, no. 8, Aug. 2004.

[10] A. Israeli and L. Rappoport, "Disjoint-access-parallel implementations of strong shared memory primitives," in *Proceedings of the 13th annual ACM symposium on Principles of Distributed Computing*, Aug. 1994.

[11] Y. Afek, G. Korland, M. Natanzon, and N. Shavit, "Scalable producer-consumer pools based on elimination-diffraction trees," in *Euro-Par 2010*, ser. Lecture Notes in Computer Science. Springer, 2010, vol. 6272, pp. 151–162.

[12] H. Sundell, A. Gidenstam, M. Papatriantafilou, and P. Tsigas, "A lock-free algorithm for concurrent bags," Department of Computer Science and Engineering, Chalmers University of Technology, Tech. Rep. 2011:01, January 2011.

[13] L. Lamport, "Specifying concurrent program modules," *ACM Trans. Program. Lang. Syst.*, vol. 5, no. 2, pp. 190–222, 1983.

[14] T. L. Harris, "A pragmatic implementation of non-blocking linked lists," in *Proceedings of the 15th International Symposium of Distributed Computing*, Oct. 2001, pp. 300–314.

[15] M. Fomitchev and E. Ruppert, "Lock-free linked lists and skip lists," in *Proceedings of the 23rd annual symposium on Principles of Distributed Computing*, Jul. 2004, pp. 50–59.

[16] D. Hendler, Y. Lev, M. Moir, and N. Shavit, "A dynamic-sized nonblocking work stealing deque," *Distributed Computing*, vol. 18, no. 3, pp. 189–207, 2006.

[17] A. Braginsky and E. Petrank, "Locality-conscious lock-free linked lists," in *ICDCN*, ser. Lecture Notes in Computer Science, M. K. Aguilera, H. Yu, N. H. Vaidya, V. Srinivasan, and R. R. Choudhury, Eds., vol. 6522. Springer, 2011, pp. 107–118.

[18] B. B. Mandelbrot, "Fractal aspects of the iteration of $z \to \lambda z(1-z)$ for complex λ and z," *Annals of the New York Academy of Sciences*, vol. 357, pp. 249–259, 1980.

[19] A. Gidenstam, M. Papatriantafilou, H. Sundell, and P. Tsigas, "Efficient and reliable lock-free memory reclamation based on reference counting," *IEEE Transactions on Parallel and Distributed Systems*, vol. 20, no. 8, pp. 1173–1187, 2009.

APPENDIX

A. ALGORITHM DETAILS

The specific fields of each array block are described in Program 1 as it is used in this implementation.

In the algorithm, there is no shared information about which array index that is currently being the next active for the *Add* or *TryRemoveAny* operation. Instead each thread is storing related information in separate memory using thread-local storage (TLS), its own index (threadID) into the global shared array, and pointers indicating the last known (by this thread) first block (threadBlock)

Program 1 The block structure and auxiliary functions.

```
1  struct blockp_t {
2      block_t * p; bool mark2 :1; bool mark1 :1;
3  };
4  struct block_t : public node_t {
5      void * nodes[BLOCK_SIZE];
6      long notifyAdd[NR_THREADS/WORD_SIZE];
7      blockp_t next;
8  };
9  void Mark1Block(block_t *block) {
10     for(;;) {
11         blockp_t next = block->next;
12         if(next.p == NULL || next.mark1 || CAS(&block->
               next,next,{next.p,next.mark2,true})) break;
13     }
14 }
15 block_t * NewBlock() {
16     block_t * block = NewNode(sizeof(block_t));
17     block->next = NULL;
18     NotifyAll(block);
19     for(int i=0;i<BLOCK_SIZE;i++) block->nodes[i]=NULL;
20     return block;
21 }
22 void NotifyAll(block_t *block) {
23     for(int i=0;i<NR_THREADS/WORD_SIZE;i++)
24         block->notifyAdd[i] = 0;
25 }
26 void NotifyStart(block_t *block, int Id) {
27     do {
28         long old = block->notifyAdd[Id/WORD_SIZE];
29     } while(!CAS(&block->notifyAdd[Id/WORD_SIZE],old,old
               |(1<<(Id%WORD_SIZE))));
30 }
31 bool NotifyCheck(block_t *block, int Id) {
32     return (block->notifyAdd[Id/WORD_SIZE]&(1<<(Id%
               WORD_SIZE)))==0;
33 }
34 void InitBag() {
35     for(int i=0;i<NR_THREADS;i++) globalHeadBlock[i]=NULL
           ;
36 }
37 void InitThread() {
38     threadBlock = globalHeadBlock[threadID];
39     threadHead = BLOCK_SIZE;
40     stealIndex = 0;
41     stealBlock = NULL; stealPrev = NULL;
42     stealHead = BLOCK_SIZE;
43 }
44 // Shared variables
45 block_t * globalHeadBlock[NR_THREADS];
46 // Thread-local storage
47 block_t * threadBlock, stealBlock, stealPrev;
48 bool foundAdd;
49 int threadHead, stealHead, stealIndex;
50 int threadID; // Unique number between 0 ... NR_THREADS
```

as well as active indices (threadHead) for inserting and removing items. In addition, each thread also keeps track of the last block (stealBlock), the corresponding index (stealHead), and its preceding block (stealPrev) used for "stealing" items from other thread's (i.e., the thread with global index stealIndex) linked lists.

When an array block gets fully empty, the block itself should be removed from the corresponding linked list. As this can happen concurrently with insertions and removals of other blocks, we apply the method introduced in [14] where blocks are first marked (using bit 0 of the next pointer) and then removed from the linked list using *CAS*. Concurrent operations that observe the mark are obliged to "help" by also trying to fulfill the full removal, and thus supporting the lock-free property. However, detection of a block to be fully empty is not straight-forward, as the first block of each linked list can have concurrent *Add* operations, adding new items directly after a stealing *TryRemoveAny* operation have found the array elements at the corresponding array indices to be empty during its

Program 2 The new Add operation.

```
1  void Add(void *item) {
2      int head = threadHead;
3      block_t * block = threadBlock;
4      for(;;) {
5          if(head==BLOCK_SIZE) {
6              block_t *oldblock = block;
7              block = NewBlock();
8              block->next=oldblock;
9              globalHeadBlock[threadID]=block;
10             threadBlock = block;
11             head = 0;
12         }
13         else if(block->nodes[head]==NULL) {
14             NotifyAll(block);
15             block->nodes[head]=item;
16             threadHead = head+1;
17             return;
18         }
19         else head++;
20     }
21 }
```

Program 3 The new TryRemoveAny operation.

```
1  void * TryRemoveAny() {
2      int head = threadHead-1;
3      block_t * block = threadBlock;
4      int round = 0;
5      for(;;) {
6          if(block == NULL || (head<0 && block->next.p ==
                 NULL)) {
7              do {
8                  int i=0;
9                  do {
10                     void *result = TryStealBlock(round);
11                     if(result!=NULL) return result;
12                     if(foundAdd) {
13                         round=0; i=0;
14                     }
15                     else if(stealBlock==NULL) i++;
16                 } while(i<NR_THREADS);
17             } while(++round<=NR_THREADS);
18             return NULL;
19         }
20         if(head<0) {
21             Mark1Block(block);
22             for(;;) {
23                 blockp_t next=DeRefLink(&block->next);
24                 if(next.mark2) Mark1Block(next.p);
25                 if(next.mark1) {
26                     if(next.p) NotifyAll(next.p);
27                     if(CAS(&globalHeadBlock[threadId],
                              block,next.p)) {
28                         block->next = {NULL,false,true};
29                         DeleteNode(block); ReScan(next);
30                         block=next.p;
31                     }
32                     else block=DeRefLink(&globalHeadBlock
                              [threadId]);
33                 }
34                 else break;
35             }
36             threadBlock = block;
37             threadHead = BLOCK_SIZE;
38             head = BLOCK_SIZE-1;
39         }
40         else {
41             void *data = block->nodes[head];
42             if(data==NULL) head--;
43             else if(CAS(&block->nodes[head],data,NULL)) {
44                 threadHead = head;
45                 return data;
46             }
47         }
48     }
49 }
```

scan. Moreover, even though blocks on second or further position in a linked list cannot have concurrent *Add* operations, the block itself might concurrently change position in the linked list, and actually become the first block. Therefore, detection of emptiness and marking for removal must be done in one atomic step that also includes the verification of the block not being the first in the linked list. To enable this, stealPrev is set to reference the previous block in the linked list, before starting the scan of the array elements of the current block. If all array elements were empty, we now need to verify that the next pointer of stealPrev is still pointing to the current block (if there exists a previous block, the current block cannot be the first) and at the same time marking the next pointer of the current block. As this cannot be done using the available single-word *CAS*, we instead introduce a second mark (bit 1 of the next pointer) indicating that the next block is marked for removal, and thus we can atomically verify the next pointer of stealPrev referencing the current block and also setting the second mark of it by using *CAS*. The further steps are then to mark the actual block of interest for removal and then proceed with the removal from the linked list, something also required to be done by any concurrent operation that have observed the second mark to be set.

As the data structure is based on array blocks where each array element can contain an item or not, these blocks are not always fully utilized. From a system perspective it is therefore necessary to maximize the overall utilization and as well provide a lower bound on minimal utilization of memory. Therefore, an essential rule for *TryRemoveAny* operations that need to "steal" items from other thread's linked lists, is to never leave a visited array block until all items (including the array block itself) have been removed, whenever this rule is possible to fulfill.

If the data structure is totally empty, the *TryRemoveAny* should terminate and return failure (e.g. NULL). However, as the data structure is highly distributed, there is no single variable for identification of global emptiness. Instead, the operation needs to scan the whole data structure step by step, in combination with some ability to detect if something has changed (i.e., concurrent *Add* operations) since it started the global scanning. Figure 3 illustrates how each individual thread can "subscribe" on pending *Add* operations on a particular block by setting the corresponding bit in a bit array. If an *Add* operation is initiated on this block, it clears the whole bit array, thus "notifying" all subscribed threads on the pending insert. However, as there can be pending inserts that actu-

ally have taken place during the scanning, but were initiated before the scanning thread started subscribing, the whole scanning procedure has to repeated globally a certain number of times to ensure global emptiness. Note that even though this implies a relatively long time for detecting global emptiness, it does not affect the time for a *TryRemoveAny* operation to find and remove items added by concurrent *Add* operations during the scanning.

For our implementation of the new lock-free bag algorithm, we have selected a slightly modified version of the lock-free memory management scheme proposed by Michael [9] which makes use of shared "hazard" pointers. The interface defined by the memory management scheme is listed in Program 4. Using this scheme we can assure that an array block can only be reclaimed when there are no local references to it from pending concurrent operations or from pointers in thread-local storage. The *ReScan* operation is an extension to the original scheme by [9]. The purpose of this operation is to force a re-scan of a deleted node, in order to avoid the problem of a normal scan possibly missing hazard pointers "moving" from one thread to another (i.e., avoiding the scenario when

Program 4 The functionality supported by the memory management scheme.

```
1  node_t * NewNode(int size);
2  void DeleteNode(node_t *node);
3  node_t * DeRefLink(node_t **link);
4  void ReleaseRef(node_t *node);
5  void ReScan(node_t *node);
```

Program 5 The auxiliary TryStealBlock function.

```
1  void * TryStealBlock(int round) {
2      int head = stealHead;
3      block_t * block = stealBlock;
4      foundAdd = false;
5      if(block==NULL) {
6          block = DeRefLink(&globalHeadBlock[stealIndex]);
7          stealBlock = block;
8          stealHead = head = 0;
9      }
10     if(head==BLOCK_SIZE) {
11         stealBlock = block = NextStealBlock(block);
12         head = 0;
13     }
14     if(block==NULL) {
15         stealIndex = (stealIndex+1)%NR_THREADS;
16         stealHead = 0;
17         stealBlock = NULL; stealPrev = NULL;
18         return NULL;
19     }
20     if(round==1) NotifyStart(block,threadId);
21     else if(round>1 && NotifyCheck(block,threadId))
           foundAdd = true;
22     for(;;) {
23         if(head==BLOCK_SIZE) {
24             stealHead = head;
25             return NULL;
26         }
27         else {
28             void *data = block->nodes[head];
29             if(data==NULL) head++;
30             else if(CAS(&block->nodes[head],data,NULL)) {
31                 stealHead = head;
32                 return data;
33             }
34         }
35     }
36  }
```

Program 6 The auxiliary NextStealBlock function.

```
1  block_t * NextStealBlock(block_t *block) {
2      blockp_t next;
3      for(;;) {
4          if(block==NULL) {
5              block = DeRefLink(&globalHeadBlock[stealIndex]);
6              break;
7          }
8          next = DeRefLink(&block->next);
9          if(next.mark2) Mark1Block(next.p);
10         if(stealPrev == NULL || next.p == NULL) {
11             if(next.mark1) {
12                 if(next.p) NotifyAll(next.p);
13                 if(CAS(&globalHeadBlock[stealIndex],block,next.p)) {
14                     block->next = {NULL,false,true};
15                     DeleteNode(block); ReScan(next);
16                 }
17                 else {
18                     stealPrev = NULL;
19                     block = DeRefLink(&globalHeadBlock[stealIndex]);
20                     continue;
21                 }
22             }
23             else stealPrev = block;
24         }
25         else {
26             if(next.mark1) {
27                 blockp_t prevnext = {block,stealPrev->next.mark2,false};
28                 if(CAS(&stealPrev->next,prevnext,next.p)) {
29                     block->next = {NULL,false,true};
30                     DeleteNode(block); ReScan(next);
31                 }
32                 else {
33                     stealPrev = NULL;
34                     block = DeRefLink(&globalHeadBlock[stealIndex]);
35                     continue;
36                 }
37             }
38             else if(block==stealBlock) {
39                 if(CAS(&stealPrev->next,block,{block,true,false})) {
40                     Mark1Block(block);
41                     continue;
42                 }
43                 else {
44                     stealPrev = NULL;
45                     block = DeRefLink(&globalHeadBlock[stealIndex]);
46                     continue;
47                 }
48             }
49             else stealPrev = block;
50         }
51         if(block == stealBlock || next.p == stealBlock) {
52             block=next.p;
53             break;
54         }
55         block=next.p;
56     }
57     return block;
58  }
```

there are first one active hazard pointer by thread i and then one by thread j with a small overlap in time where both are active, although both are missed during the concurrent scan and consequently the node is wrongly reclaimed).

In order to simplify the description of our new algorithm, we have omitted some of the details of applying the operations of the memory management [9]. In actual implementations, *ReleaseRef* calls should be inserted at appropriate places whenever a variable holding a safe pointer goes out of scope or is reassigned. The detailed descriptions of the *Add* and *TryRemoveAny* operations are listed in Programs 2 and 3 respectively, with the auxiliary functions *TryStealBlock* and *NextStealBlock* used by *TryRemoveAny* listed in Programs 5 and 6. The purpose of the *TryStealBlock* function is to continue to try stealing from the last tried index (stealHead) in the current block of stealing (stealBlock), and either return the removed item or NULL in case the current block was found to be empty. The purpose of the *NextStealBlock* function is to try removing the current block, unless it should not do so (e.g., if it was the first or last block in the list), and then advance stealBlock to the next block. If the current block could not be removed due to concurrent changes in the linked list, it returns the current block without advancing.

Understanding Bloom Filter Intersection for Lazy Address-Set Disambiguation

Mark C. Jeffrey and J. Gregory Steffan
Department of Electrical and Computer
Engineering
University of Toronto
{markj,steffan}@eecg.toronto.edu

ABSTRACT

A Bloom filter is a probabilistic bit-array-based set representation that has recently been applied to address-set *disambiguation* in systems that ease the burden of parallel programming. However, many of these systems intersect the Bloom filter bit-arrays to approximate address-set intersection and decide set disjointness. This is in contrast with the conventional and well-studied approach of making individual membership queries into the Bloom filter. In this paper we present much-needed probabilistic models for the unconventional application of testing set disjointness using Bloom filters. Consequently, we demonstrate that intersecting Bloom filters requires substantially larger bit-arrays to provide the same probability of *false set-overlap* as querying into the bit-array. For when intersection is unavoidable, we prove that partitioned Bloom filters require less space than unpartitioned. Finally, we show that for Bloom filters with a single hash function, surprisingly, intersection and querying share the same probability of false set-overlap.

Categories and Subject Descriptors

F.2.2 [**Analysis of Algorithms and Problem Complexity**]: Nonnumerical Algorithms and Problems—*computations on discrete structures*

General Terms

Design, Performance, Theory

Keywords

Bloom filters, signatures, set intersection, address-set disambiguation, transactional memory, thread-level speculation, parallelism

1. INTRODUCTION

The over-arching challenge for parallel programming stems from detecting and managing data access conflicts between parallel threads, since they can lead to invalid data and incorrect execution when improperly handled. A variety of programming models and debug tools have hence been proposed to augment locking, a conventional form of managing potential conflicts. Progress has been made in tools for finding, replaying, and avoiding concurrency bugs [18] that may result when a programmer: (i) fails to synchronize accesses to a mutable shared variable (i.e., a data race) [28]; or (ii) incorrectly reasons about atomicity, failing to enclose a set of memory accesses in a critical section (i.e., an atomicity violation) [17, 18]. Debugging in a concurrent environment is made even more challenging as the manifestation of these bugs depends on the non-deterministic interleavings of threads. Several debugging systems thus focus on deterministically replaying concurrency bugs to find their source [13,25,38]. Despite thorough testing, some bugs still make it to deployment, motivating dynamic avoidance of concurrency bugs [17]. Beyond debugging, Transactional Memory (TM) [12] and Thread-Level Speculation (TLS) [10, 15, 37] have emerged as methods of more automatically managing data access conflicts for the programmer. TM allows potentially conflicting transactions to execute concurrently, where the underlying system tracks memory accesses and detects and handles data conflicts. TLS divides a legacy sequential program into ordered speculative threads that are executed optimistically in parallel, also via an underlying system of detecting and recovering from data access conflicts.

All of these recently-proposed programming models and tools require a means of conflict detection (CD) that disambiguates streams of concurrent memory address accesses to find unsafe access interleavings (conflicts). Read- and write-sets accumulate the memory addresses read or written over *epochs* of instructions as defined by the application—including synchronization points, race-free episodes, transactions, or "chunks" of sequentially-consistent instructions [5]. In general, a conflict results when a memory address appears in the write-set of one thread and the read- or write-set of another thread. Two schedules determine when conflicts are detected: *eagerly* at the time of memory access (e.g., by checking coherence messages [26,41]), or *lazily* at the end of an epoch.

1.1 Address-Set Disambiguation Using Bloom Filters

Given this demand for runtime address-set operations, Bloom filters [1] have emerged as the address-set representation of choice for many systems in hardware TM [6,

16, 21, 32–35, 39–42], software TM [8, 19, 30, 36], TLS [6, 11], and concurrency debugging tools [13, 17, 18, 25, 28, 31, 43]. These approximate set representations provide address membership queries and set insertion in constant time, while operating on a compact, static-length bit-array. To track an address-set using a Bloom filter, addresses are hash-encoded into the large bit-array, and each thread maintains a distinct Bloom filter for each of the read- and write-sets over the course of each execution epoch. The bit-array length is designer-tunable, but the filter suffers increasing inaccuracy as length decreases; hence space and time requirements must be balanced with an acceptable probability that set membership tests falsely accept a non-member. In parallelization systems, these Bloom filter *false positives* force unnecessary conflicts among epochs, but pose no threat to correctness—e.g., their impact is limited to the re-execution of a transaction or epoch, or a false concurrency bug reported to the programmer. Hardware systems leverage Bloom filters to represent unbounded sets using statically-sized registers, and software systems benefit from fast set operations. The main concern for designers of these parallelization systems is to size the Bloom filters appropriately to achieve an acceptable false positive rate.

Despite the popularity of using Bloom filters for address-set disambiguation, few analytical models have been developed for these use-scenarios: for most recent work, the bit-arrays in Bloom filters are sized via time-consuming design space exploration, where the false positive rates are determined empirically. Eager systems use Bloom filter membership queries to detect conflicts, and the resulting false positives of individual queries follow a well-understood probability distribution [1,2,7,33]. Configuring Bloom filters for individual queries therefore requires tuning only the Bloom filter length and number of hash functions, and can be guided by the known analytical model.

1.2 Needed: Analytical Models for Lazy Applications of Address-Set Bloom Filters

In contrast with eager systems, lazy systems disambiguate finalized address-sets at the end of epochs[1], affording designers more flexibility but an expanded design space to explore. With finalized Bloom filters, there exist three different methods of determining whether address-sets are disjoint, or *deciding set disjointness*. The first method is intuitive: test every address of one set for membership in the Bloom filter of the other set [21]—we call this method *queue-of-queries*. For both the second and third approach, rather than serially querying many addresses, Bloom filters are quickly *intersected* and the result is analyzed to determine whether the input sets are disjoint [5, 6, 8, 17, 19, 25, 28, 30, 36, 43]. For the second approach, Bloom filter intersection approximates set intersection by performing the bit-wise AND of two bit-arrays, but has lower resolution (i.e., a greater probability of false conflict) than the corresponding series of queries. The third approach partitions the two bit-arrays, and the partitions are pairwise intersected. The third approach is hence called *partitioned*, while the second approach is unpartitioned—sometimes referred to as

a *true* Bloom filter [32, 33]. When the two input sets are disjoint, each disambiguation method might return a *false set-overlap*. In this context, the statistical properties of the three set-intersecting approximations, to the best of our knowledge, have neither been studied analytically nor conclusively compared in prior work.

In this paper we provide system designers with a new analytical model of the *probability of false set-overlap* for address-set Bloom filter intersection. We conclusively show which bit-array configuration admits fewer false positives, and prove that to achieve equivalent probability of false set-overlap, intersection-based usage requires Bloom filters that are at least a factor of the square root of set cardinality larger than query-based usage: for example, our models suggest that a change from unpartitioned Bloom filters to 2- or 4-way partitioning of the bit-array will yield considerable reduction of false conflicts in a number of existing parallelization systems [30, 36]. These results also reveal that for set-overlap-testing intersect-based schemes, the query-based approach should still receive serious consideration as an alternative, despite its time complexity.

Related Work: Prior work on address-set Bloom filters (a.k.a. *signatures* [6]) has optimized false positives in membership queries, but has not focused on Bloom filter intersection in particular. The work includes evaluating the impact of hash function families and parallel access to the bit-array partitions [33], optimizing the complexity of hash functions for a fixed false positive rate [42], application-specific address hashing [16], and exploiting the locality of an address stream [32]. The database community has applied Bloom filter intersection to accelerate relational join operations: approximating set intersection, and subsequently performing membership queries to the remaining bits [20]. Estimation of join cardinality has also benefited from this fast intersection [3, 27, 29]. However, unlike address-set disambiguation, database applications generally do not strive for the intersection result to be an empty set. Our work builds on these studies of Bloom filter intersection, with a focus on address-set disambiguation, and hence targeting intersections that return empty sets in the ideal case.

Contributions: This paper makes the following contributions: (i) we derive the probability distributions of false set-overlaps between two address-sets, for each of the three ways Bloom filters are applied in lazy address disambiguation; (ii) we prove that the partitioned Bloom filter configuration statistically induces fewer false conflicts than the unpartitioned configuration; (iii) we prove that for equivalent probability of false set-overlap in Bloom filters, intersection exceeds a space requirement that is larger than querying by a factor of the square root of set cardinality; (iv) we observe that, for the special case of one-way hashing, Bloom filter querying and intersection remarkably share an equivalent probability of false set-overlap.

2. BLOOM FILTERS

This section gives a brief background on the relevant aspects of Bloom filters [1]. For preliminary notation, let $[N]$ denote the set $\{1, \ldots, N\}$. A Bloom filter compactly represents a set $S = \{x_1, x_2, \ldots, x_n\}$ of n elements from some universe U. The filter is a bit-array of m bits indexed by a hash function tuple of k mutually-independent hash

---

[1]There also exist systems where finalized address-sets of a committing epoch are compared with growing address-sets of in-flight epochs. We continue to use the term "finalized set," but this could alternatively be interpreted as "nontrivial set."

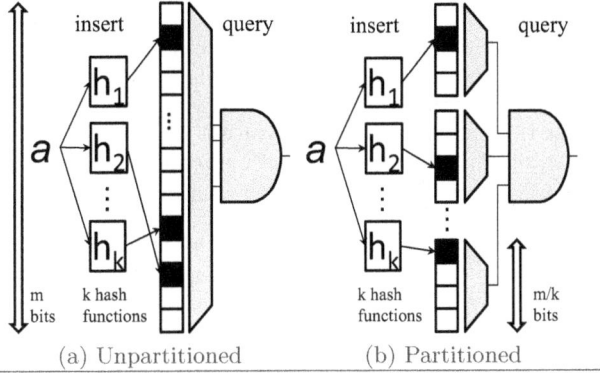

(a) Unpartitioned   (b) Partitioned

Figure 1: Bloom filter insertion and querying of address a for (a) an unpartitioned and (b) partitioned Bloom filter. In both cases, the filter has length m bits, and a tuple of k truly random hash functions. Addresses are inserted by asserting the bits indexed by the k hash values (dark boxes). A query accepts an address as a member of the set iff all k indexed bits are set to 1. Inspiration for figure is from [32].

functions $h(x) = (h_1(x), \ldots, h_k(x))$, supporting operations such as element insertion, membership queries, set union, and set intersection. Two configurations of bit indexing are widely used, called unpartitioned (or "true") and partitioned. The k-tuple hash function of an unpartitioned Bloom filter uniformly maps to the entire m-bit range of the bit-array, $h : U \rightarrow [m]^k$. In contrast, a partitioned Bloom filter distinguishes k disjoint sub-arrays of the filter, with each hash tuple value uniformly mapping to an integer $\frac{m}{k}$-bit partitioned range, $h : U \rightarrow \left[\frac{m}{k}\right]^k$ [24]. In the context of address disambiguation, S is a set of memory addresses from a v-bit address space (or universe): $S \subset U = \{0, 1, \ldots, 2^v - 1\}$.

Figure 1 illustrates the individual element operations on a Bloom filter. To initialize an empty set, all bits of the array are set to 0. Each element $x \in S$ is subsequently inserted in the filter by asserting the k bits indexed by each hash of x; the $h_i(x)$'th bit is set to 1 for $1 \leq i \leq k$. We denote the Bloom filter representation of S as $BF(S)$, which corresponds to the set of asserted bits after inserting all $x \in S$ [9, 32]. With a fully-constructed Bloom filter for S, an address $y \in U$ can be quickly tested for membership in S. The membership query accepts $y \in S$ if all of the $h_i(y)$'th bits of the array are 1, and otherwise indicates $y \notin S$.

For the remainder of this paper, we assume that the bit-array length, m, and number of hash functions, k, are constant. Let $\mathcal{H}_m = \{h | h : U \rightarrow [m]^k\}$ be the set of all hash functions mapping from the address space to the full m-bit range of a partitioned Bloom filter. Similarly, let $\mathcal{H}_{\frac{m}{k}} = \{h | h : U \rightarrow \left[\frac{m}{k}\right]^k\}$ represent the set of all hash functions from the address space to the $\frac{m}{k}$-bit sub-arrays of a partitioned Bloom filter.

2.1 Bloom Filters for Membership Queries

By encoding elements of a large universe into a compact bit-array, there is a small probability that an element y (that is not in S) has collisions on each of its k hashes with some elements in the set. Both hash *aliasing* and filter *density* (fraction of asserted bits) can lead to membership queries being falsely accepted, and so the Bloom filter actually represents a superset of the original address set: $S \subseteq BF(S)$.

In essence, the membership query "is y in S?" is not answered by no or yes, but rather no or *maybe*. The following definition formalizes this notion.

DEFINITION 1. *Let $S = \{x_1, \ldots, x_n\} \subset U$ be represented by an m-bit Bloom filter, $BF(S)$, using the k-tuple hash function $h \in (\mathcal{H}_m \cup \mathcal{H}_{\frac{m}{k}})$. When testing some element $y \notin S$ for membership in S, we define the* false positive predicate $\text{FP}_\in(S, y, h)$ *to be true when the query accepts y as a member of $BF(S)$—i.e., when $y \notin S$, but $\forall i \in [k]$, $h_i(y) = h_i(x_j)$ for some $x_j \in S$.*

This definition describes the false positive event for both unpartitioned and partitioned Bloom filters, as $h \in (\mathcal{H}_m \cup \mathcal{H}_{\frac{m}{k}})$; however, throughout the paper we will specify the Bloom filter indexing via conditioning on h. The probability of false positives for a Bloom filter is well understood and estimated in a straightforward fashion [1, 3, 32]—the reader is directed to prior work for a formal proof. Assuming the partitioned Bloom filter indexing scheme, the distribution is as follows:

LEMMA 1. [1, 24] *Let $h \in \mathcal{H}_{\frac{m}{k}}$ be a truly random k-tuple hash function. For any fixed set $S \subset U$ and element $y \notin S$, the probability that y is accepted in a membership query of partitioned $BF(S)$ is*

$$\Pr\left[\text{FP}_\in(S, y, h) \mid h \in \mathcal{H}_{\frac{m}{k}}\right] = \left(1 - \left(1 - \frac{k}{m}\right)^{|S|}\right)^k. \quad (1)$$

For unpartitioned Bloom filters, $\Pr[\text{FP}_\in(S, y, h) \mid h \in \mathcal{H}_m]$ is less than the result above, since a partitioned filter typically has more asserted bits. Notably, the two distributions asymptotically approach $\left(1 - e^{-\frac{k|S|}{m}}\right)^k$ [3][2], and the latter approximation is minimized when $k = \frac{m}{|S|} \ln 2$ [3].

2.2 Bloom Filters for Set Intersection

Beyond individual element operations, Bloom filters can be used to perform set union and intersection. In this work we focus on set intersection and its application for deciding address-set disjointness. Let $S_1, S_2 \subset U$ be two sets that are represented by Bloom filters, $BF(S_1)$ and $BF(S_2)$, that use the same m and hash functions. The filter $BF(S_1 \cap S_2)$ is computed by hash-encoding elements of the actual intersection of these sets. The Bloom filter representations of S_1 and S_2 are insufficient to accurately compute $BF(S_1 \cap S_2)$, but their *Bloom filter intersection*, $BF(S_1) \cap BF(S_2)$, is quickly computed by the bit-wise AND of their bit-arrays. Bloom filter intersection provides an approximation to set intersection that maintains the original querying property of never returning false negatives [3, 9, 29].

Guo *et al.* quantify the uncertainty in approximating set intersection with Bloom filter intersection. Assuming the unpartitioned Bloom filter configuration, the theorem by Guo is stated as a lemma toward our own contributions; readers are directed to the original work [9] for a proof.

LEMMA 2. [9] *Assuming the same m and random hash function $h \in \mathcal{H}_m$ are used in the Bloom filters of S_1, S_2, and $S_1 \cap S_2$, then $BF(S_1 \cap S_2) = BF(S_1) \cap BF(S_2)$ with probability*

$$(1 - 1/m)^{k^2 \times |S_1 - S_1 \cap S_2| \times |S_2 - S_1 \cap S_2|}.$$

---

[2]Since $(1 - k/m)^n \approx e^{-\frac{kn}{m}}$, provided $m > nk$ [3].

Apparently, the asserted Bloom filter bits of a set intersection are not necessarily equivalent to the bits asserted by Bloom filter intersection of the sets; they are equivalent with non-negligible probability.

2.3 Accuracy of the False Positive Rate

Recent work [2, 7] indicates that the "classic" analysis of the Bloom filter that proves the above Lemmas 1 and 2 is optimistic. The result attributed to Bloom (and republished in decades of subsequent work) is in fact a strict lower bound to the correct false positive probability. The new insight by Bose *et al.* and Christensen *et al.* has only focused on unpartitioned Bloom filters; applying their methods to the partitioned configuration, and subsequently repairing the Lemma by Guo *et al.* is left as future work, beyond the scope of this paper. Regardless, the approximation provided by these lemmas is sufficient for this work, as Christensen *et al.* demonstrated that the relative error diminishes with the larger m (≥ 1024 bits) typically used in parallelization systems [5, 6, 8, 13, 18, 21, 28, 32, 33, 36, 41, 42].

3. MODELING BLOOM FILTERS FOR SET DISJOINTNESS

Despite the popularity of Bloom filters in research architectures and tools, there are no previously-proposed probability distributions that model their use in deciding pairwise disjointness of sets, (a.k.a., set disambiguation). In the following sections, we (i) describe how Bloom filters are used to decide address-set disjointness, (ii) describe when they flag false conflicts among epochs, and (iii) we model and prove the probability distributions representing these unfortunate events.

3.1 Methods of Deciding Set Disjointness

This section describes the three methods of deciding set disjointness using Bloom filters: queue-of-queries, unpartitioned intersection, and partitioned intersection. We first motivate a definition of *false set-overlap*, when two disjoint sets appear to have some overlap due to Bloom filter operations. In line with Bloom's original motivation, systems implementing eager conflict detection use Bloom filter membership queries for runtime address-set comparison. At the time of accessing address y, the address is tested for membership in the read or write Bloom filters ($BF(R)$ or $BF(W)$) of other epochs (e.g., by querying incoming coherence requests). There is a probability of a false positive on each query (unnecessarily indicating an address conflict), which is modeled by Lemma 1. Since address conflicts are detected at the granularity of epochs, it becomes apparent that the probability of individual false conflicts is not of interest in parallel programming tools. Instead we wish to know the probability that entire epochs will falsely conflict, such as for lazy conflict detection schemes where the read-and write-sets are finalized. We next define two predicates which relate epoch failures to false set-overlaps.

3.1.1 Queue-of-Queries

Consider the lazy conflict detection scheme of SigTM [21], which maintains a write buffer (W) and read and write Bloom filters ($BF(R)$ and $BF(W)$) for each thread. These sets are finalized at the end of an epoch and otherwise grow monotonically. To detect conflicts at the end of a transaction, the system verifies that every member of the write-set W is not a member of all other threads' read-sets by performing membership queries into the read filters via coherence broadcasts. If any address in the write-set conflicts with the read filter of a remote transaction, the latter transaction is aborted. We use SigTM as a sample model of what we denote as the conventional approach to lazy address-set intersection—executing a *queue-of-queries* into a Bloom filter. Figure 2a illustrates this idea, where the queue of elements is the aforementioned write buffer. Each element of the write buffer (queue) is queried into the Bloom filter of some other epoch, until a conflict is found; otherwise the sets are disjoint. Supposing the two epochs did in fact access independent memory, we say that a false set-overlap occurred if one of the epochs unnecessarily aborted. The following definition formalizes false set-overlap by a queue-of-queries.

DEFINITION 2. *Let $S_1, S_2 \subset U$ be two fixed, disjoint sets, and choose S_1 to be represented by a Bloom filter of m bits and hash function $h \in (\mathcal{H}_m \cup \mathcal{H}_{\frac{m}{k}})$. We define the* false set-overlap by queries *predicate* $\mathrm{FSO}_{\in}(S_1, S_2, h)$ *to be true if, for some $x \in S_2$, $\mathrm{FP}_{\in}(S_1, x, h)$ is true.*

This definition describes when two sets would be incorrectly reported as overlapping by the conventional method of using Bloom filters for membership queries. The predicate is defined for either type of bit-indexing by hash functions, since $\mathrm{FP}_{\in}$ of Section 2 is defined for either hash function. In later sections, we will condition on the bit-indexing scheme as necessary.

3.1.2 Intersection: Partitioned and Unpartitioned

Lazy conflict detection must determine whether particular address-sets are disjoint—i.e., to ask "is their intersection empty?" Some researchers have astutely avoided the linear time required for a queue-of-queries by applying Bloom filter intersection to approximate this underlying set intersection task. Independent of the bit-indexing scheme, the bitwise AND of two bit-arrays is performed—the time-complexity of which is determined by the amount of available hardware (some researchers [36] reasonably argue that it is constant time).

On the other hand, determining set *emptiness* depends on the bit-indexing scheme. An unpartitioned Bloom filter represents an empty set if and only if all m bits of the bit-array are set to zero. Consider that if a single bit is set, it is possible (though unlikely) that some element is mapped to that same bit by all k hash values, making the filter non-empty. In contrast, partitioned Bloom filters represent an empty set if and only if *at least* one partition is empty, with all m/k bits set to zero [6]. For sufficiency, note that an empty set asserts no bits, such that all k partitions remain zero. For necessity, since inserting one element requires asserting one bit in all partitions, then if at least one partition is empty, it must be that no combination of elements can be represented by that filter—i.e., the filter is empty. Figures 2b and 2c use logic gates to illustrate the use of Bloom filter intersection to test for set-overlap.

The following definition introduces a predicate that identifies false set-overlap via Bloom filter intersection. Due to the difference in empty-set representation, partitioned and unpartitioned filters have differing statistical properties; we

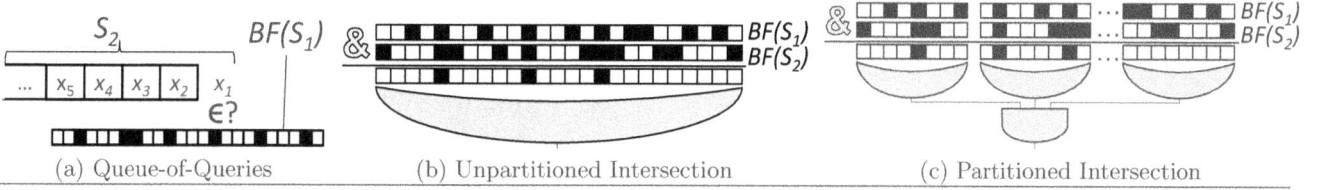

Figure 2: Three methods of testing set-overlap between sets S_1 and S_2: (a) by a queue-of-queries into the Bloom filter of S_1, such that if any element of S_2 matches in $BF(S_1)$, the sets are reported to be non-disjoint; (b) by intersecting two unpartitioned Bloom filters by bitwise AND, where any resulting asserted bits indicate non-disjoint sets; (c) by intersecting two partitioned Bloom filters, where an intersection-result consisting of at least one empty partition indicates that the input sets are disjoint.

condition on the choice of hash indexing scheme in the next section.

DEFINITION 3. *Let $S_1, S_2 \subset U$ be two fixed, disjoint sets, each represented by Bloom filters of m bits and hash function $h \in (\mathcal{H}_m \cup \mathcal{H}_{\frac{m}{k}})$. We define the* false set-overlap *by Bloom intersection predicate* $\mathrm{FSO}_\cap(S_1, S_2, h)$ *to be true, if $BF(S_1) \cap BF(S_2) \neq \emptyset$, even though $S_1 \cap S_2 = \emptyset$.*

3.2 Probability of False Set-Overlap

Having defined the conditions for three types of Bloom filter false set-overlap events, we now model their probability distributions. We begin with the probability of false set-overlap by queue-of-queries—using filters as Bloom "intended". Concerning the following theorem, fix two disjoint sets $S_1, S_2 \subset U$. The filter $BF(S_1)$ is m bits long using a truly random hash function of the partitioned bit-indexing scheme: $h \in \mathcal{H}_{\frac{m}{k}}$.

THEOREM 1. *A false set-overlap by queries of S_2 into partitioned $BF(S_1)$ is reported with probability*[3]

$$\Pr\left[\mathrm{FSO}_\in(S_1, S_2, h) \mid h \in \mathcal{H}_{\frac{m}{k}}\right]$$
$$= 1 - \left(1 - \left(1 - \left(1 - \frac{k}{m}\right)^{|S_1|}\right)^k\right)^{|S_2|}. \quad (2)$$

PROOF. Consider the contrary, between the two disjoint sets S_1 and S_2, when will a false set-overlap be avoided? Using the Bloom filter representation, the sets are correctly reported disjoint iff $(\forall x \in S_2)(x \notin BF(S_1))$, when every one of the $|S_2|$ unique queries into $BF(S_1)$ does *not* return a false positive. Model these unique queries as a sequence of up to $|S_2|$ Bernoulli trials, where a trial "success" implies a false positive on an individual query. Let random variable N be the number of unique membership queries from S_2 before one is reported a false positive. Thus N follows a geometric distribution, the number of Bernoulli failures before the first success, with probability of success $p = \Pr[\mathrm{FP}_\in(S_1, x, h)]$ for any $x \in S_2$. The two sets are deemed disjoint by Bloom filter queries if all $|S_2|$ trials fail, or if $N \geq |S_2|$. A false set-overlap

[3]Building on Lemma 1, this distribution can also be approximated by $1 - \left(1 - \left(1 - e^{-\frac{k|S_1|}{m}}\right)^k\right)^{|S_2|}$.

results if the latter is not true. Thus,

$$\Pr[\mathrm{FSO}_\in(S_1, S_2, h)]$$
$$= \Pr[N < |S_2|] \quad (3)$$
$$= \Pr[N \leq |S_2| - 1] \quad (4)$$
$$= 1 - (1 - p)^{|S_2| - 1 + 1} \quad (5)$$
$$= 1 - (1 - \Pr[\mathrm{FP}_\in(S_1, x, h)])^{|S_2|}, x \in S_2 \quad (6)$$

where Eq. (5) substitutes the geometric cumulative distribution function. Conditioning Eq. (6) on h and substituting Eq. (1) gives (2). $\square$

We now state and prove the probability that Bloom filter intersection will flag a false set-overlap[4] (for both unpartitioned and partitioned bit-indexing). Let $S_1, S_2 \subset U$ be disjoint sets. Both are represented by Bloom filters with length m bits, using the same truly random hash function tuple h. The bit-indexing scheme is conditioned in the theorem.

THEOREM 2. *A false set-overlap by Bloom filter intersection of unpartitioned $BF(S_1)$ and $BF(S_2)$ is reported with probability*

$$\Pr\left[\mathrm{FSO}_\cap \mid h \in \mathcal{H}_m\right] = 1 - \left(1 - \frac{1}{m}\right)^{k^2 |S_1||S_2|}. \quad (7)$$

For partitioned Bloom filters, a false set-overlap is reported with probability

$$\Pr\left[\mathrm{FSO}_\cap \mid h \in \mathcal{H}_{\frac{m}{k}}\right] = \left(1 - \left(1 - \frac{k}{m}\right)^{|S_1||S_2|}\right)^k. \quad (8)$$

PROOF. Concerning Eq. (7), Section 3.1.2 argues that intersection of unpartitioned Bloom filters induces a false set-overlap when some bit in the resulting bit-array is non-zero. An all-zero Bloom filter can only be created from an empty set (i.e., $BF(S) = \emptyset \iff S = \emptyset$). Therefore,

$$\Pr\left[\mathrm{FSO}_\cap \mid h \in \mathcal{H}_m\right]$$
$$= \Pr\left[\neg(BF(S_1) \cap BF(S_2) = \emptyset) \mid S_1 \cap S_2 = \emptyset, h \in \mathcal{H}_m\right] \quad (9)$$
$$= 1 - \Pr\left[BF(S_1) \cap BF(S_2) = \emptyset \mid S_1 \cap S_2 = \emptyset, h \in \mathcal{H}_m\right] \quad (10)$$

[4]Some readers may note that a membership query of y into a Bloom filter $BF(S)$ is akin to creating a new filter from y, $BF(y)$, and determining whether $BF(S) \cap BF(y)$ is empty. It is straightforward to show that Theorem 2 represents this idea, as Eq. (8) reduces to the false positive probability of Lemma 1 for $|S_2| = 1$.

We use Lemma 2 by Guo *et al.*,

$$\Pr\left[BF(S_1) \cap BF(S_2) = BF(S_1 \cap S_2) \mid h \in \mathcal{H}_m\right]$$
$$= (1 - 1/m)^{k^2 \times |S_1 - S_1 \cap S_2| \times |S_2 - S_1 \cap S_2|}$$

but assume that the sets are disjoint:

$$\Pr\left[BF(S_1) \cap BF(S_2) = \emptyset \mid S_1 \cap S_2 = \emptyset, h \in \mathcal{H}_m\right]$$
$$= (1 - 1/m)^{k^2 |S_1||S_2|}. \tag{11}$$

Substituting (11) into (10) shows (7).

Regarding Eq. (8), to avoid a false set-overlap, partitioned Bloom filters require at least one partition to be empty, with all m/k bits set to zero. Thus the negation of this statement, a false set-overlap, results when all k partitions are non-empty. Consider any one single partition: note that it operates identically to an unpartitioned Bloom filter with length m/k bits, but only a single hash function indexing the sub-array. Eq. (7) of this theorem therefore suggests that a single Bloom filter partition of length m/k and one hash function is non-empty with probability

$$1 - \left(1 - \frac{1}{m/k}\right)^{(1)^2 |S_1||S_2|}. \tag{12}$$

Looking at the entire partitioned Bloom filter, we assume that the "emptiness" of all k partitions is mutually independent. Using (12), the probability that all k partitions are non-empty is

$$\left(1 - \left(1 - \frac{k}{m}\right)^{|S_1||S_2|}\right)^k,$$

completing the proof of Eq. (8). □

4. ANALYTICAL COMPARISON OF QUERYING AND INTERSECTION

In this section we analytically compare the statistical properties and space requirements of Bloom filter intersection and querying when determining address-set disjointness. Specifically, we demonstrate (i) that partitioned Bloom filters always outperform unpartitioned Bloom filters when determining address-set disjointness by intersection; (ii) that for equivalent probability of false set-overlap (PFSO), partitioned Bloom filter intersection requires a factor $\Omega(\sqrt{|S_2|})$ more space than performing a queue-of-queries (of set S_2) into a Bloom filter.

4.1 Preliminary Inequalities

We state elementary inequalities from Mitrinović *et al.* [22, 23] used to prove the main results of the section.

LEMMA 3. [23] *Bernoulli's Inequality.*
If $-1 < x < \frac{1}{n-1}, x \neq 0$, and integer $n = 2, 3, \ldots$, then

$$1 + nx < (1 + x)^n < 1 + \frac{nx}{1 + (1-n)x}.$$

LEMMA 4. [22] *Generalization of Bernoulli's Inequality.*
If $0 < q < p$ and $-q < x < 0$, then

$$\left(1 + \frac{x}{q}\right)^q \geq \left(1 + \frac{x}{p}\right)^p.$$

LEMMA 5. *If real x is such that $0 < x < 1$ and integer $n > 1$, then $1 - x^n > 1 - x > (1 - x)^n$.*

PROOF. $x \in (0, 1) \Rightarrow x^n < x$, so evidently $1 - x^n > 1 - x$. Also, $(1 - x) \in (0, 1) \Rightarrow 1 - x > (1 - x)^n$. □

4.2 Statistical Comparison of Bit-Indexing for Bloom Filter Intersection

The following theorem asserts that partitioned Bloom filter intersection has a lower PFSO than unpartitioned. It concerns two disjoint sets $S_1, S_2 \subset U$, that are represented by Bloom filters of the same length m, with the same hash function tuple. The k hash values are truly random, and we consider $m > k > 1$, since for a single hash function, partitioned Bloom filters are effectively unpartitioned.

THEOREM 3. *Concerning false set-overlap by Bloom filter intersection, the partitioned bit-indexing scheme follows a probability distribution that is strictly less than that of an unpartitioned Bloom filter. That is, $(\forall h_{m/k} \in \mathcal{H}_{\frac{m}{k}})(\forall h_m \in \mathcal{H}_m)$,*

$$\Pr\left[\text{FSO}_\cap(S_1, S_2, h_{m/k})\right] < \Pr\left[\text{FSO}_\cap(S_1, S_2, h_m)\right].$$

PROOF. We begin by using Lemma 4, substituting $x = -1/m$, $q = 1/k$, and $p = 1$, which satisfies $0 < q < p$ and $-q < x < 0$, to see that $\left(1 - \frac{k}{m}\right)^{\frac{1}{k}} \geq \left(1 - \frac{1}{m}\right)$. Additionally, since $m > k > 1$, then by Lemma 5, $\left(1 - \frac{1}{m}\right) > \left(1 - \frac{1}{m}\right)^k$. Combining these observations,

$$\left(1 - \frac{k}{m}\right)^{\frac{1}{k}} > \left(1 - \frac{1}{m}\right)^k$$
$$\Rightarrow \left(1 - \frac{k}{m}\right)^{|S_1||S_2|} > \left(1 - \frac{1}{m}\right)^{k^2|S_1||S_2|}, \tag{13}$$

where the implication follows since $m > k > 1$, and we raise each side to the power of $(k|S_1||S_2|) > 0$. Rearranging Eq. (13), we show the main result,

$$\Pr\left[\text{FSO}_\cap(S_1, S_2, h_m)\right] = 1 - \left(1 - \frac{1}{m}\right)^{k^2|S_1||S_2|}$$
$$> 1 - \left(1 - \frac{k}{m}\right)^{|S_1||S_2|} \tag{14}$$
$$> \left(1 - \left(1 - \frac{k}{m}\right)^{|S_1||S_2|}\right)^k \tag{15}$$
$$= \Pr\left[\text{FSO}_\cap(S_1, S_2, h_{m/k})\right], \tag{16}$$

where Eq. (15) follows from Lemma 5. □

4.3 Space Comparison of Intersection and Queue-of-Queries

Given that partitioned intersection outperforms unpartitioned intersection, the following theorem thus compares the methods queue-of-queries and partitioned Bloom filter intersection for deciding set disjointness. The metric of consideration is more concrete than that in the previous theorem: we will show that the bit-array space savings of queue-of-queries is at least a factor of the square root of set cardinality, relative to partitioned Bloom filter intersection, when the respective PFSOs are equal, under reasonable conditions.

Consider the disjoint sets $S_1, S_2 \subset U$. Let $BF_q(S_1)$ be a partitioned Bloom filter of length m_q bits with a truly random k-tuple hash function $h_q \in \mathcal{H}_{\frac{m_q}{k}}$, for use in a queue-of-queries. Let partitioned Bloom filters $BF_i(S_1), BF_i(S_2)$ have length m_i bits and be indexed by the truly random k-tuple hash function $h_i \in \mathcal{H}_{\frac{m_i}{k}}$, for use in Bloom filter intersection. Assume more than one hash tuple value, $k > 1$, nontrivial sets, $|S_1|, |S_2| > 1$, and assume bit-array lengths $m_q > k$ and $m_i > d|S_1||S_2| > k$, for some constant $d \geq 1$.

THEOREM 4. *Assuming the preceding system and conditions, the bit-array space requirement of partitioned Bloom filter intersection is a factor $\Omega(\sqrt{|S_2|})$ larger than the queue-of-queries method, for equivalent PFSO. Specifically, if $k > 1$ and*

$$\Pr[\text{FSO}_\in(S_1, S_2, h_q)] = \Pr[\text{FSO}_\cap(S_1, S_2, h_i)],$$

then

$$m_i > m_q \frac{|S_2|^{\left(1 - \frac{1}{k}\right)}}{1 + \frac{k}{d}}. \tag{17}$$

PROOF. Using the theorems of Section 3.2, we first equate the stated probabilities, then using the lemmas of Section 4.1, show the inequality between m_i and m_q. The following equality is given:

$$\left(1 - \left(1 - \frac{k}{m_i}\right)^{|S_1||S_2|}\right)^k$$
$$= 1 - \left(1 - \left(1 - \left(1 - \frac{k}{m_q}\right)^{|S_1|}\right)^k\right)^{|S_2|}.$$

For clarity, let $a = |S_1|$, $b = |S_2|$, and $c_i = \left(1 - \frac{k}{m_i}\right)^a$, and likewise for c_q. Applying these substitutions, we have

$$\left(1 - c_i{}^b\right)^k = 1 - \left(1 - (1 - c_q)^k\right)^b$$

which is rearranged into

$$1 - \left(1 - c_i{}^b\right)^k = \left(1 - (1 - c_q)^k\right)^b. \tag{18}$$

Observe that $c_i, c_q \in (0, 1)$ since $m_i, m_q > k$ and $a > 1$. Therefore $(1 - c_q)^k \in (0, 1)$, so with integer $b > 1$, we may apply the left side of Bernoulli's inequality (Lemma 3) to the right hand side of Eq. (18) and have

$$1 - \left(1 - c_i{}^b\right)^k = \left(1 - (1 - c_q)^k\right)^b > 1 - b(1 - c_q)^k.$$

Rearranging and simplifying terms,

$$b(1 - c_q)^k > \left(1 - c_i{}^b\right)^k.$$

Isolate b on the left hand side, take the k'th root, then expand c_i and c_q:

$$b^{\frac{1}{k}} > \frac{1 - c_i{}^b}{1 - c_q}$$
$$= \frac{1 - \left(1 - \frac{k}{m_i}\right)^{ab}}{1 - \left(1 - \frac{k}{m_q}\right)^a}. \tag{19}$$

These steps are valid as $c_i, c_q \in (0, 1)$. Now consider the denominator of (19). Apply the left side of Bernoulli's

inequality (Lemma 3), since integer $a > 1$, and $m_q > k$. Then

$$1 - \left(1 - \frac{k}{m_q}\right)^a < \frac{ak}{m_q} \Rightarrow \frac{1}{\left(1 - \left(1 - \frac{k}{m_q}\right)^a\right)} > \frac{m_q}{ak}. \tag{20}$$

Now focus on the numerator of (19), $1 - \left(1 - \frac{k}{m_i}\right)^{ab}$. Using the right side of Lemma 3, we let $x = -\frac{k}{m_i}$, and $n = ab$, which satisfies $-1 < x < \frac{1}{n-1}$ since $m_i > k$. Thus,

$$\left(1 - \frac{k}{m_i}\right)^{ab} < 1 + \frac{ab\left(-\frac{k}{m_i}\right)}{1 + (1 - ab)\left(-\frac{k}{m_i}\right)}$$

Rearranging, $\quad 1 - \left(1 - \frac{k}{m_i}\right)^{ab} > \frac{\frac{kab}{m_i}}{1 + \frac{kab}{m_i} - \frac{k}{m_i}}$

$$> \frac{\frac{kab}{m_i}}{1 + \frac{kab}{m_i}}$$
$$= \frac{kab}{m_i + kab} \tag{21}$$

Combining inequalities (20) and (21) into (19), we have

$$b^{\frac{1}{k}} > \frac{1 - \left(1 - \frac{k}{m_i}\right)^{ab}}{1 - \left(1 - \frac{k}{m_q}\right)^a} > \frac{\frac{kab}{m_i + kab}}{\frac{ka}{m_q}}$$
$$= b \frac{m_q}{m_i + kab}$$

Rearranging, we have shown thus far that

$$m_i + abk > m_q b^{1 - \frac{1}{k}}.$$

For some constant $d \geq 1$, if designers choose $m_i > abd$, then $m_i \frac{k}{d} > abk$, thus $\left(1 + \frac{k}{d}\right) m_i > m_i + abk$. Therefore, returning $b = |S_2|$,

$$m_i > m_q \frac{|S_2|^{1 - \frac{1}{k}}}{1 + \frac{k}{d}},$$

as desired.

Regarding asymptotic notation for the space comparison, we claim that, $\forall k \geq 2$, $\frac{m_i}{m_q} = \Omega(\sqrt{|S_2|})$, or formally, $\forall k \geq 2$,

$$(\exists c, n_0 > 0)(\forall |S_2| \geq n_0) \quad \frac{m_i}{m_q} \geq c\sqrt{|S_2|}. \tag{22}$$

Here we show only the base case $k = 2$—the full proof can be found in Jeffrey's thesis [14].

For $k = 2$ and any $d \geq 1$, we have from Eq. (17),

$$\frac{m_i}{m_q} > \frac{|S_2|^{1 - \frac{1}{k}}}{1 + \frac{k}{d}} = \frac{\sqrt{|S_2|}}{1 + \frac{2}{d}}$$

which satisfies (22) for $c = \frac{1}{1 + \frac{2}{d}}$ and $n_0 > 0$. □

5. EMPIRICAL VALIDATION

In this section we empirically validate the probability distributions derived in Section 3.2. Empirical rates of false set-overlap are gathered for each of the three address-set disambiguation methods, in four discrete Bloom filter configurations. A simple experiment tests two disjoint address-sets for overlap, using the three methods discussed: queue-of-queries, and partitioned and unpartitioned Bloom filter

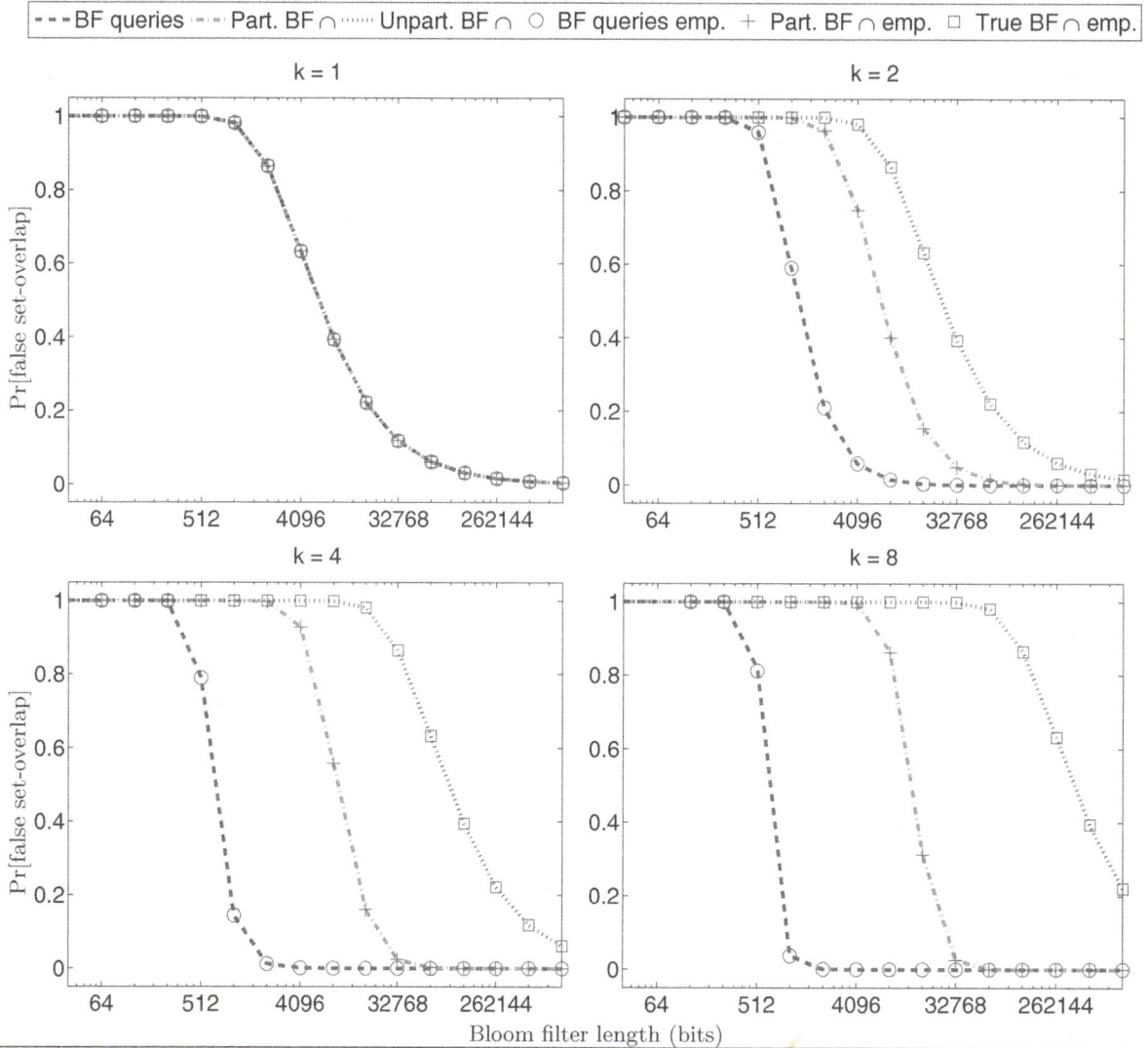

Figure 3: Probability and empirical rate of false set-overlap on the y-axis as they vary with increasing Bloom filter length on the x-axis (in log scale). Each plot represents a size k of the hash function tuple. The three curves plot the probabilistic models of false set-overlap, and are overlaid by sample points of the experimentally measured rate.

intersection. Each method returns two possible outcomes: either a false set-overlap, or disjoint sets. The experiment is repeated over 10^6 trials, and the relative frequency of false set-overlap is recorded as the empirical rate.

For a single experiment, two disjoint sets are generated, S_1 and S_2, containing random unique 32-bit integers (addresses), using the C standard library `rand` function. For a given bit-array length, m, and hash function tuple size, k, partitioned and unpartitioned Bloom filters are constructed for each of the sets, $BF_p(S_1), BF_p(S_2), BF_u(S_1), BF_u(S_2)$. Random hash functions are selected from the H_3 family [4] that approximately match the performance of ideal hash functions, for a sufficiently-random address stream [24]. To test the queue-of-queries outcome, each $x \in S_2$ is tested for membership in $BF_p(S_1)$. If at least one query returns true, the false set-overlap is recorded. Likewise, to test the Bloom filter intersection outcome, we separately intersect $BF_p(S_1) \cap BF_p(S_2)$ and $BF_u(S_1) \cap BF_u(S_2)$, and determine whether the remaining bits represent an empty set

as described in Section 3.1; otherwise a false set-overlap is recorded.

Figure 3 visualizes the false set-overlap rate as a function of Bloom filter length, m. The four plots differ only in the size of the hash function tuple: $k = 1, 2, 4, 8$. The cardinalities of the address sets were fixed to $|S_1| = |S_2| = 64$ unique elements[5] for all trials. Each set of 10^6 trials is represented by a point on the plot, having been assigned a fixed filter length. Filter lengths are shown in a log scale on the x-axis, and each length was sampled at a power-of-two to effectively show the trend of this roughly exponential decay.

---

[5] Address set cardinality is certainly application-specific; a number of earlier studies displayed average read set sizes of 26 to 67 addresses [5, 6, 32, 33, 42], but as few as 2 addresses [18, 41] and as many as 2000 addresses [32, 42]. Write set sizes are typically smaller but still vary from 1 address [5, 17, 33, 41, 42] to over 1500 [32, 42]—we choose 64-element sets as a compromise within this large space. Varying the set cardinalities will not change the general trends observed in Figure 3.

The derived theoretical distributions underlay the empirical sample points, visualizing the relationship between Bloom filter length and false set-overlap probability. It is apparent that the empirical sample points follow the theoretical distributions, validating the accuracy of our work.

6. IMPLICATIONS

Figure 3 illustrates that varying k has a different effect on each method of deciding set disjointness. For nontrivial hash function tuples (i.e., $k > 1$), the queue-of-queries method benefits from increasing k (up to a point), while the probability distribution for unpartitioned Bloom filter intersection only becomes worse. Upon close inspection of the distribution for partitioned Bloom filters, increasing k is beneficial only for filter lengths of at least 16kbits. These three patterns can also be shown analytically, by minimizing the probability distributions with respect to k. Due to space constraints, the reader is directed to Broder and Mitzenmacher [3] for an example of this process. Without proof, the optimal number of hash functions for partitioned intersection is $k^* = \frac{m}{|S_1||S_2|}\ln 2$, minimizing the false conflict probability to 2^{-k^*}.

IMPLICATION 1. *Issuing a series of Bloom filter membership queries provides set disambiguation with significantly lower space overhead than Bloom filter intersection, for larger than one-tuple hash functions.*

IMPLICATION 2. *When intersection is unavoidable for deciding pairwise set disjointness, partitioned intersection is preferable to unpartitioned as it provides the same service, with the same time-complexity, with lower (or equal) probability of false set-overlap.*

Surprisingly, for a single hash function, $k = 1$, all three methods share the same probability distribution (and empirical sample points)—this can be verified by substituting $k = 1$ for the theorems of Section 3, and the PFSO is $1 - (1 - \frac{1}{m})^{|S_1||S_2|}$. Given this equivalence, a time-complexity comparison would be helpful; unfortunately the many hardware-dependent considerations make such a study beyond the scope of this paper.

IMPLICATION 3. *Remarkably, when restricted to encoding addresses using a single hash function, Bloom filter querying and intersection share equivalent probability of false set-overlap.*

7. CONCLUSION

Motivated by the recently-popular use of Bloom filters for lazy address-set disambiguation, in this paper we introduced and conclusively compared probabilistic models for the three methods of using Bloom filters to decide set disjointness: (i) queue-of-queries, and intersection of (ii) unpartitioned and (iii) partitioned Bloom filters. We analytically and graphically demonstrated that the intersection of partitioned Bloom filters has more desirable probability of false set-overlap than their unpartitioned counterparts. We also demonstrated that partitioned intersection requires at least a factor of the square root of set cardinality more bit-array space than a queue-of-queries approach, to maintain the same probability of false set-overlap. Finally, we observed that when designers are (unfortunately) required

to use a one-tuple hash function, the queue-of-queries and intersection methods share identical probability of false set-overlap; they should use the most time-efficient strategy in such a case. The Bloom filter is indeed an excellent fit to address-set disambiguation for parallelization systems and tools, but this increasingly-common yet unconventional use for deciding set-overlap demands more study. We provide system designers with new insight in this area, easing Bloom filter design space exploration.

Acknowledgments

We thank the anonymous reviewers for their detailed comments. Bruce Francis was of monumental help through his tutorial, *Elements of Mathematical Style*, and his general feedback on our analytical work. We thank Hratch Mangassarian for the discussion on asymptotic notation, and James Tuck for initial discussion on the need for better theoretical understanding of Bloom filters in address-set disambiguation. Mark Jeffrey was supported by the NSERC Alexander Graham Bell Canada Graduate Scholarship (CGS-M).

8. REFERENCES

[1] B. H. Bloom. Space/time trade-offs in hash coding with allowable errors. *Commun. ACM*, 13(7):422–426, 1970.

[2] P. Bose, H. Guo, E. Kranakis, A. Maheshwari, P. Morin, J. Morrison, M. Smid, and Y. Tang. On the false-positive rate of Bloom filters. *Inf. Process. Lett.*, 108(4):210–213, 2008.

[3] A. Broder and M. Mitzenmacher. Network applications of Bloom filters: A survey. *Internet Mathematics*, 1:485–509, January 2004.

[4] J. L. Carter and M. N. Wegman. Universal classes of hash functions. *Journal of Computer and System Sciences*, 18(2):143 – 154, 1979.

[5] L. Ceze, J. Tuck, P. Montesinos, and J. Torrellas. Bulksc: bulk enforcement of sequential consistency. *SIGARCH Comp. Arch. News*, 35(2):278–289, 2007.

[6] L. Ceze, J. Tuck, J. Torrellas, and C. Cascaval. Bulk disambiguation of speculative threads in multiprocessors. In *International Symposium on Computer Architecture*, 2006.

[7] K. Christensen, A. Roginsky, and M. Jimeno. A new analysis of the false positive rate of a Bloom filter. *Inf. Processing Letters*, 110(21):944 – 949, 2010.

[8] J. E. Gottschlich, M. Vachharajani, and J. G. Siek. An efficient software transactional memory using commit-time invalidation. In *International Symposium on Code Generation and Optimization*, 2010.

[9] D. Guo, J. Wu, H. Chen, Y. Yuan, and X. Luo. The dynamic Bloom filters. *IEEE Transactions on Knowledge and Data Engineering*, 22:120–133, 2010.

[10] L. Hammond, M. Willey, and K. Olukotun. Data speculation support for a chip multiprocessor. In *Conference on Architectural Support for Programming Languages and Operating Systems*, October 1998.

[11] L. Han, W. Liu, and J. M. Tuck. Speculative parallelization of partial reduction variables. In *International Symposium on Code Generation and Optimization*, 2010.

[12] M. Herlihy and J. E. B. Moss. Transactional memory: architectural support for lock-free data structures. In *Intl. Symposium on Computer Architecture*, 1993.

[13] D. R. Hower and M. D. Hill. Rerun: Exploiting episodes for lightweight memory race recording. In *Intl. Symposium on Computer Architecture*, 2008.

[14] M. Jeffrey. Modeling Bloom filter intersection for address-set disambiguation. Master's thesis, University of Toronto, June 2011.

[15] V. Krishnan and J. Torrellas. A chip multiprocessor architecture with speculative multithreading. *IEEE Transactions on Computers, Special Issue on Multithreaded Architecture*, September 1999.

[16] M. Labrecque, M. Jeffrey, and J. G. Steffan. Application-specific signatures for transactional memory in soft processors. In *Intl. Symposium on Applied Reconfigurable Computing*, 2010.

[17] B. Lucia, L. Ceze, and K. Strauss. Colorsafe: architectural support for debugging and dynamically avoiding multi-variable atomicity violations. *SIGARCH Comput. Archit. News*, 38(3):222–233, 2010.

[18] B. Lucia, J. Devietti, L. Ceze, and K. Strauss. Atom-aid: Detecting and surviving atomicity violations. *IEEE Micro*, 29(1):73 –83, Jan.-Feb. 2009.

[19] M. Mehrara, J. Hao, P.-C. Hsu, and S. Mahlke. Parallelizing sequential applications on commodity hardware using a low-cost software transactional memory. In *Conference on Programming Language Design and Implementation*, 2009.

[20] L. Michael, W. Nejdl, O. Papapetrou, and W. Siberski. Improving distributed join efficiency with extended Bloom filter operations. In *International Conference on Advanced Networking and Applications*, 2007.

[21] C. C. Minh, M. Trautmann, J. Chung, A. McDonald, N. Bronson, J. Casper, C. Kozyrakis, and K. Olukotun. An effective hybrid transactional memory system with strong isolation guarantees. In *Intl. Symposium on Computer Architecture*, 2007.

[22] D. S. Mitrinović and J. E. Pečarić. Bernoulli's inequality. *Rendiconti del Circolo Matematico di Palermo*, 42:317–337, 1993.

[23] D. S. Mitrinović and P. M. Vasić. *Analytic Inequalities*. Springer-Verlag, Berlin, 1970.

[24] M. Mitzenmacher and S. Vadhan. Why simple hash functions work: exploiting the entropy in a data stream. In *SODA '08: ACM-SIAM Symposium On Discrete Algorithms*, 2008.

[25] P. Montesinos, L. Ceze, and J. Torrellas. Delorean: Recording and deterministically replaying shared-memory multiprocessor execution efficiently. In *Intl. Symposium on Computer Architecture*, 2008.

[26] K. Moore, J. Bobba, M. Moravan, M. Hill, and D. Wood. Logtm: log-based transactional memory. In *International Symposium on High-Performance Computer Architecture*, 2006.

[27] J. K. Mullin. Estimating the size of a relational join. *Information Systems*, 18(3):189 – 196, 1993.

[28] A. Muzahid, D. Suárez, S. Qi, and J. Torrellas. Sigrace: signature-based data race detection. *SIGARCH Comp. Arch. News*, 37(3):337–348, 2009.

[29] O. Papapetrou, W. Siberski, and W. Nejdl. Cardinality estimation and dynamic length adaptation for Bloom filters. *Distributed and Parallel Databases*, 28:119–156, 2010.

[30] L. Peng, L. guo Xie, X. qiang Zhang, and X. yan Xie. Conflict detection via adaptive signature for software transactional memory. In *International Conference on Computer Engineering and Technology*, 2010.

[31] G. Pokam, C. Pereira, K. Danne, R. Kassa, and A.-R. Adl-Tabatabai. Architecting a chunk-based memory race recorder in modern cmps. In *International Symposium on Microarchitecture*, 2009.

[32] R. Quislant, E. Gutierrez, O. Plata, and E. L. Zapata. Improving signatures by locality exploitation for transactional memory. In *Intl. Conference on Parallel Architectures and Compilation Techniques*, 2009.

[33] D. Sanchez, L. Yen, M. D. Hill, and K. Sankaralingam. Implementing signatures for transactional memory. In *International Symposium on Microarchitecture*, 2007.

[34] A. Shriraman, S. Dwarkadas, and M. L. Scott. Flexible decoupled transactional memory support. In *Intl. Symposium on Computer Architecture*, 2008.

[35] A. Shriraman, S. Dwarkadas, and M. L. Scott. Implementation tradeoffs in the design of flexible transactional memory support. *J. Parallel Distrib. Comput.*, 70, October 2010.

[36] M. F. Spear, M. M. Michael, and C. von Praun. Ringstm: scalable transactions with a single atomic instruction. In *Symposium on Parallelism in Algorithms and Architectures*, 2008.

[37] J. G. Steffan and T. C. Mowry. The potential for using thread-level data speculation to facilitate automatic parallelization. In *International Symposium on High-Performance Computer Architecture*, pages 2–13, 1998.

[38] J. Torrellas, L. Ceze, J. Tuck, C. Cascaval, P. Montesinos, W. Ahn, and M. Prvulovic. The bulk multicore architecture for improved programmability. *Commun. ACM*, 52(12):58–65, 2009.

[39] M. Waliullah and P. Stenstrom. Efficient management of speculative data in hardware transactional memory systems. In *International Conference on Embedded Computer Systems: Architectures, Modeling, and Simulation*, 2008.

[40] S. Wang, D. Wu, Z. Pang, and X. Yang. Software assisted transact cache to support efficient unbounded transactional memory. In *Intl. Conference on High Performance Computing and Communications*, 2008.

[41] L. Yen, J. Bobba, M. R. Marty, K. E. Moore, H. Volos, M. D. Hill, M. M. Swift, and D. A. Wood. Logtm-se: Decoupling hardware transactional memory from caches. In *International Symposium on High Performance Computer Architecture*, 2007.

[42] L. Yen, S. C. Draper, and M. D. Hill. Notary: Hardware techniques to enhance signatures. In *International Symposium on Microarchitecture*, 2008.

[43] P. Zhou, R. Teodorescu, and Y. Zhou. Hard: Hardware-assisted lockset-based race detection. In *International Symposium on High Performance Computer Architecture*, pages 121–132, 2007.

Scheduling Irregular Parallel Computations on Hierarchical Caches

Guy E. Blelloch
Carnegie Mellon University
guyb@cs.cmu.edu

Jeremy T. Fineman
Carnegie Mellon University
jfineman@cs.cmu.edu

Phillip B. Gibbons
Intel Labs Pittsburgh
phillip.b.gibbons@intel.com

Harsha Vardhan Simhadri
Carnegie Mellon University
harshas@cs.cmu.edu

ABSTRACT

For nested-parallel computations with low depth (span, critical path length) analyzing the work, depth, and *sequential* cache complexity suffices to attain reasonably strong bounds on the *parallel* runtime and cache complexity on machine models with either shared or private caches. These bounds, however, do not extend to general hierarchical caches, due to limitations in (i) the cache-oblivious (CO) model used to analyze cache complexity and (ii) the schedulers used to map computation tasks to processors. This paper presents the *parallel cache-oblivious (PCO)* model, a relatively simple modification to the CO model that can be used to account for costs on a broad range of cache hierarchies. The first change is to avoid capturing artificial data sharing among parallel threads, and the second is to account for parallelism-memory imbalances within tasks. Despite the more restrictive nature of PCO compared to CO, many algorithms have the same asymptotic cache complexity bounds.

The paper then describes a new scheduler for hierarchical caches, which extends recent work on "space-bounded schedulers" to allow for computations with arbitrary *work imbalance* among parallel subtasks. This scheduler attains provably good cache performance and runtime on parallel machine models with hierarchical caches, for nested-parallel computations analyzed using the PCO model. We show that under reasonable assumptions our scheduler is "work efficient" in the sense that the cost of the cache misses are evenly balanced across the processors—*i.e.*, the runtime can be determined within a constant factor by taking the total cost of the cache misses analyzed for a computation and dividing it by the number of processors. In contrast, to further support our model, we show that no scheduler can achieve such bounds (optimizing for both cache misses and runtime) if work, depth, and sequential cache complexity are the only parameters used to analyze a computation.

Categories and Subject Descriptors

F.2 [**Theory of Computation**]: Analysis of Algorithms and Problem Complexity; D.2.8 [**Software Engineering**]: Metrics—*complexity measures, performance measures*; D.1.3 [**Programming Techniques**]: Concurrent Programming—*Parallel programming*

General Terms

Algorithms, Theory

Keywords

Parallel hierarchical memory, Cost models, Schedulers, Analysis of parallel algorithms, Cache complexity

1. INTRODUCTION

Because of limited bandwidths on real parallel machines locality can be critical to achieving good performance for parallel programs. To account for this in the design of algorithms, many locality-aware parallel models have been suggested [2, 6, 18, 19, 23, 24]. This work has contributed significantly to our understanding of locality in parallel algorithms.

With the advent of multicores most computer users have a parallel machine on their desk or lap, and these are all based on a multi-level cache hierarchy with a 50–200X factor difference between the access time to the first level cache and main memory (whether used sequentially or in parallel). Fig. 1 shows, for example, the memory hierarchies for the current generation desktop/servers from Intel, AMD, and IBM. Correspondingly there has been significant recent work on parallel cache based locality [1, 4, 5, 7, 9, 10, 12–14, 21, 25]. The work has fallen into two main classes. One class involves designing algorithms directly for the machine and having the algorithm designer explicitly allocate tasks to processors. This includes the work by Arge et al. [4] on designing algorithms directly for a p-processor machine with one layer of private caches (the PEM), and by Valiant [25] on algorithms for a hierarchical cache with unit-size cache lines (the Multi-BSP). The other class involves dynamic parallelism in which the algorithm designer specifies the full parallelism of the computation, typically much more than is available on a real machine, and analyzes the cache cost in an abstract cost model not directly corresponding to a parallel machine. A scheduler is then responsible for dynamically mapping the computation onto the processors in a manner that bounds the cost as a function of the analyzed costs. Dynamic parallelism has important advantages, including being much simpler, potentially machine independent, and much closer to how users actually code on these machines using languages such as OpenMP, Cilk++, Intel TBB, and the Microsoft Task Parallel Library. However, the abstraction makes it harder to achieve good performance.

A pair of common abstract measures for capturing parallel cache based locality are the number of misses given a sequential ordering of a parallel computation [1, 9, 10, 21], and the depth (span, critical path length) of the computation. The cache-oblivious (CO) model (a.k.a., the ideal cache model) [20] can be used for analyzing the misses in the sequential ordering, giving a cache complexity $Q(n; M, B)$ where n is the size of the problem, M is a single cache size and B a single block size. One can show, for example, that any nested-parallel computation with sequential cache complexity Q and depth D will cause at most $Q + O(pDM/B)$ total misses when run with an appropriate scheduler on p processors, each with a private cache of size M and block size B [1]. Unfortunately, current dynamic parallelism approaches have important limitations: they either apply to hierarchies of only private or only shared caches [1,9,10,16,21], require some strict balance criteria [7,15], or require a joint algorithm/scheduler analysis [7,13–16].

In this paper we present a model and a scheduler that *enable an algorithm analysis that is independent of both the parallel machine and the scheduler, allow for irregular computations with arbitrary imbalance among tasks, and work on hierarchies of shared and private caches* (as in Fig. 1). The approach is limited to nested-parallel computations, but this includes a very broad set of algorithms, including most divide-and-conquer, data-parallel, and CREW PRAM-like algorithms.

The approach is based on three components. The first is a cache cost model (the *Parallel Cache-Oblivious (PCO)* model). As with the standard CO model the cache cost is derived in terms of a single cache size M and a single block size B giving a cache complexity $Q^*(n; M, B)$ independent of the number of processors. The model for a sequential strand of computation remains the same. When a task t forks a set of child tasks, however, the child tasks start with the same cache state; this contrasts with the standard CO analysis based on a sequential ordering of the child tasks. In particular if t fits in M all child tasks start with the cache state of the parent at the fork point, and at the join point the union of their locations are included in the cache state of the parent. If the task does not fit in M then the cache state is emptied at the fork and join points. This model ignores (incidental) data reuse among parallel subcomputations and accounts for reuse only when there is a serial relationship between instructions accessing the same data. As we show, this enables tighter bounds when mapping computations onto, for example, shared caches. For the same M and B the cache cost in the PCO model may be higher than in the CO model. For a variety of fundamental parallel algorithms, however, including quicksort, sample sort, matrix multiplication, matrix inversion, sparse-matrix multiplication, and convex hulls, the asymptotic bounds are not affected, while the higher baseline enables a provably efficient mapping to parallel hierarchies for arbitrary nested-parallel computations.

The second is a new cost metric that penalizes large imbalance in the ratio of space to parallelism in subtasks. We present a lower bound that indicates that some form of parallelism-space imbalance penalty is required. Intuitively this is because on any given parallel memory hierarchy as depicted in Fig. 1, the cache resources are linked to the processing resources: each cache is shared by a fixed number of processors. Therefore any large imbalance between space and processor requirements will require either processors to be under-utilized or caches to be over-subscribed. As in the basic PCO model, the cost $\widehat{Q}_\alpha(n; M, B)$ for inputs of size n is asymptotically equal to that of the standard sequential cache cost $Q(n; M, B)$ for many problems.

The third is a new "space-bounded scheduler" that extends recent work of Chowdhury et al. [14]. A space-bounded scheduler accepts dynamically parallel programs that have been annotated with space requirements for each recursive subcomputation called a "task." These schedulers run every task in a cache that just fits it (*i.e.*, no lower cache will fit it), and once assigned, tasks are not migrated across caches. We show that any space-bounded scheduler guarantees that the number of misses across all caches at each level i of the machine's hierarchy is at most $Q^*(n; M_i, B_i)$, where $Q^*(n; M_i, B_i)$ is the cost in the basic PCO model with problem size n, cache size M_i, and cache-line size B_i.

In contrast to previous work, we describe a space-bounded scheduler that allows parallel subtasks to be scheduled on different levels in the memory hierarchy, thus allowing significant imbalance in the sizes of tasks. Furthermore, we show that our space-bounded scheduler achieves efficient total running time, as long as the parallelism of the machine is sufficient with respect to the parallelism of the algorithm. Specifically, we show that our scheduler executes a cache-oblivious computation on a homogeneous h-level parallel memory hierarchy having p processors in time:

$$O\left(\frac{v_h \sum_{i=0}^{h} \widehat{Q}_\alpha(n; M_i, B) \cdot C_i}{p}\right),$$

where M_i is the size of each level-i cache, B is the uniform cache-line size, C_i is the cost of a level-i cache miss, and v_h is an overhead defined in Theorem 6. For any algorithms where $\widehat{Q}_\alpha(n; M, B)$ is asymptotically equal to the optimal sequential cache-oblivious cost $Q(n; M, B)$ for the problem, and under conditions where v_h is constant, this is optimal across all levels of the cache. For example, a parallel sample sort (that uses imbalanced subtasks) gives $\widehat{Q}_\alpha(n; M, B) = O((n/B)\log_M(n/B))$, which matches the optimal sequential cache complexity for sorting, implying optimality on parallel cache hierarchies using our scheduler.

2. PRELIMINARIES

Computation Model. As in most of the prior work cited in Section 1, this paper considers algorithms with nested parallelism, allowing arbitrary dynamic nesting of parallel loops and fork-join constructs but no other synchronizations. This corresponds to the class of algorithms with series-parallel dependence graphs (see Fig. 2). Computations can be decomposed into "tasks", "parallel blocks" and "strands" recursively as follows. As a base case, a *strand* is a serial sequence of instructions not containing any parallel constructs or subtasks. A *task* is formed by serially composing $k \geq 1$ strands interleaved with $(k-1)$ "parallel blocks" (denoted by $t = s_1; b_1; \ldots; s_k$). A *parallel block* is formed by composing

(a) 32-processor Intel Xeon 7500

(b) 48-processor AMD Opteron 6100

(c) 96-processor IBM z196

(d) PMH model of [3]

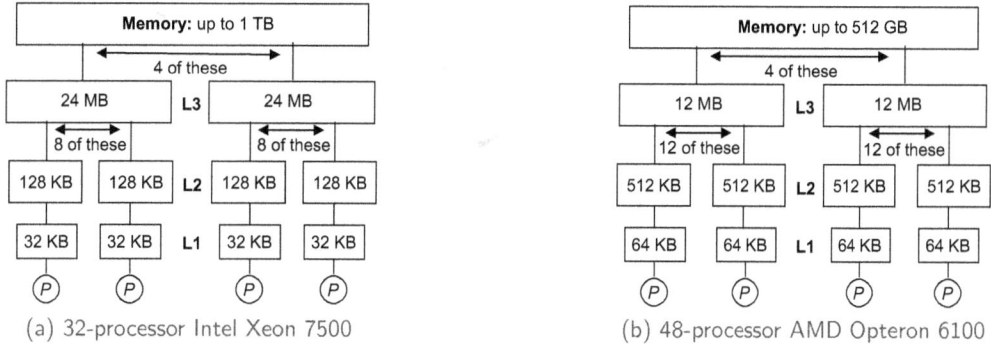

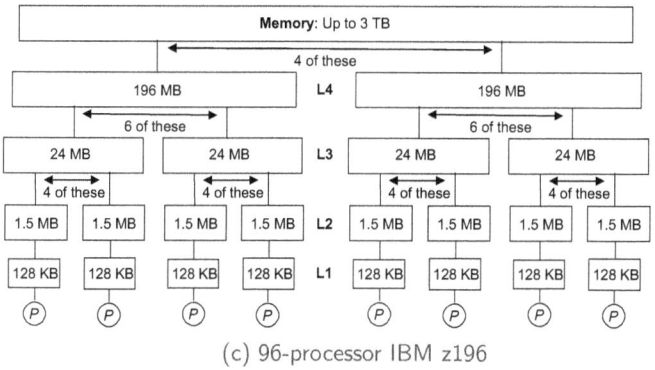

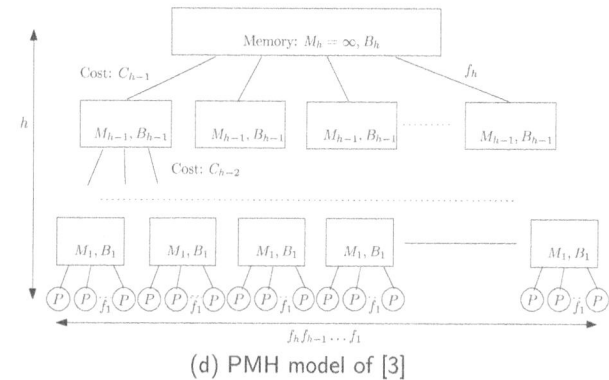

Figure 1: Memory hierarchies of current generation architectures from Intel, AMD, and IBM, plus an example abstract parallel hierarchy model. Each cache (rectangle) is shared by all processors (circles) in its subtree.

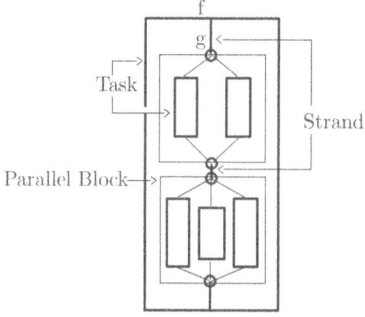

Figure 2: Decomposing the computation: tasks, strands and parallel blocks

in parallel one or more tasks with a fork point before all of them and a join point after (denoted by $b = t_1 \| t_2 \| \dots \| t_k$). A parallel block can be, for example, a parallel loop or some constant number of recursive calls. The top-level computation is a task. The *span* (a.k.a., *depth*) of a computation is the length of the longest path in the dependence graph.

The nested-parallel model assumes all strands share a single memory. We say two strands are *concurrent* if they are not ordered in the dependence graph. Concurrent reads (*i.e.*, concurrent strands reading the same memory location) are permitted, but not data races (*i.e.*, concurrent strands that read or write the same location with at least one write).

Machine Model: The Parallel Memory Hierarchy model. Following prior work addressing multi-level parallel hierarchies [3,7,10,12–14,25], we model parallel machines us-

ing a tree-of-caches abstraction. For concreteness, we use a symmetric variant of the parallel memory hierarchy (PMH) model [3] (see Fig. 1(d)), which is consistent with many other models [7,10,12–14]. A PMH consists of a height-h tree of memory units, called *caches*. We assume that each cache is an ideal cache. The leaves of the tree are at level-0 and any internal node has level one greater than its children. The leaves (level-0 nodes) are processors, and the level-h root corresponds to an infinitely large main memory. We do not assume inclusive caches, meaning that a memory location may be stored in a low-level cache without being stored at all ancestor caches. We can extend the model to support inclusive caches, but then we must assume larger cache sizes to accommodate the inclusion.

Each level in the tree is parameterized by four parameters: M_i, B_i, C_i, and f_i. We denote the *capacity* of each level-i cache by M_i. Memory transfers between a cache and its child occur at the granularity of *cache lines*. We use $B_i \geq 1$ to denote the *line size* of a level-i cache, or the size of contiguous data transferred from a level-$(i+1)$ cache to its level-i child. If a processor accesses data that is not resident in its level-1 cache, a level-1 *cache miss* occurs. More generally, a *level-$(i+1)$ cache miss* occurs whenever a level-i cache miss occurs and the requested line is not resident in the parent level-$(i+1)$ cache; once the data becomes resident in the level-$(i+1)$ cache, a level-i cache request may be serviced by loading the size-B_{i+1} line into the level-i cache. The cost of a level-i cache miss is denoted by $C_i \geq 1$, where this cost represents the amount of time to load the corresponding line into the level-i cache under full load. Thus, C_i models both the latency and the bandwidth constraints

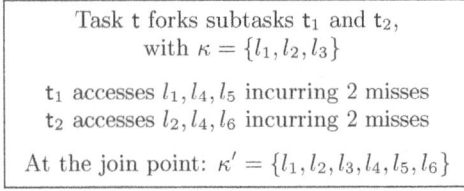

Figure 3: Example applying the PCO model (Definition 2) to a parallel block. Here, $Q^*(t; M, B; \kappa) = 4$.

of the system (whichever is worse under full load). The cost of an access at a processor that misses at all levels up to and including level-j is thus $C_j' = \sum_{i=0}^{j} C_i$. We use $f_i \geq 1$ to denote the number of level-$(i-1)$ caches below a single level-i cache, also called the **fanout**. As in [1], we assume the model maintains DAG consistent shared memory with the BACKER algorithm [11]. This is a weak consistency model and assumes that cache lines are merged on writing back to memory thus avoiding "false sharing" issues.

We assume that the number of lines in any nonleaf cache is greater than the sums of the number of lines in all its immediate children, i.e., $M_i/B_i \geq f_i M_{i-1}/B_{i-1}$ for $1 < i \leq h$, and $M_1/B_1 \geq f_1$. The miss cost C_h and line size B_h are not defined for the root of the tree as there is no level-$(h+1)$ cache. The leaves (processors) have no capacity ($M_0 = 0$), and they have $B_0 = C_0 = 1$. Also, $B_i \geq B_{i-1}$ for $0 < i < h$. Finally, we call the entire subtree rooted at a level-i cache a **level-i cluster**, and we call its child level-$(i-1)$ clusters **subclusters**. We use $p_i = \prod_{j=1}^{i} f_j$ to denote the total number of processors in a level-i cluster.

3. THE PCO MODEL

In this section, we present the Parallel Cache-Oblivious model, a simple, high-level model for algorithm analysis. As in the sequential cache-oblivious (CO) model [20], in the **Parallel Cache-Oblivious (PCO) model** there is a memory of unbounded size and a single cache with size M, linesize B (in words), and optimal (i.e., furthest into the future) replacement policy. The cache state κ consists of the set of cache lines resident in the cache at a given time. When a location in a non-resident line l is accessed and the cache is full, l replaces in κ the line accessed furthest into the future, incurring a *cache miss*.

To extend the CO model to parallel computations, one needs to define how to analyze the number of cache misses during execution of a parallel block. Analyzing using a sequential ordering of the subtasks in a parallel block (as in most prior work[1]) is problematic for mapping to even a single shared cache, as the following theorem demonstrates for the CO model:

THEOREM 1. *Consider a PMH comprised of a single cache shared by $p > 1$ processors, with cache-line size B, cache size $M \geq pB$, and a memory (i.e., $h = 2$). Then there exists a parallel block such that for any greedy scheduler[2] the number*

[1]Two prior works not using the sequential ordering are the *concurrent cache-oblivious model* [5] and the *ideal distributed cache model* [21], but both design directly for p processors and consider only a single level of private caches.

[2]In a *greedy* scheduler, a processor remains idle only if there is no ready-to-execute task.

of cache misses is nearly a factor of p larger than the cache complexity on the CO model.

PROOF. Consider a parallel block that forks off p identical tasks, each consisting of a strand reading the same set of M memory locations from M/B blocks. In the CO model, after the first M/B misses, all other accesses are hits, yielding a total cost of M/B misses in the CO model.

Any greedy schedule on p processors executes all strands at the same time, incurring simultaneous cache misses (for the same line) on each processor. Thus, the parallel block incurs $p(M/B)$ misses. □

The gap arises because a sequential ordering accounts for significant reuse among the subtasks in the block, but a parallel execution cannot exploit reuse unless the line has been loaded earlier.

To overcome this difficulty, we instead use an approach of (i) ignoring any data reuse among the subtasks and (ii) flushing the cache at each fork and join point of any task that does not fit within the cache, as follows. Let $loc(t; B)$ denote the set of distinct cache lines accessed by task t, and $S(t; B) = |loc(t; B)| \cdot B$ denote its size (also let $s(t; B) = |loc(t; B)|$ denote the size in terms of number of cache lines). Let $Q(c; M, B; \kappa)$ be the cache complexity of c in the sequential CO model when starting with cache state κ.

DEFINITION 2. *[Parallel Cache-Oblivious Model] For cache parameters M and B the **cache complexity** of a strand s, parallel block b, or task t starting at state κ is defined as:*
strand:

$$Q^*(s; M, B; \kappa) = Q(s; M, B; \kappa)$$

parallel block: *For* $b = t_1 \| t_2 \| \ldots \| t_k$,

$$Q^*(b; M, B; \kappa) = \sum_{i=1}^{k} Q^*(t_i; M, B; \kappa)$$

task: *For* $t = c_1; c_2; \ldots; c_k$,

$$Q^*(t; M, B; \kappa) = \sum_{i=1}^{k} Q^*(c_i; M, B; \kappa_{i-1}) ,$$

where $\kappa_i = \emptyset$ if $S(t; B) > M$, and $\kappa_i = \kappa \cup_{j=1}^{i} loc(c_j; B)$ if $S(t; B) \leq M$.

We use $Q^*(c; M, B)$ to denote a computation c starting with an empty cache, $Q^*(n; M, B)$ when n is a parameter of the computation, and $Q^*(c; 0, 1)$ to denote the computational work. Note that by setting M to 0, we force the analysis to count every instruction that touches even a register and hence effectively corresponds to instruction count.

Comments on the definition: Since a task t alternates between strands and parallel blocks the definition effectively clears the cache at every fork and join point in t when $S(t; B) > M$. This is perhaps more conservative than required but leads to a simple model and does not seem to affect bounds. Since in a parallel block all subtasks start with the same cache state, no sharing is assumed among parallel blocks. If an algorithms wants to share a value loaded from memory, then the load should occur before the fork. The notion of furthest in the future for Q in a strand might seem ill-defined since the future might entail parallel tasks. However, all future references fit into cache until reaching a supertask that does not fit in cache, at which point the

Problem	Span	Cache Complexity Q^*
Scan (prefix sums, etc.)	$O(\log n)$	$O(\lceil n/B \rceil)$
Matrix Transpose ($n \times m$ matrix) [20]	$O(\log(n+m))$	$O(\lceil nm/B \rceil)$
Matrix Multiplication ($\sqrt{n} \times \sqrt{n}$ matrix) [20]	$O(\sqrt{n})$	$O(\lceil n^{1.5}/B \rceil / \sqrt{M} + 1)$
Matrix Inversion ($\sqrt{n} \times \sqrt{n}$ matrix)	$O(\sqrt{n})$	$O(\lceil n^{1.5}/B \rceil / \sqrt{M} + 1)$
Quicksort [22]	$O(\log^2 n)$	$O(\lceil n/B \rceil (1 + \log\lceil n/(M+1) \rceil))$
Sample Sort [10]	$O(\log^2 n)$	$O(\lceil n/B \rceil \lceil \log_{M+2} n \rceil)$
Sparse-Matrix Vector Multiply [10] (m nonzeros, n^ϵ edge separators)	$O(\log^2 n)$	$O(\lceil m/B + n/(M+1)^{1-\epsilon} \rceil)$
Convex Hull (e.g., see [8])	$O(\log^2 n)$	$O(\lceil n/B \rceil \lceil \log_{M+2} n \rceil)$
Barnes Hut tree (e.g., see [8])	$O(\log^2 n)$	$O(\lceil n/B \rceil (1 + \log\lceil n/(M+1) \rceil))$

Table 1: Cache complexities of some algorithms analyzed in the PCO model. The bounds assume $M = \Omega(B^2)$. All algorithms are work optimal and their cache complexities match the best sequential algorithms.

cache is assumed to be flushed. Thus, there is no need to choose cache lines to evict. For a single strand the model is equivalent to the cache-oblivious model.

We believe that the PCO model is a simple, effective model for the cache analysis of parallel algorithms. It retains much of the simplicity of the ideal cache model, such as analyzing using only one level of cache. It ignores the complexities of artificial locality among parallel subtasks. Thus, it is relatively easy to analyze algorithms in the PCO model (examples are given in Section 4). Moreover, as we will show in Section 5, PCO bounds optimally map to cache miss bounds on each level of a PMH. Finally, although the PCO bounds are upper bounds, for many fundamental algorithms, they are tight: they asymptotically match the bounds given by the sequential ideal cache model, which are asymptotically optimal. Table 1 presents the PCO cache complexity of a few such algorithms, including both algorithms with polynomial span (matrix inversion) and highly imbalanced algorithms (the block transpose used in sample sort).

4. EXAMPLE PCO ANALYSIS

It is relatively easy to analyze algorithms in the PCO model. Let us consider first a simple map over an array which touches each element by recursively splitting the array in half until reaching a single element. If the algorithm for performing the map does not touch any array elements until recursing down to a single element, then each recursive task begins with an empty cache state, and hence the cache performance is $Q^*(n; M, B) = n$. An efficient implementation would instead load the middle element of the array before recursing, thus guaranteeing that a size-$\Theta(B)$ recursive subcomputation begins with a cache state containing the relevant line. We thus have the recurrence

$$Q^*(n; M, B) = \begin{cases} 2Q^*(\frac{n}{2}; M, B) + O(1) & n > B \\ O(1) & n \leq B, \end{cases}$$

which implies $Q^*(n; M, B) = O(n/B)$, matching the sequential cache complexity.

Quicksort is another algorithm that is easy to analyze in this model. A standard quicksort analysis for work [17] observes that all work can be amortized against comparisons of keys with a pivot. The probability of comparing keys of rank i and $j > i$ is at most $2/(j - i)$, i.e., the probability of selecting i or j as a pivot before any element in between. The expected work is thus $\sum_{i=1}^{n} \sum_{j>i} 2/(j-i) = \Theta(n \log n)$. Extending this analysis to either the CO or the PCO models

is identical—comparisons become free once the corresponding subarray fits in memory. Specifically, for nearby keys i and $j < i + M/3$, no paid comparison occurs if a key between $i - M/3$ and $i - 1$ is chosen before i and if $j + 1$ to $j + M/3$ is chosen before j. Summing over all keys gives expected number of paid comparisons $\sum_{i=1}^{n} \sum_{j>i+M/3} 2/(j-1) + \sum_{i=1}^{n} \sum_{j<i+M/3} 6/M = \Theta(n \log \lceil n/(M+1) \rceil + n)$. Completing the analysis (dividing this cost by B) entails observing that each recursive quicksort scans the subarray in order, and thus whenever a comparison causes a cache miss, we can charge $\Theta(B)$ comparisons against the same cache miss.

The rest of the algorithms in Table 1 can be similarly analyzed without difficulty, observing that for the original CO analyses, the cache complexities of the parallel subtasks were already analyzed independently assuming no data reuse.

5. BASIC SPACE-BOUNDED SCHEDULER

In this section we describe a class of schedulers, called space-bounded schedulers, and show (Theorem 3) that such schedulers have cache complexity on the PMH machine model that matches the PCO cache complexity. Space-bounded schedulers were introduced by Chowdhury et al. [14], but their paper does not use the PCO model and hence cannot show the same kind of optimality as Theorem 3. This section briefly describes a "greedy-space-bounded" scheduler that performs very well in terms of runtime on very balanced computations, and uses it to highlight some of the difficulties in designing a scheduler (such as the one in Section 7) that permits imbalance.

Space-Bounded Schedulers. A "space-bounded scheduler" is parameterized by a global *dilation* parameter $0 < \sigma \leq 1$ and machine parameters $\{M_i, B_i, C_i, f_i\}$. Given these parameters, we define a *level-i task* to be a task that fits within a σ fraction of the level-i cache, but not within a σ fraction of the level-$(i - 1)$ cache, i.e., $S(\mathsf{t}; B_i) \leq \sigma M_i$ and $S(\mathsf{t}; B_{i-1}) > \sigma M_{i-1}$. We call t a *maximal level-i task* if it is a level-i task but its parent (i.e., minimal containing) task is not. The top level task (no parent) is considered maximal. We call a strand a *level-i strand* if its minimal containing task is a level-i task.

A *space-bounded* scheduler [14] is one that limits the migration of tasks across caches and the number of outstanding subtasks as follows. Consider any level-i task t. Once any of t is executed by some processor below level-i cache U_i, all remaining strands of t must be executed by the same level-i cluster. We say that t is *anchored* at U_i. Moreover, at any point in time, consider the maximal level-i tasks $t_1, t_2, \ldots, t_k$ anchored to level-i cache U_i. Then $\sum_{j=1}^{k} S(t_j; B_i) \leq M_i$. That is to say, the total space used by tasks anchored to U_i does not exceed U_i's capacity. Finally, we consider strands. Whereas a task is anchored to a single cache, a level-i strand is anchored to caches along a level-i to level-1 path in the memory hierarchy. When a level-i strand is anchored to a level-$j < i$ cache, it is treated as a task that takes σM_j space, thereby preventing (many) other tasks/strands from being anchored at the same cache.

We relax the usual definition of greedy scheduler in the following: A *greedy-space-bounded scheduler* is a space-bounded scheduler in which a processor remains idle only if there is no ready-to-execute strand that can be anchored to the processor (and appropriate ancestor caches) without violating the space-bounded constraints.

Cache Bounds: PCO Cache Complexity is Optimal For Space-Bounded Schedulers. The following theorem implies that a nested-parallel computation scheduled with any space-bounded scheduler achieves optimal cache performance, with respect to the PCO model. A main idea of the proof is that each task reserves sufficient cache space and hence never needs to evict a previously loaded cache line.

THEOREM 3. *Consider a PMH and any dilation parameter $0 < \sigma \leq 1$. Let t be a level-i task. Then for all memory-hierarchy levels $j \leq i$, the number of level-j cache misses incurred by executing t with any space-bounded scheduler is at most $Q^*(t; \sigma M_j, B_j)$.*

PROOF. Let U_i be the level-i cache to which t is assigned. Observe that t uses space at most σM_i. Moreover, by definition of the space-bounded scheduler, the total space needed for tasks assigned to U_i is at most M_i, and hence no line from t need ever be evicted from U's level-i cache. Thus, an instruction x in t accessing a line ℓ does not exhibit a level-i cache miss if there is an earlier-executing instruction in t that also accesses ℓ. Any instruction serially preceding x must execute earlier than x. Hence, the parallel cache complexity $Q^*(t; \sigma M_i, B_i)$ is an upper bound on the actual number of level-i cache misses.

We next extend the proof for lower-level caches. First, let us consider a level-i strand s belonging to task t. The PCO model states that for any $M_{j<i}$, the cache complexity of a level-i strand matches the serial cache complexity of the strand beginning from an initially empty state. Consider each cache partitioned such that a level-i strand can use only the σM_j capacity of a level-$(j < i)$ cache awarded to it by the space-bounded scheduler. Then the number of misses is indeed as though the strand executed on a serial level-$(i-1)$ memory hierarchy with σM_j cache capacity at each level j. Hence, $Q^*(s; \sigma M_j, B_j)$ is an upper bound on the actual number of level-j cache misses incurred while executing the strand s. (The actual number may be less because an optimal replacement policy may not partition the caches and the cache state is not initially empty.)

Finally, to complete the proof for all memory-hierarchy levels j, we assume inductively that the theorem holds for all maximal subtasks of t. The PCO model assumes an empty initial level-j cache state for any maximal level-j subtask of t, as $S(t; B_j) > \sigma M_j$. Thus, the level-j cache complexity for t is defined as $Q^*(t; \sigma M_j, B_j) = \sum_{t' \in A(t)} Q^*(t'; \sigma M_j, B_j, \emptyset)$, where $A(t)$ is the set of all level-i strands and nearest max-

imal subtasks of t. Since the theorem holds inductively for those tasks and strands in $A(t)$, it holds for t. □

In contrast, there is no such optimality result for the CO model: Theorem 1 (showing a factor of p gap) readily extends to any greedy-space-bounded scheduler, using the same proof.

Runtime Bounds: A Simple Space-Bounded Scheduler and its Limitations. While all space-bounded schedulers achieve optimal cache complexity, they vary in total running time. Greedy-space-bounded schedulers, like the scheduler in [14], perform well for computations that are very well balanced. At a high level, a greedy-space-bounded scheduler operates on tasks anchored at each cache. These tasks are "unrolled" to produce maximal tasks, which are in turn anchored at descendant caches. If a processor P becomes idle and a strand is ready, we assume P begins working on a strand immediately (i.e., we ignore scheduler overheads). If multiple strands are available, one is chosen arbitrarily. Our main scheduler is based on a greedy-space-bounded scheduler, and an operational description of both is included in [8].

Chowdhury et al. [14] present analyses of a (nearly) greedy-space-bounded scheduler (which includes minor enhancements violating the greedy principle). These analyses are algorithm specific and rely on the balance of the underlying computation. A more general performance theorem is included in the associated technical report [8]. Along with our main theorem (Theorem 6), these analyses all use recursive application of Brent's theorem to obtain a total running time: small recursive tasks are assumed inductively to execute quickly, and the larger tasks are analyzed using Brent's theorem with respect to a single-level machine of coarser granularity.

The following are the types of informal structural restrictions imposed on the underlying algorithms to guarantee efficient scheduling with a greedy-space-bounded scheduler and previous work. For more precise, sufficient restrictions, see the technical report [8].

1. *When multiple tasks are anchored at the same cache, they should have similar structure and work. Moreover, none of them should fall on a much longer path through the computation. If this condition is relaxed, then some anchored task may fall on the critical path. It is important to guarantee each task a fair share of processing resources without leaving many processors idle.*

2. *Tasks of the same size should have the same parallelism.*

3. *The nearest maximal descendant tasks of a given task should have roughly the same size. Relaxing this condition allows two or more tasks at different levels of the memory hierarchy to compete for the same resources. Guaranteeing that each of these tasks gets enough processing resources becomes a challenge.*

In addition to these balance conditions, the previous analyses exploit preloading of tasks: the memory used by a task is assumed to be loaded (quickly) into the cache before executing the task. For array-based algorithms preloading is a reasonable requirement. When the blocks to be loaded are not contiguous, however, it may be computationally challenging to determine which blocks should be loaded. Removing the preloading requirement complicates the analysis, which then must account for high-level cache misses that may occur as a result of tasks anchored at lower-level caches.

Our new scheduler in Section 7 relaxes all of these balance conditions, allowing for more asymmetric computations. Moreover, we do not assume preloading. To facilitate analysis of less regular computations, we first define a more holistic measure of the balance of the algorithm in Section 6 and then prove our performance bounds with respect to this metric. This balance metric has the added benefit of separating the algorithm analysis from the scheduler.

6. EXTENDING PCO FOR IMBALANCE

In the PMH (or any machine with shared caches), all caches are associated with a set of processors. It therefore stands to reason that if a task needs memory M but does not have sufficient parallelism to make use of a cache of appropriate size, that either processors will sit idle or additional misses will be required. This might be true even if there is plenty of parallelism on average in the computation. The following lower-bound makes this intuition more concrete.

THEOREM 4. *(Lower Bound) Consider a PMH comprised of a single cache shared by $p > 1$ processors with parameters $B = 1$, M and C, and a memory (i.e., $h = 2$). Then for all $r \geq 1$, there exists a computation with $n = rpM$ memory accesses, $\Theta(n/p)$ span, and $Q^*(M, B) = pM$, such that for any scheduler, the runtime on the PMH is at least $nC/(C + p) \geq (1/2) \min(n, nC/p)$.*

PROOF. Consider a computation that forks off $p > 1$ parallel tasks. Each task is sequential (a single strand) and loops over touching M locations, distinct from any other task (i.e., a total of Mp locations are touched). Each task then repeats touching the same M locations in the same order a total of r times, for a total of $n = rMp$ accesses. Because M fits within the cache, only a task's first M accesses are misses and the rest are hits in the PCO model. The total cache complexity is thus only $Q^*(M, B) = Mp$ for $B = 1$ and any $r \geq 1$.

Now consider an execution (schedule) of this computation on a shared cache of size M with p processors and a miss cost of C. Divide the execution into consecutive sequences of M timesteps, called **rounds**. Because it takes 1 (on a hit) or $C \geq 1$ (on a miss) units of time for a task to access a location, no task reads the same memory location twice in the same round. Thus, a memory access costs 1 only if it is to a location in memory at the start of the round and C otherwise. Because a round begins with at most M locations in memory, the total number of accesses during a round is at most $(Mp-M)/C+M$ by a packing argument. Equivalently, in a full round, M processor steps execute at a rate of 1 access per step, and the remaining $Mp - M$ processor steps complete $1/C$ accesses per step, for an average "speed" of $1/p + (1 - 1/p)/C < 1/p + 1/C$ accesses per step. This bound holds for all rounds except the first and last. In the first round, the cache is empty, so the processor speed is $1/C$. The final round may include at most M fast steps, and the remaining steps are slow. Charging the last round's fast steps to the first round's slow steps proves an average "speed" of at most $1/p+1/C$ accesses per processor timestep. Thus, the computation requires at least $n/(p(1/p+1/C)) = nC/(C+p)$ time to complete all accesses. When $C \geq p$, this

time is at least $nC/(2C) = n/2$. When $C \leq p$, this time is at least $nC/(2p)$. □

The proof shows that even though there is plenty of parallelism overall and a fraction of at most $1/r$ of the accesses are misses in Q^*, an optimal scheduler either executes tasks (nearly) sequentially (if $C \geq p$) or incurs a cache miss on (nearly) every access (if $C \leq p$).

This indicates that some cost must be charged to account for the space-parallelism imbalance. We extend PCO with a cost metric that charges for such imbalance, but does not charge for imbalance in subtask size. When coupled with our scheduler in Section 7, the metric enables PCO bounds to effectively map to PMH runtime, even for highly-irregular computations.

The metric aims to estimate the degree of parallelism that can be utilized by a symmetric hierarchy as a function of the size of the computation. Intuitively, a computation of size S with "parallelism" $\alpha \geq 0$ should be able to use $p = O(S^\alpha)$ processors effectively. This intuition works well for algorithms where parallelism is polynomial in the size of the problem.

More formally, we define a notion of **effective cache complexity** $\widehat{Q}_\alpha(\mathsf{c})$ for a computation c based on the definition of Q^*. Just as for Q^*, $\widehat{Q}_\alpha()$ for tasks, parallel blocks and strands is defined inductively based on the composition rules described in section 2 for building a computation. (Note that since work is just a special case of Q^*, obtained by substituting $M = 0$, the following metric can be used to compute effective work just like effective cache complexity.)

DEFINITION 5. *[PCO extended for imbalance] For cache parameters M and B and parallelism α, the **effective cache complexity** of a strand s, parallel block b, or task t starting at cache state κ is defined as:*

strand: *Let t be the nearest containing task of strand s*

$$\widehat{Q}_\alpha(\mathsf{s}; M, B; \kappa) = Q^*(\mathsf{s}; M, B; \kappa) \times s(\mathsf{t}; B)^\alpha$$

parallel block: *For $\mathsf{b} = \mathsf{t}_1 \| \mathsf{t}_2 \| \dots \| \mathsf{t}_k$ in task t,*

$$\widehat{Q}_\alpha(\mathsf{b}; M, B; \kappa) =$$
$$\max \begin{cases} s(\mathsf{t}; B)^\alpha \max_i \left\{ \frac{\widehat{Q}_\alpha(\mathsf{t}_i; M, B; \kappa)}{s(\mathsf{t}_i; B)^\alpha} \right\} & \text{(depth dominated)} \\ \sum_i \widehat{Q}_\alpha(\mathsf{t}_i; M, B; \kappa) & \text{(work dominated)} \end{cases}$$

task: *For $\mathsf{t} = c_1; c_2; \dots; c_k$,*

$$\widehat{Q}_\alpha(\mathsf{t}; M, B; \kappa) = \sum_{i=1}^k \widehat{Q}_\alpha(c_i; M, B; \kappa) \ ,$$

where κ_i is defined as in Definition 2.

In the rule for parallel block, the *depth dominated* term corresponds to limiting the number of processors available to do the work on each subproblem t_i to $s(\mathsf{t}_i)^\alpha$. This throttling yields a span (depth) $\widehat{Q}_\alpha(\mathsf{t}_i)/s(\mathsf{t}_i)^\alpha$ for each task and the effective cache complexity is then the maximum of the spans over the subtasks multiplied by the number of processors for the parallel block b, which is $s(\mathsf{t}; B)^\alpha$ (see Fig. 4).

We say that an algorithm is *α-efficient* if $Q^*(n; M, B) = O(\widehat{Q}_\alpha(n; M, B))$, where n denotes the input size. This α-efficiency occurs trivially if the work term always dominates, but can also happen if sometimes the depth term dominates. The maximum α for which an algorithm is α-efficient specifies the *effective parallelism*.

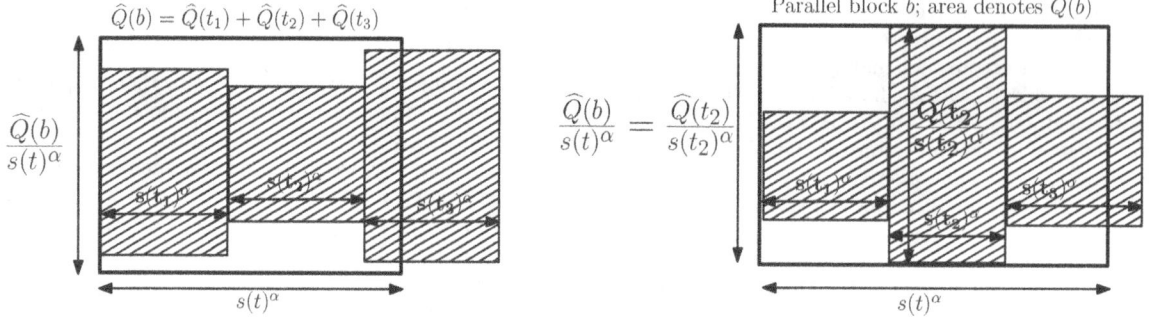

Figure 4: **Two examples of Definition 5 applied to a parallel block b = t₁ ‖ t₂ ‖ t₃ belonging to task t. The shaded rectangles represent the subtasks and the white rectangle represents the parallel block b. Subtask rectangles have fixed area ($\widehat{Q}_\alpha(t_i)$, determined recursively) and *maximum* width $s(t_i)^\alpha$. The left example is work dominated: the total area of b's subtasks is larger than any depth subterms, and determines the area $\widehat{Q}_\alpha(b) = \widehat{Q}_\alpha(t_1) + \widehat{Q}_\alpha(t_2) + \widehat{Q}_\alpha(t_3)$. The right example is depth dominated: the height of a subtask t₂ determines the height of b and hence the area is $(s(t)/s(t_2))^\alpha \widehat{Q}_\alpha(t_2)$.**

$\widehat{Q}_\alpha(\cdot)$ is an attribute of an algorithm, and as such can be analyzed irrespective of the machine and the scheduler. Appendix B of the associated report [8] illustrates the analysis for $\widehat{Q}_\alpha(\cdot)$ and effective parallelism for several algorithms. Note that, as illustrated in Fig. 4(left) and the analysis of algorithms in the report, good effective parallelism can be achieved even when there is significant work imbalance among subtasks. Finally, depth dominated term implicitly includes the span so we do not need a separate span (depth) cost in our model.

7. SCHEDULER

This section modifies the space-bounded scheduler to address some of the balance concerns discussed in Section 5. These modification restrict the space bounded scheduler, potentially forcing more processors to remain idle. These restriction, nevertheless, allow nicer provable performance guarantees.

The main performance theorem for our scheduler is the following, which is proven in Section 8. This theorem does not assume any preloading of the caches, but we do assume that all block sizes are the same (except at level 0). Here, the machine parallelism β is defined as the minimum value such that for all hierarchy levels $i > 1$, we have $f_i \leq (M_i/M_{i-1})^\beta$, and $f_1 \leq (M_1/3B_1)^\beta$. Aside from the overhead v_h (defined in the theorem), this bound is optimal in the PCO model for a PMH with 1/3-rd the given memory sizes. Here, k is a tunable constant scheduler parameter with $0 < k < 1$, discussed later in this section. Observe that the v_h overhead reduces significantly (even down to a constant) if the ratio of memory sizes is large but the fanout is small (as in the machines in Figure 1), or if $\alpha \gg \beta$.[3]

THEOREM 6. *Consider an h-level PMH with $B = B_j$ for all $1 \leq j \leq h$, and let t be a task such that $S(t; B) > f_h M_{h-1}/3$ (the desire function allocates the entire hierarchy to such a task) with effective parallelism $\alpha \geq \beta$, and let*

$\alpha' = \min\{\alpha, 1\}$. *The runtime of t is no more than:*

$$\frac{\sum_{j=0}^{h-1} \widehat{Q}_\alpha(t; M_j/3, B_j) \cdot C_j}{p_h} \cdot v_h, \quad \text{where overhead } v_h \text{ is}$$

$$v_h = 2 \prod_{j=1}^{h-1} \left(\frac{1}{k} + \frac{f_j}{(1-k)(M_j/M_{j-1})^{\alpha'}} \right).$$

Since much of the scheduler matches the greedy-space-bounded scheduler from Section 5, only the differences are highlighted here. An operational description of the scheduler can be found in the associated technical report [8].

There are three main differences between this scheduler and greedy-space-bounded scheduler from Section 5. First, we fix the dilation to $\sigma = 1/3$ instead of $\sigma = 1$. Whereas reducing σ worsens the bound in Theorem 3 (only by a constant factor for cache-oblivious algorithms), this factor of 1/3 allows us more flexibility in scheduling.

Second, to cope with tasks that may skip levels in the memory hierarchy, we associate with each cache a notion of how busy the descending cluster is, to be described more fully later. For now, we say that a cluster is *saturated* if it is "too busy" to accept new tasks, and *unsaturated* otherwise. The modification to the scheduler here is then restricting it to anchor maximal tasks only at *unsaturated* caches.

Third, to allow multiple differently sized tasks to share a cache and still guarantee fairness, we partition each of the caches, awarding ownership of specific subclusters to each task. Specifically, whenever a task t is anchored at U, t is also *allocated* some subset $\mathcal{U}_t$ of U's level-$(i-1)$ subclusters, essentially granting ownership of the clusters to t. This allocation restricts the scheduler further in that now t may execute only on $\mathcal{U}_t$ instead of all of U. This allocation is exclusive in that a cluster may be allocated to only one task at a time, and no new tasks may be anchored at any cluster $V \in \mathcal{U}_t$ except descendent tasks of t. Moreover, tasks may not skip levels through V, i.e., a new level-$(j < i-1)$ subtask of a level-$k > i$ task may not be anchored at any descendent cache of V. Tasks that skipped levels in the hierarchy before V was allocated may have already been anchored at or below V — these tasks continue running as normal, and they are the main reason for our notion of saturation.

A level-i strand is allocated every cache to which it is an-

---

[3]For example, $v_h < 10$ on the Xeon 7500 as $\alpha \to 1$.

chored, *i.e.*, exactly one cache at every level below i. In contrast, a level-i task t is anchored only to a level-i cache and allocated potentially many level-$(i-1)$ subclusters, depending on its size. We say that the size-$s = S(\mathsf{t}; B_i)$ task t *desires* $g_i(s)$ level-$(i-1)$ clusters, g_i to be specified later. When anchoring t to a level-i cache U, let q be the number of unsaturated and unallocated subclusters of U. Select the most unsaturated $\min\{q, g_i(s)\}$ of these subclusters and allocate them to t.

For each cache, there may be one anchored maximal task that is **underallocated**, meaning that it receives fewer subclusters than it desires. The only underallocated task is the most recent task that caused the cache to transition from being unsaturated to saturated. Whenever a subcluster frees up, allocate it to the underallocated task. If assigning a subcluster causes the underallocated task to achieve its desire, it is no longer underallocated, and future free subclusters become available to other tasks.

Scheduler details. We now describe the two missing details of the scheduler, namely the notion of saturation, as well as the desire function g_i, which specifies for a particular task size the number of desired subclusters.

One difficulty is trying to schedule tasks with large desires on partially assigned clusters. We continue assigning tasks below a cluster until that cluster becomes saturated. But what if the last job has large desire? To compensate, our notion of saturation leaves a bit of slack, guaranteeing that the last task scheduled can get some minimum amount of computing power. Roughly speaking, we set aside a constant fraction of the subclusters at each level as a reserve. The cluster becomes saturated when all other subclusters have been allocated. The last task scheduled, the one that causes the cluster to become saturated, may be allocated subclusters from the reserve.

There is some tradeoff in selecting the reserve constant here. If a large constant is reserved, we may only allocate a small fraction of clusters at each level, thereby wasting a large fraction of all processing power at each level. If, on the other hand, the constant is small, then the last task scheduled may run too slowly. Our analysis will count the first against the work of the computation and the second against the depth.

Designing a good function to describe saturation and the reserved subclusters is complicated by the fact that task assignments may skip levels in the hierarchy. The notion of saturation thus cannot just count the number of saturated or allocated subclusters — instead, we consider the degree to which a subcluster is utilized. For a cluster U with subclusters $V_1, V_2, \ldots, V_{f_i}$ ($f_i > 1$), define the utilization function $\mu(U)$ as follows:

$$\mu(U) = \begin{cases} \min\left\{1, \frac{1}{kf_i}\sum_{i=1}^{f_i} \mu'(V_i)\right\} & \text{if } U \text{ is a level-}(\geq 2) \\ & \quad\text{cluster} \\ \min\{1, \frac{x}{f_1 k}\} & \text{if } U \text{ is a level-1 cluster with} \\ & \quad x \text{ allocated processors} \end{cases}$$

and

$$\mu'(V) = \begin{cases} 1 & \text{if } V \text{ is allocated}, \\ \mu(V) & \text{otherwise} \end{cases},$$

where $k \in (0, 1)$, the value $(1 - k)$ specifying the fraction of processors to reserve. For a cluster U with just one subcluster V, $\mu(U) = \mu(V)$. To understand the remainder of this

section, it is sufficient to think of k as $1/2$. We say that U is saturated when $\mu(U) = 1$ and unsaturated otherwise.

It remains to define the desire function g_i for level i in the hierarchy. A natural choice for g_i is $g_i(S) = \lceil S/(M_i/f_i) \rceil = \lceil Sf_i/M_i \rceil$. That is, associate with each subcluster a $1/f_i$ fraction of the space in the level-i cache — if a task uses x times this fraction of total space, it should receive x subclusters. It turns out that this desire does not yield good scheduler performance with respect to our notion of balanced cache complexity. In particular it does not give enough parallel slackness to properly load-balance subtasks across subclusters.

Instead, we use $g_i(S) = \min\{f_i, \max\{1, \lfloor f(3S/M_i)^{\alpha'} \rfloor\}\}$, where $\alpha' = \min\{\alpha, 1\}$. What this says is that a maximal level-i task is allocated one subcluster when it has size $S(\mathsf{t}; B_i) = M_i/(3f_i^{1/\alpha'})$, and the number of subclusters allocated to t increases by a factor of 2 whenever the size of t increases by a factor of $2^{1/\alpha'}$. It reaches the maximum number of subclusters when it has size $S(\mathsf{t}; B_i) = M_{i-1}/3$. We define $g(S) = g_i(S)p_{i-1}$ if $S \in (M_{i-1}/3, M_i/3]$.

For simplicity we assumed in our model that all memory is preallocated, which includes stack space. This assumption would be problematic for algorithms with $\alpha > 1$ or for algorithms which are highly dynamic. However, it is easy to remove this restriction by allowing temporary allocation inside a task, and assume this space can be shared among parallel tasks in the analysis of Q^*. To make our bounds work this would require that for every cache we add an additional number of lines equal to the sum of the sizes of the subclusters. This augmentation would account even for the very worst case where all memory is temporarily allocated.

The analysis of this scheduler is in Section 8, summarized by Theorem 6. There are a couple of challenges that arise in the analysis. First, while it is easy to separate the run time of a task on a sequential machine in to a sum of the cache miss costs for each level, it is not as easy on a parallel machine. Periods of waiting on cache misses at several levels at multiple processors can be interleaved in a complex manner. Our **separation lemma** (lemma 9) addresses this issue by bounding the run time by the sum of its cache costs at different levels ($\widehat{Q}_\alpha(\mathsf{t}; M, B_i) \cdot C_i$).

Second, whereas a simple greedy-space-bounded scheduler applied to *balanced* tasks lends itself to an easy analysis through an inductive application of Brent's theorem, we have to tackle the problem of subtasks skipping levels in the hierarchy and partially allocated caches. At a high level, the analysis of Theorem 6 recursively decomposes a maximal level-i task into its nearest maximal descendent level-$j < i$ tasks. By inductively assuming that these tasks finish "quickly enough," we combine the subproblems with respect to the level-i cache analogous to Brent's theorem, arguing that a) when all subclusters are busy, a large amount of productive work occurs, b) and when subclusters are idle, all tasks have been allocated sufficient resources to progress at a sufficiently quick rate. Our carefully planned allocation and reservations of clusters as described earlier in this section are critical to this proof.

8. ANALYSIS OF THE SCHEDULER

This section presents the analysis of our scheduler, proving several lemmas leading up to Theorem 6. First, the following lemma implies that the capacity restriction of each cache is subsumed by the scheduling decision of only assigning tasks to unallocated, unsaturated clusters.

LEMMA 7. *Any unsaturated level-i cluster U has at least $M_i/3$ capacity available and at least one subcluster that is both unsaturated and unallocated.*

PROOF. The fact that an unsaturated cluster has an unsaturated, unallocated cluster follows from the definition. Any saturated or allocated subcluster V_i has $\mu'(V_i) = 1$. Thus, for unsaturated cluster U with subclusters $V_1, \ldots, V_{f_i}$, we have $1 > (1/kf_i)\sum_{j=1}^{f_i} \mu'(V_i) \geq (1/f_i)\sum_{j=1}^{f_i} \mu'(V_i)$, and it follows that some $\mu'(V_i) < 1$.

We now argue that if U is unsaturated, then it has at least $M_i/3$ capacity remaining. This fact is trivial for $f_i = 1$, as in that case at most one task is allocated. Suppose that tasks $t_1, t_2, \ldots, t_k$ are anchored to an unsaturated cluster and have desires $x_1, x_2, \ldots, x_k$. Since U is unsaturated $\sum_{i=1}^{k} x_i \leq f_i - 1$, which implies $x_i \leq f_i - 1$ for all i. We will show that the ratio of space to desire, $S(t_i; B)/x_i$, is at most $2M_i/3f_i$ for all tasks anchored to U, which implies $\sum_{i=1}^{k} S(t_i; B) \leq 2M_i/3$.

Since a task with desire $x \in \{1, 2, \ldots, f_i - 1\}$ has size at most $(M_i/3)((x+1)/f_i)^{1/\alpha'}$, where $\alpha' = \min\{\alpha, 1\} \leq 1$, the ratio of its space to its desire x is at most $(M_i/3x)((x+1)/f_i)^{1/\alpha'}$. Letting $q = 1/\alpha' \geq 1$, we have the space-to-desire ratio r bounded by

$$
\begin{aligned}
r &\leq \frac{M_i}{3} \cdot \frac{(x+1)^q}{x} \cdot \frac{1}{f_i^q} \leq \frac{2M_i}{3} \cdot \frac{(x+1)^q}{x+1} \cdot \frac{1}{f_i^q} \\
&\leq \frac{2M_i}{3f_i} \cdot \frac{(x+1)^{q-1}}{f_i^{q-1}} \leq \frac{2M_i}{3f_i} \qquad \square
\end{aligned}
$$

Latency added cost. Section 6 introduced effective cache complexity $\widehat{Q}_\alpha(\cdot)$, which is algorithmic measure. To analyze the scheduler, however, it is important to consider when cache misses occur. To factor in the effect of the cache miss costs, we define the latency added effective work, denoted by $\widehat{W}_\alpha^*(\cdot)$, of a computation with respect to the particular PMH. Latency added effective work is only for use in the analysis of the scheduler, and does not need to be analyzed by an algorithm designer.

The ***latency added effective work*** is similar to the effective cache complexity, but instead of counting just instructions, we add the cost of cache misses at each instruction. The cost $\rho(x)$ of an instruction x accessing location m is $\rho(x) = W(x) + C_i'$ if the scheduler causes the instruction x to fetch m from a level i cache on the given PMH. Using this per-instruction cost, we define effective work $\widehat{W}_\alpha^*(.)$ of a computation using structural induction in a manner that is deliberately similar to that of $\widehat{Q}_\alpha(.)$.

DEFINITION 8 (LATENCY ADDED COST). *For cost $\rho(x)$ of instruction x, the **latency added effective work** of a task t, or a strand s or parallel block b nested inside t is defined as:*
strand:

$$\widehat{W}_\alpha^*(s) = s(t; B)^\alpha \sum_{x \in s} \rho(x).$$

parallel block: *For $b = t_1 \| t_2 \| \ldots \| t_k$,*

$$\widehat{W}_\alpha^*(b) = \max\left\{ s(t; B)^\alpha \max_i \left\{ \frac{\widehat{W}_\alpha^*(t_i)}{s(t_i; B)^\alpha} \right\}, \sum_i \widehat{W}_\alpha^*(t_i) \right\}. \tag{1}$$

task: *For $t = c_1; c_2; \ldots; c_k$,*

$$\widehat{W}_\alpha^*(t) = \sum_{i=1}^{k} \widehat{W}_\alpha^*(c_i). \tag{2}$$

Because of the large number of parameters involved ($\{M_i, B, C_i\}_i$ etc.), it is undesirable to compute the latency added work directly for an algorithm. Instead, we will show a nice relationship between latency added work and effective work.

We first show that $\widehat{W}_\alpha^*(\cdot)$ (and $\rho(\cdot)$, on which it is based) can be decomposed into a per (cache) level costs $\widehat{W}_\alpha^{(i)}(\cdot)$ that can each be analyzed in terms of that level's parameters ($\{M_i, B, C_i\}$). We then show that these costs can be put together to provide an upper bound on $\widehat{W}_\alpha^*(\cdot)$. For $i \in [h-1]$, $\widehat{W}_\alpha^{(i)}(c)$ of a computation c is computed exactly like $\widehat{W}_\alpha^*(c)$ using a different base case: for each instruction x in c, if the memory access at x costs at least C_i', assign a cost of $\rho_i(x) = C_i$ to that node. Else, assign a cost of $\rho_i(x) = 0$. Further, we set $\rho_0(x) = W(x)$, and define $\widehat{W}_\alpha^{(0)}(c)$ in terms of $\rho_o(\cdot)$. It also follows from these definitions that $\rho(x) = \sum_{i=0}^{h-1} \rho_i(x)$ for all instructions x.

LEMMA 9. ***Separation Lemma:*** *For an h-level PMH with $B = B_j$ for all $1 \leq j \leq h$ and computation A, we have*

$$\widehat{W}_\alpha^*(A) \leq \sum_{i=0}^{h-1} \widehat{W}_\alpha^{(i)}(A).$$

PROOF. The proof is based on induction on the structure of the computation (in terms of its decomposition in to block, tasks and strands). For the base case of the induction, consider the sequential thread (or strand) s at the lowest level in the call tree. If $S(s)$ denotes the space of task immediately enclosing s, then by definition

$$
\begin{aligned}
\widehat{W}_\alpha^*(s) &= \left(\sum_{x \in s} \rho(x) \right) \cdot s(s; B)^\alpha \leq \left(\sum_{x \in s} \sum_{i=0}^{h-1} \rho_i(x) \right) \cdot s(s; B)^\alpha \\
&= \sum_{i=0}^{h-1} \left(\sum_{x \in s} \rho_i(x) \cdot s(s; B)^\alpha \right) = \sum_{i=0}^{h-1} \widehat{W}_\alpha^{(i)}(s).
\end{aligned}
$$

For a series composition of strands and blocks with in a task $t = x_1; x_2; \ldots; x_k$,

$$\widehat{W}_\alpha^*(t) = \sum_{i=1}^{k} \widehat{W}_\alpha^*(x_i) \leq \sum_{i=1}^{k} \sum_{l=0}^{h} \widehat{W}_\alpha^{(h)}(x_i) = \sum_{l=0}^{h} \widehat{W}_\alpha^{(l)}(x)$$

For a parallel block b inside task t consisting of tasks $\{t_i\}_{i=1}^m$, consider the equation 1 for $\widehat{W}_\alpha^*(b)$ which is the maximum of $m+1$ terms, the $(m+1)$-th term being a summation. Suppose that of these terms, the term that determines $\widehat{W}_\alpha^*(b)$ is the k-th term (denote this by T_k). Similarly, consider the equation 1 for evaluating each of $\widehat{W}_\alpha^{(l)}(b)$ and suppose that the k_l-th term (denoted by $T_{k_l}^{(l)}$) on the right hand side determines the value of $\widehat{W}_\alpha^{(l)}(b)$. Then,

$$\frac{\widehat{W}_\alpha^*(b)}{s(t; B)^\alpha} = T_k \leq \sum_{l=0}^{h-1} T_k^{(l)} \leq \sum_{l=0}^{h-1} T_{k_l}^{(l)} = \frac{\sum_{l=0}^{h-1} \widehat{W}_\alpha^{(l)}(b)}{s(t; B)^\alpha}, \tag{3}$$

which completes the proof. Note that we did not use the fact that some of the components were work or cache complexities. The proof only depended on the fact that $\rho(x) = $

$\sum_{i=0}^{h-1} \rho_i(x)$ and the structure of the composition rules given by equations 2, 1. ρ could have been replaced with any other kind of work and ρ_i with its decomposition. □

The previous lemma indicates that the latency added work can be separated into costs per cache level. The following lemma then relates these separated costs to effective cache complexity $\widehat{Q}_\alpha(\cdot)$.

LEMMA 10. *Consider an h-level PMH with $B = B_j$ for all $1 \le j \le h$ and a computation c. If c is scheduled on this PMH using a space-bounded scheduler with dilation $\sigma = 1/3$, then $\widehat{W}_\alpha^*(\mathsf{c}) \le \sum_{i=0}^{h-1} \widehat{Q}_\alpha(\mathsf{c}; M_i/3, B) \cdot C_i$.*

PROOF. (*Sketch*) The function $\widehat{W}_\alpha^{(i)}(\cdot)$ is monotonic in that if it is computed based on function $\rho_i'(\cdot)$ instead of $\rho_i(x)$, where $\rho_i'(x) \le \rho_i(x)$ for all instructions x, then the former estimate would be no more than the latter. It then follows from the definitions of $\widehat{W}_\alpha^{(i)}(\cdot)$ and $\rho_i(\cdot)$, that $\widehat{W}_\alpha^{(i)}(\mathsf{c}) \le \widehat{Q}_\alpha(\mathsf{c}; M_i/3, B) \cdot C_i$ for all computations c, $i \in \{0, 1, \ldots, h-1\}$. Lemma 9 then implies that for any computation c: $\widehat{W}_\alpha^*(\mathsf{c}) \le \sum_{i=0}^{h-1} \widehat{Q}_\alpha(\mathsf{c}; M_i/3, B) \cdot C_i$. □

Finally, we prove the main lemma, bounding the running time of a task with respect to the remaining utilization the clusters it has been allocated. At a high level, the analysis recursively decomposes a maximal level-i task into its nearest maximal descendent level-$j < i$ tasks. We assume inductively that these tasks finish "quickly enough." Finally, we combine the subproblems with respect to the level-i cache analogous to Brent's theorem, arguing that a) when all subclusters are busy, a large amount of productive work occurs, b) and when subclusters are idle, all tasks make sufficient progress. Whereas this analysis outline is consistent with a simple analysis of the greedy scheduler and that in [14], here we address complications that arise due to partially allocated caches and subtasks skipping levels in the hierarchy.

LEMMA 11. *Consider an h-level PMH with $B = B_j$ for all $1 \le j \le h$ and a computation to schedule with $\alpha \ge \beta$, and let $\alpha' = \min\{\alpha, 1\}$. Let N_i be a task or strand which has been assigned a set $\mathcal{U}_t$ of $q \le g_i(S(N_i; B))$ level-$(i-1)$ subclusters by the scheduler. Letting $\sum_{V \in \mathcal{U}_t}(1 - \mu(V)) = r$ (by definition, $r \le |\mathcal{U}_t| = q$), the running time of N_i is at most:*

$$\frac{\widehat{W}_\alpha^*(N_i)}{r p_{i-1}} \cdot v_i, \quad \text{where overhead } v_i \text{ is}$$

$$v_i = 2 \prod_{j=1}^{i-1}\left(\frac{1}{k} + \frac{f_i}{(1-k)(M_i/M_{i-1})^{\alpha'}}\right).$$

PROOF. We prove the claim on run time using induction on the levels.
Induction: Assume that all child maximal tasks of N_i have run times as specified above. Now look at the set of clusters $\mathcal{U}_t$ assigned to N_i. At any point in time, either:

1. all of them are saturated.

2. at least one of the subcluster is unsaturated and there are no jobs waiting in the queue $R(N_i)$. More specifically, the job on the critical path $(\chi(N_i))$ is running. Here, critical path $\chi(N_i)$ is the set of strictly ordered

immediate child subtasks that have the largest sum of effective depths. We would argue in this case that progress is being made along the critical path at a reasonable rate.

Assuming $q > 1$, we will now bound the run time required to complete N_i by bounding the number of cycles the above two phases use. Consider the first phase. A job $x \in C(N_i)$ (subtasks of N_i) when given an appropriate number of processors (as specified by the function g) can not have an overhead of more than v_{i-1}, i.e., it uses at most $\widehat{W}_\alpha^*(x)v_{i-1}$ individual processor clock cycles. Since in the first phase, at least k fraction of available subclusters under $\mathcal{U}_t$ are always allocated (at least $r p_{i-1}$ clock cycles put together) to some subtask of N_i, it can not last for more than

$$\sum_{x \in C(N_i)} \frac{1}{k} \frac{\widehat{W}_\alpha^*(x)}{r p_{i-1}} \cdot v_{i-1} < \frac{1}{k} \frac{\widehat{W}_\alpha^*(N_i)}{r p_{i-1}} \cdot v_{i-1} \text{ number of cycles.}$$

For the second phase, we argue that the critical path runs fast enough because we do not underallocate processing resources for any subtask by more than a factor of $(1-k)$ as against that indicated by the g function. Specifically, consider a job x along the critical path $\chi(N_i)$. Suppose x is a maximal level-$j(x)$ task, $j(x) < i$. If the job is allocated subclusters below a level-$j(x)$ subcluster V, then V was unsaturated at the time of allocation. Therefore, when the scheduler picked the $g_{j(x)}(S(x; B))$ most unsaturated subclusters under V (call this set $\mathcal{V}$), $\sum_{v \in \mathcal{V}} \mu(v) \ge (1-k)g_{j(x)}(S(x; B))$. When we run x on V using the subclusters $\mathcal{V}$, its run time is at most

$$\frac{\widehat{W}_\alpha^*(x)}{(\sum_{v \in \mathcal{V}} \mu(v))p_{j(x)-1}} \cdot v_{j(x)-1} < \frac{\widehat{W}_\alpha^*(x)}{(1-k)g(S(x; B_{j(x)}))} \cdot v_{j(x)-1}$$

$$= \frac{\widehat{W}_\alpha^*(x)}{s(x; B)^\alpha} \frac{s(x; B)^\alpha}{g(S(x; B_{j(x)}))} \frac{v_{j(x)-1}}{1-k}$$

time. Amongst all subtasks x of N_i, the ratio $\frac{s(x;B)^\alpha}{g(S(x;B_{j(x)}))}$ is maximum when when $S(x; B) = M_{i-1}/3$, where the ratio is $(M_{i-1}/3B)^\alpha/p_{i-1}$. Summing the run times of all jobs along the critical path would give us an upper bound for time spent in phase two. This would be at most

$$\sum_{x \in \chi(N_i)} \frac{\widehat{W}_\alpha^*(x)}{(1-k)g(S(x; B))} \cdot v_{i-1}$$

$$= \sum_{x \in \chi(N_i)} \frac{\widehat{W}_\alpha^*(x)}{s(x; B)^\alpha} \cdot \frac{s(x; B)^\alpha}{g(S(x; B))} \cdot \frac{v_{i-1}}{1-k}$$

$$\le \left(\sum_{x \in \chi(N_i)} \frac{\widehat{W}_\alpha^*(x)}{s(x; B)^\alpha}\right) \cdot \frac{(M_{i-1}/3B)^\alpha}{p_{i-1}} \cdot \frac{v_{i-1}}{1-k}$$

$$\le \frac{\widehat{W}_\alpha^*(N_i)}{s(N_i; B)^\alpha} \cdot \frac{(M_{i-1}/3B)^\alpha}{p_{i-1}} \cdot \frac{v_{i-1}}{1-k} \quad \text{(by defn. of } \widehat{W}_\alpha^*())$$

$$= \frac{\widehat{W}_\alpha^*(N_i)}{r p_{i-1}} \cdot \frac{r(M_{i-1}/3B)^\alpha}{s(N_i; B)^\alpha} \cdot \frac{v_{i-1}}{1-k}$$

$$\le \frac{\widehat{W}_\alpha^*(N_i)}{r p_{i-1}} \cdot \frac{q(M_{i-1}/3B)^\alpha}{s(N_i; B)^\alpha} \cdot \frac{v_{i-1}}{1-k}$$

$$\le \frac{\widehat{W}_\alpha^*(N_i)}{r p_{i-1}} \cdot \frac{f_i}{(1-k)(M_i/M_{i-1})^{\alpha'}} \cdot v_{i-1} \quad \text{(by defn. of } g).$$

Putting together the run times of both the phases, we have an upper bound of

$$\frac{\widehat{W}_\alpha^*(N_i)}{rp_{i-1}}v_{i-1} \cdot \left(\frac{1}{k} + \frac{f_i}{(1-k)(M_i/M_{i-1})^\alpha}\right) = \frac{\widehat{W}_\alpha^*(N_i)}{rp_{i-1}} \cdot v_i.$$

If $q = 1$, N_i would get allocated just one $(i-1)$-subcluster V, and of course, all the (yet unassigned) $(i-2)$ subclusters $\mathcal{V}$ below V. Then, we can view this scenario as N_i running on the $(i-1)$-level hierarchy. Memory accesses and cache latency costs are charged the same way as before with out modification so that the effective work of N_i would still be $\widehat{W}_\alpha^*(N_i)$. By inductive hypothesis, we know that the run time of N_i would be at most

$$\frac{\widehat{W}_\alpha^*(N_i)}{(\sum_{V\in\mathcal{V}}(1-\mu(V)))p_{i-2}} \cdot v_{i-1}$$

which is at most $\frac{\widehat{W}_\alpha^*(N_i)}{rp_{i-1}} \cdot v_i$ since $\sum_{V\in\mathcal{V}}(1-\mu(V)) \geq rf_{i-1}$ and $v_{i-1} < v_i$.

Base case ($i = 1$): N_1 has $q = r$ processors available, all under a shared cache. If $q = 1$, the claim is clearly true. If $q > 1$, since there is no further anchoring beneath the level-1 cache (since $M_0 = 0$), we can use Brent's theorem on the latency added effective work to bound the run time: $\frac{\widehat{W}_\alpha^*(N_1)}{r}$ added to the critical path length, which is at most $\frac{\widehat{W}_\alpha^*(N_1)}{s(N_1;B)^\alpha}$. This sum is at most

$$\frac{\widehat{W}_\alpha^*(N_1)}{r}\left(1 + \frac{q}{s(N_1;B)^\alpha}\right) \leq \frac{\widehat{W}_\alpha^*(N_1)}{r}\left(1 + \frac{g(S(N_1;B))}{s(N_1;B)^\alpha}\right)$$
$$\leq \frac{\widehat{W}_\alpha^*(N_1)}{r}\left(1 + \frac{S(N_1;B)^\alpha}{s(N_1;B)^\alpha} \cdot \frac{f_1}{(M_1/3)^\alpha}\right)$$
$$\leq \frac{\widehat{W}_\alpha^*(N_1)}{r} \times 2. \qquad \square$$

Theorem 6 follows from Lemmas 10 and 11, starting on a system with no utilization.

9. CONCLUSION

The paper described models that capture the "locality" of an algorithm independently of the machine or how the computation is mapped onto the machine either by hand or by a scheduler. In particular the models are just based on the structure of the program: they make no reference to processors, and use only two simple cache parameters, one capturing temporal locality (M) and one spatial locality (B), and one parallelism parameter (α). The models modify the sequential cache-oblivious model to avoid capturing false dependences and to account for memory-parallelism imbalances. The paper also developed a scheduler that can guarantee strong bounds when mapping the costs analyzed in the model to cache misses and runtime on parallel machines with tree-of-caches hierarchies. We expect the model can also be used for other types of machines with hierarchical locality.

Acknowledgments. This work is partially supported by the National Science Foundation under grant number CCF-1018188, as well as under the NSF/CRA sponsored CIFellows program. We are grateful to Intel, IBM, and Microsoft for generous gifts that have helped support this work.

10. REFERENCES

[1] U. A. Acar, G. E. Blelloch, and R. D. Blumofe. The data locality of work stealing. In *Theory of Computing Systems*, 2000.

[2] B. Alpern, L. Carter, E. Feig, and T. Selker. The uniform memory hierarchy model of computation. *Algorithmica*, 12, 1994.

[3] B. Alpern, L. Carter, and J. Ferrante. Modeling parallel computers as memory hierarchies. In *Programming Models for Massively Parallel Computers*, 1993.

[4] L. Arge, M. T. Goodrich, M. Nelson, and N. Sitchinava. Fundamental parallel algorithms for private-cache chip multiprocessors. In *SPAA*, 2008.

[5] M. A. Bender, J. T. Fineman, S. Gilbert, and B. C. Kuszmaul. Concurrent cache-oblivious B-trees. In *SPAA*, 2005.

[6] G. Bilardi, A. Pietracaprina, G. Pucci, and F. Silvestri. Network-oblivious algorithms. In *IPDPS*, 2007.

[7] G. E. Blelloch, R. A. Chowdhury, P. B. Gibbons, V. Ramachandran, S. Chen, and M. Kozuch. Provably good multicore cache performance for divide-and-conquer algorithms. In *SODA*, 2008.

[8] G. E. Blelloch, J. T. Fineman, P. B. Gibbons, and H. V. Simhadri. A cache-oblivious model for parallel memory hierarchies. Technical Report CMU-CS-10-154, Computer Science Department, Carnegie Mellon University, 2010.

[9] G. E. Blelloch and P. B. Gibbons. Effectively sharing a cache among threads. In *SPAA*, 2004.

[10] G. E. Blelloch, P. B. Gibbons, and H. V. Simhadri. Low-depth cache oblivious algorithms. In *SPAA*, 2010.

[11] R. D. Blumofe, M. Frigo, C. F. Joerg, C. E. Leiserson, and K. H. Randall. Dag-consistent distributed shared memory. In *IPPS*, 1996.

[12] R. A. Chowdhury and V. Ramachandran. The cache-oblivious gaussian elimination paradigm: theoretical framework, parallelization and experimental evaluation. In *SPAA*, 2007.

[13] R. A. Chowdhury and V. Ramachandran. Cache-efficient dynamic programming algorithms for multicores. In *SPAA*, 2008.

[14] R. A. Chowdhury, F. Silvestri, B. Blakeley, and V. Ramachandran. Oblivious algorithms for multicores and network of processors. In *IPDPS*, 2010.

[15] R. Cole and V. Ramachandran. Efficient resource oblivious scheduling of multicore algorithms. manuscript, 2010.

[16] R. Cole and V. Ramachandran. Resource oblivious sorting on multicores. In *ICALP*, 2010.

[17] T. H. Cormen, C. E. Leiserson, R. L. Rivest, and C. Stein. *Introduction to Algorithms, 2nd Edition*. MIT Press, 2001.

[18] D. Culler, R. Karp, D. Patterson, A. Sahay, K. E. Schauser, E. Santos, R. Subramonian, and T. von Eicken. Logp: towards a realistic model of parallel computation. *SIGPLAN Not.*, 28(7), 1993.

[19] P. de la Torre and C. P. Kruskal. Submachine locality in the bulk synchronous setting. In *Euro-Par, Vol. II*, 1996.

[20] M. Frigo, C. E. Leiserson, H. Prokop, and S. Ramachandran. Cache-oblivious algorithms. In *FOCS*, 1999.

[21] M. Frigo and V. Strumpen. The cache complexity of multithreaded cache oblivious algorithms. In *SPAA*, 2006.

[22] P. Kumar. Cache oblivious algorithms. In U. Meyer, P. Sanders, and J. Sibeyn, editors, *Algorithms for Memory Hierarchies*. Springer, 2003.

[23] C. E. Leiserson. Fat-Trees: Universal networks for hardware-efficient supercomputing. *IEEE Transactions on Computers*, C–34(10), 1985.

[24] L. G. Valiant. A bridging model for parallel computation. *CACM*, 33(8), 1990.

[25] L. G. Valiant. A bridging model for multi-core computing. In *ESA*, 2008.

Sharing-Aware Algorithms for Virtual Machine Colocation

Michael Sindelar
Google Inc.
1600, Amphitheatre Parkway
Mountain View, CA 94043
sindelar@google.com

Ramesh K. Sitaraman
Department of Computer
Science
University of Massachusetts
Amherst, MA 01003
ramesh@cs.umass.edu

Prashant Shenoy
Department of Computer
Science
University of Massachusetts
Amherst, MA 01003
shenoy@cs.umass.edu

ABSTRACT

Virtualization technology enables multiple virtual machines (VMs) to run on a single physical server. VMs that run on the same physical server can share memory pages that have identical content, thereby reducing the overall memory requirements on the server. We develop sharing-aware algorithms that can colocate VMs with similar page content on the same physical server to optimize the benefits of inter-VM sharing. We show that inter-VM sharing occurs in a largely hierarchical fashion, where the sharing can be attributed to VM's running the same OS platform, OS version, software libraries, or applications. We propose two hierarchical sharing models: a tree model and a more general cluster-tree model. Using a set of VM traces, we show that up to 67% percent of the inter-VM sharing is captured by the tree model and up to 82% is captured by the cluster-tree model. Next, we study two problem variants of critical interest to a virtualization service provider: the VM Maximization problem that determines the most profitable subset of the VMs that can be packed into the given set of servers, and the VM packing problem that determines the smallest set of servers that can accommodate a set of VMs. While both variants are NP-hard, we show that both admit provably good approximation schemes in the hierarchical sharing models. We show that VM maximization for the tree and cluster-tree models can be approximated in polytime to within a $(1 - \frac{1}{e})$ factor of optimal. Further, we show that VM packing can be approximated in polytime to within a factor of $O(\log n)$ of optimal for cluster-trees and to within a factor of 3 of optimal for trees, where n is the number of VMs. Finally, we evaluate our VM packing algorithm for the tree sharing model on real-world VM traces and show that our algorithm can exploit most of the available inter-VM sharing to achieve a 32% to 50% reduction in servers and a 25% to 57% reduction in memory footprint compared to sharing-oblivious algorithms.

Categories and Subject Descriptors

F.2.2 [**Analysis of Algorithms and Problem Complexity**]: Nonnumerical Algorithms and Problems—*Computations on discrete structures*; D.4.2 [**Operating Systems**]: Storage Management—*Main memory*; D.4.7 [**Operating Systems**]: Organization and Design—*Distributed systems*

General Terms

Algorithms, Management, Measurement, Theory

Keywords

Virtualization, Optimization, Page Sharing, Bin Packing

1. INTRODUCTION

Modern data centers that incorporate large server farms increasingly employ a virtualized architecture where applications run inside virtual machines (VMs) that are then hosted on physical servers. An ever-increasing range of applications utilize data center virtualization, including web hosting, enterprise applications, and e-commerce. The goal of a data center service provider, such as a cloud computing provider, is to maximize the utility that the VMs provide while conserving the required server resources such as memory and CPU.

Virtualization technology enables multiple VMs to run on the same physical server. VMs running on the same physical server share resources such as CPU and memory by utilizing a key component called the *hypervisor*. To enable the conservation of memory resources, modern hypervisors such as VMware ESX support content-based sharing of memory pages [14]. Specifically, if multiple VMs resident on the same physical server use identical pages, content-based sharing allows storing just one copy of the shared page. Thus, content-based sharing decreases the memory footprint required to host a set of VMs on a single physical server. The concept of content-based sharing was first utilized in the Disco system [1], and subsequently implemented in VMware ESX [14] where the technique was shown to save as much as 33% of the memory resources of a server. However, content-based sharing is effective only if it is complemented by algorithms that ensure that the VMs resident on each physical server contain a significant amount of sharable pages. Specifically, to truly utilize the potential of inter-VM page sharing and to significantly reduce the aggregate memory footprint, it is essential that VMs with the most shared pages are colocated in the same physical server. This underscores the importance of "sharing-aware" algorithms that "pack" VMs into servers in a manner that VM page sharing is maximized and the total memory footprint is minimized. The potential for exploiting inter-VM sharing by intelligent colocation was recognized in [16] where the authors developed a fingerprinting scheme that provides a compact representation of the memory pages in a VM. Such a scheme is an essential step in identifying VMs with a large page sharing potential. In our paper, we go further by developing formal models and algorithms for sharing-aware placement of VMs on physical servers. While we explicitly model only memory resources, other resources such as CPU and network are additional considerations in VM placement. Extending the results and techniques in this paper to multiple resources is an important direction for future work.

1.1 Our contributions

Our first contribution is the design of graph models to capture page sharing across a set of virtual machines and to empirically demonstrate the efficacy of our models to capture sharing in real systems. Our graph models of sharing form the basis of our algorithmic study and are also likely critical for future algorithmic studies in the area. We present a general sharing model and two variants of hierarchical sharing, namely the tree and the cluster-tree models. Our hierarchical models assume that shared pages between VMs can be attributed to commonality in a hierarchy of dimensions such as the OS platform, OS version, software libraries, and types of applications. Using memory traces for a mixture of diverse OSes, architectures, and software libraries, we find that a tree model can capture up to 67% of inter-VM sharing from these traces, whereas the more general cluster-tree model can capture up to 82% of the inter-VM sharing. These results demonstrate the utility of our models in capturing real-world memory sharing.

Our second contribution is the formulation and development of sharing-aware algorithms for two optimization problems that are key to a virtualization service provider: the *VM maximization* problem and the *VM packing* problem. We study these problems in the general sharing model as well as in the two hierarchical sharing models. Interestingly, we find that although the hierarchical sharing models ignore some types of sharing, thereby reducing the sharing potential, they significantly help the design of provably-good approximation algorithms for these problems. Our theoretical results are summarized in Figure 1.

Sharing Model	VM Maximization	VM Packing
General	No approx within $2^{(\log n)^\delta}$	Open
Cluster-Tree (Hierarchical)	FPTAS	$O(\log n)$-approx
Tree (Hierarchical)	FPTAS	3-approx

Figure 1: Summary of theoretical results

In the *VM maximization problem*, we are given a set of n VMs, where each VM is associated with a profit value that is earned by hosting that VM. Each VM consists of a set of memory pages. We are also given m servers, each server with a capacity of P pages. The goal of VM maximization is to determine the subset of the VMs that can be hosted on

the m servers so that the total profit earned is maximized. This problem characterizes the desire of a service provider to maximize the earned profit for a fixed set of server resources. We show that VM maximization is NP-Hard and is infeasible to even approximate well in the general sharing model where each VM can contain an arbitrary set of pages. Specifically, we show that it is infeasible to derive an approximate solution that is within a factor of $2^{(\log n)^\delta}$ of optimal, for some $\delta > 0$, assuming that 3-SAT $\notin DTIME(2^{n^{3/4+\epsilon}})$. However, we show that in the cluster-tree model and the special case of a single server, we can devise a fully-polynomial time approximation scheme (FPTAS) that yields an approximate solution that is at least a factor of $(1 - \epsilon)$ of the optimal profit, for any $\epsilon > 0$. Further, this result can be extended to obtain an approximate solution that is at least a factor of $(1 - \frac{1}{e})$ of the optimal profit for the VM maximization problem with multiple servers.

In the *VM packing problem* problem, we are given a set of VMs that must be hosted on physical servers, where each VM consists of a set of pages. The goal of this problem is to "pack" the VMs onto the smallest number of physical servers, where each server has a capacity of P pages. While VM packing is also NP-Hard, we show that we can efficiently compute an approximate solution that is within a factor of $O(\log n)$ of optimal for cluster trees and a factor 3 of optimal for trees, where n is the number of VMs. From a theoretical perspective, the VM packing problem is an interesting new generalization of the well-studied bin packing problem. Unlike bin packing, in VM packing the cumulative size of a set of items (i.e., VMs) in a bin (i.e., server) can be *smaller* than the sum of individual item sizes due to sharing. Note that if sharing is ignored, VM packing reduces to traditional bin packing.

The VM packing problem fundamentally characterizes the goals of a service provider to host a set of VMs using the least amount of server resources. The service provider will need to periodically allocate VMs to servers in a sharing-aware fashion, either as a part of the initial placement of newly-created VMs or as part of a "repacking" operation of existing VMs [16]. A periodic repacking would be necessary as both the pool of existing VMs and the sharing characteristics of individual VMs change over time, making the initial packing potentially suboptimal.

Our third contribution is an experimental evaluation of our VM packing algorithm for the tree model of sharing on actual end-user VM traces. We find that our sharing-aware algorithm reduces the number of servers required by 32% to 50% when compared to a sharing-oblivious Modified First Fit Decreasing (MFFD) bin packing algorithm. Our algorithm also significantly reduced the memory usage with the total memory footprint across all servers decreasing by 25% to 57% when compared with any sharing-oblivious algorithm. We further show that loading each server to at most 90% of memory capacity produces colocations that are stable with respect to the fluctuations in the VM's memory usage and inter-VM sharing over time.

2. VM MEMORY SHARING: PROPERTIES AND MODELS

We present three models that capture inter-VM memory page sharing with different levels of complexity. We then use real VM traces to show that a significant portion of the inter-

VM page sharing can be captured by simpler structured hierarchical models that facilitate the design of provably good sharing-aware VM colocation algorithms.

2.1 Graph models for page sharing

Our first model is the general sharing model that can accurately capture all inter-VM sharing. In this model, each VM consists of an arbitrary set of pages. One can view this as a hypergraph $G = \langle V, E \rangle$, where V is the set of VMs and each hyperedge $e \subseteq E$ denotes a memory page that is shared by all the VMs in the hyperedge. Clearly, the general sharing model can capture arbitrary sharing of pages between the VMs.

In the two hierarchical sharing models that we propose, sharing cannot be arbitrary and only some forms of sharing can be captured. First, we propose a tree model where sharing is modeled as a rooted directed tree $T = \langle V, E \rangle$ where the edges are directed away from the root and towards the leaves (See Figure 2). Each node in $v \in V$ is associated with $w(v)$ distinct pages. Each leaf corresponds to a VM and pages that are unique to that VM are associated with it. The pages associated with a non-leaf node v is shared by all the VMs that correspond to leaves of the subtree of T rooted at node v. Thus, the set of all pages in a VM is the union of all pages associated with nodes on the corresponding root-to-leaf path in T.

An example of a tree sharing model is shown in Figure 2 where one can view each level of bifurcation as representing dimensions such as OS, OS version, or software libraries. Page sharing between any two VM's is attributed to commonality in those dimensions. For instance, the pages shared across all VMs is captured in the root in the first level of the tree. VMs running the same OS platform may share a set of pages related to that OS and is captured in the second level of the tree. If they both also run the same OS version there is additional sharing captured at the third level of the tree. Even more sharing occurs if they also use the same software libraries that is captured in the fourth level of the tree. Finally, pages that are unique to the VM is captured in the corresponding leaves of the tree.

A more general version of the hierarchical sharing model is the cluster-tree model whose nodes and edges are "clustered" into super-nodes and super-edges respectively, and the super-nodes and super-edges form a rooted directed tree (See Figure 3). More formally, a cluster-tree consists of a rooted directed tree $T = \langle V, E \rangle$, where each $v \in V$ is a *super-node* and each $(u, v) \in E$ is a *super-edge*. Each super-node $v \in V$ contains a distinct set of one or more nodes denoted by $\Gamma(v)$ such that for $u \neq v$, $\Gamma(u) \cap \Gamma(v) = \emptyset$. Each super-edge $(u, v) \in E$ contains a distinct set of one or more directed edges denoted by $\Gamma(u, v)$ where $\Gamma(u, v) \subseteq \Gamma(u) \times \Gamma(v)$. The *width* of a cluster-tree denoted by k equals the $\max_{v \in V} |\Gamma(v)|$ and is assumed to be a constant. Note that setting k equal to 1 reduces a cluster-tree to the simpler tree model. Therefore, any algorithmic results for the cluster-tree model also apply to the tree model.

A cluster-tree can be used to model a more complex form of inter-VM sharing as follows. As before, each node v is associated with $w(v)$ distinct pages. Each super-node that is a leaf of T corresponds to a VM and contains a single node. Let a VM correspond to a leaf super-node that contains a single node v. All *unique* pages of that VM are associated with node v. Further, the set of *all* pages in that VM is the

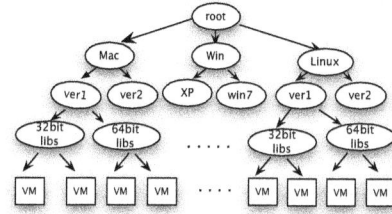

Figure 2: Tree model example

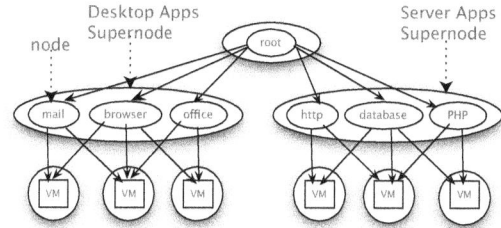

Figure 3: Cluster-Tree model example

union of all pages associated with nodes u such that either $u = v$ or u has a (directed) path to v. For instance, the leftmost VM in the cluster-tree of Figure 3 contains the unique pages associated with its leaf node, the pages associated with the "mail" and "browser" nodes that are shared with other VMs that use those desktop applications, and the pages associated with the root node that are shared with all VMs in the cluster-tree.

The cluster-tree model captures page sharing more accurately than the tree model in certain situations. As a hypothetical example, a set of VMs might be using desktop applications, while another set of VMs might be using server applications (See Figure 3). However, each VM may use only a proper subset of these applications. To capture this situation one can use a single super-node to represent desktop applications, and another super-node to represent server applications. The super-nodes contain individual nodes representing each individual application. We can then connect each leaf representing a VM to the proper subset of the nodes representing applications that the VM uses, thereby modeling the sharing more accurately. For instance, in Figure 3, the leftmost VM only uses a subset of the desktop applications, namely "mail" and "browser' but not "office". We have found that a cluster-tree with small constant width is typically sufficient for effectively capturing additional inter-VM sharing.

2.2 Empirical analysis of inter-VM sharing

Both the tree and cluster-tree hierarchical models are more structured than the general model, but they typically do not capture all of the inter-VM page sharing that exists in a set of VMs. However, using VM memory traces, we show that in practice these two models are able to capture a majority of the inter-VM sharing. The intuitive reason for their efficacy is because the structure of these models reflects how VM sharing occurs in practice. Typically the amount of memory pages that are shared between any two VMs depends on the OS platform, OS version and the software libraries utilized by those VMs. For example, more memory pages are likely to be shared between VMs running the same OS platform (e.g.,between two Mac or two Windows VMs) than between those running different OS platforms (e.g., between a Mac and a Windows VM). Similarly, there is likely to be more sharing between VMs running the same OS versions. For instance, more sharing is likely between two VMs that both run Windows XP and than two VMs that run Windows XP and Windows 7 respectively. Finally, software libraries also govern the amount of likely sharing—similar libraries and library versions will yield more sharing. As depicted in Figures 2 and 3, hierarchical models are well suited to capture such sharing by grouping VMs based on the OS platform, OS version, software library versions and so on. A limitation though is when VMs with the same OS platform and version run different overlapping subsets of application processes or have different overlapping subsets of software libraries installed on them. Sharing of this nature is not easily captured by hierarchical models.

2.2.1 Trace description

To evaluate the models and algorithms in this paper, we use a set of VM memory traces. Our dataset consists of traces from over 50 machines. We gathered memory traces from 31 volunteer machines in our department over a 9 month period. Since these volunteer machines comprised of only a subset of OS platforms and versions that we wanted to study (e.g., Windows machines and newer Linux versions were under-represented in our volunteer dataset), we setup 20 additional virtual machines in our laboratory testbed and also gathered traces from these synthetic machines, giving us the full diversity of OS platforms, OS versions, and software libraries for our study. Table 1 summarizes the various machines in our trace dataset.

OS	CPU	RAM
Mac OSX 10.5	PowerBook 6, PowerPC	1152MB
Mac OSX 10.5	i386	1GB,2GB
Centos Linux 4.4	Intel x86	1GB,2GB
Centos Linux 5.4	Intel x86	256MB
Centos Linux 5.4	Intel x86	1GB,2GB
Centos Linux 5.5	Intel x86	512MB
Centos Linux 5.5	Intel x86	1GB,2GB
Centos Linux 5.5	Intel x86 VMware	1536MB
Mac OSX 10.6	Intel x86 VMware	1536MB
Ubuntu 10.4, 10.10	Intel x86 VMWare	1536MB
Windows XP SP2	Intel x86 VMWare	1536MB
Windows 7	Intel x86 VMWare	1536MB

Table 1: Configuration of machines used to gather memory traces in our study

2.2.2 Properties of inter-VM sharing

We first consider the amount of inter-VM page sharing that is present under the general sharing model. If all virtual machines are allocated to a hypothetical physical server with infinite memory capacity, then approximately 13% of pages can be removed due to inter-VM sharing.[1] As shown in Table 2, the average sharing between pairs of Windows

---

[1] As in [16], our analysis assumes that self-shared pages—duplicated pages within a VM—are removed prior to com-

	Linux	Windows	Mac
Linux	2.24%	0.09%	0.02%
Windows		8.83%	0.16%
Mac			3.29%

Table 2: Average sharing between VM pairs across OS platforms.

	CentOs 5.5	Ubuntu 10.4	Ubuntu 10.10
CentOs 5.5	10.56%	0.37%	0.38%
Ubuntu 10.4		13.99%	4.51%
Ubuntu 10.10			13.80%

Table 3: Average sharing between VM pairs across Linux OS versions

machines was about 8.83%. Between Linux machines, the average was 2.24%. Not surprisingly, the average sharing across OS platforms (i.e., across Windows, Linux, and Mac machines) was at most 0.2%, i.e., it was an order of magnitude smaller. The inter-VM sharing increased significantly when the OS version used by the VMs were also the same. Table 3 shows the sharing observed across OS versions of the same OS platform. Since the trends are similar across OS platforms, only results for some Linux versions are shown here as a representative example. Note that while we observe 10-14% sharing across VMs running the same Linux OS versions in Table 3, the sharing drops to 4.5% for different versions of the same Linux Ubuntu distribution. Finally, we find little sharing across different Linux distributions (e.g., Centos and Ubuntu).

2.2.3 Efficacy of the tree and cluster-tree models

To study the efficacy of the tree and cluster-tree models, we selected traces from the 20 virtual machines in our laboratory testbed that comprised our synthetic data set. This provided us with a more controlled sample that represented the full diversity of OS platforms, OS versions, and software libraries. Specifically, our chosen data set represented all three OS platforms: Macs, Windows and Linux and a multitude of OS versions (Ubuntu 10.4 and 10.10, CentOS 5.5, Windows XP and 7, and Mac OS X 10.6); where available, we chose 32- and 64-bit OS versions as separate traces. The VM traces used in this experiment were carefully chosen to represent both server as well as desktop environments. Our desktop VMs comprised libraries and running processes for OpenOffice.org (v. 3.2), Firefox (v. 3), Adobe Flash (v. 10.1), and iTunes (v. 10.1), while our server VMs comprised libraries and processes for Apache 2, PHP 5, and MySQL 5.

We built hierarchical models for our chosen set of VM traces to study how much of the inter-VM sharing can be captured by these models. Our traces lend themselves naturally to a tree model which we consider first (See Figure 2). We constructed a tree with a single root that represents the set of all VMs, that has a child for each OS platform (Mac, Linux, Windows), that each have children for each OS version, which in turn have children for 32- and 64- bit versions of the software libraries. The leaves of the tree are individual VMs that run our desktop and server applications. Starting with the root, at each node v, we computed the

---

puting inter-VM sharing. Our traces contained around 9.5% self-shared pages.

	Tree	Cluster-Tree
OS	0.24%	11.37%
OS Ver	11.48%	15.68%
32- v 64-bit libs	55.27%	55.28%
Total	67.01%	82.33%

Table 4: Percentage of sharing captured in the two hierarchical models

pages that are common to all VMs that are descendants of v and associated those pages with node v. Subsequently, these pages were removed from the VMs that are descendants of v and the process was repeated recursively for each child of v. Note that that this process captures some but not all of the inter-VM sharing. Specifically, if a page p is shared between two VMs u and v but p is not present in *all* VMs that are descendants of the lowest common ancestor of u and v then page p is not captured by the tree model of sharing. However, for our VM traces, we found that the tree model captures 67% of the inter-VM sharing when compared to the general model that captures all inter-VM sharing (See Table 4).

The tree decomposition also provides insight into the amount of sharing at different levels—the amount of sharing increases as we descend down the tree. That is, only a small fraction of the sharing is attributable solely to the OS platform; a larger fraction is attributable solely to the same OS version, and a even greater amount to the architecture-dependent software libraries. At the software library level, 55% of the sharing is captured, even across VMs running different sets of applications. Thus, most of the inter-VM sharing comes from pages specific to the OS and software library versions of a VM.

One notable limitation of the tree model constructed above is that it fails to capture sharing due to 64-bit VMs that run both 32-bit and 64-bit software libraries. In the tree model of Figure 2, a VM can either use 32-bit software libraries or 64-bit software-libraries, but not both. Our cluster-tree model can be made to capture such sharing in the following manner. We convert each node of the tree to be a super-node that can contain one or more nodes. Then, we include a special node in each super-node that captures the pages that are shared between all 32-bit software libraries (in our case, 32-bit OpenOffice libraries installed on both 32- and 64-bit VMs). In this fashion, we are able to account for an additional 15% of sharing, giving a total of 82% of potentially sharable pages being captured by our cluster-tree model (See Table 4).

In summary, our hierarchical models are able to capture a significant amount of inter-VM sharing—in our analysis, a simple tree structure could account of 67% of the total sharing, while adding a small amount of complexity enabled a cluster-tree of width 2 to capture 82% of the sharing. As we show next, such hierarchical models also enable design of provably-good approximation algorithms for exploiting inter-VM sharing.

3. ALGORITHMS FOR VM COLOCATION

We study two colocation problems from the standpoint of a virtualization service provider. First, we study the *VM maximization* problem where we are given m servers that can each hold P memory pages, a set of virtual machines

$V = \{v_1, v_2, \cdots v_n\}$, and a profit function $p : V \to \mathbb{Z}^+$. Each virtual machine v_i is represented as a set P_i of pages. The goal is to find a set $V' \subseteq V$ such that V' can be packed into the m servers such that the memory capacities of the servers are not exceeded and the profit $\sum_{v_i \in V'} p(v_i)$ is maximized.

We also study the *VM packing problem* where we allocate a set of virtual machines to servers such that total number of servers is minimized, i.e., the hardware resources utilized by the service provider are minimized. Specifically, we are given a set of virtual machines $V = \{v_1, v_2, \cdots v_n\}$, where each virtual machine v_i contains a set of pages P_i. The goal is to allocate all VMs to servers such that the memory capacity P of each server is not exceeded and the total number of servers are minimized.

Both the VM maximization problem and the VM packing problem are NP-Hard, since they contain the knapsack problem and the bin-packing problem respectively as special cases when VMs do not share pages. However, as we shall see, the complexity of finding a provably approximate solution to either colocation problem is crucially dependent on the page sharing model.

3.1 General Sharing

The advantage of the general sharing model where any VM can contain any subset of pages is that all inter-VM sharing can be captured in this model. However, provably-good polytime approximation algorithms for VM colocation may not exist in the general sharing model. For instance, we can show that the VM Maximization is hard to even approximate in the general sharing model.

DEFINITION 3.1.1 (DENSEST k-SUBHYPERGRAPH PROBLEM). *Given a hypergraph $G = (V, E)$ and a parameter k, the densest k-subhypergraph problem is to find a set of k vertices with maximum number of hyperedges in the subgraph induced by this set.*

THEOREM 3.1.2 (HAJIAGHAYI ET. AL. [6]). *The densest k-subhypergraph problem is hard to approximate within a factor of $2^{(\log n)^\delta}$ for some $\delta > 0$ under the assumption that $3\text{-}SAT \notin DTIME(2^{n^{3/4+\epsilon}})$.*

THEOREM 3.1.3. *The VM Maximization problem is hard to approximate within a factor of $2^{(\log n)^\delta}$ for some $\delta > 0$ under the assumption that $3\text{-}SAT \notin DTIME(2^{n^{3/4+\epsilon}})$.*

PROOF. Let each page be a vertex in a hypergraph and each VM be a hyperedge that connects each vertex corresponding to a page contained in the VM. Further, let the profit of packing any VM be equal to 1. Then the problem of maximizing the number of VMs allocated to a server of size k is simply finding the densest k-subhypergraph. The result follows from Theorem 3.1.2. □

The complexity of approximating the VM packing problem in case of general sharing is open (See Figure 1).

3.2 Hierarchical sharing

The hierarchical sharing models do not capture all sharing that exists between VMs, but as we concluded in Section 2, it captures the majority of the sharing that exist between VMs. As we show in this section, the advantage of the hierarchical models is that it is more amenable to provably-good polytime approximation algorithms for both VM maximization and VM packing.

3.2.1 VM Maximization

We now show that in the hierarchical sharing model the VM maximization problem admits good approximation algorithms in the form of an FPTAS (fully polynomial time approximation scheme). In this section, we use the more general cluster-tree model of hierarchical sharing. The result also holds for the tree model, since the tree model is a special case of the cluster-tree model.

First, we develop a dynamic programming solution for the simpler version of the problem where we have only one server, using the left-right dynamic programming technique of [7]. We are given a cluster-tree $T = \langle V, E \rangle$ where each leaf of T represents a VM and contains a single node v whose packing yields a profit $p(v) \in \mathbb{Z}^+$. Each non-leaf is super-node consisting of at most k nodes, where k is the width of the cluster-tree. The profit values $p(v)$ are uniformly zero for any node v contained in a non-leaf super-node, i.e., profit is gained only on a leaf node which results in an entire VM being packed. Each node v is either contained in a leaf or is contained in a non-leaf super-node of T. Recall that each node v is associated with a set of $w(v)$ distinct pages. Note that the pages associated with leaves are unique to that VM and the pages associated with nodes contained in non-leaf super-nodes are potentially shared between multiple VMs. Let $\chi[c, \sigma, j, \beta]$ be the smallest size (number of pages) that must be packed into the single server to achieve a profit of at least β, with the constraint that only the subset σ of nodes contained in super-node c is packed and the remainder of the nodes are selected from trees rooted at the first j child super-nodes of super-node c.

$$\chi[c, \sigma, 0, \beta] = \begin{cases} \sum_{v \in \sigma} w(v) & \text{if } \sum_{v \in \sigma} p(v) \geq \beta \\ \infty & \text{if } \sum_{v \in \sigma} p(v) < \beta \end{cases}$$

Let c_j be the jth child of c and C' be the set of all subsets σ' of nodes in super-node c_j such that σ' and σ are compatible, i.e, for any node $v \in \sigma'$ all parents of v are included in σ. (Note that compatibility ensures that a node is packed only if its ancestors are also packed.) Thus, $\chi[c, \sigma, j, \beta]$ equals

$$\min_{0 \leq \beta' \leq \beta} \left\{ \chi[c, \sigma, j - 1, \beta - \beta'] + \min_{\sigma' \in C'} \chi[c_j, \sigma', degree(c_j), \beta'] \right\},$$

where $degree(c_j)$ is the number of children of super-node c_j. Let $B = \sum_v p(v)$ be an upper bound on the maximum achievable profit. Once the entire table $\chi[c, \sigma, j, \beta]$ is computed for all $c \in V$ and $0 \leq \beta \leq B$, we can extract the answer from the table as follows. The maximum attainable profit is simply the largest value of β such some entry $\chi[root(T), \sigma, degree(root(T)), \beta]$ is at most the server capacity P.

The run time of our dynamic programming solution can be evaluated as follows. Without loss of generality, there are $O(n)$ super-nodes and super-edges in the cluster-tree since each super-node can be assumed to have more than one child, where n is the number of VMs. The χ table has $O(2^k nB)$ entries, since each super-node contains at most k nodes, the number of super-edges is $O(n)$, and B is an upper bound on the maximum achievable profit. Each entry can be computed in $O(2^k B)$ time. Thus, the total running time of the algorithm is $O(2^{2k} nB^2)$, which is $O(nB^2)$ if we assume that the width of the cluster-tree k is a constant.

THEOREM 3.2.1. *For the single-server VM maximization*

problem in the cluster-tree sharing model, our algorithm produces a solution that is at least $(1 - \epsilon)$ of optimal with a run time of $O(n^5/\epsilon^2)$, where n is the number of VMs. That is, there exists an FPTAS for the VM maximization problem in the cluster-tree sharing model.

PROOF. We can extend the dynamic programming solution to create an FPTAS for single-server VM maximization. Analogous to the FPTAS for the knapsack problem [7], we derive an approximation by rounding the profit values of the VMs. For each node v, we round the profit values to create a new profit value $\tilde{p}(v) = \left\lfloor \frac{p(v)}{K} \right\rfloor$ for some $K = \epsilon \frac{p_{max}}{n}$, where $p_{max} = \max_v p(v)$. With the rounded profit values, the maximum profit $\tilde{B} = O(\frac{1}{\epsilon} n^2)$. The running time is then $O(n\tilde{B}^2) = O(n(\frac{1}{\epsilon} n^2)^2) = O(n^5/\epsilon^2)$.

Let $\tilde{X}$ be the solution obtained by our approximation algorithm using the rounded profit values. The profit obtained by solution $\tilde{X}$ is $\tilde{z} = \sum_{v \in \tilde{X}} p(v)$. Likewise, let $X^\star$ be the optimal solution obtaining a profit of $z^\star = \sum_{v \in X^\star} p(v)$.

$$\tilde{z} = \sum_{v \in \tilde{X}} p(v) \geq \sum_{v \in \tilde{X}} K \left\lfloor \frac{p(v)}{K} \right\rfloor \geq \sum_{v \in X^\star} K \left\lfloor \frac{p(v)}{K} \right\rfloor \quad (1)$$

$$\geq \sum_{v \in X^\star} K \left(\frac{p(v)}{K} - 1 \right) = \sum_{v \in X^\star} (p(v) - K) = z^\star - |X^\star|K, \quad (2)$$

where the last inequality in Equation 1 follows from the fact that $\tilde{X}$ is the optimal solution for the rounded profit values and hence obtains at least as much profit as $X^\star$. It follows from Equation 2 and the fact that $K = \epsilon p_{max}/n \leq \epsilon z^\star/|X^\star|$,

$$\frac{z^\star - \tilde{z}}{z^\star} \leq \frac{|X^\star|K}{z^\star} \leq \epsilon.$$

Thus, we have proven the theorem. □

We now generalize the result for the single-server VM maximization problem to the VM maximization problem where we have $m \geq 1$ physical servers for hosting the VMs. We utilize the results in [4] for the Separable Assignment Problem (SAP) where the authors show that a β-approximation for a single-server problem can be converted using LP-rounding to a $(1 - \frac{1}{e})$ β-approximation algorithm for the multi-server problem. Further, in the cases where the single server problem admits an FPTAS, the result can be strengthened to provide an approximation ratio of $(1 - \frac{1}{e})$. Thus, we can state the following theorem.

THEOREM 3.2.2. *For the multi-server VM maximization problem in the cluster-tree sharing model, there exists a poly-time algorithm that produces a solution that is at least $(1 - \frac{1}{e})$ of optimal, where n is the number of VMs and e is the transcendental number.*

3.2.2 VM packing

In the VM packing problem, we are given a set of virtual machines $V = \{v_1, v_2, \cdots v_n\}$, where each virtual machine v_i contains a set of pages P_i. The goal is to allocate all VMs to servers such that the memory capacity P of each server is not exceeded and the total number of servers are minimized.

First, we consider the VM packing problem in the cluster-tree sharing model. We can apply our algorithm for VM Maximization to derive a solution for VM packing as follows.

1. Set the profit value of all VMs to be 1. Run the VM maximization algorithm with the number of servers

m successively set to $1, 2, 2^2, \cdots 2^i, \cdots$, until at least $(1 - \frac{1}{e})n$ VMs are successfully packed by the algorithm.

2. Let m^* be the number of servers where step (1) succeeds. Repeatedly run our VM Maximization algorithm on the remainder of the unpacked VMs using m^* servers each time, until no more VMs are left.

THEOREM 3.2.3. *The above algorithm runs in polynomial time and achieves a solution that is within $O(\log n)$ factor of optimal for the VM packing problem on a cluster-tree* T *with n VMs.*

PROOF. Let OPT be the minimum number of servers needed to pack cluster-tree T. For any $m \geq OPT$, we know that our VM maximization algorithm packs at least $(1 - \frac{1}{e})n$ VMs into m servers, since each VM is assigned unit profit, the optimal profit is n, and Theorem 3.2.2 guarantees that our VM maximization algorithm achieves at least $(1 - \frac{1}{e})$ of the optimal profit. Thus, the m^* achieved in the step (1) of the above algorithm is at most $2 \cdot OPT - 2$. Each time the VM maximization algorithm is run in step (2), the number of VMs left unpacked reduces by a factor of $\frac{1}{e}$. Thus, in at most $\lceil \ln n \rceil$ rounds all VMs will be packed. The total number of servers used is at most

$$m^* \lceil \ln n \rceil \leq (2 \cdot OPT - 2) \lceil \ln n \rceil = O(\log n) \cdot OPT.$$

Our algorithm for VM packing runs in polynomial time since our polynomial time algorithm for VM Maximization is invoked $O(\log n)$ times. $\square$

For the simpler tree model, we now show that we can obtain a better approximation algorithm. Specifically, we present a 3-approximation algorithm for the VM packing problem in the tree model. We first compute a lower bound on the optimal number of servers needed to pack tree T. Next, we design a "greedy" algorithm that produces a packing solution for T that is within a factor 3 of this lower bound, and hence within a factor 3 of the optimal.

A fractional packing lower bound for the tree model.

One may think of the lower bound as the number of servers utilized by a "lower-bounding process" (LB process) that can fractionally pack VMs into servers. Since the LB process can split the pages associated with the nodes in tree T between multiple servers in a manner that a VM packing algorithm cannot, this fractional packing provides a lower bound on the number of servers that may or may not be achievable by a VM packing algorithm. Observe that the available server capacity varies as we move up the tree. The server capacity available at the root, denoted by $cap(root(\text{T}))$, is the full server capacity of P. The capacity of any node v, $cap(v)$, can be inductively defined to be the residual capacity after packing all the ancestors of v that are required to be present at the server, i.e., $cap(v) = cap(parent(v)) - w(v)$. Alternately,

$$cap(v) = P - \sum_{v' \text{ is ancestor of } v} w(v').$$

The LB process packs tree T in a bottom-up fashion as follows.

1. Pack each leaf v all by itself in a server of capacity $cap(v)$.

2. Suppose that a non-leaf node v has children v_i, $1 \leq i \leq l$. Inductively, suppose that each tree rooted at v_i, $1 \leq i \leq l$, has been packed "perfectly" by the LB process into servers of capacity $cap(v_i) = cap(v) - w(v)$ each. In a "perfect" packing all servers are full except possibly the last one. The LB process packs the tree rooted at v simply by consolidating the (at most l) partially-filled servers of its children into some number of full servers and at most one partially-filled server. This consolidation is easily achievable since the LB process is allowed to split any node across multiple servers. The full servers of its children are not repacked in any way. Finally, the server size is increased to $cap(v) = cap(v_i) + w(v)$ and a copy of v is added to each server to fill this increased capacity.

Let $size(v)$ represent the total size (in pages) required by the LB process to pack the subtree rooted at v. Note that $size(v)$ incorporates the weight of each node multiplied by the number of copies of the node that were made. Further, let the $count(v)$ denote the number of servers with capacity $cap(v)$ needed by the LB process to pack the tree rooted at v. Equivalently, $count(v)$ can be thought of as the number of copies of node v made by the LB process. The following inductive relationships hold. For each leaf v, $size(v) = w(v)$ and $count(v) = 1$. For each non-leaf node v with children v_i, $1 \leq i \leq l$,

$$count(v) = \left\lceil \frac{\sum_{i=1}^{l} size(v_i)}{cap(v) - w(v)} \right\rceil \quad (3)$$

$$size(v) = \sum_{i=1}^{l} size(v_i) + count(v) \cdot w(v) \quad (4)$$

THEOREM 3.2.4. *Any VM packing algorithm for tree* T *must pack at least $size(root(\text{T}))$ pages and utilize at least $count(root(\text{T}))$ servers.*

PROOF. We prove the theorem inductively starting from the leaves of T. In the base case, the theorem is clearly true for the leaves. Let a non-leaf node v have children v_i, $1 \leq i \leq l$. Assume inductively that any algorithm requires at least $size(v_i)$ pages to pack the trees rooted at v_i, for $1 \leq i \leq l$. Using Equation 3, we infer that any algorithm requires at least $count(v)$ copies of node v. Thus, using Equation 4, any algorithm must have size at least $size(v)$, since an additional $count(v)$ copies of v with $w(v)$ pages per copy are required. $\square$

A greedy packing algorithm.

Our algorithm GREEDY packs tree T as follows.

1. Run the LB process to compute $size(v)$ and $count(v)$ for each node in T.

2. If the $count(root(\text{T})) = 1$, then the entire tree T is packed into one server by the LB process. Likewise, the algorithm can pack the entire tree T into one server.

3. Else, if $count(root(\text{T})) \geq 1$, do the following.

   (a) Let k be the smallest count value of some node in T such that $k > 1$. Pick a node v with count k such that all its children have a count value of 1. View the set of VMs that are descendants of a child of v as a single item, resulting in as many items as the number of children of v. Note that each item fits into a single server of capacity P. Pack all items into servers of capacity P using any good bin packing algorithm, such as First Fit[2]. Now, all the VMs that are descendants of v have been packed.

(b) Remove the subtree rooted at v from T to form a new tree T$'$. Recursively, run GREEDY on T$'$.

LEMMA 3.2.5. *In step 3(a) of the* GREEDY *algorithm, the number of servers used to pack the tree rooted at v is at most $2 \cdot count(v) - 1$ servers.*

PROOF. Note that the First-Fit algorithm ensures at most one server is filled to half or less of its capacity, since any two such servers would have been combined by First-Fit into one server reducing the server count. Thus, since the LB process packs the tree rooted at v in $count(v)$ servers, our algorithm needs at most $2 \cdot count(v) - 1$ servers to pack the same contents, since otherwise two or more servers would be at most half full. □

THEOREM 3.2.6. *Algorithm* GREEDY *packs tree* T *using a number of servers that is within a factor of 3 of the optimal solution.*

PROOF. We use induction on $count(\text{root(T)})$. The base case of $count(\text{root(T)}) = 1$ is trivially true since GREEDY packs T in one server. Inductively, if $count(\text{root(T)}) > 1$, the tree T$'$ constructed in step 3(b) has a smaller count value than T. Note that the LB process constructs at least $count(v) - 1$ full servers at v. These full servers constructed by the LB process at node v will remain in its final packing of T unchanged, and is guaranteed to disappear when the tree rooted at v is removed to form T$'$. Thus,

$$count(\text{T}') \leq count(\text{T}) - count(v) + 1. \quad (5)$$

Applying the inductive hypothesis to T$'$, the algorithm packs T$'$ using at most $3 \cdot count(\text{root(T}'))$ servers. Additionally, by Lemma 3.2.5, the tree rooted at v in step 3(a) of the algorithm can be packed in $2 \cdot count(v) - 1$ servers. Thus, using Equation 5, the total number of servers used by the algorithm on tree T is at most

$$3 \cdot count(\text{T}') + 2 \cdot count(v) - 1$$
$$\leq \quad 3 \cdot (count(\text{T}) - count(v) + 1) + 2 \cdot count(v) - 1$$
$$\leq \quad 3 \cdot count(\text{root(T)}), \text{ since } count(v) \geq 2.$$

□

4. EXPERIMENTAL EVALUATION OF VM PACKING

We experimentally evaluated the performance of our algorithm GREEDY for VM packing in the tree model. To quantify the packing benefits due to real-world sharing that occurs from actual usage, we only used traces from our 31 volunteer machines (which represent "real" workloads) and

---

[2]While First Fit does not specify an order for processing the VMs, we have empirically observed that starting by placing two VMs that share the most pages in a server and consecutively picking the VM that shares the most with the most recent partially-packed server worked well in our implementation in Section 4.

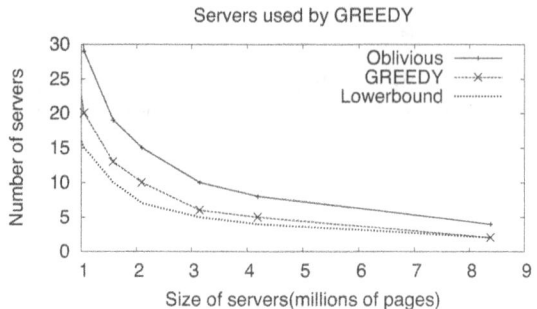

Figure 4: Comparison of server usage

did not consider the 20 laboratory VMs (which represent synthetic workloads). Since we needed a large number of traces for the VM packing experiment, we extracted 4 traces from each of the 31 volunteer machines. The traces were spaced far enough apart in time so as to not be closely correlated. We used the 124 VM traces obtained in this manner in our VM packing experiments.

We implemented GREEDY with a small twist. In step 3(a) of GREEDY when the First-Fit algorithm is applied on a set of VMs, we let our implementation of First-Fit utilize *all* available sharing between the VMs that are packed into a given server. That is, when First-Fit considers adding a new VM to a server, it assumes that any page present in the new VM that is already present in some VM in the server can be shared. Note that some of the pages shared in this fashion may not be explicitly captured in the tree model; We use this GREEDY variant since it better captures how page sharing works in actual virtualization platforms—while the sharing in the tree model guides the GREEDY VM packing, once VMs are co-located, the virtualization platform (i.e., hypervisor) will exploit *all* of the shared pages, and not just the subset identified by the tree model at packing time. Thus, this change lets our implementation capture the actual sharing benefit and not just the fraction identified by the tree model.

4.1 Server usage

The goal of VM packing is to minimize the number of servers needed to pack a given set of VMs. We compare the performance of GREEDY to that of a good sharing-oblivious algorithm. We implemented the Modified First Fit Decreasing (MFFD) algorithm [17] that is sharing-oblivious and is one of the best efficiently computable approximation schemes for bin packing. In addition, we compare GREEDY with a lower bound on the optimal number of servers required for packing the VMs. Note that the fractional packing lower bound derived in Section 3.2.2 applies to algorithms that only use the inter-VM sharing captured in the tree model. Since our implementation of GREEDY could use some additional sharing that is not captured in the tree model, it would be fairer to compare GREEDY with a lower bound derived for the general sharing model.

4.1.1 A server lower bound for general sharing

We derive two lower bounds and take the maximum of both bounds. Since these are lower bounds for general sharing, we make no assumptions about how the pages are shared. The first lower bound is a simple size bound. Let OPT

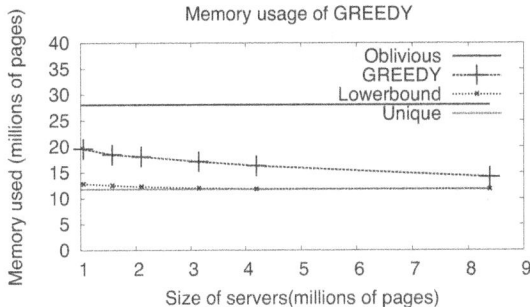

Figure 5: Comparison of memory usage

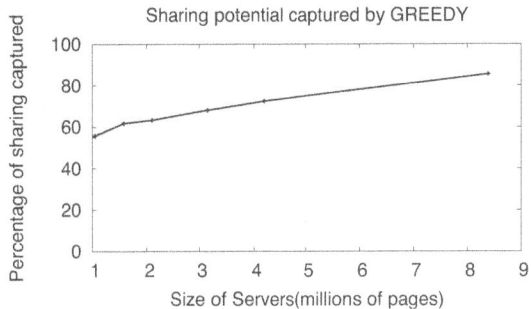

Figure 6: Realized sharing potential of GREEDY

be the smallest number of servers required to pack the given set of VMs, $V = \{v_1, v_2, \cdots v_n\}$. Let $UNIQ(V)$ be the set of unique pages contained in all the VMs in V, and let P be the server capacity. Clearly, $\lceil |UNIQ(V)|/P \rceil$ servers are needed to pack all the VMs.

Tp derive the second lower bound, we create a new set of VMs $V' = \{v_1', v_2', \cdots v_n'\}$ from the original set of VMs $V = \{v_1, v_2, \cdots v_n\}$ by removing each shared page from all but one of the VMs that contain it. Note that the optimal number of servers required to pack V' (call it OPT') is a lower bound on OPT. Further, since the VMs in V' share no pages, they can be packed with a good bin packing algorithm such as MFFD. Let $MFFD(V')$ denote the number of servers used by MFFD for the VMs in V'. From [17], we know that $MFFD(V') \leq \frac{71}{60} OPT' + 1$. Thus,

$$OPT \geq OPT' \geq \left\lceil \frac{60}{71}(MFFD(V') - 1) \right\rceil$$

Combining the two bounds, we have

$$OPT \geq \max \left\{ \lceil |UNIQ(V)|/P \rceil, \left\lceil \frac{60}{71}(MFFD(V') - 1) \right\rceil \right\}.$$

4.1.2 Results

Figure 4 shows the performance of GREEDY in comparison with the performance of sharing-oblivious MFFD (marked "Oblivious" in the figure) and the lower bound derived in Section 4.1.1. As the server memory capacity increases, we see a decrease in the number of servers and a decrease in the gap between the performance of GREEDY and the lower bound. It also shows that GREEDY is within 20% to 43% of the lower bound and 32% to 50% more efficient than the sharing-oblivious MFFD scheme. Furthermore, regardless of server size, GREEDY significantly reduces the number of servers required compared to a sharing oblivious algorithm such as MFFD. We see that as the server size increases the relative performance of GREEDY to MFFD increases from 32% to 50%, since the larger server sizes allow more sharing to be exploited by GREEDY.

4.2 Memory usage

We now show that GREEDY exploits inter-VM page sharing to decrease the total memory footprint.

4.2.1 A memory lower bound for general sharing

We derive a lower bound on the total memory footprint required for packing a set of VMs $V = \{v_1, v_2, \cdots v_n\}$ in the

general sharing model. For any $V' \subseteq V$, let $UNIQ(V')$ denote the set of unique pages contained in the VMs in set V'. For any page p, let $V_p = \{v \in V : VM\ v\ contains\ page\ p\}$. Note that each page p must have at least $\lceil |UNIQ(V_p)|/P \rceil$ replicas in any VM packing of V, where P is capacity of the server. Thus, the following expression is a lower bound on the total memory footprint of any packing of V:

$$\sum_{p \in UNIQ(V)} \lceil |UNIQ(V_p)|/P \rceil.$$

4.2.2 Results

In Figure 5, we compare the memory usage of GREEDY with that of any sharing-oblivious algorithm. Note that any sharing-oblivious algorithm uses a memory footprint that equals the sum total of the sizes of all the VMs (marked "Oblivious" in the figure). In addition, we plot the lower bound for the memory footprint of any VM packing algorithm in the general sharing model that we derived in Section 4.2.1 (marked "Lowerbound" in the figure). We also plot $|UNIQ(V)|$, the number of unique pages in the set of VMs, which is a lower bound on the memory footprint of any algorithm independent of server memory capacity (marked "Unique" in the figure).

From Figure 5, we see that as the server memory capacity increases, the gap between the performance of GREEDY and the lower bound decreases. Further, GREEDY approaches the unique pages bound (i.e., perfect sharing) as the server memory capacity increases. Furthermore, we can see that GREEDY uses substantially less memory than any sharing-oblivious algorithm, specifically it uses between 25% to 57% fewer pages.

Another metric for analyzing the performance of GREEDY is by evaluating its realized sharing potential. Sharing potential is defined as the *maximum* achievable reduction in the memory footprint for a given server memory capacity P. Note that sharing potential is a non-decreasing function of P. As P tends to infinity, sharing potential tends to the difference between the total number of pages and the total unique pages in the set of VMs. Sharing potential is hard to compute exactly, since the computing the optimal reduction is itself NP-Hard. However, we can upper bound the sharing potential by using the lower bound on the memory footprint in Section 4.2.1. The *realized* sharing potential of a VM packing algorithm is percentage of the sharing potential that is actually achieved by the algorithm. A lower bound on the realized sharing potential of a VM packing algorithm can be computed using an upper bound for the sharing po-

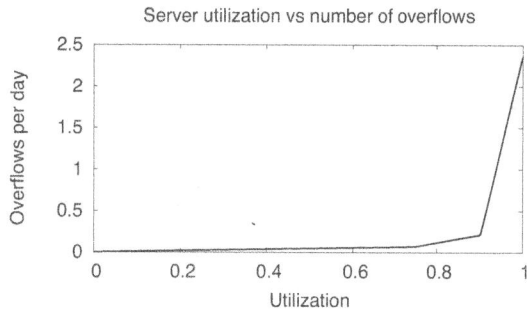

Figure 7: **Memory overflows seen at different memory utilization levels.**

tential. Using this process, we compute a lower bound on the realized sharing potential of GREEDY in Figure 6. We see that as the server memory capacity increases, GREEDY is able to realize an increasing percentage of the sharing potential, since it can pack more VMs on each server for larger server memory capacities, allowing for a larger amount of sharing to be captured. For around 4M memory pages, more than 70% of the sharing potential is realized by GREEDY.

4.3 Memory overflow

As sharing patterns and memory requirements of VMs change over time, the number of pages required on a server can become greater than its capacity, causing memory to become over-committed, a phenomenon that we term as "memory overflow". Memory overflow can cause excessive page faulting degrading the performance of the VMs. This might in turn trigger the potentially expensive operation of reallocating all the VMs in accordance with their current requirements and sharing characteristics. With this in mind, we study how stable the packings produced by GREEDY are over time. Our primary finding is that if we let GREEDY underutilize each server by a small percentage, server overflows become significantly rarer. The reason is that the extra unallocated memory capacity absorbs some of the variations caused by changing memory sharing characteristics.

We study the tradeoff between server memory utilization and overflow. For a given utilization u, $0 \leq u \leq 1$, algorithm GREEDY allocates VMs such that the memory capacity of each server is at most u times the actual server memory capacity. Using 3 physical servers with a capacity of 4194304 pages and the traces from the 31 volunteer machines, we found that almost all server overflows can be avoided by utilizing the servers to only 90% of capacity. Figure 7 shows us that for 90% utilization, we see only 3 faults over the course of a 2 week time frame. This gives an expected 4.67 days until a repacking of VMs due to overflow is required. On the other hand, fully utilizing the physical servers to 100% of its memory capacity results in 33 faults and an expected 0.42 days until reallocation is required.

5. RELATED WORK

Systems work. Content-based page sharing for virtual machines was implemented in the Disco system [1], incorporated in VMware ESX [14] and later in Xen [9]. In these systems, the hypervisor uses hashing and page comparison to identify and share identical pages running on the same

physical server. There has been recent systems work in exploiting sharing at the sub-page level by sharing portions of a page such as the Difference Engine system [5]. While we explicitly consider only page-level sharing in our work, our models and results can be extended to account for sub-page level sharing as well.

While much of the work content-based page sharing focus on effectively sharing the memory contents of VMs located on the same physical server, the potential for exploiting inter-VM sharing by intelligently colocating VMs was first studied in [16]. In [16], the authors provide a compact fingerprinting scheme using bloom filters that can identify VMs with a large sharing potential, and show that "sharing aware" placement has the potential to significantly improve memory usage. Our work takes the next step by developing formal models and provably-good algorithms for sharing-aware placement of VMs on physical servers with the goal of achieving the potential benefits of inter-VM sharing.

In our work, we have focused on optimizing memory resources, whereas the general VM colocation also incorporates other server resources such CPU, disk, and network. For instance, the VMware Distributed Resource Scheduler [13] monitors CPU, network, and memory utilization in clusters of virtual machines and use migration for load balancing. We view our work as integrating into the larger multi-resource VM colocation framework by helping incorporate sharing-aware VM placement into these systems.

Algorithmic work. There has been no prior algorithmic work in the VM maximization problem per se, though we utilize algorithmic techniques similar to that used in the closely-related knapsack problem [11]. Note that the special case of VM maximization where VMs have no shared pages is the knapsack problem. Numerous variants of the knapsack problem have been studied over the years, particularly relevant is the partially-ordered knapsack problem where the items that are packed must obey precedence constraints expressed as a partial order [7, 10]. In fact, our FPTAS for the single-server VM maximization problem for cluster-tree sharing uses the "left-right" dynamic programming technique that was developed for the tree knapsack problem in [7].

A generalization of the knapsack problem where a submodular function describes the cumulative size of any collection of items was recently studied by Fleischer and Svitkina[12]. They present a bi-criteria randomized $\left(\sqrt{\frac{n}{\log n}}, \frac{1}{2} \right)$-approximation algorithm, where a (ρ, σ)-approximation is defined as a solution where the knapsack is allowed to overflow by a factor of ρ and the profit function is guaranteed to be within a factor of σ of optimal. Furthermore, they proved a lower bound on all approximation schemes for this problem of $\frac{\rho}{\sigma} = \Omega \left(\sqrt{\frac{n}{\log n}} \right)$. While page sharing in VMs is submodular, it is much more approximable than the arbitrary submodular functions considered in [12].

A special case of VM packing where the VMs do not share any pages is the classical bin packing problem [2]. While dozens of variants of bin packing have been studied in the literature over the past decade, there is no prior algorithmic work to our knowledge that considers the interesting case where the cumulative size of the packed items can be smaller than the sum of the individual sizes due to sharing.

6. CONCLUSIONS AND OPEN PROBLEMS

In this paper, we initiated the study of sharing models and sharing-aware algorithms for VM colocation. Our work exposes the tradeoff between complex sharing models that capture all of the inter-VM sharing but are hard to exploit algorithmically, and structured hierarchical models that ignore some of the inter-VM sharing but are more amenable to provably-efficient algorithm design. Using actual VM traces, we demonstrated that hierarchical sharing models can capture a large percentage of the inter-VM sharing, making them a viable option for real-world VM colocation. Our experiments show that our VM packing algorithm exploits inter-VM sharing to substantially reduce number of servers and memory footprint and that these packings can be relatively stable over time.

Our work opens a number of exciting directions for future research. A key direction is tightening the approximation bounds, both better algorithms and lower bounds, for the VM packing problem (see Figure 1). For instance, is there an asymptotic PTAS for VM packing in the hierarchical sharing models, or even better approximation ratios? Bin packing, a special case of VM packing, has an asymptotic PTAS [3, 8], though variants are known not to have an asymptotic PTAS'es [15]. While our algorithms work in "batch mode", an important research direction is extending our work to an online setting where VM packing occurs as and when VMs are created and destroyed. Further, our work focused primarily on the server memory resource. Extending our work to multi-resource VM colocation that takes into account memory, CPU, and network resources is another important direction for future work. Finally, studying how our techniques can be applied to cloud computing platforms of the future is an interesting avenue for research. As modern data centers and cloud platforms evolve, so will the structural properties of VM sharing. Investigating these platforms may lead to new models and algorithms for reducing the operational cost of the virtualization service providers.

7. ACKNOWLEDGMENTS

We thank our shepherd Anne Benoit and the anonymous reviewers for their comments. We thank Sean Barker for his help with gathering synthetic laboratory traces and the numerous volunteers in our department for contributing memory traces for this study. The work of Michael Sindelar and Ramesh Sitaraman was supported in part by an NSF Award CNS-05-19894. Much of the work of Michael Sindelar was done while he was at UMass, Amherst. The work of Prashant Shenoy was supported in part by NSF grants OCI-1032765, CNS-0916972 and CNS-0720616.

8. REFERENCES

[1] E. Bugnion, S. Devine, and M. Rosenblum. DISCO: Running Commodity Operating Systems on Scalable Multiprocessors. In *SOSP*, pages 143–156, 1997.

[2] E. G. Coffman, Jr., M. R. Garey, and D. S. Johnson. Approximation algorithms for bin packing: A survey. In *Approximation Algorithms for NP-hard Problems*, pages 46–93, Boston, MA, USA, 1997. PWS Publishing Co.

[3] W. Fernandez de la Vega and G. Lueker. Bin packing can be solved within $1+\varepsilon$ in linear time. *Combinatorica*, 1(4):349–355, 1981.

[4] L. Fleischer, M. X. Goemans, V. S. Mirrokni, and M. Sviridenko. Tight approximation algorithms for maximum general assignment problems. In *Proceedings of the Seventeenth annual ACM-SIAM Symposium on Discrete Algorithms (SODA)*, pages 611–620, New York, NY, USA, 2006. ACM.

[5] D. Gupta, S. Lee, M. Vrable, S. Savage, A. C. Snoeren, G. Varghese, G. M. Voelker, and A. Vahdat. Difference engine: Harnessing memory redundancy in virtual machines. In *Usenix OSDI*, December 2008.

[6] M. Hajiaghayi, K. Jain, K. Konwar, L. Lau, I. Mandoiu, A. Russell, A. Shvartsman, and V. Vazirani. The minimum k-colored subgraph problem in haplotyping and DNA primer selection. In *Proceedings of the International Workshop on Bioinformatics Research and Applications (IWBRA)*, 2006.

[7] D. Johnson and K. Niemi. On knapsacks, partitions, and a new dynamic programming technique for trees. *Mathematics of Operations Research*, 8(1):1–14, 1983.

[8] N. Karmarkar and R. Karp. An efficient approximation scheme for the one-dimensional bin-packing problem. In *23rd Annual Symposium on Foundations of Computer Science*, pages 312–320. IEEE, 1982.

[9] J. Kloster, J. Kristensen, and A. Mejlholm. On the Feasibility of Memory Sharing: Content-Based Page Sharing in the Xen Virtual Machine Monitor. Master's thesis, Department of Computer Science, Aalborg University, June 2006.

[10] S. Kolliopoulos and G. Steiner. Partially ordered knapsack and applications to scheduling. *Discrete Applied Mathematics*, 155(8):889–897, 2007.

[11] S. Martello and P. Toth. *Knapsack problems: algorithms and computer implementations*. Wiley & Sons, 1990.

[12] Z. Svitkina and L. Fleischer. Submodular approximation: Sampling-based algorithms and lower bounds. In *FOCS*, pages 697–706. IEEE Computer Society, 2008.

[13] VMware. DRS performance and best practices. 2008.

[14] C. Waldspurger. Memory Resource Management in VMWare ESX Server. In *Proceedings of the Fifth Symposium on Operating System Design and Implementation (OSDI'02)*, Dec. 2002.

[15] G. Woeginger. There is no asymptotic PTAS for two-dimensional vector packing. *Information Processing Letters*, 64(6):293–297, 1997.

[16] T. Wood, G. Tarasuk-Levin, P. Shenoy, P. Desnoyers, E. Cecchet, and M. Corner. Memory buddies: Exploiting page sharing for smart colocation in virtualized data centers. In *2009 ACM SIGPLAN/SIGOPS International Conference on Virtual Execution Environments (VEE 2009)*, Washington, DC, USA, March 2009.

[17] M. Yue and L. Zhang. A simple proof of the inequality $MFFD(L) \leq 71/60\ OPT(L) + 1, L$ for MFFD bin-packing algorithm. *Acta Mathematicae Applicatae Sinica (English Series)*, 11:318–330, July 1995.

Data-Oblivious External-Memory Algorithms for the Compaction, Selection, and Sorting of Outsourced Data

Michael T. Goodrich
Dept. of Computer Science
University of California, Irvine
Irvine, CA 92697
goodrich@acm.org

ABSTRACT

We present data-oblivious algorithms in the external-memory model for compaction, selection, and sorting. Motivation for such problems comes from clients who use outsourced data storage services and wish to mask their data access patterns. We show that compaction and selection can be done data-obliviously using $O(N/B)$ I/Os, and sorting can be done, with a high probability of success, using $O((N/B)\log_{M/B}(N/B))$ I/Os.

Categories and Subject Descriptors

F.2.2 [**Analysis of Algorithms and Problem Complexity**]: Non-numerical Algorithms and Problems

General Terms

Algorithms, Theory

Keywords

External memory, data-oblivious algorithms, sorting.

1. INTRODUCTION

Online data storage is becoming a large and growing industry, in which companies provide large storage capabilities for hosting outsourced data for individual or corporate users, such as with Amazon S3 and Google Docs. The companies that provide such services typically give their users guarantees about the availability and integrity of their data, but they often have commercial interests in learning as much as possible about their users' data.

Clearly, a necessary first step towards achieving privacy is for users to store their data in encrypted form, e.g., using a secret key that is known only to the users. Simply encrypting one's data is not sufficient to achieve privacy in this context, however, since information about the content of a user's data is leaked by the pattern in which the user accesses it [9].

Problem Statement. The problem of protecting the privacy of a user's data accesses in an outsourced data storage facility can be defined in terms of *external-memory data-oblivious RAM computations*. In this framework, a group of users, who we will call "Alices," share in parallel a large data set, which is stored on a data storage server owned by Bob, who provides the Alices with an interface that supports indexed addressing of their data, so each word has a unique address. Each Alice has a CPU with a private cache, which can be used for data-dependent computations. As in the standard external-memory model (e.g., see [1]), where external storage is typically assumed to be on a disk drive, data on the external storage device is accessed and organized in contiguous blocks, with each block holding B words, where $B \geq 1$. That is, this is an adaptation of the standard external-memory model so that the external disk drive is associated with Bob and each Alice has a CPU and much smaller cache. The service provider, Bob, is trying to learn as much as possible about the content of the data shared by the Alices and he can view the sequence and location of all of their disk accesses. But he cannot see the content of what is read or written, for we assume it is encrypted using a semantically secure encryption scheme such that re-encryption of the same value is indistinguishable from an encryption of a different value (with all the Alices sharing a secret key). Moreover, Bob cannot view the content or access patterns of any private cache. We parameterize this model by assuming that each Alice has a private cache of size M, that the size of data set stored on Bob's server is N, and data is transfered between Bob's memory and any private cache in contiguous blocks of size B. Using terminology of the cryptography literature, Bob is assumed to be an *honest-but-curious* adversary [13], in that he correctly performs all protocols and does not tamper with any data, but he is nevertheless interested in learning as much as possible about the data he storing on behalf of the group of Alices.

Periodically, one of the Alices will connect to the server, Bob, to perform some computation so as to solve some combinatorial problem, $\mathcal{P}$ (like sorting or selection), on the shared data. During this connection, she has exclusive access to the data stored by Bob so that she can complete a sequence of block I/Os on his memory to solve the problem $\mathcal{P}$, and when she is finished, she disconnects her session with Bob. We say that Alice's sequence of I/Os during this session is *data-oblivious* for solving the problem $\mathcal{P}$ if the distribution of this sequence depends only on $\mathcal{P}$, N, M, and B, and the length of the access sequence itself. In particular, this distribution should be independent of the data values in the input. Put another way, this definition of a data-oblivious computation means that $\Pr(S \mid \mathcal{M}, \mathcal{P}, N, M, B)$, the probability that Bob sees an access sequence, S, conditioned on a specific initial configuration of external memory, $\mathcal{M}$, and the values of $\mathcal{P}$, N, M, and B, satisfies

$$\Pr(S \mid \mathcal{M}, \mathcal{P}, N, M, B) = \Pr(S \mid \mathcal{M}', \mathcal{P}, N, M, B),$$

for any memory configuration $\mathcal{M}' \neq \mathcal{M}$ such that $|\mathcal{M}'| = |\mathcal{M}|$. Note, in particular, that this implies that the length, $|S|$, of Alice's access sequence cannot depend on specific input values. Examples of data-oblivious access sequences for an array, A, of size N, in Bob's external memory, include the following (assuming $B = 1$):

- Simulating a circuit, $\mathcal{C}$, with its inputs taken in order from A. For instance, $\mathcal{C}$ could be a Boolean circuit or an AKS sorting network [2].

- Accessing the cells of A according to a random hash function, $h(i)$, as $A[h(1)]$, $A[h(2)]$, ..., $A[h(n)]$, or random permutation, $\pi(i)$, as $A[\pi(1)]$, $A[\pi(2)]$, ..., $A[\pi(n)]$.

Examples of computations on A that would *not* be data-oblivious include the following:

- Using the standard merge-sort or quick-sort algorithm to sort A. (Neither of these well-known algorithms is data-oblivious.)

- Using values in A as indices for a hash table, T, and accessing them as $T[h(A[1])]$, $T[h(A[2])]$, ..., $T[h(A[n])]$, where h is a random hash function. (For instance, think of what happens if all the values in A are equal and how improbable the resulting n-way collision in T would be.)

This last example is actually a little subtle. It is, in general, not data-oblivious to access a hash table, T, in this way, but note that such an access sequence *would* be data-oblivious if the elements in A are always guaranteed to be distinct. In this case, each such access in T would be to a random location and every possible sequence of such accesses in T would be equally likely for any set of distinct values in A, assuming our random hash function, h, satisfies the random oracle model (e.g., see [3]).

Related Prior Results. Data-oblivious sorting is a classic algorithmic problem, which Knuth [19] studies in some depth, since deterministic schemes give rise to sorting networks, such as the theoretically-optimal $O(n \log n)$ AKS network [2] as well as practical sorting networks [21]. Randomized data-oblivious sorting algorithms running in $O(n \log n)$ time and succeeding with high probability are likewise studied by Leighton and Plaxton [23] and Goodrich [15]. Moreover, data-oblivious sorting is finding applications to privacy-preserving secure multi-party computations [28]. For the related selection problem, Leighton *et al.* [22] give a randomized data-oblivious solution that runs in $O(n \log \log n)$ time and they give a matching lower bound for methods exclusively based on compare-exchange operations.

Chaudhry and Cormen [8] argue that data-oblivious external-memory sorting algorithms have several advantages, including good load-balancing and the avoidance of poor performance on "bad" inputs. They give a data-oblivious sorting algorithm for the parallel disk model and analyze its performance experimentally [7]. But their method is size-limited and does not achieve the optimal I/O complexity of previous external-memory sorting algorithms (e.g., see [1]), which use $O((N/B) \log_{M/B}(N/B))$ I/Os. None of the previous external-memory sorting algorithms that use $O((N/B) \log_{M/B}(N/B))$ I/Os are data-oblivious, however.

Goodrich and Mitzenmacher [16] show that any RAM algorithm, $\mathcal{A}$, can be simulated in a data-oblivious fashion in the external-memory model so that each memory access performed by $\mathcal{A}$ has an overhead of $O(\min\{\log^2(N/B), \log^2_{M/B}(N/B) \log_2 N\})$ amortized I/Os in the simulation, and which is data-oblivious with high probability (w.v.h.p.)[1], which both improves and extends a result

of Goldreich and Ostrovsky [14] to the I/O model. The overhead of the Goodrich-Mitzenmacher simulation is optimal for the case when N/B is polynomial in M/B and is based on an "inner loop" use of a deterministic data-oblivious sorting algorithm that uses $O((N/B) \log^2_{M/B}(N/B))$ I/Os, but this result is not optimal in general.

Our Results. We give data-oblivious external-memory algorithms for compaction, selection, quantile computation, and sorting of outsourced data. Our compaction and selection algorithms use $O(N/B)$ I/Os and our sorting algorithm uses $O((N/B) \log_{M/B}(N/B))$ I/Os, which is asymptotically optimal [1]. All our algorithms are randomized and succeed with high probability. Our results also imply that one can improve the expected amortized overhead for a randomized external-memory data-oblivious RAM simulation to be $O(\log_{M/B}(N/B) \log_2 N)$.

Our main result is for the sorting problem, as we are not aware of any asymptotically-optimal oblivious external-memory sorting algorithm prior to our work. Still, our other results are also important, in that our sorting algorithm is based on our algorithms for selection and quantiles, which in turn are based on new methods for data-oblivious data compaction. We show, for instance, that efficient compaction leads to a selection algorithm that uses $O(n)$ I/Os, and succeed w.v.h.p., where $n = O(N/B)$. Interestingly, this result beats a lower bound for the complexity of parallel selection networks, of $\Omega(n \log \log n)$, due to Leighton *et al.* [22]. Our selection result doesn't invalidate their lower bound, however, for their lower bound is for circuits that only use compare-exchange operations, whereas our algorithm uses other "blackbox" primitive operations besides compare-exchange, including addition, subtraction, data copying, and random functions. Thus, our result demonstrates the power of using operations other than compare-exchange in a data-oblivious selection algorithm.

Our algorithms are based on a number of new techniques for data-oblivious algorithm design, including the use of a recent data structure by Goodrich and Mitzenmacher [17], known as the invertible Bloom lookup table. We show in this paper how this data structure can be used in a data-oblivious way to solve the compaction problem, which in turn leads to efficient methods for selection, quantiles, and sorting. Our methods also use a butterfly-like routing network and a "shuffle-and-deal" technique reminiscent of Valiant-Brebner routing [27], so as to avoid data-revealing access patterns.

Given the motivation of our algorithms from outsourced data privacy, we make some reasonable assumptions regarding the computational models used by some of our algorithms. For instance, for some of our results, we assume that $B \geq \log^\epsilon(N/B)$, which we call the *wide-block* assumption. This is, in fact, equivalent or weaker than several similar assumptions in the external-memory literature (e.g., see [4, 24]). In addition, we sometimes also use a weak *tall-cache* assumption that $M \geq B^{1+\epsilon}$, for some small constant $\epsilon > 0$, which is also common in the external-memory literature (e.g., see [6, 11]).

2. INVERTIBLE BLOOM FILTERS

As mentioned above, one of the tools we use in our algorithms involves a data-oblivious use of the invertible Bloom lookup table of Goodrich and Mitzenmacher [17], which is itself based on the invertible Bloom filter data structure of Eppstein and Goodrich [10].

An invertible Bloom lookup table, $\mathcal{B}$, is a randomized data structure storing a set of key-value pairs. It supports the following operations (among others):

- insert(x, y): insert the key-value pair, (x, y), into $\mathcal{B}$. This operation always succeeds, assuming that keys are distinct.

---

[1] In this paper, we take the phrase "with high probability" to mean that the probability is at least $1 - 1/(N/B)^d$, for a given constant $d \geq 1$.

- delete(x, y): remove the key-value pair, (x, y), from $\mathcal{B}$. This operation assumes (x, y) is in $\mathcal{B}$.

- get(x): lookup and return the value, y, associated with the key, x, in $\mathcal{B}$. This operation may fail, with some probability.

- listEntries: list all the key-value pairs being stored in $\mathcal{B}$. With low probability, this operation may return a partial list along with an "list-incomplete" error condition.

When an invertible-map Bloom lookup table $\mathcal{B}$ is first created, it initializes a table, T, of a specified capacity, m, which is initially empty. The table T is the main storage used to implement $\mathcal{B}$. Each of the cells in T stores a constant number of fields, each of which is a single memory word or block. Insertions and deletions can proceed independent of the capacity m and can even create situations where the number, n, of key-value pairs in $\mathcal{B}$ can be much larger than m. Nevertheless, the space used for B remains $O(m)$. The get and listEntries methods, on the other hand, only guarantee good probabilistic success when $n < m$.

Like a traditional Bloom filter [5], an invertible Bloom lookup table uses a set of k random hash functions, $h_1, h_2, \ldots, h_k$, defined on the universe of keys, to determine where items are stored. In this case, we also assume that, for any x, the $h_i(x)$ values are distinct, which can be achieved by a number of methods, including partitioning. Each cell contains three fields:

- a `count` field, which counts the number of entries that have been mapped to this cell,

- a `keySum` field, which is the sum of all the keys that have been mapped to this cell,

- a `valueSum` field, which is the sum of all the values that have been mapped to this cell.

Given these fields, which are all initially set to 0, performing the insert operation is fairly straightforward:

- insert(x, y):
   for each (distinct) $h_i(x)$ value, for $i = 1, \ldots, k$ **do**
      add 1 to $T[h_i(x)]$.`count`
      add x to $T[h_i(x)]$.`keySum`
      add y to $T[h_i(x)]$.`valueSum`

The delete method is basically the reverse of that above. The listEntries method is similarly simple[2]:

- listEntries:
   while there is an $i \in [1, m]$ s. t. $T[i]$.`count` = 1 **do**
      output ($T[i]$.`keySum`, $T[i]$.`valueSum`)
      call delete($T[i]$.`keySum`)

It is a fairly straightforward exercise to implement this method in $O(m)$ time, say, by using a link-list-based priority queue of cells in T indexed by their `count` fields and modifying the delete method to update this queue each time it deletes an entry from $\mathcal{B}$. If, at the end of the while-loop, all the entries in T are empty, then we say that the method succeeded.

Lemma 1 (Goodrich and Mitzenmacher) [17]: *Given an invertible Bloom lookup table, T, of size $m = \lceil \delta k n \rceil$, holding at most n key-value pairs, the listEntries method succeeds with probability $1 - 1/n^c$, where $c \geq 1$ is any given constant and $k \geq 2$ and $\delta \geq 2$ are constant depending on c.*

---

[2]We describe this method in a destructive fashion—if one wants a non-destructive method, then one should first create a copy of the table T as a backup.

The important observation about the functioning of the invertible Bloom lookup table, for the purposes of this paper, is that the sequence of memory locations accessed during an insert(x, y) method is oblivious to the value y and the number of items already stored in the table. That is, the locations accessed in performing an insert method depend only on the key, x. The listEntries method, on the other hand, is not oblivious to keys or values.

3. DATA-OBLIVIOUS COMPACTION

In this section, we describe efficient data-oblivious algorithms for compaction. In this problem, we are given an array, A, of N cells, at most R of which are marked as "distinguished" (e.g., using a marked bit or a simple test) and we want to produce an array, D, of size $O(R)$ that contains all the distinguished items from A. Note that this is the fundamental operation done during disk defragmentation, which is a natural operation that one would want to do in an outsourced file system, since users of such systems are charged for the space they use.

We say that such a compaction algorithm is *order-preserving* if the distinguished items in A remain in their same relative order in D. In addition, we say that a compaction algorithm is *tight* if it compacts A to an array D of size exactly R. If this size of D is merely $O(R)$, and we allow for some empty cells in D, then we say that the compaction is *loose*. Of course, we can always use a data-oblivious sorting algorithm, such as with the following suboptimal result, to perform a tight order-preserving compaction.

Lemma 2 (Goodrich and Mitzenmacher) [16]: *Given an array A of size N, one can sort A with a deterministic data-oblivious algorithm that uses $O((N/B) \log^2_{M/B}(N/B))$ I/Os, assuming $B \geq 1$ and $M \geq 2B$.*

In the remainder of this section, we give several compaction algorithms, which exhibit various trade-offs between performance and the compaction properties listed above. Incidentally, each of these algorithms is used in at least one of our algorithms for selection, quantiles, and sorting.

Data Consolidation. Each of our compaction algorithms uses a data-oblivious consolidation preprocessing operation. In this operation, we are given an array A of size N such that at most $R \leq N$ elements in A are marked as "distinguished." The output of this step is an array, A', of $\lceil N/B \rceil$ blocks, such that $\lfloor R/B \rfloor$ blocks in A' are completely full of distinguished elements and at most one block in A' is partially full of distinguished elements. All other blocks in A' are completely empty of distinguished elements. This consolidation step uses $O(N/B)$ I/Os, assuming only that $B \geq 1$ and $M \geq 2B$, and it is order-preserving with respect to the distinguished elements in A.

We start by viewing A as being subdivided into $\lceil N/B \rceil$ blocks of size B each (it is probably already stored this way in Bob's memory). We then scan the blocks of A from beginning to end, keeping a block, x, in Alice's memory as we go. Initially, we just read in the first block of A and let x be this block. Each time after this that we scan a block, y, of A, from Bob's memory, if the distinguished elements from x and y in Alice's memory can form a full block, then we write out to Bob's memory a full block to A' of the first B distinguished elements in $x \cup y$, maintaining the relative order of these distinguished elements. Otherwise, we merge the fewer than B distinguished elements in Alice's memory into the single block, x, again, maintaining their relative order, and we write out an empty block to A' in Bob's memory. We then repeat. When we are done scanning A, we write out x to Bob's memory; hence, the access pattern for this method is a simple scan of A and A', which is clearly data-oblivious. Thus, we have the following.

Lemma 3: *Suppose we are given an array A of size N, with at most R of its elements marked as distinguished. We can deterministically consolidate A into an array A' of $\lceil N/B \rceil$ blocks of size B each with a data-oblivious algorithm that uses $\lceil N/B \rceil$ I/Os, such that all but possibly the last block in A' are completely full of distinguished elements or completely empty of distinguished elements. This computation assumes that $B \geq 1$ and $M \geq 2B$, and it preserves the relative order of distinguished elements.*

Tight Order-Preserving Compaction for Sparse Arrays. The semi-oblivious property of the invertible Bloom lookup table allows us to efficiently perform tight order-preserving compaction in a data-oblivious fashion, provided the input array is sufficiently sparse. Given the consolidation preprocessing step (Lemma 3), we describe this result in the RAM model (which could be applied to blocks that are viewed as memory words for the external-memory model), with $n = N/B$ and $r = R/B$.

Theorem 4: *Suppose we are given an array, A, of size n, holding at most $r \leq n$ distinguished items. We can perform a tight order-preserving compaction of the distinguished items from A into an array D of size r in a data-oblivious fashion in the RAM model in $O(n + r \log^2 r)$ time. This method succeeds with probability $1 - 1/r^c$, for any given constant $c \geq 1$.*

PROOF. We create an invertible Bloom lookup table, T, of size $3r$. Then we map each entry, $A[i]$, into T using the key-value pair $(i, A[i])$. Note that the insertion algorithm begins by reading k cells of T whose locations in this case depend only on i (recall that k is the number of hash functions). If the entry $A[i]$ is distinguished, then this operation involves changing the fields of these cells in T according to the invertible Bloom lookup table insertion method and then writing them back to T. If, on the other hand, $A[i]$ is not distinguished, then we return the fields back to each cell $T[h_j(i)]$ unchanged (but re-encrypted so that Bob cannot tell of the cells were changed or not). Since the memory accesses in T are the same independent of whether $A[i]$ is distinguished or not, each key we use is merely an index i, and insertion into an invertible Bloom lookup table is oblivious to all factors other than the key, this insertion algorithm is data-oblivious. Given the output from this insertion phase, which is the table T, of size $O(r)$, we then perform a RAM simulation of the listEntries method to list out the distinguished items in T, using the simulation result of Goodrich and Mitzenmacher [16]. The simulation algorithm performs the actions of a RAM computation in a data-oblivious fashion such that each step of the RAM computation has an amortized time overhead of $O(\log^2 r)$. Thus, simulating the listEntries method in a data-oblivious fashion takes $O(r \log^2 r)$ time and succeeds with probability $1 - 1/r^c$, for any given constant $c > 0$, by Lemma 1. The size of the output array, D, is exactly r. Note that, at this point, the items in the array D are not necessarily in the same relative order that they were in A. So, to make this compaction operation order-preserving, we complete the algorithm by performing a data-oblivious sorting of D, using each item's original position in A as its key, say by Lemma 2. $\square$

Thus, we can perform tight data-oblivious compaction for sparse arrays, where r is $O(n/\log^2 n)$, in linear time. Performing this method on an array that is not sparse, however, would result in an $O(n \log^2 n)$ running time. Nevertheless, we can perform such an action on a dense array faster than this.

Tight Order-Preserving Compaction. Let us now show how to perform a tight order-preserving compaction for a dense array in a data-oblivious fashion using $O((N/B) \log_{M/B}(N/B))$ I/Os. We begin by performing a data consolidation preprocessing operation (Lemma 3). This allows us to describe our compaction algorithm at the block level, for an array, A, of n blocks, where $n = \lceil N/B \rceil$, and a private memory of size $m = O(M/B)$.

Let us define a routing network, $\mathcal{R}$, for performing this action, in such a way that $\mathcal{R}$ is somewhat like a butterfly network (e.g., see [21]). There are $\lceil \log n \rceil$ levels, $L_0, L_1, \ldots$, to this network, with each level, L_i, consisting of n cells (corresponding to the positions in A). Cell j of level L_i is connected to cell j and cell $j - 2^i$ of level L_{i+1}. (See Figure 1.)

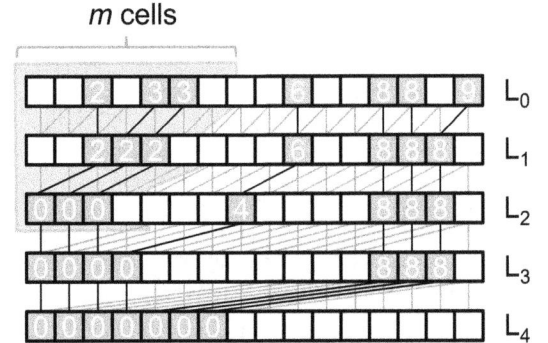

Figure 1: A butterfly-like compaction network. Occupied cells are shaded and labeled with the remaining distance that the block for that cell needs to move to the left. In addition, a block of m cells on level L_0 is highlighted to show that its destination on a level $O(\log m)$ away is of size roughly $m/2$.

Initially, each occupied cell on level L_0 is labeled with the number of cells that it needs to be moved to the left to create a tight compaction. Note that such a labeling can easily be produced by a single left-to-right data-oblivious scan of the array A. For each occupied cell j on level L_i, labeled with distance label, d_j, we route the contents of cell j to cell $j - (d_j \bmod 2^{i+1})$, which, by a simple inductive argument, is either cell j or $j - 2^i$ on level L_{i+1}. We then update the distance label for this cell to be $d_j \leftarrow d_j - (d_j \bmod 2^{i+1})$, and continue.

Lemma 5: *If we start with a valid set of distance labels on level L_0, there will be no collisions at any internal level of the network $\mathcal{R}$.*

PROOF. Notice that we can cause a collision between two cells, j and k, in going from level i to level $i + 1$, only if $k = j + 2^i$ and $(d_j \bmod 2^{i+1}) = 0$ and $(d_k \bmod 2^{i+1}) = 2^i$. So suppose such a pair of colliding cells exists. Then $(d_k - d_j) \bmod 2^{i+1} = 2^i$. Also, note that there are $d_k - d_j$ empty cells between k and j, by the definition of these distance labels. Thus, there are at least 2^i empty cells between j and k; hence, $k \geq j + 2^i + 1$, which is a contradiction. So no such pair of colliding cells exists. $\square$

Thus, we can route the elements of A to their final destinations in $O(n \log n)$ scans. We can, in fact, route elements faster than this, by considering cells $2m - 1$ at a time, starting at a cell $jm + 1$ on level L_0. In this case, there are m possible destination cells at level L_l with index at least $jm + 1$, where $l = i + \log m - 1$. So we can route all these m cells with destinations among these cells on level L_l in internal memory with a single scan of these cells. We can then move this "window" of $2m-1$ cells to the right by m cells and repeat this routing. At the level L_l we note that these consecutive m cells are now independent of one other, and the connection pattern of the previous $\log m - 1$ levels will be repeated for cells that are at distance m apart. Thus, we can repeat the same routing for level L_l (after a simple shuffle that brings together cells that are m apart). Therefore, we can route the cells from L_0 to level $L_{\log n}$ using $O(n \log n / \log m) = O((N/B) \log_{M/B}(N/B))$ I/Os. Moreover, since we are simulating a circuit, the sequence of I/Os is data-oblivious.

Theorem 6: *Given an array A of N cells such that at most $R \leq N$ of the cells in A are distinguished, we can deterministically perform a tight order-preserving compaction of A in a data-oblivious fashion using $O((N/B) \log_{M/B}(N/B))$ I/Os, assuming $B \geq 1$ and $M \geq 3B$.*

Note that we can also use this method "in reverse" to expand any compact array to a larger array in an order-preserving way. In this case, each element would be given an expansion factor, which would be the number of cells it should be moved to the right (with these factors forming a non-decreasing sequence).

Loose Compaction. Suppose we are now given an array A of size N, such that at most $R < N/4$ of the elements in A are marked as "distinguished" and we want to map the distinguished elements from A into an array D, of size $5R$ using an algorithm that is data-oblivious.

We begin by performing the data consolidation algorithm of Lemma 3, to consolidate the distinguished elements of A to be full or empty block-sized cells (save the last one), where we consider a cell "empty" if it stores a null value that is different from any input value. So let us view A as a set of $n = \lceil N/B \rceil$ cells and let us create an array, C, of size $4r$ block-sized cells, for $r = \lceil R/B \rceil$.

Define an *A-to-C thinning pass* to be a sequential scan of A such that, for each $A[i]$, we choose an index $j \in [1, 4r]$ uniformly at random, read the cell $C[j]$, and if it's empty, $A[i]$ is distinguished, and we have yet to successfully write $A[i]$ to C (which can be indicated with a simple bit associated with $A[i]$), then we write $A[i]$ to the cell $C[j]$. Otherwise, if $C[j]$ is nonempty or $A[i]$ is not distinguished, then we write the old value of $C[j]$ back to the cell $C[j]$. Thus, the memory accesses made by an A-to-C thinning pass are data-oblivious and the time to perform such a pass is $O(n)$.

We continue our algorithm by performing c_0 rounds of A-to-C thinning passes, where c_0 is a constant determined in the analysis, so the probability that any block of A is unsuccessfully copied into C is at most $1/2^{2c_0}$. We then consider regions of A of size $\lceil c_1 \log n \rceil = O(\log(N/B))$, where c_1 is another constant determined in the analysis, so that each such region has at most $(c_1 \log n)/2$ occupied cells w.v.h.p. In particular, we assign these values according to the following.

Lemma 7: *Consider a region of $c_1 \log(N/B)$ blocks of A, such that each block is unsuccessfully copied into C independently with probability at most $1/2^{2c_0}$. The number of blocks of A that still remain in this region is over $(c_1/2) \log(N/B)$ with probability at most $(N/B)^{-c_1}$, provided $c_0 \geq 3$.*

PROOF. The expected number of blocks that still remain is at most $(c_1/2^{2c_0}) \log(N/B)$. Thus, if we let X denote the number blocks that still remain, then, by a Chernoff bound (e.g., Lemma 22 from the appendix) and the fact that $c_0 \geq 3$, we have he following:

$$\Pr\left(X > (c_1/2) \log(N/B)\right) \quad < \quad 2^{-(c_1/2) \log(N/B)(2c_0-3)}$$
$$< \quad 2^{-c_1 \log(N/B)}$$
$$= \quad (N/B)^{-c_1}.$$

□

So this lemma gives us a lower bound for c_0. In addition, if we take $c_1 = d+2$, then the probability that there is any of our regions of size $c_1 \log(N/B)$ blocks with more than $c_1 \log(N/B)/2$ blocks still remaining is at most $(N/B)^{-(d+1)}$, which gives us a high probability of success.

Since c_1 is a constant and the number of blocks we can fit in memory is $m = M/B \geq \log^{\epsilon^2}(N/B) = \log^{\epsilon^2} n$, by our wide-block and tall-cache assumptions, we can apply the data-oblivious sorting algorithm of Lemma 2 to sort each of the $O(n/\log n)$ regions using $O(\log n)$ I/Os a piece, putting every distinguished element before any unmarked elements. Thus, the overall number of I/Os for such a step is linear. Then, we compact each such region to its first $(c_1/2) \log n$ blocks. This action therefore halves the size of the array, A. So we then repeat the above actions for the smaller array. We continue these reductions until the number of the remaining set of blocks is less than $n/\log_m^2 n$, at which point we completely compress the remaining array A by using the data-oblivious sorting algorithm of Lemma 2 on the entire array. This results in array of size at most r, which we concatenate to the array, C, of size $4r$, to produce a compacted array of size $5r$. Therefore, we have the following.

Theorem 8: *Given an array, A, of size N, such that at most $R < N/4$ of A's elements are marked as distinguished, we can compress the distinguished elements in A into an array B of size $5R$ using a data-oblivious algorithm that uses $O(N/B)$ I/Os and succeeds with probability at least $1 - 1/(N/B)^d$, for any given constant $d \geq 1$, assuming $B \geq \log^{\epsilon}(N/B)$ and $M \geq B^{1+\epsilon}$, for some constant $\epsilon > 0$.*

PROOF. To establish the claim on the number of I/Os for this algorithm, note that the I/Os needed for all the iterations are proportional to the geometric sum,

$$n + n/2 + n/4 + \cdots + n/\log_m^2 n,$$

which is $O(n) = O(N/B)$. In addition, when we complete the compression using the deterministic sorting algorithm of Lemma 2, we use

$$O((n/\log_m^2 n) \log_m^2(n/\log_m^2 n)) = O(n) = O(N/B)$$

I/Os, under our weak wide-block and tall-cache assumptions. Thus, the entire algorithm uses $O(N/B)$ I/Os and succeeds with very high probability. □

Incidentally, we can also show that it is also possible to perform loose compaction without the wide-block and tall-cache assumptions, albeit with a slightly super-linear number of I/Os. Specifically, we prove the following in the full version of this paper.

Theorem 9: *Given an array, A, of size N, such that at most $R < N/4$ of A's elements are marked as distinguished, we can compress the distinguished elements in A into an array B of size $4.25R$ using a data-oblivious algorithm that uses $O((N/B) \log^*(N/B))$ I/Os and succeeds with probability at least $1 - 1/(N/B)^d$, for any given constant $d \geq 1$, assuming only that $B \geq 1$ and $M \geq 2B$.*

4. SELECTION AND QUANTILES

Selection. Suppose we are given an array A of n comparable items and want to find the kth smallest element in A. For each element a_i in A, we mark a_i as distinguished with probability $1/n^{1/2}$. Assuming that there are at most $n^{1/2} + n^{3/8}$ distinguished items, we then compress all the distinguished items in A to an array, C, of size $n^{1/2} + n^{3/8}$ using the method of Theorem 4, which runs in $O(n)$ time in this case and, as we prove, succeeds with high probability. We then sort the items in C using a data-oblivious algorithm, which can be done in $O(n^{1/2} \log^2 n)$ time by Lemma 2, considering empty cells as holding $+\infty$. We then scan this sorted array, C. During this scan, we save in our internal registers, items, x' and y', with ranks $\lceil k/n^{1/2} - n^{3/8} \rceil$ and $|C| - \lceil (n-k)/n^{1/2} - 2n^{3/8} \rceil$, respectively, in C, if they exist. If x' (resp., y') does not exist, then we set $x' = -\infty$ (resp., $y' = +\infty$). We then scan A to find x'' and y'', the smallest and largest elements in A, respectively. Then we set $x = \max\{x', x''\}$ and $y = \min\{y', y''\}$. We show below that, w.v.h.p., the kth smallest element is contained in the range $[x, y]$ and there are $O(n^{7/8})$ items of A in this range.

Lemma 10: *There are more than $n^{1/2} + n^{3/8}$ elements in C with probability at most $e^{-n^{1/4}/3}$, and fewer than $n^{1/2} - n^{3/8}$ elements in C with probability at most $e^{-n^{1/4}/2}$.*

PROOF. Let X denote the number of elements of A chosen to belong to C. Noting that each element of A is chosen independently with probability $1/n^{1/2}$ to belong to C, by a standard Chernoff bound (e.g., see [25], Theorem 4.4),

$$
\begin{aligned}
\Pr(X > n^{1/2} + n^{3/8}) &= \Pr(X > (1 + n^{-1/8})n^{1/2}) \\
&\leq e^{-n^{1/4}/3},
\end{aligned}
$$

since $E(X) = n^{1/2}$. Also, by another standard Chernoff bound (e.g., see [25], Theorem 4.5),

$$
\begin{aligned}
\Pr(X < n^{1/2} - n^{3/8}) &= \Pr(X < (1 - n^{-1/8})n^{1/2}) \\
&\leq e^{-n^{1/4}/2}.
\end{aligned}
$$

$\square$

Recall that we then performed a scan, where we save in our internal registers, items, x' and y', with ranks $\lceil k/n^{1/2} - n^{3/8} \rceil$ and $|C| - \lceil (n-k)/n^{1/2} - n^{3/8} \rceil$, respectively, in C, if they exist. If x' (resp., y') does not exist, then we set $x' = -\infty$ (resp., $y' = +\infty$). We then scan A to find x'' and y'', the smallest and largest elements in A, respectively. Then we set $x = \max\{x', x''\}$ and $y = \min\{y', y''\}$.

Lemma 11: *With probability at least $1 - 2e^{-n^{1/8}/9} - e^{-4n^{3/8}/5} - e^{-n^{1/4}/3} - e^{n^{1/4}/2}$, the kth smallest element of A is contained in the range $[x, y]$ and there are at most $8n^{7/8}$ items of A in the range $[x, y]$.*

PROOF. Let us first suppose that $k \leq 2n^{7/8}$. In this case, we pick the smallest element in A for x, in which case $k \geq x$.

So, to consider the remaining possibility that $x > k$, for $k > 2n^{7/8}$. We can model the number of elements of A less than or equal to x as the sum, X, of $k' = k/n^{1/2} - n^{3/8}$ independent geometric random variables with parameter $p = n^{-1/2}$. The probability that k is less than or equal to x is bounded by

$$
\Pr(X > k) = \Pr(X > (n^{1/2} + t)k'),
$$

where $t = n^{7/8}/(k/n^{1/2} - n^{3/8})$; hence, $t \geq n^{3/8}$ and $k' > n^{3/8}$. If $t/n^{1/2} < 1/2$, then, by a Chernoff bound (e.g., Lemma 23 from the appendix), we have the following:

$$
\begin{aligned}
\Pr(X > k) &< e^{-(t^2/n)k'/3} \\
&< e^{-n^{1/8}/3}.
\end{aligned}
$$

Similarly, if $t/n^{1/2} \geq 1/2$, then

$$
\begin{aligned}
\Pr(X > k) &< e^{-(t/n^{1/2})k'/9} \\
&< e^{-n^{1/8}/9}.
\end{aligned}
$$

Thus, in either case, the probability that the kth smallest element is greater than x is bounded by this latter probability. By a symmetric argument, assuming $|C| \geq n^{1/2} - n^{3/8}$, the probability that there are the more than $(n-k)$ elements of A greater than y, for $k < n - 2n^{7/8}$, is also bounded by this latter probability (note that, for $k \geq n - 2n^{7/8}$, it is trivially true that the kth smallest element is less than or equal to y). So, with probability at least $1 - 2e^{-n^{1/8}/9} - e^{-n^{1/4}/2}$, the kth smallest element is contained in the range $[x, y]$.

Let us next consider the number of elements of A in the range $[x, y]$. First, note that, probability at least $1 - e^{n^{1/4}/3}$, there are at most $n' = 4n^{3/8}$ elements of the random sample, C, in this range; hence, we can model the number of elements of A in this range as being bounded by the sum, Y, of n' geometric random variables with parameter $p = 1/n^{1/2}$. Thus, by a Chernoff bound (e.g., Lemma 23 from the appendix), we have the following:

$$
\begin{aligned}
\Pr(Y > 8n^{7/8}) &= \Pr(Y > (n^{1/2} + n^{1/2})n') \\
&< e^{-n'/5} \\
&= e^{-4n^{3/8}/5}.
\end{aligned}
$$

This gives us the lemma. $\square$

So, we make an addition scan of A to mark the elements in A that are in the range $[x, y]$, and we then compress these items to an array, D, of size $O(n^{7/8})$, using the method of Theorem 4, which runs in $O(n)$ time in this case. In addition, we can determine the rank, $r(x)$, of x in A. Thus, we have just reduced the problem to returning the item in D with rank $k - r(x) + 1$. We can solve this problem by sorting D using the oblivious sorting method of Lemma 2 followed by a scan to obliviously select the item with this rank. Therefore, we have the following:

Theorem 12: *Given an integer, $1 \leq k \leq n$, and an array, A, of n comparable items, we can select the kth smallest element in A in $O(n)$ time using a data-oblivious algorithm that succeeds with probability at least $1 - n^{-d}$, for any given constant $d > 0$.*

Note that the running time (with a very-high success probability) of this method beats the $\Omega(n \log \log n)$ lower bound of Leighton *et al.* [22], which applies to any high-success-probability randomized data-oblivious algorithm based on the exclusive use of compare-exchange as the primitive data-manipulation operation. Our method is data-oblivious, but it also uses primitive operations of copying, summation, and random hashing. Thus, Theorem 12 demonstrates the power of using these primitives in data-oblivious algorithms. In addition, by substituting data-oblivious external-memory compaction and sorting steps for the internal-memory methods used above, we get the following:

Theorem 13: *Given an integer, $1 \leq k \leq N$, and an array, A, of N comparable items, we can select the kth smallest element in A using $O(N/B)$ I/Os with a data-oblivious external-memory algorithm that succeeds with probability at least $1 - (N/B)^{-d}$, for any given constant $d > 0$, assuming only that $B \geq 1$ and $M \geq 2B$.*

Quantiles. Let us now consider the problem of selecting q quantile elements from an array A using an external-memory data-oblivious algorithm, for the case when $q \leq (M/B)^{1/4}$, which will be sufficient for this algorithm to prove useful for our external-memory sorting algorithm, which we describe in Section 5.

If $(M/B) > (N/B)^{1/4}$, then we sort A using the deterministic data-oblivious algorithm of Lemma 2, which uses $O(N/B)$ I/Os in this case. Then we simply read out the elements at ranks that are multiples of $N/(q+1)$, rounded to integer ranks.

Let us therefore suppose instead that $(M/B) \leq (N/B)^{1/4}$; so $q \leq (N/B)^{1/16}$. In this case, we randomly choose each element of A to belong to a random subset, C, with probability $1/N^{1/4}$. With high probability, there are at most $N^{3/4} \pm N^{1/2}$ such elements, so we can compact them into an array, C, of capacity $N^{3/4} + N^{1/2}$ by Theorem 4, using $O(N/B)$ I/Os. We then sort this array and compact it down to capacity $N^{3/4} + N^{1/2}$, using Lemma 2, and let $|C|$ denote its actual size (which we remember in private memory). We then scan this sorted array, C, and read into Alice's memory every item, x_i, with rank that is a multiple of $(\hat{n}/(q+1)) - N^{1/2}$, rounded to integer ranks, where $\hat{n} = N^{3/4}$, with the exception that x_1 is the smallest element in A. We also select items at ranks, $y_i = |C| - (N^{3/4} - N^{3/4}i/(q+1) - 2N^{1/2})$, rounded to integer ranks, with the exception that y_q is the largest element in A. Let $[x_i, y_i]$ denote each such pair of such items, which, as we show below, will surround a value, $\hat{n}/(q+1)$, with high probability. In addition, as we also show in the analysis, there are at most $8N^{3/4}$ elements of A in each interval $[x_i, y_i]$, with high probability. That is, there are at most $O(N^{13/16})$ elements of A in any interval $[x_i, y_i]$, with high probability. Storing all the $[x_i, y_i]$ intervals in Alice's memory, we scan A to identify for each element in A if it is contained in such an interval $[x_i, y_i]$, marking it with i in this case, or if it is outside every such interval. During this scan we also maintain counts (in Alice's memory) of how many elements of A fall between each consecutive pair of intervals, $[x_i, y_i]$ and $[x_{i+1}, y_{i+1}]$, and how many elements fall inside each interval $[x_i, y_i]$. We then compact all the elements of A that are inside such intervals into an array D of size $O(N^{13/16})$ using Theorem 4, using $O(N/B)$ I/Os, and we pad this array with dummy elements so the number of elements of D in each interval $[x_i, y_i]$ is exactly $\lceil 8N^{3/4} \rceil$. We then sort D using the data-oblivious method of Lemma 2. Next, for each subarray of D of size $\lceil 8N^{3/4} \rceil$ we use the selection algorithm of Theorem 13 to select the k_ith smallest element in this subarray, where k_i is the value that will return the ith quantile for A (based on the counts we computed during our scans of A).

Lemma 14: *The number of elements of A in C is more than $N^{3/4} + N^{1/2}$ with probability at most $e^{-N^{1/4}/3}$, and the number of elements of A in C is less than $N^{3/4} - N^{1/2}$ with probability at most $e^{-N^{1/4}/2}$.*

PROOF. Let X denote the number of elements of A chosen to belong to C. Noting that each element of A is chosen independently with probability $1/N^{1/4}$ to belong to C, by a standard Chernoff bound (e.g., see [25], Theorem 4.4),

$$\Pr(X > N^{3/4} + N^{1/2}) = \Pr(X > (1 + N^{-1/4})N^{3/4})$$
$$\leq e^{-N^{1/4}/3},$$

since $E(X) = n^{1/2}$. Also, by another standard Chernoff bound (e.g., see [25], Theorem 4.5),

$$\Pr(X < N^{3/4} - N^{1/2}) = \Pr(X < (1 - N^{-1/4})N^{3/4})$$
$$\leq e^{-N^{1/4}/2}.$$

$\square$

We then compress these elements into an array, C, of size assumed to be at most $N^{3/4} + N^{1/2}$ by Theorem 4, using $O(N/B)$

I/Os, which will fail with probability at most $1/N^{3c/4}$, for any given constant $c > 0$. Given the array C, we select items at ranks $x_i = (\hat{n}i/(q+1)) - N^{1/2}$, rounded to integer ranks. where $\hat{n} = N^{3/4}$. We also select items at ranks, $y_i = |C| - (N^{3/4} - N^{3/4}i/(q+1) - 2N^{1/2})$, rounded to integer ranks. Let $[x_i, y_i]$ denote each such pair, with the added convention that we take x_1 to be the smallest element in A and y_q to be the largest element in A.

Lemma 15: *There are more than $8N^{3/4}$ elements of A in any interval $[x_i, y_i]$ with probability at most $e^{-N^{1/2}/9} + 2e^{-N^{1/4}/3}$.*

PROOF. Let us assume that $N^{3/4} - N^{1/2} \leq |C| \leq N^{3/4} + N^{1/2}$, which hold with probability at least $1 - 2e^{-N^{1/4}/3}$. Thus, there are at most $4N^{1/2}$ elements in C that are in any $[x_i, y_i]$ pair, other than the first or last. Thus, in such a general case, the number of elements, X, from A in this interval has expected value $E(X) \leq 4N^{3/4}$. In addition, since X is the sum of geometric random variables with parameter $1/N^{1/4}$,

$$\Pr(X > 8N^{3/4}) = \Pr(X > (N^{1/4} + N^{1/4})4N^{1/2})$$
$$\leq e^{-N^{1/2}/9}.$$

The probability bounds for the first and last intervals are proved by a similar argument. $\square$

In addition, note that there are at most $(N/B)^{1/16}$ intervals, $[x_i, y_i]$. Also, we have the following.

Lemma 16: *Interval $[x_k, y_k]$ contains the kth quantile with probability at least $1 - 2e^{-N^{1/4}/3}$.*

PROOF. Let us consider the probability that the kth quantile is less than x_k. In the random sample, x_k has rank $\hat{n}k/(q+1) - N^{1/2} = N^{3/4}k/(q+1) - N^{1/2}$. Thus, the number, X, of elements from A less than this number has expected value $E(X) = Nk/(q+1) - N^{3/4}$. Since X is the sum of geometric random variables with parameter $N^{-1/4}$, we can bound $\Pr(X > Nk/(q+1))$ by

$$\Pr\left(X > (N^{1/4} + \tau) \cdot \left(\frac{N^{3/4}k}{q+1} - N^{1/2}\right)\right)$$
$$\leq e^{-(\tau N^{-1/4})^2(N^{3/4}k/(q+1) - N^{1/2})/3}$$
$$= e^{-\tau^2 N^{-1/2}(N^{3/4}k/(q+1) - n^{1/2})/3},$$

where $\tau = N^{3/4}/(N^{3/4}k/(q+1) - N^{1/2})$, which greater than 1. So

$$\Pr(X > Nk(q+1)) \leq e^{-\tau N^{-1/2}N^{3/4}/3}$$
$$< e^{-N^{1/4}/3}.$$

By a symmetric argument, the kth quantile is more than y_k by this same probability. $\square$

Thus, each of the intervals, $[x_k, y_k]$, contains the kth quantile with probability at least $1 - 2qe^{-N^{1/4}/3}$. Therefore, we have the following.

Theorem 17: *Given an array, A, of N comparable items, we can select the $q \leq (M/B)^{1/4}$ quantiles in A using $O(N/B)$ I/Os with a data-oblivious external-memory algorithm that succeeds with probability at least $1 - (N/B)^{-d}$, for any given constant $d > 0$, assuming only that $B \geq 1$ and $M \geq 2B$.*

5. DATA-OBLIVIOUS SORTING

Consider now the sorting problem, where we are given an array, A, of N comparable items stored as key-value pairs and we want to output an array C of size N holding the items from A in key order. For inductive reasons, however, we allow both A and C to be arrays of size $O(N)$ that have N non-empty cells, with the requirement that the items in non-empty cells in the output array C be given in non-decreasing order.

We begin by computing q quantiles for the items in A using Theorem 17, for $q = (M/B)^{1/4}$. We then would like to distribute the items of A distributed between all these quantiles to $q+1$ subarrays of size $O(N/q)$ each. Let us think of each subgroup (defined by the quantiles) in A as a separate color, so that each item in A is given a specific color, $1, 2, \ldots, q+1$, with there being $\lceil N/(q+1) \rceil$ items of each color.

Multi-way Data Consolidation. To prepare for this distribution, we do a $(q+1)$-way consolidation of A, so that the items in each block of size B in the consolidated array A' are all of the same color. We perform this action as follows. Read into Alice's memory the first $q+1$ blocks of A, and separate them into $q+1$ groups, one for each color. While there is a group of items with the same color of size at least B, output a block of these items to A'. Once we have output q' such blocks, all the remaining colors in Alice's memory have fewer than B members. So we then output $q+1-q'$ empty blocks to A', keeping the "left over" items in Alice's memory. We then repeat this computation for the next $q+1$ blocks of A, and the next, and so on. When we complete the scan of A, all the blocks in A' will be completely full of items of the same color or they will be completely empty. We finish this $(q+1)$-way consolidation, then, by outputting $(q+1)$ blocks, each containing as many items of the same color as possible. These last blocks are the only partially-full blocks in A'. Thus, all the blocks of A' are monochromatic and all but these last blocks of A' are full.

Shuffle-and-Deal Data Distribution. Our remaining goal, then, is to distribute the (monochromatic) blocks of A' to $q+1$ separate arrays, $C_1, \ldots, C_{q+1}$, one for each color. Unfortunately, doing this as a straightforward scan of A' may encounter the colors in a non-uniform fashion. To probabilistically avoid this "hot spot" behavior, we apply a *shuffle-and-deal* technique, where we perform a random permutation to the $n' = O(N/B)$ blocks in A' in a fashion somewhat reminiscent of Valiant-Brebner routing [27]. The random permutation algorithm we use here is the well-known algorithm (e.g., see Knuth [20]), where, for $i = 1, 2, \ldots, n'$, we swap block i and a random block chosen uniformly from the range $[i, n']$. This is the "shuffle," and even though the adversary, Bob, can see us perform this shuffle, note that the choices we make do not depend on data values. Given this shuffled deck of blocks in A', we then perform a series of scans to "deal" the blocks of A' to the $q+1$ arrays.

We do this "deal" as follows. We read in the next $(M/B)^{3/4}$ blocks of A'. Note that, w.v.h.p., there should now be at most $O((M/B)^{1/2})$ blocks of each color now in Alice's memory. So we write out $c(M/B)^{1/2}$ blocks to each C_i in Bob's memory, including as many full blocks as possible and padding with empty blocks as needed (to keep accesses being data-oblivious), for a constant c determined in the analysis. Then, we apply Theorem 8, which implies a success with high probability, to compact each C_i to have size $O(N/q) = O(N/(M/B)^{1/4})$ each, which is $O(N/(qB))$ blocks. We then repeat the above computation for each subarray, C_i.

Data-Oblivious Failure Sweeping. We continue in this manner until we have formed $O(n^{1/2})$ subarrays of size $O(n^{1/2})$ each,

where $n = N/B$. At this point, we then recursively call our sorting algorithm to produce a padded sorting of each of the subarrays. Of course, since we are recursively solving smaller problems, whose success probability depends on their size, some of these may fail to correctly produce a padded sorting of their inputs. Let us assume that at most $O(n^{1/4})$ of these recursive sorts fail, however, and apply Theorem 6 to deterministically compact all of these subarrays into a single array, D, of size $O(n^{3/4})$, in $O(n \log_m n)$ time, where $m = M/B$. We then apply the deterministic data-oblivious sorting method of Lemma 2 to D, and then we perform a reversal of Theorem 6 to expand these sorted elements back to their original subarrays. This provides a data-oblivious version of the failure sweeping technique [12] and gives us a padded sorting of A w.v.h.p.

Finally, after we have completed the algorithm for producing a padded sorting of A, we perform a tight order-preserving compaction for all of A using Theorem 6. Given appropriate probabilistic guarantees, given below, this completes the algorithm.

Lemma 18: *Given $(M/B)^{3/4}$ blocks of A', read in from consecutive blocks from a random permutation, more than $c(M/B)^{1/2}$ of these blocks are of color, χ, for a given color, χ, with probability less than $(N/B)^{-d}$, for $c > 2de/\epsilon^2$, where ϵ is the constant used in the wide-block and tall-cache assumptions.*

PROOF. Let X be the number of blocks among $(M/B)^{3/4}$ blocks chosen independently without replacement from A' that are of color χ and let Y be the number of blocks among $(M/B)^{3/4}$ blocks chosen independently with replacement from A' that are of color χ. By a theorem (4) of Hoeffding [18],

$$\Pr(X > c(M/B)^{1/2}) \leq \Pr(Y > c(M/B)^{1/2}).$$

Thus, since $E(Y) = (M/B)^{1/2}$, then, by a Chernoff bound (e.g., Lemma 22 from the appendix),

$$\Pr(Y > c(M/B)^{1/2}) \leq 2^{-c(M/B)^{1/2}} \leq (N/B)^d,$$

for $c > 2de/\epsilon^2$. $\square$

This bound applies to any $(M/B)^{3/4}$ blocks we read in from A', and any specific color, χ. Thus, we have the following.

Corollary 19: *For each set of $(M/B)^{3/4}$ blocks of A', read in from consecutive blocks from the constructed random permutation, more than $c(M/B)^{1/2}$ of these blocks are of any color, χ, with probability less than $(N/B)^{-d}$, for $c > 2d'e/\epsilon^2$, where ϵ is the constant used in the wide-block and tall-cache assumptions and $d' \geq d+1$.*

PROOF. There are $(N/B)/(M/B)^{3/4}$ sets of $(M/B)^{3/4}$ blocks of A' read in from consecutive blocks from the constructed random permutation. In addition, there are $(M/B)^{1/16}$ colors. Thus, by the above lemma and the union bound, the probability that any of these sets overflow a color χ is at most

$$\frac{N/B}{(M/B)^{3/4}} \cdot \frac{1}{(N/B)^{d'}} \cdot (M/B)^{1/16} \leq (N/B)^{-d},$$

for $d' \geq d+1$. $\square$

So we write out $c(M/B)^{1/2}$ blocks to each C_i, including as many full blocks as possible and padding with empty blocks as needed. We then repeat the quantile computation and shuffle-and-deal computation on each of the C_i's.

At the point when subproblem sizes become of size $O(n^{1/2})$, we then switch to a recursive computation, which we claim inductively succeeds with probability $1 - 1/n^{d/2}$, for any given constant $d \geq 2$, for $n = N/B$.

Lemma 20: *There are more than $n^{1/4}$ failing recursive subproblems with probability at most $2^{-n^{1/4}}$.*

PROOF. Each of the recursive calls fails independently. Thus, if we let X denote the number of failing recursive calls, then $E(X) \le n^{1/2}/n^{d/2} = n^{-(d-1)/2}$. Thus, by a Chernoff bound (e.g., Lemma 22 from the appendix),

$$
\begin{aligned}
\Pr(X > n^{1/4}) &= \Pr(X > n^{1/4+(d-1)/2} \cdot n^{(d-1)/2}) \\
&\le 2^{-n^{1/4}}.
\end{aligned}
$$

□

Thus, the failure sweeping step in our sorting algorithm succeeds with high probability, which completes the analysis and gives us the following.

Theorem 21: *Given an array, A, of size N, we can perform a data-oblivious sorting of A with an algorithm that succeeds with probability $1 - 1/(N/B)^d$ and uses $O((N/B)\log_{M/B}(N/B))$ I/Os, for any given constant $d \ge 1$, assuming that $B \ge \log^\epsilon(N/B)$ and $M \ge B^{1+\epsilon}$, for some small constant $\epsilon > 0$.*

Acknowledgments

We would like to thank Pawel Pszona for some helpful comments regarding an earlier version of this paper. This research was supported in part by the National Science Foundation under grants 0724806, 0713046, 0847968, and 0953071.

6. REFERENCES

[1] A. Aggarwal and J. S. Vitter. The input/output complexity of sorting and related problems. *Commun. ACM*, 31:1116–1127, 1988.

[2] M. Ajtai, J. Komlós, and E. Szemerédi. An $O(n \log n)$ sorting network. In *Proc. 15th Annu. ACM Sympos. Theory Comput.*, pages 1–9, 1983.

[3] M. Bellare and P. Rogaway. Random oracles are practical: a paradigm for designing efficient protocols. In *1st ACM Conf. on Computer and Communications Security (CCS)*, pages 62–73, 1993.

[4] M. A. Bender, E. D. Demaine, and M. Farach-Colton. Cache-oblivious B-trees. *SIAM J. Comput.*, 35(2):341–358, 2005.

[5] B. H. Bloom. Space/time trade-offs in hash coding with allowable errors. *Commun. ACM*, 13(7):422–426, 1970.

[6] G. S. Brodal. Cache-oblivious algorithms and data structures. In T. Hagerup and J. Katajainen, editors, *SWAT*, volume 3111 of *LNCS*, pages 3–13. Springer, 2004.

[7] G. Chaudhry and T. H. Cormen. Oblivious vs. distribution-based sorting: An experimental evaluation. In G. S. Brodal and S. Leonardi, editors, *ESA*, volume 3669 of *LNCS*, pages 317–328. Springer, 2005.

[8] G. Chaudhry and T. H. Cormen. Slabpose columnsort: A new oblivious algorithm for out-of-core sorting on distributed-memory clusters. *Algorithmica*, 45(3):483–508, 2006.

[9] S. Chen, R. Wang, X. Wang, and K. Zhang. Side-channel leaks in web applications: a reality today, a challenge tomorrow. In *Proceedings of the 31st IEEE Symposium on Security and Privacy*, 2010.

[10] D. Eppstein and M. T. Goodrich. Straggler identification in round-trip data streams via Newton's identities and invertible Bloom filters. *IEEE Transactions on Knowledge and Data Engineering*, 23:297–306, 2011.

[11] M. Frigo, C. E. Leiserson, H. Prokop, and S. Ramachandran. Cache-oblivious algorithms. In *40th IEEE Symp. on Foundations of Computer Science (FOCS)*, page 285, 1999.

[12] M. Ghouse and M. T. Goodrich. Fast randomized parallel methods for planar convex hull construction. *Comput. Geom. Theory Appl.*, 7:219–236, 1997.

[13] O. Goldreich, S. Micali, and A. Wigderson. How to play ANY mental game. In *STOC '87: Proceedings of the nineteenth annual ACM symposium on Theory of computing*, pages 218–229, New York, NY, USA, 1987. ACM.

[14] O. Goldreich and R. Ostrovsky. Software protection and simulation on oblivious RAMs. *J. ACM*, 43(3):431–473, 1996.

[15] M. T. Goodrich. Randomized Shellsort: A simple oblivious sorting algorithm. In *Proceedings of the ACM-SIAM Symposium on Discrete Algorithms (SODA)*, pages 1–16. SIAM, 2010.

[16] M. T. Goodrich and M. Mitzenmacher. MapReduce parallel cuckoo hashing and oblivious RAM simulations. *CoRR*, abs/1007.1259, 2010.

[17] M. T. Goodrich and M. Mitzenmacher. Invertible Bloom lookup tables. *ArXiv e-prints*, January 2011. 1101.2245.

[18] W. Hoeffding. Probability inequalities for sums of bounded random variables. *Journal of the American Statistical Association*, 58(301):13–30, Mar. 1963.

[19] D. E. Knuth. *Sorting and Searching*, volume 3 of *The Art of Computer Programming*. Addison-Wesley, Reading, MA, 1973.

[20] D. E. Knuth. *Seminumerical Algorithms*, volume 2 of *The Art of Computer Programming*. Addison-Wesley, Reading, MA, 3rd edition, 1998.

[21] F. T. Leighton. *Introduction to Parallel Algorithms and Architectures: Arrays, Trees, Hypercubes.* Morgan-Kaufmann, San Mateo, CA, 1992.

[22] F. T. Leighton, Y. Ma, and T. Suel. On probabilistic networks for selection, merging, and sorting. *Theory Comput. Syst.*, 30(6):559–582, 1997.

[23] T. Leighton and C. G. Plaxton. Hypercubic sorting networks. *SIAM J. Comput.*, 27(1):1–47, 1998.

[24] K. Mehlhorn and U. Meyer. External-memory breadth-first search with sublinear I/O. In *10th European Symposium on Algorithms (ESA)*, pages 723–735, 2002.

[25] M. Mitzenmacher and E. Upfal. *Probability and Computing: Randomized Algorithms and Probabilistic Analysis.* Cambridge University Press, New York, NY, USA, 2005.

[26] K. Mulmuley. *Computational Geometry: An Introduction Through Randomized Algorithms.* Prentice Hall, Englewood Cliffs, NJ, 1993.

[27] L. G. Valiant and G. J. Brebner. Universal schemes for parallel communication. In *13th ACM Symposium on Theory of Computing (STOC)*, pages 263–277, 1981.

[28] G. Wang, T. Luo, M. T. Goodrich, W. Du, and Z. Zhu. Bureaucratic protocols for secure two-party sorting, selection, and permuting. In *5th ACM Symp. on Information, Computer and Comm. Security (ASIACCS)*, pages 226–237, 2010.

APPENDIX

A. SOME CHERNOFF BOUNDS

Several of our proofs make use of Chernoff bounds (e.g., see [25] for other examples), which, for the sake of completeness, we review in this subsection. We begin with the following Chernoff bound, which is a simplification of a well-known bound.

Lemma 22: *Let $X = X_1 + X_2 + \cdots + X_n$ be the sum of independent 0-1 random variables, such that $X_i = 1$ with probability p_i, and let $\mu \geq E(X) = \sum_{i=1}^{n} p_i$. Then, for $\gamma > 2e$,*

$$\Pr(X > \gamma\mu) < 2^{-\gamma\mu \log(\gamma/e)}.$$

PROOF. By a standard Chernoff bound (e.g., see [25]) and the fact that $\gamma > 2e$,

$$\begin{aligned}
\Pr(X > \gamma\mu) &< \left(\frac{e^{\gamma-1}}{\gamma^\gamma}\right)^\mu \\
&\leq \left(\frac{e}{\gamma}\right)^{\gamma\mu} \\
&= 2^{-\gamma\mu \log(\gamma/e)}.
\end{aligned}$$

$\square$

There are other simplified Chernoff bounds similar to that of Lemma 22 (e.g., see [25, 26]), but they typically omit the $\log(\gamma/e)$ term (where the log is base-2, of course). We include it here, since it is useful for large γ, which will be the case for some of our uses. Nevertheless, we sometimes leave off the $\log(\gamma/e)$ term, as well, in applying Lemma 22, if that aids simplicity, since $\log(\gamma/e) > 1$ for $\gamma > 2e$.

In addition, we also need a Chernoff bound for the sum, X, of n independent geometric random variables with parameter p, that is, for X being a negative binomial random variable with parameters n and p. Recall that a geometric random variable with parameter p is a discrete random variable that is equal to j with probability $q^{j-1}p$, where $q = 1 - p$. Thus, $E(X) = \alpha n$, where $\alpha = 1/p$.

Lemma 23: *Let $X = X_1 + X_2 + \cdots + X_n$ be the sum of n independent geometric random variables with parameter p. Then we have the following:*

- *If $0 < t < \alpha/2$, then $\Pr(X > (\alpha + t)n) \leq e^{-(tp)^2 n/3}$.*
- *If $t \geq \alpha/2$, then $\Pr(X > (\alpha + t)n) \leq e^{-tpn/9}$.*
- *If $t \geq \alpha$, then $\Pr(X > (\alpha + t)n) \leq e^{-tpn/5}$.*
- *If $t \geq 2\alpha$, then $\Pr(X > (\alpha + t)n) \leq e^{-tpn/3}$.*
- *If $t \geq 3\alpha$, then $\Pr(X > (\alpha + t)n) \leq e^{-tpn/2}$.*

PROOF. We follow the approach of Mulmuley [26], who uses the Chernoff technique (e.g., see [25]) to prove a similar result for the special case when $p = 1/2$ and $t \geq 6$ (albeit with a slight flaw, which we fix). For $0 < \lambda < \ln(1/(1-p))$,

$$\begin{aligned}
E\left(e^{\lambda X_i}\right) &= \sum_{j=1}^{\infty} e^{\lambda j} \Pr(X_i = j) \\
&= \sum_{j=1}^{\infty} e^{\lambda j} q^{j-1} p \\
&= pe^\lambda \sum_{j=0}^{\infty} (e^\lambda q)^j \\
&= \frac{pe^\lambda}{1 - e^\lambda q}.
\end{aligned}$$

Applying the Chernoff technique, then,

$$\begin{aligned}
\Pr(X > (\alpha + t)n) &\leq e^{-\lambda(\alpha+t)n}\left(\frac{pe^\lambda}{1 - e^\lambda q}\right)^n \\
&= p^n \left(\frac{e^{-\lambda(\alpha+t-1)}}{1 - e^\lambda q}\right)^n.
\end{aligned}$$

Let $\beta = p/(1-p)$ and observe that we can satisfy the condition that $0 < \lambda < \ln(1/(1-p))$ by setting

$$e^\lambda = 1 + \frac{\beta t}{\alpha + t}.$$

By substitution and some calculation, note that

$$e^{-\lambda} = 1 - \frac{\beta t}{\alpha + t + \beta t}$$

and

$$1 - e^\lambda q = \frac{p}{1 + tp}.$$

Thus, we can bound $\Pr(X > (\alpha + t)n)$ by

$$\begin{aligned}
&p^n \left(1 - \frac{\beta t}{\alpha + t + \beta t}\right)^{(\alpha+t-1)n} \left(\frac{1 + tp}{p}\right)^n \\
&= \left(1 - \frac{\beta t}{\alpha + t + \beta t}\right)^{(\alpha+t-1)n} (1 + tp)^n.
\end{aligned}$$

Moreover, since $1 - x \leq e^{-x}$, for all x,

$$\left(1 - \frac{\beta t}{\alpha + t + \beta t}\right)^{(\alpha+t-1)} \leq e^{-\frac{\beta t(\alpha+t-1)}{\alpha+t+\beta t}} = e^{-tp}.$$

Therefore,

$$\Pr(X > (\alpha + t)n) \leq e^{-tpn} (1 + tp)^n.$$

Unfortunately, if we use the well-known inequality, $1 + x \leq e^x$, with $x = tp$, to bound the "$1 + tp$" term in the above equation, we get a useless result. So, instead, we use better approximations:

- If $0 < x < 1$, then we can use a truncated Maclaurin series to bound

$$\ln(1+x) \leq x - \frac{x^2}{2} + \frac{x^3}{3}.$$

Thus,

$$1 + x \leq e^{x - \frac{x^2}{2} + \frac{x^3}{3}},$$

which implies that, for $0 < t < \alpha/2$,

$$\begin{aligned}
\Pr(X > (\alpha + t)n) &\leq \left(\frac{e^{(tp)^3/3}}{e^{(tp)^2/2}}\right)^n \\
&\leq e^{-(tp)^2 n/3}.
\end{aligned}$$

- The remaining bounds follow from the following facts, which are easily verified:
  1. If $x \geq 1/2$, then $1 + x < e^{x/(1+1/8)}$.
  2. If $x \geq 1$, then $1 + x < e^{x/(1+1/4)}$.
  3. If $x \geq 2$, then $1 + x < e^{x/(1+1/2)}$.
  4. If $x \geq 3$, then $1 + x < e^{x/2}$.

$\square$

Incidentally, the bound for $t \geq 3\alpha$ fixes a slight flaw in a Chernoff bound proof by Mulmuley [26].

Author Index

www.ingramcontent.com/pod-product-compliance
Lightning Source LLC
Chambersburg PA
CBHW082104220326
41598CB00066BA/5264